TABLE OF CONTENTS
Color coded for your convenience

CASUAL DINING & FAST FOOD
Enjoy the savings and convenience of your favorite Casual & Family Restaurants plus Fast Food and Carryout.

www.entertainment.com/dine

DINING OUT
Explore dining at the best Fine Dine and "Out on the Town" restaurants in your area.

www.entertainment.com/dine

TRAVEL & HOTELS
Your best source for travel savings! Save on Hotels, Car Rentals, Cruises, Condos and entire Vacation Packages.

www.entertainment.com/travel

ENTERTAINMENT & SPORTS
Save on the latest Movies, Live Shows, Concerts, Sporting Events, Museums and activities.

www.entertainment.com/fun

RETAIL & SERVICES
Savings for everything from Apparel to Flowers. Also visit our Top Web Deals section online at www.entertainment.com.

www.entertainment.com/shop

FIND IT FAST!

Your Featured Offers . . . . *now at the front of each section*

Section Indexes . . . . *front of each section*

Neighborhood Index *(includes Printable Coupons!)* . . . *after Retail & Services section*

Alphabetical Index . . . . *after Neighborhood Index*

Rules of Use/Membership Information. . . . . *in back of book*

S0-FFZ-626

Start using your discounts today!

YOU MUST REGISTER ONLINE TO FULLY ACTIVATE YOUR MEMBERSHIP

Use your Entertainment® membership card for:

- **Dining Out:** Save at restaurants in the Dining Out section simply by presenting the card.

- **Exclusive Online Savings:** Register at www.entertainment.com/register to access even more savings online.

- **Travel Savings:** Enjoy hotel and car rental savings plus package deals. See the Travel & Hotels section for more details.

Fully activate your membership online at www.entertainment.com/register

Enjoy additional savings and incredible benefits year-round.

Fully activate your membership online at
www.entertainment.com/register

DON'T MISS OUT

EVEN MORE SAVINGS AND TOOLS ONLINE
at www.entertainment.com

- Print **50% off** and **2-for-1 discounts** not found in your book.

NEW
- Get **Repeat Savings™**. Save again and again at participating merchants.

NEW
- **$1000s in travel savings**—hotels, car rentals, new package deals and more.

- Order **discounted tickets** for movies, sporting events, concerts and more at www.entertainment.com/tickets.

- Purchase **discounted restaurant certificates/cards** for hundreds of restaurants across the country at www.entertainment.com/dine. Great for a night on the town or as a gift.

NEW
- Access **savings from top online retailers**. We have added hundreds of offers, so when you shop online start at entertainment.com.

- **Find it fast**—get driving directions, maps and offers near you. Search by merchant or by type of merchant.

NEW DISCOUNTS ADDED DAILY!

You must register your membership card at
www.entertainment.com/register
to get these exclusive member benefits and savings!

Privacy Policy: Please see our Privacy Policy on www.entertainment.com.

Introducing...

Find a place you like?

Now you can go back and save up to *20% once per month.** Just look for ![repeat savings] on the coupon and at www.entertainment.com for participating merchants.

HOW IT WORKS

STEP 1—**Select an offer.** Go to www.entertainment.com to find your Repeat Savings™ offers. Participating merchants in your book are also designated with ![repeat savings] on the coupon.

STEP 2—**Print.** Print the offer found at www.entertainment.com every month.

STEP 3—**Save.** Redeem your printable offer at Repeat Savings™ merchants each month.

Repeat each month for 20% savings!

*Most offers are up to 20% off (maximum discount $25) and available one time per month.

CLICK

PRINT

SAVE

REPEAT

You must register your Membership Card at
www.entertainment.com/register
to get this feature.

...and Now Easier to Use!

WHAT'S NEAR ME?
Check out our improved Neighborhood Index now including Printable Offers that you can access and print at entertainment.com. Also included in the Index Section at the back of the book is our Alphabetical Index!

SIMPLE ORGANIZATION
We have added a color bar with the name of the section on most pages to make it easier to find. Each section will start off with some of our most popular merchants followed by the section index and other great offers.

SAVINGS ON RESTAURANT CERTIFICATES/CARDS
Purchase restaurant certificates and cards for hundreds of restaurants across the country at www.entertainment.com/dine. Great for a night on the town or as a gift.

ORDER MOVIE, EVENTS & ATTRACTIONS TICKETS AT www.entertainment.com/tickets
Now order discount tickets online for many movies, concerts, sporting events, theater and special events. Listings are updated daily, so check back often.

TOP WEB DEALS
We have tripled the number of offers available at online retailers, bringing you the best of the Web. Listings are updated daily, so check back often.

You must register your Membership Card at
www.entertainment.com/register
to get this feature.

SAVINGS FOR YOU AND ALL THAT YOU DO

Teens

> Gaming, Music, Movies. It's got all the savings.

SAVE OVER $150

Families

> It's our guide to weekend activities for the family.

SAVE OVER $65

Life Tastes Good ™

www.simondelivers.com

$20 OFF
Your First Order
of $100 or more

$100 minimum purchase (not including alcohol, tobacco, or delivery fee) is required.
**Redeemable
www.simondelivers.com**
valid now thru 12/31/07
Code: HAPPEN20

Free Delivery
with any order of
$80 or more

$100 minimum purchase (not including alcohol, tobacco, or delivery fee) is required.
**Redeemable
www.simondelivers.com**
valid now thru 12/31/06
Code: HAPPEN1

Free Delivery
with any order of
$80 or more

$100 minimum purchase (not including alcohol, tobacco, or delivery fee) is required.
**Redeemable
www.simondelivers.com**
valid 01/01/07 thru 02/28/07
Code: HAPPEN2

Free Delivery
with any order of
$80 or more

$100 minimum purchase (not including alcohol, tobacco, or delivery fee) is required.
**Redeemable
www.simondelivers.com**
valid 03/01/07 thru 04/30/07
Code: HAPPEN3

Free Delivery
with any order of
$80 or more

$100 minimum purchase (not including alcohol, tobacco, or delivery fee) is required.
**Redeemable
www.simondelivers.com**
valid 05/01/07 thru 06/30/07
Code: HAPPEN4

Free Delivery
with any order of
$80 or more

$100 minimum purchase (not including alcohol, tobacco, or delivery fee) is required.
**Redeemable
www.simondelivers.com**
valid 07/01/07 thru 09/30/07
Code: HAPPEN5

Free Delivery
with any order of
$80 or more

$100 minimum purchase (not including alcohol, tobacco, or delivery fee) is required.
**Redeemable
www.simondelivers.com**
valid 10/01/07 thru 12/31/07
Code: HAPPEN6

AA1

www.simondelivers.com

Offer validity is governed by the Rules of Use and excludes defined holidays. Offers are not valid with other discount offers, unless specified. Coupons void if purchased, sold or bartered. Discounts exclude tax, tip and/or alcohol, where applicable.

Offer validity is governed by the Rules of Use and excludes defined holidays. Offers are not valid with other discount offers, unless specified. Coupons void if purchased, sold or bartered. Discounts exclude tax, tip and/or alcohol, where applicable.

Offer validity is governed by the Rules of Use and excludes defined holidays. Offers are not valid with other discount offers, unless specified. Coupons void if purchased, sold or bartered. Discounts exclude tax, tip and/or alcohol, where applicable.

Offer validity is governed by the Rules of Use and excludes defined holidays. Offers are not valid with other discount offers, unless specified. Coupons void if purchased, sold or bartered. Discounts exclude tax, tip and/or alcohol, where applicable.

Offer validity is governed by the Rules of Use and excludes defined holidays. Offers are not valid with other discount offers, unless specified. Coupons void if purchased, sold or bartered. Discounts exclude tax, tip and/or alcohol, where applicable.

Offer validity is governed by the Rules of Use and excludes defined holidays. Offers are not valid with other discount offers, unless specified. Coupons void if purchased, sold or bartered. Discounts exclude tax, tip and/or alcohol, where applicable.

Offer validity is governed by the Rules of Use and excludes defined holidays. Offers are not valid with other discount offers, unless specified. Coupons void if purchased, sold or bartered. Discounts exclude tax, tip and/or alcohol, where applicable.

CASUAL DINING & FAST FOOD

Find It Fast!
This section's index, found after the featured offers, lists offers by neighborhood!

OVER 490 OFFERS

plus more at
www.entertainment.com/dine

CHECK OUT THESE FEATURED OFFERS IN THE FRONT OF THIS SECTION:

i'm lovin' it™

www.mcdonalds.com

CASUAL DINING & FAST FOOD

---

 *ONE QUARTER POUNDER WITH CHEESE®

i'm lovin' it

Enjoy one complimentary
*QUARTER POUNDER WITH
CHEESE® when a second
*QUARTER POUNDER WITH
CHEESE® is purchased.

*weight before cooking - 4oz (113.4 gms); Not valid with any other offers

valid anytime after breakfast hours
One coupon per customer visit

Valid now thru 11/1/07
See reverse side for details   **A1**

 FREE BIG MAC®

i'm lovin' it

Enjoy one complimentary BIG
MAC® when a second BIG
MAC® is purchased.

Not valid with any other offers

valid anytime after breakfast hours

One coupon per customer visit

Valid now thru 11/1/07
See reverse side for details   **A2**

 MCGRIDDLES® BREAKFAST SANDWICH

Enjoy one complimentary
MCGRIDDLES® BREAKFAST
SANDWICH when a second
MCGRIDDLES® BREAKFAST
SANDWICH is purchased.

Not valid with any other offers

valid anytime during breakfast hours
One coupon per customer visit

Valid now thru 11/1/07
See reverse side for details   **A3**

CASUAL DINING & FAST FOOD

 entertainment.

NACHOS BELLGRANDE

Enjoy one complimentary NACHOS BELLGRANDE when a second NACHOS BELLGRANDE of equal or greater value is purchased.

Coupon code HPBELG

valid anytime

Valid now thru November 1, 2007 See reverse side for details A4

Valid at All Participating Border Foods Locations

www.borderfoods.com

Offer validity is governed by the Rules of Use and excludes defined holidays. Offers are not valid with other discount offers, unless specified. Coupons void if purchased, sold or bartered. Discounts exclude tax, tip and/or alcohol, where applicable.

HUNGRY FOR SAVINGS?

Classic Italian

LOCATE YOUR QUIZNOS SUB® AT WWW.QUIZNOS.COM OR 1-866-4-TOASTED.

FREE SUB!
BUY ANY SIZE TOASTY® COMBO AND GET A SECOND SUB OF EQUAL OR LESSER VALUE FREE

Valid through 12/31/07

Toasty Combo includes any size sub, small fountain drink and choice of chips, side salad or cookie. Free sub must be of equal or lesser value than sub purchased in the Toasty Combo. Free product includes a sub only, not a Toasty Combo. Not valid on delivery orders. This original coupon must be surrendered when ordering. Limit one coupon per person per visit. May not be combined with any other offer or coupon. Taxes not included. No cash value (unless prohibited by law, then cash value is $.005). Value of promotional item(s) varies by location. No substitutions. Void if copied or transferred and where prohibited. Valid in participating U.S. locations only. Offer validity is governed by the Rules of Use and excludes defined holidays. Coupons void if purchased, sold or bartered.

KIDS EAT FREE!
WITH PURCHASE OF ANY SIZE TOASTY® COMBO

Valid through 12/31/07

One free Quiz Kidz® Meal per each adult Toasty Combo purchased. Toasty Combo includes any size sub, small fountain drink and choice of chips, side salad or cookie. Not valid on delivery orders. This original coupon must be surrendered when ordering. Limit one coupon per person per visit. May not be combined with any other offer or coupon. Taxes not included. No cash value (unless prohibited by law, then cash value is $.005). Value of promotional item(s) varies by location. No substitutions. Void if copied or transferred and where prohibited. Valid in participating U.S. stores only. Offer validity is governed by the Rules of Use and excludes defined holidays. Coupons void if purchased, sold or bartered.

FREE CHIPS & DRINK!
FREE SMALL FOUNTAIN DRINK AND CHIPS WITH PURCHASE OF ANY REGULAR OR LARGE SUB

Valid through 12/31/07

Not valid on delivery orders, Real Deal™ menu or limited time offers. This original coupon must be surrendered when ordering. Limit one coupon per person per visit. May not be combined with any other offer or coupon. Taxes not included. No cash value (unless prohibited by law, then cash value is $.005). Value of promotional item(s) varies by location. No substitutions. Void if copied or transferred and where prohibited. Valid in participating U.S. locations only. Offer validity is governed by the Rules of Use and excludes defined holidays. Coupons void if purchased, sold or bartered.

$10 OFF!
ANY CATERING ORDER OVER $35 OR $5 OFF ANY CATERING ORDER OVER $20

Valid through 12/31/07

Not valid on delivery orders. This original coupon must be surrendered when ordering. Limit one coupon per order. May not be combined with any other offer or coupon. Taxes not included. No cash value (unless prohibited by law, then cash value is $.005). Value of promotional item(s) varies by location. No substitutions. Void if copied or transferred and where prohibited. Valid in participating U.S. stores only. Offer validity is governed by the Rules of Use and excludes defined holidays. Coupons void if purchased, sold or bartered.

Copyright 2006 QIP Holder LLC. All rights reserved. "Quiznos" and related marks are property of QIP Holder LLC.

TRY SOME OF THESE FAVORITES
Visit WWW.QUIZNOS.COM for the full menu

TOASTY® SUBS

Steak

Black Angus Steak on Rosemary Parmesan Bread
Black Angus steak, mozzarella, cheddar, mushrooms, sautéed onions, Honey Bourbon Mustard and Zesty Grille Sauce

Turkey

Turkey Ranch & Swiss
Turkey, Swiss, lettuce, tomato, red onion, Ranch Dressing

Turkey Bacon Guacamole
Turkey, bacon, guacamole, mozzarella, lettuce, tomato, red onion, Ranch Dressing

Smoked Turkey on Rosemary Parmesan Bread
Smoked turkey, Swiss, lettuce, tomato, red onion, Roasted Red Pepper Sauce

Chicken

Mesquite Chicken with Bacon
Mesquite chicken, bacon, cheddar, lettuce, tomato, red onion, Ranch Dressing

Chicken Carbonara
Chicken, bacon, mozzarella, mushrooms, Creamy Bacon Alfredo Sauce

Honey Mustard Chicken with Bacon on Italian Ciabatta Bread
Chicken, bacon, Swiss, lettuce, tomato, red onion, Honey Mustard Dressing

Signature Classics

Classic Italian
Salami, pepperoni, capicola, ham, mozzarella, lettuce, tomato, red onion, black olives, Red Wine Vinaigrette Dressing

The Traditional
Roast Beef, turkey, ham, cheddar, lettuce, tomato, red onion, black olives, Ranch Dressing

Double Bacon BLT
Double portion of hickory-smoked bacon, with tomato, shredded lettuce, mayonnaise

Clubs

Honey Bacon Club
Ham, turkey, bacon, Swiss, lettuce, tomato, red onion, Honey-French Dressing

Classic Club with Bacon
Turkey, ham, bacon, cheddar, lettuce, tomato, mayonnaise

Real Deal™ EVERYDAY VALUE MENU
Honey-Cured Ham
Deli Tuna
Steakhouse Beef Dip
Oven Roasted Turkey
Roast Beef
Meatball

Lite Selection

Honey Bourbon Chicken on Wheat Bread
Chicken, lettuce, tomato, red onion, Honey Bourbon Mustard

Turkey Lite on Wheat Bread
Turkey, lettuce, tomato, red onion, Fat-Free Red Wine

Veggie

Veggie
Guacamole, black olives, lettuce, tomato, red onion, mushrooms, mozzarella, cheddar, Red Wine Vinaigrette Dressing

CRAVEABLE SALADS

Roadhouse Ranch
Roast beef, bacon, cheddar, special recipe salad blend, cherry tomatoes, BBQ Sauce, Ranch Dressing

Honey Mustard Chicken
Chicken, bacon, cheddar, special recipe salad blend, cherry tomatoes, Honey Mustard Dressing

Black & Bleu
Black Angus steak strips, bleu cheese crumbles, red onion, special recipe salad blend, cherry tomatoes, Balsamic Vinaigrette Dressing

Roman Chicken
Chicken, parmesan, asiago and Romano cheese, special recipe salad blend, cherry tomatoes, Peppercorn Caesar Dressing

TOASTED GOURMET BREAD BOWLS™

Country French Chicken
Oven roasted chicken topped with broccoli cheese soup & melted cheddar cheese

Signature Steak 'N Chili
Tender steak topped with hearty chili & melted cheddar cheese

Southwest Chicken
Roasted chicken topped with creamy southwestern chicken corn chowder & melted cheddar cheese

SIGNATURE SOUPS
Broccoli Cheese
Chicken Noodle
Chicken & Corn Chowder
Chili

Served with Crackers

 **JUST FOR QUIZ KIDZ®**

Includes Quiz Kidz sub, drink, cookie, snack and a surprise!

Pizza Cheesy™
Pizza Pepperoni™
Toasty® Turkey & Cheese
Cheesy Toasted Cheese
Toasty® Ham & Cheese

All menu items subject to change
Check in-store menu board or visit WWW.QUIZNOS.COM for current menu

PIZZA HUT® MENU
GATHER 'ROUND THE GOOD STUFF!®

Supreme Pan Pizza

PICK YOUR CRUST!
- Pan Pizza
- Thin 'N Crispy
- Stuffed Crust
- Hand-Tossed

Crust Types May Vary By Location.

CREATE YOUR OWN!
Toppings:
Pepperoni, Beef Topping, Chicken, Bacon, Italian Sausage, Pork Topping, Ham, Black Olives, Red Onions, Tomatoes, Extra Cheese, Fresh Mushrooms, Green Peppers, Pineapple

Toppings May Vary By Location.

PICK YOUR RECIPE!
- Meat Lover's®
- Pepperoni Lover's®
- Cheese Lover's
- Veggie Lover's®
- Super Supreme
- Supreme

Recipes May Vary By Location.

MORE FOR YOUR MEAL!
- Breadsticks
- Buffalo Wings
- Drinks
- Baked Cinnamon Sticks

Side Items May Vary By Location.

For complete nutritional information, contact your local Pizza Hut restaurant or go to www.pizzahut.com. Prices, participation, delivery areas and charges may vary. Credit card availability may vary by location. The Pizza Hut name, logos and related marks are trademarks of Pizza Hut, Inc. ©2006 Pizza Hut, Inc.

Large Any Way You Want It

$10.99 Monday and Tuesday

$11.99 Wednesday through Sunday

Up to 3 Toppings, Specialty or Supreme. Super Supreme $1 more.
Valid on Pan, Thin 'N Crispy and Hand-Tossed Style Pizza (where available).
Only at participating locations. One coupon per order. Not valid with other offers. No duplication of toppings. Delivery areas and charges may vary. 1/20 cent cash redemption value. ©2006 Pizza Hut, Inc.

E2   Expires 12/31/07   A73

Family Feeding Frenzy

Buy 2 Medium Pizzas Any Way You Want Them & 10 Breadsticks for

$19.99

and get a FREE Pepsi® 2-Liter

Up to 3 Toppings, Specialty or Supreme. Super Supreme $1 more.
Valid on Pan, Thin 'N Crispy and Hand-Tossed Style Pizza (where available).
May substitute for 2-Liter.
Only at participating locations. One coupon per order. Not valid with other offers. No duplication of toppings. Delivery areas and charges may vary. 1/20 cent cash redemption value. PEPSI and PEPSI-COLA are registered trademarks of PepsiCo, Inc. ©2006 Pizza Hut, Inc.

E3   Expires 12/31/07   A73   A6

Family Feeding Frenzy

Buy 2 Medium Pizzas Any Way You Want Them & 10 Breadsticks for

$19.99

 and get a FREE Pepsi® 2-Liter

Up to 3 Toppings, Specialty or Supreme. Super Supreme $1 more.
Valid on Pan, Thin 'N Crispy® and Hand-Tossed Style Pizza (where available).
May substitute for 2-Liter.

Only at participating locations. One coupon per order. Not valid with other offers. No duplication of toppings. Delivery areas and charges may vary. 1/20 cent cash redemption value. PEPSI and PEPSI-COLA are registered trademarks of PepsiCo. ©2006 Pizza Hut, Inc.

Expires 12/31/07

E4   A73

Large Any Way You Want It

$10.99 $11.99
Monday and Tuesday | Wednesday through Sunday

Up to 3 Toppings, Specialty or Supreme. Super Supreme $1 more.
Valid on Pan, Thin 'N Crispy® and Hand-Tossed Style Pizza (where available).

Only at participating locations. One coupon per order. Not valid with other offers. No duplication of toppings. Delivery areas and charges may vary. 1/20 cent cash redemption value. ©2006 Pizza Hut, Inc.

Expires 12/31/07

E5   A73

Prices, participation, delivery areas and charges may vary. Credit card availability may vary by location.
The Pizza Hut name, logos and related marks are trademarks of Pizza Hut, Inc. ©2006 Pizza Hut, Inc.

Casual Dining & Fast Food Index

Multiple Locations

A & W	B52-B54
Angeno's	B60
Au Bon Pain	B34-B36
NEW Auntie Anne's	B55-B57
Baja Sol Tortilla Grill	B16-B18
Ben & Jerry's Ice Cream	B28-B30
Big Apple Bagels	B100-B101
Bobby & Steve's Auto World	B288
Camille's	B31-B33
NEW Carbone's	B61-B63
Chanticlear Pizza	B19-B21, B308
kids Culver's Frozen Custard	B4-B6
Domino's Pizza	B7-B9
Eddington's	B46-B47
kids Embers America Restaurant	B72
NEW Figaro's Pizza	B145
kids KarmelKorn	B43-B45
NEW Krispy Kreme Doughnuts	B15
NEW Linwood Pizza	B168
Long John Silver's	B257-B258
kids Orange Julius®	B25-B27
Pannekoeken Huis	B71
Papa John's Pizza	B22-B24
Pizza Man	B204
Pizza N' Pasta	B37-B39
Pizza Ranch	B206
NEW Quizno's Sub®	A5
Rocco's Pizza	B222
Roly Poly	B42
kids Snuffy's Malt Shop	B228
kids Steak Escape	B40-B41
kids Taco John's	B10-B12
kids TCBY	B232-B233
Wing Street	B254

Minnesota

Albertville
kids Rosetti's Pizza & Pasta	B223

Andover
Big Bite Pizza	B277
NEW Marco's Pizza	B175
The Meadows Restaurant & Sports Bar	B183

(continued)
State of Bean	B456
NEW Tasty Pizza	B231

Anoka
NEW Anoka Coffee Shop	B91
Diamonds Sports Bar & Grill	B132
Durkin's Pub	B135
NEW Fatso's	B142
Jackson Street Grill & Bar	B162
NEW Main Street Central Perk	B392
Spectators Grille & Bar	B68
Zebra Pizza & Tacos	B479

Belle Plaine
Duets	B134

Bethel
NEW Fatboys Bar & Grill	B141

Burnsville
Chinese Gourmet Restaurant	B311
kids Honeybaked Ham	B365-B367
J's Family Restaurant	B376
Maya Mexican Restaurante	B180
NEW Nina's Grill	B414
Q-Sharks Cafe	B431
NEW Renegades Bar & Grill	B218
Shooters Billiard Parlor & Cafe	B447

Cambridge
Cafe Caffeine	B297

Cedar
NEW Hunter's Inn Bar & Grill	B371

Champlin
5-8 Grill & Bar	B86
Enjoy China	B140

Chanhassen
NEW Aroma Cafe'	B265
NEW CJ's Coffee & Wine Bar	B113
NEW MaggieMoo's	B51
Pizzaioli Pizzamaker	B428

Chaska
Chaska Bakery	B309
NEW Coffee Cats Cafe	B315
NEW Heartbreakers Bar & Grill	B155

NEW **New Merchants Added This Year** kids **Great Place for Kids!**

Casual Dining & Fast Food Index

Circle Pines
- Miller's on Main............ B186

Cologne
- NEW J & D's 212 Club............ B375

Eden Prairie
- Coffee Oasis.............. B317
- NEW Detello's Pizza & Pasta....... .B131
- NEW Eden Restaurant............ B136
- Higher Grounds............ B362
- NEW Leonardo's............ B64-B66
- NEW Little Sushi on the Prairie...... .B169
- Qdoba Mexican Grill............ B67
- Red Moon Restaurant.......... B214

Elk River
- Big Vinny's Subs............. B281
- The Grille at Elk River Country Club....... B154
- NEW Northwoods Bar & Grill....... B198
- NEW Sarpino's Pizza............ B225

Excelsior
- NEW Cafe Lettieris............ B298
- Pizza Prima............ B205

Faribault
- NEW Dusek's Bakery............ B342

Forest Lake
- NEW Brick House Eatery.......... B108
- Country Home Bakery & Deli..... B325

Hamel
- NEW Rascal's Bar & Restaurant....... B213
- Rose Garden............ B440

Hopkins
- Boston Garden............ B289
- Country Glazed Ham Shop...... B324
- kids The Depot............ B130
- kids Honeybaked Ham......... B365-B367
- Jack Yee's Restaurant.......... B378
- Munkabeans & Sunshine...... B410
- Nick's Ice Cream & Popcorn..... B196
- NEW Tuttle's Shady Oak Grill....... B244
- Wanderer's Chinese Cuisine...... B251

Inver Grove Heights
- In the Spirit of Coffee, Cards & Gifts........ B372-B373
- Jersey's Bar & Grill.......... B381
- NEW Lastrack Family Restaurant..... B166
- NEW Turitto's Pizza & Subs......... B242

Jordan
- Cup of Knowledge........... B328

Lakeland
- Common Grounds Coffee House.... B320

Lakeville
- Babe's Sports Bar & Grill....... B93
- Blue Sky Creamery.......... B105
- NEW Cafe' Pierre............. B302
- Daddio's Take-N-Bake......... B332
- NEW Pizza Prima & Pasta.......... B427
- kids Tacoville............ B462

Long Lake
- The Red Rooster........... B216

Mankato
- Roadhouse 169 Bar & Grill...... B220

Maple Plain
- kids Pete's Pizza............ B423

Minneapolis
- 101 Blu............ B69
- NEW 1st of Thai Restaurant.......... B85
- Adrian's Tavern............ B259
- NEW Ambrosia Coffee........... B260
- kids American Pie......... B87,B261
- Amy's Classic Confections........ B262
- Anodyne @ 43rd........... B264
- Athen's Cafe............. B92
- Audubon Coffee......... B268-B269
- Auntie Em's............ B270
- The Backyard Bar & Grill........ B94
- NEW Bahn Thai Cuisine............ B273
- Be-Bop Sports Bar & Grill........ B96
- Betsy's Back Porch Coffee....... B274
- Betty's Bikes & Buns.......... B275
- Beyond Juice............ B99
- Big Daddy's Pizza........... B278
- NEW Big Dipper............ B279

NEW **New Merchants Added This Year** **Great Place for Kids!**

CASUAL DINING & FAST FOOD INDEX

- Big Stop Deli B280
- Blondies Sports Grill and Bar B104
- Blue Eyes Cafe B286
- Blue Moon Coffee Cafe B287
- Boston's B481-B484
- Bruck's Espresso Bar B293
- The Bulldog Restaurant B110
- Bunkers Music Bar & Grill B111
- Bunny's B112
- C. McGee's Deli B294
- Cafe Limon B299
- Cafe of the Americas B301
- Cafe Tatta Bunna B300
- Camden Coffee Company B304-B305
- The Cardinal Restaurant & Bar B115
- Cedar Inn Bar & Grill B306
- Cedar Market & Deli B307
- Charley's Grilled Subs B118
- Charly's Polleria Restaurant B116
- Chicago Deli Cafe & Grille B117
- Cinema Grill B123
- Coffee & Tea LTD. B124
- Col. Muzzy's Texas BBQ B319
- Crescent Moon Bakery B327
- Crystal Cafe & Grill B126
- Cupcake B127
- Cuppa Java B329-B330
- Cuzzy's B331
- Daily Grind B333
- Denny's 5th Ave. Bakery B336
- Diamonds Coffee Shoppe B337
- The Dinkytowner B133
- The District B84
- East African Taste Restaurant B343
- 8th Street Grill B137
- El Nuevo Rodeo B138
- El Paraiso Mexican Restaurant B139
- El Rey Bakery B344
- El Tequila Restaurante B345
- Eli's Food & Cocktails B77
- Espresso 22 .... B346
- Espresso Royale Cafe B348
- Fire Roast Mountain Cafe B349
- The Fish House B350

- Flashback Cafe
  & Cocktail Lounge B144
- Franklin Market & Deli B352
- Franklin Street Bakery B353
- Fresco Juice Company B146
- Freshens B147
- Gabby's Saloon & Eatery B148
- Great Steak & Potato Co. B153, B360
- Harold's Chicken B361
- Harvey's Bar & Grill B79
- Heavenly Daze Coffee B156
- Hollywood Scoops B363
- Holy Land Deli B364
- House of Java B369
- Hunan Restaurant B370
- Imperial Room B76
- International Business Cafe B374
- Jamaica Jamaica B163
- Java Restaurant B380
- Jerusalem's Restaurant B382
- Jimbo's B383
- JJ's Clubhouse B161
- JT's Restaurant & Pizza Parlor B377
- KinhDo Restaurant B165
- La Bodega Tapas Bar B78
- La Casita B70
- La Pinata B386
- Legends Bar & Grill B167
- Lone Tree Bar & Grill B170
- Loring Park Coffee House
  & Wine Bar B172
- MacKenzie B75
- Mady's Bowl and Lounge B390
- Mama Donato's B393
- Mama Taught Me How To
  Cook Soul Food Eatery! B394
- Mama's Bakery, Pizza
  & Salad Bar B395
- Manny's Tortas B396
- Marble Slab Creamery B174
- Margarita Bella B176
- Marina Grill & Deli B397
- Marino's Deli B398
- Marla's Indian
  & Caribbean Cuisine B177
- Martini's B178

NEW New Merchants Added This Year   **kids** Great Place for Kids!

Casual Dining & Fast Food Index

Marysburg Books B399-B400
Maxwell's B179
Mayslack's B181
(kids) Mel-O-Glaze Bakery B401
Mell's Beauty Bar B80
Mexico Y Mexico B402
Mias Pizza B403
Milda's Cafe B185
Ming's Palace B406
Mings Garden Restaurant B187,B407
Minneapolis Town Hall Brewery B188
Mochalini's B189
Mojos Pizza B408
Moose Bar & Grill B190
Muddy Paws Cheesecake B191
The Neighborhood
  Ice Cream Shoppe B411-B412
Nestle Tollhouse
  Cafe by Chip B193-B194
Nino's Pizza Plus B197
North Country Co-op B415
(NEW) Northern Espresso Cafe B416
(kids) Old Fashion Donut Shoppe B417
Pair of Dice Pizza B419
Panaderia El Rey B421
(NEW) Papa's Pizza and Pasta B199
Park Cafe B422
(kids) Park Tavern Lounge & Lanes B200
Pasquale's Sports Bar
  & Restaurant B201
Ping's Szechuan Star B202
(NEW) Pizza Flame B203
Pizza Magic B424
Pizzeria Uno B207
Plan B Coffeehouse B429
Porter's Bar and Grill B210
(NEW) Pretzel Time B211
Pupuseria El Rincon
  Salva Doreno B430
Qdoba Mexican Grill B67
Queen Of Cakes B432
Rail Station Bar & Grill B212
Rand Deli & Catering B433
The Red Pepper B215,B435
Red Sea Restaurant B217
The Refuge B83

Restaurante Guayaquil B219,B436
Riverside Restaurant B438
Rocky Rococo B439
Rosen's City Tavern B82
Sally's Saloon & Eatery B224
Scandia Bake Shop B441
Scoops Pub B226
Scoreboard Pizza B442
2nd Moon Coffee Cafe B443
Shaw's Bar & Grill B445
Shell's Cafe B446
Sindbad Cafe & Market B448
(kids) Soho Cafe B451
The Sportsman's Pub B229
Spring Street Tavern B230
(kids) Square Peg Diner B454
(NEW) Sun Ray Restaurant B457
Sweet Taste of Italy B458-B460
Taraccino Coffee B463
The Tea Garden B235
Tea Source B236
TJ's of Edina B234
Tortilla Ria Mexican Cafe B466
Tropicana B241
(NEW) Twisted Shamrock Pub & Grill B467
(NEW) Two Stooges Sports Bar & Grill B245
Ubah Restaurant B468
(NEW) Uptown Pizza B246
Vescio's B247
Vientiane Restaurant B470
Villa Pizza B249
Village Blend B472
Waberi Somalian Restaurant B474
The Wagon Grill B250
Waldo's Bar & Grill B475
(NEW) The Well Sports Tavern & Grill B252
Wing Joint B477
Wolves Den Native Coffee B255
Zebra Pizza & Tacos B479

Minnetonka

General Store Cafe B150
Glen Lake Coffee Co. B356-B357

Mound

(NEW) Tokyo Express B465

(NEW) **New Merchants Added This Year** (kids) **Great Place for Kids!**

CASUAL DINING & FAST FOOD INDEX

NORTHFIELD
- The Mock Turtle B464

OSSEO
- *NEW* Boston's B481-B484
- *NEW* Chin Yung B120
- Country Glazed Ham Shop B324
- Gator's Garden Cafe B149
- The Lookout Bar & Grill B171
- *NEW* MaggieMoo's B51
- Mongkok B409
- Qdoba Mexican Grill B67
- Segue Cafe B444
- Yarn Cafe B478

PRIOR LAKE
- City Perks Coffee House B313

RED WING
- Andy's Sports Bar & Grill B263
- *kids* Bev's Cafe B276
- *NEW* The Galley Room B354

ROCHESTER
- *kids* Great Steak & Potato Co. B153,B360

ROGERS
- *NEW* Luna Blu B389

ROSEMOUNT
- McDivot's Sports Pub & Eatery B182

SAINT FRANCIS
- Boulevard Coffee B290
- *NEW* Tasty Pizza B231

SAINT PAUL
- 5-8 Tavern & Grill B81
- *NEW* Ambrosia Coffee B260
- American Sports Cafe & Nightclub. . . B88
- *kids* Andy's Garage B89
- *kids* Aroma's Pizza & Cafe B266
- *NEW* Artists' Grind B267
- Aurelio's. B271
- Avalon Tearoom
  & Pastry Shoppe. B272
- Bascali's Brick Oven. B95
- *NEW* The Bean Factory B97
- The Bird Nightclub. B102
- Black Bear Crossings B282

- Blink Bonnie B283
- Blondies Cafe B103
- *NEW* Blue Cat Coffee & Tea B284-B285
- Boca Chica. B106
- *NEW* Brewberry's Coffee Shop B107
- Brothers Coffee B291
- Bru House Coffee Shop B292
- Cabin Fever B295
- Capital City Market Cafe & Bar B114
- China Wok Restaurant. B310
- Chocolat Celeste. B121
- *NEW* Chula Vista B122
- Cinema Espresso B312
- Classic Pizza. B314
- Coffee Cottage B316
- Copper Dome Restaurant B321
- Cora's Best Chicken Wings. B322
- Cosmic's Cafe B323
- *NEW* Creative Catering B326
- CuppaChiodo's B128
- *NEW* Dar's Double Scoop B335
- Don Panchos Bakery B338
- Dorothy Ann Bakery & Cafe. B339
- Dugout Bar B341
- Espresso Donut Co. B347
- 5 Star Cafe B351
- *kids* Flaherty's Pub & Grill B143
- *NEW* Genghis Grill B151-B152
- Giuseppe's B355
- Golden's Cafe & Deli B358
- Grandma Rita's Cafe B359
- *kids* Honeybaked Ham. B365-B367
- Hong Wong B368
- Hunan Garden
  Chinese Restaurant B158
- In the Spirit of Coffee,
  Cards & Gifts B372-B373
- J.R. Mac's Bar & Grill B159-B160
- Jade Island Cuisine B379
- Kalli's Popcorn Shop. B384
- *NEW* La Casita B70
- *NEW* Leonardo's B64-B66
- Limu Coffee. B387
- *NEW* Lori's Coffee House B388
- The Mediterranean Cruise Cafe B184

NEW **New Merchants Added This Year**   *kids* **Great Place for Kids!**

CASUAL DINING & FAST FOOD INDEX

- [NEW] Midway Rendezvous Cafe....... B404
- [NEW] Mim's Cafe B405
- Muddy Paws Cheesecake B191
- [NEW] The Neighborhood Cafe........ B192
- New York Burrito B413
- Over The Rainbow.......... B418
- Paisano's Pizza & Hot Hoagies B420
- Pizza Pazza............... B425
- Pizza Planet.............. B426
- Plums Neighborhood Grill & Bar......... B208-B209
- [NEW] Razs Cafe B434
- Roberts Sports Bar & Entertainment.......... B221
- [NEW] Salsarita's Fresh Cantina B58-B59
- Skinners Pub & Eatery B227
- The Smooth Grind........... B449
- [NEW] Snelling Cafe B450
- Sojourner's Cafe......... B452-B453
- St. Paul Bagelry & Deli B455
- The Tea Garden B235
- Tea Source B236
- Tiffany's Sports Lounge........ B238
- Valley Sports Pub & Grill B469
- Villa Pizza................ B249
- Villa Roma Pizzaria........... B471
- [kids] Wabasha Deli B473
- [kids] West Side Lanes............ B476
- The Whiskey Rack........... B253
- [kids] [NEW] Zobota Cafe.............. B256

SAVAGE
- Buffalo Tap B109
- [NEW] Cactus Grill Mexican Buffet B296
- Spectators Grille & Bar B68
- Tin Shed Tavern & Pizza........ B239
- [NEW] Tropical Smoothie Cafe B240

SHAKOPEE
- Coffee Ta Cream............ B318
- Taco Loco B461
- [NEW] Thailand View............. B237
- Turtle's Bar & Grill........... B243
- Zuppa Cucina B480

SOUTH SAINT PAUL
- [NEW] The Coop Restaurant B125

- [kids] Judes Coffee & Eatery......... B164
- [NEW] Restaurante La Rancherita B437

STILLWATER
- Angel O'Malley's B90
- Charlie's Irish Pub........... B119
- The Daily Grind B129,B334
- Darla's Grill & Malt Shop B73-B74
- Dreamcoat Cafe............ B340
- [NEW] Mai Thai Cafe B173

VICTORIA
- Victoria House............. B248

WACONIA
- [NEW] Beef 'O' Brady's Family Sports Pub.............. B485
- Hopper's Bar & Grill.......... B157

WASECA
- The Daily Grind B129,B334
- [NEW] Katie O'Leary's Beef & Brew B385

WAYZATA
- Beanhaven Cafe............ B98
- Caffe de Lago B303
- Maggie's Restaurant B391

WISCONSIN

HUDSON
- Darla's Grill & Malt Shop B73-B74

OTHER
- [kids] Blimpie Subs & Salads.......... B48
- [NEW] Cold Stone Creamery B13-B14
- Dairy Queen® B49-B50
- [kids] McDonald's®......... A1-A3,B1-B3
- [NEW] Nick-N-Willy's Take-N-Bake...... B195
- [kids] Pizza Hut A6
- [kids] Taco Bell® A4

Register at
entertainment.com/register
to access even more of these
great savings!

[NEW] **New Merchants Added This Year**   [kids] **Great Place for Kids!**

McDonald's®

Enjoy one complimentary BIG MAC® when a second BIG MAC® is purchased.
See reverse for Offer Details.

See Reverse Side for Locations

Valid now thru November 1, 2007

B1

McDonald's®

Enjoy one complimentary MEDIUM SOFT DRINK OR DASANI® BOTTLED WATER when one PREMIUM SALAD is purchased at regular price.
See reverse for Offer Details.

See Reverse Side for Locations

Valid now thru November 1, 2007

B2

McDonald's®

Enjoy one complimentary SAUSAGE McMUFFIN® WITH EGG SANDWICH when a second SAUSAGE McMUFFIN® WITH EGG SANDWICH is purchased.
See reverse for Offer Details.

See Reverse Side for Locations

Valid now thru November 1, 2007

B3

CASUAL DINING & FAST FOOD

McDonald's®

i'm lovin' it

Valid at participating restaurants in Minnesota & Western Wisconsin

Cash value 1/20 of 1 cent

®2006 McDonald's Corporation

Offer Details: Valid anytime after breakfast hours. Not valid with any other offers. One coupon per customer visit.

00072458

Offer validity is governed by the Rules of Use and excludes defined holidays. Offers are not valid with other discount offers, unless specified. Coupons void if purchased, sold or bartered. Discounts exclude tax, tip and/or alcohol, where applicable.

McDonald's®

i'm lovin' it

Valid at participating restaurants in Minnesota & Western Wisconsin

Cash value 1/20 of 1 cent

®2006 McDonald's Corporation

Offer Details: Valid anytime after breakfast hours. Not valid with any other offers; Excludes Fruit & Walnut Salad and side salad. One coupon per customer visit.

00072473

Offer validity is governed by the Rules of Use and excludes defined holidays. Offers are not valid with other discount offers, unless specified. Coupons void if purchased, sold or bartered. Discounts exclude tax, tip and/or alcohol, where applicable.

McDonald's®

i'm lovin' it

Valid at participating restaurants in Minnesota & Western Wisconsin

Cash value 1/20 of 1 cent

®2006 McDonald's Corporation

Offer Details: Valid anytime during breakfast hours. Not valid with any other offers. One coupon per customer visit.

00072487

Offer validity is governed by the Rules of Use and excludes defined holidays. Offers are not valid with other discount offers, unless specified. Coupons void if purchased, sold or bartered. Discounts exclude tax, tip and/or alcohol, where applicable.

Culver's Frozen Custard

Enjoy one complimentary DOUBLE BUTTERBURGER CHEESE SANDWICH when a second DOUBLE BUTTERBURGER CHEESE SANDWICH of equal or greater value is purchased.
See reverse for Offer Details.

Valid at All Participating Locations

Valid now thru November 1, 2007

B4

Culver's Frozen Custard

Enjoy one complimentary MEDIUM FROZEN CUSTARD SHAKE OR MALT when a second MEDIUM FROZEN CUSTARD SHAKE OR MALT of equal or greater value is purchased.
See reverse for Offer Details.

Valid at All Participating Locations

Valid now thru November 1, 2007

B5

Culver's Frozen Custard

Enjoy one complimentary TWO SCOOP SUNDAE when a second TWO SCOOP SUNDAE of equal or greater value is purchased.
See reverse for Offer Details.

Valid at All Participating Locations

Valid now thru November 1, 2007

B6

CASUAL DINING & FAST FOOD

Culver's Frozen Custard
- Fresh, never frozen, lean ground chuck blend
- 5%-10% leaner than a national brand burger
- Lightly toasted buttered bun for an old-fashioned flavor
- Always fresh, cooked to order

Valid at All Participating Locations

Offer Details: Valid anytime. Not valid with any other discounts or promotions; Limit one coupon per person per visit at Participating Culver's Frozen Custard Restaurants.

00095313

Offer validity is governed by the Rules of Use and excludes defined holidays. Offers are not valid with other discount offers, unless specified. Coupons void if purchased, sold or bartered. Discounts exclude tax, tip and/or alcohol, where applicable.

Culver's Frozen Custard
- Every guest who chooses Culver's leaves happy!
- Visit www.culvers.com to locate a Culver's® near you
- Frozen Custard...It's Better Than Ice Cream

Valid at All Participating Locations

Offer Details: Valid anytime. Not valid with any other discounts or promotions; Limit one coupon per person per visit at Participating Culver's Frozen Custard Restaurants.

00664877

Offer validity is governed by the Rules of Use and excludes defined holidays. Offers are not valid with other discount offers, unless specified. Coupons void if purchased, sold or bartered. Discounts exclude tax, tip and/or alcohol, where applicable.

Culver's Frozen Custard
- "Premium ice cream"
- Made in small batches
- Always served fresh
- Chocolate, vanilla & a flavor of the day, everyday!
- Visit www.culvers.com to locate a Culver's® near you

Valid at All Participating Locations

Offer Details: Valid anytime. Not valid with any other discounts or promotions; Limit one coupon per person per visit at Participating Culver's Frozen Custard Restaurants.

00664882

Offer validity is governed by the Rules of Use and excludes defined holidays. Offers are not valid with other discount offers, unless specified. Coupons void if purchased, sold or bartered. Discounts exclude tax, tip and/or alcohol, where applicable.

Domino's Pizza

Enjoy one complimentary LARGE ORIGINAL OR THIN CRUST PIZZA when a second LARGE ORIGINAL OR THIN CRUST PIZZA of equal or greater value is purchased.
See reverse for Offer Details.
Tracking Code: 400

FREE LARGE ORIGINAL OR THIN CRUST PIZZA

www.dominos.com

Valid at All Participating Locations

Valid now thru November 1, 2007

B7

Domino's Pizza

Enjoy one complimentary LARGE ORIGINAL OR THIN CRUST PIZZA when a second LARGE ORIGINAL OR THIN CRUST PIZZA of equal or greater value is purchased.
See reverse for Offer Details.
Tracking Code: 400

FREE LARGE ORIGINAL OR THIN CRUST PIZZA

www.dominos.com

Valid at All Participating Locations

Valid now thru November 1, 2007

B8

Domino's Pizza

Enjoy one complimentary LARGE ORIGINAL OR THIN CRUST PIZZA & BREAD SIDE ITEM when a second LARGE ORIGINAL OR THIN CRUST PIZZA & BREAD SIDE ITEM of equal or greater value is purchased.
See reverse for Offer Details.
Tracking Code: 652

FREE LG., ORIG. OR THIN CRUST PIZZA & BREAD

www.dominos.com

Valid at All Participating Locations

Valid now thru November 1, 2007

B9

Domino's Pizza
- Try our delicious side items, Buffalo Wings, Chicken Kickers, bread sticks, dessert CinnaStix & Cheesy Bread
- Don't forget our 2x Tuesday special!
- Call 1-800-DOMINOS to find the location that delivers to your area
- Please mention coupon when ordering

Valid at All Participating Locations

00663509

Offer Details: Valid anytime. Carry out only. Offer valid on regular price pizza only; Valid holidays.

Offer validity is governed by the Rules of Use and excludes defined holidays. Offers are not valid with other discount offers, unless specified. Coupons void if purchased, sold or bartered. Discounts exclude tax, tip and/or alcohol, where applicable.

Domino's Pizza
- Try our delicious side items, Buffalo Wings, Chicken Kickers, bread sticks, dessert CinnaStix & Cheesy Bread
- Don't forget our 2x Tuesday special!
- Call 1-800-DOMINOS to find the location that delivers to your area
- Please mention coupon when ordering

Valid at All Participating Locations

00663509

Offer Details: Valid anytime. Carry out only. Offer valid on regular price pizza only; Valid holidays.

Offer validity is governed by the Rules of Use and excludes defined holidays. Offers are not valid with other discount offers, unless specified. Coupons void if purchased, sold or bartered. Discounts exclude tax, tip and/or alcohol, where applicable.

Domino's Pizza
- Try our delicious side items, Buffalo Wings, Chicken Kickers, bread sticks, dessert CinnaStix & Cheesy Bread
- Don't forget our 2x Tuesday special!
- Call 1-800-DOMINOS to find the location that delivers to your area
- Please mention coupon when ordering

Valid at All Participating Locations

Offer Details: Valid anytime. Carry out only. Offer valid on regular price pizza only; Valid holidays.

00663513

Offer validity is governed by the Rules of Use and excludes defined holidays. Offers are not valid with other discount offers, unless specified. Coupons void if purchased, sold or bartered. Discounts exclude tax, tip and/or alcohol, where applicable.

Taco John's

Enjoy one complimentary CHICKEN OR BEEF MEAT & POTATO BURRITO when a second CHICKEN OR BEEF MEAT & POTATO BURRITO of equal or greater value is purchased.
See reverse for Offer Details.

See Reverse Side for Locations

Valid now thru November 1, 2007   B10

Taco John's

Enjoy one complimentary CHICKEN OR BEEF SOFT SHELL TACO when a second CHICKEN OR BEEF SOFT SHELL TACO of equal or greater value is purchased.
See reverse for Offer Details.

See Reverse Side for Locations

Valid now thru November 1, 2007   B11

Taco John's

Enjoy one complimentary SUPER BURRITO when a second SUPER BURRITO of equal or greater value is purchased.
See reverse for Offer Details.

See Reverse Side for Locations

Valid now thru November 1, 2007   B12

Taco John's
- Valid at listed locations only

MINNESOTA
Blaine
12497 Hwy. 65 & 242
(763)754-3723

515 Northtown Dr.
(763)784-9302

Brooklyn Center
1361 Brookdale Ctr.
(763)561-8000

Cambridge
225 2nd Ave. NE
(763)689-4553

Faribault
1431 N.W. 4th St.
(507)334-3287

Forest Lake
32 Southlake Ave.
(651)464-7590

Hutchinson
134 - 4th Ave. NW
(320)587-3424

New Brighton
2040 Silver Lake Rd.
(651)636-8065

North St. Paul
2201 11th Ave. E
(651)770-0913

Oak Park Heights
5910 Neal Ave. N.
(651)439-7771

Oakdale
1010 Gershwin Ave. N
(651)738-6831

Princeton
301 S LaGrande Ave.
(763)389-5478

Ramsey
6401 Hwy. 10 N.W.
(763)433-9099

St. Paul
3338 Rice St.
(651)483-5776

888 E. Maryland Ave.
(651)774-8307

White Bear Lake
4430 S. Lake St.
(651)653-5997

WISCONSIN
Hudson
710 11th St.
(715)386-5522

Menomonie
1212 N Broadway
(715)235-4477

Rice Lake
2410 S Main St.
(715)234-3011

Offer Details: Valid anytime. One coupon per customer per visit.

00097876

Offer validity is governed by the Rules of Use and excludes defined holidays. Offers are not valid with other discount offers, unless specified. Coupons void if purchased, sold or bartered. Discounts exclude tax, tip and/or alcohol, where applicable.

Taco John's
- Valid at listed locations only

MINNESOTA
Blaine
12497 Hwy. 65 & 242
(763)754-3723

515 Northtown Dr.
(763)784-9302

Brooklyn Center
1361 Brookdale Ctr.
(763)561-8000

Cambridge
225 2nd Ave. NE
(763)689-4553

Faribault
1431 N.W. 4th St.
(507)334-3287

Forest Lake
32 Southlake Ave.
(651)464-7590

Hutchinson
134 - 4th Ave. NW
(320)587-3424

New Brighton
2040 Silver Lake Rd.
(651)636-8065

North St. Paul
2201 11th Ave. E
(651)770-0913

Oak Park Heights
5910 Neal Ave. N.
(651)439-7771

Oakdale
1010 Gershwin Ave. N
(651)738-6831

Princeton
301 S LaGrande Ave.
(763)389-5478

Ramsey
6401 Hwy. 10 N.W.
(763)433-9099

St. Paul
3338 Rice St.
(651)483-5776

888 E. Maryland Ave.
(651)774-8307

White Bear Lake
4430 S. Lake St.
(651)653-5997

WISCONSIN
Hudson
710 11th St.
(715)386-5522

Menomonie
1212 N Broadway
(715)235-4477

Rice Lake
2410 S Main St.
(715)234-3011

Offer Details: Valid anytime. One coupon per customer per visit.

00097877

Offer validity is governed by the Rules of Use and excludes defined holidays. Offers are not valid with other discount offers, unless specified. Coupons void if purchased, sold or bartered. Discounts exclude tax, tip and/or alcohol, where applicable.

Taco John's
- Valid at listed locations only

MINNESOTA
Blaine
12497 Hwy. 65 & 242
(763)754-3723

515 Northtown Dr.
(763)784-9302

Brooklyn Center
1361 Brookdale Ctr.
(763)561-8000

Cambridge
225 2nd Ave. NE
(763)689-4553

Faribault
1431 N.W. 4th St.
(507)334-3287

Forest Lake
32 Southlake Ave.
(651)464-7590

Hutchinson
134 - 4th Ave. NW
(320)587-3424

New Brighton
2040 Silver Lake Rd.
(651)636-8065

North St. Paul
2201 11th Ave. E
(651)770-0913

Oak Park Heights
5910 Neal Ave. N.
(651)439-7771

Oakdale
1010 Gershwin Ave. N
(651)738-6831

Princeton
301 S LaGrande Ave.
(763)389-5478

Ramsey
6401 Hwy. 10 N.W.
(763)433-9099

St. Paul
3338 Rice St.
(651)483-5776

888 E. Maryland Ave.
(651)774-8307

White Bear Lake
4430 S. Lake St.
(651)653-5997

WISCONSIN
Hudson
710 11th St.
(715)386-5522

Menomonie
1212 N Broadway
(715)235-4477

Rice Lake
2410 S Main St.
(715)234-3011

Offer Details: Valid anytime. One coupon per customer per visit.

00097878

Offer validity is governed by the Rules of Use and excludes defined holidays. Offers are not valid with other discount offers, unless specified. Coupons void if purchased, sold or bartered. Discounts exclude tax, tip and/or alcohol, where applicable.

Cold Stone Creamery

Enjoy one complimentary LOVE IT (regular) OR GOTTA HAVE IT (large) ICE CREAM when a second LOVE IT (regular) OR GOTTA HAVE IT (large) ICE CREAM of equal or greater value is purchased.
See reverse for Offer Details.
Tracking Code: plu # 80

Valid at all Minnesota locations

Valid now thru November 1, 2007

B13

Cold Stone Creamery

Enjoy $4 OFF any SIGNATURE CAKE (excludes petite cakes).
See reverse for Offer Details.
Tracking Code: plu # 79

Valid at all Minnesota locations

Valid now thru November 1, 2007

B14

Krispy Kreme Doughnuts

Enjoy ONE DOZEN ORIGINAL GLAZED when a second DOZEN ORIGINAL GLAZED of equal or greater value is purchased.
See reverse for Offer Details.

See Reverse Side for Locations

Valid now thru November 1, 2007

B15

CASUAL DINING & FAST FOOD

Cold Stone Creamery

- Cold Stone Creamery® offers the best in smooth & creamy ice cream, made fresh daily in every store
- Choose your favorite mix-ins, including fresh baked brownies, fruits, pie filling, candies, cookies & nuts
- Ice Cream Creations™ are mixed on a cold granite stone, then served in a fresh-baked waffle cone or bowl
- Come & indulge today!

Valid at all Minnesota locations

00702704

Offer Details: Valid anytime.

Offer validity is governed by the Rules of Use and excludes defined holidays. Offers are not valid with other discount offers, unless specified. Coupons void if purchased, sold or bartered. Discounts exclude tax, tip and/or alcohol, where applicable.

Cold Stone Creamery

- Cold Stone Creamery® offers the best in smooth & creamy ice cream, made fresh daily in every store
- Choose your favorite mix-ins, including fresh baked brownies, fruits, pie filling, candies, cookies & nuts
- Ice Cream Creations™ are mixed on a cold granite stone, then served in a fresh-baked waffle cone or bowl
- Come & indulge today!

Valid at all Minnesota locations

00702758

Offer Details: Valid anytime.

Offer validity is governed by the Rules of Use and excludes defined holidays. Offers are not valid with other discount offers, unless specified. Coupons void if purchased, sold or bartered. Discounts exclude tax, tip and/or alcohol, where applicable.

Krispy Kreme Doughnuts

14989 Florence Trail
Apple Valley, MN
(952)891-4828

3388 River Rapids Dr.
Coon Rapids, MN
(763)576-0871

12950 Technology Dr.
Eden Prairie, MN
(952)914-9511

7851 Elm Creek Blvd.
Maple Grove, MN
(763)416-6060

1825 Suburban
St. Paul, MN
(651)739-8888

Offer Details: Valid anytime.

00701130

Offer validity is governed by the Rules of Use and excludes defined holidays. Offers are not valid with other discount offers, unless specified. Coupons void if purchased, sold or bartered. Discounts exclude tax, tip and/or alcohol, where applicable.

Baja Sol Tortilla Grill

Enjoy one complimentary ENTREE & SOFT DRINK when a second ENTREE & SOFT DRINK of equal or greater value is purchased.

See reverse for Offer Details.

Valid now thru November 1, 2007

See Reverse Side for Locations

B16

Baja Sol Tortilla Grill

Enjoy one complimentary ENTREE & SOFT DRINK when a second ENTREE & SOFT DRINK of equal or greater value is purchased.

See reverse for Offer Details.

Valid now thru November 1, 2007

See Reverse Side for Locations

B17

Baja Sol Tortilla Grill

Enjoy one complimentary ENTREE & SOFT DRINK when a second ENTREE & SOFT DRINK of equal or greater value is purchased.

See reverse for Offer Details.

Valid now thru November 1, 2007

See Reverse Side for Locations

B18

CASUAL DINING & FAST FOOD

Baja Sol Tortilla Grill
- The freshest Mex under the sun!
- Unlimited hot chips & fresh salsa bar w/ every entree purchase!
- Fresh made tortillas
- Skinless chicken breast & choice sirloin steak
- Fresh vegetables- made to order
- Catering available

BAJA SOL
TORTILLA GRILL

Minneapolis
1730 New Brighton Blvd.
(The Quarry)
(612)788-3000

2300 Hennepin Ave.
(Uptown)
(612)374-9900

City Center 40 S. 7th St., #93
(Skyway level)
(612)332-2505

U.S. Bank Plaza Atrium
200 S. 6th St.
(612)333-2003

Rochester
1141 6th St. N.W.
(Barlow Plaza)
(507)529-8892

Roseville
2100 Snelling Ave. N.
(Har Mar Mall)
(651)697-9000

St. Louis Park
4997 Excelsior Rd,
(Miracle Mile)
(952)926-9097

00663152

Offer Details: Valid anytime.

Offer validity is governed by the Rules of Use and excludes defined holidays. Offers are not valid with other discount offers, unless specified. Coupons void if purchased, sold or bartered. Discounts exclude tax, tip and/or alcohol, where applicable.

Baja Sol Tortilla Grill
- The freshest Mex under the sun!
- Unlimited hot chips & fresh salsa bar w/ every entree purchase!
- Fresh made tortillas
- Skinless chicken breast & choice sirloin steak
- Fresh vegetables- made to order
- Catering available

BAJA SOL
TORTILLA GRILL

Minneapolis
1730 New Brighton Blvd.
(The Quarry)
(612)788-3000

2300 Hennepin Ave.
(Uptown)
(612)374-9900

City Center 40 S. 7th St., #93
(Skyway level)
(612)332-2505

U.S. Bank Plaza Atrium
200 S. 6th St.
(612)333-2003

Rochester
1141 6th St. N.W.
(Barlow Plaza)
(507)529-8892

Roseville
2100 Snelling Ave. N.
(Har Mar Mall)
(651)697-9000

St. Louis Park
4997 Excelsior Rd,
(Miracle Mile)
(952)926-9097

00663152

Offer Details: Valid anytime.

Offer validity is governed by the Rules of Use and excludes defined holidays. Offers are not valid with other discount offers, unless specified. Coupons void if purchased, sold or bartered. Discounts exclude tax, tip and/or alcohol, where applicable.

Baja Sol Tortilla Grill
- The freshest Mex under the sun!
- Unlimited hot chips & fresh salsa bar w/ every entree purchase!
- Fresh made tortillas
- Skinless chicken breast & choice sirloin steak
- Fresh vegetables- made to order
- Catering available

BAJA SOL
TORTILLA GRILL

Minneapolis
1730 New Brighton Blvd.
(The Quarry)
(612)788-3000

2300 Hennepin Ave.
(Uptown)
(612)374-9900

City Center 40 S. 7th St., #93
(Skyway level)
(612)332-2505

U.S. Bank Plaza Atrium
200 S. 6th St.
(612)333-2003

Rochester
1141 6th St. N.W.
(Barlow Plaza)
(507)529-8892

Roseville
2100 Snelling Ave. N.
(Har Mar Mall)
(651)697-9000

St. Louis Park
4997 Excelsior Rd,
(Miracle Mile)
(952)926-9097

00663152

Offer Details: Valid anytime.

Offer validity is governed by the Rules of Use and excludes defined holidays. Offers are not valid with other discount offers, unless specified. Coupons void if purchased, sold or bartered. Discounts exclude tax, tip and/or alcohol, where applicable.

Chanticlear Pizza
Enjoy any MEDIUM PIZZA at 50% off the regular price.
See reverse for Offer Details.

Up to $8.00 Value

www.chanticlearpizza.com

See Reverse Side for Locations

Valid now thru November 1, 2007

B19

Chanticlear Pizza
Enjoy one complimentary LARGE PIZZA when a second LARGE PIZZA of equal or greater value is purchased.
See reverse for Offer Details.

Up to $20.00 Value

Chanticlear Pizza®

www.chanticlearpizza.com

See Reverse Side for Locations

Valid now thru November 1, 2007

B20

Chanticlear Pizza
Enjoy one complimentary MEDIUM PIZZA when a second MEDIUM PIZZA of equal or greater value is purchased.
See reverse for Offer Details.

Up to $16.00 Value

Chanticlear Pizza®

www.chanticlearpizza.com

See Reverse Side for Locations

Valid now thru November 1, 2007

B21

CASUAL DINING & FAST FOOD

Chanticlear Pizza

- Delicious Pizza Every Time!™
- The area's best thin crust pizza!
- Ask about our nightly specials

Chanticlear Pizza®

Andover
1573 154th Ave. N.W.
(763)434-6554

Anoka
440 Bunker Lake Blvd. N.W.
(Bunker Lake Blvd. & Ferry St.)
(763)421-4242

Arden Hills
3551 Lexington Ave.
(651)490-1313

Blaine
914 125th Ln. N.E.
(1 mi. E. of Blaine High School, off of Hwy. 242)
(763)754-0800

Champlin
11632 Winnetka Ave. N.
(763)427-6300

Coon Rapids
2835 Northdale Blvd.
(1 Mile W. of Coon Rapids High School)
(763)757-2020

Crystal
6236 Bass Lake Rd.
(Bass Lake Rd. & Hwy. 81)
(763)535-0777

Eden Prairie
8793 Columbine Rd.
(Hwy. 212 & Anderson Lakes Pkwy.)
(952)252-2222

Elk River
19328 Hwy. 169 N.W.
(763)274-2225

Fridley
1262 E. Moore Lake Dr.
(763)571-9595

Ham Lake
18015 Ulysses St.
(181st Ave. & Hwy. 65)
(763)434-3333

Inver Grove
9034 Cahill Ave.
(651)451-7677

Lino Lakes
7771 Lake Dr.
(651)786-7022

Maple Grove
9511 Black Oats Ln.
(E. of Wal-Mart Supercenter, behind McDonalds)
(763)494-9949

Monticello
9375 Deegan Ave.
(763)295-7774

New Hope
9428A 36th Ave.
(Hwy. 169 & 36th Ave.)
(763)593-1313

Rogers
14000 Northdale Blvd.
(763)494-9990

Vadnais Heights
1032 E. Hwy. 96
(651)255-5000

Offer Details: Valid anytime. Carryout only. One coupon per customer per visit; Not valid with any other offer.

00650679

Offer validity is governed by the Rules of Use and excludes defined holidays. Offers are not valid with other discount offers, unless specified. Coupons void if purchased, sold or bartered. Discounts exclude tax, tip and/or alcohol, where applicable.

Chanticlear Pizza

- Delicious Pizza Every Time!™
- The area's best thin crust pizza!
- Ask about our nightly specials

Chanticlear Pizza®

Andover
1573 154th Ave. N.W.
(763)434-6554

Anoka
440 Bunker Lake Blvd. N.W.
(Bunker Lake Blvd. & Ferry St.)
(763)421-4242

Arden Hills
3551 Lexington Ave.
(651)490-1313

Blaine
914 125th Ln. N.E.
(1 mi. E. of Blaine High School, off of Hwy. 242)
(763)754-0800

Champlin
11632 Winnetka Ave. N.
(763)427-6300

Coon Rapids
2835 Northdale Blvd.
(1 Mile W. of Coon Rapids High School)
(763)757-2020

Crystal
6236 Bass Lake Rd.
(Bass Lake Rd. & Hwy. 81)
(763)535-0777

Eden Prairie
8793 Columbine Rd.
(Hwy. 212 & Anderson Lakes Pkwy.)
(952)252-2222

Elk River
19328 Hwy. 169 N.W.
(763)274-2225

Fridley
1262 E. Moore Lake Dr.
(763)571-9595

Ham Lake
18015 Ulysses St.
(181st Ave. & Hwy. 65)
(763)434-3333

Inver Grove
9034 Cahill Ave.
(651)451-7677

Lino Lakes
7771 Lake Dr.
(651)786-7022

Maple Grove
9511 Black Oats Ln.
(E. of Wal-Mart Supercenter, behind McDonalds)
(763)494-9949

Monticello
9375 Deegan Ave.
(763)295-7774

New Hope
9428A 36th Ave.
(Hwy. 169 & 36th Ave.)
(763)593-1313

Rogers
14000 Northdale Blvd.
(763)494-9990

Vadnais Heights
1032 E. Hwy. 96
(651)255-5000

Offer Details: Valid anytime. One coupon per customer per visit; Not valid with any other offer.

00702411

Offer validity is governed by the Rules of Use and excludes defined holidays. Offers are not valid with other discount offers, unless specified. Coupons void if purchased, sold or bartered. Discounts exclude tax, tip and/or alcohol, where applicable.

Chanticlear Pizza

- Delicious Pizza Every Time!™
- The area's best thin crust pizza!
- Ask about our nightly specials

Chanticlear Pizza®

Andover
1573 154th Ave. N.W.
(763)434-6554

Anoka
440 Bunker Lake Blvd. N.W.
(Bunker Lake Blvd. & Ferry St.)
(763)421-4242

Arden Hills
3551 Lexington Ave.
(651)490-1313

Blaine
914 125th Ln. N.E.
(1 mi. E. of Blaine High School, off of Hwy. 242)
(763)754-0800

Champlin
11632 Winnetka Ave. N.
(763)427-6300

Coon Rapids
2835 Northdale Blvd.
(1 Mile W. of Coon Rapids High School)
(763)757-2020

Crystal
6236 Bass Lake Rd.
(Bass Lake Rd. & Hwy. 81)
(763)535-0777

Eden Prairie
8793 Columbine Rd.
(Hwy. 212 & Anderson Lakes Pkwy.)
(952)252-2222

Elk River
19328 Hwy. 169 N.W.
(763)274-2225

Fridley
1262 E. Moore Lake Dr.
(763)571-9595

Ham Lake
18015 Ulysses St.
(181st Ave. & Hwy. 65)
(763)434-3333

Inver Grove
9034 Cahill Ave.
(651)451-7677

Lino Lakes
7771 Lake Dr.
(651)786-7022

Maple Grove
9511 Black Oats Ln.
(E. of Wal-Mart Supercenter, behind McDonalds)
(763)494-9949

Monticello
9375 Deegan Ave.
(763)295-7774

New Hope
9428A 36th Ave.
(Hwy. 169 & 36th Ave.)
(763)593-1313

Rogers
14000 Northdale Blvd.
(763)494-9990

Vadnais Heights
1032 E. Hwy. 96
(651)255-5000

Offer Details: Valid anytime. One coupon per customer per visit; Not valid with any other offer.

00650671

Offer validity is governed by the Rules of Use and excludes defined holidays. Offers are not valid with other discount offers, unless specified. Coupons void if purchased, sold or bartered. Discounts exclude tax, tip and/or alcohol, where applicable.

Papa John's Pizza

Enjoy any LARGE PIZZA when a second any LARGE PIZZA of equal or greater value is purchased.
See reverse for Offer Details.

FREE LARGE PIZZA

PIZZA
PAPA JOHN's
Better Ingredients.
Better Pizza.

Valid now thru November 1, 2007

Valid at All Participating Locations

B22

Papa John's Pizza

Enjoy any LARGE PIZZA when a second any LARGE PIZZA of equal or greater value is purchased.
See reverse for Offer Details.

FREE LARGE PIZZA

PIZZA
PAPA JOHN's
Better Ingredients.
Better Pizza.

Valid now thru November 1, 2007

Valid at All Participating Locations

B23

Papa John's Pizza

Enjoy any LARGE PIZZA when a second any LARGE PIZZA of equal or greater value is purchased.
See reverse for Offer Details.

FREE LARGE PIZZA

PIZZA
PAPA JOHN's
Better Ingredients.
Better Pizza.

Valid now thru November 1, 2007

Valid at All Participating Locations

B24

CASUAL DINING & FAST FOOD

Papa John's Pizza

PIZZA PAPA JOHN'S®
Better Ingredients.
Better Pizza.
Valid at All Participating Locations

Offer Details: Valid anytime. Valid on regular price pizza only; Not valid with any other discounts or promotions.

00676788

Offer validity is governed by the Rules of Use and excludes defined holidays. Offers are not valid with other discount offers, unless specified. Coupons void if purchased, sold or bartered. Discounts exclude tax, tip and/or alcohol, where applicable.

Papa John's Pizza

PIZZA PAPA JOHN'S®
Better Ingredients.
Better Pizza.
Valid at All Participating Locations

Offer Details: Valid anytime. Valid on regular price pizza only; Not valid with any other discounts or promotions.

00676788

Offer validity is governed by the Rules of Use and excludes defined holidays. Offers are not valid with other discount offers, unless specified. Coupons void if purchased, sold or bartered. Discounts exclude tax, tip and/or alcohol, where applicable.

Papa John's Pizza

PIZZA PAPA JOHN'S®
Better Ingredients.
Better Pizza.
Valid at All Participating Locations

Offer Details: Valid anytime. Valid on regular price pizza only; Not valid with any other discounts or promotions.

00676788

Offer validity is governed by the Rules of Use and excludes defined holidays. Offers are not valid with other discount offers, unless specified. Coupons void if purchased, sold or bartered. Discounts exclude tax, tip and/or alcohol, where applicable.

ONE MEDIUM ORANGE JULIUS® DRINK

Orange Julius®

Enjoy one complimentary MEDIUM ORANGE JULIUS® DRINK when a second MEDIUM ORANGE JULIUS® DRINK of equal or greater value is purchased.

See reverse for Offer Details.

Valid now thru November 1, 2007

See Reverse Side for Locations

B25

ONE LARGE PRETZEL

Orange Julius®

Enjoy one complimentary LARGE PRETZEL when a second LARGE PRETZEL of equal or greater value is purchased.

See reverse for Offer Details.

Valid now thru November 1, 2007

See Reverse Side for Locations

B26

Up To $5.00 Value

Orange Julius®

Enjoy one complimentary MENU ITEM when a second MENU ITEM of equal or greater value is purchased.

See reverse for Offer Details.

Valid now thru November 1, 2007

See Reverse Side for Locations

B27

CASUAL DINING & FAST FOOD

Orange Julius®
- "The Magic IS IN THE DRINK"®
- Many fruit flavors to choose from
- Creations with your choice of nutrifiers
- Smoothies
- Hot dogs & pretzels

Julius

Northtown Mall
Blaine, MN
(763) 780-2807

77 Brookdale Ctr.
Brooklyn Center, MN
(763) 566-5676

915 County Rd. 42
(Burnsville Ctr.)
Burnsville, MN
(952) 435-7628

Maplewood Mall
Maplewood, MN
(651) 770-7605

172 Rosedale Ctr.
Roseville, MN
(651) 636-2693

K105 41st St. Ave. & Division
(Crossroads Shpg. Ctr.)
St. Cloud, MN
(320) 252-5347

Offer Details: Valid anytime. One coupon/card per customer per visit.

00110436

Offer validity is governed by the Rules of Use and excludes defined holidays. Offers are not valid with other discount offers, unless specified. Coupons void if purchased, sold or bartered. Discounts exclude tax, tip and/or alcohol, where applicable.

Orange Julius®
- "Real Fruit, Real Refreshing!"
- So much more than just orange-many fruit flavors to choose from
- Premium Fruit Smoothies & Julius Originals
- Hot dogs & pretzels

Julius

Northtown Mall
Blaine, MN
(763) 780-2807

77 Brookdale Ctr.
Brooklyn Center, MN
(763) 566-5676

915 County Rd. 42
(Burnsville Ctr.)
Burnsville, MN
(952) 435-7628

Maplewood Mall
Maplewood, MN
(651) 770-7605

172 Rosedale Ctr.
Roseville, MN
(651) 636-2693

Offer Details: Valid anytime. One coupon/card per customer per visit.

00499236

Offer validity is governed by the Rules of Use and excludes defined holidays. Offers are not valid with other discount offers, unless specified. Coupons void if purchased, sold or bartered. Discounts exclude tax, tip and/or alcohol, where applicable.

Orange Julius®
- "The Magic IS IN THE DRINK"®
- Many fruit flavors to choose from
- Creations with your choice of nutrifiers
- Smoothies
- Hot dogs & pretzels

Julius

Blaine
Northtown Mall
(763) 780-2807

Brooklyn Center
77 Brookdale Ctr.
(763) 566-5676

Burnsville
915 County Rd. 42
(Burnsville Ctr.)
(952) 435-7628

Golden Valley
7724 Olson Memorial Hwy.
(Hwy. 55 & Winnetka)
(763) 544-1279

Maplewood
Maplewood Mall
(651) 770-7605

Minneapolis
716 Washington Ave. S.E.
(612) 378-1010

Roseville
172 Rosedale Ctr.
(651) 636-2693

St. Cloud
K105 41st St. Ave. & Division
(Crossroads Shpg. Ctr.)
(320) 252-5347

Offer Details: Valid anytime. One coupon/card per customer per visit.

00110437

Offer validity is governed by the Rules of Use and excludes defined holidays. Offers are not valid with other discount offers, unless specified. Coupons void if purchased, sold or bartered. Discounts exclude tax, tip and/or alcohol, where applicable.

REGULAR CONE / CUP

Ben & Jerry's Ice Cream

Enjoy one complimentary REGULAR CONE/CUP when a second REGULAR CONE/CUP of equal or greater value is purchased.

See reverse for Offer Details.

REPEAT SAVINGS

Valid now thru November 1, 2007

See Reverse Side for Locations

B28

SHAKE OR SMOOTHIE

Ben & Jerry's Ice Cream

Enjoy one complimentary SHAKE OR SMOOTHIE when a second SHAKE OR SMOOTHIE of equal or greater value is purchased.

See reverse for Offer Details.

REPEAT SAVINGS

Valid now thru November 1, 2007

See Reverse Side for Locations

B29

FREE SUNDAE

Ben & Jerry's Ice Cream

Enjoy one complimentary SUNDAE when a second SUNDAE of equal or greater value is purchased.

See reverse for Offer Details.

REPEAT SAVINGS

Valid now thru November 1, 2007

See Reverse Side for Locations

B30

CASUAL DINING & FAST FOOD

Ben & Jerry's Ice Cream
- Vermont's finest ice cream
- Ice cream cakes
- World's best birthday parties
- Catering services for all occasions
- Gift certificates
- Store tours
- Education program

BEN&JERRY'S
ICE CREAM & FROZEN YOGURT SCOOP SHOP

5134 Southdale Ctr.
(Center Ct.)
Edina, MN
(952)929-4167

3070 Excelsior Blvd.
(next to Whole Foods)
Minneapolis, MN
(612)927-9900

702 Washington Ave. S.E.
Minneapolis, MN
(612)378-9099

976 Grand Ave.
(1 block E. of Victoria)
St. Paul, MN
(651)292-1770

00601908

Offer Details: Valid anytime.

Offer validity is governed by the Rules of Use and excludes defined holidays. Offers are not valid with other discount offers, unless specified. Coupons void if purchased, sold or bartered. Discounts exclude tax, tip and/or alcohol, where applicable.

Ben & Jerry's Ice Cream
- Vermont's finest ice cream
- Ice cream cakes
- World's best birthday parties
- Catering services for all occasions
- Gift certificates
- Store tours
- Education program

BEN&JERRY'S
ICE CREAM & FROZEN YOGURT SCOOP SHOP

5134 Southdale Ctr.
(Center Ct.)
Edina, MN
(952)929-4167

3070 Excelsior Blvd.
(next to Whole Foods)
Minneapolis, MN
(612)927-9900

702 Washington Ave. S.E.
Minneapolis, MN
(612)378-9099

976 Grand Ave.
(1 block E. of Victoria)
St. Paul, MN
(651)292-1770

00601912

Offer Details: Valid anytime.

Offer validity is governed by the Rules of Use and excludes defined holidays. Offers are not valid with other discount offers, unless specified. Coupons void if purchased, sold or bartered. Discounts exclude tax, tip and/or alcohol, where applicable.

Ben & Jerry's Ice Cream
- Vermont's finest ice cream
- Ice cream cakes
- World's best birthday parties
- Catering services for all occasions
- Gift certificates
- Store tours
- Education program

BEN&JERRY'S
ICE CREAM & FROZEN YOGURT SCOOP SHOP

5134 Southdale Ctr.
(Center Ct.)
Edina, MN
(952)929-4167

3070 Excelsior Blvd.
(next to Whole Foods)
Minneapolis, MN
(612)927-9900

702 Washington Ave. S.E.
Minneapolis, MN
(612)378-9099

976 Grand Ave.
(1 block E. of Victoria)
St. Paul, MN
(651)292-1770

00601915

Offer Details: Valid anytime.

Offer validity is governed by the Rules of Use and excludes defined holidays. Offers are not valid with other discount offers, unless specified. Coupons void if purchased, sold or bartered. Discounts exclude tax, tip and/or alcohol, where applicable.

FREE SANDWICH

Camille's

Enjoy one complimentary SANDWICH when a second SANDWICH of equal or greater value is purchased.
See reverse for Offer Details.

Camille's sidewalk cafe

Valid now thru November 1, 2007

See Reverse Side for Locations

B31

FREE CUP OF SOUP OR SMOOTHIE

Camille's

Enjoy one complimentary CUP OF SOUP OR SMOOTHIE when a second CUP OF SOUP OR SMOOTHIE of equal or greater value is purchased.
See reverse for Offer Details.

Camille's sidewalk cafe

Valid now thru November 1, 2007

See Reverse Side for Locations

B32

FREE SALAD

Camille's

Enjoy one complimentary SALAD when a second SALAD of equal or greater value is purchased.
See reverse for Offer Details.

Camille's sidewalk cafe

Valid now thru November 1, 2007

See Reverse Side for Locations

B33

CASUAL DINING & FAST FOOD

Camille's
- Eat, relax, enjoy!
- We cater to your every desire
- Sandwiches, grilled paninis & wraps
- Salads & soups
- Smoothies
- Expresso
- Catering

Camille's sidewalk cafe

2010 S.E. Delaware Ave.
Ankeny, IA
(515)963-7722
6925 Mills Civic Pkwy.
#140
West Des Moines, IA
(515)457-7080

1450 109th Ave. NE
130
Blaine, MN
(763)792-6687
712 Mainstreet
Hopkins, MN
(952)938-1366

150 S. 5th St., #200
(Fifth St. Towers)
Minneapolis, MN
(612)333-4429
13301 60th St. N
Oak Park Heights, MN
(651)275-3867

Offer Details: Valid anytime.

00110513

Offer validity is governed by the Rules of Use and excludes defined holidays. Offers are not valid with other discount offers, unless specified. Coupons void if purchased, sold or bartered. Discounts exclude tax, tip and/or alcohol, where applicable.

Camille's
- Eat, relax, enjoy!
- We cater to your every desire
- Sandwiches, grilled paninis & wraps
- Salads & soups
- Smoothies
- Espresso
- Catering

Camille's sidewalk cafe

2010 S.E. Delaware Ave.
Ankeny, IA
(515)963-7722
6925 Mills Civic Pkwy.
#140
West Des Moines, IA
(515)457-7080

1450 109th Ave. NE
130
Blaine, MN
(763)792-6687
712 Mainstreet
Hopkins, MN
(952)938-1366

150 S. 5th St., #200
(Fifth St. Towers)
Minneapolis, MN
(612)333-4429
13301 60th St. N
Oak Park Heights, MN
(651)275-3867

Offer Details: Valid anytime.

00110514

Offer validity is governed by the Rules of Use and excludes defined holidays. Offers are not valid with other discount offers, unless specified. Coupons void if purchased, sold or bartered. Discounts exclude tax, tip and/or alcohol, where applicable.

Camille's
- Eat, relax, enjoy!
- We cater to your every desire
- Sandwiches, grilled paninis & wraps
- Salads & soups
- Smoothies
- Espresso
- Catering

Camille's sidewalk cafe

2010 S.E. Delaware Ave.
Ankeny, IA
(515)963-7722
6925 Mills Civic Pkwy.
#140
West Des Moines, IA
(515)457-7080

1450 109th Ave. NE
130
Blaine, MN
(763)792-6687
712 Mainstreet
Hopkins, MN
(952)938-1366

150 S. 5th St., #200
(Fifth St. Towers)
Minneapolis, MN
(612)333-4429
13301 60th St. N
Oak Park Heights, MN
(651)275-3867

Offer Details: Valid anytime.

00110515

Offer validity is governed by the Rules of Use and excludes defined holidays. Offers are not valid with other discount offers, unless specified. Coupons void if purchased, sold or bartered. Discounts exclude tax, tip and/or alcohol, where applicable.

entertainment
entertainment.com

Au Bon Pain
Enjoy one complimentary SANDWICH when a second SANDWICH of equal or greater value is purchased.
See reverse for Offer Details.

FREE SANDWICH

au bon pain

www.abpmncatering.com
See Reverse Side for Locations

Valid now thru November 1, 2007   B34

---

entertainment
entertainment.com

Au Bon Pain
Enjoy one complimentary COFFEE when a second COFFEE of equal or greater value is purchased.
See reverse for Offer Details.

FREE COFFEE

au bon pain

www.abpmncatering.com
See Reverse Side for Locations

Valid now thru November 1, 2007   B35

---

entertainment
entertainment.com

Au Bon Pain
Enjoy 20% off any CATERING SERVICES - maximum discount $100.00.
See reverse for Offer Details.

Up To $100.00 Value

au bon pain

www.abpmncatering.com
See Reverse Side for Locations

Valid now thru November 1, 2007   B36

CASUAL DINING & FAST FOOD

Au Bon Pain
- Planning an event? Ask our consultants for ideas!
- Go to www.abpmncatering.com

au bon pain

8405 Lyndale Ave. S.
Bloomington, MN
(952)252-6333

225 S. 6th St.
Minneapolis, MN
(612)341-4420

40 S. 7th St. Ste. 225
(City Center)
Minneapolis, MN
(612)259-0101

733 Marquette Ave., Ste. 241
Minneapolis, MN
(612)343-5252

Offer Details: Valid anytime.

00662745

Offer validity is governed by the Rules of Use and excludes defined holidays. Offers are not valid with other discount offers, unless specified. Coupons void if purchased, sold or bartered. Discounts exclude tax, tip and/or alcohol, where applicable.

Au Bon Pain
- Planning an event? Ask our consultants for ideas!
- Go to www.abpmncatering.com

au bon pain

8405 Lyndale Ave. S.
Bloomington, MN
(952)252-6333

225 S. 6th St.
Minneapolis, MN
(612)341-4420

40 S. 7th St. Ste. 225
(City Center)
Minneapolis, MN
(612)259-0101

733 Marquette Ave., Ste. 241
Minneapolis, MN
(612)343-5252

Offer Details: Valid anytime.

00662754

Offer validity is governed by the Rules of Use and excludes defined holidays. Offers are not valid with other discount offers, unless specified. Coupons void if purchased, sold or bartered. Discounts exclude tax, tip and/or alcohol, where applicable.

Au Bon Pain
- Planning an event? Ask our consultants for ideas!
- Go to www.abpmncatering.com

au bon pain

8405 Lyndale Ave. S.
Bloomington, MN
(952)252-6333

225 S. 6th St.
Minneapolis, MN
(612)341-4420

40 S. 7th St. Ste. 225
(City Center)
Minneapolis, MN
(612)259-0101

733 Marquette Ave., Ste. 241
Minneapolis, MN
(612)343-5252

Offer Details: Valid anytime.

00662755

Offer validity is governed by the Rules of Use and excludes defined holidays. Offers are not valid with other discount offers, unless specified. Coupons void if purchased, sold or bartered. Discounts exclude tax, tip and/or alcohol, where applicable.

Pizza N' Pasta

Enjoy any one PIZZA at 50% off the regular price - maximum discount $11.00.
See reverse for Offer Details.

Up To $11.00 Value

Valid now thru November 1, 2007

See Reverse Side for Locations

B37

Pizza N' Pasta

Enjoy any one PIZZA at 50% off the regular price - maximum discount $11.00.
See reverse for Offer Details.

Up To $11.00 Value

Valid now thru November 1, 2007

See Reverse Side for Locations

B38

Pizza N' Pasta

Enjoy one complimentary PASTA ENTREE when a second PASTA ENTREE of equal or greater value is purchased.
See reverse for Offer Details.

Up To $8.00 Value

Valid now thru November 1, 2007

See Reverse Side for Locations

B39

CASUAL DINING & FAST FOOD

Pizza N' Pasta

Burnsville
12629 Nicollet Ave. S.
(952)894-7302
Chaska
105 W. 2nd St.
(952)448-7100
Eagan
4250 Lexington Ave. S.
(651)681-0000

Lakeville
16060 Cedar Ave.
(952)432-4200
Northfield
550 Professional Dr.
(507)645-9200
Prior Lake
5115 Gateway S.E.
(952)226-4200

Rosemount
15092 Claret Ave.
(651)423-3500
Shakopee
584 Marshall
(952)496-0000

Offer Details: Valid anytime. Carry out only; Sorry, no delivery.

00626426

Offer validity is governed by the Rules of Use and excludes defined holidays. Offers are not valid with other discount offers, unless specified. Coupons void if purchased, sold or bartered. Discounts exclude tax, tip and/or alcohol, where applicable.

Pizza N' Pasta

Burnsville
12629 Nicollet Ave. S.
(952)894-7302
Chaska
105 W. 2nd St.
(952)448-7100
Eagan
4250 Lexington Ave. S.
(651)681-0000

Lakeville
16060 Cedar Ave.
(952)432-4200
Northfield
550 Professional Dr.
(507)645-9200
Prior Lake
5115 Gateway S.E.
(952)226-4200

Rosemount
15092 Claret Ave.
(651)423-3500
Shakopee
584 Marshall
(952)496-0000

Offer Details: Valid anytime. Carry out only; Sorry, no delivery.

00626426

Offer validity is governed by the Rules of Use and excludes defined holidays. Offers are not valid with other discount offers, unless specified. Coupons void if purchased, sold or bartered. Discounts exclude tax, tip and/or alcohol, where applicable.

Pizza N' Pasta

Burnsville
12629 Nicollet Ave. S.
(952)894-7302
Chaska
105 W. 2nd St.
(952)448-7100
Eagan
4250 Lexington Ave. S.
(651)681-0000

Lakeville
16060 Cedar Ave.
(952)432-4200
Northfield
550 Professional Dr.
(507)645-9200
Prior Lake
5115 Gateway S.E.
(952)226-4200

Rosemount
15092 Claret Ave.
(651)423-3500
Shakopee
584 Marshall
(952)496-0000

Offer Details: Valid anytime. Carry out only; Sorry, no delivery.

00626432

Offer validity is governed by the Rules of Use and excludes defined holidays. Offers are not valid with other discount offers, unless specified. Coupons void if purchased, sold or bartered. Discounts exclude tax, tip and/or alcohol, where applicable.

Steak Escape

Enjoy one complimentary SANDWICH when a second SANDWICH of equal or greater value is purchased.
See reverse for Offer Details.

FREE SANDWICH

STEAK ESCAPE®

Valid now thru November 1, 2007

See Reverse Side for Locations

B40

Steak Escape

Enjoy one complimentary SMASHED POTATO when a second SMASHED POTATO of equal or greater value is purchased.
See reverse for Offer Details.

ONE SMASHED POTATO

STEAK ESCAPE®

Valid now thru November 1, 2007

See Reverse Side for Locations

B41

Roly Poly

Enjoy one complimentary MENU ITEM when a second MENU ITEM of equal or greater value is purchased.
See reverse for Offer Details.

Up To $6.00 Value

ROLY POLY

Valid now thru November 1, 2007

See Reverse Side for Locations

B42

CASUAL DINING & FAST FOOD

Steak Escape
- The Steak Escape has proven that fast food can be fresh, delicious, made-to-order & a great experience

STEAK ESCAPE.

505 Northtown Dr.
(Northtown Mall)
Blaine, MN
(763)780-0251

1361 Brookdale Ctr.
(Brookdale Center)
Brooklyn Center, MN
(763)561-8000

1600 Miller Trunk Hwy
(Miller Hill Mall)
Duluth, MN
(218)722-3326

8251 Flying Cloud Dr.
(Eden Prairie Center)
Eden Prairie, MN
(952)914-5400

2500 13th Ave. E
Hibbing, MN
(218)262-5052

5910 Neal Ave. N.
Oak Park Hgts., MN
(651)439-7771

Offer Details: Valid anytime.

00107888

Offer validity is governed by the Rules of Use and excludes defined holidays. Offers are not valid with other discount offers, unless specified. Coupons void if purchased, sold or bartered. Discounts exclude tax, tip and/or alcohol, where applicable.

Steak Escape
- The Steak Escape has proven that fast food can be fresh, delicious, made-to-order & a great experience

STEAK ESCAPE.

505 Northtown Dr.
(Northtown Mall)
Blaine, MN
(763)780-0251

1361 Brookdale Ctr.
(Brookdale Center)
Brooklyn Center, MN
(763)561-8000

1600 Miller Trunk Hwy
(Miller Hill Mall)
Duluth, MN
(218)722-3326

8251 Flying Cloud Dr.
(Eden Prairie Center)
Eden Prairie, MN
(952)914-5400

2500 13th Ave. E
Hibbing, MN
(218)262-5052

5910 Neal Ave. N.
Oak Park Hgts., MN
(651)439-7771

Offer Details: Valid anytime.

00107889

Offer validity is governed by the Rules of Use and excludes defined holidays. Offers are not valid with other discount offers, unless specified. Coupons void if purchased, sold or bartered. Discounts exclude tax, tip and/or alcohol, where applicable.

Roly Poly
- Hot & cold sandwiches
- Hearty soups
- Chips & cookies
- Party platters & box lunches
- Delivery available

ROLY POLY

10950 Club West Pkwy.
Blaine, MN
(763)784-1712

121 Willow Bend
(Crystal Shpg. Ctr.)
Crystal, MN
(763)533-0377

7733 Flying Cloud Dr.
Eden Praire, MN
(952)224-3604

2211 11th Ave. E.
North St. Paul, MN
(651)777-7727

Offer Details: Valid anytime.

00108427

Offer validity is governed by the Rules of Use and excludes defined holidays. Offers are not valid with other discount offers, unless specified. Coupons void if purchased, sold or bartered. Discounts exclude tax, tip and/or alcohol, where applicable.

KarmelKorn

Enjoy one complimentary FLAVORED SNACKER when a second FLAVORED SNACKER of equal or greater value is purchased.
See reverse for Offer Details.

ONE FLAVORED SNACKER

Valid now thru November 1, 2007

See Reverse Side for Locations

B43

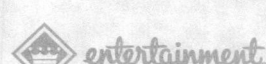

KarmelKorn

Enjoy one POPCORN OR KANISTER ORDER at 50% off the regular price - maximum discount $4.00.
See reverse for Offer Details.

50% OFF

Valid now thru November 1, 2007

See Reverse Side for Locations

B44

KarmelKorn

Enjoy one complimentary LARGE PRETZEL when a second LARGE PRETZEL of equal or greater value is purchased.
See reverse for Offer Details.

ONE LARGE PRETZEL

Valid now thru November 1, 2007

See Reverse Side for Locations

B45

CASUAL DINING & FAST FOOD

KarmelKorn
- A variety of fresh popped flavors
- Party & gift tins
- "We're popping it fresh"®

KARMELKORN®

320 Northtown Dr.
Blaine, MN
(763)780-2807

Brookdale Center
Brooklyn Center, MN
(763)566-5676

915 County Rd. 42
Burnsville, MN
(952)435-7628

Maplewood Mall
Maplewood, MN
(651)770-7605

172 Rosedale Ctr.
Roseville, MN
(651)636-2693

105K 41st St. Ave.
& Division
(Crossroads Shpg. Ctr.)
St. Cloud, MN
(320)252-5347

Offer Details: Valid anytime. One coupon/card per customer per visit.

00102818

Offer validity is governed by the Rules of Use and excludes defined holidays. Offers are not valid with other discount offers, unless specified. Coupons void if purchased, sold or bartered. Discounts exclude tax, tip and/or alcohol, where applicable.

KarmelKorn
- A variety of fresh popped flavors
- Party & gift tins
- "We're popping it fresh"®

KARMELKORN®

320 Northtown Dr.
Blaine, MN
(763)780-2807

Brookdale Center
Brooklyn Center, MN
(763)566-5676

915 County Rd. 42
Burnsville, MN
(952)435-7628

Maplewood Mall
Maplewood, MN
(651)770-7605

172 Rosedale Ctr.
Roseville, MN
(651)636-2693

105K 41st St. Ave.
& Division
(Crossroads Shpg. Ctr.)
St. Cloud, MN
(320)252-5347

Offer Details: Valid anytime. One coupon/card per customer per visit.

00102819

Offer validity is governed by the Rules of Use and excludes defined holidays. Offers are not valid with other discount offers, unless specified. Coupons void if purchased, sold or bartered. Discounts exclude tax, tip and/or alcohol, where applicable.

KarmelKorn
- "We're popping it fresh"®

KARMELKORN®

320 Northtown Dr.
Blaine, MN
(763)780-2807

Brookdale Center
Brooklyn Center, MN
(763)566-5676

915 County Rd. 42
Burnsville, MN
(952)435-7628

Maplewood Mall
Maplewood, MN
(651)770-7605

172 Rosedale Ctr.
Roseville, MN
(651)636-2693

Offer Details: Valid anytime. One coupon/card per customer per visit.

00499535

Offer validity is governed by the Rules of Use and excludes defined holidays. Offers are not valid with other discount offers, unless specified. Coupons void if purchased, sold or bartered. Discounts exclude tax, tip and/or alcohol, where applicable.

entertainment.com

Eddington's

Enjoy one complimentary REGULAR BOWL when a second REGULAR BOWL of equal or greater value is purchased.
See reverse for Offer Details.

FREE REGULAR BOWL

EDDINGTON'S SOUP & SALAD HOUSE

Valid now thru November 1, 2007

See Reverse Side for Locations

B46

---

entertainment.com

Eddington's

Enjoy one complimentary REGULAR BOWL when a second REGULAR BOWL of equal or greater value is purchased.
See reverse for Offer Details.

FREE REGULAR BOWL

EDDINGTON'S SOUP & SALAD HOUSE

Valid now thru November 1, 2007

See Reverse Side for Locations

B47

---

entertainment.com

Blimpie Subs & Salads

Enjoy one complimentary SIX INCH REGULAR SUB OR REGULAR SALAD when a second SIX INCH REGULAR SUB OR REGULAR SALAD of equal or greater value is purchased.
See reverse for Offer Details.

SUB OR SALAD

Blimpie SUBS & SALADS

Valid now thru November 1, 2007

Valid at Participating Locations

B48

CASUAL DINING & FAST FOOD

Eddington's
- Unfast food fast!
- Homemade soups are our specialty
- Garden fresh salad bar
- Delicious sandwiches & wraps
- Freshly baked breadsticks
- Baked potatoes

Coon Rapids
13111 Riverdale Dr.
(763)323-9222

Edina
5125 Edina Industrial Blvd.
(Open Mon.-Fri.)
(952)896-1148

Minneapolis
155 5th Ave. S. Ste. 105
(2nd St. S. & 5th Ave. S. Cerresota Bldg. Open Mon.-Fri.)
(612)259-0092

296 Pillsbury Center
(Downtown Minneapolis, open Mon.-Fri.)
(612)338-5747

Minnetonka
12987 Ridgedale Dr.
(Open Mon.-Sat.)
(952)591-9586

Roseville
2100 Snelling Ave. N.
(Har Mar Mall, open Mon.-Sat.)
(651)697-9794

St. Paul
56 E. 6th St., Ste. 208
(Norwest Bank Bldg.-Skyway, open Mon.-Fri.)
(651)228-0427

Offer Details: Valid anytime. All you can eat bowls excluded; No substitutes.

00000057

Offer validity is governed by the Rules of Use and excludes defined holidays. Offers are not valid with other discount offers, unless specified. Coupons void if purchased, sold or bartered. Discounts exclude tax, tip and/or alcohol, where applicable.

Eddington's
- Unfast food fast!
- Homemade soups are our specialty
- Garden fresh salad bar
- Delicious sandwiches & wraps
- Freshly baked breadsticks
- Baked potatoes

Coon Rapids
13111 Riverdale Dr.
(763)323-9222

Edina
5125 Edina Industrial Blvd.
(Open Mon.-Fri.)
(952)896-1148

Minneapolis
155 5th Ave. S. Ste. 105
(2nd St. S. & 5th Ave. S. Cerresota Bldg. Open Mon.-Fri.)
(612)259-0092

296 Pillsbury Center
(Downtown Minneapolis, open Mon.-Fri.)
(612)338-5747

Minnetonka
12987 Ridgedale Dr.
(Open Mon.-Sat.)
(952)591-9586

Roseville
2100 Snelling Ave. N.
(Har Mar Mall, open Mon.-Sat.)
(651)697-9794

St. Paul
56 E. 6th St., Ste. 208
(Norwest Bank Bldg.-Skyway, open Mon.-Fri.)
(651)228-0427

Offer Details: Valid anytime. All you can eat bowls excluded; No substitutes.

00000057

Offer validity is governed by the Rules of Use and excludes defined holidays. Offers are not valid with other discount offers, unless specified. Coupons void if purchased, sold or bartered. Discounts exclude tax, tip and/or alcohol, where applicable.

Blimpie Subs & Salads
- Famous for fresh-sliced meats & cheese
- Large variety of hot & cold subs
- Ask about our 3-ft. or 5-ft. Blimpie Blast Sub for parties & catered services

Blimpie
SUBS & SALADS

Valid at Participating Locations

Offer Details: Valid anytime.

00408630

Offer validity is governed by the Rules of Use and excludes defined holidays. Offers are not valid with other discount offers, unless specified. Coupons void if purchased, sold or bartered. Discounts exclude tax, tip and/or alcohol, where applicable.

entertainment.
entertainment.com

Dairy Queen®
$2 off a purchase of a DQ® CHILLABRATION™ CAKE.
See reverse for Offer Details.

$2.00 Value

Dairy Queen

Valid now thru November 1, 2007

Valid only at participating Dairy Queen locations in Minnesota, South Dakota & North Dakota   B49

---

entertainment.
entertainment.com

Dairy Queen®
Enjoy one complimentary BLIZZARD® when a second BLIZZARD® of equal or greater value is purchased.
See reverse for Offer Details.

ONE BLIZZARD®

Dairy Queen

Valid now thru November 1, 2007

Valid only at participating Dairy Queen locations in Minnesota, South Dakota & North Dakota   B50

---

entertainment.
entertainment.com

MaggieMoo's
Enjoy any ICE CREAM ORDER at 50% off the regular price.
See reverse for Offer Details.

Up To $5.00 Value

MaggieMoo's®
ICE CREAM AND TREATERY

www.maggiemoos.com
See Reverse Side for Locations

REPEAT SAVINGS™

Valid now thru November 1, 2007   B51

CASUAL DINING & FAST FOOD

Dairy Queen®

Valid only at participating Dairy Queen locations in Minnesota, South Dakota & North Dakota

Offer Details: Valid anytime.

00666596

Offer validity is governed by the Rules of Use and excludes defined holidays. Offers are not valid with other discount offers, unless specified. Coupons void if purchased, sold or bartered. Discounts exclude tax, tip and/or alcohol, where applicable.

Dairy Queen®

Valid only at participating Dairy Queen locations in Minnesota, South Dakota & North Dakota

Offer Details: Valid anytime.

00666595

Offer validity is governed by the Rules of Use and excludes defined holidays. Offers are not valid with other discount offers, unless specified. Coupons void if purchased, sold or bartered. Discounts exclude tax, tip and/or alcohol, where applicable.

MaggieMoo's

- Award-winning ice cream made fresh on site with the freshest ingredients
- We hand-fold your favorite nuts, candy or fruit in our ice cream right in front of you
- Smoothies, milkshakes, cakes, treats & more
- Birthday & group parties

MaggieMoo's® ICE CREAM AND TREATERY

600 Market St., Ste. 160
Chanhassen, MN
(952)949-6667

12115 Elm Creek Blvd.
Maple Grove, MN
(763)424-9900

Offer Details: Valid anytime.

00695688

Offer validity is governed by the Rules of Use and excludes defined holidays. Offers are not valid with other discount offers, unless specified. Coupons void if purchased, sold or bartered. Discounts exclude tax, tip and/or alcohol, where applicable.

entertainment
entertainment.com

A & W
Enjoy ONE BURGER when a second BURGER of equal or greater value is purchased.
See reverse for Offer Details.

FREE BURGER

A&W
ALL AMERICAN FOOD™

See Reverse Side for Locations

Valid now thru November 1, 2007 B52

---

entertainment
entertainment.com

A & W
Enjoy ONE ROOT BEER FLOAT when a second ROOT BEER FLOAT of equal or greater value is purchased.
See reverse for Offer Details.

FREE ROOT BEER FLOAT

A&W
ALL AMERICAN FOOD™

See Reverse Side for Locations

Valid now thru November 1, 2007 B53

---

entertainment
entertainment.com

A & W
Enjoy ONE HOT DOG when a second HOT DOG of equal or greater value is purchased.
See reverse for Offer Details.

FREE HOT DOG

A&W
ALL AMERICAN FOOD™

See Reverse Side for Locations

Valid now thru November 1, 2007 B54

CASUAL DINING & FAST FOOD

A & W

A&W
ALL AMERICAN FOOD™

Mall of America
(S. Food Ct. 3rd floor)
Bloomington, MN
(952)858-8436

12759 Riverdale Blvd.
(Riverdale Shpg. Plaza)
Coon Rapids, MN
(763)576-1265

404 Wilson Ave.
Faribault, MN
(507)334-9379

Apache Mall
Rochester, MN
(507)288-1248

5820 Tower St.
(Hwy. 55)
Rockford, MN
(763)477-4430

230 Pine Cone Rd.
Sartell, MN
(320)240-6840

Offer Details: Valid anytime.

00102871

Offer validity is governed by the Rules of Use and excludes defined holidays. Offers are not valid with other discount offers, unless specified. Coupons void if purchased, sold or bartered. Discounts exclude tax, tip and/or alcohol, where applicable.

A & W

A&W
ALL AMERICAN FOOD™

Mall of America
(S. Food Ct. 3rd floor)
Bloomington, MN
(952)858-8436

12759 Riverdale Blvd.
(Riverdale Shpg. Plaza)
Coon Rapids, MN
(763)576-1265

404 Wilson Ave.
Faribault, MN
(507)334-9379

Apache Mall
Rochester, MN
(507)288-1248

5820 Tower St.
(Hwy. 55)
Rockford, MN
(763)477-4430

230 Pine Cone Rd.
Sartell, MN
(320)240-6840

Offer Details: Valid anytime.

00102872

Offer validity is governed by the Rules of Use and excludes defined holidays. Offers are not valid with other discount offers, unless specified. Coupons void if purchased, sold or bartered. Discounts exclude tax, tip and/or alcohol, where applicable.

A & W

A&W
ALL AMERICAN FOOD™

Mall of America
(S. Food Ct. 3rd floor)
Bloomington, MN
(952)858-8436

12759 Riverdale Blvd.
(Riverdale Shpg. Plaza)
Coon Rapids, MN
(763)576-1265

404 Wilson Ave.
Faribault, MN
(507)334-9379

Apache Mall
Rochester, MN
(507)288-1248

5820 Tower St.
(Hwy. 55)
Rockford, MN
(763)477-4430

230 Pine Cone Rd.
Sartell, MN
(320)240-6840

Offer Details: Valid anytime.

00102873

Offer validity is governed by the Rules of Use and excludes defined holidays. Offers are not valid with other discount offers, unless specified. Coupons void if purchased, sold or bartered. Discounts exclude tax, tip and/or alcohol, where applicable.

Auntie Anne's

Enjoy one complimentary ORDER of AUNTIE ANNE'S STIX & MEDIUM SODA FOUNTAIN DRINK when a second ORDER of AUNTIE ANNE'S STIX & MEDIUM SODA FOUNTAIN DRINK of equal or greater value is purchased.

See reverse for Offer Details.

Valid now thru November 1, 2007

ORDER OF AUNTIE ANNE'S STIX & MEDIUM SODA

Auntie Anne's
PRETZEL PERFECT

Valid at All Participating Locations

B55

Auntie Anne's

Enjoy ONE PRETZEL DOG & MEDIUM SODA FOUNTAIN DRINK when a second PRETZEL DOG & MEDIUM SODA FOUNTAIN DRINK of equal or greater value is purchased.

See reverse for Offer Details.

Valid now thru November 1, 2007

ONE PRETZEL DOG & MEDIUM SODA FOUNTAIN DRINK

Auntie Anne's
PRETZEL PERFECT

Valid at All Participating Locations

B56

Auntie Anne's

Enjoy ONE PRETZEL, MEDIUM SODA FOUNTAIN DRINK & DIP when a second PRETZEL, MEDIUM SODA FOUNTAIN DRINK & DIP of equal or greater value is purchased.

See reverse for Offer Details.

Valid now thru November 1, 2007

ONE PRETZEL, MED. SODA FOUNTAIN DRINK & DIP

Auntie Anne's
PRETZEL PERFECT

Valid at All Participating Locations

B57

Auntie Anne's
- Hand-Rolled Soft Pretzels baked fresh in full view of our customers
- Don't forget a dipping sauce for your pretzel
- Compliment your Pretzel with our Old Fashioned Lemonade™
- Store hours vary, call for information

AuntieAnne's™
PRETZEL PERFECT
Valid at All Participating Locations

Offer Details: Valid anytime. Valid at participating locations; Free items must be of equal or lesser value; One coupon per person, one time only; Not good with any other offer; Tax extra where applicable; Not a cash substitute; Duplicated or altered coupons will not be accepted.

00701333

Offer validity is governed by the Rules of Use and excludes defined holidays. Offers are not valid with other discount offers, unless specified. Coupons void if purchased, sold or bartered. Discounts exclude tax, tip and/or alcohol, where applicable.

Auntie Anne's
- Hand-Rolled Soft Pretzels baked fresh in full view of our customers
- Don't forget a dipping sauce for your pretzel
- Compliment your Pretzel with our Old Fashioned Lemonade™
- Store hours vary, call for information

AuntieAnne's™
PRETZEL PERFECT
Valid at All Participating Locations

Offer Details: Valid anytime. Valid at participating locations; Free items must be of equal or lesser value; One coupon per person, one time only; Not good with any other offer; Tax extra where applicable; Not a cash substitute; Duplicated or altered coupons will not be accepted.

00701346

Offer validity is governed by the Rules of Use and excludes defined holidays. Offers are not valid with other discount offers, unless specified. Coupons void if purchased, sold or bartered. Discounts exclude tax, tip and/or alcohol, where applicable.

Auntie Anne's
- Hand-Rolled Soft Pretzels baked fresh in full view of our customers
- Don't forget a dipping sauce for your pretzel
- Compliment your Pretzel with our Old Fashioned Lemonade™
- Store hours vary, call for information

AuntieAnne's™
PRETZEL PERFECT
Valid at All Participating Locations

Offer Details: Valid anytime. Valid at participating locations; Free items must be of equal or lesser value; One coupon per person, one time only; Not good with any other offer; Tax extra where applicable; Not a cash substitute; Duplicated or altered coupons will not be accepted.

00701348

Offer validity is governed by the Rules of Use and excludes defined holidays. Offers are not valid with other discount offers, unless specified. Coupons void if purchased, sold or bartered. Discounts exclude tax, tip and/or alcohol, where applicable.

entertainment.com

Salsarita's Fresh Cantina
Enjoy one complimentary ENTREE when a second ENTREE of equal or greater value is purchased.
See reverse for Offer Details.

REPEAT SAVINGS

FREE ENTREE

Salsarita's Fresh Cantina

9000 Hudson Rd. Ste. 622, Woodbury, MN
(651) 203-2600

Valid now thru November 1, 2007   B58

---

entertainment.com

Salsarita's Fresh Cantina
Enjoy one complimentary ENTREE when a second ENTREE of equal or greater value is purchased.
See reverse for Offer Details.

REPEAT SAVINGS

FREE ENTREE

Salsarita's Fresh Cantina

9000 Hudson Rd. Ste. 622, Woodbury, MN
(651) 203-2600

Valid now thru November 1, 2007   B59

---

entertainment.com

Angeno's
Enjoy one complimentary MENU ITEM when a second MENU ITEM of equal or greater value is purchased or for those who prefer - any one pizza at 50% off the regular price - maximum discount $6.00.
See reverse for Offer Details.

Up To $6.00 Value

Angeno's PIZZA AND PASTA

See Reverse Side for Locations

Valid now thru November 1, 2007   B60

CASUAL DINING & FAST FOOD

Salsarita's Fresh Cantina
- New healthy, fresh & hot
- Tacos, burritos, quesadillas, nachos & salads
- Catering available-any event, any size

Salsarita's
Fresh Cantina

9000 Hudson Rd. Ste. 622
Woodbury, MN
(651) 203-2600

Offer Details: Valid anytime.

00695687

Offer validity is governed by the Rules of Use and excludes defined holidays. Offers are not valid with other discount offers, unless specified. Coupons void if purchased, sold or bartered. Discounts exclude tax, tip and/or alcohol, where applicable.

Salsarita's Fresh Cantina
- New healthy, fresh & hot
- Tacos, burritos, quesadillas, nachos & salads
- Catering available-any event, any size

Salsarita's
Fresh Cantina

9000 Hudson Rd. Ste. 622
Woodbury, MN
(651) 203-2600

Offer Details: Valid anytime.

00695687

Offer validity is governed by the Rules of Use and excludes defined holidays. Offers are not valid with other discount offers, unless specified. Coupons void if purchased, sold or bartered. Discounts exclude tax, tip and/or alcohol, where applicable.

Angeno's
- Thin crust
- Deep dish
- Double crust
- Full line of pastas
- Banquet room available
- Salads
- Wine & beer

Angeno's
PIZZA AND PASTA

3060 Brookdale Dr.
(Xerxes & Brookdale Dr.)
Brooklyn Park, MN
(763) 560-0481

13588 80th Circle
Maple Grove, MN
(763) 420-8200

3355 Plymouth Blvd., Suite 100
(1/2 block east of Mann Theater)
Plymouth, MN
(763) 559-8866

13575 Northdale Blvd.
Rogers, MN
(763) 428-9819

Offer Details: Valid anytime. One coupon per customer per visit; Not valid on delivery.

00061518

Offer validity is governed by the Rules of Use and excludes defined holidays. Offers are not valid with other discount offers, unless specified. Coupons void if purchased, sold or bartered. Discounts exclude tax, tip and/or alcohol, where applicable.

FREE LARGE TWO TOPPING PIZZA

Carbone's

Enjoy one complimentary LARGE TWO-TOPPING PIZZA when a second LARGE TWO-TOPPING PIZZA of equal or greater value is purchased.
See reverse for Offer Details.

REPEAT SAVINGS™

Valid now thru November 1, 2007

See Reverse Side for Locations

B61

FREE LARGE TWO TOPPING PIZZA

Carbone's

Enjoy one complimentary LARGE TWO-TOPPING PIZZA when a second LARGE TWO-TOPPING PIZZA of equal or greater value is purchased.
See reverse for Offer Details.

REPEAT SAVINGS™

Valid now thru November 1, 2007

See Reverse Side for Locations

B62

FREE LARGE TWO TOPPING PIZZA

Carbone's

Enjoy one complimentary LARGE TWO-TOPPING PIZZA when a second LARGE TWO-TOPPING PIZZA of equal or greater value is purchased.
See reverse for Offer Details.

REPEAT SAVINGS™

Valid now thru November 1, 2007

See Reverse Side for Locations

B63

CASUAL DINING & FAST FOOD

Carbone's

MINNESOTA
Albertville
5986 Main Ave.
(763)497-1497

Bloomington
1834 E. Old Shakopee Rd.
(952)888-5663

Coon Rapids
8525 Cottonwood St. N.W.
(763)717-0327

Eagan
1665 Yankee Doodle Rd.
(651)452-6000

Inver Grove Hgts.
6432 Cahill Ave.
(651)450-7832

Mahtomedi
960 Mahtomedi Ave.
(651)426-5222

Maplewood
2655 White Bear Ave.
(651)770-0075

Minneapolis
4724 Cedar Ave.
(612)724-0063

North Branch
6427 Ash St.
(651)277-5555

Oakdale
705 Century Ave. S.
(651)501-0822

Plymouth
1400 County Rd. 101
(763)473-1477

Savage
4046 County Rd. 42
(952)746-6656

White Bear Lake
1350 Hwy. 96
(651)429-7609

WISCONSIN
Hudson
212 Locust St.
(715)386-8228

New Richmond
244 S. Knowles Ave.
(715)246-0011

Roberts
110 W. Main St.
(715)749-9000

Somerset
220 Main St.
(715)247-4992

00697681

Offer Details: Valid anytime. Dine-in or carry out.

Offer validity is governed by the Rules of Use and excludes defined holidays. Offers are not valid with other discount offers, unless specified. Coupons void if purchased, sold or bartered. Discounts exclude tax, tip and/or alcohol, where applicable.

Carbone's

MINNESOTA
Albertville
5986 Main Ave.
(763)497-1497

Bloomington
1834 E. Old Shakopee Rd.
(952)888-5663

Coon Rapids
8525 Cottonwood St. N.W.
(763)717-0327

Eagan
1665 Yankee Doodle Rd.
(651)452-6000

Inver Grove Hgts.
6432 Cahill Ave.
(651)450-7832

Mahtomedi
960 Mahtomedi Ave.
(651)426-5222

Maplewood
2655 White Bear Ave.
(651)770-0075

Minneapolis
4724 Cedar Ave.
(612)724-0063

North Branch
6427 Ash St.
(651)277-5555

Oakdale
705 Century Ave. S.
(651)501-0822

Plymouth
1400 County Rd. 101
(763)473-1477

Savage
4046 County Rd. 42
(952)746-6656

White Bear Lake
1350 Hwy. 96
(651)429-7609

WISCONSIN
Hudson
212 Locust St.
(715)386-8228

New Richmond
244 S. Knowles Ave.
(715)246-0011

Roberts
110 W. Main St.
(715)749-9000

Somerset
220 Main St.
(715)247-4992

00697681

Offer Details: Valid anytime. Dine-in or carry out.

Offer validity is governed by the Rules of Use and excludes defined holidays. Offers are not valid with other discount offers, unless specified. Coupons void if purchased, sold or bartered. Discounts exclude tax, tip and/or alcohol, where applicable.

Carbone's

MINNESOTA
Albertville
5986 Main Ave.
(763)497-1497

Bloomington
1834 E. Old Shakopee Rd.
(952)888-5663

Coon Rapids
8525 Cottonwood St. N.W.
(763)717-0327

Eagan
1665 Yankee Doodle Rd.
(651)452-6000

Inver Grove Hgts.
6432 Cahill Ave.
(651)450-7832

Mahtomedi
960 Mahtomedi Ave.
(651)426-5222

Maplewood
2655 White Bear Ave.
(651)770-0075

Minneapolis
4724 Cedar Ave.
(612)724-0063

North Branch
6427 Ash St.
(651)277-5555

Oakdale
705 Century Ave. S.
(651)501-0822

Plymouth
1400 County Rd. 101
(763)473-1477

Savage
4046 County Rd. 42
(952)746-6656

White Bear Lake
1350 Hwy. 96
(651)429-7609

WISCONSIN
Hudson
212 Locust St.
(715)386-8228

New Richmond
244 S. Knowles Ave.
(715)246-0011

Roberts
110 W. Main St.
(715)749-9000

Somerset
220 Main St.
(715)247-4992

00697681

Offer Details: Valid anytime. Dine-in or carry out.

Offer validity is governed by the Rules of Use and excludes defined holidays. Offers are not valid with other discount offers, unless specified. Coupons void if purchased, sold or bartered. Discounts exclude tax, tip and/or alcohol, where applicable.

FREE LARGE PIZZA

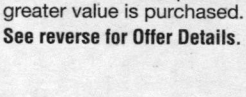

Leonardo's
Enjoy one complimentary LARGE PIZZA when a second LARGE PIZZA of equal or greater value is purchased.
See reverse for Offer Details.

REPEAT SAVINGS

leonardo's PIZZA

www.leos-pizza.com
See Reverse Side for Locations

Valid now thru November 1, 2007

B64

50% OFF

Leonardo's
Enjoy one LARGE SPECIALTY PIZZA at 50% off the regular price.
See reverse for Offer Details.

REPEAT SAVINGS

leonardo's PIZZA

www.leos-pizza.com
See Reverse Side for Locations

Valid now thru November 1, 2007

B65

FREE SALAD

Leonardo's
Enjoy one complimentary SALAD when a second SALAD of equal or greater value is purchased.
See reverse for Offer Details.

REPEAT SAVINGS

leonardo's PIZZA

www.leos-pizza.com
See Reverse Side for Locations

Valid now thru November 1, 2007

B66

CASUAL DINING & FAST FOOD

Leonardo's

leonardo's PIZZA

7875 150th St. W.
Apple Valley, MN
(952)431-2200

16506 W. 78th St.
Eden Prairie, MN
(952)975-0700

8362 Tamarack Village
#123
Woodbury, MN
(651)578-0100

Offer Details: Valid anytime.

00672595

Offer validity is governed by the Rules of Use and excludes defined holidays. Offers are not valid with other discount offers, unless specified. Coupons void if purchased, sold or bartered. Discounts exclude tax, tip and/or alcohol, where applicable.

Leonardo's

leonardo's PIZZA

7875 150th St. W.
Apple Valley, MN
(952)431-2200

16506 W. 78th St.
Eden Prairie, MN
(952)975-0700

8362 Tamarack Village
#123
Woodbury, MN
(651)578-0100

Offer Details: Valid anytime.

00672632

Offer validity is governed by the Rules of Use and excludes defined holidays. Offers are not valid with other discount offers, unless specified. Coupons void if purchased, sold or bartered. Discounts exclude tax, tip and/or alcohol, where applicable.

Leonardo's

leonardo's PIZZA

7875 150th St. W.
Apple Valley, MN
(952)431-2200

16506 W. 78th St.
Eden Prairie, MN
(952)975-0700

8362 Tamarack Village
#123
Woodbury, MN
(651)578-0100

Offer Details: Valid anytime.

00672633

Offer validity is governed by the Rules of Use and excludes defined holidays. Offers are not valid with other discount offers, unless specified. Coupons void if purchased, sold or bartered. Discounts exclude tax, tip and/or alcohol, where applicable.

entertainment.
entertainment.com

Qdoba Mexican Grill
Enjoy one complimentary ENTREE when a second ENTREE of equal or greater value is purchased.
See reverse for Offer Details.
Tracking Code: Promo #169

FREE ENTRÉE

Qdoba
MEXICAN GRILL
www.qdoba.com

See Reverse Side for Locations

Valid now thru November 1, 2007   B67

---

entertainment.
entertainment.com

Spectators Grille & Bar
Enjoy one complimentary LUNCH OR DINNER ENTREE when a second LUNCH OR DINNER ENTREE of equal or greater value is purchased.
See reverse for Offer Details.

Up To $9.00 Value

Spectators Grille & Bar

See Reverse Side for Locations

Valid now thru November 1, 2007   B68

---

entertainment.
entertainment.com

101 Blu
Enjoy one complimentary LUNCH OR DINNER ENTREE when a second LUNCH OR DINNER ENTREE of equal or greater value is purchased.
See reverse for Offer Details.

Up To $10.00 Value

101 blu
Uptown Bar and Restaurant

REPEAT SAVINGS

3001 Hennepin Ave., Minneapolis, MN
(612) 821-0008

Valid now thru November 1, 2007   B69

CASUAL DINING & FAST FOOD

Qdoba Mexican Grill
- What are you going to love at Qdoba?

Qdoba
MEXICAN GRILL

11611 Leona Rd.
Eden Prairie, MN
(952)941-3800

12107 Elm Creek Blvd.
Maple Grove, MN
(763)494-0115

4712 Excelsior Blvd.
St. Louis Park, MN
(952)926-5600

Offer Details: Valid anytime.

00654810

Offer validity is governed by the Rules of Use and excludes defined holidays. Offers are not valid with other discount offers, unless specified. Coupons void if purchased, sold or bartered. Discounts exclude tax, tip and/or alcohol, where applicable.

Spectators Grille & Bar
- Upscale sportsbar with great food & service
- 22 TV's for your favorite sporting events, including 4 big screens
- Express lunch menu
- Patio dining

Spectators
Grille & Bar

6415 Hwy. 10
(Sunfish Commons)
Ramsey, MN
(763)433-2615

5715 Egan Dr.
Savage, MN
(952)226-5800

Offer Details: Valid anytime.

00504546

Offer validity is governed by the Rules of Use and excludes defined holidays. Offers are not valid with other discount offers, unless specified. Coupons void if purchased, sold or bartered. Discounts exclude tax, tip and/or alcohol, where applicable.

101 Blu
- We provide a variety of appetizers for a lighter fare
- Menus changed often & weekly specials are available
- Enjoy our Euro Bistro Cuisine, an eclectic menu with dishes from around the world
- Extensive lunch & dinner menus
- Lunch: 11 a.m.-4 p.m.
- Dinner: 4 p.m.-11 p.m.
- Happy hour 4-7 p.m. nightly
- A variety of DJs with a mix of musical genres play nightly at 8 p.m.

101 blu
Uptown
Bar and Restaurant

3001 Hennepin Ave.
(Calhoun Square)
Minneapolis, MN
(612)821-0008

Offer Details: Valid anytime.

00660623

Offer validity is governed by the Rules of Use and excludes defined holidays. Offers are not valid with other discount offers, unless specified. Coupons void if purchased, sold or bartered. Discounts exclude tax, tip and/or alcohol, where applicable.

La Casita

Enjoy one complimentary LUNCH OR DINNER ENTREE when a second LUNCH OR DINNER ENTREE of equal or greater value is purchased.
See reverse for Offer Details.

Up To $9.00 Value

La Casita
MEXICAN RESTAURANT

Valid now thru November 1, 2007 — See Reverse Side for Locations — B70

Pannekoeken Huis

Enjoy one complimentary DINNER ENTREE when a second DINNER ENTREE of equal or greater value is purchased.
See reverse for Offer Details.

FREE DINNER ENTREE

Pannekoeken Huis

Valid now thru November 1, 2007 — See Reverse Side for Locations — B71

Embers America Restaurant

Enjoy one complimentary ENTREE when a second ENTREE of equal or greater value is purchased.
See reverse for Offer Details.

Up To $9.00 Value

embers®
•FAMILY RESTAURANTS•

Valid now thru November 1, 2007 — See Reverse Side for Locations — B72

CASUAL DINING & FAST FOOD

La Casita
- Best Margaritas - Minneapolis St. Paul Magazine
- Best Happy Hour - Roseville Review
- Happy hour: 3 p.m.-6 p.m. daily
- Children's menu
- Full bar
- Delivery, catering, & in-house banquets available

La Casita
MEXICAN RESTAURANT

5085 Central Ave.
Columbia Hgts., MN
(763) 571-7784

1925 Perimeter Rd.
Roseville, MN
(651) 287-4055

Offer Details: Valid anytime. Dine in only; Specials excluded.

00108858

Offer validity is governed by the Rules of Use and excludes defined holidays. Offers are not valid with other discount offers, unless specified. Coupons void if purchased, sold or bartered. Discounts exclude tax, tip and/or alcohol, where applicable.

Pannekoeken Huis
- The original dutch oven pancake
- Breakfast, lunch & dinner
- Special kids menu

Pannekoeken Huis

1845 E. County Rd. D.
Maplewood, MN
(651) 779-7844

13705 27th Ave. N.
Plymouth, MN
(763) 559-5177

5721 Egan Ave.
Savage, MN
(952) 226-4795

4995 Excelsior Blvd.
St. Louis Park, MN
(952) 920-2120

Offer Details: Valid any evening. Dine in only; Specials excluded.

00622920

Offer validity is governed by the Rules of Use and excludes defined holidays. Offers are not valid with other discount offers, unless specified. Coupons void if purchased, sold or bartered. Discounts exclude tax, tip and/or alcohol, where applicable.

Embers America Restaurant

embers
·FAMILY RESTAURANTS·

222 Chestnut
Chaska, MN
(952) 448-4093

5400 Central Ave. N.E.
Fridley, MN
(763) 571-8637

7700 Nicollet Ave.
(494 & Nicollet Ave.)
Richfield, MN
(612) 866-4411

13105 Main St.
Rogers, MN
(763) 428-4176

Offer Details: Valid anytime.

00108139

Offer validity is governed by the Rules of Use and excludes defined holidays. Offers are not valid with other discount offers, unless specified. Coupons void if purchased, sold or bartered. Discounts exclude tax, tip and/or alcohol, where applicable.

entertainment.
entertainment.com

Darla's Grill & Malt Shop

Enjoy one complimentary LUNCH OR DINNER ENTREE when a second LUNCH OR DINNER ENTREE of equal or greater value is purchased.
See reverse for Offer Details.

REPEAT SAVINGS

Up To $7.00 Value

Darla's Grill & Malt Shop

See Reverse Side for Locations

Valid now thru November 1, 2007

B73

---

entertainment.
entertainment.com

Darla's Grill & Malt Shop

Enjoy one complimentary LUNCH OR DINNER ENTREE when a second LUNCH OR DINNER ENTREE of equal or greater value is purchased.
See reverse for Offer Details.

REPEAT SAVINGS

Up To $7.00 Value

Darla's Grill & Malt Shop

See Reverse Side for Locations

Valid now thru November 1, 2007

B74

CASUAL DINING & FAST FOOD

---

entertainment.
entertainment.com

MacKenzie

Enjoy one complimentary LUNCH OR DINNER ENTREE when a second LUNCH OR DINNER ENTREE of equal or greater value is purchased or for those who prefer - any one pizza at 50% off the regular price.
See reverse for Offer Details.

REPEAT SAVINGS

Up To $7.00 Value

AN AMERICAN BAR
MACKENZIE
WITH A SCOTCH FLAVOR

www.mackenziepub.com

918 Hennepin Ave., Minneapolis, MN
(612)333-7268

Valid now thru November 1, 2007

B75

Darla's Grill & Malt Shop
- Darla's takes pride in being a smoke-free, kid-friendly, family-owned restaurant
- Open daily
- Hand-dipped Brown's premium ice cream
- We have a full menu
- We received a 4-star rating by the Star Tribune
- We've been featured on Good Morning America & TLC's "A Wedding Story"

00617494

Darla's Grill & Malt Shop

131 S. Main St.
Stillwater, MN
(651)439-9294

840 Carmichael
Hudson, WI
(715)386-5994

Offer Details: Valid anytime.

Offer validity is governed by the Rules of Use and excludes defined holidays. Offers are not valid with other discount offers, unless specified. Coupons void if purchased, sold or bartered. Discounts exclude tax, tip and/or alcohol, where applicable.

Darla's Grill & Malt Shop
- Darla's takes pride in being a smoke-free, kid-friendly, family-owned restaurant
- Open daily
- Hand-dipped Brown's premium ice cream
- We have a full menu
- We received a 4-star rating by the Star Tribune
- We've been featured on Good Morning America & TLC's "A Wedding Story"

00617494

Darla's Grill & Malt Shop

131 S. Main St.
Stillwater, MN
(651)439-9294

840 Carmichael
Hudson, WI
(715)386-5994

Offer Details: Valid anytime.

Offer validity is governed by the Rules of Use and excludes defined holidays. Offers are not valid with other discount offers, unless specified. Coupons void if purchased, sold or bartered. Discounts exclude tax, tip and/or alcohol, where applicable.

MacKenzie
- An American bar with a Scotch flavor
- Sandwiches, salads, soups & homemade pizza
- Outdoor seating - or join us inside!
- 5 TV's showing football, basketball, baseball, hockey & NASCAR
- Credit cards accepted
- Upstairs available for private parties

00599780

MACKENZIE — AN AMERICAN BAR WITH A SCOTCH FLAVOR

918 Hennepin Ave.
Minneapolis, MN
(612)333-7268

Offer Details: Valid anytime.

Offer validity is governed by the Rules of Use and excludes defined holidays. Offers are not valid with other discount offers, unless specified. Coupons void if purchased, sold or bartered. Discounts exclude tax, tip and/or alcohol, where applicable.

Imperial Room

Enjoy one complimentary DINNER ENTREE when a second DINNER ENTREE of equal or greater value is purchased.
See reverse for Offer Details.

Up To $9.00 Value

The Imperial Room

417 1st Ave. N., Minneapolis, MN
(612) 376-7676

Valid now thru November 1, 2007   B76

Eli's Food & Cocktails

Enjoy one complimentary LUNCH OR DINNER ENTREE when a second LUNCH OR DINNER ENTREE is purchased.
See reverse for Offer Details.

Up To $19.00 Value

Eli's Food & Cocktails

1225 Hennepin Ave., Minneapolis, MN
(612) 332-9997

Valid now thru November 1, 2007   B77

La Bodega Tapas Bar

Enjoy one complimentary LUNCH OR DINNER ENTREE when a second LUNCH OR DINNER ENTREE of equal or greater value is purchased.
See reverse for Offer Details.

Up To $9.00 Value

La Bodega Tapas Bar

3005 Lyndale Ave S, Minneapolis, MN
(612) 823-2661

Valid now thru November 1, 2007   B78

CASUAL DINING & FAST FOOD

Imperial Room
- Half off happy hour 3:30 p.m.-8 p.m., Tue.-Fri., Sat. 5 p.m.-8 p.m. Select appetizers
- Nightly drink specials starting at 9
- Tue. open mic
- Thurs. live music 5-9 p.m. & happy hour 'til 12 a.m..
- Featured entrees nightly

00620378

The Imperial Room

417 1st Ave. N.
Minneapolis, MN
(612)376-7676

Offer Details: Valid any evening.

Offer validity is governed by the Rules of Use and excludes defined holidays. Offers are not valid with other discount offers, unless specified. Coupons void if purchased, sold or bartered. Discounts exclude tax, tip and/or alcohol, where applicable.

Eli's Food & Cocktails
- Weekly specials
- Weekend brunch
- Martini menu & full bar
- Delicious appetizers
- Soups, salads & sandwiches
- Entrees, pasta, burgers & dogs

00703541

Eli's
FOOD & COCKTAILS

1225 Hennepin Ave.
Minneapolis, MN
(612)332-9997

Offer Details: Valid anytime.
Tipping should be 15% to 20% of TOTAL bill before discount

Offer validity is governed by the Rules of Use and excludes defined holidays. Offers are not valid with other discount offers, unless specified. Coupons void if purchased, sold or bartered. Discounts exclude tax, tip and/or alcohol, where applicable.

La Bodega Tapas Bar
- Best new wine bar - Minneapolis/St. Paul Magazine
- Live music & flamenco dancing Wed-Sat
- Only tapas bar in the Twin Cities
- Open noon to 1 am daily

00461121

La Bodega
TAPAS BAR

3005 Lyndale Ave S
(near corner of Lake St.)
Minneapolis, MN
(612)823-2661

Offer Details: Valid anytime. Friday & Saturday seating before 6:00 p.m. or after 9:00 p.m..

Offer validity is governed by the Rules of Use and excludes defined holidays. Offers are not valid with other discount offers, unless specified. Coupons void if purchased, sold or bartered. Discounts exclude tax, tip and/or alcohol, where applicable.

Harvey's Bar & Grill

Enjoy one complimentary DINNER ENTREE when a second DINNER ENTREE of equal or greater value is purchased.
See reverse for Offer Details.

Up To $9.00 Value

106 N. 3rd St., Minneapolis, MN
(612)343-5930

Valid now thru November 1, 2007

B79

Mell's Beauty Bar

Enjoy one complimentary DINNER ENTREE when a second DINNER ENTREE of equal or greater value is purchased.
See reverse for Offer Details.

Up To $12.00 Value

www.mellsbeautybar.com

606 Washington Ave. N., Minneapolis, MN
(612)338-1680

Valid now thru November 1, 2007

B80

5-8 Tavern & Grill

Enjoy one complimentary LUNCH OR DINNER ENTREE when a second LUNCH OR DINNER ENTREE of equal or greater value is purchased.
See reverse for Offer Details.

Up To $7.00 Value

5·8 TAVERN AND GRILL
Maplewood

2289 Minnehaha Ave., Maplewood, MN
(651)735-5858

Valid now thru November 1, 2007

B81

CASUAL DINING & FAST FOOD

Harvey's Bar & Grill

- Bar food with a flair!
- Harvey's nachos can't be beat
- Everything from salads & wraps to New York strip
- Casual yet classy atmosphere
- Call for entertainment schedule

00491686

106 N. 3rd St.
Minneapolis, MN
(612) 343-5930

Offer Details: Valid any evening. Dine in only.

Offer validity is governed by the Rules of Use and excludes defined holidays. Offers are not valid with other discount offers, unless specified. Coupons void if purchased, sold or bartered. Discounts exclude tax, tip and/or alcohol, where applicable.

Mell's Beauty Bar

- Full service bar, restaurant & licensed beauty salon
- Voted "Best Martini 2003" by citysearch.com
- Choose between a relaxing chair massage or basic manicure for $15 with a drink of your choice
- Delicious appetizers & gourmet pizzas

00586183

606 Washington Ave. N.
Minneapolis, MN
(612) 338-1680

Offer Details: Valid any evening.

Offer validity is governed by the Rules of Use and excludes defined holidays. Offers are not valid with other discount offers, unless specified. Coupons void if purchased, sold or bartered. Discounts exclude tax, tip and/or alcohol, where applicable.

5-8 Tavern & Grill

- Home of the Juicy Lucy & The Best Burger Basket in the Twin Cities
- Burgers, sandwiches & walleye
- Friendly service, great food & modest prices
- Casual family dining

00661240

2289 Minnehaha Ave.
(1.25 mi. north of I-94 on McKnight)
Maplewood, MN
(651) 735-5858

Offer Details: Valid anytime. Dine in only; Specials excluded; This location only.

Offer validity is governed by the Rules of Use and excludes defined holidays. Offers are not valid with other discount offers, unless specified. Coupons void if purchased, sold or bartered. Discounts exclude tax, tip and/or alcohol, where applicable.

Rosen's City Tavern

Enjoy one complimentary LUNCH OR DINNER ENTREE when a second LUNCH OR DINNER ENTREE of equal or greater value is purchased.
See reverse for Offer Details.

Up To $8.00 Value

ROSEN'S CITY TAVERN IN THE DISTRICT

430 1st Ave. N., Minneapolis, MN
(612)338-1926

Valid now thru November 1, 2007

B82

The Refuge

Enjoy one complimentary LUNCH OR DINNER ENTREE when a second LUNCH OR DINNER ENTREE of equal or greater value is purchased.
See reverse for Offer Details.

Up To $7.00 Value

THE REFUGE BAR & GRILL

430 1st Ave. N., Minneapolis, MN
(612)333-8100

Valid now thru November 1, 2007

B83

The District

Enjoy one complimentary LUNCH OR DINNER ENTREE when a second LUNCH OR DINNER ENTREE of equal or greater value is purchased.
See reverse for Offer Details.

Up To $7.00 Value

THE DISTRICT Est. 1996 Warehouse Brewing Co.

430 1st Ave. N., Minneapolis, MN
(612)333-2739

Valid now thru November 1, 2007

B84

CASUAL DINING & FAST FOOD

Rosen's City Tavern

- All new atmosphere & upscale menu - everything from sandwiches to pastas to steaks & more!
- Great happy hour daily with appetizer & drink specials
- Outdoor seating & party/banquet facilities
- Sunday brunch during Vikings home games

ROSEN'S CITY TAVERN IN THE DISTRICT

430 1st Ave. N.
(Warehouse District)
Minneapolis, MN
(612)338-1926

Offer Details: Valid anytime. Valid after 7:30 p.m. on Target Center Event nights.

00087883

Offer validity is governed by the Rules of Use and excludes defined holidays. Offers are not valid with other discount offers, unless specified. Coupons void if purchased, sold or bartered. Discounts exclude tax, tip and/or alcohol, where applicable.

The Refuge

- Appetizers, sandwiches, burgers & salads
- Located down the block from the Target Center

THE REFUGE BAR & GRILL

430 1st Ave. N.
(Warehouse District)
Minneapolis, MN
(612)333-8100

Offer Details: Valid anytime. Valid after 7:30 p.m. on Target Center Event nights.

00303966

Offer validity is governed by the Rules of Use and excludes defined holidays. Offers are not valid with other discount offers, unless specified. Coupons void if purchased, sold or bartered. Discounts exclude tax, tip and/or alcohol, where applicable.

The District

- Appetizers, burgers, sandwiches, pastas, stir fry & more
- Great happy hour daily with appetizer & drink specials

THE DISTRICT Est. 1996
Warehouse Brewing Co.

430 1st Ave. N.
(Warehouse District)
Minneapolis, MN
(612)333-2739

Offer Details: Valid anytime. Valid after 7:30 p.m. on Target Center Event nights.

00216481

Offer validity is governed by the Rules of Use and excludes defined holidays. Offers are not valid with other discount offers, unless specified. Coupons void if purchased, sold or bartered. Discounts exclude tax, tip and/or alcohol, where applicable.

1st of Thai Restaurant

Enjoy one complimentary DINNER ENTREE when a second DINNER ENTREE of equal or greater value is purchased.

See reverse for Offer Details.

Up To $8.00 Value

1st of Thai Restaurant

Valid now thru November 1, 2007

10100 6th Ave. N., Plymouth, MN
(763) 591-6085

B85

5-8 Grill & Bar

Enjoy one complimentary LUNCH OR DINNER ENTREE when a second LUNCH OR DINNER ENTREE of equal or greater value is purchased.

See reverse for Offer Details.

Up To $7.00 Value

5•8 GRILL AND BAR
Champlin

Valid now thru November 1, 2007

6251 Douglas Ct., Champlin, MN
(763) 425-5858

B86

American Pie

Enjoy one complimentary LUNCH OR DINNER ENTREE when a second LUNCH OR DINNER ENTREE of equal or greater value is purchased or for those who prefer - any one pizza at 50% off the regular price - maximum discount $7.00.

See reverse for Offer Details.

Up To $7.00 Value

American Pie

Valid now thru November 1, 2007

6529 Nicollet Ave. S., Richfield, MN
(612) 243-3661

B87

CASUAL DINING & FAST FOOD

1st of Thai Restaurant
- We use only the freshest ingredients
- Made to order
- Thai, Vietnamese & Chinese cuisine
- Open daily

1st of Thai Restaurant

10100 6th Ave. N.
Plymouth, MN
(763)591-6085

Offer Details: Valid any evening. Dine in only.

00670923

Offer validity is governed by the Rules of Use and excludes defined holidays. Offers are not valid with other discount offers, unless specified. Coupons void if purchased, sold or bartered. Discounts exclude tax, tip and/or alcohol, where applicable.

5-8 Grill & Bar
- Casual family dining
- Home of the Juicy Lucy & The Best Burger Basket in the Twin Cities
- Sandwiches, bugers & walleye
- Friendly service, great food & modest prices

5·8 GRILL AND BAR
Champlin

6251 Douglas Ct.
(1.5 mi. east of Hwy. 169 on the corner of 109th & Douglas)
Champlin, MN
(763)425-5858

Offer Details: Valid anytime. Dine in only; Specials excluded; This location only.

00659574

Offer validity is governed by the Rules of Use and excludes defined holidays. Offers are not valid with other discount offers, unless specified. Coupons void if purchased, sold or bartered. Discounts exclude tax, tip and/or alcohol, where applicable.

American Pie
- All of our food is baked to perfection
- We deliver, serving Richfield, Bloomington, Edina & S. Minneapolis

American Pie

6529 Nicollet Ave. S.
Richfield, MN
(612)243-3661

Offer Details: Valid anytime.

00569096

Offer validity is governed by the Rules of Use and excludes defined holidays. Offers are not valid with other discount offers, unless specified. Coupons void if purchased, sold or bartered. Discounts exclude tax, tip and/or alcohol, where applicable.

American Sports Cafe & Nightclub

Enjoy one complimentary DINNER ENTREE when a second DINNER ENTREE of equal or greater value is purchased.

See reverse for Offer Details.

Up To $8.00 Value

AMERICAN SPORTS CAFE & NIGHTCLUB

2554 Como Ave., St. Paul, MN
(651) 646-1339

Valid now thru November 1, 2007

B88

Andy's Garage

Enjoy one complimentary LUNCH OR DINNER ENTREE when a second LUNCH OR DINNER ENTREE of equal or greater value is purchased.

See reverse for Offer Details.

Up To $5.00 Value

Andy's GARAGE

www.andysgaragecafe.com

1825 University Ave., St. Paul, MN
(651) 917-2332

Valid now thru November 1, 2007

B89

Angel O'Malley's

Enjoy any FOOD/BEVERAGE ORDER at 50% off the regular price - maximum discount $5.00.

See reverse for Offer Details.

Up To $5.00 Value

Angel O'Malley's

904 S. 4th St., Stillwater, MN
(651) 430-9654

Valid now thru November 1, 2007

B90

CASUAL DINING & FAST FOOD

American Sports Cafe & Nightclub

- Located just west of 280 on Como
- TVs, pool & darts
- Restaurant & bar hours: 11 am-1 am

AMERICAN SPORTS CAFE & NIGHTCLUB

2554 Como Ave.
(280 & Como)
St. Paul, MN
(651)646-1339

Offer Details: Valid any evening.

00461089

Offer validity is governed by the Rules of Use and excludes defined holidays. Offers are not valid with other discount offers, unless specified. Coupons void if purchased, sold or bartered. Discounts exclude tax, tip and/or alcohol, where applicable.

Andy's Garage

- Good food, good fun!
- American grill - deli sandwiches, soups, ice cream & desserts
- Entertainment Saturday nights
- Written up in Minneapolis/St. Paul magazine & City Pages

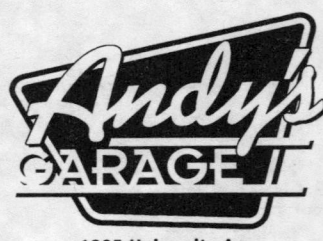

Andy's Garage

1825 University Ave.
St. Paul, MN
(651)917-2332

Offer Details: Valid anytime.

00459813

Offer validity is governed by the Rules of Use and excludes defined holidays. Offers are not valid with other discount offers, unless specified. Coupons void if purchased, sold or bartered. Discounts exclude tax, tip and/or alcohol, where applicable.

Angel O'Malley's

- Fresh "create your own" sandwiches
- Homemade soups, salads & pastries
- Gourmet coffees & teas
- Special occasion cakes

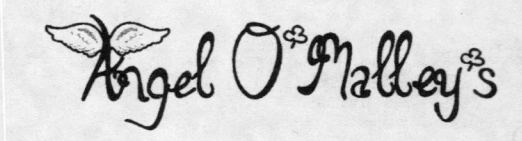

Angel O'Malley's

904 S. 4th St.
Stillwater, MN
(651)430-9654

Offer Details: Valid anytime.

00502092

Offer validity is governed by the Rules of Use and excludes defined holidays. Offers are not valid with other discount offers, unless specified. Coupons void if purchased, sold or bartered. Discounts exclude tax, tip and/or alcohol, where applicable.

CASUAL DINING & FAST FOOD

Anoka Coffee Shop
Enjoy one complimentary ENTREE when a second ENTREE of equal or greater value is purchased.
See reverse for Offer Details.

REPEAT SAVINGS

Valid now thru November 1, 2007

Up To $7.00 Value

Anoka Coffee Shop

530 W. Main, Anoka, MN
(763) 421-9749

B91

Athen's Cafe
Enjoy one complimentary LUNCH OR DINNER ENTREE when a second LUNCH OR DINNER ENTREE of equal or greater value is purchased.
See reverse for Offer Details.

REPEAT SAVINGS

Valid now thru November 1, 2007

Up To $8.00 Value

ATHENS Cafe

4080 W. Broadway, Robbinsdale, MN
(763) 504-0757

B92

Babe's Sports Bar & Grill
Enjoy one complimentary LUNCH OR DINNER ENTREE when a second LUNCH OR DINNER ENTREE of equal or greater value is purchased.
See reverse for Offer Details.

Valid now thru November 1, 2007

Up To $8.00 Value

Babe's SportsBar & Grill
THE BEST of BOTH

20685 Holyoke Ave., Lakeville, MN
(952) 469-5200

B93

Anoka Coffee Shop
- Sandwiches, salads & burgers
- Delicious breakfasts!
- Checks & cash accepted only

Anoka Coffee Shop

530 W. Main
Anoka, MN
(763) 421-9749

Offer Details: Valid anytime.

00610776

Offer validity is governed by the Rules of Use and excludes defined holidays. Offers are not valid with other discount offers, unless specified. Coupons void if purchased, sold or bartered. Discounts exclude tax, tip and/or alcohol, where applicable.

Athen's Cafe
- Located in Robbinsdale Town Center Mall
- Featuring authentic Greek cuisine
- Huge portions and sampler platters featuring lamb kebob, chicken & lamb gyros, falafel, stuffed grape leaves, spinach pie, hummus, rice, greek salad & pita bread
- Many vegetarian entrees

ATHENS Cafe

4080 W. Broadway
(Hwy. 81 & 41st St.)
Robbinsdale, MN
(763) 504-0757

Offer Details: Valid anytime.

00290468

Offer validity is governed by the Rules of Use and excludes defined holidays. Offers are not valid with other discount offers, unless specified. Coupons void if purchased, sold or bartered. Discounts exclude tax, tip and/or alcohol, where applicable.

Babe's Sports Bar & Grill
- Live entertainment every Friday & Saturday night - no cover
- Serving great food and drinks
- Open daily at 11:00 am

Babe's SportsBar & Grill
THE BEST of BOTH

20685 Holyoke Ave.
Lakeville, MN
(952) 469-5200

Offer Details: Valid anytime.

00491648

Offer validity is governed by the Rules of Use and excludes defined holidays. Offers are not valid with other discount offers, unless specified. Coupons void if purchased, sold or bartered. Discounts exclude tax, tip and/or alcohol, where applicable.

The Backyard Bar & Grill

Enjoy one complimentary LUNCH OR DINNER ENTREE when a second LUNCH OR DINNER ENTREE of equal or greater value is purchased.
See reverse for Offer Details.

$10.00 VALUE

The Backyard Bar & Grill

Valid now thru November 1, 2007

1500 E. 78th St., Richfield, MN
(612) 798-0002

B94

Bascali's Brick Oven

Enjoy one complimentary LUNCH OR DINNER ENTREE when a second LUNCH OR DINNER ENTREE of equal or greater value is purchased.
See reverse for Offer Details.

Up To $9.00 Value

BASCALI'S *Wood Fired Italian* **BRICK OVEN**

Valid now thru November 1, 2007

1552 Como Ave, St. Paul, MN
(651) 645-6617

B95

Be-Bop Sports Bar & Grill

Enjoy one complimentary LUNCH OR DINNER ENTREE when a second LUNCH OR DINNER ENTREE of equal or greater value is purchased.
See reverse for Offer Details.

Up To $8.00 Value

BEBOP NIGHTCLUB — SPORTS BAR & GRILL — BLAINE, MN

Valid now thru November 1, 2007

1009 109th Ave. N.E., Blaine, MN
(763) 754-2424

B96

CASUAL DINING & FAST FOOD

The Backyard Bar & Grill
- A place to share some laughs & experience great food & service
- Our menu offers something for everyone
- Daily drink & food specials
- Happy hour 3 p.m.-6 p.m. & 10 p.m.-close
- Kids menu available

The Backyard Bar & Grill

1500 E. 78th St.
Richfield, MN
(612) 798-0002

Offer Details: Valid anytime. Dine in only; Specials excluded.

00614914

Offer validity is governed by the Rules of Use and excludes defined holidays. Offers are not valid with other discount offers, unless specified. Coupons void if purchased, sold or bartered. Discounts exclude tax, tip and/or alcohol, where applicable.

Bascali's Brick Oven
- "Simply Italian"
- Beer & wine selection to compliment your meal
- Convenient to State Fair Grounds & Como Zoo

BASCALI'S
Wood Fired Italian
BRICK OVEN

1552 Como Ave
(Como & Snelling)
St. Paul, MN
(651) 645-6617

Offer Details: Valid anytime.

00455465

Offer validity is governed by the Rules of Use and excludes defined holidays. Offers are not valid with other discount offers, unless specified. Coupons void if purchased, sold or bartered. Discounts exclude tax, tip and/or alcohol, where applicable.

Be-Bop Sports Bar & Grill
- Serving great food & drinks daily at 11 a.m.
- Softball leagues
- Volleyball leagues
- Flag football, boot hockey, broom ball, plus many more activities

BEBOP NIGHTCLUB
SPORTS BAR & GRILL

BLAINE, MN
1009 109th Ave. N.E.
Blaine, MN
(763) 754-2424

Offer Details: Valid anytime.

00502602

Offer validity is governed by the Rules of Use and excludes defined holidays. Offers are not valid with other discount offers, unless specified. Coupons void if purchased, sold or bartered. Discounts exclude tax, tip and/or alcohol, where applicable.

entertainment.com

The Bean Factory
Enjoy one complimentary MENU ITEM when a second MENU ITEM of equal or greater value is purchased.
See reverse for Offer Details.

Up To $5.00 Value

Valid now thru November 1, 2007

See Reverse Side for Locations

B97

---

entertainment.com

Beanhaven Cafe
Enjoy one complimentary MENU ITEM when a second MENU ITEM of equal or greater value is purchased.
See reverse for Offer Details.

$8.00 Value

Beanhaven CAFE

Valid now thru November 1, 2007

18154 Minnetonka Blvd., Deephaven, MN
(952) 475-8488

B98

---

entertainment.com

Beyond Juice
Enjoy one complimentary MENU ITEM when a second MENU ITEM of equal or greater value is purchased.
See reverse for Offer Details.

Up To $7.00 Value

Beyond Juice
Meal in a Cup

www.beyondjuice.com

Valid now thru November 1, 2007

See Reverse Side for Locations

B99

CASUAL DINING & FAST FOOD

The Bean Factory
- Roasted a day at a time
- Full service coffee shop with plenty of seating
- Fresh roasted coffee makes a great gourmet gift
- The lowest roasted bean price in the Twin Cities
- Sandwiches & soups
- J & S Coffee
- Live music
- Gift baskets available

1342 Thomas Ave.
St. Paul, MN

1518 Randolph Ave.
St. Paul, MN
(651) 699-7788

Offer Details: Valid anytime.

00108688

Offer validity is governed by the Rules of Use and excludes defined holidays. Offers are not valid with other discount offers, unless specified. Coupons void if purchased, sold or bartered. Discounts exclude tax, tip and/or alcohol, where applicable.

Beanhaven Cafe
- Breakfast served all day
- Fresh baked muffins & bagels
- Homemade soups
- Hot & cold sandwiches
- Casual catering

Beanhaven CAFE

18154 Minnetonka Blvd.
Deephaven, MN
(952) 475-8488

Offer Details: Valid anytime.

00605050

Offer validity is governed by the Rules of Use and excludes defined holidays. Offers are not valid with other discount offers, unless specified. Coupons void if purchased, sold or bartered. Discounts exclude tax, tip and/or alcohol, where applicable.

Beyond Juice
- A health alternative to fast food
- Free delivery within the Skyway system
- Open 6 a.m.-5 p.m. Mon.-Fri.

Beyond Juice — Meal in a Cup

200 S. 6th St. # 288
(US Bank plaza)
Minneapolis, MN
(612) 371-8000

625 Marquette Ave. S.
(North Star Center)
Minneapolis, MN
(612) 371-8000

Offer Details: Valid anytime.

00633382

Offer validity is governed by the Rules of Use and excludes defined holidays. Offers are not valid with other discount offers, unless specified. Coupons void if purchased, sold or bartered. Discounts exclude tax, tip and/or alcohol, where applicable.

Big Apple Bagels

Enjoy one complimentary SANDWICH when a second SANDWICH of equal or greater value is purchased.

See reverse for Offer Details.

FREE SANDWICH

Big Apple BAGELS
Get Fresh With Us™

See Reverse Side for Locations

Valid now thru November 1, 2007 B100

Big Apple Bagels

Enjoy SIX BAGELS when a second SIX BAGELS of equal or greater value is purchased.

See reverse for Offer Details.

BAGELS

Big Apple BAGELS
Get Fresh With Us™

See Reverse Side for Locations

Valid now thru November 1, 2007 B101

The Bird Nightclub

Enjoy one complimentary DINNER ENTREE when a second DINNER ENTREE of equal or greater value is purchased.

See reverse for Offer Details.

REPEAT SAVINGS

Up To $8.00 Value

THE BIRD NIGHTCLUB

3035 White Bear Ave., Maplewood, MN
(651) 779-2266

Valid now thru November 1, 2007 B102

CASUAL DINING & FAST FOOD

Big Apple Bagels
- Bagels, cream cheese
- Sandwiches
- Espresso drinks
- Deli party trays

Big Apple BAGELS
Get Fresh With Us

229 E. Main St.
Anoka, MN
(763)323-3321

7501 145th St. W
Apple Valley, MN
(952)432-3699

1380 Duckwood Dr.
Eagan, MN
(651)681-9726

508 S Lake St.
Forest Lake, MN
(651)464-4997

1690 White Bear Ave.
Maplewood, MN
(651)770-4900

Offer Details: Valid anytime. BAB's Choice Bagels 20 cents extra.

00410342

Offer validity is governed by the Rules of Use and excludes defined holidays. Offers are not valid with other discount offers, unless specified. Coupons void if purchased, sold or bartered. Discounts exclude tax, tip and/or alcohol, where applicable.

Big Apple Bagels
- Bagels, cream cheese
- Sandwiches
- Espresso drinks
- Deli party trays

Big Apple BAGELS
Get Fresh With Us

229 E. Main St.
Anoka, MN
(763)323-3321

7501 145th St. W
Apple Valley, MN
(952)432-3699

1380 Duckwood Dr.
Eagan, MN
(651)681-9726

508 S Lake St.
Forest Lake, MN
(651)464-4997

1690 White Bear Ave.
Maplewood, MN
(651)770-4900

Offer Details: Valid anytime. BAB's Choice Bagels 20 cents extra.

00410345

Offer validity is governed by the Rules of Use and excludes defined holidays. Offers are not valid with other discount offers, unless specified. Coupons void if purchased, sold or bartered. Discounts exclude tax, tip and/or alcohol, where applicable.

The Bird Nightclub
- Full menu - burgers, sandwiches, appetizers & more
- Dancing every night (ages 18+ Thurs. & Sat.)

THE BIRD
NIGHTCLUB

3035 White Bear Ave.
(2 blocks S of 694 on White Bear Ave.)
Maplewood, MN
(651)779-2266

Offer Details: Valid any evening.

00468070

Offer validity is governed by the Rules of Use and excludes defined holidays. Offers are not valid with other discount offers, unless specified. Coupons void if purchased, sold or bartered. Discounts exclude tax, tip and/or alcohol, where applicable.

Blondies Cafe

Enjoy one complimentary MENU ITEM when a second MENU ITEM of equal or greater value is purchased.

See reverse for Offer Details.

Up To $7.00 Value

Blondies CAFE

www.blondiescafe.com

454 Snelling Ave. S., St. Paul, MN
(651) 204-0152

B103

Valid now thru November 1, 2007

Blondies Sports Grill and Bar

Enjoy one complimentary LUNCH OR DINNER ENTREE when a second LUNCH OR DINNER ENTREE of equal or greater value is purchased.

See reverse for Offer Details.

Up To $10.00 Value

Blondies SPORTS GRILL & BAR

7495 Brooklyn Blvd., Minneapolis, MN
(763) 560-9000

B104

Valid now thru November 1, 2007

Blue Sky Creamery

Enjoy one complimentary MENU ITEM when a second MENU ITEM of equal or greater value is purchased.

See reverse for Offer Details.

Up To $5.00 Value

BLUE SKY CREAMERY

17671 Glasgow Ave., Lakeville, MN
(952) 953-9953

B105

Valid now thru November 1, 2007

CASUAL DINING & FAST FOOD

Blondies Cafe
- Sandwiches & salads
- Freshly made soups
- Homemade desserts & pastries
- Espresso drinks

Blondies CAFE

454 Snelling Ave. S.
St. Paul, MN
(651)204-0152

Offer Details: Valid anytime.

00632128

Offer validity is governed by the Rules of Use and excludes defined holidays. Offers are not valid with other discount offers, unless specified. Coupons void if purchased, sold or bartered. Discounts exclude tax, tip and/or alcohol, where applicable.

Blondies Sports Grill and Bar
- Casual dining with a sports flair
- Patio dining - 20 tables!
- Full bar with 14 beers on tap
- NTN Trivia & QB1 on 41 screens, interactive sports games & food service from 11 am - 12 pm
- Open 365 days a year

Blondies SPORTS GRILL & BAR

7495 Brooklyn Blvd.
Minneapolis, MN
(763)560-9000

Offer Details: Valid anytime.

00374876

Offer validity is governed by the Rules of Use and excludes defined holidays. Offers are not valid with other discount offers, unless specified. Coupons void if purchased, sold or bartered. Discounts exclude tax, tip and/or alcohol, where applicable.

Blue Sky Creamery
- Featuring Nitro Ice Cream

BLUE SKY CREAMERY

17671 Glasgow Ave.
Lakeville, MN
(952)953-9953

Offer Details: Valid anytime.

00611331

Offer validity is governed by the Rules of Use and excludes defined holidays. Offers are not valid with other discount offers, unless specified. Coupons void if purchased, sold or bartered. Discounts exclude tax, tip and/or alcohol, where applicable.

Boca Chica

Enjoy one complimentary DINNER ENTREE when a second DINNER ENTREE of equal or greater value is purchased.

See reverse for Offer Details.

Up $ To **8** .00 Value

The Mexican Experience
Boca Chica
RESTAURANTE & LIQUORS

11 Cesar Chavez St., St. Paul, MN
(651) 222-8499

Valid now thru November 1, 2007

B106

Brewberry's Coffee Shop

Enjoy any FOOD/BEVERAGE ORDER at 50% off the regular price - maximum discount $5.00.

See reverse for Offer Details.

Up $ To **5** .00 Value

BREWBERRYS
Neighborhood COFFEE
Saint Paul, Minnesota

475 Fairview Ave. S., St. Paul, MN
(651) 699-1117

Valid now thru November 1, 2007

B107

Brick House Eatery

Enjoy one complimentary MENU ITEM when a second MENU ITEM of equal or greater value is purchased.

See reverse for Offer Details.

Up $ To **6** .00 Value

BRICK HOUSE EATERY

REPEAT SAVINGS

56 Broadway Ave. E., Forest Lake, MN
(651) 464-7574

Valid now thru November 1, 2007

B108

CASUAL DINING & FAST FOOD

Boca Chica

- Remember your fantastic Mexican vacation saying "I'll be back"? Experience those same feelings at your next fiesta at Boca Chica
- The best authentic Mexican food in town

The Mexican Experience

Boca Chica
RESTAURANTE & LIQUORS

11 Cesar Chavez St.
St. Paul, MN
(651) 222-8499

Offer Details: Valid Sunday thru Friday evenings. Sunday brunch excluded. Not valid on Saturday; Present coupon before ordering; One coupon per customer per visit; Not valid on Mexican/American holidays.

00014671

Offer validity is governed by the Rules of Use and excludes defined holidays. Offers are not valid with other discount offers, unless specified. Coupons void if purchased, sold or bartered. Discounts exclude tax, tip and/or alcohol, where applicable.

Brewberry's Coffee Shop

- Gourmet espresso drinks
- Soups, sandwiches & salads
- Pastries, muffins, scones & cookies
- Granitas & Italian sodas
- Voted "Favorite Coffee Shop 2006" - MN Women's Press
- Bulk coffee beans
- Free Wi-fi
- Open daily

BREWBERRYS Neighborhood COFFEE
Saint Paul, Minnesota

475 Fairview Ave. S.
(at Randolph near St. Kate's)
St. Paul, MN
(651) 699-1117

Offer Details: Valid anytime.

00701423

Offer validity is governed by the Rules of Use and excludes defined holidays. Offers are not valid with other discount offers, unless specified. Coupons void if purchased, sold or bartered. Discounts exclude tax, tip and/or alcohol, where applicable.

Brick House Eatery

- Grilled paninis
- Build your own sandwich
- Soups & salads
- Gourmet espresso drinks
- Kids menu
- Smoothies & 16 flavors of ice cream
- Outdoor patio with a beautiful view of Forest Lake
- Try our homemade brownie ice cream sandwich

BRICK HOUSE EATERY

56 Broadway Ave. E.
(downtown Forest Lake)
Forest Lake, MN
(651) 464-7574

Offer Details: Valid anytime.

00703666

Offer validity is governed by the Rules of Use and excludes defined holidays. Offers are not valid with other discount offers, unless specified. Coupons void if purchased, sold or bartered. Discounts exclude tax, tip and/or alcohol, where applicable.

entertainment.
entertainment.com

Buffalo Tap
Enjoy any FOOD ORDER at 50% off the regular price - maximum discount $5.00.
See reverse for Offer Details.

REPEAT SAVINGS

Valid now thru November 1, 2007

Up To $5.00 Value

BUFFALO TAP
Famous BURGERS & WINGS
www.buffalotap.com

4990 W. 123rd St., Savage, MN
(952)808-7317

B109

---

entertainment.
entertainment.com

The Bulldog Restaurant
Enjoy one complimentary LUNCH OR DINNER ENTREE when a second LUNCH OR DINNER ENTREE of equal or greater value is purchased.
See reverse for Offer Details.

REPEAT SAVINGS

Valid now thru November 1, 2007

Up To $8.00 Value

THE BULLDOG
restaurant

2549 Lyndale Ave. S., Minneapolis, MN
(612)872-8893

B110

---

entertainment.
entertainment.com

Bunkers Music Bar & Grill
Enjoy one complimentary ENTREE when a second ENTREE of equal or greater value is purchased.
See reverse for Offer Details.

REPEAT SAVINGS

Valid now thru November 1, 2007

Up To $8.00 Value

BUNKERS
MUSIC BAR & GRILL

761 N. Washington, Minneapolis, MN
(612)338-8188

B111

CASUAL DINING & FAST FOOD

Buffalo Tap
- Beat the stampede!
- Famous burgers & wings
- Wings from mild to wild
- Coldest beer in town
- Everything served in a frosted mug

BUFFALO·TAP
Famous
BURGERS & WINGS

4990 W. 123rd St.
Savage, MN
(952)808-7317

00471921

Offer Details: Valid anytime. Dine in only.

Offer validity is governed by the Rules of Use and excludes defined holidays. Offers are not valid with other discount offers, unless specified. Coupons void if purchased, sold or bartered. Discounts exclude tax, tip and/or alcohol, where applicable.

The Bulldog Restaurant
- Friendly staff - great service
- 20 tap beers from around the world
- Proud to be serving Chicago-style Vienna beef hot dogs
- Choose from our delicious sandwiches, including vegetarian
- Enjoy our jukebox which has a variety of all-time favorite music
- Golden tee, darts, multiple flat screen TV's

THE BULLDOG
restaurant

2549 Lyndale Ave. S.
Minneapolis, MN
(612)872-8893

00568943

Offer Details: Valid anytime.

Offer validity is governed by the Rules of Use and excludes defined holidays. Offers are not valid with other discount offers, unless specified. Coupons void if purchased, sold or bartered. Discounts exclude tax, tip and/or alcohol, where applicable.

Bunkers Music Bar & Grill
- Live music 7 days a week!
- Happy hour 3 p.m.-7 p.m.
- Lunches & daily blue plate specials
- Lunch available Mon.-Sat. 11 a.m.-4 p.m.

BUNKERS
MUSIC BAR & GRILL

761 N. Washington
Minneapolis, MN
(612)338-8188

00650613

Offer Details: Valid anytime.

Offer validity is governed by the Rules of Use and excludes defined holidays. Offers are not valid with other discount offers, unless specified. Coupons void if purchased, sold or bartered. Discounts exclude tax, tip and/or alcohol, where applicable.

Bunny's

Enjoy one complimentary LUNCH OR DINNER ENTREE when a second LUNCH OR DINNER ENTREE of equal or greater value is purchased.
See reverse for Offer Details.

Up To $9.00 Value

5916 Excelsior Blvd., Minneapolis, MN
(952)922-9515

Valid now thru November 1, 2007

B112

CJ's Coffee & Wine Bar

Enjoy one complimentary MENU ITEM when a second MENU ITEM of equal or greater value is purchased.
See reverse for Offer Details.

Up To $5.00 Value

www.cjscoffeeandwine.com
600 Market St., Ste. 170, Chanhassen, MN
(952)949-8744

Valid now thru November 1, 2007

B113

Capital City Market Cafe & Bar

Enjoy one complimentary DINNER ENTREE when a second DINNER ENTREE of equal or greater value is purchased.
See reverse for Offer Details.

Up To $15.00 Value

411 Minnesota St., St. Paul, MN
(651)605-0266

Valid now thru November 1, 2007

B114

CASUAL DINING & FAST FOOD

Bunny's
- Great sandwiches, soups & salads
- Full bar service
- Open daily

BUNNY'S
BAR & GRILL

5916 Excelsior Blvd.
Minneapolis, MN
(952)922-9515

Offer Details: Valid anytime. Dine in only; Breakfast excluded; Specials excluded.

00054198

Offer validity is governed by the Rules of Use and excludes defined holidays. Offers are not valid with other discount offers, unless specified. Coupons void if purchased, sold or bartered. Discounts exclude tax, tip and/or alcohol, where applicable.

CJ's Coffee & Wine Bar
- Open daily
- Panini sandwiches
- Soups
- Bakery items
- Appetizers
- Desserts
- Live music Fri. & Sat.
- Artisan roasted espresso
- Smoke free
- Free Wifi
- Beer & wine

CJ's
COFFEE & WINE BAR

600 Market St., Ste. 170
Chanhassen, MN
(952)949-8744

Offer Details: Valid anytime. Excludes alcoholic beverages.

00695691

Offer validity is governed by the Rules of Use and excludes defined holidays. Offers are not valid with other discount offers, unless specified. Coupons void if purchased, sold or bartered. Discounts exclude tax, tip and/or alcohol, where applicable.

Capital City Market Cafe & Bar
- Our lunch & dinner menu feature fresh garden salads, delicious homemade soups, sandwiches & daily specials
- Breakfast & lunch is quick deli-style service
- Dinner is full service in a relaxed setting
- Happy hour Mon.-Sat. from 4 p.m.-7 p.m.

CAPITAL CITY
MARKETCAFE & BAR

411 Minnesota St.
St. Paul, MN
(651)605-0266

Offer Details: Valid any evening.
Tipping should be 15% to 20% of TOTAL bill before discount

00637581

Offer validity is governed by the Rules of Use and excludes defined holidays. Offers are not valid with other discount offers, unless specified. Coupons void if purchased, sold or bartered. Discounts exclude tax, tip and/or alcohol, where applicable.

entertainment
entertainment.com

The Cardinal Restaurant & Bar

Enjoy one complimentary ENTREE when a second ENTREE of equal or greater value is purchased.
See reverse for Offer Details.

REPEAT SAVINGS

Valid now thru November 1, 2007

Up To $7.00 Value

the CARDINAL RESTAURANT & BAR

www.cardinaltavern.com

2920 E. 38th St., Minneapolis, MN
(612)724-5837

B115

---

entertainment
entertainment.com

Charly's Polleria Restaurant

Enjoy one complimentary LUNCH OR DINNER ENTREE when a second LUNCH OR DINNER ENTREE of equal or greater value is purchased.
See reverse for Offer Details.

REPEAT SAVINGS

Valid now thru November 1, 2007

Up To $12.00 Value

CHARLY'S POLLERIA RESTAURANT

2851 Central Ave. N.E., Minneapolis, MN
(612)789-9535

B116

---

entertainment
entertainment.com

Chicago Deli Cafe & Grille

Enjoy one complimentary ENTREE when a second ENTREE of equal or greater value is purchased.
See reverse for Offer Details.

REPEAT SAVINGS

Valid now thru November 1, 2007

Up To $10.00 Value

CHICAGO DELI CAFE & GRILLE

4810 Chicago Ave. S., Minneapolis, MN
(612)822-8362

B117

CASUAL DINING & FAST FOOD

The Cardinal Restaurant & Bar

- Burgers, sandwiches & homemade specials
- Serving breakfast, lunch & dinner
- Darts & pool
- Patio

the CARDINAL
RESTAURANT & BAR

2920 E. 38th St.
Minneapolis, MN
(612) 724-5837

Offer Details: Valid anytime. Combination dinners excluded.

00654805

Offer validity is governed by the Rules of Use and excludes defined holidays. Offers are not valid with other discount offers, unless specified. Coupons void if purchased, sold or bartered. Discounts exclude tax, tip and/or alcohol, where applicable.

Charly's Polleria Restaurant

- Ecuadorian cuisine
- Rotisserie chicken & more
- Beer & wine
- 2-for-1 Happy hour 3 p.m.-7 p.m. daily
- Parking in rear

CHARLY'S POLLERIA RESTAURANT

2851 Central Ave. N.E.
Minneapolis, MN
(612) 789-9535

Offer Details: Valid anytime.

00693162

Offer validity is governed by the Rules of Use and excludes defined holidays. Offers are not valid with other discount offers, unless specified. Coupons void if purchased, sold or bartered. Discounts exclude tax, tip and/or alcohol, where applicable.

Chicago Deli Cafe & Grille

- Serving breakfast, lunch & dinner
- Breakfast & lunch specials available
- Try our famous gyros!
- Great sandwiches & Greek dinners
- Homemade pastries
- Delivery available

CHICAGO DELI
CAFE & GRILLE

4810 Chicago Ave. S.
Minneapolis, MN
(612) 822-8362

Offer Details: Valid anytime.

00626872

Offer validity is governed by the Rules of Use and excludes defined holidays. Offers are not valid with other discount offers, unless specified. Coupons void if purchased, sold or bartered. Discounts exclude tax, tip and/or alcohol, where applicable.

Charley's Grilled Subs

Enjoy one complimentary MENU ITEM when a second MENU ITEM of equal or greater value is purchased.

See reverse for Offer Details.

Up To $7.00 Value

Charley's Grilled Subs

N344, Bloomington, MN
(952) 854-2246

B118

Valid now thru November 1, 2007

Charlie's Irish Pub

Enjoy one complimentary MENU ITEM when a second MENU ITEM of equal or greater value is purchased.

See reverse for Offer Details.

Up To $10.00 Value

Charlie's Irish Pub

101 S. Water St., Stillwater, MN
(651) 439-6000

B119

Valid now thru November 1, 2007

Chin Yung

Enjoy one complimentary DINNER ENTREE when a second DINNER ENTREE of equal or greater value is purchased.

See reverse for Offer Details.

Up To $8.00 Value

Chin Yung Chinese Restaurant

金蓉

13704 - 83rd Way N., Maple Grove, MN
(763) 420-8940

B120

Valid now thru November 1, 2007

CASUAL DINING & FAST FOOD

Charley's Grilled Subs

- Charley's has delicious subs-something for everyone!
- Salads
- Deli favorites

Charley's
GRILLED SUBS

N344
(Mall of America)
Bloomington, MN
(952)854-2246

Offer Details: Valid anytime.

00563451

Offer validity is governed by the Rules of Use and excludes defined holidays. Offers are not valid with other discount offers, unless specified. Coupons void if purchased, sold or bartered. Discounts exclude tax, tip and/or alcohol, where applicable.

Charlie's Irish Pub

- Located in the rear of the Water Street Inn on the river front in historic downtown Stillwater

Charlie's Irish 🍀 Pub

101 S. Water St.
Stillwater, MN
(651)439-6000

Offer Details: Valid anytime.

00609078

Offer validity is governed by the Rules of Use and excludes defined holidays. Offers are not valid with other discount offers, unless specified. Coupons void if purchased, sold or bartered. Discounts exclude tax, tip and/or alcohol, where applicable.

Chin Yung

- Family friendly environment
- Our menu is made to order
- Family owned & operated for over 12 years
- Open daily

CHIN YUNG
CHINESE RESTAURANT

13704 - 83rd Way N.
(Rice Lake Plaza)
Maple Grove, MN
(763)420-8940

Offer Details: Valid any evening. House specials excluded; Dine in only. Tipping should be 15% to 20% of TOTAL bill before discount

00682092

Offer validity is governed by the Rules of Use and excludes defined holidays. Offers are not valid with other discount offers, unless specified. Coupons void if purchased, sold or bartered. Discounts exclude tax, tip and/or alcohol, where applicable.

entertainment.com

Chocolat Celeste
Enjoy one complimentary MENU ITEM when a second MENU ITEM of equal or greater value is purchased.
See reverse for Offer Details.

REPEAT SAVINGS

Valid now thru November 1, 2007

Up To $5.00 Value

Chocolat Céleste

www.chocolatceleste.com
2506 University Ave. W., St. Paul, MN
(651) 644-3823

B121

---

entertainment.com

Chula Vista
Enjoy one complimentary LUNCH OR DINNER ENTREE when a second LUNCH OR DINNER ENTREE of equal or greater value is purchased.
See reverse for Offer Details.

REPEAT SAVINGS

Valid now thru November 1, 2007

Up To $11.00 Value

Chula Vista MEXICAN RESTAURANT

1741 S. Robert St., St. Paul, MN
(651) 552-8457

B122

---

entertainment.com

Cinema Grill
Enjoy one complimentary ENTREE when a second ENTREE of equal or greater value is purchased.
See reverse for Offer Details.

Valid now thru November 1, 2007

Up To $10.00 Value

CINEMA GRILL

www.newhopecinemagrill.com
2749 Winnetka Ave. N., New Hope, MN
(763) 417-0017

B123

CASUAL DINING & FAST FOOD

Chocolat Celeste
- Fresh cream truffles
- Ingredient chocolates from around the world
- Delivery throughout the U.S.
-

www.chocolatceleste.com

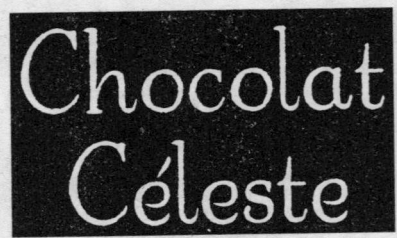

Chocolat Céleste

2506 University Ave. W.
St. Paul, MN
(651) 644-3823

Offer Details: Valid anytime.

00517496

Offer validity is governed by the Rules of Use and excludes defined holidays. Offers are not valid with other discount offers, unless specified. Coupons void if purchased, sold or bartered. Discounts exclude tax, tip and/or alcohol, where applicable.

Chula Vista
- Visit Chula Vista authentic Mexican cuisine, a unique atmosphere
- Many Mexican favorites & some American favorites too!
- Variety of delicious desserts
- Happy hour specials

Chula Vista
MEXICAN RESTAURANT

1741 S. Robert St.
St. Paul, MN
(651) 552-8457

Offer Details: Valid anytime.

00676757

Offer validity is governed by the Rules of Use and excludes defined holidays. Offers are not valid with other discount offers, unless specified. Coupons void if purchased, sold or bartered. Discounts exclude tax, tip and/or alcohol, where applicable.

Cinema Grill
- Enjoy dinner & a great movie
- Casual food, beer, wine & desserts served by our friendly staff
- 1st run movies
- Seating at tables in comfortable swivel chairs
- Children's birthday packages
- Group, school & corporate parties

Cinema Grill

2749 Winnetka Ave. N.
New Hope, MN
(763) 417-0017

Offer Details: Valid anytime.

00690713

Offer validity is governed by the Rules of Use and excludes defined holidays. Offers are not valid with other discount offers, unless specified. Coupons void if purchased, sold or bartered. Discounts exclude tax, tip and/or alcohol, where applicable.

Coffee & Tea LTD.

Enjoy one complimentary MENU ITEM when a second MENU ITEM of equal or greater value is purchased.
See reverse for Offer Details.

Valid now thru November 1, 2007

Up To $5.00 Value

COFFEE & TEA LTD

www.coffeeandtealtd.com

See Reverse Side for Locations

B124

The Coop Restaurant

Enjoy one complimentary LUNCH OR DINNER ENTREE when a second LUNCH OR DINNER ENTREE of equal or greater value is purchased.
See reverse for Offer Details.

Valid now thru November 1, 2007

Up To $7.00 Value

THE COOP RESTAURANT

157 3rd Ave. S., S. St. Paul, MN
(651)455-7566

B125

CASUAL DINING & FAST FOOD

Crystal Cafe & Grill

Enjoy one complimentary ENTREE when a second ENTREE of equal or greater value is purchased.
See reverse for Offer Details.

Valid now thru November 1, 2007

Up To $6.00 Value

Crystal Cafe & Grill

2732 Douglas Dr. N., Crystal, MN
(763)595-0655

B126

Coffee & Tea LTD.
- Largest selection of daily roasted coffees
- Large selection of teas
- Mail order available nationwide
- All coffees & teas available by the cup
- All Coffees roasted at our Minneapolis store
- Expresso, cappuccino, coffee, tea, chai & iced beverages

COFFEE & TEA LTD

2000 NE Court, Sears
(Mall of America)
Bloomington, MN
(952)854-2883

2730 W 43rd St.
Minneapolis, MN
(612)920-6344

www.coffeeandtealtd.com

00378787

Offer Details: Valid anytime.

Offer validity is governed by the Rules of Use and excludes defined holidays. Offers are not valid with other discount offers, unless specified. Coupons void if purchased, sold or bartered. Discounts exclude tax, tip and/or alcohol, where applicable.

The Coop Restaurant
- Burgers, chicken & bbq ribs & more
- Serving customers for over 40 yrs.
- Open 11 a.m.-9 p.m. daily
- Call-in orders welcome

THE COOP
RESTAURANT

157 3rd Ave. S.
(corner of 3rd & S. View Blvd., 1 mi. S. of 494)
S. St. Paul, MN
(651)455-7566

00695298

Offer Details: Valid anytime.

Offer validity is governed by the Rules of Use and excludes defined holidays. Offers are not valid with other discount offers, unless specified. Coupons void if purchased, sold or bartered. Discounts exclude tax, tip and/or alcohol, where applicable.

Crystal Cafe & Grill
- Open daily for breakfast & lunch
- We serve the best pancakes in town!
- Daily specials

Crystal Cafe & Grill

2732 Douglas Dr. N.
Crystal, MN
(763)595-0655

00698475

Offer Details: Valid anytime. Dine in only; Specials excluded.

Offer validity is governed by the Rules of Use and excludes defined holidays. Offers are not valid with other discount offers, unless specified. Coupons void if purchased, sold or bartered. Discounts exclude tax, tip and/or alcohol, where applicable.

Cupcake

Enjoy one complimentary MENU ITEM when a second MENU ITEM of equal or greater value is purchased.
See reverse for Offer Details.

Up To $7.00 Value

cupcake®

Valid now thru November 1, 2007

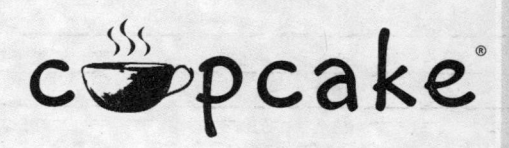

3338 University Ave. S.E., Minneapolis, MN
(612)378-4818

B127

CuppaChiodo's

Enjoy one complimentary MENU ITEM when a second MENU ITEM of equal or greater value is purchased.
See reverse for Offer Details.

Up To $7.00 Value

CuppaChiodo's
Sandwiches, Desserts & More

Valid now thru November 1, 2007

2020 Silver Lake Rd., New Brighton, MN
(651)631-3094

B128

The Daily Grind

Enjoy any BEVERAGE ORDER at 50% off the regular price - maximum discount $5.00.
See reverse for Offer Details.

Up To $5.00 Value

the daily grind

Valid now thru November 1, 2007

100 N. State St., Waseca, MN
(507)835-9186

B129

CASUAL DINING & FAST FOOD

Cupcake
- Coffee shop & bakery
- Breakfast & lunch

cupcake

3338 University Ave. S.E.
Minneapolis, MN
(612)378-4818

Offer Details: Valid anytime.

00590720

Offer validity is governed by the Rules of Use and excludes defined holidays. Offers are not valid with other discount offers, unless specified. Coupons void if purchased, sold or bartered. Discounts exclude tax, tip and/or alcohol, where applicable.

CuppaChiodo's
- Espresso drinks & teas
- Sandwiches, panninis & wraps
- Salads
- Frozen custard, smoothies & Italian sodas
- Desserts & pastries
- Kids meals
- Open daily
- Outside patio

CuppaChiodo's
Coffee & Frozen Custard
Sandwiches, Desserts & More

2020 Silver Lake Rd.
New Brighton, MN
(651)631-3094

Offer Details: Valid anytime.

00633456

Offer validity is governed by the Rules of Use and excludes defined holidays. Offers are not valid with other discount offers, unless specified. Coupons void if purchased, sold or bartered. Discounts exclude tax, tip and/or alcohol, where applicable.

The Daily Grind
- Fruit smoothies
- Italian sodas
- House coffee, cappuccino & lattes
- Iced coffee drinks

the daily grind

100 N. State St.
Waseca, MN
(507)835-9186

Offer Details: Valid anytime.

00670976

Offer validity is governed by the Rules of Use and excludes defined holidays. Offers are not valid with other discount offers, unless specified. Coupons void if purchased, sold or bartered. Discounts exclude tax, tip and/or alcohol, where applicable.

CASUAL DINING & FAST FOOD

---

entertainment.com

The Depot

Enjoy one complimentary MENU ITEM when a second MENU ITEM is purchased.
See reverse for Offer Details.

Up To $5.00 Value

the DepoT coffee House

Valid now thru November 1, 2007

9451 Excelsior, Hopkins, MN
(952)938-2204

B130

---

entertainment.com

Detello's Pizza & Pasta

Enjoy one complimentary DINNER ENTREE when a second DINNER ENTREE of equal or greater value is purchased or for those who prefer - any one pizza at 50% off the regular price.
See reverse for Offer Details.

Up To $8.00 Value

Detello's PIZZA & PASTA

Valid now thru November 1, 2007

6207 Dell Rd., Eden Prairie, MN
(952)934-0333

B131

---

entertainment.com

Diamonds Sports Bar & Grill

Enjoy one complimentary LUNCH OR DINNER ENTREE when a second LUNCH OR DINNER ENTREE of equal or greater value is purchased.
See reverse for Offer Details.

Up To $8.00 Value

DIAMONDS SPORTS BAR & GRILL

REPEAT SAVINGS

www.diamonds-sportsbar.com

Valid now thru November 1, 2007

7550 Hwy. 10 NW, Ramsey, MN
(763)576-1696

B132

The Depot
- Specializing in coffees, teas, sandwiches & soups
- Fun center
- Live music & events

the Depot coffee house

9451 Excelsior
Hopkins, MN
(952)938-2204

Offer Details: Valid anytime.

00312104

Offer validity is governed by the Rules of Use and excludes defined holidays. Offers are not valid with other discount offers, unless specified. Coupons void if purchased, sold or bartered. Discounts exclude tax, tip and/or alcohol, where applicable.

Detello's Pizza & Pasta
- All items are prepared daily in our kitchen
- 20+ Toppings & 3 crusts to choose from
- Try our famous homemade garlic bread
- Family owned & operated for 20 years
- Great selection of fresh salads, homemade pastas & delicious pizza

Detello's PIZZA & PASTA

6207 Dell Rd.
(corner of Hwy. 62 & Hwy. 101)
Eden Prairie, MN
(952)934-0333

Offer Details: Valid any evening. Dine in only; Specials excluded. Tipping should be 15% to 20% of TOTAL bill before discount

00691544

Offer validity is governed by the Rules of Use and excludes defined holidays. Offers are not valid with other discount offers, unless specified. Coupons void if purchased, sold or bartered. Discounts exclude tax, tip and/or alcohol, where applicable.

Diamonds Sports Bar & Grill
- Come to Diamonds, a sports complex with a full service bar & restaurant & a 6000 sq. ft. patio!
- Come for the food, stay for the nightly entertainment starting at 8:30pm (Sun.-Thurs. DJ, Fri. & Sat. live bands)
- Diamonds has 3 softball fields, 4 volleyball courts, darts & pool too!
- So come & see us!
- For delivery call (763) 323-8898

DIAMONDS SPORTS BAR & GRILL

7550 Hwy. 10 NW
(4 mi. W of Anoka)
Ramsey, MN
(763)576-1696

Offer Details: Valid anytime.

00500065

Offer validity is governed by the Rules of Use and excludes defined holidays. Offers are not valid with other discount offers, unless specified. Coupons void if purchased, sold or bartered. Discounts exclude tax, tip and/or alcohol, where applicable.

The Dinkytowner

Enjoy one complimentary ENTREE when a second ENTREE of equal or greater value is purchased.
See reverse for Offer Details.

Up To $7.00 Value

412 1/2 14th Ave. SE, Minneapolis, MN
(612)362-0437

Valid now thru November 1, 2007

B133

Duets

Enjoy one complimentary MENU ITEM when a second MENU ITEM of equal or greater value is purchased.
See reverse for Offer Details.

Up To $5.00 Value

108 West Main St., Belle Plaine, MN
(952)873-2239

Valid now thru November 1, 2007

B134

Durkin's Pub

Enjoy one complimentary LUNCH OR DINNER ENTREE when a second LUNCH OR DINNER ENTREE of equal or greater value is purchased.
See reverse for Offer Details.

Up To $6.00 Value

Durkin's Pub
Est. 1947

227 E. Main St., Anoka, MN
(763)712-0476

Valid now thru November 1, 2007

B135

CASUAL DINING & FAST FOOD

The Dinkytowner
- Serving breakfast anytime
- Nightly entertainment - DJs, live music
- Beer and wine
- Pool tables
- Open 7 days a week
- Open from the early morning to late night

00455805

412 1/2 14th Ave. SE
(Dinkytown)
Minneapolis, MN
(612)362-0437

Offer Details: Valid anytime. Present coupon/card before ordering.

Offer validity is governed by the Rules of Use and excludes defined holidays. Offers are not valid with other discount offers, unless specified. Coupons void if purchased, sold or bartered. Discounts exclude tax, tip and/or alcohol, where applicable.

Duets
- Coffee & espresso
- Deli, bakery & ice cream
- Music & more
- Mon. - Fri. 7 a.m. - 7 p.m.
- Sat. 7 a.m. - 5 p.m., Sun. 8 a.m. - 2 p.m.

00492042

108 West Main St.
Belle Plaine, MN
(952)873-2239

Offer Details: Valid anytime.

Offer validity is governed by the Rules of Use and excludes defined holidays. Offers are not valid with other discount offers, unless specified. Coupons void if purchased, sold or bartered. Discounts exclude tax, tip and/or alcohol, where applicable.

Durkin's Pub
- Great selection of appetizers, sandwiches, burgers, soups, salads & more
- Full service bar
- Live entertainment
- Open 7 days a week

00520545

Est. 1947

227 E. Main St.
(Historic downtown Anoka)
Anoka, MN
(763)712-0476

Offer Details: Valid anytime.

Offer validity is governed by the Rules of Use and excludes defined holidays. Offers are not valid with other discount offers, unless specified. Coupons void if purchased, sold or bartered. Discounts exclude tax, tip and/or alcohol, where applicable.

Eden Restaurant

Enjoy one complimentary ENTREE when a second ENTREE of equal or greater value is purchased.
See reverse for Offer Details.

Up To $6.00 Value

Eden Restaurant

Valid now thru November 1, 2007

7130 Shady Oak Rd., Edens Prairie, MN
(952)944-9603

B136

8th Street Grill

Enjoy one complimentary DINNER ENTREE when a second DINNER ENTREE of equal or greater value is purchased.
See reverse for Offer Details.

Up To $12.00 Value

Valid now thru November 1, 2007

800 Marquette Ave., Minneapolis, MN
(612)349-5717

B137

El Nuevo Rodeo

Enjoy one complimentary LUNCH OR DINNER ENTREE when a second LUNCH OR DINNER ENTREE of equal or greater value is purchased.
See reverse for Offer Details.

Up To $14.00 Value

El Nuevo Rodeo

Valid now thru November 1, 2007

2709 E. Lake St., Minneapolis, MN
(612)728-0101

B138

CASUAL DINING & FAST FOOD

Eden Restaurant
- Specializing in Vietnamese cuisine
- Hours: Mon.-Fri. 11 a.m.-2 p.m., Closed Sat. & Sun.
- Celebrating 20 years in business

00695717

Eden Restaurant

7130 Shady Oak Rd.
Edens Prairie, MN
(952)944-9603

Offer Details: Valid anytime.

Offer validity is governed by the Rules of Use and excludes defined holidays. Offers are not valid with other discount offers, unless specified. Coupons void if purchased, sold or bartered. Discounts exclude tax, tip and/or alcohol, where applicable.

8th Street Grill
- Open Mon.-Wed. 7 a.m.-midnight, Thurs.-Fri. 7 a.m.-1 a.m., Sat. 11 a.m.-1 a.m.
- Featuring great burgers, huge Caesar salads & much more
- Great Happy Hour from 3 p.m.-7 p.m.
- Heated outdoor seating

00280791

Marquette Ave.
8th ST. GRILL

800 Marquette Ave.
Minneapolis, MN
(612)349-5717

Offer Details: Valid any evening.

Offer validity is governed by the Rules of Use and excludes defined holidays. Offers are not valid with other discount offers, unless specified. Coupons void if purchased, sold or bartered. Discounts exclude tax, tip and/or alcohol, where applicable.

El Nuevo Rodeo

00694262

El Nuevo Rodeo

2709 E. Lake St.
Minneapolis, MN
(612)728-0101

Offer Details: Valid anytime.

Offer validity is governed by the Rules of Use and excludes defined holidays. Offers are not valid with other discount offers, unless specified. Coupons void if purchased, sold or bartered. Discounts exclude tax, tip and/or alcohol, where applicable.

El Paraiso Mexican Restaurant

Enjoy one complimentary LUNCH OR DINNER ENTREE when a second LUNCH OR DINNER ENTREE of equal or greater value is purchased.
See reverse for Offer Details.

REPEAT SAVINGS

Valid now thru November 1, 2007

Up To $13.00 Value

El Paraiso
Mexican Restaurant

3501 Nicollet Ave. S., Minneapolis, MN
(612) 823-4707

B139

Enjoy China

Enjoy one complimentary DINNER ENTREE when a second DINNER ENTREE of equal or greater value is purchased.
See reverse for Offer Details.

REPEAT SAVINGS

Valid now thru November 1, 2007

Up To $9.00 Value

ENJOY CHINA
RESTAURANT
Szechuan, Mandarin & Cantonese Cuisine

樂 華

11440 Marketplace Dr., Champlin, MN
(763) 712-1869

B140

Fatboys Bar & Grill

Enjoy one complimentary LUNCH OR DINNER ENTREE when a second LUNCH OR DINNER ENTREE of equal or greater value is purchased.
See reverse for Offer Details.

REPEAT SAVINGS

Valid now thru November 1, 2007

Up To $14.00 Value

Fatboys
BAR & GRILL

www.fatboysmn.com

21383 Ulysses St. N.E., East Bethel, MN
(763) 434-8181

B141

CASUAL DINING & FAST FOOD

El Paraiso Mexican Restaurant
- Authentic Mexican food
- We specialize in seafood
- Live Mariachi weekends
- Beer/wine

El Paraiso
Mexican Restaurant

3501 Nicollet Ave. S.
Minneapolis, MN
(612)823-4707

Offer Details: Valid anytime.

00693171

Offer validity is governed by the Rules of Use and excludes defined holidays. Offers are not valid with other discount offers, unless specified. Coupons void if purchased, sold or bartered. Discounts exclude tax, tip and/or alcohol, where applicable.

Enjoy China
- Szechwan, Mandarin & Cantonese cuisine
- Mon.-Thurs. 11 a.m-9 p.m.
- Fri. & Sat. 11 a.m.-10 p.m.
- Sun. 12 p.m.-9 p.m.
- Lunch buffet
- Take out available
- Beer & wine

ENJOY CHINA
RESTAURANT
Szechuan, Mandarin & Cantonese Cuisine

樂 華

11440 Marketplace Dr.
(Champlin Marketplace, Hwy. 169 & 114th Ave.)
Champlin, MN
(763)712-1869

Offer Details: Valid any evening. Dine in only.
Tipping should be 15% to 20% of TOTAL bill before discount

00624963

Offer validity is governed by the Rules of Use and excludes defined holidays. Offers are not valid with other discount offers, unless specified. Coupons void if purchased, sold or bartered. Discounts exclude tax, tip and/or alcohol, where applicable.

Fatboys Bar & Grill
- Motorcycle themed restaurant
- Delicious sandwiches, burgers & steaks
- Great appetizers
- Lunch buffet Mon.-Fri.
- Happy hour Mon.-Fri. with 2 for 1's

Fatboys
BAR & GRILL

21383 Ulysses St. N.E.
East Bethel, MN
(763)434-8181

Offer Details: Valid anytime. Dine in only; Specials excluded.

00695866

Offer validity is governed by the Rules of Use and excludes defined holidays. Offers are not valid with other discount offers, unless specified. Coupons void if purchased, sold or bartered. Discounts exclude tax, tip and/or alcohol, where applicable.

Fatso's

Enjoy one complimentary LUNCH OR DINNER ENTREE when a second LUNCH OR DINNER ENTREE of equal or greater value is purchased.
See reverse for Offer Details.

Up To $8.00 Value

www.fatsosnightclub.com

1922 First Ave., Anoka, MN
(763)433-2299

Valid now thru November 1, 2007

B142

Flaherty's Pub & Grill

Enjoy one complimentary LUNCH OR DINNER ENTREE when a second LUNCH OR DINNER ENTREE of equal or greater value is purchased.
See reverse for Offer Details.

Up To $8.00 Value

Flaherty's Pub & Grill

www.flahertysbowl.com

1273 W. County Rd. E., Arden Hills, MN
(651)633-1777

Valid now thru November 1, 2007

B143

Flashback Cafe & Cocktail Lounge

Enjoy one complimentary LUNCH OR DINNER ENTREE when a second LUNCH OR DINNER ENTREE of equal or greater value is purchased.
See reverse for Offer Details.

Up To $8.00 Value

Flashback CAFE & COCKTAIL LOUNGE

2520 26th Ave. S., Minneapolis, MN
(612)721-6211

Valid now thru November 1, 2007

B144

CASUAL DINING & FAST FOOD

Fatso's
- Best burgers on Earth!
- Take the ultimate Fatso challenge - eat our 2 lb. burger & get your face in the book of Fatso's
- Great selection of appetizers
- Corporate events & catering

1922 First Ave.
(downtown Anoka)
Anoka, MN
(763)433-2299

Offer Details: Valid anytime. Dine in only; Specials excluded.

00691527

Offer validity is governed by the Rules of Use and excludes defined holidays. Offers are not valid with other discount offers, unless specified. Coupons void if purchased, sold or bartered. Discounts exclude tax, tip and/or alcohol, where applicable.

Flaherty's Pub & Grill
- Birthday parties, company parties
- Cosmic & moonlight bowling
- 36 bowling lanes
- Bumper bowling
- Large game room
- Live bands November thru March on Fridays & Saturdays

1273 W. County Rd. E.
(Snelling & County Rd. E.)
Arden Hills, MN
(651)633-1777

Offer Details: Valid anytime.

00520841

Offer validity is governed by the Rules of Use and excludes defined holidays. Offers are not valid with other discount offers, unless specified. Coupons void if purchased, sold or bartered. Discounts exclude tax, tip and/or alcohol, where applicable.

Flashback Cafe & Cocktail Lounge

2520 26th Ave. S.
Minneapolis, MN
(612)721-6211

Offer Details: Valid anytime. Dine in only.
Tipping should be 15% to 20% of TOTAL bill before discount

00700927

Offer validity is governed by the Rules of Use and excludes defined holidays. Offers are not valid with other discount offers, unless specified. Coupons void if purchased, sold or bartered. Discounts exclude tax, tip and/or alcohol, where applicable.

Figaro's Pizza

FREE PIZZA

Enjoy any one complimentary PIZZA when a second PIZZA of equal or greater value is purchased.

See reverse for Offer Details.

FIGARO'S PIZZA

Valid now thru November 1, 2007

See Reverse Side for Locations

B145

Fresco Juice Company

Up To $5.00 Value

Enjoy one complimentary FOOD/BEVERAGE ORDER when a second FOOD/BEVERAGE ORDER of equal or greater value is purchased.

See reverse for Offer Details.

REPEAT SAVINGS

FRESCO JUICE COMPANY

1426 W Lake St., Minneapolis, MN
(612)825-6556

Valid now thru November 1, 2007

B146

Freshens

ONE YOGURT OR ICE CREAM CUP OR CONE

Enjoy one complimentary YOGURT OR ICE CREAM CUP OR CONE when a second YOGURT OR ICE CREAM CUP OR CONE of equal or greater value is purchased.

See reverse for Offer Details.

REPEAT SAVINGS

Freshëns PREMIUM YOGURT & ICE CREAM

Valid now thru November 1, 2007

See Reverse Side for Locations

B147

CASUAL DINING & FAST FOOD

Figaro's Pizza
- We deliver!
- We bake or you bake!
- Pizza, calzones, salads, breadsticks & more
- Fun kids pizzas
- Open for lunch & dinner

FIGARO'S PIZZA

726 Martin St.
(and Hwy. 10)
Big Lake, MN
(763)262-7437

10400 Baltimore St. N.E.
Blaine, MN
(763)398-6800

262 Travelers Trail
Burnsville, MN
(952)895-9100

2211 11th Ave. E.
North St. Paul, MN
(651)748-9999

Offer Details: Valid anytime.

00109294

Offer validity is governed by the Rules of Use and excludes defined holidays. Offers are not valid with other discount offers, unless specified. Coupons void if purchased, sold or bartered. Discounts exclude tax, tip and/or alcohol, where applicable.

Fresco Juice Company
- Located in Uptown near the corner of Lake & Hennepin
- Specializing in real fruit smoothies
- Fresh vegetable juices
- Fresh fruit juices
- Hot drinks & healthy goodies

FRESCO JUICE COMPANY

1426 W Lake St.
Minneapolis, MN
(612)825-6556

Offer Details: Valid anytime.

00278509

Offer validity is governed by the Rules of Use and excludes defined holidays. Offers are not valid with other discount offers, unless specified. Coupons void if purchased, sold or bartered. Discounts exclude tax, tip and/or alcohol, where applicable.

Freshens
- Frozen yogurt
- Hard ice cream
- Fruit smoothies
- Pretzels
- CinnaMonster cinnamon rolls

Freshëns PREMIUM YOGURT & ICE CREAM

N126 N. Garden
(Mall of America)
Bloomington, MN
(952)858-9812

S336 South Ave.
(Mall of America)
Bloomington, MN
(952)858-9814

120 S. 6th St.
(One Financial Plaza)
Minneapolis, MN
(612)338-8066

Offer Details: Valid anytime.

00593017

Offer validity is governed by the Rules of Use and excludes defined holidays. Offers are not valid with other discount offers, unless specified. Coupons void if purchased, sold or bartered. Discounts exclude tax, tip and/or alcohol, where applicable.

Gabby's Saloon & Eatery

Enjoy one complimentary ENTREE when a second ENTREE of equal or greater value is purchased.
See reverse for Offer Details.

Up To $11.00 Value

1900 Marshall St. NE, Minneapolis, MN
(612)788-8239

Valid now thru November 1, 2007

B148

Gator's Garden Cafe

Enjoy one complimentary LUNCH OR DINNER ENTREE when a second LUNCH OR DINNER ENTREE of equal or greater value is purchased.
See reverse for Offer Details.

Up To $11.00 Value

13001 62nd Place, Maple Grove, MN
(763)553-9711

Valid now thru November 1, 2007

B149

General Store Cafe

Enjoy any FOOD/BEVERAGE ORDER at 50% off the regular price - maximum discount $5.00.
See reverse for Offer Details.

Up To $5.00 Value

14401 Hwy. 7, Minnetonka, MN
(952)979-9156

Valid now thru November 1, 2007

B150

CASUAL DINING & FAST FOOD

Gabby's Saloon & Eatery

- Unique night club/sports bar on the river
- Sports bar downstairs, big screen TV's, game room & patio bar open seven days a week
- Night club upstairs, DJ's and live music open 7 PM - 1 AM Mon - Sun

gabby's saloon & eatery

1900 Marshall St. NE
Minneapolis, MN
(612) 788-8239

Offer Details: Valid anytime. Dine in only. Excludes appetizers and daily specials.

00228194

Offer validity is governed by the Rules of Use and excludes defined holidays. Offers are not valid with other discount offers, unless specified. Coupons void if purchased, sold or bartered. Discounts exclude tax, tip and/or alcohol, where applicable.

Gator's Garden Cafe

- Enjoy appetizers to ribs inside Gator's Garden Cafe or on the patio.
- The Garden Cafe offers a bright, open atmosphere.
- We offer a full menu and beverage service.
- All size groups are welcome.
- The entertainment complex also features a high energy nightclub, state of the art bowling center, banquet facility and volleyball courts.

Gator's Garden Café

13001 62nd Place
Maple Grove, MN
(763) 553-9111

Offer Details: Valid anytime.
Tipping should be 15% to 20% of TOTAL bill before discount

00084595

Offer validity is governed by the Rules of Use and excludes defined holidays. Offers are not valid with other discount offers, unless specified. Coupons void if purchased, sold or bartered. Discounts exclude tax, tip and/or alcohol, where applicable.

General Store Cafe

- Everything is homemade
- Lunch served from 11 a.m.-2 p.m. weekdays - soups, salads & sandwiches
- Desserts & coffee served weekdays from 9:30 a.m.-9 p.m.
- Espresso drinks, smoothies & ice cream

GENERAL STORE Café

14401 Hwy. 7
(located in the General Store of Minnetonka)
Minnetonka, MN
(952) 979-9156

Offer Details: Valid anytime.

00584558

Offer validity is governed by the Rules of Use and excludes defined holidays. Offers are not valid with other discount offers, unless specified. Coupons void if purchased, sold or bartered. Discounts exclude tax, tip and/or alcohol, where applicable.

entertainment.com

Genghis Grill
Enjoy one complimentary LUNCH OR DINNER ENTREE when a second LUNCH OR DINNER ENTREE of equal or greater value is purchased.
See reverse for Offer Details.

REPEAT SAVINGS

Valid now thru November 1, 2007

Up To $13.00 Value

GENGHIS GRILL
THE MONGOLIAN STIR FRY

www.genghisgrill.com
1304 Town Centre Dr., Eagan, MN
(651) 452-2363

B151

---

entertainment.com

Genghis Grill
Enjoy one complimentary LUNCH OR DINNER ENTREE when a second LUNCH OR DINNER ENTREE of equal or greater value is purchased.
See reverse for Offer Details.

REPEAT SAVINGS

Valid now thru November 1, 2007

Up To $13.00 Value

GENGHIS GRILL
THE MONGOLIAN STIR FRY

www.genghisgrill.com
1304 Town Centre Dr., Eagan, MN
(651) 452-2363

B152

---

entertainment.com

Great Steak & Potato Co.
Enjoy one complimentary MENU ITEM when a second MENU ITEM of equal or greater value is purchased.
See reverse for Offer Details.

REPEAT SAVINGS

Valid now thru November 1, 2007

Up To $6.00 Value

THE GREAT STEAK & POTATO COMPANY

See Reverse Side for Locations

B153

CASUAL DINING & FAST FOOD

Genghis Grill
- Mongolian stir fry
- Build your own bowl

GENGHIS GRILL
THE MONGOLIAN STIR FRY

1304 Town Centre Dr.
Eagan, MN
(651)452-2363

Offer Details: Valid anytime.
Tipping should be 15% to 20% of TOTAL bill before discount

00695260

Offer validity is governed by the Rules of Use and excludes defined holidays. Offers are not valid with other discount offers, unless specified. Coupons void if purchased, sold or bartered. Discounts exclude tax, tip and/or alcohol, where applicable.

Genghis Grill
- Mongolian stir fry
- Build your own bowl

GENGHIS GRILL
THE MONGOLIAN STIR FRY

1304 Town Centre Dr.
Eagan, MN
(651)452-2363

Offer Details: Valid anytime.
Tipping should be 15% to 20% of TOTAL bill before discount

00695260

Offer validity is governed by the Rules of Use and excludes defined holidays. Offers are not valid with other discount offers, unless specified. Coupons void if purchased, sold or bartered. Discounts exclude tax, tip and/or alcohol, where applicable.

Great Steak & Potato Co.
- America's #1 grilled sandwiches
- Great steak
- Chicken Philly
- Ham Explosion
- Turkey Philly
- Veggie Delight
- Baked potato
- Low-carb wraps
- Fresh cut fries
- Grilled salad

THE GREAT STEAK & POTATO COMPANY

388 South Ave.
(Mall of America)
Bloomington, MN
(952)858-8263

333 Apache Dr. S.W. #198
Rochester, MN
(507)536-9162

Offer Details: Valid anytime.

00443709

Offer validity is governed by the Rules of Use and excludes defined holidays. Offers are not valid with other discount offers, unless specified. Coupons void if purchased, sold or bartered. Discounts exclude tax, tip and/or alcohol, where applicable.

The Grille at Elk River Country Club

Enjoy one complimentary ENTREE when a second ENTREE of equal or greater value is purchased.
See reverse for Offer Details.

REPEAT SAVINGS

Valid now thru November 1, 2007

Up To $7.00 Value

The Grille at ELK RIVER COUNTRY CLUB

20015 Elk Lake Rd., Elk River, MN
(763)441-4163

B154

Heartbreakers Bar & Grill

Enjoy one complimentary LUNCH OR DINNER ENTREE when a second LUNCH OR DINNER ENTREE of equal or greater value is purchased or for those who prefer - any one pizza at 50% off the regular price.
See reverse for Offer Details.

REPEAT SAVINGS

Valid now thru November 1, 2007

Up To $8.00 Value

Heartbreakers BAR & GRILL

222 Pioneer Trail, Chaska, MN
(952)448-2743

B155

CASUAL DINING & FAST FOOD

Heavenly Daze Coffee

Enjoy one complimentary MENU ITEM when a second MENU ITEM of equal or greater value is purchased.
See reverse for Offer Details.

REPEAT SAVINGS

Valid now thru November 1, 2007

Up To $5.00 Value

Heavenly Daze Coffee

1853 Washington Ave. S., Minneapolis, MN
(612)341-1106

B156

The Grille at Elk River Country Club

- Public always welcome!
- Serving a full menu of breakfast, lunch & dinner
- After golfing on our scenic 18 hole golf course, stop in for delicious salads, sandwiches, burgers & more
- Banquet, wedding & meeting facilities available

The Grille at ELK RIVER COUNTRY CLUB

20015 Elk Lake Rd.
Elk River, MN
(763) 441-4163

Offer Details: Valid anytime.

00472541

Offer validity is governed by the Rules of Use and excludes defined holidays. Offers are not valid with other discount offers, unless specified. Coupons void if purchased, sold or bartered. Discounts exclude tax, tip and/or alcohol, where applicable.

Heartbreakers Bar & Grill

- Lousy food - warm beer
- Appetizers & soups
- Sandwiches, hoagies & wraps
- Pizza
- Burgers, chicken & fish

Heartbreakers BAR & GRILL

222 Pioneer Trail
Chaska, MN
(952) 448-2743

Offer Details: Valid anytime.

00700416

Offer validity is governed by the Rules of Use and excludes defined holidays. Offers are not valid with other discount offers, unless specified. Coupons void if purchased, sold or bartered. Discounts exclude tax, tip and/or alcohol, where applicable.

Heavenly Daze Coffee

- Full espresso bar
- Roasted fresh locally
- Soups, sandwiches & smoothies
- Selection of teas & desserts
- Comfortable, relaxing non-smoking atmosphere

Heavenly Daze Coffee

1853 Washington Ave. S.
(Across from University of Minnesota Law School)
Minneapolis, MN
(612) 341-1106

Offer Details: Valid anytime.

00493286

Offer validity is governed by the Rules of Use and excludes defined holidays. Offers are not valid with other discount offers, unless specified. Coupons void if purchased, sold or bartered. Discounts exclude tax, tip and/or alcohol, where applicable.

Hopper's Bar & Grill

Enjoy one complimentary LUNCH OR DINNER ENTREE when a second LUNCH OR DINNER ENTREE of equal or greater value is purchased.

See reverse for Offer Details.

Up To $5.00 Value

Hoppers
Bar & Grill

119 S. Olive St., Waconia, MN
(952) 442-1149

Valid now thru November 1, 2007

B157

Hunan Garden Chinese Restaurant

Enjoy one complimentary ENTREE when a second ENTREE of equal or greater value is purchased.

See reverse for Offer Details.

Up To $10.00 Value

HUNAN GARDEN

380 Cedar St., St. Paul, MN
(651) 224-7588

Valid now thru November 1, 2007

B158

J.R. Mac's Bar & Grill

Enjoy one complimentary LUNCH OR DINNER ENTREE when a second LUNCH OR DINNER ENTREE of equal or greater value is purchased.

See reverse for Offer Details.

Up To $7.00 Value

J.R. MAC'S

1420 W. 7th St., St. Paul, MN
(651) 224-8482

Valid now thru November 1, 2007

B159

CASUAL DINING & FAST FOOD

Hopper's Bar & Grill

- Home of the coldest beer on earth!
- Happy Hour prices from 10 a.m.-6 p.m. Mon.-Fri.
- Located across from the Waconia Theatre
- Sandwiches, burgers & pizza
- Live music Fri. & Sat. nights at 9 p.m.

Hoppers
Bar & Grill

119 S. Olive St.
Waconia, MN
(952)442-1149

Offer Details: Valid anytime.

00527303

Offer validity is governed by the Rules of Use and excludes defined holidays. Offers are not valid with other discount offers, unless specified. Coupons void if purchased, sold or bartered. Discounts exclude tax, tip and/or alcohol, where applicable.

Hunan Garden Chinese Restaurant

- This gracious Chinese restaurant features traditional Hunan & Szechuan cuisine.
- Vegetarian entrees available upon request.
- Located in downtown St. Paul, Hunan Garden offers excellent food & a comfortable atmosphere.
- Full bar & banquet facilities available.
- Tues, Wed & Thurs live entertainment.
- Hours: Mon-Thurs 11am-9:30pm, Fri & Sat 11am-10:30pm, Sun 3-9:30pm.

HUNAN GARDEN

380 Cedar St.
(corner of 6th & Cedar)
St. Paul, MN
(651)224-7588

Offer Details: Valid any evening. Dine in only.
Tipping should be 15% to 20% of TOTAL bill before discount

00044353

Offer validity is governed by the Rules of Use and excludes defined holidays. Offers are not valid with other discount offers, unless specified. Coupons void if purchased, sold or bartered. Discounts exclude tax, tip and/or alcohol, where applicable.

J.R. Mac's Bar & Grill

- Great food - Great fun
- Party room available
- Full service bar

J.R. MAC'S

1420 W. 7th St.
(W. 7th & Otto St.)
St. Paul, MN
(651)224-8482

Offer Details: Valid anytime.

00529150

Offer validity is governed by the Rules of Use and excludes defined holidays. Offers are not valid with other discount offers, unless specified. Coupons void if purchased, sold or bartered. Discounts exclude tax, tip and/or alcohol, where applicable.

J.R. Mac's Bar & Grill

Enjoy one complimentary LUNCH OR DINNER ENTREE when a second LUNCH OR DINNER ENTREE of equal or greater value is purchased.

See reverse for Offer Details.

Up To $7.00 Value

J.R. MAC'S

1420 W. 7th St., St. Paul, MN
(651) 224-8482

Valid now thru November 1, 2007

B160

JJ's Clubhouse

Enjoy one complimentary LUNCH OR DINNER ENTREE when a second LUNCH OR DINNER ENTREE of equal or greater value is purchased or for those who prefer - any one pizza at 50% off the regular price.

See reverse for Offer Details.

Up To $9.00 Value

JJ's Clubhouse
SPORTS BAR & GRILL

6400 Wayzata Blvd., Golden Valley, MN
(763) 595-8771

Valid now thru November 1, 2007

B161

Jackson Street Grill & Bar

Enjoy one complimentary DINNER ENTREE when a second DINNER ENTREE of equal or greater value is purchased.

See reverse for Offer Details.

Up To $8.00 Value

JACKSON STREET GRILL & BAR

227 Jackson St., Anoka, MN
(763) 323-8083

Valid now thru November 1, 2007

B162

CASUAL DINING & FAST FOOD

J.R. Mac's Bar & Grill
- Great food - Great fun
- Party room available
- Full service bar

00529150

J.R. MAC'S

1420 W. 7th St.
(W. 7th & Otto St.)
St. Paul, MN
(651) 224-8482

Offer Details: Valid anytime.

Offer validity is governed by the Rules of Use and excludes defined holidays. Offers are not valid with other discount offers, unless specified. Coupons void if purchased, sold or bartered. Discounts exclude tax, tip and/or alcohol, where applicable.

JJ's Clubhouse
- Dining in a casual, sports bar atmosphere
- Watch your favorite sporting event on one of our many T.V.'s, or enjoy a game of darts
- Great burgers & chicken sandwiches
- Patio seating available
- Come try our brunch menu on Saturday & Sunday mornings

00322158

JJ's Clubhouse
SPORTS BAR & GRILL

6400 Wayzata Blvd.
(N Frontage Rd. of 394 & Louisiana)
Golden Valley, MN
(763) 595-8771

Offer Details: Valid anytime. Dine in only. Valid also on Saturday & Sunday brunch.

Offer validity is governed by the Rules of Use and excludes defined holidays. Offers are not valid with other discount offers, unless specified. Coupons void if purchased, sold or bartered. Discounts exclude tax, tip and/or alcohol, where applicable.

Jackson Street Grill & Bar
- Burgers & sandwiches
- Soups & salads
- Delicious house specialties & appetizers
- Kid's menu

00547398

JACKSON STREET GRILL & BAR

227 Jackson St.
Anoka, MN
(763) 323-8083

Offer Details: Valid any evening.

Offer validity is governed by the Rules of Use and excludes defined holidays. Offers are not valid with other discount offers, unless specified. Coupons void if purchased, sold or bartered. Discounts exclude tax, tip and/or alcohol, where applicable.

CASUAL DINING & FAST FOOD

Jamaica Jamaica

Up To $12.00 Value

Enjoy one complimentary LUNCH OR DINNER ENTREE when a second LUNCH OR DINNER ENTREE of equal or greater value is purchased.
See reverse for Offer Details.

REPEAT SAVINGS

JAMAICA JAMAICA

Valid now thru November 1, 2007

3765 Bloomington Ave. S., Minneapolis, MN
(612)721-0264

B163

Judes Coffee & Eatery

Up To $5.00 Value

Enjoy one complimentary MENU ITEM when a second MENU ITEM of equal or greater value is purchased.
See reverse for Offer Details.

REPEAT SAVINGS

Jude's Coffee & Eatery

Valid now thru November 1, 2007

421 Marie Ave., S. St. Paul, MN
(651)450-1555

B164

KinhDo Restaurant

Up To $7.00 Value

Enjoy one complimentary LUNCH OR DINNER ENTREE when a second LUNCH OR DINNER ENTREE of equal or greater value is purchased.
See reverse for Offer Details.

KINHDO

Valid now thru November 1, 2007

2709 Winnetka Ave. N., New Hope, MN
(763)544-8440

B165

Jamaica Jamaica
- Come to Jamaica Jamaica for authentic Jamaican cuisine
- Jerk chicken, pork, wings & shrimp
- Curry goat & oxtail
- Curry vegetables & much more
- Spicy or mild
- Open Tues.-Sat.
- We take reservations!

Jamaica Jamaica

3765 Bloomington Ave. S.
(corner of 38th & Bloomington)
Minneapolis, MN
(612)721-0264

Offer Details: Valid anytime. Dine in only.

00568838

Offer validity is governed by the Rules of Use and excludes defined holidays. Offers are not valid with other discount offers, unless specified. Coupons void if purchased, sold or bartered. Discounts exclude tax, tip and/or alcohol, where applicable.

Judes Coffee & Eatery
- Specialty coffee
- Soups & sandwiches

Jude's Coffee & Eatery

421 Marie Ave.
S. St. Paul, MN
(651)450-1555

Offer Details: Valid anytime.

00573370

Offer validity is governed by the Rules of Use and excludes defined holidays. Offers are not valid with other discount offers, unless specified. Coupons void if purchased, sold or bartered. Discounts exclude tax, tip and/or alcohol, where applicable.

KinhDo Restaurant

KinhDo

2709 Winnetka Ave. N.
New Hope, MN
(763)544-8440

Offer Details: Valid anytime.

00184052

Offer validity is governed by the Rules of Use and excludes defined holidays. Offers are not valid with other discount offers, unless specified. Coupons void if purchased, sold or bartered. Discounts exclude tax, tip and/or alcohol, where applicable.

CASUAL DINING & FAST FOOD

Lastrack Family Restaurant

Enjoy one complimentary ENTREE when a second ENTREE of equal or greater value is purchased.
See reverse for Offer Details.

Up To $10.00 Value

LASTRACK Family RESTAURANT

6370 Concord Blvd., Inver Grove Hgts., MN
(651)455-4518

REPEAT SAVINGS

Valid now thru November 1, 2007

B166

Legends Bar & Grill

Enjoy one complimentary LUNCH OR DINNER ENTREE when a second LUNCH OR DINNER ENTREE of equal or greater value is purchased.
See reverse for Offer Details.

Up To $9.00 Value

est. 1990
LEGENDS
BAR & GRILL

825 E. Hennepin Ave., Minneapolis, MN
(612)331-8781

REPEAT SAVINGS

Valid now thru November 1, 2007

B167

Linwood Pizza

Enjoy one complimentary LARGE PIZZA when a second LARGE PIZZA of equal or greater value is purchased.
See reverse for Offer Details.

FREE LARGE PIZZA

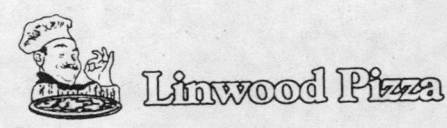

Linwood Pizza

See Reverse Side for Locations

REPEAT SAVINGS

Valid now thru November 1, 2007

B168

Lastrack Family Restaurant
- Fresh ground coffee
- Breakfast served all day
- Homemade soups
- Sandwiches & burgers
- Soups & salads
- Entrees

LASTRACK
Family
RESTAURANT

6370 Concord Blvd.
Inver Grove Hgts., MN
(651)455-4518

Offer Details: Valid anytime.

00695294

Offer validity is governed by the Rules of Use and excludes defined holidays. Offers are not valid with other discount offers, unless specified. Coupons void if purchased, sold or bartered. Discounts exclude tax, tip and/or alcohol, where applicable.

Legends Bar & Grill
- Friendly, warm, casual atmosphere
- Legends' gourmet burgers
- Italian specialties
- Homemade soups
- Specialty sandwiches served on fresh-baked breads
- And much more!

est. 1990

LEGENDS
BAR & GRILL

825 E. Hennepin Ave.
Minneapolis, MN
(612)331-8781

Offer Details: Valid anytime.

00665757

Offer validity is governed by the Rules of Use and excludes defined holidays. Offers are not valid with other discount offers, unless specified. Coupons void if purchased, sold or bartered. Discounts exclude tax, tip and/or alcohol, where applicable.

Linwood Pizza
- Gourmet pizzas
- Always fresh ingredients, never frozen
- "Not your average Joe's"

Linwood Pizza

#21 121st N.W.
Coon Rapids, MN
(763)767-0363
303 Credit Union Dr. #1
Isanti, MN
(763)444-6900

12925 Lake Blvd.
Lindstrom, MN
(651)257-1166
21831 Viking Blvd.
Linwood, MN
(651)462-8414

365 S. Dana Ave.
Rush City, MN
(320)358-1022

Offer Details: Valid anytime. Dine-in or carry out.

00681654

Offer validity is governed by the Rules of Use and excludes defined holidays. Offers are not valid with other discount offers, unless specified. Coupons void if purchased, sold or bartered. Discounts exclude tax, tip and/or alcohol, where applicable.

entertainment.
entertainment.com

Little Sushi on the Prairie
Enjoy one complimentary LUNCH OR DINNER ENTREE when a second LUNCH OR DINNER ENTREE of equal or greater value is purchased.
See reverse for Offer Details.

REPEAT SAVINGS

Valid now thru November 1, 2007

Up To $15.00 Value

Little Sushi on the Prairie
www.littlesushiontheprairie.com

8353 Crystal View Rd., Eden Prairie, MN
(952)944-0962

B169

---

entertainment.
entertainment.com

Lone Tree Bar & Grill
Enjoy one complimentary ENTREE when a second ENTREE of equal or greater value is purchased.
See reverse for Offer Details.

REPEAT SAVINGS

Valid now thru November 1, 2007

Up To $10.00 Value

Lone Tree
BAR & GRILLE

528 Hennepin Ave., Minneapolis, MN
(612)338-1730

B170

---

entertainment.
entertainment.com

The Lookout Bar & Grill
Enjoy one complimentary LUNCH OR DINNER ENTREE when a second LUNCH OR DINNER ENTREE of equal or greater value is purchased.
See reverse for Offer Details.

REPEAT SAVINGS

Valid now thru November 1, 2007

Up To $13.00 Value

The Lookout
Catering
BAR & GRILL
www.lookoutbarandgrill.com

8672 Pineview Ln. N., Maple Grove, MN
(763)424-4365

B171

CASUAL DINING & FAST FOOD

Little Sushi on the Prairie

- Open daily
- We specialize in sushi
- Tempura & teriyaki specialties
- Pork, chicken & steak entrees
- Beer & wine available
- Great review in the Star Tribune

Little Sushi on the Prairie

8353 Crystal View Rd.
(between Punch & Chevy's)
Eden Prairie, MN
(952)944-0962

Offer Details: Valid anytime. Combination dishes excluded; Dine in only. Tipping should be 15% to 20% of TOTAL bill before discount

00690586

Offer validity is governed by the Rules of Use and excludes defined holidays. Offers are not valid with other discount offers, unless specified. Coupons void if purchased, sold or bartered. Discounts exclude tax, tip and/or alcohol, where applicable.

Lone Tree Bar & Grill

- Prime the pump with great appetizers or select one of our top ten burgers
- Excellent wings & chili or go for one of the Lone Tree specialties

Lone Tree

BAR & GRILLE

528 Hennepin Ave.
Minneapolis, MN
(612)338-1730

Offer Details: Valid anytime. Dine in only. Not valid for carry out.

00215642

Offer validity is governed by the Rules of Use and excludes defined holidays. Offers are not valid with other discount offers, unless specified. Coupons void if purchased, sold or bartered. Discounts exclude tax, tip and/or alcohol, where applicable.

The Lookout Bar & Grill

- Come for the food.... stay for the fun!
- Appetizers, sandwiches, seafood, pasta, broasted chicken & more
- Catering & banquets available
- Patio with kid's play area
- Visit our website for entertainment schedules

The Lookout

Catering
BAR & GRILL
Established 1958

8672 Pineview Ln. N.
Maple Grove, MN
(763)424-4365

Offer Details: Valid anytime. Dine in only.

00588951

Offer validity is governed by the Rules of Use and excludes defined holidays. Offers are not valid with other discount offers, unless specified. Coupons void if purchased, sold or bartered. Discounts exclude tax, tip and/or alcohol, where applicable.

Loring Park Coffee House & Wine Bar

Enjoy one complimentary MENU ITEM when a second MENU ITEM of equal or greater value is purchased.

See reverse for Offer Details.

Up $7.00 Value

www.loringparkcoffeehouse.com

1301 Harmon Place, Minneapolis, MN
(612) 332-9094

Valid now thru November 1, 2007

B172

Mai Thai Cafe

Enjoy one complimentary LUNCH OR DINNER ENTREE when a second LUNCH OR DINNER ENTREE of equal or greater value is purchased.

See reverse for Offer Details.

Up $10.00 Value

MAI THAI CAFÉ
Excite your taste senses with our exquisite cuisine.

1501 Stillwater Blvd., Stillwater, MN
(651) 275-0359

Valid now thru November 1, 2007

B173

Marble Slab Creamery

Enjoy one complimentary ORIGINAL SIZE or BIG DIPPER SIZE ICE CREAM when a second ORIGINAL SIZE or BIG DIPPER SIZE ICE CREAM of equal or greater value is purchased.

See reverse for Offer Details.

Up $7.00 Value

www.marbleslabcreamery.com

1450 109th Ave. N.E., #100, Blaine, MN
(763) 786-4601

Valid now thru November 1, 2007

B174

CASUAL DINING & FAST FOOD

Loring Park Coffee House & Wine Bar
- Fresh soups, salads & sandwiches
- Baked goods & desserts
- Gourmet pizzas
- Study stations with free wireless access

00596641

Coffee House
loring park

1301 Harmon Place
Minneapolis, MN
(612)332-9094

Offer Details: Valid anytime.

Offer validity is governed by the Rules of Use and excludes defined holidays. Offers are not valid with other discount offers, unless specified. Coupons void if purchased, sold or bartered. Discounts exclude tax, tip and/or alcohol, where applicable.

Mai Thai Cafe
- Specializing in Thai food with an American twist
- We don't add additional MSG
- We can make it mild but we're known for hot-hot-hot!

00701080

MAI THAI CAFÉ
Excite your taste senses with our exquisite cuisine.

1501 Stillwater Blvd.
Stillwater, MN
(651)275-0359

Offer Details: Valid anytime.

Offer validity is governed by the Rules of Use and excludes defined holidays. Offers are not valid with other discount offers, unless specified. Coupons void if purchased, sold or bartered. Discounts exclude tax, tip and/or alcohol, where applicable.

Marble Slab Creamery
- Super premium ice cream made fresh daily in our store
- Waffle cones, cookies & brownies made from scratch
- We feature a variety of mixin's which include candy, fruits, nuts & more
- Try our delicious shakes, malts & banana splits

00617718

MARBLE SLAB CREAMERY®

1450 109th Ave. N.E., #100
(near Super Target)
Blaine, MN
(763)786-4601

Offer Details: Valid anytime.

Offer validity is governed by the Rules of Use and excludes defined holidays. Offers are not valid with other discount offers, unless specified. Coupons void if purchased, sold or bartered. Discounts exclude tax, tip and/or alcohol, where applicable.

Marco's Pizza

Enjoy one complimentary MENU ITEM when a second MENU ITEM of equal or greater value is purchased.

See reverse for Offer Details.

FREE MENU ITEM

Marco's PIZZA

Valid now thru November 1, 2007

2280 Bunker Lake Blvd. NW, Andover, MN
(763) 755-1910

B175

Margarita Bella

Enjoy one complimentary LUNCH OR DINNER ENTREE when a second LUNCH OR DINNER ENTREE of equal or greater value is purchased.

See reverse for Offer Details.

Up To $14.00 Value

MARGARITA BELLA
RESTAURANT & BAR

Valid now thru November 1, 2007

1032 3rd Ave. N.E., Minneapolis, MN
(612) 331-7955

B176

Marla's Indian & Caribbean Cuisine

Enjoy one complimentary LUNCH OR DINNER ENTREE when a second LUNCH OR DINNER ENTREE of equal or greater value is purchased.

See reverse for Offer Details.

Up To $15.00 Value

marla's
INDIAN & CARIBBEAN
cuisine

Valid now thru November 1, 2007

1123 W. Lake St., Minneapolis, MN
(612) 823-2866

B177

CASUAL DINING & FAST FOOD

Marco's Pizza
- Fast delivery!
- We bake, you bake
- Gourmet and traditional pizzas
- Pasta & calzones
- Toasted subs
- Kids menu

Marco's
P I Z Z A
2280 Bunker Lake Blvd. NW
Andover, MN
(763)755-1910

Offer Details: Valid anytime.

00695116

Offer validity is governed by the Rules of Use and excludes defined holidays. Offers are not valid with other discount offers, unless specified. Coupons void if purchased, sold or bartered. Discounts exclude tax, tip and/or alcohol, where applicable.

Margarita Bella
- We proudly serve fresh food daily
- Come & join us for happy hour
- Enjoy authentic Mexican cuisine

MARGARITA BELLA
RESTAURANT & BAR

1032 3rd Ave. N.E.
Minneapolis, MN
(612)331-7955

Offer Details: Valid anytime.

00611083

Offer validity is governed by the Rules of Use and excludes defined holidays. Offers are not valid with other discount offers, unless specified. Coupons void if purchased, sold or bartered. Discounts exclude tax, tip and/or alcohol, where applicable.

Marla's Indian & Caribbean Cuisine
- Specializing in Indian & Caribbean cuisine
- Vegetarian & vegan entrees
- Cozy, eclectic atmosphere with friendly service
- Strong beer & wine
- Catering available

Marla's
INDIAN & CARIBBEAN
Cuisine

1123 W. Lake St.
Minneapolis, MN
(612)823-2866

Offer Details: Valid anytime. Buffet excluded; Dine in only.
Tipping should be 15% to 20% of TOTAL bill before discount

00691692

Offer validity is governed by the Rules of Use and excludes defined holidays. Offers are not valid with other discount offers, unless specified. Coupons void if purchased, sold or bartered. Discounts exclude tax, tip and/or alcohol, where applicable.

Martini's

Enjoy one complimentary LUNCH OR DINNER ENTREE when a second LUNCH OR DINNER ENTREE of equal or greater value is purchased.
See reverse for Offer Details.

Up $ To **19**.00 Value

MARTINI'S
www.millenium-hotels.com

1313 Nicollet Mall, Minneapolis, MN
(612)359-2240

Valid now thru November 1, 2007

B178

Maxwell's

Enjoy one complimentary DINNER ENTREE when a second DINNER ENTREE of equal or greater value is purchased.
See reverse for Offer Details.

Up $ To **10**.00 Value

Maxwell's AMERICAN PUB

1201 Washington Ave. S., Minneapolis, MN
(612)338-1980

Valid now thru November 1, 2007

B179

Maya Mexican Restaurante

Enjoy one complimentary LUNCH OR DINNER ENTREE when a second LUNCH OR DINNER ENTREE of equal or greater value is purchased.
See reverse for Offer Details.

Up $ To **11**.00 Value

MEXICAN MAYA

1400 County Rd. 42, Burnsville, MN
(952)892-3350

Valid now thru November 1, 2007

B180

CASUAL DINING & FAST FOOD

Martini's

- "Shake things up" by stopping by Martini's Lounge & enjoying one of our distinctive gins or vodkas
- Select a Martini from one of our 400 plus Martini recipes
- Relax in our contemporary setting & people watch as you enjoy an appetizer or sandwich

MARTINI'S

1313 Nicollet Mall
Minneapolis, MN
(612)359-2240

Offer Details: Valid anytime.

00507067

Offer validity is governed by the Rules of Use and excludes defined holidays. Offers are not valid with other discount offers, unless specified. Coupons void if purchased, sold or bartered. Discounts exclude tax, tip and/or alcohol, where applicable.

Maxwell's

- Casual, American comfort foods
- Incredible nightly drink specials
- In the shadow of the Metrodome

Maxwell's AMERICAN PUB

1201 Washington Ave. S.
(Just W. of Seven Corners)
Minneapolis, MN
(612)338-1980

Offer Details: Valid any evening. Dine in only; Dome & Guthrie events excluded.

00665275

Offer validity is governed by the Rules of Use and excludes defined holidays. Offers are not valid with other discount offers, unless specified. Coupons void if purchased, sold or bartered. Discounts exclude tax, tip and/or alcohol, where applicable.

Maya Mexican Restaurante

- Authentic Mexican cuisine from the Central Pacific region
- Award winning soups
- Best "Ethnic Food Award"
- Happy hour 3 p.m.-6 p.m. & 10 p.m. to close
- Open daily

MEXICAN MAYA

1400 County Rd. 42
Burnsville, MN
(952)892-3350

Offer Details: Valid anytime.

00617962

Offer validity is governed by the Rules of Use and excludes defined holidays. Offers are not valid with other discount offers, unless specified. Coupons void if purchased, sold or bartered. Discounts exclude tax, tip and/or alcohol, where applicable.

entertainment.com

Mayslack's

Enjoy one complimentary LUNCH OR DINNER ENTREE when a second LUNCH OR DINNER ENTREE of equal or greater value is purchased.
See reverse for Offer Details.

Up To **$11.00** Value

www.mayslacks.com

1428 4th St. N.E., Minneapolis, MN
(612) 789-9862

Valid now thru November 1, 2007

B181

---

entertainment.com

McDivot's Sports Pub & Eatery

Enjoy one complimentary LUNCH OR DINNER ENTREE when a second LUNCH OR DINNER ENTREE of equal or greater value is purchased.
See reverse for Offer Details.

Up To **$8.00** Value

McDivot's
Sports Pub and Eatery

14550 S. Robert Trail, Rosemount, MN
(651) 322-1333

Valid now thru November 1, 2007

B182

CASUAL DINING & FAST FOOD

---

entertainment.com

The Meadows Restaurant & Sports Bar

Enjoy one complimentary ENTREE when a second ENTREE of equal or greater value is purchased.
See reverse for Offer Details.

Up To **$13.00** Value

The Meadows Restaurant sports bar

REPEAT SAVINGS

www.themeadowsrestaurant.com

17646 Central Ave., Ham Lake, MN
(763) 434-4970

Valid now thru November 1, 2007

B183

Mayslack's

- Home of the world-famous roast beef sandwich
- Serving great food since 1955
- Great local live music every Thurs., Fri., & Sat.

Mayslack's
IN HISTORIC N.E. MINNEAPOLIS

1428 4th St. N.E.
Minneapolis, MN
(612) 789-9862

Offer Details: Valid anytime.

00578935

Offer validity is governed by the Rules of Use and excludes defined holidays. Offers are not valid with other discount offers, unless specified. Coupons void if purchased, sold or bartered. Discounts exclude tax, tip and/or alcohol, where applicable.

McDivot's Sports Pub & Eatery

- 360 degree sports bar
- Karaoke Sun. & Wed.
- Happy hour Mon.-Thurs. 3 p.m-6 p.m

McDivot's
Sports Pub and Eatery

14550 S. Robert Trail
Rosemount, MN
(651) 322-1333

Offer Details: Valid anytime. Dine in only. Not valid with any other discounts or promotions.

00596727

Offer validity is governed by the Rules of Use and excludes defined holidays. Offers are not valid with other discount offers, unless specified. Coupons void if purchased, sold or bartered. Discounts exclude tax, tip and/or alcohol, where applicable.

The Meadows Restaurant & Sports Bar

- Open for breakfast at 6 a.m. daily
- Great brick oven pizza
- Everything from sandwiches & burgers to pasta, steaks & more
- Kid's menu
- Specializing in groups up to 50

The Meadows
Restaurant sports bar

17646 Central Ave.
(Hwy. 65 & Crosstown)
Ham Lake, MN
(763) 434-4970

Offer Details: Valid anytime. Buffet excluded; Dine in only; Specials excluded.

00665216

Offer validity is governed by the Rules of Use and excludes defined holidays. Offers are not valid with other discount offers, unless specified. Coupons void if purchased, sold or bartered. Discounts exclude tax, tip and/or alcohol, where applicable.

The Mediterranean Cruise Cafe

Enjoy one complimentary DINNER ENTREE when a second DINNER ENTREE of equal or greater value is purchased.

See reverse for Offer Details.

Up To $10.00 Value

www.medcruisecafe.com

3945 Sibley Memorial Highway, Eagan, MN
(651)452-5991

Valid now thru November 1, 2007

B184

Milda's Cafe

Enjoy one complimentary ENTREE when a second ENTREE of equal or greater value is purchased.

See reverse for Offer Details.

Up To $6.00 Value

1720 Glenwood Ave. North, Minneapolis, MN
(612)377-9460

Valid now thru November 1, 2007

B185

Miller's on Main

Enjoy one complimentary LUNCH OR DINNER ENTREE when a second LUNCH OR DINNER ENTREE of equal or greater value is purchased.

See reverse for Offer Details.

Up To $10.00 Value

REPEAT SAVINGS

www.millersonmain.com

8001 Lake Dr., Lino Lakes, MN
(651)783-7106

Valid now thru November 1, 2007

B186

CASUAL DINING & FAST FOOD

The Mediterranean Cruise Cafe
- Family owned restaurant since 1979
- Featuring the best of delicious & authentic homemade Mediterranean & American dishes: shish kabobs, lamb shanks, stir-fry, steaks, seafood & gyros
- We offer a full service bar, catering, weddings, take-out menus, live entertainment & belly dancing Thurs.-Sat.
- We have great food & great prices
- Open daily 11 a.m.-11 p.m.

00001076

THE MEDITERRANEAN CRUISE CAFE

3945 Sibley Memorial Highway
(Cedar Ave. S. & Hwy. 13 N., 5 min. S. of Mall of America)
Eagan, MN
(651)452-5991

Offer Details: Valid any evening. Dine in only.

Offer validity is governed by the Rules of Use and excludes defined holidays. Offers are not valid with other discount offers, unless specified. Coupons void if purchased, sold or bartered. Discounts exclude tax, tip and/or alcohol, where applicable.

Milda's Cafe
- Home cooking at its finest!
- Delicious daily specials
- Try our famous Pasties (meat pie sealed in a homemade crust) served Mon., Wed. & Fri.
- Delicious homemade cinnamon & caramel rolls
- Breakfast served all day
- Always good food & great service at a reasonable price
- Open Mon.-Fri. 6 a.m.-3 p.m., Sat. 6 a.m.-1 p.m.
- Closed last Saturday of each month, Sundays & holidays

00628078

Milda's Cafe

1720 Glenwood Ave. North
Minneapolis, MN
(612)377-9460

Offer Details: Valid anytime. Dine in only.

Offer validity is governed by the Rules of Use and excludes defined holidays. Offers are not valid with other discount offers, unless specified. Coupons void if purchased, sold or bartered. Discounts exclude tax, tip and/or alcohol, where applicable.

Miller's on Main
- Best appetizers, sandwiches, salads & dinners in the area
- Remember our famous take-out chicken for your next party!

MILLER'S on MAIN

8001 Lake Dr.
Lino Lakes, MN
(651)783-7106

Offer Details: Valid anytime. Dine in only; Specials excluded.

00461258

Offer validity is governed by the Rules of Use and excludes defined holidays. Offers are not valid with other discount offers, unless specified. Coupons void if purchased, sold or bartered. Discounts exclude tax, tip and/or alcohol, where applicable.

Mings Garden Restaurant

Enjoy one complimentary LUNCH ENTREE when a second LUNCH ENTREE of equal or greater value is purchased.
See reverse for Offer Details.

Up To $5.00 Value

Ming's Garden Restaurant

Valid now thru November 1, 2007

4190 Vinewood Ln. #113, Plymouth, MN
(763)559-3131

B187

Minneapolis Town Hall Brewery

Enjoy one complimentary LUNCH OR DINNER ENTREE when a second LUNCH OR DINNER ENTREE of equal or greater value is purchased.
See reverse for Offer Details.

Up To $13.00 Value

MINNEAPOLIS Town Hall BREWERY
Est. 1997

Valid now thru November 1, 2007

1430 Washington Ave. S., Minneapolis, MN
(612)339-8696

B188

Mochalini's

Enjoy one complimentary MENU ITEM when a second MENU ITEM of equal or greater value is purchased.
See reverse for Offer Details.

Up To $6.00 Value

mochalini's
www.mochadelites.com

Valid now thru November 1, 2007

12517 Central Ave. N.E., Blaine, MN
(763)862-3771

B189

CASUAL DINING & FAST FOOD

Mings Garden Restaurant
- Located between TJ Maxx & Rainbow Foods
- Fine Chinese dining
- Sun-Thur 11:30am-9:30pm
- Fri & Sat 11:30am-10pm

Ming's Garden Restaurant

4190 Vinewood Ln. #113
(between Rainbow Foods & TJ Maxx)
Plymouth, MN
(763)559-3131

Offer Details: Valid during luncheon hours. Dine in only; Buffet excluded.

00198881

Offer validity is governed by the Rules of Use and excludes defined holidays. Offers are not valid with other discount offers, unless specified. Coupons void if purchased, sold or bartered. Discounts exclude tax, tip and/or alcohol, where applicable.

Minneapolis Town Hall Brewery
- Welcome to Minneapolis Town Hall Brewery, an upscale bar with a relaxing, classic old world atmosphere.
- Come for our great pastas & variety of specials & stay to be part of the busy nightlife crowd in the late evening
- We have 9 beers brewed on site: 5 regular, 2 seasonal, & 2 cask & always have classic tunes, like James Taylor, in the background

Minneapolis Town Hall Brewery
Est. 1997

1430 Washington Ave. S.
Minneapolis, MN
(612)339-8696

Offer Details: Valid anytime.
Tipping should be 15% to 20% of TOTAL bill before discount

00505578

Offer validity is governed by the Rules of Use and excludes defined holidays. Offers are not valid with other discount offers, unless specified. Coupons void if purchased, sold or bartered. Discounts exclude tax, tip and/or alcohol, where applicable.

Mochalini's
- Gourmet espresso drinks
- Smoothies & frozen coffee
- Grilled panini & wrap sandwiches
- Create your own pasta
- Soups & salads
- Desserts & pastries
- Delicious breakfast croissant sandwiches & burritos
- Open daily

mochalini's

12517 Central Ave. N.E.
Blaine, MN
(763)862-3771

Offer Details: Valid anytime.

00637533

Offer validity is governed by the Rules of Use and excludes defined holidays. Offers are not valid with other discount offers, unless specified. Coupons void if purchased, sold or bartered. Discounts exclude tax, tip and/or alcohol, where applicable.

CASUAL DINING & FAST FOOD

Moose Bar & Grill

Enjoy one complimentary LUNCH OR DINNER ENTREE when a second LUNCH OR DINNER ENTREE of equal or greater value is purchased or for those who prefer - any one pizza at 50% off the regular price.
See reverse for Offer Details.

Up To $12.00 Value

MOOSE BAR & GRILL
NE MINNEAPOLIS

356 Monroe St., Minneapolis, MN
(612) 623-4999

Valid now thru November 1, 2007

B190

Muddy Paws Cheesecake

Enjoy one complimentary MENU ITEM when a second MENU ITEM of equal or greater value is purchased.
See reverse for Offer Details.

Up To $6.00 Value

MuddyPaws CheeseCake
www.muddypawscheesecake.com
See Reverse Side for Locations

Valid now thru November 1, 2007

B191

The Neighborhood Cafe

Enjoy one complimentary ENTREE when a second ENTREE of equal or greater value is purchased.
See reverse for Offer Details.

Up To $8.00 Value

THE NEIGHBORHOOD CAFÉ

1570 Selby Ave., St. Paul, MN
(651) 644-8887

Valid now thru November 1, 2007

B192

Moose Bar & Grill

- There is something for everyone at this traditional neighborhood saloon
- We have great homemade food, soups & pizza
- For your entertainment, enjoy darts, pool tables, Golden Tee, S.S. Bowling & large-screen TVs while you enjoy our delicious appetizers
- Full service bar, karaoke, catering, meeting facilities & take out available
- Open 365 days a year

NE MINNEAPOLIS
356 Monroe St.
Minneapolis, MN
(612)623-4999

Offer Details: Valid anytime.
Tipping should be 15% to 20% of TOTAL bill before discount

00633482

Offer validity is governed by the Rules of Use and excludes defined holidays. Offers are not valid with other discount offers, unless specified. Coupons void if purchased, sold or bartered. Discounts exclude tax, tip and/or alcohol, where applicable.

Muddy Paws Cheesecake

- "Life Is Short...Eat Cheesecake!"
- More flavors than anyone else in the world - 117 & counting
- Available by the slice or whole
- Cheesecake made from scratch to order
- Nationwide shipping
- Full cafe menu at our Hennepin/Uptown location only

2528 Hennepin Ave. S.
Minneapolis, MN
(612)377-4441

740 Snelling Ave. N.
St. Paul, MN
(651)458-1625

Offer Details: Valid anytime.

00594557

Offer validity is governed by the Rules of Use and excludes defined holidays. Offers are not valid with other discount offers, unless specified. Coupons void if purchased, sold or bartered. Discounts exclude tax, tip and/or alcohol, where applicable.

The Neighborhood Cafe

- Serving breakfast, lunch & late night Fri. & Sat.
- Best homemade hashbrowns in town
- Serving Dunn Bros. Coffee
- Patio seating
- Free wi-fi

THE NEIGHBORHOOD CAFÉ
1570 Selby Ave.
St. Paul, MN
(651)644-8887

Offer Details: Valid anytime. Dine in only.
Tipping should be 15% to 20% of TOTAL bill before discount

00677716

Offer validity is governed by the Rules of Use and excludes defined holidays. Offers are not valid with other discount offers, unless specified. Coupons void if purchased, sold or bartered. Discounts exclude tax, tip and/or alcohol, where applicable.

entertainment.com

Nestle Tollhouse Cafe by Chip

Enjoy one complimentary COOKIE when a second COOKIE of equal or greater value is purchased.
See reverse for Offer Details.

FREE COOKIE

283 E. Broadway, Bloomington, MN
(952) 853-0272

Valid now thru November 1, 2007

B193

---

entertainment.com

Nestle Tollhouse Cafe by Chip

Enjoy one complimentary REGULAR SIZE COFFEE when a second REGULAR SIZE COFFEE of equal or greater value is purchased.
See reverse for Offer Details.

ONE REGULAR SIZE COFFEE

283 E. Broadway, Bloomington, MN
(952) 853-0272

Valid now thru November 1, 2007

B194

---

entertainment.com

Nick-N-Willy's Take-N-Bake

Buy any SIGNATURE PIZZA at regular price, get a free MEDIUM 1-TOPPING PIZZA.
See reverse for Offer Details.

FREE MEDIUM 1-TOPPING PIZZA

www.nicknwillys.com

See Reverse Side for Locations

Valid now thru November 1, 2007

B195

CASUAL DINING & FAST FOOD

Nestle Tollhouse Cafe by Chip
- Cookies
- Smoothies
- Cookie cakes
- Brownies
- Lattes & cappucinos
- Espressos
- Ice-cream

283 E. Broadway
Bloomington, MN
(952)853-0272

Offer Details: Valid anytime.

00654870

Offer validity is governed by the Rules of Use and excludes defined holidays. Offers are not valid with other discount offers, unless specified. Coupons void if purchased, sold or bartered. Discounts exclude tax, tip and/or alcohol, where applicable.

Nestle Tollhouse Cafe by Chip
- Cookies
- Smoothies
- Cookie cakes
- Brownies
- Lattes & cappucinos
- Espressos
- Ice-cream

283 E. Broadway
Bloomington, MN
(952)853-0272

Offer Details: Valid anytime.

00654855

Offer validity is governed by the Rules of Use and excludes defined holidays. Offers are not valid with other discount offers, unless specified. Coupons void if purchased, sold or bartered. Discounts exclude tax, tip and/or alcohol, where applicable.

Nick-N-Willy's Take-N-Bake
- Made FRESH in our kitchen, baked PERFECTLY in your oven
- See our full menu & a complete list of locations at nicknwillys.com

Valid at Participating Locations   www.nicknwillys.com

Offer Details: Valid anytime. Take-N-Bake pizzas only; Not valid with any other offer or in-store special.

00702974

Offer validity is governed by the Rules of Use and excludes defined holidays. Offers are not valid with other discount offers, unless specified. Coupons void if purchased, sold or bartered. Discounts exclude tax, tip and/or alcohol, where applicable.

Nick's Ice Cream & Popcorn

Enjoy one complimentary MENU ITEM when a second MENU ITEM of equal or greater value is purchased.
See reverse for Offer Details.

Up To $5.00 Value

Nick's Ice Cream & Popcorn

Valid now thru November 1, 2007

12727 Wayzata Blvd., Minnetonka, MN
(952)546-9757

B196

Nino's Pizza Plus

Enjoy one complimentary ENTREE when a second ENTREE of equal or greater value is purchased or for those who prefer - any one pizza at 50% off the regular price.
See reverse for Offer Details.

Up To $10.00 Value

Nino's Pizza Plus

Valid now thru November 1, 2007

4729 Lyndale Ave. N., Minneapolis, MN
(612)529-3820

B197

Northwoods Bar & Grill

Enjoy one complimentary LUNCH OR DINNER ENTREE when a second LUNCH OR DINNER ENTREE of equal or greater value is purchased.
See reverse for Offer Details.

Up To $7.00 Value

NORTHWOODS BAR & GRILL

www.rileynorthwoods.com

Valid now thru November 1, 2007

19735 Iguana St. #103, Elk River, MN
(763)274-2380

B198

CASUAL DINING & FAST FOOD

Nick's Ice Cream & Popcorn
- 28 different ice cream flavors to choose from!
- Fruit smoothies, shakes & malts
- Sundaes
- Flavored popcorn
- A variety of popcorn tins
- Now serving hot dogs

Nick's
Ice Cream & Popcorn

12727 Wayzata Blvd.
(Ridgedale Mall)
Minnetonka, MN
(952)546-9757

Offer Details: Valid anytime.

00518954

Offer validity is governed by the Rules of Use and excludes defined holidays. Offers are not valid with other discount offers, unless specified. Coupons void if purchased, sold or bartered. Discounts exclude tax, tip and/or alcohol, where applicable.

Nino's Pizza Plus
- Our Italian specialties include pastas & pizzas
- Appetizers
- Desserts

Nino's Pizza Plus

4729 Lyndale Ave. N.
Minneapolis, MN
(612)529-3820

Offer Details: Valid anytime.

00605086

Offer validity is governed by the Rules of Use and excludes defined holidays. Offers are not valid with other discount offers, unless specified. Coupons void if purchased, sold or bartered. Discounts exclude tax, tip and/or alcohol, where applicable.

Northwoods Bar & Grill
- Great appetizers & pizza
- Delicious burgers & sandwiches
- Kids & senior menu
- Happy hour Mon.-Fri. 4 p.m.-7 p.m.
- All-you-can-eat fish on Thurs.
- Darts, pull tabs & pool
- Live music & Karaoke

NORTHWOODS BAR & GRILL

19735 Iguana St. #103
Elk River, MN
(763)274-2380

Offer Details: Valid anytime. Dine in only; Specials excluded.
Tipping should be 15% to 20% of TOTAL bill before discount

00692604

Offer validity is governed by the Rules of Use and excludes defined holidays. Offers are not valid with other discount offers, unless specified. Coupons void if purchased, sold or bartered. Discounts exclude tax, tip and/or alcohol, where applicable.

Papa's Pizza and Pasta

Enjoy one complimentary LUNCH OR DINNER ENTREE when a second LUNCH OR DINNER ENTREE of equal or greater value is purchased or for those who prefer - any one pizza at 50% off the regular price - maximum discount $10.00.
See reverse for Offer Details.

Valid now thru November 1, 2007

Up To $10.00 Value

Papa's Pizza and Pasta

www.papaspizzaandpasta.com

4159 Thomas Ave. N., Minneapolis, MN
(612)521-7272

B199

Park Tavern Lounge & Lanes

Enjoy one complimentary MENU ITEM when a second MENU ITEM of equal or greater value is purchased.
See reverse for Offer Details.

Valid now thru November 1, 2007

Up To $5.00 Value

Park Tavern LOUNGE & LANES

3401 Louisiana Avenue, St Louis Park, MN
(952)929-6810

B200

Pasquale's Sports Bar & Restaurant

Enjoy one complimentary LUNCH OR DINNER ENTREE when a second LUNCH OR DINNER ENTREE of equal or greater value is purchased or for those who prefer - any one pizza at 50% off the regular price.
See reverse for Offer Details.

Valid now thru November 1, 2007

Up To $9.00 Value

PASQUALE'S

151 Northtown Dr., Blaine, MN
(763)780-4777

B201

CASUAL DINING & FAST FOOD

Papa's Pizza and Pasta
- "Everybody Eats When They Come To My House"
- East coast tomato pie, pizza & hoagies
- We make all our own sauces
- Homemade cheesecake
- Closed Sundays

00670538

Papa's Pizza and Pasta

4159 Thomas Ave. N.
Minneapolis, MN
(612) 521-7272

Offer Details: Valid anytime.

Offer validity is governed by the Rules of Use and excludes defined holidays. Offers are not valid with other discount offers, unless specified. Coupons void if purchased, sold or bartered. Discounts exclude tax, tip and/or alcohol, where applicable.

Park Tavern Lounge & Lanes
- Great food
- Casual atmosphere
- Cocktails
- 20 new AMF lanes

00000671

Park Tavern LOUNGE & LANES

3401 Louisiana Avenue
St Louis Park, MN
(952) 929-6810

Offer Details: Valid anytime. Dine in only; Not valid on delivery.

Offer validity is governed by the Rules of Use and excludes defined holidays. Offers are not valid with other discount offers, unless specified. Coupons void if purchased, sold or bartered. Discounts exclude tax, tip and/or alcohol, where applicable.

Pasquale's Sports Bar & Restaurant
- Famous for our gourmet pizza, Mama Mia Pasta & sandwiches
- Mon-Sat 11am-11pm, Sun 11:30am-10pm
- Sports bar open until 1am daily

00080592

PASQUALE'S

151 Northtown Dr.
(Northtown Mall)
Blaine, MN
(763) 780-4777

Offer Details: Valid anytime. Friday's excluded.

Offer validity is governed by the Rules of Use and excludes defined holidays. Offers are not valid with other discount offers, unless specified. Coupons void if purchased, sold or bartered. Discounts exclude tax, tip and/or alcohol, where applicable.

Ping's Szechuan Star

Enjoy one complimentary LUNCH OR DINNER ENTREE when a second LUNCH OR DINNER ENTREE of equal or greater value is purchased.
See reverse for Offer Details.

Up To $12.00 Value

1401 Nicollet Avenue, Minneapolis, MN
(612) 874-9404

B202

Valid now thru November 1, 2007

Pizza Flame

Enjoy one complimentary DINNER ENTREE when a second DINNER ENTREE of equal or greater value is purchased or for those who prefer - any one pizza at 50% off the regular price.
See reverse for Offer Details.

Up To $9.00 Value

pizza flame
COON RAPIDS

See Reverse Side for Locations

B203

Valid now thru November 1, 2007

CASUAL DINING & FAST FOOD

Pizza Man

Enjoy any one complimentary PIZZA when a second PIZZA of equal or greater value is purchased.
See reverse for Offer Details.

Up To $14.00 Value

PIZZA MAN DELIVERS

See Reverse Side for Locations

B204

Valid now thru November 1, 2007

Ping's Szechuan Star

- Experience Oriental cuisine featuring spicy Szechuan as well as Cantonese, Mandarin and Hunan dishes.
- Peking Duck is always available, no pre-orders needed.
- The contemporary and stylish dining room features full bar service including an extensive list of wines by the glass.

00301899

PING'S
Szechuan
BAR & GRILL
1401 Nicollet Avenue
Minneapolis, MN
(612) 874-9404

Offer Details: Valid anytime. Buffet excluded; Dine in only. Special menu excluded; Chinese New Year excluded.

Tipping should be 15% to 20% of TOTAL bill before discount

Offer validity is governed by the Rules of Use and excludes defined holidays. Offers are not valid with other discount offers, unless specified. Coupons void if purchased, sold or bartered. Discounts exclude tax, tip and/or alcohol, where applicable.

Pizza Flame

- Simply The Best!
- 3 Crust styles
- Try our famous house specials
- Delicious pastas & fresh salads
- Beer & wine available
- Banquet facilities - Coon Rapids
- Dine-in, carry out & delivery available

00107819

pizza flame
COON RAPIDS

2016 105th Ave. N.W.
Coon Rapids, MN
(763) 757-5100

317 Osborne Rd.
(1 Block S. of Coon Rapids Blvd.)
Fridley, MN
(763) 786-7772

Offer Details: Valid any evening. Dine-in or carry out.

Offer validity is governed by the Rules of Use and excludes defined holidays. Offers are not valid with other discount offers, unless specified. Coupons void if purchased, sold or bartered. Discounts exclude tax, tip and/or alcohol, where applicable.

Pizza Man

- The best pizza in town. It's that simple

00102532

11011 61st St. N.E.
Albertville, MN
(763) 497-2501

2744 Douglas Dr. N.
Crystal, MN
(763) 525-9905

13451 Business Ctr. Dr.
(next to Holiday Gas Station & the fairgrounds)
Elk River, MN
(763) 441-8191

619 Locust St.
Monticello, MN
(763) 295-3737

Offer Details: Valid anytime. Carry out only.

Offer validity is governed by the Rules of Use and excludes defined holidays. Offers are not valid with other discount offers, unless specified. Coupons void if purchased, sold or bartered. Discounts exclude tax, tip and/or alcohol, where applicable.

Pizza Prima

Enjoy any one complimentary PIZZA when a second PIZZA of equal or greater value is purchased.
See reverse for Offer Details.

Up To $17.00 Value

PIZZA PRIMA
Take N Bake
Est. 2003

23770 Hwy. 7, Shorewood, MN
(952) 474-4333

Valid now thru November 1, 2007

B205

Pizza Ranch

Enjoy any one complimentary PIZZA when a second PIZZA of equal or greater value is purchased.
See reverse for Offer Details.

FREE PIZZA

The Pizza Ranch®
"Home of the Pizza Lover's Pizza"®

See Reverse Side for Locations

Valid now thru November 1, 2007

B206

Pizzeria Uno

Enjoy one complimentary LARGE PIZZA when a second LARGE PIZZA of equal or greater value is purchased.
See reverse for Offer Details.

Up To $18.00 Value

PIZZERIA UNO
EST. 1943
CHICAGO BAR & GRILL

6740 France Ave., Edina, MN
(952) 925-5005

Valid now thru November 1, 2007

B207

CASUAL DINING & FAST FOOD

Pizza Prima
- Delicious Take & Bake Pizza
- We offer traditional & gourmet pizzas
- Homemade sauce, fresh 3-blend sauce & hand-tossed dough

PIZZA PRIMA
Take N Bake
Est. 2003

23770 Hwy. 7
Shorewood, MN
(952)474-4333

00603718

Offer Details: Valid anytime.

Offer validity is governed by the Rules of Use and excludes defined holidays. Offers are not valid with other discount offers, unless specified. Coupons void if purchased, sold or bartered. Discounts exclude tax, tip and/or alcohol, where applicable.

Pizza Ranch
- "Home of the Pizza Lover's Pizza"
- Good things, every day!

The Pizza Ranch

1338 Babcock Blvd. E.
Delano, MN
(763)972-5992
2408 9th St. E.
Glencoe, MN
(320)864-4010

425 Merger St.
Norwood, MN
(952)467-4010
224 1st St. W.
Waconia, MN
(952)442-3321

00110257

Offer Details: Valid anytime. Carry out only.

Offer validity is governed by the Rules of Use and excludes defined holidays. Offers are not valid with other discount offers, unless specified. Coupons void if purchased, sold or bartered. Discounts exclude tax, tip and/or alcohol, where applicable.

Pizzeria Uno
- Pizzeria Uno... a fine restaurant specializing in Chicago style deep dish pizza made from the finest meats, spices, vegetables & cheeses
- Delicious pastas, sandwiches, soups & burgers available too
- Stop in for a unique dining experience often imitated but never quite duplicated

PIZZERIA UNO
EST. 1943
CHICAGO BAR & GRILL℠

6740 France Ave.
Edina, MN
(952)925-5005

00213977

Offer Details: Valid anytime. Dine-in or carry out; Sorry, no delivery. One coupon per customer per visit; Present coupon before ordering.

Offer validity is governed by the Rules of Use and excludes defined holidays. Offers are not valid with other discount offers, unless specified. Coupons void if purchased, sold or bartered. Discounts exclude tax, tip and/or alcohol, where applicable.

entertainment
entertainment.com

Plums Neighborhood Grill & Bar

Enjoy one complimentary LUNCH OR DINNER ENTREE when a second LUNCH OR DINNER ENTREE of equal or greater value is purchased.
See reverse for Offer Details.

REPEAT SAVINGS

Up $ **9** ^{00} Value
To

Plums
NEIGHBORHOOD GRILL & BAR

480 S. Snelling Ave., St. Paul, MN
(651)699-2227

Valid now thru November 1, 2007

B208

---

entertainment
entertainment.com

Plums Neighborhood Grill & Bar

Enjoy one complimentary LUNCH OR DINNER ENTREE when a second LUNCH OR DINNER ENTREE of equal or greater value is purchased.
See reverse for Offer Details.

REPEAT SAVINGS

Up $ **9** ^{00} Value
To

Plums
NEIGHBORHOOD GRILL & BAR

480 S. Snelling Ave., St. Paul, MN
(651)699-2227

Valid now thru November 1, 2007

B209

---

entertainment
entertainment.com

Porter's Bar and Grill

Enjoy one complimentary LUNCH OR DINNER ENTREE when a second LUNCH OR DINNER ENTREE of equal or greater value is purchased.
See reverse for Offer Details.

REPEAT SAVINGS

Up $ **10** ^{00} Value
To

PORTER'S
Bar & Grill

www.porters.citysearch.com

2647 Nicollet Ave. S, Minneapolis, MN
(612)872-0808

Valid now thru November 1, 2007

B210

CASUAL DINING & FAST FOOD

Plums Neighborhood Grill & Bar
- Great food
- Sunday breakfast buffet
- Homemade soups
- Full bar service
- Dine on our beautiful patio

00529053

Plums
NEIGHBORHOOD GRILL & BAR

480 S. Snelling Ave.
(Snelling Ave. & Randolph Ave.)
St. Paul, MN
(651)699-2227

Offer Details: Valid anytime.

Offer validity is governed by the Rules of Use and excludes defined holidays. Offers are not valid with other discount offers, unless specified. Coupons void if purchased, sold or bartered. Discounts exclude tax, tip and/or alcohol, where applicable.

Plums Neighborhood Grill & Bar
- Great food
- Sunday breakfast buffet
- Homemade soups
- Full bar service
- Dine on our beautiful patio

00529053

Plums
NEIGHBORHOOD GRILL & BAR

480 S. Snelling Ave.
(Snelling Ave. & Randolph Ave.)
St. Paul, MN
(651)699-2227

Offer Details: Valid anytime.

Offer validity is governed by the Rules of Use and excludes defined holidays. Offers are not valid with other discount offers, unless specified. Coupons void if purchased, sold or bartered. Discounts exclude tax, tip and/or alcohol, where applicable.

Porter's Bar and Grill
- Serving great char-broiled sizzling steaks, chops, Tex Mex, & BBQ ribs
- Sandwiches & burgers
- Make sure to catch our 2 happy hours: 3:30 p.m.-7:30 p.m. & 10 p.m.-close daily for half price mixed drinks & tap beers
- Sat. & Sun. half price Bloody Marys & screwdrivers plus breakfast entrees from 11 a.m.-3:00 p.m.

00389654

PORTER'S Bar & Grill

2647 Nicollet Ave. S
Minneapolis, MN
(612)872-0808

Offer Details: Valid anytime. Dine in only.

Offer validity is governed by the Rules of Use and excludes defined holidays. Offers are not valid with other discount offers, unless specified. Coupons void if purchased, sold or bartered. Discounts exclude tax, tip and/or alcohol, where applicable.

Pretzel Time

Enjoy one complimentary PRETZEL when a second PRETZEL of equal or greater value is purchased.
See reverse for Offer Details.

FREE PRETZEL

PRETZEL TIME

384 W. Market St., Bloomington, MN
(952)854-7980

Valid now thru November 1, 2007

B211

Rail Station Bar & Grill

Enjoy one complimentary ENTREE when a second ENTREE of equal or greater value is purchased.
See reverse for Offer Details.

Up To $14.00 Value

The Rail Station Bar & Grill
www.railstationbarandgrill.com

3675 Minnehaha Ave. S., Minneapolis, MN
(612)729-3663

Valid now thru November 1, 2007

B212

Rascal's Bar & Restaurant

Enjoy one complimentary LUNCH OR DINNER ENTREE when a second LUNCH OR DINNER ENTREE of equal or greater value is purchased.
See reverse for Offer Details.

Up To $14.00 Value

RASCAL'S BAR & RESTAURANT
MEDINA ENTERTAINMENT CENTER
www.medinaentertainment.com

500 Hwy. 55, Medina, MN
(763)478-6661

Valid now thru November 1, 2007

B213

CASUAL DINING & FAST FOOD

PRETZEL TIME

Pretzel Time

384 W. Market St.
(Mall of America W. Market)
Bloomington, MN
(952) 854-7980

Offer Details: Valid anytime.

00702655

Offer validity is governed by the Rules of Use and excludes defined holidays. Offers are not valid with other discount offers, unless specified. Coupons void if purchased, sold or bartered. Discounts exclude tax, tip and/or alcohol, where applicable.

Rail Station Bar & Grill

- Come to the Rail Station for breakfast, lunch or dinner
- All of our sauces, soups & salad dressings are made from scratch
- Enjoy one of our great burgers, steaks, chops or savory pasta or seafood
- Our delicious hand-battered mushrooms were written up by the Star Tribune
- Seasonal outdoor dining
- Kids menu available
- Minneapolis' only heated & air-conditioned smoking car

The Rail Station
Bar & Grill

3675 Minnehaha Ave. S.
Minneapolis, MN
(612) 729-3663

Offer Details: Valid anytime. Dine in only; Specials excluded.
Tipping should be 15% to 20% of TOTAL bill before discount

00622040

Offer validity is governed by the Rules of Use and excludes defined holidays. Offers are not valid with other discount offers, unless specified. Coupons void if purchased, sold or bartered. Discounts exclude tax, tip and/or alcohol, where applicable.

Rascal's Bar & Restaurant

- Open daily serving a large made-from-scratch menu
- Happy Hour Mon.-Fri.
- 12 Lane bowling center with Extreme Cosmic on weekends
- Full banquet/wedding facilities for 10-1500 people
- Join us in The Ballroom for the greatest local & national acts

RASCALS BAR & RESTAURANT
MEDINA ENTERTAINMENT CENTER

500 Hwy. 55
Medina, MN
(763) 478-6661

Offer Details: Valid anytime. Dine in only; Brunch included; Specials excluded. National acts/special events excluded.
Tipping should be 15% to 20% of TOTAL bill before discount

00698682

Offer validity is governed by the Rules of Use and excludes defined holidays. Offers are not valid with other discount offers, unless specified. Coupons void if purchased, sold or bartered. Discounts exclude tax, tip and/or alcohol, where applicable.

Red Moon Restaurant

Enjoy one complimentary DINNER ENTREE when a second DINNER ENTREE of equal or greater value is purchased.
See reverse for Offer Details.

REPEAT SAVINGS

Up To $8.00 Value

RED MOON CHINESE CAFE

Valid now thru November 1, 2007

582 Prairie Center Dr., Eden Prairie, MN
(952)941-6556

B214

The Red Pepper

Enjoy one complimentary DINNER ENTREE when a second DINNER ENTREE of equal or greater value is purchased.
See reverse for Offer Details.

Up To $7.00 Value

THE RED PEPPER
Chinese Restaurant

Valid now thru November 1, 2007

See Reverse Side for Locations

B215

The Red Rooster

Enjoy one complimentary LUNCH OR DINNER ENTREE when a second LUNCH OR DINNER ENTREE of equal or greater value is purchased.
See reverse for Offer Details.

Up To $9.00 Value

RED ROOSTER

Valid now thru November 1, 2007

1830 W Wayzata Blvd., Long Lake, MN
(952)473-4089

B216

CASUAL DINING & FAST FOOD

Red Moon Restaurant
- Cantonese & Szechuan cuisine
- Family owned & operated
- You come in as our guests - we will treat you right

RED MOON CHINESE CAFE

582 Prairie Center Dr.
(Tower Square, behind McDonalds)
Eden Prairie, MN
(952)941-6556

Offer Details: Valid any evening. Buffet excluded; Dine in only.

00667594

Offer validity is governed by the Rules of Use and excludes defined holidays. Offers are not valid with other discount offers, unless specified. Coupons void if purchased, sold or bartered. Discounts exclude tax, tip and/or alcohol, where applicable.

The Red Pepper
- Specializing in Szechuan & Hunan cuisine
- Try our Hong Kong Steak, Crispy Walleye & Szechuan Duck in Plum Sauce

THE RED PEPPER
Chinese Restaurant

187 Cheshire Lane
Plymouth, MN
(763)404-1770

2902 W 66th St.
Richfield, MN
(612)869-6817

Offer Details: Valid any evening. Dine in only; Family dinners & specialties excluded.

00001138

Offer validity is governed by the Rules of Use and excludes defined holidays. Offers are not valid with other discount offers, unless specified. Coupons void if purchased, sold or bartered. Discounts exclude tax, tip and/or alcohol, where applicable.

The Red Rooster
- A great family place!
- Casual, relaxed atmosphere
- Dinners from prime rib to jumbo shrimp
- Hot & cold sandwiches
- Burgers
- Full service bar
- Open daily

RED ROOSTER

1830 W Wayzata Blvd.
Long Lake, MN
(952)473-4089

Offer Details: Valid anytime. Dine in only.

00002367

Offer validity is governed by the Rules of Use and excludes defined holidays. Offers are not valid with other discount offers, unless specified. Coupons void if purchased, sold or bartered. Discounts exclude tax, tip and/or alcohol, where applicable.

entertainment.
entertainment.com

Red Sea Restaurant

Enjoy one complimentary LUNCH OR DINNER ENTREE when a second LUNCH OR DINNER ENTREE of equal or greater value is purchased.
See reverse for Offer Details.

REPEAT SAVINGS™

Up To $9.00 Value

RED SEA RESTAURANT & BAR

320 Cedar St., Minneapolis, MN
(612) 333-1644

Valid now thru November 1, 2007 — B217

---

entertainment.
entertainment.com

Renegades Bar & Grill

Enjoy one complimentary LUNCH OR DINNER ENTREE when a second LUNCH OR DINNER ENTREE of equal or greater value is purchased.
See reverse for Offer Details.

REPEAT SAVINGS™

Up To $10.00 Value

Renegades Bar & Grill

3809 W. Hwy. 13, Burnsville, MN
(952) 707-8427

Valid now thru November 1, 2007 — B218

---

entertainment.
entertainment.com

Restaurante Guayaquil

Enjoy one complimentary ENTREE when a second ENTREE of equal or greater value is purchased.
See reverse for Offer Details.

REPEAT SAVINGS™

Up To $11.00 Value

RESTAURANTE GUAYAQUIL

1526 E. Lake St., Minneapolis, MN
(612) 722-2346

Valid now thru November 1, 2007 — B219

CASUAL DINING & FAST FOOD

Red Sea Restaurant
- African & American cuisine
- Casual atmosphere
- Chicken wings
- Burgers
- Lamb, beef & chicken
- Entrees can be made mild or spicy
- Full bar service
- Imported & domestic wines
- Breakfast served daily

RED SEA RESTAURANT & BAR

320 Cedar St.
Minneapolis, MN
(612)333-1644

Offer Details: Valid anytime. Combination dinners excluded.

00662097

Offer validity is governed by the Rules of Use and excludes defined holidays. Offers are not valid with other discount offers, unless specified. Coupons void if purchased, sold or bartered. Discounts exclude tax, tip and/or alcohol, where applicable.

Renegades Bar & Grill
- Serving delicious sandwiches, burgers & entrees
- Happy hour 3 p.m.-6 p.m. daily - 2 for 1
- Live music

Renegades Bar & Grill

3809 W. Hwy. 13
Burnsville, MN
(952)707-8427

Offer Details: Valid anytime.

00685015

Offer validity is governed by the Rules of Use and excludes defined holidays. Offers are not valid with other discount offers, unless specified. Coupons void if purchased, sold or bartered. Discounts exclude tax, tip and/or alcohol, where applicable.

Restaurante Guayaquil
- Delicious Ecuadorian dishes, great service right in the heart of Minneapolis
- Authentic lunch & dinner menu
- Variety of breakfast entrees - some authentic, some not, but all are good!

RESTAURANTE GUAYAQUIL

1526 E. Lake St.
(Corner of Bloomington & Lake)
Minneapolis, MN
(612)722-2346

Offer Details: Valid anytime.

00568808

Offer validity is governed by the Rules of Use and excludes defined holidays. Offers are not valid with other discount offers, unless specified. Coupons void if purchased, sold or bartered. Discounts exclude tax, tip and/or alcohol, where applicable.

entertainment
entertainment.com

Roadhouse 169 Bar & Grill

Enjoy one complimentary LUNCH OR DINNER ENTREE when a second LUNCH OR DINNER ENTREE of equal or greater value is purchased.

See reverse for Offer Details.

REPEAT SAVINGS

Up To $8.00 Value

THE ROADHOUSE 169 BAR & GRILL — MANKATO, MINNESOTA

1006 N. River Dr., Mankato, MN
(507) 387-7511

Valid now thru November 1, 2007

B220

---

entertainment
entertainment.com

Roberts Sports Bar & Entertainment

Enjoy one complimentary LUNCH OR DINNER ENTREE when a second LUNCH OR DINNER ENTREE of equal or greater value is purchased.

See reverse for Offer Details.

REPEAT SAVINGS

Up To $8.00 Value

ROBERT'S SPORTS BAR & ENTERTAINMENT

www.robertssportsbar.com

2400 County Rd. H2, Moundsview, MN
(763) 786-1144

Valid now thru November 1, 2007

B221

---

entertainment
entertainment.com

Rocco's Pizza

Enjoy any one PIZZA at 50% off the regular price.

See reverse for Offer Details.

Up To $12.00 Value

ROCCO'S PIZZA

www.roccospizza.com

See Reverse Side for Locations

REPEAT SAVINGS

Valid now thru November 1, 2007

B222

CASUAL DINING & FAST FOOD

Roadhouse 169 Bar & Grill

- Burgers & sandwiches
- Open daily for lunch & dinner
- Visa & Mastercard accepted
- Gift certificates available
- Dine-in or call ahead for take-out

00637489

THE ROADHOUSE 169 BAR & GRILL
MANKATO, MINNESOTA

1006 N. River Dr.
(1-1/2 blks. S. of Mankato Harley Davidson on 169)
Mankato, MN
(507) 387-7511

Offer Details: Valid anytime.

Offer validity is governed by the Rules of Use and excludes defined holidays. Offers are not valid with other discount offers, unless specified. Coupons void if purchased, sold or bartered. Discounts exclude tax, tip and/or alcohol, where applicable.

Roberts Sports Bar & Entertainment

- Hoagies, pizza burgers, salads & more
- Full bar
- Visit our website for entertainment schedule
- Cigar shop & lounge
- Enjoy a 10% discount on accessories in The Cigar Shop at Roberts with this coupon

00577234

ROBERT'S SPORTS BAR & ENTERTAINMENT

Pizza Planet Express

2400 County Rd. H2
Moundsview, MN
(763) 786-1144

Offer Details: Valid anytime. Dine in only.

Offer validity is governed by the Rules of Use and excludes defined holidays. Offers are not valid with other discount offers, unless specified. Coupons void if purchased, sold or bartered. Discounts exclude tax, tip and/or alcohol, where applicable.

Rocco's Pizza

- We have won 5 national awards!
- All locations open at 4 p.m. daily
- Home of the 20" Super Heavy Weight Pizza

ROCCO'S PIZZA

Cottage Grove
7422 E. Point Douglas Rd.
(651) 459-5575

Little Canada
2750 Lake Shore Ave.
(651) 483-4435

Oakdale
1951 Geneva Ave. N
(651) 738-9091

St. Paul
1215 Randolph Ave.
(651) 698-3439

West St. Paul
120 W. Annapolis St.
(651) 450-9577

White Bear Lake
2018 E. Co. Rd. F
(651) 407-8432

Woodbury
8470 City Center Dr.
(651) 714-1104

00355046

Offer Details: Valid anytime. Carry out only.

Offer validity is governed by the Rules of Use and excludes defined holidays. Offers are not valid with other discount offers, unless specified. Coupons void if purchased, sold or bartered. Discounts exclude tax, tip and/or alcohol, where applicable.

CASUAL DINING & FAST FOOD

Rosetti's Pizza & Pasta

Enjoy one complimentary DINNER ENTREE when a second DINNER ENTREE of equal or greater value is purchased or for those who prefer - any one pizza at 50% off the regular price - maximum discount $8.00.

See reverse for Offer Details.

Up To $8.00 Value

Rosetti's Pizza & Pasta

5600 LaCentre Ave., Albertville, MN
(763)497-7440

Valid now thru November 1, 2007

B223

Sally's Saloon & Eatery

Enjoy one complimentary DINNER ENTREE when a second DINNER ENTREE of equal or greater value is purchased.

See reverse for Offer Details.

Up To $9.00 Value

"COME FOR THE FOOD"
Sally's Saloon & Eatery
"STAY FOR THE PARTY!!"
"THE PARTY'S AT SALLY'S!!"

www.sallyssaloon.com

712 Washington Ave. S. E., Minneapolis, MN
(612)331-3231

Valid now thru November 1, 2007

B224

Sarpino's Pizza

Enjoy any one complimentary PIZZA when a second PIZZA of equal or greater value is purchased.

See reverse for Offer Details.

Up To $16.00 Value

Sarpino's™ Pizzeria

www.sarpinos-usa.com

9175 Quaday Ave. N.E., Otsego, MN
(763)441-6200

Valid now thru November 1, 2007

B225

Rosetti's Pizza & Pasta
- Handmade pizza on a stone hearth oven
- Wide selection of fresh pizzas and pastas
- All entrees made to order
- Beer and wine available
- Locally owned & operated
- Lunch buffet
- Catering & banquet room available

Rosetti's
Pizza & Pasta

5600 LaCentre Ave.
(Next to Coburn's)
Albertville, MN
(763) 497-7440

Offer Details: Valid any evening. Delivery excluded; Dine in only.

Offer validity is governed by the Rules of Use and excludes defined holidays. Offers are not valid with other discount offers, unless specified. Coupons void if purchased, sold or bartered. Discounts exclude tax, tip and/or alcohol, where applicable.

00568086

Sally's Saloon & Eatery
- Fast, Friendly Service
- Casual American Comfort Food
- Outrageous Nightly Drink Specials
- Game Room

"COME FOR THE FOOD"
Sally's
Saloon & Eatery
"THE PARTY'S AT SALLY'S!!"
"STAY FOR THE PARTY!!"

712 Washington Ave. S.E.
(located on East Bank, U of M)
Minneapolis, MN
(612) 331-3231

Offer Details: Valid any evening. Dine in only; U of M events excluded.

Offer validity is governed by the Rules of Use and excludes defined holidays. Offers are not valid with other discount offers, unless specified. Coupons void if purchased, sold or bartered. Discounts exclude tax, tip and/or alcohol, where applicable.

00519013

Sarpino's Pizza

Sarpino's™
Pizzeria

9175 Quaday Ave. N.E.
Otsego, MN
(763) 441-6200

Offer Details: Valid anytime. Carry out only.

Offer validity is governed by the Rules of Use and excludes defined holidays. Offers are not valid with other discount offers, unless specified. Coupons void if purchased, sold or bartered. Discounts exclude tax, tip and/or alcohol, where applicable.

00677747

Scoops Pub

Enjoy one complimentary LUNCH OR DINNER ENTREE when a second LUNCH OR DINNER ENTREE of equal or greater value is purchased.
See reverse for Offer Details.

Up To $7.00 Value

482 Northdale Blvd., Coon Rapids, MN
(763) 757-7600

Valid now thru November 1, 2007

B226

Skinners Pub & Eatery

Enjoy one complimentary LUNCH OR DINNER ENTREE when a second LUNCH OR DINNER ENTREE of equal or greater value is purchased.
See reverse for Offer Details.

Up To $6.00 Value

SKINNER'S PUB and EATERY

919 Randolph Ave., St. Paul, MN
(651) 291-0146

Valid now thru November 1, 2007

B227

Snuffy's Malt Shop

Enjoy one complimentary REGULAR HAMBURGER when a second REGULAR HAMBURGER of equal or greater value is purchased.
See reverse for Offer Details.

REGULAR HAMBURGER

Snuffy's malt shop
* MALTS *
* HAMBURGERS *
* FRENCH FRIES *

See Reverse Side for Locations

Valid now thru November 1, 2007

B228

CASUAL DINING & FAST FOOD

Scoops Pub
- Great selection of appetizers
- Salads, sandwiches, burgers & pizza
- Kids meals
- Daily specials
- Pool & darts
- Full bar

Scoop's pub

482 Northdale Blvd.
Coon Rapids, MN
(763) 757-7600

Offer Details: Valid anytime. Dine in only; Specials excluded.

00659057

Offer validity is governed by the Rules of Use and excludes defined holidays. Offers are not valid with other discount offers, unless specified. Coupons void if purchased, sold or bartered. Discounts exclude tax, tip and/or alcohol, where applicable.

Skinners Pub & Eatery
- Great burgers & sandwiches
- Homemade soups & salads
- We feature Pizza Factory brand pizzas
- Delicious fried chicken
- Full bar

SKINNER'S PUB and EATERY

919 Randolph Ave.
St. Paul, MN
(651) 291-0146

Offer Details: Valid anytime. Dine in only.

00617579

Offer validity is governed by the Rules of Use and excludes defined holidays. Offers are not valid with other discount offers, unless specified. Coupons void if purchased, sold or bartered. Discounts exclude tax, tip and/or alcohol, where applicable.

Snuffy's Malt Shop
- Family oriented
- 50's Malt shop atmosphere
- Great burgers - winner of the Readers Award for Twin Cities Best Burgers
- Written up in the New York Times!

Snuffy's malt shop

4502 Valley View Rd.
Edina, MN
(952) 920-0949

17519 Minnetonka Blvd.
Minnetonka, MN
(952) 475-1850

1125 W Larpenteur Ave.
St. Paul, MN
(651) 488-0241

244 Cleveland Ave. S
St. Paul, MN
(651) 690-1846

Offer Details: Valid anytime.

00000883

Offer validity is governed by the Rules of Use and excludes defined holidays. Offers are not valid with other discount offers, unless specified. Coupons void if purchased, sold or bartered. Discounts exclude tax, tip and/or alcohol, where applicable.

The Sportsman's Pub

Enjoy one complimentary ENTREE when a second ENTREE of equal or greater value is purchased.
See reverse for Offer Details.

Valid now thru November 1, 2007

Up To $7.00 Value

The Sportsmans Pub

www.sportsmanspub.com

2124 Como Ave., SE, Minneapolis, MN
(612)379-8407

B229

Spring Street Tavern

Enjoy one complimentary LUNCH OR DINNER ENTREE when a second LUNCH OR DINNER ENTREE of equal or greater value is purchased.
See reverse for Offer Details.

Valid now thru November 1, 2007

Up To $9.00 Value

Northeast Minneapolis SPRING STREET TAVERN

355 Monroe St. N.E., Minneapolis, MN
(612)627-9123

B230

Enjoy one complimentary LUNCH OR DINNER ENTREE when a second LUNCH OR DINNER ENTREE of equal or greater value is purchased or for those who prefer - any one pizza at 50% off the regular price.
See reverse for Offer Details.

Valid now thru November 1, 2007

Up To $12.00 Value

TASTY PIZZA — THE TASTIEST IN TOWN — SINCE 1963

See Reverse Side for Locations

B231

CASUAL DINING & FAST FOOD

The Sportsman's Pub
- Famous burgers
- Spicy Chili
- Pizza
- Original sandwiches

The Sportsmans Pub

2124 Como Ave., SE
Minneapolis, MN
(612) 379-8407

Offer Details: Valid anytime.

00573406

Offer validity is governed by the Rules of Use and excludes defined holidays. Offers are not valid with other discount offers, unless specified. Coupons void if purchased, sold or bartered. Discounts exclude tax, tip and/or alcohol, where applicable.

Spring Street Tavern
- Breakfast served all day
- Open Mon.-Sat. at 8 a.m., Sun. at 9 a.m.
- Bloody Mary bar Sat. & Sun. til 3 p.m.
- Burgers & sandwiches
- Vegetarian items
- Items on our menu made from scratch
- Live music Thurs. nights & Sun. afternoons

Northeast Minneapolis
SPRING STREET TAVERN

355 Monroe St. N.E.
Minneapolis, MN
(612) 627-9123

Offer Details: Valid anytime.
Tipping should be 15% to 20% of TOTAL bill before discount

00578993

Offer validity is governed by the Rules of Use and excludes defined holidays. Offers are not valid with other discount offers, unless specified. Coupons void if purchased, sold or bartered. Discounts exclude tax, tip and/or alcohol, where applicable.

- The tastiest in town
- Italian & American cuisine in a sports bar atmosphere
- We feature all major sporting events on 14 TV's
- Full bar
- Fun for the whole family!

TASTY PIZZA
THE TASTIEST IN TOWN · SINCE 1965

Tasty Pizza
13827 Round Lake Blvd.
Andover, MN
(763) 421-3893

Tasty Pizza
3220 NW Bridge St.
St. Francis, MN
(763) 753-4988

Offer Details: Valid anytime. Dine in only.

00110456

Offer validity is governed by the Rules of Use and excludes defined holidays. Offers are not valid with other discount offers, unless specified. Coupons void if purchased, sold or bartered. Discounts exclude tax, tip and/or alcohol, where applicable.

entertainment.com

TCBY

Enjoy one complimentary HAND SCOOPED OR SOFT SERVE YOGURT CUP when a second HAND SCOOPED OR SOFT SERVE YOGURT CUP of equal or greater value is purchased.
See reverse for Offer Details.

FREE HAND SCOOPED OR SOFT SERVE YOGURT CUP

"TCBY"® Treats

Valid now thru November 1, 2007

See Reverse Side for Locations

B232

---

entertainment.com

TCBY

Enjoy one complimentary SHIVER OR SMOOTHIE when a second SHIVER OR SMOOTHIE of equal or greater value is purchased.
See reverse for Offer Details.

FREE SHIVER OR SMOOTHIE

"TCBY"® Treats

Valid now thru November 1, 2007

See Reverse Side for Locations

B233

CASUAL DINING & FAST FOOD

---

entertainment.com

TJ's of Edina

Enjoy one complimentary ENTREE when a second ENTREE of equal or greater value is purchased.
See reverse for Offer Details.

Up To $6.00 Value

TJ's of Edina
Restaurant Pizzeria

REPEAT SAVINGS

Valid now thru November 1, 2007

7100 Amundson Ave., Edina, MN
(952) 941-2005

B234

TCBY

- "The Country's Best Yogurt"
- Sugar free yogurt available
- Sundaes, smoothies, parfaits, cakes, pies, & more

"TCBY"® Treats

6415 Labeaux #C80
(Albertville Premium Outlets)
Albertville, MN
(763)497-7077

1480 Southdale Ctr.
(Southdale Ctr.)
Edina, MN
(952)920-2253

4231 Winnetka Ave. N.
New Hope, MN
(763)537-9344

120 Rosedale Ctr.
(Rosedale Ctr.)
Roseville, MN
(651)635-9868

Offer Details: Valid anytime.

00110147

Offer validity is governed by the Rules of Use and excludes defined holidays. Offers are not valid with other discount offers, unless specified. Coupons void if purchased, sold or bartered. Discounts exclude tax, tip and/or alcohol, where applicable.

TCBY

- "The Country's Best Yogurt"
- Sugar free yogurt available
- Sundaes, smoothies, parfaits, cakes, pies, & more

"TCBY"® Treats

6415 Labeaux #C80
(Albertville Premium Outlets)
Albertville, MN
(763)497-7077

1480 Southdale Ctr.
(Southdale Ctr.)
Edina, MN
(952)920-2253

4231 Winnetka Ave. N.
New Hope, MN
(763)537-9344

120 Rosedale Ctr.
(Rosedale Ctr.)
Roseville, MN
(651)635-9868

Offer Details: Valid anytime.

00110148

Offer validity is governed by the Rules of Use and excludes defined holidays. Offers are not valid with other discount offers, unless specified. Coupons void if purchased, sold or bartered. Discounts exclude tax, tip and/or alcohol, where applicable.

TJ's of Edina

TJ's of Edina
Restaurant Pizzeria

7100 Amundson Ave.
Edina, MN
(952)941-2005

Offer Details: Valid anytime.

00241530

Offer validity is governed by the Rules of Use and excludes defined holidays. Offers are not valid with other discount offers, unless specified. Coupons void if purchased, sold or bartered. Discounts exclude tax, tip and/or alcohol, where applicable.

entertainment
entertainment.com

The Tea Garden
Enjoy one complimentary MENU ITEM when a second MENU ITEM of equal or greater value is purchased.
See reverse for Offer Details.

REPEAT SAVINGS

Valid now thru November 1, 2007

Up To $5.00 Value

the tea garden

www.teagardeninc.com
See Reverse Side for Locations

B235

---

entertainment
entertainment.com

Tea Source
Enjoy one complimentary MENU ITEM when a second MENU ITEM of equal or greater value is purchased.
See reverse for Offer Details.

REPEAT SAVINGS

Valid now thru November 1, 2007

Up To $5.00 Value

TEA SOURCE

See Reverse Side for Locations

B236

CASUAL DINING & FAST FOOD

---

entertainment
entertainment.com

Thailand View
Enjoy one complimentary LUNCH OR DINNER ENTREE when a second LUNCH OR DINNER ENTREE of equal or greater value is purchased.
See reverse for Offer Details.

REPEAT SAVINGS

Valid now thru November 1, 2007

Up To $13.00 Value

Thailand View Restaurant

1135 First Ave. E., Shakopee, MN
(952) 403-0305

B237

The Tea Garden

🍃 the tea garden

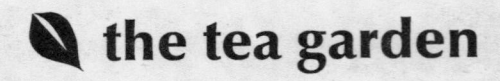

2601 Hennepin Ave. S.
Minneapolis, MN
(612) 377-1700

1692 Grand Ave.
St. Paul, MN
(651) 690-3495

Offer Details: Valid anytime.

00527276

Offer validity is governed by the Rules of Use and excludes defined holidays. Offers are not valid with other discount offers, unless specified. Coupons void if purchased, sold or bartered. Discounts exclude tax, tip and/or alcohol, where applicable.

Tea Source

TEA SOURCE

2908 Pentagon Dr. N.E.
(St. Anthony Shpg. Ctr.)
St. Anthony, MN
(612) 788-4842

752 Cleveland Ave. S.
St. Paul, MN
(651) 690-9822

Offer Details: Valid anytime.

00620592

Offer validity is governed by the Rules of Use and excludes defined holidays. Offers are not valid with other discount offers, unless specified. Coupons void if purchased, sold or bartered. Discounts exclude tax, tip and/or alcohol, where applicable.

Thailand View

- Thai taste is mouth-watering & can be exceptional medicine that satisfies your health & hunger
- You will be served with a warm heart that Thai people are known for

Thailand View Restaurant

1135 First Ave. E.
Shakopee, MN
(952) 403-0305

Offer Details: Valid anytime.
Tipping should be 15% to 20% of TOTAL bill before discount

00686183

Offer validity is governed by the Rules of Use and excludes defined holidays. Offers are not valid with other discount offers, unless specified. Coupons void if purchased, sold or bartered. Discounts exclude tax, tip and/or alcohol, where applicable.

Tiffany's Sports Lounge

Enjoy one complimentary LUNCH OR DINNER ENTREE when a second LUNCH OR DINNER ENTREE of equal or greater value is purchased.
See reverse for Offer Details.

Up To $9.00 Value

2051 Ford Pkwy, St. Paul, MN
(651) 690-4747

Valid now thru November 1, 2007

B238

Tin Shed Tavern & Pizza

Enjoy one complimentary ENTREE when a second ENTREE of equal or greater value is purchased or for those who prefer - any one pizza at 50% off the regular price.
See reverse for Offer Details.

Up To $8.00 Value

www.tinshedtavern.com
12250 Zinran Ave. S., Savage, MN
(952) 736-2444

Valid now thru November 1, 2007

B239

Tropical Smoothie Cafe

Enjoy one complimentary MENU ITEM when a second MENU ITEM of equal or greater value is purchased.
See reverse for Offer Details.

Up To $6.00 Value

REPEAT SAVINGS

8330 Egan Dr., Savage, MN
(952) 226-1633

Valid now thru November 1, 2007

B240

CASUAL DINING & FAST FOOD

Tiffany's Sports Lounge
- Come join us at Tiffany's!
- Celebrating over 30 years of friendship, laughter, & service in the Highland Village

00510828

2051 Ford Pkwy
St. Paul, MN
(651) 690-4747

Offer Details: Valid anytime. Dine in only.

Offer validity is governed by the Rules of Use and excludes defined holidays. Offers are not valid with other discount offers, unless specified. Coupons void if purchased, sold or bartered. Discounts exclude tax, tip and/or alcohol, where applicable.

Tin Shed Tavern & Pizza
- Breakfast, lunch & dinner
- Pizza & pasta
- Pizza by the slice at lunch
- Sandwiches & more
- Banquet facilities available
- Full bar

12250 Zinran Ave. S.
(101 & Zinran in Eagle Valley Shpg. Ctr.)
Savage, MN
(952) 736-2444

00542118

Offer Details: Valid anytime. Breakfast included; Dine in only.

Offer validity is governed by the Rules of Use and excludes defined holidays. Offers are not valid with other discount offers, unless specified. Coupons void if purchased, sold or bartered. Discounts exclude tax, tip and/or alcohol, where applicable.

Tropical Smoothie Cafe
- Smoothies - low-fat, dessert, power, weight-gain & meal replacement
- Gourmet wraps
- Specialty sandwiches
- Breads
- Salads
- Breakfast

8330 Egan Dr.
Savage, MN
(952) 226-1633

Offer Details: Valid anytime.

00700428

Offer validity is governed by the Rules of Use and excludes defined holidays. Offers are not valid with other discount offers, unless specified. Coupons void if purchased, sold or bartered. Discounts exclude tax, tip and/or alcohol, where applicable.

Tropicana

Enjoy one complimentary MENU ITEM when a second MENU ITEM of equal or greater value is purchased.
See reverse for Offer Details.

Up To $5.00 Value

328 W. Market, Bloomington, MN
(952) 858-8111

Valid now thru November 1, 2007

B241

Turitto's Pizza & Subs

Enjoy any one PIZZA at 50% off the regular price - maximum discount $7.00.
See reverse for Offer Details.

Up To $7.00 Value

6611 Concord St. E., Inver Grove Hts., MN
(651) 455-6363

Valid now thru November 1, 2007

B242

Turtle's Bar & Grill

Enjoy one complimentary LUNCH OR DINNER ENTREE when a second LUNCH OR DINNER ENTREE of equal or greater value is purchased.
See reverse for Offer Details.

Up To $9.00 Value

132 1st Ave. E, Shakopee, MN
(952) 445-9668

Valid now thru November 1, 2007

B243

CASUAL DINING & FAST FOOD

Tropicana
- Tropicana smoothies
- Swensen's ice cream
- TCBY yogurt
- Tropicana juices

00585580

Tropicana
SMOOTHIES, JUICES & MORE

328 W. Market
(Mall Of America)
Bloomington, MN
(952)858-8111

Offer Details: Valid anytime.

Offer validity is governed by the Rules of Use and excludes defined holidays. Offers are not valid with other discount offers, unless specified. Coupons void if purchased, sold or bartered. Discounts exclude tax, tip and/or alcohol, where applicable.

Turitto's Pizza & Subs
- Traditional & specialty pizzas
- Submarines & sandwiches

00695696

Turitto's
PIZZA SUBMARINES

6611 Concord St. E.
Inver Grove Hts., MN
(651)455-6363

Offer Details: Valid anytime. Dine-in or carry out.

Offer validity is governed by the Rules of Use and excludes defined holidays. Offers are not valid with other discount offers, unless specified. Coupons void if purchased, sold or bartered. Discounts exclude tax, tip and/or alcohol, where applicable.

Turtle's Bar & Grill
- Fantastic food, homeade pizzas
- Great burgers, chicken, & ribs
- Two full service bars - one non-smoking
- 16 different beers on tap
- Turtle's is your auto racing headquarters

00205043

Turtle's
BAR & GRILL

132 1st Ave. E
Shakopee, MN
(952)445-9668

Offer Details: Valid anytime. Dine in only.

Offer validity is governed by the Rules of Use and excludes defined holidays. Offers are not valid with other discount offers, unless specified. Coupons void if purchased, sold or bartered. Discounts exclude tax, tip and/or alcohol, where applicable.

Tuttle's Shady Oak Grill

Enjoy one complimentary LUNCH OR DINNER ENTREE when a second LUNCH OR DINNER ENTREE of equal or greater value is purchased or for those who prefer - any one pizza at 50% off the regular price.
See reverse for Offer Details.

Up To $8.00 Value

Tuttle's SHADY OAK GRILL

107 Shady Oak Rd., Hopkins, MN
(952)938-4090

Valid now thru November 1, 2007

B244

Two Stooges Sports Bar & Grill

Enjoy one complimentary LUNCH OR DINNER ENTREE when a second LUNCH OR DINNER ENTREE of equal or greater value is purchased.
See reverse for Offer Details.

REPEAT SAVINGS

Up To $10.00 Value

Two Stooges SPORTS BAR & GRILL — FRIDLEY, MN

7178 University Ave., N.E., Fridley, MN
(763)574-1399

Valid now thru November 1, 2007

B245

Uptown Pizza

Enjoy any one complimentary PIZZA when a second PIZZA of equal or greater value is purchased.
See reverse for Offer Details.

REPEAT SAVINGS

FREE PIZZA

UPTOWN PIZZA

www.uptownpizzampls.com

323 W. Lake St., Minneapolis, MN
(612)823-7203

Valid now thru November 1, 2007

B246

CASUAL DINING & FAST FOOD

Tuttle's Shady Oak Grill

Tuttle's
SHADY OAK GRILL

107 Shady Oak Rd.
Hopkins, MN
(952) 938-4090

Offer Details: Valid anytime. Dine in only.
Tipping should be 15% to 20% of TOTAL bill before discount

00701018

Offer validity is governed by the Rules of Use and excludes defined holidays. Offers are not valid with other discount offers, unless specified. Coupons void if purchased, sold or bartered. Discounts exclude tax, tip and/or alcohol, where applicable.

Two Stooges Sports Bar & Grill

- Delicious appetizers, sandwiches, burgers, pastas & more
- Great happy hour with food & drink discounts
- Try our fantastic daily specials for lunch or dinner
- 14 Plasma TV's & 161 in. HD big screen
- Parties & banquets from 30-300 guests
- 43 World class pool tables & 8 dart boards
- Karaoke & live music

SPORTS BAR Two Stooges FRIDLEY, MN & GRILL

7178 University Ave., N.E.
Fridley, MN
(763) 574-1399

00695823

Offer Details: Valid anytime. Dine in only; Specials excluded.

Offer validity is governed by the Rules of Use and excludes defined holidays. Offers are not valid with other discount offers, unless specified. Coupons void if purchased, sold or bartered. Discounts exclude tax, tip and/or alcohol, where applicable.

Uptown Pizza

- Traditional New York style pizza
- Ask about specialites
- Native to Uptown for 30 years

UPTOWN PIZZA

323 W. Lake St.
Minneapolis, MN
(612) 823-7203

00685719

Offer Details: Valid anytime. Carry out only.

Offer validity is governed by the Rules of Use and excludes defined holidays. Offers are not valid with other discount offers, unless specified. Coupons void if purchased, sold or bartered. Discounts exclude tax, tip and/or alcohol, where applicable.

Vescio's

Enjoy one complimentary ENTREE when a second ENTREE of equal or greater value is purchased.
See reverse for Offer Details.

Up $ To **8** 00 Value

VESCIO'S ITALIAN RESTAURANT

406 14th Ave. SE, Minneapolis, MN
(612) 378-1747

Valid now thru November 1, 2007

B247

Victoria House

Enjoy one complimentary LUNCH OR DINNER ENTREE when a second LUNCH OR DINNER ENTREE of equal or greater value is purchased.
See reverse for Offer Details.

Up $ To **17** 00 Value

Victoria HOUSE

1715 Steiger Lake Lane, Victoria, MN
(952) 443-2858

Valid now thru November 1, 2007

B248

CASUAL DINING & FAST FOOD

Villa Pizza

Enjoy one complimentary SLICE OF NEOPOLITAN PIZZA when a second SLICE OF NEOPOLITAN PIZZA of equal or greater value is purchased.
See reverse for Offer Details.

REPEAT SAVINGS

ONE SLICE NEOPOLITAN PIZZA

Villa Pizza

See Reverse Side for Locations

Valid now thru November 1, 2007

B249

Vescio's

- Traditional Italian dining with a touch of class
- Pizza, pasta, sandwiches & salads
- Beer & wine
- We accept reservations
- Celebrating over 40 years in Dinkytown™

VESCIO'S ITALIAN RESTAURANT

406 14th Ave. SE
(U of M Campus, Dinkytown)
Minneapolis, MN
(612)378-1747

Offer Details: Valid Sunday thru Friday (Saturday seating after 9 p.m.). Dine in only. Not valid with any other coupons, offers or specials; Holidays excluded; Not valid on University of Minnesota game nights.

00059651

Offer validity is governed by the Rules of Use and excludes defined holidays. Offers are not valid with other discount offers, unless specified. Coupons void if purchased, sold or bartered. Discounts exclude tax, tip and/or alcohol, where applicable.

Victoria House

- Visit Victoria House to experience a casual yet elegant dining atmosphere.
- Sample any one of our specialties...
- Cajun Filet Mignon, World-Famous Pepperoni Soup, Pecan Walleye, or Minnesota Chicken stuffed with parmesan, swiss and monterey cheeses and portabella mushrooms, served on a bed of wild rice.
- Only a short drive west from the Twin Cities on Hwy. 5.

Victoria HOUSE

1715 Steiger Lake Lane
Victoria, MN
(952)443-2858

Offer Details: Valid anytime.
Tipping should be 15% to 20% of TOTAL bill before discount

00486258

Offer validity is governed by the Rules of Use and excludes defined holidays. Offers are not valid with other discount offers, unless specified. Coupons void if purchased, sold or bartered. Discounts exclude tax, tip and/or alcohol, where applicable.

Villa Pizza

- Celebrating 40 years of freshness
- Pasta, stromboli, pizza & salads
- Pizza by the slice
- "Very villa, very good"®

Villa Pizza

216 E. Broadway	340 N. Garden	3001 White Bear Ave.
(Mall of America)	*(Mall of America)*	*(Maplewood Mall food court)*
Bloomington, MN	Bloomington, MN	Maplewood, MN
(952)854-4361	(952)858-8312	(651)748-4138

Offer Details: Valid anytime.

00634881

Offer validity is governed by the Rules of Use and excludes defined holidays. Offers are not valid with other discount offers, unless specified. Coupons void if purchased, sold or bartered. Discounts exclude tax, tip and/or alcohol, where applicable.

The Wagon Grill

Enjoy one complimentary LUNCH OR DINNER ENTREE when a second LUNCH OR DINNER ENTREE of equal or greater value is purchased.
See reverse for Offer Details.

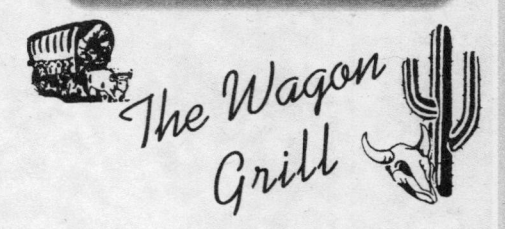

Up To $7.00 Value

The Wagon Grill

4135 W. Broadway N., Robbinsdale, MN
(763) 561-5026

Valid now thru November 1, 2007

B250

Wanderer's Chinese Cuisine

Enjoy one complimentary DINNER ENTREE when a second DINNER ENTREE of equal or greater value is purchased.
See reverse for Offer Details.

Up To $11.00 Value

WANDERER'S GARDEN
Chinese Restaurant and Bar

13059 Ridgedale Dr., Minnetonka, MN
(952) 544-2808

Valid now thru November 1, 2007

B251

The Well Sports Tavern & Grill

Enjoy one complimentary LUNCH OR DINNER ENTREE when a second LUNCH OR DINNER ENTREE of equal or greater value is purchased.
See reverse for Offer Details.

Up To $8.00 Value

THE WELL
SPORTS TAVERN & GRILL
COON RAPIDS

www.wellsportstavern.com

35 Coon Rapids Blvd., Coon Rapids, MN
(763) 792-0800

Valid now thru November 1, 2007

B252

CASUAL DINING & FAST FOOD

The Wagon Grill
- Serving breakfast, lunch & dinner
- Delicious salads, sandwiches & burgers
- Try our grilled panini sandwiches
- Kids & senior choices
- Open daily

The Wagon Grill

4135 W. Broadway N.
(downtown Robbinsdale)
Robbinsdale, MN
(763)561-5026

Offer Details: Valid anytime. Dine in only.

00661050

Offer validity is governed by the Rules of Use and excludes defined holidays. Offers are not valid with other discount offers, unless specified. Coupons void if purchased, sold or bartered. Discounts exclude tax, tip and/or alcohol, where applicable.

Wanderer's Chinese Cuisine
- Wide variety of Chinese dishes - both meat & vegetarian
- Famous for our Sesame Chicken & Wor Shu Duck
- Full service bar

WANDERER'S GARDEN
Chinese Restaurant and Bar

13059 Ridgedale Dr.
(Ridge Square)
Minnetonka, MN
(952)544-2808

Offer Details: Valid any evening. Buffet excluded; Dine in only.

00399062

Offer validity is governed by the Rules of Use and excludes defined holidays. Offers are not valid with other discount offers, unless specified. Coupons void if purchased, sold or bartered. Discounts exclude tax, tip and/or alcohol, where applicable.

The Well Sports Tavern & Grill
- Casual neighborhood sports tavern & grill
- 100% Angus burgers & full size wings
- 14 Flat screen TVs
- Great appetizers & delicious sandwiches
- Daily happy hour - food & drink specials
- Pull tabs
- Vikings, Twins, Timberwolves & Wild food & drink specials
- Smoking permitted

THE WELL
SPORTS TAVERN & GRILL
COON RAPIDS

35 Coon Rapids Blvd.
Coon Rapids, MN
(763)792-0800

Offer Details: Valid anytime. Dine in only; Specials excluded.

00681244

Offer validity is governed by the Rules of Use and excludes defined holidays. Offers are not valid with other discount offers, unless specified. Coupons void if purchased, sold or bartered. Discounts exclude tax, tip and/or alcohol, where applicable.

The Whiskey Rack

Enjoy one complimentary LUNCH OR DINNER ENTREE when a second LUNCH OR DINNER ENTREE of equal or greater value is purchased.
See reverse for Offer Details.

REPEAT SAVINGS

Up To $8.00 Value

2112 E. 11th Ave., N. St. Paul, MN
(651)779-0243

Valid now thru November 1, 2007

B253

Wing Street

Enjoy one complimentary 10 WING OR 20 WING ORDER when a second 10 WING OR 20 WING ORDER of equal or greater value is purchased.
See reverse for Offer Details.
Tracking Code: FS

ONE 10 WING OR 20 WING ORDER

WingStreet
www.pizzahutmn.com

See Reverse Side for Locations

Valid now thru November 1, 2007

B254

CASUAL DINING & FAST FOOD

Wolves Den Native Coffee

Enjoy one complimentary MENU ITEM when a second MENU ITEM of equal or greater value is purchased.
See reverse for Offer Details.

Up To $5.00 Value

WOLVES DEN
NATIVE COFFEE

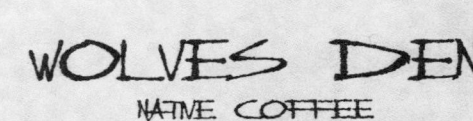

REPEAT SAVINGS

1201 E. Franklin Ave., Minneapolis, MN
(612)871-6373

Valid now thru November 1, 2007

B255

The Whiskey Rack
- Full lunch & dinner menu
- Great happy hour specials 3 p.m.-6 p.m. Mon.-Fri.
- Pool, darts & pull tabs

The Whiskey Rack

2112 E. 11th Ave.
(adjacent to Target Greatland at Hwy. 36 & McKnight)
N. St. Paul, MN
(651)779-0243

Offer Details: Valid anytime. Dine in only; Specials excluded.

00614783

Offer validity is governed by the Rules of Use and excludes defined holidays. Offers are not valid with other discount offers, unless specified. Coupons void if purchased, sold or bartered. Discounts exclude tax, tip and/or alcohol, where applicable.

Wing Street
- 2 Ways to wing it: bone-in or bone-out
- Meatier, tastier wings that come in 6 intense flavors
- Go to www.pizzahutmn.com to order online

WingStreet

Apple Valley
14844 Granada Dr.
(651)488-8888

Bloomington
3701 W. Old Shakopee Rd. #200
(651)488-8888

Eagan
2135 Cliff Rd.
(651)488-8888

Edina
6805 B York Ave.
(651)488-8888

Falcon Heights
1544 Larpenteur Ave. W.
(651)488-8888

Maple Grove
6326 Vinewood Ln.
(651)488-8888

Plymouth
187 Cheshire Ln. #200
(651)488-8888

Rochester
1105 7th St. N.W.
(507)252-1212

840 S. Broadway
(507)285-5000

Offer Details: Valid anytime.

00663324

Offer validity is governed by the Rules of Use and excludes defined holidays. Offers are not valid with other discount offers, unless specified. Coupons void if purchased, sold or bartered. Discounts exclude tax, tip and/or alcohol, where applicable.

Wolves Den Native Coffee
- Organic, free trade native coffee
- Espresso, cappuccino, etc.
- Soups & sandwiches
- Indian tacos
- Open daily
- Catering
- Wireless internet
- Meeting room available at no charge

WOLVES DEN
NATIVE COFFEE

1201 E. Franklin Ave.
Minneapolis, MN
(612)871-6373

Offer Details: Valid anytime.

00654841

Offer validity is governed by the Rules of Use and excludes defined holidays. Offers are not valid with other discount offers, unless specified. Coupons void if purchased, sold or bartered. Discounts exclude tax, tip and/or alcohol, where applicable.

FREE MENU ITEM

Zobota Cafe

Enjoy one complimentary MENU ITEM when a second MENU ITEM of equal or greater value is purchased.
See reverse for Offer Details.
Tracking Code: Hap06/07

ZÖBOTA CAFÉ

Located at Como Park Zoo & Conservatory in St. Paul

1225 Estabrook Dr., St. Paul, MN
(651) 487-2121

Valid now thru November 1, 2007 B256

FREE COMBO MEAL

Long John Silver's

Enjoy one complimentary COMBO MEAL when a second COMBO MEAL of equal or greater value is purchased.
See reverse for Offer Details.

See Reverse Side for Locations

Valid now thru November 1, 2007 B257

FREE COMBO MEAL

Long John Silver's

Enjoy one complimentary COMBO MEAL when a second COMBO MEAL of equal or greater value is purchased.
See reverse for Offer Details.

See Reverse Side for Locations

Valid now thru November 1, 2007 B258

CASUAL DINING & FAST FOOD

Zobota Cafe

- Open year-round
- Sandwiches, Salads & Daily Chef's Specialty Entrees
- Kid's Menu
- Indoor/Outdoor Seating
- Air Conditioned in Summer
- Located in the Visitor Center
- Unique Space Available for Weddings & Special Events
- See Attractions Section for Como Town Coupon

ZOBOTA CAFÉ

Located at Como Park Zoo & Conservatory in St. Paul

1225 Estabrook Dr.
St. Paul, MN
(651) 487-2121

Offer Details: Valid anytime.

00696507

Offer validity is governed by the Rules of Use and excludes defined holidays. Offers are not valid with other discount offers, unless specified. Coupons void if purchased, sold or bartered. Discounts exclude tax, tip and/or alcohol, where applicable.

Long John Silver's

4240 Pheasant Ridge Dr.
Blaine, MN
(763) 259-0762

378 South Ave.
(S. Food Ct., 3rd floor)
Bloomington, MN
(952) 858-9436

12759 Riverdale Blvd.
(Riverdale Village Shpg. Plaza)
Coon Rapids, MN
(763) 576-1265

17750 Kenwood Trail
Lakeville, MN
(952) 898-1213

13910 Grove Dr.
Maple Grove, MN
(763) 494-9268

2219 Hwy. 10
Mounds View, MN
(763) 785-0676

Offer Details: Valid anytime.

00110429

Offer validity is governed by the Rules of Use and excludes defined holidays. Offers are not valid with other discount offers, unless specified. Coupons void if purchased, sold or bartered. Discounts exclude tax, tip and/or alcohol, where applicable.

Long John Silver's

4240 Pheasant Ridge Dr.
Blaine, MN
(763) 259-0762

378 South Ave.
(S. Food Ct., 3rd floor)
Bloomington, MN
(952) 858-9436

12759 Riverdale Blvd.
(Riverdale Village Shpg. Plaza)
Coon Rapids, MN
(763) 576-1265

17750 Kenwood Trail
Lakeville, MN
(952) 898-1213

13910 Grove Dr.
Maple Grove, MN
(763) 494-9268

2219 Hwy. 10
Mounds View, MN
(763) 785-0676

Offer Details: Valid anytime.

00110429

Offer validity is governed by the Rules of Use and excludes defined holidays. Offers are not valid with other discount offers, unless specified. Coupons void if purchased, sold or bartered. Discounts exclude tax, tip and/or alcohol, where applicable.

entertainment.com — Up To $6.00 Value

Adrian's Tavern

Enjoy one complimentary LUNCH OR DINNER ENTREE when a second LUNCH OR DINNER ENTREE of equal or greater value is purchased.

valid anytime

B259

Offer validity is governed by the Rules of Use and excludes defined holidays. Offers are not valid with other discount offers, unless specified.

Valid now thru November 1, 2007

---

entertainment.com — Up To $5.00 Value

Ambrosia Coffee

www.ambrosiaespresso.com

Enjoy one complimentary MENU ITEM when a second MENU ITEM of equal or greater value is purchased.

valid anytime

B260

Offer validity is governed by the Rules of Use and excludes defined holidays. Offers are not valid with other discount offers, unless specified.

Valid now thru November 1, 2007

---

entertainment.com — Up To $7.00 Value

American Pie

Enjoy one complimentary LUNCH OR DINNER ENTREE when a second LUNCH OR DINNER ENTREE of equal or greater value is purchased or for those who prefer - any one pizza at 50% off the regular price - maximum discount $7.00.

valid anytime

B261

Offer validity is governed by the Rules of Use and excludes defined holidays. Offers are not valid with other discount offers, unless specified.

Valid now thru November 1, 2007

---

entertainment.com — Up To $5.00 Value

Amy's Classic Confections

Enjoy any FOOD ORDER at 50% off the regular price - maximum discount $5.00.

valid anytime

B262

Offer validity is governed by the Rules of Use and excludes defined holidays. Offers are not valid with other discount offers, unless specified.

Valid now thru November 1, 2007

---

entertainment.com — Up To $7.00 Value

Andy's Sports Bar & Grill

Enjoy one complimentary LUNCH OR DINNER ENTREE when a second LUNCH OR DINNER ENTREE of equal or greater value is purchased.

valid anytime

Offers not valid holidays and subject to Rules of Use
Tipping should be 15% to 20% of the total bill before discount

B263

Offer validity is governed by the Rules of Use and excludes defined holidays. Offers are not valid with other discount offers, unless specified.

Valid now thru November 1, 2007

---

entertainment.com — Up To $5.00 Value

Anodyne

Enjoy any BEVERAGE ORDER at 50% off the regular price - maximum discount $5.00.

valid anytime

B264

Offer validity is governed by the Rules of Use and excludes defined holidays. Offers are not valid with other discount offers, unless specified.

Valid now thru November 1, 2007

AMBROSIA COFFEE

- Organic & fair-trade coffee
- Soups, salads & sandwiches
- Smoothies & ice blended glaciers
- Pastries & breakfast

1278 Lone Oak Rd. *(Next to Hampton Inn),*
Eagan, MN
(651)681-8188

7373 France Ave. S. *(Centennial Lakes Medical Bldg.),* **Edina, MN**
(952)831-6232

430 1st Ave. N. *(Corner of 1st Ave. & 5th St., in the Kickernick Bldg. Lobby),* **Minneapolis, MN**
(612)338-7005

00694650

Adrian's Tavern

- Delicious burgers
- Friendly service
- Located near the corner of 48th & Chicago
- Families welcome

4812 Chicago Ave. S
Minneapolis, MN
(612)824-4011

00276897

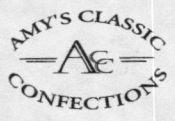

AMY'S CLASSIC CONFECTIONS

- Specialists in unique candy baskets & gifts
- Custom made for any occasion
- Select from a large variety of pre-made baskets or custom design your own
- We will assist you in creating an extraordinary gift that will be truly enjoyed & remembered
- B.T. McElrath chocolates, gourmet Jelly Bellies & fresh-popped popcorn

601 Marquette Ave.
(6 Quebec Building)
Minneapolis, MN
(612)436-0016

00633366

American Pie

- All of our food is baked to perfection
- We deliver, serving Richfield, Bloomington, Edina & S. Minneapolis

6529 Nicollet Ave. S.
Richfield, MN
(612)243-3661

00569096

Amodyne

- Open daily
- Breakfast served all day
- Fresh soup, scones & desserts
- Open mike 1st Friday of every month
- Live music on weekends
- Eclectic espresso, coffee & tea menu
- Comfortable smoke-free atmosphere

4301 Nicollet Ave.
(43rd & Nicollet)
Minneapolis, MN
(612)824-4300

00459880

ANDYS Sports Bar & Grill

- Daily specials Mon.-Sat.
- Best burgers & hot wings in town
- 9 p.m.-10:30 p.m. Wed. nights 2-for-1
- Fri. night is trivia night at 7:30 p.m.

529 Plum St.
Red Wing, MN
(651)388-4471

00701849

entertainment.com — Up to $5.00 Value

Aroma Café

Enjoy one complimentary MENU ITEM when a second MENU ITEM of equal or greater value is purchased.

valid anytime

B265

Offer validity is governed by the Rules of Use and excludes defined holidays. Offers are not valid with other discount offers, unless specified.

Valid now thru November 1, 2007

---

entertainment.com — Up to $6.00 Value

AROMA'S PIZZA & CAFE

Enjoy one complimentary MENU ITEM when a second MENU ITEM of equal or greater value is purchased.

valid anytime

B266

Offer validity is governed by the Rules of Use and excludes defined holidays. Offers are not valid with other discount offers, unless specified.

Valid now thru November 1, 2007

---

entertainment.com — Up to $5.00 Value

Artists' Grind

Enjoy one complimentary MENU ITEM when a second MENU ITEM of equal or greater value is purchased.

valid anytime

B267

Offer validity is governed by the Rules of Use and excludes defined holidays. Offers are not valid with other discount offers, unless specified.

Valid now thru November 1, 2007

---

entertainment.com — Up to $5.00 Value

Audubon Coffee

Enjoy one complimentary MENU ITEM when a second MENU ITEM of equal or greater value is purchased.

valid anytime

B268

Offer validity is governed by the Rules of Use and excludes defined holidays. Offers are not valid with other discount offers, unless specified.

Valid now thru November 1, 2007

---

entertainment.com — Up to $5.00 Value

Audubon Coffee

Enjoy one complimentary MENU ITEM when a second MENU ITEM of equal or greater value is purchased.

valid anytime

B269

Offer validity is governed by the Rules of Use and excludes defined holidays. Offers are not valid with other discount offers, unless specified.

Valid now thru November 1, 2007

---

entertainment.com — Up to $5.00 Value

Auntie Em's

www.auntieemsbooks.com

Enjoy one complimentary MENU ITEM when a second MENU ITEM of equal or greater value is purchased.

valid anytime

B270

Offer validity is governed by the Rules of Use and excludes defined holidays. Offers are not valid with other discount offers, unless specified.

Valid now thru November 1, 2007

AROMA'S PIZZA & CAFE

- Good food & lots of it
- Visit us on the first floor of the Carriage Hill Plaza

350 St. Peter
(Carriage Hill Plaza)
St. Paul, MN
(651)293-9040

00369902

Aroma Café

- Coffee & espresso drinks
- Smoothies/blended coffee drinks
- Gourmet soups
- Fresh salads
- Fresh pastries daily
- Relaxing atmosphere
- Free wireless internet
- Gift cards available

7868 Century Blvd.
(off Hwy. 5 & Century Blvd.)
Chanhassen, MN
(952)448-9089

00671037

Audubon Coffee

- Come for the coffee, stay for the gossip
- Now accepting regulars
- Yummy soups, sandwiches, and, oh yeah, coffee

2852 Johnson St. N.E.
Minneapolis, MN
(612)781-0427

00573478

Artists' Grind

- Organic espresso drinks
- Deli sandwiches, soups & tamales
- Pastries
- Italian Gelato
- Teas & hot cider
- Bulk coffee beans
- Art gallery & gift items

2399 University Ave. W.
St. Paul, MN
(651)641-1656

00677752

Aunt Gus's

- Full service espresso bar, smoothies, bakery & snacks
- Books for toddlers thru young adults
- Gifts
- Special events & book fairs

5 W. Diamond Lake Rd.
Minneapolis, MN
(612)798-1827

00634749

Audubon Coffee

- Come for the coffee, stay for the gossip
- Now accepting regulars
- Yummy soups, sandwiches, and, oh yeah, coffee

2852 Johnson St. N.E.
Minneapolis, MN
(612)781-0427

00573478

AURELIO'S

Up To $18.00 Value

Enjoy any one complimentary PIZZA when a second PIZZA of equal or greater value is purchased.

valid anytime

B271

Valid now thru November 1, 2007

Offer validity is governed by the Rules of Use and excludes defined holidays. Offers are not valid with other discount offers, unless specified.

Avalon Tearoom & Pastry Shoppe

Up To $7.00 Value

Enjoy one complimentary MENU ITEM when a second MENU ITEM of equal or greater value is purchased.

Special events excluded

valid anytime

B272

Valid now thru November 1, 2007

Offer validity is governed by the Rules of Use and excludes defined holidays. Offers are not valid with other discount offers, unless specified.

Bahn Thai Cuisine

Up To $10.00 Value

Enjoy one complimentary LUNCH OR DINNER ENTREE when a second LUNCH OR DINNER ENTREE of equal or greater value is purchased.

Dine in only; Specials excluded; Buffet excluded

valid anytime

Tipping should be 15% to 20% of TOTAL bill before discount

B273

Valid now thru November 1, 2007

Offer validity is governed by the Rules of Use and excludes defined holidays. Offers are not valid with other discount offers, unless specified.

Betsy's BACK PORCH coffee
bp
Nurture your Nature

Up To $5.00 Value

Enjoy one complimentary MENU ITEM when a second MENU ITEM of equal or greater value is purchased.

valid anytime

B274

Valid now thru November 1, 2007

Offer validity is governed by the Rules of Use and excludes defined holidays. Offers are not valid with other discount offers, unless specified.

Betty's BIKES & BUNS

Up To $5.00 Value

www.bettysbikesandbuns.com

Enjoy one complimentary MENU ITEM when a second MENU ITEM of equal or greater value is purchased.

valid anytime

B275

Valid now thru November 1, 2007

Offer validity is governed by the Rules of Use and excludes defined holidays. Offers are not valid with other discount offers, unless specified.

Bev's Cafe

Up To $5.00 Value

Enjoy one complimentary MENU ITEM when a second MENU ITEM of equal or greater value is purchased.

valid anytime

Tipping should be 15% to 20% of TOTAL bill before discount

B276

Valid now thru November 1, 2007

Offer validity is governed by the Rules of Use and excludes defined holidays. Offers are not valid with other discount offers, unless specified.

Avalon Tearoom & Pastry Shoppe

- 80 Varieties of bulk loose leaf teas, freshly brewed
- Soups, specialty sandwiches & salads
- Scrumptious scones & pastries
- Quiche
- Call ahead to schedule your afternoon tea for any occasion, including birthday parties or bridal showers
- Children's tea parties
- Gift shop with hundreds of tea-related items; English Bone China, cards & books

2179 4th St.
White Bear Lake, MN
(651)653-3822

00575386

AURELIO'S

- Stuffed pizza
- Spinach pie
- Calabrese
- Pastas- 1/4 lb. meat balls
- Sandwiches
- Antipasto salads
- Open for lunch
- Beer served

2827 Hamline Ave.
Roseville, MN
(651)636-1730

00659502

Betsy's Back Porch Coffee
Nurture your Nature

- Gourmet coffee & tea
- Pastries
- Soups & sandwiches
- Fireplace
- Entertainment
- Non-smoking atmosphere

5447 Nicollet Ave.
(Diamond Lake & Nicollet)
Minneapolis, MN
(612)827-8283

00500905

Bahn Thai Cuisine

- Grand opening 2005
- Authentic Thai cuisine
- Made to order, spice to your liking
- Always & only the freshest ingredients
- Meat & vegetarian choices
- Credit cards accepted

4108 Lancaster Ln. N.
Plymouth, MN
(763)559-9030

00682078

Bev's Cafe

- Soups & salads
- Delicious burgers & sandwiches
- Pasta dinners
- Chicken, fish & pork chops
- To go orders available

221 Bush St.
(near St. James Hotel)
Red Wing, MN
(651)388-5227

00468750

Betty's Bikes & Buns

- Fresh baked cookies, scones, cinnamon twists & buns
- Our coffee is great!
- Spunky help
- Motorcycle parking

600 E. Hennepin
Minneapolis, MN
(612)378-4988

00613711

Big Bite Pizza

Up To $6.00 Value

Enjoy any one PIZZA at 50% off the regular price.

Carry out only

valid anytime

B277

Offer validity is governed by the Rules of Use and excludes defined holidays. Offers are not valid with other discount offers, unless specified.

Valid now thru November 1, 2007

Big Daddy's Pizza

50% OFF

WE'RE BIG ON EVERYTHING!

Enjoy any one PIZZA at 50% off the regular price.

Carry out only

valid anytime

B278

Offer validity is governed by the Rules of Use and excludes defined holidays. Offers are not valid with other discount offers, unless specified.

Valid now thru November 1, 2007

Big Dipper

Up To $5.00 Value

Enjoy one complimentary MENU ITEM when a second MENU ITEM of equal or greater value is purchased.

valid anytime

B279

Offer validity is governed by the Rules of Use and excludes defined holidays. Offers are not valid with other discount offers, unless specified.

Valid now thru November 1, 2007

Big Stop Deli

BUY ONE GET ONE FREE

Enjoy one complimentary MENU ITEM when a second MENU ITEM of equal or greater value is purchased.

valid anytime

B280

Offer validity is governed by the Rules of Use and excludes defined holidays. Offers are not valid with other discount offers, unless specified.

Valid now thru November 1, 2007

Big Vinny's Sandwiches

Up To $5.00 Value

Enjoy one complimentary MENU ITEM when a second MENU ITEM of equal or greater value is purchased.

valid anytime

B281

Offer validity is governed by the Rules of Use and excludes defined holidays. Offers are not valid with other discount offers, unless specified.

Valid now thru November 1, 2007

Black Bean Crossings Coffee House Cafe

Up To $6.00 Value

Enjoy one complimentary MENU ITEM when a second MENU ITEM of equal or greater value is purchased.

valid anytime

B282

Offer validity is governed by the Rules of Use and excludes defined holidays. Offers are not valid with other discount offers, unless specified.

Valid now thru November 1, 2007

Big Daddy's Pizza

- Award-winning family recipes
- Premium cheese
- Pizza, pastas, calzone
- Wings, mozzarella sticks, chicken strips, garlic toast & more

10980 Hwy. 65 #110
Blaine, MN
(763) 755-5252

00612452

Big Bite Pizza

- 3 crusts & 19 toppings to choose from
- Pastas, salads, wings & more
- Free delivery
- Cash, check or credit cards accepted

13656 Crosstown Blvd. N.W.
(Bunker Lake Blvd. & Crosstown Blvd.)
Andover, MN
(763) 754-9999

00568209

Big Stop DELI

1800 26th Ave.
Minneapolis, MN
(612) 529-4238

00634801

Big Dipper

- Delicious homemade ice cream
- Over 30 flavors to choose from
- Malts & sundaes

10904 Baltimore St. #107, Blaine, MN
(763) 786-4463
1250 126th Ave. #100, Blaine, MN
(763) 755-7630

00695465

- Open all year round
- Gourmet coffees, teas & specialty drinks
- Delicious deli sandwiches, salads, soups, fresh baked pastries, homemade desserts & more
- Banquet facilities, community meeting rooms and catering available

1360 North Lexington Parkway
(in Como Park)
St. Paul, MN
(651) 488-4920

00492606

Big Vinny's Sandwiches

- 6 inch & 12 inch subs
- White, wheat & focaccia bread
- Hot oven baked

9100 Park Ave.
(located inside Godfather's Pizza)
Otsego, MN
(763) 241-9000

00524691

FREE MENU ITEM

Blink Bonnie
Signature Sandwiches
Free Delivery in the Metro Area
Subs

Enjoy one complimentary MENU ITEM when a second MENU ITEM of equal or greater value is purchased.

valid anytime

B283

Offer validity is governed by the Rules of Use and excludes defined holidays. Offers are not valid with other discount offers, unless specified.

Valid now thru November 1, 2007

Up To $5.00 Value

BLUE CAT COFFEE & TEA

Enjoy any FOOD/BEVERAGE ORDER at 50% off the regular price - maximum discount $5.00.

valid anytime

B284

Offer validity is governed by the Rules of Use and excludes defined holidays. Offers are not valid with other discount offers, unless specified.

Valid now thru November 1, 2007

Up To $5.00 Value

BLUE CAT COFFEE & TEA

Enjoy any FOOD/BEVERAGE ORDER at 50% off the regular price - maximum discount $5.00.

valid anytime

B285

Offer validity is governed by the Rules of Use and excludes defined holidays. Offers are not valid with other discount offers, unless specified.

Valid now thru November 1, 2007

Up To $5.00 Value

Blue Eyes Café

Enjoy one complimentary MENU ITEM when a second MENU ITEM of equal or greater value is purchased.

valid anytime

B286

Offer validity is governed by the Rules of Use and excludes defined holidays. Offers are not valid with other discount offers, unless specified.

Valid now thru November 1, 2007

Up To $5.00 Value

BLUE MOON COFFEE CAFE

Enjoy one complimentary MENU ITEM when a second MENU ITEM of equal or greater value is purchased.

valid anytime

B287

Offer validity is governed by the Rules of Use and excludes defined holidays. Offers are not valid with other discount offers, unless specified.

Valid now thru November 1, 2007

$5.00 VALUE

Bobby & Steve's
Auto Repair Experts
Auto World
Minneapolis

Enjoy $5.00 off any OIL CHANGE.

valid anytime

B288

Offer validity is governed by the Rules of Use and excludes defined holidays. Offers are not valid with other discount offers, unless specified.

Valid now thru November 1, 2007

BLUE CAT COFFEE & TEA

- Coffee & Espresso
- Loose leaf teas
- Sandwiches & soups
- Smoothies & iced drinks
- Pastries
- In the heart of District Del Sol on St. Pauls W. side
- Open Mon. - Sat.

151 Cesar Chavez
(Concord St. just East of Robert St.)
St. Paul, MN
(651)291-7676

00676753

Blink Bonnie
Signature Sandwiches Subs

- Gourmet sub sandwiches
- Soups
- Salads
- Free delivery
- We cater - box lunches & party subs

237 E. 7th St.
(Union Depot)
St. Paul, MN
(651)229-0000

00582578

Blue Eyes Café

- Vietnamese & American cuisine
- Serving coffee, sandwiches, rice & more
- Open for breakfast, brunch, lunch & dinner 7 days a week

2424 Nicollet Ave. S.
Minneapolis, MN
(612)870-1035

00573369

BLUE CAT COFFEE & TEA

- Coffee & Espresso
- Loose leaf teas
- Sandwiches & soups
- Smoothies & iced drinks
- Pastries
- In the heart of District Del Sol on St. Pauls W. side
- Open Mon. - Sat.

151 Cesar Chavez
(Concord St. just East of Robert St.)
St. Paul, MN
(651)291-7676

00676753

Bobby & Steve's Auto World
Minneapolis
Auto Repair Experts

3828 Central Ave. NE, Columbia Heights, MN
(763)788-1113

1221 Washington Ave. S., Minneapolis, MN
(612)333-8900

304 W. 61st St., Minneapolis, MN
(612)861-6133

7920 France Ave. S., Minneapolis, MN
(952)831-8833

00322471

BLUE MOON COFFEE CAFE

- Smoke-free
- Open every day including holidays
- Teas, wide variety of coffee, bulk beans
- Pastries, sandwiches
- Ice cream novelties

3822 E Lake St.
Minneapolis, MN
(612)721-9230

00414388

BOSTON GARDEN

Up To $5.00 Value

www.bostoneddy.com

Enjoy one complimentary MENU ITEM when a second MENU ITEM of equal or greater value is purchased or when dining alone - one MENU ITEM at 50% off the regular price - maximum discount $3.00.

Dine in only; Sorry, no delivery

valid anytime

B289

Offer validity is governed by the Rules of Use and excludes defined holidays. Offers are not valid with other discount offers, unless specified.

Valid now thru November 1, 2007

BOULEVARD COFFEE

FREE MENU ITEM

Enjoy one complimentary MENU ITEM when a second MENU ITEM of equal or greater value is purchased.

valid anytime

B290

Offer validity is governed by the Rules of Use and excludes defined holidays. Offers are not valid with other discount offers, unless specified.

Valid now thru November 1, 2007

Brothers Coffee

Up To $5.00 Value

roasted fresh everyday

Enjoy one complimentary MENU ITEM when a second MENU ITEM of equal or greater value is purchased.

valid anytime

B291

Offer validity is governed by the Rules of Use and excludes defined holidays. Offers are not valid with other discount offers, unless specified.

Valid now thru November 1, 2007

The BRU HOUSE Coffee Shop

Up To $5.00 Value

Enjoy any BEVERAGE ORDER at 50% off the regular price.

valid anytime

B292

Offer validity is governed by the Rules of Use and excludes defined holidays. Offers are not valid with other discount offers, unless specified.

Valid now thru November 1, 2007

Brucks Cafe

Up To $5.00 Value

Enjoy one complimentary MENU ITEM when a second MENU ITEM of equal or greater value is purchased.

valid anytime

B293

Offer validity is governed by the Rules of Use and excludes defined holidays. Offers are not valid with other discount offers, unless specified.

Valid now thru November 1, 2007

C. McGee's DELI

Up To $5.00 Value

Enjoy one complimentary MENU ITEM when a second MENU ITEM of equal or greater value is purchased.

valid anytime

B294

Offer validity is governed by the Rules of Use and excludes defined holidays. Offers are not valid with other discount offers, unless specified.

Valid now thru November 1, 2007

BOULEVARD COFFEE

- Espresso drinks
- Drive thru
- Pastries
- Breakfast sandwiches
- Teas
- Fruit smoothies
- Iced blended coffees

23212 St. Francis Blvd #1300
(St. Francis City Centre)
St. Francis, MN
(763)213-8133

00659106

BOSTON GARDEN

- Pizza, pasta, subs
- Breakfast
- Strong beer, wine
- Locally owned, full service

1019 Main St., Hopkins, MN
(952)933-7827
www.bostoneddy.com

00000178

The BRU HOUSE Coffee Shop

- "Voted Best Place For A Cup Of Coffee", six times!! (Lillie News)
- Specialty coffees & exotic teas
- Soups, salads & sandwiches
- Pastries
- Beer & wine available

1431-A Silver Lake Rd.
(1/2 mi. N. of 694)
New Brighton, MN
(651)631-1112

00571271

Brothers Coffee

roasted fresh everyday

- We roast our own coffee beans here daily!
- Cappuccino & espresso
- Cold press coffee & coffee beans
- Smoothies & Italian sodas
- Iced & Chai tea
- Frozen espresso drinks
- Free internet access

3090 Courthouse Ln.
(Hwy. 55 & Lone Oak Rd.)
Eagan, MN
(651)454-9400

00622016

C. McGee's DELI

- Voted #1 deli in City Pages
- Eat in, take out, or delivery available
- Hours: 7-5 Monday-Thursday, 7-4 Friday, closed weekends
- Breakfast coffee bar!

800 N Washington Ave. N
Minneapolis, MN
(612)288-0606

00000113

Brucks Cafe

1810 Riverside Ave., #104
Minneapolis, MN
(612)339-0876

00653143

entertainment.com — Up To $5.00 Value

cabin fever café

Enjoy one complimentary MENU ITEM when a second MENU ITEM of equal or greater value is purchased.

valid anytime

B295

Offer validity is governed by the Rules of Use and excludes defined holidays. Offers are not valid with other discount offers, unless specified.

Valid now thru November 1, 2007

---

entertainment.com — Up To $9.00 Value

Cactus Grill Mexican Buffet

Enjoy one complimentary DINNER BUFFET when a second DINNER BUFFET of equal or greater value is purchased.

valid any evening

B296

Offer validity is governed by the Rules of Use and excludes defined holidays. Offers are not valid with other discount offers, unless specified.

Valid now thru November 1, 2007

---

entertainment.com — Up To $5.00 Value

Antiques & Coffee
- Cafe Caffeiné -

Enjoy one complimentary MENU ITEM when a second MENU ITEM of equal or greater value is purchased.

valid anytime

B297

Offer validity is governed by the Rules of Use and excludes defined holidays. Offers are not valid with other discount offers, unless specified.

Valid now thru November 1, 2007

---

entertainment.com — Up To $6.00 Value

Café Lettieri's
Cappuccino • Panini • Gelato

Enjoy one complimentary MENU ITEM when a second MENU ITEM of equal or greater value is purchased.

valid anytime

B298

Offer validity is governed by the Rules of Use and excludes defined holidays. Offers are not valid with other discount offers, unless specified.

Valid now thru November 1, 2007

---

entertainment.com — Up To $7.00 Value

Gourmet - Deli   Gourmet - Coffee
café LIMÓN
Soups • Salads • Sandwiches

Enjoy one complimentary MENU ITEM when a second MENU ITEM of equal or greater value is purchased.

valid anytime

B299

Offer validity is governed by the Rules of Use and excludes defined holidays. Offers are not valid with other discount offers, unless specified.

Valid now thru November 1, 2007

---

entertainment.com — Up To $5.00 Value

CAFE TATTA BUNNA

Enjoy one complimentary MENU ITEM when a second MENU ITEM of equal or greater value is purchased.

valid anytime

B300

Offer validity is governed by the Rules of Use and excludes defined holidays. Offers are not valid with other discount offers, unless specified.

Valid now thru November 1, 2007

Cactus Grill Mexican Buffet

- Authentic Mexican food

3995 Egan Dr.
(intersection of 42 & Huntington)
Savage, MN
(952)808-7734

00702036

Café Lettieri's
Cappuccino • Panini • Gelato

- Dine-in & drive-thru
- Locally roasted coffee
- Breakfast sandwiches
- Panini
- Savory soups
- Gelato (ice cream in season)
- Cappuccino
- Great Italian food & freshly brewed coffee

19215 Hwy. 7
Shorewood, MN
(952)470-9343

00635837

Tatta Bunna

- "A Cup Above the Rest"
- Fresh coffee
- Finest Southern pastries
- Exotic teas
- Hottest sandwiches & soup
- Best salads
- Internet access
- Catering & Joe-to-go

2100 Plymouth Ave. N.
(inside Mpls. Urban League)
Minneapolis, MN
(612)529-8305

00575475

Cabin Fever Café

- Soups
- Sandwiches
- Fresh baked goods
- Specialty coffees
- Serving breakfast & lunch

243 W. 7th St.
St. Paul, MN
(651)290-2909

00619402

Antiques & Coffee
- Cafe Caffeiné -

- Gourmet coffee, espresso, lattes, mochas, & more
- In-house coffee roastery
- Smoothies
- Fresh desserts & pastries
- 3 level antique emporium
- New & used bookstore attached

109 South Adams St.
Cambridge, MN
(763)552-0109

00573290

café LIMÓN
Gourmet - Deli   Gourmet - Coffee
Soups • Salads • Sandwiches

- Gourmet deli
- Soups, salads & sandwiches
- Gourmet coffee drinks

611 W. Lake St.
Minneapolis, MN
(612)823-5149

00671011

Up To $5.00 Value

CAFÉ OF THE AMERICAS

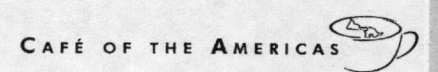

www.americas.org
Enjoy any BEVERAGE ORDER at 50% off the regular price.

valid anytime

B301

Offer validity is governed by the Rules of Use and excludes defined holidays. Offers are not valid with other discount offers, unless specified.

Valid now thru November 1, 2007

Up To $6.00 Value

Café Pierre

Enjoy one complimentary MENU ITEM when a second MENU ITEM of equal or greater value is purchased.

valid anytime

B302

Offer validity is governed by the Rules of Use and excludes defined holidays. Offers are not valid with other discount offers, unless specified.

Valid now thru November 1, 2007

Up To $5.00 Value

caffe' de Lago

Enjoy one complimentary MENU ITEM when a second MENU ITEM of equal or greater value is purchased.

valid anytime

B303

Offer validity is governed by the Rules of Use and excludes defined holidays. Offers are not valid with other discount offers, unless specified.

Valid now thru November 1, 2007

Up To $7.00 Value

Camden Coffee COMPANY

Enjoy one complimentary MENU ITEM when a second MENU ITEM of equal or greater value is purchased.

valid anytime

B304

Offer validity is governed by the Rules of Use and excludes defined holidays. Offers are not valid with other discount offers, unless specified.

Valid now thru November 1, 2007

Up To $7.00 Value

Camden Coffee COMPANY

Enjoy one complimentary MENU ITEM when a second MENU ITEM of equal or greater value is purchased.

valid anytime

B305

Offer validity is governed by the Rules of Use and excludes defined holidays. Offers are not valid with other discount offers, unless specified.

Valid now thru November 1, 2007

Up To $7.00 Value

CEDAR INN
BAR AND GRILL

Enjoy one complimentary LUNCH OR DINNER ENTREE when a second LUNCH OR DINNER ENTREE of equal or greater value is purchased.

Dine in only

valid anytime

B306

Offer validity is governed by the Rules of Use and excludes defined holidays. Offers are not valid with other discount offers, unless specified.

Valid now thru November 1, 2007

Café Pierre

- Coffee & espresso
- Made to order sandwiches & pizzas
- Ice creams, gelati-da & pastries
- Live music on Fridays

7704 160th St. W.
Lakeville, MN
(952) 431-1227

00671875

Café of the Americas

- Homemade food with a Latin accent
- Full catering menu
- Fair Trade & organic coffee
- Conveniently located on the 21 & 7 bus lines

3019 Minnehaha Ave.
(1/2 blk. S. of Lake St.)
Minneapolis, MN
(612) 276-0803

00654884

Camden Coffee COMPANY

- Organic fair trade coffee
- Pastries made daily
- Hot & cold drinks
- Soups & sandwiches
- Wi-Fi & computer access on-site
- Live music on Fri. nights
- Revolving art show

1500 44th Ave. N.
Minneapolis, MN
(612) 521-1161

00695273

Caffe' de Lago

- Locally roasted coffee
- Loose leaf teas
- Soups, sandwiches, pastries & desserts
- Cozy, warm atmosphere & friendly staff
- Seconds from Lake Minnetonka

17623 Minnetonka Blvd.
Minnetonka, MN
(952) 404-3868

00568081

Cedar Inn
BAR AND GRILL

- Burgers & sandwiches
- Buffalo wings & broasted chicken
- Appetizers
- Side orders
- Wide screen TV
- Darts
- Pool table

4155 Cedar Ave. S.
Minneapolis, MN
(612) 729-9785

00614961

Camden Coffee COMPANY

- Organic fair trade coffee
- Pastries made daily
- Hot & cold drinks
- Soups & sandwiches
- Wi-Fi & computer access on-site
- Live music on Fri. nights
- Revolving art show

1500 44th Ave. N.
Minneapolis, MN
(612) 521-1161

00695273

Cedar Market & Deli
Fine Greek Foods

Up To $5.00 Value

Enjoy one complimentary MENU ITEM when a second MENU ITEM of equal or greater value is purchased.

valid anytime

B307

Chanticlear Pizza

Up To $10.00 Value

www.chanticlearpizza.com
Enjoy any LARGE PIZZA at 50% off the regular price.

Carryout only

valid anytime

One coupon per customer per visit; Not valid with any other offer

B308

CHASKA BAKERY
Serving the Twin Cities Since 1886

Up To $5.00 Value

Enjoy any BAKED GOODS ORDER at 50% off the regular price.

valid anytime

B309

CHINA WOK

Up To $6.00 Value

Enjoy one complimentary ENTREE when a second ENTREE of equal or greater value is purchased.

Dine in only

valid any evening
Tipping should be 15% to 20% of TOTAL bill before discount

B310

CHINESE GOURMET RESTAURANT
Taste the Good Fortune.
中華飯店

Up To $8.00 Value

Enjoy one complimentary DINNER ENTREE when a second DINNER ENTREE of equal or greater value is purchased.

Dine in only

valid any evening
Tipping should be 15% to 20% of TOTAL bill before discount

B311

---

cinema ESPRESSO
DVD COFFEE HOUSE

FREE MENU ITEM

Enjoy one complimentary MENU ITEM when a second MENU ITEM of equal or greater value is purchased.

valid anytime

B312

Chanticlear Pizza

Coupons void if purchased, sold or bartered. Discounts exclude tax, tip and/or alcohol, where applicable.

Andover
1573 154th Ave. N.W.
(763)434-6554

Anoka
440 Bunker Lake Blvd. N.W.
(Bunker Lake Blvd. & Ferry St.)
(763)421-4242

Arden Hills
3551 Lexington Ave.
(651)490-1313

Blaine
914 125th Ln. N.E.
(1 mi. E. of Blaine High School, off of Hwy. 242)
(763)754-0800

Champlin
11632 Winnetka Ave. N.
(763)427-6300

Coon Rapids
2835 Northdale Blvd.
(1 Mile W. of Coon Rapids High School)
(763)757-2020

Crystal
6236 Bass Lake Rd.
(Bass Lake Rd. & Hwy. 81)
(763)535-0777

Eden Prairie
8793 Columbine Rd.
(Hwy. 212 & Anderson Lakes Pkwy.)
(952)252-2222

Elk River
19328 Hwy. 169 N.W.
(763)274-2225

Fridley
1262 E. Moore Lake Dr.
(763)571-9595

Ham Lake
18015 Ulysses St.
(181st Ave. & Hwy. 65)
(763)434-3333

Inver Grove
9034 Cahill Ave.
(651)451-7677

Lino Lakes
7771 Lake Dr.
(651)786-7022

Maple Grove
9511 Black Oaks Ln.
(E. of Wal-Mart Supercenter, behind McDonalds)
(763)494-9949

Monticello
9375 Deegan Ave.
(763)295-7774

New Hope
9428A 36th Ave.
(Hwy. 169 & 36th Ave.)
(763)593-1313

Rogers
14000 Northdale Blvd.
(763)494-9990

Vadnais Heights
1032 E. Hwy. 96
(651)255-5000

00650676

Cedar Market & Deli
Fine Greek Foods

- Authentic Greek food
- Delicious fresh soups & Greek salads
- Vegetarian dishes: Spinach pie
- Baklava
- Come visit us & see our market. We have grocery items from the Middle East, Turkey, Greece & Pakistan
- We accept Visa & Mastercard

1710 E. Old Shakopee Rd.
(Corner of Old Cedar Ave. & Old Shakopee Rd.)
Bloomington, MN
(952)888-2121

00568097

China Wok

- Cantonese & Szechuan specialties
- Located in Shannon Square Shopping Center
- Call ahead for fast service
- Open Mon-Fri 11am-9pm, Sat noon-9pm, & Sun 4-8pm

3673 Lexington Ave.
Arden Hills, MN
(651)482-0442

00138363

Chaska Bakery
Serving the Twin Cities Since 1886

- Homemade pies
- Homemade cookies
- Gourmet pastries
- Fresh baked bread or rolls
- Kolachia & coffee cakes
- Danish & muffins
- Gourmet coffee
- Wedding cakes
- Cakes for all occasions
- Sweets table for any occasion
- European delicacies
- Special orders
- Photo cakes

500 Chestnut St. N.
Chaska, MN
(952)448-2201

00631373

---

cinema ESPRESSO
DVD COFFEE HOUSE

- Gourmet espresso drinks
- Hot, cold & blended coffee drinks
- Power & soda drinks
- Smoothies
- Pastries
- DVD rentals

5936 Lexington Ave. N.
Shoreview, MN
(651)255-1893

00656144

CHINESE GOURMET RESTAURANT
Taste the Good Fortune.
中華飯店

- Mandarin style cuisine
- Lunch specials from 11 a.m.-3 p.m.
- Variety of delicious entrees & appetizers
- Serving beer & wine
- Sun.-Thurs. 11 a.m.-10 p.m.
- Fri. & Sat. 11 a.m.-10:30 p.m.

12901 Aldrich Ave. S
(35W & Burnsville Pkwy.)
Burnsville, MN
(952)894-1717

00059370

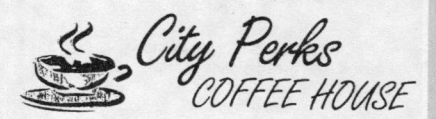

City Perks COFFEE HOUSE

Up To $5.00 Value

Enjoy one complimentary MENU ITEM when a second MENU ITEM of equal or greater value is purchased.

valid anytime

B313

Offer validity is governed by the Rules of Use and excludes defined holidays. Offers are not valid with other discount offers, unless specified.

Valid now thru November 1, 2007

Classic Pizza and Ice Cream

Up To $8.00 Value

Enjoy one complimentary MENU ITEM when a second MENU ITEM of equal or greater value is purchased or for those who prefer - any one pizza at 50% off the regular price.

Dine-in or carry out

valid anytime

B314

Offer validity is governed by the Rules of Use and excludes defined holidays. Offers are not valid with other discount offers, unless specified.

Valid now thru November 1, 2007

---

coffee cats café

www.coffeecatscafe.com

Up To $5.00 Value

Enjoy one complimentary MENU ITEM when a second MENU ITEM of equal or greater value is purchased.

valid anytime

B315

Offer validity is governed by the Rules of Use and excludes defined holidays. Offers are not valid with other discount offers, unless specified.

Valid now thru November 1, 2007

COFFEE cottage

Up To $5.00 Value

Enjoy one complimentary MENU ITEM when a second MENU ITEM of equal or greater value is purchased.

valid anytime

B316

Offer validity is governed by the Rules of Use and excludes defined holidays. Offers are not valid with other discount offers, unless specified.

Valid now thru November 1, 2007

Coffee Oasis

Up To $6.00 Value

Enjoy one complimentary MENU ITEM when a second MENU ITEM of equal or greater value is purchased.

valid anytime

B317

Offer validity is governed by the Rules of Use and excludes defined holidays. Offers are not valid with other discount offers, unless specified.

Valid now thru November 1, 2007

Coffee Ta Cream

Up To $5.00 Value

Enjoy one complimentary MENU ITEM when a second MENU ITEM of equal or greater value is purchased.

valid anytime

B318

Offer validity is governed by the Rules of Use and excludes defined holidays. Offers are not valid with other discount offers, unless specified.

Valid now thru November 1, 2007

Classic Pizza and Ice Cream

- Great pizza
- Hoagies
- Salads
- Bridgeman's Ice Cream

466 Hamline Ave. S.
(Hamline Ave. & Randolph Ave.)
St. Paul, MN
(651)699-7263

00527011

COFFEE cottage

- Locally owned coffee house
- The best coffee staff in the White Bear Lake area
- Try one of our famous cinnamon twists
- Enjoy our unique gift area with a variety of fun items
- We get our coffee beans from Alakef in Duluth, MN

88 Stillwater Rd.
Mahtomedi, MN
(651)407-0942

00605000

Coffee Ta Cream

- Coffee
- Salads & sandwiches
- Ice cream
- Desserts

1157 Shakopee Town Square
Shakopee, MN
(952)445-9008

00609402

City Perks COFFEE HOUSE

- We serve a full line of fresh roasted coffees, espresso drinks & loose-leaf teas
- Fresh-baked breads, muffins, pastries, cookies, cakes, soups & sandwiches
- Smoothies, iced coffee & tea drinks

16210 Eagle Creek Ave.
(next to the library)
Prior Lake, MN
(952)226-2489

00461901

caribou coffee cafe

- Gourmet coffee & specialty espresso drinks
- Delicious fresh-made sandwiches, melts, wraps, soups & salads
- Fresh baked muffins & scones
- Smoothies & ice cream
- Comfy couches & fireplace
- Beautiful relaxing view of lake & wildlife

2940 N. Chestnut St.
(Hwy. 41 & Pioneer Trail, behind Dairy Queen)
Chaska, MN
(952)448-7331

00670583

Coffee Oasis

- Enjoy our drive-thru window or our smoke-free environment!
- Hours: Mon-Fri. 6 a.m.-3 p.m., Sat. 7 a.m.-2 p.m., Sun. 8 a.m.-12 p.m.
- Espresso, lattes & mochas
- Bulk coffees
- Muffins, scones & cookies

8439 Joiner Way
(next to Applebee's)
Eden Prairie, MN
(952)996-9900

00367278

COL. MUZZY'S TEXAS BBQ

Up To $6.00 Value

Enjoy one complimentary MENU ITEM when a second MENU ITEM of equal or greater value is purchased.

valid anytime

B319

Valid now thru November 1, 2007

Offer validity is governed by the Rules of Use and excludes defined holidays. Offers are not valid with other discount offers, unless specified.

CommonGrounds Coffee

Up To $5.00 Value

Enjoy one complimentary MENU ITEM when a second MENU ITEM of equal or greater value is purchased.

valid anytime

B320

Valid now thru November 1, 2007

Offer validity is governed by the Rules of Use and excludes defined holidays. Offers are not valid with other discount offers, unless specified.

The Copper Dome Restaurant

Up To $6.00 Value

Enjoy one complimentary MENU SELECTION when a second MENU SELECTION of equal or greater value is purchased.

valid anytime Tuesday thru Saturday

B321

Valid now thru November 1, 2007

Offer validity is governed by the Rules of Use and excludes defined holidays. Offers are not valid with other discount offers, unless specified.

Cora's Best Chicken Wings

Up To $5.00 Value

Enjoy one complimentary MENU ITEM when a second MENU ITEM of equal or greater value is purchased.

valid anytime

B322

Valid now thru November 1, 2007

Offer validity is governed by the Rules of Use and excludes defined holidays. Offers are not valid with other discount offers, unless specified.

Cosmic's Cafe

Up To $5.00 Value

Enjoy one complimentary MENU ITEM when a second MENU ITEM of equal or greater value is purchased.

valid anytime

B323

Valid now thru November 1, 2007

Offer validity is governed by the Rules of Use and excludes defined holidays. Offers are not valid with other discount offers, unless specified.

COUNTRY GLAZED HAM SHOP
GOURMET SANDWICHES & MEATS

Up To $6.00 Value

Enjoy one complimentary MENU ITEM when a second MENU ITEM of equal or greater value is purchased.

Delivery excluded

valid anytime

B324

Valid now thru November 1, 2007

Offer validity is governed by the Rules of Use and excludes defined holidays. Offers are not valid with other discount offers, unless specified.

Common Grounds Coffee

- Specialty coffees, teas & cocoa
- Soups & sandwiches
- Candy, fudge & ice cream
- Smoothies & Hawaiian Ice

350 S. St. Croix Trail
Lakeland, MN
(651)436-7338

00609315

Col. Muzzy's Texas BBQ

- Beef brisket
- Pulled pork
- Smoked chicken
- Smoked sausage
- BBQ ribs
- Gyros
- Hot dogs
- Hamburgers

336 N. Garden
(Mall Of America)
Bloomington, MN
(952)858-8788

00585560

Cora's Best Chicken Wings

- Best chicken wings in town
- Regular & Hot & Spicy
- Value meals
- 2 Great locations

1143 Payne Ave., St. Paul, MN
(651)776-0020

168 Concord St., St. Paul, MN
(651)221-0020

00387645

The Copper Dome Restaurant

- Ideal family restaurant
- Breakfast served anytime 7 days, lunch & dinner 11-closing
- Tues. - Fri. 6:30 a.m. - 2 p.m., Sat. & Sun. 7 a.m. - 2 p.m., closed Mon. except holiday
- Omelets, waffles & pancakes

1333 Randolph Avenue
Saint Paul, MN
(651)690-0993

00000027

Country Glazed Ham Shop

- Gourmet sandwiches
- Breads baked fresh daily from New French Bakery
- Soups & desserts made from scratch daily
- Box lunches, party trays & catering available
- We deliver!

7924 Main St., Maple Grove, MN
(763)420-5069

14200 Wayzaka Blvd., Minnetonka, MN
(952)591-0494

00104786

Cosmic's Cafe

- Gourmet coffee drinks
- Sandwiches & snacks
- Ice Rages
- Numi teas
- Pool
- Internet access
- Free WiFi

189 N. Snelling Ave.
St. Paul, MN
(651)645-0106

00667289

COUNTRY HOME
Bakery & Deli

Up To **$5.00** Value

Enjoy any FOOD/BEVERAGE ORDER at 50% off the regular price - maximum discount $5.00.

valid anytime

B325

Valid now thru November 1, 2007

Offer validity is governed by the Rules of Use and excludes defined holidays. Offers are not valid with other discount offers, unless specified.

CREATIVE CATERING

Up To **$9.00** Value

Enjoy one complimentary MENU ITEM when a second MENU ITEM of equal or greater value is purchased.

Carry out only

valid anytime

B326

Valid now thru November 1, 2007

Offer validity is governed by the Rules of Use and excludes defined holidays. Offers are not valid with other discount offers, unless specified.

Crescent Moon Bakery

Up To **$5.00** Value

Enjoy any BAKED GOODS ORDER at 50% off the regular price - maximum discount $5.00.

valid anytime

B327

Valid now thru November 1, 2007

Offer validity is governed by the Rules of Use and excludes defined holidays. Offers are not valid with other discount offers, unless specified.

Cup of Knowledge

Up To **$5.00** Value

Enjoy one complimentary MENU ITEM when a second MENU ITEM of equal or greater value is purchased.

valid anytime

B328

Valid now thru November 1, 2007

Offer validity is governed by the Rules of Use and excludes defined holidays. Offers are not valid with other discount offers, unless specified.

Cuppa Java

Up To **$6.00** Value

www.cuppajava.com

Enjoy one complimentary MENU ITEM when a second MENU ITEM of equal or greater value is purchased.

valid anytime

B329

Valid now thru November 1, 2007

Offer validity is governed by the Rules of Use and excludes defined holidays. Offers are not valid with other discount offers, unless specified.

Cuppa Java

Up To **$6.00** Value

www.cuppajava.com

Enjoy one complimentary MENU ITEM when a second MENU ITEM of equal or greater value is purchased.

valid anytime

B330

Valid now thru November 1, 2007

Offer validity is governed by the Rules of Use and excludes defined holidays. Offers are not valid with other discount offers, unless specified.

CREATIVE CATERING

- All meals are homemade & prepared fresh each day
- Delicious sandwiches, fresh salads & daily soups
- Lunch served Mon.-Fri., dinner Mon.-Thurs. after 4 p.m.
- Our dinner selection changes daily
- Full catering service
- Free delivery for orders over $50

3470 Lexington Ave. N.
Shoreview, MN
(651)486-0700

00677737

COUNTRY HOME
Bakery & Deli

- Full line of breads, rolls, fine danishes, donuts, assorted pastries, & special order products
- Specializing in cakes for all occasions
- Forest Lake area's only complete bakery & deli
- Soups, wraps, & sandwiches

20 N Lake St.
Forest Lake, MN
(651)464-6060

00447802

Cup of Knowledge

- Coffee, espresso, tea, baked goods & soup
- Used books

106 E. First St.
Jordan, MN
(952)492-6430

00518725

Crescent Moon Bakery

2339 Central Ave. N.E.
Minneapolis, MN
(612)782-0169

00620612

Cuppa Java

- On the corner of Penn & Cedar Lake Rd.
- Sandwiches & soups
- Malts, smoothies & coffee drinks
- Bagels, muffins & scones

400 Penn Ave. S.
(Near 394 & Penn in Bryn Mawr)
Minneapolis, MN
(612)374-4806

00532703

Cuppa Java

- On the corner of Penn & Cedar Lake Rd.
- Sandwiches & soups
- Malts, smoothies & coffee drinks
- Bagels, muffins & scones

400 Penn Ave. S.
(Near 394 & Penn in Bryn Mawr)
Minneapolis, MN
(612)374-4806

00532703

entertainment.com — Up To $8.00 Value

Cuzzy's

www.cuzzys.com

Enjoy one complimentary ENTREE when a second ENTREE of equal or greater value is purchased.

valid anytime

B331

Offer validity is governed by the Rules of Use and excludes defined holidays. Offers are not valid with other discount offers, unless specified.

---

entertainment.com — FREE MENU ITEM

Daddio's TAKE-N-BAKE

Enjoy one complimentary MENU ITEM when a second MENU ITEM of equal or greater value is purchased.

valid anytime

B332

Offer validity is governed by the Rules of Use and excludes defined holidays. Offers are not valid with other discount offers, unless specified.

---

entertainment.com — Up To $5.00 Value

Daily Grind

Enjoy one complimentary MENU ITEM when a second MENU ITEM of equal or greater value is purchased.

valid anytime

B333

Offer validity is governed by the Rules of Use and excludes defined holidays. Offers are not valid with other discount offers, unless specified.

---

entertainment.com — Up To $5.00 Value

THE DAILY GRIND

Enjoy one complimentary MENU ITEM when a second MENU ITEM of equal or greater value is purchased.

valid anytime

B334

Offer validity is governed by the Rules of Use and excludes defined holidays. Offers are not valid with other discount offers, unless specified.

entertainment.com — Up To $5.00 Value

Dar's Double Scoop

Ice Cream & Coffee Shop

Enjoy any ICE CREAM ORDER at 50% off the regular price - maximum discount $5.00.

valid anytime

B335

Offer validity is governed by the Rules of Use and excludes defined holidays. Offers are not valid with other discount offers, unless specified.

---

entertainment.com — Up To $5.00 Value

DENNY'S 5th Avenue Bakery

Enjoy any BAKED GOODS ORDER at 50% off the regular price.

valid anytime

B336

Offer validity is governed by the Rules of Use and excludes defined holidays. Offers are not valid with other discount offers, unless specified.

Daddio's TAKE-N-BAKE

- We make it fresh! You make it hot!
- Specialty pizzas & Mexican meals available
- We also feature pastas, breadsticks, wraps & salads
- Cinnamums & cookies for dessert

17665 Glasgow Ave.
Lakeville, MN
(952)431-9900

00632234

Cuzzy's

- Burgers
- Full bar
- In downtown Minneapolis

507 Washington Ave. N
Minneapolis, MN
(612)339-6211

00474411

THE DAILY GRIND

- The oldest coffee shop in town & the only one with a river view
- Espresso milk shakes-famous since 1992
- Gourmet coffee
- Fresh baked goods
- We are smoke free

317 S. Main St.
Stillwater, MN
(651)430-3207

00613406

Daily Grind

- Gourmet coffees, lattes, mochas & more
- Teas & fruit smoothies
- Fresh pastries

4080 W. Broadway #129
Robbinsdale, MN
(763)537-6305

00564948

DENNY'S 5th Avenue Bakery

- Photo cakes & cakes for all occasions
- Specialty breads
- Family owned & operated
- Full service bakery
- Wedding cakes
- Donuts, brownies & pastries
- Hours Mon.-Fri. 5 a.m.-6 p.m., Sat. 5 a.m.-4 p.m.

7840 5th Ave. S.
Bloomington, MN
(952)881-4445

00577218

Dar's Double Scoop
Ice Cream & Coffee Shop

- 44 Flavors of premium ice cream
- Sundaes, floats & malts
- Coffee, tea & cappuccino

1046 Rice St.
St. Paul, MN
(651)487-4073

00695099

DIAMONDS Coffee Shoppe

Up To $5.00 Value

Enjoy any FOOD/BEVERAGE ORDER at 50% off the regular price - maximum discount $5.00.

valid anytime

B337

Offer validity is governed by the Rules of Use and excludes defined holidays. Offers are not valid with other discount offers, unless specified.

Valid now thru November 1, 2007

DON PANCHOS BAKERY PANADERIA

Up To $5.00 Value

Enjoy any BAKED GOODS ORDER at 50% off the regular price.

valid anytime

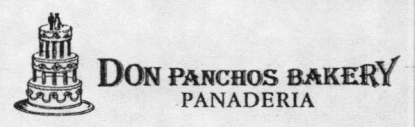

B338

Offer validity is governed by the Rules of Use and excludes defined holidays. Offers are not valid with other discount offers, unless specified.

Valid now thru November 1, 2007

Dorothy Ann BAKERY & CAFE
"A Tradition of Good Taste."

Up To $5.00 Value

Enjoy one complimentary MENU ITEM when a second MENU ITEM of equal or greater value is purchased or when dining alone - one MENU ITEM at 50% off the regular price - maximum discount $3.00.

valid anytime

B339

Offer validity is governed by the Rules of Use and excludes defined holidays. Offers are not valid with other discount offers, unless specified.

Valid now thru November 1, 2007

DREAMCOAT CAFE

Up To $7.00 Value

www.dreamcoatcafe.com

Enjoy one complimentary MENU ITEM when a second MENU ITEM of equal or greater value is purchased.

valid anytime

B340

Offer validity is governed by the Rules of Use and excludes defined holidays. Offers are not valid with other discount offers, unless specified.

Valid now thru November 1, 2007

DUGOUT BAR

Up To $7.00 Value

Enjoy one complimentary MENU ITEM when a second MENU ITEM of equal or greater value is purchased.

valid anytime

B341

Offer validity is governed by the Rules of Use and excludes defined holidays. Offers are not valid with other discount offers, unless specified.

Valid now thru November 1, 2007

DUSEK'S BAKERY

50% OFF

Enjoy any BAKED GOODS ORDER at 50% off the regular price - maximum discount $5.00.

valid anytime

B342

Offer validity is governed by the Rules of Use and excludes defined holidays. Offers are not valid with other discount offers, unless specified.

Valid now thru November 1, 2007

DON PANCHOS BAKERY
PANADERIA

- Pastries, cookies & cakes
- Bread, rolls & donuts
- Other delicious desserts
- Hours 6 am - 8 pm Monday - Friday
- Saturday & Sunday 6 am - 6 pm. Only closed Christmas & New Years

140 Concord St.
St. Paul, MN
(651)225-8744

00414604

DIAMONDS Coffee Shoppe

- Your atomic coffee stop
- Breakfast sandwiches
- Full coffee bar
- Soups, salads & sandwiches
- Separate smoking lounge
- Open early 7 days a week - 'til midnight on weekends!
- Catch us on the way downtown!

1618 Central Ave. N.E.
Minneapolis, MN
(612)789-5282

00516607

DREAMCOAT CAFÉ

- Gourmet coffees
- Soups & sandwiches
- In house bakery
- Ice cream
- Live music

215 S Main St.
Stillwater, MN
(651)430-0615

00402704

Dorothy Ann
"A Tradition of Good Taste."

- Sandwiches, salads, soups, specialty coffees
- Fresh baked breads, donuts, pastries, tortes, bagels, muffins, bars, dinner rolls & cookies
- Wedding cakes

1705-1 Weir Dr.
Woodbury, MN
(651)731-3323

00061933

DUSEK'S BAKERY

- Serving the surrounding Faribault area since 1932
- Full service bakery
- All products made from scratch
- Delivery service
- Cakes for all occasions: birthdays, weddings & anniversaries
- Open Tues.-Sat. 5 a.m.-5 p.m.

223 Central Ave.
(downtown Faribault)
Faribault, MN
(507)334-6495

00677972

DUGOUT BAR

- Fast, friendly service
- Gameroom, Golden Tee & pool tables
- Pull tabs
- Cities best live music weekends - call for schedule
- Nightly drink specials
- Variety of appetizers
- Great sandwiches & burgers

96 Mahtomedi Ave.
Mahtomedi, MN
(651)429-8640

00575408

entertainment.com — Up To $10.00 Value

East African Taste Restaurant

Enjoy one complimentary LUNCH OR DINNER ENTREE when a second LUNCH OR DINNER ENTREE of equal or greater value is purchased.

valid anytime

Tipping should be 15% to 20% of TOTAL bill before discount

B343

Offer validity is governed by the Rules of Use and excludes defined holidays. Offers are not valid with other discount offers, unless specified.

Valid now thru November 1, 2007

---

entertainment.com — 50% OFF

El Rey Bakery

Enjoy up to 2 DOZEN DONUTS at 50% off the regular price.

valid anytime

B344

Offer validity is governed by the Rules of Use and excludes defined holidays. Offers are not valid with other discount offers, unless specified.

Valid now thru November 1, 2007

---

entertainment.com — Up To $14.00 Value

EL TEQUILA RESTAURANTE

Enjoy one complimentary LUNCH OR DINNER ENTREE when a second LUNCH OR DINNER ENTREE of equal or greater value is purchased.

Dine in only

valid anytime

Tipping should be 15% to 20% of TOTAL bill before discount   B345

Offer validity is governed by the Rules of Use and excludes defined holidays. Offers are not valid with other discount offers, unless specified.

Valid now thru November 1, 2007

---

entertainment.com — Up To $5.00 Value

ESPRESSO 22

Enjoy one complimentary MENU ITEM when a second MENU ITEM of equal or greater value is purchased.

valid anytime

B346

Offer validity is governed by the Rules of Use and excludes defined holidays. Offers are not valid with other discount offers, unless specified.

Valid now thru November 1, 2007

---

entertainment.com — Up To $5.00 Value

Espresso Donut Co

Enjoy one complimentary MENU ITEM when a second MENU ITEM of equal or greater value is purchased.

valid anytime

B347

Offer validity is governed by the Rules of Use and excludes defined holidays. Offers are not valid with other discount offers, unless specified.

Valid now thru November 1, 2007

---

entertainment.com — FREE MENU ITEM

ESPRESSO ROYALE CAFE

Enjoy one complimentary MENU ITEM when a second MENU ITEM of equal or greater value is purchased.

valid anytime

B348

Offer validity is governed by the Rules of Use and excludes defined holidays. Offers are not valid with other discount offers, unless specified.

Valid now thru November 1, 2007

El Rey Bakery

- An American bakery featuring pies, donuts, sweet rolls & coffee cakes
- Cakes for all occasions
- Everything made fresh daily

2914 Pentagon Dr.
(Off Hwy. 88)
Minneapolis, MN
(612)706-2730

00588725

East African Taste Restaurant

- Experience the authentic taste of East Africa
- Try Ittoo Lukkuu Dorowot (chicken) with a glass of wine or beer

2405 Central Ave. N.E.
Minneapolis, MN
(612)789-2805

00617800

ESPRESSO 22

- Espresso & other coffee drinks
- Sandwiches & homemade soup
- Muffins & cookies

1501 University Ave. S.E.
Minneapolis, MN
(612)378-9555

00577841

EL TEQUILA RESTAURANTE

- Authentic Mexican cuisine
- All dishes made from scratch
- Breakfast served all day
- Try our King Burritos!
- Our menu offers something for everyone
- Kids menu

835 45th N.E.
(Central Plaza Mall)
Hilltop, MN
(763)574-2460

00660643

ESPRESSO ROYALE CAFE

411 14th S.E.
Minneapolis, MN
(612)623-8127

00689818

Espresso Donut Co

- Treat yourself!
- Espresso beverages
- Roasted fresh coffee on site
- The best of the best ice cream
- Fresh daily baked donuts
- All-natural smoothies
- Gift baskets
- Call in orders welcome
- Large orders taken in advance for your next meeting!

2070 Eagle Creek Ln., #500
(corner of Valley Creek Rd. & County Rd. 19)
Woodbury, MN
(651)436-4001

00613665

Fireroast Mountain Café

entertainment.com — Up To $7.00 Value

Enjoy one complimentary MENU ITEM when a second MENU ITEM of equal or greater value is purchased.

valid anytime

B349

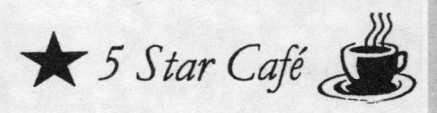

Offer validity is governed by the Rules of Use and excludes defined holidays. Offers are not valid with other discount offers, unless specified.

Valid now thru November 1, 2007

The Fish House

entertainment.com — Up To $9.00 Value

Enjoy one complimentary MENU ITEM when a second MENU ITEM of equal or greater value is purchased.

valid anytime

B350

Offer validity is governed by the Rules of Use and excludes defined holidays. Offers are not valid with other discount offers, unless specified.

Valid now thru November 1, 2007

---

5 Star Café

entertainment.com — Up To $5.00 Value

Enjoy one complimentary MENU ITEM when a second MENU ITEM of equal or greater value is purchased.

valid anytime

B351

Offer validity is governed by the Rules of Use and excludes defined holidays. Offers are not valid with other discount offers, unless specified.

Valid now thru November 1, 2007

Franklin MARKET & DELI

entertainment.com — Up To $6.00 Value

Enjoy one complimentary MENU ITEM when a second MENU ITEM of equal or greater value is purchased.

valid anytime

B352

Offer validity is governed by the Rules of Use and excludes defined holidays. Offers are not valid with other discount offers, unless specified.

Valid now thru November 1, 2007

Franklin Street Bakery

Old World Flavor

entertainment.com — Up To $5.00 Value

Enjoy any BAKED GOODS ORDER at 50% off the regular price - maximum discount $5.00.

valid anytime

B353

Offer validity is governed by the Rules of Use and excludes defined holidays. Offers are not valid with other discount offers, unless specified.

Valid now thru November 1, 2007

---

the Galley Room
kitchenware & coffee bar

entertainment.com — Up To $5.00 Value

Enjoy any FOOD/BEVERAGE ORDER at 50% off the regular price - maximum discount $5.00.

valid anytime

B354

Offer validity is governed by the Rules of Use and excludes defined holidays. Offers are not valid with other discount offers, unless specified.

Valid now thru November 1, 2007

The Fish House

- One bite & you're hooked
- Chicken & fish dinners
- Catfish, orange roughy, perch, walleye & red snapper
- Delicious sides

2221 W. Broadway
Minneapolis, MN
(612)588-9622

00585971

Fireroast Mountain Café

3800 37th Ave. S.
Minneapolis, MN
(612)724-9895

00695275

Franklin MARKET & DELI

- Gyros, chicken sandwiches, chicken wings
- Market

1519 E. Franklin Ave.
Minneapolis, MN
(612)871-9009

00654902

★ 5 Star Café

- Foul Mudammas Fava Beans
- Frappe Freeze Crunch
- Freshly roasted coffee
- Gourmet coffee, juices & homemade chai tea
- Sandwiches, soup & great selection of pastries

2469 W. 7th St.
St. Paul, MN
(651)696-0909

00517528

the Galley Room
kitchenware & coffee bar

323 Main St.
Red Wing, MN
(651)338-7313

00701040

FRANKLIN STREET BAKERY

- Breads
- Desserts, cakes & cupcakes
- Full espresso bar
- Sandwiches
- Special order desserts
- Seasonal patio seating
- Mon.-Fri. 6 a.m-6 p.m
- Sat. & Sun. 8 a.m.-5 p.m.

1020 E. Franklin Ave.
(corner of Franklin & 11th Ave.)
Minneapolis, MN
(612)871-3109

00653002

entertainment
entertainment.com

Up To **$10.00** Value

GIUSEPPE'S
ITALIAN RISTORANTE

Enjoy one complimentary MENU SELECTION when a second MENU SELECTION of equal or greater value is purchased.

Take out excluded; Saturday evenings excluded

valid Monday thru Friday evenings after 5 p.m., Saturday noon - 5 p.m.   B355

Offer validity is governed by the Rules of Use and excludes defined holidays. Offers are not valid with other discount offers, unless specified.

Valid now thru November 1, 2007

---

entertainment
entertainment.com

Up To **$5.00** Value

Glen Lake Coffee Company

Enjoy one complimentary MENU ITEM when a second MENU ITEM of equal or greater value is purchased.

valid anytime

B356

Offer validity is governed by the Rules of Use and excludes defined holidays. Offers are not valid with other discount offers, unless specified.

Valid now thru November 1, 2007

---

entertainment
entertainment.com

Up To **$5.00** Value

Glen Lake Coffee Company

Enjoy one complimentary MENU ITEM when a second MENU ITEM of equal or greater value is purchased.

valid anytime

B357

Offer validity is governed by the Rules of Use and excludes defined holidays. Offers are not valid with other discount offers, unless specified.

Valid now thru November 1, 2007

---

entertainment
entertainment.com

50% OFF

GOLDEN'S CAFE & DELI

www.goldensdeli.com

Enjoy any FOOD ORDER at 50% off the regular price - maximum discount $5.00.

valid anytime

Not valid with catering   B358

Offer validity is governed by the Rules of Use and excludes defined holidays. Offers are not valid with other discount offers, unless specified.

Valid now thru November 1, 2007

---

entertainment
entertainment.com

FREE MENU ITEM

Grandma Rita's
C A F E

Enjoy one complimentary MENU ITEM when a second MENU ITEM of equal or greater value is purchased.

valid anytime

B359

Offer validity is governed by the Rules of Use and excludes defined holidays. Offers are not valid with other discount offers, unless specified.

Valid now thru November 1, 2007

---

entertainment
entertainment.com

Up To **$6.00** Value

THE GREAT STEAK & POTATO COMPANY

Enjoy one complimentary MENU ITEM when a second MENU ITEM of equal or greater value is purchased.

valid anytime

B360

Offer validity is governed by the Rules of Use and excludes defined holidays. Offers are not valid with other discount offers, unless specified.

Valid now thru November 1, 2007

Glen Lake Coffee Company

- Coffee, espresso & iced drinks
- Sandwiches & soups
- Waffles
- Freshly roasted coffee beans

14725 Excelsior Blvd.
Minnetonka, MN
(952)933-3323

00573381

GIUSEPPE'S
ITALIAN RISTORANTE

- A little bit of Italy tucked away in New Brighton
- Beer & wine
- Homemade Southern Italian
- Earth baked bread
- M-F 10:30-9:00, Sat 12-9
- Closed Sunday

1435 Silver Lake Rd.
(1/2 mile north of I-694)
New Brighton, MN
(651)631-2744

00000428

GOLDEN'S CAFE & DELI

- Fresh squeezed lemonade
- Hot bagel sandwiches
- Farmer's market fresh since 1984
- Hours for deli: Mon. - Fri. 11 a.m. - 2 p.m.
- Hours for farmer's market: 6 a.m. - noon

St. Paul Farmer's Market 275 E. Fourth St.
St. Paul, MN
(651)224-8888

00515811

Glen Lake Coffee Company

- Coffee, espresso & iced drinks
- Sandwiches & soups
- Waffles
- Freshly roasted coffee beans

14725 Excelsior Blvd.
Minnetonka, MN
(952)933-3323

00573381

THE GREAT STEAK & POTATO COMPANY

- America's #1 grilled sandwiches
- Great steak
- Chicken Philly
- Ham Explosion
- Turkey Philly
- Veggie Delight
- Baked potato
- Low-carb wraps
- Fresh cut fries
- Grilled salad

388 South Ave. *(Mall of America)*, Bloomington, MN
(952)858-8263
333 Apache Dr. S.W. #198, Rochester, MN
(507)536-9162

00443709

Grandma Rita's CAFE

- Sandwiches, soups & salads
- Espresso drinks
- Nachos, tacos & burritos
- Pizza & pastries
- Open for breakfast & lunch

327 W. 7th St.
St. Paul, MN
(651)224-9235

00632012

HAROLD'S CHICKEN

Up To $7.00 Value

Enjoy one complimentary MENU ITEM when a second MENU ITEM of equal or greater value is purchased.

valid anytime

B361

Offer validity is governed by the Rules of Use and excludes defined holidays. Offers are not valid with other discount offers, unless specified.

Valid now thru November 1, 2007

HIGHER GROUNDS

Up To $5.00 Value

Enjoy any BEVERAGE ORDER at 50% off the regular price.

valid anytime

B362

Offer validity is governed by the Rules of Use and excludes defined holidays. Offers are not valid with other discount offers, unless specified.

Valid now thru November 1, 2007

HOLLYWOOD Scoops
44 Flavors — icecream parlor

FREE MENU ITEM

Enjoy one complimentary MENU ITEM when a second MENU ITEM of equal or greater value is purchased.

valid anytime

B363

Offer validity is governed by the Rules of Use and excludes defined holidays. Offers are not valid with other discount offers, unless specified.

Valid now thru November 1, 2007

HOLY LAND

Up To $7.00 Value

Enjoy one complimentary LUNCH OR DINNER ENTREE when a second LUNCH OR DINNER ENTREE of equal or greater value is purchased.

valid anytime
Tipping should be 15% to 20% of TOTAL bill before discount

B364

Offer validity is governed by the Rules of Use and excludes defined holidays. Offers are not valid with other discount offers, unless specified.

Valid now thru November 1, 2007

THE HONEYBAKED HAM COMPANY
Est. 1957

FREE COMBO MEAL

Enjoy one complimentary COMBO MEAL when a second COMBO MEAL of equal or greater value is purchased.

valid anytime

B365

Offer validity is governed by the Rules of Use and excludes defined holidays. Offers are not valid with other discount offers, unless specified.

Valid now thru November 1, 2007

THE HONEYBAKED HAM COMPANY
Est. 1957

FREE SANDWICH

Enjoy one complimentary SANDWICH when a second SANDWICH of equal or greater value is purchased.

valid anytime

B366

Offer validity is governed by the Rules of Use and excludes defined holidays. Offers are not valid with other discount offers, unless specified.

Valid now thru November 1, 2007

HIGHER GROUNDS

- Gourmet Coffees
- Espresso smoothies
- Fruit smoothies
- Italian sodas
- Chai

8916 Aztec Dr.
(inside the Cloud 9 Carwash complex)
Eden Prairie, MN
(952)697-4021

00657044

HAROLD'S CHICKEN

- Opened in 1950 by Harold Pierce
- He aspired to provide the best fish & chicken in Chicago
- It has now grown to over 80 locations with this being the first location in Minnesota
- We are proud to serve you!
- Serving great chicken since 1950
- Phone ahead for faster service

2117 W. Broadway Ave.
Minneapolis, MN
(612)529-0112

00634840

HOLY LAND

- Bakery, groceries & Lebanese deli
- The biggest, tastiest gyro in town
- Fine Greek & Lebanese food
- Pocket & flat pita bread
- Falafel sandwiches, kubben, taboulesh salads, lamb & chicken kabobs, dolmades, spanakopita & many other delicious dishes

2513 Central Ave. NE
Minneapolis, MN
(612)781-2627

00354991

HOLLYWOOD Scoops

- 44 Flavors of Cedar Crest Ice Cream
- Popcorn
- Nachos
- Soft drinks
- Malts, shakes & sundaes
- Candy
- 3,000 Tunes on the juke box

681 Winnetka Ave. N.
(next door to Great Photos Fast!)
Golden Valley, MN
(763)545-2663

00695088

THE HONEYBAKED HAM COMPANY

1905 County Rd. 42 *(at CR-5)*,
Burnsville, MN
(952)435-8000

12965 Ridgedale Dr. *(across from Ridgedale Mall)*, Minnetonka, MN
(952)540-1048

2401 Fairview Ave. N. *(across from Rosedale Ctr.)*, Roseville, MN
(651)631-8211

For locations nationwide, call
(800)394-4424

00585262

THE HONEYBAKED HAM COMPANY

1905 County Rd. 42 *(at CR-5)*,
Burnsville, MN
(952)435-8000

12965 Ridgedale Dr. *(across from Ridgedale Mall)*, Minnetonka, MN
(952)540-1048

2401 Fairview Ave. N. *(across from Rosedale Ctr.)*, Roseville, MN
(651)631-8211

For locations nationwide, call
(800)394-4424

00585248

1 LB. SALAD

THE HONEYBAKED HAM COMPANY
Est. 1957

Enjoy one complimentary 1 LB. SALAD when a second 1 LB. SALAD of equal or greater value is purchased.

valid anytime

B367

Offer validity is governed by the Rules of Use and excludes defined holidays. Offers are not valid with other discount offers, unless specified.

Valid now thru November 1, 2007

Up To $8.00 Value

HONG WONG
FINE CHINESE CUISINE

Enjoy one complimentary DINNER ENTREE when a second DINNER ENTREE of equal or greater value is purchased.

Dine in only; Buffet excluded

valid any evening

B368

Offer validity is governed by the Rules of Use and excludes defined holidays. Offers are not valid with other discount offers, unless specified.

Valid now thru November 1, 2007

Up To $5.00 Value

HOUSE OF JAVA

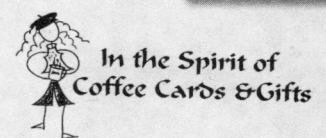

Enjoy one complimentary MENU ITEM when a second MENU ITEM of equal or greater value is purchased.

valid anytime

B369

Offer validity is governed by the Rules of Use and excludes defined holidays. Offers are not valid with other discount offers, unless specified.

Valid now thru November 1, 2007

Up To $6.00 Value

Hunan RESTAURANT

Enjoy one complimentary DINNER ENTREE when a second DINNER ENTREE of equal or greater value is purchased.

Dine in only; Buffet excluded

valid any evening

B370

Offer validity is governed by the Rules of Use and excludes defined holidays. Offers are not valid with other discount offers, unless specified.

Valid now thru November 1, 2007

Up To $12.00 Value

HUNTER'S INN
BAR & Grill

Enjoy one complimentary LUNCH OR DINNER ENTREE when a second LUNCH OR DINNER ENTREE of equal or greater value is purchased.

valid anytime
Offers not valid holidays and subject to Rules of Use
Tipping should be 15% to 20% of the total bill before discount

B371

Offer validity is governed by the Rules of Use and excludes defined holidays. Offers are not valid with other discount offers, unless specified.

Valid now thru November 1, 2007

Up To $5.00 Value

In the Spirit of Coffee Cards & Gifts

Enjoy one complimentary MENU ITEM when a second MENU ITEM of equal or greater value is purchased.

valid anytime

B372

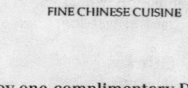

Offer validity is governed by the Rules of Use and excludes defined holidays. Offers are not valid with other discount offers, unless specified.

Valid now thru November 1, 2007

HONG WONG
FINE CHINESE CUISINE

- There are 3 main factors in dominating Chinese cooking - color, aroma & taste
- We do the best to achieve that goal by combining skill and the freshest ingredients

2139 Cliff Road
(Cedar Cliff Shopping Center)
Eagan, MN
(651) 452-0086

00001015

THE HONEYBAKED HAM COMPANY

1905 County Rd. 42 *(at CR-5)*,
Burnsville, MN
(952) 435-8000

12965 Ridgedale Dr. *(across from Ridgedale Mall)*, **Minnetonka, MN**
(952) 540-1048

2401 Fairview Ave. N. *(across from Rosedale Ctr.)*, **Roseville, MN**
(651) 631-8211

For locations nationwide, call
(800) 394-4424

00585265

Hunan RESTAURANT

- Authentic Peking, Szechuan, Cantonese & Hunan cuisine
- We serve wine and beer for your dining pleasure
- Special banquet & catering service available
- Closed Sunday

8066 Morgan Circle
(off 80th St. behind Wendy's)
Bloomington, MN
(952) 881-2280

00000623

HOUSE OF JAVA

- Gourmet espresso drinks
- Fresh soups
- Delicious sandwiches
- Internet access with wireless available
- Smoothies & teas
- Fresh roasted coffee beans
- Desserts & muffins
- Breakfast sandwiches
- Gift items

3320 Brookdale Dr.
(Xerxes Ave. & Brookdale Dr.)
Brooklyn Park, MN
(763) 503-5749

00636388

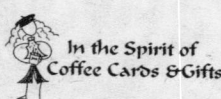

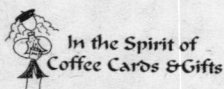

In the Spirit of Coffee Cards & Gifts

- Dunn Bros.™ coffee
- Homemade cookies & scones
- Godiva™ chocolates
- Dippin' Dots™
- Ice cream
- Lattes, smoothies, chai tea & iced drinks
- Boyd's Bears™, candles, greeting cards, Ty™ products & a variety of gift items
- Home keeping decor
- Books, music & balloons!

5828 Blaine Ave. E., Inver Grove Hgts., MN
(651) 451-0722

2230 Eagle Creek Ln., Woodbury, MN
(651) 998-0456

00606486

HUNTER'S INN
BAR & Grill

- Great appetizers
- Delicious burgers, wraps & sandwiches
- Pizza
- Flavorful steaks

20454 Hwy. 65
East Bethel, MN
(763) 434-3331

00695459

Coupons void if purchased, sold or bartered. Discounts exclude tax, tip and/or alcohol, where applicable.

In the Spirit of Coffee Cards & Gifts

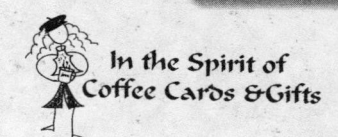

Up To $5.00 Value

Enjoy one complimentary MENU ITEM when a second MENU ITEM of equal or greater value is purchased.

valid anytime

B373

Offer validity is governed by the Rules of Use and excludes defined holidays. Offers are not valid with other discount offers, unless specified.

Valid now thru November 1, 2007

INTERNATIONAL BUSINESS CAFE

Up To $6.00 Value

Enjoy one complimentary MENU ITEM when a second MENU ITEM of equal or greater value is purchased.

valid anytime

B374

Offer validity is governed by the Rules of Use and excludes defined holidays. Offers are not valid with other discount offers, unless specified.

Valid now thru November 1, 2007

J&D's In Club

Up To $7.00 Value

Enjoy one complimentary LUNCH OR DINNER ENTREE when a second LUNCH OR DINNER ENTREE of equal or greater value is purchased.

valid anytime

B375

Offer validity is governed by the Rules of Use and excludes defined holidays. Offers are not valid with other discount offers, unless specified.

Valid now thru November 1, 2007

JJ's Family Restaurant

Up To $9.00 Value

Enjoy one complimentary ENTREE when a second ENTREE of equal or greater value is purchased.

valid anytime

B376

Offer validity is governed by the Rules of Use and excludes defined holidays. Offers are not valid with other discount offers, unless specified.

Valid now thru November 1, 2007

JT's Restaurant & Pizza Parlor

Up To $8.00 Value

Enjoy one complimentary LUNCH OR DINNER ENTREE when a second LUNCH OR DINNER ENTREE of equal or greater value is purchased or for those who prefer - any one pizza at 50% off the regular price.

Dine in only; Specials excluded

valid anytime

Tipping should be 15% to 20% of TOTAL bill before discount

B377

Offer validity is governed by the Rules of Use and excludes defined holidays. Offers are not valid with other discount offers, unless specified.

Valid now thru November 1, 2007

JACK YEE'S RESTAURANT

Up To $7.00 Value

Enjoy one complimentary DINNER ENTREE when a second DINNER ENTREE of equal or greater value is purchased.

Dine in only; Buffet excluded

valid any evening

B378

Offer validity is governed by the Rules of Use and excludes defined holidays. Offers are not valid with other discount offers, unless specified.

Valid now thru November 1, 2007

INTERNATIONAL BUSINESS CAFE

1300 Nicollet Mall, Ste. 2090
Minneapolis, MN
(612)333-6033

00694666

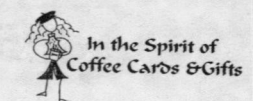

In the Spirit of Coffee Cards & Gifts

- Dunn Bros.™ coffee
- Homemade cookies & scones
- Godiva™ chocolates
- Dippin' Dots™
- Ice cream
- Lattes, smoothies, chai tea & iced drinks
- Boyd's Bears™, candles, greeting cards, Ty™ products & a variety of gift items
- Home keeping decor
- Books, music & balloons!

5828 Blaine Ave. E., Inver Grove Hgts., MN
(651)451-0722

2230 Eagle Creek Ln., Woodbury, MN
(651)998-0456

00606486

J's Family Restaurant

- Open Mon-Fri 7am-9pm, Sat-Sun 8am-9pm
- Breakfast served until 1:30pm
- Serving wine & strong beer
- Italian-American cuisine
- Kids menu

2913 E. Cliff Rd.
(corner of Cliff Rd. & River Hills Dr.)
Burnsville, MN
(952)890-2669

00476419

J & D's 2 n C lub

- Home of the Almost World Famous Hamburger
- Coldest beer anywhere!
- Home style cooking

505 Lake St. W.
Cologne, MN
(952)466-3328

00670534

JACK YEE'S RESTAURANT

- Enjoy the best New York style Chinese food
- Downtown Hopkins
- Specializing in Szechuan & Mandarin cuisine
- Also serving beer & wine
- Sun-Thurs 11am-10pm, Fri & Sat 11am-11pm
- Free parking ramp in rear

1016 Mainstreet
Hopkins, MN
(952)935-8621

00000258

JT's Restaurant & Pizza Parlor

8492 Central Ave. N.E.
Springlake Park, MN
(763)792-2888

00680051

entertainment.com — Up To $8.00 Value

Jade Island Chinese Cuisine 青岛

Enjoy one complimentary LUNCH OR DINNER ENTREE when a second LUNCH OR DINNER ENTREE of equal or greater value is purchased.

Dine in only; Buffet excluded

valid anytime

B379

Offer validity is governed by the Rules of Use and excludes defined holidays. Offers are not valid with other discount offers, unless specified.

Valid now thru November 1, 2007

---

entertainment.com — Up To $8.00 Value

JAVA RESTAURANT

Enjoy one complimentary ENTREE when a second ENTREE of equal or greater value is purchased.

valid anytime

B380

Offer validity is governed by the Rules of Use and excludes defined holidays. Offers are not valid with other discount offers, unless specified.

Valid now thru November 1, 2007

---

entertainment.com — Up To $8.00 Value

Jersey's BAR & GRILL

Enjoy one complimentary LUNCH OR DINNER ENTREE when a second LUNCH OR DINNER ENTREE of equal or greater value is purchased.

valid anytime

B381

Offer validity is governed by the Rules of Use and excludes defined holidays. Offers are not valid with other discount offers, unless specified.

Valid now thru November 1, 2007

entertainment.com — Up To $8.00 Value

Jerusalem's Restaurant

Enjoy one complimentary DINNER ENTREE when a second DINNER ENTREE of equal or greater value is purchased.

valid any evening

Not valid for appetizers & side orders; Not valid with any other specials

B382

Offer validity is governed by the Rules of Use and excludes defined holidays. Offers are not valid with other discount offers, unless specified.

Valid now thru November 1, 2007

---

entertainment.com — Up To $6.00 Value

Jimbo's

Enjoy one complimentary DINNER ENTREE when a second DINNER ENTREE of equal or greater value is purchased or for those who prefer - any one pizza at 50% off the regular price - maximum discount $6.00.

Sorry, no delivery

valid any evening

B383

Offer validity is governed by the Rules of Use and excludes defined holidays. Offers are not valid with other discount offers, unless specified.

Valid now thru November 1, 2007

---

entertainment.com — Up To $5.00 Value

Kalli's POPCORN SHOP

Enjoy one complimentary MENU ITEM when a second MENU ITEM of equal or greater value is purchased.

valid anytime

B384

Offer validity is governed by the Rules of Use and excludes defined holidays. Offers are not valid with other discount offers, unless specified.

Valid now thru November 1, 2007

JAVA RESTAURANT

- Serving the finest Middle-Eastern & American foods since 1974
- Fresh ingredients
- Moderate prices
- Carry out available
- Belly dancing on weekends

2801 Nicollet Ave.
(28th & Nicollet)
Minneapolis, MN
(612) 870-7871

00000130

Jade Island Chinese Cuisine 青岛

- Beer & wine available
- Major credit cards accepted
- Featuring Mandarin, Hunan, Szechuan & Cantonese cuisine

7534 149 St. W.
Apple Valley, MN
(952) 891-3333

00593032

Jerusalem's Restaurant

- Middle Eastern cuisine from scratch
- Pocket sandwiches
- Voted Best Middle Eastern cuisine 6 years in a row
- Voted best vegetarian restaurant
- Beer & wine available
- Free parking
- Belly dancing
- Outdoor patio

1518 Nicollet Ave.
Minneapolis, MN
(612) 871-8883

00000721

Jersey's BAR & GRILL

- Good food, good friends, good times
- Delicious appetizers
- Soups & salads
- Sandwiches & burgers
- Chicken, ribs & steak
- Full bar service
- Children's menu

6449 Concord Blvd.
Inver Grove, MN
(651) 455-4561

00516654

Kelli's POPCORN SHOP

- Come visit our 50's style ice cream parlor & popcorn shop!
- Ice cream - hard & soft!
- Shakes & malts
- Slushes & freezes
- Buttery white & flavored popcorn available in a variety of sizes
- Gift tins for all occasions
- See you tomorrow!

14861 Granada Dr.
(downtown Apple Valley)
Apple Valley, MN
(952) 432-3311

00547386

JIMBO'S

- Video store downstairs

8550 Van Buren
(Hwy 10 at Van Buren, 2 blks. E. of Northtown)
Blaine, MN
(763) 784-0939

00002278

entertainment.com

Up To $7.00 Value

Katie O'Leary's
BEEF & BREW

Enjoy one complimentary LUNCH OR DINNER ENTREE when a second LUNCH OR DINNER ENTREE of equal or greater value is purchased.

Dine in only

valid anytime

B385

Offer validity is governed by the Rules of Use and excludes defined holidays. Offers are not valid with other discount offers, unless specified.

Valid now thru November 1, 2007

---

entertainment.com

$7.00 Value

La Pinata

Enjoy one complimentary ENTREE when a second ENTREE of equal or greater value is purchased.

valid anytime

Tipping should be 15% to 20% of TOTAL bill before discount

B386

Offer validity is governed by the Rules of Use and excludes defined holidays. Offers are not valid with other discount offers, unless specified.

Valid now thru November 1, 2007

---

entertainment.com

Up To $5.00 Value

LIMU COFFEE

Enjoy one complimentary MENU ITEM when a second MENU ITEM of equal or greater value is purchased.

valid anytime

B387

Offer validity is governed by the Rules of Use and excludes defined holidays. Offers are not valid with other discount offers, unless specified.

Valid now thru November 1, 2007

---

entertainment.com

FREE MENU ITEM

Lori's Coffee House

Enjoy one complimentary MENU ITEM when a second MENU ITEM of equal or greater value is purchased.

valid anytime

B388

Offer validity is governed by the Rules of Use and excludes defined holidays. Offers are not valid with other discount offers, unless specified.

Valid now thru November 1, 2007

---

entertainment.com

Up To $5.00 Value

Luna Blu Coffee Co

www.lunablucoffe.com

Enjoy one complimentary MENU ITEM when a second MENU ITEM of equal or greater value is purchased.

valid anytime

B389

Offer validity is governed by the Rules of Use and excludes defined holidays. Offers are not valid with other discount offers, unless specified.

Valid now thru November 1, 2007

---

entertainment.com

Up To $7.00 Value

Mady's
Bowl & Lounge

Enjoy one complimentary MENU ITEM when a second MENU ITEM of equal or greater value is purchased.

valid anytime

Tipping should be 15% to 20% of TOTAL bill before discount

B390

Offer validity is governed by the Rules of Use and excludes defined holidays. Offers are not valid with other discount offers, unless specified.

Valid now thru November 1, 2007

La Pinata

- Delicious broiled chicken
- Tacos, burritos, enchiladas & more
- Sandwiches
- Kid's meals

2520 Hillsboro Ave. N.
Golden Valley, MN
(763) 253-3300

00606506

Katie O'Leary's
BEEF & BREW

- Beer
- Burgers
- Cocktails
- Appetizers
- Live music Sat.
- Happy hour specials

117 2nd Ave. N.E.
Waseca, MN
(507) 835-2000

00670971

Lori's Coffee House

- Gourmet organic coffee
- Soups & sandwiches
- Pastries

1441 Cleveland Ave. N.
St. Paul, MN
(651) 647-9007

00682022

LIMU COFFEE

- Espresso cafe & imported coffees
- Ethiopian coffee ceremonies
- Premium gourmet coffees

500 5th Ave. NW, Ste. 109
New Brighton, MN
(612) 788-3459

00605055

Mady's
Bowl & Lounge

- Featuring hand dipped pork tenderloin & onion rings
- Serving from 11am-11pm 7 days a week

3919 Central Ave. NE
Minneapolis, MN
(763) 789-9104

00000077

Luna Blu Coffee Co.

- '2005 Golden Cup Award' winner
- Gourmet coffee & espresso drinks
- Soups & sandwiches
- Smoothies
- Premium homemade ice cream
- Baked goods
- Free Wi-Fi & XM radio
- Satellite tv

101 Marketplace 14165 James Rd. #112
(Just N. of I94 at the N.E. corner of County Rd.
144 & Hwy. 101)
Rogers, MN
(763) 428-0760

00690651

MAGGIE'S Restaurant

entertainment.com — Up To $5.00 Value

Enjoy one complimentary BREAKFAST or MENU SELECTION when a second BREAKFAST or MENU SELECTION of equal or greater value is purchased or for those who prefer - any one pizza at 50% off the regular price.

Sorry, no delivery with coupon

valid anytime

B391

Valid now thru November 1, 2007

Offer validity is governed by the Rules of Use and excludes defined holidays. Offers are not valid with other discount offers, unless specified.

MAIN STREET CENTRAL PERK & ICE CREAM

entertainment.com — Up To $5.00 Value

Enjoy one complimentary MENU ITEM when a second MENU ITEM of equal or greater value is purchased.

valid anytime

B392

Valid now thru November 1, 2007

Offer validity is governed by the Rules of Use and excludes defined holidays. Offers are not valid with other discount offers, unless specified.

Mama Donato's
Cucina Italiana
Pizza & Pasta

entertainment.com — Up To $7.00 Value

Enjoy one complimentary ENTREE when a second ENTREE of equal or greater value is purchased.

Dine in only; Specials excluded

valid anytime

Offers not valid holidays and subject to Rules of Use
Tipping should be 15% to 20% of the total bill before discount

B393

Valid now thru November 1, 2007

Offer validity is governed by the Rules of Use and excludes defined holidays. Offers are not valid with other discount offers, unless specified.

"Mama Taught Me How To Cook" Soul Food Eatery!

entertainment.com — Up To $13.00 Value

Enjoy one complimentary LUNCH OR DINNER ENTREE when a second LUNCH OR DINNER ENTREE of equal or greater value is purchased.

valid anytime

B394

Valid now thru November 1, 2007

Offer validity is governed by the Rules of Use and excludes defined holidays. Offers are not valid with other discount offers, unless specified.

MAMA'S Bakery Pizza Salad Bar

entertainment.com — Up To $7.00 Value

Enjoy one complimentary MENU ITEM when a second MENU ITEM of equal or greater value is purchased or for those who prefer - any one pizza at 50% off the regular price - maximum discount $7.00.

valid anytime

B395

Valid now thru November 1, 2007

Offer validity is governed by the Rules of Use and excludes defined holidays. Offers are not valid with other discount offers, unless specified.

Manny's Tortas
GOURMET MEXICAN SANDWICHES

entertainment.com — Up To $7.00 Value

Enjoy one complimentary MENU ITEM when a second MENU ITEM of equal or greater value is purchased.

valid anytime

B396

Valid now thru November 1, 2007

Offer validity is governed by the Rules of Use and excludes defined holidays. Offers are not valid with other discount offers, unless specified.

Main Street Central Perk & Ice Cream

207 E. Main St.
(historic downtown Anoka)
Anoka, MN
(763) 427-7266

00695055

"Mama Taught Me How To Cook" Soul Food Eatery!

- If you like soul food, you'll love us!
- Featuring all your "down home" favorites including our house special: Bar B Q Ham Hocks, greens, pinto beans, ribs, fried okra, pig feet, sweet-potato pie, peach cobbler & we even have chittlins
- Come see what else we got!

2520 Kenzie Terrace N.E.
(corners of Lowry Ave. N.E. & Stinson Pkwy.)
Minneapolis, MN
(612) 781-3280

00692373

Manny's Tortas
GOURMET MEXICAN SANDWICHES

- On the corner of Lake & Bloomington in Mercado Central
- Mexican sandwiches (tortas)
- Desserts (postres)
- A wide variety of coffee
- Mexican hot chocolate
- Beer & wine available
- Extended summer hours: Fri. & Sat. till 3:00 a.m.

1515 E Lake St. #103
Minneapolis, MN
(612) 728-5408

00363447

MAGGIE'S Restaurant

- Maggie's Restaurant--a Wayzata tradition--specializing in Italian and American cuisine
- Open for breakfast, lunch, and dinner 7 days a week
- Conveniently located in the Village Shoppes of Wayzata--ample free parking

844 E Lake St.
(Village Shoppes)
Wayzata, MN
(952) 476-0840

00000481

Mama Donato's
Cucina Italiana
Pizza & Pasta

- Joseph & Julie's homemade Italian food
- Pizza & pasta
- Delicious sandwiches
- Fresh salads
- Kids menu
- Homemade desserts
- Try us for your next party

4705 36th Ave. N.
Crystal, MN
(763) 521-1113

00693532

MAMA'S Bakery Pizza Salad Bar

- Mama's homemade bakery
- Salad bar
- Pizza
- Gourmet coffee
- Giant dessert bars

800 Nicollet Mall
Minneapolis, MN
(612) 767-1681

00685724

Marina Grill & Deli
GREEK • MEDITERRANEAN • AMERICAN

Up To $5.00 Value

Enjoy one complimentary MENU ITEM when a second MENU ITEM of equal or greater value is purchased.

Buffet excluded

valid anytime

B397

Valid now thru November 1, 2007

Offer validity is governed by the Rules of Use and excludes defined holidays. Offers are not valid with other discount offers, unless specified.

Marino's Deli
NORTHEAST MINNEAPOLIS

Up To $6.00 Value

Enjoy one complimentary MENU ITEM when a second MENU ITEM of equal or greater value is purchased.

valid anytime

B398

Valid now thru November 1, 2007

Offer validity is governed by the Rules of Use and excludes defined holidays. Offers are not valid with other discount offers, unless specified.

Marysburg Books
Coffee Emporium & Wine Bar

Up To $7.00 Value

www.marysburgbooks.com

Enjoy one complimentary MENU ITEM when a second MENU ITEM of equal or greater value is purchased.

valid anytime

B399

Valid now thru November 1, 2007

Offer validity is governed by the Rules of Use and excludes defined holidays. Offers are not valid with other discount offers, unless specified.

Marysburg Books
Coffee Emporium & Wine Bar

Up To $7.00 Value

www.marysburgbooks.com

Enjoy one complimentary MENU ITEM when a second MENU ITEM of equal or greater value is purchased.

valid anytime

B400

Valid now thru November 1, 2007

Offer validity is governed by the Rules of Use and excludes defined holidays. Offers are not valid with other discount offers, unless specified.

Mel-O-Glaze Bakery

Up To $5.00 Value

Enjoy any BAKED GOODS ORDER at 50% off the regular price.

valid anytime

B401

Valid now thru November 1, 2007

Offer validity is governed by the Rules of Use and excludes defined holidays. Offers are not valid with other discount offers, unless specified.

Mexico y Mexico Restaurante

Up To $7.00 Value

Enjoy one complimentary MENU ITEM when a second MENU ITEM of equal or greater value is purchased.

valid anytime

B402

Valid now thru November 1, 2007

Offer validity is governed by the Rules of Use and excludes defined holidays. Offers are not valid with other discount offers, unless specified.

Marino's Deli
NORTHEAST MINNEAPOLIS

- Italian entrees hot ready to eat or cold ready for your oven
- Specialty hoagies
- Homemade Italian sausage, meatballs & sauce
- Gourmet meats & cheeses
- Italian bakery goods & desserts
- Open Mon.-Sat. 11 a.m.-8 p.m.
- Catering for all occasions-large or small

1946 Johnson St. N. E.
Minneapolis, MN
(612) 781-0970

00002321

Martysburg Books
Coffee Emporium & Wine Bar

- Serving wine & gourmet espresso beverages, food, pastries & desserts in the warehouse district of downtown Minneapolis
- Book & writers clubs
- Study groups
- Open mic night
- Local performing artists
- Special events
- Conference room available

304 Washington Ave. N., Ste. 100
(corner of Washington & 3rd Ave. N.)
Minneapolis, MN
(612) 340-0078

00573363

Mexico y Mexico Restaurante

- Authentic Mexican food
- Breakfast daily
- All food is made from scratch
- Catering
- Coffee shop
- Beer & wine bar
- Friendly service for the whole family
- Open daily

1831 Central Ave. N.E.
Minneapolis, MN
(612) 781-0200

00620040

Marina Grill & Deli
GREEK • MEDITERRANEAN • AMERICAN

- Greek, Mediterranean & American cuisine
- Catering available
- Open daily

2424 University Ave. N.E.
Minneapolis, MN
(612) 788-0461

00670532

Martysburg Books
Coffee Emporium & Wine Bar

- Serving wine & gourmet espresso beverages, food, pastries & desserts in the warehouse district of downtown Minneapolis
- Book & writers clubs
- Study groups
- Open mic night
- Local performing artists
- Special events
- Conference room available

304 Washington Ave. N., Ste. 100
(corner of Washington & 3rd Ave. N.)
Minneapolis, MN
(612) 340-0078

00573363

Mel-O-Glaze Bakery

- Baking it right since 1961
- Large assortment of baked goods including: bread, cookies, muffins, pies & pastries
- Specializing in "award winning" donuts!

4800 28th Ave. S.
(Minnehaha Pkwy.)
Minneapolis, MN
(612) 729-9316

00580811

Mia's Pizza

Up to $12.00 Value

Enjoy one complimentary MENU ITEM when a second MENU ITEM of equal or greater value is purchased.

valid anytime

B403

Valid now thru November 1, 2007

Offer validity is governed by the Rules of Use and excludes defined holidays. Offers are not valid with other discount offers, unless specified.

Midway Rendevous Cafe

Up to $5.00 Value

Enjoy one complimentary MENU ITEM when a second MENU ITEM of equal or greater value is purchased.

valid anytime

B404

Valid now thru November 1, 2007

Offer validity is governed by the Rules of Use and excludes defined holidays. Offers are not valid with other discount offers, unless specified.

Mim's Cafe

Up to $9.00 Value

Enjoy one complimentary MENU ITEM when a second MENU ITEM of equal or greater value is purchased.

valid anytime

Tipping should be 15% to 20% of TOTAL bill before discount

B405

Valid now thru November 1, 2007

Offer validity is governed by the Rules of Use and excludes defined holidays. Offers are not valid with other discount offers, unless specified.

Ming's Palace

Up to $8.00 Value

Enjoy one complimentary LUNCH OR DINNER ENTREE when a second LUNCH OR DINNER ENTREE of equal or greater value is purchased.

valid anytime

Buffet & combination dinners excluded

B406

Valid now thru November 1, 2007

Offer validity is governed by the Rules of Use and excludes defined holidays. Offers are not valid with other discount offers, unless specified.

Ming's Garden Restaurant

Up to $8.00 Value

Enjoy one complimentary DINNER ENTREE when a second DINNER ENTREE of equal or greater value is purchased.

Dine in only; Buffet excluded

valid any evening

B407

Valid now thru November 1, 2007

Offer validity is governed by the Rules of Use and excludes defined holidays. Offers are not valid with other discount offers, unless specified.

MoJo's Pizza

Up to $16.00 Value

Enjoy any one complimentary PIZZA when a second PIZZA of equal or greater value is purchased.

valid anytime

B408

Valid now thru November 1, 2007

Offer validity is governed by the Rules of Use and excludes defined holidays. Offers are not valid with other discount offers, unless specified.

Midway Rendevous Cafe

- Macciato
- Espresso
- Latte
- Frappucino
- Teas
- Pastries
- Cold drinks

518 N. Snelling Ave.
St. Paul, MN
(651)645-7572

00687190

Mia's Pizza
Take & Bake
traditional & gourmet

- Traditional & gourmet pizza
- 6 & 12 inch subs
- Great salads
- Buffalo wings, chicken bites, cheese bread & more
- Take & bake pizza
- Desserts
- Credit cards accepted

12065 Hanson Blvd. N.W.
(121st & Hanson Blvd.)
Coon Rapids, MN
(763)754-5777

00634965

MING'S PALACE

- Specializing in Szechuan & Cantonese food
- Newly decorated location
- Buffet not included
- Hours: Mon.-Sat. 11:00 a.m.-9:00 p.m., closed Sunday

4004 Minnehaha Ave. S
Minneapolis, MN
(612)724-8883

00155679

Mim's Cafe

- Middle Eastern & American cuisine
- Shawarma
- Falefel
- Burgers

1435 Cleveland Ave. N.
St. Paul, MN
(651)646-0456

00682075

MoJo's Pizza

- Pizza
- Pasta
- Hot subs, calzones & buffalo wings
- We have something for everyone!
- Delivery or carry out

8565 Edinburgh Ctr. Dr., Brooklyn Park, MN
(763)424-2295

6522 University Ave. N.E., Fridley, MN
(763)572-8500

00636119

Ming's Garden
Restaurant

- Located between TJ Maxx & Rainbow Foods
- Fine Chinese dining
- Sun-Thur 11:30am-9:30pm
- Fri & Sat 11:30am-10pm

4190 Vinewood Ln. #113
(between Rainbow Foods & TJ Maxx)
Plymouth, MN
(763)559-3131

00001008

Mongkok

Up To **$11.00** Value

Enjoy one complimentary LUNCH OR DINNER ENTREE when a second LUNCH OR DINNER ENTREE of equal or greater value is purchased.

valid anytime
Tipping should be 15% to 20% of TOTAL bill before discount

B409

Offer validity is governed by the Rules of Use and excludes defined holidays. Offers are not valid with other discount offers, unless specified.

---

monkabeans and sunshine cafe

Up To **$5.00** Value

Enjoy one complimentary MENU ITEM when a second MENU ITEM of equal or greater value is purchased.

valid anytime

B410

Offer validity is governed by the Rules of Use and excludes defined holidays. Offers are not valid with other discount offers, unless specified.

---

the neighborhood ice cream shoppe

Up To **$5.00** Value

Enjoy one complimentary MENU ITEM when a second MENU ITEM of equal or greater value is purchased.

valid anytime

B411

Offer validity is governed by the Rules of Use and excludes defined holidays. Offers are not valid with other discount offers, unless specified.

---

the neighborhood ice cream shoppe

Up To **$5.00** Value

Enjoy one complimentary MENU ITEM when a second MENU ITEM of equal or greater value is purchased.

valid anytime

B412

Offer validity is governed by the Rules of Use and excludes defined holidays. Offers are not valid with other discount offers, unless specified.

NEW YORK BURRITO GOURMET WRAPS

FREE MENU ITEM

Enjoy one complimentary MENU ITEM when a second MENU ITEM of equal or greater value is purchased.

valid anytime

B413

Offer validity is governed by the Rules of Use and excludes defined holidays. Offers are not valid with other discount offers, unless specified.

Nina's GRILL

Up To **$7.00** Value

Enjoy one complimentary DINNER ENTREE when a second DINNER ENTREE of equal or greater value is purchased.

valid any evening
Tipping should be 15% to 20% of TOTAL bill before discount

B414

Offer validity is governed by the Rules of Use and excludes defined holidays. Offers are not valid with other discount offers, unless specified.

monkabeans and sunshine cafe

- Breakfasts, sandwiches & pizza
- Ice cream & malts
- Coffees, teas & lattes
- Live music & open mic
- Call ahead for quick outdoor seating

**1206 Main St.
Hopkins, MN
(952)938-9056**

Coupons void if purchased, sold or bartered.
Discounts exclude tax, tip and/or alcohol, where applicable.

00701424

Mongkok

- Everything freshly made - no MSG!
- Asian food - Thai, Japanese, sushi & Chinese
- Catering available

8085 Wedgewood Lane N.
(across from Cub Foods)
**Maple Grove, MN
(763)416-4454**

Coupons void if purchased, sold or bartered.
Discounts exclude tax, tip and/or alcohol, where applicable.

00457731

---

the neighborhood ice cream shoppe

- Over 40 flavors of ice cream
- Cones & sundaes
- Frozen coffee drinks
- Malts & smoothies
- Custom ice cream cakes

**6137 Kellogg Ave.
Edina, MN
(952)922-9597**

Coupons void if purchased, sold or bartered.
Discounts exclude tax, tip and/or alcohol, where applicable.

00526292

---

the neighborhood ice cream shoppe

- Over 40 flavors of ice cream
- Cones & sundaes
- Frozen coffee drinks
- Malts & smoothies
- Custom ice cream cakes

**6137 Kellogg Ave.
Edina, MN
(952)922-9597**

Coupons void if purchased, sold or bartered.
Discounts exclude tax, tip and/or alcohol, where applicable.

00526292

Nina's Grill

- Try our Russian cuisine or American favorites
- Come in for great burgers & sandwiches
- Full bar service
- Golden Tee & billiards
- Visit our market next door for groceries, souvenirs & music from Russia

**2510 Horizon Dr.
Burnsville, MN
(952)846-4007**

Coupons void if purchased, sold or bartered.
Discounts exclude tax, tip and/or alcohol, where applicable.

00685717

NEW YORK BURRITO - GOURMET WRAPS

- One bite & you will be hooked!
- Gourmet wraps-Thai peanut chicken, cajun chicken, marinated steak & more
- Now serving cold beer
- 12 Flavors of Blue Bunny Ice Cream
- Traditional smothered burritos, quesadillas & fajitas

**925 County Rd. E.
Vadnais Heights, MN
(651)787-9999**

Coupons void if purchased, sold or bartered.
Discounts exclude tax, tip and/or alcohol, where applicable.

00610703

entertainment.com — Up To $5.00 Value

North Country Co-op

Enjoy one complimentary MENU ITEM when a second MENU ITEM of equal or greater value is purchased.

valid anytime

B415

Valid now thru November 1, 2007

Offer validity is governed by the Rules of Use and excludes defined holidays. Offers are not valid with other discount offers, unless specified.

---

entertainment.com — FREE MENU ITEM

NORTHERN Espresso·Café
Relax · Laugh · Enjoy

Enjoy one complimentary MENU ITEM when a second MENU ITEM of equal or greater value is purchased.

valid anytime

B416

Valid now thru November 1, 2007

Offer validity is governed by the Rules of Use and excludes defined holidays. Offers are not valid with other discount offers, unless specified.

---

entertainment.com — Up To $5.00 Value

Old-Fashion DONUT SHOPPE

Enjoy any BAKED GOODS ORDER at 50% off the regular price - maximum discount $5.00.

valid anytime

B417

Valid now thru November 1, 2007

Offer validity is governed by the Rules of Use and excludes defined holidays. Offers are not valid with other discount offers, unless specified.

---

entertainment.com — Up To $7.00 Value

Over The Rainbow

Enjoy one complimentary LUNCH OR DINNER ENTREE when a second LUNCH OR DINNER ENTREE of equal or greater value is purchased.

valid anytime

B418

Valid now thru November 1, 2007

Offer validity is governed by the Rules of Use and excludes defined holidays. Offers are not valid with other discount offers, unless specified.

---

entertainment.com — FREE PIZZA

Pair of Dice Pizza

Enjoy any one complimentary PIZZA when a second PIZZA of equal or greater value is purchased.

valid anytime

B419

Valid now thru November 1, 2007

Offer validity is governed by the Rules of Use and excludes defined holidays. Offers are not valid with other discount offers, unless specified.

---

entertainment.com — Up To $6.00 Value

PAISANO'S Pizza & Hot Hoagies

Enjoy one complimentary MENU ITEM when a second MENU ITEM of equal or greater value is purchased.

valid anytime

B420

Valid now thru November 1, 2007

Offer validity is governed by the Rules of Use and excludes defined holidays. Offers are not valid with other discount offers, unless specified.

NORTHERN Espresso · Café
Relax · Laugh · Enjoy

- Gourmet coffee drinks
- Soups, sandwiches & salads
- Fresh baked pastries
- 12 Flavors of Carusos Gelato
- Bagels & cream cheese
- Meeting room & childrens play area

10950 Club West Pkwy.
Blaine, MN
(763)784-1291

00695129

Over The Rainbow

- Corner of North Dale and Minnihaha.
- Delicious appetizers, burgers, sandwiches and salads.
- DJ dancing Friday's and Saturdays.
- Karoke on Thursday's and Sunday's.

719 N. Dale St.
St. Paul, MN
(651)487-5070

00491425

PAISANO'S Pizza & Hot Hoagies

- Specializing in great pizza & hoagies
- Open 7 days a week

619 Selby Ave.
St. Paul, MN
(651)224-3350

00375432

North Country Co-op

- Organic, fair-trade coffee
- Salad bar & soups
- Sushi
- Pizza-by-the-slice
- Sandwiches
- Democratically member-owned & operated since 1971
- Full line grocery store
- Variety of ethnic & American items

1929 S. 5th St.
Minneapolis, MN
(612)338-3110

00654799

Old Fashion DONUT SHOPPE

- Open: Mon. thru Fri. 5:30 a.m.-1:30 p.m.
- Sat. 7 a.m.-12 p.m.

2720 N. Douglas Dr.
Crystal, MN
(763)544-1680

00057886

Pair of Dice Pizza

- 16" Or 12" pizza, original thin crust
- Wings - Buffalo, plain & BBQ
- Bread sticks & thick-sliced bread
- Cheese sticks
- Cole slaw
- BBQ rib tips
- French fries with great sides - ranch, blue cheese, parmesan & crushed red pepper

2715 W. Broadway
Minneapolis, MN
(612)522-3423

00577472

PANADERIA EL REY BAKERY

Up To **$5.00** Value

Enjoy one BAKED GOODS ORDER at 50% off the regular price - maximum discount $5.00.

valid anytime

B421

Offer validity is governed by the Rules of Use and excludes defined holidays. Offers are not valid with other discount offers, unless specified.

Valid now thru November 1, 2007

PARK Café

Up To **$6.00** Value

Enjoy one complimentary MENU ITEM when a second MENU ITEM of equal or greater value is purchased.

valid anytime

Tipping should be 15% to 20% of TOTAL bill before discount

B422

Offer validity is governed by the Rules of Use and excludes defined holidays. Offers are not valid with other discount offers, unless specified.

Valid now thru November 1, 2007

PETE'S Pizza

50% OFF

Enjoy any one PIZZA at 50% off the regular price - maximum discount $7.00.

Delivery excluded

valid anytime

B423

Offer validity is governed by the Rules of Use and excludes defined holidays. Offers are not valid with other discount offers, unless specified.

Valid now thru November 1, 2007

PIZZA MAGIC

Up To **$12.00** Value

Enjoy any one complimentary PIZZA when a second PIZZA of equal or greater value is purchased.

valid anytime

B424

Offer validity is governed by the Rules of Use and excludes defined holidays. Offers are not valid with other discount offers, unless specified.

Valid now thru November 1, 2007

Pizza Pazza

"Pizza with Personality"

Up To **$7.00** Value

Enjoy one complimentary MENU ITEM when a second MENU ITEM of equal or greater value is purchased or for those who prefer - any one pizza at 50% off the regular price.

valid anytime

B425

Offer validity is governed by the Rules of Use and excludes defined holidays. Offers are not valid with other discount offers, unless specified.

Valid now thru November 1, 2007

PIZZA PLANET Express / ROBERT'S

FREE PIZZA

Enjoy any one PIZZA at 50% off the regular price.

Delivery excluded

valid anytime

B426

Offer validity is governed by the Rules of Use and excludes defined holidays. Offers are not valid with other discount offers, unless specified.

Valid now thru November 1, 2007

PARK Cafe

- Open Mon.-Fri. from 7 a.m.-2 p.m.
- Featuring salad bar & pizza by the slice
- Full catering service
- Homemade bakery
- Gourmet coffee
- Deli sandwiches
- Mexican food

300 S. 6th St.
(Hennepin County Government Ctr.)
Minneapolis, MN
(612)349-5700

00280822

PANADERIA EL REY BAKERY

- Located near the corner of Lake & Nicollet
- Open 6 a.m. - 10 p.m., 365 days a year
- Specializing in Mexican pastries, as well as American & European
- We offer a variety of breads, cakes & cookies
- Cappuccino & hot chocolate available

3041 Nicollet Ave.
Minneapolis, MN
(612)827-2730

00276140

PIZZA MAGIC

- 16 toppings to choose from
- 3 crusts
- Cheese bread, breadsticks, chicken wings
- Create your own magic!

4351 Central Ave. N.E.
Columbia Heights, MN
(763)788-3610

00516508

PETE'S Pizza

- Thin crust, hand tossed & deep dish
- Pastas, calzones & appetizers
- Try one of our delicious specialty pizzas

4902 W. Hwy. 12
Maple Plain, MN
(763)479-2221

00515614

ROBERT'S

- Pizza, hoagies, salads & more
- Visit our website for the entertainment schedule

2400 County Rd. H2
Moundsview, MN
(763)786-1144

00585561

Pizza Pazza

- Limited delivery area
- Also serving hot hoagies, subs, wings, salads & cheese bread
- Open Mon.-Thurs. 11 a.m.-11 p.m., Fri. & Sat. 11 a.m.-1 a.m., Sun. noon-8 p.m.

1556 Selby Ave.
(Selby Ave. & Snelling Ave.)
St. Paul, MN
(651)644-4077

00526890

PIZZA PRIMA & PASTA
Italian Eatery

Up To $8.00 Value

Enjoy one complimentary LUNCH OR DINNER ENTREE when a second LUNCH OR DINNER ENTREE of equal or greater value is purchased or for those who prefer - any one pizza at 50% off the regular price - maximum discount $8.00.

Dine-in or carry out

valid anytime

B427

Offer validity is governed by the Rules of Use and excludes defined holidays. Offers are not valid with other discount offers, unless specified.

Valid now thru November 1, 2007

PIZZAIOLI PIZZAMAKER

50% OFF

Enjoy any one PIZZA at 50% off the regular price.

valid anytime

B428

Offer validity is governed by the Rules of Use and excludes defined holidays. Offers are not valid with other discount offers, unless specified.

Valid now thru November 1, 2007

Plan B Coffeehouse
Where even nerds are cool

Up To $5.00 Value

Enjoy one complimentary MENU ITEM when a second MENU ITEM of equal or greater value is purchased.

valid anytime

B429

Offer validity is governed by the Rules of Use and excludes defined holidays. Offers are not valid with other discount offers, unless specified.

Valid now thru November 1, 2007

Pupuseria
El Rincón Salva Doreño

Up To $5.00 Value

Enjoy one complimentary MENU ITEM when a second MENU ITEM of equal or greater value is purchased.

valid anytime

B430

Offer validity is governed by the Rules of Use and excludes defined holidays. Offers are not valid with other discount offers, unless specified.

Valid now thru November 1, 2007

Q-SHARKS CAFÉ

Up To $5.00 Value

qsharksbilliards.com

Enjoy one complimentary MENU ITEM when a second MENU ITEM of equal or greater value is purchased.

valid anytime

B431

Offer validity is governed by the Rules of Use and excludes defined holidays. Offers are not valid with other discount offers, unless specified.

Valid now thru November 1, 2007

Queen of Cakes

Up To $5.00 Value

www.queen-of-cakes.com

Enjoy any BAKED GOODS ORDER at 50% off the regular price.

valid anytime

B432

Offer validity is governed by the Rules of Use and excludes defined holidays. Offers are not valid with other discount offers, unless specified.

Valid now thru November 1, 2007

PIZZAIOLI
PIZZAMAKER

- Real pizza
- Fully baked & fully great
- Also offering half baked - started in our oven, finished in yours
- Delivery available

588 W. 78th St.
(next to Oasis Market)
Chanhassen, MN
(952)949-9777

Coupons void if purchased, sold or bartered. Discounts exclude tax, tip and/or alcohol, where applicable.

00520924

PIZZA PRIMA & PASTA
ITALIAN EATERY

- Fresh pizza with homemade sauce
- Homemade pastas
- Hot & cold hoagies

20198 Heritage Dr.
Lakeville, MN
(952)469-8800

Coupons void if purchased, sold or bartered. Discounts exclude tax, tip and/or alcohol, where applicable.

00671863

Pupuseria
El Rincón Salva Doreño

- Pupusas, yuca frita, sopa de pata, de Res y de pollo, carne asada, bistec
- Ethnic desserts
- Empanadas
- Platanos fritos
- Nuegados

1515 E. Lake St. #104
(Mercado Central)
Minneapolis, MN
(612)728-5442

Coupons void if purchased, sold or bartered. Discounts exclude tax, tip and/or alcohol, where applicable.

00500973

Plan B Coffeehouse
Where even nerds are cool

- Where nerds are cool
- People-watching
- Liquid stimulants
- Art
- Night and Day
- Boys and Girls

2717 Hennepin Ave. S
Minneapolis, MN
(612)872-1419

Coupons void if purchased, sold or bartered. Discounts exclude tax, tip and/or alcohol, where applicable.

00447743

Queen of Cakes

- Cakes for all occasions
- Wedding cakes are our specialty
- Last minute cake orders welcome
- Fresh cakes always available

7027 Amundson Ave.
Edina, MN
(952)942-7628

Coupons void if purchased, sold or bartered. Discounts exclude tax, tip and/or alcohol, where applicable.

00580722

Q-SHARKS CAFÉ

- Signature sandwiches
- Shirks Pizza
- 100% beef hot dogs
- Pretzels
- Nachos
- Freshly ground coffee
- Slushies
- Party facilities for 6 - 150

1927 W. Burnsville Pkwy.
(Valley Ridge Ctr.)
Burnsville, MN
(952)736-8284

Coupons void if purchased, sold or bartered. Discounts exclude tax, tip and/or alcohol, where applicable.

00522659

Rand Deli & Catering

Up To $5.00 Value

Enjoy any FOOD/BEVERAGE ORDER at 50% off the regular price.

valid anytime

B433

Offer validity is governed by the Rules of Use and excludes defined holidays. Offers are not valid with other discount offers, unless specified.

Valid now thru November 1, 2007

Razs Cafe

FREE MENU ITEM

Enjoy one complimentary MENU ITEM when a second MENU ITEM of equal or greater value is purchased.

valid anytime

B434

Offer validity is governed by the Rules of Use and excludes defined holidays. Offers are not valid with other discount offers, unless specified.

Valid now thru November 1, 2007

THE RED PEPPER
Chinese Restaurant

Up To $7.00 Value

Enjoy one complimentary DINNER ENTREE when a second DINNER ENTREE of equal or greater value is purchased.

Dine in only; Family dinners & specialties excluded

valid any evening
Tipping should be 15% to 20% of TOTAL bill before discount

B435

Offer validity is governed by the Rules of Use and excludes defined holidays. Offers are not valid with other discount offers, unless specified.

Valid now thru November 1, 2007

RESTAURANTE GUAYAQUIL

Up To $11.00 Value

Enjoy one complimentary ENTREE when a second ENTREE of equal or greater value is purchased.

valid anytime

B436

Offer validity is governed by the Rules of Use and excludes defined holidays. Offers are not valid with other discount offers, unless specified.

Valid now thru November 1, 2007

Restaurante La Rancherita

Up To $8.00 Value

Enjoy one complimentary LUNCH OR DINNER ENTREE when a second LUNCH OR DINNER ENTREE of equal or greater value is purchased.

valid anytime
Offers not valid holidays and subject to Rules of Use
Tipping should be 15% to 20% of the total bill before discount

B437

Offer validity is governed by the Rules of Use and excludes defined holidays. Offers are not valid with other discount offers, unless specified.

Valid now thru November 1, 2007

Riverside
RESTAURANT

Up To $10.00 Value

Enjoy one complimentary LUNCH OR DINNER ENTREE when a second LUNCH OR DINNER ENTREE of equal or greater value is purchased.

valid anytime

B438

Offer validity is governed by the Rules of Use and excludes defined holidays. Offers are not valid with other discount offers, unless specified.

Valid now thru November 1, 2007

RAZ'S CAFE

- Gourmet coffee drinks
- Ice cream
- Soups
- Sandwiches
- Pastries
- Bulk coffee
- Teas
- Smoothies
- Italian soda
- Credit cards accepted

1049 B West Hwy. 96
Shoreview, MN
(651)766-6965

00672034

RESTAURANTE GUAYAQUIL

- Delicious Ecuadorian dishes, great service right in the heart of Minneapolis
- Authentic lunch & dinner menu
- Variety of breakfast entrees - some authentic, some not, but all are good!

1526 E. Lake St.
(Corner of Bloomington & Lake)
Minneapolis, MN
(612)722-2346

00568808

Riverside RESTAURANT

- Somalian, Arabian & American cuisine
- Buffet daily 11 a.m.-4 p.m.

329 Cedar Ave. S.
Minneapolis, MN
(612)332-4555

00653408

Rand Deli Catering

- A wide variety of sandwiches & salads made fresh daily
- Homemade soups
- Hot sandwiches & other items
- Scones made from scratch everyday

527 Marquette Ave., #205
(Rand Tower, Skyway level)
Minneapolis, MN
(612)333-6425

00633435

THE RED PEPPER
Chinese Restaurant

- Specializing in Szechuan & Hunan cuisine
- Try our Hong Kong Steak, Crispy Walleye & Szechuan Duck in Plum Sauce

187 Cheshire Lane, Plymouth, MN
(763)404-1770
2902 W 66th St., Richfield, MN
(612)869-6817

00001138

Restaurante La Rancherita

- Authentic Mexican cuisine
- Everything made to order
- Join us for "Seafood Weekends"

100 S. 7th Ave.
South St. Paul, MN
(651)455-1714

00696303

Rocky Rococo Pizza and Pasta

ONE REGULAR SLICE & MEDIUM DRINK

Enjoy ONE REGULAR SLICE & MEDIUM DRINK when a second REGULAR SLICE & MEDIUM DRINK of equal or greater value is purchased.

valid anytime
Tipping should be 15% to 20% of TOTAL bill before discount

B439

Offer validity is governed by the Rules of Use and excludes defined holidays. Offers are not valid with other discount offers, unless specified.

Valid now thru November 1, 2007

Rose Garden
CHINESE-VIETNAMESE RESTAURANT

Up To $10.00 Value

Enjoy one complimentary LUNCH OR DINNER ENTREE when a second LUNCH OR DINNER ENTREE of equal or greater value is purchased.

valid anytime
Tipping should be 15% to 20% of TOTAL bill before discount

B440

Offer validity is governed by the Rules of Use and excludes defined holidays. Offers are not valid with other discount offers, unless specified.

Valid now thru November 1, 2007

Scandia Bake Shop

Up To $5.00 Value

www.scandiabakeshop.com

Enjoy any BAKED GOODS ORDER at 50% off the regular price - maximum discount $5.00.

valid anytime

B441

Offer validity is governed by the Rules of Use and excludes defined holidays. Offers are not valid with other discount offers, unless specified.

Valid now thru November 1, 2007

SCOREBOARD PIZZA

Up To $5.00 Value

Enjoy one complimentary MENU ITEM when a second MENU ITEM of equal or greater value is purchased or for those who prefer - any one pizza at 50% off the regular price.

Dine in only; Sorry, no delivery

valid anytime
Tipping should be 15% to 20% of TOTAL bill before discount

B442

Offer validity is governed by the Rules of Use and excludes defined holidays. Offers are not valid with other discount offers, unless specified.

Valid now thru November 1, 2007

2ND MOON COFFEE CAFE

Up To $5.00 Value

Enjoy one complimentary MENU ITEM when a second MENU ITEM of equal or greater value is purchased.

valid anytime

B443

Offer validity is governed by the Rules of Use and excludes defined holidays. Offers are not valid with other discount offers, unless specified.

Valid now thru November 1, 2007

Segue

Up To $5.00 Value

Taste and See...

www.seguecafe.com

Enjoy any BEVERAGE ORDER at 50% off the regular price.

valid anytime

B444

Offer validity is governed by the Rules of Use and excludes defined holidays. Offers are not valid with other discount offers, unless specified.

Valid now thru November 1, 2007

Rose Garden
CHINESE-VIETNAMESE RESTAURANT

- Delicious Chinese & Vietnamese dishes
- Pork, beef, chicken, seafood & vegetarian available
- Open daily

714 Hwy. 55
Medina, MN
(763)478-8044

00579848

Rocky Rococo
PIZZA AND PASTA

- Every one of Rocky's Award-Winning Pan-Style pizza is prepared with Amore
- 3 separate dough rises for each pizza gives you the biggest, tastiest pizza in town
- Plus, Rocky's rectangular pan pizza doesn't cut corners, so it's 20% bigger than conventional round pizzas!

7540 Brooklyn Blvd.
Brooklyn Park, MN
(763)560-5451

00472405

SCOREBOARD PIZZA

- Cold beer, sandwiches, broasted chicken
- Come & watch your favorite sports event or game on our TV's
- Family neighborhood hot spot! Open 7 days a week

6816 Humboldt Ave N
Brooklyn Center, MN
(763)566-4455

00002279

Scandia Bake Shop

- Quality & taste since 1951
- Scandinavian specialties include Marzipan tortes & Kvansa cakes
- We also feature donuts, danishes, coffee cakes & gourmet coffee
- New items include sandwiches & soups
- Try our fabulous wedding cakes such as chocolate marble white cake or butter cream made with real butter

5011 34th Ave. S.
Minneapolis, MN
(612)724-8353

00631850

Segue
Taste and See...

- Gourmet espresso & coffee
- Live music on weekends
- Soups & sandwiches
- Casual, relaxed atmosphere
- Taste & see...Psalm 34:8

11271 96th Ave. N.
(Zachary Sq. Mall just off County Rd. 81 & Zachary Ln.)
Maple Grove, MN
(763)424-3940

00579936

2ND MOON COFFEE CAFE

- Smoke-free
- Open everyday including holidays
- Tea, wide variety of coffee, bulk beans
- Pastries, sandwiches
- Ice cream novelties

2225 E Franklin
Minneapolis, MN
(612)343-4255

00414396

Shaw's
BAR & GRILL

Up To **$6.00** Value

Enjoy one complimentary MENU ITEM when a second MENU ITEM of equal or greater value is purchased.

valid anytime

B445

Offer validity is governed by the Rules of Use and excludes defined holidays. Offers are not valid with other discount offers, unless specified.

Valid now thru November 1, 2007

Shell's Café

Up To **$6.00** Value

Enjoy one complimentary MENU ITEM when a second MENU ITEM of equal or greater value is purchased.

valid anytime

B446

Offer validity is governed by the Rules of Use and excludes defined holidays. Offers are not valid with other discount offers, unless specified.

Valid now thru November 1, 2007

Shooters
Billiard Parlor, Café & Pro-shop

Up To **$9.00** Value

www.shootersbilliardclub.com

Enjoy one complimentary LUNCH OR DINNER ENTREE when a second LUNCH OR DINNER ENTREE of equal or greater value is purchased.

valid anytime
Tipping should be 15% to 20% of TOTAL bill before discount

B447

Offer validity is governed by the Rules of Use and excludes defined holidays. Offers are not valid with other discount offers, unless specified.

Valid now thru November 1, 2007

Sindbad

Up To **$10.00** Value

Enjoy one complimentary LUNCH OR DINNER ENTREE when a second LUNCH OR DINNER ENTREE of equal or greater value is purchased.

valid anytime

B448

Offer validity is governed by the Rules of Use and excludes defined holidays. Offers are not valid with other discount offers, unless specified.

Valid now thru November 1, 2007

Smooth Grind
SMOOTHIES • COFFEE • TEA

Up To **$6.00** Value

www.smoothgrind.com

Enjoy one complimentary MENU ITEM when a second MENU ITEM of equal or greater value is purchased.

valid anytime

B449

Offer validity is governed by the Rules of Use and excludes defined holidays. Offers are not valid with other discount offers, unless specified.

Valid now thru November 1, 2007

Snelling Cafe
Cafe & Deli

Up To **$5.00** Value

Enjoy one complimentary MENU ITEM when a second MENU ITEM of equal or greater value is purchased.

valid anytime

B450

Offer validity is governed by the Rules of Use and excludes defined holidays. Offers are not valid with other discount offers, unless specified.

Valid now thru November 1, 2007

Shell's Café

- Boxed lunches
- From burgers to melts to specialty sandwiches-made to order
- Assorted salads
- Jumbo cookies & ice cream
- Breakfast & lunch

1550 American Blvd.
(U.S. Bank Mortgage Building)
Bloomington, MN
(952)854-3382

00615522

Shaw's
BAR & GRILL

- "Home of the Shaw Burger"
- Dine in or take-out
- Open daily 10 a.m. - 1 a.m.
- Full service menu 11 a.m. - 10 p.m.
- Live music Wednesday - Sunday
- Happy Hour 3-7, 7 days a week
- 1/2 price appetizers & dollar off drinks

1528 University
(16th & University in Northeast)
Minneapolis, MN
(612)781-4405

00516622

Sinbad

- Located between 25th & 26th on Nicollet Ave., S.
- Specializing in Mediterranean and Middle Eastern cuisine
- Be sure to check out our complete line of Middle Eastern groceries, bulk foods and Arabic newspapers & magazines too!

2528 Nicollet Ave. S
Minneapolis, MN
(612)871-6505

00276050

Shooters
Billiard Parlor, Café & Pro-shop

- 57-table billiard parlor
- Full menu cafe - open late nights
- Billiard pro-shop with over 600 cues
- Billiard parlor hours: 10am-6am
- Ladies Night every Monday

1934 E. Hwy. 13
(Hwy. 13 & Cliff Rd.)
Burnsville, MN
(952)894-1100

00466277

Snelling Cafe
Cafe & Deli

- Gourmet coffees
- Sandwiches
- Baked goods
- Smoothies
- Juices
- Billiards & foosball

638 Snelling Ave. N.
St. Paul, MN
(651)644-1933

00672918

Smooth Grind

- Certified fair trade coffees - locally roasted
- Espresso bar, gourmet coffees & teas
- Smoothies
- Soups, salads & sandwiches
- Pastries, scones & muffins
- Unique local art & gift items

2723 Lexington Ave.
(1 block N. of County Rd. C on Lexington)
Roseville, MN
(651)490-0490

00523440

Soho Cafe

Up To $5.00 Value

Enjoy one complimentary MENU ITEM when a second MENU ITEM of equal or greater value is purchased.

valid anytime

B451

Offer validity is governed by the Rules of Use and excludes defined holidays. Offers are not valid with other discount offers, unless specified.

Valid now thru November 1, 2007

Sojourner's Café

Up To $5.00 Value

Enjoy any FOOD/BEVERAGE ORDER at 50% off the regular price.

valid anytime

B452

Offer validity is governed by the Rules of Use and excludes defined holidays. Offers are not valid with other discount offers, unless specified.

Valid now thru November 1, 2007

Sojourner's Café

Up To $5.00 Value

Enjoy any FOOD/BEVERAGE ORDER at 50% off the regular price.

valid anytime

B453

Offer validity is governed by the Rules of Use and excludes defined holidays. Offers are not valid with other discount offers, unless specified.

Valid now thru November 1, 2007

Square Peg Diner

Up To $7.00 Value

www.squarepegdiner.com

Enjoy one complimentary ENTREE when a second ENTREE of equal or greater value is purchased.

Dine in only

valid anytime
Tipping should be 15% to 20% of TOTAL bill before discount

B454

Offer validity is governed by the Rules of Use and excludes defined holidays. Offers are not valid with other discount offers, unless specified.

Valid now thru November 1, 2007

Saint Paul Bagelry

Up To $6.00 Value

Enjoy one complimentary MENU ITEM when a second MENU ITEM of equal or greater value is purchased.

valid anytime

B455

Offer validity is governed by the Rules of Use and excludes defined holidays. Offers are not valid with other discount offers, unless specified.

Valid now thru November 1, 2007

State of Bean Coffeehouse

Up To $5.00 Value

Enjoy one complimentary MENU ITEM when a second MENU ITEM of equal or greater value is purchased.

valid anytime

B456

Offer validity is governed by the Rules of Use and excludes defined holidays. Offers are not valid with other discount offers, unless specified.

Valid now thru November 1, 2007

Sojourner's Café

- Christian Coffee Shop
- Espresso
- Cappuccino
- Koinonia
- A resting place for the weary soul

1406 White Bear Ave.
St. Paul, MN
(651) 771-9614

00396364

Soho Cafe

- Pizza by the slice
- Chicken wings
- Stromboli, calzones & pasta
- Salads
- Hot hoagies & pita sandwiches
- Delicious gyros

2532 S. Hennepin Ave.
Minneapolis, MN
(612) 377-7996

00582420

Square Peg Diner

- Casual breakfast & lunch
- Breakfast served all day
- Burgers & sandwiches
- Catering available from coffee & snacks to full dinners

2021 E. Hennepin Ave.
(2 blocks E. of Stinson)
Minneapolis, MN
(612) 378-0855

00575462

Sojourner's Café

- Christian Coffee Shop
- Espresso
- Cappuccino
- Koinonia
- A resting place for the weary soul

1406 White Bear Ave.
St. Paul, MN
(651) 771-9614

00396364

State of Bean Coffeehouse

- Gourmet espresso drinks
- Soups & baked good
- Fresh roasted coffee beans to order
- Smoothies & our signature "Ice-blended Bean Freeze"
- Pick up our 3/4 gallon coffee to go!

1573 154th Ave. #101
Andover, MN
(763) 434-2326

00634828

Saint Paul Bagelry

- Deli sandwiches
- Breakfast sandwiches all day
- Soups
- All bagels & cream cheese made fresh each day
- Fresh ground coffee & espresso drinks
- Fruit smoothies
- Catering menu available
- Senior & student discounts

1702 N. Lexington Ave.
(Larpenteur & Lexington in Lexington Plaza)
Roseville, MN
(651) 488-1700

00652235

entertainment.com Up To $11.00 Value

Sun Ray Restaurant

Enjoy one complimentary LUNCH OR DINNER ENTREE when a second LUNCH OR DINNER ENTREE of equal or greater value is purchased.

valid anytime

Tipping should be 15% to 20% of TOTAL bill before discount

B457

Offer validity is governed by the Rules of Use and excludes defined holidays. Offers are not valid with other discount offers, unless specified.

Valid now thru November 1, 2007

---

entertainment.com 50% OFF

Sweet Taste of Italy

www.sweettasteofitaly.com
Enjoy any one PIZZA at 50% off the regular price.

valid anytime

B458

Offer validity is governed by the Rules of Use and excludes defined holidays. Offers are not valid with other discount offers, unless specified.

Valid now thru November 1, 2007

---

entertainment.com Up To $5.00 Value

Sweet Taste of Italy

www.sweettasteofitaly.com
Enjoy one complimentary MENU ITEM when a second MENU ITEM of equal or greater value is purchased.

Specials excluded

valid anytime

B459

Offer validity is governed by the Rules of Use and excludes defined holidays. Offers are not valid with other discount offers, unless specified.

Valid now thru November 1, 2007

---

entertainment.com FREE PIZZA

Sweet Taste of Italy

www.sweettasteofitaly.com
Enjoy any one complimentary PIZZA when a second PIZZA of equal or greater value is purchased.

valid anytime

B460

Offer validity is governed by the Rules of Use and excludes defined holidays. Offers are not valid with other discount offers, unless specified.

Valid now thru November 1, 2007

---

entertainment.com Up To $7.00 Value

Taco Logo
Authentic Mexican Fast Food

Enjoy one complimentary MENU ITEM when a second MENU ITEM of equal or greater value is purchased.

valid anytime

B461

Offer validity is governed by the Rules of Use and excludes defined holidays. Offers are not valid with other discount offers, unless specified.

Valid now thru November 1, 2007

---

entertainment.com Up To $5.00 Value

tacoville

Enjoy one complimentary MENU ITEM when a second MENU ITEM of equal or greater value is purchased.

valid anytime

B462

Offer validity is governed by the Rules of Use and excludes defined holidays. Offers are not valid with other discount offers, unless specified.

Valid now thru November 1, 2007

Sweet Taste of Italy

- "American Twist on Italian Favorites"
- Spaghetti, lasagna, ravioli, gondolas & more...
- Dine in, carry out & catering

9576 Noble Parkway, Brooklyn Park, MN
(763)493-4733

6023 42nd Ave. N., Crystal, MN
(763)533-6554

Coupons void if purchased, sold or bartered.
Discounts exclude tax, tip and/or alcohol, where applicable.

00581298

Sun Ray Restaurant

128 W. Lake St.
Minneapolis, MN
(612)823-1127

Coupons void if purchased, sold or bartered.
Discounts exclude tax, tip and/or alcohol, where applicable.

00685725

Sweet Taste of Italy

- "American Twist on Italian Favorites"
- Spaghetti, lasagna, ravioli, gondolas & more...
- Dine in, carry out & catering

9576 Noble Parkway, Brooklyn Park, MN
(763)493-4733

6023 42nd Ave. N., Crystal, MN
(763)533-6554

Coupons void if purchased, sold or bartered.
Discounts exclude tax, tip and/or alcohol, where applicable.

00580928

Sweet Taste of Italy

- "American Twist on Italian Favorites"
- Spaghetti, lasagna, ravioli, gondolas & more...
- Dine in, carry out & catering

9576 Noble Parkway, Brooklyn Park, MN
(763)493-4733

6023 42nd Ave. N., Crystal, MN
(763)533-6554

Coupons void if purchased, sold or bartered.
Discounts exclude tax, tip and/or alcohol, where applicable.

00515684

---

tacoville

- Located on I-35 & Hwy 70 behind the Lakeville McStop
- The Home of the Lakeville Taco

11276 210th Street W
Lakeville, MN
(952)469-1913

Coupons void if purchased, sold or bartered.
Discounts exclude tax, tip and/or alcohol, where applicable.

00000124

Taco Loco
Authentic Mexican Fast Food

- Tacos, burritos & tortas
- Side orders
- Jarritos
- Desserts
- Party meals available

835 1st Ave. W.
Shakopee, MN
(952)445-5055

Coupons void if purchased, sold or bartered.
Discounts exclude tax, tip and/or alcohol, where applicable.

00607780

Taraccino Coffee

Up To $5.00 Value

www.taracinnocoffee.com

Enjoy one complimentary MENU ITEM when a second MENU ITEM of equal or greater value is purchased.

valid anytime

Excludes gelato & Black Cat products

B463

Offer validity is governed by the Rules of Use and excludes defined holidays. Offers are not valid with other discount offers, unless specified.

Valid now thru November 1, 2007

The Mock Turtle
Bits of Britain & Fine Teas

Up To $5.00 Value

Enjoy one complimentary MENU ITEM when a second MENU ITEM of equal or greater value is purchased.

valid anytime

B464

Offer validity is governed by the Rules of Use and excludes defined holidays. Offers are not valid with other discount offers, unless specified.

Valid now thru November 1, 2007

Tokyo Express
Japanese Restaurant

Up To $9.00 Value

Enjoy one complimentary DINNER ENTREE when a second DINNER ENTREE of equal or greater value is purchased.

Specials excluded; Dine in only

valid any evening

B465

Offer validity is governed by the Rules of Use and excludes defined holidays. Offers are not valid with other discount offers, unless specified.

Valid now thru November 1, 2007

Tortilla Ria Mexican Cafe

Up To $6.00 Value

Enjoy one complimentary MENU ITEM when a second MENU ITEM of equal or greater value is purchased.

valid anytime

Valid at Bloomington location only

B466

Offer validity is governed by the Rules of Use and excludes defined holidays. Offers are not valid with other discount offers, unless specified.

Valid now thru November 1, 2007

Twisted Shamrock Pub & Grill

Up To $9.00 Value

www.twistedshamrock.com

Enjoy one complimentary DINNER ENTREE when a second DINNER ENTREE of equal or greater value is purchased.

Dine in only; Specials excluded

valid any evening

Tipping should be 15% to 20% of TOTAL bill before discount

B467

Offer validity is governed by the Rules of Use and excludes defined holidays. Offers are not valid with other discount offers, unless specified.

Valid now thru November 1, 2007

UBAH Restaurant

Up To $8.00 Value

Enjoy one complimentary ENTREE when a second ENTREE of equal or greater value is purchased.

valid anytime

B468

Offer validity is governed by the Rules of Use and excludes defined holidays. Offers are not valid with other discount offers, unless specified.

Valid now thru November 1, 2007

The MOCK TURTLE
BITS OF BRITAIN & FINE TEAS

- Fine teas
- Pots of tea or cups to go
- Food & retail items from Great Britain: cheeses, chocolates, scones & desserts & biscuits (cookies)
- Tea pots & tea paraphernalia
- Teapot warmers, infusers & the like
- Real Double Devon cream
- Jams & jellies

**220 Division St.
Northfield, MN
(507) 664-9680**

00586058

Taraccino Coffee

- "The way neighborhood coffee should be..."
- Home of Nord East Mud
- Our own roasted beans!
- Featuring Caruso's Gelato
- On site baking
- Non-smoking
- Wireless internet access
- Delicious smoothies

**224 E. Hennepin Ave.
Minneapolis, MN
(612) 617-0292**

00549027

TORTILLA RIA MEXICAN CAFE

- Come for lunch or dinner
- Open daily
- Happy Hour 3-6 p.m.
- Full Mexican menu
- Beverages & tap beer

**7909 Southtown Ctr.
(between Applebee's & Kohl's)
Bloomington, MN
(952) 881-7004**

00546808

TOKYO EXPRESS
Japanese Restaurant

- Open daily
- Authentic Japanese cuisine
- All dishes made to order
- Vegetarian choices
- Drive thru available for pickup
- No MSG

**5205 Shoreline Dr.
(Next to Stonegate Plaza)
Mound, MN
(952) 472-5999**

00683954

UBAH RESTAURANT

- East African & American cuisine
- Breakfast, lunch & dinner

**411 Cedar Ave. S.
Minneapolis, MN
(612) 333-9119**

00654875

Twisted Shamrock Pub & Grill

- Casual dining
- Full bar
- Pool table, darts, foosball
- 3 Rental halls
- Banquets, weddings, business meetings, special occasions & holiday parties
- Live entertainment on the weekends

**4947 W. Broadway
(N.E. of County Rd. 81 & Hwy. 100)
Crystal, MN
(763) 537-5576**

00692583

entertainment
entertainment.com

Up To **$7⁰⁰** Value

The Valley Sports Pub & Grill
Eagan, Mn

Enjoy one complimentary LUNCH OR DINNER ENTREE when a second LUNCH OR DINNER ENTREE of equal or greater value is purchased.

valid anytime

B469

Offer validity is governed by the Rules of Use and excludes defined holidays. Offers are not valid with other discount offers, unless specified.

Valid now thru November 1, 2007

---

entertainment
entertainment.com

Up To **$9⁰⁰** Value

Vientiane Restaurant

Enjoy one complimentary DINNER ENTREE when a second DINNER ENTREE of equal or greater value is purchased.

Dine in only

valid any evening
Tipping should be 15% to 20% of TOTAL bill before discount

B470

Offer validity is governed by the Rules of Use and excludes defined holidays. Offers are not valid with other discount offers, unless specified.

Valid now thru November 1, 2007

---

entertainment
entertainment.com

Up To **$7⁰⁰** Value

Villa Roma Pizzaria

Enjoy any one PIZZA at 50% off the regular price.

Specials excluded; Delivery excluded

valid anytime

B471

Offer validity is governed by the Rules of Use and excludes defined holidays. Offers are not valid with other discount offers, unless specified.

Valid now thru November 1, 2007

---

entertainment
entertainment.com

Up To **$8⁰⁰** Value

Village Blend
A taste of community.

www.villageblend.com

Enjoy one complimentary MENU ITEM when a second MENU ITEM of equal or greater value is purchased.

valid anytime

B472

Offer validity is governed by the Rules of Use and excludes defined holidays. Offers are not valid with other discount offers, unless specified.

Valid now thru November 1, 2007

---

entertainment
entertainment.com

Up To **$5⁰⁰** Value

Wabasha Deli & Cafe

Enjoy one complimentary MENU ITEM when a second MENU ITEM of equal or greater value is purchased.

valid anytime

B473

Offer validity is governed by the Rules of Use and excludes defined holidays. Offers are not valid with other discount offers, unless specified.

Valid now thru November 1, 2007

---

entertainment
entertainment.com

Up To **$8⁰⁰** Value

Waberi Somalian Restaurant

Enjoy one complimentary LUNCH OR DINNER ENTREE when a second LUNCH OR DINNER ENTREE of equal or greater value is purchased.

valid anytime
Tipping should be 15% to 20% of TOTAL bill before discount

B474

Offer validity is governed by the Rules of Use and excludes defined holidays. Offers are not valid with other discount offers, unless specified.

Valid now thru November 1, 2007

Vientiane Restaurant

- Chinese, Thai & Lao cuisine

5600 Bass Lake Rd.
Crystal, MN
(763) 537-5575

00580870

Valet

- Brats, burgers, coneys & tacos
- Sandwiches, soups & salads
- Play a game of pool or Golden Tee

3385 Sibley Memorial Hwy.
Eagan, MN
(651) 454-2760

00594716

Village Blend
A taste of community.

- A taste of community
- Coffee & wine cafe
- Soups, wraps, sandwiches & salads
- Gourmet pizzas
- Desserts & pastries
- Live music
- Broadband internet & wireless

2900 Pentagon Blvd.
(Located in St. Anthony Shopping Ctr. off Hwy. 88)
Minneapolis, MN
(612) 781-7940

00575598

Villa Roma Pizzaria

- Gourmet pizzas with over 20 topping choices
- Sandwiches, calzones, pizzas and more
- All made fresh with our delicious homemade sauce

603 W. 7th St.
St. Paul, MN
(651) 228-9319

00493369

Waberi Somalian Restaurant

- Authentic Somalian food
- Spaghetti & rice
- Chicken & steak
- Sambusa - delicious beef & onion in a wrap
- Keykey is another tasty choice for your meal
- Try some kackac for dessert

3205 Cedar Ave. S.
Minneapolis, MN
(612) 722-5505

00631846

Wabasha Deli & Cafe

- Full breakfast menu including: pancakes, omelets, french toast, specialty breakfast & sandwiches
- Lunch service
- Hot & cold sandwiches
- Delicious soups & salads

32 E. Fillmore Ave.
St. Paul, MN
(651) 291-8868

00573392

Waldo's Bar & Grill

Up To $5.00 Value

Enjoy one complimentary MENU ITEM when a second MENU ITEM of equal or greater value is purchased.

valid anytime

B475

Offer validity is governed by the Rules of Use and excludes defined holidays. Offers are not valid with other discount offers, unless specified.

West Side Lanes

Up To $5.00 Value

www.westsidelanes.com

Enjoy one complimentary MENU ITEM when a second MENU ITEM of equal or greater value is purchased or when dining alone - one MENU ITEM at 50% off the regular price - maximum discount $3.00.

valid anytime
Tipping should be 15% to 20% of TOTAL bill before discount

B476

Offer validity is governed by the Rules of Use and excludes defined holidays. Offers are not valid with other discount offers, unless specified.

Wing Joint

Up To $7.00 Value

Enjoy one complimentary MENU ITEM when a second MENU ITEM of equal or greater value is purchased.

Specials excluded

valid anytime

B477

Offer validity is governed by the Rules of Use and excludes defined holidays. Offers are not valid with other discount offers, unless specified.

YARN CAFE

Up To $6.00 Value

www.yarn-cafe.com

Enjoy one complimentary MENU ITEM when a second MENU ITEM of equal or greater value is purchased.

valid anytime

B478

Offer validity is governed by the Rules of Use and excludes defined holidays. Offers are not valid with other discount offers, unless specified.

Zebra Pizza & Tacos

FREE PIZZA

www.zebrapizza.com

Enjoy any one complimentary PIZZA when a second PIZZA of equal or greater value is purchased.

valid anytime

B479

Offer validity is governed by the Rules of Use and excludes defined holidays. Offers are not valid with other discount offers, unless specified.

Zuppa Cucina

Gourmet Soups, Salads and Sandwiches

Up To $7.00 Value

Enjoy one complimentary MENU ITEM when a second MENU ITEM of equal or greater value is purchased.

valid anytime

B480

Offer validity is governed by the Rules of Use and excludes defined holidays. Offers are not valid with other discount offers, unless specified.

West Side Lanes

- Appetizers, soups, salads, sandwiches & burgers
- Bowling birthday parties & special event parties
- Banquet hall rental for birthdays, weddings, anniversary or company parties
- NTN Trivia & QBI available in the Lounge

1625 S. Robert St.
W. St. Paul, MN
(651) 451-6222

00143504

Waldo's Bar & Grill

4601 Lyndale Ave. N.
Minneapolis, MN
(612) 522-9840

00515699

YARN CAFE

- Gourmet coffee & espresso
- Pastries & fabulous truffles
- Salads & sandwiches
- Gourmet cheeses
- Beer & wine
- Largest yarn selection around!
- Knitting groups & classes
- Knit by the fire enjoying coffee, wine & great company

12688 Bass Lake Rd.
(494 & Bass Lake Rd.)
Maple Grove, MN
(763) 478-2899

00652126

Wing Joint

- Seasoned chicken wings
- Smoked hickory ribs
- Great selections of appetizers
- Broasted chicken
- Buffalo "hot" wings
- Burgers
- Old fashioned malts

10603 University NE
(across from Walgreens)
Blaine, MN
(763) 755-3735

00634817

Zuppa Cucina
Gourmet Soups, Salads and Sandwiches

- Gourmet soups, salads & sandwiches
- Wraps
- Gourmet pizzas

1667 E. 17th Ave., Ste. 104
Shakopee, MN
(952) 445-3737

00522937

Zebra Pizza & Tacos

- Family owned & operated
- Honor competitor coupons
- Wings, tacos, nachos, & more
- Dessert pizza

2110 Northdale Blvd. N.W.,
Coon Rapids, MN
(763) 755-0590

14031 St. Francis Blvd., Ramsey, MN
(763) 323-7303

00573301

Boston's
THE GOURMET PIZZA
RESTAURANT & SPORTS BAR

Valid now thru November 1, 2007 — Up To $8.00 Value

Boston's
THE GOURMET PIZZA
RESTAURANT & SPORTS BAR

Free Appetizer or Dessert with the purchase of 2 entrees.

One offer per party, per visit

valid anytime

See reverse side for details

B481

Valid now thru November 1, 2007 — Up To $8.00 Value

Boston's
THE GOURMET PIZZA
RESTAURANT & SPORTS BAR

Free Appetizer or Dessert with the purchase of 2 entrees.

One offer per party, per visit

valid anytime

See reverse side for details

B482

Valid now thru November 1, 2007 — Up To $10.00 Value

Boston's
THE GOURMET PIZZA
RESTAURANT & SPORTS BAR

Enjoy $10 off with a minimum purchase of forty dollars (excluding tax, tip, and alcoholic beverages).

One offer per party, per visit

valid anytime

See reverse side for details

B483

Valid now thru November 1, 2007 — Up To $5.00 Value

Boston's
THE GOURMET PIZZA
RESTAURANT & SPORTS BAR

Enjoy $5 off with a minimum purchase of fifteen dollars (excluding tax, tip and alcoholic beverages).

One offer per party, per visit

valid anytime

See reverse side for details

B484

Boston's
THE GOURMET PIZZA
RESTAURANT & SPORTS BAR

Boston's
THE GOURMET PIZZA
RESTAURANT & SPORTS BAR

12794 Riverdale Blvd., Coon Rapids, MN
(763)421-2100
12109 Main St. W., Maple Grove, MN
(763)315-4334

Boston's
THE GOURMET PIZZA
RESTAURANT & SPORTS BAR

12794 Riverdale Blvd., Coon Rapids, MN
(763)421-2100
12109 Main St. W., Maple Grove, MN
(763)315-4334

Offer validity is governed by the Rules of Use and excludes defined holidays. Offers are not valid with other discount offers, unless specified. Coupons void if purchased, sold or bartered. Discounts exclude tax, tip and/or alcohol, where applicable.

Boston's
THE GOURMET PIZZA
RESTAURANT & SPORTS BAR

12794 Riverdale Blvd., Coon Rapids, MN
(763)421-2100
12109 Main St. W., Maple Grove, MN
(763)315-4334

Offer validity is governed by the Rules of Use and excludes defined holidays. Offers are not valid with other discount offers, unless specified. Coupons void if purchased, sold or bartered. Discounts exclude tax, tip and/or alcohol, where applicable.

Boston's
THE GOURMET PIZZA
RESTAURANT & SPORTS BAR

12794 Riverdale Blvd., Coon Rapids, MN
(763)421-2100
12109 Main St. W., Maple Grove, MN
(763)315-4334

Offer validity is governed by the Rules of Use and excludes defined holidays. Offers are not valid with other discount offers, unless specified. Coupons void if purchased, sold or bartered. Discounts exclude tax, tip and/or alcohol, where applicable.

Boston's
THE GOURMET PIZZA
RESTAURANT & SPORTS BAR

12794 Riverdale Blvd., Coon Rapids, MN
(763)421-2100
12109 Main St. W., Maple Grove, MN
(763)315-4334

Offer validity is governed by the Rules of Use and excludes defined holidays. Offers are not valid with other discount offers, unless specified. Coupons void if purchased, sold or bartered. Discounts exclude tax, tip and/or alcohol, where applicable.

entertainment.

BEEF 'O' BRADY'S
Est. 1985
Family Sports Pubs

$5 off $15

813 Marketplace Dr.
Waconia, MN
(952)442-8767

✂ Please remove certificate and present before bill is totaled.

Valid now thru November 1, 2007
See reverse side for details

$5.00 VALUE

Enjoy $5 off with a minimum purchase of fifteen dollars (excluding tax, tip and alcoholic beverages).
valid anytime
813 Marketplace Dr., Waconia, MN, (952)442-8767

Tipping should be 15% to 20% of TOTAL bill before discount

BEEF 'O' BRADY'S
Est. 1985
Family Sports Pubs

00703702

B485

Beef 'O' Brady's Family Sports Pub

BEEF'S STARTERS

Potato Skins 4.99
Loaded with flavor, our potato skins are topped with crisp, fried bacon and shredded cheddar-jack cheese. Served with sour cream.

New Queso Dip & Chips 3.99
Spicy Mexican cheese dip blended with seasoned beef, diced jalapeños and tomatoes. Served with crispy tortilla chips.

BURGERS

The 'O' Brady Burger 6.49
Our own special recipe. Seasoned with a unique blend of herbs and spices, topped with melted provolone cheese, and served with mayonnaise, lettuce, tomato, pickle and onion.

New Black & Bleu Burger 6.79
A "knockout" of a burger. Our seasoned Steak Burger is blackened and smothered in our creamy Bleu cheese, lettuce and tomato, then topped with fried onion rings.

'O' BRADY'S BASKETS

Wing Basket 7.29
Our famous Buffalo-style chicken wings accompanied with our tasty french fries & creamy cole slaw. Served with your choice of Jim's legendary Buffalo-style sauce, Honey BBQ, Garlic, Teriyaki or Caribbean Jerk.

Fish n' Chips 7.49
You'll fall for this hook, line and sinker. Delicious cod filets fried golden brown served with our tasty french fries, creamy cole slaw, lemon wedge and your choice of tartar sauce or malt vinegar.

SANDWICHES

Roast Beef Garlic Melt 6.99
So good, you won't want to share. Garlic bread topped with our premium roast beef, sliced onions, and provolone cheese. Served hot & pressed.

Watterson 6.79
Named after one of our *first* customers. You'll order this one again. Premium roast beef and Swiss on grilled rye with mayonnaise, lettuce, tomato, pickle and onion.

Menu Sampler - Prices and menu subject to change.

---

813 Marketplace Dr.
Waconia, MN
(952)442-8767

Beef 'O' Brady's Est. 1985
Family Sports Pubs

Name _____ Phone _____
Address _____
State _____ ZIP _____ Birthday _____ Anniversary _____
Email Address _____

Offer validity is governed by the Rules of Use and excludes defined holidays. Offers are not valid with other discount offers, unless specified. Coupons void if purchased, sold or bartered. Discounts exclude tax, tip and/or alcohol, where applicable.

DINING OUT

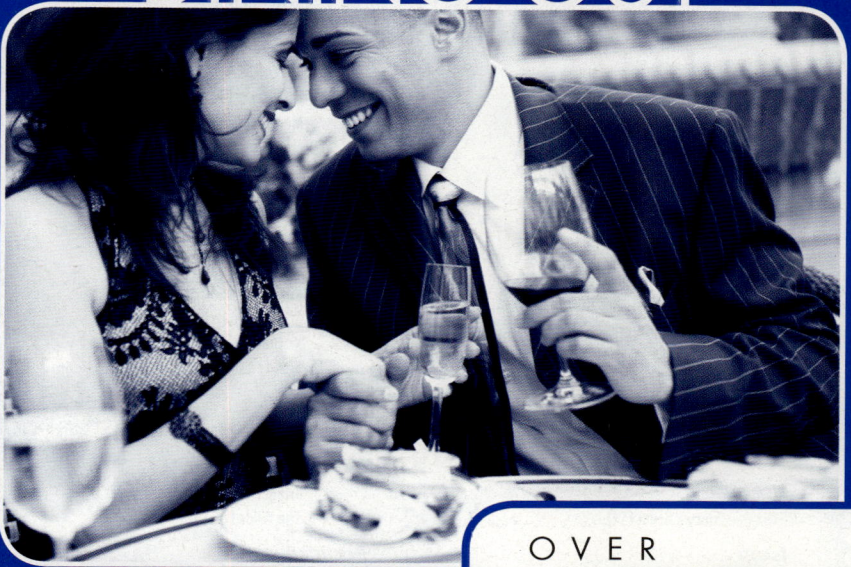

Find It Fast!
This section's index lists offers by neighborhood!

OVER **60** OFFERS

plus more at
www.entertainment.com/dine

CHECK OUT THESE FEATURED OFFERS IN THE FRONT OF THIS SECTION:

The Melting Pot — a fondue restaurant

Woody's Grille

KIKUGAWA AT RIVERPLACE

Tanners Steakhouse & Bar

jP american bistro

NaaR Grille — A New Twist in Mediterranean Cuisine

THE Woodbury BROILER BAR

Seasons RESTAURANT

Dining Out Index
(Card # is indicated in parentheses)

Minnesota

Afton
- Afton House Inn (74) C23

Andover
- NEW Tanners Steakhouse & Bar (30) C4

Burnsville
- Dakota County Steakhouse (80) C44

Champlin
- El Toro (121) C15

Chaska
- NEW Pine Street Grille (20) C39
- Playoffs Sports Bar & Grill (105) C40
- NEW Seasons Restaurant (19) C8

Eden Prairie
- NEW Naar (17) C6

Gaylord
- NEW Woody's Grille (23) C2

Hopkins
- Stacy's Grille (54) C26

Isanti
- Wintergreens (66) C42

Minneapolis
- America's Harvest (70) C58
- NEW Antoine's Creole Maison (21) C28
- Atlas Grill (7) C19
- Beach House Bar & Grille (116) C12
- Cafe Northstar (29) C29
- Chez Daniel Bistro (14) C30
- Cornell's (114) C43
- Creekside Cafe (37) C55
- NEW Crystal Bistro (40) C48
- da Afghan (77) C50
- Dashen Ethiopian
  Restaurant & Bar (87) C31
- El Azteca (27) C14
- NEW Elsie's Restaurant & Bar (51) C25
- Erte (18) C17
- Fridley Crab House (32) C13
- Harmony's (58) C33
- Hopscotch Grill (2) C11
- Jewel of India (120) C21
- jP American Bistro (43) C5
- Kikugawa at Riverplace (108) C3
- Kips An Authentic Irish
  Pub & Restaurant (12) C53
- Kokomo's Island Cafe (96) C10
- NEW Koyi Sushi (26) C35
- Little Tel-Aviv
  Cafe & Restaurant (46) C45
- Lombard's (34) C46
- MacTavish's (33) C49
- NEW Mairin's Table
  Neighborhood Bistro (49) C36
- NEW The Melting Pot (91) C1
- Nic's on Nicollet (13) C38
- Northern Shores (4) C22
- NEW Rix Bar & Grill (50) C59
- Rudolph's Bar-B-Que (16) C9
- St. Petersburg Restaurant
  and Vodka Bar (47) C41
- NEW Woody's Grille (23) C2

Osseo
- NEW Kay's Wine Bar & Bistro (15) C34

Prior Lake
- Trigger's (5) C18
- The Wilds Pub (57) C54

Rochester
- Grand Grill (68) C32
- Lord Essex Tavern (36) C56
- Shady Hill Grille (38) C57
- NEW Westfire Grille (52) C60

Saint Paul
- Carousel Restaurant (22) C24
- McGuires (45) C37
- Nickelby's Maplewood Grill (110) . . . C51
- NEW The Woodbury Broiler Bar (25) C7

Saint Paul Park
- Harborside Restaurant
  & Lounge (101) C20

Stillwater
- NEW Murasaki Japanese
  Restaurant (48) C16
- NEW Nacho Mama's (39) C47
- St. Croix Crab House
  Music Cafe (72) C52
- Water Street Inn (104) C27

NEW New Merchants Added This Year   **kids** Great Place for Kids!

Card No. 91

The Melting Pot
a fondue restaurant
www.meltingpot.com

REPEAT SAVINGS

Up To **$23.00** Value

The Melting Pot is the country's premier fondue restaurant. Here fondue transforms into a memorable dining experience where you can dip into something different.

*E*njoy one complimentary LUNCH OR DINNER ENTREE when a second LUNCH OR DINNER ENTREE of equal or greater value is purchased.

Friday & Saturday seating before 6 p.m. or after 9 p.m.

valid anytime

Reservations recommended

80 S. 9th St. (corner of 9th & Marquette), **Minneapolis, MN** (612)338-9900

00695719

The French Quarter — $20
Andouille sausage along with shrimp, choice tenderloin, and boneless breast of chicken, rolled in a Cajun spice blend.

Teriyaki Sirloin — $20
Teriyaki-marinated choice sirloin.

Breast of Chicken — $16
Boneless breast of chicken.

Shrimp & Sirloin — $20
Shrimp paired with teriyaki-marinated choice sirloin.

Twin Lobster Tails — Market Price
Two succulent lobster tails served with Garlic Dijon Butter.

The Vegetarian — $20
An array of fresh seasonal vegetables, tofu, artichoke hearts, Portobello mushrooms, and our own Spinach and Gorgonzola Ravioli.

Menu Sampler - Prices and menu subject to change.

Offer validity is governed by the Rules of Use and excludes defined holidays. Offers are not valid with other discount offers, unless specified. Coupons void if purchased, sold or bartered. Discounts exclude tax, tip and/or alcohol, where applicable. Tipping should be 15% to 20% of the total bill before discount.

C1

Card No. 23

Woody's Grille

REPEAT SAVINGS

Up To **$16.00** Value

*E*njoy one complimentary DINNER ENTREE when a second DINNER ENTREE of equal or greater value is purchased.

valid Sat.-Thurs. evenings

6399 City West Pkwy., Eden Prairie, MN (952)944-8799
220 Carlson Pkwy., Plymouth, MN (763)476-1011

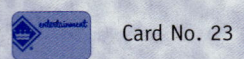

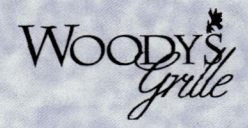

00694274

Woody's was named one of the "Best Neighborhood" restaurants in the Twin Cities. A popular gathering place for breakfast, lunch & dinner, Woody's is a casual restaurant in a soft, warm, yet energetic setting. It's distinctive menu is considered Ethnic-American. Our mission is to serve you good food & plenty of it - at a reasonable price.

Pasta

Fettuccine Fornello
Sautéed chicken breast, broccoli florets, portabella mushrooms, vine-ripened tomatoes and Old Smokehouse bacon tossed in a garlic cream sauce 15.45

Four-Cheese Pasta
Mozzarella, Jack, Cheddar and Pecorino Romano cheese sauce tossed with penne pasta 10.45 with Italian sausage 12.95

From The Grille

Chicken Forte
Pan-seared chicken breast topped with Black Forest ham, spinach, vine-ripened tomatoes, melted Swiss cheese and a mushroom Marsala wine sauce. Served with a fresh mozzarella tomato salad and grilled asparagus 17.45

Home-Style Meatloaf
Thick-sliced meatloaf, grilled and topped with sautéed buttered mushrooms and sweet onions. Served with sweet, roasted red pepper mashed potatoes, seasonal vegetables and gravy 15.45

Chicken Marsala
Lightly breaded chicken breast sautéed golden brown and served with roasted garlic mashed potatoes, seasonal vegetables and a mushroom Marsala wine sauce 15.45

Menu Sampler - Prices and menu subject to change.

Offer validity is governed by the Rules of Use and excludes defined holidays. Offers are not valid with other discount offers, unless specified. Coupons void if purchased, sold or bartered. Discounts exclude tax, tip and/or alcohol, where applicable. Tipping should be 15% to 20% of the total bill before discount.

C2

KIKUGAWA AT RIVERPLACE

Card No. 108

Up To $20.00 Value

Located in Riverplace just across the Mississippi from downtown Minneapolis, Kikugawa offers delicious Japanese cuisine. Our menu includes seafood, beef & chicken dishes expertly prepared. We have a fabulous sushi bar available as well. Enjoy full bar service & validated parking in the Riverplace ramp.

*E*njoy one complimentary DINNER ENTREE when a second DINNER ENTREE of equal or greater value is purchased.

valid Sunday thru Friday evenings

Friday seating before 6 p.m. or after 9 p.m.

43 Main St. (Riverplace), Minneapolis, MN
(612) 378-3006

00633273

TEMPURA AND YAKIMONO

Fantasy Tempura — 19.75
A combination of seafood, including shrimp and scallops, chicken and zesty beef with seasonal vegetables

Salmon Teriyaki — 18.50
Regal salmon basted with Kikugawa's tasty teriyaki sauce and broiled to perfection

NABEMONO-TABLE COOKERY

Yosenabe — 20.00
Shrimp, crab meat, clams, fresh fish, beef, chicken and select vegetables come together in all their flavors and subtle complexity in a superb Japanese "bouillabaisse"

Chicken Mizutaki — 17.50
The freshest chicken slices and vegetables cooked table-side in a light broth and served with dipping sauce. A light and healthy meal!

ENTREES

Vegetable Tempura — 12.50
A classic in Japanese cuisine. Fresh vegetables coated with a light batter

Yaki Niku — 17.50
Marinated, broiled beef and selected vegetables

Menu Sampler - Prices and menu subject to change.

Offer validity is governed by the Rules of Use and excludes defined holidays. Offers are not valid with other discount offers, unless specified. Coupons void if purchased, sold or bartered. Discounts exclude tax, tip and/or alcohol, where applicable. Tipping should be 15% to 20% of the total bill before discount.

Card No. 30

Tanners
Steakhouse & Bar

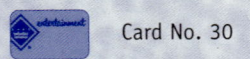

www.tannerssteakhouse.com

Up To $16.00 Value

*E*njoy one complimentary LUNCH OR DINNER ENTREE when a second LUNCH OR DINNER ENTREE of equal or greater value is purchased.

Specials excluded; Dine in only

valid anytime

13655 Martin St. (located just off Hwy. 10), Andover, MN
(763)767-1500

00700835

Join us in Andover & discover why Tanners Steakhouse has quickly become a local favorite. We offer a lively bar atmosphere or a cozy dining experience. Our extensive, from scratch, menu not only features Choice cut steaks, but also a unique variety of dishes. Our exclusive daily specials & exceptional, friendly service keep guests coming back time & time again.

FAMILY OWNED BRINGING YOU THE BEST OF THE BEST

PRIME RIB
(AFTER 4PM DAILY)
Seasoned, slow roasted, served with au jus.
Calf Cut - 12 ounce 15.99
Bull Cut - 18 ounce 19.99

TENDERLOIN FILET
An 8 ounce house cut Tenderloin Filet wrapped in bacon. This one will melt in your mouth! Market Price

TANNERS FAVORITES

CAJUN BLEU BEEF TIPS
Blackened beef tips and mushrooms topped with crumbled Maytag bleu cheese and broiled to perfection. Served with mashed potatoes and fresh sauteed vegetables. 13.99

HICKORY SMOKED RIBS
Our ribs are first rubbed with a blend of our own spices and cured. Then hickory smoked in house. Finally finished on the grill and basted with our signature BBQ sauce.
Full Rack Platter 18.99
Half Rack Platter 14.99

CHIPOTLE MEATLOAF
Traditional meatloaf with a spicy twist! Hearty homemade meatloaf served with mashed potatoes. Try it smothered with Chipotle ketchup brown sauce or with the sauce on the side. 10.99

FRESH SEAFOOD

ASIAN GLAZED SALMON
Grilled Atlantic salmon basted with an Asian sesame sauce. Served with teriyaki almond green beans and mashed potatoes. 16.99

SANDWICHES

PULLED PORK SANDWICH
Our pulled pork sandwich is simmered in a light barley beer for over 10 hours and mixed with our homemade BBQ sauce. Served on a homestyle bun. 7.99

Menu Sampler - Prices and menu subject to change.

Offer validity is governed by the Rules of Use and excludes defined holidays. Offers are not valid with other discount offers, unless specified. Coupons void if purchased, sold or bartered. Discounts exclude tax, tip and/or alcohol, where applicable. Tipping should be 15% to 20% of the total bill before discount.

jP american bistro

Card No. 43

Up To $29.00 Value

*E*njoy one complimentary DINNER ENTREE when a second DINNER ENTREE of equal or greater value is purchased.

valid Sunday-Friday

Reservations recommended

2937 Lyndale Ave. S., Minneapolis, MN (612)824-9300

00588250

Located in the Lyn-Lake area, jP is a charming bistro with an eclectic wine list & American menu grounded in French & Italian technique. An open kitchen & historic architecture create a memorable dining experience. Available for private gatherings is a 35-seat wine room, artfully designed. Voted one of the top 20 restaurants in the Twin Cities.

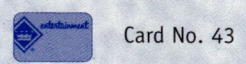

PIZZA WITH SAN MARZANO TOMATO SAUCE, BASIL AND HOUSE-MADE MOZZARELLA

BISTRO HOUSE SALAD WITH BABY GREENS, BALSAMIC VINAIGRETTE AND MANCHEGO

JP'S RUSTIC PIZZA WITH APPLEWOOD SMOKED BACON, CASHEW/CURRANT PESTO AND PECORINO-ROMANO

BISTRO CALAMARI WITH THAI DIPPING SAUCE

SEARED RARE SUSHI-GRADE TUNA MARINATED IN SWEET INDONESIAN SOY SAUCE ON YUKON GOLD POTATO PURÉE WITH ORGANIC BROCCOLI

HOUSE-MADE FETTUCINE TOSSED WITH BRAISED BERKSHIRE PORK, SWEET ONION CONFIT, TOMATO AND VACCHE-ROSSE PARMIGIANO

MEYER LEMON MASCARPONE TART IN A PISTACHIO CRUST WITH RASPBERRY SORBET

CARAMELIZED BANANA CREAM PIE

SONNY'S ICE CREAM AND SORBETS

Menu Sampler - Prices and menu subject to change.

Offer validity is governed by the Rules of Use and excludes defined holidays. Offers are not valid with other discount offers, unless specified. Coupons void if purchased, sold or bartered. Discounts exclude tax, tip and/or alcohol, where applicable. Tipping should be 15% to 20% of the total bill before discount.

NaaR Grille

A New Twist in Mediterranean Cuisine™

www.naargrille.com

At Naar Grille we pledge to provide you with superb service, unique, unforgettable & exciting entertainment. We want to earn your next visit by providing the best dining experience through guest service excellence. Our menu changes continuously with new dishes from the Mediterranean & other parts of the world.

Card No. 17

Up to $22.00 Value

REPEAT SAVINGS

*E*njoy one complimentary LUNCH OR DINNER ENTREE when a second LUNCH OR DINNER ENTREE of equal or greater value is purchased.

valid anytime

11528 Leona Rd., Eden Prairie, MN (952)946-6227

00690538

Entrees

NaaR-Kabobs - Signature NaaR favorite, including choice cuts of lamb, beef, shrimp, or chicken seasoned to perfection with a blend of Mediterranean spices, intricately skewered with vegetables including Portabella mushrooms; served with rice, Mediterranean salad and apricot pistachio sauce
Beef or Shrimp $20   Chicken or Lamb $20

Arugula Squash Ravioli - Pasta with a savory butternut and acorn squash center; served with roasted cauliflower sauce and sprinkled with toasted almonds, sautéed arugula and spinach. The flavors are especially appealing to the vegetarian palate $18

Gyro - Tender mixture of rotisserie beef and lamb pressed with herbs and spices, thinly sliced; served with vegetable skewers, rice and Mediterranean salad $16

Filet Mignon - Grilled 8 oz. tenderloin arranged with a signature blend of Mediterranean potatoes and mushrooms; paired with a flavorful classic ratatouille and scented with white truffles $30

Roasted Chicken Breast - Garlic and lemon chicken breast with fresh figs, coriander scented rice, and vegetable skewers; finished with lemon thyme sauce and flavorful chicken confit $18

Norwegian Salmon - Poached in herbs and extra virgin olive oil, laid on Moroccan couscous, and topped with a pepedew, garbanzo, and fava bean relish $18

Seafood Pasta - Hand rolled linguini tossed with pan-seared shrimp, scallops and lobster with pomodoro sauce. Finished with freshly grated Manchango cheese $22

Menu Sampler - Prices and menu subject to change.

Offer validity is governed by the Rules of Use and excludes defined holidays. Offers are not valid with other discount offers, unless specified. Coupons void if purchased, sold or bartered. Discounts exclude tax, tip and/or alcohol, where applicable. Tipping should be 15% to 20% of the total bill before discount.

THE Woodbury BROILER BAR

www.thebroilerbar.com

Card No. 25

Up To **$15.00** Value

$\mathcal{E}$njoy one complimentary DINNER ENTREE when a second DINNER ENTREE of equal or greater value is purchased.

valid any evening

9900 Valley Creek Rd. (Intersection of Valley Creek & Cty. Rd. 19), Woodbury, MN (651)578-8118

00695794

HOUSE DISHES

SOUTHWESTERN ENCHILADAS
Flour tortillas rolled with Shredded Chicken smothered with a Roasted Chipotle Pepper sauce and melted cheese. Served with Rice, beans, shredded lettuce, tomatoes and sour cream. $11.95

BROILER BAR SOUTHWESTERN FAJITAS
These are traditional Fajitas with the twist of Zucchini, Squash, Carrots with traditional peppers and onions.
Veggie $9.95   Chicken $12.95   Beef $12.95   Shrimp $14.95 and Combo $13.95

PASTA

CHIPOTLE CHICKEN ALFREDO
Spicy Cajun Grilled Chicken, sliced and served atop Fettuccine with our Creamy Chipotle Alfredo Sauce. We top the whole dish off with a dollop of Bearnaise Sauce. $13.95

TERIYAKI BROILED STEAK LO MEIN
A smooth blend of Teriyaki, Ginger, Garlic and Honey, Char Broiled to order and served on a generous portion of our Veggie Lo Mein. $14.95

BROILER BAR CHOPHOUSE SPECIALTIES

BROILER BAR SIGNATURE STEAK
12 oz Sirloin rubbed with House Recipe Seasonings and topped with Bearnaise Sauce, Grilled to Perfection and Served with a side of Our Creamy Fettucine Alfredo. $16.95

CLASSIC FILET MIGNON
Sixteen ounces of butter knife tenderness and mouth-watering flavor, done perfectly to your liking! Served with Bearnaise sauce and a side of our Bruschetta Tomato Linguini. $32.95

BROILER BAR PETITE FILET
An eight ounce portion of our Classic Filet Mignon. Served with Bernaise sauce and our Bruschetta Tomato Linguini. $20.95

HAND-CUT RIBEYE
Hand-Cut Ribeye, seasoned and Char Broiled. Topped with Caramelized Onions and our Bleu Cheese seasoned butter. Served with Garlic Mashed potatoes and Broiler Veggies $23.95

ROADHOUSE TWIN PORK CHOPS
Two Hearty Fire-Grilled Rib Chops seasoned with a special Cajun blend. Served with a side of French Fries and Broiler Veggies or Chipotle Alfredo. $16.95

Menu Sampler - Prices and menu subject to change.

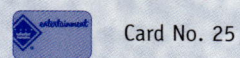

Offer validity is governed by the Rules of Use and excludes defined holidays. Offers are not valid with other discount offers, unless specified. Coupons void if purchased, sold or bartered. Discounts exclude tax, tip and/or alcohol, where applicable. Tipping should be 15% to 20% of the total bill before discount.

Seasons
RESTAURANT

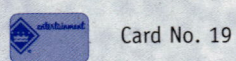

Card No. 19

Up To $34.00 Value

Seasons Restaurant features dramatic three-story windows overlooking Lake McKnight. Our chef prepares an array of composed salads, hors d'oeuvres, soup of the day & imported & domestic cheeses to accompany your entree. We strive to offer you a legendary dining experience with a variety of menu options & excellent service. Enjoy our outdoor patios seasonally.

Enjoy one complimentary ENTREE when a second ENTREE of equal or greater value is purchased.

Brunch included; Buffet included

valid anytime

Reservations required

1 Oak Ridge Dr., Chaska, MN (952)368-3100

00691375

Black Angus New York Strip Steak
Mushroom Ragout, Mashed Potatoes
$34.00

Cumin Smoked Ribs
Chitpotle Watermelon Bar B Que, Pickled Watermelon Salad, French Fries
$26.00

Pan Seared Crab Cake
Fresh Field Greens, Coleslaw, Saffron Rémoulade
$21.00

Halibut
Macadamia Crusted, Banana Butter, Wild Rice
$24.00

Butternut Squash and Roasted Wild Mushroom Ravioli
Tossed with Marinara Sauce, Fresh Spinach and Parmesan Cheese
$24.00

Menu Sampler - Prices and menu subject to change.

Offer validity is governed by the Rules of Use and excludes defined holidays. Offers are not valid with other discount offers, unless specified. Coupons void if purchased, sold or bartered. Discounts exclude tax, tip and/or alcohol, where applicable. Tipping should be 15% to 20% of the total bill before discount.

C8

RUDOLPHS
— Established 1975 —
www.rudolphsribs.com

Card No. 16

Up To $18.00 Value

Rudolph's has been the Twin Cities most honored bar-b-que producer for over 30 years. Their unrivaled spare ribs & distinctive cole slaw leave Rudy's loyal fans clamoring for more. No bones about it, whether it's spare ribs, baby backs or bar-b-que brisket, the scene at Rudolph's is legendary. Takeout & Rib Ticklin' Catering is available.

*E*njoy one complimentary LUNCH OR DINNER ENTREE when a second LUNCH OR DINNER ENTREE of equal or greater value is purchased.

Dine in only

valid anytime

For holidays-see Rules of Use; Not valid on carry-out

1933 Lyndale Ave. S. (Lyndale & Franklin), **Minneapolis, MN (612)871-8969**

00287736

Appetizers & Pizzas

Citizen Cornbread	Fresh baked topped with honey maple butter	$6
Dracula Wings	Bar-b-que spiced chicken wings seared on the broiler	$8
The Academy	One pound of smoked rib tips	$8
The Big Chill	Hummus, fiery feta cheese, red pepper hummus, kalamata olives and warm pita bread	$8
Some Like 'Em Hot Wings	Tossed in Buffalo sauce, bleu cheese dressing and celery or served plain	$9
Popeye	Spinach and artichoke dip with warm pita bread	$7
The Poseidon Adventure	Parmesan-crusted sea scallops, Sam Adams poached jumbo shrimp in a skillet	$10
Mystic Pizza	Black beans, corn, smoked chicken, mozzarella and cheddar cheese	$8
Hopalong Pizza	Bar-b-que chicken, smoked Gouda, red onion and bar-b-que sauce	$8

Entrees
Served with your choice of creamy cole slaw or salad

New York Strip Steak	Steak butter and onion strings with Idaho baked potato	$21
Tenderloin Medallions	Three medallions, garlic mashed potatoes and whiskey peppercorn sauce	$19
Ribeye	Grilled onions and mushrooms with Idaho baked potato	$22
Smoked Brisket	Slow smoked beef brisket with bar-b-que sauce. Served with garlic mashed potatoes	$13
Pecan Crusted Walleye	Pressed into a pecan-studded crumb and sautéed. Served with dirty rice	$17
Herb Crusted Chicken	Two breasts of chicken, mustard bar-b-que sauce with garlic mashed potatoes	$14
Kabobs	One scallop skewer, one jumbo shrimp skewer and one tenderloin medallion skewer. Served with dirty rice	$19
Pork Chops	Bar-b-que seasoned. Served with garlic mashed potatoes	$13
Smoked Lamb Chops	Braised cabbage. Served with garlic mashed potatoes	2 for $19 .... 3 for $27

Menu Sampler - Prices and menu subject to change.

Offer validity is governed by the Rules of Use and excludes defined holidays. Offers are not valid with other discount offers, unless specified. Coupons void if purchased, sold or bartered. Discounts exclude tax, tip and/or alcohol, where applicable. Tipping should be 15% to 20% of the total bill before discount.

Kokomo's Island Cafe

Card No. 96

REPEAT SAVINGS — Up To **$20.00** Value

Welcome to Kokomo's Island Cafe! Stroll through cascading palm canopies & playful waterfalls then indulge your taste buds as you choose from a tasty array of mouthwatering dishes. Our menu is a delightful tropical festival of flavors. Our party pavilion is available for private parties.

Enjoy one complimentary LUNCH OR DINNER ENTREE when a second LUNCH OR DINNER ENTREE of equal or greater value is purchased.

valid anytime

Mall of America, Bloomington, MN (952)698-3072

00623957

PASTA & NOODLES

Dragon Master's Golden Noodles — 11.95
Rich, spicy Coconut Curry Sauce tossed with linguine and peppers, broccoli, onion, garlic and fire-grilled chicken

Lime Fusion Shrimp — 15.95
Tender shrimp sautéed in Lime and Garlic Sauce, with sweet peppers, onion, snap peas and tossed with fettuccine

LANDLUBBERS ENTREES

Key West Lime Chicken — 15.95
Spicy, lime marinated, fire grilled, double chicken breast, served with Bahama Mama's Yams & Sugar Snap Peas

Black Pearl Ribs — 15.95
Jumbo bones, fire-grilled with teriyaki glaze, served with Bahama Mama Yams & Sugar Snap Peas

SEASIDE ENTREES

Surfin' Grilled Salmon — 16.95
Sizzlin' Atlantic Salmon topped with Red Pepper Sauce & served with Garlic Mashed Potatoes and Caribbean Succotash

Jerk Blackened Grouper — 13.95
Grouper seasoned with Cajun seasonings, pan-seared & lightly brushed with Pineapple Sweet & Sour Sauce, served over *Koko's* Crunchy Yellow Rice and Lava Black Beans

Castaway Tilapia — 15.95
Tilapia baked the "island way" in a banana leaf, with *Kokos* Crunchy Yellow Rice, vegetables, garlic & lime, served with Lava Black Beans

Paradise Shrimp Skewers — 18.95
Fire-grilled jumbo shrimp seasoned with *Tiki Dust*, served with Chimmichurri Sauce, *Koko's* Crunchy Yellow Rice & Sugar Snap Peas

Tiki-*Koko* Shrimp — 15.95
Jumbo shrimp, butterflied & fried with a coconut crust, Pineapple Sweet & Sour Sauce, Bahama Mama's Yams and Caribbean Corn Succotash

---

Menu Sampler - Prices and menu subject to change.

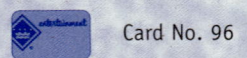

Offer validity is governed by the Rules of Use and excludes defined holidays. Offers are not valid with other discount offers, unless specified. Coupons void if purchased, sold or bartered. Discounts exclude tax, tip and/or alcohol, where applicable. Tipping should be 15% to 20% of the total bill before discount.

HOPSCOTCH GRILL
@ GAMEWORKS

Card No. 2

Up To $18.00 Value

*E*njoy one complimentary LUNCH OR DINNER ENTREE when a second LUNCH OR DINNER ENTREE of equal or greater value is purchased.

valid anytime

600 Hennepin Ave. Ste. 110 (Block E, downtown),
Minneapolis, MN (612)656-7300

00663380

Join us at the Hopscotch Grill in downtown Minneapolis' Block E. Savor a delicious New York strip or hand rubbed ribs. For lighter fare, choose from many sandwich favorites, pizza, pasta & burgers. Located inside Gameworks, we're an easy find that you'll be glad you discovered!

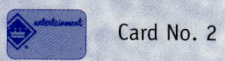

RIBS & SHRIMP COMBO
Our version of surf & turf! A half slab of our fabulous ribs teamed up with skewers of marinated shrimp • 17.99

♡ GRILLED CHICKEN BREAST
A fresh 10-oz. chicken breast seasoned to your liking and char-grilled for a great healthy choice • 10.99
Choose Your Flavor:
**House-Blend Lemon Pepper
Sweet and Spicy BBQ
Classic Teriyaki
Spicy Jerk**

FISH & CHIPS
A perfect comfort food choice! A generous plate of hand-dipped beer battered whitefish fillets, flash-fried to a golden brown. Served with fries and coleslaw • 10.99

TRI-TIP STACKER
The best tasting sandwich around. Thinly sliced Tri-Tip basted in our signature BBQ sauce and stacked tall on a toasted hoagie roll • 9.99

TRI-TIP STEAK
An incredible steak! Our 12-oz. Choice cut is marinated, grilled to your preference and basted with our signature BBQ sauce • 15.99

MEATLOAF
A generous portion of the American classic, slowly roasted with the perfect blend of seasonings • 11.99

Menu Sampler - Prices and menu subject to change.

Offer validity is governed by the Rules of Use and excludes defined holidays. Offers are not valid with other discount offers, unless specified. Coupons void if purchased, sold or bartered. Discounts exclude tax, tip and/or alcohol, where applicable. Tipping should be 15% to 20% of the total bill before discount.

The Beach House
BAR AND GRILLE
www.beachhousebarandgrille.com

Card No. 116

Up To $20.00 Value

The Beach House Bar & Grille offers an all-American cuisine with a Caribbean flair. Steaks, salads, wood-fired pizzas & seafood are just a few of our menu selections. Relax & enjoy your favorite game on our plasma TVs during happy hour. Open air dining & patio seating available. Lunch & dinner served daily. Happy hour specials. Weekend breakfast buffet.

Enjoy one complimentary LUNCH OR DINNER ENTREE when a second LUNCH OR DINNER ENTREE of equal or greater value is purchased.

Dine in only

valid anytime

6900 Lakeland Ave. N., Brooklyn Park, MN
(763) 566-6700

00650656

WOOD FIRED PIZZAS

JERK CHICKEN
Guava barbecue, smoke gouda, red onion and cilantro. 8.50

PEPPERONI
Mozzarella, oregano and parmesan. 7.50

SANDWICHES & WRAPS

ISLAND CLUB
On toasted white pullman with rotisserie turkey, bacon, lettuce, tomato and mayo. 8.50

CUBAN
Ham, provolone, salami, pulled pork, pickles and provolone cheese, grill-pressed on a hoagie bun. 8.95

GRILLED JERK CHICKEN
Lettuce, tomato and cheddar on a griddled sweet roll. 9.50

FRIED WALLEYE SANDWICH
Tartar sauce and cheddar cheese on a griddled sweet roll. 9.95

ENTREES

WOOD GRILLED FILET MIGNON
Loaded mashed potatoes. 19.95

BARBECUE ROTISSERIE CHICKEN
One half chicken with Island spice rub, glazed with guava barbecue and served with mashed potatoes and a grilled vegetable skewer. 12.50

FRIED SHRIMP PLATTER
Served with spicy-creamy cocktail sauce, lemon and rasta fries. 14.95

ROTISSERIE SPARE RIBS
Slow cooked with guava barbecue, served with rasta fries. Half Rack 11.95 Full Rack 16.95

Menu Sampler - Prices and menu subject to change.

Offer validity is governed by the Rules of Use and excludes defined holidays. Offers are not valid with other discount offers, unless specified. Coupons void if purchased, sold or bartered. Discounts exclude tax, tip and/or alcohol, where applicable. Tipping should be 15% to 20% of the total bill before discount.

Fridley Crab House

Card No. 32

Up To $13.00 Value

REPEAT SAVINGS

*E*njoy one complimentary LUNCH OR DINNER ENTREE when a second LUNCH OR DINNER ENTREE of equal or greater value is purchased.

Brunch excluded; Dine in only; Specials excluded

valid anytime

6161 Hwy. 65 N.E., Fridley, MN (763)571-3444

00568985

We are proud to offer our guests the finest selection of North Atlantic & Arctic oceans. Our crab is harvested fresh by the most talented & adventurous fisherman in the world, so you many enjoy this "delicacy of kings". We also offer phenomenal live music for your enjoyment. Kids menu available.

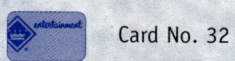

The BB King Sandwich (toasted Swirl bread)
Bacon, Bacon, Bleu Cheese, lettuce, tomato & Monterey Jack cheese.

Grilled Top Sirloin Sandwich (toasted French roll)
If you're craving a steak sandwich, this is it! Grilled to your liking.

Juicy Lucy in the Sky (grilled Swirl bread)
Half-pound beefsteak, tomatoes, grilled onion & our special sauce!

Three Dog Night
Lobster, shrimp & scallops sautéed, served with toasted garlic cream sauce and fresh pasta.

Golden Alaskan King Crab Legs
1 ½ pounds "lemon steamed," served with sweet butter.

Alaskan Snow Crab Legs
1 ½ pounds "lemon steamed," served with drawn butter.

The Crab Trio
½ pound each: Alaskan Snow Crab, Dungeness Crab, & Golden Alaskan King Crab.

The Lobster Twins
Two twin lobster tails, broiled, served with sweet butter.

Lobster Chops
Split lobster tail with jumbo sea scallops, char-broiled.

Three Shrimp Feast
Breaded Gulf shrimp, Parrot Bay Coconut shrimp & colossal stuffed shrimp.

Canadian Walleye
You tell us: grilled, pan-fried or beer battered!

Menu Sampler - Prices and menu subject to change.

Offer validity is governed by the Rules of Use and excludes defined holidays. Offers are not valid with other discount offers, unless specified. Coupons void if purchased, sold or bartered. Discounts exclude tax, tip and/or alcohol, where applicable. Tipping should be 15% to 20% of the total bill before discount.

El Azteca
Authentic Mexican Food

Card No. 27

REPEAT SAVINGS

Up To $12.00 Value

We welcome you to El Azteca the midwest headquarters for authentic mexican cuisine. Sample our delicious fajitas or our savory enchiladas in our family friendly atomosphere. We offer a full bar with the best margaritas in town.

*E*njoy one complimentary LUNCH OR DINNER ENTREE when a second LUNCH OR DINNER ENTREE of equal or greater value is purchased.

Dine in only; This location only

valid anytime

3500 Vicksburg Ln. #500, Plymouth, MN
(763)550-1570

00659300

Shrimp Fajitas 11.00
Tender shrimp with bell peppers and green onions. Served with guacamole, beans with cheese & tomatoes & flour or corn tortillas

Beef or Chicken Fajitas 9.75
Tender sliced beef or chicken with bell peppers and green onions. Served with guacamole, beans with cheese & tomatoes & flour or corn tortillas

Steak a la Tampiqueña 10.50
Ribeye steak cooked with onions. Served with rice, beans, tortilla & a salad

T-bone steak 12.00
Grilled T-bone steak with onions, tomato, bell peppers & mushrooms. Served with rice, beans & tortillas

Burritos Mexicanos 9.50
Two burritos filled with choice of steak or chicken fajitas & topped with nacho sauce, lettuce, sour cream, tomatoes.

Chilaquiles Mexicanos 7.00
Corn tortillas cooked with chicken & our own special sauce. Topped with nacho cheese garnished with guacamole salad

Taquitos Mexicanos 7.25
Four deep-fried, rolled, corn tortillas – two stuffed with chicken & two with beef tips. Served with guacamole & sour cream

Quesadilla Rellena 7.00
Two flour tortillas, grilled & stuffed with cheese, chopped beef or chicken. Served with guacamole salad & sour cream

Chimichanga 9.00
Two flour tortillas deep-fried & filled with beef tips & fried beans. Topped with nacho cheese, garnished with guacamole salad

Enchilada Supreme 7.50
Supreme combination consisting of one chicken, one bean, one cheese & one beef enchilada. Topped with ranchero sauce, lettuce, tomatoes & sour cream

---

Menu Sampler - Prices and menu subject to change.

Offer validity is governed by the Rules of Use and excludes defined holidays. Offers are not valid with other discount offers, unless specified. Coupons void if purchased, sold or bartered. Discounts exclude tax, tip and/or alcohol, where applicable. Tipping should be 15% to 20% of the total bill before discount.

EL TORO

Card No. 121

REPEAT SAVINGS

Up To **$12.00** Value

*E*njoy one complimentary LUNCH OR DINNER ENTREE when a second LUNCH OR DINNER ENTREE of equal or greater value is purchased.

Dine in only

valid anytime

10901 Douglas Dr., Champlin, MN (763)425-9307

00659387

Welcome to El Toro, authentic Mexican cuisine at it's finest. Enjoy our casual family friendly environment while sipping on the best margaritas in town. Daily lunch & dinner specials.

Mixed Fajitas 10.75
Same as above with both beef & chicken

Texas Fajitas 12.00
Tender sliced beef, chicken & shrimp with bell peppers and green onions. Served with guacamole, beans with cheese & tomato & flour or corn tortillas

Carne Asada 9.75
Tender roast beef served with beans, guacamole salad and three tortillas

Steak Ranchero 10.50
Steak with salsa ranchero sauce. Served with rice & beans

Carnitas Dinner 9.75
Fried pork served with rice, beans, guacamole salad & three tortillas

Steak a la Tampiqueña 10.50
Ribeye steak cooked with onions. Served with rice, beans, tortilla & a salad

Enchiladas Rancheras 8.50
Two cheese enchiladas with shredded pork cooked with onions, tomatoes & bell peppers. Served with guacamole salad & choice of rice or beans

Pollo Asado 9.50
Three pieces of chicken topped with onions & served with rice & beans

Yolandas 7.50
Three chicken enchiladas topped with ranchero sauce. Served with rice & guacamole salad

Burritos Deluxe 8.50
Two burritos, one chicken with beans & one beef with beans topped with lettuce, tomatoes & sour cream. Served with choice of rice or beans

Burrito Ruleta 6.00
Burritos filled with chicken & topped with nacho sauce. Served with rice & pico de gallo

Tacos de Carne Asada 8.50
Three folded corn tortillas filled with carne asada. Served with tomatillo sauce, pico de gallo & charro beans

Menu Sampler - Prices and menu subject to change.

Offer validity is governed by the Rules of Use and excludes defined holidays. Offers are not valid with other discount offers, unless specified. Coupons void if purchased, sold or bartered. Discounts exclude tax, tip and/or alcohol, where applicable. Tipping should be 15% to 20% of the total bill before discount.

C15

MURASAKI
JAPANESE STEAKHOUSE & SUSHI BAR

Card No. 48

Up to $22.00 Value

Murasaki (Japanese for purple) is a lovely Japanese Steakhouse just N. of Hwy. 36 on MN 5. Enjoy teppanyaki with your family while the chef cooks your meal before your eyes. You can also sit in the main dining room & savor sushi, sashimi, tempura & much more. Open daily for lunch & dinner.

Enjoy one complimentary DINNER ENTREE when a second DINNER ENTREE of equal or greater value is purchased.

Sushi excluded; Dine in only

valid any evening

1491 Stillwater Blvd., Stillwater, MN (651)439-1376

00701592

COMBINATION DINNERS

MURASAKI SPECIAL DINNER $29.95
Lobster – Filet Mignon – Hibachi Shrimp – Teriyaki Chicken

GEISHA DINNER $28.95
Lobster – Hibachi Shrimp – Hibachi Scallops

EMPEROR DINNER $27.95
Lobster – Filet Mignon – Teriyaki Chicken

VEGETARIAN DINNER $14.95
Variety of garden fresh vegetables and deep fried tofu (bean curd)

ENTRÉES

FILET MIGNON DINNER $21.95
8 ounces of Filet Mignon (add 4 ounces $6.00)

HIBACHI SHRIMP DINNER $17.95

CHICKEN TERIYAKI DINNER $14.95

HIBACHI SCALLOPS DINNER $22.95

LOBSTER TAIL DINNER $28.95

HIBACHI TUNA DINNER $25.95

Menu Sampler - Prices and menu subject to change.

Offer validity is governed by the Rules of Use and excludes defined holidays. Offers are not valid with other discount offers, unless specified. Coupons void if purchased, sold or bartered. Discounts exclude tax, tip and/or alcohol, where applicable. Tipping should be 15% to 20% of the total bill before discount.

erté

Card No. 18

Up To $18.00 Value

REPEAT SAVINGS

Enjoy one complimentary DINNER ENTREE when a second DINNER ENTREE of equal or greater value is purchased.

Valid Sunday-Friday evenings

323 13th Ave. N.E., Minneapolis, MN (612)623-4211

00650295

THE HOUSE $17
erté's signature 10 oz. coulotte cut sirloin, recommended MR-M – served with erté's bronze steak sauce. his bronze sculptures are perfection just like this steak and sauce!

FILET MIGNON $22
8 oz. Angus beef... this is an incredible steak, words can't describe it so we'll leave it at that - enjoy!

PORKETTA $21
spicy sausage stuffed pork tenderloin with sun dried tomato and basil bread pudding, accompanied by a Chianti buerre rouge sauce.......go ahead, you know you want to yell it.......Su-eeeeee (t)

CHICKEN SALTIMBOCCA $15
this is not a dance... it's breast of chicken folded with prosciutto, provolone & herbs- finished with Madeira butter sauce. now... start dancing!

SHRIMP SCAMPI $17
a true classic – jumbo shrimp sautéed with garlic & butter – deglazed with pernod & served on rice pilaf

PORK CHOPS $15
the Irish say, "hunger is a good sauce"...we agree, now finish that with Lissa's secret brown sugar-scotch sauce on 2 grilled t-bone pork chops, marinated in Guinness and.....you'll just hunger for more... the Irish are very clever

STAR PRAIRIE RAINBOW TROUT $14.5
super fresh, sunflower crusted trout griddled with maple caramelized shallots and served with wild rice cakes   these trout were raised in spring feed ponds at the base of a Wisconsin valley, alongside the picturesque Apple River – you'll write home about this one.

BOWSTRING WALLEYE $18
memories of "going up north" fishing for walleye on bowstring lake brings back this favorite family recipe of cornmeal- parmesan crusted walleye, sautéed & served with wild rice cakes and our homemade tartar sauce. this big one didn't get away

---

Menu Sampler - Prices and menu subject to change.

Offer validity is governed by the Rules of Use and excludes defined holidays. Offers are not valid with other discount offers, unless specified. Coupons void if purchased, sold or bartered. Discounts exclude tax, tip and/or alcohol, where applicable. Tipping should be 15% to 20% of the total bill before discount.

Trigger's
at the MINNESOTA HORSE & HUNT CLUB

www.mnhorseandhunt.com/trigr_idy.htm

Few things can match the atmosphere of our four-star restaurant with its panoramic views & beautiful, handcrafted fieldstone fireplaces. We specialize in fine dishes from the fields, forests & streams of the upper midwest & Canada. Come & enjoy a retreat away from the cities.

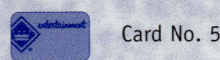

Card No. 5

Up to $25.00 Value — REPEAT SAVINGS

Enjoy one complimentary LUNCH OR DINNER ENTREE when a second LUNCH OR DINNER ENTREE is purchased.

valid Sunday thru Friday

2920 E. 220th St. (30 mi. S. of the Twin Cities),
Prior Lake, MN (952) 447-2272

00666665

STARTERS

BILL'S SMOKED PHEASANT QUESADILLAS
Bill created the smoked pheasant Quesadillas on a hunting trip, and it became a staple for a quick lunch or snack ever since. 12 inch Tortilla shell filled with smoked pheasant and green chilis topped with shredded cheddar jack cheese served with sour cream and salsa.
$9.50

DINNER ENTREES

LONG TOM PHEASANT
Long Tom Farm is where Bill and his partners hunt deer, ducks and of course, pheasant. Until now you had to hunt all day to enjoy this item. Boneless Beer battered Pheasant Breast, deep fried with sweet chili sauce for dipping.
$22.95

BOB'S WALLEYE
Bob Woodruff, a fishing guide on the Ontario border for over forty years, cooked a lot walleye, and he cooked it very well. Walleye pike your way; grilled, sauteed or beer battered served with tarter sauce.
$19.95

ARGENTINE MIXED GRILL
6oz Ribeye Steak
1 half order of Beef Andouille Sausage
1 Bone Short Rib with Chimichurri dipping sauce
$24.95

Menu Sampler - Prices and menu subject to change.

Offer validity is governed by the Rules of Use and excludes defined holidays. Offers are not valid with other discount offers, unless specified. Coupons void if purchased, sold or bartered. Discounts exclude tax, tip and/or alcohol, where applicable. Tipping should be 15% to 20% of the total bill before discount.

C18

ATLAS GRILL

www.atlasgrill.com

Card No. 7

Up To $20.00 Value

Atlas Grill & Clubroom is an approachable, elegant downtown Minneapolis restaurant. Our chef & staff have received critical acclaim for our fine food & gracious, unobtrusive service from newspapers & event magazines alike. In the evening, it becomes not only a place for a lovely dinner after work, but is available as a unique & memorable special event venue.

*E*njoy one complimentary DINNER ENTREE when a second DINNER ENTREE of equal or greater value is purchased.

valid any evening

200 S. 6th St., Minneapolis, MN (612)332-4200

00667425

Entrees

Fire Roasted Chilean Sea Bass — 18.95
With Calamata Olive Artichoke and Cilantro Relish

Atlas Chicken — 15.95
Lightly Breaded and Served with a Citrus Beurre Blanc Sauce

Gulf Shrimp — 19.95
Marinated in Garlic and Basil, Served With Basmati Rice

Atlantic Salmon — 18.95
Pan Seared & Served with Lemon, Saffron, Tarragon Infusion Sauce

Tenderloin Brochette Fire Roasted — 20.95
Tenderloin with Grilled Vegetables & Saffron Basmati Rice

Vegetarian Platter Sautéed — 14.95
Vegetables, Roasted Eggplant Puree & Basmati Rice

Menu Sampler - Prices and menu subject to change.

Offer validity is governed by the Rules of Use and excludes defined holidays. Offers are not valid with other discount offers, unless specified. Coupons void if purchased, sold or bartered. Discounts exclude tax, tip and/or alcohol, where applicable. Tipping should be 15% to 20% of the total bill before discount.

C19

Harborside Restaurant
at Willie's Hidden Harbor

Card No. 101

Up To $20.00 Value

REPEAT SAVINGS

*E*njoy one complimentary DINNER ENTREE when a second DINNER ENTREE of equal or greater value is purchased.

valid any evening

388 9th Ave. W., St. Paul Park, MN (651)459-2129

00626905

Join us at Harborside Restaurant for a fabulous voyage! In the summer dock your boat & come on in! Casual fine dining in a fun nautical atmosphere. Handicap accessible & our banquet room seats up to 325. Make time to visit our Ship Store.

Entrees
Includes soup or salad and choice of potato.

SIZZLING PEPPER STEAK
Sirloin Steak topped with sautéed peppers, onions, and mushrooms
14 ounce sirloin   16.95   or   8 ounce sirloin   11.95

SNOW CRAB LEGS
Steamed Snow Crab Legs served with butter   19.95

GARLIC SHRIMP
Broiled with a garlic butter sauce   15.95

THE CATFISH
Farm raised and southern fried   13.95

THE SEAFARER
Baked Fish with toasted almonds and lemon butter   9.95

THE YACHT
4pc Broasted Chicken   12.95   THE DINGY   2pc   9.95

COMBOS

THE MARINER
1/2 Rack BBQ'd Ribs and Broasted Chicken (2pc)   14.95

CAPTAIN HOOK
1/2 Rack BBQ'd Ribs and Fried Shrimp (4pc)   15.95

STEAK & LAKE
8 ounce Steak and Fried Catfish   15.95

Menu Sampler - Prices and menu subject to change.

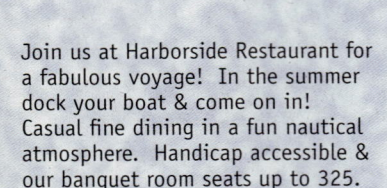

Offer validity is governed by the Rules of Use and excludes defined holidays. Offers are not valid with other discount offers, unless specified. Coupons void if purchased, sold or bartered. Discounts exclude tax, tip and/or alcohol, where applicable. Tipping should be 15% to 20% of the total bill before discount.

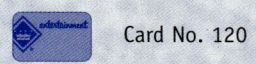

JEWEL OF INDIA
Authentic Indian Cuisine

Card No. 120

Up To $17.00 Value

Welcome to Jewel of India, where we feature authentic Indian fare. Our cuisine is prepared using a perfect blend of Indian spices and ingredients, and is a delightful escape from the main stream.

*E*njoy one complimentary LUNCH OR DINNER ENTREE when a second LUNCH OR DINNER ENTREE of equal or greater value is purchased.

valid anytime

Saturday's excluded

1427 Washington Ave. S, Minneapolis, MN
(612) 339-0002

00262864

Shrimp Curry or Vindaloo 12.95
Fresh shrimp prepared in a light sauce. Served mild or hot.

Tandoori Chicken 9.95
Spring Chicken marinated in yogurt with fresh spices and lemon then barbecued in the tandoor.

Chicken Curry or Vindaloo 9.95
Fresh chicken, delicately prepared in light gravy served mild or hot.

Lamb Curry or Vindaloo 10.95
Lamb prepared in flavorful onion and tomato sauce.

Kashmir Rogan Josh 11.95

Shrimp Green Masala 12.95
Fresh, large, shrimp cooked with bell pepper, poppy seeds and coriander in the Chef's special sauce.

Chana Masala 7.95
A delicious combination of chickpeas, onions, and tomatoes in a rich sauce.

Navratan Korma 9.95
A royal entrée. Nine garden fresh vegetables, gently simmered in a spice-laced cream sauce.

Menu Sampler - Prices and menu subject to change.

Offer validity is governed by the Rules of Use and excludes defined holidays. Offers are not valid with other discount offers, unless specified. Coupons void if purchased, sold or bartered. Discounts exclude tax, tip and/or alcohol, where applicable. Tipping should be 15% to 20% of the total bill before discount.

Northern Shores Grille

Card No. 4

REPEAT SAVINGS — Up To **$31.00** Value

*E*njoy one complimentary DINNER ENTREE when a second DINNER ENTREE of equal or greater value is purchased.

valid any evening

30 S. 7th St. (Downtown Marriott), **Minneapolis, MN**
(612) 349-4026

00407292

We are excited about our new restaurant, Northern Shores Grille, specializing in exquisite regional cuisine. Enjoy a casual dining experience blending upper Midwestern & Minnesota cuisine, & have created dishes that will surprise & delight. We are a very unique restaurant & would love for you to be our guest.

Steaks

All Steaks are cooked to your desired doneness and topped with Tomato Onion Relish and a Red Wine Chocolate Reduction, served with your choice of Oven Roasted Potato Spears or Whipped Potatoes

8 oz. Sirloin Steak –	$16
10 oz. Strip Steak –	$25
8 oz. Filet Mignon Steak –	$26

Savor the Season

A three course, seasonally inspired dinner including salad, entrée, and dessert. This satisfying sensory delight changes periodically, please ask your server about tonight's selection..................$21

Entrées

Signature Walleye Pike –
Walleye Pike crusted in Brioche served with Mushrooms, Haricot Vert, and Lobster Oil, accompanied by Whipped Potatoes $21

Wild Cedar Plank Salmon – [Organic]
Salmon Filet with Fingerling Potatoes, Haricot Vert, Roma Tomatoes, and Champagne Vinaigrette $18

Grilled Pork Chop –
Pork Chop with Maple Mustard Sauce served with Oven Roasted Potato Spears and Roasted Pear Chutney...$18

Fried Chicken –
Fried Chicken served with Whipped Potatoes, Seasonal Vegetables, and Fresh Baked Biscuits.....................$16

Grilled Chicken – [low cholesterol]
Grilled Chicken with Roasted Tomato Sauce, Black Pepper Fettuccine with Basil Pesto and Sun Dried Tomatoes and Fresh Steamed Asparagus $16

Menu Sampler - Prices and menu subject to change.

Offer validity is governed by the Rules of Use and excludes defined holidays. Offers are not valid with other discount offers, unless specified. Coupons void if purchased, sold or bartered. Discounts exclude tax, tip and/or alcohol, where applicable. Tipping should be 15% to 20% of the total bill before discount.

The Historic AFTON HOUSE INN 1867

www.aftonhouseinn.com

Casual fine dining in the Wheel or Pennington room on the St. Croix River. Enjoy a full dinner menu along with our entrees prepared tableside. 25 Room inn with in-room jacuzzis & fireplaces. Private & public cruises May-Oct.

Card No. 74

$20.00 Value

Enjoy one complimentary DINNER ENTREE when a second DINNER ENTREE of equal or greater value is purchased.

valid Sunday-Friday

3291 S. St. Croix Tr., Afton, MN (651)436-8883

00613992

Walleye Cakes served with Pepper Salsa and Sliced Cucumbers $10.95

Artichoke and Lump Crab Dip **served with Grilled Ciabatta Bread $10.95**

Afton House Inn Caesar Salad $7.50 per person
Our Signature Salad prepared for at least two or more. Fresh Romaine, Baked Croutons, Shredded Parmesan and Dressing Made from Scratch. Prepared at your Table. Served with a Parmesan Cheese Crisp.

Parmesan, Apple and Apricot Salad elevated in an amazing Five Herb Dressing $7.95

King Salmon Stuffed with Crab, Lobster and Brie Cheese over Sticky Rice served with Lemon Butter Sauce $17.95

Almond Crusted Walleye served with Potato Purée and a Browned Almond Butter Sauce $20.95

Chicken Roulade Stuffed with Chicken Mousse, Walnuts and Spinach, served Over Caramelized Apples and a Rosemary Pan Jus $17.95

Pork Porterhouse – Pepper and Clove Crusted, Flame Broiled and served with Garlic Mashed Potatoes, Seasonal Vegetables and a Wild Berry Glaze $26.95

Honey Bourbon Butter Filet with Lump Crab Meat, Potato Gratin and Green Oil $29.95

Menu Sampler - Prices and menu subject to change.

Offer validity is governed by the Rules of Use and excludes defined holidays. Offers are not valid with other discount offers, unless specified. Coupons void if purchased, sold or bartered. Discounts exclude tax, tip and/or alcohol, where applicable. Tipping should be 15% to 20% of the total bill before discount.

C23

CAROUSEL

Card No. 22

Up To $26.00 Value

REPEAT SAVINGS

*E*njoy one complimentary DINNER ENTREE when a second DINNER ENTREE of equal or greater value is purchased.

valid any evening

11 E. Kellogg Blvd. (Radisson Riverfront Hotel St. Paul), St. Paul, MN (651)605-0190

00492609

The Twin Cities' only revolving restaurant offers an outstanding view of the Mississippi River and skyline. Exceptional gourmet dining features chicken, steak and seafood specialties. Choose a fine wine to compliment your dinner. Please call for reservations.

ENTREES

MINNESOTA WALLEYE-$25.00
Crispy Wild Rice Breading on a Walleye Filet, lightly sautéed and topped with Beurre Blanc.

COQ A VIN-$24.00
Roasted Bone-in Chicken Breast served with the Traditional Mushroom and Red Wine Sauce.

SEARED SEA BASS-$26.00
Chilean Sea Bass Baked to perfection, topped with Herb Maitre d' Butter and Julienne Vegetables.

COCONUT PRAWNS-$30.00
Four Prawns Breaded with a Sweet Coconut batter and served with a Spicy Jamaican Sauce.

SPECIALTIES

GRILLED PORTERHOUSE-$39.00
Twenty-Two Ounce Charbroiled Porterhouse Steak cooked to your desired temperature. Please leave us a little more time for well-done.

NEW ENGLAND SEAFOOD PLATE-$39.00
If Seafood is your craving, then this is your plate. Includes Two Prawns served Scampi style, One Broiled Cold Water Lobster Tail, and King Crab Legs.

Menu Sampler - Prices and menu subject to change.

Offer validity is governed by the Rules of Use and excludes defined holidays. Offers are not valid with other discount offers, unless specified. Coupons void if purchased, sold or bartered. Discounts exclude tax, tip and/or alcohol, where applicable. Tipping should be 15% to 20% of the total bill before discount.

Card No. 51

Elsie's
RESTAURANT & BAR

Up To $23.00 Value

*E*njoy one complimentary DINNER ENTREE when a second DINNER ENTREE of equal or greater value is purchased.

Dine in only

valid any evening

729 Marshall St. NE, Minneapolis, MN (612)378-9701

00499946

Sandwiches

Choice Top Sirloin Steak Sandwich
6 oz Steak served on Toast $8.95

Italian Beef Hoagie
Italian Beef Sauteed Onions & Sweet Peppers,
Mozzarella Cheese & Au Jus $7.25

Dinners

Broiled Canadian Walleye
Served with Lemon and Tartar sauce
$15.95

Deep Fried Shrimp
Lightly Breaded & Fried to a Golden Brown
served with Cocktail & Tartar sauce. $15.95

Prime Cut Top Sirloin
USDA Choice 8 oz Steak
$15.95

Chicken Cordon Bleu
Chicken breasts with sliced Ham & Swiss Cheese
$12.95

Menu Sampler - Prices and menu subject to change.

Offer validity is governed by the Rules of Use and excludes defined holidays. Offers are not valid with other discount offers, unless specified. Coupons void if purchased, sold or bartered. Discounts exclude tax, tip and/or alcohol, where applicable. Tipping should be 15% to 20% of the total bill before discount.

C25

Stacy's Grille

Card No. 54

Up To $22.00 Value

Stacy's Grille is a cozy, contemporary restaurant where classic American cuisine is infused with local Minnesota flavor. Enjoy a variety of dinner entrees designed to please the most discriminating palate. A picturesque view of our pond & fountain provide the perfect backdrop for gatherings. Our impeccable service will make your time here an experience to remember.

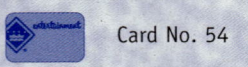

Enjoy one complimentary DINNER ENTREE when a second DINNER ENTREE of equal or greater value is purchased.

valid any evening

5801 Opus Pkwy. (Minneapolis Marriott Southwest), Minnetonka, MN (952)352-6268

00493424

Appetizers

Stacy's Crab Cake
Cucumber noodles, tomato-horseradish sauce 12.00

Stacy's Specialties

Pan Fried Walleye
Panko battered walleye with shallot and Bermuda onion relish lightly drizzled with lemon beurre blanc. Served with roasted parsley potatoes and baby carrots 18.00

Entrees

New York Strip
Herb and wine marinated strip steak with garlic mashed potatoes, balsamic reduction and onion rings 24.00

Black n' Bleu Halibut
Pan seared halibut topped with gorgonzola-mint veloute sauce. Accompanied by tomato marmalade and roasted new potatoes 22.00

Chicken Marsala
Pan seared medallions of chicken tossed with ziti pasta layered with spinach and oven dried tomatoes in a brown marsala sauce 17.00

Menu Sampler - Prices and menu subject to change.

Offer validity is governed by the Rules of Use and excludes defined holidays. Offers are not valid with other discount offers, unless specified. Coupons void if purchased, sold or bartered. Discounts exclude tax, tip and/or alcohol, where applicable. Tipping should be 15% to 20% of the total bill before discount.

Water Street Inn

Est. 1890

www.waterstreetinn.us

Card No. 104

Up to $22.00 Value

REPEAT SAVINGS

Enjoy one complimentary ENTREE when a second ENTREE of equal or greater value is purchased.

valid anytime

101 S. Water St. (just N. of the historic Lift Bridge),
Stillwater, MN (651)439-6000

00613761

Experience the best of historic downtown Stillwater at the only hotel-restaurant on the river! Fine & casual dining overlooking the St. Croix. Breakfast, lunch & dinner served daily. Dine, stay, enjoy the view at the Water Street Inn. Wedding & conference facilities available for up to 300 people.

Entrées

PORK TENDERLOIN
Seared pork tenderloin dressed with a rum-pecan demiglace, over braised red cabbage and apple confit.
Served with seasonal vegetables and mashed potatoes.
$19.95

SEA BASS
Delicate grilled sea bass, topped with a rich cream sauce and succulent pieces of lobster.
Served with roasted shallot risotto.
$26.95

IRISH WHISKEY STEAK
A delicious Irish specialty. Grilled beef medallions, marinated in fresh herbs, olive oil and Irish Whiskey.
Served with seasonal vegetables and mashed potatoes.
$21.95

WATER STREET DUCK
Savory duck breast sautéed with a raspberry and Port reduction.
Served with Southern-style grits.
$20.95

STILLWATER STEAK & SHRIMP
A perfectly grilled sirloin paired with delicious jumbo shrimp.
Served with a marinated mushroom and cognac cream sauce.
$25.95

HICKORY-SMOKED RIBS
Tender pork ribs, hickory-smoked in house.
Served with our homemade barbecue sauce.
$18.95

LOBSTER TAIL
A traditional 8-ounce tail, roasted to perfection, accompanied by drawn butter and lemon.
Served with seasonal vegetables and wild rice pilaf.
$26.95

Menu Sampler - Prices and menu subject to change.

Offer validity is governed by the Rules of Use and excludes defined holidays. Offers are not valid with other discount offers, unless specified. Coupons void if purchased, sold or bartered. Discounts exclude tax, tip and/or alcohol, where applicable. Tipping should be 15% to 20% of the total bill before discount.

Card No. 21

Antoine's Creole Maison

REPEAT SAVINGS — Up To $17.00 Value

*E*njoy one complimentary ENTREE when a second ENTREE of equal or greater value is purchased.

valid anytime

2819 Hennepin Ave. S., Minneapolis, MN
(612) 871-2262

00692334

In the name of my grandfather, Antoine George & the rest of my family, we would like to welcome you to Antoine's Creole Maison Restaurant. Everyone cooked in my home, & goodness, did we enjoy eating the great food that you will experience here. Enjoy a glass of wine or beer while you savor our home-style Louisiana French Creole Cuisine. Hope to see you soon!

"Blue Monday" Red Beans and Rice with Andouille Sausage $14.99
Every Monday we began the week working either in the fields or just cleaning our home. What a relief it was to relax and enjoy this classic Louisiana mainstay. Now we enjoy it on any given day of the week.
Served over long-grain white rice with buttered French bread

Catfish $16.99
A 7 oz well seasoned filet, dredged in flour and deep fried.
Served with country-style potato salad and French bread

Poboys $13.69 each
Fried Shrimp or Fried Catfish
Served on French bread with shredded lettuce and slices of tomatoes. Served with country fries and a sweet pickle

Shrimp Creole $15.99
Medium sized shrimp and vegetables, simmered in a Creole tomato and bay leaf sauce.
Served over white rice with buttered French bread

Jambalaya $14.95
Spicy tomato sauce and vegetables mixed with long-grain white rice, chicken strips, baby shrimp and smoked sausage.
Served with buttered French bread

Menu Sampler - Prices and menu subject to change.

Offer validity is governed by the Rules of Use and excludes defined holidays. Offers are not valid with other discount offers, unless specified. Coupons void if purchased, sold or bartered. Discounts exclude tax, tip and/or alcohol, where applicable. Tipping should be 15% to 20% of the total bill before discount.

cafe northstar
CROWNE PLAZA NORTHSTAR HOTEL

Card No. 29

Up To **$20.00** Value

Cafe Northstar is a full service restaurant, sporting a European personality with a Scandinavian flair. Located in the Crowne Plaza Northstar Hotel, which is in the heart of the financial & retail district of downtown Minneapolis. "The Place to Meet".

Enjoy one complimentary ENTREE when a second ENTREE of equal or greater value is purchased.

valid anytime

618 Second Ave. S. (Inside the Crowne Plaza Northstar Hotel), **Minneapolis, MN (612)338-2288**

00544370

Main Courses

Seared Breast of Chicken... $12.95
Served over Garlic Mashed Potatoes with Lemon, Capers and Mushrooms.

Vegetarian Puff... $10.95
A fresh alternative –
Prepared with Portabella Mushroom, Tomatoes, Potatoes, Asparagus, Squash, and Green Onion, topped with a Puff Pastry Shell and presented on a bed of fresh Mesclun.

Grilled New York Strip Steak... $19.95
Served with Garlic Mashed Potatoes and a Mushroom Port Wine Sauce.

Veal Marsala... $18.95
A classic Veal dish, Wild Mushrooms, and Onions in a Marsala Sauce. Served with Angel Hair Pasta and Asparagus.

Pasta Primavera with Shrimp... $14.95
Shrimp, sautéed in Butter are added to pasta and Braised Vegetables.

Pumpkin Seed Crusted Tuna... $16.95
Crusted Tuna Steak served with Pineapple Salsa and Angel Hair Pasta.

Menu Sampler - Prices and menu subject to change.

Offer validity is governed by the Rules of Use and excludes defined holidays. Offers are not valid with other discount offers, unless specified. Coupons void if purchased, sold or bartered. Discounts exclude tax, tip and/or alcohol, where applicable. Tipping should be 15% to 20% of the total bill before discount.

Chez Daniel Bistro
"Just East of France"

Card No. 14

Up To $18.00 Value

*E*njoy one complimentary DINNER ENTREE when a second DINNER ENTREE of equal or greater value is purchased.

Sunday brunch excluded

valid any evening

Not valid on holidays

2800 W. 80th St. (Embassy Suites), **Bloomington, MN**
(952)888-4447

00086690

"Just East of France" you will find our Bistro. Join us for a fabulous dining experience. We feature the classic French entrees served to perfection. Top your evening off with our delicious desserts.

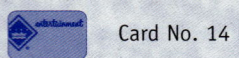

ENTREES

Grilled New York Strip
sauce diable, house potato
...$ 28.00

10 oz. Seared Filet Mignon
shiitake-spinach saute, amish blue cheese butter...$ 30.00 Petit 6 oz. $ 25.00

Hazelnut Crusted Rack of Lamb
dijon, wild rice pilaf, blackberry demi glace...$ 28.00

Pan Seared Scarlet Snapper
crawfish risotto, vanilla-bourbon broth...$ 24.00

Moroccan Duck Breast
blackberry glace, house potato
$ 23.00

Seafood Spaghetti Noir
shrimp, clam, carrot, basil, chorizo cream...$ 22.00

Oven Roasted ½ Chicken
lavender jus, lemon marmalade potato puree ...$ 21.00

Chicken Penne Pasta
broccoli, garlic, lemon, red chili flakes, chablis butter sauce...$ 21.00

Grilled Salmon & Scallops
strawberry-mustard seed buerre blanc, potato puree...$ 27.00

Broiled Walleye
capers, tomato, gremolata, wild rice pilaf, brown butter...$ 23.00

Seared Pork Tenderloin
spiced pear gravy, house potato...$ 26.00

Menu Sampler - Prices and menu subject to change.

Offer validity is governed by the Rules of Use and excludes defined holidays. Offers are not valid with other discount offers, unless specified. Coupons void if purchased, sold or bartered. Discounts exclude tax, tip and/or alcohol, where applicable. Tipping should be 15% to 20% of the total bill before discount.

C30

Guaranteed Best Rate*
More listings online and over the phone!

Schaumburg

AMERISUITES SCHAUMBURG
1851 Mcconnor Pkwy, Schaumburg.
COMFORT SUITES SCHAUMBURG
1100 E Higgins Rd, Schaumburg.
LA QUINTA INN SCHAUMBURG
1730 E Higgins Rd, Schaumburg.

Springfield

AMERICA'S BEST INN SPRINGFIELD
500 N 1st St, Springfield.
RAMADA LTD SPRINGFIELD SOUTH
5970 S 6th Street Rd, Springfield.
RENAISSANCE SPRINGFIELD HOTEL
701 E Adams St, Springfield.

Indiana

Indianapolis

ADAM'S MARK INDIANAPOLIS, IN
2544 Executive Dr, Indianapolis.
BAYMONT INN & STES IND AIRPORT
2650 Executive Dr, Indianapolis.
BEST VALUE INN & SUITES
520 E Thompson Rd, Indianapolis.
LA QUINTA INN INDIANAPOLIS N
3880 W 92nd St, Indianapolis.
OMNI SEVERIN HOTEL
40 Jackson Pl, Indianapolis.
RADISSON HOTEL CITY CENTRE
31 W Ohio St, Indianapolis.

RADISSON INDIANAPOLIS AIRPORT
2500 S High School Rd, Indianapolis.
WYNDHAM INDIANAPOLIS
251 Pennsylvania Pkwy, Indianapolis.

Iowa

For this state's listings go to entertainment.com/travel

Kansas

Overland Park

CLUBHOUSE INN AND SUITES OVERLAND PARK
10610 Marty St, Overland Park.
DAYS INN OVERLAND PARK
4401 W 107th St, Overland Park.
DOUBLETREE HOTEL - OVERLAND PARK
10100 College Blvd, Overland Park.

Kentucky

Lexington

KNIGHTS INN NORTH
1935 Stanton Way, Lexington.
LA QUINTA INN LEXINGTON
1919 Stanton Way, Lexington.
RED ROOF INN LEXINGTON
100 Canebrake Dr, Lexington.

Louisville

BRECKINRIDGE INN
2800 Breckenridge Ln, Louisville.

CLARION HOTEL & CONF CENTER
9700 Bluegrass Pkwy, Louisville.
THE GALT HOUSE HOTEL
140 N 4th St, Louisville.

Louisiana

New Orleans

AMBASSADOR NEW ORLEANS
535 Tchoupitoulas St, New Orleans.
BARONNE PLAZA
201 Baronne St, New Orleans.
BEST WESTERN ST CHRISTOPHER
114 Magazine St, New Orleans.
BIENVILLE HOUSE HOTEL
320 Decatur St, New Orleans.
COTTON EXCHANGE HOTEL
231 Carondelet St, New Orleans.
COUNTRY INN & STES NEW ORLEANS
315 Magazine St, New Orleans.
DAUPHINE ORLEANS
415 Dauphine St, New Orleans.
DOUBLETREE HOTEL DOWNTOWN
300 Canal St, New Orleans.
FRENCH QUARTER COURTYARD
1101 N Rampart St, New Orleans.
GARDEN DISTRICT HOTEL
2203 Saint Charles Ave, New Orleans.
HAMPTON INN NEW ORLEANS
12340 I-10 Service Rd, New Orleans.
HISTORIC FRENCH MARKET INN
501 Decatur St, New Orleans.
HOTEL LE CIRQUE
#2 Lee Circle, New Orleans.

New Orleans – rates from $99

Visit New Orleans to help this great American city re-build.

New Orleans has something for everyone. Enjoy the rich flavors of an authentic Creole dinner in one of the world famous restaurants. Head to the renowned Audubon Zoo or ride past alligators on a swamp tour. Step back in time at one of the beautiful Southern plantations. Go on a midnight Ghost Tour or visit one of the many haunted historical landmarks. Don't forget to check out the never-ending nightlife of the infamous French Quarter.

Call: 800-50-HOTELS or book online at www.entertainment.com/travel

---

Discounts subject to availability.
*See Rebate Rules on page E31-E32 and Program Rules on page E33.

Guaranteed Best Rate*

Book at www.entertainment.com/travel or call 1-800-50-HOTEL

THE OUTRIGGER REEF ON THE BEACH
2169 Kalia Rd, Honolulu.

TURTLE BAY RESORT
57 091 Kamehameha Highway, Kahuku.

WAIKIKI BEACH MARRIOTT RESORT
2552 Kalakaua Ave, Honolulu.

WAIKIKI GATEWAY HOTEL
2070 Kalakaua Ave, Honolulu.

WAIKIKI RESORT HOTEL
130 Liliuokalani Ave, Honolulu.

WAIKIKI SAND VILLA HOTEL
23475 Ala Wai Blvd., Honolulu.

Idaho

Boise

AMERISUITES TOWN SQUARE MALL
925 N Milwaukee St, Boise.

RED LION PARK CENTER SUITES
424 East Park Centers Suites, Boise.

SHILO INN BOISE AIRPORT
4111 Broadway Ave, Boise.

SHILO INN RIVERSIDE
3031 W Main St, Boise.

Illinois

Arlington Heights

AMERISUITES ARLINGTON HEIGHTS
2111 S Arlington Heights Rd, Arlington Heights.

LA QUINTA INN CHICAGO ARLINGTON HEIGHTS
1415 W Dundee Rd, Arlington Heights.

RED ROOF INN CHICAGO ARLINGTON HEIGHTS
22 S Algonquin Rd, Arlington Heights.

Chicago

AMALFI HOTEL CHICAGO
20 W Kinzie St, Chicago.

BEST WESTERN GRANT PARK
1100 S Michigan Ave, Chicago.

BEST WESTERN INN OF CHICAGO
162 E Ohio St, Chicago.

BEST WESTERN RIVER NORTH
125 W Ohio St, Chicago.

CLUB QUARTERS, CENTRAL LOOP
111 W Adams St, Chicago.

CLUB QUARTERS, WACKER AT MICHIGAN
75 E Wacker Dr, Chicago.

COMFORT INN & SUITES DOWNTOWN
15 E Ohio St, Chicago.

CONGRESS PLAZA HOTEL
520 S Michigan Ave, Chicago.

COURTYARD BY MARRIOTT CHICAGO DOWNTOWN
30 E Hubbard St, Chicago.

DAYS INN GOLD COAST DOWNTOWN
1816 N Clark St, Chicago.

DOUBLETREE GUEST SUITES
198 E Delaware Pl, Chicago.

DRAKE HOTEL
140 E Walton Pl, Chicago.

ESSEX INN
800 S Michigan Ave, Chicago.

FAIRFIELD INN & STES DOWNTOWN
216 E Ontario St, Chicago.

FITZPATRICK CHICAGO HOTEL
166 E Superior St, Chicago.

Shop & Book more hotels at entertainment.com/travel

HAMPTON INN & SUITES CHICAGO
33 W Illinois St, Chicago.

HILTON CHICAGO- MICHIGAN AVE CULTURAL MILE
720 S Michigan Ave, Chicago.

HILTON GARDEN INN CHICAGO DNTN MAGNIF. MILE
10 E Grand Ave, Chicago.

HOTEL 71
71 E Wacker Dr, Chicago.

HOTEL ALLEGRO CHICAGO - A KIMPTON HOTEL
171 W Randolph St, Chicago.

HYATT REGENCY - CHICAGO
151 E Wacker Dr, Chicago.

HYATT REGENCY MCCORMICK PLACE
2233 S King Dr, Chicago.

LE MERIDIEN CHICAGO
521 N Rush St, Chicago.

LENOX SUITES HOTEL
616 N Rush St, Chicago.

MILLENNIUM KNICKERBOCKER HOTEL CHICAGO
163 E Walton Pl, Chicago.

OMNI AMBASSADOR EAST
1301 N State Pkwy, Chicago.

PALMER HOUSE HILTON
17 E Monroe St, Chicago.

RADISSON HOTEL & STES CHICAGO
160 E Huron St, Chicago.

RAMADA INN LAKE SHORE
4900 S Lake Shore Dr, Chicago.

RED ROOF INN CHICAGO DOWNTOWN
162 E Ontario St, Chicago.

SENECA HOTEL & SUITES
200 E Chestnut St, Chicago.

SHERATON CHICAGO HOTEL AND TOWERS
301 E North Water St, Chicago.

SOFITEL CHICAGO WATER TOWER
20 E Chestnut St, Chicago.

SWISSOTEL CHICAGO
323 E Wacker Dr, Chicago.

TALBOTT HOTEL
20 E Delaware Pl, Chicago.

THE RAPHAEL CHICAGO HOTEL
201 E Delaware Pl, Chicago.

THE TREMONT CHICAGO HOTEL
100 E Chestnut St, Chicago.

THE WESTIN CHICAGO RIVER NORTH
320 N Dearborn St, Chicago.

TRAVELODGE HOTEL DOWNTOWN
65 E Harrison St, Chicago.

WHITEHALL HOTEL
105 E Delaware Pl, Chicago.

WYNDHAM CHICAGO
633 N Saint Clair St, Chicago.

Des Plaines

BEST WESTERN OHARE
10300 W Higgins Rd, Des Plaines.

CHICAGO O'HARE HOTEL
1450 E Touhy Ave, Des Plaines.

HYATT REGENCY O'HARE
9300 Bryn Mawr Ave, Des Plaines.

Elk Grove

BEST WESTERN CHICAGO WEST
1600 Oakton St, Elk Grove Village.

COMFORT INN O'HARE AIRPORT
2550 Landmeier Rd, Elk Grove Village.

DAYS INN O'HARE AIRPORT WEST
1920 E Higgins Rd, Elk Grove Village.

E17

You can access **25,000** hotels in over **700** cities. See sample listings above.
Shop and Book more hotels at www.entertainment.com/travel

Guaranteed Best Rate*
More listings online and over the phone!

ASTON MAUI KAANAPALI VILLAS
45 Kai Ala Dr, Lahaina.

ASTON PAKI MAUI
3615 Lower Honoapiilani Rd, Lahaina.

EMBASSY VACATION RESORT (KAANAPALI)
104 Kaanapali Shores Pl, Lahaina.

GRAND WAILEA RESORT
3850 Wailea Alanui Dr, Kihei.

HYATT REGENCY MAUI RESORT & SPA
200 Nohea Kai Dr, Lahaina.

KAANAPALI BEACH HOTEL
2525 Kaanapali Pkwy, Lahaina.

KAHANA SUNSET
4909 Lower Honoapiilani Rd, Lahaina.

MAUI COAST HOTEL
2259 S Kihei Rd, Kihei.

OHANA MAUI ISLANDER HOTEL
660 Wainee St, Lahaina.

OUTRIGGER MAUI ELDORADO
2661 Kekaa Dr, Lahaina.

OUTRIGGER PALMS AT WAILEA
3200 Wailea Alanui Dr, Kihei.

OUTRIGGER ROYAL KAHANA
4365 Lower Honoapiilani Rd, Lahaina.

ROYAL LAHAINA RESORT
2780 Kekaa Dr, Lahaina.

SHERATON MAUI RESORT
2605 Kaanapali Pkwy, Lahaina.

THE WESTIN MAUI RESORT & SPA
2365 Kaanapali Pkwy, Lahaina.

THE WHALER ON KAANAPALI BEACH
2481 Kaanapali Pkwy, Lahaina.

Oahu

AQUA KUHIO VILLAGE
2463 Kuhio Ave, Honolulu.

AQUA MARINA HOTEL A CONDOTEL
1700 Ala Moana Blvd, Honolulu.

ASTON CORAL REEF HOTEL
2299 Kuhio Ave, Honolulu.

ASTON WAIKIKI BEACH TOWER
2470 Kalakaua Ave, Honolulu.

ASTON WAIKIKI BEACHSIDE HOTEL
2452 Kalakaua Ave, Honolulu.

ASTON WAIKIKI SUNSET
229 Paoakalani Ave, Honolulu.

CASTLE ISLAND COLONY
445 Seaside Ave, Honolulu.

CASTLE WAIKIKI SHORE
2161 Kalia Rd, Honolulu.

CONTINENTAL SURF HOTEL
2426 Kuhio Ave, Honolulu.

DOUBLETREE ALANA WAIKIKI HOTEL
1956 Ala Moana Blvd, Honolulu.

HAWAII POLO INN & TOWER
1696 Ala Moana Blvd, Honolulu.

HILTON HAWAIIAN VILLAGE BEACH RESORT & SPA
2005 Kalia Rd, Honolulu.

HONOLULU AIRPORT HOTEL
3401 N Nimitz Hwy, Honolulu.

HYATT REGENCY WAIKIKI RESORT & SPA
2424 Kalakaua Ave, Honolulu.

MARC SUITES WAIKIKI
412 Lewers St, Honolulu.

MIRAMAR AT WAIKIKI
2345 Kuhio Ave, Honolulu.

OCEAN RESORT HOTEL WAIKIKI
175 Paoakalani Ave, Honolulu.

OHANA EAST
150 Kaiulani Ave, Honolulu.

OHANA ISLANDER WAIKIKI
270 Lewers St, Honolulu.

OHANA MAILE SKY COURT
2058 Kuhio Ave, Honolulu.

OHANA REEF LANAI
225 Saratoga Rd, Honolulu.

OHANA ROYAL ISLANDER
2164 Kalia Rd, Honolulu.

OHANA WAIKIKI MALIA
2211 Kuhio Ave, Honolulu.

OHANA WAIKIKI SURF EAST
422 Royal Hawaiian Ave, Honolulu.

OHANA WAIKIKI WEST
2330 Kuhio Ave, Honolulu.

OUTRIGGER LUANA WAIKIKI
2045 Kalakaua Ave, Honolulu.

OUTRIGGER WAIKIKI ON THE BEACH
2335 Kalakaua Ave, Honolulu.

PARK SHORE WAIKIKI
2586 Kalakaua Ave, Honolulu.

QUEEN KAPIOLANI HOTEL
150 Kapahulu Ave, Honolulu.

RENAISSANCE ILIKAI WAIKIKI
1777 Ala Moana Blvd, Honolulu.

RESORTQUEST WAIKIKI BEACH HOTEL
2570 Kalakaua Ave, Honolulu.

SHERATON MOANA SURFRIDER
2365 Kalakaua Ave, Honolulu.

SHERATON WAIKIKI
2255 Kalakaua Ave, Honolulu.

Honolulu— rates from $99

For those who love the sophistication of the city but yearn for the pleasures of nature's most abundant beauty, Honolulu is an island city to return to again and again. Waikiki continues to serve as home base for endless possibilities for day trips full of cultural and scenic eco-adventures, from Diamond Head, Waikiki, the Marina or travel to surfings' famous North Shore.

Call: 800-50-HOTELS or book online at www.entertainment.com/travel

E16

Discounts subject to availability.
*See Rebate Rules on page E31-E32 and Program Rules on page E33.

Guaranteed Best Rate*

Book at www.entertainment.com/travel or call 1-800-50-HOTEL

SPA ATLANTIS RESORT & SPA
1350 N Ocean Blvd, Pompano Beach.

Sarasota

BEST WESTERN GOLDEN HOST
4675 N Tamiami Trl, Sarasota.

HILTON GARDEN INN SARASOTA
8270 N Tamiami Trl, Sarasota.

THE HELMSLEY SANDCASTLE
1540 Ben Franklin Dr, Sarasota.

St. Augustine

DAYS INN ST AUGUSTINE BEACH
541 A1a Beach Blvd, St. Augustine.

REGENCY INN & SUITES
331 A1a Beach Blvd, St. Augustine.

ST AUGUSTINE BEACHFRONT RESORT
300 A1a Beach Blvd, St. Augustine.

St. Petersburg

ALDEN BEACH RESORT
5900 Gulf Blvd, St. Petersburg.

BEST WESTERN BEACHFRONT RESORT
6200 Gulf Blvd, St. Petersburg.

SOUTH BEACH CONDO HOTEL
11360 Gulf Blvd, St. Petersburg.

Tampa

ASHLEY PLAZA HOTEL
111 W Fortune St, Tampa.

BEST WESTERN WESTSHORE
1200 N West Shore Blvd, Tampa.

CLARION HOTEL TAMPA WESTSHORE
5303 W Kennedy Blvd, Tampa.

COMFORT INN CONFERENCE CENTER
820 E Busch Blvd, Tampa.

LA QUINTA INN TAMPA AIRPORT
4730 W Spruce St, Tampa.

QUORUM HOTEL TAMPA WESTSHORE
700 N West Shore Blvd, Tampa.

SAILPORT WATERFRONT SUITES
2506 N Rocky Point Dr, Tampa.

West Palm Beach

BEST WESTERN PALM BCH LAKE INN
1800 Palm Beach Lakes Blvd, West Palm Beach.

COMFORT INN PALM BEACH LAKES
1901 Palm Beach Lakes Blvd, West Palm Beach.

MARRIOTT WEST PALM BEACH HOTEL
1001 Okeechobee Blvd, Palm Beach.

PGA NATIONAL RESORT AND SPA
400 Avenue Of Champions, Palm Beach.

RADISSON SUITE INN AIRPORT
1808 S Australian Ave, West Palm Beach.

WELLESLEY INN WEST PALM BEACH
1910 Palm Beach Lakes Blvd, West Palm Beach.

Georgia

Atlanta

AMERISUITES PERIMETER
1005 Crestline Pkwy Ne, Atlanta.

BEST WESTERN GRANADA SUITE HTL
1302 W Peachtree St Nw, Atlanta.

Shop & Book more hotels at entertainment.com/travel

COMFORT INN BUCKHEAD NORTH
5793 Roswell Rd Ne, Atlanta.

DAYS INN DOWNTOWN ATLANTA
300 Spring St Nw, Atlanta.

DOUBLETREE GUEST SUITES
6120 Peachtree Dunwoody Rd Ne, Atlanta.

THE WESTIN PEACHTREE PLAZA
210 Peachtree St Nw, Atlanta.

Savannah

HYATT REGENCY SAVANNAH
2 Base Dr, Savannah.

LA QUINTA INN SAVANNAH (I-95)
6 Gateway Blvd S, Savannah.

LA QUINTA INN SAVANNAH MIDTOWN
6805 Abercorn St, Savannah.

Hawaii

Big Island

ASTON SHORES AT WAIKOLOA
69-1035 Keana Pl, Waikoloa.

CASTLE HILO HAWAIIAN HOTEL
71 Banyan Dr, Hilo.

HAPUNA BEACH PRINCE HOTEL
62 100 Kaunaoa Dr, Kamuela.

HAWAII NANILOA HOTEL
93 Banyan Dr, Hilo.

HILO SEASIDE HOTEL
126 Banyan Dr, Hilo.

HILTON WAIKOLOA VILLAGE
425 Waikioloa Beach Drive, Waikoloa.

KONA SEASIDE HOTEL
75-5646 Palani Rd, Kailua Kona.

MAUNA KEA BEACH HOTEL
62-100 Mauna Kea Beach Dr, Kamuela.

OUTRIGGER KEAUHOU BEACH RESORT
78-6740 Alii Dr, Kailua Kona.

ROYAL KONA RESORT
75 5852 Alii Dr, Kailua Kona.

SHERATON KEAUHOU BAY RESORT & SPA
78-128 Ehukai St, Kailua Kona.

WAIKOLOA BEACH MARRIOTT
69-275 Waikoloa Beach Dr, Waikoloa.

Kauai

ALOHA BEACH RESORT HOTEL
3-5920 Kuhio Hwy, Kapaa.

BEST WESTERN PLANTATION HALE
484 Kuhio Hwy, Kapaa.

HYATT REGENCY KAUAI RESORT&SPA
1571 Poipu Rd, Koloa.

KAUAI SANDS HOTEL
420 Papaloa Rd, Kapaa.

OUTRIGGER KIAHUNA PLANTATION
2253 Poipu Rd, Koloa.

SHERATON KAUAI RESORT
2440 Hoonani Rd, Koloa.

Maui

ASTON AT PAPAKEA RESORT
3543 Lower Honoapiilani Rd, Lahaina.

ASTON AT THE MAUI BANYAN
2575 S Kihei Rd, Kihei.

ASTON KAANAPALI SHORES
3445 Honoapiilani Hwy, Lahaina.

ASTON MAHANA AT KAANAPALI
110 Kaanapali Shores Pl, Lahaina.

E15

You can access **25,000** hotels in over **700** cities. See sample listings above.
Shop and Book more hotels at www.entertainment.com/travel

Guaranteed Best Rate*
More listings online and over the phone!

THE REGISTRY RESORT & CLUB
475 Seagate Dr, Naples.

Orlando

AMERISUITES UNIVERSAL
5895 Caravan Ct, Orlando.

BEST WESTERN AIRPORT INN
8101 Aircenter Ct, Orlando.

BEST WESTERN MOVIELAND
6233 International Dr, Orlando.

BEST WESTERN PLAZA INTL
8738 International Dr, Orlando.

BUENA VISTA SUITES
8203 World Center Dr, Orlando.

CARIBE ROYALE SUITES & VILLAS
8101 World Center Dr, Orlando.

CLARION HOTEL UNIVERSAL
7299 Universal Blvd, Orlando.

COMFORT INN LAKE BUENA VISTA
8442 Palm Pkwy, Orlando.

COMFORT INN NEAR UNIVERSAL
6101 W Sand Lake Rd, Orlando.

COMFORT SUITES NEAR UNIVERSAL
5617 Major Blvd, Orlando.

COMFORT SUITES ORLANDO
9350 Turkey Lake Rd, Orlando.

COURTYARD LBV @ VISTA CENTER
8501 Palm Pkwy, Orlando.

DAYS INN ORLANDO AIRPORT
2323 Mccoy Rd, Orlando.

DOUBLETREE CASTLE HOTEL
8629 International Dr, Orlando.

EMBASSY VAC.RESORT@GRAND BEACH
8317 Lake Bryan Beach Blvd, Orlando.

HOLIDAY INN & STES UNIVERSAL
5905 S Kirkman Rd, Orlando.

HOLIDAY INN SUNSPREE RESORT
13351 State Road 535, Orlando.

HOWARD JOHNSON INN INTL DRIVE
6603 International Dr, Orlando.

HOWARD JOHNSON PLAZA UNIVERSAL
7050 S Kirkman Rd, Orlando.

I-DRIVE INN
6323 International Dr, Orlando.

LA QUINTA INN ORLANDO ARPRT W.
7931 Daetwyler Dr, Orlando.

LA QUINTA INN/SUITES AIRPORT N
7160 N Frontage Rd, Orlando.

ORLANDO GRAND PLAZA HOTEL
7400 International Dr, Orlando.

PARC CORNICHE CONDO SUITE HTL
6300 Parc Corniche Dr, Orlando.

QUALITY SUITES UNVRSL ORLANDO
7400 Canada Ave, Orlando.

RADISSON BARCELO HOTEL
8444 International Dr, Orlando.

RADISSON LAKE BUENA VISTA
8686 Palm Pkwy, Orlando.

RADISSON PLAZA HOTEL
60 S Ivanhoe Blvd, Orlando.

RODEWAY INN INTERNATIONAL
6327 International Dr, Orlando.

SHERATON SAFARI
12205 S Apopka Vineland Rd, Orlando.

SHERATON STUDIO CITY HOTEL
5905 International Dr, Orlando.

THE ENCLAVE SUITES AT ORLANDO
6165 Carrier Dr, Orlando.

THE PEABODY
9801 International Dr, Orlando.

UNIVERSAL'S HARD ROCK HOTEL
5800 Universal Blvd, Orlando.

UNIVERSAL'S PORTOFINO BAY
5601 Universal Blvd, Orlando.

UNIVERSAL'S ROYAL PACIFIC RSRT
6300 Hollywood Way, Orlando.

WESTGATE LAKES RESORT & SPA
10,000 Turkey Lake Road, Orlando.

WYNDHAM ORLANDO RESORT
8001 International Dr, Orlando.

Palm Beach

THE BREAKERS
1 S County Rd, Palm Beach.

Panama City

EDGEWATER BEACH RESORT
11212 Front Beach Rd, Panama City Beach.

LONG BEACH RESORT
10511 Front Beach Rd, Panama City Beach.

RAMADA LIMITED PANAMA CITY BCH
12907 Front Beach Rd, Panama City Beach.

Pompano Beach

OCEAN POINT RESORT
1208 N Ocean Blvd, Pompano Beach.

PARADISE BEACH RESORT
1380 S Ocean Blvd, Pompano Beach.

Orlando - rates from $49

Orlando will satisfy every vacationer's dreams. From theme park adventures and nightlife, to World class hotels with pampering spas and award winning golf courses, and endless sunshine to enjoy the nearby beaches and shopping extravaganzas, Orlando offers nonstop fun for families, couples or business travelers alike.

Call: 800-50-HOTELS or book online at www.entertainment.com/travel

E14

Discounts subject to availability.
*See Rebate Rules on page E31-E32 and Program Rules on page E33.

Guaranteed Best Rate*

Book at www.entertainment.com/travel or call 1-800-50-HOTEL

MAGICAL MEMORIES VILLAS
5075 W Irlo Bronson Memorial Hwy, Kissimmee.

MAINSTAY SUITES MAINGATE
4786 W Irlo Bronson Memorial Hwy, Kissimmee.

QUALITY SUITES MAINGATE EAST
5876 W Irlo Bronson Memorial Hwy, Kissimmee.

RADISSON RESORT PARKWAY
2900 Parkway Blvd, Kissimmee.

RADISSON WORLDGATE RESORT
3011 Maingate Ln, Kissimmee.

RAMADA INN RESORT
2950 Reedy Creek Blvd, Kissimmee.

RAMADA PLAZA & INN GATEWAY
7470 Highway 192 West, Kissimmee.

REGENCY EXPRESS INN & SUITES
2407 W Vine St, Kissimmee.

SERALAGO HOTEL & SUITES MAIN GATE EAST
5678 W Irlo Bronson Memorial Hwy, Kissimmee.

STAR ISLAND RESORT AND CLUB
5000 Avenue Of The Stars, Kissimmee.

WESTGATE TOWERS
7600 W Irlo Bronson Memorial Hwy, Kissimmee.

WESTGATE VACATION VILLAS
2770 N Old Lake Wilson Rd, Kissimmee.

Lake Buena Vista

BEST WESTERN IN THE WALT DISNEY WORLD RESORT
2000 Hotel Plaza Blvd, Orlando.

DOUBLETREE GUEST SUITES
2305 Hotel Plaza Blvd, Orlando.

GROSVENOR RESORT
1850 Hotel Plaza Blvd, Orlando.

HILTON WALT DISNEY WORLD
1751 Hotel Plaza Blvd, Orlando.

WALT DISNEY SWAN RESORT
1200 Epcot Resort Blvd, Orlando.

WALT DISNEY WORLD DOLPHIN
1500 Epcot Resort Blvd, Orlando.

WYNDHAM PALACE RESORT & SPA
1900 N Buena Vista Dr, Orlando.

Lantana

THE RITZ CARLTON PALM BEACH
100 S. Ocean Avenue, Palm Beach.

Long Island

COMFORT INN MEDFORD
2695 Route 112, Medford.

Madison

DAYS INN MADISON FL
Hwy-53 & I-10 Exit 37, Madison.

Marco Island

HILTON MARCO ISLAND BEACH RST
560 S Collier Blvd, Marco Island.

MARCO BEACH OCEAN RESORT
480 S Collier Blvd, Marco Island.

RADISSON MARCO ISLAND
600 S Collier Blvd, Marco Island.

Miami

BAYMONT INN & STES MIA AIRPORT
3501 Nw Le Jeune Road, Miami.

Shop & Book more hotels at entertainment.com/travel

CLARION HOTEL & SUITES
100 Se 4th St, Miami.

DAYS INN MIAMI AIRPORT NORTH
4767 Nw 36th St, Miami.

DAYS INN MIAMI CIVIC CENTER
1050 Nw 14th St, Miami.

GOLDEN GLADES INN CONF CENTER
16500 Nw 2nd Ave, Miami.

HILTON MIAMI AIRPORT
5101 Blue Lagoon Dr, Miami.

LA QUINTA INN MIAMI AIRPORT N.
7401 Nw 36th St, Miami.

MIAMI MARRIOTT BISCAYNE BAY
1633 N Bayshore Dr, Miami.

RIANDE CONTINENTAL BAYSIDE
146 Biscayne Blvd, Miami.

Miami Beach

BEST WESTERN SOUTH BEACH
1050 Washington Ave, Miami Beach.

BISCAYA HOTEL
4000 Alton Rd, Miami Beach.

CASABLANCA RESORT
6345 Collins Ave, Miami Beach.

CATALINA HOTEL & BEACH CLUB
1732 Collins Ave, Miami Beach.

COLONY HOTEL
736 Ocean Dr, Miami Beach.

DEAUVILLE BEACH RESORT
6701 Collins Ave, Miami Beach.

FAIRFIELD INN & STES MIAMI BCH
4101 Collins Ave, Miami Beach.

FONTAINEBLEAU RESORT
4441 Collins Ave, Miami Beach.

HADDON HALL HOTEL SOUTH BEACH
1500 Collins Ave, Miami Beach.

HOWARD JOHNSON PLAZA CARIBBEAN
3737 Collins Ave, Miami Beach.

HOWARD JOHNSON PLAZA DEZERLAND
8701 Collins Ave, Miami Beach.

LE MERIDIEN SUNNY ISLES BEACH
18683 Collins Ave, North Miami Beach.

LOEWS MIAMI BEACH
1601 Collins Ave, Miami Beach.

MARCO POLO RAMADA PLAZA
19201 Collins Ave, North Miami Beach.

NEWPORT BEACHSIDE RESORT
16701 Collins Ave, North Miami Beach.

RIANDE CONTINENTAL SOUTH BEACH
1825 Collins Ave, Miami Beach.

RIU FLORIDA BEACH
3101 Collins Ave, Miami Beach.

SEACOAST SUITES
5101 Collins Ave, Miami Beach.

TRUMP INT'L SONESTA BEACH RSRT
18101 Collins Ave, North Miami Beach.

TUDOR HOTEL AND SUITES
1111 Collins Ave, Miami Beach.

VILLA CAPRI
3010 Collins Ave, Miami Beach.

Naples

QUALITY INN & STE GOLF RESORT
4100 Golden Gate Pkwy, Naples.

THE HAWTHORN SUITES OF NAPLES
3557 Pine Ridge Rd, Naples.

E13

You can access 25,000 hotels in over 700 cities. See sample listings above.
Shop and Book more hotels at www.entertainment.com/travel

Guaranteed Best Rate*
More listings online and over the phone!

HOWARD JOHNSON OCEANS EDGE RST
700 N Fort Lauderdale Beach Blvd, Ft. Lauderdale.

LA QUINTA INN CYPRESS CREEK
999 W Cypress Creek Rd, Ft. Lauderdale.

OCEAN MANOR RESORT
4040 Galt Ocean Dr, Ft. Lauderdale.

PELICAN BEACH RESORT
2000 N Atlantic Blvd, Ft. Lauderdale.

RAMADA INN AIRPORT CRUISEPORT
2275 W State Road 84, Ft. Lauderdale.

RAMADA PLAZA BEACH RESORT
4060 Galt Ocean Dr, Ft. Lauderdale.

RED CARPET INN AIRPORT
2460 W State Road 84, Ft. Lauderdale.

RIVERSIDE HOTEL
620 E Las Olas Blvd, Ft. Lauderdale.

SEA CLUB RESORT
619 N Fort Lauderdale Beach Blvd, Ft. Lauderdale.

SHERATON YANKEE CLIPPER
1140 Seabreeze Blvd, Ft. Lauderdale.

SHERATON YANKEE TRADER
321 N Ft Lauderdale Beach Bl, Ft. Lauderdale.

Ft. Myers

BEST WESTERN INN & STES CORAL BRIDGE/FT MYERS
9200 College Pkwy, Ft. Myers.

COUNTRY INN & SUITES FT MYERS - SANIBEL GATE
13901 Shell Point Plz, Ft. Myers.

LA QUINTA INN FT MYERS
4850 S Cleveland Ave, Ft. Myers.

Ft. Myers Beach

DIAMONDHEAD BEACH RESORT
2000 Estero Blvd, Ft. Myers Beach.

LANI KAI BEACHFRONT
1400 Estero Blvd, Ft. Myers Beach.

OUTRIGGER BEACH RESORT
6200 Estero Blvd, Ft. Myers Beach.

Hollywood

LA QUINTA INN/SUITES AIRPORT
2620 N 26th Ave, Hollywood.

RAMADA INN HOLLYWOOD BEACH RST
101 N Ocean Dr, Hollywood.

RAMADA PLAZA DOWNTOWN HOLLYWOOD
1925 Harrison St, Hollywood.

WHITE SANDS INN
5501 N Ocean Dr, Hollywood.

Jacksonville

LA QUINTA INN JAX AIRPORT N
812 Dunn Ave, Jacksonville.

OMNI JACKSONVILLE HOTEL
245 Water St, Jacksonville.

RADISSON HOTEL JACKSONVILLE BUTLER BLVD.
4700 Salisbury Road, Jacksonville.

RADISSON RIVERWALK
1515 Prudential Dr, Jacksonville.

Kissimmee

AMERICAN VACATION HOMES
2983 Vineland Rd, Kissimmee.

BEST WESTERN MAINGATE EAST
4018 W Vine St, Kissimmee.

COMFORT SUITES MAINGATE EAST
2775 Florida Plaza Blvd, Kissimmee.

DAYS SUITES AT OLD TOWN
5820 W Irlo Bronson Memorial Hwy, Kissimmee.

ECONOLODGE MAINGATE RESORT
7514 W Irlo Bronson Memorial Hwy, Kissimmee.

ENDLESS SUMMER VACATION HOMES
1154 W Osceola Pkwy, Kissimmee.

FANTASY WORLD CLUB VILLAS
5005 Kyngs Heath Rd, Kissimmee.

GLOBAL VACATION HOMES
2833 Shea Ct Ofc Address, Kissimmee.

HOLIDAY INN MAINGATE WEST
7601 Black Lake Rd, Kissimmee.

HOLIDAY VILLAS
2928 Vineland Rd, Kissimmee.

HOMEWOOD SUITES DISNEY WORLD
3100 Parkway Blvd, Kissimmee.

HOMEWOOD SUITES DISNEY WORLD
3501 W Vine St, Kissimmee.

HOWARD JOHNSON MAINGATE EAST
6051 W Irlo Bronson Memorial Hwy, Kissimmee.

HOWARD JOHNSON MAINGATE RESORT
8660 W Irlo Bronson Memorial Hwy, Kissimmee.

LA QUINTA INN LAKESIDE
7769 W Irlo Bronson Memorial Hwy, Kissimmee.

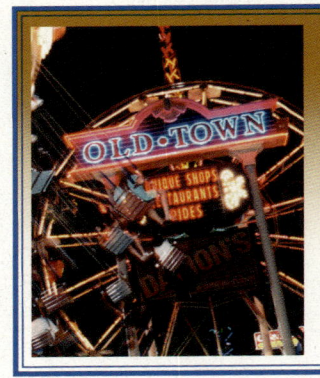

Kissimmee— rates from $39

When you stay in Kissimmee for your next Florida vacation, you are in the center of all the fun. Located in the center of all the major theme parks, dinner shows, sport venues and outdoor activities, Kissimmee vacations are jam-packed with endless options.

Call: 800-50-HOTELS or book online at www.entertainment.com/travel

Discounts subject to availability.
*See Rebate Rules on page E31-E32 and Program Rules on page E33.

Guaranteed Best Rate*

Book at www.entertainment.com/travel or call 1-800-50-HOTEL

JURYS WASHINGTON
1500 New Hampshire Ave Nw, Washington.

L'ENFANT PLAZA HOTEL
480 Lenfant Plz Sw, Washington.

LINCOLN SUITES DOWNTOWN
1823 L St Nw, Washington.

PRESIDENT INN
1600 New York Ave Ne, Washington.

RIVER INN
924 25th St Nw, Washington.

ST GREGORY HOTEL & SUITES
2033 M St Nw, Washington.

THE CAPITOL HILL SUITES
200 C St Se, Washington.

TRAVELODGE GATEWAY
1917 Bladensburg Rd Ne, Washington.

WASHINGTON PLAZA
10 Thomas Cir Nw, Washington.

WASHINGTON SUITES GEORGETOWN
2500 Pennsylvania Ave Nw, Washington.

WYNDHAM WASHINGTON, DC
1400 M St Nw, Washington.

Florida

Boca Raton

BOCA RATON BRIDGE HOTEL
999 E Camino Real, Boca Raton.

BOCA RATON PLAZA HTL & STES
2901 N Federal Hwy, Boca Raton.

HILTON GARDEN INN BOCA RATON
8201 Congress Ave, Boca Raton.

Championsgate

OMNI ORLANDO AT CHAMPIONSGATE
1500 Masters Blvd, Davenport.

Clearwater

BEST WESTERN SEA WAKE BEACH
691 S Gulfview Blvd, Clearwater Beach.

LA QUINTA INN CLEARWATER
21338 Us Highway 19 N, Clearwater.

QUALITY HOTEL ON THE BEACH
655 S Gulfview Blvd, Clearwater Beach.

RADISSON HOTEL CLEARWATER CENTRAL
20967 Us Highway 19 N, Clearwater.

SEA STONE RESORT
445 Hamden Dr, Clearwater Beach.

SHEPHARDS BEACH RESORT
619 S Gulfview Blvd, Clearwater Beach.

SUPER 8 CLEARWATER AIRPORT
13260 34th St N, Clearwater.

Cocoa Beach

COMFORT INN & SUITES RESORT
3901 N Atlantic Ave, Cocoa Beach.

HILTON COCOA BEACH OCEANFRONT
1550 N Atlantic Ave, Cocoa Beach.

LA QUINTA INN COCOA BEACH
1275 N Atlantic Ave, Cocoa Beach.

Davenport

INTEGRA BAHAMA BAY RESORT
400 Gran Bahama Blvd, Davenport.

SUPERIOR HOLIDAY HOMES
2700 Sand Mine Rd, Davenport.

Shop & Book more hotels at entertainment.com/travel

Daytona Beach

BAHAMA HOUSE
2001 S. Atlantic Ave, Daytona.

BERMUDA HOUSE
2560 N Atlantic Ave, Daytona.

DAYTONA INN BEACH RESORT
219 S Atlantic Ave, Daytona.

HAWAIIAN INN OCEANFRONT RESORT
2301 S Atlantic Ave, Daytona.

OCEAN SANDS BEACH RESORT
1024 N Atlantic Ave, Daytona.

OCEANSIDE INN
1909 S Atlantic Ave, Daytona.

PLAZA OCEAN CLUB
640 N Atlantic Ave, Daytona.

SUNTERRA DAYTONA BEACH REGENCY
400 N. Atlantic Ave, Daytona.

Deerfield Beach

COMFORT INN OCEANSIDE
50 S A1a, Deerfield Beach.

COMFORT SUITES DEERFIELD BEACH
1040 E Newport Center Dr, Deerfield Beach.

RAMADA INN DEERFIELD BEACH
1250 W Hillsboro Blvd, Deerfield Beach.

Florida Keys

COCONUT CAY RESORT & MARINA
7196 Overseas Hwy, Marathon.

COMFORT INN KEY WEST
3824 N Roosevelt Blvd, Key West.

FAIRFIELD INN KEY WEST
2400 N Roosevelt Blvd, Key West.

HAWKS CAY RESORT
61 Hawks Cay Blvd, Marathon.

HOWARD JOHNSON RESORT
Bayside At Mm 102 Overseas H, Key Largo.

HYATT KEY WEST RESORT & MARINA
601 Front St, Key West.

INN AT KEY WEST
3420 N Roosevelt Blvd, Key West.

KEY COLONY BAY HOTEL
13351 Overseas Hwy, Marathon.

MARINA DEL MAR OCEANSIDE
527 Caribbean Blvd, Key Largo.

MARINER'S CLUB KEY LARGO
97501 Overseas Hwy, Key Largo.

OCEAN KEY RESORT
Zero Duval Street, Key West.

QUALITY INN & SUITES
3850 N Roosevelt Blvd, Key West.

RADISSON HOTEL KEY WEST
3820 N Roosevelt Blvd, Key West.

RAMADA LIMITED
99751 Overseas Hwy, Key Largo.

SHERATON KEY WEST
2001 S Roosevelt Blvd, Key West.

Ft. Lauderdale

BEST WESTERN OAKLAND PARK INN
3001 N Federal Hwy, Ft. Lauderdale.

BONAVENTURE RESORT & SPA
250 Racquet Club Rd, Ft. Lauderdale.

CLARION LAUDERDALE BEACH RST
4660 N Ocean Dr, Ft. Lauderdale.

EL PALACIO HOTEL AND RESORT
4900 Powerline Rd, Ft. Lauderdale.

FORT LAUDERDALE BEACH RESORT
4221 N. Ocean Blvd/A1a, Ft. Lauderdale.

E11

You can access 25,000 hotels in over 700 cities. See sample listings above.
Shop and Book more hotels at www.entertainment.com/travel

Guaranteed Best Rate*
More listings online and over the phone!

FOREST SUITES RESORT
1 Lake Pkwy, South Lake Tahoe.

Sunnyvale

MAPLE TREE INN
711 E El Camino Real, Sunnyvale.

QUALITY INN CIVIC CENTER
852 W El Camino Real, Sunnyvale.

WILD PALMS - JOIE DE VIVRE
910 E Fremont Ave, Sunnyvale.

Ventura

COUNTRY INN & SUITES VENTURA
298 S Chestnut St, Ventura.

LA QUINTA INN VENTURA
5818 Valentine Rd, Ventura.

SHORES INN & SUITES
1059 S Seaward Ave, Ventura.

Colorado

Boulder

MILLENNIUM HARVEST HOUSE
1345 28th St, Englewood.

Colorado Springs

CHEYENNE MOUNTAIN RESORT
3225 Broadmoor Valley Rd, Colorado Springs.

THE ACADEMY HOTEL
8110 N Academy Blvd, Colorado Springs.

WYNDHAM COLORADO SPRINGS
5580 Tech Center Dr, Colorado Springs.

Denver

COMFORT INN & SUITES
4685 Quebec St, Denver.

COURTYARD DENVER SOUTH
8320 S Valley Hwy, Englewood.

GRAND HYATT DENVER
1750 Welton St, Denver.

GUESTHOUSE HOTEL STAPLETON
3737 Quebec St, Denver.

LA QUINTA INN CHERRY CREEK
1975 S Colorado Blvd, Denver.

LA QUINTA INN DENVER DOWNTOWN
3500 Fox St, Denver.

LA QUINTA INN/STES TECH CTR
7077 S Clinton St, Englewood.

RAMADA INN DOWNTOWN DENVER
1150 E Colfax Ave, Denver.

RED LION DENVER CENTRAL
4040 Quebec St, Denver.

Connecticut

For this state's listings go to entertainment.com/travel

Delaware

For this state's listings go to entertainment.com/travel

District Of Columbia

Washington D.C.

BEACON HOTEL WASHINGTON DC
1615 Rhode Island Ave Nw, Washington.

BEST WESTERN CAPITOL SKYLINE
10 I St Sw, Washington.

CARLYLE SUITES
1731 New Hampshire Ave Nw, Washington.

CHURCHILL HOTEL
1914 Connecticut Ave Nw, Washington.

CLUB QUARTERS
839 17th St Nw, Washington.

COMFORT INN CONVENTION CENTER/DOWNTOWN
1201 13th St Nw, Washington.

CONNECTICUT AVENUE DAYS INN
4400 Connecticut Ave Nw, Washington.

COURTYARD WASHINGTON NORTHWEST
1900 Connecticut Ave Nw, Washington.

FOUR POINTS WASHINGTON D.C.
1201 K St Nw, Washington.

HOLIDAY INN GEORGETOWN
2101 Wisconsin Ave Nw, Washington.

HOTEL HELIX
1430 Rhode Island Ave Nw, Washington.

JURYS NORMANDY INN
2118 Wyoming Ave Nw, Washington.

Washington D.C. - rates from $60

Our nation's capital offers year round experiences for all types of visitors. DC offers a diverse selection of restaurants from cafes to bistros to hip new restaurants, world renowned shopping, world class performers and free musical concerts. Visitors will enjoy exploring historic neighborhoods and visiting the famous sites, inspiring monuments and museums - many of which offer free admission. Don't miss the festivals and events during Cherry Blossom season from late March through early April!

Call: 800-50-HOTELS or book online at www.entertainment.com/travel

E10

Discounts subject to availability.
*See Rebate Rules on page E31-E32 and Program Rules on page E33.

Guaranteed Best Rate*

Book at www.entertainment.com/travel or call 1-800-50-HOTEL

HERITAGE MARINA HOTEL
2550 Van Ness Ave, San Francisco.
HILTON FISHERMAN'S WHARF
2620 Jones St, San Francisco.
HILTON SAN FRANCISCO
333 Ofarrell St, San Francisco.
HOTEL NIKKO SAN FRANCISCO
222 Mason St, San Francisco.
HYATT AT FISHERMAN'S WHARF
555 N Point St, San Francisco.
KING GEORGE HOTEL UNION SQUARE
334 Mason St, San Francisco.
LA QUINTA INN SAN FRANCISCO
1050 Van Ness Ave, San Francisco.
MARRIOTT FISHERMAN'S WHARF
1250 Columbus Ave, San Francisco.
MONARCH
1015 Geary St, San Francisco.
PAN PACIFIC HOTEL - SAN FRANCISCO
500 Post St, San Francisco.
POWELL HOTEL
28 Cyril Magnin St, San Francisco.
RADISSON FISHERMAN'S WHARF
250 Beach St, San Francisco.
RADISSON MIYAKO
1625 Post St, San Francisco.
RAMADA PLAZA DOWNTOWN
1231 Market St, San Francisco.
RENAISSANCE PARC 55
55 Cyril Magnin St, San Francisco.
SAVOY HOTEL
580 Geary St, San Francisco.
SHERATON FISHERMANS WHARF
2500 Mason St, San Francisco.
SIR FRANCIS DRAKE HOTEL - A KIMPTON HOTEL
450 Powell St, San Francisco.
THE MAXWELL, A JOIE DE VIVRE BOUTIQUE HOTEL
386 Geary St, San Francisco.
THE WESTIN ST FRANCIS
335 Powell St, San Francisco.
TUSCAN INN FISHERMAN'S WHARF
425 N Point St, San Francisco.
VILLA FLORENCE HOTEL - A KIMPTON HOTEL
225 Powell St, San Francisco.
WHARF INN
2601 Mason St, San Francisco.
YORK HOTEL
940 Sutter St, San Francisco.

San Francisco International Airport

BEST WESTERN GROSVENOR HOTEL
380 S Airport Blvd, South San Francisco.
CLARION SAN FRANCISCO AIRPORT
401 E Millbrae Ave, Millbrae.
COMFORT INN AIRPORT
1390 El Camino Real, Millbrae.
EMBASSY SUITES SFO AIRPORT
150 Anza Blvd, Burlingame.
FOUR POINTS SAN FRANCISCO
264 S Airport Blvd, South San Francisco.
GOOD NITE INN SFO
245 S Airport Blvd, South San Francisco.
HYATT REGENCY SFO AIRPORT
1333 Bayshore Hwy, Burlingame.

Shop & Book more hotels at entertainment.com/travel

LA QUINTA INN SFO AIRPORT
20 Airport Blvd, South San Francisco.
QUALITY SUITES MILLBRAE
250 El Camino Real, Millbrae.
SHERATON GATEWAY SAN FRANCISCO AIRPORT HOTEL
600 Airport Blvd, Burlingame.
TRAVELODGE SFO AIRPORT NORTH
326 S Airport Blvd, South San Francisco.

San Jose

COMFORT INN SAN JOSE
875 N 13th St, San Jose.
HYATT SAINTE CLAIRE
302 S Market St, San Jose.
HYATT SAN JOSE
1740 N 1st St, San Jose.
WYNDHAM SAN JOSE
1350 N 1st St, San Jose.

San Luis Obispo

BEST WESTERN ROYAL OAK HOTEL
214 Madonna Rd, San Luis Obispo.
TRAVELODGE SAN LUIS OBISPO
1825 Monterey St, San Luis Obispo.
TRAVELODGE SAN LUIS OBISPO
345 Marsh St, San Luis Obispo.

Santa Ana

DOUBLETREE CLUB ORANGE COUNTY
7 Hutton Centre Dr, Santa Ana.
QUALITY SUITES JOHN WAYNE AP
2701 Hotel Terrace Dr., Santa Ana.
SANTA ANA PLAZA HOTEL
1600 E 1st St, Santa Ana.

Santa Barbara

BEST WESTERN PEPPER TREE INN
3850 State St, Santa Barbara.
HOTEL OCEANA SANTA BARBARA
202 W Cabrillo Blvd, Santa Barbara.
SANDPIPER LODGE
3525 State St, Santa Barbara.
THE SANDMAN INN
3714 State St, Santa Barbara.

Santa Clara

GUESTHOUSE INN & SUITES
2930 El Camino Real, Santa Clara.
HOWARD JOHNSON INN SANTA CLARA
2499 El Camino Real, Santa Clara.
RAMADA LIMITED SANTA CLARA
1655 El Camino Real, Santa Clara.

Santa Monica

RADISSON HUNTLEY SANTA MONICA
1111 2nd St, Santa Monica.
THE GEORGIAN HOTEL
1415 Ocean Ave, Santa Monica.
VENICE ON THE BEACH HOTEL
2819 Ocean Front Walk, Santa Monica.

South Lake Tahoe

3 PEAKS RESORT & BEACH CLUB
931 Park Ave, South Lake Tahoe.
EMBASSY SUITES RESORT
4130 Lake Tahoe Blvd, South Lake Tahoe.

You can access **25,000** hotels in over **700** cities. See sample listings above.
Shop and Book more hotels at www.entertainment.com/travel

Guaranteed Best Rate*
More listings online and over the phone!

HARBORVIEW INN
550 W Grape St, San Diego.

HAWTHORN SUITES SAN DIEGO
1335 Hotel Cir S, San Diego.

HILTON LA JOLLA TORREY PINES
10950 N Torrey Pines Rd, La Jolla.

HILTON SAN DIEGO RESORT
1775 E Mission Bay Dr, San Diego.

HOTEL LA JOLLA AT THE SHORES
7955 La Jolla Shores Dr, La Jolla.

HOWARD JOHNSON SEA WORLD
3330 Rosecrans St, San Diego.

HUMPHREY'S HALF MOON & SUITES
2303 Shelter Island Dr, San Diego.

HYATT REGENCY ISLANDIA
1441 Quivira Rd, San Diego.

HYATT REGENCY LA JOLLA
3777 La Jolla Village Dr, San Diego.

KINGS INN
1333 Hotel Cir S, San Diego.

MANCHESTER GRAND HYATT
1 Market Pl, San Diego.

MISSION VALLEY RESORT
875 Hotel Cir S, San Diego.

OCEAN PARK INN
710 Grand Ave, San Diego.

OLD TOWN WESTERN INN & SUITES
3889 Arista St, San Diego.

OLYMPIC RESORT
6111 El Camino Real, Carlsbad.

PARADISE POINT RESORT & SPA NOBLE HSE RESORT
1404 Vacation Rd, San Diego.

RADISSON HARBOR VIEW
1646 Front St, San Diego.

RADISSON LA JOLLA
3299 Holiday Ct, La Jolla.

RAMADA INN & SUITES CARLSBAD
751 Macadamia Dr, Carlsbad.

RAMADA INN & SUITES GASLAMP
830 6th Ave, San Diego.

RAMADA INN SAN DIEGO CONF CTR
5550 Kearny Mesa Rd, San Diego.

RAMADA PLAZA HOTEL CIRCLE SOUTH
2151 Hotel Cir S, San Diego.

RED LION HANALEI HOTEL
2270 Hotel Cir N, San Diego.

SAN DIEGO MARRIOTT LA JOLLA
4240 La Jolla Village Dr, La Jolla.

SEA LODGE ON LA JOLLA SHORES BEACH
8110 Camino Del Oro, La Jolla.

SHELTER POINTE HOTEL
1551 Shelter Island Dr, San Diego.

SHERATON SAN DIEGO HTL MARINA
1380 Harbor Island Dr, San Diego.

SHERATON SUITES SAN DIEGO
701 A St, San Diego.

SOMMERSET SUITES
606 Washington St, San Diego.

SUPER 8 MOTEL SEA WORLD ZOO
445 Hotel Cir S, San Diego.

THE DANA ON MISSION BAY - SEA WORLD
1710 W Mission Bay Dr, San Diego.

TOWN & COUNTRY RESORT
500 Hotel Cir N, San Diego.

WYNDHAM EMERALD PLAZA
400 W Broadway, San Diego.

San Francisco

ADANTE HOTEL
610 Geary St, San Francisco.

ALEXANDER INN & SUITES
415 Ofarrell St, San Francisco.

BEST INN FISHERMANS WHARF
2850 Van Ness Ave, San Francisco.

BEST WESTERN AMERICANIA
121 7th St, San Francisco.

BEST WESTERN MIYAKO INN
1800 Sutter St, San Francisco.

BRITTON
112 7th St, San Francisco.

CARTWRIGHT HOTEL
524 Sutter St, San Francisco.

CATHEDRAL HILL HOTEL
1101 Van Ness Ave, San Francisco.

CHANCELLOR HOTEL UNION SQUARE.
433 Powell St, San Francisco.

CLUB QUARTERS IN SAN FRANCISCO
424 Clay St, San Francisco.

COMFORT INN BY THE BAY
2775 Van Ness Ave, San Francisco.

EDWARDIAN SAN FRANCISCO HOTEL
1668 Market St, San Francisco.

GRAND HYATT SAN FRANCISCO
345 Stockton St, San Francisco.

GROSVENOR SUITES
899 Pine St, San Francisco.

HANDLERY HOTEL
351 Geary Street, San Francisco.

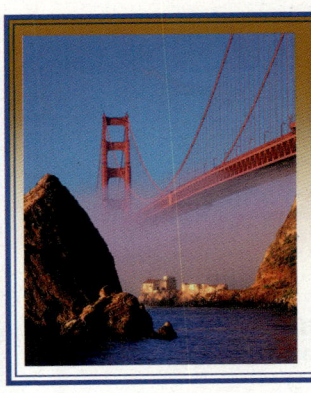

San Francisco— rates from $79

Cosmopolitan flair, spectacular scenery cultural diversity makes San Francisco one of the top destinations in the world. Perennial favorites include Fisherman's Wharf, Chinatown, cable cars, the Golden Gate Bridge and the mission district. Its shopping hub, Union Square, anchors a who's who of world-famous stores.

Call: 800-50-HOTELS or book online at www.entertainment.com/travel

E8

Discounts subject to availability.
*See Rebate Rules on page E31-E32 and Program Rules on page E33.

Guaranteed Best Rate*

Book at www.entertainment.com/travel or call 1-800-50-HOTEL

Orange

BEST VALUE INN ANAHEIM
3101 W Chapman Ave, Orange.

DOUBLETREE ANAHEIM ORANGE CNTY
100 The City Dr S, Orange.

HAWTHORN SUITES ORANGE
720 The City Dr S, Orange.

Palm Springs

7 SPRINGS INN & SUITES
950 N Indian Canyon Dr, Palm Springs.

PALM SPRINGS RIVIERA RESORT
1600 N Indian Canyon Dr, Palm Springs.

QUALITY INN-PALM SPRINGS
1269 E Palm Canyon Dr, Palm Springs.

ROYAL SUN INN
1700 S Palm Canyon Dr, Palm Springs.

Pismo Beach

BEST WESTERN SHORE CLIFF
2555 Price St, Pismo Beach.

COTTAGE INN BY THE SEA
2351 Price St, Pismo Beach.

ROSE GARDEN INN PISMO BEACH
230 Five Cities Dr, Pismo Beach.

SPYGLASS INN
2705 Spyglass Dr, Pismo Beach.

Redding

LA QUINTA INN REDDING
2180 Hilltop Dr, Redding.

RAMADA LIMITED REDDING
1286 Twin View Blvd, Redding.

RED LION HOTEL REDDING
1830 Hilltop Dr, Redding.

Sacramento

GOOD NITE INN SACRAMENTO
25 Howe Ave, Sacramento.

LA QUINTA INN SACRAMENTO DWTWN
200 Jibboom St, Sacramento.

RED LION HOTEL SACRAMENTO
1401 Arden Way, Sacramento.

SHERATON GRAND SACRAMENTO
1230 J St, Sacramento.

THE CLARION HOTEL
2600 Auburn Blvd, Sacramento.

VAGABOND INN SACRAMENTO MIDTWN
1319 30th St, Sacramento.

San Diego

BAHIA RESORT HOTEL
998 W Mission Bay Dr, San Diego.

BEST WESTERN BLUE SEA LODGE
707 Pacific Beach Dr, San Diego.

BEST WESTERN MISSION BAY
2575 Clairemont Dr, San Diego.

BEST WESTERN SEVEN SEAS
411 Hotel Cir S, San Diego.

BRISTOL HOTEL
1055 1st Ave, San Diego.

CALIFORNIA SUITES HOTEL
5415 Clairemont Mesa Blvd, San Diego.

CATAMARAN RESORT AND SPA
3999 Mission Blvd, San Diego.

COMFORT INN & SUITES ZOO SEA WORLD
2485 Hotel Circle Pl, San Diego.

COMFORT INN GASLAMP
660 G St, San Diego.

COMFORT SUITES
631 Camino Del Rio S, San Diego.

DAYS INN & SUITES SEAWORLD
3350 Rosecrans St, San Diego.

DAYS INN DOWNTOWN SAN DIEGO
833 Ash St, San Diego.

DAYS INN HOTEL CIRCLE
543 Hotel Cir S, San Diego.

DAYS INN MISSION BAY
4540 Mission Bay Dr, San Diego.

DOUBLETREE CLUB
1515 Hotel Cir S, San Diego.

DOUBLETREE DEL MAR
11915 El Camino Real, San Diego.

DOUBLETREE MISSION VALLEY
7450 Hazard Center Dr, San Diego.

EMBASSY SUITES SAN DIEGO BAY
601 Pacific Hwy, San Diego.

EMPRESS HOTEL
7766 Fay Ave, La Jolla.

ESTANCIA LA JOLLA HOTEL & SPA
9700 N Torrey Pines Rd, La Jolla.

FOUR POINTS SHERATON SAN DIEGO
8110 Aero Dr, San Diego.

GOOD NITE INN QUALCOMM STADIUM
4545 Waring Rd, San Diego.

GOOD NITE INN SEA WORLD
3880 Greenwood St, San Diego.

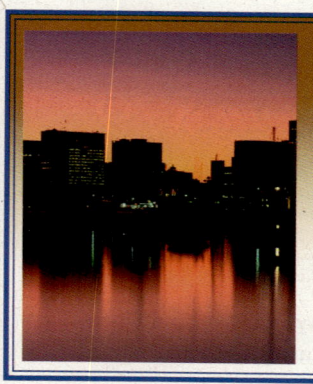

San Diego– rates from $45

San Diego is renowned for its idyllic climate, 70 miles of pristine beaches and a dazzling array of world-class family attractions. Popular attractions include the world-famous San Diego Zoo and Wild Animal Park, Sea World San Diego and LEGOLAND California. San Diego offers an expansive variety of things to see and do, appealing to guests of all ages from around the world.

Call: 800-50-HOTELS or book online at www.entertainment.com/travel

E7

You can access **25,000** hotels in over **700** cities. See sample listings above.
Shop and Book more hotels at www.entertainment.com/travel

Guaranteed Best Rate*
More listings online and over the phone!

HOLLYWOOD ROOSEVELT
7000 Hollywood Blvd, Los Angeles.

HYATT WEST HOLLYWOOD
8401 W Sunset Blvd, West Hollywood.

LE MONTROSE SUITE HOTEL
900 Hammond St, West Hollywood.

RAMADA - HOLLYWOOD NEAR UNIVERSAL STUDIOS
1160 N Vermont Ave, Los Angeles.

RAMADA PLAZA HOTEL & SUITES - WEST HOLLYWOOD
8585 Santa Monica Blvd, West Hollywood.

Indian Wells

INDIAN WELLS RESORT HOTEL
76661 Us Highway 111, Indian Wells.

MIRAMONTE RESORT
45000 Indian Wells Ln, Indian Wells.

RENAISSANCE ESMERALDA RESORT
44400 Indian Wells Ln, Indian Wells.

Inglewood

ADVENTURER ALL SUITE HOTEL LAX
4200 W Century Blvd, Inglewood.

BEST WESTERN SUITES HOTEL
5005 W Century Blvd, Inglewood.

COMFORT INN & SUITES LAX
4922 W Century Blvd, Inglewood.

RAMADA LTD LAX AIRPORT EAST
4300 W Century/I-405, Inglewood.

La Mesa

RAMADA LTD LA MESA CA
7911 University Ave, La Mesa.

Long Beach

GUESTHOUSE HOTEL LONG BEACH
5325 E Pacific Coast Hwy, Long Beach.

QUEEN MARY HOTEL
1126 Queens Hwy, Long Beach.

THE COAST LONG BEACH HOTEL
700 Queensway Dr, Long Beach.

Los Angeles

BEST WESTERN DRAGON GATE INN
818 N Hill St, Los Angeles.

BEST WESTERN REDONDO BEACH
1850 S Pacific Coast Hwy, Redondo Beach.

COMFORT INN LA CITY CENTER
1710 W 7th St, Los Angeles.

ELAN HOTEL MODERN
8435 Beverly Blvd, Los Angeles.

LE MERIDIEN BEVERLY HILLS
465 S La Cienega Blvd, Los Angeles.

LUXE HOTEL SUNSET BOULEVARD
11461 W Sunset Blvd, Los Angeles.

MILLENNIUM BILTMORE
506 S Grand Ave, Los Angeles.

MIYAKO HOTEL LOS ANGELES
328 E 1st St, Los Angeles.

NEW OTANI
120 S Los Angeles St, Los Angeles.

PORTOFINO HOTEL & YACHT CLUB-NOBLE HSE HOTEL
260 Portofino Way, Redondo Beach.

QUALITY INN & SUITES
1901 W Olympic Blvd, Los Angeles.

REDONDO PIER INN
206 S Pacific Coast Hwy, Redondo Beach.

THE WESTIN BONAVENTURE
404 S Figueroa St, Los Angeles.

800-50-HOTEL (6835)
Call & Book 25,000 Hotels!

WILSHIRE GRAND LOS ANGELES
930 Wilshire Blvd, Los Angeles.

YOURSTAY WILSHIRE APARTMENTS
348 Hauser Blvd, Los Angeles.

Los Angeles International Airport

CLARION HOTEL LAX AIRPORT
5249 W Century Blvd, Los Angeles.

EMBASSY SUITES LAX INT'L AIRPORT S.
1440 E. Imperial Ave., El Segundo.

FOUR POINTS SHERATON LAX
9750 Airport Blvd, Los Angeles.

HACIENDA LAX AIRPORT
525 N Sepulveda Blvd, El Segundo.

LAX PLAZA HOTEL
6333 Bristol Pkwy, Culver City.

RADISSON AT LAX AIRPORT
6225 W Century Blvd, Los Angeles.

RADISSON LOS ANGELES WESTSIDE
6161 W Centinela Ave, Culver City.

SUNBURST SPA & SUITES MOTEL
3900 Sepulveda Blvd, Culver City.

TRAVELODGE LAX SOUTH
1804 E Sycamore Ave, El Segundo.

Lynnwood

TRAVELODGE LYNWOOD CENTURY FWY
11401 Long Beach Blvd, Lynnwood.

Marina Del Rey

MARINA DEL REY HOTEL
13534 Bali Way, Marina Del Rey.

MARINA INTERNATIONAL HOTEL
4200 Admiralty Way, Marina Del Rey.

RAMADA LIMITED MARINA DEL RAY
3130 Washington Blvd, Marina Del Rey.

Newport Beach

BEST WESTERN NEWPORT BEACH INN
6208 W Pacific Coast Hwy, Newport Beach.

RADISSON NEWPORT BEACH
4545 Macarthur Blvd, Newport Beach.

SUTTON PLACE HOTEL
4500 Macarthur Blvd, Newport Beach.

Oakland

DAYS INN OAKLAND AIRPORT
8350 Edes Ave, Oakland.

FAIRFIELD INN & SUITES
8452 Edes Ave, Oakland.

JACK LONDON INN
444 Embarcadero W, Oakland.

PARK PLAZA HOTEL
150 Hegenberger Rd, Oakland.

Oceanside

LA QUINTA INN OCEANSIDE
937 N Coast Hwy, Oceanside.

OCEANSIDE MARINA SUITES
2008 Harbor Dr N, Oceanside.

RAMADA LIMITED OCEANSIDE
1440 Mission Ave, Oceanside.

Ontario

AMERISUITES ONTARIO MILLS
4760 Mills Cir, Ontario.

RAMADA LIMITED ONTARIO
1841 E G St, Ontario.

RODEWAY INN ONTARIO AIRPORT
4075 E Guasti Rd, Ontario.

Discounts subject to availability.
*See Rebate Rules on page E31-E32 and Program Rules on page E33.

Guaranteed Best Rate*

Book at www.entertainment.com/travel or call 1-800-50-HOTEL

RODEWAY INN MAINGATE
1211 S West Pl, Anaheim.

ROYAL PACIFIC INN
916 S Beach Blvd, Anaheim.

SHERATON HOTEL
900 S Disneyland Dr, Anaheim.

SUPER 8 DISNEYLAND DRIVE
915 S Disneyland Dr, Anaheim.

SUPER 8 MOTEL DISNEYLAND
415 W Katella Ave, Anaheim.

TROPICANA INN & SUITES
1540 S Harbor Blvd, Anaheim.

Bakersfield

BEST WESTERN HILL HOUSE
700 Truxtun Ave, Bakersfield.

DAYS INN BAKERSFIELD
4500 Buck Owens Blvd, Bakersfield.

LA QUINTA INN/STES BAKERSFIELD
3232 Riverside Dr, Bakersfield.

RED LION HOTEL BAKERSFIELD
2400 Camino Del Rio Ct, Bakersfield.

Beverly Hills

BEST WESTERN BEVERLY PAVILION
9360 Wilshire Blvd, Beverly Hills.

BEVERLY TERRACE
469 N Doheny Dr, Beverly Hills.

CENTURY WILSHIRE
10776 Wilshire Blvd, Los Angeles.

LUXE HOTEL RODEO DRIVE
360 N Rodeo Dr, Beverly Hills.

Buena Park

BEST WESTERN INN SUITES
7555 Beach Blvd, Buena Park.

EMBASSY SUITES BUENA PARK
7762 Beach Blvd, Buena Park.

KNOTTS BERRY FARM RESORT HOTEL
7675 Crescent Ave, Buena Park.

Burbank

RAMADA INN BURBANK
2900 N San Fernando Blvd, Burbank.

SAFARI INN, A COAST HOTEL
1911 W Olive Ave, Burbank.

TRAVELODGE BURBANK GLENDALE
1112 N Hollywood Way, Burbank.

Capistrano Beach

CAPISTRANO SEASIDE INN
34862 Pacific Coast Hwy, Capistrano Beach.

DOUBLETREE GUEST SUITES DOHENY BEACH
34402 Pacific Coast Hwy, Capistrano Beach.

Carlsbad

GRAND PACIFIC PALISADES
5805 Armada Dr, Carlsbad.

Carmel/Monterey

BEST WESTERN CARMEL MISSION
3665 Rio Rd, Carmel.

BLUE LAGOON INN
2362 Fremont St, Monterey.

CARMEL VALLEY RANCH
1 Old Ranch Rd, Carmel.

COAST SANTA CRUZ HOTEL
175 W Cliff Dr, Santa Cruz.

COMFORT INN MUNRAS
1262 Munras Ave, Monterey.

Shop & Book more hotels at entertainment.com/travel

CONTINENTAL INN
414 Ocean St, Santa Cruz.

HYATT REGENCY MONTEREY
1 Old Golf Course Rd, Monterey.

MARIPOSA INN
1386 Munras Ave, Monterey.

PORTOLA PLAZA HOTEL
2 Portola Plz, Monterey.

RAMADA LIMITED CARMEL HILL
1182 Cass St, Monterey.

RAMADA LIMITED MONTEREY BAY
2058 Fremont St, Monterey.

SANTA CRUZ BEACH INN
600 Riverside Ave, Santa Cruz.

TRAVELODGE MONTEREY BAY
2030 Fremont St, Monterey.

Chula Vista

GOOD NITE CHULA VISTA
225 Bay Blvd, Chula Vista.

LA QUINTA INN CHULA VISTA
150 Bonita Rd, Chula Vista.

VAGABOND INN CHULA VISTA
230 Broadway, Chula Vista.

Coronado

HOTEL DEL CORONADO - A KSL LUXURY RESORT
1500 Orange Ave, Coronado.

LA AVENIDA ON CORONADO ISLAND
1315 Orange Ave, Coronado.

LOEWS CORONADO BAY RESORT
4000 Coronado Bay Rd, Coronado.

Costa Mesa

HILTON COSTA MESA
3050 Bristol St, Costa Mesa.

LA QUINTA INN JOHN WAYNE ARPRT
1515 S Coast Dr, Costa Mesa.

RAMADA LTD & STES COSTA MESA
1680 Superior Ave, Costa Mesa.

Fresno

DAYS INN FRESNO
4061 N Blackstone Ave, Fresno.

LA QUINTA INN FRESNO
2926 Tulare St, Fresno.

RADISSON HOTEL & CONF CENTER
2233 Ventura St, Fresno.

Fullerton

ANAHEIM PARK HOTEL
222 W Houston Ave, Fullerton.

CHASE SUITE HOTEL FULLERTON
2932 Nutwood Ave, Fullerton.

FOUR POINTS BY SHERATON FULLERTON/ANAHEIM
1500 S Raymond Ave, Fullerton.

Garden Grove

CROWNE PLAZA GARDEN GROVE RST
12021 Harbor Blvd, Garden Grove.

HYATT REGENCY ORANGE COUNTY
11999 Harbor Blvd, Garden Grove.

RAMADA PLAZA HOTEL ANAHEIM
10022 Garden Grove Blvd, Garden Grove.

Hollywood

HOLLYWOOD METROPOLITAN HOTEL
5825 W Sunset Blvd, Los Angeles.

E5

You can access 25,000 hotels in over 700 cities. See sample listings above.
Shop and Book more hotels at www.entertainment.com/travel

Guaranteed Best Rate*
More listings online and over the phone!

RAMADA FOOTHILLS INN & SUITES
6944 E Tanque Verde Rd, Tucson.

THE LODGE AT VENTANA CANYON
6200 N Club House Ln, Tucson.

WESTWARD LOOK RESORT
245 E Ina Rd, Tucson.

Arkansas
Little Rock

BAYMONT INN & STES LITTLE RK W
1010 Breckenridge Dr, Little Rock.

COMFORT INN & SUITES AIRPORT
4301 E Roosevelt Rd, Little Rock.

THE PEABODY LITTLE ROCK
3 Statehouse Plz, Little Rock.

California
Anaheim

ALAMO INN & SUITES
1140 W Katella Ave, Anaheim.

ANABELLA HOTEL DISNEYLAND
1030 W Katella Ave, Anaheim.

ANAHEIM AT THE PARK TRAVELODGE
1166 W Katella Ave, Anaheim.

ANAHEIM ECONO LODGE
871 S Harbor Blvd, Anaheim.

ANAHEIM FANTASY INN & SUITES
425 W Katella Ave, Anaheim.

ANAHEIM PLAZA HOTEL
1700 S Harbor Blvd, Anaheim.

ANAHEIM RAMADA
1331 E Katella Ave, Anaheim.

ANAHEIM VAGABOND EXECUTIVE INN
2145 S Harbor Blvd, Anaheim.

ANAHEIM-BUENA PARK TRAVELODGE
705 S Beach Blvd, Anaheim.

BEST WESTERN - PAVILIONS
1176 W Katella Ave, Anaheim.

BEST WESTERN ANAHEIM INN
1630 S Harbor Blvd, Anaheim.

BEST WESTERN PARK PLACE INN
1544 S Harbor Blvd, Anaheim.

BEST WESTERN RAFFLES INN
2040 S Harbor Blvd, Anaheim.

BEST WESTERN STOVALL'S INN
1110 W Katella Ave, Anaheim.

CAROUSEL INN & SUITES
1530 S Harbor Blvd, Anaheim.

CLARION HOTEL ANAHEIM RESORT
616 W Convention Way, Anaheim.

COAST ANAHEIM HOTEL
1855 S Harbor Blvd, Anaheim.

COMFORT INN MAINGATE
2171 S Harbor Blvd, Anaheim.

DAYS INN & SUITES ANAHEIM CONV. CTR.
2029 S. Harbor Blvd., Anaheim.

DAYS INN MAINGATE CONV CENTER
620 W Orangewood Ave, Anaheim.

DAYS INN SUITES AT DISNEYLAND
1111 S Harbor Blvd, Anaheim.

DESERT PALMS HOTEL & SUITES
631 W Katella Ave, Anaheim.

DISNEY GRAND CALIFORNIAN HOTEL
1600 S Disneyland Dr, Anaheim.

DISNEY'S PARADISE PIER HOTEL
1717 S Disneyland Dr, Anaheim.

DISNEYLAND HOTEL
1150 W Magic Way, Anaheim.

HILTON ANAHEIM
777 W Convention Way, Anaheim.

HOWARD JOHNSON PLAZA ANAHEIM
1380 S Harbor Blvd, Anaheim.

LA QUINTA INN & SUITES ANAHEIM
1752 S Clementine St, Anaheim.

PARK VUE INN
1570 S Harbor Blvd, Anaheim.

PARKSIDE INN AND SUITES
1830 S West St, Anaheim.

PENNY SLEEPER INN
1441 S Manchester Ave, Anaheim.

PORTOFINO INN DISNEYLAND CONVN
1831 S Harbor Blvd, Anaheim.

RADISSON MAINGATE
1850 S Harbor Blvd, Anaheim.

RAMADA INN MAINGATE ANAHEIM
1650 S Harbor Blvd, Anaheim.

RAMADA LIMITED MAIN GATE NORTH
921 S Harbor Blvd, Anaheim.

RAMADA LIMITED SUITES DISNEYLAND
2141 S Harbor Blvd, Anaheim.

RAMADA PLAZA ANAHEIM RESORT
515 W Katella Ave, Anaheim.

Anaheim– rates from $49

Book Now & Save!! Orange County on Sale - Experience OC just like the TV Show!!

No Place like Southern California evokes the stereotype of California's good life quite the way Orange County does: The theme parks of Anaheim, namely Disneyland & Knott's Berry Farm, lure millions of visitors. Million-dollar mansions dot the coast line and lush golf courses line beaches. The area supports fine dining, upscale shopping, and several outstanding visual and performing-arts establishments.

Call: 800-50-HOTELS or book online at www.entertainment.com/travel

Photo Credit: Micky Jones

E4

Discounts subject to availability.
*See Rebate Rules on page E31-E32 and Program Rules on page E33.

Guaranteed Best Rate*

Book at www.entertainment.com/travel or call 1-800-50-HOTEL

United States of America

Alabama

Birmingham

BAYMONT INN & STES BIRMINGHAM
513 Cahaba Park Cir, Birmingham.

COMFORT INN BIRMINGHAM
195 Oxmoor Rd, Birmingham.

HOWARD JOHNSON EXPRESS INN
275 Oxmoor Rd, Birmingham.

Alaska

Anchorage

BEST VALUE INN EXECUTIVE STES
4360 Spenard Rd, Anchorage.

BEST WESTERN BARRATT INN
4616 Spenard Rd, Anchorage.

CLARION SUITES ANCHORAGE
325 W 8th Ave, Anchorage.

Arizona

Chandler

PRIME HOTEL & SUITES CHANDLER
7475 W Chandler Blvd, Chandler.

RED ROOF PHOENIX CHANDLER
7400 W Boston St, Chandler.

SAN MARCOS GOLF & CONFERENCE RESORT
1 N San Marcos Pl, Chandler.

Flagstaff

HIGHLAND COUNTRY INN
223 S Milton Rd, Flagstaff.

QUALITY INN FLAGSTAFF-LUCKY LN
2500 E Lucky Ln, Flagstaff.

RADISSON WOODLANDS
1175 W Route 66, Flagstaff.

Mesa

BEST WESTERN DOBSON RANCH INN
1666 S Dobson Rd, Mesa.

LA QUINTA INN & SUITES - MESA
902 W Grove Ave, Mesa.

WESTGATE PAINTED MOUNTAIN RST
6302 E Mckellips Rd, Mesa.

Phoenix

BEST WESTERN AIRPORT INN
2425 S 24th St, Phoenix.

COMFORT INN PHOENIX
5050 N Black Canyon Hwy, Phoenix.

EMBASSY SUITES PHOENIX AIRPORT
1515 N 44th St, Phoenix.

HOTEL SAN CARLOS - DOWNTOWN CONVENTION CENTER
202 N Central Ave, Phoenix.

LA QUINTA INN PHOENIX NORTH
2510 W Greenway Rd, Phoenix.

POINTE HILTON SQUAW PEAK
7677 N 16th St, Phoenix.

POINTE HILTON TAPATIO CLIFFS
11111 N 7th St, Phoenix.

Shop & Book more hotels at entertainment.com/travel

RAMADA INN DOWNTOWN PHOENIX
401 N 1st St, Phoenix.

RAMADA LIMITED AIRPORT NORTH
4120 E Van Buren St, Phoenix.

RAMADA PLAZA HOTEL & STES-PHOENIX METROCENTER
12027 N 28th Dr, Phoenix.

SIERRA SUITES PHOENIX BILTMORE
5235 N 16th St, Phoenix.

SUNSHINE HOTEL AND RESORT
3600 N 2nd Ave, Phoenix.

WYNDHAM PHOENIX - DOWNTOWN
50 E Adams St, Phoenix.

Scottsdale

AMERISUITES SCOTTSDALE OLD TWN
7300 E 3rd Ave, Scottsdale.

BEST WESTERN PAPAGO INN
7017 E Mcdowell Rd, Scottsdale.

CHAPARRAL SUITES RESORT
5001 N Scottsdale Rd, Scottsdale.

DAYS INN FASHION SQUARE MALL
4710 N Scottsdale Rd, Scottsdale.

FAIRFIELD INN BY MARRIOTT SCOTTSDALE DOWNTOWN
5101 N Scottsdale Rd, Scottsdale.

HOSPITALITY SUITE RESORT
409 N Scottsdale Rd, Scottsdale.

LA QUINTA INN/STES SCOTTSDALE
8888 E Shea Blvd, Scottsdale.

MILLENNIUM RESORT SCOTTSDALE MCCORMICK RANCH
7401 N Scottsdale Rd, Scottsdale.

RADISSON RESORT & SPA
7171 N Scottsdale Rd, Scottsdale.

RAMADA LIMITED SCOTTSDALE
6935 E 5th Ave, Scottsdale.

SCOTTSDALE LINKS RESORT
16858 N Perimeter Dr, Scottsdale.

SCOTTSDALE PLAZA RESORT
7200 N Scottsdale Rd, Scottsdale.

THE SCOTTSDALE RESORT
7700 E Mccormick Pkwy, Scottsdale.

Sedona

BEST WESTERN INN OF SEDONA
1200 W Highway 89a, Sedona.

L'AUBERGE DE SEDONA
301 Lauberge Ln, Sedona.

SEDONA SUMMIT RESORT
500 Navoti Dr, Sedona.

Tempe

EXECUTIVE SUITES EXTENDED STAY
1635 N Scottsdale Rd, Tempe.

FIESTA INN RESORT
2100 S Priest Dr, Tempe.

HAWTHORN SUITES TEMPE
2301 E Southern Ave, Tempe.

Tucson

AMERISUITES TUCSON AIRPORT
6885 S Tucson Blvd, Tucson.

LA QUINTA INN TUCSON EAST
6404 E Broadway Blvd, Tucson.

LOEWS VENTANA CANYON RESORT
7000 N Resort Dr, Tucson.

OMNI TUCSON NATIONAL RESORT
2727 W Club Dr, Tucson.

E3

You can access **25,000** hotels in over **700** cities. See sample listings above.
Shop and Book more hotels at www.entertainment.com/travel

Up To $200 Rebate Available!

Guaranteed Best Rate* Hotel Program

HERE'S HOW TO SAVE...

1. See **"sample"** listings on pages E3–E29. To access the full list of hotels, call **1-800-50-HOTEL (1-800-504-6835)** for savings of up to $100.*

   OR

   Go to **www.entertainment.com/travel** and book online to save up to $200.*

2. Book your trip by phone or online. Obtain your online booking confirmation via e-mail for the link to your free travel coupons.

3. Don't forget to mail in your rebate form after your stay.

BOOK BY PHONE

SAVE UP TO $100 MORE*
when you book by phone at
1-800-50-HOTEL
(1-800-504-6835)

–OR–

BOOK ONLINE

SAVE UP TO $200 MORE*
when you book online at
www.entertainment.com/travel

*See Rebate Rules on pages E31–E32 and Program Rules on page E33.

Guaranteed Best Rate*...at Over 25,000 Hotels Worldwide!

PLUS!

When you book:

- **Get up to $200 in additional savings**

  See next page for details.

- **Get FREE online coupons for your travel destination**

  Enjoy valuable Entertainment® discounts for restaurants, theme parks, attractions and sporting events.

Go to entertainment.com/travel or call 1-800-50-HOTEL to check for rates and availability.

Great Hotel Deals at Popular Travel Destinations

*See Rebate Rules on pages E31–E32 and Program Rules of Use on page E33.

Turn Page for Sample Listings!

TravelSmith®

INDISPENSABLE, EASY-CARE CLOTHES AND ACCESSORIES

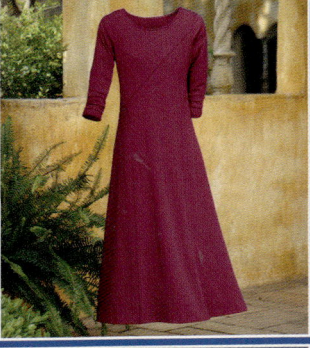

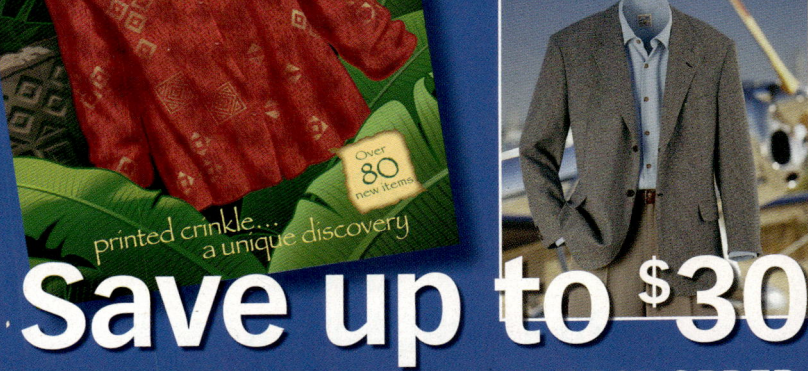

printed crinkle... a unique discovery

Over 80 new items

Save up to $30
OFF YOUR FIRST ORDER

$10 off
Any purchase of $50 or more

or $30 off
Any purchase of $150 or more

HOW TO REDEEM: Place your order at **TravelSmith.com** or call **800-950-1600** to order or request a free catalog. Enter or mention code 75023953 in the "Source Code" box when prompted during the check out process.

OFFER CONDITIONS: Offer is valid off new customer's first order. TravelSmith reserves the right to verify Entertainment® membership. Coupons are non-transferable, may not be republished or resold, and can be used only once per new customer. Not valid on prior purchases, pending orders, or with any other discounts, coupons, certificates, or promotions. This does not apply to shipping and handling or applicable sales tax or gift certificates. Coupons cannot be used at outlet stores or warehouse events.

Valid now thru December 31, 2007
Offer validity is governed by the Rules of Use. Coupons void if purchased, sold or bartered.

D87

WHY STAY IN A HOTEL?

amazing condo vacation deals!

LOW PRICES & SPACIOUS ROOMS

Stay at a breathtaking **Cancún resort** for as little as
$93 a night, $649 a week

Experience fabulous **Orlando** from
$379 a week…just $54 a night!

Spend a week in **Europe** starting at
$76 a night, $529 a week

Or vacation in:
**THE CARIBBEAN
LATIN AMERICA
ROCKY MOUNTAINS
PALM SPRINGS
LAS VEGAS
LAKE TAHOE**
and more!

**CALL TODAY
To Book These Incredible Values!***
800-822-1890

For more offers and destinations, or to book online, visit condodirect.com/entertainment

condodirect
VACATION RENTAL DEALS

*Subject to availability. Prices are representative, in U.S. dollars, vary according to unit, location, and date, and are subject to local taxes where applicable. All confirmations are final and nonrefundable. FL SOT#10224; WA SOT# 601 765 244; CST# 2030985-50; NV SOT# 2003-0412. Other terms and conditions apply. **Valid now through December 31, 2007 and subject to advance reservations.** Offer validity is governed by the Rules of Use. Coupons void if purchased, sold, or bartered.

D86

floridaticketstation™.com
Come Play In Our Backyard!

ORLANDO

Visit Us Online & Save Up To
50% OFF
Theme Parks • Dinner Shows • Water Parks

Enter Coupon Code FTSEG01

$10 Off†
Regular Price Plus Tax

Universal Orlando®
Stay & Play Plus* Water Park Pass
Limit 2 per customer.
Redeemable only at www.floridaticketstation.com/entertainment
Expires 12/31/07.

Enter Coupon Code FTSEG02

FREE Self Parking
With a purchase of any multi-day Universal Orlando® theme park ticket
$9 Value. Limit 1 per customer.
Redeemable only at www.floridaticketstation.com/entertainment
Expires 12/31/07.

Enter Coupon Code FTSEG03

$10 Off†
Regular Price Plus Tax

ANY ticket order of $200 or more
Limit 1 per customer.
Redeemable only at www.floridaticketstation.com/entertainment
Expires 12/31/07.

Enter Coupon Code FTSEG04

Save $88†
Arabian Nights Dinner Show Family of 4 Fun Pack, just $75.
Limit 1 per customer.
Redeemable only at www.floridaticketstation.com/entertainment
Expires 12/31/07.

---

*Valid for up to seven consecutive days including first day any portion of this ticket is used. Ticket is nontransferable and valid during regular operation hours. Parking is not included. No discounts on food or merchandise. Some restrictions apply and benefits are subject to change without notice. Coupons for Universal Orlando Theme Park tickets or parking valid only at www.floridaticketstation.com/entertainment. † These coupons not combinable with any other coupons, offers, promotions or discounts. Coupons and benefits subject to change without notice. Universal elements and all related Indicia TM & © 2006 Universal Studios. © 2006 Universal Orlando. All rights reserved.

visit us at www.floridaticketstation.com/entertainment

Valid now thru December 31, 2007

Offer validity is governed by the Rules of Use and excludes defined holidays. Offers are not valid with other discount offers, unless specified. Coupons void if purchased, sold or bartered. Discounts exclude tax, tip and/or alcohol, where applicable.

:::
floridavacationstation™.com
You Bought the Book... Now Book the FUN!

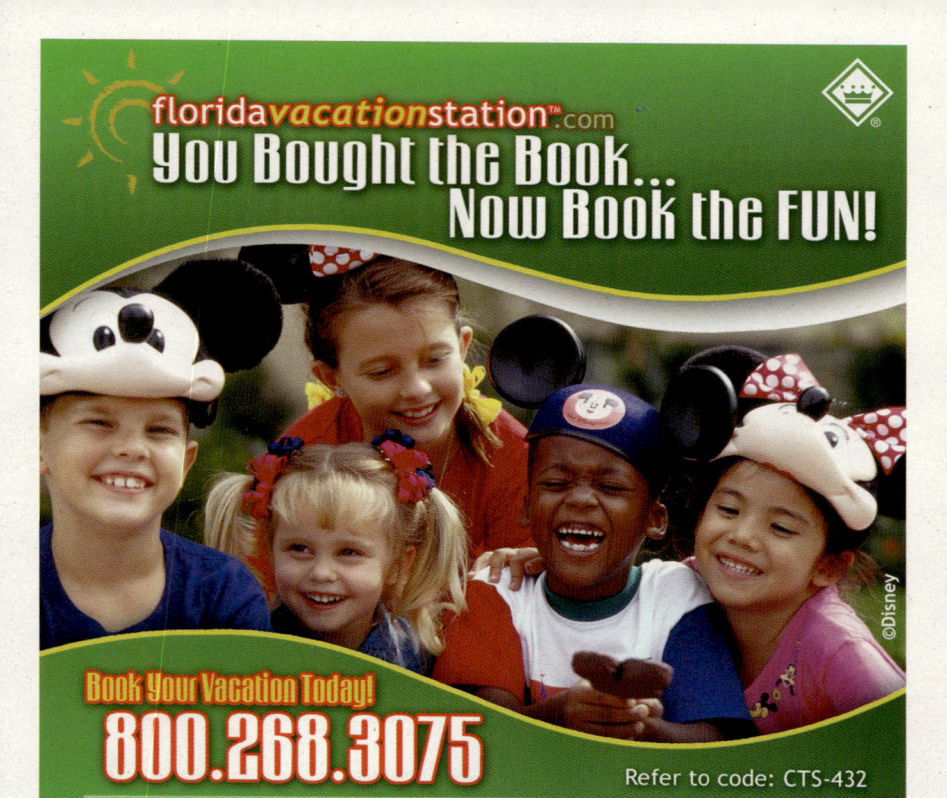

Book Your Vacation Today!
800.268.3075

Refer to code: CTS-432

©Disney

Orlando Family Fun Getaway

FROM **$179**

Retail Value $407. Save Over 60%!

3-days/2-nights in Orlando
Two Adult Disney
Touch of Magic passes

Terms & Conditions Apply.
Call 800.268.3075 or visit our web site for details.
Offer Expires 12/31/07.

Florida Beach & Fun Pack

FROM **$579**

Retail Value $967. Save Over 40%!

3-days/2-nights in Orlando
3-days/2-nights in Daytona
Two 1-day Disney tickets
4-day Thrifty Car Rental

Call 800.268.3075 or visit our web site for details.
Offer Expires 12/31/07.

SLEEP INN Inn & Suites   Radisson   COUNTRY INNS & SUITES BY CARLSON   QUALITY   RAMADA WORLDWIDE

visit us at www.floridavacationstation.com/entertainment
As to Disney's artwork, logos and properties ©Disney

This advertising material is being used for the purpose of soliciting sales of a vacation ownership plan.

Valid now thru December 31, 2007

Offer validity is governed by the Rules of Use and excludes defined holidays. Offers are not valid with other discount offers, unless specified. Coupons void if purchased, sold or bartered. Discounts exclude tax, tip and/or alcohol, where applicable.

D85

Share more
special moments

4 days and 3 nights in Orlando, Florida, for only **$199**[*]

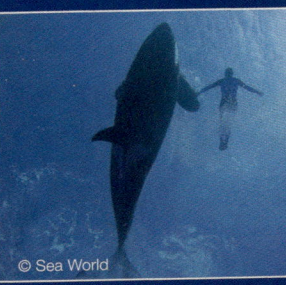

Walt Disney World® Resort

© Universal Orlando®

© Sea World

Disney *Touch of Magic*
- Accommodations at an Orlando-area hotel
- Two one-day *Touch of Magic* Tickets to *Walt Disney World*® Theme Park of your choice plus one visit to either *Disney's Blizzard Beach* Water Park, *Disney's Typhoon Lagoon* Water Park, *DisneyQuest*® Indoor Interactive Theme Park® (General admission; does not include prize play games) or *Downtown Disney*® Pleasure Island
- Meal & Movie Deal for two at *Downtown Disney*® area

Universal Stay and Play
- Accommodations at an Orlando-area hotel
- Two Star or Adventurer passes to either Universal Studios® or Universal's Islands of Adventure® theme parks, and the nighttime entertainment* of Universal CityWalk®
- Meal & Movie Deal® for two at Universal CityWalk®

SeaWorld® Anytime
- Accommodations at an Orlando-area hotel
- Two SeaWorld Anytime passes®
- Dinner for two at Dine with Shamu (reservations required)

Simply choose a package that features your favorite Orlando attractions and we'll take care of the rest. There's no better way to get away.

Call 800-396-1883 for details and reservations.
Mention reservation code ENT06.

You dream it. We plan it. You live it.

Sheraton
VACATION OWNERSHIP

These are not complete details of participation. Additional restrictions apply. Please call 800-396-1883 for a complete list of details and restrictions. This offer expires December 31, 2007. Retail value of this package is up to $690, depending on season. This offer is designed for individuals and families with a combined annual household income of at least $50,000. Attendance at a resort preview and sales presentation is required. This offer does not include transportation, taxes, tips, telephone calls or other items of a personal nature. SVO Vistana Villages, Inc., is the developer and an equal opportunity credit lender. This offer is subject to change without notice.

Sheraton Vacation Ownership is not operated by nor an affiliate of Universal Studios. Universal elements and all related indicia TM & © 2006 Universal Studios. © 2006 Universal Orlando. All rights reserved. Other terms and conditions apply.

As to Disney artwork, logo and properties: ©Disney

*The SeaWorld Anytime Pass is valid for unlimited visits to SeaWorld Orlando during regularly scheduled park hours for up to six consecutive days from date of first visit at no extra charge. Parking is not included. Must exchange valid SeaWorld Orlando paid admission ticket on first visit to receive pass. Non-transferable. Offer subject to change without notice. Restrictions may apply.

This offer is void where prohibited by law and/or where registration or licensing requirements have not been met.

This advertising material is being used for the purpose of soliciting sales of Timeshare Interests.

SVOTSA3858   © 2006 Starwood Vacation Ownership   D84 03/06

3-Day/2-Night American Escape Getaway!

Only $49.95!
Retail Value of up to $200 per night!*

A $49.95 Vacation Getaway for Two!

This **Entertainment**® **Member** special features hotel accommodations for two people to <u>your choice</u> of one of the following great vacation destinations:

- Boyne Mountain, MI • Daytona Beach, FL • Wisconsin Dells, WI
- Orlando, FL • Myrtle Beach, SC • St. Augustine, FL
- Smoky Mountains, TN • Miami, FL • Branson, MO • Las Vegas, NV

greatvacation! DESTINATIONS

Call 1-800-569-3316

(Mon–Fri, 9am to 9pm, EST). Please reference <u>Offer Code GVD052.</u>
For more details on this offer please visit www.greatvacationdestinations.com

*Retail value based on destination choice and travel dates. Attendance at a 90-120 minute vacation ownership presentation at a Great Vacation Destinations Partner Resort may be required depending on your state of residence. Great Vacation Destinations is a wholly owned subsidiary and a registered trademark of Bluegreen® Corporation. Valid through 12/31/07 and subject to advance reservations.

THIS ADVERTISING MATERIAL IS BEING USED FOR THE PURPOSE OF SOLICITING THE SALE OF TIMESHARE INTERESTS.

Great Places, Great Values, Great Vacations!

Valid now thru December 31, 2007

Offer validity is governed by the Rules of Use and excludes defined holidays. Offers are not valid with other discount offers, unless specified. Coupons void if purchased, sold or bartered. Discounts exclude tax, tip and/or alcohol, where applicable.

D83

It's not the places you go,
it's the places you'll come back to

Sunterra offers a variety of spacious and fully-equipped accommodations in some of the most desirable vacation destinations imaginable.

As a special offer for Entertainment® Members, we have discounted vacation packages available to these remarkable destinations...

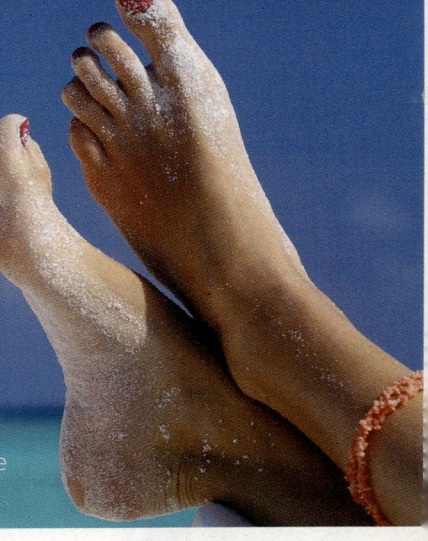

- Williamsburg, VA
- Orlando, FL
- Sedona, AZ
- Branson, MO
- Scottsdale, AZ
- Daytona Beach, FL
- Las Vegas, NV
- St. Maarten, Carib
- South Lake Tahoe, CA

Packages start at just $199 for 4 wonderful days and 3 exciting nights!

That's not per person or per day...that's the entire price of your studio suite accommodations on site at one of our beautiful resorts. Additional packages available for 5-night and 7-night stays ($349 and $499 respectively)!

This is an unbeatable price...and it's all for you, the valued Entertainment® Member.

Call 800.840.5937
M to F, 8 a.m.–9 p.m. PST **Mention code: ZEB07**

Visit our website at: **www.sunterragetaways.com**
to view our outstanding properties.

This offer is valid through June 30, 2008, and subject to advance reservations and availability. Prices do not include transportation and no pets are allowed on site at the resorts.

Offer validity is governed by the Rules of Use and excludes defined holidays. Offers are not valid with other discount offers, unless specified. Coupons void if purchased, sold or bartered. Discounts exclude tax, tip and/or alcohol, where applicable.

Sunterra®

D82

Save big on your next vacation with US.

Save $50
off Las Vegas Vacations for Two

Must book by Nov. 30, 2007
Travel by Dec. 16, 2007

Use promo code **ENT LAS**

Save $200
off an Orlando Vacation for Four

Must book by July 31, 2007
Travel by August 31, 2007

Use promo code **ENT MCO**

Save $300
off a Beach Vacation for Four
(Caribbean, Mexico or Hawaii)

Must book and travel by June 30, 2007

Use promo code **ENT BEACH**

Cinderella Castle [Magic Kingdom®]

Trust US Airways Vacations to help make your dreams of a fabulous vacation come true. With air and hotel packages to the best destinations on the planet, US Airways Vacations is your one-stop shop for the perfect vacation with big savings.

Book today at **www.entertainment.com/usairwaysvacations** or call **800-341-8725**.

As to Disney artwork, logos and properties ©Disney

usairwaysvacations.com

A STAR ALLIANCE MEMBER

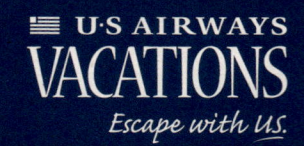

US AIRWAYS VACATIONS
Escape with US.

Flights may be provided by US Airways Express (operated by Air Midwest, Air Wisconsin, Chautauqua, Colgan, Mesa, Piedmont, PSA, Republic Airways, Trans States), or on America West, America West Express (operated by Mesa Airlines) or United®.
*Terms and conditions: Las Vegas: Promotion is $25 off per person to LAS air-inclusive packages. Maximum $100 discount per package. Minimum $300 per person package price. Must enter promo code ENT LAS or mention when calling to receive discount. Orlando: Promotion is $50 off per person to MCO air-inclusive packages. Maximum discount $200 per package. Minimum $480 per person package price. Must enter promo code ENT MCO or mention when calling to receive discount. Beach: Promotion is $75 off per person to Beach air-inclusive packages for the following destinations: ACA, SJD, CUN, CZM, GDL, GYM, ZLO, MZT, MEX, PVR, ZIH, HNL, KOA, LIH, OGG, ANV, AUA, FPO, GGT, NAS, TCB, BGI, GCM, PLS, LRM, SDQ, PUJ, MBJ, SXM, SVU, SKB, UVF, STT, STX. Maximum discount $300 per package. Minimum $640 per person package price. Must enter promo code ENT BEACH or mention when calling to receive discount. Additional restrictions and blackout dates apply. ©2006 US Airways Vacations USV06-1011. Offer validity is governed by the Rules of Use and excludes defined holidays. Coupons void if purchased, sold or bartered.

LEGOLAND CALIFORNIA

Coupon entitles bearer to $6 off up to six one-day full-price admissions. Valid only on the day of purchase at LEGOLAND. Not valid with any other discounts or offers. Children 2 and under are admitted free. Original coupon must be exchanged at the ticket booth at the time of ticket purchase. Restrictions apply. Prices and hours subject to change without notice. **Not for resale.** Expires 12/31/2007 NEBP

A-1361   C-2361

LEGO, LEGOLAND, the LEGO logo and the brick configuration are trademarks of the LEGO Group.
©2006 The LEGO Group.

Offer validity is governed by the Rules of Use and excludes defined holidays. Offers are not valid with other discount offers, unless specified. Coupons void if purchased, sold or bartered. Discounts exclude tax, tip and/or alcohol, where applicable.

Westgate Daytona Beach
This resort is on the famous Daytona Beach and offers one and two bedroom oceanfront villas. Located near the Speedway and all of the attractions Daytona has to offer.

Westgate Towers, Town Center & Vacation Villas • Kissimmee, FL
One and two bedroom villas located one mile from Walt Disney World Resort. Kids Club & family activities. Amenities include pools, spa, sand volleyball, video arcade and much more.

Westgate Lakes Resort & Spa • Orlando, FL
Family resort located minutes from International Drive and all attractions. Spacious studio - four bedroom suites with whirlpool tubs. European spa, fitness center, restaurant, deli, water sports and more.

Westgate Palace • Orlando, FL
Directly off International Drive overlooking Wet 'n Wild this resort offers two bedroom suites for any budget.

Westgate Blue Tree at Lake Buena Vista • Lake Buena Vista, FL
One mile from the Walt Disney World Resort and Downtown Disney entrance. One and two bedroom villas and an array of recreational amenities including pool, tennis and mini golf.

Westgate River Ranch • River Ranch, FL
This Resort Ranch offers everything from an airport to a rodeo and features horseback riding, boating, restaurant, swimming pool, campfire, barbecue and Western saloon with live Country and Western entertainment.

Westgate South Beach
One and Two Bedroom villas located beachfront and in the heart of all the action that Miami has to offer.

Westgate Smoky Mountains • Gatlinburg, TN
Located in the heart of the Smoky's and offering studio, one and two bedroom mid-rise villas. Only minutes from Downtown Gatlinburg and the famous Pigeon Forge.

Westgate Flamingo Bay • Las Vegas, NV
A short drive off the strip you will find the private oasis of Westgate Flamingo Bay, offering spacious one and two bedroom villas.

Westgate Park City Resort & Spa
Situated at the base of the Canyons Resort, this resort boasts an award winning restaurant and full service European spa. Accommodations include studio to four bedroom villas.

Westgate Historic Williamsburg
Located five minutes from Historic Williamsburg, this charming resort offers efficiency accommodations.

Westgate Branson Wood • Branson, MO
145 acres tucked away on the moutainside, right in the Heart of Branson. Resort offers 2 outdoor swimming pools, 1 indoor swimming pool, exercise facility, and many more on-site activities.

Westgate Emerald Pointe • Hollister, MO
Located in the Ozark Mountains, just minutes away from the high energy excitement of Branson. This resort offers spacious one and two bedroom villas with fully equipped kitchen and washer/dryer.

ENT4509

Offer validity is governed by the Rules of Use and excludes defined holidays. Offers are not valid with other discount offers, unless specified. Coupons void if purchased, sold or bartered. Discounts exclude tax, tip and/or alcohol, where applicable.

PLANET HOLLYWOOD

Not valid with any other offers or discounts. One coupon per table. Excludes tax and gratuity. Valid at participating Planet Hollywood locations.

1 01900 15195 3

Offer validity is governed by the Rules of Use and excludes defined holidays. Offers are not valid with other discount offers, unless specified. Coupons void if purchased, sold or bartered. Discounts exclude tax and tip where applicable.

PLANET HOLLYWOOD

Not valid with any other offers or discounts. One coupon per table. Excludes tax and gratuity. Valid at participating Planet Hollywood locations.

1 01900 15195 3

Offer validity is governed by the Rules of Use and excludes defined holidays. Offers are not valid with other discount offers, unless specified. Coupons void if purchased, sold or bartered. Discounts exclude tax and tip where applicable.

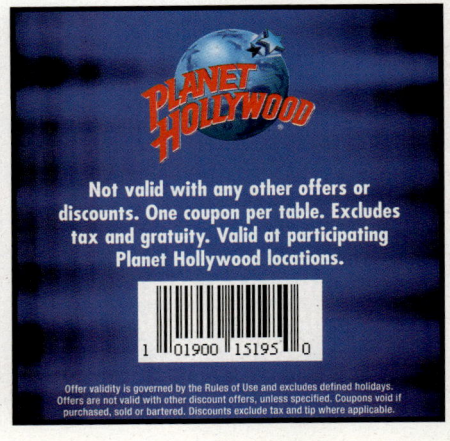

SAVE UP TO $36!

LEGOLAND CALIFORNIA

Save $6 on one-day admission
to LEGOLAND® California for up to six guests.

LEGOLAND® California is built for a full day of real family fun with more than 50 rides, shows and attractions. The fun is located in the seaside village of Carlsbad, California, 30 minutes north of San Diego, one hour south of Anaheim. For days and hours of operation call (760) 918-LEGO or visit www.LEGOLAND.com

Valid now thru December 31, 2007
See reverse side for details.

D77

Save up to 50% off Published Rates!**

Call: 1-888-501-9994 and mention your special Entertainment® booking code: **ENT4509**

**All reservations are subject to availability. Not valid for group bookings and cannot be combined with other offers.

Westgate Resorts

www.westgatedestinations.com

Valid now thru December 31, 2007
See reverse side for details.

D78

PLANET HOLLYWOOD

$5 OFF ANY FOOD, BEVERAGE OR MERCHANDISE PURCHASE OF $20 OR MORE

Valid now thru December 31, 2007
See reverse side for details.

D79

PLANET HOLLYWOOD

$5 OFF ANY FOOD, BEVERAGE OR MERCHANDISE PURCHASE OF $20 OR MORE

Valid now thru December 31, 2007
See reverse side for details.

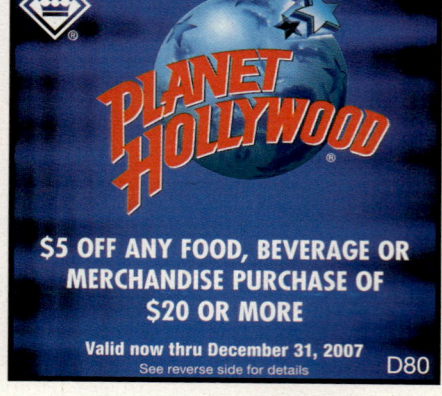

D80

SuperShuttle — YOUR AIRPORT RIDE

- TO or FROM the airport and your home, office or hotel
- Service 24 hours every day

ExecuCar — YOUR PRIVATE RIDE

ExecuCar locations in bold.

- Your private ride TO or FROM the airport
- Service 24 hours every day

Austin, Baltimore, Boulder, Burbank, **Dallas/Ft. Worth**, **Denver**, **Los Angeles/Orange County**, Miami, Minneapolis/St. Paul, New York, Ontario, Palm Beach, **Phoenix/Scottsdale**, Sacramento, **San Francisco**, **Tampa**, Washington, D.C.

Book online at www.supershuttle.com and use discount code PGESC or call 1-800-BLUE-VAN (258-3826) and present this coupon to the driver when you are picked up. Good for transportation to or from the airport. Not valid in conjunction with any other discount offer. 24-hour advance reservation requested.

Offer validity is governed by the Rules of Use and excludes defined holidays. Offers are not valid with other discount offers, unless specified. Coupons void if purchased, sold or bartered. Discounts exclude tax, tip and/or alcohol, where applicable.

PETSMART

PetsHotel with Doggie Day Camp

Please visit petshotel.com or call 1-877-4-PetSmart for current locations and more information. Simply call any of our locations to book your reservation and bring in this certificate to receive offer.

4 15108 56461 1

Valid through 12/31/07 only at PetSmart PetsHotel in U.S. For first-time customers only. Minimum two nights' stay required. Must present coupon with purchase. Limit one coupon per customer and transaction. Void if copied. Not redeemable for cash or credit. Non-transferable. Not valid with any other discount or offer. Based on availability. Current vaccinations required. Call or visit your local PetSmart PetsHotel for more details. PetSmart reserves the right to refuse or limit this service. ©2006 PetSmart Store Support Group, Inc. All rights reserved.

Offer validity is governed by the Rules of Use and excludes defined holidays. Offers are not valid with other discount offers, unless specified. Coupons void if purchased, sold or bartered. Discounts exclude tax, tip and/or alcohol, where applicable.

CRUISE AMERICA RV RENTAL & SALES

TERMS AND CONDITIONS

1. Reservations must be made in advance through Cruise America®. Call 1-800-327-7799 (U.S., Alaska and Canada).
2. Give the reservationist your special Entertainment® coupon code ENT1207 when you call.
3. One coupon per rental; must be presented with payment.
4. Offer subject to vehicle availability, renter restrictions, standard contract provisions and other fees which may apply.
5. Coupon value in U.S. currency for U.S. transactions and Canadian currency for Canadian transactions.
6. Not valid with other discount offers or hot deals.
7. Valid for U.S. and Canadian residents only.

Offer validity is governed by the Rules of Use and excludes defined holidays. Offers are not valid with other discount offers, unless specified. Coupons void if purchased, sold or bartered. Discounts exclude tax, tip and/or alcohol, where applicable.

SuperShuttle®   ExecuCar®

$2 OFF PER PERSON PER DIRECTION on SuperShuttle®
Up to $28.00 value

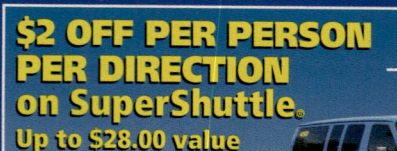

—or—

$5 OFF PER RIDE on ExecuCar® Private Sedan Services
Up to $10.00 value

Your Airport Ride

Book online at: supershuttle.com and use code PGESC

Valid now thru December 31, 2007   See reverse side for details   D74

PETSMART™

PetSmart PetsHotel®
with Doggie Day Camp℠

- Superior day and overnight care with personalized attention for dogs and cats
- PetSmart® safety-certified caregivers on-site 24/7
- Veterinarians always on-call

save $10 on your pet's next stay

Valid now thru December 31, 2007
See reverse side for details

D75

SAVE UP TO $200.00

CRUISE AMERICA
RV RENTAL & SALES

Save Up To $200 Off A Rental

Valid for $50.00 off a 3-6 day Motorhome rental -or-
Valid for $100.00 off a 7-13 day Motorhome rental -or-
Valid for $200.00 off a 14 day or more Motorhome rental

Valid now thru December 31, 2007
See reverse side for details

D76

IT'S AN ENTIRE UNIVERSE OF ACTION, THRILLS AND EXCITEMENT!

At Universal Orlando® Resort you'll find two amazing theme parks, nonstop nightlife and more, all in one convenient location. Jump into the action of the movies at Universal Studios®. Feel the rush of adrenaline at Universal's Islands of Adventure®. And enjoy live music, casual and fine dining, dancing, movies and more at Universal CityWalk®. Universal Orlando Resort—a one-of-a-kind vacation for today's kind of family.

Universal elements and all related indicia TM & © 2006 Universal Studios. © 2006 Universal Orlando. All rights reserved. 236103/0306/EP

UNIVERSAL Orlando RESORT

*Offer valid through December 31, 2007. Coupon redeemable only at www.universalorlando.com/entertainment with promotional code UNENTBOOK5. Limit four (4) people per coupon. Coupon has no cash value. Offer not valid with any other offers, specials, discounts, or for separately ticketed events, such as Halloween Horror Nights and Rock the Universe. Parking not included. No discounts on food or merchandise. Additional restrictions may apply. Offer subject to change without notice. Universal elements and all related indicia TM & © 2006 Universal Studios. © 2006 Universal Orlando. All rights reserved.

Offer validity is governed by the Rules of Use and excludes defined holidays. Offers are not valid with other discount offers, unless specified. Coupon void if purchased, sold or bartered. Discounts exclude tax, tip and/or alcohol, where applicable.

UNIVERSAL Orlando RESORT

*Offer valid through December 31, 2007. No copies or reproductions of coupon will be accepted. Coupon redeemable only at the Universal Orlando Resort front gate ticket windows. Limit four (4) people per coupon. Coupon has no cash value. Offer not valid with any other offers, specials, discounts, or for separately ticketed events, such as Halloween Horror Nights and Rock the Universe. Parking not included. No discounts on food or merchandise. Additional restrictions may apply. Offer subject to change without notice. Universal elements and all related indicia TM & © 2006 Universal Studios. © 2006 Universal Orlando. All rights reserved.

2 0 0 6 0 2 0 0 7

Offer validity is governed by the Rules of Use and excludes defined holidays. Offers are not valid with other discount offers, unless specified. Coupon void if purchased, sold or bartered. Discounts exclude tax, tip and/or alcohol, where applicable.

UNIVERSAL Orlando RESORT

* Offer valid through December 31, 2007. Present to server when ordering. Not valid for Meal Deal, or with any other offers, specials or discounts. Alcohol not included. This coupon cannot be used for any other application without authorization from Universal Orlando Resort Food Services. Offer and benefits subject to change without notice. Universal elements and all related indicia TM & © 2006 Universal Studios. © 2006 Universal Orlando. All rights reserved.

Offer validity is governed by the Rules of Use and excludes defined holidays. Offers are not valid with other discount offers, unless specified. Coupon void if purchased, sold or bartered. Discounts exclude tax, tip and/or alcohol, where applicable.

UNIVERSAL Orlando RESORT

*Savings are per reservation and not valid with any other Universal Orlando® Resort offer. $50 savings is based on a 4 or 5 night minimum hotel and ticket vacation. $100 savings is based on a 6 night minimum hotel and ticket vacation. Ticket and room nights must be booked by December 16, 2007, and travel completed by December 27, 2007. **Not valid for separately ticketed concerts and special events. Some venues require ages 21 or older for admission. Photo ID required. Does not include admission to Universal Cineplex. Subject to availability. Restrictions apply and benefits are subject to change without notice. Universal Parks & Resorts Vacations℠ is registered with the State of Florida as a seller of travel. Registration number ST-24215. Universal elements and all related indicia TM & © 2006 Universal Studios. © 2006 Universal Orlando. All rights reserved.

Offer validity is governed by the Rules of Use and excludes defined holidays. Offers are not valid with other discount offers, unless specified. Coupon void if purchased, sold or bartered. Discounts exclude tax, tip and/or alcohol, where applicable.

A BETTER VACATION FOR TODAY'S FAMILY

UNIVERSAL Orlando RESORT

$8 OFF*
2-Day/2-Park Adult or Child Ticket to Universal Studios Florida® and Universal's Islands of Adventure®

Redeem at any Universal Orlando® Resort front gate ticket window.

Valid now thru December 31, 2007
See reverse side for details
D70

$5 OFF*
1-Day/1-Park Adult or Child Ticket to Universal Studios Florida® or Universal's Islands of Adventure®

Visit www.universalorlando.com/entertainment and enter promotional code UNENTBOOK5 to receive $5 savings.

Valid now thru December 31, 2007
See reverse side for details
D71

SAVE UP TO $100*
on a Universal Orlando® Resort Vacation!

Book a 4-5 night vacation and save $50 OR book a 6 night or more vacation and save $100*!

- Choose hotel accommodations at one of our 3 magnificently themed on-site resorts or one of the many Orlando area hotels.
- Your vacation also includes admission to both Universal Orlando theme parks with unlimited park-to-park access and a CityWalk Party Pass**.
- Use promotional code UNENTBOOK4 to receive $50 savings and promotional code UNENTBOOK6 to receive $100 savings.

Visit univacations.com/entertainment or call 1-877-289-8750 to book today!

Valid now thru December 27, 2007
See reverse side for details
D72

15% OFF*
all food and non-alcoholic beverage purchases at ONE (1) of the following restaurants:

Universal Studios®
Cafe La Bamba
Universal Studios' Classic Monsters Cafe

Universal's Islands of Adventure®
Circus McGurkus Cafe Stoo-pendous™
Pizza Predattoria®

Not valid for Meal Deal, or with any other offers, specials or discounts.

Valid now thru December 31, 2007
See reverse side for details
D73

1. SeaWorld Orlando
2. SeaWorld San Diego
3. SeaWorld San Antonio
4. Busch Gardens Tampa Bay
5. Busch Gardens Williamsburg
6. Adventure Island Tampa Bay
7. Water Country USA Williamsburg
8. Sesame Place Philadelphia

The Worlds of Busch Gardens
EUROPE — WILLIAMSBURG, VA
AFRICA — TAMPA BAY, FL

Not valid with any other discount, special event or special pricing, or on purchase of multi-park, multi-day, annual or season passes. NOT FOR SALE. Valid at Busch Gardens in Tampa Bay, FL and Williamsburg, VA.

©2006 Busch Entertainment Corporation. All rights reserved.

A13778   C13777

Offer validity is governed by the Rules of Use. Coupons void if purchased, sold or bartered.

Valid now thru December 31, 2007

SeaWorld ADVENTURE PARKS
Orlando, San Antonio, & San Diego

Not valid with any other discount, special event or special pricing, or on purchase of multi-park, multi-day, annual or season passes. NOT FOR SALE. Valid at SeaWorld in Orlando, FL, San Antonio, TX and San Diego, CA.

©2006 Busch Entertainment Corporation. All rights reserved.

A13778   C13777

Offer validity is governed by the Rules of Use. Coupons void if purchased, sold or bartered.

Valid now thru December 31, 2007

SESAME PLACE
Langhorne, PA

Not valid with any other discount, special event or special pricing, or on purchase of multi-park, multi-day, annual or season passes. NOT FOR SALE. Valid at Sesame Place in Langhorne, PA.

©2006 Busch Entertainment Corporation. All rights reserved.
©2006 Sesame Workshop. "Sesame Street" and its logo are trademarks of Sesame Workshop. All rights reserved.

A13778   C13777

Offer validity is governed by the Rules of Use. Coupons void if purchased, sold or bartered.

Valid now thru December 31, 2007

Adventure Island
TAMPA BAY, FL

Water Country USA
WILLIAMSBURG, VA

Not valid with any other discount, special event, special pricing, or on purchase of multi-park, multi-day, annual or season passes. NOT FOR SALE. Valid at Adventure Island in Tampa Bay, FL and Water Country USA in Williamsburg, VA

©2006 Busch Entertainment Corporation. All rights reserved.

A13778   C13777

Offer validity is governed by the Rules of Use. Coupons void if purchased, sold or bartered.

Valid now thru December 31, 2007

Memories for a Lifetime

Save $5.00 on Admission to SeaWorld

Present coupon at any ticket window at time of purchase during regular park operating hours. One coupon good for up to six (6) admissions during one park visit.

seaworld.com

D66

Save $5.00 on Admission to Busch Gardens

Present coupon at any ticket window at time of purchase during regular park operating hours. One coupon good for up to six (6) admissions during one park visit.

buschgardens.com

D67

Save $5.00 on Admission to Adventure Island and Water Country USA

Present coupon at any ticket window at time of purchase during regular park operating hours. One coupon good for up to six (6) admissions during one park visit.

adventureisland.com, watercountryusa.com

D68

Save $5.00 on Admission to Sesame Place

Present coupon at any ticket window at time of purchase during regular park operating hours. One coupon good for up to six (6) admissions during one park visit. Not valid on weekends July 2–August 28, 2007.

sesameplace.com

D69

For more details, call your travel agent, call 1-800-CARNIVAL or visit www.carnival.com

Terms and Conditions:
Certificate may be redeemed at any travel agent and is valid on selected 3, 4, 5, 7 day or longer Carnival cruises departing prior to December 31, 2007.
- Applies to new individual bookings only. Limit one certificate per stateroom.
- Offer is capacity controlled and space may be limited on certain cruises. Certain restrictions apply. Specific cruises may be excluded at any time. Christmas and New Year's cruises will not be available.
- Applies to purchases at the available rates for stateroom categories 6A through 12 (excluding 6E and 9A).
- Offer is combinable with Carnival's Super Saver program.
- Offer is not combinable with any other discount, promotional offer or groups.
- Savings for single occupancy bookings is $50 for 7 day or longer cruises and $25 for 3, 4 and 5 day cruises.
- Only original certificates will be accepted. Reproductions will not be accepted.
- Certificate has no cash value and savings amount is expressed in U.S. dollars.
- Certificate must be submitted with deposit payment. Savings amount may not be deducted from deposit amount.
- Ships registered: Panama and the Bahamas.

TRAVEL AGENT INFORMATION: Request fare code CPEP when making reservations. Please include this completed certificate with deposit. Travel agent commission is based on discounted rate.

Guest Name _____
Booking Number _____
Ship _____ Sailing Date _____
Travel Agency Name _____
Travel Agency Phone Number _____

Offer validity is governed by the Rules of Use and excludes defined holidays. Offers are not valid with other discount offers, unless specified. Coupons void if purchased, sold or bartered. Discounts exclude tax, tip and/or alcohol, where applicable.

ENT1207

For more details, call your travel agent, call 1-800-CARNIVAL or visit www.carnival.com

Terms and Conditions:
Certificate may be redeemed at any travel agent and is valid on selected 3, 4, 5, 7 day or longer Carnival cruises departing prior to December 31, 2007.
- Applies to new individual bookings only. Limit one certificate per stateroom.
- Offer is capacity controlled and space may be limited on certain cruises. Certain restrictions apply. Specific cruises may be excluded at any time. Christmas and New Year's cruises will not be available.
- Applies to purchases at the available rates for stateroom categories 6A through 12 (excluding 6E and 9A).
- Offer is combinable with Carnival's Super Saver program.
- Offer is not combinable with any other discount, promotional offer or groups.
- Savings for single occupancy bookings is $50 for 7 day or longer cruises and $25 for 3, 4 and 5 day cruises.
- Only original certificates will be accepted. Reproductions will not be accepted.
- Certificate has no cash value and savings amount is expressed in U.S. dollars.
- Certificate must be submitted with deposit payment. Savings amount may not be deducted from deposit amount.
- Ships registered: Panama and the Bahamas.

TRAVEL AGENT INFORMATION: Request fare code CPEP when making reservations. Please include this completed certificate with deposit. Travel agent commission is based on discounted rate.

Guest Name _____
Booking Number _____
Ship _____ Sailing Date _____
Travel Agency Name _____
Travel Agency Phone Number _____

Offer validity is governed by the Rules of Use and excludes defined holidays. Offers are not valid with other discount offers, unless specified. Coupons void if purchased, sold or bartered. Discounts exclude tax, tip and/or alcohol, where applicable.

ENT1207

For more details, call your travel agent, call 1-800-CARNIVAL or visit www.carnival.com

Terms and Conditions:
Certificate may be redeemed at any travel agent and is valid on selected 3, 4, 5, 7 day or longer Carnival cruises departing prior to December 31, 2007.
- Applies to new individual bookings only. Limit one certificate per stateroom.
- Offer is capacity controlled and space may be limited on certain cruises. Certain restrictions apply. Specific cruises may be excluded at any time. Christmas and New Year's cruises will not be available.
- Applies to purchases at the available rates for stateroom categories 6A through 12 (excluding 6E and 9A).
- Offer is combinable with Carnival's Super Saver program.
- Offer is not combinable with any other discount, promotional offer or groups.
- Savings for single occupancy bookings is $50 for 7 day or longer cruises and $25 for 3, 4 and 5 day cruises.
- Only original certificates will be accepted. Reproductions will not be accepted.
- Certificate has no cash value and savings amount is expressed in U.S. dollars.
- Certificate must be submitted with deposit payment. Savings amount may not be deducted from deposit amount.
- Ships registered: Panama and the Bahamas.

TRAVEL AGENT INFORMATION: Request fare code CPEP when making reservations. Please include this completed certificate with deposit. Travel agent commission is based on discounted rate.

Guest Name _____
Booking Number _____
Ship _____ Sailing Date _____
Travel Agency Name _____
Travel Agency Phone Number _____

Offer validity is governed by the Rules of Use and excludes defined holidays. Offers are not valid with other discount offers, unless specified. Coupons void if purchased, sold or bartered. Discounts exclude tax, tip and/or alcohol, where applicable.

ENT1207

Carnival
The Fun Ships

Save up to an extra $100 per stateroom on a fabulous 7 day or longer Carnival cruise or up to an extra $50 per stateroom on the newest, largest and most popular 3, 4 and 5 day fleet. This special savings is combinable with our low Super Saver rates...

it's your best vacation value!

SAVE UP TO $100 PER STATEROOM

Valid now thru December 31, 2007
See reverse side for details

D63

Carnival
The Fun Ships

Save up to an extra $100 per stateroom on a fabulous 7 day or longer Carnival cruise or up to an extra $50 per stateroom on the newest, largest and most popular 3, 4 and 5 day fleet. This special savings is combinable with our low Super Saver rates...

it's your best vacation value!

SAVE UP TO $100 PER STATEROOM

Valid now thru December 31, 2007
See reverse side for details

D64

Carnival
The Fun Ships

Save up to an extra $100 per stateroom on a fabulous 7 day or longer Carnival cruise or up to an extra $50 per stateroom on the newest, largest and most popular 3, 4 and 5 day fleet. This special savings is combinable with our low Super Saver rates...

it's your best vacation value!

SAVE UP TO $100 PER STATEROOM

Valid now thru December 31, 2007
See reverse side for details

D65

Mention offer PC# 983441 and CDP# 205521

If there's a Hertz Local Edition® location in your neighborhood, call and ask us to come and get you.

Advance reservations are required as blackout periods may apply. This offer is subject to NeverLost-equipped vehicle availability. This offer is redeemable at participating Hertz locations in the U.S. and Canada, has no cash value and may not be used with any other CDP#, coupon, discount, rate or promotion. Hertz age, driver, credit, and daily, weekly or weekend rate qualifications for the renting location apply and the car must be returned to that location. Discounts apply to time and mileage only. Taxes, tax reimbursement, fees and optional service charges, such as refueling, are not subject to discount. Call for details.

Offer validity is governed by the Rules of Use.
Coupons void if purchased, sold or bartered.

Mention offer PC# 983404 and CDP# 205521

If there's a Hertz Local Edition® location in your neighborhood, call and ask us to come and get you.

Advance reservations are required as blackout periods may apply. This offer is redeemable at participating Hertz locations in the U.S. and Canada, subject to vehicle availability. Not all vehicles, vehicle equipment and services are available at all locations. This coupon has no cash value, and may not be used with any other CDP#, coupon, discount, rate or promotion. Hertz age, driver, credit and weekly rate qualifications for the renting location apply and the car must be returned to that location. Taxes, tax reimbursement, fees and optional service charges, such as refueling, are not subject to discount. Discounts apply to time and mileage only. Call for details.

Offer validity is governed by the Rules of Use.
Coupons void if purchased, sold or bartered.

Mention offer PC# 983566 and CDP# 205521

If there's a Hertz Local Edition® location in your neighborhood, call and ask us to come and get you.

Advance reservations are required as blackout periods may apply. This offer is redeemable at participating Hertz locations in the U.S. and Canada and is subject to availability of SIRIUS-equipped vehicles. This coupon has no cash value, and may not be used with any other CDP#, coupon, discount, rate or promotion. Hertz age, driver, credit and rate qualifications for the renting location apply and the car must be returned to that location. Taxes, tax reimbursement, fees and optional service charges, such as refueling, are not subject to discount. Discounts apply to time and mileage only. Call for details.

Offer validity is governed by the Rules of Use.
Coupons void if purchased, sold or bartered.

Mention offer PC# 983555 and CDP# 205521

If there's a Hertz Local Edition® location in your neighborhood, call and ask us to come and get you.

Advance reservations are required as blackout periods may apply. It is redeemable at participating Hertz locations in the U.S., Canada and Puerto Rico, subject to vehicle availability. This coupon has no cash value, and may not be used with any other CDP#, coupon, discount, rate or promotion. Hertz age, driver, credit and monthly rate qualifications for the renting location apply and the car must be returned to that location. Taxes, tax reimbursement, fees and optional service charges, such as refueling, are not subject to discount. Discounts apply to time and mileage only. Call for details.

Offer validity is governed by the Rules of Use.
Coupons void if purchased, sold or bartered.

Mention offer PC# 983426 and CDP# 205521

If there's a Hertz Local Edition® location in your neighborhood, call and ask us to come and get you.

Advance reservations are required as blackout periods may apply. This offer is redeemable at participating Hertz locations in the U.S., Canada and Puerto Rico, subject to vehicle availability. Highest obtainable upgrade is to a premium class car. Brand and model not guaranteed. This coupon has no cash value, and may not be used with any other CDP#, coupon, discount, rate or promotion. Hertz age, driver, credit and daily, weekend and weekly rate qualifications for the renting location apply and the car must be returned to that location. Discounts apply to time and mileage only. Call for details.

Offer validity is governed by the Rules of Use.
Coupons void if purchased, sold or bartered.

Mention offer PC# 983430 and CDP# 205521

If there's a Hertz Local Edition® location in your neighborhood, call and ask us to come and get you.

Advance reservations are required as blackout periods may apply. This offer is redeemable at participating Hertz locations in the U.S., Canada and Puerto Rico, subject to vehicle availability. This coupon has no cash value and may not be used with any other CDP#, coupon, discount, rate or promotion. Hertz age, driver, credit and weekend rate qualifications for the renting location apply and the car must be returned to that location. Taxes, tax reimbursement, fees and optional service charges, such as refueling, are not subject to discount. Discounts apply to time and mileage only. Call for details.

Offer validity is governed by the Rules of Use.
Coupons void if purchased, sold or bartered.

$30 Off

HERTZ FUN COLLECTION
HERTZ PRESTIGE COLLECTION
WEEKLY RENTALS

- Go to hertz.com for our lowest rates.
- Enter your rental location, date and arrival information
- Click "Yes" I have a Discount (CDP), Coupon or other Offer
- Enter your **Discount Plan #205521** and **PC# 983404**

For phone reservations:
Call 1-888-999-7125
or call your travel agent.

See reverse side for details

Valid now thru June 30, 2008   D57

---

2 Free Days

HERTZ NEVERLOST®
When renting a Neverlost-equipped vehicle for at least 3 days

- Go to hertz.com for our lowest rates.
- Enter your rental location, date and arrival information
- Click "Yes" I have a Discount (CDP), Coupon or other Offer
- Enter your **Discount Plan #205521** and **PC# 983441**

For phone reservations:
Call 1-888-999-7125
or call your travel agent.

See reverse side for details

Valid now thru June 30, 2008   D58

$50 Off

A MONTHLY RENTAL
When renting a midsize/intermediate or higher class vehicle

- Go to hertz.com for our lowest rates.
- Enter your rental location, date and arrival information
- Click "Yes" I have a Discount (CDP), Coupon or other Offer
- Enter your **Discount Plan #205521** and **PC# 983555**

For phone reservations:
Call 1-888-999-7125
or call your travel agent.

See reverse side for details

Valid now thru June 30, 2008   D59

---

2 Free Days

SIRIUS SATELLITE RADIO
When renting a SIRIUS-equipped vehicle for at least 3 days.

- Go to hertz.com for our lowest rates.
- Enter your rental location, date and arrival information
- Click "Yes" I have a Discount (CDP), Coupon or other Offer
- Enter your **Discount Plan #205521** and **PC# 983566**

For phone reservations:
Call 1-888-999-7125
or call your travel agent.

See reverse side for details

Valid now thru June 30, 2008   D60

Save $5 a Day

ON YOUR WEEKEND RENTAL OF
MID-SIZE AND HIGHER CAR CLASSES
Up to $20 off, minimum two day weekend rentals

- Go to hertz.com for our lowest rates.
- Enter your rental location, date and arrival information
- Click "Yes" I have a Discount (CDP), Coupon or other Offer
- Enter your **Discount Plan #205521** and **PC# 983430**

For phone reservations:
Call 1-888-999-7125
or call your travel agent.

See reverse side for details

Valid now thru June 30, 2008   D61

FREE

ONE CAR CLASS UPGRADE
When renting a compact through full-size class car
in the U.S., Canada and Puerto Rico for a day, weekend or week

- Go to hertz.com for our lowest rates.
- Enter your rental location, date and arrival information
- Click "Yes" I have a Discount (CDP), Coupon or other Offer
- Enter your **Discount Plan #205521** and **PC# 983426**

For phone reservations:
Call 1-888-999-7125
or call your travel agent.

See reverse side for details

Valid now thru June 30, 2008   D62

We're in the neighborhood

Mention offer PC# 983430 and CDP# 205521

If there's a Hertz Local Edition® location in your neighborhood, call and ask us to come and get you.

Advance reservations are required as blackout periods may apply. This offer is redeemable at participating Hertz locations in the U.S., Canada and Puerto Rico, subject to vehicle availability. This coupon has no cash value and may not be used with any other CDP#, coupon, discount, rate or promotion. Hertz age, driver, credit and weekend rate qualifications for the renting location apply and the car must be returned to that location. Taxes, tax reimbursement, fees and optional service charges, such as refueling, are not subject to discount. Discounts apply to time and mileage only. Call for details.

Offer validity is governed by the Rules of Use.
Coupons void if purchased, sold or bartered.

Mention offer PC# 983415 and CDP# 205521

If there's a Hertz Local Edition® location in your neighborhood, call and ask us to come and get you.

Advance reservations are required as blackout periods may apply. This offer is redeemable at participating Hertz locations in the U.S., Canada, and Puerto Rico, subject to vehicle availability. This coupon has no cash value and may not be used with any other CDP#, coupon, discount, rate or promotion. Hertz age, driver, credit and weekly rate qualifications for the renting location apply and the car must be returned to that location. Taxes, tax reimbursement, fees and optional service charges, such as refueling, are not subject to discount. Discounts apply to time and mileage only. Call for details.

Offer validity is governed by the Rules of Use.
Coupons void if purchased, sold or bartered.

Mention offer PC# 983426 and CDP# 205521

If there's a Hertz Local Edition® location in your neighborhood, call and ask us to come and get you.

Advance reservations are required as blackout periods may apply. This offer is redeemable at participating Hertz locations in the U.S., Canada and Puerto Rico, subject to vehicle availability. Highest obtainable upgrade is to a premium class car. Brand and model not guaranteed. This coupon has no cash value, and may not be used with any other CDP#, coupon, discount, rate or promotion. Hertz age, driver, credit and daily, weekly and weekend rate qualifications for the renting location apply and the car must be returned to that location. Discounts apply to time and mileage only. Call for details.

Offer validity is governed by the Rules of Use.
Coupons void if purchased, sold or bartered.

Mention offer PC# 983511 and CDP# 205521

Surrender this coupon at the time and place of rental. This offer is redeemable at participating Hertz locations in Europe, subject to higher car class availability by country and at time of rental. Upgrades are not guaranteed at time of reservation. Blackout periods may apply. Reservations must be made in the U.S. at least 24 hours prior to vehicle pickup. This coupon has no cash value and may not be used with any other CDP#, coupon, discount, Tour Rates or other rates or promotions. Offer void where prohibited by law, taxed or otherwise restricted. Renter must meet all Hertz qualifications, standards and requirements, including those relating to age, driving license and credit in effect at the time and place of rental. Car must be returned to renting location.

Offer validity is governed by the Rules of Use.
Coupons void if purchased, sold or bartered.

Special Offers Plus Discounts. Save Up to 25%
visit entertainment.com/hertz for low web rates too.

$20 Off

A WEEKLY RENTAL OF MID-SIZE AND HIGHER CAR CLASSES

- Go to hertz.com for our lowest rates.
- Enter your rental location, date and arrival information
- Click "Yes" I have a Discount (CDP), Coupon or other Offer
- Enter your Discount Plan #205521 and PC# 983415

For phone reservations:
Call 1-888-999-7125
or call your travel agent.

Hertz

See reverse side for details
Valid now thru June 30, 2008   D53

Save $5 a Day

ON YOUR WEEKEND RENTAL OF MID-SIZE AND HIGHER CAR CLASSES
Up to $20 off, minimum two day weekend rentals

- Go to hertz.com for our lowest rates.
- Enter your rental location, date and arrival information
- Click "Yes" I have a Discount (CDP), Coupon or other Offer
- Enter your Discount Plan #205521 and PC# 983430

For phone reservations:
Call 1-888-999-7125
or call your travel agent.

Hertz

See reverse side for details
Valid now thru June 30, 2008   D54

FREE

UPGRADE IN EUROPE
Minimum 3 day rental of economy through full-size manual shift vehicles at Hertz non-prepaid Affordable Rates

- Go to hertz.com for our lowest rates.
- Enter your rental location, date and arrival information
- Click "Yes" I have a Discount (CDP), Coupon or other Offer
- Enter your Discount Plan #205521 and PC# 983511

For phone reservations:
Call 1-888-999-7125
or call your travel agent.

Hertz

See reverse side for details
Valid now thru June 30, 2008   D55

FREE

ONE CAR CLASS UPGRADE
When renting a compact through full-size class car in the U.S., Canada and Puerto Rico for a day, weekend or week

- Go to hertz.com for our lowest rates.
- Enter your rental location, date and arrival information
- Click "Yes" I have a Discount (CDP), Coupon or other Offer
- Enter your Discount Plan #205521 and PC# 983426

For phone reservations:
Call 1-888-999-7125
or call your travel agent.

Hertz

See reverse side for details
Valid now thru June 30, 2008   D56

Terms and Conditions.
One coupon per National rental and void once redeemed. Original coupon must be presented at counter upon arrival. Renter must meet standard age, driver and credit requirements. 24-hour advance reservation required. Blackout dates may apply. May not be combined with other discounts or promotions, except your Entertainment® discount. Valid only at participating National locations. Offer not valid in Manhattan, N.Y., or San Jose, CA. Valid for two free car class upgrades from the car class reserved. Valid now through 6/30/08. ©2006-2008 Vanguard Car Rental USA Inc. All rights reserved. 1832d-AN-106

Offer validity is governed by the Rules of Use and excludes defined holidays. Offers are not valid with other discount offers, unless specified. Coupons void if purchased, sold or bartered. Discounts exclude tax, tip and/or alcohol, where applicable.

Terms and Conditions.
One coupon per National rental and void once redeemed. Original coupon must be presented at counter upon arrival. Discount applies to base rate only, which does not include taxes (including GST/VAT), governmentally-authorized or imposed surcharges, license recoupment/air tax recovery and concession recoupment fees, airport and airport facility fees, fuel, additional driver fee, one-way rental charge or optional items. Not valid on truck rentals in Canada. Renter must meet standard age, driver and credit requirements. 24-Hour advance reservations required. Blackout dates may apply. May not be combined with other discounts or promotions, except your Entertainment® discount. Availability is limited. Valid only at participating National locations. Some countries may convert coupon value into local currency. Valid now through 6/30/08. ©2006-2008 Vanguard Car Rental USA Inc. All rights reserved. 1832d-AN-106

Offer validity is governed by the Rules of Use and excludes defined holidays. Offers are not valid with other discount offers, unless specified. Coupons void if purchased, sold or bartered. Discounts exclude tax, tip and/or alcohol, where applicable.

Terms and Conditions.
One coupon per National rental and void once redeemed. Original coupon must be presented at counter upon arrival. Free day is prorated against base rate of entire rental period, which does not include taxes, governmentally-authorized or imposed surcharges, license recoupment/air tax recovery and concession recoupment fees, airport and airport facility fees, fuel, additional driver fee, one-way rental charge or optional items. Weekend rental requires a 3-day minimum (5-day maximum) rental with a Saturday overnight keep. Vehicle must not be picked up before weekend rates are available on Thursday and must not be returned before the immediately following Sunday. Vehicles must be returned no later than the immediately following Monday on or before the time the rental began or higher extra day rates may apply. Renter must meet standard age, driver and credit requirements. 24-hour advance reservation required. Blackout dates may apply. May not be combined with other discounts or promotions, except your Entertainment® discount. Subject to availability and good only at participating National locations. Offer not valid in Manhattan, N.Y., or San Jose, CA. Valid now through 6/30/08. ©2006-2008 Vanguard Car Rental USA Inc. All rights reserved. 1832d-AN-106

Offer validity is governed by the Rules of Use and excludes defined holidays. Offers are not valid with other discount offers, unless specified. Coupons void if purchased, sold or bartered. Discounts exclude tax, tip and/or alcohol, where applicable.

Terms and Conditions.
One coupon per National rental and void once redeemed. Original coupon must be presented at counter upon arrival. Discount applies to base rate only, which does not include taxes (including VAT), governmentally-authorized or imposed surcharges, license recoupment/air tax recovery and concession recoupment fees, airport and airport facility fees, fuel, additional driver fee, one-way rental charge or optional items. Renter must meet standard age, driver and credit requirements. 24-hour advance reservation required. Blackout dates may apply. May not be combined with other discounts or promotions, except your Entertainment® discount. Subject to availability and valid only at participating National locations. Some countries may convert coupon value into local currency. Valid now through 6/30/08. ©2006-2008 Vanguard Car Rental USA Inc. All rights reserved. 1832d-AN-106

Offer validity is governed by the Rules of Use and excludes defined holidays. Offers are not valid with other discount offers, unless specified. Coupons void if purchased, sold or bartered. Discounts exclude tax, tip and/or alcohol, where applicable.

Terms and Conditions.
One coupon per National rental and void once redeemed. Original coupon must be presented at counter upon arrival. Discount applies to base rate only, which does not include taxes, governmentally-authorized or imposed surcharges, license recoupment/air tax recovery and concession recoupment fees, airport and airport facility fees, fuel, additional driver fee, one-way rental charge or optional items. Renter must meet standard age, driver and credit requirements. 24-Hour advance reservation required. Blackout dates may apply. May not be combined with other discounts or promotions, except your Entertainment® discount. Subject to availability and valid only at participating National locations. Valid now through 6/30/08. ©2006-2008 Vanguard Car Rental USA Inc. All rights reserved. 1832d-AN-106

Offer validity is governed by the Rules of Use and excludes defined holidays. Offers are not valid with other discount offers, unless specified. Coupons void if purchased, sold or bartered. Discounts exclude tax, tip and/or alcohol, where applicable.

Terms and Conditions.
One coupon per National rental and void once redeemed. Original coupon must be presented at counter upon arrival. Renter must meet standard age, driver and credit requirements. 24-hour advance reservation required. Blackout dates may apply. May not be combined with other discounts or promotions, except your Entertainment® discount. Valid only at participating National locations. Offer not valid in Manhattan, N.Y., or San Jose, CA. Valid for two free car class upgrades from the car class reserved. Valid now through 6/30/08. ©2006-2008 Vanguard Car Rental USA Inc. All rights reserved. 1832d-AN-106

Offer validity is governed by the Rules of Use and excludes defined holidays. Offers are not valid with other discount offers, unless specified. Coupons void if purchased, sold or bartered. Discounts exclude tax, tip and/or alcohol, where applicable.

$15 OFF WEEKLY RENTAL

In addition to your standard Entertainment® discount. Reserve a compact car or larger for a minimum of 5 days in the United States, Canada, Latin America, or the Caribbean.

Request Coupon I.D. ND16 and Contract I.D. 5004607.

Book online at **entertainment.com/national** or call **1-888-575-6279**.

National
Green means go.

Valid now thru June 30, 2008
See reverse side for details
D47

TWO CAR CLASS UPGRADE!

In addition to your standard Entertainment® discount. Reserve a compact through a midsize car in the United States or Canada.

Request Coupon I.D. NU41 and Contract I.D. 5004607.

Book online at **entertainment.com/national** or call **1-888-575-6279**.

National
Green means go.

Valid now thru June 30, 2008
See reverse side for details
D48

$20 OFF WEEKLY RENTAL

In addition to your standard Entertainment® discount. Reserve a midsize car or larger for a minimum of 5 days in the United States, Latin America, or the Caribbean.

Request Coupon I.D. ND17 and Contract I.D. 5004607.

Book online at **entertainment.com/national** or call **1-888-575-6279**.

National
Green means go.

Valid now thru June 30, 2008
See reverse side for details
D49

ONE FREE WEEKEND DAY

In addition to your standard Entertainment® discount. Reserve a midsize car or larger for a minimum of 3 days (maximum 5 days) in the United States.

Request Coupon I.D. NF14 and Contract I.D. 5004607.

Book online at **entertainment.com/national** or call **1-888-575-6279**.

National
Green means go.

Valid now thru June 30, 2008
See reverse side for details
D50

TWO CAR CLASS UPGRADE!

In addition to your standard Entertainment® discount. Reserve a compact through midsize car in the United States or Canada.

Request Coupon I.D. NU41 and Contract I.D. 5004607.

Book online at **entertainment.com/national** or call **1-888-575-6279**.

National
Green means go.

Valid now thru June 30, 2008
See reverse side for details
D51

$50 OFF MONTHLY RENTAL

In addition to your standard Entertainment® discount. Reserve a midsize car or larger in the United States. Valid for a rental of at least 29 days. (Maximum 330 days)

Request Coupon I.D. ND18 and Contract I.D. 5004607.

Book online at **entertainment.com/national** or call **1-888-575-6279**.

National
Green means go.

Valid now thru June 30, 2008
See reverse side for details
D52

DRIVE AND SAVE.

Get the best rates at entertainment.com/national or call 1-888-575-6279.

National — Green means go.

National features GM vehicles like this Chevrolet Impala.

Terms and Conditions.
One coupon per National rental and void once redeemed. Original coupon must be presented at counter upon arrival. Free day is prorated against base rate of entire rental period, which does not include taxes, governmentally-authorized or imposed surcharges, license recoupment/air tax recovery and concession recoupment fees, airport and airport facility fees, fuel, additional driver fee, one-way rental charge or optional items. Weekend rental requires a 3-day minimum (5-day maximum) rental with a Saturday overnight keep. Vehicle must not be picked up before weekend rates are available on Thursday and must not be returned before the immediately following Sunday. Vehicles must be returned no later than the immediately following Monday on or before the time the rental began or higher extra day rates may apply. Renter must meet standard age, driver and credit requirements. 24-hour advance reservation required. Blackout dates may apply. May not be combined with other discounts or promotions, except your Entertainment® discount. Subject to availability and good only at participating National locations. Offer not valid in Manhattan, N.Y., or San Jose, CA. Valid now through 6/30/08. ©2006-2008 Vanguard Car Rental USA Inc. All rights reserved. 1832c-AN-106

Offer validity is governed by the Rules of Use and excludes defined holidays. Offers are not valid with other discount offers, unless specified. Coupons void if purchased, sold or bartered. Discounts exclude tax, tip and/or alcohol, where applicable.

Terms and Conditions.
One coupon per National rental and void once redeemed. Original coupon must be presented at counter upon arrival. Discount applies to base rate only, which does not include taxes (including VAT), governmentally-authorized or imposed surcharges, license recoupment/air tax recovery and concession recoupment fees, airport and airport facility fees, fuel, additional driver fee, one-way rental charge or optional items. Renter must meet standard age, driver and credit requirements. 24-hour advance reservation required. Blackout dates may apply. May not be combined with other discounts or promotions, except your Entertainment® discount. Subject to availability and valid only at participating National locations. Some countries may convert coupon value into local currency. Valid now through 6/30/08. ©2006-2008 Vanguard Car Rental USA Inc. All rights reserved. 1832c-AN-106

Offer validity is governed by the Rules of Use and excludes defined holidays. Offers are not valid with other discount offers, unless specified. Coupons void if purchased, sold or bartered. Discounts exclude tax, tip and/or alcohol, where applicable.

Terms and Conditions.
One coupon per National rental and void once redeemed. Original coupon must be presented at counter upon arrival. Free day is prorated against base rate for entire rental period, which does not include taxes (including VAT/GST), other governmentally-authorized or imposed surcharges, license recoupment/air tax recovery and concession recoupment fees, airport and airport facility fees, fuel, additional driver fee, one-way rental charge, or optional items. Not valid on truck rentals in Canada. Renter must meet standard age, driver and credit requirements. Blackout dates may apply. May not be combined with other discounts or promotions, except your Entertainment® discount. Subject to availability and valid only at participating National locations. 24-Hour advance reservations required. Offer not valid in Manhattan, N.Y., or San Jose, CA. Valid now through 6/30/08. ©2006-2008 Vanguard Car Rental USA Inc. All rights reserved. 1832c-AN-106

Offer validity is governed by the Rules of Use and excludes defined holidays. Offers are not valid with other discount offers, unless specified. Coupons void if purchased, sold or bartered. Discounts exclude tax, tip and/or alcohol, where applicable.

Terms and Conditions.
One coupon per National rental and void once redeemed. Original coupon must be presented at counter upon arrival. Renter must meet standard age, driver and credit requirements. 24-hour advance reservation required. Blackout dates may apply. May not be combined with other discounts or promotions, except your Entertainment® discount. Valid only at participating National locations. Offer not valid in Manhattan, N.Y., or San Jose, CA. Valid for two free car class upgrades from the car class reserved. Valid now through 6/30/08. ©2006-2008 Vanguard Car Rental USA Inc. All rights reserved. 1832c-AN-106

Offer validity is governed by the Rules of Use and excludes defined holidays. Offers are not valid with other discount offers, unless specified. Coupons void if purchased, sold or bartered. Discounts exclude tax, tip and/or alcohol, where applicable.

UPGRADE THE CAR, NOT THE PRICE.

Enjoy special offers and upgrades from National. Get the best rates at entertainment.com/national or call 1-888-575-6279.

National — Green means go.

National features GM vehicles like this Pontiac G6.

$20 OFF WEEKLY RENTAL

In addition to your standard Entertainment® discount. Reserve a midsize car or larger for a minimum of 5 days in the United States, Latin America, or the Caribbean.

Request Coupon I.D. ND17 and Contract I.D. 5004607.

Book online at **entertainment.com/national** or call **1-888-575-6279**.

National — Green means go.

Valid now thru June 30, 2008
See reverse side for details

D43

ONE FREE WEEKEND DAY

In addition to your standard Entertainment® discount. Reserve a midsize car or larger for a minimum of 3 days (maximum 5 days) in the United States.

Request Coupon I.D. NF14 and Contract I.D. 5004607.

Book online at **entertainment.com/national** or call **1-888-575-6279**.

National — Green means go.

Valid now thru June 30, 2008
See reverse side for details

D44

TWO CAR CLASS UPGRADE!

In addition to your standard Entertainment® discount. Reserve a compact through midsize car in the United States or Canada.

Request Coupon I.D. NU41 and Contract I.D. 5004607.

Book online at **entertainment.com/national** or call **1-888-575-6279**.

National — Green means go.

Valid now thru June 30, 2008
See reverse side for details

D45

ONE FREE DAY

In addition to your standard Entertainment® discount. Reserve a midsize car or larger for a minimum of 5 days in the United States, Canada, Latin America, or the Caribbean.

Request Coupon I.D. NF15 and Contract I.D. 5004607.

Book online at **entertainment.com/national** or call **1-888-575-6279**.

National — Green means go.

Valid now thru June 30, 2008
See reverse side for details

D46

Coupon 1

One coupon per Alamo rental and void once redeemed. Original coupon must be presented at counter upon arrival. Discount applies to base rate, which does not include taxes, other governmentally-authorized or imposed surcharges, license recoupment/air tax recovery and concession recoupment fees, airport and airport facility fees, fuel, additional driver fee, one-way rental charge, or optional items. Offer is subject to standard rental conditions. Blackout dates may apply. Not valid with any other discount or promotional rate, except your Entertainment® discount. Subject to availability and valid only at participating Alamo locations. 24-Hour advance reservations required. Valid now through 6/30/08. ©2006-2008 Vanguard Car Rental USA Inc. All rights reserved. 1832b- AN-106

ALAMO® FEATURES GM VEHICLES.

Offer validity is governed by the Rules of Use and excludes defined holidays. Offers are not valid with other discount offers, unless specified. Coupons void if purchased, sold or bartered. Discounts exclude tax, tip and/or alcohol, where applicable.

Coupon 2

One coupon per Alamo rental and void once redeemed. Original coupon must be presented at counter upon arrival. Discount applies to base rate, which does not include taxes (including VAT), other governmentally-authorized or imposed surcharges, license recoupment/air tax recovery and concession recoupment fees, airport and airport facility fees, fuel, additional driver fee, one-way rental charge, or optional items. Offer is subject to standard rental conditions. Blackout dates may apply. Not valid with any other discount or promotional rate, except your Entertainment® discount. Subject to availability and valid only at participating Alamo locations. 24-Hour advance reservations required. Some countries may convert coupon value into local currency. Valid now through 6/30/08. ©2006-2008 Vanguard Car Rental USA Inc. All rights reserved. 1832b-AN-106

ALAMO® FEATURES GM VEHICLES.

Offer validity is governed by the Rules of Use and excludes defined holidays. Offers are not valid with other discount offers, unless specified. Coupons void if purchased, sold or bartered. Discounts exclude tax, tip and/or alcohol, where applicable.

Coupon 3

One coupon per Alamo rental and void once redeemed. Original coupon must be presented at counter upon arrival. Discount applies to base rate, which does not include taxes (including VAT), other governmentally-authorized or imposed surcharges, license recoupment/air tax recovery and concession recoupment fees, airport and airport facility fees, fuel, additional driver fee, one-way rental charge, or optional items. Offer is subject to standard rental conditions. Blackout dates may apply. Not valid with any other discount or promotional rate, except your Entertainment® discount. Subject to availability and valid only at participating Alamo locations. 24-Hour advance reservations required. Some countries may convert coupon value into local currency. Valid now through 6/30/08. ©2006-2008 Vanguard Car Rental USA Inc. All rights reserved. 1832b-AN-106

ALAMO® FEATURES GM VEHICLES.

Offer validity is governed by the Rules of Use and excludes defined holidays. Offers are not valid with other discount offers, unless specified. Coupons void if purchased, sold or bartered. Discounts exclude tax, tip and/or alcohol, where applicable.

Coupon 4

One coupon per Alamo rental and void once redeemed. Original coupon must be presented at counter upon arrival. Discount applies to base rate, which does not include taxes, other governmentally-authorized or imposed surcharges, license recoupment/air tax recovery and concession recoupment fees, airport and airport facility fees, fuel, additional driver fee, one-way rental charge, or optional items. Offer is subject to standard rental conditions.Blackout dates may apply. Not valid with any other discount or promotional rate, except your Entertainment® discount. Subject to availability and valid only at participating Alamo locations. 24-Hour advance reservations required. Valid now through 6/30/08. ©2006-2008 Vanguard Car Rental USA Inc. All rights reserved. 1832b-AN-106

ALAMO® FEATURES GM VEHICLES.

Offer validity is governed by the Rules of Use and excludes defined holidays. Offers are not valid with other discount offers, unless specified. Coupons void if purchased, sold or bartered. Discounts exclude tax, tip and/or alcohol, where applicable.

Coupon 5

One coupon per Alamo rental and void once redeemed. Original coupon must be presented at counter upon arrival.Discount applies to base rate, which does not include taxes, other governmentally-authorized or imposed surcharges, license recoupment/air tax recovery and concession recoupment fees, airport and airport facility fees, fuel, additional driver fee, one-way rental charge, or optional items. Offer is subject to standard rental conditions.Blackout dates may apply. Not valid with any other discount or promotional rate, except your Entertainment® discount. Subject to availability and valid only at participating Alamo locations. 24-Hour advance reservations required. Valid now through 6/30/08. ©2006-2008 Vanguard Car Rental USA Inc. All rights reserved. 1832b-AN-106

ALAMO® FEATURES GM VEHICLES.

Offer validity is governed by the Rules of Use and excludes defined holidays. Offers are not valid with other discount offers, unless specified. Coupons void if purchased, sold or bartered. Discounts exclude tax, tip and/or alcohol, where applicable.

Coupon 6

One coupon per Alamo rental and void once redeemed. Original coupon must be presented at counter upon arrival. In Europe, the Middle East, and Africa, upgrade is subject to availability at time of rental pickup and requires a 5-day minimum rental. Offer is subject to standard rental conditions. Blackout dates may apply. 24-Hour advance reservations required. Not valid with any other discount or promotional rate, except your Entertainment® discount. Offer valid only at participating Alamo locations. Valid for a free one car class upgrade from the car class reserved (same transmission in Europe, the Middle East and Africa). Offer not valid in Manhattan, N.Y., or San Jose, CA. Valid now through 6/30/08. ©2006-2008 Vanguard Car Rental USA Inc. All rights reserved. 1832b-AN-106

ALAMO® FEATURES GM VEHICLES.

Offer validity is governed by the Rules of Use and excludes defined holidays. Offers are not valid with other discount offers, unless specified. Coupons void if purchased, sold or bartered. Discounts exclude tax, tip and/or alcohol, where applicable.

UP TO $20 OFF

In addition to your standard Entertainment® discount, reserve a compact car or larger in the United States, Latin America, or the Caribbean.

Request I.D. Number 7012170 and:

Coupon Code	Days	$ OFF
AD25	2	$10
AD26	3	$15
AD27	4	$20

entertainment.com/alamo
1-800-237-0984.

Alamo

Valid now thru June 30, 2008
See reverse side for details

D37

$50 OFF
A MONTHLY RENTAL

In addition to your standard Entertainment® discount, reserve a midsize car or larger in the United States. Valid for a rental of at least 29 days. (Maximum 330 Days)

Request Coupon Code AD29 and I.D. Number 7012170.

entertainment.com/alamo
1-800-237-0984.

Alamo

Valid now thru June 30, 2008
See reverse side for details

D38

$25 OFF
MINIMUM 3-DAY RENTAL

In addition to your standard Entertainment® discount, reserve a convertible, minivan, or sport utility vehicle for a minimum of 3 days in the United States.

Request Coupon Code AD28 and I.D. Number 7012170.

entertainment.com/alamo
1-800-237-0984.

Alamo

Valid now thru June 30, 2008
See reverse side for details

D39

UP TO $20 OFF

In addition to your standard Entertainment® discount, reserve a compact car or larger in the United States, Latin America, or the Caribbean.

Request I.D. Number 7012170 and:

Coupon Code	Days	$ OFF
AD25	2	$10
AD26	3	$15
AD27	4	$20

entertainment.com/alamo
1-800-237-0984.

Alamo

Valid now thru June 30, 2008
See reverse side for details

D40

FREE UPGRADE

In addition to your standard Entertainment® discount, reserve a compact through midsize car in the United States, Canada, Europe, Middle East or Africa.

In the U.S. or Canada, **request Coupon Code AU38 and I.D. Number 7012170.** In Europe, the Middle East or Africa, **request Coupon Code AU12 and I.D. Number 7012170.**

entertainment.com/alamo
1-800-237-0984.

Alamo

Valid now thru June 30, 2008
See reverse side for details

D41

$25 OFF
MINIMUM 3-DAY RENTAL

In addition to your standard Entertainment® discount, reserve a convertible, minivan, or sport utility vehicle for a minimum of 3 days in the United States.

Request Coupon Code AD28 and I.D. Number 7012170.

entertainment.com/alamo
1-800-237-0984.

Alamo

Valid now thru June 30, 2008
See reverse side for details

D42

ALL ROADS LEAD TO
ALAMO COUNTRY.

OFFICIAL RENTAL CAR OF THE AMERICAN VACATION
Alamo

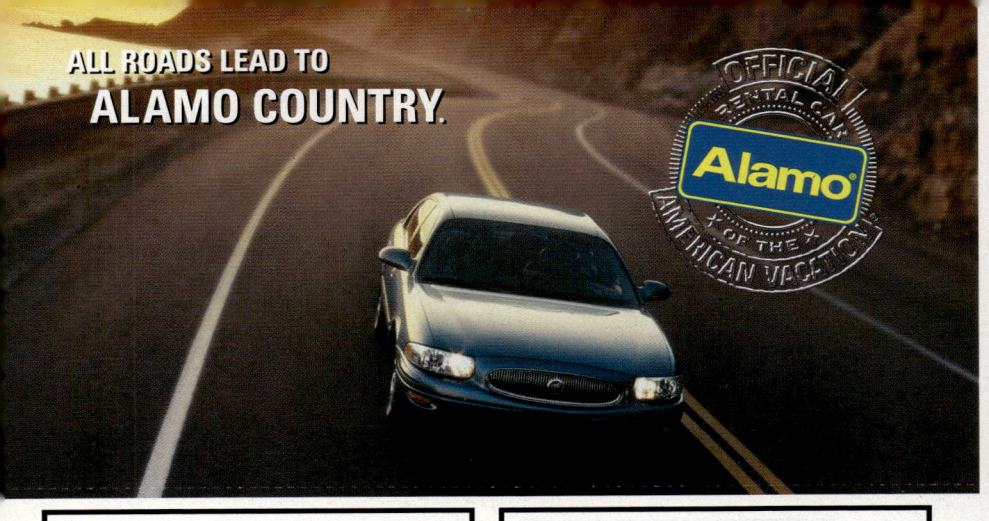

One coupon per Alamo rental and void once redeemed. Original coupon must be presented at counter upon arrival. Free day is prorated against base rate for entire rental period, which does not include taxes (including VAT/GST), other governmentally-authorized or imposed surcharges, license recoupment/air tax recovery and concession recoupment fees, airport and airport facility fees, fuel, additional driver fee, one-way rental charge, or optional items. Not valid on truck rentals in Canada. Offer is subject to standard rental conditions. Blackout dates may apply. Not valid with any other discount or promotional rate, except your Entertainment® discount. Subject to availability and valid only at participating Alamo locations. 24-Hour advance reservations required. Offer not valid in Manhattan, N.Y., or San Jose, CA. Valid now through 6/30/08. ©2006-2008 Vanguard Car Rental USA Inc. All rights reserved. 1832a-AN-106

ALAMO® FEATURES GM VEHICLES.

Offer validity is governed by the Rules of Use and excludes defined holidays. Offers are not valid with other discount offers, unless specified. Coupons void if purchased, sold or bartered. Discounts exclude tax, tip and/or alcohol, where applicable.

One coupon per Alamo rental and void once redeemed. Original coupon must be presented at counter upon arrival. Discount applies to base rate, which does not include taxes (including VAT), other governmentally-authorized or imposed surcharges, license recoupment/ air tax recovery and concession recoupment fees, airport and airport facility fees, fuel, additional driver fee, one-way rental charge, or optional items. Offer is subject to standard rental conditions. Blackout dates may apply. Not valid with any other discount or promotional rate, except your Entertainment® discount. Subject to availability and valid only at participating Alamo locations. 24-Hour advance reservations required. Some countries may convert coupon value into local currency. Valid now through 6/30/08. ©2006-2008 Vanguard Car Rental USA Inc. All rights reserved. 1832a-AN-106

ALAMO® FEATURES GM VEHICLES.

Offer validity is governed by the Rules of Use and excludes defined holidays. Offers are not valid with other discount offers, unless specified. Coupons void if purchased, sold or bartered. Discounts exclude tax, tip and/or alcohol, where applicable.

One coupon per Alamo rental and void once redeemed. Original coupon must be presented at counter upon arrival. Discount applies to base rate, which does not include taxes, other governmentally-authorized or imposed surcharges, license recoupment/air tax recovery and concession recoupment fees, airport and airport facility fees, fuel, additional driver fee, one-way rental charge, or optional items. Offer is subject to standard rental conditions. Blackout dates may apply. Not valid with any other discount or promotional rate, except your Entertainment® discount. Subject to availability and valid only at participating Alamo locations. 24-Hour advance reservations required. Valid now through 6/30/08. ©2006-2008 Vanguard Car Rental USA Inc. All rights reserved. 1832a-AN-106

ALAMO® FEATURES GM VEHICLES.

Offer validity is governed by the Rules of Use and excludes defined holidays. Offers are not valid with other discount offers, unless specified. Coupons void if purchased, sold or bartered. Discounts exclude tax, tip and/or alcohol, where applicable.

One coupon per Alamo rental and void once redeemed. Original coupon must be presented at counter upon arrival. In Europe, the Middle East, and Africa, upgrade is subject to availability at time of rental pickup and requires a 5-day minimum rental. Offer is subject to standard rental conditions. Blackout dates may apply. 24-Hour advance reservations required. Not valid with any other discount or promotional rate, except your Entertainment® discount. Offer valid only at participating Alamo locations. Valid for a free one car class upgrade from the car class reserved (same transmission in Europe, the Middle East and Africa). Offer not valid in Manhattan, N.Y., or San Jose, CA. Valid now through 6/30/08. ©2006-2008 Vanguard Car Rental USA Inc. All rights reserved. 1832a-AN-106

ALAMO® FEATURES GM VEHICLES.

Offer validity is governed by the Rules of Use and excludes defined holidays. Offers are not valid with other discount offers, unless specified. Coupons void if purchased, sold or bartered. Discounts exclude tax, tip and/or alcohol, where applicable.

ALL ROADS LEAD TO ALAMO COUNTRY.®

Book by phone or, for best rates, book online at entertainment.com/alamo or call 1-800-237-0984.

UP TO $20 OFF

In addition to your standard Entertainment® discount, reserve a compact car or larger in the United States, Latin America, or the Caribbean.

Request I.D. Number 7012170 and:

Coupon Code	Days	$ OFF
AD25	2	$10
AD26	3	$15
AD27	4	$20

entertainment.com/alamo
1-800-237-0984

Valid now thru June 30, 2008
See reverse side for details

D33

ONE FREE DAY

In addition to your standard Entertainment® discount, reserve a compact car or larger for a minimum of 5 days in the United States, Canada, Latin America, or the Caribbean.

Request Coupon Code AF18 and I.D. Number 7012170.

entertainment.com/alamo
1-800-237-0984

Valid now thru June 30, 2008
See reverse side for details

D34

FREE UPGRADE

In addition to your standard Entertainment® discount, reserve a compact through midsize car in the United States, Canada, Europe, Middle East or Africa.

In the U.S. or Canada, **request Coupon Code AU38 and I.D. Number 7012170.** In Europe, the Middle East or Africa, **request Coupon Code AU12 and I.D. Number 7012170.**

entertainment.com/alamo
1-800-237-0984

Valid now thru June 30, 2008
See reverse side for details

D35

$25 OFF
MINIMUM 3-DAY RENTAL

In addition to your standard Entertainment® discount, reserve a convertible, minivan, or sport utility vehicle for a minimum of 3 days in the United States.

Request Coupon Code AD28 and I.D. Number 7012170.

entertainment.com/alamo
1-800-237-0984

Valid now thru June 30, 2008
See reverse side for details

D36

TERMS AND CONDITIONS
Offer applies to vehicles reserved in advance at standard weekly rates for a minimum of 6 days at participating North American locations. Rates are as posted at time of reservation at enterprise.com or by calling 1-888-446-9952. Rental must be 26 days or less and end on or before 06/30/08. Discount may vary by location and time of rental. Discount does not apply to taxes, surcharges, tax reimbursement, airport access and related fees, excess mileage fees, vehicle licensing fees, and optional products and services, including damage waiver at $30 or less per day. Check your auto policy and/or credit card agreement for rental vehicle coverage. Original coupon must be redeemed at the time of rental and may not be used in conjunction with any other coupon, offer or discounted rates. Normal rental qualifications apply. Vehicles subject to availability. Other restrictions, including holiday and blackout dates, may apply. Void where prohibited. Pickup and drop-off service is subject to geographic and other restrictions. Cash value: 1/100¢.

Offer validity is governed by the Rules of Use and excludes defined holidays. Offers are not valid with other discount offers, unless specified. Coupons void if purchased, sold or bartered. Discounts exclude tax, tip and/or alcohol, where applicable.

Valid now thru June 30, 2008

TERMS AND CONDITIONS
Offer applies to vehicles reserved in advance at standard weekly rates for a minimum of 6 days at participating North American locations. Rates are as posted at time of reservation at enterprise.com or by calling 1-888-446-9952. Rental must be 26 days or less and end on or before 06/30/08. Discount may vary by location and time of rental. Discount does not apply to taxes, surcharges, tax reimbursement, airport access and related fees, excess mileage fees, vehicle licensing fees, and optional products and services, including damage waiver at $30 or less per day. Check your auto policy and/or credit card agreement for rental vehicle coverage. Original coupon must be redeemed at the time of rental and may not be used in conjunction with any other coupon, offer or discounted rates. Normal rental qualifications apply. Vehicles subject to availability. Other restrictions, including holiday and blackout dates, may apply. Void where prohibited. Pickup and drop-off service is subject to geographic and other restrictions. Cash value: 1/100¢.

Offer validity is governed by the Rules of Use and excludes defined holidays. Offers are not valid with other discount offers, unless specified. Coupons void if purchased, sold or bartered. Discounts exclude tax, tip and/or alcohol, where applicable.

Valid now thru June 30, 2008

TERMS AND CONDITIONS
Offer applies to vehicles reserved in advance at standard daily rates for up to 7 days at participating North American locations. Weekly rates may be available depending on length of rental or for longer rental needs. Rates are as posted at time of reservation at enterprise.com or by calling 1-888-446-9952. Discount may vary by location and time of rental. Rental must end by 06/30/08. Discount does not apply to taxes, surcharges, tax reimbursement, airport access and related fees, excess mileage fees, vehicle licensing fees, and optional products and services, including damage waiver at $30 or less per day. Check your auto policy and/or credit card agreement for rental vehicle coverage. Original coupon must be redeemed at the time of rental and may not be used in conjunction with any other coupon, offer or discounted rates. Normal rental qualifications apply. Vehicles subject to availability. Other restrictions, including holiday and blackout dates, may apply. Void where prohibited. Pickup and drop-off service is subject to geographic and other restrictions. Cash value: 1/100¢.

Offer validity is governed by the Rules of Use and excludes defined holidays. Offers are not valid with other discount offers, unless specified. Coupons void if purchased, sold or bartered. Discounts exclude tax, tip and/or alcohol, where applicable.

Valid now thru June 30, 2008

TERMS AND CONDITIONS
Offer valid on reservations made in advance for an Economy through Full-size vehicle at standard daily or weekly rates at participating North American airport locations. The upgrade request will be sent to Enterprise along with your reservation of the lower class car. The upgrade car class will not appear on your reservation, but will be applied at no extra charge upon arrival at the rental counter if a car in the next higher class is available. Rental must be for 26 days or less and end by 06/30/08. Offer may not be used in conjunction with any other coupon, offer or discounted rate. Vehicles are subject to availability. Other restrictions may apply. Pick-up and drop-off service is subject to geographic and other restrictions. Normal rental qualifications apply. Void where prohibited.

Offer validity is governed by the Rules of Use and excludes defined holidays. Offers are not valid with other discount offers, unless specified. Coupons void if purchased, sold or bartered. Discounts exclude tax, tip and/or alcohol, where applicable.

Valid now thru June 30, 2008

TERMS AND CONDITIONS
Offer valid for one (1) 24-hour day's time charge for a vehicle reserved in advance at standard weekend rates for a rental starting on Friday and ending on the following Monday at participating North American locations. Up to two additional days may be added at standard daily rates. Offer not valid at airport locations. All rates are as posted at time of reservation at enterprise.com or by calling 1-888-446-9952. Rental must end on or before 06/30/08. Offer does not apply to taxes, surcharges, recovery fees and optional products and services, including damage waiver at $30 or less per day. Check your auto policy and/or credit card agreement for rental vehicle coverage. Original coupon must be redeemed at the time of rental and may not be used in conjunction with any other coupon, offer or discounted rates. Normal rental qualifications apply. Vehicles subject to availability. Other restrictions, including holiday and blackout dates, may apply. Pickup and drop-off service is subject to geographic and other restrictions. Void where prohibited. Cash value: 1/100¢. ERAC Employees: Please RECOMPUTE the Rental Rate, discounting the one weekend day amount when closing the contract.

Offer validity is governed by the Rules of Use and excludes defined holidays. Offers are not valid with other discount offers, unless specified. Coupons void if purchased, sold or bartered. Discounts exclude tax, tip and/or alcohol, where applicable.

Valid now thru June 30, 2008

TERMS AND CONDITIONS
Offer valid on reservations made in advance for an Economy through Full-size vehicle at standard daily or weekly rates at participating North American airport locations. The upgrade request will be sent to Enterprise along with your reservation of the lower class car. The upgrade car class will not appear on your reservation, but will be applied at no extra charge upon arrival at the rental counter if a car in the next higher class is available. Rental must be for 26 days or less and end by 06/30/08. Offer may not be used in conjunction with any other coupon, offer or discounted rate. Vehicles are subject to availability. Other restrictions may apply. Pick-up and drop-off service is subject to geographic and other restrictions. Normal rental qualifications apply. Void where prohibited.

Offer validity is governed by the Rules of Use and excludes defined holidays. Offers are not valid with other discount offers, unless specified. Coupons void if purchased, sold or bartered. Discounts exclude tax, tip and/or alcohol, where applicable.

Valid now thru June 30, 2008

Up To 20% Off
Standard Weekly Rates

- Offer requires a minimum 6-day rental.
- Visit us at enterprise.com or call (888) 446-9952 and reference customer **#ETBX7B**.
- Discount will be applied at time of reservation.
- Discount may vary by location and time of rental.
- Coupon must be presented at time of rental.

Enterprise rent-a-car
Pick Enterprise. We'll pick you up.®

Valid now thru June 30, 2008
See reverse side for details
D27

Up To 20% Off
Standard Weekly Rates

- Offer requires a minimum 6-day rental.
- Visit us at enterprise.com or call (888) 446-9952 and reference customer **#ETBX7B**.
- Discount will be applied at time of reservation.
- Discount may vary by location and time of rental.
- Coupon must be presented at time of rental.

Enterprise rent-a-car
Pick Enterprise. We'll pick you up.®

Valid now thru June 30, 2008
See reverse side for details
D28

One Free Upgrade

- Valid on Economy through Full-size vehicles.
- Visit us at enterprise.com or call (888) 446-9952 and reference customer **#ETBX7D**.
- Upgrade will be applied at the time of rental.
- Coupon must be presented at time of rental.

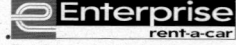

Enterprise rent-a-car
Pick Enterprise. We'll pick you up.®

Valid now thru June 30, 2008
See reverse side for details
D29

Up To 20% Off
Standard Daily Rates

- Visit us at enterprise.com or call (888) 446-9952 and reference customer **#ETBX7A**.
- No minimum length of rental required.
- Discount will be applied at time of reservation.
- Discount may vary by location and time of rental.
- Coupon must be presented at time of rental.

Enterprise rent-a-car
Pick Enterprise. We'll pick you up.®

Valid now thru June 30, 2008
See reverse side for details
D30

One Free Upgrade

- Valid on Economy through Full-size vehicles.
- Visit us at enterprise.com or call (888) 446-9952 and reference customer **#ETBX7D**.
- Upgrade will be applied at the time of rental.
- Coupon must be presented at time of rental.

Enterprise rent-a-car
Pick Enterprise. We'll pick you up.®

Valid now thru June 30, 2008
See reverse side for details
D31

One Free Weekend Day

- Not valid at airports.
- Rental must begin on Friday and end the following Monday. Add up to two additional days at Standard Daily Rates.
- Visit us at enterprise.com or call (888) 446-9952 and reference customer **#ETBX7C**.
- Free day will be applied upon return of vehicle.
- Coupon must be presented at time of rental.

Enterprise rent-a-car
Pick Enterprise. We'll pick you up.®

Valid now thru June 30, 2008
See reverse side for details
D32

Great Cars, Low Rates, Free Pickup

And Over 5,800 Locations In North America.

Enterprise rent-a-car
Pick Enterprise. We'll pick you up.®

Reserve online at enterprise.com or call 1 888 446-9952.

TERMS AND CONDITIONS
Offer applies to vehicles reserved in advance at standard daily rates for up to 7 days at participating North American locations. Weekly rates may be available depending on length of rental or for longer rental needs. Rates are as posted at time of reservation at enterprise.com or by calling 1-888-446-9952. Discount may vary by location and time of rental. Rental must end by 06/30/08. Discount does not apply to taxes, surcharges, tax reimbursement, airport access and related fees, excess mileage fees, vehicle licensing fees, and optional products and services, including damage waiver at $30 or less per day. Check your auto policy and/or credit card agreement for rental vehicle coverage. Original coupon must be redeemed at the time of rental and may not be used in conjunction with any other coupon, offer or discounted rates. Normal rental qualifications apply. Vehicles subject to availability. Other restrictions, including holiday and blackout dates, may apply. Void where prohibited. Pickup and drop-off service is subject to geographic and other restrictions. Cash value: 1/100¢.

Offer validity is governed by the Rules of Use and excludes defined holidays. Offers are not valid with other discount offers, unless specified. Coupons void if purchased, sold or bartered. Discounts exclude tax, tip and/or alcohol, where applicable.
Valid now thru June 30, 2008

TERMS AND CONDITIONS
Offer applies to vehicles reserved in advance at standard daily rates for up to 7 days at participating North American locations. Weekly rates may be available depending on length of rental or for longer rental needs. Rates are as posted at time of reservation at enterprise.com or by calling 1-888-446-9952. Discount may vary by location and time of rental. Rental must end by 06/30/08. Discount does not apply to taxes, surcharges, tax reimbursement, airport access and related fees, excess mileage fees, vehicle licensing fees, and optional products and services, including damage waiver at $30 or less per day. Check your auto policy and/or credit card agreement for rental vehicle coverage. Original coupon must be redeemed at the time of rental and may not be used in conjunction with any other coupon, offer or discounted rates. Normal rental qualifications apply. Vehicles subject to availability. Other restrictions, including holiday and blackout dates, may apply. Void where prohibited. Pickup and drop-off service is subject to geographic and other restrictions. Cash value: 1/100¢.

Offer validity is governed by the Rules of Use and excludes defined holidays. Offers are not valid with other discount offers, unless specified. Coupons void if purchased, sold or bartered. Discounts exclude tax, tip and/or alcohol, where applicable.
Valid now thru June 30, 2008

TERMS AND CONDITIONS
Offer applies to vehicles reserved in advance at standard weekly rates for a minimum of 6 days at participating North American locations. Rates are as posted at time of reservation at enterprise.com or by calling 1-888-446-9952. Rental must be 26 days or less and end on or before 06/30/08. Discount may vary by location and time of rental. Discount does not apply to taxes, surcharges, tax reimbursement, airport access and related fees, excess mileage fees, vehicle licensing fees, and optional products and services, including damage waiver at $30 or less per day. Check your auto policy and/or credit card agreement for rental vehicle coverage. Original coupon must be redeemed at the time of rental and may not be used in conjunction with any other coupon, offer or discounted rates. Normal rental qualifications apply. Vehicles subject to availability. Other restrictions, including holiday and blackout dates, may apply. Void where prohibited. Pickup and drop-off service is subject to geographic and other restrictions. Cash value: 1/100¢.

Offer validity is governed by the Rules of Use and excludes defined holidays. Offers are not valid with other discount offers, unless specified. Coupons void if purchased, sold or bartered. Discounts exclude tax, tip and/or alcohol, where applicable.
Valid now thru June 30, 2008

TERMS AND CONDITIONS
Offer valid for one (1) 24-hour day's time charge for a vehicle reserved in advance at standard weekend rates for a rental starting on Friday and ending on the following Monday at participating North American locations. Up to two additional days may be added at standard daily rates. Offer not valid at airport locations. All rates are as posted at time of reservation at enterprise.com or by calling 1-888-446-9952. Rental must end on or before 06/30/08. Offer does not apply to taxes, surcharges, recovery fees and optional products and services, including damage waiver at $30 or less per day. Check your auto policy and/or credit card agreement for rental vehicle coverage. Original coupon must be redeemed at the time of rental and may not be used in conjunction with any other coupon, offer or discounted rates. Normal rental qualifications apply. Vehicles subject to availability. Other restrictions, including holiday and blackout dates, may apply. Pickup and drop-off service is subject to geographic and other restrictions. Void where prohibited. Cash value: 1/100¢. ERAC Employees: Please RECOMPUTE the Rental Rate, discounting the one weekend day amount when closing the contract.

Offer validity is governed by the Rules of Use and excludes defined holidays. Offers are not valid with other discount offers, unless specified. Coupons void if purchased, sold or bartered. Discounts exclude tax, tip and/or alcohol, where applicable.
Valid now thru June 30, 2008

Great Cars, Low Rates, Free Pickup

And Over 5,800 Locations In North America.

Enterprise rent-a-car
Pick Enterprise. We'll pick you up.®

Reserve online at enterprise.com or call 1 888 446-9952.

Up To 20% Off
Standard Daily Rates

- Visit us at enterprise.com or call (888) 446-9952 and reference customer #ETBX7A.
- No minimum length of rental required.
- Discount will be applied at time of reservation.
- Discount may vary by location and time of rental.
- Coupon must be presented at time of rental.

Enterprise rent-a-car
Pick Enterprise. We'll pick you up.®

Valid now thru June 30, 2008
See reverse side for details   D23

Up To 20% Off
Standard Daily Rates

- Visit us at enterprise.com or call (888) 446-9952 and reference customer #ETBX7A.
- No minimum length of rental required.
- Discount will be applied at time of reservation.
- Discount may vary by location and time of rental.
- Coupon must be presented at time of rental.

Enterprise rent-a-car
Pick Enterprise. We'll pick you up.®

Valid now thru June 30, 2008
See reverse side for details   D24

One Free Weekend Day

- Not valid at airports.
- Rental must begin on Friday and end the following Monday. Add up to two additional days at Standard Daily Rates.
- Visit us at enterprise.com or call (888) 446-9952 and reference customer #ETBX7C.
- Free day will be applied upon return of vehicle.
- Coupon must be presented at time of rental.

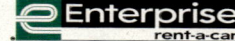

Enterprise rent-a-car
Pick Enterprise. We'll pick you up.®

Valid now thru June 30, 2008
See reverse side for details   D25

Up To 20% Off
Standard Weekly Rates

- Offer requires a minimum 6-day rental.
- Visit us at enterprise.com or call (888) 446-9952 and reference customer #ETBX7B.
- Discount will be applied at time of reservation.
- Discount may vary by location and time of rental.
- Coupon must be presented at time of rental.

Enterprise rent-a-car
Pick Enterprise. We'll pick you up.®

Valid now thru June 30, 2008
See reverse side for details   D26

Terms and Conditions: Coupon valid at participating Budget locations in the contiguous U.S. on an intermediate (group C) through a full-size four-door (group E) car. Dollars off applies to the time and mileage charges only on a minimum two-day weekend rental. A Saturday night stayover is required. Coupon must be surrendered at time of rental; one coupon per rental. Offer may not be used in conjunction with any other coupon, promotion or offer, except your Entertainment® discount. Weekend rental period begins Thursday noon and car must be returned by Monday 11:59 p.m. or higher rate will apply. Offer subject to vehicle availability at the time of rental and may not be available on some rates at some times. **An advance reservation is required.** Taxes, concession recovery fees, customer facility charges ($10/contract in CA), optional items and other surcharges may apply and are extra. For reservations made on budget.com, dollars off will be applied at time of rental, subject to vehicle availability. Renter must meet Budget age, driver and credit requirements. Minimum age may vary by location. An additional daily surcharge may apply for renters under 25 years old. **Rental must begin by 6/30/08.**

For Budget CSR Use Only
- In CPN, enter **MUGZ548** for a 2-day rental
  MUGZ549 for a 3-day rental
  MUGZ550 for a 4-day rental
- In BCD, enter **X443030**
- Attach to COUPON tape

At checkout:
- Complete this information
  RA #: _____
  Operator ID: _____
  Rental Location: _____
  BCD #: _____

©2006 Budget Rent A Car System, Inc.
Budget features Ford, Lincoln and Mercury vehicles.

Offer validity is governed by the Rules of Use and excludes defined holidays.
Coupons void if purchased, sold or bartered.

Terms and Conditions: Coupon valid on premium (group G), luxury (group H), convertible (group K), passenger van (group P), sports (group S), specialty (group X), sport utility vehicle (groups F, L, W and Z) and minivan (group V) cars. Dollars off applies to the daily time and mileage charges only on a minimum five-day rental period that includes a Saturday night stayover. Taxes, concession recovery fees, customer facility charges ($10/contract in CA), optional items and other surcharges may apply and are extra. Coupon must be surrendered at time of rental; one coupon per rental. Offer may not be used in conjunction with any other coupon, promotion or offer, except your Entertainment® discount. **An advance reservation is required.** Coupon valid at participating Budget locations in the contiguous U.S. Offer subject to vehicle availability at the time of rental, and may not be available on some rates at some times. For reservations made on budget.com, dollars off will be applied at time of rental, subject to vehicle availability. Renter must meet Budget age, driver and credit requirements. Minimum age may vary by location. An additional daily surcharge may apply for renters under 25 years old. **Rental must begin by 6/30/08.**

For Budget CSR Use Only
At checkout:
- In CPN, enter **MUGZ551**
- In BCD, enter **X443030**
- Complete this information
  RA #: _____
  Operator ID: _____
  Rental Location: _____
- Attach to COUPON tape

COUPON # MUGZ551

©2006 Budget Rent A Car System, Inc.
Budget features Ford, Lincoln and Mercury vehicles.

Offer validity is governed by the Rules of Use and excludes defined holidays.
Coupons void if purchased, sold or bartered.

Terms and Conditions: Coupon valid for $50 off a monthly or Mini-Lease rentals at participating Budget locations in the contiguous U.S. Offer applies to a minimum 30-day rental period of an intermediate (group C) through a full-size four-door (group E) car. Offer of $50 off a long-term rental applies to the time and mileage charges on the first month of a minimum 30- and a maximum 330-consecutive-day rental. Taxes, concession recovery fees, customer facility charges ($10/contract in CA), optional items and other surcharges may apply and are extra. Coupon must be surrendered at time of rental; one coupon per rental period. **An advance reservation is required.** Offer is subject to vehicle availability at time of rental and may not be available on some rates some times Offer may not be used in conjunction with any other coupon, promotion or offer, except your Entertainment® discount. For reservations made on budget.com, dollars off will be applied at time of rental, subject to vehicle availability. Renter must meet Budget age, driver and credit requirements. Minimum age may vary by location. An additional daily surcharge may apply for renters under 25 years old. **Rental must begin by 6/30/08.**

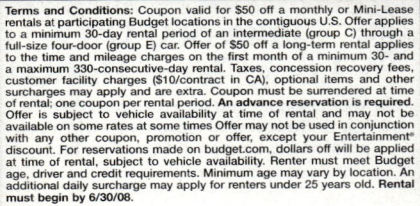

For Budget CSR Use Only
- In CPN, enter **MUGZ557**
- In BCD, enter **X443030**
- Attach to COUPON tape
At checkout:
- Complete this information
  RA #: _____
  Operator ID: _____
  Rental Location: _____
  BCD #: _____

COUPON # MUGZ557

©2006 Budget Rent A Car System, Inc.
Budget features Ford, Lincoln and Mercury vehicles.

Offer validity is governed by the Rules of Use and excludes defined holidays.
Coupons void if purchased, sold or bartered.

Terms and Conditions: Coupon valid for a one-time, one-car group upgrade on an intermediate (group C) through a full-size four-door (group E) car. Maximum upgrade to premium (group G). Offer valid on daily, weekend, weekly and monthly rates only. The upgraded car is subject to vehicle availability at the time of rental and may not be available on some rates at some times. Coupon valid at participating Budget locations in the contiguous U.S. Coupon must be surrendered at time of rental; one coupon per rental. **A 24-hour advance reservation is required using this coupon.** Offer may not be used in conjunction with any other coupon, promotion or offer, except your Entertainment® discount. For reservations made on budget.com, upgrade will be applied at time of rental, subject to vehicle availability. Renter must meet Budget age, driver and credit requirements. Minimum age may vary by location. An additional daily surcharge may apply for renters under 25 years old. **Rental must begin by 6/30/08.**

For Budget CSR Use Only
- Assign customer a car one group higher than car group reserved
- In CPN, enter **UUGZ105**
- In BCD, enter **X443030**
- Attach to COUPON tape
At checkout:
- Complete this information
  RA #: _____
  Operator ID: _____
  Rental Location: _____
  BCD #: _____

COUPON # UUGZ105

©2006 Budget Rent A Car System, Inc.
Budget features Ford, Lincoln and Mercury vehicles.

Offer validity is governed by the Rules of Use and excludes defined holidays.
Coupons void if purchased, sold or bartered.

Terms and Conditions: Coupon valid on an intermediate (group C) through a full-size four-door (group E) car. Dollars off applies to the time and mileage charges only on a minimum five-day rental. Taxes, concession recovery fees, customer facility charges ($10/contract in CA), optional items and other surcharges may apply and are extra. Coupon must be surrendered at time of rental; one coupon per rental. **An advance reservation is required.** May not be used in conjunction with any other coupon, promotion or offer, except your Entertainment® discount. Coupon valid at participating Budget locations in the contiguous U.S. Offer subject to vehicle availability at time of rental and may not be available on some rates at some times. For reservations made on budget.com, dollars off will be applied at time of rental; subject to vehicle availability. Renter must meet Budget age, driver and credit requirements. Minimum age may vary by location. An additional daily surcharge may apply for renters under 25 years old. **Rental must begin by 6/30/08.**

For Budget CSR Use Only
- In CPN, enter **MUGZ547**
- In BCD, enter **X443030**
- Attach to COUPON tape
At checkout:
- Complete this information
  RA #: _____
  Operator ID: _____
  Rental Location: _____
  BCD #: _____

COUPON # MUGZ547

©2006 Budget Rent A Car System, Inc.
Budget features Ford, Lincoln and Mercury vehicles.

Offer validity is governed by the Rules of Use and excludes defined holidays.
Coupons void if purchased, sold or bartered.

Terms and Conditions: Offer applies to one day free of the daily time and mileage charges on a minimum five-day consecutive rental at weekly rates with a Saturday night stayover on an intermediate (group C) through a full-size four-door (group E) car. Taxes, concession recovery fees, customer facility charges ($10/contract in CA), optional items and other surcharges may apply and are extra. Coupon must be surrendered at time of rental; one coupon per rental and cannot be used for one-way rentals. Offer may not be used in conjunction with any other coupon, promotion or offer, except your Entertainment® discount. Coupon valid at participating Budget locations in the contiguous U.S. (excluding the New York Metro area). **An advance reservation is required.** Offer may not be available during holiday and other blackout periods. Offer is subject to vehicle availability at the time of rental and may not be available on some rates at some times. For reservations made on budget.com, free day will be applied at time of rental, subject to vehicle availability. Renter must meet Budget age, driver and credit requirements. Minimum age may vary by location. An additional daily surcharge may apply for renters under 25 years old. **Rental must begin by 6/30/08.**

For Budget CSR Use Only
- In CPN, enter **TUGZ336**
- In BCD, enter **X443030**
- Attach to COUPON tape
At checkout:
- Complete this information
  RA #: _____
  Operator ID: _____
  Rental Location: _____
  BCD #: _____

COUPON # TUGZ336

©2006 Budget Rent A Car System, Inc.
Budget features Ford, Lincoln and Mercury vehicles.

Offer validity is governed by the Rules of Use and excludes defined holidays.
Coupons void if purchased, sold or bartered.

Save $25 On A Weekly Rental

Get your discount and take an extra $25 off a weekly rental when you present this coupon at time of rental.

Offer valid on premium (group G) cars or higher through 6/30/08.

Mention **BCD # X443030** and **CPN # MUGZ551**

For reservations, contact your travel agent or visit Budget at www.entertainment.com/budget or call 1-888-724-6212

Budget.

Valid now thru June 30, 2008
Subject to Terms and Conditions on reverse side. D17

Save Up To $20 On A Weekend Rental

Get your discount plus an extra $10 to $20 off a weekend rental when you present this coupon at time of rental.

Offer valid on intermediate through full-size four-door cars through 6/30/08.

Mention **BCD # X443030** and
CPN # MUGZ2548 for a 2-day rental
CPN # MUGZ2549 for a 3-day rental
CPN # MUGZ2550 for a 4-day rental

For reservations, contact your travel agent or visit Budget at www.entertainment.com/budget or call 1-888-724-6212

Budget.

Valid now thru June 30, 2008
Subject to Terms and Conditions on reverse side. D18

Free Upgrade

Get your discount plus an upgrade when you present this coupon at time of rental.
Offer valid on an intermediate through full-size four-door car through 6/30/08.

Mention **BCD # X443030** and **CPN # UUGZ105**

For reservations, contact your travel agent or visit Budget at www.entertainment.com/budget or call 1-888-724-6212

Budget.

Valid now thru June 30, 2008
Subject to Terms and Conditions on reverse side. D19

Take $50 Off A Long-Term Rental

Get your discount and take an extra $50 off a monthly or Budget mini-lease rental when you present this coupon at time of rental.

Offer valid on intermediate through full-size four-door cars through 6/30/08.

Mention **BCD # X443030** and **CPN # MUGZ557**

For reservations, contact your travel agent or visit Budget at www.entertainment.com/budget or call 1-888-724-6212

Budget.

Valid now thru June 30, 2008
Subject to Terms and Conditions on reverse side. D20

Free Day On A Weekly Rental

Get your discount plus a free day when you present this coupon at time of rental.

Offer valid on intermediate through full-size four-door cars through 6/30/08.

Mention **BCD # X443030** and **CPN # TUGZ336**

For reservations, contact your travel agent or visit Budget at www.entertainment.com/budget or call 1-888-724-6212

Budget.

Valid now thru June 30, 2008
Subject to Terms and Conditions on reverse side. D21

Save $20 On A Weekly Rental

Get your discount and take an extra $20 off a weekly rental when you present this coupon at time of rental.

Offer valid on intermediate through full-size four-door cars through 6/30/08.

Mention **BCD # X443030** and **CPN # MUGZ547**

For reservations, contact your travel agent or visit Budget at www.entertainment.com/budget or call 1-888-724-6212

Budget.

Valid now thru June 30, 2008
Subject to Terms and Conditions on reverse side. D22

So many great ways to save.
That's Budget.

Terms and Conditions: Coupon valid on an intermediate (group C) through a full-size four-door (group E) car. Dollars off applies to the time and mileage charges only on a minimum five-day rental. Taxes, concession recovery fees, customer facility charges ($10/contract in CA), optional items and other surcharges may apply and are extra. Coupon must be surrendered at time of rental; one coupon per rental. **An advance reservation is required.** May not be used in conjunction with any other coupon, promotion or offer, except your Entertainment® discount. Coupon valid at participating Budget locations in the contiguous U.S. Offer subject to vehicle availability at time of rental and may not be available on some rates at some times. For reservations made on budget.com, dollars off will be applied at time of rental; subject to vehicle availability. Renter must meet Budget age, driver and credit requirements. Minimum age may vary by location. An additional daily surcharge may apply for renters under 25 years old. **Rental must begin by 6/30/08.**

For Budget CSR Use Only
- In CPN, enter **MUGZ547**
- In BCD, enter **X443030**
- Attach to COUPON tape

At checkout:
- Complete this information
  RA #: _____
  Operator ID: _____
  Rental Location: _____
  BCD #: _____

COUPON # MUGZ547

© 2006 Budget Rent A Car System, Inc.
Budget features Ford, Lincoln and Mercury vehicles.

Budget budget.com

Offer validity is governed by the Rules of Use and excludes defined holidays.
Coupons void if purchased, sold or bartered.

Terms and Conditions: Offer of one weekend day free applies to the time and mileage charges only of the third consecutive day of a minimum three-day weekend rental on an intermediate (group C) through a full-size four-door (group E) car. Taxes, concession recovery fees, customer facility charges ($10/contract in CA), optional items and other surcharges may apply and are extra. Weekend rental period begins Thursday noon and car must be returned by Monday 11:59 p.m. or a higher rate will apply. Saturday night stayover is required. Coupon must be surrendered at time of rental and cannot be used for one-way rentals; one coupon per rental. Offer may not be used in conjunction with any other coupon, promotion or offer, except with your Entertainment® discount. Coupon valid at participating Budget locations in the contiguous U.S. (excluding the New York Metro area). **An advance reservation is required.** Offer may not be available during holiday and other blackout periods. Offer is subject to vehicle availability at the time of rental and may not be available on some rates at some times. For reservations made on budget.com, free day will be applied at time of rental, subject to vehicle availability. Renter must meet Budget age, driver and credit requirements. Minimum age may vary by location. An additional daily surcharge may apply for renters under 25 years old. **Rental must begin by 6/30/08.**

For Budget CSR Use Only
- In CPN, enter **TUGZ427**
- In BCD, enter **X443030**
- Attach to COUPON tape

At checkout:
- Complete this information
  RA #: _____
  Operator ID: _____
  Rental Location: _____
  BCD #: _____

COUPON # TUGZ427

© 2006 Budget Rent A Car System, Inc.
Budget features Ford, Lincoln and Mercury vehicles.

Budget budget.com

Offer validity is governed by the Rules of Use and excludes defined holidays.
Coupons void if purchased, sold or bartered.

Terms and Conditions: Coupon valid at participating Budget locations in the contiguous U.S. on an intermediate (group C) through a full-size four-door (group E) car. Dollars off applies to the time and mileage charges only on a minimum two-day weekend rental. A Saturday night stayover is required. Coupon must be surrendered at time of rental; one coupon per rental. Offer may not be used in conjunction with any other coupon, promotion or offer, except your Entertainment® discount. Weekend rental period begins Thursday noon and car must be returned by Monday 11:59 p.m. or higher rate will apply. Offer may not be available on some rates at some times. **An advance reservation is required.** Taxes, concession recovery fees, customer facility charges ($10/contract in CA), optional items and other surcharges may apply and are extra. For reservations made on budget.com, dollars off will be applied at time of rental, subject to vehicle availability. Renter must meet Budget age, driver and credit requirements. Minimum age may vary by location. An additional daily surcharge may apply for renters under 25 years old. **Rental must begin by 6/30/08.**

For Budget CSR Use Only
- In CPN, enter **MUGZ548** for a 2-day rental
  MUGZ549 for a 3-day rental
  MUGZ550 for a 4-day rental
- In BCD, enter **X443030**
- Attach to COUPON tape

At checkout:
- Complete this information
  RA #: _____
  Operator ID: _____
  Rental Location: _____
  BCD #: _____

© 2006 Budget Rent A Car System, Inc.
Budget features Ford, Lincoln and Mercury vehicles.

Budget budget.com

Offer validity is governed by the Rules of Use and excludes defined holidays.
Coupons void if purchased, sold or bartered.

Terms and Conditions: Coupon valid for a one-time, one-car group upgrade on an intermediate (group C) through a full-size four-door (group E) car. Maximum upgrade to premium (group G). Offer valid on daily, weekend, weekly and monthly rates only. The upgraded car is subject to vehicle availability at the time of rental and may not be available on some rates at some times. Coupon valid at participating Budget locations in the contiguous U.S. Coupon must be surrendered at time of rental; one coupon per rental. **A 24-hour advance reservation is required using this coupon.** Offer may not be used in conjunction with any other coupon, promotion or offer, except your Entertainment® discount. For reservations made on budget.com, upgrade will be applied at time of rental, subject to vehicle availability. Renter must meet Budget age, driver and credit requirements. Minimum age may vary by location. An additional daily surcharge may apply for renters under 25 years old. **Rental must begin by 6/30/08.**

For Budget CSR Use Only
- Assign customer a car one group higher than car group reserved
- In CPN, enter **UUGZ105**
- In BCD, enter **X443030**
- Attach to COUPON tape

At checkout:
- Complete this information
  RA #: _____
  Operator ID: _____
  Rental Location: _____
  BCD #: _____

COUPON # UUGZ105

© 2006 Budget Rent A Car System, Inc.
Budget features Ford, Lincoln and Mercury vehicles.

Budget budget.com

Offer validity is governed by the Rules of Use and excludes defined holidays.
Coupons void if purchased, sold or bartered.

Budget has more ways than ever to save!

FREE Weekend Day

Get your discount plus a free day when you present this coupon at time of rental.

Offer valid on intermediate through full-size four-door cars through 6/30/08.

Mention BCD # X443030 and CPN # TUGZ427

For reservations, contact your travel agent or visit Budget at www.entertainment.com/budget or call 1-888-724-6212

Budget

Valid now thru June 30, 2008
Subject to Terms and Conditions on reverse side. D13

Save $20 On A Weekly Rental

Get your discount and take an extra $20 off a weekly rental when you present this coupon at time of rental.

Offer valid on intermediate through full-size four-door cars through 6/30/08.

Mention BCD # X443030 and CPN # MUGZ547

For reservations, contact your travel agent or visit Budget at www.entertainment.com/budget or call 1-888-724-6212

Budget

Valid now thru June 30, 2008
Subject to Terms and Conditions on reverse side. D14

Free Upgrade

Get your discount plus an upgrade when you present this coupon at time of rental.

Offer valid when you rent an intermediate through full-size four-door car through 6/30/08.

Mention BCD # X443030 and CPN # UUGZ105

For reservations, contact your travel agent or visit Budget at www.entertainment.com/budget or call 1-888-724-6212

Budget

Valid now thru June 30, 2008
Subject to Terms and Conditions on reverse side. D15

Save Up To $20 On A Weekend Rental

Get your discount plus an extra $10 to $20 off a weekend rental when you present this coupon at time of rental.

Offer valid on intermediate through full-size four-door cars through 6/30/08.

**Mention BCD # X443030 and
CPN # MUGZ548** for a 2-day rental
CPN # MUGZ549 for a 3-day rental
CPN # MUGZ550 for a 4-day rental

For reservations, contact your travel agent or visit Budget at www.entertainment.com/budget or call 1-888-724-6212

Budget

Valid now thru June 30, 2008
Subject to Terms and Conditions on reverse side. D16

Terms and Conditions: Coupon valid on premium (group G), luxury (group H), convertible (group K), passenger van (group P), sports car (group S), specialty car (group X), sport utility vehicle (groups F, W, L and Z) and minivan (group V) cars. Dollars off applies to the daily time and mileage charges only on a minimum five-day rental period that includes a Saturday night stayover. Taxes, concession recovery fees, customer facility charges ($10/contract in CA), optional items and other surcharges may apply and are extra. Coupon must be surrendered at time of rental; one coupon per rental. Offer may not be used in conjunction with any other coupon, promotion or offer, except your Entertainment® discount. **An advance reservation is required.** Coupon valid at participating Avis locations in the contiguous U.S. and Canada. Offer subject to vehicle availability at the time of rental, and may not be available on some rates at some times. Renter must meet Avis age, driver and credit requirements. Minimum age may vary by location. An additional daily surcharge may apply for renters under 25 years old. **Rental must begin by 6/30/08.**

Rental Sales Agent Instructions
At checkout:
- In AWD, enter **B790072**
- In CPN, enter **MUGA116**
- Complete this information:
  RA #: _____
  Rental Location: _____
- Attach to COUPON tape

COUPON # **MUGA116**

© 2006 Avis Rent A Car System, LLC

AVIS · We try harder.® · avis.com

Offer validity is governed by the Rules of Use and excludes defined holidays.
Coupons void if purchased, sold or bartered.

Terms and Conditions: Coupon valid on an intermediate (group C) through a full-size four-door (group E) car. Dollars off applies to the daily time and mileage charges only on a minimum five-day rental period. Taxes, concession recovery fees, customer facility charges ($10/contract in CA), optional items and other surcharges may apply and are extra. Coupon must be surrendered at time of rental; one coupon per rental. Offer may not be used in conjunction with any other coupon, promotion or offer, except your Entertainment® discount. **An advance reservation is required.** Coupon valid at participating Avis locations in the contiguous U.S. and Canada. Offer subject to vehicle availability at the time of rental, and may not be available on some rates at some times. For reservations made on avis.com, dollars off will be applied at time of rental, subject to vehicle availability. Renter must meet Avis age, driver and credit requirements. Minimum age may vary by location. An additional daily surcharge may apply for renters under 25 years old. **Rental must begin by 6/30/08.**

Rental Sales Agent Instructions
At checkout:
- In AWD, enter **B790072**
- In CPN, enter **MUGA115**
- Complete this information:
  RA #: _____
  Rental Location: _____
- Attach to COUPON tape

COUPON # **MUGA115**

© 2006 Avis Rent A Car System, LLC

AVIS · We try harder.® · avis.com

Offer validity is governed by the Rules of Use and excludes defined holidays.
Coupons void if purchased, sold or bartered.

Terms and Conditions: Coupon valid for a one-time, one-car group upgrade on an intermediate (group C) through a full-size four-door (group E) car. Maximum upgrade to premium (group G). Offer valid on daily, weekend, weekly and monthly rates only. The upgraded car is subject to vehicle availability at the time of rental, and may not be available on some rates and at some times. Coupon valid at participating Avis locations in the contiguous U.S. and Canada. Coupon must be surrendered at time of rental; one coupon per rental. May not be used in conjunction with any other coupon, promotion or offer, except your Entertainment® discount. **A 24-hour advance reservation is required,** using this coupon. For reservations made on avis.com, upgrade will be applied at time of rental, subject to vehicle availability Renter must meet Avis age, driver and credit requirements. Minimum age may vary by location. An additional daily surcharge may apply for renters under 25 years old. **Rental must begin by 6/30/08.**

Rental Sales Agent Instructions
At checkout:
- In AWD, enter **B790072**
- Assign customer a car one group higher than car group reserved.
  Upgrade to no higher than Group G. Charge for car group reserved.
- In CPN, enter **UUGA298**
- Complete this information:
  RA #: _____
  Rental Location: _____
- Attach to COUPON tape

COUPON # **UUGA298**

© 2006 Avis Rent A Car System, LLC

AVIS · We try harder.® · avis.com

Offer validity is governed by the Rules of Use and excludes defined holidays.
Coupons void if purchased, sold or bartered.

Terms and Conditions: Offer of one weekend day free applies to the time and mileage charges only of the third consecutive day of a minimum three-day weekend rental on an intermediate (group C) through a full-size four-door (group E) car. Taxes, concession recovery fees, customer facility charges ($10/contract in CA), optional items and other surcharges may apply and are extra. Weekend rental period begins Thursday and car must be returned by Monday 11:59 p.m. or a higher rate will apply. A Saturday night stayover is required. Coupon must be surrendered at time of rental; one coupon per rental and cannot be used for one-way rentals. May not be used in conjunction with any other coupon, promotion or offer, except your Entertainment® discount. Coupon valid at participating Avis locations in the contiguous U.S. and Canada, except the New York Metro area. **An advance reservation is required.** Offer may not be available during holiday and other blackout periods. Offer subject to vehicle availability at the time of rental, and may not be available on some rates and at some times. For reservations made on avis.com, free day will be applied at time of rental, subject to vehicle availability. Renter must meet Avis age, driver and credit requirements. Minimum age may vary by location. An additional daily surcharge may apply for renters under 25 years old. **Rental must begin by 6/30/08.**

Rental Sales Agent Instructions
At checkout:
- In AWD, enter **B790072**
- In CPN, enter **TUGA074**
- Complete this information:
  RA #: _____
  Rental Location: _____
- Attach to COUPON tape

COUPON # **TUGA074**

© 2006 Avis Rent A Car System, LLC

AVIS · We try harder.® · avis.com

Offer validity is governed by the Rules of Use and excludes defined holidays.
Coupons void if purchased, sold or bartered.

Terms and Conditions: Coupon valid for $50 off monthly or Mini-Lease rental at participating Avis locations in the contiguous U.S. and Canada. Offer applies to a minimum 30-day rental period of an intermediate (group C) through a full-size four-door (group E) car. Offer of $50 off a long-term rental applies to the time and mileage charges on the first month of a minimum 30 and maximum 330 consecutive day rental. Taxes, concession recovery fees, customer facility charges ($10/contract in CA), optional items and other surcharges may apply and are extra. Coupon must be surrendered at time of rental; one coupon per rental. **An advance reservation is required.** May not be used in conjunction with any other coupon, promotion or offer, except your Entertainment® discount. Offer subject to vehicle availability at the time of rental, and may not be available on some rates and at some times. For reservations made on avis.com, dollars off will be applied at time of rental, subject to vehicle availability. Renter must meet Avis age, driver and credit requirements. Minimum age may vary by location. An additional daily surcharge may apply for renters under 25 years old. **Rental must begin by 6/30/08.**

Rental Sales Agent Instructions
At checkout:
- In AWD, enter **B790072**
- In CPN, enter **MUGG080**
- Complete this information:
  RA #: _____
  Rental Location: _____
- Attach to COUPON tape

COUPON # **MUGG080**

© 2006 Avis Rent A Car System, LLC

AVIS · We try harder.® · avis.com

Offer validity is governed by the Rules of Use and excludes defined holidays.
Coupons void if purchased, sold or bartered.

Terms and Conditions: Offer applies to one day free of the daily time and mileage charges on a minimum five consecutive day rental period on weekly rates with a Saturday night stayover on an intermediate (group C) through full-size four-door (group E) car. Taxes, concession recovery fees, customer facility charges ($10/contract in CA), optional items and other surcharges may apply and are extra. Coupon must be surrendered at time of rental and cannot be used for one-way rentals; one coupon per rental. Offer may not be used in conjunction with any other coupon, promotion or offer, except your Entertainment® discount. **An advance reservation is required.** Coupon valid at participating Avis locations in the contiguous U.S. and Canada, excluding the NY Metro area. Offer may not be available during holiday and other blackout periods. Offer subject to vehicle availability at the time of rental, and may not be available on some rates and at some times. For reservations made on avis.com, free day will be applied at time of rental, subject to vehicle availability. Renter must meet Avis age, driver and credit requirements. Minimum age may vary by location. An additional daily surcharge may apply for renters under 25 years old. **Rental must begin by 6/30/08.**

Rental Sales Agent Instructions
At checkout:
- In AWD, enter **B790072**
- In CPN, enter **TUGG008**
- Complete this information:
  RA #: _____
  Rental Location: _____
- Attach to COUPON tape

COUPON # **TUGG008**

© 2006 Avis Rent A Car System, LLC

AVIS · We try harder.® · avis.com

Offer validity is governed by the Rules of Use and excludes defined holidays.
Coupons void if purchased, sold or bartered.

$20 off a weekly rental

Rent a car for a minimum of five days and you can get $20 off.

For reservations, visit www.entertainment.com/avis or call 1-800-245-8572

To save every time you rent, always provide your **Avis Worldwide Discount (AWD) # B790072**

Be sure to mention the coupon # MUGA115

AVIS We try harder. avis.com

Valid now thru June 30, 2008
See reverse side for details

D7

$25 off a weekly rental

Rent a car for a minimum of five days and you can get $25 off. Includes luxury and premium vehicles, SUVs, minivans and convertibles.

For reservations, visit www.entertainment.com/avis or call 1-800-245-8572

To save every time you rent, always provide your **Avis Worldwide Discount (AWD) # B790072**

Be sure to mention the coupon # MUGA116

AVIS We try harder. avis.com

Valid now thru June 30, 2008
See reverse side for details

D8

FREE weekend day

Rent a car for three or more days and you can get a weekend day free.

For reservations, visit www.entertainment.com/avis or call 1-800-245-8572

To save every time you rent, always provide your **Avis Worldwide Discount (AWD) # B790072**

Be sure to mention the coupon # TUGA074

AVIS We try harder. avis.com

Valid now thru June 30, 2008
See reverse side for details

D9

FREE car upgrade

Rent a car and receive a one-time one-car group upgrade. An advance reservation with request for upgrade is required.

For reservations, visit www.entertainment.com/avis or call 1-800-245-8572

To save every time you rent, always provide your **Avis Worldwide Discount (AWD) # B790072**

Be sure to mention the coupon # UUGA298

AVIS We try harder. avis.com

Valid now thru June 30, 2008
See reverse side for details

D10

FREE day on a weekly rental

Rent a car for a minimum of five days and you can get a free day.

For reservations, visit www.entertainment.com/avis or call 1-800-245-8572

To save every time you rent, always provide your **Avis Worldwide Discount (AWD) # B790072**

Be sure to mention the coupon # TUGG008

AVIS We try harder. avis.com

Valid now thru June 30, 2008
See reverse side for details

D11

$50 off a long-term rental

Rent a car for a minimum of 30 days and receive $50 off.

For reservations, visit www.entertainment.com/avis or call 1-800-245-8572

To save every time you rent, always provide your **Avis Worldwide Discount (AWD) # B790072**

Be sure to mention the coupon # MUGG080

AVIS We try harder. avis.com

Valid now thru June 30, 2008
See reverse side for details

D12

Your choice of savings from Avis!

- **$25 off a five-day rental**
- **$20 off a five-day rental**
- **A free upgrade**
- **A free weekend day**

And more! See coupons on next page.

AVIS
We try harder.®

Terms and Conditions: Coupon valid on an intermediate (group C) through a full-size four-door (group E) car. Dollars off applies to the daily time and mileage charges only on a minimum five-day rental period. Taxes, concession recovery fees, customer facility charges ($10/contract in CA), optional items and other surcharges may apply and are extra. Coupon must be surrendered at time of rental; one coupon per rental. Offer may not be used in conjunction with any other coupon, promotion or offer, except your Entertainment® discount. **An advance reservation is required.** Coupon valid at participating Avis locations in the contiguous U.S. and Canada. Offer subject to vehicle availability at the time of rental, and may not be available on some rates at some times. For reservations made on avis.com, dollars off will be applied at time of rental, subject to vehicle availability. Renter must meet Avis age, driver and credit requirements. Minimum age may vary by location. An additional daily surcharge may apply for renters under 25 years old. **Rental must begin by 6/30/08.**

Rental Sales Agent Instructions
At checkout:
- In AWD, enter B790072
- In CPN, enter MUGA115
- Complete this information:
  RA #: _____
  Rental Location: _____
- Attach to COUPON tape

COUPON # MUGA115
©2006 Avis Rent A Car System, LLC

AVIS *We try harder.®*
avis.com

Offer validity is governed by the Rules of Use and excludes defined holidays.
Coupons void if purchased, sold or bartered.

Terms and Conditions: Coupon valid on premium (group G), luxury (group H), convertible (group K), passenger van (group P), sports car (group S), specialty car (group X), sport utility vehicle (groups F, W, L and Z) and minivan (group V) cars. Dollars off applies to the daily time and mileage charges only on a minimum five-day rental period that includes a Saturday night stayover. Taxes, concession recovery fees, customer facility charges ($10/contract in CA), optional items and other surcharges may apply and are extra. Coupon must be surrendered at time of rental; one coupon per rental. Offer may not be used in conjunction with any other coupon, promotion or offer, except your Entertainment® discount. **An advance reservation is required.** Coupon valid at participating Avis locations in the contiguous U.S. and Canada. Offer subject to vehicle availability at the time of rental, and may not be available on some rates at some times. For reservations made at avis.com, dollars off will be applied at time of rental; subject to vehicle availability. Renter must meet Avis age, driver and credit requirements. Minimum age may vary by location. An additional daily surcharge may apply for renters under 25 years old. **Rental must begin by 6/30/08.**

Rental Sales Agent Instructions
At checkout:
- In AWD, enter B790072
- In CPN, enter MUGA116
- Complete this information:
  RA #: _____
  Rental Location: _____
- Attach to COUPON tape

COUPON # MUGA116
©2006 Avis Rent A Car System, LLC

AVIS *We try harder.®*
avis.com

Offer validity is governed by the Rules of Use and excludes defined holidays.
Coupons void if purchased, sold or bartered.

Terms and Conditions: Offer of one weekend day free applies to the time and mileage charges only of the third consecutive day of a minimum three-day weekend rental on an intermediate (group C) through a full-size four-door (group E) car. Taxes, concession recovery fees, customer facility charges ($10/contract in CA), optional items and other surcharges may apply and are extra. Weekend rental period begins Thursday and car must be returned by Monday 11:59 p.m. or a higher rate will apply. A Saturday night stayover is required. Coupon must be surrendered at time of rental; one coupon per rental and cannot be used for one-way rentals. May not be used in conjunction with any other coupon, promotion or offer, except your Entertainment® discount. Coupon valid at participating Avis locations in the contiguous U.S. and Canada, except the New York Metro area. **An advance reservation is required.** Offer may not be available during holiday and other blackout periods. Offer subject to vehicle availability at the time of rental, and may not be available on some rates at some times. For reservations made on avis.com, free day will be applied at time of rental, subject to vehicle availability. Renter must meet Avis age, driver and credit requirements. Minimum age may vary by location. An additional daily surcharge may apply for renters under 25 years old. **Rental must begin by 6/30/08.**

Rental Sales Agent Instructions
At checkout:
- In AWD, enter B790072
- In CPN, enter TUGA074
- Complete this information:
  RA #: _____
  Rental Location: _____
- Attach to COUPON tape

COUPON # TUGA074
©2006 Avis Rent A Car System, LLC

AVIS *We try harder.®*
avis.com

Offer validity is governed by the Rules of Use and excludes defined holidays.
Coupons void if purchased, sold or bartered.

Terms and Conditions: Coupon valid for a one-time, one-car group upgrade on an intermediate (group C) through a full-size four-door (group E) car. Maximum upgrade to premium (group G). Offer valid on daily, weekend, weekly and monthly rates only. The upgraded car is subject to vehicle availability at the time of rental, and may not be available on some rates and at some times. Coupon valid at participating Avis locations in the contiguous U.S. and Canada. Coupon must be surrendered at time of rental; one coupon per rental. May not be used in conjunction with any other coupon, promotion or offer, except your Entertainment® discount. **A 24-hour advance reservation is required, using this coupon.** For reservations made on avis.com, upgrade will be applied at time of rental, subject to vehicle availability. Renter must meet Avis age, driver and credit requirements. Minimum age may vary by location. An additional daily surcharge may apply for renters under 25 years old. **Rental must begin by 6/30/08.**

Rental Sales Agent Instructions
At checkout:
- In AWD, enter B790072
- Assign customer a car one group higher than car group reserved. Upgrade to no higher than Group G. Charge for car group reserved.
- In CPN, enter UUGA298
- Complete this information:
  RA #: _____
  Rental Location: _____
- Attach to COUPON tape

COUPON # UUGA298
©2006 Avis Rent A Car System, LLC

AVIS *We try harder.®*
avis.com

Offer validity is governed by the Rules of Use and excludes defined holidays.
Coupons void if purchased, sold or bartered.

We try harder
to make your money go farther.

$25 off a weekly rental

Rent a car for a minimum of five days and you can get $25 off.

For reservations, visit
www.entertainment.com/avis or call
1-800-245-8572

To save every time you rent, always provide your Avis Worldwide Discount (AWD) # B790072

Be sure to mention the coupon # MUGA116

AVIS
We try harder.
avis.com

Valid now thru June 30, 2008
See reverse side for details

D3

$20 off a weekly rental

Rent a car for a minimum of five days and you can get $20 off.

For reservations, visit
www.entertainment.com/avis or call
1-800-245-8572

To save every time you rent, always provide your Avis Worldwide Discount (AWD) # B790072

Be sure to mention the coupon # MUGA115

AVIS
We try harder.
avis.com

Valid now thru June 30, 2008
See reverse side for details

D4

FREE car upgrade

Rent a car and receive a one-time one car group upgrade. An advance reservation with request for upgrade is required.

For reservations, visit
www.entertainment.com/avis or call
1-800-245-8572

To save every time you rent, always provide your Avis Worldwide Discount (AWD) # B790072

Be sure to mention the coupon # UUGA298

AVIS
We try harder.
avis.com

Valid now thru June 30, 2008
See reverse side for details

D5

FREE weekend day

Rent a car for three or more days and you can get a weekend day free.

For reservations, visit
www.entertainment.com/avis or call
1-800-245-8572

To save every time you rent, always provide your Avis Worldwide Discount (AWD) # B790072

Be sure to mention the coupon # TUGA074

AVIS
We try harder.
avis.com

Valid now thru June 30, 2008
See reverse side for details

D6

Hotwire.com — Save Big
Deep discounts on travel

Flights $20 OFF
DISCOUNT AIRFARE

Major airlines use Hotwire to fill their empty seats

Hotels $10 OFF
ANY HOTEL

Top hotels use Hotwire to fill their unsold rooms

Car Rentals $5 OFF
ANY RENTAL CAR

Uniting lonely rental cars with savvy travelers

Packages $50 OFF
ANY PACKAGE

Air + hotel packages save you time

To redeem your mail-in rebate:*

1. Visit http://www.hotwire.com/rebate.jsp to book your trip.
   You must book and complete travel between **8/1/06** and **12/31/07** to qualify.
2. Print your booking confirmation and mail it with your signed original rebate form (this page) and a copy of your Entertainment® Card to:

   Hotwire Entertainment® Mail-In Rebate
   P.O. Box 2870
   San Francisco, CA 94126-2870

3. Your rebate will appear on your credit card statement 6 to 8 weeks after we receive your proper documentation.

Questions? Contact Hotwire Customer Care at 1-866-HOTWIRE.

Sign to redeem: _____

*Applies only to travel booked between 08/01/06 and 12/31/07 at www.hotwire.com/rebate.jsp and completed between 08/01/06 and 12/31/07. Does not apply to cruise or non-Clearance/non-FlexSaver air bookings. Form must be postmarked within 30 days of booking and received no later than ten days thereafter. Rebate open to legal US residents age 18 or older at time of booking. Rebates will be credited to the same card used for Hotwire booking. If Hotwire is unable to complete the credit for any reason, Hotwire will not be obligated to fulfill the credit in any other form. Original signed forms only; copies or reproductions will not be accepted. Fraudulent submission may result in federal prosecution under mail-fraud statutes. Hotwire is not responsible for lost, late, damaged, misdirected, incomplete, incorrect, illegible or postage-due mail. Void where prohibited, taxed or restricted. One rebate per Hotwire booking, per customer per year, and per Entertainment® Card number. Offer rights not assignable or transferable. Rebate may not be combined with other offers. Hotwire reserves the right to verify identification. Hotwire's decision will be final in all matters relating to this rebate.

Valid now thru December 31, 2007

Offer validity is governed by the Rules of Use and excludes defined holidays. Offers are not valid with other discount offers, unless specified. Coupons void if purchased, sold or bartered. Discounts exclude tax, tip and/or alcohol, where applicable.

You must be a registered member at entertainment.com to take advantage of this great offer.

SAVE 5% OFF
ANY FARE WORLDWIDE FOR UP TO SIX (6) PASSENGERS

AA American Airlines®

One promo code may be used for up to six (6) times on the same intinerary. All published fare rules apply. Offer may be redeemed online only at www.entertainment.com/aa and your unique promo code will be assigned once you visit the site.

Valid on reservations booked now thru December 31, 2007

Offer validity is governed by the Rules of Use and excludes defined holidays. Offers are not valid with other discount offers, unless specified. Coupons void if purchased, sold or bartered. Discounts exclude tax, tip and/or alcohol, where applicable.

D1

AmericanAirlines
We know why you fly®

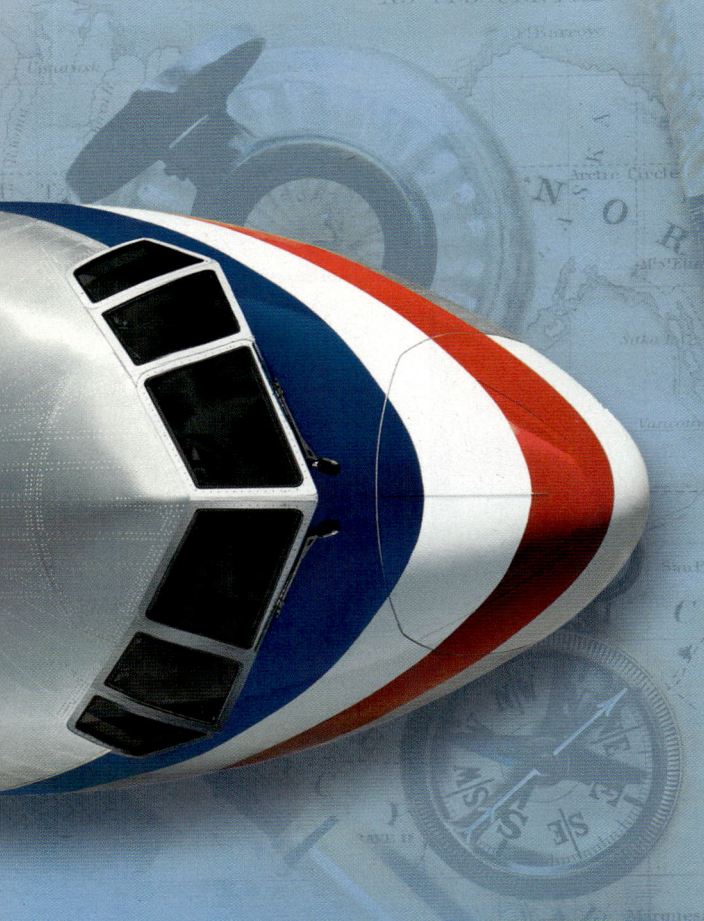

AA.com®

TRAVEL & HOTELS

Make your travel arrangements at
www.entertainment.com/travel

OVER 85 OFFERS

plus more at
www.entertainment.com/travel

Transportation
Alamo	D33-D42
American Airlines	D1
Avis	D3-D12
Budget Car Rental	D13-D22
Carnival Cruise Line	D63-D65
Cruise America	D76
Enterprise Rent-A-Car	D23-D32
Hertz	D53-D62
National Car Rental	D43-D52
SuperShuttle	D74

Lodging & Vacation
CondoDirect	D86
Florida Vacation Station	D85
Great Vacation Destinations	D83
Guaranteed Best Rate	E3-E30
Hotel Chain Savings	E48-E50
Hotels at HalfPrice	E35-E46
Hotwire.com	D2
PetSmart PetsHotel	D75
Sheraton Vacation Ownership	D84
Sunterra	D82
US Airways	D81
Westgate Resorts	D78

Attractions & Vacation Wear
Adventure Island — Water Country USA	D68
Busch Gardens	D67
Legoland	D77
Planet Hollywood	D79-D80
SeaWorld	D66
Sesame Place	D69
TravelSmith	D87
Universal Orlando Resort	D70-D73

How "Buy-One-Get-One-Free" Dining Offers Work

When two or more people dine together, the least expensive entrée or meal ordered is complimentary up to the maximum value stated on the offer.

Up To $16.00 Value

Dinner for two, buy-one-get-one-free value $16.00*

Member's Order:
1 Steak Entrée $17.00
1 Roast Beef Entrée $15.00

Save the cost of the LEAST expensive entrée $15.00

Member's Order:
1 Steak Entrée $17.00
1 Fish Entrée $20.00

Save the MAXIMUM value $16.00

Example

Example

Note: Offers may be subject to additional conditions or restrictions. Please reference the Rules of Use in the back of your book and each individual offer.

*Maximum values vary. Some are higher, some are lower. All are clearly printed on each offer.

DINE & SAVE™

Enjoy dining and saving at the best fine dine and casual restaurants in your area.

It's easy!*

CASUAL DINING & FAST FOOD

For Casual Dining & Fast Food offers, remove the coupon or certificate from your book and present it to the merchant before your bill is totaled. The merchant will retain the coupon and subtract the discount amount from the bill.

DINING OUT

For Dining Out offers (with a ⬛ symbol located in the upper right-hand corner of the offer page), present your Membership Card before your bill is totaled to receive your discount. The merchant will remove the card number from the back of your Membership Card to indicate you have used the offer.

*For complete program details, please refer to the Rules of Use page located in the back of your book. For offer information, please refer to each individual offer.

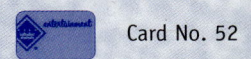

WESTFIRE GRILLE
www.westfiregrille.com

Card No. 52

Up To $18.00 Value

We're not just your ordinary hangout. We strive daily to make your visit to Westfire Grille a great one. 10 High-definition big-screen TVs.

*E*njoy one complimentary LUNCH OR DINNER ENTREE when a second LUNCH OR DINNER ENTREE of equal or greater value is purchased.

valid anytime

2043 Superior Dr. N.W., Rochester, MN (507)424-3390

00694141

Entrées

Entrées include tossed garden greens and a warm breadstick.
Potato choices include: Garlic Mashed, Baked, Waffle Fries, our fresh vegetable of the day.

Top Sirloin Steak Dinner
USDA choice sirloin, broiled your way with pesto garlic butter topped with onion straws. $13.95

New York Sirloin Steak
Aged center-cut New York strip, broiled your way. $16.95

Coconut Shrimp
Hand breaded butterfly shrimp with real coconut in the breading. $14.95

BBQ Pork Ribs
A rack of baby back ribs, roasted slow and slathered with our house BBQ sauce. $16.95
1/2 Rack $12.95

Fish N' Chips
Deep fried loin of cod. $11.95

Walleye Dinner
Minnesota favorite, pan fried or broiled to perfection topped with sliced almonds & a butter wine sauce
$14.95

Steak & Shrimp
Top sirloin steak and 3 hand breaded fried or broiled jumbo shrimp $17.95

Menu Sampler - Prices and menu subject to change.

Offer validity is governed by the Rules of Use and excludes defined holidays. Offers are not valid with other discount offers, unless specified. Coupons void if purchased, sold or bartered. Discounts exclude tax, tip and/or alcohol, where applicable. Tipping should be 15% to 20% of the total bill before discount.

Rix Bar & Grill

Card No. 50

Up To **$16.00** Value

*E*njoy one complimentary LUNCH OR DINNER ENTREE when a second LUNCH OR DINNER ENTREE of equal or greater value is purchased.

valid anytime

2203 44th Ave. N., Minneapolis, MN (612)588-2228

00695412

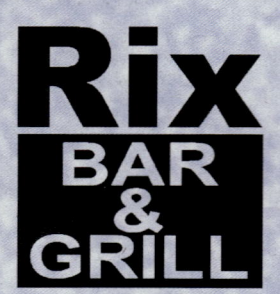

People all over the Twin Cities know about our award winning burgers, but our menu also includes a unique selection of appetizers, salads, sandwiches, dinners & desserts. Whether its brunch on Sat. & Sun., or lunch or dinner any day of the week; every dish that comes out of our open kitchen is made with fresh, quality, often local ingredients.

Our Award Winning Burgers!

Big Rix — 10
Two beef patties, jalapeno bacon, sharp cheddar cheese, caramelized onions, lettuce and a spicy sauce on a jumbo butter roll.

Western Chipotle B.B.Q. — 8
Hickory smoked bacon, cheddar cheese, and chipotle BBQ sauce.

Sandwiches

Cajun Meatloaf — 9
Seasoned meatloaf topped with black olives and served with mayonnaise and spicy honey mustard on texas toast.

Ham Stacker — 8
Grilled slices of thick honey pit ham smothered in swiss cheese and served on texas toast with mayo and our spicy honey mustard

Entrees

Caribbean Pork Chop — 16
A thick 10oz chop seasoned with caribbean jerk spices and served on a bed of sweet potato fries and our fresh vegetable of the day

Garlic – Lime Chicken — 14
Boneless chicken breasts seasoned with eight spices and pan fried in garlic oil and lime juice served with garlic mashed potatoes and our vegetable of the day

Pesto Cream Pasta — 13
Linguini noodles, artichokes, mushrooms and seared chicken breast in a creamy pesto sauce.

Menu Sampler - Prices and menu subject to change.

Offer validity is governed by the Rules of Use and excludes defined holidays. Offers are not valid with other discount offers, unless specified. Coupons void if purchased, sold or bartered. Discounts exclude tax, tip and/or alcohol, where applicable. Tipping should be 15% to 20% of the total bill before discount.

America's Harvest

The Northland Inn
AN EXECUTIVE CONFERENCE CENTER

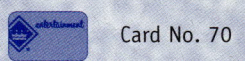

Card No. 70

Up to $27.00 Value

The America's Harvest Restaurant located in the Northland Inn provides only the best quality in Americana dining. Our seemingly endless salad & dessert buffets compliment & are included with the outstanding regional dishes prepared by Executive Chef Jack Shapansky & his team.

Enjoy one complimentary DINNER ENTREE when a second DINNER ENTREE of equal or greater value is purchased.

valid any evening

7025 Northland Dr. (Northland Inn), Brooklyn Park, MN
(763) 536-3333
(800) 441-6422

00597493

Seared Pork Rib Chop
Mango and Cider Meat Glaze
Fried Apple & Herb Grits
Sautéed Swiss Chard
$24.95

Pan-fried Walleye
Two Filets of Walleye dredged in Pistachios and seasoned flour and fried in whole butter
Lemon Honey Mayonnaise
Fresh Vegetables and Risotto Cakes
$25.95

Wadsworth's Grilled Strip Steak
14 oz. USDA Choice, Bone-in Sirloin of Beef Steak
On a Black Bean Salsa
Roasted Red Pepper in Olive Oil
Roasted Fingerling Potatoes
$28.95

Mediterranean Roasted Breast of Chicken
Orzo, Tomato, Artichoke Hearts and Mushrooms
Caper and Garlic Butter
Sautéed Asparagus
$23.95

Shrimp and Scallop Stuffed Portabella Mushroom
on a Bed Spinach Linguine tossed in a Tomato, Fresh Herbs and Balsamic Vinaigrette
Roasted Spring Onion
$26.95

Oven Roasted Chilean Sea Bass
Wrapped in a Banana Leaf filled with Green Papaya Slaw, Roasted Ripe Plantains and Spiced Butter
Served with Pineapple Salsa
$26.95

Roasted Rack of Australian Lamb
With Seasoned Barley and Grilled Vegetables and Roast Garlic Pecan Sauce
$27.95

Sliced Grilled Steak "Au Poivre"
Marinated in Herbs, Mustard and Cracked Black Pepper with Fresh Vegetables and Mashed Potatoes
$24.95

Menu Sampler - Prices and menu subject to change.

Offer validity is governed by the Rules of Use and excludes defined holidays. Offers are not valid with other discount offers, unless specified. Coupons void if purchased, sold or bartered. Discounts exclude tax, tip and/or alcohol, where applicable. Tipping should be 15% to 20% of the total bill before discount.

C58

Shady Hill Grille

www.soldiersfield.com

Card No. 38

REPEAT SAVINGS — Up To $15.00 Value

The Shady Hill Grille's Executive Chef David Tator will tantalize your taste buds with his fabulous menu featuring midwest-aged, hand-cut steaks, chicken, pork, seafood, and pasta entrees at reasonable prices. Located at the Best Western Soldiers Field, our warm atmosphere and friendly staff will keep you coming back.

Enjoy one complimentary LUNCH OR DINNER ENTREE when a second LUNCH OR DINNER ENTREE of equal or greater value is purchased.

valid anytime

401 6th St. SW (Best Western Soldiers Field), **Rochester, MN** (507)288-0206

00454901

STEAKS

FILET MIGNON - A 6 ounce Steer Filet cut from the heart of the Tenderloin and finished with Sauteed Mushrooms ... 13.45

STRIP STEAK AL FORNO - A 10 ounce Robust Italian Style Strip Steak seasoned with Fresh Garlic and Rosemary and grilled to order with a Parmesan Crust ... 14.95

CHICKEN ENTREES

CHICKEN PICATTA - Tender Breast of Chicken sauteed, then finished in a sauce of White Wine, Parsley, Capers, and Lemon Juice ... 9.95

BABCOCK PORK ENTREES

APPLE CIDER PORK - Babcock's Finest Pork Loin, In-House Smoked and served with an Apple Cider Sauce ... 8.95

SEAFOOD

WALLEYE ALMONDINE - Minnesota's Finest Freshwater Fish dressed in a coat of Ground Almonds and Fried to a Golden Brown ... 14.95

PASTA

LOUISIANA CHICKEN WITH RED CHILI PEPPER LINGUINI - Tender Chicken Strips coated with Cajun Seasoning and Sauteed - blended with a Cajun Cream Sauce and served atop Red Chili Pepper Linguini ... 10.95

Menu Sampler - Prices and menu subject to change.

Offer validity is governed by the Rules of Use and excludes defined holidays. Offers are not valid with other discount offers, unless specified. Coupons void if purchased, sold or bartered. Discounts exclude tax, tip and/or alcohol, where applicable. Tipping should be 15% to 20% of the total bill before discount.

THE Lord Essex LOUNGE

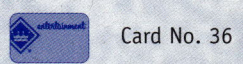

www.kahler.com

Card No. 36

Up To $18.00 Value

Lord Essex Tavern offers traditional English pub appetizers and entrees in an elegant, rich atmosphere. We are open Mon-Fri 11 a.m.-10 p.m. and Sat 5 p.m.-10 p.m.

*E*njoy one complimentary LUNCH OR DINNER ENTREE when a second LUNCH OR DINNER ENTREE of equal or greater value is purchased.

valid anytime

20 Second Ave. SW (Kahler Grand Hotel), Rochester, MN
(507) 282-2581

00454840

Buckingham Chicken Pot Pye 8.95
Rich Chicken Stew in a Puff Pastry
Small House Salad

Strip Sirloin Steak, 8 oz. 10.95
Grilled Onions, sautéed Mushrooms, on Crusted Roll

Heartland Shepherd's Pye 8.95
Choice Beef Tips braised in Ale layered with Wild Rice, Sweet Kernel Corn
Small House Salad

Walleye Fish Sandwich 7.95
Batter-Fried Walleye Pike topped with Cheddar Cheese & served with our special Tartar Sauce

Roasted Breast of Chicken 13.95
Boursin Dressing

Milk Fed Veal Parmigiana 17.95
With Pasta, Tomato Sauce

Herb Crusted Swordfish 17.95
Broiled

Menu Sampler - Prices and menu subject to change.

Offer validity is governed by the Rules of Use and excludes defined holidays. Offers are not valid with other discount offers, unless specified. Coupons void if purchased, sold or bartered. Discounts exclude tax, tip and/or alcohol, where applicable. Tipping should be 15% to 20% of the total bill before discount.

C56

CREEK SIDE CAFE

Card No. 37

Up to $17.00 Value

Creekside Cafe is dining at its best! International elegance with a variety of tastes and influences from around the world, overlooking 25 acres of preserved picturesque marshlands. We feature a wonderful wine list, and there is no need to dress up - casual dress is welcome.

*E*njoy one complimentary DINNER ENTREE when a second DINNER ENTREE of equal or greater value is purchased.

valid any evening

3131 Campus Dr. (Radisson Hotel & Conference Center), Plymouth, MN (763)559-6288

00463737

Pastas

Pesto Ravioli — $14.75
Garlic, basil and parmesan cheese stuffed in a spinach striped pasta shell, tossed in a chive alfredo sauce.

Shrimp Scampi a la Radisson — $12.75
With roasted tomatoes, parmesan cheese and herbed bread crumbs.

Entrees

New York Strip Steak — $26.00
Hand cut, char broiled and topped with Maitre D' Hotel butter

Grilled Ahi Tuna — $21.50
With roasted red pepper coulis.

Chicken Breast Oscar — $21.75
A grilled boneless chicken breast, topped with blue crab meat, grilled Asparagus and sauce béarnaise.

Medallions of Beef Tenderloin — $26.50
Grilled and served with sautéed fresh spinach, sweet onions, shiitake Mushrooms and Roma tomatoes.

Menu Sampler - Prices and menu subject to change.

Offer validity is governed by the Rules of Use and excludes defined holidays. Offers are not valid with other discount offers, unless specified. Coupons void if purchased, sold or bartered. Discounts exclude tax, tip and/or alcohol, where applicable. Tipping should be 15% to 20% of the total bill before discount.

C55

THE Wilds PUB
RESTAURANT & BAR
www.golfthewilds.com

Located at the premier Wilds Golf Club, we're always open to the public. Minutes from the Twin Cities, join us for casual lunch and fine dining. Our fair weather patio offers breathtaking views of the 18th green and the Minneapolis skyline. We host banquets up to 350 guests & have the largest Sun. brunch buffet south of the river.

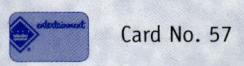

Card No. 57

REPEAT SAVINGS

Up To **$22.00** Value

*E*njoy one complimentary LUNCH OR DINNER ENTREE when a second LUNCH OR DINNER ENTREE of equal or greater value is purchased.

valid anytime

Sunday brunch and all-you-can-eat specials excluded; Friday & Saturday seating before 6 p.m. or after 8:30 p.m.

3151 Wilds Ridge, Prior Lake, MN (952) 445-3500

00479864

Vegetarian Pasta
Fresh Red and Green Peppers, Zucchini, Carrots, Mushrooms, Asparagus and Linguini tossed in our Spicy Marinara Sauce with grated Parmesan Cheese.... **$10.95**

Wilds Pasta Delarose
If you love pasta, this is an award winner! Fettucini Pasta with Pepperoni, Italian Sausage, Black Olives and Onion tossed in our own Delarose Sauce.... **$12.95**

Grilled Salmon
A wonderfully unique selection! Fresh Atlantic Salmon seasoned and grilled to perfection. Topped with fresh Basil Cream Sauce.... **$17.95**
Recommended Wine: Red Zinfandel

Baked Chicken and Mushroom Strudel
Julienne Chicken, sliced Mushrooms and Onions flavored with Sherry Cream Sauce, wrapped in Phyllo Dough and baked to a golden brown. Served with mixed Wild Rice.... **$13.95**
Recommended Wines: Chardonnay or White Zinfandel

"The Pub Club"
Stacks of Turkey, Ham, Bacon, Cheddar and Swiss Cheese layered with Lettuce, Tomato and Mayo on toasted White Bread.... **$8.95**

Minnesota Walleye Sandwich
Fresh Walleye broiled or in a golden brown Beer Batter. Served on a toasted Hoagie Roll with a zesty Cajun Creole Mayo.... **$9.95**

Menu Sampler - Prices and menu subject to change.

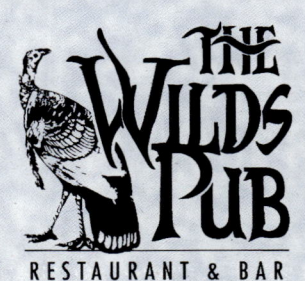

Offer validity is governed by the Rules of Use and excludes defined holidays. Offers are not valid with other discount offers, unless specified. Coupons void if purchased, sold or bartered. Discounts exclude tax, tip and/or alcohol, where applicable. Tipping should be 15% to 20% of the total bill before discount.

Kip's Authentic Irish Pub and Restaurant
est. 2005

Card No. 12

Up To $15.00 Value

*E*njoy one complimentary LUNCH OR DINNER ENTREE when a second LUNCH OR DINNER ENTREE of equal or greater value is purchased.

Dine in only; Brunch excluded

valid anytime

9970 Wayzata Blvd. (located adjacent to the Marriot Minneapolis, West Hwy. 169 & 394), **St. Louis Park, MN**
(952)367-5070

00674340

SANDWICHES

Grilled Chicken Sandwich
With caramelized onions, tomato, brie cheese and herb mayonnaise. 8.95

MAIN COURSES

Chicken Pot Pie
Slow-roasted chicken and simmered baby veggies with creamy, steamy sauce. All neatly wrapped in a golden pie crust. 12.95

Finn McCool's Rib-eye Steak
Peppercorn crusted with Irish whiskey sauce, champ and tiny string beans. 21.95

Doyle's Grilled Minnesota Walleye
Fresh walleye grilled and served with boiled red potatoes and tiny string beans. 14.95

Bangers and Mash
Irish style sausage, mashed potatoes, pan gravy and fried onions. 10.95

Shepherd's Pie
Choice ground beef, garden vegetables and our special mashed potatoes makes this warm-hearted favorite. 10.95

Menu Sampler - Prices and menu subject to change.

Offer validity is governed by the Rules of Use and excludes defined holidays. Offers are not valid with other discount offers, unless specified. Coupons void if purchased, sold or bartered. Discounts exclude tax, tip and/or alcohol, where applicable. Tipping should be 15% to 20% of the total bill before discount.

ST. CROIX Crab House MUSIC CAFE

www.stcroixmusiccafe.com

We are proud to offer our guests the finest selection of the North Atlantic and Arctic Oceans. Our crab is harvested fresh by the most talented and adventurous fishermen in the world, so that you may enjoy this "delicacy of kings". After your memorable dining experience, stay to drink in the sounds of our phenomenal live music.

Card No. 72

Up To $13.00 Value

*E*njoy one complimentary DINNER ENTREE when a second DINNER ENTREE of equal or greater value is purchased.

valid any evening

317 S. Main St. (downtown Stillwater), **Stillwater, MN**
(651)439-0024

00476089

Crab, Crab & Lobster

Golden Alaskan King Crab Legs 23.95
  1-1/2 pounds "Lemon steamed" and served with sweet butter
Dungeness Sweet Crab Legs (Seasonal) 19.95
  1-1/2 pounds "Garlic Grilled" and served with hot butter
New! Lobster Chops 15.95
  Split lobster tails with jumbo sea scallops, served char broiled

Steaks & Chops

14 oz. Center Cut Sirloin 9.89
  Our house steak, fresh cut and extra lean, served with mushrooms
New! Two Pork Loin Chops 11.95
  Boneless center cut pork chops served BBQ, Cajun or Blackened

Seafood in every bite Pasta

New! Blackened Chicken Pasta .... Half 7.29 Full 9.89
  Aztec Alfredo sauce with fresh linguini noodles

Simply Caesars & Soups

New! Shrimp Tenderloin Caesar .... Half 5.99 Full 7.59
  Our Classic Caesar topped with battered shrimp tenderloins

Burgers, Chicken & Sandwiches

New! French Riviera on a grilled French roll 6.89
  Thinly sliced roast beef with sautéed mushrooms and red onions

Menu Sampler - Prices and menu subject to change.

Offer validity is governed by the Rules of Use and excludes defined holidays. Offers are not valid with other discount offers, unless specified. Coupons void if purchased, sold or bartered. Discounts exclude tax, tip and/or alcohol, where applicable. Tipping should be 15% to 20% of the total bill before discount.

C52

Nickelby's Maplewood Grill

Card No. 110

Up To **$14.00** Value

Thank you for joining us! All of Nickelby's entrees include our complete salad bar and two homemade soups. Banquet facilities available for wedding receptions for up to 250 people and meeting space for up to 300 people. We feature the Minnesota Comedy Club in the lounge Friday and Saturday evenings.

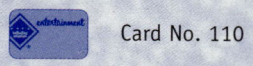

Enjoy one complimentary DINNER ENTREE when a second DINNER ENTREE of equal or greater value is purchased.

valid any evening

1780 E. County Rd. D, Maplewood, MN (651) 770-2811

00465990

PASTAS

Fettuccine Alfredo Traditional garlic cream sauce with fresh parmesan $11.95
 With chicken $13.95
 With shrimp $15.95

Chicken Marsala Fusilli with sundried tomatoes & mushrooms in marsala cream $13.95

Main Entrees

Petite New York Strip 6oz cooked to order $12.95

Grilled Pork Chops 2-10oz center cut $15.95

Chicken Breast Stuffed with herb cream cheese and tomato basil sauce $13.95

Mesquite Smoked Chicken Made with roasted red pepper sauce $13.95

Sautéed Catfish Served with tomato pepper relish $13.95

Menu Sampler - Prices and menu subject to change.

Offer validity is governed by the Rules of Use and excludes defined holidays. Offers are not valid with other discount offers, unless specified. Coupons void if purchased, sold or bartered. Discounts exclude tax, tip and/or alcohol, where applicable. Tipping should be 15% to 20% of the total bill before discount.

C51

da Afghan Restaurant

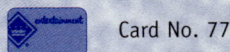

www.daafghan.com

Card No. 77

Up to $14.00 Value

Voted "Best Middle Eastern Restaurant" by City Pages & The Twin Cities Reader. Naturally raised lamb. Fine dining in a casual atmosphere. Serving a good selection of wine & beer. Please call for directions. Reservations suggested on weekends.

Enjoy one complimentary DINNER ENTREE when a second DINNER ENTREE of equal or greater value is purchased.

valid any evening

Friday & Saturday seating before 6:00 p.m. and after 8:00 p.m.; Sampler for two excluded

929 W 80th St., Bloomington, MN (952)888-5824

00272855

Appetizers

Combination Appetizers
Four lamb ribs, two spinach pies, two potato pies and two smbosas. Served with mint, cucumber and yogurt dressing.

Entrees

Kabeli Palow with Chicken or Lamb　　with lamb 14.95　　with chicken 12.95
Sauteed lamb or chicken cooked in a tomato and onion sauce until very tender. Served with basmati rice that is seasoned with tomatoes, onions, black cardamom and Afghani spices. Topped with a julienne of shaved carrots, raisins and slivered almonds.

Lamb or Chicken Karaee　　with lamb 15.95　　with chicken 14.95
Garden vegetables with tender chunks of lamb or chicken delicately seasoned and slowly stir fried to the best flavored and served over basmati rice.
Choice of extra hot, hot or mild

Combination Pasta of Mantou and Aushok
Try both of our pastas. A half serving each of Mantou and Aushok.

Afghani Delights

Spring Lamb Chops　　19.95
Four lightly seasoned spring lamb chops charbroiled to perfection. Served with the vegetable of the day and basmati rice.

Afghani Style Filet Mignon Steak - 9oz.　　19.95
A tender filet mignon steak marinated with garlic and spices. A veal stock sauce seasoned with black pepper and spices blankets and steak. Served with fresh vegetables and basmati rice that has been cooked with tomatoes and onions and then topped with a julienne of carrots, raisins and slivered almonds.

Vegetarian

Afghani Spinach Pie　　9.95
A large homemade Afghani hand tossed dough crust filled with spinach, green onions, and unique spices. The pie is lightly brushed with olive oil, baked and served with homemade yogurt sauce.

Menu Sampler - Prices and menu subject to change.

Offer validity is governed by the Rules of Use and excludes defined holidays. Offers are not valid with other discount offers, unless specified. Coupons void if purchased, sold or bartered. Discounts exclude tax, tip and/or alcohol, where applicable. Tipping should be 15% to 20% of the total bill before discount.

C50

MacTavish's
Your Neighborhood Restaurant

Card No. 33

Up To **$18.00** Value

Situated within the clubhouse at Edinburgh USA, MacTavish's restaurant offers a view of our world class golf course. Enjoy everything MacTavish's has to offer, from a delicious array of appetizers, sandwiches & salads to choice steaks, seafood & pasta entrees. Visit us at www.mactavishs.com.

Enjoy one complimentary LUNCH OR DINNER ENTREE when a second LUNCH OR DINNER ENTREE of equal or greater value is purchased.

Brunch excluded; Dine in only

valid anytime

Not valid with any other discount offer

Edinburgh USA - 8700 Edinbrook Crossing, Brooklyn Park, MN (763)315-8535

00467720

Starters

Lemon Grass Shrimp — 9.50
Shrimp sautéed in our dragon sauce, served on a bed of baby greens, carrots, celery and Gorgonzola cheese dip

Dragon Wings — 8.25
Crispy wings in a sweet and spicy sauce with cucumbers and blue cheese dressing

Sandwiches

Havana Pork — 8.25
Chili roasted shaved pork, smoked ham, Swiss cheese, pickles, Dijon mustard, chipotle lime aioli on grilled French bread, French fries

Pan Toscano — 9.95
Braised roast beef, caramelized onions, roasted peppers, provolone cheese, classic aioli on rustic Italian bread, French fries

Entrées

Seafood Fettuccini — 13.95
Rock crab, bay scallops, Tiger shrimp and pasta ribbons tossed with roasted garlic Alfredo sauce

Grilled Salmon Fillet — 14.50
Fresh Atlantic salmon finished with artichoke hearts, grape tomatoes, garlic and wine, wild rice pilaf

Steaks
Charbroiled Aged USDA Choice Cuts

Served with a cup of soup or garden salad, fresh vegetables and choice of baked potato, French fries, buttermilk chive mashed potatoes, roasted garlic scalloped potatoes or wild rice pilaf

Filet Mignon-7oz.	Top Sirloin-9oz.	Hand-Cut Ribeye-16oz.
Cabernet Sauce	Onion Hay	Herb Butter
21.95	15.95	20.95

Combination Plates

Served with a cup of soup or garden salad, fresh vegetables and choice of baked potato, French fries, buttermilk chive mashed potatoes, roasted garlic scalloped potatoes or wild rice pilaf

Charbroiled Sirloin Steak and Lodge Walleye - 16.50
Charbroiled Sirloin Steak and Shrimp Scampi or Lemon Grass Shrimp - 16.95

Menu Sampler - Prices and menu subject to change.

Offer validity is governed by the Rules of Use and excludes defined holidays. Offers are not valid with other discount offers, unless specified. Coupons void if purchased, sold or bartered. Discounts exclude tax, tip and/or alcohol, where applicable. Tipping should be 15% to 20% of the total bill before discount.

Crystal Bistro
Finest Mediterranean & Continental Restaurant

Card No. 40

Up To $13.00 Value

Welcome to Crystal Bistro, offering the finest in Afghan cuisine. Family owned & operated, we proudly feature our authentic family recipes. Sample our delicious kabobs, pastas & tender organic lamb. Beer & wine available to compliment your meal. Open for lunch & dinner, closed Mondays.

*E*njoy one complimentary DINNER ENTREE when a second DINNER ENTREE of equal or greater value is purchased.

Dine in only

valid any evening

Reservations recommended

6408 Bass Lake Rd., Crystal, MN (763)533-4900

00701793

Kabobs
All Kabobs marinated with garlic, onions & herbs. Served with vegetables and basmati rice.

Lamb Kabob $13.95
Beef or chicken Kabob $12.95

Kofta Kabob
Freshly grounded beef char broiled mixed with spices. $11.95

Mixed Grill
Shrimp, chicken, and beef $14.95

Pasta

Mantu
Steamed pastry shells stuffed with ground beef, onions, and mixed afghani spices. Topped off with tomato, yogurt, and zety garlic sauce. $12.95

Avshak
Homemade steamed pasta filled with fresh chopped sautéed spinach and green onions. Topped off with tomato, yogurt, and garlic sauce. $12.95

Entrees

Kabli Palaw
Choice of sautéed lamb or chicken with basmati rice. Topped off with julienne of carrots, raisons & sliced almonds with chicken $12.95

Chicken Curry
Boneless chicken in a curry sauce served on basmati rice with stewed potatoes. $11.95

Lamp chops
Thress lightly seasoned lamb chops char broiled. $18.95

Menu Sampler - Prices and menu subject to change.

Offer validity is governed by the Rules of Use and excludes defined holidays. Offers are not valid with other discount offers, unless specified. Coupons void if purchased, sold or bartered. Discounts exclude tax, tip and/or alcohol, where applicable. Tipping should be 15% to 20% of the total bill before discount.

C48

Nacho Mama's

Card No. 39

Up to $24.00 Value

REPEAT SAVINGS

*E*njoy one complimentary LUNCH OR DINNER ENTREE when a second LUNCH OR DINNER ENTREE of equal or greater value is purchased.

valid anytime

312 S. Main St., Stillwater, MN (651)439-9544

00701702

Visit us in downtown Stillwater for delicious Mexican cuisine with some twists! You'll love our warm dinner atmosphere. Enjoy any one of our entrees including a traditional chimichanga or unusual pulled BBQ pork burrito. See you soon!

Pulled BBQ Pork Burrito $13
Stuffed with pulled pork, beans, and cheese then grilled and basted with Tequilla bbq sauce.

Avocado and Arugula Salad $11
with fresh spinach and papaya then drizzled with honey-lime vinaigrette.

Beef Tenderloin $24
Two four ounce tenderloin steaks wrapped with jalapeño bacon and served with a roasted red pepper and roasted yellow pepper puree.

Carna Asada with Blackened Corn $16
grilled skirt steak sliced and served with pico and tortillas

Stuffed Chorizo Flank Steak Roulade $17
with roasted red pepper-garlic coulis

Sea Bass Stuffed with Tequilla-Lime Shrimp $23
topped with chili-lime butter and pico de Gallo

Tilapia Fillet and Shrimp $22
fire roasted, and filled with black bean and corn salsa then baked in a banana leaf.

Menu Sampler - Prices and menu subject to change.

Offer validity is governed by the Rules of Use and excludes defined holidays. Offers are not valid with other discount offers, unless specified. Coupons void if purchased, sold or bartered. Discounts exclude tax, tip and/or alcohol, where applicable. Tipping should be 15% to 20% of the total bill before discount.

Lombard's

Card No. 34

Up to $19.00 Value

www.selectminneapolis.com

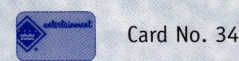

Come visit Lombard's Restaurant located in the Crowne Plaza Minneapolis North. We offer a wide variety of entrees. We also have an extensive beer & wine list.

Enjoy one complimentary DINNER ENTREE when a second DINNER ENTREE of equal or greater value is purchased.

Dine in only; Brunch excluded; Specials excluded

valid any evening

Reservations recommended

2200 Freeway Blvd., Brooklyn Ctr., MN (763)566-8000

00672082

Sandwiches and Wraps

Lombard's Half-Pound Burger: A thick and Juicy Half-Pound Burger Served with Lettuce, Tomato and Onions on a Fresh Baked Bun. $6.99 / 7.29 with cheese.

New Orleans Wrap: Cajun Spiced Chicken, Canadian bacon, Pepper Cheese and Onions. Served in a Red Pepper Wrap. $7.99

Chicken Salad Croissant: Fresh Baked Croissant stuffed with our Homemade Chicken Salad. $6.99

Entrees

Pasta Bella: Linguini Pasta, Bermuda Onion, Tomato, Ripe Olive and Artichoke Hearts Sautéed with fresh herbs, Garlic, White Wine and Olive Oil. $7.99

Walleye Almondine: Sautéed Filet of Walleye topped with an Almond Buerre Blanc. served with Wild Rice. $15.99

Salmon Dill: A 6-Ounce Salmon Filet Sautéed to perfection topped with a Dill Chardonnay Sauce served with a Rice Medley. $15.99

Dijon Chicken: Sautéed Chicken Breast topped with Garlic Herbed Bread crumbs served with a Shaker Sauce. $14.99

Pork Tenderloin: Sautéed and Cooked to perfection. Topped with a Rosemary Bordelaise Sauce. $15.99

New York: A 10-ounce New York Steak Grilled to the temperature of your liking topped with a Sundried Tomato Butter. $25.99

Menu Sampler - Prices and menu subject to change.

Offer validity is governed by the Rules of Use and excludes defined holidays. Offers are not valid with other discount offers, unless specified. Coupons void if purchased, sold or bartered. Discounts exclude tax, tip and/or alcohol, where applicable. Tipping should be 15% to 20% of the total bill before discount.

C46

Card No. 46

Little Tel-Aviv
Café & Restaurant
www.LittleTelAviv.com

REPEAT SAVINGS

Up To **$15.00** Value

*E*njoy one complimentary ENTREE when a second ENTREE of equal or greater value is purchased.

valid anytime

3238 W. Lake St. (Calhoun Village), Minneapolis, MN
(612) 929-1111

Come in & experience the taste of Israel & Morocco in a warm & inviting setting. We look forward to seeing you soon. Conveniently located in Calhoun Village.

00568933

Entrees

All entrees are served with a small dinner salad and crispy, flavored flat bread sticks.

Israeli Platter - Select four Deli Salads, served with a warm pita bread. — 8.75

Moroccan-Style Mahi Mahi - Sautéed with garlic, red bell pepper, fresh cilantro, and tomato. Served with warm garbanzo beans. — 14.95

Moroccan Couscous - Covered with marinara and topped with homemade walleye cakes. — 14.25

Tuna Steak - Grilled 8oz. tuna steak. Served with a baked potato, and roasted vegetables. — 17.25

Israeli-Style Walleye - Fillet of walleye stuffed with fresh herbs, mushrooms, and onions. Served on a bed of pasta and covered with a rich creamy spinach sauce. — 14.95

Fish and Chips - Crispy fried walleye. Served with French fries. — 12.95

Menu Sampler - Prices and menu subject to change.

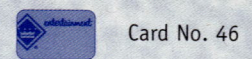

Offer validity is governed by the Rules of Use and excludes defined holidays. Offers are not valid with other discount offers, unless specified. Coupons void if purchased, sold or bartered. Discounts exclude tax, tip and/or alcohol, where applicable. Tipping should be 15% to 20% of the total bill before discount.

DAKOTA COUNTY STEAKHOUSE

Card No. 80

Up To $19.00 Value

REPEAT SAVINGS

*E*njoy one complimentary LUNCH OR DINNER ENTREE when a second LUNCH OR DINNER ENTREE of equal or greater value is purchased.

Brunch excluded

valid anytime

14201 Nicollet Ave. (inside Holiday Inn of Burnsville), Burnsville, MN (952)435-2100

00594786

Located at County Rd. 42 & Hwy. 35 in the Holiday Inn of Burnsville, Dakota County Steakhouse offers delicious food in a quiet, comfortable atmosphere. Featuring BBQ ribs, prime rib, chicken & seafood. On the lighter side, enjoy some soup, a refreshing salad or a sandwich for lunch.

Sandwiches

»» Country Club House ««
Stacked High with Grilled Chicken, Sliced Smoked Ham, Cheddar Cheese, Bacon, Lettuce, Tomato and Mayo
Served on your choice of Bread with French Fries
$8.50

Buck Hill Burger
Generous 1/2 Pound Burger Grilled with Bacon, Mushrooms, and your choice of Swiss or Cheddar Cheese
Served on a Pub Bun with French Fries
$7.95

»» Prime Rib Sandwich ««
A 6oz. Cut of Prime with Sautéed Mushrooms and Pepper Jack Cheese
Served on a Hoagie Bun with French Fries
$10.95

Specialties

Filet Mignon
The Most Tender Steak of All (8oz)
$21.95

Steak Fajita
10 Ounce Gilled Sirloin Topped with Onions, Peppers, Black Olives and Pepper Jack Cheese
$15.95

»» Barbecued Baby Back Ribs ««
Our Famous Rack of Tender Baby Back Ribs, Slow Roasted and Grilled with Our Special BBQ Sauce
$16.95

Kings Walleye Pike
A Minnesota Favorite!
Sautéed with Toasted Almonds or Golden Deep Fried
$14.95

Pastas

Seafood Alfredo
Tender Bow Tie Pasta Tossed with Shrimp, Scallops and Our Creamy Alfredo Sauce
$13.95

Menu Sampler - Prices and menu subject to change.

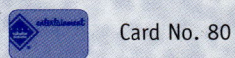

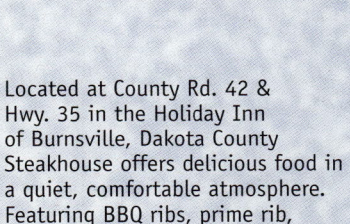

Offer validity is governed by the Rules of Use and excludes defined holidays. Offers are not valid with other discount offers, unless specified. Coupons void if purchased, sold or bartered. Discounts exclude tax, tip and/or alcohol, where applicable. Tipping should be 15% to 20% of the total bill before discount.

CORNELL'S

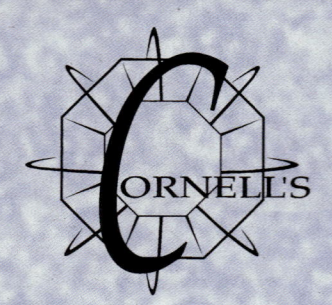

Card No. 114

Up To $15.00 Value

REPEAT SAVINGS

Cornell's is a beautiful atrium restaurant set in a tropical atmosphere. Dine amidst the foliage & water fountains in a casual setting. Our menu features a variety of items suiting the simple to the most sophisticated palates. Enjoy.

*E*njoy one complimentary LUNCH OR DINNER ENTREE when a second LUNCH OR DINNER ENTREE of equal or greater value is purchased.

valid anytime

425 S. 7th St. (Minneapolis Hilton), **Minneapolis, MN**
(612)333-3111

00396890

Sandwiches

Hot Turkey Sandwich
Fresh roast turkey breast served open faced on sourdough bread with mashed potatoes smothered with turkey gravy. $7.25

Chicken Tacos
Spiced chicken, onion, and cilantro in warm tortilla shell. Served with lettuce, fresh roasted salsa, sour cream and red chili rice. $7.95

Pasta

Farfalle
Bowtie pasta tossed with tomato, fresh basil, mushrooms and garlic. Finished with a rich cream sauce. $8.95

Cajun Pasta
Spicy Andouille sausage, and grilled chicken breast sauteed with julienne peppers, onions and tomatoes. Tossed with tomato cream sauce. $9.95

Entrees

Bacon Wrapped Stuffed Shrimp
Five jumbo shrimp stuffed with monterey jack cheese and wrapped with bacon. Served with vegetable of the day and choice of potato. $13.95

Walleye
Served the way you like it, blackened, broiled or lemon peppered. $13.95

Filet of Salmon
Served the way you like it. Grilled, blackened, or lemon peppered. With vegetable of the day and choice of potato. $13.95

Gourmet Pizza

BBQ Chicken Pizza
Grilled chicken, BBQ sauce, red onion and mozzarella cheese.
Small $7.95
Large $13.95

Menu Sampler - Prices and menu subject to change.

Offer validity is governed by the Rules of Use and excludes defined holidays. Offers are not valid with other discount offers, unless specified. Coupons void if purchased, sold or bartered. Discounts exclude tax, tip and/or alcohol, where applicable. Tipping should be 15% to 20% of the total bill before discount.

WinterGreens
GOLF • GRILL • DINING

Card No. 66

Up To $20.00 Value

*E*njoy one complimentary DINNER ENTREE when a second DINNER ENTREE of equal or greater value is purchased.

valid any evening

306 Credit Union Dr., Isanti, MN (763)444-8422

00588574

Relax & unwind in our casual Northwood¿s dining room. Serving certified Angus steaks, seafood & hearty pastas in a smoke free environment. Full bar & wine list available. Located in Isanti, 30 mi. N. of the cities on Hwy. 65.

From the Grill

12-oz. Top Sirloin 16.99
Grilled Certified Angus Beef® sirloin steak cooked just the way you like it, our customers' favorite.

20-oz. Ribeye 21.99
Grilled Certified Angus Beef® bone-in rib eye served your way.

Pork Porterhouse Chop 11.99
Grilled pork porterhouse chop served with a side of sweet pork sauce.

Salmon 13.99
Grilled salmon fillet served with a side of lemon butter sauce.

Pasta Entrées

Chicken Parmigiana 12.99
Spaghetti with breaded chicken topped with tomato sauce, Mozzarella and Parmesan cheeses.

Garlic Shrimp & Linguini 13.99
Pasta topped with shrimp, sautéed in garlic butter, and sprinkled with Parmesan cheese and roma tomatoes.

Pasta Pollo 12.99
Pasta topped wtih grilled chicken & broccoli florets in a Pesto & Parmesan sauce.

Menu Sampler - Prices and menu subject to change.

Offer validity is governed by the Rules of Use and excludes defined holidays. Offers are not valid with other discount offers, unless specified. Coupons void if purchased, sold or bartered. Discounts exclude tax, tip and/or alcohol, where applicable. Tipping should be 15% to 20% of the total bill before discount.

ST. PETERSBURG
RESTAURANT AND VODKA BAR

Card No. 47

Up To **$19.00** Value

www.myvodkabar.com

With our own exquisite menu selections, full bar & nearly 100 vodkas, St. Petersburg is the place for fine dining anytime. And with our extensive facilities, it's the place for your wedding, holiday party or special event. We cordially invite you to experience traditional Russian hospitality, excellent choice of dishes & our extensive selection of Russian vodka.

*E*njoy one complimentary LUNCH OR DINNER ENTREE when a second LUNCH OR DINNER ENTREE of equal or greater value is purchased.

Specials excluded; Dining room only; Special events excluded

valid anytime

Not valid with any other discount offer

3610 France Ave. N., Robbinsdale, MN (763)587-1787

00523500

Appetizers

Seafood Blintzes
Crepes with salmon and crab filling, topped with shrimp and lobster sauce $9

Roasted Eggplant Dip
Roasted eggplant with garlic aioli and grilled pita bread $6

Main Course

Salmon Romanoff
Chablis poached Norwegian Salmon fillet topped with cream-dill sauce. Served with rice pilaf and vegetables du Jour $17

Walleye St. Petersburg
Sautéed walleye fillet with shrimp, scallops and tomato-lobster coulis. Served with rice pilaf and vegetables du Jour $18

Fillet Mignon
Fillet Mignon, demi glace, potato nest and vegetables du Juor $25

Cherry Chicken
Marinated grilled chicken breast, vodka cherry demi glace. Served with rice pilaf and vegetables du Jour $14

Roast Duck with Apples
Crispy, half duck with cranberry glaze, rice pilaf and roasted apples $18

Menu Sampler - Prices and menu subject to change.

Offer validity is governed by the Rules of Use and excludes defined holidays. Offers are not valid with other discount offers, unless specified. Coupons void if purchased, sold or bartered. Discounts exclude tax, tip and/or alcohol, where applicable. Tipping should be 15% to 20% of the total bill before discount.

PLAYOFFS
SPORTS BAR & GRILL

Card No. 105

REPEAT SAVINGS

Up To **$17.00** Value

*E*njoy one complimentary ENTREE when a second ENTREE of equal or greater value is purchased.

valid anytime

2 River Bend Place, Chaska, MN (952)466-3323

00631297

Come to Playoffs for championship food, fun & good times! Everything on the menu is prepared from scratch. The eclectic menu features something for everyone - from Blackened Mahi Mahi to pastas, steaks, burgers, wraps, sandwiches & more. We offer full bar service & have 10 TVs for the game! Children's menu available. Serving breakfast, lunch & dinner.

ENTREES

BLACKENED MAHI MAHI Dusted in our homemade Cajun spice braised and served with seven spice butter sauce. $16.95

CHICKEN TORTELLINI Tortellini in a mushroom cream sauce with sautéed chicken breast, sprinkled with Parmesan cheese. $11.95

ASIAN CHICKEN PASTA Tender chicken breast sautéed in olive oil with garlic, onions, ginger, teriyaki and broccoli topped with parmesan. $11.95

SANDWICHES

WALLEYE SANDWICH Deep fried walleye served on a hoagie bun. $8.95

PHILLY CHEESE STEAK Thinly sliced roast beef with sautéed green peppers, onions and mushrooms, all under melted Swiss cheese. $8.95

BURGERS

PLAYOFF BURGER Charbroiled beef patty with American and Swiss cheeses, bacon, lettuce, onions, mushrooms and of course, onion rings and French fries. $8.95

Menu Sampler - Prices and menu subject to change.

Offer validity is governed by the Rules of Use and excludes defined holidays. Offers are not valid with other discount offers, unless specified. Coupons void if purchased, sold or bartered. Discounts exclude tax, tip and/or alcohol, where applicable. Tipping should be 15% to 20% of the total bill before discount.

PINE grille STREET

Card No. 20

Up to $16.00 Value

REPEAT SAVINGS

Visit Pine Street Grille in the historic Chaska Mill Building. Whether your enjoying a dinner by the fireplace or on the deck, this is a great place to relax & get together with your friends & family. Banquet facilities available.

*E*njoy one complimentary LUNCH OR DINNER ENTREE when a second LUNCH OR DINNER ENTREE of equal or greater value is purchased.

valid anytime

500 Pine St., Ste. 101, Chaska, MN (952)368-9222

00691394

APPETIZERS

Bruschetta
Our grilled French bread topped with tomatoes, basil, garlic, and parmasean cheese, served with a balsamic sauce
$6

Deep Fried Calamari
Crispy, breaded fried calamari served with a creamy lemon mayonnaise
Small=$6 Large=$10

SALADS

Chinese Chicken Salad
Grilled marinated chicken with Asian vegetables served on a bed of Napa cabbage and tossed with a sesame, ginger, and soy vinaigrette
$11

PASTA

Tortellini
Cheese stuffed tortellini pasta with sun dried tomatoes and a medley of mushrooms in a cheesy white sauce
$11

ENTREES

Shepherds Pie
a generous portion of homemade beef stew topped with seasoned mashed potatoes and baked to a golden brown
$14

12 oz Ribeye with Sauteed Mushrooms
tender and smothered in a medley of juicy mushrooms
$18

SANDWICHES

Grilled Chicken Sandwich
Grilled marinated chicken breast with avocado, tomato, lettuce, and Dijon mayonnaise on ciabiatta
$8

Grilled Vegetable Sandwich
Grilled marinated portabella mushroom, roasted red bell pepper, grilled red onion, and herbed feta cheese on ciabiatta bread
$7

Menu Sampler - Prices and menu subject to change.

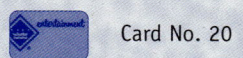

Offer validity is governed by the Rules of Use and excludes defined holidays. Offers are not valid with other discount offers, unless specified. Coupons void if purchased, sold or bartered. Discounts exclude tax, tip and/or alcohol, where applicable. Tipping should be 15% to 20% of the total bill before discount.

Nic's Nicollet

www.millenium-hotels.com

Card No. 13

REPEAT SAVINGS

Up To $19.00 Value

*E*njoy one complimentary LUNCH OR DINNER ENTREE when a second LUNCH OR DINNER ENTREE of equal or greater value is purchased.

Sunday Brunch included

valid anytime

1313 Nicollet Mall, Minneapolis, MN (612)359-2260

00507053

Spectacular sixteen foot Soup & Salad Bar for lunch & dinner. For lunch, choose from a wide selection of sandwiches & our featured Entree's. For dinner, choose from our selection of sandwiches, choice beef & fresh seafood complemented by our unique wine list.

Starters

Smoked Salmon and Artichoke Dip — 9
A warm blend of smoked salmon, artichoke hearts and parmesan cheese served in a sourdough boulie with sliced baguette

Salads

Salad Bar — 8
Something for everyone on our salad bar: crisp greens, fresh salad toppings, and a selection of salads and soups

Entrees

Chicken Oscar — 16
Sautéed chicken breast topped with snow crabmeat, asparagus and sauce hollandaise

Nic's Delmonico Steak — 21
Grilled new york strip basted with butter and topped with an onion ring accompanied by a salmon stuffed portabella mushroom cap

Friday Night Fish Fry — 11
Beer battered cod
French fries
Coleslaw
All you care to eat
Includes our salad bar

Saturday Night Prime Rib
Roast prime rib of beef au jus
Baked potato
Fresh vegetable
Includes our salad bar
Kings cut — 16
Queens cut — 13

Menu Sampler - Prices and menu subject to change.

Offer validity is governed by the Rules of Use and excludes defined holidays. Offers are not valid with other discount offers, unless specified. Coupons void if purchased, sold or bartered. Discounts exclude tax, tip and/or alcohol, where applicable. Tipping should be 15% to 20% of the total bill before discount.

C38

McGuires

Card No. 45

Up To **$19.00** Value

Terrific food served daily in the upscale, casual ambience of "historic" McGuires, a local landmark & a great place for excellent food, cocktails & a fun outdoor patio. Come in & enjoy our evening specials. Entertainment members also recieve a free dessert of your choice - just show your Entertainment card!

Enjoy one complimentary DINNER ENTREE when a second DINNER ENTREE of equal or greater value is purchased.

Dine in only; Specials excluded; Brunch included

valid any evening

1201 W. County Rd. E. (located between Snelling & Lexington), **Arden Hills, MN (651)636-4123**

00659491

Salads

Cobb Salad – A Delicious Blend of Fresh, Mixed Greens Layered with Black Olives, Boiled Eggs, Guacamole, Diced Tomatoes, Bacon Bits, and Crumbled Bleu Cheese. *$8.99*

FROM THE GRILL

Orange Chipotle Chicken – An 8 oz. Chicken Breast Broiled and Basted with Our Own Orange-Chipotle BBQ Sauce. Not too spicy, Just Enough to Add a Little Zing. *$14.99*

McGuire's Top Sirloin Special – USDA Choice Cuts of Top Butt Sirloin; Available in Three Sizes, All Grilled to Your Preference; Prepared Three Styles: *Special* (with Sautéed Onions and Bell Peppers) or Prepared *Traditional* (with Mushrooms and Onions) or *Al Forno* (Rubbed with Garlic, Thyme, Cracked Black Pepper and Kosher Salt).

    8 Ounce Petite……………………………………..$15.49
    10 Ounce Classic………………………………….$16.99
    16 Ounce King……………………………………..$18.99

Combination Entrees

Steak and Lobster – 8 oz. USDA Choice 'Petite' Top Sirloin Prepared Three styles *Special* (with Sautéed Onions and Bells) or Prepared *Traditional* (with Mushrooms and Onions) or *Al Forno* (Rubbed with Garlic, Thyme Cracked Black Pepper and Kosher Salt) Grilled to Your Preference and a Whole *8oz.* Lobster Tail Split and) Oven Broiled. Served with Lemon and Drawn Butter. *$27.99*

From The Sea

Sherried Scallops – Sea Scallops Sautéed with Onion and Garlic. Deglazed with White Wine and Finished in a Subtle Cream Sauce. Served with **PITA BREAD**. *$18.99*

Menu Sampler - Prices and menu subject to change.

Offer validity is governed by the Rules of Use and excludes defined holidays. Offers are not valid with other discount offers, unless specified. Coupons void if purchased, sold or bartered. Discounts exclude tax, tip and/or alcohol, where applicable. Tipping should be 15% to 20% of the total bill before discount.

Mairin's Table

Neighborhood Bistro

Card No. 49

Up To $19.00 Value

Join us at Mairin's Table, located in N.E. Minneapolis, for delightful cuisine & atmosphere. Savor our smoked salmon stuffed mushrooms as an appetizer, before any of our delicious main courses.

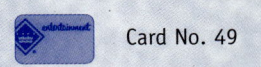

*E*njoy one complimentary LUNCH OR DINNER ENTREE when a second LUNCH OR DINNER ENTREE of equal or greater value is purchased.

valid anytime

23 N.E. 4th St., Minneapolis, MN (612)746-4272

00693264

Sandwiches

French Dip   9
Crusty bread and tender beef served with sautéed peppers and onions au jus.

BLT   8
Jalapeno smoked bacon, lettuce, and tomato served on your choice of sour dough or whole grain bread.

Main Courses

Portabella Pomedoro (Vegetarian)   **13**
Grilled portabella mushrooms in red sauce, served on fettuccine.

Shrimp and Scallops   18
Bay shrimp and sea scallops sautéed in a béarnaise cream, served over pasta.

Sirloin   19
Seared and topped with toasted coriander and ginger compound butter.

Moroccan Kabob   10
Skewered Kefta served on couscous with marinated carrots.

Menu Sampler - Prices and menu subject to change.

Offer validity is governed by the Rules of Use and excludes defined holidays. Offers are not valid with other discount offers, unless specified. Coupons void if purchased, sold or bartered. Discounts exclude tax, tip and/or alcohol, where applicable. Tipping should be 15% to 20% of the total bill before discount.

C36

KOY SUSHI

Card No. 26

Up To $17.00 Value

REPEAT SAVINGS

Enjoy one complimentary LUNCH OR DINNER ENTREE when a second LUNCH OR DINNER ENTREE of equal or greater value is purchased.

valid anytime

122 N. 4th St., Minneapolis, MN (612)375-9811

00695415

Savor delicious cold or hot appetizers while we prepare for you our fresh sushi rolls. If sushi is not for you, choose from a variety of delicious entrees - chicken, steak or seafood. Parking is available at the ramp on 2nd Ave. N. & 4th St. N. Visit soon!

CHEF'S ROLLS

SALMON TEMPURA ROLL
Tempura battered salmon and avocado roll, topped with spicy mayo and sweet sauce
$12.00

DRAGON ROLL
Cooked tuna, masago and spicy mayo inside, topped with unagi and avocado
$13.00

HIGH ROLLER
Spicy crab, cucumber and unagi, topped with salmon and avocado and mixed with a little bit of crunchy
$17.00

CRUNCHY ROLL
Shrimp tempura, tobiko, crunchy tempura and masago
$10.00

RAINBOW ROLL
California roll inside, topped with tuna, salmon and yellowtail
$12.00

KING ROLL
California roll inside, topped with unagi and avocado
$12.00

Menu Sampler - Prices and menu subject to change.

Offer validity is governed by the Rules of Use and excludes defined holidays. Offers are not valid with other discount offers, unless specified. Coupons void if purchased, sold or bartered. Discounts exclude tax, tip and/or alcohol, where applicable. Tipping should be 15% to 20% of the total bill before discount.

C35

Kay's Wine Bar & Bistro

Card No. 15

REPEAT SAVINGS — Up To $20.00 Value

Experience the first "chef driven" restaurant in Maple Grove, a perfect alternative to the typical chain restaurant. We offer carefully selected wines, all available by the glass, to compliment our bistro menu which changes bi-weekly.

*E*njoy one complimentary DINNER ENTREE when a second DINNER ENTREE of equal or greater value is purchased.

Dine in only

valid any evening

7924 Main St. N., Maple Grove, MN (763)420-5069

00687781

Small Plates and Starters

Trio of Crostini: $5
White Bean & Rosemary
Roasted Tomato & Caramelized Onion
Artichoke & Aged Gouda

Black Pepper & Cognac Shrimp $6

Entrees

Penne al Telefono $9

Creole Gulf Shrimp, Andouille Sausage Dirty Rice $14

Duroc Pork Rib Chop, Caramelized Onion Pan Sauce, $16
Applewood Smoked Bacon & Aged Cheddar Grits,
Sautéed Fresh Green Beans

Menu Sampler - Prices and menu subject to change.

Offer validity is governed by the Rules of Use and excludes defined holidays. Offers are not valid with other discount offers, unless specified. Coupons void if purchased, sold or bartered. Discounts exclude tax, tip and/or alcohol, where applicable. Tipping should be 15% to 20% of the total bill before discount.

Harmony's

Card No. 58

Up To $20.00 Value

REPEAT SAVINGS

The Minneapolis Hilton & Towers is located in the heart of downtown Minneapolis, connected via skyway to the Minneapolis Convention Center, Orchestra Hall & downtown shopping attractions. Harmony's offers casual dining in a European sidewalk atmosphere. Join us for a wonderful meal, we look forward to serving you.

*E*njoy one complimentary DINNER ENTREE when a second DINNER ENTREE of equal or greater value is purchased.

valid any evening

1001 Marquette Ave. (Minneapolis Hilton), **Minneapolis, MN (612)397-4927**

00510546

PASTA

Lobster Ravioli — 15.00
With Jumbo Sea Scallops and Lobster Cream and Julienne of Fresh Basil

Grilled Chicken with Penne — 12.00
Tender Pieces of Chicken Breast in a Roasted Red Pepper Coulis, With Fresh Vegetables

ENTRÉES

Sautéed Walleye with Rice Pilaf and Seasonal Vegetables — 15.50

Apple Rosemary Roast Pork Loin — 14.75
Tender Slices of Centercut Roast with Port Demi-Glacé served with Potatoes Dauphinois.

Classic Chicken Oscar — 18.00
Sautéed Chicken Breast with Fresh Asparagus, Crab Meat and Hollandaise Sauce Served with Fresh Vegetable and Potatoes Dauphinois

Tournedos of Beef — 20.00
Twin 4 oz. Filets of Beef served with Béarnaise Sauce and Potato Dauphinois

Breast of Duck — 14.50
Plump, moist and fire-roasted with a Cranberry-Orange Glaze Served with Rice Pilaf

Menu Sampler - Prices and menu subject to change.

Offer validity is governed by the Rules of Use and excludes defined holidays. Offers are not valid with other discount offers, unless specified. Coupons void if purchased, sold or bartered. Discounts exclude tax, tip and/or alcohol, where applicable. Tipping should be 15% to 20% of the total bill before discount.

· GRAND GRILL ·
www.kahler.com

The Grand Grill offers extensive breakfast, lunch, and dinner menus. Fare ranges from light and casual to delicious dinner entrees. Hours are M-F 6:30 a.m.-9:00 p.m. and Sat-Sun 7:00 a.m.-9:00 p.m.

Card No. 68

Up To $17.00 Value

REPEAT SAVINGS

*E*njoy one complimentary LUNCH OR DINNER ENTREE when a second LUNCH OR DINNER ENTREE of equal or greater value is purchased.

valid anytime

20 2nd Ave. SW (Kahler Grand Hotel), **Rochester, MN**
(507) 280-6200

00455297

SANDWICHES

THE GRAND GRILL WALLEYE . $8.95
A light and crispy battered filet topped with cheddar cheese on a grilled kaiser bun with lettuce and tomato. A Minnesota favorite!

FRESH ROAST TURKEY $6.95
Hand carved all white turkey on thick bread with redskin mashed potatoes and smothered in rich giblet gravy

VEGGIE SANDWICH ♥ $6.95
Lettuce, tomato, onion, cucumber, fresh basil & baby swiss cheese

♥ indicates a lowfat, low calorie option

DINNER ENTREES

HERB CRUSTED RACK OF PORK $13.95
The prime rib of pork slowly roasted with an herb crust

LEMON PEPPER SHRIMP . . . $15.95
Tender plump shrimp sauteed in garlic butter and tossed with lemon pepper seasoning

NORTH ATLANTIC SALMON . . $14.95
Broiled salmon filet with a fresh dill cream sauce

PASTABILITIES

CHICKEN PARMESAN $9.95
A lightly breaded breast of chicken topped with a zesty tomato sauce and parmesan cheese, served on a bed of spaghetti

Menu Sampler - Prices and menu subject to change.

Offer validity is governed by the Rules of Use and excludes defined holidays. Offers are not valid with other discount offers, unless specified. Coupons void if purchased, sold or bartered. Discounts exclude tax, tip and/or alcohol, where applicable. Tipping should be 15% to 20% of the total bill before discount.

C32

DASHEN ETHIOPIAN RESTAURANT & BAR

Card No. 87

Up To $12.00 Value
REPEAT SAVINGS

Come experience the taste of Ethiopia. Over 40 delicious dishes to choose from. We have an extensive vegetarian menu & full bar. In addition to street parking, we have a lot in the back for your convenience.

*E*njoy one complimentary LUNCH OR DINNER ENTREE when a second LUNCH OR DINNER ENTREE of equal or greater value is purchased.

valid anytime

2713 E. Lake St., Minneapolis, MN (612)724-8868

00622207

Vegetarian

| የአተር ክክ | Yater Kik | $ 7.95 |

Yellow split peas cooked with fresh garlic, ginger, onion, & curry sauce.

| ጥቅል ጎመን | Tikel Gommen | $ 8.25 |

A combination of potatoes with cabbage, carrot, onion, pepper, fresh garlic, mild curry & our house spice.

| ጎመን | Gommen | $ 8.50 |

Collard Green, onions, fresh garlic, vegetable oil & jalapenos.

Main Dish

| ልዩ ጥብስ | Leyu Tibs | $ 10.95 |

Cubes of lamb, cooked with onions & seasoned butter.

| ዶሮ ወጥ | Doro Wat | $ 8.95 |

Chicken drumstick & thigh, cooked in 'Berbere' & onion sauce, served with cheese & boiled egg.

| ዓሣ ጉላሽ | Asa Gulash | $ 9.95 |

Chunks of filet fish cooked with onion, tomato, garlic and 'Awaze' sauce.

| ጎመን በሲጋ | Gommen Be Siga | $ 9.95 |

Spinach & beef cooked with butter, garlic, onion, & green pepper.

Menu Sampler - Prices and menu subject to change.

Offer validity is governed by the Rules of Use and excludes defined holidays. Offers are not valid with other discount offers, unless specified. Coupons void if purchased, sold or bartered. Discounts exclude tax, tip and/or alcohol, where applicable. Tipping should be 15% to 20% of the total bill before discount.

C31

Guaranteed Best Rate*

Book at www.entertainment.com/travel or call 1-800-50-HOTEL

HOTEL MONACO
333 Saint Charles Ave, New Orleans.
HOTEL MONTELEONE
214 Royal St, New Orleans.
HOTEL PROVINCIAL
1024 Chartres St, New Orleans.
HYATT REGENCY NEW ORLEANS
Poydras At Loyola Avenue, New Orleans.
IBERVILLE SUITES
910 Iberville St, New Orleans.
LA QUINTA INN & STES DOWNTOWN
301 Camp St, New Orleans.
LE PAVILLON HOTEL
833 Poydras St, New Orleans.
MAISON DUPUY
1001 Toulouse St, New Orleans.
PARC ST. CHARLES
500 Saint Charles Ave, New Orleans.
QUEEN & CRESCENT HOTEL
344 Camp St, New Orleans.
RAMADA PLAZA INN ON BOURBON
541 Bourbon St, New Orleans.
ROYAL ST. CHARLES HOTEL
135 Saint Charles Ave, New Orleans.
SHERATON NEW ORLEANS
500 Canal St, New Orleans.
ST LOUIS HOTEL
730 Bienville St, New Orleans.
THE RITZ-CARLTON NEW ORLEANS
921 Canal St, New Orleans.

Maine

For this state's listings go to entertainment.com/travel

Maryland

Annapolis

DAYS INN & SUITES ANNAPOLIS
2451 Riva Rd, Annapolis.
HISTORIC INNS OF ANNAPOLIS
58 State Cir, Annapolis.
THE O'CALLAGHAN HOTEL
174 West St, Annapolis.

Baltimore

BEST INN BALTIMORE
6510 Frankford Ave, Baltimore.
BROOKSHIRE SUITES
120 E Lombard St, Baltimore.
DAYS INN INNER HARBOR
100 Hopkins Pl, Baltimore.
MOUNT VERNON HOTEL
24 W Franklin St, Baltimore.
PEABODY COURT A CLARION HOTEL
612 Cathedral St, Baltimore.
RADISSON HOTEL AT CROSS KEYS
100 Village Sq, Baltimore.
RADISSON PLAZA LORD BALTIMORE
20 W Baltimore St, Baltimore.
THE HARBOR COURT HOTEL
550 Light St, Baltimore.
TREMONT PLAZA
222 Saint Paul St, Baltimore.
WYNDHAM BALTIMORE - INNER HARBOR
101 W Fayette St, Baltimore.

Cheverly

COMFORT INN CAPITOL GATEWAY
6205 Annapolis Rd, Hyattsville.

Shop & Book more hotels at entertainment.com/travel

HOWARD JOHNSON CHEVERLY
5811 Annapolis Rd, Hyattsville.
RAMADA INN NEW CARROLLTON/DC AREA
8500 Annapolis Rd, Hyattsville.

Linthicum Heights

COMFORT SUITES BWI AIRPORT
815 Elkridge Landing Rd, Linthicum Heights.
HAMPTON INN BWI/BALTIMORE
829 Elkridge Landing Rd, Linthicum Heights.
MICROTEL INN & SUITES BWI
1170 Winterson Rd, Linthicum Heights.

Ocean City

CAROUSEL RESORT HOTEL & CONDOS
11700 Coastal Hwy, Ocean City.
CLARION RESORT FONTAINEBLEAU
10100 Coastal Hwy, Ocean City.
PRINCESS BAYSIDE RESORT
4801 Coastal Hwy, Ocean City.

Massachusetts

Boston

BEST WESTERN ROUNDHOUSE SUITES
891 Massachusetts Ave, Boston.
BOSTON OMNI PARKER HOUSE HOTEL
60 School St, Boston.
BOSTON PARK PLAZA HOTEL
64 Arlington St, Boston.
CLUB QUARTERS
161 Devonshire St, Boston.
COPLEY SQUARE HOTEL
47 Huntington Ave, Boston.
HAMPTON INN & SUITES BOSTON
811 Massachusetts Ave, Boston.
JURYS BOSTON HOTEL
350 Stuart St, Boston.
MIDTOWN HOTEL
220 Huntington Ave, Boston.
RAMADA INN BOSTON
800 William T Morrissey Blvd, Boston.
RADISSON HOTEL BOSTON
200 Stuart St, Boston.
THE COLONNADE
120 Huntington Ave, Boston.
THE LANGHAM BOSTON
250 Franklin St, Boston.

Cambridge

BEST WESTERN HOTEL TRIA
220 Alewife Brook Pkwy, Cambridge.
HYATT REGENCY CAMBRIDGE
575 Memorial Dr, Cambridge.
RADISSON HOTEL CAMBRIDGE
777 Memorial Dr, Cambridge.

Revere

COMFORT INN & SUITES BOSTON/AIRPORT
85 American Legion Hwy, Revere.
HAMPTON INN LOGAN AIRPORT
230 Lee Burbank Hwy, Revere.
RODEWAY INN
309 American Legion Hwy, Revere.

Michigan

Detroit

HOTEL PONTCHARTRAIN/ COBO CENTER
2 Washington Blvd, Detroit.
OMNI DETROIT HOTEL AT RIVER PLACE
1000 River Place Dr, Detroit.

E19

You can access **25,000** hotels in over **700** cities. See sample listings above.
Shop and Book more hotels at www.entertainment.com/travel

Guaranteed Best Rate*
More listings online and over the phone!

RESIDENCE INN BY MARRIOTT DETROIT DEARBORN
5777 Southfield Fwy, Detroit.

Wayne County International Airport

BAYMONT INN & SUITES DET APRT
9000 Wickham Rd, Romulus.
FAIRFIELD INN DETROIT AIRPORT
31119 Flynn Dr, Romulus.
QUALITY INN METRO AIRPORT
7600 Merriman Rd, Romulus.

Minnesota

Brooklyn Park

SLEEP INN MINNEAPOLIS ST.PAUL
7011 Northland Cir N, Minneapolis.

Minneapolis

BAYMONT INN & STES BLOOMINGTON
7815 Nicollet Ave S, Minneapolis.
CLARION HOTEL AIRPORT
5151 American Blvd W, Minneapolis.
HOLIDAY INN EXPRESS HTL & STES
225 S 11th St, Minneapolis.
MILLENNIUM HOTEL
1313 Nicollet Ave, Minneapolis.
MINNEAPOLIS HILTON
1001 Marquette Ave, Minneapolis.
RADISSON HOTEL METRODOME
615 Washington Ave Se, Minneapolis.

Minneapolis/St. Paul International Airport

AMERISUITES MALL OF AMERICA
7800 International Dr, Minneapolis.
COMFORT INN AIRPORT
1321 E 78th St, Minneapolis.
COUNTRY INN MALL OF AMERICA
2221 Killebrew Dr, Minneapolis.
DAYS INN MALL OF AMERICA ARPT
1901 Killebrew Dr, Minneapolis.
HOSPITALITY INN & SUITES
1601 American Blvd E, Minneapolis.

Richfield

AMERICINN AIRPORT/MALL OF AMERICA
1200 E 78th St, Minneapolis.

St. Paul

COURTYARD MINNEAPOLIS AIRPORT
1352 Northland Dr, St. Paul.
FAIRFIELD INN & STES MSP ARPT
1330 Northland Dr, St. Paul.
RADISSON CITY CENTER ST PAUL
411 Minnesota St, St. Paul.

Mississippi

Biloxi

CASINO MAGIC BILOXI
195 Beach Blvd, Biloxi.
GULF BEACH RESORT
2428 Beach Blvd, Biloxi.
IMPERIAL PALACE HOTEL & CASINO
850 Bayview Ave, Biloxi.

800-50-HOTEL (6835)
Call & Book 25,000 Hotels!

Missouri

Clayton

CROWNE PLAZA CLAYTON
7750 Carondelet Ave, St. Louis.

Kansas City

BAYMONT INN & SUITES SOUTH
8601 Hillcrest Rd, Kansas City.
BEST WESTERN SEVILLE PLAZA
4309 Main St, Kansas City.
HYATT REGENCY CROWN CENTER
2345 Mcgee St, Kansas City.

Maryland Heights

BAYMONT INN & SUITES WESTPORT
12330 Dorsett Rd, Maryland Heights.
BEST WESTERN WESTPORT
2434 Old Dorsett Rd, Maryland Heights.
DRURY INN & SUITES WESTPORT
12220 Dorsett Rd, Maryland Heights.

St. Louis

ADAM'S MARK ST.LOUIS
315 Chestnut St, St. Louis.
CLUBHOUSE INN & SUITES
1970 Craig Rd, St. Louis.
HILTON ST. LOUIS AT THE BALLPARK
1 S Broadway, St. Louis.
MILLENNIUM HOTEL ST. LOUIS
200 S 4th St, St. Louis.
RADISSON DOWNTOWN ST LOUIS
200 N 4th St, St. Louis.
SHERATON WESTPORT LAKESIDE
191 Westport Plaza Drive, St. Louis.
THE MAYFAIR, A WYNDHAM HOTEL
806 Saint Charles St, St. Louis.

Montana

For this state's listings go to entertainment.com/travel

Nebraska

Omaha

BEST WESTERN SETTLE INN
650 N 109th Ct, Omaha.
CLARION HOTEL WEST
4888 S 118th St, Omaha.
OMAHA EXECUTIVE INN & SUITES
3650 S 72nd Str At 1-80, Omaha.

Nevada

Henderson

SUNSET STATION HOTEL & CASINO
1301 W Sunset Rd, Henderson.

Las Vegas

ALADDIN RESORT & CASINO
3667 Las Vegas Blvd S, Las Vegas.
AMERICAS BEST VALUE INN & STES
167 E Tropicana Ave, Las Vegas.
BALLYS LAS VEGAS
3645 Las Vegas Blvd S, Las Vegas.
BELLAGIO
3600 Las Vegas Blvd S, Las Vegas.
BEST WESTERN MARDI GRAS
3500 Paradise Rd, Las Vegas.
BOARDWALK HOTEL & CASINO
3750 Las Vegas Blvd S, Las Vegas.

Discounts subject to availability.
*See Rebate Rules on page E31-E32 and Program Rules on page E33.

Guaranteed Best Rate*

Book at www.entertainment.com/travel or call 1-800-50-HOTEL

CAESARS PALACE
3570 Las Vegas Blvd S, Las Vegas.

CIRCUS CIRCUS HOTEL & CASINO
2880 Las Vegas Blvd S, Las Vegas.

CLARION HOTEL & SUITES
325 E Flamingo Rd, Las Vegas.

EMERALD SUITES HOTEL
9145 Las Vegas Blvd S, Las Vegas.

EXCALIBUR HOTEL CASINO
3850 Las Vegas Blvd S, Las Vegas.

FLAMINGO LAS VEGAS
3555 Las Vegas Blvd S, Las Vegas.

GOLD COAST HOTEL & CASINO
4000 W Flamingo Rd, Las Vegas.

GOLDEN NUGGET HOTEL & CASINO
129 Fremont St, Las Vegas.

GOLDEN PALM CASINO HOTEL
3111 W Tropicana Ave, Las Vegas.

HARD ROCK HOTEL & CASINO
4455 Paradise Rd, Las Vegas.

HARRAHS HOTEL & CASINO
3475 Las Vegas Blvd S, Las Vegas.

HAWTHORN INN AND SUITES
910 S Boulder Hwy, Henderson.

HILTON LAS VEGAS
3000 Paradise Rd, Las Vegas.

HOTEL SAN REMO CASINO RESORT
115 E Tropicana Ave, Las Vegas.

IMPERIAL PALACE HOTEL AND CASINO
3535 Las Vegas Blvd S, Las Vegas.

LAS VEGAS HILTON
3000 Paradise Rd, Las Vegas.

LUXOR HOTEL AND CASINO
3900 Las Vegas Blvd S, Las Vegas.

MANDALAY BAY RESORT AND CASINO
3950 Las Vegas Blvd S, Las Vegas.

MGM GRAND HOTEL AND CASINO
3799 Las Vegas Blvd S, Las Vegas.

MONTE CARLO RESORT & CASINO
3770 Las Vegas Blvd S, Las Vegas.

MONTELAGO VILLAGE RESORT
30 Strada Di Villaggio, Henderson.

NEW FRONTIER
3120 Las Vegas Blvd S, Las Vegas.

NEW YORK NEW YORK HTL & CASINO
3790 Las Vegas Blvd S, Las Vegas.

PARIS LAS VEGAS
3655 Las Vegas Blvd S, Las Vegas.

PARK PLAZA LADY LUCK
206 N 3rd St, Las Vegas.

RIVIERA HOTEL & CASINO
2901 Las Vegas Blvd S, Las Vegas.

SAHARA HOTEL & CASINO
2535 Las Vegas Blvd S, Las Vegas.

STARDUST RESORT & CASINO
3000 Las Vegas Blvd S, Las Vegas.

STRATOSPHERE TOWER HOTEL
2000 Las Vegas Blvd S, Las Vegas.

SUMMER BAY RESORT LAS VEGAS
100 Winnick Ave, Las Vegas.

SUNCOAST HOTEL & CASINO
9090 Alta Dr, Las Vegas.

THE MIRAGE
3400 Las Vegas Blvd S, Las Vegas.

THE ORLEANS HOTEL & CASINO
4500 W Tropicana Ave, Las Vegas.

THE PALMS CASINO RESORT
4321 W Flamingo Rd, Las Vegas.

TREASURE ISLAND AT THE MIRAGE
3300 Las Vegas Blvd S, Las Vegas.

TROPICANA RESORT & CASINO
3801 Las Vegas Blvd S, Las Vegas.

TUSCANY SUITES & CASINO
255 E Flamingo Rd, Las Vegas.

Laughlin

FLAMINGO LAUGHLIN
1900 S Casino Dr, Laughlin.

HARRAH'S LAUGHLIN
2900 S Casino Dr, Laughlin.

RAMADA EXPRESS HOTEL CASINO
2121 S Casino Dr, Laughlin.

Reno

ATLANTIS CASINO RESORT SPA - RENO
3800 S Virginia St, Reno.

CAESARS TAHOE
55 Highway 50, Stateline.

CIRCUS CIRCUS HOTEL & CASINO RENO
500 N Sierra St, Reno.

ELDORADO HOTEL CASINO
345 N Virginia St, Reno.

GOLDEN PHOENIX HOTEL AND CASINO
255 N Sierra St, Reno.

HARRAHS LAKE TAHOE
Highway 50, Stateline.

HARRAHS RENO
219 N Center, Reno.

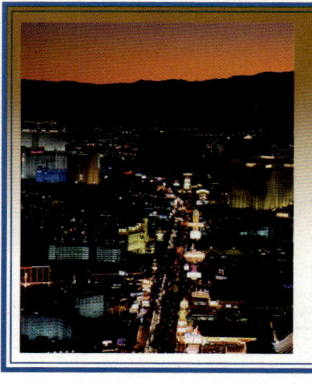

Las Vegas– rates from $29

Vacation, convention, holiday or weekend jaunt, Las Vegas is non-stop entertainment. Vegas is one of the most popular destinations no matter what the season.

Call: 800-50-HOTELS or book online at www.entertainment.com/travel

E21

You can access **25,000** hotels in over **700** cities. See sample listings above.
Shop and Book more hotels at www.entertainment.com/travel

Guaranteed Best Rate*
More listings online and over the phone!

HORIZON CASINO RESORT
50 Highway 50, Stateline.

LA QUINTA INN RENO
4001 Market St, Reno.

PEPPERMILL
2707 S Virginia St, Reno.

RENO HILTON
2500 E 2nd St, Reno.

SANDS REGENCY
345 N Arlington Ave, Reno.

SILVER LEGACY RESORT CASINO
407 N Virginia St, Reno.

THE RIDGE TAHOE
400 Ridge Club Drive, Stateline.

New Hampshire
For this state's listings go to entertainment.com/travel

New Jersey

Atlantic City

BALLYS ATLANTIC CITY
Park Place And Boardwalk, Atlantic City.

BORGATA HOTEL CASINO AND SPA
1 Borgata Way, Atlantic City.

CAESARS ATLANTIC CITY
2100 Pacific Ave, Atlantic City.

FLAGSHIP ALL SUITE HOTEL
60 N Maine Ave, Atlantic City.

HILTON CASINO ATLANTIC CITY
Boston At The Boradwalk, Atlantic City.

HOWARD JOHNSON ATLANTIC CITY
Chelsea/Pacific Avenue, Atlantic City.

QUALITY INN ATLANTIC CITY
500 N Albany Ave, Atlantic City.

RESORTS ATLANTIC CITY
1133 Boardwalk, Atlantic City.

ROYAL SUITES ATLANTIC PALACE
New York Ave. & Boardwalk, Atlantic City.

SANDS CASINO HOTEL
Indiana And Brighton Park, Atlantic City.

SHERATON ATLANTIC CITY
2 Miss America Way, Atlantic City.

TROPICANA CASINO & RESORT
Brighton Ave And Boardwalk, Atlantic City.

Newark

COMFORT SUITES NEWARK
1348 Mccarter Hwy, Newark.

HOWARD JOHNSON NEWARK AIRPORT
20 Frontage Rd, Newark.

RAMADA INN NEWARK INTL AIRPORT
550 Us Highway 1 And 9, Newark.

Secaucus

AMERISUITES SECAUCUS
575 Park Plaza Dr, Secaucus.

MEADOWLANDS PLAZA HOTEL
40 Wood Ave, Secaucus.

PRIME STES SECAUCUS MEADOWLAND
350 State Rt 3, Secaucus.

800-50-HOTEL
(6835)
Call & Book 25,000 Hotels!

New Mexico

Albuquerque

BAYMONT INN & STES ALBUQUERQUE
7439 Pan American Fwy N.E., Albuquerque.

HILTON
1901 University Blvd Ne, Albuquerque.

LA QUINTA ALBUQUERQUE AIRPORT
2116 Yale Blvd Se, Albuquerque.

LA QUINTA ALBUQUERQUE NORTH
5241 San Antonio Dr Ne, Albuquerque.

RADISSON HOTEL CONF. CENTER
2500 Carlisle Blvd Ne, Albuquerque.

SLEEP INN AIRPORT
2300 International Ave Se, Albuquerque.

Santa Fe

ELDORADO HOTEL & SPA
309 W San Francisco St, Santa Fe.

FORT MARCY HOTEL SUITES
320 Artist Rd, Santa Fe.

LA QUINTA INN SANTE FE
4298 Cerrillos Rd, Santa Fe.

PARK INN & SUITES
2907 Cerrillos Rd, Santa Fe.

RADISSON SANTA FE
750 N Saint Francis Dr, Santa Fe.

SANTA FE SAGE INN
725 Cerrillos Rd, Santa Fe.

New York

Albany

BEST WESTERN ALBANY AIRPORT
200 Wolf Rd, Albany.

DESMOND HOTEL & CONFERENCE CTR
660 Albany Shaker Rd, Albany.

HOWARD JOHNSON ALBANY
1614 Central Ave, Albany.

Buffalo

ADAM'S MARK BUFFALO
120 Church St, Buffalo.

BEST WESTERN NORSTAR INN
4630 Genesee St, Buffalo.

HYATT REGENCY BUFFALO
2 Fountain Plz, Buffalo.

RAMADA LIMITED BUFFALO AIRPORT
48 Freeman Rd, Buffalo.

SLEEP INN AMHERST
75 Inn Keepers Ln, Buffalo.

JFK International Airport

HOWARD JOHNSON JAMAICA
15395 Rockaway Blvd, Jamaica.

RADISSON JFK AIRPORT
I35-30 140th Street, Jamaica.

RAMADA PLAZA HOTEL JFK AIRPORT
Jfk International Airport, Jamaica.

New York

QUALITY HOTEL ON BROADWAY
215 W 94th St, New York.

New York City/Manhattan

ALGONQUIN HOTEL
59 W 44th St, New York.

AMERITANIA HOTEL
230 W 54th St, New York.

AMSTERDAM COURT HOTEL
226 W 50th St, New York.

E22

Discounts subject to availability.
*See Rebate Rules on page E31-E32 and Program Rules on page E33.

Guaranteed Best Rate*

Book at www.entertainment.com/travel or call 1-800-50-HOTEL

BENTLEY HOTEL
500 E 62nd St, New York.
CARNEGIE SUITES
229 W 58th St, New York.
DOUBLETREE METROPOLITAN HOTEL
569 Lexington Ave, New York.
EDISON
228 W 47th St, New York.
FLATOTEL
135 W 52nd St, New York.
GRAND HYATT NEW YORK
Park Ave At Grand Central St, New York.
HELMSLEY MIDDLETOWNE HOTEL
148 E 48th St, New York.
HELMSLEY PARK LANE
36 Central Park S, New York.
HILTON NEW YORK
1335 Avenue Of The Americas, New York.
HOLIDAY INN MARTINIQUE
49 W 32nd St, New York.
HOLIDAY INN MIDTOWN 57TH ST
440 W 57th St, New York.
HOTEL BELLECLAIRE
250 W 77th St, New York.
HOTEL METRO
45 W 35th St, New York.
HOTEL PENNSYLVANIA
401 7th Ave, New York.
LE PARKER MERIDIEN
118 W 57th St, New York.
MANHATTAN BROADWAY
273 W 38th St, New York.
MANSFIELD HOTEL
12 W 44th St, New York.

MILFORD PLAZA
270 W 45th St, New York.
MILLENNIUM BROADWAY
145 W 44th St, New York.
ON THE AVE HOTEL
2178 Broadway At 77th Street, New York.
PARAMOUNT
235 W 46th St, New York.
PARK CENTRAL NEW YORK HOTEL
870 7th Ave, New York.
RADISSON LEXINGTON HOTEL
511 Lexington Ave, New York.
RAMADA PLAZA NEW YORKER
481 8th Ave, New York.
SALISBURY HOTEL
123 W 57th St, New York.
SHERATON MANHATTAN HOTEL
790 7th Ave, New York.
SHERATON NEW YORK HTL & TOWERS
811 7th Ave, New York.
SKYLINE HOTEL
725 10th Ave, New York.
ST JAMES TIMES SQUARE
109 W 45th St, New York.
THE ALEX HOTEL
205 E 45th St, New York.
THE AVALON
16 E 32nd St, New York.
THE BELVEDERE HOTEL
319 W 48th St, New York.
THE MUSE
130 W 46th St, New York.
THE NEW YORK HELMSLEY HOTEL
212 E 42nd St, New York.

THE ROOSEVELT HOTEL
45 E 45th St, New York.
THE TIME HOTEL
224 W 49th St, New York.
THIRTY THIRTY
30 E 30th St, New York.
W HOTEL NEW YORK
541 Lexington Ave, New York.
WARWICK NEW YORK
65 W 54th St, New York.
WASHINGTON JEFFERSON HOTEL
318 W 51st St, New York.
WELLINGTON
871 7th Ave, New York.

Niagara Falls

DAYS INN AT THE FALLS, NIAGARA FALLS NY
443 Main St, Niagara Falls.
FALLSIDE HOTEL & CONF CENTRE
401 Buffalo Ave, Niagara Falls.
FOUR POINTS BY SHERATON NIAGARA FALLS
114 Buffalo Ave, Niagara Falls.
HOWARD JOHNSON CLOSEST TO FALL
454 Main St, Niagara Falls.
QUALITY HOTEL AND SUITES
240 Rainbow Blvd, Niagara Falls.
RAMADA INN BY THE FALLS
219 4th St, Niagara Falls.
TRAVELODGE HOTEL FALLSVIEW
201 Rainbow Blvd, Niagara Falls.

New York– rates from $79

Superb architecture, the world's greatest theatre district, some of the most renowned galleries and museums anywhere, eclectic neighborhoods, cultural events and fantastic restaurants and shopping—New York City has it all.

Call: 800-50-HOTELS or book online at www.entertainment.com/travel

You can access **25,000** hotels in over **700** cities. See sample listings above.
Shop and Book more hotels at www.entertainment.com/travel

Guaranteed Best Rate*
More listings online and over the phone!

Rochester
CLARION RIVERSIDE HOTEL
120 E Main St, Rochester.
PARK PLAZA ROCHESTER AIRPORT
175 Jefferson Rd, Rochester.
WELLESLEY INN ROCHESTER SOUTH
797 E Henrietta Rd, Rochester.

North Carolina
Charlotte
COMFORT INN EXECUTIVE PARK
5822 Westpark Dr, Charlotte.
COMFORT SUITES - AIRPORT
3424 Mulberry Church Rd, Charlotte.
QUALITY INN EXECUTIVE PARK
440 Griffith Rd, Charlotte.

Durham
CLARION HOTEL RTP
4912 S Miami Blvd, Durham.
MILLENNIUM HOTEL DURHAM
2800 Campus Walk Ave, Durham.
QUALITY INN & SUITES DURHAM
3710 Hillsborough Rd, Durham.

Raleigh
AMERISUITES RALEIGH WAKE FORST
1105 Navaho Dr, Raleigh.
ECONO LODGE RALEIGH NORTH
2641 Appliance Ct, Raleigh.
LA QUINTA INN RALEIGH CRABTREE
2211 Summit Park Ln, Raleigh.

North Dakota
For this state's listings go to entertainment.com/travel

Ohio
Cincinnati
HYATT REGENCY CINCINNATI
151 W 5th St, Cincinnati.
MILLENNIUM HOTEL
141 W 6th St, Cincinnati.
TERRACE HOTEL CINCINNATI
15 W 6th St, Cincinnati.

Cleveland
COMFORT INN DOWNTOWN CLEVELAND
1800 Euclid Ave, Cleveland.
HOLIDAY INN EXPRESS DOWNTOWN
629 Euclid Ave, Cleveland.
RADISSON HOTEL GATEWAY
651 Huron Rd E, Cleveland.

Columbus
BEST WESTERN COLUMBUS NORTH
888 E Dublin Granville Rd, Columbus.
CONCOURSE HOTEL
4300 International Gtwy, Columbus.

Dublin
AMERISUITES COLUMBUS DUBLIN
6161 Parkcenter Cir, Dublin.

800-50-HOTEL
(6835)
Call & Book
25,000 Hotels!

BAYMONT INN & SUITES DUBLIN
6145 Parkcenter Cir, Dublin.
MARRIOTT COLUMBUS NORTHWEST
5605 Paul G Blazer Memorial, Dublin.
SHERATON SUITES COLUMBUS
201 Hutchinson Ave, Columbus.

Kent
KENT INN & CONFERENCE CENTER
4363 State Route 43, Kent.

Oklahoma
Oklahoma City
AMERISUITES OKLAHOMA CITY ARPT
1818 S Meridian Ave, Oklahoma City.
BILTMORE HOTEL OKLAHOMA
401 S Meridian Ave, Oklahoma City.
LA QUINTA INN/STES OKC AIRPORT
800 S Meridian Ave, Oklahoma City.

Tulsa
BAYMONT INN & SUITES TULSA
4530 East Kelly Drive, Tulsa.
LA QUINTA INN TULSA EAST
10829 E 41st St, Tulsa.
RADISSON INN
2201 N 77th East Ave, Tulsa.

Oregon
Eugene
A SECRET GARDEN B&B
1910 University St, Eugene.
BEST VALUE INN EUGENE
1140 W 6th Ave, Eugene.
CAMPUS INN & SUITES EUGENE
390 E Broadway, Eugene.

Gresham
FOUR POINTS BY SHERATON PORTLAND EAST
1919 Ne 181st Ave, Portland.

Portland
AVALON HOTEL AND SPA
0455 Sw Hamilton Ct, Portland.
BANFIELD MOTEL
1525 Ne 37th Ave, Portland.
BEST VALUE INN AND SUITES-PORTLAND
4911 Ne 82nd Ave, Portland.
BEST WESTERN INN AT THE MEADOW
1215 N Hayden Meadows Dr, Portland.
BEST WESTERN PONY SOLDIER INN AIRPORT
9901 Ne Sandy Blvd, Portland.
COMFORT SUITES PORTLAND ARPT
12010 Ne Airport Way, Portland.
COURTYARD BY MARRIOTT PORTLAND DNTN-LLOYD CTR
435 Ne Wasco St, Portland.
FAIRFIELD INN BY MARRIOTT PORTLAND AIRPORT
11929 Ne Airport Way, Portland.
HILTON PORTLAND & EXECUTIVE TOWER
921 Sw 6th Ave, Portland.
INN AT THE CONVENTION CENTER
420 Ne Holladay St, Portland.
QUALITY INN PORTLAND AIRPORT
8247 Ne Sandy Blvd, Portland.
VALUE INN PORTLAND
10450 Sw Barbur Blvd, Eugene.

Discounts subject to availability.
*See Rebate Rules on page E31-E32 and Program Rules on page E33.

Guaranteed Best Rate*

Book at www.entertainment.com/travel or call 1-800-50-HOTEL

Tigard

BRIDGEPORT VALUE INN
17993 Sw Lower Boones Ferry Rd, Portland.
COURTYARD BY MARRIOTT PORTLAND TIGARD
15686 Sw Sequoia Pkwy, Portland.
HOWARD JOHNSON EXP INN TIGARD
11460 Sw Pacific Hwy, Portland.

Pennsylvania

Harrisburg

BAYMONT INN & STES HARRISBURG
990 Eisenhower Blvd, Harrisburg.
HOWARD JOHNSON HARRISBURG
473 Eisenhower Blvd, Harrisburg.
WYNDHAM HARRISBURG HERSHEY
4650 Lindle Rd, Harrisburg.

Lancaster

HOTEL BRUNSWICK
151 N Queen St, Lancaster.
HOWARD JOHNSON INN LANCASTER
2100 Us Hwy 30 East, Lancaster.
LANCASTER HOST RESORT & CONFERENCE CENTER
2300 Lincoln Hwy E, Lancaster.

Philadelphia

CLUB QUARTERS
1628 Chestnut St, Philadelphia.
COMFORT INN DOWNTOWN HISTORIC
100 N Columbus Blvd, Philadelphia.
HILTON GARDEN INN PHILADELPHIA
1100 Arch St, Philadelphia.
HOTEL WINDSOR
1700 Benjamin Franklin Parkw, Philadelphia.
LOEWS PHILADELPHIA
1200 Market St, Philadelphia.
THE LATHAM HOTEL
135 S 17th St, Philadelphia.
THE RADISSON PLAZA WARWICK
1701 Locust St, Philadelphia.
WYNDHAM PHILADELPHIA
17th & Race St., Philadelphia.

Pittsburgh

COMFORT INN & SUITES
2898 Banksville Rd, Pittsburgh.
RADISSON PITTSBURGH GREENTREE
101 Radisson Dr, Pittsburgh.
RAMADA PLAZA SUITES DOWNTOWN
1 Bigelow Sq, Pittsburgh.

Rhode Island

For this state's listings go to entertainment.com/travel

South Carolina

Charleston

CHARLESTON RIVERVIEW HOTEL
170 Lockwood Blvd, Charleston.
COMFORT INN RIVERVIEW
144 Bee St, Charleston.

Shop & Book more hotels at entertainment.com/travel

THE FRANCIS MARION HOTEL
387 King St, Charleston.

Columbia

BAYMONT INN & SUITES COLUMBIA
1538 Horseshoe Dr, Columbia.
CAROLINIAN HOTEL
7510 Two Notch Rd, Columbia.
HOWARD JOHNSON INN COLUMBIA
200 Zimalcrest Dr, Columbia.

Hilton Head Island

COMFORT INN HILTON HEAD ISLAND
2 Tanglewood Dr, Hilton Head.
HILTON HEAD PLAZA HOTEL
36 S Forest Beach Dr, Hilton Head.
QUALITY INN & SUITES
200 Museum St, Hilton Head.

Myrtle Beach

COMPASS COVE OCEANFRONT RESORT
2311 S Ocean Blvd, Myrtle Beach.
M GRANDE RESORT AND SPA
2701 S Ocean Blvd, Myrtle Beach.
OCEAN DUNES RESORT & VILLAS
201 75th Ave N, Myrtle Beach.
PATRICIA GRAND RESORT HOTEL
2710 N Ocean Blvd, Myrtle Beach.
POINDEXTER OCEANFRONT RESORT
1702 N Ocean Blvd, Myrtle Beach.
SAND DUNES RESORT HOTEL
201 74th Ave N, Myrtle Beach.
SANDS OCEAN CLUB RESORT
9550 Shore Dr, Myrtle Beach.
SEACREST OCEANFRONT RESORT
803 S Ocean Blvd, Myrtle Beach.

South Dakota

Rapid City

FOOTHILLS INN
1625 N Lacrosse St, Rapid City.
RADISSON HOTEL MT. RUSHMORE
445 Mount Rushmore Rd, Rapid City.
RAMADA INN RAPID CITY
1721 N Lacrosse St, Rapid City.

Tennessee

Chattanooga

DAYS INN DOWNTOWN CHATTANOOGA
101 E 20th St, Chattanooga.
LA QUINTA INN CHATTANOOGA
7015 Shallowford Rd, Chattanooga.
RAMADA LIMITED CHATTANOOGA
6650 Ringgold Rd, Chattanooga.

Gatlinburg

PARK VISTA GATLINBURG RESORT
705 Cherokee Orchard Rd, Gatlinburg.
SIDNEY JAMES MOUNTAIN LODGE
610 Historic Nature Trl, Gatlinburg.
WESTGATE SMOKY MOUNTAIN RESORT
915 Garden Rd, Gatlinburg.

E25

You can access **25,000** hotels in over **700** cities. See sample listings above.
Shop and Book more hotels at www.entertainment.com/travel

Guaranteed Best Rate*
More listings online and over the phone!

Independence

AMERISUITES INDEPENDENCE
6025 Jefferson Dr, Independence.
CLARION HOTEL & CONF CENTER
5300 Rockside Rd, Independence.
DAYS INN INDEPENDENCE
5555 Brecksville Rd, Independence.

Knoxville

BAYMONT INN & STES KNOXVILLE E
7210 Saddlerack St, Knoxville.
BUDGET INNS OF AMERICA
323 N Cedar Bluff Rd, Knoxville.
CLUBHOUSE INN & STES KNOXVILLE
208 Market Place Blvd, Knoxville.

Memphis

BAYMONT INN & SUITES AIRPORT
3005 Millbranch Rd, Memphis.
MEMPHIS PLAZA HOTEL & SUITES
6101 Shelby Oaks Dr, Memphis.
RADISSON HOTEL DOWNTOWN
185 Union Ave, Memphis.

Nashville

AIRPORT RAMADA INN & SUITES
2425 Atrium Way, Nashville.
AMERISUITES OPRYLAND
220 Rudy Cir, Nashville.
COMFORT INN DOWNTOWN
1501 Demonbreun St, Nashville.
DAYS INN DOWNTOWN NASHVILLE
211 N 1st St, Nashville.
GAYLORD OPRYLAND HOTEL
2800 Opryland Dr, Nashville.
RADISSON OPRYLAND HOTEL
2401 Music Valley Dr, Nashville.
THE HOTEL PRESTON
733 Briley Pkwy, Nashville.

Pigeon Forge

HOLIDAY INN PIGEON FORGE
308 Henderson Chapel Rd, Pigeon Forge.
HOWARD JOHNSON PIGEON FORGE
2826 Parkway, Pigeon Forge.
RESORTQUEST GOLFVIEW RESORT
610 Dollywood Ln, Pigeon Forge.

Texas

Arlington

AMERISUITES ARLINGTON
2380 Road To Six Flags, Arlington.
COUNTRY INN & SUITES ARLINGTON
1075 Wet N Wild Way, Arlington.
HAWTHORN SUITES
2401 Brookhollow Plaza Dr, Arlington.
QUALITY INN & SUITES
1607 N Watson Rd, Arlington.
WINGATE INN ARLINGTON
1024 Brookhollow Plaza Dr, Arlington.

Austin

BRADFORD HOMESUITES AUSTIN
10001 N Capital Of Texas Hwy, Austin.
NORTH AUSTIN PLAZA HOTEL & STE
6911 Ih-35 North, Austin.

800-50-HOTEL (6835)
Call & Book 25,000 Hotels!

RADISSON HOTEL & SUITES AUSTIN
111 E Cesar Chavez St, Austin.

Corpus Christi

QUALITY INN AND SUITES
3202 E Surfside Blvd, Corpus Christi.
RADISSON CORPUS CHRISTI BEACH
3200 E Surfside Blvd, Corpus Christi.
RAMADA INN BAYFRONT
601 N Water St, Corpus Christi.

Dallas

AMERISUITES NEAR THE GALLERIA
5229 Spring Valley Rd, Dallas.
AMERISUITES PARK CENTRAL
12411 N Central Expy, Dallas.
BEST WESTERN MARKET CENTER
2023 Market Center Blvd, Dallas.
HOTEL LAWRENCE
302 S Houston St, Dallas.

HYATT REGENCY DALLAS REUNION
300 Reunion Blvd E, Dallas.
RADISSON DALLAS LOVE FIELD
1241 W Mockingbird Ln, Dallas.
STONELEIGH
2927 Maple Ave, Dallas.

Dallas/Ft. Worth Airport

CLARION DFW AIRPORT SOUTH
4440 W Airport Fwy, Irving.
HYATT REGENCY DFW
2332 S International Pkwy, Irving.
RADISSON HOTEL DFW SOUTH
4600 W Airport Fwy, Irving.

El Paso

AMERISUITES EL PASO AIRPORT
6030 Gateway Blvd E, El Paso.
BAYMONT INN & STES EL PASO W.
7620 N Mesa St, El Paso.
LA QUINTA INN EL PASO LOMALAND
11033 Gateway Blvd W, El Paso.
RAMADA SUITES EL PASO
8250 Gateway Blvd E, El Paso.

Ft. Worth

AMERISUITES FORT WORTH CITYVW
5900 Cityview Blvd, Ft. Worth.
BEST WESTERN INNSUITES HOTEL
2000 Beach St, Ft. Worth.
FORT WORTH PLAZA HOTEL
1701 Commerce St, Ft. Worth.
LA QUINTA INN & STES FTW S.W.
4900 Bryant Irving Road, Ft. Worth.

Galveston

INN AT THE WATERPARK
2525 Jones Dr, Galveston.
LA QUINTA INN GALVESTON
1402 Seawall Blvd, Galveston.
RAMADA LIMITED GALVESTON
2300 Seawall Blvd, Galveston.

Houston

HEARTHSIDE SUITES HOUSTON 290
12925 Northwest Fwy, Houston.
HOTEL DEREK
2525 West Loop S, Houston.
HOTEL ICON
220 Main Street, Houston.

E26

Discounts subject to availability.
***See Rebate Rules on page E31-E32 and Program Rules on page E33.**

Guaranteed Best Rate*

Book at www.entertainment.com/travel or call 1-800-50-HOTEL

MARRIOTT WEST LOOP GALLERIA
1750 West Loop S, Houston.

OMNI HOUSTON HOTEL
4 Riverway, Houston.

SHERATON HOUSTON BROOKHOLLOW
3000 North Loop W, Houston.

THE WOODLANDS RESORT & CONFERENCE CENTER
2301 N. Millbend Drive The Woodlands, Tx, Houston.

Houston Intercontinental Airport

AMERISUITES IAH GREENSPOINT
300 Ronan Park Pl, Houston.

COMFORT SUITES BUSH AIRPORT
15555 John F Kennedy Blvd, Houston.

REGENCY INN & SUITES BUSH INTERCONTINENTAL
15420 W. Hardy Road, Houston.

WYNDHAM GREENSPOINT
12400 Greenspoint Drive, Houston.

San Antonio

AMERISUITES RIVERWALK
601 S Saint Marys St, San Antonio.

BEST WESTERN ALAMO SUITES DOWNTOWN
102 El Paso St, San Antonio.

BEST WESTERN LACKLAND/KELLYUSA
6815 W Us Highway 90, San Antonio.

ECONO LODGE CENTRAL
6015 W Ih 10, San Antonio.

EL TROPICANO RIVERWALK - A CLARION HOTEL
110 Lexington Ave, San Antonio.

HAWTHORN SUITES RIVERWALK
830 N Saint Marys St, San Antonio.

HOMEWOOD SUITES RIVERWALK
432 W Market St, San Antonio.

HOTEL VALENCIA RIVERWALK
150 E Houston St, San Antonio.

LA MANSION DEL RIO HOTEL
112 College St, San Antonio.

MENGER HOTEL
204 Alamo Plz, San Antonio.

OMNI SAN ANTONIO
9821 Colonnade Blvd, San Antonio.

RADISSON MARKET SQUARE
502 W Durango Blvd, San Antonio.

RADISSON RESORT HILL COUNTRY
9800 Westover Hills Blvd, San Antonio.

RIVERWALK PLAZA
100 Villita St, San Antonio.

THE CROCKETT HOTEL
320 Bonham, San Antonio.

WOODFIELD SUITES DOWNTOWN
100 W Durango Blvd, San Antonio.

South Padre Island

COMFORT SUITES BEACHSIDE
912 Padre Blvd, South Padre Island.

LA QUINTA INN/STES BEACH RESRT
7000 Padre Blvd, South Padre Island.

SHERATON SOUTH PADRE ISLAND
310 Padre Blvd, South Padre Island.

Utah

Park City

FOX POINT AT REDSTONE
6975 N 2200 W, Park City.

PARK PLAZA RESORT
2060 Sidewinder Dr, Park City.

Shop & Book more hotels at entertainment.com/travel

PROSPECTOR SQUARE LODGE
1940 Prospector Ave, Park City.

Salt Lake City

AIRPORT INN HOTEL
2333 W North Temple, Salt Lake City.

FOOTHILLS INN
154 W. 600 South, Salt Lake City.

LITTLE AMERICA HOTEL
500 S Main St, Salt Lake City.

MICROTEL INN & SUITES AIRPORT
61 Tommy Thompson Rd, Salt Lake City.

RED LION HOTEL SALT LAKE
161 W 600 S, Salt Lake City.

SHILO INN HOTEL CITY CENTER
206 S West Temple, Salt Lake City.

SKY HARBOR SUITES
1876 W North Temple, Salt Lake City.

Vermont

For this state's listings go to entertainment.com/travel

Virginia

Alexandria

COURTYARD BY MARRIOTT ALEXANDRIA
2700 Eisenhower Ave, Alexandria.

DAYS INN ALEXANDRIA VA
110 S Bragg St, Alexandria.

HILTON OLD TOWN ALEXANDRIA
1767 King St, Alexandria.

Arlington

HILTON CRYSTAL CITY
2399 Jefferson Davis Hwy, Arlington.

MARRIOTT CRYSTAL GATEWAY
1700 Jefferson Davis Hwy, Arlington.

Richmond

COMFORT INN EXECUTIVE CENTER
7201 W Broad St, Richmond.

DAYS INN RICHMOND VA
5701 Chamberlayne Rd, Richmond.

QUALITY INN WEST END
8008 W Broad St, Richmond.

Virginia Beach

LA QUINTA INN VIRGINIA BEACH
192 Newtown Rd, Virginia Beach.

RAMADA PLAZA RESORT OCEANFRONT
5700 Atlantic Ave, Virginia Beach.

THE ATRIUM RESORT
315 21st & Arctic Avenue, Virginia Beach.

Williamsburg

KING'S CREEK PLANTATION
191 Cottage Cove Ln, Williamsburg.

KINGSGATE RESORT
619 Georgetown Cres, Williamsburg.

QUARTERPATH INN
620 York St, Williamsburg.

Washington

Bellevue

COAST BELLEVUE HOTEL
625 116th Ave Ne, Bellevue.

HYATT REGENCY BELLEVUE
900 Bellevue Way Ne, Bellevue.

RED LION BELLEVUE INN
11211 Main St, Bellevue.

You can access 25,000 hotels in over 700 cities. See sample listings above.
Shop and Book more hotels at www.entertainment.com/travel

Guaranteed Best Rate*
More listings online and over the phone!

Seattle

BEST WESTERN EXECUTIVE INN
200 Taylor Ave N, Seattle.
COMFORT SUITES SEATTLE CENTER
601 Roy St, Seattle.
DAYS INN DOWNTOWN SEATTLE
2205 7th Ave, Seattle.
EXECUTIVE PACIFIC PLAZA HOTEL
400 Spring St, Seattle.
GRAND HYATT SEATTLE
721 Pine St, Seattle.
INN AT QUEEN ANNE
505 1st Ave N, Seattle.
MARRIOTT COURTYARD LAKE UNION
925 Westlake Ave N, Seattle.
MEDITERRANEAN INN
425 Queen Anne Ave N, Seattle.
QUALITY INN & SUITES SEATTLE
225 Aurora Ave N, Seattle.
RAMADA INN DOWNTOWN SEATTLE
2200 5th Ave, Seattle.
RED LION HOTEL ON 5TH AVENUE
1415 5th Ave, Seattle.
RENAISSANCE SEATTLE HOTEL
515 Madison St, Seattle.
SHERATON
1400 6th Ave, Seattle.
SILVER CLOUD HOTEL BROADWAY
1100 Broadway, Seattle.
SILVER CLOUD INN - LAKE UNION
1150 Fairview Ave N, Seattle.
SIXTH AVENUE INN
2000 6th Ave, Seattle.
THE EDGEWATER-A NOBLE HOUSE HOTEL
2411 Alaskan Way Pier 67, Seattle.
THE MARQUEEN HOTEL
600 Queen Anne Ave N, Seattle.
THE PARAMOUNT, A COAST HOTEL
724 Pine St, Seattle.
THE ROOSEVELT, A COAST HOTEL
1531 7th Ave, Seattle.
THE WARWICK SEATTLE HOTEL
401 Lenora St, Seattle.
THE WESTIN SEATTLE
1900 5th Ave, Seattle.
TRAVELODGE BY THE SPACE NEEDLE
200 6th Ave N, Seattle.

TRAVELODGE SEATTLE CITY CENTER
2213 8th Ave, Seattle.
UNIVERSITY INN
4140 Roosevelt Way Ne, Seattle.
VANCE HOTEL
620 Stewart St, Seattle.

Seattle/Tacoma International Airport

LA QUINTA INN SEA-TAC
2824 S 188th St, Seattle.
PRIME HOTEL SEA-TAC AIRPORT
18118 International Blvd, Seattle.
RADISSON HOTEL SEATTLE AIRPORT
17001 International Blvd, Seattle.
RAMADA INN & SUITES SEATAC
16720 International Blvd, Seattle.
RED LION HOTEL SEATTLE AIRPORT
18220 International Blvd, Seattle.

800-50-HOTEL
(6835)
Call & Book 25,000 Hotels!

RED LION HOTEL SEATTLE SOUTH
11244 Tukwila International Blvd, Seattle.
RED ROOF INN SEATTLE
16838 International Blvd, Seattle.

Spokane

HOWARD JOHNSON INN SPOKANE
211 S Division St, Spokane.
RAMADA INN & SUITES SPOKANE
9601 N Newport Hwy, Spokane.
RED LION RIVER INN - SPOKANE
700 N Division St, Spokane.

Vancouver

GUEST HOUSE MOTEL
11504 Ne 2nd St, Vancouver.
HEATHMAN LODGE
7801 Ne Greenwood Dr, Vancouver.
HILTON VANCOUVER WASHINGTON
301 W 6th St, Vancouver.

RAMADA INN VANCOUVER
9107 Ne Vancouver Mall Dr, Vancouver.
RED LION HOTEL AT THE QUAY
100 Columbia St, Vancouver.
RED LION INN AT SALMON CREEK
1500 Ne 134th St, Vancouver.
SHILO INN - HAZEL DELL
13206 Ne Highway 99, Vancouver.
SHILO INN - VANCOUVER (DOWNTOWN)
401 E 13th St, Vancouver.

West Virginia

For this state's listings go to entertainment.com/travel

Wisconsin

Milwaukee

BEST WESTERN INN TOWNE HOTEL
710 N Old World 3rd St, Milwaukee.
RADISSON MILWAUKEE AIRPORT
6331 S 13th St, Milwaukee.
WYNDHAM MILWAUKEE
139 E Kilbourn Ave, Milwaukee.

Wyoming

Jackson

BEST WESTERN LODGE AT JACKSON HOLE
80 Scott Ln, Jackson.

Jackson Hole

GRAND VISTA LODGING
400 East Snow King, Jackson.

Canada

British Columbia

Victoria

BEST WESTERN CARLTON PLAZA
642 Johnson St, Victoria.
DELTA VICTORIA OCEAN POINTE RESORT
45 Songhees Road, Victoria.
HOTEL GRAND PACIFIC
463 Belleville St, Victoria.
LAUREL POINT INN
680 Montreal St, Victoria.

Discounts subject to availability.
*See Rebate Rules on page E31-E32 and Program Rules on page E33.

Guaranteed Best Rate*

Book at www.entertainment.com/travel or call 1-800-50-HOTEL

QUEEN VICTORIA HOTEL & SUITES
655 Douglas Street, Victoria.
RAMADA HUNTINGDON HOTEL & STES
330 Quebec Street, Victoria.

Whistler
PAN PACIFIC WHISTLER MOUNTAINSIDE
4320 Sundial Cres, Whistler.
THE COAST WHISTLER HOTEL
4005 Whistler Way, Whistler.
WHISTLER PINNACLE HOTEL
4319 Main St, Whistler.

Ontario
Niagara Falls
ASTON MICHAEL'S INN BY THE FALLS
5599 River Rd, Niagara Falls.
BEST WESTERN FIRESIDE HOTEL
4067 River Rd, Niagara Falls.
BROCK PLAZA HOTEL
5685 Falls Avenue, Niagara Falls.
CLARION HOTEL BY THE FALLS
6045 Stanley Avenue, Niagara Falls.
COURTYARD NIAGARA FALLS
5950 Victoria Avenue, Niagara Falls.
DAYS INN & STES NIAGARA FALLS
5068 Centre Street, Niagara Falls.
DAYS INN CLIFTON HILL CASINO
5657 Victoria Avenue, Niagara Falls.
HOWARD JOHNSON BY THE FALLS
5905 Victoria Ave, Niagara Falls.
IMPERIAL HOTEL AND SUITES
5851 Victoria Ave, Niagara Falls.
OLD STONE INN
5425 Robinson St, Niagara Falls.
QUALITY INN CLIFTON HILL
4946 Clifton Hill, Niagara Falls.
RED CARPET INN & STES FALLSWAY
5334 Kitchener Street, Niagara Falls.
SHERATON ON THE FALLS
5875 Falls Ave, Niagara Falls.

Toronto
30 CARLTON ST.
30 Carlton St., Toronto.
33 GERRARD ST W
33 Gerrard St W, Toronto.
METROPOLITAN HOTEL
108 Chestnut St, Toronto.

Québec
Montreal
BEST WESTERN VILLE MARIE
3407 Peel Street, Montreal.
DELTA MONTREAL
475 Du President-Kennedy Ave, Montreal.
HOTEL DE LA MONTAGNE
1430 De La Montagne, Montreal.
HOTEL LE CANTLIE SUITES
1110 Sherbrooke St W, Montreal.
HOTEL MARITIME PLAZA MONTREAL
1155 Rue Guy, Montreal.
(800)50-HOTEL
HOTEL OMNI MONT-ROYAL
1050 Sherbrooke Street West, Montreal.
MARRIOTT CHATEAU CHAMPLAIN
1050 De La Gauchetiere, Montreal.

Shop & Book more hotels at entertainment.com/travel

Mexico
Baja California
Cabo San Lucas
RIU PALACE CABO SAN LUCAS ALL INCLUSIVE
Camino Vieja A San Jose Del, Cabo San Lucas.
VILLA DEL PALMAR RESORT & SPA
Km 0 5 Camino Viejo A San Jo, Cabo San Lucas.
VILLA LA ESTANCIA
Camino Viejo A San Jose Km 6, Cabo San Lucas.

Jalisco
Nuevo Vallarta
ALL INCLUSIVE SAMBA VALLARTA BY PUEBLO BONITO
Avenida Y Costera La Playa S, Nuevo Vallarta.
MARIVAL RESORT & SUITES
Boulevard Nuevo Vallarta, Nuevo Vallarta.
VILLA DEL PALMAR FLAMINGOS
Paseo Cocoteros 750 S, Nuevo Vallarta.

Puerto Vallarta
HOWARD JOHNSON NAUTILUS
Paseo De La Marina Sur No 21, Puerto Vallarta.
LA JOLLA DE MISMALOYA HOTEL
Zona Hotelera Sur Km 11.5, Puerto Vallarta.
MELIA PUERTO VALLARTA ALL INCLUSIVE
Paseo De La Marina Sur Lote, Puerto Vallarta.
VELAS VALLARTA SUITE RESORT
Paseo De La Marina 585, Puerto Vallarta.

Quintana Roo
Cancun
CASAMAGNA MARRIOTT RESORT
Blvd. Kulkukan, Cancun.
GRAN MELIA CANCUN
Blvd. Kukulcan Km 16.5, Cancun.
J W MARRIOTT CANCUN RESORT&SPA
Blvd. Kukulkan Km 14.5, Cancun.
MIRAMAR MISION CANCUN
Blvd Kukulkan Km 9.5, Cancun.
MOON PALACE GOLF & SPA RESORT
Carretera Cancun-Chetumal, Cancun.
OASIS CANCUN ALL INCLUSIVE
Avenida Kukulkan, Cancun.

Carribean
Puerto Rico
San Juan
RADISSON AMBASSADOR PLAZA
1369 Ashford Avenue, Condado, San Juan.
SAN JUAN BEACH
1045 Ashford Ave, San Juan.
WYNDHAM CONDADO PLAZA HOTEL
999 Ashford Avenue, San Juan.

E29

**You can access 25,000 hotels in over 700 cities. See sample listings above.
Shop and Book more hotels at www.entertainment.com/travel**

International Destinations

ARUBA
Oranjestad
Palm Beach
Eagle Beach
Aruba

BAHAMAS
Nassau
Freeport
Lucaya
Cable Beach
Paradise Island

BARBADOS
St. James
Christ Church

BELGIUM
Bruxelles

CAYMAN ISLANDS
Seven Mile Beach
Collier's Bay East
Grand Cayman

DOMINICAN REPUBLIC
Punta Cana
Santo Domingo
Puerto Plata
Higuey

EGYPT
Cairo

FRANCE
Paris
Lille
Lourdes
Nice
Lyon
Avignon
Vedene
Montpellier
Marseille
Cannes

GERMANY
Berlin
Heidelberg
Munchen
Frankfurt Urt Am Main
Wiesbaden
Oberding
Kelsterbach
Hamburg
Koln

GREECE
Thessaloniki
Athina

GREAT BRITAIN
London
Edinburgh
Inverness
Glasgow
Canterbury
Bath
Crawley
Dundee
Slough
West Drayton
Horley
Brighton

HONG KONG
Tsim Sha Tsui
Lantau Island
Shatin

IRELAND
Dublin
Cork
Galway
Limerick

ITALY
Rome
Venice
Florence
Sorrento
Naples
Milano
Venezia

JAMAICA
Ocho Rios
Montego Bay
Negril
Oracabessa
Rose Hall

MEXICO
Puerto Vallarta
Nuevo Vallarta
Ixtapa
Playa Del Carmen
Riviera Maya
Cabo San Lucas
Cancun
Los Cabos
Bucerias
Acapulco
Mexico City
Mazatlan Sinaloa
Guadalajara
Cozumel
Mazatlan

NETHERLANDS
Amsterdam
Naarden
Maastricht
Hoofddorp
Schiphol-Rijk
Bruxelles

NORWAY
Bergen
Oslo

POLAND
Warsaw
Krakow

SPAIN
Barcelona
Madrid
Sant Josep De Sa Talaia
Sevilla
Granada
Valencia
Bilbao

VIRGIN ISLANDS
St. Thomas
Christiansted
Charlotte Amalie
Red Hook St. Thomas

Call 800-50-Hotel or visit www.entertainment.com/travel to book one of these or 700 other cities internationally.

GUARANTEED BEST RATE–REBATE CERTIFICATE

Name _____

Hotel _____

Date of Stay ____/____/____ to ____/____/____
             (month/day/year)   (month/day/year)

Booking Number _____

Fill out this rebate form and mail it to: REBATE
                                              807 SOUTH JACKSON ROAD
                                              SUITE B
                                              PHARR, TX 78577

You may print another form for your next trip at our web site:
www.entertainment.com/travel

See reverse side for Rebate Rules of Use

GUARANTEED BEST RATE–REBATE CERTIFICATE

Name _____

Hotel _____

Date of Stay ____/____/____ to ____/____/____
             (month/day/year)   (month/day/year)

Booking Number _____

Fill out this rebate form and mail it to: REBATE
                                              807 SOUTH JACKSON ROAD
                                              SUITE B
                                              PHARR, TX 78577

You may print another form for your next trip at our web site:
www.entertainment.com/travel

See reverse side for Rebate Rules of Use

GUARANTEED BEST RATE–REBATE CERTIFICATE

Name _____

Hotel _____

Date of Stay ____/____/____ to ____/____/____
             (month/day/year)   (month/day/year)

Booking Number _____

Fill out this rebate form and mail it to: REBATE
                                              807 SOUTH JACKSON ROAD
                                              SUITE B
                                              PHARR, TX 78577

You may print another form for your next trip at our web site:
www.entertainment.com/travel

See reverse side for Rebate Rules of Use

E31

REBATE RULES OF USE

1. You must book and confirm a Guaranteed Best Rate hotel to be eligible for offer. No call-in or faxed rebates will be accepted.
2. The Rebate is only valid for reservations booked and prepaid through this program.
3. Rebate Levels are as follows[†]:

1-800-50-HOTEL call reservations only:
 2 Nights – $10 Rebate
 3 or 4 Nights – $20 Rebate
 5, 6, or 7 Nights – $30 Rebate
 8 or 9 Nights – $50 Rebate, and
 10 Nights – $100 Rebate

Online reservation rebates only:
 2 Nights – $20 Rebate
 3 or 4 Nights – $40 Rebate
 5, 6, or 7 Nights – $60 Rebate
 8 or 9 Nights – $100 Rebate, and
 10 Nights – $200 Rebate

4. After Checkout, please cut out and mail this completed form to:
 Rebate
 807 S. Jackson Road, Suite B
 Pharr, TX 78577
5. Not valid with any other offer, including, but not limited to, frequent flyer miles.
6. Form must be mailed in to collect rebates. Rebates will be credited back to your credit card.
7. One rebate per booking number.
8. The envelope must be postmarked within 60 days after your checkout date.
9. "Booking" means a completed stay booked on one calendar day.
10. Our interpretation of the rules of this offer is final.

[†]All rebates are in U.S. funds.

REBATE RULES OF USE

1. You must book and confirm a Guaranteed Best Rate hotel to be eligible for offer. No call-in or faxed rebates will be accepted.
2. The Rebate is only valid for reservations booked and prepaid through this program.
3. Rebate Levels are as follows[†]:

1-800-50-HOTEL call reservations only:
 2 Nights – $10 Rebate
 3 or 4 Nights – $20 Rebate
 5, 6, or 7 Nights – $30 Rebate
 8 or 9 Nights – $50 Rebate, and
 10 Nights – $100 Rebate

Online reservation rebates only:
 2 Nights – $20 Rebate
 3 or 4 Nights – $40 Rebate
 5, 6, or 7 Nights – $60 Rebate
 8 or 9 Nights – $100 Rebate, and
 10 Nights – $200 Rebate

4. After Checkout, please cut out and mail this completed form to:
 Rebate
 807 S. Jackson Road, Suite B
 Pharr, TX 78577
5. Not valid with any other offer, including, but not limited to, frequent flyer miles.
6. Form must be mailed in to collect rebates. Rebates will be credited back to your credit card.
7. One rebate per booking number.
8. The envelope must be postmarked within 60 days after your checkout date.
9. "Booking" means a completed stay booked on one calendar day.
10. Our interpretation of the rules of this offer is final.

[†]All rebates are in U.S. funds.

REBATE RULES OF USE

1. You must book and confirm a Guaranteed Best Rate hotel to be eligible for offer. No call-in or faxed rebates will be accepted.
2. The Rebate is only valid for reservations booked and prepaid through this program.
3. Rebate Levels are as follows[†]:

1-800-50-HOTEL call reservations only:
 2 Nights – $10 Rebate
 3 or 4 Nights – $20 Rebate
 5, 6, or 7 Nights – $30 Rebate
 8 or 9 Nights – $50 Rebate, and
 10 Nights – $100 Rebate

Online reservation rebates only:
 2 Nights – $20 Rebate
 3 or 4 Nights – $40 Rebate
 5, 6, or 7 Nights – $60 Rebate
 8 or 9 Nights – $100 Rebate, and
 10 Nights – $200 Rebate

4. After Checkout, please cut out and mail this completed form to:
 Rebate
 807 S. Jackson Road, Suite B
 Pharr, TX 78577
5. Not valid with any other offer, including, but not limited to, frequent flyer miles.
6. Form must be mailed in to collect rebates. Rebates will be credited back to your credit card.
7. One rebate per booking number.
8. The envelope must be postmarked within 60 days after your checkout date.
9. "Booking" means a completed stay booked on one calendar day.
10. Our interpretation of the rules of this offer is final.

[†]All rebates are in U.S. funds.

Guaranteed Best Rate Program

Rules of Use

- Rate is guaranteed at the time of reservation to be the best rate for the room type at the same hotel on the dates booked. If you find a lower rate available for the same dates at the same hotel, within 24 hours of booking the reservation with us, call 1-800-50-HOTEL (1-800-504-6835) and we will either refund the difference or cancel the reservation without a cancellation fee. **Subject to availability.** Bed type and smoking preferences cannot be guaranteed.

- You will be required to prepay with a major credit card.

- To change or cancel your reservation, call 1-800-50-HOTEL (1-800-504-6835). A fee will be applied to your credit card for any change or cancellation.

- The cancellation fee as of May 1, 2006, is $25 USD, which is subject to change. In addition, if you do not change or cancel your reservation before the cancellation policy period applicable to the hotel you reserved, which varies by hotel (usually 24 to 72 hours prior to your date of arrival), you will be subject to a charge of one-night's room rate, tax recovery charges, service fees and additional fees that may vary by hotel or property. Please request information on the applicable cancellation fees prior to making your reservation. No refunds will be made for no-shows or early checkouts.

- Some peak seasonal dates may not be discounted, and the rate guarantee does not apply to special events such as New Year's Eve and the Super Bowl.

- Guaranteed Best Rate Program hotels are not subject to any additional discounts, except the rebate. See Page E32.

- All rates are quoted and billed in U.S. funds unless otherwise specified.

All information was current at the time of printing and is expected to be in effect through the expiration of the Entertainment® book. However, changes beyond our control may affect the information prior to the expiration. Please note that Entertainment Publications, Inc. cannot guarantee the level of services offered at a property and/or if services are operational at the time of visit. Services may be closed due to seasonality reasons and/or may be closed for renovation.

The Privacy Policy for the Guaranteed Best Rate Program is located at www.entertainment.com/GBR.

Hotels at HalfPrice®

Save 50% off full-priced rates
or 10% off the best promotional rate
available to the public.

Here's how...

1. Find your city and choose a hotel. See listings on pages E35–E46 or go to www.entertainment.com/travel.

2. Call the hotel directly using the number listed to make advance reservations.
   - Identify yourself as an **Entertainment**® Member.
   - Check to see if the Entertainment® rate* is available for your travel dates.
   - Receive a confirmation number and retain it for your records.

3. Present your Entertainment® membership card at check-in.

*Discount subject to availability. See the Rules of Use on page E47 for full program details.

Your Key to Savings

$ Indicates the hotel's full-priced (rack) room rate before the discount.

$	=	Up to $60
$$	=	$61–$100
$$$	=	$101–$150
$$$$	=	$151 and Up

R30 Indicates reservations only accepted within 30 days of arrival.

U.S. funds. (Canadian hotels are in Canadian funds.)
(Rates subject to change. Hotel rates may fluctuate throughout the year due to seasonal factors.)

Contact the hotels directly for Entertainment® Membership rate availability.
50% off full-priced (rack) room rates or 10% off the best promotional rate—subject to availability.

Check out our ✦FEATURED PROPERTIES

United States of America

Alabama
See entertainment.com/travel for this state's hotel listings and savings.

Alaska
Anchorage

COAST INTERNATIONAL INN, $$$
3333 International Airport Rd., Anchorage. Valid for any room. Valid September thru May. R30. (907)243-2233, (800)544-0986

DAYS INN DOWNTOWN, $$$
321 E. 5th Ave., Anchorage. Valid for any room. Valid September thru May. (907)276-7226

HOWARD JOHNSON PLAZA HOTEL, $$$
239 W. 4th Ave., Anchorage. Valid for any room. Valid September thru May. (907)793-5500, (800)545-7665

Arizona
Phoenix

HOMEWOOD SUITES PHOENIX, $$$$
2536 W. Beryl Ave., Phoenix. Valid for one suite. (602)674-8900

RADISSON PHOENIX AIRPORT, $$$$
3333 E. University Dr., Phoenix. Valid for one standard room. Valid May 15 thru January 13. R30. (602)437-8400

TRAVELODGE SUITES HOTEL, $$
3101 N. 32nd St., Phoenix. Valid for one suite. (602)956-4900, (800)950-1688

Scottsdale

DAYS INN, $$$
4710 N. Scottsdale Rd., Scottsdale. Valid for any room. Valid May thru December. (480)947-5411

SCOTTSDALE MARRIOTT AT McDOWELL MOUNTAINS, $$$$$
16770 N. Perimeter, Scottsdale. Valid for one suite. (480)502-3836

THE SCOTTSDALE PLAZA RESORT, $$$$
7200 N. Scottsdale Rd., Scottsdale. Valid for any room or suite. R30. (480)948-5000, (800)832-2025

Tucson

LA QUINTA INN AIRPORT, $$$
7001 S Tucson Blvd., Tucson. Valid for any room. Special events excluded. (210)302-7206, (800)531-5900

RESIDENCE INN - TUCSON, $$$
6477 E. Speedway Blvd., Tucson. Valid for any room. Valid April 15 thru December 15. R30. (520)721-0991

Arkansas
See entertainment.com/travel for this state's hotel listings and savings.

California
Anaheim

ANAHEIM QUALITY INN MAINGATE, $$$
2200 S. Harbor Blvd., Anaheim. Valid for any room. Dec 20-31 & Labor Day wknd excl. Holidays & special events excl. R30. (714)750-5211, (800)479-5210

BEST WESTERN ANAHEIM INN, $$$
1630 S. Harbor Blvd., Anaheim. Valid for any room. (714)774-1050, (800)854-8175

DESERT INN & SUITES, $$$
1600 S. Harbor Blvd., Anaheim. Valid for any room. R30. (714)772-5050, (866)433-0228

DESERT PALMS HOTEL & SUITES, $$$$
631 W. Katella Ave., Anaheim. Valid for any room. Valid September thru May. (714)535-1133, (888)521-6420

PARK INN ANAHEIM, $$$$
1520 S. Harbor Blvd., Anaheim. Valid for any room. (714)635-7275, (800)670-7275

THE ANABELLA HOTEL, $$$$
1030 W. Katella Ave., Anaheim. Valid for any room. Suites & Concierge Rooms excl. (714)905-1050, (800)863-4888

TROPICANA INN & SUITES, $$$$
1540 S. Harbor Blvd., Anaheim. Valid for one deluxe room. Valid September thru May. Holidays & conventions excluded. (714)635-4082, (800)828-4898

Big Bear Lake

BIG BEAR LAKEFRONT LODGE, $$$$
40360 Lake View Drive, Big Bear Lake. Valid for any room. Suites excluded. Valid Sunday thru Thursday. (909)866-8271

SNOW LAKE LODGE, $$$$
41579 Big Bear Blvd., Big Bear. Valid for one condo. Holidays excl. (714)777-3700, (800)854-2324

Buena Park

KNOTTS BERRY FARM RESORT HOTEL, $$$$
7675 Crescent Ave., Buena Park. Valid for any room or suite. (714)226-0798, (866)752-2444

Carmel/Monterey

CAROUSEL MOTEL, $$$$
110 Riverside Ave., Santa Cruz. Valid for any room. Valid Sunday thru Friday September thru June. (831)425-7090

DEER HAVEN INNS & SUITES, $$$
740 Crocker Ave., Pacific Grove. Valid for any room. Valid Sunday thru Thursday. Special events & holidays excl. (831)655-6325, (800)525-3373

HIDDEN VALLEY INN, $$$$
102 W. Carmel Valley Rd., Carmel Valley. Valid for any room. Valid November thru March & Sunday-Thursday April thru October. Special events excluded. (831)659-5361, (800)367-3336

✦ LIGHTHOUSE LODGE & SUITES $$$$
1249 Lighthouse Ave., Pacific Grove. Valid for any room or suite. Valid October thru June. Special events excl. R30. (831)655-2111, (800)858-1249

Carpinteria

BEST WESTERN CARPINTERIA INN, $$$$
4558 Carpinteria Ave., Carpinteria. Valid for any room. Valid October - April & Sunday thru Thursday May - September. (805)684-0473

✦ HOLIDAY INN EXPRESS SANTA BARBARA/CARPINTERIA $$$
5606 Carpinteria Ave., Carpinteria. Valid for one suite. (805)566-9499, (888)409-8300

Chico

BEST WESTERN HERITAGE INN - CHICO, $$
25 Heritage Lane, Chico. Valid for one standard room. (530)894-8600

SAFARI INN, $
2352 Esplanade, Chico. Valid for one standard room. (530)343-3201

Dana Point

✦ HOLIDAY INN EXPRESS HOTEL & SUITES $$$$
34280 Pacific Coast Hwy., Dana Point. Valid for any room. June 15-Sept 15, holidays & New Year's Eve excl. (800)232-3262

Fairfield

ECONOLODGE INN & SUITES - FAIRFIELD/NAPA, $$
4625 Central Way, Fairfield. Valid for any room. (707)864-2426

Fresno

BEST WESTERN VILLAGE INN, $$
3110 N. Blackstone Ave., Fresno. Valid for any room. (559)226-2110, (800)722-8878

PICCADILLY INN EXPRESS, $$$
5113 E. McKinley, Fresno. Valid for any room. (559)456-1418, (800)445-2428

QUALITY INN, $$$
4278 W. Ashlan Ave., Fresno. Valid for any room. (559)275-2727

Hollywood

✦ BEST WESTERN SUNSET PLAZA HOTEL $$$
8400 Sunset Blvd., West Hollywood. Valid for any room. (323)654-0750, (800)421-3652

LE MONTROSE SUITE HOTEL, $$$$
900 Hammond St., West Hollywood. Valid for one suite. Special events excl. R30. (310)855-1115, (800)776-0666

✦ RAMADA INN HOLLYWOOD NEAR UNIVERSAL STUDIOS $$$$
1160 N. Vermont Ave., Hollywood. Valid for any room or suite. Special events excl. (323)315-1800, (800)800-9733

Los Angeles

CARLYLE INN, $$$$
1119 S. Robertson Blvd., Los Angeles. Valid for any room. Valid Sunday thru Thursday. July-Aug, special events & holidays excl. (310)275-4445, (800)322-7595

HOTEL SOFITEL, $$$$
8555 Beverly Blvd., Los Angeles. Valid for any room. Suites excluded. (310)278-5444, (800)521-7772

Discount subject to availability. Please read the **Rules of Use** on page E47.

Hotels at Half Price

OMNI LOS ANGELES HOTEL AT CALIFORNIA PLAZA, $$$$
251 S. Olive St., Los Angeles. Valid for one deluxe room. (213)617-3300, (800)THE-OMNI

SPORTSMEN'S LODGE HOTEL, $$$$
12825 Ventura Blvd., North Hollywood. Valid for any poolview room. Valid Friday, Saturday, Sunday & holidays. (818)769-4700, (800)821-8511

THE ORLANDO, $$$$
8384 W. Third St., Los Angeles. Valid for any room. (323)658-6600, (800)62H-OTEL

Los Angeles International Airport

+ **TRAVELODGE HOTEL AT LAX $$**
5547 W. Century Blvd., Los Angeles. Valid for any room. (800)421-3939

WESTIN LOS ANGELES AIRPORT, $$$$
5400 W. Century Blvd., Los Angeles. Valid for any room. R30. (310)216-5858

Milpitas

HILTON GARDEN INN, $$
30 Ranch Dr., Milpitas. Valid for any room or suite. Valid Friday, Saturday & Sunday. (408)719-1313

LARKSPUR LANDING, $$$
40 Ranch Dr., Milpitas. Valid for any room or suite. Valid Friday, Saturday & Sunday. (408)719-1212

Napa Valley

CALISTOGA GOLDEN HAVEN SPA & RESORT, $$$
1713 Lake St., Calistoga. Valid for any room. Economy rooms excl. Valid Sunday thru Thursday October thru June. R30. (707)942-6793

THE CHABLIS INN, $$$$
3360 Solano Ave., Napa. Valid for one standard room. Valid Sunday thru Thursday November - June. (707)257-1944, (800)443-3490

Novato

BEST WESTERN NOVATO OAKS INN, $$$
215 Alameda del Prado, Novato. Valid for one standard room. Valid October thru May. R30. (415)883-4400, (800)625-7466

INN MARIN, $$$$
250 Entrada Dr., Novato. Valid for any room. Suites excluded. Valid November thru May & Sunday thru Thursday June thru October. (415)883-5952, (800)652-6565

Oakland

CLARION HOTEL OAKLAND AIRPORT, $$$
500 Hegenberger Rd., Oakland. Valid for any room. (510)562-5311

WOODFIN SUITE HOTEL, $$$$
5800 Shellmound St., Emeryville. Valid for one suite. (510)601-5880, (888)433-9042

Ontario

RODEWAY INN - ONTARIO AIRPORT/MILLS MALL, $$
4075 E. Guasti Rd., Ontario. Valid for any room. Special events excluded. (909)390-8886

SHERATON, $$$$
429 N. Vineyard Ave., Ontario. Valid for any room. April 27-May 1 & October 27-November 1 excl. (909)937-8000, (800)582-2946

Palm Springs

HILTON PALM SPRINGS RESORT, $$$$
400 E. Tahquitz Way, Palm Springs. Valid for any room or suite. Min 2 nts stay on holidays & holiday wknds. Valid May thru January. (760)320-6868, (800)522-6900

RESIDENCE INN PALM DESERT, $$$$
38-305 Cook Street, Palm Desert. Valid for one studio room. (760)776-0050

Rancho Cordova

QUALITY INN & SUITES-RANCHOCORDOVA/SACRAMENTO, $$$
3240 Matherfield Rd., Rancho Cordova. Valid for any room. Special events excluded. (916)363-3344

Sacramento

GOVERNORS INN, $$$
210 Richards Blvd., Sacramento. Valid for any room. Valid Friday, Saturday & Sunday. (916)448-7224

HOLIDAY INN SACRAMENTO NORTHEAST, $$$$
5321 Date Ave., Sacramento. Valid for any room. Suites excluded. (916)338-5800, (800)338-2810

San Diego

+ **BEST VALUE INN - MISSION BAY/SEAWORLD $$$**
4545 Mission Bay Dr., San Diego. Valid for any room. Holidays & special events excl. (858)483-4222

+ **BEST WESTERN ISLAND PALMS HOTEL & MARINA $$$$**
2051 Shelter Island Dr., San Diego. Valid for marina view room or suite. (619)222-0561, (800)345-9995

+ **DAYS INN HOTEL CIRCLE/SEA WORLD $$$**
543 Hotel Circle S., San Diego. Valid for one deluxe room. (619)297-8800, (800)227-4743

+ **HOLIDAY INN SAN DIEGO BAYSIDE $$$$**
4875 N. Harbor Dr., San Diego. Valid for one deluxe room. R30. (619)224-3621, (800)662-8899

+ **HUMPHREY'S HALF MOON INN & SUITES $$$$**
2303 Shelter Island Dr., San Diego. Valid for one junior suite. R30. (619)224-3411, (800)542-7400

+ **PACIFIC TERRACE HOTEL $$$$**
610 Diamond St., San Diego. Valid for any room. Valid Sunday thru Thursday September 15 thru May 31. R30. (858)581-3500, (800)344-3370

+ **THE DANA ON MISSION BAY $$$$**
1710 W. Mission Bay Dr., San Diego. Valid for one marina view room. R30. (619)222-6440, (800)345-9995

+ **TOWN & COUNTRY RESORT HOTEL $$$$**
500 Hotel Circle N., San Diego. Valid for any room. Holiday wknds excl. (619)291-7131, (800)772-8527

San Francisco

COMFORT INN BY THE BAY, $$$$
2775 Van Ness Ave., San Francisco. Valid for any room. July, Aug & Special events excl. (415)928-5000

FRANCISCO BAY INN, $$$
1501 Lombard St., San Francisco. Valid for one deluxe room. (415)474-3030, (800)410-7007

MARK HOPKINS INTER-CONTINENTAL, $$$$
One Nob Hill, San Francisco. Valid for one standard room. R30. (415)392-3434

OMNI SAN FRANCISCO HOTEL, $$$$
500 California St. at Montomery, San Francisco. Valid for one deluxe room. (415)677-9494, (800)THE-OMNI

THE CARTWRIGHT HOTEL ON UNION SQUARE, $$$$
524 Sutter Street, San Francisco. Valid for any room. (415)421-2865, (888)919-9779

THE PICKWICK HOTEL, $$$$
85 Fifth St., San Francisco. Valid for any room. (415)421-7500, (800)227-3282

San Francisco International Airport

DOUBLETREE HOTEL SAN FRANCISCO AIRPORT, $$$$
835 Airport Blvd., Burlingame. Valid for any room. (650)344-5500

San Jose

CROWNE PLAZA, $$$$
282 Almaden Blvd., San Jose. Valid for any room. (408)998-0400

HOTEL DE ANZA, $$$$
233 W. Santa Clara St., San Jose. Valid for any room. Valid Thursday thru Sunday & Holidays. New Year's Eve excl. (408)286-1000, (800)843-3700

HOTEL VALENCIA SANTANA ROW, $$$$
355 Santana Row, San Jose. Valid for any room. R30. (408)551-0010, (866)842-0100

WYNDHAM SAN JOSE HOTEL, $$$$
1350 N. First St., San Jose. Valid for one standard room. (408)453-6200, (800)WYN-DHAM

Santa Ana

COMFORT SUITES, $$$
2620 Hotel Terrace Dr., Santa Ana. Valid for one suite. (714)966-5200, (800)592-4776

DOUBLETREE CLUB HOTEL, $$$$
7 Hutton Centre Dr., Santa Ana. Valid for one standard room. (714)751-2400

EMBASSY SUITES SANTA ANA-OCAN, $$$$
1325 E. Dyer Rd., Santa Ana. Valid for any room. (714)241-3800

E36 — Discount subject to availability. Please read the **Rules of Use** on page E47.

Remember to identify yourself as an Entertainment® Member.

Contact the hotels directly for Entertainment® Membership rate availability.
50% off full-priced (rack) room rates or **10% off the best promotional rate** — subject to availability.

Check out our ✦ **FEATURED PROPERTIES**

Santa Barbara

✦ **CABRILLO INN AT THE BEACH, $$$$**
931 E. Cabrillo Blvd., Santa Barbara. Valid for one oceanview room. Valid Sunday thru Thursday. July & Aug excl. (805)966-1641, (800)648-6708

FESS PARKER'S DOUBLE TREE RESORT, $$$$
633 E. Cabrillo Blvd., Santa Barbara. Valid for one standard room. Valid Sunday thru Friday. R30. (805)564-4333

SANTA BARBARA INN, $$$$
901 E. Cabrillo Blvd., Santa Barbara. Valid for any room. Valid Sunday thru Thursday. Special events excluded. R30. (805)966-2285, (800)231-0431

Santa Clara

CANDLEWOOD SUITES SILICON VALLEY, SAN JOSE, $$$$
481 El Camino Real, Santa Clara. Valid for one studio suite. Max stay 6 nts. (408)241-9305

SIERRA SUITES HOTEL-SANTA CLARA, $$$$
3915 Rivermark Plaza, Santa Clara. Valid for one suite. (408)486-0800, (800)474-3772

Sonoma County

BEST WESTERN DRY CREEK INN, $$$
198 Dry Creek Rd., Healdsburg. Valid for any room. Valid Sunday thru Thursday October thru June. Holiday weekends excl. R30. (707)433-0300, (800)222-5784

FLAMINGO CONFERENCE RESORT & SPA, $$$$
2777 Fourth St., Santa Rosa. Valid for any room or suite. Valid Sunday thru Thursday October thru June. (707)545-8530, (800)848-8300

South Lake Tahoe

BEST WESTERN TIMBER COVE LODGE MARINA RESORT, $$$
3411 Lake Tahoe Blvd., South Lake Tahoe. Valid for any room. Valid Sunday thru Thursday. Dec. 25-Jan. 2, Holidays, & special event periods excluded. (530)541-6722, (800)972-8558

QUALITY INN & SUITES, $$$
3838 Lake Tahoe Blvd., South Lake Tahoe. Valid for any room. Valid Sunday thru Thursday. Weekends & Holiday periods excl. (530)541-5400, (800)245-6343

✦ **TAHOE CHALET INN $$$$**
3860 Hwy. 50, South Lake Tahoe. Valid for any room. Minimum stay 2 nights. Dec. 26-Jan. 1 & holidays excl. R30. (530)544-3311, (800)821-2656

TAHOE SEASONS RESORT, $$$$
3901 Saddle Rd., South Lake Tahoe. Valid for one suite. Holidays excluded. R30. (530)541-6700, (800)874-8770

Sunnyvale

LARKSPUR LANDING, $$
748 N. Mathilda Ave., Sunnyvale. Valid for any room or suite. Valid Friday, Saturday & Sunday. (408)733-1212

SUNDOWNER INN, $$$$
504 Ross Dr., Sunnyvale. Valid for any room. (408)734-9900, (800)223-9901

Visalia

LAMP LITER INN, $$$
3300 W. Mineral King Ave., Visalia. Valid for any room. (559)732-4511, (800)662-6692

Yosemite National Park

THE PINES RESORT, $$$
54432 North Shore Road, Bass Lake. Valid for any room. Valid September thru May. Holidays excl. Min. stay 2 nights on wknds. (559)642-3121, (800)350-7463

THE REDWOODS IN YOSEMITE, $$$$
8038 Chilnualna Falls Rd., Wawona. Valid for any room. Min stay 2 nts. Valid September thru May. Holidays excluded. (209)375-6666

Colorado

Aspen/Snowmass Area

CRESTWOOD CONDOMINIUMS, $$$
400 Wood Rd., Snowmass Village. Valid for one condo. Holidays excl. R30. (970)923-2450, (800)356-5949

SNOWFLAKE INN, $$$$
221 E. Hyman Ave., Aspen. Valid for 1-bedroom suite w/kitchen. (970)925-3221

Aurora/Denver International Airport

CRYSTAL INN, $$$
3300 N. Ouray St., Aurora. Valid for one standard room. Special events excluded. R30. (303)340-3800, (888)890-3800

LA QUINTA INN AURORA, $$
1011 S Abilene St, Aurora. Valid for any room. Special events excluded. (210)302-7206, (800)531-5900

Avon/Beaver Creek

SHERATON MOUNTAIN VISTA, $$$$
160 W Beaver Creek Blvd, Avon. Valid for one deluxe room. R30. (970)748-6000, (888)627-8098

THE CHARTER AT BEAVER CREEK, $$$$
120 Offerson Road, Beaver Creek. Valid for one unit. R30. (970)949-6660, (800)525-6660

Colorado Springs

APOLLO PARK EXECUTIVE SUITES, $$$
805 S. Circle Dr. #2-B, Colorado Springs. Valid for one suite. (719)634-0286, (800)279-3620

COLORADO SPRINGS HAMPTON INN, $$$
7245 Commerce Center Dr., Colorado Springs. Valid for any room. Valid September thru May. R30. (719)593-9700

Copper

✦ **COPPER ONE LODGE $$$$**
155 Copper Mountain Rd., Copper. Valid for one deluxe room. Martin Luther King & President's wks, Spring Break & Dec 17-Jan 2 excl. (303)791-3680, (800)801-7356

COPPER SPRINGS LODGE, $$$$
105 Wheeler Circle, Copper. Valid for one deluxe room. Martin Luther King & President's wks, Spring Break & Dec 17-Jan 2 excl. (303)791-3680, (800)801-7356

Denver

CANDLEWOOD SUITES DENVER LAKEWOOD, $$$$
895 Tabor St., Golden. Valid for one studio suite. Max stay 6 nts. (303)232-7171

LA QUINTA INN CHERRY CREEK, $$
1975 S Colorado Blvd, Denver. Valid for any room. Special events excluded. (210)302-7206, (800)531-5900

RED LION DENVER DOWNTOWN, $$$$
1975 Bryant St., Denver. Valid for any room. Special events excluded. (303)433-8331, (800)388-5381

SHERATON DENVER TECH CENTER, $$$$
7007 S. Clinton St., Englewood. Valid for one standard room. (303)799-6200

Keystone

CINNAMON RIDGE, $$$$
85 Oro Grande, Keystone. Valid for one deluxe room. Martin Luther King & President's wks, Spring Break & Dec 17-Jan 2 excl. (303)791-3680, (800)801-7356

✦ **THE SPRINGS LODGE $$$$**
0052 Hunki Dori Ct., Keystone. Valid for one deluxe room. Martin Luther King & President's wks, Spring Break & Dec 17-Jan 2 excl. (303)791-3680, (800)801-7356

Vail

LION SQUARE LODGE, $$$$
660 W. Lionshead Place, Vail. Valid for one unit. R30. (970)476-2281, (800)525-5788

MONTANEROS, $$$$
641 W. Lionshead Circle, Vail. Valid for one unit. R30. (970)476-2491, (800)444-8245

Westminster

LA QUINTA INN WESTMINSTER MALL, $$
8701 Turnpike Dr, Westminster. Valid for any room. Special events excluded. (210)302-7206, (800)531-5900

OMNI INTERLOCKEN RESORT, $$$$
500 Interlocken Blvd., Broomfield. Valid for one deluxe room. (303)438-6600, (800)THE-OMNI

Connecticut

See entertainment.com/travel for this state's hotel listings and savings.

Delaware

See entertainment.com/travel for this state's hotel listings and savings.

District Of Columbia

Washington D.C.

BEACON HOTEL & CORPORATE QUARTERS, $$$$
1615 Rhode Island Ave. NW, Washington. Valid for any room. Valid Friday, Saturday, Sunday and holidays. (202)296-2100, (800)821-4367

Discount subject to availability. Please read the **Rules of Use** on page E47.

Hotels at Half Price

BEST WESTERN NEW HAMPSHIRE SUITES, $$$$
1121 New Hampshire Ave. NW, Washington. Valid for one suite. Valid Friday, Saturday & Sunday June thru February. (202)457-0565

GEORGETOWN SUITES, $$$$
1111 30th St. NW., Washington. Valid for one suite. April, May & October excluded. (202)298-7800, (800)348-7203

Florida

Boca Raton

DOUBLETREE GUEST SUITES, $$$$
701 N.W. 53rd St., Boca Raton. Valid for one suite. (561)997-9500

HOLIDAY INN EXPRESS BOCA RATON WEST, $$$
8144 W. Glades Rd., Boca Raton. Valid for any room. Dec 20-Jan 1 & Feb1-April 15 excl. R30. (561)482-7070

Cape Canaveral

VENTURA RESORT RENTALS, $$$$
7400 Ridgewood Ave., Cape Canaveral. Valid for one condo. (407)273-8770, (800)311-9736

Ft. Lauderdale

SHERATON YANKEE TRADER HOTEL, $$$$
321 N. Ft. Lauderdale Beach Blvd., Ft. Lauderdale. Valid for any room or suite. (954)467-1111, (888)627-7108

WELLESLEY INN, $$$
13600 NW 2nd St., Sunrise. Valid for one standard room. Holidays excl. (954)845-9929

Kissimmee

COUNTRY INN & SUITES MAINGATE, $$$
5001 Calypso Cay Way, Kissimmee. Valid for any room. Holidays excl. R30. (407)997-1400

✦ **KNIGHTS INN MAINGATE $**
7475 W. Irlo Bronson Memorial Hwy., Kissimmee. Valid for any room. (407)396-4200, (800)944-0062

OAK PLANTATION RESORT, $$$$
4090 Enchanted Oaks Circle, Kissimmee. Valid for any room. R30. (407)847-8200, (866)804-8200

✦ **QUALITY SUITES AT DISNEY'S MAINGATE $$$$**
5876 W. Irlo Bronson Hwy (US 192), Kissimmee. Valid for one 1 or 2 bedroom suites. (407)396-8040, (800)848-4148

TRAVELODGE HOTEL - MAINGATE EAST, $$$$
5711 W. Irlo Bronson Memorial Hwy., Kissimmee. Valid for any room. (407)396-4222

VILLAS OF SOMERSET, $$$$
2928 Vineland Rd., Kissimmee. Valid for one villa. (407)397-0700, (800)344-3959

Lake Buena Vista

✦ **WALT DISNEY WORLD SWAN & DOLPHIN $$$$**
1500 Epcot Resorts Blvd., Lake Buena Vista. Valid for any room. Dec 25-Jan 1 excl. (800)227-1500

Miami

CANDLEWOOD SUITES MIAMI AIRPORT WEST, $$$
8855 NW 27th St., Miami. Valid for one studio suite. Max stay 6 nts. (305)591-9099

COMFORT INN & SUITES HOTEL, $$$
5301 N.W. 36th St., Miami. Valid for one standard room. Jan 26-March 15 excl. R30. (305)871-6000

LA QUINTA INN & SUITES AIRPORT WEST, $$$
8730 NW 27th St, Miami. Valid for any room. Special events excluded. (210)302-7206, (800)531-5900

Miami Beach

BOULEVARD HOTEL, $$$$
740 Ocean Dr., Miami Beach. Valid for any room. (305)532-0376

MARSEILLES HOTEL, $$$$
1741 Collins Ave., Miami Beach. Valid for any room. (305)503-1442, (800)829-3003

Orlando

✦ **HOLIDAY HOMES OF ORLANDO $$$$**
9521 S. Orange Blossom Trail, Ste. 103, Orlando. Valid for 3- or 4-bedroom home with private pool. Holidays excl. (407)240-5527, (800)288-2187

HOLIDAY INN ORLANDO INT'L AIRPORT, $$$$
5750 TG Lee Blvd., Orlando. Valid for any room. (407)851-6400, (800)206-2747

MASTER'S INN INTERNATIONAL DRIVE, $$
8222 Jamaican Ct., Orlando. Valid for any room. (407)345-1172, (800)633-3434

RADISSON INN LAKE BUENA VISTA, $$$
8686 Palm Pkwy., Orlando. Valid for any room. Max stay 7 nts. (407)239-8400

✦ **SHERATON'S VISTANA RESORT $$$$**
8800 Vistana Centre Dr., Orlando. Valid for any room. R30. (407)239-3100, (866)208-0003

✦ **VENTURA RESORT RENTALS $$$$**
5946 Curry Ford Rd., Orlando. Valid for one home or condo. (407)273-8770, (800)247-8417

Plantation

✦ **SHERATON SUITES PLANTATION $$$$**
311 N. University Dr., Plantation. Valid for one suite. (954)424-3300, (800)325-3535

St. Petersburg

✦ **TRADEWINDS ISLAND GRAND BEACH RESORT $$$$**
5500 Gulf Blvd., St. Pete Beach. Valid for any room. Standard Rooms & Holiday periods excl. R30. (727)363-2212, (877)300-5520

✦ **TRADEWINDS SANDPIPER HOTEL & SUITES $$$$**
6000 Gulf Blvd., St. Pete Beach. Valid for any room. Standard Rooms & Holiday periods excl. R30. (727)363-2212, (877)300-5520

Tampa

CHASE SUITE HOTEL BY WOODFIN, $$$$
3075 N. Rocky Point Dr., Tampa. Valid for one suite. (813)281-5677, (877)433-9644

LA QUINTA INN & SUITES U.S.F., $$$
3701 E Fowler, Tampa. Valid for any room. Special events excluded. (210)302-7206, (800)531-5900

SHERATON SUITES - TAMPA AIRPORT, $$$$
4400 W. Cypress St., Tampa. Valid for any one suite. (813)873-8675

Georgia

See entertainment.com/travel for this state's hotel listings and savings.

Hawaii

Big Island

HILO SEASIDE HOTEL, $$$
126 Banyan Way, Hilo. Valid for any room. Standard garden rooms excl. (808)935-0821, (800)560-5557

KONA SEASIDE HOTEL, $$$
76-5646 Palani Rd., Kailua-Kona. Valid for any room. Standard rooms excl. (808)329-2455, (800)560-5558

RESORTQUEST KONA BY THE SEA, $$$$
75-6106 Alii Drive, Kailua-Kona. Valid for any room. Dec 23 - Jan 3 & Feb 18 - 21 excl. (403)444-4136, (866)774-2924

RESORTQUEST SHORES AT WAIKOLOA, $$$$
69-1035 Keana Place, Waikoloa. Valid for any room. Dec 23-Jan 3 & Feb 18-21 excl. (403)444-4136, (866)774-2924

✦ **RESORTQUEST WAIKOLOA COLONY VILLAS $$$$**
69-555 Waikoloa Beach Dr., Waikoloa. Valid for any room. Dec 23-Jan 3 & Feb 18-21 excl. (403)444-4136, (866)774-2924

Kauai

HANALEI BAY RESORT, $$$$
5380 Honoiki Rd., Princeville. Valid for any room. Dec 23-Jan 3 & Feb 18-21 excl. (403)444-4136, (866)774-2924

HILTON KAUAI BEACH RESORT, $$$$
4331 Kauai Beach Dr., Lihue. Valid for any room. (808)245-1955, (888)805-3843

✦ **KAUAI SANDS HOTEL $$$**
420 Papaloa Rd., Wailua. Valid for any room. Standard rooms excl. (808)822-4951, (800)560-5553

RESORTQUEST AT POIPU KAI, $$$$
1775 Poipu Rd., Koloa. Valid for any room. Dec 23-Jan 3 & Feb 18-21 excl. (403)444-4136, (866)774-2924

✦ **RESORTQUEST ISLANDER ON THE BEACH $$$$**
4-484 Kuhio Hwy., Kapaa. Valid for any room. Dec 23-Jan 3 & Feb 18-21 excl. (403)444-4136, (866)774-2924

Discount subject to availability. Please read the **Rules of Use** on page E47.

Remember to identify yourself as an Entertainment® Member.

Contact the hotels directly for Entertainment® Membership rate availability. **50% off full-priced (rack) room rates** or **10% off the best promotional rate**— subject to availability.

Check out our ✦FEATURED PROPERTIES

✦ **RESORTQUEST WAIMEA PLANTATION COTTAGES $$$$**
9400 Kaumualii Hwy., #367, Waimea. Valid for any room. Dec 23-Jan 3 & Feb 18-21 excl. (403)444-4136, (866)774-2924

Maui

ASTON MAUI LU, $$$
575 South Kihei Rd., Kihei. Valid for any room. Dec 23-Jan 3 & Feb 18-21 excl. (403)444-4136, (866)774-2924

MAUI SEASIDE HOTEL, $$$
100 W. Kaahumanu Ave., Kahului. Valid for any room. Standard rooms excl. (808)877-3311, (800)560-5552

✦ **MAUI SUNSET $$$**
1032 S. Kihei Rd., Kihei. Valid for one condo. R30. (425)454-9923, (800)233-3310

RESORTQUEST AT PAPAKEA RESORT, $$$$
3543 Lower Honoapiilani Rd., Kaanapali. Valid for any room. Dec 23-Jan 3 & Feb 18-21 excl. (403)444-4136, (866)774-2924

✦ **RESORTQUEST AT THE MAUI BANYAN $$$$**
2575 South Kihei Rd., Kihei. Valid for any room. Dec 23-Jan 3 & Feb 18-21 excl. (403)444-4136, (866)774-2924

✦ **RESORTQUEST KAANAPALI SHORES $$$$**
3445 Lower Honoapiilani Rd., Kaanapali. Valid for any room. Dec 23-Jan 3 & Feb 18-21 excl. (403)444-4136, (866)774-2924

RESORTQUEST MAHANA AT KAANAPALI, $$$$
110 Kaanapali Shores Place, Kaanapali. Valid for any room. Min stay 3 nts. Dec 23-Jan 3 & Feb 18-21 excl. (403)444-4136, (866)774-2924

RESORTQUEST MAUI HILL, $$$$
2881 South Kihei Rd., Kihei. Valid for any room. Dec 23-Jan 3 & Feb 18-21 excl. (403)444-4136, (866)774-2924

✦ **RESORTQUEST MAUI KAANAPALI VILLAS $$$$**
45 Kai Ala Dr., Kaanapali. Valid for any room. Dec 23-Jan 3 & Feb 18-21 excl. (403)444-4136, (866)774-2924

RESORTQUEST PAKI MAUI, $$$$
3615 Lower Honopiilani Rd., Kaanapali. Valid for any room. Dec 23 - Jan 3 & Feb 18 - 21 excl. (403)444-4136, (866)774-2924

Oahu

ASTON HONOLULU PRINCE, $$$
415 Nahua St., Honolulu. Valid for any room. Dec 23-Jan 3 & Feb 18-21 excl. (403)444-4136, (866)774-2924

RESORTQUEST AT THE EXECUTIVE CENTRE HOTEL, $$$$
1088 Bishop Street, Honolulu. Valid for any room. Dec 23 - Jan 3 & Feb 18 - 21 excl. (403)444-4136, (866)774-2924

RESORTQUEST AT THE WAIKIKI BANYAN, $$$$
201 Ohua Ave., Honolulu. Valid for any room. Dec 23-Jan 3 & Feb 18-21 excl. (403)444-4136, (866)774-2924

RESORTQUEST COCONUT PLAZA HOTEL, $$$$
450 Lewers St., Honolulu. Valid for any room. Dec 23-Jan 3 & Feb 18-21 excl. (403)444-4136, (866)774-2924

RESORTQUEST PACIFIC MONARCH, $$$$
2427 Kuhio Ave., Honolulu. Valid for any room. Dec 23-Jan 3 & Feb 18-21 excl. (403)444-4136, (866)774-2924

✦ **RESORTQUEST WAIKIKI BEACH HOTEL $$$$**
2570 Kalakaua Ave., Honolulu. Valid for any room. Dec 23-Jan 3 & Feb 18-21 excl. (403)444-4136, (866)774-2924

RESORTQUEST WAIKIKI BEACH TOWER, $$$$
2470 Kalakaua Ave., Honolulu. Valid for any room. Dec 23-Jan 3 & Feb 18-21 excl. (403)444-4136, (866)774-2924

RESORTQUEST WAIKIKI BEACHSIDE HOTEL, $$$$
2452 Kalakaua Ave., Honolulu. Valid for any room. Dec 23-Jan 3 & Feb 18-21 excl. (403)444-4136, (866)774-2924

RESORTQUEST WAIKIKI CIRCLE HOTEL, $$$$
2464 Kalakaua Ave., Honolulu. Valid for any room. Dec 23-Jan 3 & Feb 18-21 excl. (403)444-4136, (866)774-2924

RESORTQUEST WAIKIKI JOY HOTEL, $$$
320 Lewers Street, Honolulu. Valid for any room. Dec 23-Jan 3 & Feb 18-21 excl. (403)444-4136, (866)774-2924

✦ **RESORTQUEST WAIKIKI SUNSET $$$$**
229 Paoakalani Ave., Honolulu. Valid for any room. Dec 23-Jan 3 & Feb 18-21 excl. (403)444-4136, (866)774-2924

Idaho

Boise

BEST WESTERN AIRPORT INN, $$
2660 Airport Way, Boise. Valid for any room. Valid September thru May. R30. (208)384-5000, (800)727-5004

BEST WESTERN NORTHWEST LODGE, $$
6989 Federal Way, Boise. Valid for any room. Valid September thru May. R30. (208)287-2300, (866)385-6343

HOLIDAY INN BOISE AIRPORT, $$$
3300 Vista Ave., Boise. Valid for any room. R30. (208)343-4900

RED LION, $$$$
1800 Fairview Ave., Boise. Valid for any room. Suites excluded. R30. (208)344-7691

RESIDENCE INN BY MARRIOTT - BOISE CENTRAL, $$$
1401 Lusk Ave., Boise. Valid for one studio suite. R30. (208)344-1200

Coeur d'Alene

GUESTHOUSE INN, $$
330 W Appleway Dr., Coeur d'Alene. Valid for any room. (208)765-3011

LA QUINTA INN & SUITES, $$
2209 E. Sherman Ave, Coeur d' Alene. Valid for any room. Suites excluded. Valid September thru May. Special events excl. (208)667-6777, (800)531-5900

Idaho Falls

RED LION HOTEL ON THE FALLS, $$$
475 River Parkway, Idaho Falls. Valid for any room. Valid September thru May. R30. (208)523-8000, (800)325-4000

Illinois

Chicago

BEST WESTERN GRANT PARK HOTEL, $$$$
1100 S. Michigan Ave., Chicago. Valid for any room. (312)922-2900, (800)472-6875

DAYS INN GOLD COAST, $$$$
1816 N. Clark, Chicago. Valid for any room. Valid Sunday thru Thursday. Special events & holidays excl. (312)664-3040

HILTON CHICAGO, $$$$
720 S. Michigan Ave., Chicago. Valid for any room. (312)922-4400

HOMEWOOD SUITES BY HILTON CHICAGO-DOWNTOWN, $$$$
40 E. Grand Ave., Chicago. Valid for one suite. R30. (312)644-2222

OMNI CHICAGO HOTEL, $$$$
676 N. Michigan Ave., Chicago. Valid for one suite. (312)944-6664, (800)THE-OMNI

Indiana

Indianapolis

HAMPTON INN NORTHEAST, $$
6817 E. 82nd St., Indianapolis. Valid for any room. R30. (317)576-0220

MARRIOTT INDIANAPOLIS EAST, $$$$
7202 E. 21st St., Indianapolis. Valid for any room. Advance purchase rates excl. (317)352-1231

MARTEN HOUSE HOTEL & LILLY CONFERENCE CENTER, $$$
1801 W. 86th St., Indianapolis. Valid for any room. Special events excl. (317)872-4111, (800)736-5634

Iowa

Cedar Rapids

BEST WESTERN COOPERS MILL HOTEL & RESTAURANT, $$
100 F Ave. NW, Cedar Rapids. Valid for any room. R30. (319)366-5323, (800)858-5511

CROWNE PLAZA FIVE SEASONS, $$$
350 1st Ave. N.E., Cedar Rapids. Valid for one standard room. Special events excl. R30. (319)363-8161

Des Moines

CHASE SUITE HOTEL, $$$
11428 Forest Ave., Clive. Valid for one suite. (515)223-7700, (888)433-6140

Discount subject to availability. Please read the **Rules of Use** on page E47.

E39

Go to **entertainment.com/travel** for more listings.

Hotels at Half Price

SHERATON, $$$$
1800 50th St., West Des Moines. Valid for any room. (515)223-1800

VALLEY WEST INN, $$$
3535 Westown Pkwy, W. Des Moines. Valid for any room. Aug. 1-26 excl. Suites excluded. (515)225-2524, (800)833-6755

Kansas

Overland Park

CHASE SUITE HOTEL BY WOODFIN, $$$$
6300 W. 110th St., Overland Park. Valid for one suite. (913)491-3333, (888)433-9765

HAMPTON INN, $$$
10591 Metcalf Frontage, Overland Park. Valid for any room. Valid Friday, Saturday & Sunday September thru May. R30. (913)341-1551

Wichita

HILTON WICHITA AIRPORT, $$$$
2098 Airport Rd., Wichita. Valid for one standard room. (316)945-5272, (800)247-4458

THE INN AT TALLGRASS, $$$$
2280 N. Tara, Wichita. Valid for one suite. (316)684-3466

Kentucky

See entertainment.com/travel for this state's hotel listings and savings.

Louisiana

New Orleans

EMBASSY SUITES HOTEL, $$$$
315 Julia St., New Orleans. Valid for one suite. R30. (504)525-1993

HOLIDAY INN CHATEAU LEMOYNE, $$$$
301 Rue Dauphine, New Orleans. Valid for any room. R30. (504)581-1303, (800)747-3279

HOTEL PROVINCIAL, $$$$
1024 Rue Chartres, New Orleans. Valid for any room. R30. (504)581-4995, (800)535-7922

LA QUINTA INN BULLARD, $$
12001 I-10 Service Rd, New Orleans. Valid for any room. Special events excluded. (210)302-7206, (800)531-5900

OMNI ROYAL ORLEANS, $$$$
612 St. Louis St., New Orleans. Valid for one deluxe room. Valid Sunday thru Thursday. Mardi Gras, Dec 31-Jan 3 & special events excl. (504)529-5333, (800)THE-OMNI

Maine

See entertainment.com/travel for this state's hotel listings and savings.

Maryland

See entertainment.com/travel for this state's hotel listings and savings.

Massachusetts

Boston

COPLEY SQUARE HOTEL, $$$$
47 Huntington Ave., Boston. Valid for any room. (617)536-9000, (800)225-7062

MIDTOWN HOTEL, $$$$
220 Huntington Ave., Boston. Valid for any room. Sept & Oct excl. R30. (617)262-1000, (800)343-1177

Michigan

See entertainment.com/travel for this state's hotel listings and savings.

Minnesota

Duluth

HAWTHORN SUITES AT WATERFRONT PLAZA, $$$$
325 Lake Ave. S, Duluth. Valid for one suite. Valid Sunday thru Thursday September thru June. R30. (218)727-4663, (877)766-2665

INN ON LAKE SUPERIOR, $$$
350 Canal Park Dr., Duluth. Valid for one standard room. Valid Sunday thru Thursday October thru June. (218)726-1111, (888)668-4352

RADISSON HOTEL DULUTH HARBORVIEW, $$$
505 W. Superior St., Duluth. Valid for one std dbl, dlx or hillside dbl dlx room. Holidays excl. Valid Sunday thru Thursday October thru May. R30. (218)727-8981

Eagan

✦ HILTON GARDEN INN - EAGAN $$$
1975 Rahncliff Ct., Eagan. Valid for any room. Valid September thru May. Stay 'n Fly pkgs excl. R30. (651)686-4605, (800)500-4232

✦ HOLIDAY INN EXPRESS - EAGAN $$$
1950 Rahncliff Ct., Eagan. Valid for any room or suite. Valid September thru May. Stay 'n Fly pkgs excl. R30. (651)681-9266, (800)681-5290

Maplewood

BEST WESTERN MAPLEWOOD INN, $$$
1780 E. County Rd. D, Maplewood. Valid for any room. R30. (651)770-2811, (888)770-2811

Minneapolis

HAMPTON INN, $$$
4201 American Blvd., Bloomington. Valid for any room. R30. (952)835-6643

HILTON GARDEN INN BLOOMINGTON, $$$
8100 Bridge Rd., Bloomington. Valid for any room. Valid September thru May. R30. (952)831-1012, (800)645-2319

HOLIDAY INN METRODOME, $$$$
1500 Washington Ave. S, Minneapolis. Valid for one double room. Max stay 7 nts. (612)333-4646

LE BOURGET AERO SUITES, $$$$
7770 Johnson Ave. S, Bloomington. Valid for any room. R30. (952)893-9999, (800)449-0409

PARK PLAZA HOTEL, $$$$
4460 W. 78th St. Circle, Bloomington. Valid for any room. R30. (952)831-3131, (800)814-7000

Rochester

COURTYARD ROCHESTER, $$$
161 13th Ave. SW, Rochester. Valid for any room. Valid September thru May. R30. (507)536-0040, (800)504-1035

HOLIDAY INN CITY CENTER, $$$
220 S. Broadway, Rochester. Valid for any room. Valid Friday & Saturday. R30. (507)288-3231, (800)241-1597

St. Paul

HAMPTON INN SHOREVIEW, $$$
1000 Gramsie Rd., Shoreview. Valid for any room. Valid September thru May. R30. (651)482-0402, (877)233-3194

HOLIDAY INN RIVER CENTRE, $$$$
175 W. 7th St., St. Paul. Valid for any room. (651)225-1515

HOLIDAY INN ST. PAUL NORTH, $$$$
1201 W. Country Rd. E., St. Paul. Valid for any room. Poolside rooms & suites excl. R30. (651)636-4123

RADISSON CITY CENTER HOTEL ST. PAUL, $$$$
411 Minnesota St., St. Paul. Valid for any room. (651)291-8800

Mississippi

See entertainment.com/travel for this state's hotel listings and savings.

Missouri

Branson

✦ BRANSON'S BEST $$
3150 Green Mountain Dr., Branson. Valid for one standard room. (417)336-2378, (800)404-5013

SAVANNAH HOUSE, $$
165 Expressway Ln., Branson. Valid for one standard room. (417)336-3132, (800)383-3132

✦ SETTLE INN RESORT & CONFERENCE CENTER $$
3050 Green Mountain Dr., Branson. Valid for one standard room. (417)335-4700, (800)677-6906

WHISPERING HILLS INN, $$
2346 Shepherd of the Hills Expy, Branson. Valid for one standard room. (417)335-4922, (888)485-8030

Kansas City

CLARION HOTEL SPORTS COMPLEX, $$$
9103 E. 39th St., Kansas City. Valid for one standard room. R30. (816)737-0200, (877)425-2746

Montana

Great Falls

CRYSTAL INN, $$$
3701 31st St. SW, Great Falls. Valid for one standard room. Special events excluded. R30. (406)727-7788, (866)727-7788

E40   Discount subject to availability. Please read the **Rules of Use** on page E47.

Remember to identify yourself as an Entertainment® Member.

Contact the hotels directly for Entertainment® Membership rate availability. **50% off full-priced (rack) room rates** or **10% off the best promotional rate**—subject to availability.

Check out our FEATURED PROPERTIES

LA QUINTA INN & SUITES, $$
600 River Drive S., Great Falls. Valid for any room or suite. Valid September thru May. Spa suites excluded. Special events excluded. (406)761-2600, (800)531-5900

Kalispell

LA QUINTA INN & SUITES, $$$
255 Montclair Dr., Kalispell. Valid for any room. Valid Oct 1 thru June 14. Holidays & special events excl. R30. (406)257-5255, (800)531-5900

RED LION KALISPELL CENTER, $$$
20 N. Main, Kalispell. Valid for any room. Valid September thru June 1. R30. (406)751-5050, (800)325-4000

Missoula

DOUBLETREE HOTEL MISSOULA EDGEWATER, $$$$
100 Madison, Missoula. Valid for any room. R30. (406)728-3100

RED LION INN, $$$$
700 W. Broadway, Missoula. Valid for any room. R30. (406)728-3300

Nebraska

Omaha

CROWNE PLAZA, $$$
655 N 108th Ave, Omaha. Valid for one standard room. (402)496-0850

LA QUINTA INN OMAHA, $$
3330 N 104th Ave, Omaha. Valid for any room. Special events excluded. (210)302-7206, (800)531-5900

RESIDENCE INN BY MARRIOTT - OMAHA, $$$
6990 Dodge St., Omaha. Valid for one studio suite. Valid Friday, Saturday & Sunday. R30. (402)553-8898

Nevada

Las Vegas

ALEXIS PARK RESORT, $$$$
375 E. Harmon, Las Vegas. Valid for any room. (702)796-3322, (800)582-2228

CARRIAGE HOUSE, $$$$
105 E. Harmon, Las Vegas. Valid for one suite. Valid Sunday thru Thursday. Special events & holidays excl. (702)798-1020, (800)221-2301

TERRIBLE'S HOTEL & CASINO, $$$$
4100 Paradise Rd., Las Vegas. Valid for any room. (702)733-7000, (800)640-9777

THE JOCKEY CLUB, $$$$
3700 Las Vegas Blvd. S., Las Vegas. Valid for one condo. Holidays excl. (714)777-3700, (800)854-2324

Reno

DAYS INN, $$
701 E. 7th St., Reno. Valid for any room. Valid Sunday thru Thursday. Special events & holiday wknds excl. (775)786-4070

LA QUINTA INN AIRPORT, $$
4001 Market St, Reno. Valid for any room. Special events excluded. (210)302-7206, (800)531-5900

New Hampshire
See entertainment.com/travel for this state's hotel listings and savings.

New Jersey
See entertainment.com/travel for this state's hotel listings and savings.

New Mexico

Albuquerque

CLUBHOUSE INN & SUITES, $$$
1315 Menaul Blvd. NE, Albuquerque. Valid for any room. R30. (505)345-0010

LE BARON COURTYARD & SUITES, $$
2120 Menual Blvd. N.E., Albuquerque. Valid for standard or double room. Valid Sunday thru Thursday. Special events & holidays excl. (505)884-0250

RADISSON HOTEL & CONFERENCE CENTER, $$$
2500 Carlisle N.E., Albuquerque. Valid for any room. Balloon Fiesta week excl. (505)888-3311

Santa Fe

LA QUINTA INN SANTA FE, $$$
4298 Cerrillos Rd, Santa Fe. Valid for any room. Special events excluded. (210)302-7206, (800)531-5900

RADISSON HOTEL SANTA FE, $$$$
750 N. St. Francis Dr., Santa Fe. Valid for any room or suite. Max stay 5 nights. R30. (505)982-5591

New York

Albany

HOLIDAY INN TURF ON WOLF ROAD, $$$$
205 Wolf Rd., Albany. Valid for any room. Valid Friday, Saturday, Sunday & holidays September thru June. (518)458-7250

REGENCY INN & SUITES, $$$
416 Southern Blvd., Albany. Valid for any room. Aug excl. (518)462-6555, (866)864-3629

New York City/Manhattan

AFFINIA DUMONT, $$$$
150 E. 34th Street, New York. Valid for one suite. Valid Friday, Saturday & Sunday. R30. (212)320-8019, (866)AFF-INIA

AFFINIA MANHATTAN, $$$$
371 Seventh Avenue, New York. Valid for one suite. Valid Friday, Saturday & Sunday. R30. (212)320-8026, (866)AFF-INIA

TRAVEL INN HOTEL, $$$$
515 W. 42th St., New York. Valid for any room. (212)695-7171

WELLINGTON HOTEL, $$$$
871 Seventh Ave. at 55th St., New York. Valid for any room or suite. R30. (212)247-3900, (800)652-1212

North Carolina
See entertainment.com/travel for this state's hotel listings and savings.

North Dakota

Bismarck

BEST WESTERN RAMKOTA HOTEL, $$$
800 S. 3rd St., Bismarck. Valid for any room. Special events excluded. R30. (701)258-7700

RADISSON HOTEL BISMARCK, $$
605 E. Broadway Ave., Bismarck. Valid for any room. Valid Friday, Saturday & Sunday. Special events excluded. R30. (701)255-6000

Grand Forks

HOLIDAY INN GRAND FORKS, $$
1210 N 43rd St., Grand Forks. Valid for one standard room. Valid Sunday thru Thursday September - February & April - June. (701)772-7131

Ohio
See entertainment.com/travel for this state's hotel listings and savings.

Oklahoma
See entertainment.com/travel for this state's hotel listings and savings.

Oregon

Clackamas

BEST WESTERN SUNNYSIDE INN, $$
12855 SE 97th, Portland. Valid for any room. Jacuzzi suites excl. Valid Friday, Saturday & Sunday. (503)652-1500, (800)547-8400

DAYS INN PORTLAND SOUTH, $$
9717 SE Sunnyside Rd., Clackamas. Valid for any room. Valid Friday, Saturday & Sunday. (503)654-1699, (800)241-1699

MONARCH HOTEL & CONFERENCE CENTER, $$$$
12566 SE 93rd Ave, Clackamas. Valid for any room. Jacuzzi suites excluded. Valid weekends/holidays. R30. (503)652-1515, (800)492-8700

Eugene

LA QUINTA INN & SUITES, $$
155 Day Island Rd., Eugene. Valid for any room or suite. Spa suites excluded. (541)344-8335, (800)531-5900

VALLEY RIVER INN, $$$$
1000 Valley River Way, Eugene. Valid for one deluxe room. R30. (541)743-1000, (800)543-8266

Grants Pass

HOLIDAY INN EXPRESS GRANTS PASS, $$$
105 NE Agness Ave., Grants Pass. Valid for any room. Valid September thru May. Special events excluded. R30. (541)471-6144, (800)838-7666

RIVERSIDE INN RESORT & CONFERENCE CENTER, $$$
971 S.E. 6th Ave., Grants Pass. Valid for one standard room. Valid September-May & Sunday thru Thursday June-August. R30. (541)476-6873, (800)334-4567

Discount subject to availability. Please read the **Rules of Use** on page E47.

Go to **entertainment.com/travel** for more listings.

Hotels at Half Price®

Hillsboro

COURTYARD PORTLAND HILLSBORO, $$$
3050 NW Stucki Place, Hillsboro. Valid for any room. Suites excluded. Valid Friday, Saturday, Sunday & holidays. (503)690-1800

LARKSPUR LANDING, $$
3133 NE Shute Rd., Hillsboro. Valid for any room or suite. Valid Friday, Saturday & Sunday. (503)681-2121

Lake Oswego

HILTON GARDEN INN, $$$
14850 Kruse Oaks Dr., Lake Oswego. Valid for any room. Whirlpool rooms excl. R30. (503)684-8900

RESIDENCE INN BY MARRIOTT - PORTLAND SOUTH, $$$$
15200 S.W. Bangy Rd., Lake Oswego. Valid for one studio suite. Valid weekends/holidays. (503)684-2603

Lincoln City

+ CROWN PACIFIC INN $$$
50 N.E. Bechill St., Depoe Bay. Valid for any room. Valid October thru May & Sunday thru Thursday June thru September. Spa rooms excluded. Holidays excl. (541)765-7773, (877)765-7773

+ CROWN PACIFIC INN EXPRESS $$$
1070 SE 1st St., Lincoln City. Valid for any room. Suites excluded. Valid October thru May & valid Sunday thru Thursday June thru September. Holidays excl. (541)994-7559, (800)359-7559

+ EDGECLIFF MOTEL $$
3733 SW Hwy. 101, Lincoln City. Valid for any room. Valid September 15 thru June 15. Honeymoon Suite & Holidays excl. (541)996-2055, (888)750-3636

+ INN AT SPANISH HEAD RESORT HOTEL $$$$
4009 S.W. Hwy. 101, Lincoln City. Valid for any room. Valid Sunday thru Thursday September thru June. Min stay 2 nts. (541)996-2161, (800)452-8127

THE ASHLEY INN, $$$
3430 NE Hwy 101, Lincoln City. Valid for any room. June 15 thru Sept 15 & Holidays excl. (541)996-7500, (888)427-4539

Newport

BEST WESTERN AGATE BEACH INN, $$$
3019 N. Coast Hwy., Newport. Valid for any room. Suites excluded. Valid September 15 thru June 15. Holidays & school vacation periods excluded. R30. (541)265-9411, (800)547-3310

VALU INN/NEWPORT, $$
531 S.W. Fall St., Newport. Valid for any room. Max stay 3 nts. (541)265-6203, (800)443-7777

Portland

5TH AVENUE SUITES, $$$$
506 S.W. Washington at 5th Ave., Portland. Valid for one room or suite. (503)222-0001

BEST WESTERN AT THE MEADOWS, $$$
1215 N. Hayden Meadows Dr., Portland. Valid for any room. Max stay 3 nts. R30. (503)286-9600

FOUR POINTS SHERATON PORTLAND DOWNTOWN, $$$$
50 S.W. Morrison, Portland. Valid for any room. R30. (503)221-0711, (888)627-8263

HILTON PORTLAND & EXECUTIVE TOWER, $$$$
921 SW Sixth Ave., Portland. Valid for any room. Valid weekends/holidays. New Year's Eve excl. (503)226-1611

RADISSON HOTEL PORTLAND AIRPORT, $$$$
6233 NE 78th Ct., Portland. Valid for one standard room. Special events excluded. (503)251-2000, (800)994-7878

RED LION HOTEL PORTLAND - CONVENTION CENTER, $$$
1021 N.E. Grand Ave., Portland. Valid for any room. Suites excluded. (503)235-2100, (800)343-1822

SHERATON PORTLAND AIRPORT HOTEL, $$$$
8235 NE Airport Way, Portland. Valid for any room. R30. (503)281-2500, (800)808-9497

THE BENSON, A COAST HOTEL, $$$$
309 S.W. Broadway, Portland. Valid for any room. R30. (503)228-2000

THRIFTLODGE, $$
949 E. Burnside St., Portland. Valid for any room. (503)234-8411

Rockaway Beach

+ SURFSIDE RESORT $$$
101 NW 11th St., Rockaway Beach. Valid for any room. Valid September 15 thru June 15. Holidays excluded. (503)355-2312, (800)243-7786

Seaside

SAND & SEA, $$$$
475 S. Prom, Seaside. Valid for one condo. Min stay 2 nts. Valid September 15 thru June 30. Holidays & school vacations excl. (503)738-8441, (800)628-2371

THE TIDES, $$$$
2316 Beach Dr., Seaside. Valid for one condo. Valid September 15 thru June 15. Holidays & school breaks excl. Min stay 2 nts. (503)738-6317, (800)548-2846

Sunriver

SUNRIVER RESORT, $$$$
1 Center Dr., Sunriver. Valid for any room or suite. Dec 21-Jan 1 & June 23-Aug 24 excl. (541)593-1000, (800)547-3922

THE PINES AT SUNRIVER, $$$
Meadow Rd., Sunriver. Valid for one condo. Min stay 2 nts. R30. (888)333-1962

Tolovana Park

INN AT CANNON BEACH, $$$$
3215 S. Hemlock, Cannon Beach. Valid for any room. Valid September 15 thru June 30. Min stay 2 nts. Holidays & special events excl. (503)436-9085, (800)321-6304

TOLOVANA INN, $$$
3400 S. Hemlock, Tolovana Park. Valid for any room. Min stay 2 nts. Valid September 15 thru June 15. Holidays & school vacations excl. R30. (503)436-2211, (800)333-8890

Pennsylvania

Harrisburg

WYNDHAM HARRISBURG HERSHEY, $$$$
4650 Lindle Rd., Harrisburg. Valid for one standard room. July & August excl. (717)564-5511, (800)WYN-DHAM

Philadelphia

HOLIDAY INN EXPRESS MIDTOWN, $$$
1305 Walnut St., Philadelphia. Valid for any room. Valid Friday, Saturday, Sunday & holidays. New Year's Eve excl. Penn relays, Army-Navy & Greek wknds excl. (215)735-9300

OMNI HOTEL AT INDEPENDENCE PARK, $$$$
401 Chestnut St., Philadelphia. Valid for one deluxe room. Valid Friday, Saturday, Sunday & holidays. (215)925-0000, (800)THE-OMNI

Rhode Island

See entertainment.com/travel for this state's hotel listings and savings.

South Carolina

See entertainment.com/travel for this state's hotel listings and savings.

South Dakota

Rapid City

BEST WESTERN RAMKOTA HOTEL, $$
2111 LaCrosse St., Rapid City. Valid for any room. Valid September 16 thru June 14. R30. (605)343-8550

HOTEL ALEX JOHNSON, $$$
523 6th St., Rapid City. Valid for one standard room. Valid October 15 thru April. (605)342-1210

Sioux Falls

BEST WESTERN RAMKOTA HOTEL, $$
3200 W. Maple, Sioux Falls. Valid for any room. R30. (605)336-0650

CLUBHOUSE HOTEL & SUITES, $$$
2320 S. Louise Ave., Sioux Falls. Valid for any room. Suites excluded. Valid Sunday thru Thursday September thru May. Special events excluded. R30. (605)361-8700

Tennessee

See entertainment.com/travel for this state's hotel listings and savings.

Texas

Dallas

ARISTOCRAT HOTEL, $$$$
1933 Main St., Dallas. Valid for any room. (214)741-7700, (800)231-4235

CROWNE PLAZA - DALLAS MARKET CENTER, $$$$
7050 Stemmons Fwy., Dallas. Valid for any room. R30. (214)630-8500

Discount subject to availability. Please read the **Rules of Use** on page E47.

Remember to identify yourself as an Entertainment® Member.

Contact the hotels directly for Entertainment® Membership rate availability. **50% off full-priced (rack) room rates** or 10% off the best promotional rate — subject to availability.

Check out our ★FEATURED PROPERTIES

HAMPTON INN ADDISON, $$$
4505 Beltway Dr., Addison. Valid for any room. (972)991-2800

OMNI DALLAS HOTEL AT PARK WEST, $$$$
1590 LBJ Fwy., Dallas. Valid for one deluxe room. (972)869-4300, (800)THE-OMNI

Houston

COURTYARD HOUSTON, $$$
2504 N. Loop West, Houston. Valid for any room. (713)688-7711

OMNI HOUSTON HOTEL WESTSIDE, $$$$
13210 Katy Freeway, Houston. Valid for one deluxe room. (281)558-8338, (800)THE-OMNI

RESIDENCE INN MEDICAL CENTER/ RELIANT PARK, $$$
7710 Main, Houston. Valid for one studio suite. Valid Friday, Saturday & Sunday. R30. (713)660-7993

WESTIN OAKS, $$$$
5011 Westheimer, Houston. Valid for any room. Valid Friday, Saturday & Sunday. (713)960-8100

Houston Intercontinental Airport

COUNTRY INN & SUITES, $$$
15555 B JFK Blvd., Houston. Valid for any room. (281)987-2400

HILTON GARDEN INN BUSH INTERCONTINENTAL, $$$$
15400 John F. Kennedy Blvd., Houston. Valid for any room. R30. (281)449-4148

WYNDHAM GREENSPOINT HOTEL, $$$$
12400 Greenspoint Dr., Houston. Valid for one standard room. (281)875-2222, (866)933-7829

New Braunfels

THE HOTEL FAUST, $$$$
240 S. Seguin Ave., New Braunfels. Valid for any room. Suites excluded. (830)625-7791

San Antonio

HOTEL VALENCIA RIVERWALK, $$$$
150 E. Houston St., San Antonio. Valid for any room. (210)227-9700, (866)842-0100

LA QUINTA INN SEAWORLD/INGRAM PARK, $$$
7134 NW Loop 410, San Antonio. Valid for any room. Special events excluded. (210)302-7206, (800)531-5900

RODEWAY INN DOWNTOWN, $$
900 N. Main Ave., San Antonio. Valid for any double room. Valid Sunday thru Thursday. (210)223-2951

Utah

Cedar City

BEST WESTERN TOWN & COUNTRY, $$
189 N. Main St., Cedar City. Valid for one deluxe double room. Valid October thru May. Special events & holidays excl. R30. (435)586-9900, (800)493-4089

CRYSTAL INN, $$$
1575 W. 200 North, Cedar City. Valid for one standard room. Special events excluded. R30. (435)586-8888, (888)787-6661

Park City

COPPERBOTTOM INN, $$
1637 Shortline Rd., Park City. Valid for any room. Min stay 2 nts. Valid April 1 thru December 1. R30. (435)655-3315, (888)727-5248

GABLES HOTEL, $$$
1335 Lowell Ave., Park City. Valid for one suite. Min stay 2 nts. Valid April 25 thru November 14. R30. (435)655-3315, (800)443-1045

Provo

HAMPTON INN - PROVO, $$$
1511 S. 40 E., Provo. Valid for any room. Valid September thru May. Holidays & special events excl. R30. (801)377-6396

MARRIOTT PROVO, $$$$
101 W. 100 N., Provo. Valid for any room. Suites excluded. Valid Friday, Saturday & Sunday. R30. (801)377-4700

Salt Lake City

BAYMONT INN & SUITES SALT LAKE CITY AIRPORT, $$
2080 W. North Temple, Salt Lake City. Valid for one standard room. (801)355-0088

CHASE SUITE HOTEL BY WOODFIN, $$$$
765 E. 400 South, Salt Lake City. Valid for one suite. (801)532-5511, (888)433-6071

HILTON SALT LAKE AIRPORT, $$$$
5151 Wiley Post Way, Salt Lake City. Valid for one standard room. Valid Friday, Saturday & Sunday. (801)539-1515

HILTON SALT LAKE CITY CENTER, $$$$
255 S. West Temple, Salt Lake City. Valid for one standard room. Suites excluded. (801)328-2000

LA QUINTA INN & SUITES AIRPORT, $$
4905 W. Wiley Post Way, Salt Lake City. Valid for any room. Special events excluded. (210)302-7206, (800)531-5900

QUALITY INN AIRPORT, $$
1659 W. North Temple, Salt Lake City. Valid for any room. (801)533-9000

Vermont

See entertainment.com/travel for this state's hotel listings and savings.

Virginia

See entertainment.com/travel for this state's hotel listings and savings.

Washington

Bellevue

DOUBLETREE HOTEL BELLEVUE, $$$$
300 - 112th Ave. S.E., Bellevue. Valid for any room. Suites excl. (425)455-1300

LARKSPUR LANDING, $$
15805 SE 37th St., Bellevue. Valid for any room or suite. Valid Friday, Saturday & Sunday. (425)373-1212

RED LION BELLEVUE INN, $$$$
11211 Main St., Bellevue. Valid for one deluxe room. R30. (425)455-5240, (800)421-8193

Everett

BEST WESTERN CASCADIA INN, $$$
2800 Pacific Ave., Everett. Valid for any room. (425)258-4141, (800)822-5876

QUALITY INN HOTEL & CONFERENCE CENTER, $$$
101 - 128th St. SE, Everett. Valid for any room. Suites excluded. Max stay 3 nts. Valid October thru May and Sunday thru Thursday June thru September. R30. (425)337-2900, (800)256-8137

Kent

DAYS INN SOUTH SEATTLE/KENT, $$
1711 W. Meeker St., Kent. Valid for any room. July-Aug excl. (253)854-1950

TOWNE PLACE SUITES SEATTLE SOUTH CENTER, $$
18123 72nd Ave. S., Kent. Valid for one suite. (253)796-6000

Leavenworth

DER RITTERHOF MOTOR INN, $$$
190 Hwy. 2, Leavenworth. Valid for any room. Valid October thru June. Festivals excl. R30. (509)548-5845, (800)255-5845

QUALITY INN & SUITES - LEAVENWORTH, $$$
185 Hwy. 2, Leavenworth. Valid for any room. Holidays & special events excl. R30. (509)548-7992, (800)693-1225

Ocean Shores

THE CANTERBURY INN, $$$$
643 Ocean Shores Blvd., Ocean Shores. Valid for any room. Valid Sunday thru Thursday. Holidays & school vacation periods excluded. (360)289-3317, (800)562-6678

THE POLYNESIAN, $$$
615 Ocean Shores Blvd., Ocean Shores. Valid for any room. Minimum stay 2 nights. Valid Sunday thru Thursday. Holidays & school vacation periods excluded. (360)289-3361, (800)562-4836

THE SANDS RESORT, $$$$
801 Ocean Shores Blvd. NW, Ocean Shores. Valid for any room. Minimum stay 2 nts. Valid Sunday thru Thursday. Holidays & school vacation periods excluded. (360)289-2444, (800)841-4001

Olympia

RAMADA GOVERNOR HOUSE, $$$
621 S. Capitol Way, Olympia. Valid for any room. Special events excluded. (360)352-7700

RED LION HOTEL OLYMPIA, $$$
2300 Evergreen Park Dr., Olympia. Valid for any room. Max stay 4 nts. R30. (360)943-4000, (800)325-4000

Discount subject to availability. Please read the **Rules of Use** on page E47.   E43

Go to **entertainment.com/travel** for more listings.

Hotels at HalfPrice

Seattle

CROWNE PLAZA SEATTLE, $$$$
1113 6th Ave., Seattle. Valid for one standard room. Suites excl. (206)464-1980, (800)521-2762

EXECUTIVE HOTEL PACIFIC, $$$$
400 Spring St., Seattle. Valid for one standard room. Max stay 7 nts. R30. (206)623-3900, (800)426-1165

RAMADA INN DOWNTOWN SEATTLE, $$$
2200 5th Ave., Seattle. Valid for any room. Valid Sunday thru Thursday. August excl. (206)441-9785

THE ROOSEVELT, A COAST HOTEL, $$$$
1531 Seventh Ave, Seattle. Valid for any room. (206)621-1200

TRAVELODGE BY THE SPACE NEEDLE, $$$
200 6th Ave. N., Seattle. Valid for any room. Valid September thru May. (206)441-7878

Seattle/Tacoma International Airport

HILTON SEATTLE AIRPORT & CONFERENCE CENTER, $$$$
17620 International Blvd., Seattle. Valid for any room. R30. (206)244-4800

LA QUINTA INN SEA-TAC INT'L, $$$
2824 S 188th St., Seattle. Valid for any room. Special events excluded. (210)302-7206, (800)531-5900

RED LION HOTEL SEATTLE AIRPORT, $$$$
18220 International Blvd., Seattle. Valid for any room. Max stay 4 nts. Parking pkgs excl. R30. (206)246-5535, (800)325-4000

Spokane

BEST WESTERN PEPPERTREE AIRPORT INN, $$$
3711 S. Geiger Blvd., Spokane. Valid for any room. Family & spa suites excluded. Valid September thru May. (509)624-4655, (800)799-3933

BROADWAY INN & SUITES, $$
6309 E. Broadway, Spokane. Valid for any room. Suites excluded. Special events excluded. (509)535-7185

LA QUINTA INN & SUITES, $$
3808 N Sullivan Rd. Bldg 34, Spokane Valley. Valid for any room. Suites excluded. Valid September thru June. Special events excl. (509)893-0955, (800)531-5900

RED LION RIVER INN, $$$
700 N. Division St., Spokane. Valid for any room. R30. (509)326-5577, (800)325-4000

THE RIDPATH HOTEL, $$$
515 W. Sprague Avenue, Spokane. Valid for any room. Valentines Day & New Years excluded. R30. (509)838-2711, (800)325-4000

Vancouver

HEATHMAN LODGE, $$$
7801 NE Greenwood Dr., Vancouver. Valid for one standard room. Suites excluded. Valid Friday, Saturday & Sunday. (360)254-3100, (888)475-3100

RED LION HOTEL AT THE QUAY, $$$
100 Columbia St., Vancouver. Valid for any room. R30. (360)694-8341

RESIDENCE INN BY MARRIOTT - PORTLAND NORTH, $$$
8005 N.E. Parkway Dr., Vancouver. Valid for one studio room. Valid Friday, Saturday & Sunday. R30. (360)253-4800

West Virginia
See entertainment.com/travel for this state's hotel listings and savings.

Wisconsin
See entertainment.com/travel for this state's hotel listings and savings.

Wyoming
See entertainment.com/travel for this state's hotel listings and savings.

Canada

Alberta

Banff

BANFF PARK LODGE RESORT & CONFERENCE CENTRE, $$$
222 Lynx St., Banff. Valid for any room. Valid Sunday thru Friday October thru June. Dec 27-Jan 2 excl. (403)762-4433, (800)661-9266

BANFF ROCKY MOUNTAIN RESORT, $$$$
1029 Banff Ave., Banff. Valid for any room. Valid Sunday thru Thursday October thru May 19. Holiday periods excl. (403)762-5531, (800)661-9563

BUMPER'S INN, $$
603 Banff Ave., Banff. Valid for any room. Valid October thru May. (403)762-3386, (800)661-3518

Calgary

BEST WESTERN HOSPITALITY INN, $$$
135 Southland Dr. SE Southland Drive/MacLeod Trail, Calgary. Valid for any room. Suites excl. Valid September 15 thru June 15 Friday thru Sunday. (403)278-5050, (877)278-5050

✦ **CARRIAGE HOUSE INN $$$$**
9030 MacLeod Trail South, Calgary. Valid for any room. Executive rooms excl. (403)253-1101, (800)661-9566

DELTA BOW VALLEY, $$$
209 4th Ave. S.E., Calgary. Valid for any room. Valid Friday, Saturday, Sunday & holidays. (403)266-1980

HAMPTON INN & SUITES, $$$$
2231 Banff Trail NW, Calgary. Valid for any room. (403)289-9800, (888)432-6777

HOLIDAY INN EXPRESS HOTEL & SUITES, $$$$
12025 Lake Fraser Dr. SE, Calgary. Valid for any room or suite. Stampede week & special events excl. (403)225-3000, (877)429-4377

SANDMAN CALGARY DOWNTOWN, $$$
888 - 7th Ave., SW, Calgary. Valid for any room. (403)237-8626, (800)726-3626

SHERATON SUITES CALGARY EAU CLAIRE, $$$$
255 Barclay Parade SW, Calgary. Valid for one suite. (403)266-7200, (888)784-8370

THE COAST PLAZA HOTEL & CONFERENCE CENTRE, $$$$
1316 - 33 St. NE, Calgary. Valid for any room. Special events excl. R30. (403)248-8888, (800)661-1464

Edmonton

ARGYLL PLAZA HOTEL, $$$
9933 - 63 Ave., Edmonton. Valid for one suite. (780)438-5876, (866)203-2930

CHATEAU LOUIS HOTEL & CONFERENCE CENTRE, $$$
11727 Kingsway, Edmonton. Valid for any room. Valid for queen & twin rooms. Specialty suites excl. Valid Friday, Saturday, Sunday & holidays. R30. (780)452-7770, (800)661-9843

CROWNE PLAZA - CHATEAU LACOMBE, $$$$
10111 Bellamy Hill, Edmonton. Valid for any room or suite. (780)428-6611, (800)661-8801

DAYS INN, $$$
10041 - 106 St., Edmonton. Valid for any room. R30. (780)423-1925, (800)267-2191

DELTA EDMONTON CENTRE SUITE HOTEL, $$$$
10222 102nd Street, Edmonton. Valid for one suite. (780)429-3900

SANDMAN HOTEL EDMONTON, $$$
17635 Stony Plain Rd., Edmonton. Valid for any room. (780)483-1385, (800)726-3626

THE FAIRMONT HOTEL MACDONALD, $$$$
10065-100 St., Edmonton. Valid for any room. Specialty suites excl. Valid Friday & Saturday. (780)424-5181, (800)441-1414

Jasper

ASTORIA HOTEL, $$$
404 Connaught Dr., Jasper. Valid for any room. Valid October thru May. (780)852-3351, (800)661-7343

THE FAIRMONT JASPER PARK LODGE, $$$$
Old Lodge Rd., Jasper. Valid for one deluxe or jr suite. Valid October 15 thru April 30. Holidays excl. Min 2 nts stay. Rates not available to groups or convention delegates. (780)852-3301

British Columbia

Cranbrook

SANDMAN INN CRANBROOK, $$$
405 Cranbrook St., Cranbrook. Valid for any room. (250)426-4236, (800)726-3626

THE PRESTIGE ROCKY MTN. RESORT & CONV. CTR., $$$$
209 Van Horne St. S., Cranbrook. Valid for any room. (250)417-0444

Discount subject to availability. Please read the **Rules of Use** on page E47.

Remember to identify yourself as an Entertainment® Member.

Contact the hotels directly for Entertainment® Membership rate availability. 50% off full-priced (rack) room rates or 10% off the best promotional rate—subject to availability.

Check out our FEATURED PROPERTIES

Harrison Hot Springs

HARRISON HOT SPRINGS RESORT & SPA, $$$$
100 Esplanade Ave., Harrison Hot Springs. Valid for any room. Valid Sunday thru Thursday. (604)796-2244, (800)663-2266

Kamloops

EXECUTIVE INN, $$$
540 Victoria St., Kamloops. Valid for one deluxe room. (250)372-2281, (800)663-2837

PLAZA HERITAGE HOTEL, $$$
405 Victoria St., Kamloops. Valid for any room or suite. (250)377-8075, (877)977-5292

Kelowna

HOLIDAY INN EXPRESS, $$$$
2429 Hwy. 97 North, Kelowna. Valid for one standard room. Valid October thru June. (250)763-0500, (800)465-0200

LAKE OKANAGAN RESORT, $$$$
2751 Westside Rd., Kelowna. Valid for one standard room. Valid September 16 thru June 17. (250)769-3511, (800)663-3273

Nelson

PRESTIGE LAKEVIEW INN, $$$$
1301 Front St., Nelson. Valid for any room. (250)352-3595, (877)737-8443

THE PRESTIGE LAKESIDE RESORT & CONVENTION CTR, $$$$
701 Lakeside Drive, Nelson. Valid for any room. (250)352-7222

Penticton

SANDMAN HOTEL PENTICTON, $$$
939 Burnaby Ave. W., Penticton. Valid for any room. (250)493-7151, (800)726-3626

Princeton

A.P. GUEST RANCH, $$$$
Box 1148, Hwy 5A # 4220, Merritt. Valid for any room. Holidays excl. (250)378-6520

SANDMAN INN PRINCETON, $$$
102 Frontage Rd., Princeton. Valid for any room. (250)295-6923, (800)726-3626

Richmond

BEST WESTERN ABERCORN INN, $$$
9260 Bridgeport Rd., Richmond. Valid for any room. (604)270-7576, (800)663-0085

HILTON VANCOUVER AIRPORT HOTEL, $$$$
5911 Minoru Blvd., Richmond. Valid for any room. (604)273-6336

HOLIDAY INN INTERNATIONAL - VANCOUVER AIRPORT, $$$$
10720 Cambie Rd., Richmond. Valid for any room. (604)821-1818, (888)831-3388

MARRIOTT VANCOUVER AIRPORT, $$$$
7571 Westminster Hwy., Richmond. Valid for any room. (604)276-2112, (877)323-8888

SANDMAN HOTEL VANCOUVER AIRPORT, $$$$
3233 St. Edwards Dr., Richmond. Valid for any room. (604)303-8888, (800)726-3626

Vancouver

EMPIRE LANDMARK HOTEL & CONFERENCE CENTRE, $$$$
1400 Robson St., Vancouver. Valid for any room. (604)687-0511, (800)830-6144

FAIRMONT HOTEL VANCOUVER, $$$$
900 West Georgia St., Vancouver. Valid for any room. (604)684-3131

PACIFIC PALISADES HOTEL, $$$$
1277 Robson St., Vancouver. Valid for any room or suite. Labor Day weekend excl. (604)688-0461, (800)663-1815

✦ **PAN PACIFIC HOTEL VANCOUVER $$$$**
#300-999 Canada Place, Vancouver. Valid for any room. (604)662-8111, (800)663-1515

RENAISSANCE VANCOUVER HOTEL HARBOURSIDE, $$$$
1133 West Hastings St., Vancouver. Valid for any room. (604)689-9211, (800)905-8582

WEDGEWOOD HOTEL & SPA, $$$$
845 Hornby St., Vancouver. Valid for executive room or suite. Max stay 3 nts. (604)689-7777, (800)663-0666

WESTIN GRAND VANCOUVER, $$$$
433 Robson St., Vancouver. Valid for any room. Valid anytime. (604)602-1999, (888)680-9393

Victoria

DELTA VICTORIA OCEAN POINTE RESORT & SPA, $$$$
45 Songhees Rd., Victoria. Valid for any room. Valid September thru June. (250)360-2999

✦ **PAUL'S MOTOR INN $$$**
1900 Douglas St., Victoria. Valid for any room. (250)382-9231

✦ **ROYAL SCOT SUITE HOTEL $$$$**
425 Quebec St., Victoria. Valid for any room or suite. (250)388-5463, (800)663-7515

✦ **THE LAUREL POINT INN $$$$**
680 Montreal Street, Victoria. Valid for any room or suite. (250)386-8721, (800)663-7667

✦ **VICTORIA REGENT HOTEL $$$$**
1234 Wharf St., Victoria. Valid for any room or suite. R30. (250)386-2211, (800)663-7472

Whistler

CRYSTAL LODGE, $$$$
4154 Village Green, Whistler Village. Valid for any room. Suites excl. R30. (604)932-2221, (800)667-3363

DELTA WHISTLER VILLAGE SUITES, $$$$
4308 Main St., Whistler. Valid for one suite. Valid May thru November & Sunday thru Thursday December thru April. (604)905-3987, (888)299-3987

TANTALUS RESORT LODGE, $$$$
4200 Whistler Way, Whistler. Valid for one condo. Valid May thru November & Sunday thru Thursday December thru April. (604)932-4146

Manitoba

Winnipeg

CARLTON INN, $$
220 Carlton St., Winnipeg. Valid for any room. (204)942-0881, (877)717-2885

DELTA WINNIPEG, $$$$
350 St. Mary Ave., Winnipeg. Valid for any room. (204)942-0551

HOLIDAY INN WINNIPEG SOUTH, $$$$
1330 Pembina Hwy., Winnipeg. Valid for one standard room. Business Class floors & suites excl. (204)452-4747, (800)423-1337

RAMADA MARLBOROUGH HOTEL, $$$
331 Smith St., Winnipeg. Valid for any room. Special events & holidays excl. (204)942-6411, (800)667-7666

Ontario

Lester B. Pearson International Airport

DELTA TORONTO AIRPORT WEST, $$$$
5444 Dixie Rd., Toronto. Valid for any room. (905)624-1144, (800)737-3211

WYNDHAM BRISTOL PLACE-TORONTO AIRPORT, $$$$
950 Dixon Rd., Toronto. Valid for one standard room. (416)675-9444, (800)996-3426

Niagara Falls

BEST WESTERN CAIRN CROFT HOTEL, $$$$
6400 Lundy's Lane, Niagara Falls. Valid for any room. Valid October thru June. R30. (905)356-1161, (800)263-2551

DOUBLETREE RESORT LODGE & SPA FALLSVIEW, $$$
6039 Fallsview Blvd., Niagara Falls. Valid for any room. Valid Sunday thru Thursday October 15 thru May. (905)358-3817

Ottawa

CROWNE PLAZA HOTEL OTTAWA, $$$$
101 Lyon St., Ottawa. Valid for any room or suite. (613)237-3600, (800)227-6963

DELTA OTTAWA HOTEL & SUITES, $$$$
361 Queen St., Ottawa. Valid for any room or suite. (613)238-6000

EMBASSY WEST HOTEL & CONFERENCE CENTRE, $$$$
1400 Carling Ave., Ottawa. Valid for any room. (613)729-4331, (800)267-8696

Toronto

DAYS INN & CONFERENCE CENTER-TORONTO DOWNTOWN, $$$$
30 Carlton St., Toronto. Valid for any room. Valid Sunday thru Thursday. Dec 30- Jan 1, holidays & special events excl. (416)977-6655

HOLIDAY INN HOTEL & SUITES TORONTO - MARKHAM, $$$$
7095 Woodbine Ave., Markham. Valid for any room. (905)474-0444, (800)387-3303

Discount subject to availability. Please read the **Rules of Use** on page E47.   E45

Go to **entertainment.com/travel** for more listings.

Hotels at Half Price

+ **HOWARD JOHNSON HOTEL TORONTO/MARKHAM $$$$**
555 Cochrane Dr., Markham. Valid for any room. Special events excl. (905)479-5000, (877)703-4656

VALHALLA INN TORONTO, $$$$
1 Valhalla Inn Rd., Toronto. Valid for any room. (416)239-2391, (800)268-2500

WESTIN HARBOUR CASTLE, $$$$
1 Harbour Square, Toronto. Valid for any room. Suites & executive club floor excluded. (416)869-1600

Québec

Montreal

DAYS INN MONTREAL DOWNTOWN, $$$$
215 René-Levesque E., Montreal. Valid for any room. (514)393-3388, (800)668-3872

HOLIDAY INN MONTREAL - MIDTOWN, $$$$
420 Sherbrooke St. W., Montreal. Valid for any room. (514)842-6111, (800)387-3042

HÔTEL GOUVERNEUR PLACE DUPUIS, $$$
1415 St-Hubert St., Montreal. Valid for any room. Suites excluded. (514)842-4881, (888)910-1111

HÔTEL LE CANTLIE SUITES, $$$$
1110 Sherbrooke St. W., Montreal. Valid for any room. (514)842-2000, (800)567-1110

Saskatchewan

Regina

RAMADA HOTEL & CONVENTION CENTRE, $$$
1818 Victoria Ave. E., Regina. Valid for any room. Suites excluded. (306)569-1666, (800)667-6500

SANDMAN HOTEL, SUITES & SPA - REGINA, $$$
1800 Victoria Ave. E., Regina. Valid for any room. (306)757-2444, (800)726-3626

Saskatoon

DELTA BESSBOROUGH, $$$$
601 Spadina Cresent E., Saskatoon. Valid for any room. (306)244-5521

SANDMAN HOTEL SASKATOON, $$$
310 Circle Dr. W., Saskatoon. Valid for any room. (306)477-4844, (800)726-3626

SASKATOON INN HOTEL & CONFERENCE CENTRE, $$$$
2002 Airport Dr., Saskatoon. Valid for any room. (306)242-1440, (800)667-8789

Mexico

Distrito Federal

Mexico City

CAMINO REAL MEXICO, $$$$
Mariano Escobedo No. 700, Col. Anzures, Mexico City. Valid for one standard room. Valid Friday, Saturday & Sunday. 52-55-5263-8888

HOTEL FONTAN MEXICO, $$
Paseo de la Reforma #24, Col. Centro, Mexico City. Valid for any room. 52-55-55185460

Guerrero

Acapulco

CAMINO REAL ACAPULCO DIAMANTE, $$$$
Baja Catita S/N Carr. Escenica Km.14, Acapulco. Valid for one superior sea view room. 52-744-435-1010

Jalisco

Puerto Vallarta

CLUB EMBARCADERO PACIFICO HOTEL & VILLAS, $$$
Paseo de la Marina s/n Marina Vallarta, Puerto Vallarta. Valid for any room or suite. 52-322-221-11-77

SHERATON BUGANVILIAS RESORT & CONV. CENTER, $$$$
Blvd. Fco. Medina Ascencio #999, Puerto Vallarta. Valid for any room. (818)842-6155, (800)433-5451

VALLARTA TORRE, $$$$
Paseo de las Garzas #168, Puerto Vallarta. Valid for one condo. Min stay 2 nts. R30. (888)333-1962

Quintana Roo

Cancun

BEACH PALACE, $$$$
Blvd. Kukulcan KM 11.5, Zona Hotelera, Cancun. Valid for one suite. 52-998-891-4110, (800)635-1836

HOLIDAY INN EXPRESS, $$$
Paseo Pok-Ta-Pok, Lotes 21 y 22, Cancun. Valid for any room. July, August, Holy week & holidays excl. 52-998-8832200, 800-465-4329

HOTEL PLAZA CARIBE, $$
Ave. Tulum Esq. Uxmal Lote 19, Cancun. Valid for any room. Valid Aug 16 thru July 15. Christmas & Easter excl. 52-998-8841377

OMNI CANCUN HOTEL & VILLAS, $$$$
Blvd. Kukulkan, L-48, KM. 16.5, M. 53, Cancun. Valid for one deluxe room. Dec 26 - Jan 2 & Holidays excl. 52-998-881-0600, 800-446-8977

Caribbean

Antigua/Barbuda

Mamora Bay

ST. JAMES'S CLUB, $$$$
P.O. Box 63, Mamora Bay. Valid for any room. Christmas, New Year's, President's & Easter Weeks excl. Bonus: 25% off the all-inclusive rate. (268)460-5000, (800)345-0356

Bahamas

Freeport

XANADU BEACH RESORT & MARINA, $$$
P.O. Box F42438 Grand Bahama Island, Freeport. Valid for any room. Superior rooms excl. Thanksgiving & New Year's excl. (242)352-6782

Grand Bahama Island

CHILLINGSWORTH COURT, $$$$
Bahamia North Freeport, Grand Bahama Island. Valid for one condo. (513)621-5278

PORT LUCAYA RESORT AND YACHT CLUB, $$$
Bell Channel Bay PO Box F-42452, Grand Bahama Island. Valid for any room. R30. (242)373-6618, (800)582-2921

New Providence

NASSAU BEACH HOTEL, $$$
P.O. Box N-7756, Cable Beach, Nassau, New Providence. Valid for any room. Suites excl. Holidays excl. (242)327-7711, (888)627-7282

Barbados

Christ Church

SEA BREEZE BEACH HOTEL, $$$$
Maxwell Coast Rd. Barbados, Christ Church. Valid for any room. (246)428-2825

Saint Maarten/St. Martin

Baie Nettle

LE FLAMBOYANT RESORT, $$$$
Rte. Des Terres Basses, Baie Nettle–F.W.I. Valid for one deluxe room. Valid April 16 thru December 17. 59-0590-87-6000

Cupecoy

SUMMIT RESORT HOTEL, $$$$
42 Jordan Rd., Box 4046, Cupecoy. Valid for one studio suite. (718)518-7470

Trinidad & Tobago

Black Rock

LE GRAND COURLAN RESORT & SPA, $$$$
P.O. Box 25 Stonehaven Bay, Black Rock. Valid for any room. Valid April thru December. Christmas holiday excl. (868)639-9667

Virgin Islands

St. Thomas

POINT PLEASANT RESORT, $$$$
6600 Estate Smith Bay #4, St. Thomas. Valid for one suite. Dec 20-Jan 2 excl. (340)775-7200, (800) 524-2300

Discount subject to availability. Please read the **Rules of Use** on page E47.

Remember to identify yourself as an Entertainment® Member.

Hotels at HalfPrice®

Rules of Use

- The Entertainment® 50% discount applies only to full-priced (rack) room rates, not to any other discount, Internet or daily rate; 10% discount applies only to the promotional rate available to the general public. Rates cannot be used in conjunction with any other discounts, including daily rates or rates found on the Internet.

- Entertainment® rates do not apply to walk-ins, group/convention rates, packages, travel agency bookings, special amenities, taxes/fees, meal plans or Internet rates, and cannot be combined with any other discount rate programs. All rates are subject to availability.

- **Availability**—Reservations with the Entertainment® rate are accepted until the hotel projects to be 80% or more occupied. As a result, the discount may not be available for your entire stay because occupancy varies on a daily basis.

- Due to limited availability, hotels offering discounts on "any room" may exclude special rooms such as suites, concierge and premium rooms.

- Only one room can be discounted per Entertainment® membership card and the card is non-transferable.

- Hotels participate in the program on an individual basis. You must call the number listed for the hotel and state that you are an **"Entertainment Member"** to be eligible for the Entertainment® rate, if available.

- Remaining flexible with your travel dates may offer the greatest opportunity for the Entertainment® rate. Discounts may not be available for every night of your stay, especially if traveling during peak seasons, holiday weeks, conventions or special events such as Mardi Gras, Race Weekends & New Year's Eve.

- If the Entertainment® rate is not available, check alternate dates, call back closer to your travel date, or contact other hotels listed in the area. Be sure to register your Entertainment® membership card and view a complete listing of participating hotels on **www.entertainment.com/travel**.

- Be sure to ask for the hotel's policy on deposits, cancellations and late arrival guarantees.

- The Guaranteed Best Rate rebate is not applicable to Hotels at HalfPrice® bookings.

- **Advance reservations are required and you must present your Entertainment® membership card at check-in to obtain your discount.**

All information was current at the time of printing and is expected to be in effect through the expiration of the Entertainment® book. However, changes beyond our control may affect the information prior to the expiration. Please note that Entertainment Publications, Inc. cannot guarantee the level of services offered at a property and/or if services will be operational at the time of visit. Services may be closed due to seasonality reasons and/or may be closed for renovation.

ENTERTAINMENT PUBLICATIONS DOES NOT CONTROL ANY HOTEL'S MANAGEMENT POLICY.

UP TO 20% OFF

GREAT CHAINS

How to Save
1. Call the Hotel of Your Choice
2. Give the ID Number
3. Receive Your Savings

Best Western
(800) 441-1114
ID# 00162370

Red Roof Inn — ACCOR hotels
(888) 503-7695
ID# 534795

Days Inn
(800) 268-2195
ID# 1000 000181

Travelodge
(800) 545-5545
ID# 1000 000181

Wingate Inn — Built For Business
(877) 202-8814
ID# 1000 000181

La Quinta Inns · Inn & Suites
(800) 533-6821
ID# LQValue

Knights Inn
(800) 682-1071
ID# 1000 000181

Howard Johnson — Go anywhere. Stay here.
(800) 769-0939
ID# 1000 000181

IMPORTANT: Valid only at participating locations. Discount rates apply to regular (rack) non-discounted room rates and are subject to program room availability. Advance reservations required. Blackout dates and other restrictions may apply. This program cannot be used in conjunction with any other discount promotional room rate. The toll-free numbers listed are valid only for booking the promotional rate that accompanies the ID# listed. Not valid for group travel. **Expires December 31, 2007.**

GREAT SAVINGS

INTERCONTINENTAL HOTELS GROUP

- INTERCONTINENTAL HOTELS & RESORTS
- CROWNE PLAZA HOTELS & RESORTS
- HOTEL indigo
- Holiday Inn HOTELS · RESORTS
- Holiday Inn EXPRESS
- STAYBRIDGE SUITES
- CANDLEWOOD SUITES

(877) 580-2943
ID# 100219193

Radisson
(866) 851-7575
ID# 80478437

COUNTRY INN & SUITES BY CARLSON
(866) 851-7575
ID# 80478437

RAMADA WORLDWIDE
(800) 462-8035
ID# 1000 000181

AmeriHost Inn
(800) 996-2087
ID# 1000 000181

SUPER 8 MOTEL
(800) 889-9706
ID# 1000 000181

Turn Page for More Chains More Savings

E49

GREAT CHAINS — GREAT SAVINGS

UP TO 20% OFF

Comfort Inn
(800) 533-2100
ID# 00803210

Comfort Suites
(800) 533-2100
ID# 00803210

Quality
(800) 533-2100
ID# 00803210

Sleep Inn
(800) 533-2100
ID# 00803210

Clarion
(800) 533-2100
ID# 00803210

MainStay Suites
(800) 533-2100
ID# 00803210

Econo Lodge
(800) 533-2100
ID# 00803210

Rodeway Inn
(800) 533-2100
ID# 00803210

Suburban Extended Stay Hotel
BY CHOICE HOTELS
(800) 533-2100
ID# 00803210

Cambria Suites™
BY CHOICE HOTELS
(800) 533-2100
ID# 00803210

IMPORTANT: Valid only at participating locations. Discount rates apply to regular (rack) non-discounted room rates and are subject to program room availability. Advance reservations required. Blackout dates and other restrictions may apply. This program cannot be used in conjunction with any other discount promotional room rate. The toll-free numbers listed are valid only for booking the promotional rate that accompanies the ID# listed. Not valid for group travel. **Expires December 31, 2007.**

ENTERTAINMENT & SPORTS

Order discount movie and event tickets online at www.entertainment.com/tickets
...see details on back

OVER 180 OFFERS

plus more at www.entertainment.com/fun

CHECK OUT THESE FEATURED OFFERS IN THE FRONT OF THIS SECTION:

- Minnesota Timberwolves
- Minnesota Twins
- Mann Theatres
- Water Park of America — Water, Woods & Wild Life
- Underwater Adventures Aquarium — Mall of America
- Great Clips IMAX Theatre at the Minnesota Zoo
- Marcus Theatres
- Crown Theatres — crowntheatres.com

www.entertainment.com/tickets

Your source for discounted movie, events & attractions tickets

DISCOUNTED EVENTS & ATTRACTIONS TICKETS

Now order discount tickets online for many concerts, sporting events, theater and special events. Listings are updated daily, so check back often!

A GREAT GIFT IDEA!

DISCOUNTED MOVIE TICKETS

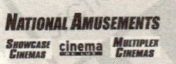

REGAL ENTERTAINMENT GROUP   AMC THEATRES   CINEMARK The Best Seat In Town   NATIONAL AMUSEMENTS SHOWCASE CINEMAS / cinema / MULTIPLEX CINEMAS   Carmike Cinemas

AMC Theatres	Clearview Cinema	Malco Cinemas
Brenden Cinema	Consolidated Theatres	Mulone Cinema
Carmike	Crown Theatres	National Amusements
Chakeres	Destinta Theater	Pacific Theatres
CinemaStar	Dipson Theater	Regal Entertainment Group
Cinemagic	Lockport Cinema	The Bridge
Cinemark		

**LISTINGS ARE UPDATED DAILY AT
www.entertainment.com/tickets
SO CHECK BACK OFTEN!**

Order forms and additional movie offers can be found at the back of this section

ENTERTAINMENT & SPORTS

www.timberwolves.com

🎭 entertainment | **50% OFF**

Minnesota Timberwolves

Enjoy up to FOUR $24 TICKETS at 50% off the regular price.

valid for any Monday thru Thursday game during the 2006-2007 regular season

Tickets subject to availablility; Not valid for groups, playoffs or other promotions; Redeemable at Ticketmaster outlets, phones & internet as well as the Target Center box office
WOLVES06

Valid now thru November 1, 2007
See reverse side for details   F1

🎭 entertainment | **50% OFF**

Minnesota Timberwolves

Enjoy up to FOUR $24 TICKETS at 50% off the regular price.

valid for any Monday thru Thursday game during the 2006-2007 regular season

Tickets subject to availablility; Not valid for groups, playoffs or other promotions; Redeemable at Ticketmaster outlets, phones & internet as well as the Target Center box office
WOLVES06

Valid now thru November 1, 2007
See reverse side for details   F2

www.timberwolves.com

To get a 2006-2007 schedule or information on Timberwolves Fan Plans call (612) 337- DUNK or check out our website at www.timberwolves.com

Offer validity is governed by the Rules of Use and excludes defined holidays. Offers are not valid with other discount offers, unless specified. Coupons void if purchased, sold or bartered. Discounts exclude tax, tip and/or alcohol, where applicable.

To get a 2006-2007 schedule or information on Timberwolves Fan Plans call (612) 337- DUNK or check out our website at www.timberwolves.com

Offer validity is governed by the Rules of Use and excludes defined holidays. Offers are not valid with other discount offers, unless specified. Coupons void if purchased, sold or bartered. Discounts exclude tax, tip and/or alcohol, where applicable.

A TWINS GAME THROUGH THE EYES OF A YOUNGSTER. C'MON, YOU REMEMBER.

THIS IS TWINS TERRITORY

800-33-TWINS
twinsbaseball.com

ENTERTAINMENT & SPORTS

---

entertainment | ONE UPPER CLUB LEVEL TICKET

MINNESOTA Twins

Enjoy one complimentary UPPER CLUB LEVEL TICKET when you purchase a second UPPER CLUB LEVEL TICKET of equal value.

valid for 2007 regular season home games

Redeem at Twins Pro Shops or Twins Box Office at least 24 hrs. prior to game, or by mail at least 7 days prior to game; Quantities limited, subject to ticket availability; Not valid for premium home games AA

Valid now thru November 1, 2007
See reverse side for details   F3

---

entertainment | ONE UPPER CLUB LEVEL TICKET

MINNESOTA Twins

Enjoy one complimentary UPPER CLUB LEVEL TICKET when you purchase a second UPPER CLUB LEVEL TICKET of equal value.

valid for 2007 regular season home games

Redeem at Twins Pro Shops or Twins Box Office at least 24 hrs. prior to game, or by mail at least 7 days prior to game; Quantities limited, subject to ticket availability; Not valid for premium home games AA

Valid now thru November 1, 2007
See reverse side for details   F4

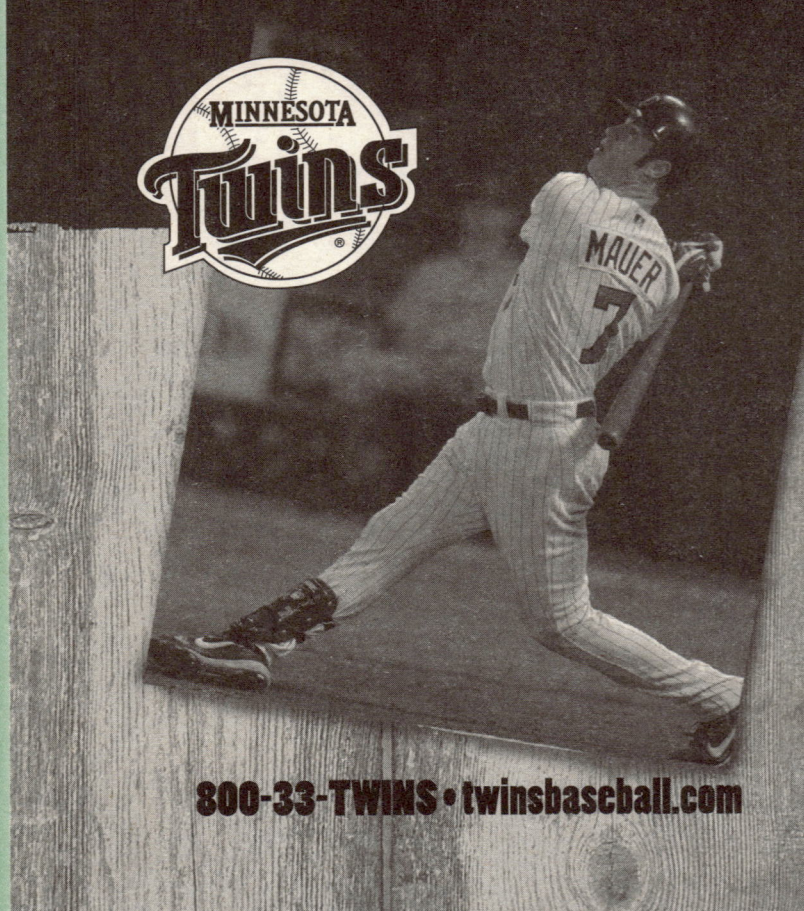

MINNESOTA TWINS

800-33-TWINS • twinsbaseball.com

MAIL TO MINNESOTA TWINS
SDS 12-1466 P.O. Box 86 Minneapolis, MN 55486-1466
Valid for 2007 regular season home games at the Metrodome
Ticket Pricing Information
Please call (612)33-TWINS or outstate 1-800-33-TWINS

Enclosed is my check for $_____ (ticket) + $5.00 (mail handling) per order=_____
payable to Minnesota Twins.
Visa, MasterCard, American Express, Discover, Diners Club

CC#:_____ Exp:_____
More than one coupon may be submitted together as one order for total mail handling charge of $5.00.
Please complete to validate:

Game Choice:_____
Name:_____
Address:_____
City:_____ State:_____ ZIP:_____
Day Phone:_____ Night Phone:_____
Signature:_____

Not valid for group or other promotions. Service fees per ticket apply if redeemed at Twins Pro-Shop. Call for game times and dates. 612-33-TWINS or outstate 1-800-33-TWINS. Coupon valid for one game only. www.twinsbaseball.com

Offer validity is governed by the Rules of Use and excludes defined holidays. Offers are not valid with other discount offers, unless specified. Coupons void if purchased, sold or bartered. Discounts exclude tax, tip and/or alcohol, where applicable.

MAIL TO MINNESOTA TWINS
SDS 12-1466 P.O. Box 86 Minneapolis, MN 55486-1466
Valid for 2007 regular season home games at the Metrodome
Ticket Pricing Information
Please call (612)33-TWINS or outstate 1-800-33-TWINS

Enclosed is my check for $_____ (ticket) + $5.00 (mail handling) per order=_____
payable to Minnesota Twins.
Visa, MasterCard, American Express, Discover, Diners Club

CC#:_____ Exp:_____
More than one coupon may be submitted together as one order for total mail handling charge of $5.00.
Please complete to validate:

Game Choice:_____
Name:_____
Address:_____
City:_____ State:_____ ZIP:_____
Day Phone:_____ Night Phone:_____
Signature:_____

Not valid for group or other promotions. Service fees per ticket apply if redeemed at Twins Pro-Shop. Call for game times and dates. 612-33-TWINS or outstate 1-800-33-TWINS. Coupon valid for one game only. www.twinsbaseball.com

Offer validity is governed by the Rules of Use and excludes defined holidays. Offers are not valid with other discount offers, unless specified. Coupons void if purchased, sold or bartered. Discounts exclude tax, tip and/or alcohol, where applicable.

THEATER BONUS

See details on certificate below

Great Savings!

MANN Theatres

ENTERTAINMENT & SPORTS

Please remove certificate to redeem.

---

entertainment

THEATER BONUS

Enjoy TWO ADMISSIONS at $6.00 each.

valid 7 days a week

Restrictions May apply - please call your local theatre; REDEEM AT THEATRE BOX OFFICE

MANN Theatres

Valid now thru November 1, 2007   See reverse side for details   F5

Mann Theatres

Baxter
Brainerd/Baxter Movies 10 at Westgate
(218)828-6228

Champlin
Champlin Cinema 14
(Hwy. 169 and 117th Ave.)
(763)712-9955

Cottage Grove
Cottage Grove Drive In
(seasonal)
(651)458-5965

Grand Rapids
Grand Rapids Cinema 8
(218)326-4400

Hibbing
Hibbing Cinema 8
(218)262-3382

Plymouth
Plymouth Cinema 12
(Vicksburg & Hwy. 55)
(763)551-0000

St. Louis Park
St. Louis Park Cinema 6
(Hwy. 100 & Excelsior Blvd.)
(952)927-9611

St. Paul
Grandview 1 & 2
(Grand & Fairview)
(651)698-3344

Highland 1 & 2
(Cleveland & Ford Pkwy)
(651)698-3085

Mann Theatres

Baxter
Brainerd/Baxter Movies 10 at Westgate
(218)828-6228

Champlin
Champlin Cinema 14
(Hwy. 169 and 117th Ave.)
(763)712-9955

Cottage Grove
Cottage Grove Drive In
(seasonal)
(651)458-5965

Grand Rapids
Grand Rapids Cinema 8
(218)326-4400

Hibbing
Hibbing Cinema 8
(218)262-3382

Plymouth
Plymouth Cinema 12
(Vicksburg & Hwy. 55)
(763)551-0000

St. Louis Park
St. Louis Park Cinema 6
(Hwy. 100 & Excelsior Blvd.)
(952)927-9611

St. Paul
Grandview 1 & 2
(Grand & Fairview)
(651)698-3344

Highland 1 & 2
(Cleveland & Ford Pkwy)
(651)698-3085

Offer validity is governed by the Rules of Use and excludes defined holidays. Offers are not valid with other discount offers, unless specified. Coupons void if purchased, sold or bartered. Discounts exclude tax, tip and/or alcohol, where applicable.

Water Park of America

America's Biggest Indoor Water Park

- Just 5 Minutes from the Airport
- Adjacent to Mall of America
- Phone: 877-75 SLIDE

SURF MINNESOTA!

ENTERTAINMENT & SPORTS

entertainment

FREE ADMISSION

Enjoy one complimentary ADMISSION when a second ADMISSION of equal or greater value is purchased.

valid anytime

On availability basis

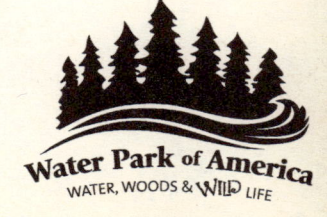

Water Park of America
WATER, WOODS & WILD LIFE

Valid now thru November 1, 2007 — See reverse side for details — F6

Water Park of America
WATER, WOODS & WILD LIFE

- Twist & turn in America's highest indoor water slides
- Clear, enclosed slide 90' above the Twin Cities skyline
- 403 Grand Lodge water park accommodations
- Wave Pool
- Surf Rider stand-up surfing
- America's longest indoor family raft ride
- Devil's Cave river ride
- Tube & body slides
- 3,500 SF interactive play structure
- Zero entry depth children's pool
- Kayak course
- Sports activity pool
- 5,800 SF Northern Lights family arcade
- Split Rock Grille
- Sleepy Eye Cafe
- General admission prices are available

877-75 SLIDE
1700 East American Blvd. | Bloomington, MN 55425
www.waterparkofamerica.com

Water Park of America
WATER, WOODS & WILD LIFE

1700 E. American Blvd.
Bloomington, MN
(952)854-8900

Offer validity is governed by the Rules of Use and excludes defined holidays. Offers are not valid with other discount offers, unless specified. Coupons void if purchased, sold or bartered. Discounts exclude tax, tip and/or alcohol, where applicable.

WORLD'S LARGEST UNDERGROUND AQUARIUM

WORLD'S BEST Discovery Channel SHARK ENCOUNTER

See over 4,500 living sea creatures and touch real sharks! With ocean tanks winding under the Mall of America, the Underwater Adventures Aquarium has been named the "World's Best Shark Encounter" by the Discovery Channel.

www.sharky.tv • 952-883-0202

Underwater Adventures AQUARIUM
MALL OF AMERICA

ENTERTAINMENT & SPORTS

---

entertainment — FREE ADMISSION

Underwater Adventures AQUARIUM
MALL OF AMERICA

Enjoy one complimentary ADMISSION when a second ADMISSION of equal or greater value is purchased.

Not valid toward group rates or classes

valid anytime

Not valid Saturdays Memorial Day-Labor Day

Valid now thru November 1, 2007
See reverse side for details

F7

---

entertainment — FREE TICKET

Underwater Adventures AQUARIUM
MALL OF AMERICA

Enjoy one complimentary PLUNGE TICKET when a second PLUNGE TICKET of equal or greater value is purchased.

valid anytime

Not valid Saturdays Memorial Day-Labor Day

Valid now thru November 1, 2007
See reverse side for details

F8

WORLD'S LARGEST UNDERGROUND AQUARIUM

See over 4,500 living sea creatures and touch real sharks! With ocean tanks winding under the Mall of America, the Underwater Adventures Aquarium has been named the "World's Best Shark Encounter" by the Discovery Channel.

www.sharky.tv • 952-883-0202

Underwater Adventures AQUARIUM
MALL OF AMERICA

WORLD'S BEST Discovery SHARK ENCOUNTER

Underwater Adventures
120 E. Broadway
(Mall of America)
Bloomington, MN
(952)883-0202

Offer validity is governed by the Rules of Use and excludes defined holidays. Offers are not valid with other discount offers, unless specified. Coupons void if purchased, sold or bartered. Discounts exclude tax, tip and/or alcohol, where applicable.

Underwater Adventures
120 E. Broadway
(Mall of America)
Bloomington, MN
(952)883-0202

Offer validity is governed by the Rules of Use and excludes defined holidays. Offers are not valid with other discount offers, unless specified. Coupons void if purchased, sold or bartered. Discounts exclude tax, tip and/or alcohol, where applicable.

Entertainment & Sports Index

Attractions

Minnesota

Andover
- (kids) Bunker Beach G30

Chaska
- Minnesota Landscape Arboretum G157

Minneapolis
- (kids) Brooklyn Center Community Center G135
- (kids) Crystal Recreation Dept.. .... G147
- Grand Rios Indoor Water Park G27
- (kids) Nascar Silicon Motor Speedway G32
- The Park at MOA G22
- Richfield Municipal Pool & Waterslide G163
- St. Louis Park Outdoor Aquatic Park G149
- (kids) St. Louis Park Rec Center G150
- (kids) Underwater Adventures Aquarium F7-F8
- Water Park of America F6

Saint Paul
- Battle Creek Waterworks Family Aquatic Center........ G146
- Cascade Bay Water Park G28
- NEW Como Town G29
- (kids) Eagles Nest Indoor Playground G148
- Minnesota Zoo G26
- (kids) Tamarack Nature Center G151
- (kids) Tropics Indoor Water Park.. .... G31

Shakopee
- Canterbury Park G37

Wisconsin

Osceola
- Osceola & St. Croix Valley Railway. G143

Concerts/Performance

Minnesota

Chanhassen
- Chanhassen Fireside Theatre G41
- Chanhassen Dinner Theatre........ G42

Hamel
- NEW Medina Entertainment Center G129

Minneapolis
- Acme Comedy Co............. G43
- Brave New Workshop G165
- ComedySportz G123
- (kids) Greater Twin Cities Youth Symphonies.......... G124
- The Guthrie Theater............ G45
- Minnesota Dance Theatre G125
- Plymouth Playhouse G126

Saint Paul
- Great American History Theatre..... G40
- The Minnesota Opera G46
- NEW Mounds Theatre.............. G130
- Ordway Center for the Performing Arts......... G48-G50
- Saint Paul Chamber Orchestra....... G44
- NEW Starting Gate Productions........ G134

Other
- (kids) NEW Disney Live G38
- Metropolitan Boys Choir & Choralaires G164

Golf

Minnesota

Alexandria
- Arrowwood Golf Club G74

Annandale
- Southbrook Golf Club G71

Belle Plaine
- Valley View Golf Course G59

Buffalo
- Buffalo Heights Golf Course....... G66

Cannon Falls
- The Summit Golf Club G69

Chaska
- Dahlgreen Golf Club............ G54
- Golf Zone G81

Cottage Grove
- All Seasons Golf............. G78

NEW **New Merchants Added This Year**   (kids) **Great Place for Kids!**

ENTERTAINMENT & SPORTS INDEX

Farmington
- Southern Hills Golf Club G61

Forest Lake
- Castlewood Golf Course G64

Glencoe
- Glencoe Country Club G55

Isanti
- Wintergreens Indoor Golf G90

Lester Prairie
- Shadowbrooke Golf Course G70

Minneapolis
- NEW B&V Golf Course. G79
- Begin Oaks Golf Course G80
- Braemar Golf Dome. G68
- kids Grand Slam U.S.A. G82
- kids Spring Lake Amusement Park G88

Minnetonka
- The Bunker Indoor Golf Center G65

Montgomery
- Montgomery Golf Club G73

Monticello
- NEW Riverwood National Driving Range. G141
- NEW Riverwood National Golf Course. . . . G60
- NEW Vintage Driving Range G89
- NEW Vintage Golf Course. G75

Onamia
- Izatys Golf & Yacht Club - The Sanctuary G57

Owatonna
- Hidden Creek Golf Club G56

Redwood Falls
- Redwood Falls Golf Club. G58

Rogers
- Northern Palms Driving Range G85

Saint Paul
- Brightwood Hills. G67
- The Bunker Indoor Golf Center G65
- Como Park Golf Course G87
- kids Grand Slam U.S.A. G82
- Island Lake Golf Center G84
- kids Lava Links. G77

- Phalen Park Golf Course G72
- Roseville Cedarholm Golf Course . . . G86

Sauk Centre
- Greystone Golf Club. G83

Wayzata
- Orono Golf Course. G62

WISCONSIN

River Falls
- Kilkarney Hills Golf Course G63

Saint Croix Falls
- NEW St. Croix Falls Mini Golf & Go-Karts G144

HEALTH & BEAUTY

MINNESOTA

Chaska
- kids Chaska Community Center G145

MOVIES

MULTIPLE LOCATIONS
- kids CEC Theatres G13-G15
- kids Crown Theatres G10-G11
- kids Mann Theatres F5,G1-G5
- kids Marcus Theatres. G7-G9
- kids NEW Regal Entertainment Group . . . G169-G174

MINNESOTA

Minneapolis
- The Bell Auditorium G162
- NEW Cinema Grill Theater G51
- Riverview Theater. G52

Saint Paul
- kids Great Clips IMAX Theatre G6

OTHER
- NEW Carmike Cinemas G12

MUSEUMS

MINNESOTA

Minneapolis
- American Swedish Institute G158
- The Bakken Museum G167

NEW **New Merchants Added This Year**   kids **Great Place for Kids!**

Entertainment & Sports Index

The Bell Museum
   of Natural History G159
NEW Dinosaur Walk MOA G36
NEW Hennepin History Museum G168
kids Walker Art Center G47

Saint Paul
Fort Snelling G160
kids Gibbs Museum of Pioneer
   & Dakotah Life G161

Recreational Sports

Multiple Locations
NEW Pump It Up G133
kids Ramsey County
   Parks & Recreation G100
NEW USA Karate G92

Minnesota
Andover
NEW Adventure Park G128
NEW Ollie & Co. Indoor Skate Park G131

Anoka
NEW Super Bowl G114

Burnsville
kids Adventure Zone G93
kids Burnsville Ice Center G97
kids Pro-Kart Indoor Racing G33
Q-Sharks G104
Shooters Billiards G106

Eden Prairie
Brunswick Zone G108
Eden Prairie Community Center G94

Excelsior
kids **NEW** Country Club Lanes G111

Hamel
Medina Lanes G113

Hopkins
NEW Tuttle's Bowling, Bar & Grill G137

Minneapolis
Airport Bowl G109
kids Cheap Skate G98
Classic Bowl G115
Gameworks G34

kids **NEW** Kids' Time of Northtown G95
kids Lariat Lanes G112
Lyn-Del Lanes G139
NEW Memory Lanes G138
kids Park Tavern Lounge & Lanes G117
NEW PlayZone Arcade G23
NEW Plymouth Ice Center G132
kids Roller Garden G101
kids Rollerdome G102
kids Skateville G103
kids Texa-Tonka Lanes G120
kids 3rd Lair G96
NEW Two Stooges Billiards G107

Osseo
NEW Eddies Billiards G140
kids Maple Grove Community Center G91
kids Pro-Kart Indoor Racing G33
kids Sundance Golf and Bowl G119

Saint Paul
Flaherty's Arden Bowl G110
kids John Rose Minnesota Oval G99
kids Midway Pro Bowl G116
Minnesota Swarm G25
kids St. Bernard's Bowling Lanes G118
kids Vertical Endeavors G76
kids West Side Lanes G121
kids Wooddale Recreation Center G142

Shakopee
Rack N' Roll Billiards G105

Willernie
kids Wildwood Bowl G122

Wisconsin
Centuria
NEW McKenzie Lanes G53

Retail

Minnesota
Minneapolis
NEW Toy Store G24

NEW New Merchants Added This Year   **kids** Great Place for Kids!

ENTERTAINMENT & SPORTS INDEX

SPECIAL EVENTS

MULTIPLE LOCATIONS
- **kids** Smuckers Stars on Ice G39

OTHER
- Dodge's World's Toughest Rodeo G127
- **kids** Minnesota Renaissance Festival G35
- **kids** Trail of Terror G166

SPORTING EVENTS

MINNESOTA

Minneapolis
- **kids** Minnesota Lynx G17-G18
- U of M Athletics G153-G156

Saint Paul
- **kids** Minnesota Thunder Pro Soccer G21
- Rice And Arlington Batting Cages G152

OTHER
- **kids** Minnesota Timberwolves F1-F2, G16
- **kids** Minnesota Twins F3-F4, G19-G20

OTHER
- **NEW** Stages Theatre Company G136

Register at
entertainment.com/register
to access even more of these great savings!

NEW New Merchants Added This Year   **kids** Great Place for Kids!

entertainment.
entertainment.com

Mann Theatres

Enjoy TWO ADMISSIONS at $6.00 each.
See reverse for Offer Details.

THEATER BONUS

MANN Theatres

Valid now thru November 1, 2007   See Reverse Side for Locations   G1

---

entertainment.
entertainment.com

Mann Theatres

Enjoy TWO ADMISSIONS at $6.00 each.
See reverse for Offer Details.

THEATER BONUS

MANN Theatres

Valid now thru November 1, 2007   See Reverse Side for Locations   G2

---

entertainment.
entertainment.com

Mann Theatres

Enjoy TWO ADMISSIONS at $6.00 each.
See reverse for Offer Details.

THEATER BONUS

MANN Theatres

Valid now thru November 1, 2007   See Reverse Side for Locations   G3

ENTERTAINMENT & SPORTS

Mann Theatres

MANN Theatres

Baxter
Brainerd/Baxter Movies 10
at Westgate
(218)828-6228

Champlin
Champlin Cinema 14
(Hwy. 169 and 117th Ave.)
(763)712-9955

Cottage Grove
Cottage Grove Drive In
(seasonal)
(651)458-5965

Grand Rapids
Grand Rapids Cinema 8
(218)326-5440

Hibbing
Hibbing Cinema 8
(218)262-3382

Plymouth
Plymouth Cinema 12
(Vicksburg & Hwy. 55)
(763)551-0000

St. Louis Park
St. Louis Park Cinema 6
(Hwy. 100 & Excelsior Blvd.)
(952)927-9611

St. Paul
Grandview 1 & 2
(Grand & Fairview)
(651)698-3344

Highland 1 & 2
(Cleveland & Ford Pkwy)
(651)698-3085

Offer Details: Valid 7 days a week. Restrictions May apply - please call your local theatre; REDEEM AT THEATRE BOX OFFICE.

00001258

Offer validity is governed by the Rules of Use and excludes defined holidays. Offers are not valid with other discount offers, unless specified. Coupons void if purchased, sold or bartered. Discounts exclude tax, tip and/or alcohol, where applicable.

Mann Theatres

MANN Theatres

Baxter
Brainerd/Baxter Movies 10
at Westgate
(218)828-6228

Champlin
Champlin Cinema 14
(Hwy. 169 and 117th Ave.)
(763)712-9955

Cottage Grove
Cottage Grove Drive In
(seasonal)
(651)458-5965

Grand Rapids
Grand Rapids Cinema 8
(218)326-5440

Hibbing
Hibbing Cinema 8
(218)262-3382

Plymouth
Plymouth Cinema 12
(Vicksburg & Hwy. 55)
(763)551-0000

St. Louis Park
St. Louis Park Cinema 6
(Hwy. 100 & Excelsior Blvd.)
(952)927-9611

St. Paul
Grandview 1 & 2
(Grand & Fairview)
(651)698-3344

Highland 1 & 2
(Cleveland & Ford Pkwy)
(651)698-3085

Offer Details: Valid 7 days a week. Restrictions May apply - please call your local theatre; REDEEM AT THEATRE BOX OFFICE.

00001258

Offer validity is governed by the Rules of Use and excludes defined holidays. Offers are not valid with other discount offers, unless specified. Coupons void if purchased, sold or bartered. Discounts exclude tax, tip and/or alcohol, where applicable.

Mann Theatres

MANN Theatres

Baxter
Brainerd/Baxter Movies 10
at Westgate
(218)828-6228

Champlin
Champlin Cinema 14
(Hwy. 169 and 117th Ave.)
(763)712-9955

Cottage Grove
Cottage Grove Drive In
(seasonal)
(651)458-5965

Grand Rapids
Grand Rapids Cinema 8
(218)326-5440

Hibbing
Hibbing Cinema 8
(218)262-3382

Plymouth
Plymouth Cinema 12
(Vicksburg & Hwy. 55)
(763)551-0000

St. Louis Park
St. Louis Park Cinema 6
(Hwy. 100 & Excelsior Blvd.)
(952)927-9611

St. Paul
Grandview 1 & 2
(Grand & Fairview)
(651)698-3344

Highland 1 & 2
(Cleveland & Ford Pkwy)
(651)698-3085

Offer Details: Valid 7 days a week. Restrictions May apply - please call your local theatre; REDEEM AT THEATRE BOX OFFICE.

00001258

Offer validity is governed by the Rules of Use and excludes defined holidays. Offers are not valid with other discount offers, unless specified. Coupons void if purchased, sold or bartered. Discounts exclude tax, tip and/or alcohol, where applicable.

entertainment.com

Mann Theatres
Enjoy TWO ADMISSIONS at $6.00 each.
See reverse for Offer Details.

THEATER BONUS

Mann Theatres

Valid now thru November 1, 2007

See Reverse Side for Locations

G4

---

entertainment.com

Mann Theatres
Enjoy TWO ADMISSIONS at $6.00 each.
See reverse for Offer Details.

THEATER BONUS

Mann Theatres

Valid now thru November 1, 2007

See Reverse Side for Locations

G5

---

entertainment.com

Great Clips IMAX Theatre
Enjoy one complimentary ADMISSION when a second ADMISSION of equal or greater value is purchased.
See reverse for Offer Details.

FREE ADMISSION

Great Clips IMAX THEATRE
AT THE MINNESOTA ZOO
www.imax.com/minnesota

12000 Zoo Blvd., Apple Valley, MN
(952) 431-IMAX

Valid now thru November 1, 2007

G6

ENTERTAINMENT & SPORTS

Mann Theatres

MANN *Theatres*

Baxter
Brainerd/Baxter Movies 10 at Westgate
(218)828-6228

Champlin
Champlin Cinema 14
(Hwy. 169 and 117th Ave.)
(763)712-9955

Cottage Grove
Cottage Grove Drive In
(seasonal)
(651)458-5965

Grand Rapids
Grand Rapids Cinema 8
(218)326-5440

Hibbing
Hibbing Cinema 8
(218)262-3382

Plymouth
Plymouth Cinema 12
(Vicksburg & Hwy. 55)
(763)551-0000

St. Louis Park
St. Louis Park Cinema 6
(Hwy. 100 & Excelsior Blvd.)
(952)927-9611

St. Paul
Grandview 1 & 2
(Grand & Fairview)
(651)698-3344

Highland 1 & 2
(Cleveland & Ford Pkwy)
(651)698-3085

Offer Details: Valid 7 days a week. Restrictions May apply - please call your local theatre; REDEEM AT THEATRE BOX OFFICE.

00001258

Offer validity is governed by the Rules of Use and excludes defined holidays. Offers are not valid with other discount offers, unless specified. Coupons void if purchased, sold or bartered. Discounts exclude tax, tip and/or alcohol, where applicable.

Mann Theatres

MANN *Theatres*

Baxter
Brainerd/Baxter Movies 10 at Westgate
(218)828-6228

Champlin
Champlin Cinema 14
(Hwy. 169 and 117th Ave.)
(763)712-9955

Cottage Grove
Cottage Grove Drive In
(seasonal)
(651)458-5965

Grand Rapids
Grand Rapids Cinema 8
(218)326-5440

Hibbing
Hibbing Cinema 8
(218)262-3382

Plymouth
Plymouth Cinema 12
(Vicksburg & Hwy. 55)
(763)551-0000

St. Louis Park
St. Louis Park Cinema 6
(Hwy. 100 & Excelsior Blvd.)
(952)927-9611

St. Paul
Grandview 1 & 2
(Grand & Fairview)
(651)698-3344

Highland 1 & 2
(Cleveland & Ford Pkwy)
(651)698-3085

Offer Details: Valid 7 days a week. Restrictions May apply - please call your local theatre; REDEEM AT THEATRE BOX OFFICE.

00001258

Offer validity is governed by the Rules of Use and excludes defined holidays. Offers are not valid with other discount offers, unless specified. Coupons void if purchased, sold or bartered. Discounts exclude tax, tip and/or alcohol, where applicable.

Great Clips IMAX Theatre

- Call for showtimes & availability: 952-431-IMAX (4629) Toll-free: 877-660-IMAX
- 12,000 Watts of digital surround sound
- 6-Story high screen
- Stadium seating

Great Clips® IMAX® THEATRE

AT THE MINNESOTA ZOO
12000 Zoo Blvd.
(at the Minnesota Zoo)
Apple Valley, MN
(952)431-IMAX

Offer Details: Valid anytime. Valid only at the Great Clips IMAX® Theatre at the Minnesota Zoo Box Office; Subject to seat availability; No valid for the first 2 weeks of a full-length Hollywood film.

00487145

Offer validity is governed by the Rules of Use and excludes defined holidays. Offers are not valid with other discount offers, unless specified. Coupons void if purchased, sold or bartered. Discounts exclude tax, tip and/or alcohol, where applicable.

entertainment
entertainment.com

Marcus Theatres
Enjoy up to FOUR ADMISSIONS at $6.50 each.
See reverse for Offer Details.

UP TO 4 ADMISSIONS AT $6.50 EACH

MARCUS THEATRES
www.marcustheatres.com

See Reverse Side for Locations

Valid now thru November 1, 2007   G7

---

entertainment
entertainment.com

Marcus Theatres
Enjoy up to FOUR ADMISSIONS at $6.50 each.
See reverse for Offer Details.

UP TO 4 ADMISSIONS AT $6.50 EACH

MARCUS THEATRES
www.marcustheatres.com

See Reverse Side for Locations

Valid now thru November 1, 2007   G8

---

entertainment
entertainment.com

Marcus Theatres
Enjoy up to FOUR ADMISSIONS at $6.50 each.
See reverse for Offer Details.

UP TO 4 ADMISSIONS AT $6.50 EACH

MARCUS THEATRES
www.marcustheatres.com

See Reverse Side for Locations

Valid now thru November 1, 2007   G9

ENTERTAINMENT & SPORTS

Marcus Theatres

- Visit us online for movie showtimes & to sign up for movie showtimes to be e-mailed to you!

570 Freeport
Elk River, MN
(763)441-1234

1325 S. Frontage Rd.
Hastings, MN
(651)438-9700

5677 Hadley Ave. N.
Oakdale, MN
(651)770-4994

15280 Carrousel Way
Rosemount, MN
(651)322-4600

1116 Shakopee Town Sq.
Shakopee, MN
(952)445-5300

Shakopee Town Sq. Mall
Shakopee, MN
(952)445-4742

Offer Details: Valid anytime. Evening promotional code: GVPEV65; Matinee promotional code: GVPTV65.

00084228

Offer validity is governed by the Rules of Use and excludes defined holidays. Offers are not valid with other discount offers, unless specified. Coupons void if purchased, sold or bartered. Discounts exclude tax, tip and/or alcohol, where applicable.

Marcus Theatres

- Visit us online for movie showtimes & to sign up for movie showtimes to be e-mailed to you!

570 Freeport
Elk River, MN
(763)441-1234

1325 S. Frontage Rd.
Hastings, MN
(651)438-9700

5677 Hadley Ave. N.
Oakdale, MN
(651)770-4994

15280 Carrousel Way
Rosemount, MN
(651)322-4600

1116 Shakopee Town Sq.
Shakopee, MN
(952)445-5300

Shakopee Town Sq. Mall
Shakopee, MN
(952)445-4742

Offer Details: Valid anytime. Evening promotional code: GVPEV65; Matinee promotional code: GVPTV65.

00084228

Offer validity is governed by the Rules of Use and excludes defined holidays. Offers are not valid with other discount offers, unless specified. Coupons void if purchased, sold or bartered. Discounts exclude tax, tip and/or alcohol, where applicable.

Marcus Theatres

- Visit us online for movie showtimes & to sign up for movie showtimes to be e-mailed to you!

570 Freeport
Elk River, MN
(763)441-1234

1325 S. Frontage Rd.
Hastings, MN
(651)438-9700

5677 Hadley Ave. N.
Oakdale, MN
(651)770-4994

15280 Carrousel Way
Rosemount, MN
(651)322-4600

1116 Shakopee Town Sq.
Shakopee, MN
(952)445-5300

Shakopee Town Sq. Mall
Shakopee, MN
(952)445-4742

Offer Details: Valid anytime. Evening promotional code: GVPEV65; Matinee promotional code: GVPTV65.

00084228

Offer validity is governed by the Rules of Use and excludes defined holidays. Offers are not valid with other discount offers, unless specified. Coupons void if purchased, sold or bartered. Discounts exclude tax, tip and/or alcohol, where applicable.

entertainment
entertainment.com

Crown Theatres

Present this coupon at theatre box office and pay the MATINEE PRICE. Maximum of two tickets purchased per coupon.
See reverse for Offer Details.

REDEEM AT THEATRE

CROWN THEATRES
crowntheatres.com

Valid now thru November 1, 2007 — See Reverse Side for Locations — G10

---

entertainment
entertainment.com

Crown Theatres

Present this coupon at theatre box office and pay the MATINEE PRICE. Maximum of two tickets purchased per coupon.
See reverse for Offer Details.

REDEEM AT THEATRE

CROWN THEATRES
crowntheatres.com

Valid now thru November 1, 2007 — See Reverse Side for Locations — G11

---

entertainment
entertainment.com

Carmike Cinemas

Valid for up to twelve (12) tickets at $5.50 each. Not valid for the first two weeks on SONY picture films. Coupon must be redeemed through Entertainment Publications, Inc. per order form instructions on back.
See reverse for Offer Details.

DISCOUNT MOVIE TICKETS

Carmike Cinemas

Valid now thru November 1, 2007 — Valid at All Participating Locations — G12

ENTERTAINMENT & SPORTS

Crown Theatres

- Get treated like royalty at Crown Theatres
- Visit crowntheatres.com for locations & show times

CROWN THEATRES
crowntheatres.com

CONNECTICUT
Greenwich
2 Railroad Ave.
(203)869-4030
Hartford
330 New Park Ave.
(860)236-6677
Norwalk
542 Westport Ave.
(203)846-8797
South Norwalk
64 N. Main St.
(203)899-7979

Stamford
118 Summer St.
(203)323-1690
5 Landmark Sq.
(203)324-3100
Trumbull
100 Quary Rd.
(203)365-6500
ILLINOIS
Glenview
1850 Tower Rd.
(847)729-9600

Skokie
7000 Carpenter Rd.
(Village Crossing Shpg.Ctr.)
(847)673-8486
MARYLAND
Annapolis
1020 Annapolis Mall
(410)224-1145

2474 Solomons Island Rd.
(Annapolis Harbour Shpg. Ctr.)
(410)224-1145
MINNESOTA
Minneapolis
600 Hennepin Ave. S.
(612)338-5900

Offer Details: Valid anytime. Redeem at Theatre Box Office; Not valid holidays & subject to rules of use; Not valid with any other discount offer unless specified; Coupon VOID if purchased, sold, or bartered for cash; Not valid on "No Pass" movies.

00213508

Offer validity is governed by the Rules of Use and excludes defined holidays. Offers are not valid with other discount offers, unless specified. Coupons void if purchased, sold or bartered. Discounts exclude tax, tip and/or alcohol, where applicable.

Crown Theatres

- Get treated like royalty at Crown Theatres
- Visit crowntheatres.com for locations & show times

CROWN THEATRES
crowntheatres.com

CONNECTICUT
Greenwich
2 Railroad Ave.
(203)869-4030
Hartford
330 New Park Ave.
(860)236-6677
Norwalk
542 Westport Ave.
(203)846-8797
South Norwalk
64 N. Main St.
(203)899-7979

Stamford
118 Summer St.
(203)323-1690
5 Landmark Sq.
(203)324-3100
Trumbull
100 Quary Rd.
(203)365-6500
ILLINOIS
Glenview
1850 Tower Rd.
(847)729-9600

Skokie
7000 Carpenter Rd.
(Village Crossing Shpg.Ctr.)
(847)673-8486
MARYLAND
Annapolis
1020 Annapolis Mall
(410)224-1145

2474 Solomons Island Rd.
(Annapolis Harbour Shpg. Ctr.)
(410)224-1145
MINNESOTA
Minneapolis
600 Hennepin Ave. S.
(612)338-5900

Offer Details: Valid anytime. Redeem at Theatre Box Office; Not valid holidays & subject to rules of use; Not valid with any other discount offer unless specified; Coupon VOID if purchased, sold, or bartered for cash; Not valid on "No Pass" movies.

00213508

Offer validity is governed by the Rules of Use and excludes defined holidays. Offers are not valid with other discount offers, unless specified. Coupons void if purchased, sold or bartered. Discounts exclude tax, tip and/or alcohol, where applicable.

Carmike Cinemas

- Tickets available by mail order only. You will receive tickets to present at the box office for admission. Please note ticket usage restrictions on coupons.
- Ticket orders fulfilled by availability. Ticket prices are subject to change without notice.
- All checks or money orders must be made payable to: **Entertainment Publications, Inc.** Price per ticket is on the front of this coupon. Check/money order must include *total cost of tickets ordered* **plus** shipping and handling of $2.25 for orders valued at $39.99 or less and $5.50 for orders valued at $40.00 or more. Do not send cash.
- Mail payment and completed coupons to: ENTERTAINMENT PUBLICATIONS, INC.
  c/o TICKETS
  P.O. BOX 539
  DUNCAN, SC 29334-5390
- Allow three weeks for delivery of tickets. Note expiration dates on tickets received. They may vary. Tickets may not be exchanged or returned for refund.
- Call 1-877-814-5292 only if you have ordered more than three weeks ago and have not received your order.

Number of movie tickets you wish to order with this coupon: _____
Name: _____
Address: _____
Daytime Phone (____) _____
City: _____ State: _____ ZIP: _____
E-Mail Address: _____

Offer Details: Valid anytime.

00656185

Offer validity is governed by the Rules of Use and excludes defined holidays. Offers are not valid with other discount offers, unless specified. Coupons void if purchased, sold or bartered. Discounts exclude tax, tip and/or alcohol, where applicable.

entertainment.
entertainment.com

CEC Theatres
Enjoy up to TWO ADMISSIONS at $5.50 each.
See reverse for Offer Details.

DISCOUNT MOVIE TICKETS

CEC Theatres
Movie Excellence Since 1955

Valid now thru November 1, 2007

See Reverse Side for Locations

G13

---

entertainment.
entertainment.com

CEC Theatres
Enjoy up to TWO ADMISSIONS at $5.50 each.
See reverse for Offer Details.

DISCOUNT MOVIE TICKETS

CEC Theatres
Movie Excellence Since 1955

Valid now thru November 1, 2007

See Reverse Side for Locations

G14

---

entertainment.
entertainment.com

CEC Theatres
Enjoy up to TWO ADMISSIONS at $5.50 each.
See reverse for Offer Details.

DISCOUNT MOVIE TICKETS

CEC Theatres
Movie Excellence Since 1955

Valid now thru November 1, 2007

See Reverse Side for Locations

G15

ENTERTAINMENT & SPORTS

CEC Theatres

- For all CEC showtimes, visit us at www.cectheatres.com
- Minnesota, Wisconsin & North Dakota locations

CEC Theatres
Movie Excellence Since 1955

WEST ACRES 14 - Fargo, ND
(701)461-8902

CENTURY 10 - Fargo, ND
(701)461-8902

SAFARI 7 - Moorhead, MN
(701)461-8902

PARKWOOD 18 - St. Cloud, MN
(320)253-4328

LAKES 10 - Duluth, MN
(218)729-0335

SUPERIOR 7 - Superior, WI
(218)729-0335

AMIGO 9 - Bemidji, MN
(218)759-0324

CINEMA 9 - Hudson, WI
(715)386-1420

WINONA 7 - Winona, MN
(501)452-1643

LAKE 7 - Rice Lake, WI
(715)234-2691

CINEMA 7 - Albert Lea, MN
(507)373-7933

MARSHALL 6 - Marshall, MN
(507)532-6262

CINEMA 6 - Virginia, MN
(218)741-6954

CINEMA 6 - Faribault, MN
(507)332-0633

CROSSROADS 6 - St. Cloud, MN (320)253-4328

CINEMA 6 - Breckenridge, MN
(218)643-3851

DULUTH 10 - Duluth, MN
(218)729-0335

Offer Details: Valid Sunday thru Friday only. Not valid when "pass list suspended" or when "no discounts" appears in ads or is posted at the box office; Note: Additional $0.50 charge for the movies playing on the UltraScreen®.

00473675

Offer validity is governed by the Rules of Use and excludes defined holidays. Offers are not valid with other discount offers, unless specified. Coupons void if purchased, sold or bartered. Discounts exclude tax, tip and/or alcohol, where applicable.

CEC Theatres

- For all CEC showtimes, visit us at www.cectheatres.com
- Minnesota, Wisconsin & North Dakota locations

CEC Theatres
Movie Excellence Since 1955

WEST ACRES 14 - Fargo, ND
(701)461-8902

CENTURY 10 - Fargo, ND
(701)461-8902

SAFARI 7 - Moorhead, MN
(701)461-8902

PARKWOOD 18 - St. Cloud, MN
(320)253-4328

LAKES 10 - Duluth, MN
(218)729-0335

SUPERIOR 7 - Superior, WI
(218)729-0335

AMIGO 9 - Bemidji, MN
(218)759-0324

CINEMA 9 - Hudson, WI
(715)386-1420

WINONA 7 - Winona, MN
(501)452-1643

LAKE 7 - Rice Lake, WI
(715)234-2691

CINEMA 7 - Albert Lea, MN
(507)373-7933

MARSHALL 6 - Marshall, MN
(507)532-6262

CINEMA 6 - Virginia, MN
(218)741-6954

CINEMA 6 - Faribault, MN
(507)332-0633

CROSSROADS 6 - St. Cloud, MN (320)253-4328

CINEMA 6 - Breckenridge, MN
(218)643-3851

DULUTH 10 - Duluth, MN
(218)729-0335

Offer Details: Valid Sunday thru Friday only. Not valid when "pass list suspended" or when "no discounts" appears in ads or is posted at the box office; Note: Additional $0.50 charge for the movies playing on the UltraScreen®.

00473675

Offer validity is governed by the Rules of Use and excludes defined holidays. Offers are not valid with other discount offers, unless specified. Coupons void if purchased, sold or bartered. Discounts exclude tax, tip and/or alcohol, where applicable.

CEC Theatres

- For all CEC showtimes, visit us at www.cectheatres.com
- Minnesota, Wisconsin & North Dakota locations

CEC Theatres
Movie Excellence Since 1955

WEST ACRES 14 - Fargo, ND
(701)461-8902

CENTURY 10 - Fargo, ND
(701)461-8902

SAFARI 7 - Moorhead, MN
(701)461-8902

PARKWOOD 18 - St. Cloud, MN
(320)253-4328

LAKES 10 - Duluth, MN
(218)729-0335

SUPERIOR 7 - Superior, WI
(218)729-0335

AMIGO 9 - Bemidji, MN
(218)759-0324

CINEMA 9 - Hudson, WI
(715)386-1420

WINONA 7 - Winona, MN
(501)452-1643

LAKE 7 - Rice Lake, WI
(715)234-2691

CINEMA 7 - Albert Lea, MN
(507)373-7933

MARSHALL 6 - Marshall, MN
(507)532-6262

CINEMA 6 - Virginia, MN
(218)741-6954

CINEMA 6 - Faribault, MN
(507)332-0633

CROSSROADS 6 - St. Cloud, MN (320)253-4328

CINEMA 6 - Breckenridge, MN
(218)643-3851

DULUTH 10 - Duluth, MN
(218)729-0335

Offer Details: Valid Sunday thru Friday only. Not valid when "pass list suspended" or when "no discounts" appears in ads or is posted at the box office; Note: Additional $0.50 charge for the movies playing on the UltraScreen®.

00473675

Offer validity is governed by the Rules of Use and excludes defined holidays. Offers are not valid with other discount offers, unless specified. Coupons void if purchased, sold or bartered. Discounts exclude tax, tip and/or alcohol, where applicable.

entertainment.com

Minnesota Timberwolves
Enjoy up to FOUR $24 TICKETS at 50% off the regular price.
See reverse for Offer Details.
Tracking Code: WOLVES06

50% OFF

Valid now thru November 1, 2007

To get a 2006-2007 schedule or information on Timberwolves Fan Plans call (612) 337-DUNK or check out our website at www.timberwolves.com

G16

---

entertainment.com

Minnesota Lynx
Enjoy up to 4 TICKETS at 50% off the regular price.
See reverse for Offer Details.
Tracking Code: LYNX07

50% OFF

Valid now thru November 1, 2007

600 1st Ave. N., Minneapolis, MN
(612) 673-8400

G17

---

entertainment.com

Minnesota Lynx
Enjoy up to 4 TICKETS at 50% off the regular price.
See reverse for Offer Details.
Tracking Code: LYNX07

50% OFF

Valid now thru November 1, 2007

600 1st Ave. N., Minneapolis, MN
(612) 673-8400

G18

ENTERTAINMENT & SPORTS

Minnesota Timberwolves

To get a 2006-2007 schedule or information on Timberwolves Fan Plans call (612) 337- DUNK or check out our website at www.timberwolves.com

Offer Details: Valid for any Monday thru Thursday game during the 2006-2007 regular season. Tickets subject to availablility; Not valid for groups, playoffs or other promotions; Redeemable at Ticketmaster outlets, phones & internet as well as the Target Center box office.

00090518

Offer validity is governed by the Rules of Use and excludes defined holidays. Offers are not valid with other discount offers, unless specified. Coupons void if purchased, sold or bartered. Discounts exclude tax, tip and/or alcohol, where applicable.

Minnesota Lynx

- To get a 2007 schedule or information on Lynx tickets, call (612)673-8400 or check out our website at www.wnba.com/lynx

600 1st Ave. N.
(Target Ctr.)
Minneapolis, MN
(612)673-8400

Offer Details: Valid for any game. On availability basis; Not valid for groups or other promotions; Redeem at Target Center Box Office or any Ticketmaster outlet, phones and internet; Valid for tickets priced at $20 or less.

00476173

Offer validity is governed by the Rules of Use and excludes defined holidays. Offers are not valid with other discount offers, unless specified. Coupons void if purchased, sold or bartered. Discounts exclude tax, tip and/or alcohol, where applicable.

Minnesota Lynx

- To get a 2007 schedule or information on Lynx tickets, call (612)673-8400 or check out our website at www.wnba.com/lynx

600 1st Ave. N.
(Target Ctr.)
Minneapolis, MN
(612)673-8400

Offer Details: Valid for any game. On availability basis; Not valid for groups or other promotions; Redeem at Target Center Box Office or any Ticketmaster outlet, phones and internet; Valid for tickets priced at $20 or less.

00476173

Offer validity is governed by the Rules of Use and excludes defined holidays. Offers are not valid with other discount offers, unless specified. Coupons void if purchased, sold or bartered. Discounts exclude tax, tip and/or alcohol, where applicable.

entertainment
entertainment.com

Minnesota Twins
Enjoy one complimentary UPPER CLUB LEVEL TICKET when you purchase a second UPPER CLUB LEVEL TICKET of equal value.
See reverse for Offer Details.
Tracking Code: AA

ONE UPPER CLUB LEVEL TICKET

MINNESOTA Twins
www.twinsbaseball.com

Valid now thru November 1, 2007

See Reverse Side for Locations

G19

---

entertainment
entertainment.com

Minnesota Twins
Enjoy one complimentary UPPER CLUB LEVEL TICKET when you purchase a second UPPER CLUB LEVEL TICKET of equal value.
See reverse for Offer Details.
Tracking Code: AA

ONE UPPER CLUB LEVEL TICKET

MINNESOTA Twins
www.twinsbaseball.com

Valid now thru November 1, 2007

See Reverse Side for Locations

G20

---

entertainment
entertainment.com

Minnesota Thunder Pro Soccer
Enjoy one complimentary GENERAL ADMISSION TICKET when a second GENERAL ADMISSION TICKET of equal or greater value is purchased.
See reverse for Offer Details.

Up To $12.00 Value

MINNESOTA THUNDER

www.mnthunder.com
1158 Concordia Ave., St. Paul, MN
(651) 917-8326

Valid now thru November 1, 2007

G21

ENTERTAINMENT & SPORTS

Minnesota Twins

- To get a 2007 pocket schedule call 612-33-TWINS
- Pro Shop locations: Apple Valley (Southport Ctr.) 952-891-2934; Roseville (Rosedale Market Place) 651-635-0777; Minnetonka (Ridge Sq.) 952-546-0815
- Service fee applies when redeemed at Pro Shop locations

00002427

MAIL TO MINNESOTA TWINS
SDS 12-1466 P.O. Box 86 Minneapolis, MN 55486-1466
Valid for 2007 regular season home games at the Metrodome
Ticket Pricing Information
Please call (612)33-TWINS or outstate 1-800-33-TWINS

Enclosed is my check for $_____ (ticket) + $5.00 (mail handling) per order=_____
payable to Minnesota Twins.
Visa, MasterCard, American Express, Discover, Diners Club
CC#:_____ Exp:_____
More than one coupon may be submitted together as one order for total mail handling charge of $5.00.
Please complete to validate:
Game Choice:_____
Name:_____
Address:_____
City:_____ State:_____ ZIP:_____
Day Phone:_____ Night Phone:_____
Signature:_____

Not valid for group or other promotions. Service fees per ticket apply if redeemed at Twins Pro-Shop. Call for game times and dates. 612-33-TWINS or outstate 1-800-33-TWINS. Coupon valid for one game only. www.twinsbaseball.com

Offer Details: Valid for 2007 regular season home games. Redeem at Twins Pro Shops or Twins Box Office at least 24 hrs. prior to game, or by mail at least 7 days prior to game; Quantities limited, subject to ticket availability; Not valid for premium home games.

Offer validity is governed by the Rules of Use and excludes defined holidays. Offers are not valid with other discount offers, unless specified. Coupons void if purchased, sold or bartered. Discounts exclude tax, tip and/or alcohol, where applicable.

Minnesota Twins

- To get a 2007 pocket schedule call 612-33-TWINS
- Pro Shop locations: Apple Valley (Southport Ctr.) 952-891-2934; Roseville (Rosedale Market Place) 651-635-0777; Minnetonka (Ridge Sq.) 952-546-0815
- Service fee applies when redeemed at Pro Shop locations

00002427

MAIL TO MINNESOTA TWINS
SDS 12-1466 P.O. Box 86 Minneapolis, MN 55486-1466
Valid for 2007 regular season home games at the Metrodome
Ticket Pricing Information
Please call (612)33-TWINS or outstate 1-800-33-TWINS

Enclosed is my check for $_____ (ticket) + $5.00 (mail handling) per order=_____
payable to Minnesota Twins.
Visa, MasterCard, American Express, Discover, Diners Club
CC#:_____ Exp:_____
More than one coupon may be submitted together as one order for total mail handling charge of $5.00.
Please complete to validate:
Game Choice:_____
Name:_____
Address:_____
City:_____ State:_____ ZIP:_____
Day Phone:_____ Night Phone:_____
Signature:_____

Not valid for group or other promotions. Service fees per ticket apply if redeemed at Twins Pro-Shop. Call for game times and dates. 612-33-TWINS or outstate 1-800-33-TWINS. Coupon valid for one game only. www.twinsbaseball.com

Offer Details: Valid for 2007 regular season home games. Redeem at Twins Pro Shops or Twins Box Office at least 24 hrs. prior to game, or by mail at least 7 days prior to game; Quantities limited, subject to ticket availability; Not valid for premium home games.

Offer validity is governed by the Rules of Use and excludes defined holidays. Offers are not valid with other discount offers, unless specified. Coupons void if purchased, sold or bartered. Discounts exclude tax, tip and/or alcohol, where applicable.

Minnesota Thunder Pro Soccer

- For more information, call (651) 917-8326 or visit our website
- All Minnesota Thunder home games are at James Griffin Stadium in St. Paul

MINNESOTA THUNDER

1158 Concordia Ave.
St. Paul, MN
(651)917-8326

Offer Details: Valid for any regular season home game. Redeem at Minnesota Thunder box office only. Not valid with any other discount offer.

00470396

Offer validity is governed by the Rules of Use and excludes defined holidays. Offers are not valid with other discount offers, unless specified. Coupons void if purchased, sold or bartered. Discounts exclude tax, tip and/or alcohol, where applicable.

entertainment.
entertainment.com

The Park at MOA
Enjoy one 20-POINT PASS when a 85-POINT PASS is purchased.
See reverse for Offer Details.
Tracking Code: 674

FREE 20-POINT PASS

THE PARK AT MOA
MALL OF AMERICA™

Valid now thru November 1, 2007

5000 Center Ct., Bloomington, MN
(952)883-8600

G22

---

entertainment.
entertainment.com

PlayZone Arcade
Enjoy $5 WORTH OF TOKENS when $5 WORTH OF TOKENS are purchased.
See reverse for Offer Details.

FREE $5 WORTH OF TOKENS

PlayZone Arcade
MALL OF AMERICA

Valid now thru November 1, 2007

5000 Center Ct., Bloomington, MN
(952)883-8600

G23

ENTERTAINMENT & SPORTS

---

entertainment.
entertainment.com

Toy Store
Enjoy 20% off the regular price of any PURCHASE (sale items excluded) - maximum discount $25.00.
See reverse for Offer Details.

Up To $25.00 Value

TOY STORE

REPEAT SAVINGS™

Valid now thru November 1, 2007

5000 Center Ct., Bloomington, MN
(952)883-8600

G24

The Park at MOA
- The Park at MOA is the largest indoor amusement park in America
- It's seven acres of year round excitement - & it's all yours!
- Over 30 rides & attractions, including our spinning roller coaster, Timberland Twister!
- It all adds up to a world of fun for the whole family

00700510

THE PARK AT MOA
MALL OF AMERICA™
5000 Center Ct.
Bloomington, MN
(952)883-8600

Offer Details: Valid anytime. Holidays excluded; Coupon has no cash value; Not for resale; Must present at time of purchase. Not valid with any other discount offer.

Offer validity is governed by the Rules of Use and excludes defined holidays. Offers are not valid with other discount offers, unless specified. Coupons void if purchased, sold or bartered. Discounts exclude tax, tip and/or alcohol, where applicable.

PlayZone Arcade
- The Park at MOA is the largest indoor amusement park in America
- It's seven acres of year-round excitement & it's all yours!
- Over 30 rides & attractions, including our spinning roller coaster, Timberland Twister!
- It all adds up to a world of fun for the whole family

00701411

PLAYZONE ARCADE
MALL OF AMERICA
5000 Center Ct.
Bloomington, MN
(952)883-8600

Offer Details: Valid anytime.

Offer validity is governed by the Rules of Use and excludes defined holidays. Offers are not valid with other discount offers, unless specified. Coupons void if purchased, sold or bartered. Discounts exclude tax, tip and/or alcohol, where applicable.

Toy Store
- The Park at MOA is the largest indoor amusement park in America
- It's seven acres of year-round excitement & it's all yours
- Over 30 rides & attractions including our spinning roller coaster, Timberland Twister!
- It all adds up to a world of fun for the whole family

00698118

TOY STORE
5000 Center Ct.
Bloomington, MN
(952)883-8600

Offer Details: Valid anytime.

Offer validity is governed by the Rules of Use and excludes defined holidays. Offers are not valid with other discount offers, unless specified. Coupons void if purchased, sold or bartered. Discounts exclude tax, tip and/or alcohol, where applicable.

entertainment
entertainment.com

Minnesota Swarm

Enjoy one complimentary LOWER LEVEL ADMISSION when a second LOWER LEVEL ADMISSION of equal or greater value is purchased.

See reverse for Offer Details.

Up To $25.00 Value

SWARM LACROSSE
MINNESOTA

www.mnswarm.com

Valid now thru November 1, 2007

175 W. Kellogg Blvd., St. Paul, MN
(651) 222-9453

G25

---

entertainment
entertainment.com

Minnesota Zoo

Enjoy one complimentary CHILD'S ADMISSION when an ADULT ADMISSION is purchased.

See reverse for Offer Details.

CHILD'S ADMISSION

MINNESOTA ZOO
Changing how you see the world

Valid now thru November 1, 2007

13000 Zoo Blvd., Apple Valley, MN
(952) 431-9500

G26

---

entertainment
entertainment.com

Grand Rios Indoor Water Park

Enjoy one complimentary GENERAL ADMISSION when a second GENERAL ADMISSION of equal or greater value is purchased.

See reverse for Offer Details.

REPEAT SAVINGS

GENERAL ADMISSION

Grand Rios
INDOOR WATER PARK

www.grandrios.com

Valid now thru November 1, 2007

6900 Lakeland Ave. N., Brooklyn Park, MN
(763) 367-5847

G27

ENTERTAINMENT & SPORTS

Minnesota Swarm
- To get a 2007 schedule or information on Swarm season tickets, call 651-222-9453 or visit our website www.mnswarm.com

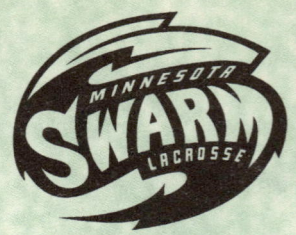

00623779

MINNESOTA SWARM LACROSSE

175 W. Kellogg Blvd.
St. Paul, MN
(651) 222-9453

Offer Details: Valid anytime. Tickets subject to availability. Not valid for groups, playoffs or other promotions. Redeemable at the Xcel Energy Center box office only..

Offer validity is governed by the Rules of Use and excludes defined holidays. Offers are not valid with other discount offers, unless specified. Coupons void if purchased, sold or bartered. Discounts exclude tax, tip and/or alcohol, where applicable.

Minnesota Zoo
- Bringing entertainment, education & conservation to life
- More than 2000 animals representing 390 species
- Open 363 days a year - closed Thanksgiving & December 25

00666148

MINNESOTA ZOO
Changing how you see the world

13000 Zoo Blvd.
Apple Valley, MN
(952) 431-9500

Offer Details: Valid anytime.

Offer validity is governed by the Rules of Use and excludes defined holidays. Offers are not valid with other discount offers, unless specified. Coupons void if purchased, sold or bartered. Discounts exclude tax, tip and/or alcohol, where applicable.

Grand Rios Indoor Water Park
- Lazy river & four story water tower
- Hurricane plunge & body tube slides
- Coconut Island, spas & activity pools
- Birthday parties & 3800 sq ft. arcade
- Please call ahead for availability (763) 367-5847

00653333

Grand Rios INDOOR WATER PARK

6900 Lakeland Ave. N.
Brooklyn Park, MN
(763) 367-5847

Offer Details: Valid anytime. On availability basis.

Offer validity is governed by the Rules of Use and excludes defined holidays. Offers are not valid with other discount offers, unless specified. Coupons void if purchased, sold or bartered. Discounts exclude tax, tip and/or alcohol, where applicable.

entertainment
entertainment.com

Cascade Bay Water Park
Enjoy up to 4 ADMISSIONS at 50% off the regular price.
See reverse for Offer Details.

REPEAT SAVINGS™

50% OFF

Cascade Bay

Valid now thru November 1, 2007

1360 Civic Center Dr., Eagan, MN
(651) 675-5577

G28

---

entertainment
entertainment.com

Como Town
Enjoy one complimentary 10 TICKET PACKAGE when a second 10 TICKET PACKAGE of equal or greater value is purchased.
See reverse for Offer Details.
Tracking Code: Hap06/07

FREE 10 TICKET PACKAGE

Como Town

The Family Amusement Park at
Como Park Zoo & Conservatory in St. Paul
www.comotown.com

Valid now thru November 1, 2007

1301 Midway Pkwy., St. Paul, MN
(651) 487-2121

G29

---

entertainment
entertainment.com

Bunker Beach
Enjoy one complimentary ADMISSION when a second ADMISSION of equal or greater value is purchased.
See reverse for Offer Details.

FREE ADMISSION

Bunker Beach

www.bunkerbeach.com

Valid now thru November 1, 2007

Bunker Hills Regional Park, Coon Rapids, MN
(763) 767-2895

G30

ENTERTAINMENT & SPORTS

Cascade Bay Water Park
- Float down the lazy river, splash in the zero depth leisure pool or tackle any one of the 5 waterslides
- Large concessions & play areas
- Open from early June until late August

00624198

1360 Civic Center Dr.
Eagan, MN
(651)675-5577

Offer Details: Valid after 4 p.m. Mon.-Sat., all day Sun.. Valid after 4 p.m. Mon.-Sat., all day Sun..

Offer validity is governed by the Rules of Use and excludes defined holidays. Offers are not valid with other discount offers, unless specified. Coupons void if purchased, sold or bartered. Discounts exclude tax, tip and/or alcohol, where applicable.

Como Town
- All new rides
- Interactive playground
- Como Town Theater
- Caricature artists & face painters
- Snacks & food
- Gifts & souvenirs
- Open Memorial Day-Labor Day
- Hours: Sun-Thur 10 am-8 pm & Fri-Sat 10 am-9 pm
- Open weekends-Spring & Fall 10 a.m.-6 p.m.
- See food section for Zobota Cafe coupon

00697166

The Family Amusement Park at Como Park Zoo & Conservatory in St. Paul
1301 Midway Pkwy.
St. Paul, MN
(651)487-2121

Offer Details: Valid Memorial Day-Labor Day; weekends Spring & Fall.

Offer validity is governed by the Rules of Use and excludes defined holidays. Offers are not valid with other discount offers, unless specified. Coupons void if purchased, sold or bartered. Discounts exclude tax, tip and/or alcohol, where applicable.

Bunker Beach
- Formally Bunker Hills Wave Pool
- 2 Tower waterslides
- Kid friendly adventure spray pool
- Minnesota's only wave pool
- Birthday parties & groups welcome

00581314

Bunker Hills Regional Park
(Hwy. 242 & Foley Blvd.)
Coon Rapids, MN
(763)767-2895

Offer Details: Valid anytime.

Offer validity is governed by the Rules of Use and excludes defined holidays. Offers are not valid with other discount offers, unless specified. Coupons void if purchased, sold or bartered. Discounts exclude tax, tip and/or alcohol, where applicable.

entertainment
entertainment.com

Tropics Indoor Water Park

Enjoy one complimentary ADMISSION when a second ADMISSION of equal or greater value is purchased.
See reverse for Offer Details.

Up To $8.00 Value

Tropics
INDOOR WATER PARK
SHOREVIEW COMMUNITY CENTER

www.shorevewcommunitycenter.com

4580 Victoria St. N., Shoreview, MN
(651)490-4700

Valid now thru November 1, 2007

G31

---

entertainment
entertainment.com

Nascar Silicon Motor Speedway

Enjoy one complimentary RACE TICKET when a second RACE TICKET of equal or greater value is purchased.
See reverse for Offer Details.

ONE RACE TICKET

NASCAR SILICON MOTOR SPEEDWAY
Racing so real you can feel it...

www.smsonline.com

352 South Ave., Bloomington, MN
(952)854-7700

Valid now thru November 1, 2007

G32

---

entertainment
entertainment.com

Pro-Kart Indoor Racing

Enjoy one complimentary TICKET when a second TICKET of equal or greater value is purchased.
See reverse for Offer Details.

Up To $14.00 Value

Pro Kart Indoors

See Reverse Side for Locations

Valid now thru November 1, 2007

G33

ENTERTAINMENT & SPORTS

Tropics Indoor Water Park

- Slide down our twisting two story waterslide
- Scamper in our zero depth beach
- Slam dunk with our water basketball
- Climb on our giant sea creatures
- Call for hours! (651)490-4700

00504790

Tropics
INDOOR WATER PARK
SHOREVIEW COMMUNITY CENTER

4580 Victoria St. N.
Shoreview, MN
(651)490-4700

Offer Details: Valid anytime.

Offer validity is governed by the Rules of Use and excludes defined holidays. Offers are not valid with other discount offers, unless specified. Coupons void if purchased, sold or bartered. Discounts exclude tax, tip and/or alcohol, where applicable.

Nascar Silicon Motor Speedway

- Personal coaching
- Gift certificates
- Group events
- Leagues & competitions
- A variety of packages

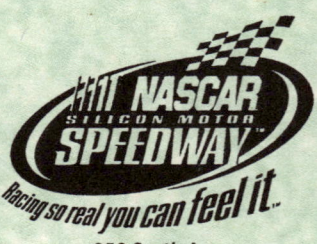

00502464

NASCAR SILICON MOTOR SPEEDWAY
Racing so real you can feel it.

352 South Ave.
(Mall of America)
Bloomington, MN
(952)854-7700

Offer Details: Valid Monday thru Friday.

Offer validity is governed by the Rules of Use and excludes defined holidays. Offers are not valid with other discount offers, unless specified. Coupons void if purchased, sold or bartered. Discounts exclude tax, tip and/or alcohol, where applicable.

Pro-Kart Indoor Racing

- Corporate events
- Bachelor parties
- Private events
- Open daily
- European-style indoor go-karting

Pro Kart Indoors

12500 Chowen Ave. S
Burnsville, MN
(952)808-7223

11700 Troy Ln.
Maple Grove, MN
(763)428-1333

Offer Details: Valid anytime.

00491677

Offer validity is governed by the Rules of Use and excludes defined holidays. Offers are not valid with other discount offers, unless specified. Coupons void if purchased, sold or bartered. Discounts exclude tax, tip and/or alcohol, where applicable.

entertainment.com

Gameworks

Enjoy one complimentary $10 GAME PLAY CREDIT CARD when a second $10 GAME PLAY CREDIT CARD of equal or greater value is purchased.
See reverse for Offer Details.

$10 GAME PLAY CREDIT CARD

GAMEWORKS
EAT • DRINK • PARTY • PLAY

Valid now thru November 1, 2007

600 Hennepin Ave., Ste. 110, Minneapolis, MN
(612)656-7300

G34

---

entertainment.com

Minnesota Renaissance Festival

Enjoy one complimentary ADMISSION when a second ADMISSION of equal or greater value is purchased.
See reverse for Offer Details.

FREE ADMISSION

www.renaissancefest.com

Valid now thru November 1, 2007

3 Miles south of Shakopee on 169

G35

---

entertainment.com

Dinosaur Walk MOA

Enjoy one complimentary ADMISSION when a second ADMISSION of equal or greater value is purchased.
See reverse for Offer Details.

FREE ADMISSION

Dinosaur Walk
Mall of America

REPEAT SAVINGS

Valid now thru November 1, 2007

376 N. Garden, Bloomington, MN
(952)854-6451

G36

ENTERTAINMENT & SPORTS

Gameworks
- Eat, drink, party & play
- The best game plan for any event - corporate, team-building, holiday parties, business meetings, bar/bat mitzvahs, prom/grad nights & birthdays!

GAMEWORKS
EAT · DRINK · PARTY + PLAY

600 Hennepin Ave., Ste. 110
(Block E)
Minneapolis, MN
(612)656-7300

Offer Details: Valid anytime.

00667420

Offer validity is governed by the Rules of Use and excludes defined holidays. Offers are not valid with other discount offers, unless specified. Coupons void if purchased, sold or bartered. Discounts exclude tax, tip and/or alcohol, where applicable.

Minnesota Renaissance Festival
- 9 a.m.-7 p.m. rain or shine!
- Call 1-800-966-8215 for more information

3 Miles south of Shakopee on 169

Offer Details: Valid for all weekends in August.

00355586

Offer validity is governed by the Rules of Use and excludes defined holidays. Offers are not valid with other discount offers, unless specified. Coupons void if purchased, sold or bartered. Discounts exclude tax, tip and/or alcohol, where applicable.

Dinosaur Walk MOA

Dinosaur Walk
Mall of America

376 N. Garden
Bloomington, MN
(952)854-6451

Offer Details: Valid anytime.

00703751

Offer validity is governed by the Rules of Use and excludes defined holidays. Offers are not valid with other discount offers, unless specified. Coupons void if purchased, sold or bartered. Discounts exclude tax, tip and/or alcohol, where applicable.

entertainment
entertainment.com

Canterbury Park
Enjoy one complimentary LIVE HORSE RACING ADMISSION when a second LIVE HORSE RACING ADMISSION of equal or greater value is purchased.
See reverse for Offer Details.

FREE ADMISSION

CANTERBURY PARK

Valid now thru November 1, 2007

1100 Canterbury Rd., Shakopee, MN
(952)445-7223

G37

---

entertainment
entertainment.com

Disney Live
Enjoy up to 8 full price tickets at 50% off the regular price. Redeemable at the box office or at www.entertainment.com/tickets.
See reverse for Offer Details.

50% OFF

Disney Live!
PRODUCED BY FELD ENTERTAINMENT
www.disneylive.com

Valid now thru November 1, 2007

Visit entertainment.com/hotline for additional details such as dates, times, locations and prices.

G38

---

entertainment
entertainment.com

Smuckers Stars on Ice
Enjoy UP TO 4 RESERVED TICKETS at 50% off the regular price.
See reverse for Offer Details.

50% OFF

SMUCKER'S STARS on ICE

www.starsonice.com

Valid now thru November 1, 2007

Visit www.starsonice.com for show dates, performance times & locations

G39

ENTERTAINMENT & SPORTS

Canterbury Park
- Live racing mid-May thru early Sept.
- Racing on Thurs. & Fri. evenings, Sat., Sun. & holidays in the afternoon
- Card Club & Casino Games Room open 24 hours a day, year round
- For more info. call (952)445-7223
- Children under 17 are always free

00526710

1100 Canterbury Rd.
(Hwy. 169 at Canterbury Rd.)
Shakopee, MN
(952)445-7223

Offer Details: Valid anytime.

Offer validity is governed by the Rules of Use and excludes defined holidays. Offers are not valid with other discount offers, unless specified. Coupons void if purchased, sold or bartered. Discounts exclude tax, tip and/or alcohol, where applicable.

Disney Live

Disney Live!

PRODUCED BY FELD ENTERTAINMENT

Visit entertainment.com/hotline for additional details such as dates, times, locations and prices.

00700846

Offer Details: Valid for scheduled performances Monday thru Thursday matinee and evening & Friday matinee. Not valid on front row & VIP seating, no double discounts. Tour subject to change.

Offer validity is governed by the Rules of Use and excludes defined holidays. Offers are not valid with other discount offers, unless specified. Coupons void if purchased, sold or bartered. Discounts exclude tax, tip and/or alcohol, where applicable.

Smuckers Stars on Ice
- Don't miss Olympic Gold Medalists Alexei Yagudin, Jamie Sale & David Pelletier, World Champion & 6 time U.S. National Champion Todd Eldredge & more of skating's biggest & brightest stars from the 2006 Winter Olympic Games when Smucker's Stars on Ice appears for one performance only!

00476661

SMUCKER'S STARS on ICE

Visit www.starsonice.com for show dates, performance times & locations

Offer Details: Valid for performances November 15, 2006 thru April 30, 2007 only. Valid for all tickets $50 or under. Redeem at Box Office or to redeem on-line, use redemption code EPS; No refunds or exchanges; Date, time & cast subject to change; Tickets subject to availability; Not valid on ticket presales or previously purchased tickets; Not valid with any other discount offer.

Offer validity is governed by the Rules of Use and excludes defined holidays. Offers are not valid with other discount offers, unless specified. Coupons void if purchased, sold or bartered. Discounts exclude tax, tip and/or alcohol, where applicable.

entertainment
entertainment.com

Great American History Theatre

Enjoy one complimentary ADMISSION when a second ADMISSION of equal or greater value is purchased.
See reverse for Offer Details.

REPEAT SAVINGS

Valid now thru November 1, 2007

FREE ADMISSION

GREAT AMERICAN History Theatre

www.historytheatre.com

30 E. 10th St., St. Paul, MN
(651)292-4323

G40

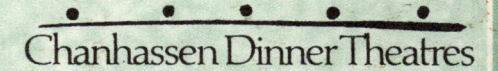

---

entertainment
entertainment.com

Chanhassen Fireside Theatre

Enjoy $7.50 off the regular price of up to six tickets for Dinner & Show.
See reverse for Offer Details.

Valid now thru November 1, 2007

Up To $45.00 Value

Chanhassen Dinner Theatres
Fireside Theatre

501 West 78th Street, Chanhassen, MN
(952)934-1525

G41

---

entertainment
entertainment.com

Chanhassen Dinner Theatre

Enjoy $7.50 off the regular price of up to six tickets for Dinner & Show.
See reverse for Offer Details.

Valid now thru November 1, 2007

Up To $45.00 Value

Chanhassen Dinner Theatres
Main Dinner Theatre

501 W 78th St., Chanhassen, MN
(952)934-1525

G42

ENTERTAINMENT & SPORTS

Great American History Theatre

- Real People, Real Stories, Real Great Theatre!
- Premier producer of new works
- Call for a season brochure or visit our website
- 2006-07 season Sept.-May

00630581

GREAT AMERICAN
History Theatre

30 E. 10th St.
(downtown St. Paul between Cedar St. & Wabasha St.)
St. Paul, MN
(651)292-4323

Offer Details: Valid anytime. On availability basis; Redeem at Box Office Only; Not valid for Lutefisk Champ & Other Frozen Holiday Tales or Raw Stages.

Offer validity is governed by the Rules of Use and excludes defined holidays. Offers are not valid with other discount offers, unless specified. Coupons void if purchased, sold or bartered. Discounts exclude tax, tip and/or alcohol, where applicable.

Chanhassen Fireside Theatre

00229759

Procedures and conditions of use:

1. ONE COUPON PER PARTY (max. 6 per party). Savings as follows:

	1st ticket	2nd ticket	3rd ticket	4th ticket	5th ticket	6th ticket
Sun.-Fri. evenings	$7.50 off	$7.50 off	$7.50 off	$7.50 off	$7.50 off	$7.50 off

2. Advance reservations and payment required prior to performance. When making reservations you MUST identify yourself as a HAPPENINGS® Club member to use this special offer.

3. Coupon cannot be used in conjunction with other discounts, on holidays, holiday eves., for the Holiday Show, matinees, or during the last week of any performance run.

4. Call box office early to obtain best seating and availability for coupon redemption. (When a sell-out is PROJECTED, no further coupons will be accepted for that performance).

5. HAPPENINGS® reservations must be made through the Chanhassen Dinner Theatres box office only.

Offer Details: Valid any performance Sunday thru Friday evenings. On availabilty basis, matinees excluded; Procedures and conditions of use on reverse side.

Offer validity is governed by the Rules of Use and excludes defined holidays. Offers are not valid with other discount offers, unless specified. Coupons void if purchased, sold or bartered. Discounts exclude tax, tip and/or alcohol, where applicable.

Chanhassen Dinner Theatre

- Enjoy a relaxing dinner theatre with the best in Broadway musicals complemented by choice of entree & quality service.

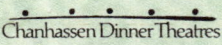

00229769

Chanhassen Dinner Theatres
Main Dinner Theatre
IMPORTANT NOTICE!

Procedures and conditions of use:

1. ONE COUPON PER PARTY (max. 6 per party). $7.50 off per ticket, Sun.-Fri. evenings.

2. Advance reservations and payment required prior to performance. When making reservations you MUST identify yourself as a HAPPENINGS® Club member to use this special offer.

3. Coupon cannot be used in conjunction with other discounts, on holidays, holiday eves., for the Holiday Show, matinees, or during the last week of any performance run.

4. Call box office early to obtain best seating and availability for coupon redemption. (When a sell-out is PROJECTED, no further coupons will be accepted for that performance).

5. HAPPENINGS® reservations must be made through the Chanhassen Dinner Theatres box office only.

Offer Details: Any performance Sunday thru Friday evenings. On availability basis, matinees excluded; Procedures and conditions of use on reverse.

Offer validity is governed by the Rules of Use and excludes defined holidays. Offers are not valid with other discount offers, unless specified. Coupons void if purchased, sold or bartered. Discounts exclude tax, tip and/or alcohol, where applicable.

entertainment
entertainment.com

Acme Comedy Co.
Enjoy up to four complimentary ADMISSIONS when you purchase up to four ADMISSIONS of equal or greater value.
See reverse for Offer Details.

Up To $52.00 Value

acme COMEDY CO.

www.acmecomedycompany.com

See Reverse Side for Locations

Valid now thru November 1, 2007

G43

---

entertainment
entertainment.com

Saint Paul Chamber Orchestra
Enjoy ONE COMPLIMENTARY ADMISSION when ONE ADULT ADMISSION of equal or greater value is purchased - maximum discount $65.00.
See reverse for Offer Details.

FREE ADMISSION

spco
THE SAINT PAUL CHAMBER ORCHESTRA
www.thespco.org

The Historic Hamm Building 3rd Floor 408 St. Peter St., St. Paul, MN
(651) 291-1144

Valid now thru November 1, 2007

G44

---

entertainment
entertainment.com

The Guthrie Theater
Enjoy one complimentary ADMISSION when a second ADMISSION of equal or greater value is purchased.
See reverse for Offer Details.

FREE ADMISSION

GUTHRIE
www.guthrietheater.org

See Reverse Side for Locations

Valid now thru November 1, 2007

G45

ENTERTAINMENT & SPORTS

Acme Comedy Co.
- Minneapolis' premier comedy nightclub
- Shows at 8 p.m. Tues.-Thurs. and 8 p.m. & 10:30 p.m. on Fri.

00404833

acme COMEDY CO.

708 N 1st St.
Minneapolis, MN
(612)338-6393

Please call for directions

Offer Details: Valid Tuesday thru Friday. Not valid on special events; Call for reservations.

Offer validity is governed by the Rules of Use and excludes defined holidays. Offers are not valid with other discount offers, unless specified. Coupons void if purchased, sold or bartered. Discounts exclude tax, tip and/or alcohol, where applicable.

Saint Paul Chamber Orchestra
- All offers are subject to availability
- Admission is not guaranteed
- Call (651)291-1144 for a free copy of the 2006-2007 calendar listing concert times & locations

00087390

SPCO THE SAINT PAUL CHAMBER ORCHESTRA

Enjoy the SPCO at Ordway Center. Valid for any regularly scheduled SPCO subscription concert at Ordway Center Sept. 2006 - May 2007. All offers are subject to availability. Admission is not guaranteed Call (651)291-1144 for a free copy of the 2006-2007 calendar listing concert times & locations

Name:_____
Address:_____
City/State/ZIP:_____
Day Phone:_____ Eve. Phone:_____

The Historic Hamm Building
3rd Floor
408 St. Peter St.
St. Paul, MN
(651)291-1144

Offer Details: Valid for any performance at Ordway Center for the 2006-2007 season. On availability basis; No advance reservations; Redeemable 1 hour before performance only in person at box office.

Offer validity is governed by the Rules of Use and excludes defined holidays. Offers are not valid with other discount offers, unless specified. Coupons void if purchased, sold or bartered. Discounts exclude tax, tip and/or alcohol, where applicable.

The Guthrie Theater

00283236

GUTHRIE

818 S. 2nd St.
Minneapolis, MN
(612)377-2224

No advance reservations or other discounts accepted with this offer

Redeem at the Guthrie Box Office in person on day of performance only

Offer Details: Valid for Tues. or Wed. performances of Lost in Yonkers, Edgardo Mine & Major Barbara only. Not valid with any other discounts or promotions; Subject to availability.

Offer validity is governed by the Rules of Use and excludes defined holidays. Offers are not valid with other discount offers, unless specified. Coupons void if purchased, sold or bartered. Discounts exclude tax, tip and/or alcohol, where applicable.

entertainment
entertainment.com

The Minnesota Opera
Enjoy up to 4 TICKETS at 50% off the regular price.
See reverse for Offer Details.

50% OFF

THE MINNESOTA OPERA

www.mnopera.org

Valid now thru November 1, 2007

Ordway Center for the Performing Arts 345 Washington St., St. Paul, MN
(651) 224-4222

G46

---

entertainment
entertainment.com

Walker Art Center
Enjoy up to 4 ADULT GALLERY ADMISSIONS at 50% off the regular price.
See reverse for Offer Details.
Tracking Code: 45

REPEAT SAVINGS

GALLERY ADMISSIONS

www.walkerart.org

Valid now thru November 1, 2007

1750 Hennepin Ave., Minneapolis, MN
(612) 375-7600

G47

---

entertainment
entertainment.com

Ordway Center for the Performing Arts
Enjoy up to 2 ADMISSIONS at 50% off the regular price.
See reverse for Offer Details.

50% OFF

Ordway Center for the Performing Arts

Valid now thru November 1, 2007

345 Washington St., St. Paul, MN
(651) 224-4222

G48

ENTERTAINMENT & SPORTS

The Minnesota Opera
- La donna del lago
- The Tales of Hoffmann
- The Grapes of Wrath
- Lakme
- The Marriage of Figaro

THE MINNESOTA OPERA

Ordway Center for the Performing Arts 345 Washington St.
St. Paul, MN
(651)224-4222

Offer Details: Valid for all weeknight performances. Good for all levels subject to availability; Redeemable only thru the MN Opera Ticket Office; 620 N. First St., Minneapolis, MN 55401 (612)333-6669; All performances held at Ordway Center for the Performing Arts; 345 Washington St., Saint Paul, MN 55102; vaild for the 2006-2007 season - Aug. 28, 2006-May 12, 2007.

00507770

Offer validity is governed by the Rules of Use and excludes defined holidays. Offers are not valid with other discount offers, unless specified. Coupons void if purchased, sold or bartered. Discounts exclude tax, tip and/or alcohol, where applicable.

Walker Art Center
- Visit the Minneapolis Sculpture Garden, the Walker's contemporary art exhibitions, the Walker's shop & restaurants
- Minutes from downtown Minneapolis
- Kids 12 & under are always free

1750 Hennepin Ave.
Minneapolis, MN
(612)375-7600

Offer Details: Valid anytime.

00459228

Offer validity is governed by the Rules of Use and excludes defined holidays. Offers are not valid with other discount offers, unless specified. Coupons void if purchased, sold or bartered. Discounts exclude tax, tip and/or alcohol, where applicable.

Ordway Center for the Performing Arts

Ordway Center for the Performing Arts

345 Washington St.
St. Paul, MN
(651)224-4222

Offer Details: Valid for Rob Curto's FORRO' FOR ALL Tues., Oct. 3, 2006 7:30 p.m.. Subject to availability. Prior ticket purchases excluded; Regular service fees apply.

00703672

Offer validity is governed by the Rules of Use and excludes defined holidays. Offers are not valid with other discount offers, unless specified. Coupons void if purchased, sold or bartered. Discounts exclude tax, tip and/or alcohol, where applicable.

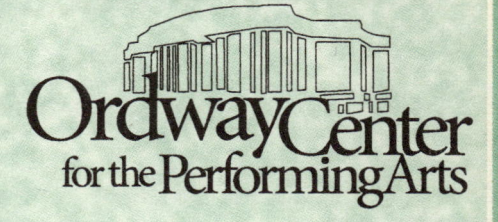

entertainment.
entertainment.com

Ordway Center for the Performing Arts

Enjoy up to 2 ADMISSIONS at 50% off the regular price.
See reverse for Offer Details.

50% OFF

Ordway Center
for the Performing Arts

345 Washington St., St. Paul, MN
(651) 224-4222

Valid now thru November 1, 2007

G49

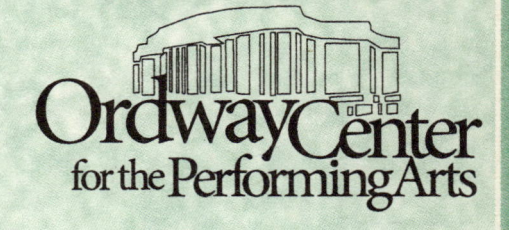

---

entertainment.
entertainment.com

Ordway Center for the Performing Arts

Enjoy up to 2 ADMISSIONS at 50% off the regular price.
See reverse for Offer Details.

50% OFF

Ordway Center
for the Performing Arts

345 Washington St., St. Paul, MN
(651) 224-4222

Valid now thru November 1, 2007

G50

---

entertainment.
entertainment.com

Cinema Grill Theater

Enjoy one complimentary ADMISSION when a second ADMISSION of equal or greater value is purchased.
See reverse for Offer Details.

FREE ADMISSION

CINEMA GRILL

www.newhopecinemagrill.com

2749 Winnetka Ave. N., New Hope, MN
(763) 417-0017

Valid now thru November 1, 2007

G51

ENTERTAINMENT & SPORTS

Ordway Center for the Performing Arts

OrdwayCenter
for the Performing Arts

345 Washington St.
St. Paul, MN
(651) 224-4222

00703676

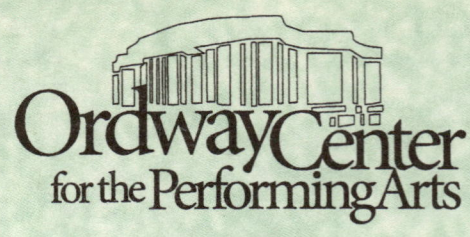

Offer Details: Valid for Illstyle & Peace: Same Spirit Different Movement, Sun. Oct. 15, 2006, 5 p.m.. Subject to availability. Prior ticket purchases excluded; Regular service fees apply.

Offer validity is governed by the Rules of Use and excludes defined holidays. Offers are not valid with other discount offers, unless specified. Coupons void if purchased, sold or bartered. Discounts exclude tax, tip and/or alcohol, where applicable.

Ordway Center for the Performing Arts

OrdwayCenter
for the Performing Arts

345 Washington St.
St. Paul, MN
(651) 224-4222

00703679

Offer Details: Valid for Chicago The Musical, Jan. 16 & 17, 2007, Gallery Seating. Subject to availability. Prior ticket purchases excluded; Regular service fees apply.

Offer validity is governed by the Rules of Use and excludes defined holidays. Offers are not valid with other discount offers, unless specified. Coupons void if purchased, sold or bartered. Discounts exclude tax, tip and/or alcohol, where applicable.

Cinema Grill Theater

- Enjoy dinner and a great movie
- Casual food, beer, wine & desserts served by our friendly staff
- 1st run movies
- Seating at tables in comfortable swivel chairs
- Children's birthday packages
- Group, school & corporate parties

2749 Winnetka Ave. N.
New Hope, MN
(763) 417-0017

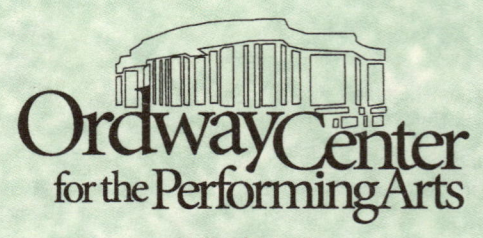

00690664

Offer Details: Valid Sunday thru Thursday.

Offer validity is governed by the Rules of Use and excludes defined holidays. Offers are not valid with other discount offers, unless specified. Coupons void if purchased, sold or bartered. Discounts exclude tax, tip and/or alcohol, where applicable.

entertainment.
entertainment.com

Riverview Theater

Enjoy one complimentary ADMISSION when a second ADMISSION of equal or greater value is purchased.
See reverse for Offer Details.

FREE ADMISSION

Riverview Theater

www.riverviewtheater.com
3800 42nd Ave. S, Minneapolis, MN
(612) 729-7369

Valid now thru November 1, 2007

G52

---

entertainment.
entertainment.com

McKenzie Lanes

Enjoy up to 4 GAMES (open bowling) at 50% off the regular price.
See reverse for Offer Details.

REPEAT SAVINGS

50% OFF

McKenzie Lanes

75 State Hwy. 35, Centuria, WI
(715) 646-2228

Valid now thru November 1, 2007

G53

---

entertainment.
entertainment.com

Dahlgreen Golf Club

Enjoy one complimentary GREEN FEE when a second GREEN FEE of equal or greater value is purchased.
See reverse for Offer Details.

REPEAT SAVINGS

FREE GREEN FEE

DAHLGREEN GOLF CLUB

www.dahlgreen.com
6940 Dahlgren Rd., Chaska, MN
(952) 448-7463

Valid now thru November 1, 2007

G54

ENTERTAINMENT & SPORTS

Riverview Theater
- Classic 50's theater with original decor
- Stadium seating & digital sound
- Real butter on our popcorn
- Matinees & children's admission $2.00

00455025

Riverview Theater

3800 42nd Ave. S
(10 blocks E of Hiawatha Ave.)
Minneapolis, MN
(612)729-7369

Offer Details: Valid anytime.

Offer validity is governed by the Rules of Use and excludes defined holidays. Offers are not valid with other discount offers, unless specified. Coupons void if purchased, sold or bartered. Discounts exclude tax, tip and/or alcohol, where applicable.

McKenzie Lanes
- 8 Lanes
- Birthday parties
- Extreme bowling Fri. & Sat. nights
- Bumper bowling
- Leagues

00671965

McKenzie Lanes

75 State Hwy. 35
Centuria, WI
(715)646-2228

Offer Details: Valid anytime.

Offer validity is governed by the Rules of Use and excludes defined holidays. Offers are not valid with other discount offers, unless specified. Coupons void if purchased, sold or bartered. Discounts exclude tax, tip and/or alcohol, where applicable.

Dahlgren Golf Club
- Located 5 mi. W. of downtown Chaska
- Take Hwy. 212 W. 4 1/2 mi. to County Rd. 43, left for 1/2 mi. to Dahlgren Rd., right to the clubhouse
- Company outings welcome

00600940

DAHLGREN GOLF CLUB

www.dahlgreen.com
6940 Dahlgren Rd.
Chaska, MN
(952)448-7463

Offer Details: Valid anytime Monday thru Friday, Saturday & Sunday after 2 p.m..

Offer validity is governed by the Rules of Use and excludes defined holidays. Offers are not valid with other discount offers, unless specified. Coupons void if purchased, sold or bartered. Discounts exclude tax, tip and/or alcohol, where applicable.

GREEN FEE
Glencoe COUNTRY CLUB

Enjoy one complimentary GREEN FEE when a second GREEN FEE of equal or greater value is purchased.

valid anytime

Please present ENTERTAINMENT® Membership Card to obtain discount. Not valid holidays & subject to Rules of Use. Not valid with other discount offers unless specified

G55

Valid now thru November 1, 2007

Offer validity is governed by the Rules of Use and excludes defined holidays. Offers are not valid with other discount offers, unless specified.

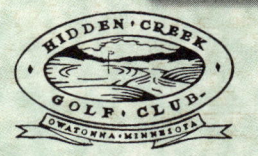

FREE GREEN FEE
HIDDEN CREEK GOLF CLUB — OWATONNA · MINNESOTA

www.hiddencreekmn.com

Enjoy one complimentary GREEN FEE when 3 GREEN FEES of equal or greater value are purchased.

valid anytime

Golf cart required

G56

Valid now thru November 1, 2007

Offer validity is governed by the Rules of Use and excludes defined holidays. Offers are not valid with other discount offers, unless specified.

Up To $80.00 Value
IZATYS GOLF & YACHT CLUB

www.izatys.com

Enjoy one complimentary GREEN FEE when THREE GREEN FEES of equal or greater value are purchased.

valid anytime

Please present ENTERTAINMENT® Membership Card to obtain discount. Not valid holidays & subject to Rules of Use. Not valid with other discount offers unless specified

G57

Valid now thru November 1, 2007

Offer validity is governed by the Rules of Use and excludes defined holidays. Offers are not valid with other discount offers, unless specified.

FREE GREEN FEE
REDWOOD FALLS GOLF CLUB

Enjoy one complimentary GREEN FEE when a second GREEN FEE of equal or greater value is purchased.

valid anytime except Wednesday & Thursday afternoons

Golf cart required; Please present ENTERTAINMENT® Membership Card to obtain discount. Not valid holidays & subject to Rules of Use. Not valid with other discount offers unless specified

G58

Valid now thru November 1, 2007

Offer validity is governed by the Rules of Use and excludes defined holidays. Offers are not valid with other discount offers, unless specified.

FREE GREEN FEE
VALLEY VIEW GOLF CLUB

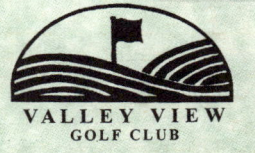

www.vvgolf.com

Enjoy one complimentary GREEN FEE when a second GREEN FEE of equal or greater value is purchased.

valid Mon.-Thurs. anytime, Fri.-Sun. after 12:00 p.m.

G59

Valid now thru November 1, 2007

Offer validity is governed by the Rules of Use and excludes defined holidays. Offers are not valid with other discount offers, unless specified.

FREE GREEN FEE
RIVERWOOD NATIONAL

www.riverwoodnational.com

Enjoy one complimentary GREEN FEE when a second GREEN FEE of equal or greater value is purchased.

Valid Monday thru Friday

Golf cart required; Not valid during leagues and tournaments

G60

Valid now thru November 1, 2007

Offer validity is governed by the Rules of Use and excludes defined holidays. Offers are not valid with other discount offers, unless specified.

HIDDEN CREEK GOLF CLUB

- 18 Hole Scottish links style course
- 100% Bentgrass tees, fairways & greens
- 4 Sets of tees to accommodate golfers of any skill level
- 1-888-MOR-GOLF

4989 E. Rose St.
Owatonna, MN
(507)444-9229

00598465

REDWOOD FALLS GOLF CLUB

101 E. Oak, PO Box 384
Redwood Falls, MN
(507)627-8901

00087678

RIVERWOOD NATIONAL

10247 95th St. N.E.
(3 Minutes N. of I-94 & The Outlets of Albertville off County Rd. 19)
Otsego, MN
(763)271-5000

00694134

Glencoe COUNTRY CLUB

- We provide 18 holes of uninterrupted play, PGA golf professional on-staff, driving range, putting green, group & individual lessons, a fully stocked pro shop, and banquet facilities.
- Affordable golfing for the whole family.

1325 1st St. E
Glencoe, MN
(320)864-3023

00472648

IZATYS GOLF & YACHT CLUB

- Top designer John Harbottle has created the Sanctuary, an 18-hole course, designated as a wildlife sanctuary by the National Audobon Society.
- This course is 6,646 yards which includes native trees, marsh hazards, and pot bunkers.
- Izatys is a beautiful resort 90 miles north of the Twin Cities.

40005 85th Ave.
Onamia, MN
(320)532-3101

00463237

VALLEY VIEW GOLF CLUB

- Welcome to Valley View Golf Club. The magnificent views of the Minnesota River Valley provide a spectacular setting for this challenging 6,300 yard par 71, 18-hole championship course built in 1991.

23795 Laredo Ave.
Belle Plaine, MN
(952)873-4653

00492047

entertainment.com — FREE GREEN FEE

Southern Hills Golf Club

Enjoy one complimentary GREEN FEE when a second GREEN FEE of equal or greater value is purchased.

valid Monday thru Friday

Please present ENTERTAINMENT® Membership Card to obtain discount. Not valid holidays & subject to Rules of Use. Not valid with other discount offers unless specified; Not valid with any other discounts or promotions

G61

Offer validity is governed by the Rules of Use and excludes defined holidays. Offers are not valid with other discount offers, unless specified.

Valid now thru November 1, 2007

---

entertainment.com — FREE GREEN FEE

ORONO PUBLIC GOLF

Enjoy one complimentary GREEN FEE when a second GREEN FEE of equal or greater value is purchased.

valid weekdays, excluding holidays

Please present ENTERTAINMENT® Membership Card to obtain discount. Not valid holidays & subject to Rules of Use. Not valid with other discount offers unless specified

G62

Offer validity is governed by the Rules of Use and excludes defined holidays. Offers are not valid with other discount offers, unless specified.

Valid now thru November 1, 2007

---

entertainment.com — FREE GREEN FEE

KILKARNEY HILLS GOLF CLUB

www.kilkarneyhills.com

Enjoy one complimentary GREEN FEE when a second GREEN FEE of equal or greater value is purchased.

valid anytime Monday thru Friday; valid Saturday, Sunday & Holidays after 2 p.m.

Golf cart required; Please present ENTERTAINMENT® Membership Card to obtain discount. Not valid with other discount offers unless specified

G63

Offer validity is governed by the Rules of Use and excludes defined holidays. Offers are not valid with other discount offers, unless specified.

Valid now thru November 1, 2007

---

entertainment.com — FREE GREEN FEE

Castlewood Forest Lake Public Golf Course

Enjoy one complimentary 9 HOLE GREEN FEE when a second 9 HOLE GREEN FEE of equal or greater value is purchased.

valid anytime Monday thru Friday

Reservations required; On availability basis; Please present ENTERTAINMENT® Membership Card to obtain discount. Not valid holidays & subject to Rules of Use. Not valid with other discount offers unless specified

G64

Offer validity is governed by the Rules of Use and excludes defined holidays. Offers are not valid with other discount offers, unless specified.

Valid now thru November 1, 2007

---

entertainment.com — Up To $34.00 Value

THE BUNKER INDOOR GOLF CENTER

Enjoy one complimentary hour of golf when a second hour of golf of equal or greater value is purchased.

valid Monday thru Friday October thru April, anytime May thru September

Please present ENTERTAINMENT® Membership Card to obtain discount. Not valid holidays & subject to Rules of Use. Not valid with other discount offers unless specified; Valid for Foursomes only

Card #155

G65

Offer validity is governed by the Rules of Use and excludes defined holidays. Offers are not valid with other discount offers, unless specified.

Valid now thru November 1, 2007

---

entertainment.com — ONE ROUND OF GOLF

Buffalo Heights Golf Course

Enjoy one complimentary ROUND OF GOLF when a second ROUND OF GOLF of equal or greater value is purchased.

valid anytime

Please present ENTERTAINMENT® Membership Card to obtain discount. Not valid holidays & subject to Rules of Use. Not valid with other discount offers unless specified

G66

Offer validity is governed by the Rules of Use and excludes defined holidays. Offers are not valid with other discount offers, unless specified.

Valid now thru November 1, 2007

ORONO PUBLIC GOLF

- Built in 1924, this beautiful 9 hole course offers small, elevated greens, mature trees, water & track that can be tailored to a variety of skill levels.

265 Orono Orchard Rd.
Orono, MN
(952) 473-9904

00276974

CASTLEWOOD FOREST LAKE PUBLIC GOLF COURSE

7050 Scandia Trail North
Forest Lake, MN
(651) 464-6233

00002210

Buffalo Heights Golf Course

- Buffalo Heights Golf Course features a 9 hole golf course with PGA Pros on staff.
- We are open daily, April through October from 7 a.m. till 9 p.m.
- Reservations are recommended.

905 S. Hwy. 25
Buffalo, MN
(763) 682-2854

00154718

Southern Hills Golf Club

18950 Chippendale Ave.
Farmington, MN
(651) 463-4653

00408264

KILKARNEY HILLS GOLF CLUB

- Leagues
- Computer V.S.G.A. handicapping
- Complete practice facilities
- Lessons available
- Banquet facilities available

163 Radio Rd.
River Falls, WI
(715) 425-8501

00503903

THE BUNKER INDOOR GOLF CENTER

- Where are you golfing this winter in Minnesota?
- We have 12 full swing golf simulators at each location
- Play year round on your choice of over 30 world championship golf courses!
- Drive, chip & putt
- Play with your own clubs
- Hit regulation balls

14900 Hwy. 7 W, Minnetonka, MN
(952) 936-9595

1811 S. Robert St., West St. Paul, MN
(651) 552-6011

00491735

Coupons void if purchased, sold or bartered. Discounts exclude tax, tip and/or alcohol, where applicable.

ROUND OF GOLF

entertainment.com

BRIGHTWOOD Hills GOLF COURSE

Enjoy one complimentary ROUND OF GOLF when a second ROUND OF GOLF of equal or greater value is purchased.

valid Monday thru Friday during open golf

No walk alongs; Please present ENTERTAINMENT® Membership Card to obtain discount. Not valid holidays & subject to Rules of Use. Not valid with other discount offers unless specified

G67

Offer validity is governed by the Rules of Use and excludes defined holidays. Offers are not valid with other discount offers, unless specified.

Valid now thru November 1, 2007

Up To $7.00 Value

entertainment.com

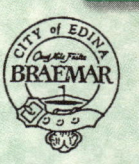

CITY OF EDINA BRAEMAR

Enjoy THE INDOOR DRIVING RANGE at 50% off the regular price.

Specials excluded

valid anytime

Please present ENTERTAINMENT® Membership Card to obtain discount. Not valid holidays & subject to Rules of Use. Not valid with other discount offers unless specified

G68

Offer validity is governed by the Rules of Use and excludes defined holidays. Offers are not valid with other discount offers, unless specified.

Valid now thru November 1, 2007

FREE GREEN FEE

entertainment.com

The Summit Golf Club

www.summitgolfclub.com

Enjoy one complimentary GREEN FEE when a second GREEN FEE of equal or greater value is purchased.

valid Monday thru Thursday

Golf cart required

G69

Offer validity is governed by the Rules of Use and excludes defined holidays. Offers are not valid with other discount offers, unless specified.

Valid now thru November 1, 2007

Up To $19.00 Value

entertainment.com

SHADOWBROOKE

www.shadowbrooke.com

Enjoy one complimentary GREEN FEE when a second GREEN FEE of equal or greater value is purchased.

valid Monday thru Friday

Not valid on tournaments

G70

Offer validity is governed by the Rules of Use and excludes defined holidays. Offers are not valid with other discount offers, unless specified.

Valid now thru November 1, 2007

FREE GREEN FEE

entertainment.com

Southbrook GOLF CLUB

www.southbrookgolf.com

Enjoy one complimentary GREEN FEE of equal or greater value is purchased.

valid Mon. - Fri. anytime & Sat. & Sun. after 1 p.m.

G71

Offer validity is governed by the Rules of Use and excludes defined holidays. Offers are not valid with other discount offers, unless specified.

Valid now thru November 1, 2007

FREE GREEN FEE

entertainment.com

Phalen Park Golf Course

ci.stpaul.mn.us

Enjoy one complimentary GREEN FEE when a second GREEN FEE of equal or greater value is purchased.

valid Mon.-Fri. afer 9 a.m. & Sat. & Sun. after 2 p.m.

Not valid during leagues and tournaments

G72

Offer validity is governed by the Rules of Use and excludes defined holidays. Offers are not valid with other discount offers, unless specified.

Valid now thru November 1, 2007

CITY OF EDINA BRAEMAR

- Open November-mid April
- Professional teaching staff
- Weekends by the 1/2 hour
- Mon-Fri by the bucket

7420 Braemar Blvd.
(West of Braemar Golf Course)
Edina, MN
(952)826-6744

00000046

BRIGHTWOOD Hills GOLF COURSE

- Brightwood Hills features a 9-hole par 30 course.

1975 Silver Lake Road
New Brighton, MN
(651)638-2150

00002205

SHADOWBROOKE

- Contemporary golf in a relaxed country setting
- Lush fairways, plush greens, challenging water & spectacular 3-level putting green
- 18-Hole, par- 71 course

3192 State Hwy. 7 *(25 minutes west of Excelcior at intersection State Hwy. 7 & Co. Rd. 1)*, **Lester Prairie, MN**
(320)395-4250
www.shadowbrook.com

00397351

The Summit golf club

- Ranked 8th in the nation, 1st in Minnesota by Golf Digest for best new affordable golf course
- Toll free: (877)582-4653
- Bentgrass fairways, tees & greens
- 25 Minutes S. of the Metro on Hwy. 52 then 2 mi. W. on 19

31286 Hwy. 19 Blvd.
Cannon Falls, MN
(507)263-4648

00588634

Phalen Park Golf Course

- 18 Holes par 70/71
- Full service golf shop
- Lake Phalen
- Driving range & banquet facilities

1615 Phalen Dr.
St. Paul, MN
(651)778-0413

00582776

Southbrook GOLF CLUB

- 18 Hole championship course
- Par 72
- Fully stocked pro shop
- Full service year round restaurant
- Tee time recommended
- 45 Minutes W. on Hwy. 55 from the Twin Cities
- 1-877-292-9630

511 Morrison Ave. S.
(1 mile S.W. of Annandale)
Annandale, MN
(320)274-2341

00588845

FREE GREEN FEE — Montgomery Golf Club

www.montgomerygolfclub.com

Enjoy one complimentary GREEN FEE when a second GREEN FEE of equal or greater value is purchased.

valid anytime

Golf cart required; Not valid with any other discounts or promotions; Please present ENTERTAINMENT® Membership Card to obtain discount. Not valid holidays & subject to Rules of Use. Not valid with other discount offers unless specified. G73

Valid now thru November 1, 2007

Offer validity is governed by the Rules of Use and excludes defined holidays. Offers are not valid with other discount offers, unless specified.

Up To $29.00 Value — Arrowwood Resort & Conference Center

Enjoy one complimentary GREEN FEE when a second GREEN FEE of equal or greater value is purchased.

valid Monday thru Friday

Please present ENTERTAINMENT® Membership Card to obtain discount. Not valid holidays & subject to Rules of Use. Not valid with other discount offers unless specified. G74

Valid now thru November 1, 2007

Offer validity is governed by the Rules of Use and excludes defined holidays. Offers are not valid with other discount offers, unless specified.

FREE GREEN FEE — Vintage Golf Course (EST. 2000)

www.riverwoodnational.com

Enjoy one complimentary GREEN FEE when a second GREEN FEE of equal or greater value is purchased.

Valid Mon.-Fri.

valid Mon.-Fri.; Not valid during leagues and tournaments G75

Valid now thru November 1, 2007

Offer validity is governed by the Rules of Use and excludes defined holidays. Offers are not valid with other discount offers, unless specified.

Up To $13.00 Value — Vertical Endeavors Minnesota Rock Gym

www.verticalendeavors.com

Enjoy one complimentary WEEK DAY DAILY ENTRY when a second WEEK DAY DAILY ENTRY of equal or greater value is purchased.

valid Monday thru Friday only

G76

Valid now thru November 1, 2007

Offer validity is governed by the Rules of Use and excludes defined holidays. Offers are not valid with other discount offers, unless specified.

MINI-GOLF — Lava Links

www.lavalinks.net

Enjoy ONE ROUND OF MINIATURE GOLF when a second ROUND OF MINIATURE GOLF of equal or greater value is purchased.

valid anytime

Not valid with any other discounts or promotions G77

Valid now thru November 1, 2007

Offer validity is governed by the Rules of Use and excludes defined holidays. Offers are not valid with other discount offers, unless specified.

Up To $10.00 Value — all seasons golf

Enjoy one complimentary GREEN FEE when a second GREEN FEE of equal or greater value is purchased.

valid anytime

G78

Valid now thru November 1, 2007

Offer validity is governed by the Rules of Use and excludes defined holidays. Offers are not valid with other discount offers, unless specified.

Arrowwood
RESORT & CONFERENCE CENTER

- Challenging & scenic 18 hole golf course surrounded by lakes & water
- All new pro shop & clubhouse to compliment the course
- Adjacent to beautiful Arrowwood Resort & Conference Center, with marina, horse back riding, outdoor tennis, indoor/outdoor pool & many other amenities

**2100 Arrowwood Ln.
Alexandria, MN
(320)762-8337**

00525913

*Coupons void if purchased, sold or bartered.
Discounts exclude tax, tip and/or alcohol, where applicable.*

MONTGOMERY Golf Club

- Montgomery Golf Club... just minutes from the Twin Cities you can enjoy our beautiful 18 hole course
- We have a spacious driving range, with senior citizen & junior rates available
- We offer 3 year memberships starting at $1150 as well as corporate memberships
- Visit soon!

**900 Rogers Dr.
Montgomery, MN
(507)364-5602**

00547415

*Coupons void if purchased, sold or bartered.
Discounts exclude tax, tip and/or alcohol, where applicable.*

VERTICAL ENDEAVORS

- Enjoy rock climbing at the region's premier indoor facility. Routes for all ages & abilities. Participants MUST sign a Vertical Endeavors liability waiver & rules agreement. Participants under 18 must have the form signed by a parent or legal guardian. Call (651)776-1430 for reservations

**834 Arcade St.
(below Seeger Square - entrance off Forest St.)
St. Paul, MN
(651)776-1430**

00144472

VINTAGE GOLF COURSE

**10444 95th St. N.E.
Otsego, MN
(763)271-5000**

00694611

---

all seasons golf

**7552 W. Point Douglas Rd.
Cottage Grove, MN
(651)459-2135**

00525815

Lava LINKS

- Tropical indoor 18 hole miniature golf course
- Video arcade
- Laser tag
- Snack bar
- Birthday packages available

**1655 W. County Rd. B2
(Crossroads Mall (across from Pavillion Place UA Theater)
Roseville, MN
(651)628-9956**

00237530

B&V Golf Course

Up To $5.00 Value

Enjoy one complimentary GREEN FEE when a second GREEN FEE of equal or greater value is purchased.

valid anytime

G79

Offer validity is governed by the Rules of Use and excludes defined holidays. Offers are not valid with other discount offers, unless specified.

Valid now thru November 1, 2007

BEGIN OAKS GOLF

FREE GREEN FEE

www.beginoaksgolf.com

Enjoy one complimentary GREEN FEE when a second GREEN FEE of equal or greater value is purchased.

valid Monday thru Friday

Golf cart required

G80

Offer validity is governed by the Rules of Use and excludes defined holidays. Offers are not valid with other discount offers, unless specified.

Valid now thru November 1, 2007

GOLF ZONE — RAIN·SNOW·SHINE YEAR·ROUND FUN

FREE GREEN FEE

www.yourgolfzone.com

Enjoy one complimentary GREEN FEE when a second GREEN FEE of equal or greater value is purchased.

valid anytime

On availability basis

G81

Offer validity is governed by the Rules of Use and excludes defined holidays. Offers are not valid with other discount offers, unless specified.

Valid now thru November 1, 2007

GRAND SLAM U.S.A.

50% OFF

Enjoy up to 4 ROUNDS of MINIATURE GOLF at 50% off the regular price.

valid anytime

One coupon per customer per visit

G82

Offer validity is governed by the Rules of Use and excludes defined holidays. Offers are not valid with other discount offers, unless specified.

Valid now thru November 1, 2007

GreyStone GOLF CLUB

FREE GREEN FEE

www.greystonegc.net

Enjoy one complimentary GREEN FEE when 3 GREEN FEES of equal or greater value are purchased.

valid anytime

G83

Offer validity is governed by the Rules of Use and excludes defined holidays. Offers are not valid with other discount offers, unless specified.

Valid now thru November 1, 2007

Island Lake Golf Center

Up To $14.00 Value

Enjoy one complimentary GREEN FEE when a second GREEN FEE of equal or greater value is purchased.

valid anytime

Not valid during leagues and tournaments

G84

Offer validity is governed by the Rules of Use and excludes defined holidays. Offers are not valid with other discount offers, unless specified.

Valid now thru November 1, 2007

BEGIN OAKS GOLF

- "It's like being up north without the drive"
- Premiere 9 hole, par 34 course
- Large lighted grass driving range
- Lessons available

5635 Yucca Ln. N.
(S. of County Rd. 47 & W. of Northwest Blvd.)
Plymouth, MN
(763)559-7574

Coupons void if purchased, sold or bartered.
Discounts exclude tax, tip and/or alcohol, where applicable.

00612591

B&V Golf Course

- 9 Holes
- Full driving range
- Grass tees
- Practice greens

4155 Hwy. 101
(Hwy. 55 & Hwy. 101)
Plymouth, MN
(763)478-6443

Coupons void if purchased, sold or bartered.
Discounts exclude tax, tip and/or alcohol, where applicable.

00591305

GRAND SLAM U.S.A.

- 18 hole indoor mini golf
- Also available: Laser tag, video arcade, basketball, mega playzone, spaceball & snack bar
- Call for birthday party information & discount packages

2941 Coon Rapids Blvd., Coon Rapids, MN
(763)427-1959

3984 Sibley Memorial Hwy., Eagan, MN
(651)452-6539

Coupons void if purchased, sold or bartered.
Discounts exclude tax, tip and/or alcohol, where applicable.

00407622

GOLF ZONE — RAIN·SNOW·SHINE
YEAR-ROUND FUN

- 9 Hole pitch & putt
- 27 Hole real grass mini-putt
- Fully heated driving stalls
- Full length driving range
- Tee it up year round

825 Flying Cloud Dr.
Chaska, MN
(952)445-1500

Coupons void if purchased, sold or bartered.
Discounts exclude tax, tip and/or alcohol, where applicable.

00667301

Island Lake Golf Center

1000 Red Fox Rd.
Shoreview, MN
(651)787-0383

Coupons void if purchased, sold or bartered.
Discounts exclude tax, tip and/or alcohol, where applicable.

00348382

GreyStone GOLF CLUB

- A Tom Lehman Signature Course
- Full dining room in The Greystone Grill
- Lots available, join the Greystone community!
- Full driving range & practice facility
- I-94 to Sauk Centre exit, right on U.S. 71, course is 4 mi. N. on the right side

10548 Andrews Dr.
Sauk Centre, MN
(320)351-4653

Coupons void if purchased, sold or bartered.
Discounts exclude tax, tip and/or alcohol, where applicable.

00599995

Northern Palms Golf Center

Up to $12.00 Value

entertainment.com

www.palmsgolfcenter.com

Enjoy one complimentary 1/2 HOURLY PLAY SESSION when a second 1/2 HOURLY PLAY SESSION of equal or greater value is purchased.

valid anytime

G85

Valid now thru November 1, 2007

Offer validity is governed by the Rules of Use and excludes defined holidays. Offers are not valid with other discount offers, unless specified.

Roseville Cedarholm Golf Course

FREE GREEN FEE

entertainment.com

www.ci.roseville.mn.us/parks

Enjoy one complimentary GREEN FEE when a second GREEN FEE of equal or greater value is purchased.

valid anytime

G86

Valid now thru November 1, 2007

Offer validity is governed by the Rules of Use and excludes defined holidays. Offers are not valid with other discount offers, unless specified.

Como Park Golf Course

FREE GREEN FEE

entertainment.com

ci.stpaul.mn.us

Enjoy one complimentary GREEN FEE when a second GREEN FEE of equal or greater value is purchased.

valid Mon.-Fri. after 9 a.m. & Sat. & Sun. after 2 p.m.

Not valid during leagues and tournaments; Golf cart required

G87

Valid now thru November 1, 2007

Offer validity is governed by the Rules of Use and excludes defined holidays. Offers are not valid with other discount offers, unless specified.

Spring Lake Park Amusement

FREE ROUND OF MINIATURE GOLF

entertainment.com

Enjoy one complimentary ROUND OF MINIATURE GOLF when a second ROUND OF MINIATURE GOLF of equal or greater value is purchased.

valid anytime

Thru Labor Day weekend

G88

Valid now thru November 1, 2007

Offer validity is governed by the Rules of Use and excludes defined holidays. Offers are not valid with other discount offers, unless specified.

Vintage Golf Course

FREE BUCKET OF BALLS

entertainment.com

DRIVING RANGE

www.riverwoodnational.com

Enjoy one complimentary BUCKET OF BALLS when a second BUCKET OF BALLS of equal or greater value is purchased.

valid anytime

G89

Valid now thru November 1, 2007

Offer validity is governed by the Rules of Use and excludes defined holidays. Offers are not valid with other discount offers, unless specified.

WinterGreens Golf • Grill • Dining

Up to $25.00 Value

entertainment.com

Enjoy one complimentary HOURLY PLAY SESSION when a second HOURLY PLAY SESSION of equal or greater value is purchased.

valid Monday thru Friday

G90

Valid now thru November 1, 2007

Offer validity is governed by the Rules of Use and excludes defined holidays. Offers are not valid with other discount offers, unless specified.

ROSEVILLE
Cedarholm Golf Course

- 10 minutes from downtown St. Paul & Minneapolis
- 9 holes
- Par 3
- Players of all abilities welcome
- Quick yet challenging course

2323 Hamline Ave.
(at Hwy. 36)
Roseville, MN
(651)633-8337

00577299

SPRING LAKE PARK AMUSEMENT

- Mini golf

1066 NE Hwy. 10
(corner of Hwy. 65 and County Rd. 10)
Spring Lake Park, MN
(763)786-4994

00000811

WinterGreens
GOLF • GRILL • DINING

- Keep golfing all year long
- Open 9 a.m.-10 p.m. daily
- State of the art simulators
- Over 45 courses
- Bring your clubs or use ours
- Full bar & grill
- Short 30 minute drive
- N. on Hwy. 65

306 Credit Union Dr.
Isanti, MN
(763)444-8422

00579823

NORTHERN Palms

- Year-round state-of-the-art, open air driving range
- 40 Heated, lighted hitting stations
- Sand filled turf
- Golf instruction

14160 James Rd.
Rogers, MN
(763)428-9299

00607615

Como Park Golf Course

- 18 Holes par 70
- Clubhouse with panoramic view
- Full service golf shop

1431 N. Lexington Pkwy.
St. Paul, MN
(651)488-9673

00582782

VINTAGE GOLF COURSE
EST. 2000
DRIVING RANGE

10444 95th St. N.E.
(3 mi. N. of I94 & The Outlets at Albertville, off County Rd. 19)
Otsego, MN
(763)271-5000

00693436

entertainment.com — Up To $6.00 Value

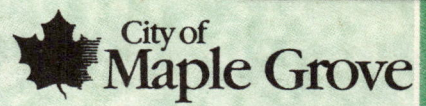

City of Maple Grove
Parks & Recreation

www.ci.maple-grove.mn.us/

Enjoy one complimentary LEISURE POOL, INDOOR PLAYGROUND or OPEN ICESKATE ADMISSION when a second LEISURE POOL, INDOOR PLAYGROUND or OPEN ICESKATE ADMISSION of equal or greater value is purchased.

valid anytime

G91

Offer validity is governed by the Rules of Use and excludes defined holidays. Offers are not valid with other discount offers, unless specified.

Valid now thru November 1, 2007

---

entertainment.com — 50% OFF

USA KARATE
THE POWERFUL ALTERNATIVE

www.usa-karate.net

Enjoy any 8 KARATE LESSONS at 50% off the regular price.

valid anytime

G92

Offer validity is governed by the Rules of Use and excludes defined holidays. Offers are not valid with other discount offers, unless specified.

Valid now thru November 1, 2007

---

entertainment.com — ADMISSION

ADVENTURE ZONE

Enjoy one complimentary ADMISSION when a second ADMISSION of equal or greater value is purchased.

valid anytime

G93

Offer validity is governed by the Rules of Use and excludes defined holidays. Offers are not valid with other discount offers, unless specified.

Valid now thru November 1, 2007

---

entertainment.com — FREE ADMISSION

Eden Prairie Community Center
EDEN PRAIRIE — LIVE • WORK • DREAM

Enjoy one complimentary ADMISSION when a second ADMISSION of equal or greater value is purchased.

valid anytime

G94

Offer validity is governed by the Rules of Use and excludes defined holidays. Offers are not valid with other discount offers, unless specified.

Valid now thru November 1, 2007

entertainment.com — 50% OFF

Kids' Time

Enjoy up to 4 HOURLY PLAY SESSIONS at 50% off the regular price.

valid anytime

G95

Offer validity is governed by the Rules of Use and excludes defined holidays. Offers are not valid with other discount offers, unless specified.

Valid now thru November 1, 2007

---

entertainment.com — Up To $12.00 Value

3rd Lair
SKATEPARK–SKATESHOP

www.3rdlair.com

Enjoy one complimentary SESSION when a second SESSION of equal or greater value is purchased.

Special events excluded

valid Sun.-Fri.

G96

Offer validity is governed by the Rules of Use and excludes defined holidays. Offers are not valid with other discount offers, unless specified.

Valid now thru November 1, 2007

USA KARATE
THE POWERFUL ALTERNATIVE

MINNESOTA
Anoka
3507 Round Lake Blvd. N.W.
(Andover)
(763)427-0440

Brooklyn Ctr.
6070 Shingle Creek Pkwy.
(763)566-5579

Burnsville
14021 Grand Ave.
(952)892-6565

Chanhassen
460 W. 79th St.
(952)906-2969

Crosslake
34330 County Rd. 3
(218)692-3415

Maple Grove
13604 N. 80th Circle
(763)420-8333

Plymouth
3900 Vinewood Ln. N.
(763)519-1115

Shakopee
1353 Heather St.
(952)233-5323

Stillwater
105 New England Place
(651)439-0093

Woodbury
2110 Eagle Creek Ln.
(651)998-0960

WISCONSIN
Hudson
832 Carmichael Rd.
(715)377-8201

Coupons void if purchased, sold or bartered. Discounts exclude tax, tip and/or alcohol, where applicable.

00691173

Eden Prairie Community Center

16700 Valley View Rd.
Eden Prairie, MN
(952)949-8470

Coupons void if purchased, sold or bartered. Discounts exclude tax, tip and/or alcohol, where applicable.

00652963

3rd Lair
SKATEPARK–SKATESHOP

- Largest indoor skate park in the midwest
- All ages & skill levels welcome
- Party room available for special events & birthday parties
- Lessons & park rental available
- Fully stocked pro shop for all skate board & inline needs
- For more info., call 763-79-SKATE

850 Florida Ave. S.
Golden Valley, MN
(763)79S-KATE

Coupons void if purchased, sold or bartered. Discounts exclude tax, tip and/or alcohol, where applicable.

00518572

City of Maple Grove
Parks & Recreation

12951 Weaver Lake Rd.
Maple Grove, MN
(763)494-6500

Coupons void if purchased, sold or bartered. Discounts exclude tax, tip and/or alcohol, where applicable.

00252198

ADVENTURE ZONE

- Season passes available
- Private sessions; open play sessions
- Adventure Zone is the best game in town for paint ball!
- Pro shop
- Gun rental

Burnsville, MN
(952)890-7961

Coupons void if purchased, sold or bartered. Discounts exclude tax, tip and/or alcohol, where applicable.

00477963

Kids' Time

- No reservations needed
- A variety of games, crafts & activities
- A fun place for kids 17 months-11 yrs.
- State licensed
- Snacks & food

80 N.W. Coon Rapids Blvd.
(just W. of Northtown Mall)
Coon Rapids, MN
(763)780-9651

Coupons void if purchased, sold or bartered. Discounts exclude tax, tip and/or alcohol, where applicable.

00698446

entertainment.com — FREE ADMISSION

BURNSVILLE ICE CENTER

Enjoy one complimentary ADMISSION FOR PUBLIC SKATING with this coupon.

Skate rental not included

valid anytime

One coupon per customer per visit

G97

Valid now thru November 1, 2007

Offer validity is governed by the Rules of Use and excludes defined holidays. Offers are not valid with other discount offers, unless specified.

---

entertainment.com — Up To $6.00 Value

Cheap Skate

www.cheapskatecr.com

Enjoy one complimentary ROLLER SKATING ADMISSION when a second ROLLER SKATING ADMISSION of equal or greater value is purchased.

valid anytime

G98

Valid now thru November 1, 2007

Offer validity is governed by the Rules of Use and excludes defined holidays. Offers are not valid with other discount offers, unless specified.

---

entertainment.com — FREE ADMISSION

JOHN ROSE MINNESOTA OVAL — ROSEVILLE USA

Enjoy one complimentary ADMISSION when a second ADMISSION of equal or greater value is purchased.

Good toward general in-line or ice skating; Call for skate times 651 415-2170

valid during public sessions

G99

Valid now thru November 1, 2007

Offer validity is governed by the Rules of Use and excludes defined holidays. Offers are not valid with other discount offers, unless specified.

---

entertainment.com — BUY ONE GET ONE FREE

RAMSEY COUNTY PARKS & RECREATION DEPARTMENT

www.co.ramsey.mn.us/parks

Enjoy one complimentary ADMISSION FOR PUBLIC SKATING when a second ADMISSION FOR PUBLIC SKATING of equal or greater value is purchased.

Skate rental excluded

valid anytime

G100

One coupon per customer per visit

Valid now thru November 1, 2007

Offer validity is governed by the Rules of Use and excludes defined holidays. Offers are not valid with other discount offers, unless specified.

---

entertainment.com — SKATING ADMISSION

ROLLER GARDEN

Enjoy one complimentary ROLLER SKATING ADMISSION when you purchase a second ADMISSION of equal or greater value.

valid during public sessions

Except for special events & private parties

G101

Valid now thru November 1, 2007

Offer validity is governed by the Rules of Use and excludes defined holidays. Offers are not valid with other discount offers, unless specified.

---

entertainment.com — Up To $6.00 Value

ROLLERBLADE ROLLERDOME

www.roller-dome.com

Enjoy one complimentary IN-LINE SKATING ADMISSION when a second IN-LINE SKATING ADMISSION of equal or greater value is purchased.

valid anytime

G102

Valid now thru November 1, 2007

Offer validity is governed by the Rules of Use and excludes defined holidays. Offers are not valid with other discount offers, unless specified.

Cheap Skate

- Family entertainment center
- Videos, music & live cam
- Arcade, concessions, in-line skate rentals, lessons
- Birthday parties, private parties & group events

3075 Coon Rapids Blvd
(6 miles W. of Hwy. 610/252)
Coon Rapids, MN
(763)427-8980

00499926

RAMSEY COUNTY
PARKS & RECREATION DEPARTMENT

Valid at All Participating Locations

00002090

ROLLERDOME

900 South 5th Street, Minneapolis, MN
(612)825-3663
METRODOME
612-825-3663
www.roller-dome.com

00001126

BURNSVILLE ICE CENTER

251 Civic Center Parkway
Burnsville, MN
(952)895-4651

00000839

JOHN ROSE MINNESOTA OVAL — ROSEVILLE USA

- The largest outdoor skating/summer in-line skating facility in North America
- Plan your special event at our facility
- Banquet facilities available - call (651) 415-2131

2661 Civic Center Dr.
(near intersection County Rd. C & Lexington)
Roseville, MN
(651)415-2170

00000074

ROLLER GARDEN

- Birthday party specials
- Private parties
- 12 yrs & under sessions
- Adult-only sessions
- Christian comtemporary music session
- Video arcade & snack bar

5622 West Lake Street, St. Louis Park, MN
(952)929-5518
(952)922-RINK

00000305

entertainment.com — FREE ADMISSION

Skateville

Enjoy one complimentary ADMISSION when a second ADMISSION of equal or greater value is purchased.

valid anytime

Not valid for private parties or special promotions

G103

Offer validity is governed by the Rules of Use and excludes defined holidays. Offers are not valid with other discount offers, unless specified.

Valid now thru November 1, 2007

---

entertainment.com — 50% OFF

Q-SHARKS BILLIARDS & PRO-SHOP

www.qsharksbilliards.com

Enjoy up to 4 HOURLY PLAY SESSIONS at 50% off the regular price.

valid anytime

G104

Offer validity is governed by the Rules of Use and excludes defined holidays. Offers are not valid with other discount offers, unless specified.

Valid now thru November 1, 2007

---

entertainment.com — 50% OFF

Rack N Roll BILLIARDS
Shakopee, MN

Enjoy up to 4 HOURLY PLAY SESSIONS at 50% off the regular price.

valid anytime

G105

Offer validity is governed by the Rules of Use and excludes defined holidays. Offers are not valid with other discount offers, unless specified.

Valid now thru November 1, 2007

---

entertainment.com — 4 HOURLY PLAY SESSIONS

Shooters

Enjoy up to 4 HOURLY PLAY SESSIONS at 50% off the regular price.

valid anytime

G106

Offer validity is governed by the Rules of Use and excludes defined holidays. Offers are not valid with other discount offers, unless specified.

Valid now thru November 1, 2007

---

entertainment.com — 50% OFF

Two Stooges BILLIARDS
Fridley, MN

www.two-stooges.com

Enjoy up to 4 HOURLY PLAY SESSIONS at 50% off the regular price.

valid anytime

G107

Offer validity is governed by the Rules of Use and excludes defined holidays. Offers are not valid with other discount offers, unless specified.

Valid now thru November 1, 2007

---

entertainment.com — UP TO 4 GAMES

Brunswick Zone™

Enjoy up to 4 GAMES (open bowling) at 50% off the regular price.

valid anytime

G108

Offer validity is governed by the Rules of Use and excludes defined holidays. Offers are not valid with other discount offers, unless specified.

Valid now thru November 1, 2007

Q-SHARKS BILLIARDS & PRO-SHOP

- 30 Diamond professional tables
- Pro-shop
- Authorized Jacoby & Samsara dealers
- Fine selection of cues & accessories
- 12 TV's
- Cafe & refreshments
- Larger game room
- Open 7 days - Sun.-Thurs. 11 a.m-4 a.m., Fri. & Sat. 11 a.m.-5 a.m.

1927 W. Burnsville Pkwy.
Burnsville, MN
(952)736-8284

00522670

Shooters

1934 Hwy. 13 E.
Burnsville, MN
(952)894-1100

00609965

Brunswick Zone

- Cosmic Bowling
- 40 Lanes
- Full service bar available
- Banquet room
- Birthday parties

12200 Singletree Ln.
Eden Prairie, MN
(952)941-0445

00626881

Skateville

- Rollerskating, regular sessions only

201 South River Ridge Circle
Burnsville, MN
(952)890-0988

00058992

Rack A Roll BILLIARDS
Shakopee, Mn

- Sunday & Monday - beginners
- Tuesday - 9 ball tournament
- Wednesdays - ladies night, ladies play free. D.J & karaoke from 8 p.m. - 1 a.m.
- Thursday - open 8 ball tournament
- 21 tables
- Ping-pong, video games, pinball, pro-shop, foosball, darts & snack shop
- Friday night tournament "Coffee Pot Open", 1 a.m. sign-up & 1:30 a.m. start

1111 Shakopee Town Sq.
Shakopee, MN
(952)403-9999

00519072

Two Stooges BILLIARDS
Fridley, Mn

- Brand new bar & full service restaurant
- 43 World class tables
- 8 Dart boards
- 14 Plasma TV's
- Leagues & tournaments
- Texas hold'em 6 nights a week
- Ladies nights on Sun. & Tues.
- Karaoke & live music
- Full service pro shop
- Banquet & party facilities

7178 University Ave. N.E.
Fridley, MN
(763)574-1399

00696501

UP TO THREE LINES

AIRPORT BOWL

Enjoy UP TO 3 LINES of OPEN BOWLING when you purchase the SAME NUMBER at regular adult prices.

valid anytime

One coupon per customer per visit

G109

Valid now thru November 1, 2007

Offer validity is governed by the Rules of Use and excludes defined holidays. Offers are not valid with other discount offers, unless specified.

50% OFF

Flaherty's Arden Bowl — COSMIC BOWLING at Brunswick

www.flahertysbowl.com

Enjoy up to 4 GAMES (open bowling) at 50% off the regular price.

valid anytime

G110

Valid now thru November 1, 2007

Offer validity is governed by the Rules of Use and excludes defined holidays. Offers are not valid with other discount offers, unless specified.

UP TO 3 LINES

Country Club Lanes

Enjoy up to THREE LINES of OPEN BOWLING when you purchase the SAME NUMBER at regular adult rates.

valid anytime

One coupon per customer per visit

G111

Valid now thru November 1, 2007

Offer validity is governed by the Rules of Use and excludes defined holidays. Offers are not valid with other discount offers, unless specified.

THREE LINES OF OPEN BOWLING

Lariat Lanes

www.lariatlanes.com

Enjoy UP TO THREE LINES OF OPEN BOWLING when you purchase the SAME NUMBER at regular adult rates.

valid anytime

Not valid for atomic bowling

G112

Valid now thru November 1, 2007

Offer validity is governed by the Rules of Use and excludes defined holidays. Offers are not valid with other discount offers, unless specified.

UP TO THREE LINES

MEDINA LANES

www.medinaentertainment.com

Enjoy UP TO THREE LINES of OPEN BOWLING when you purchase the SAME NUMBER at regular adult prices.

valid anytime

G113

Valid now thru November 1, 2007

Offer validity is governed by the Rules of Use and excludes defined holidays. Offers are not valid with other discount offers, unless specified.

UP TO 3 LINES OF OPEN BOWLING

Super Bowl

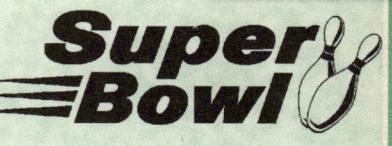

www.superbowlmn.com

Enjoy up to 3 LINES OF OPEN BOWLING when you purchase the same number at regular adult prices.

valid anytime

G114

Valid now thru November 1, 2007

Offer validity is governed by the Rules of Use and excludes defined holidays. Offers are not valid with other discount offers, unless specified.

Flaherty's Arden Bowl COSMIC BOWLING

- Birthday parties & company parties
- Cosmic & moonlight bowling
- Full service pub & grille
- 36 lanes
- Bumper bowling
- Large game room

1273 W. County Rd. E.
(Suelling & County Rd. E.)
Arden Hills, MN
(651)633-1777

00528470

Lariat Lanes

6320 Penn Avenue South
Minneapolis, MN
(612)866-5311

00000318

Super Bowl

- 24 Lanes
- Cosmic glow in the dark bowling
- Full service Pub 300 Lounge
- Pizza, burgers & snacks
- Pro shop
- We specialize in birthday & company parties
- Visit our website for specials & directions

6720 Riverdale Dr. N.W.
(near Hwy. 10 on Sunfish Lake Blvd.)
Ramsey, MN
(763)421-7779

00703419

AIRPORT BOWL

7711 - 14th Avenue South
Minneapolis, MN
(612)866-7577

00000044

Country Club Lanes

5601 Manitou Road
Tonka Bay, MN
(952)474-5959

00000491

MEDINA LANES

500 Hwy. 55
Hamel, MN
(763)478-6661

00054449

entertainment.com — UP TO 3 LINES OF OPEN BOWLING

Classic Bowl

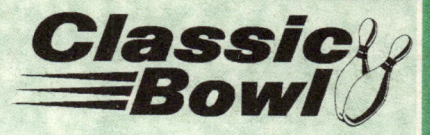

www.classicbowlmn.com

Enjoy up to 3 LINES OF OPEN BOWLING when you purchase the same number at regular adult prices.

valid anytime

G115

Offer validity is governed by the Rules of Use and excludes defined holidays. Offers are not valid with other discount offers, unless specified.

Valid now thru November 1, 2007

---

entertainment.com — UP TO THREE LINES

MIDWAY PRO BOWL

Enjoy UP TO THREE LINES of OPEN BOWLING when you purchase the same number at regular adult rates.

valid anytime

One coupon per customer per visit

G116

Offer validity is governed by the Rules of Use and excludes defined holidays. Offers are not valid with other discount offers, unless specified.

Valid now thru November 1, 2007

---

entertainment.com — UP TO THREE LINES

Park Tavern
LOUNGE & LANES

Enjoy UP TO THREE LINES of OPEN BOWLING when you purchase the SAME NUMBER at regular adult prices.

valid anytime

G117

Offer validity is governed by the Rules of Use and excludes defined holidays. Offers are not valid with other discount offers, unless specified.

Valid now thru November 1, 2007

---

entertainment.com — UP TO THREE LINES

ST. BERNARD'S LANES

Enjoy up to THREE LINES OF OPEN BOWLING when you purchase the SAME NUMBER at regular adult rates.

valid anytime

G118

Offer validity is governed by the Rules of Use and excludes defined holidays. Offers are not valid with other discount offers, unless specified.

Valid now thru November 1, 2007

---

entertainment.com — UP TO THREE LINES

Sundance
GOLF & BOWL
"All Season Family Sports Center"

www.sundancegolfbowl.com

Enjoy UP TO THREE LINES of OPEN BOWLING when you purchase the SAME NUMBER at regular adult rates.

valid anytime

G119

Offer validity is governed by the Rules of Use and excludes defined holidays. Offers are not valid with other discount offers, unless specified.

Valid now thru November 1, 2007

---

entertainment.com — UP TO THREE LINES

Texa-Tonka Lanes

Enjoy UP TO THREE LINES of OPEN BOWLING when you purchase the SAME NUMBER at regular adult prices.

valid anytime

G120

Offer validity is governed by the Rules of Use and excludes defined holidays. Offers are not valid with other discount offers, unless specified.

Valid now thru November 1, 2007

MIDWAY PRO BOWL

- Featuring 32 lanes for your bowling enjoyment with AMF Magiscore
- Full service cocktail lounge
- Snack bar
- Full service pro bowling shop

**1556 University Ave.
St. Paul, MN
(651)646-1396**

Classic Bowl

- 24 Lanes
- Cosmic glow in the dark bowling
- Full service Chasers Lounge with pool tables & darts
- Pizza, burgers & snacks
- Pro shop
- We specialize in birthday & company parties
- Visit our website for specials & directions

11707 Round Lake Blvd.
(corner of Coon Rapids Blvd. & Round Lake Blvd.)
**Coon Rapids, MN
(763)421-4402**

ST. BERNARD'S LANES

167 W Geranium
(off Rice St.)
**St. Paul, MN
(651)489-2677**

Park Tavern LOUNGE & LANES

- Large game room
- Big screen TV
- Full liquor service
- Great food
- 9am-12:30pm

**3401 Louisiana Avenue
St Louis Park, MN
(952)929-6810**

Texa-Tonka Lanes

**8200 Minnetonka Blvd
St. Louis Park, MN
(952)935-3427**

Sundance GOLF & BOWL
"All Season Family Sports Center"

- 18 hole golf, driving range
- 24 lanes w/ automatic scoring
- Sports bar & restaurant
- Banquets & meetings

15240 - 113th Ave. N
(Located halfway between Osseo & Rogers on Cty. Rd. 121, North of Cty. Rd. 81)
**Maple Grove, MN
(763)420-4800**

entertainment.com — UP TO THREE LINES

West Side Lanes

www.westsidelanes.com

Enjoy UP TO THREE LINES of OPEN BOWLING when you purchase the SAME NUMBER at regular adult rates.

valid anytime during open bowling

G121

Offer validity is governed by the Rules of Use and excludes defined holidays. Offers are not valid with other discount offers, unless specified.

Valid now thru November 1, 2007

---

entertainment.com — Up To $6.00 Value

Wildwood Bowl

Enjoy up to TWO LINES during OPEN BOWLING (availability basis) when a second person pays for the same number.

valid anytime

G122

Offer validity is governed by the Rules of Use and excludes defined holidays. Offers are not valid with other discount offers, unless specified.

Valid now thru November 1, 2007

---

entertainment.com — FREE ADMISSION

the interactive improv experience — comedysportz

www.comedysportzTC.com

Enjoy one complimentary ADMISSION when a second ADMISSION of equal or greater value is purchased.

Valid for any shows on Thursday, Friday 10:30 p.m. or Saturday 10:30 p.m.

G123

Offer validity is governed by the Rules of Use and excludes defined holidays. Offers are not valid with other discount offers, unless specified.

Valid now thru November 1, 2007

---

entertainment.com — FREE ADMISSION

Greater Twin Cities Youth Symphonies

www.gtcys.org

Enjoy one complimentary ADMISSION when a second ADMISSION of equal or greater value is purchased.

valid anytime

One coupon/card per customer per visit

G124

Offer validity is governed by the Rules of Use and excludes defined holidays. Offers are not valid with other discount offers, unless specified.

Valid now thru November 1, 2007

---

entertainment.com — FREE ADMISSION

Minnesota Dance Theatre

www.dancethatdares.com

Enjoy one complimentary ADMISSION when a second ADMISSION of equal or greater value is purchased.

valid anytime

Redeem at Box Office Only; On availability basis

G125

Offer validity is governed by the Rules of Use and excludes defined holidays. Offers are not valid with other discount offers, unless specified.

Valid now thru November 1, 2007

---

entertainment.com — FREE ADMISSION

PLYMOUTH PLAYHOUSE Presents

www.plymouthplayhouse.com

Enjoy one complimentary ADMISSION when a second ADMISSION of equal or greater value is purchased.

valid Sunday, Wednesday & Thursday

On availability basis

G126

Offer validity is governed by the Rules of Use and excludes defined holidays. Offers are not valid with other discount offers, unless specified.

Valid now thru November 1, 2007

WILDWOOD Bowl

- 8 Lane Bowling Center
- Great food
- Video games
- Live music every Friday & Saturday night

310 Stillwater Rd.
Willernie, MN
(651)426-0213

Coupons void if purchased, sold or bartered.
Discounts exclude tax, tip and/or alcohol, where applicable.

00399696

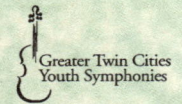

Greater Twin Cities Youth Symphonies

- Concerts for kids by kids
- Call GTCYS for a season brochure or visit www.gtcys.org
- Marlene Pauley, Artistic Director
- Presented by the Symphony, GTCYS' most advanced orchestra

528 Hennepin Ave. Suite 404
Minneapolis, MN
(612)870-7611

Coupons void if purchased, sold or bartered.
Discounts exclude tax, tip and/or alcohol, where applicable.

00468234

PLYMOUTH PLAYHOUSE Presents

2705 Annapolis Ln. (Hwy. 55 & 494)
(Best Western Kelly Inn)
Plymouth, MN
(763)553-1600

Advanced reservations & payment required prior to performance. When making reservations, you MUST identify yourself as Happenings® member to use this special offer.

Reservations must be made through the Plymouth Playhouse Theatre Box Office only. Call box office early to obtain best seating & availability for coupon redemption (when a sell-out is projected, no further coupons will be accepted).

Coupons void if purchased, sold or bartered.
Discounts exclude tax, tip and/or alcohol, where applicable.

00225712

West Side Lanes

- 20 lanes & bumpers available
- Plan a bowling birthday party
- Lounge, snack bar, NTN Trivia
- Banquet room available for special occasions
- We can help with fund-raising activities

1625 S. Robert St.
W. St. Paul, MN
(651)451-6222

Coupons void if purchased, sold or bartered.
Discounts exclude tax, tip and/or alcohol, where applicable.

00138390

---

comedysportz
the interactive improv experience

- Comedy show for the whole family
- Interactive, improv experience
- Corporate entertainment & private parties at our location or yours
- Improv workshops
- Call for reservations
- Show times: Thurs. 8 p.m., Fri. 10:30 p.m.. & Sat. 10:30 p.m.

3001 Hennepin Ave. S.
(2nd floor, Calhoun Sq.)
Minneapolis, MN
(612)870-1230

Coupons void if purchased, sold or bartered.
Discounts exclude tax, tip and/or alcohol, where applicable.

00504077

Minnesota Dance Theatre

- 40 Years of tradition
- Training tomorrow's dancers today
- Performing for over 25,000 people annually
- For concert information & performance times, visit our website at www.dancethatdares.com

528 Hennopia Ave. 6th Fl.
Minneapolis, MN
(612)338-0627

Coupons void if purchased, sold or bartered.
Discounts exclude tax, tip and/or alcohol, where applicable.

00597699

entertainment.com

Up To $29.00 Value

DODGE WORLD'S TOUGHEST BULLS & BRONCS

www.bullsandbroncs.com

Enjoy one complimentary ADULT ADMISSION when a second ADULT ADMISSION of equal or greater value is purchased.

valid for Friday, February 2, 2007 show only

Not valid with any other discount offer

G127

Offer validity is governed by the Rules of Use and excludes defined holidays. Offers are not valid with other discount offers, unless specified.

Valid now thru November 1, 2007

---

entertainment.com

FREE ADMISSION

Adventure Park

www.adventureparkinc.com

Enjoy one complimentary ADMISSION when a second ADMISSION of equal or greater value is purchased.

valid anytime

G128

Offer validity is governed by the Rules of Use and excludes defined holidays. Offers are not valid with other discount offers, unless specified.

Valid now thru November 1, 2007

---

entertainment.com

FREE ADMISSION

MEDINA ENTERTAINMENT CENTER
Rascals Bar & Restaurant

www.medinaentertainment.com

Enjoy one complimentary ADMISSION when a second ADMISSION of equal or greater value is purchased.

National acts/special events excluded

valid anytime

G129

Offer validity is governed by the Rules of Use and excludes defined holidays. Offers are not valid with other discount offers, unless specified.

Valid now thru November 1, 2007

---

entertainment.com

FREE ADMISSION

www.moundstheatre.org

Enjoy one complimentary ADMISSION when a second ADMISSION of equal or greater value is purchased.

valid anytime

On availability basis; Redeem at Box Office Only

G130

Offer validity is governed by the Rules of Use and excludes defined holidays. Offers are not valid with other discount offers, unless specified.

Valid now thru November 1, 2007

---

entertainment.com

FREE SESSION

Ollie & Co. Indoor Skateboard Park
Come Skate with Us

www.ollieindoorskatepark.com

Enjoy ONE SESSION when a second SESSION of equal or greater value is purchased.

valid anytime

G131

Offer validity is governed by the Rules of Use and excludes defined holidays. Offers are not valid with other discount offers, unless specified.

Valid now thru November 1, 2007

---

entertainment.com

FREE PUBLIC OPEN SKATING ADMISSION

PLYMOUTH ICE Center

www.ci.plymouth.mn.us

Enjoy one complimentary PUBLIC OPEN SKATING ADMISSION when a second PUBLIC OPEN SKATING ADMISSION of equal or greater value is purchased.

valid anytime

G132

Offer validity is governed by the Rules of Use and excludes defined holidays. Offers are not valid with other discount offers, unless specified.

Valid now thru November 1, 2007

Adventure Park

- Jungle themed indoor park for ages 1-12
- Bamboo hut snack bar
- Come & play anytime, anyday
- Perfect for birthday parties & field trips
- Toddlers area
- Open daily

14200 Lincoln St. NE
(2 blks. W. of Hwy. 65)
Ham Lake, MN
(763)757-3000

00695445

- A variety of childrens & adult professional live stage productions
- Call us or visit our website for available showtimes
- Home of Starting Gate productions

1029 Hudson Rd.
St. Paul, MN
(651)772-2253

00696502

Plymouth Ice Center

- Open daily year round
- Concessions
- Call for birthday party information
- Check out our all-ages Learn to Skate School
- Skate rental
- Skating hotline (763)509-5255 - call for open skating hours

3650 Plymouth Blvd.
(adjacent to Plymouth Lifetime Fitness)
Plymouth, MN
(763)509-5250

00690706

Dodge World's Toughest Bulls & Broncs

- Rodeo dates - Fri. Feb. 2, 2007 & Sat. Feb. 3, 2007
- Top cowboys & cowgirls compete in bareback riding, saddle bronc riding, bull riding & much more
- Call 1-866-XCELTIX for group sales information & all other events at the XCEL Energy Center

Xcel Energy Center, 199 W. Kellogg Blvd.,
St. Paul, MN 55102

00486414

Medina Entertainment Center

- Midwest largest dance floor
- Rascal's Bar & Restaurant full service dining
- 12 Lane bowling center with Extreme Cosmic on weekends
- Full banquet/wedding facilities for 10-1,500 people
- Stay next door at Medina Inn - (763)478-9770

500 Hwy. 55
Medina, MN
(763)478-6661

00698855

Ollie & Co. Indoor Skateboard Park

- North Metros newest premier skate park
- Skate park
- BMX biking
- In-line skating
- Board & helmet rentals
- Birthday packages available
- Park rental
- Open daily year round
- Proudly hosting monthly competitions

13835 Aberdeen St.
Ham Lake, MN
(763)767-5757

00700421

entertainment.com

ONE POP-IN PLAYTIME ADMISSION

PUMP IT UP
"THE INFLATABLE PARTY ZONE"

www.pumpitupparty.com

Enjoy one complimentary POP-IN PLAYTIME ADMISSION when a second POP-IN PLAYTIME ADMISSION of equal or greater value is purchased.

valid anytime

G133

Valid now thru November 1, 2007

Offer validity is governed by the Rules of Use and excludes defined holidays. Offers are not valid with other discount offers, unless specified.

---

entertainment.com

FREE ADMISSION

STARTING GATE PRODUCTIONS
www.startinggate.org

www.startinggate.org

Enjoy one complimentary ADMISSION when a second ADMISSION of equal or greater value is purchased.

valid anytime

On availability basis

G134

Valid now thru November 1, 2007

Offer validity is governed by the Rules of Use and excludes defined holidays. Offers are not valid with other discount offers, unless specified.

---

entertainment.com

FREE ADMISSION

CITY OF BROOKLYN CENTER
COMMUNITY CENTER
Indoor Pool & Waterslide

Enjoy one complimentary GENERAL ADMISSION with or without water slide when you purchase a second ADMISSION of equal or greater value.

valid anytime

G135

Valid now thru November 1, 2007

Offer validity is governed by the Rules of Use and excludes defined holidays. Offers are not valid with other discount offers, unless specified.

---

entertainment.com

FREE ADMISSION

stages theatre company
our world is magical!

www.stagestheatre.org

Enjoy one complimentary ADMISSION when a second ADMISSION of equal or greater value is purchased.

valid anytime

One coupon/card per customer per visit

G136

Valid now thru November 1, 2007

Offer validity is governed by the Rules of Use and excludes defined holidays. Offers are not valid with other discount offers, unless specified.

---

entertainment.com

50% OFF

Tuttle's
Bowling, Bar & Grill

Enjoy up to 4 GAMES (open bowling) at 50% off the regular price.

valid anytime

G137

Valid now thru November 1, 2007

Offer validity is governed by the Rules of Use and excludes defined holidays. Offers are not valid with other discount offers, unless specified.

---

entertainment.com

50% OFF

Memory Lanes

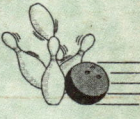

Enjoy up to 4 GAMES (open bowling) at 50% off the regular price.

valid anytime

Not valid with any other discounts or promotions

G138

Valid now thru November 1, 2007

Offer validity is governed by the Rules of Use and excludes defined holidays. Offers are not valid with other discount offers, unless specified.

STARTING GATE PRODUCTIONS
www.startinggate.org

- High quality professional productions for a diverse audience
- Known for our technical excellence
- Visit our website for information & show times
- Performing in the historic Mounds Theatre, located in the Daytons Bluff neighborhood

1029 Hudson Rd.
(Mounds Theatre)
St. Paul, MN
(651)645-3503

00698420

☆☆ Our World is Magical!
stages theatre company

- Ticket office hours: Tues.-Sat. 12 p.m.-6 p.m.
- Visit our website for ticket & production information
- Theatre classes available!

1111 Mainstreet
(in the Hopkins Center for the Arts)
Hopkins, MN
(952)979-1111

00692238

Memory Lanes

2520 26th Ave. S.
Minneapolis, MN
(612)721-6211

00701083

PUMP IT UP
The Inflatable Party Zone

1182 E. Cliff Rd., Burnsville, MN
(952)707-9386

7406 Washington Ave., Eden Prairie, MN
(952)400-4230

13941 Lincoln Dr. N.E. #400, Ham Lake, MN
(763)757-9000

7045 6th St. N., Oakdale, MN
(651)735-1556

3500 Holly Ln. N. #65, Plymouth, MN
(763)553-0340

00691171

BROOKLYN CENTER
COMMUNITY CENTER
Indoor Pool & Waterslide

6301 Shingle Creek Pkwy, Minneapolis, MN
(763)569-3400

Water Slide schedule (subject to change):
Mon. & Fri. 5 p.m.-8 p.m., Wed. 6 p.m.-8 p.m., Sat. 1 p.m.-8 p.m., Sun. 1 p.m.-5 p.m.

Open Swim schedule: Mon., Wed. & Fri. 9 a.m.-9 p.m. (adults only 9 a.m.-1 p.m.), Tues. & Thurs. 9 a.m.-4 p.m. (adults only 9 a.m.-1 p.m.), Sat. 1 p.m.-8 p.m., Sun 1 p.m.-5 p.m.

Children under age 6 must be accompanied by an adult in the pool

00000772

Tuttle's
Bowling, Bar & Grill

107 Shady Oak Rd.
Hopkins, MN
(952)938-4090

00700914

entertainment.com — 50% OFF

Lyn-Del Lanes
and Pro Shop

Enjoy up to 4 GAMES (open bowling) at 50% off the regular price.

Bumper bowling excluded

valid anytime

G139

Offer validity is governed by the Rules of Use and excludes defined holidays. Offers are not valid with other discount offers, unless specified.

Valid now thru November 1, 2007

---

entertainment.com — 50% OFF

Eddie's Billiards

Enjoy up to 4 HOURLY PLAY SESSIONS at 50% off the regular price.

valid anytime

G140

Offer validity is governed by the Rules of Use and excludes defined holidays. Offers are not valid with other discount offers, unless specified.

Valid now thru November 1, 2007

---

entertainment.com — FREE BUCKET OF BALLS

Riverwood National Driving Range

Enjoy one complimentary BUCKET OF BALLS when a second BUCKET OF BALLS of equal or greater value is purchased.

valid anytime

G141

Offer validity is governed by the Rules of Use and excludes defined holidays. Offers are not valid with other discount offers, unless specified.

Valid now thru November 1, 2007

---

entertainment.com — TENNIS ADMISSION

Wood Dale Recreation Center

Enjoy one complimentary TENNIS CLUB GUEST PASS when a second TENNIS CLUB GUEST PASS of equal or greater value is purchased.

Private parties & special events excluded

valid anytime

Call for court availability

G142

Offer validity is governed by the Rules of Use and excludes defined holidays. Offers are not valid with other discount offers, unless specified.

Valid now thru November 1, 2007

entertainment.com — Up To $24.00 Value

Osceola & St. Croix Valley Railway

www.mtmuseum.org

Enjoy UP TO 4 ADMISSIONS at 50% off the regular price.

valid Saturday, Sunday & holidays Memorial weekend thru Labor day

Not valid with any other discounts or promotions; Not valid on family, group, or charter rates

G143

Offer validity is governed by the Rules of Use and excludes defined holidays. Offers are not valid with other discount offers, unless specified.

Valid now thru November 1, 2007

---

entertainment.com — 50% OFF

St. Croix Falls MINI GOLF & GO-KARTS

Enjoy up to 4 ROUNDS of MINIATURE GOLF at 50% off the regular price.

valid anytime

G144

Offer validity is governed by the Rules of Use and excludes defined holidays. Offers are not valid with other discount offers, unless specified.

Valid now thru November 1, 2007

Eddie's Billiards

- "Get Behind the 8 Ball..."
- 26 Pool tables
- Video games
- Smoking available for ages 18 & over
- Leagues
- Cue repair
- Diamond tables

**11211 96th Ave. N.
Maple Grove, MN
(763)493-4830**

00672924

Wooddale Recreation Center

- Large modern facility
- Tennis club
- Roller rink
- Call for court availability

**2122 Wooddale Drive
Woodbury, MN
(651)735-6214**

00002087

St. Croix Falls Mini Golf & Go-Karts

- 18 Hole mini golf
- Fifth mile go-kart track
- Open daily in summer
- Group discounts - Call for reservations

**1971 U.S. Hwy. 8
St. Croix Falls, WI
(715)483-1627**

00671881

Lyn-Del Lanes and Pro Shop

- Open bowling daily
- Pro-shop
- Family atmosphere
- Bumpers for kids
- League openings
- Call for parties
- Pizza
- Hot dogs
- Soda
- Appetizers
- Atm machines

**9336 Lyndale Ave. S.
Bloomington, MN
(952)881-4232**

00694635

Riverwood National Driving Range

10247 95th St. N.E.
(3 min. N. of I-94 & The Outlets of Albertville, off County Rd. 19)
**Otsego, MN
(763)271-5000**

00694148

Osceola & St. Croix Valley Railway

- Board at the Historic 1916 Osceola Depot
- Operating Saturdays, Sundays & holidays Memorial weekend - Labor Day weekend
- Located in the Scenic St. Croix River Valley
- 90 Minute or 50 minute round trip rates
- Limited seating is available on a first come, first serve basis, call for reservations

**114 Depot Rd., Osceola, WI
(715)755-3570
www.mtmuseum.org**

00312219

*Coupons void if purchased, sold or bartered.
Discounts exclude tax, tip and/or alcohol, where applicable.*

entertainment.com — FREE ADMISSION

Chaska Community Center

Enjoy one complimentary ADMISSION when a second ADMISSION of equal or greater value is purchased.

valid anytime

G145

Valid now thru November 1, 2007

Offer validity is governed by the Rules of Use and excludes defined holidays. Offers are not valid with other discount offers, unless specified.

---

entertainment.com — FREE ADMISSION

Battle Creek Waterworks
Ramsey County Parks & Recreation Department
Family Aquatic Center

Enjoy one complimentary ADMISSION when a second ADMISSION of equal or greater value is purchased.

valid anytime

Not valid with any other discount offer

G146

Valid now thru November 1, 2007

Offer validity is governed by the Rules of Use and excludes defined holidays. Offers are not valid with other discount offers, unless specified.

entertainment.com — Up To $6.00 Value

City of Crystal

Enjoy one complimentary DAILY POOL, WATERSLIDE OR COMBINATION ADMISSION when a second DAILY POOL, WATERSLIDE OR COMBINATION ADMISSION of equal or greater value is purchased.

valid anytime

G147

Valid now thru November 1, 2007

Offer validity is governed by the Rules of Use and excludes defined holidays. Offers are not valid with other discount offers, unless specified.

---

entertainment.com — FREE ADMISSION

Eagles Nest Indoor Playground
City of New Brighton Parks & Recreation

www.newbrightonmn.gov

Enjoy one complimentary ADMISSION when a second ADMISSION of equal or greater value is purchased.

valid anytime

G148

Valid now thru November 1, 2007

Offer validity is governed by the Rules of Use and excludes defined holidays. Offers are not valid with other discount offers, unless specified.

---

entertainment.com — Up To $14.00 Value

CITY OF ST. LOUIS PARK
Outdoor Aquatic Park

www.stlouispark.org

Enjoy up to 4 ADMISSIONS at 50% off the regular price.

valid anytime

G149

Valid now thru November 1, 2007

Offer validity is governed by the Rules of Use and excludes defined holidays. Offers are not valid with other discount offers, unless specified.

---

entertainment.com — Up To $6.00 Value

CITY OF ST. LOUIS PARK
Rec Center

www.stlouispark.org

Enjoy up to 4 INDOOR ICE SKATING ADMISSIONS at 50% off the regular price.

valid anytime

G150

Valid now thru November 1, 2007

Offer validity is governed by the Rules of Use and excludes defined holidays. Offers are not valid with other discount offers, unless specified.

Battle Creek WATERWORKS
Ramsey County Parks & Recreation Department
Family Aquatic Center

- Shallow pool with zero depth beach entry
- Interactive Water Play system specially designed for children & family fun
- Activity pool featuring a swim area, lily pad water walk & a 3-story high twisting waterslide
- Children's sand/water play area
- Restrooms, changing area & concessions/vending

2401 Upper Afton Rd.
Maplewood, MN
(651)501-6340

00659614

Eagles Nest Indoor Playground
City of New Brighton Parks & Recreation

400 - 10th St. NW
New Brighton, MN
(651)638-2130

00206008

CITY OF ST. LOUIS PARK
Rec Center

- Indoor arena open year-round
- Open skating/open hockey
- Indoor ice skating
- Skate sharpening & skate rental available
- Call ahead for schedule (952)924-2567 x6

3700 Monterey Dr.
St. Louis Park, MN
(952)924-2540

00449243

CHASKA COMMUNITY CENTER

- Indoor pool with waterslide & rope swing
- Indoor track
- Gymnasium
- Ice arena
- Exercise weight equipment
- Steam & sauna room
- Indoor playground
- Cafe Grill
- Virtual golf
- Theatre auditorium

1661 Parkridge Dr.
Chaska, MN
(952)448-5633

00000450

CITY of CRYSTAL

- Birthday party specials
- Group rates by reservation
- Private pool/Waterslide rental
- Swimming lessons available

4800 Douglas Dr.
Minneapolis, MN
(763)531-0052

00252028

CITY OF ST. LOUIS PARK
Outdoor Aquatic Park

- Sand & water play area, 0 depth entry for little shavers
- Daring drop slides & 3-story waterslides
- Picnic area & gazebo
- Concessions - hotdogs, ice cream, soda, chips & more!

3700 Monterey Dr.
St. Louis Park, MN
(952)924-2540

00449257

Coupons void if purchased, sold or bartered. Discounts exclude tax, tip and/or alcohol, where applicable.

entertainment.com — Up To $15.00 Value

TAMARACK NATURE CENTER

www.co.ramsey.mn.us/parks/tamarack

Enjoy one complimentary ADMISSION when a second ADMISSION of equal or greater value is purchased.

Special events excluded

valid anytime

Reservations required

G151

Offer validity is governed by the Rules of Use and excludes defined holidays. Offers are not valid with other discount offers, unless specified.

Valid now thru November 1, 2007

---

entertainment.com — 50% OFF UP TO 10 TOKENS

Enjoy up to 10 TOKENS at 50% off the regular price.

valid anytime

G152

Offer validity is governed by the Rules of Use and excludes defined holidays. Offers are not valid with other discount offers, unless specified.

Valid now thru November 1, 2007

---

entertainment.com — FREE ADMISSION

Enjoy one complimentary ADMISSION when a second ADMISSION of equal or greater value is purchased.

valid for: baseball & wrestling, men's & women's gymnastics, women's hockey, volleyball, soccer & softball

Redeemable for regular season, on-campus events only

G153

Offer validity is governed by the Rules of Use and excludes defined holidays. Offers are not valid with other discount offers, unless specified.

Valid now thru November 1, 2007

---

entertainment.com — FREE ADMISSION

Enjoy one complimentary ADMISSION when a second ADMISSION of equal or greater value is purchased.

2006-2007 Regular season schedule only

valid for women's non-conference basketball

G154

Offer validity is governed by the Rules of Use and excludes defined holidays. Offers are not valid with other discount offers, unless specified.

Valid now thru November 1, 2007

---

entertainment.com — FREE ADMISSION

Enjoy one complimentary ADMISSION when a second ADMISSION of equal or greater value is purchased.

valid for Gopher Football games on Sept. 16 & Oct. 21

Schedule subject to change

G155

Offer validity is governed by the Rules of Use and excludes defined holidays. Offers are not valid with other discount offers, unless specified.

Valid now thru November 1, 2007

---

entertainment.com — FREE ADMISSION

Enjoy one complimentary ADMISSION when a second ADMISSION of equal or greater value is purchased.

2006-2007 Regular season schedule only

valid for men's non-conference basketball

G156

Offer validity is governed by the Rules of Use and excludes defined holidays. Offers are not valid with other discount offers, unless specified.

Valid now thru November 1, 2007

- Baseball & softball
- Private lessons
- Training room
- Clinics
- Party room rentals
- Turf field available to rent

1500 N. Rice St.
(between Larpenteur & Maryland at Nebraska)
St. Paul, MN
(651) 558-2117

00652263

TAMARACK NATURE CENTER

- Summer day camp programs, birthday parties, ski lessons, apple cidering, maple syruping, parent-child classes, school groups & weekend family programs
- Meeting space available
- Call for information & schedules

5287 Otter Lake Rd.
(2 miles North of Hwy 96 & 35E)
White Bear Township, MN
(651) 407-5350

00496323

- Redeem at ticket office on day of game, at the game site

4 Oak St. S. E.
(Mariucci Arena)
Minneapolis, MN
(612) 624-8080

00546660

- Redeem at ticket office on day of game, at the game site
- Ticket office is located in the east lobby of Mariucci Arena

4 Oak St. S. E.
(Mariucci Arena)
Minneapolis, MN
(612) 624-8080

00546656

- Redeem at ticket office on day of game, at the game site
- Schedule subject to change

4 Oak St. S. E.
(Mariucci Arena)
Minneapolis, MN
(612) 624-8080

00546666

- Redeem at the ticket office in the east lobby of Mariucci Arena, or on the day of game at the Metrodome box office
- Schedule subject to change

4 Oak St. S. E.
(Mariucci Arena)
Minneapolis, MN
(612) 624-8080

00546662

Coupons void if purchased, sold or bartered. Discounts exclude tax, tip and/or alcohol, where applicable.

entertainment.com
Up To $7.00 Value

UNIVERSITY OF MINNESOTA

Minnesota Landscape ARBORETUM

www.arboretum.umn.edu

Enjoy one complimentary ADMISSION when a second ADMISSION of equal or greater value is purchased.

valid anytime

G157

Valid now thru November 1, 2007

Offer validity is governed by the Rules of Use and excludes defined holidays. Offers are not valid with other discount offers, unless specified.

---

entertainment.com
FREE ADMISSION

The American Swedish Institute

www.americanswedishinst.org

Enjoy one complimentary ADMISSION when a second ADMISSION of equal or greater value is purchased.

valid anytime

G158

Valid now thru November 1, 2007

Offer validity is governed by the Rules of Use and excludes defined holidays. Offers are not valid with other discount offers, unless specified.

---

entertainment.com
50% OFF

BELL MUSEUM of Natural History

www.umn.edu/bellmuse

Enjoy up to 4 ADMISSIONS at 50% off the regular price - maximum discount $6.00.

valid anytime

G159

Valid now thru November 1, 2007

Offer validity is governed by the Rules of Use and excludes defined holidays. Offers are not valid with other discount offers, unless specified.

---

entertainment.com
BUY ONE GET ONE FREE

MINNESOTA HISTORICAL SOCIETY

www.mnhs.org

Enjoy one complimentary ADMISSION when a second ADMISSION of equal or greater value is purchased.

valid anytime

Valid at Fort Snelling, Comstock House, Folsom House, Forest History Center, Grand Mound, Harkin Store, James J. Hill House, Oliver H. Kelly Farm, Charles A. Lindbergh House, Lower Sioux Agency, Sibley House & Split Rock Lighthouse

G160

Valid now thru November 1, 2007

Offer validity is governed by the Rules of Use and excludes defined holidays. Offers are not valid with other discount offers, unless specified.

---

entertainment.com
Up To $10.00 Value

GIBBS MUSEUM OF PIONEER & DAKOTAH LIFE

www.rchs.com

Enjoy up to 4 ADMISSIONS at 50% off the regular price.

valid anytime

Not valid for Hallows Eve program

G161

Valid now thru November 1, 2007

Offer validity is governed by the Rules of Use and excludes defined holidays. Offers are not valid with other discount offers, unless specified.

---

entertainment.com
Up To $7.00 Value

Minnesota Film Arts

the BELL

www.mnfilmarts.org

Enjoy one complimentary ADMISSION when a second ADMISSION of equal or greater value is purchased.

valid anytime

G162

Valid now thru November 1, 2007

Offer validity is governed by the Rules of Use and excludes defined holidays. Offers are not valid with other discount offers, unless specified.

The American Swedish Institute

- Valid during museum hours: Tues., Thurs. - Sat. 12-4 p.m., Wed. 12-8 p.m., Sun. 1-5 p.m
- Explore the museum of Swedish-American art, culture and history located within the former home of Swedish immigrant and newspaper publisher Swan Turnblad
- The 33 room castle is on the National Register of Historic Places

2600 Park Ave.
Minneapolis, MN
(612) 871-4907

00496658

MINNESOTA HISTORICAL SOCIETY

Hwy. 55 & Hwy. 5
Minneapolis, MN
(612) 726-1171

00507084

---

the BELL
Minnesota Film Arts

- Documentaries, foreign & independent films
- Since 1962
- Minneapolis/St. Paul International Film Festival
- See schedule at www.mnfilmarts.org

10 Church St. S.E.
Minneapolis, MN
(612) 331-3134

00621970

UNIVERSITY OF MINNESOTA
Minnesota Landscape ARBORETUM

- Premier botanical garden with over 1,000 acres, 32 display gardens, & extensive plant collections
- Guided tours, conservatory, gift shop, restaurant, hiking, cross country ski trails
- Open year round

3675 Arboretum Dr.
(9 miles west of I-494, on Hwy. 5 in Chanhassen)
Chaska, MN
(952) 443-1400

00508788

BELL MUSEUM
of Natural History

- A small, friendly museum connecting people with the natural world
- Featuring art & science exhibits, Minnesota wildlife dioramas, & a children's Touch & See room

10 Church St. S.E.
(on the U of M Minneapolis Campus)
Minneapolis, MN
(612) 624-7083

00500072

GIBBS MUSEUM
OF PIONEER & DAKOTAH LIFE

- Early Minnesota pioneer family
- Reconstructed pioneer sod house
- Furnished 19th century farm house
- One room country schoolhouse
- Native American Dakotah culture
- Dakotah bark lodge & teepees
- Special events Sat. & Sun.
- Open May 1 thru October 31

2097 W. Larpenteur Ave.
(Corner of Cleveland & Larpenteur)
Falcon Heights, MN
(651) 646-8629

00504264

entertainment.com — FREE ADMISSION

Richfield Municipal Pool & Waterslide

Enjoy one complimentary ADMISSION when a second ADMISSION of equal or greater value is purchased.

valid anytime

G163

Offer validity is governed by the Rules of Use and excludes defined holidays. Offers are not valid with other discount offers, unless specified.

Valid now thru November 1, 2007

---

entertainment.com — FREE ADMISSION

Metropolitan Boys Choir / The Metropolitan Choralaires

Enjoy one complimentary ADMISSION when a second ADMISSION of equal or greater value is purchased.

valid for the Holiday Concert & the Spring Benefit Concert for the 2006-07 season

G164

Offer validity is governed by the Rules of Use and excludes defined holidays. Offers are not valid with other discount offers, unless specified.

Valid now thru November 1, 2007

---

entertainment.com — Up To $50.00 Value

Brave New Workshop

www.bravenewworkshop.com

Enjoy up to 4 ADMISSIONS at 50% off the regular price.

valid Wednesday thru Friday at 8 p.m. & Saturdays at 10 p.m.

Valid at the Minneapolis location only; Not valid December 18 thru 31

G165

Offer validity is governed by the Rules of Use and excludes defined holidays. Offers are not valid with other discount offers, unless specified.

Valid now thru November 1, 2007

---

entertainment.com — Up To $15.00 Value

Trail of Terror

Enjoy one complimentary ADMISSION when a second ADMISSION of equal or greater value is purchased.

valid anytime

G166

Offer validity is governed by the Rules of Use and excludes defined holidays. Offers are not valid with other discount offers, unless specified.

Valid now thru November 1, 2007

---

entertainment.com — 50% OFF

The Bakken Museum

Enjoy up to 4 ADMISSIONS at 50% off the regular price.

valid anytime

G167

Offer validity is governed by the Rules of Use and excludes defined holidays. Offers are not valid with other discount offers, unless specified.

Valid now thru November 1, 2007

---

entertainment.com — 50% OFF

Hennepin History Museum
THE HISTORICAL SOCIETY OF HENNEPIN COUNTY

Enjoy up to 4 ADMISSIONS at 50% off the regular price.

valid anytime

G168

Offer validity is governed by the Rules of Use and excludes defined holidays. Offers are not valid with other discount offers, unless specified.

Valid now thru November 1, 2007

Metropolitan Boys Choir / Metropolitan Choralaires

- We'd love to have you join us for our 35th Anniversary Season!
- Please call (612)827-6501 for further information

00509542

Richfield Municipal Pool & Waterslide

630 E. 66th St.
Richfield, MN
(612)861-9355

00666222

Trail of Terror

- Heated indoor maze, haunted hay ride & Club Scream!
- Call 1-800-966-8215 for more information
- Phantoms Feast - a freaky five course meal - make your reservations today!

3 Miles south of Shakopee on 169

00355568

Brave New Workshop

- Founded by Dudley Riggs in 1958 - Alumni include Louie Anderson & Al Franken
- Longest running satirical comedy theatre in the U.S.
- Like a "live version of Saturday Night Live...only funnier!"
- Uptown Minneapolis with lots of restaurants, shops & pubs nearby
- We serve beer, wine & espresso drinks

2605 Hennepin Ave.
Minneapolis, MN
(612)332-6620

00366861

Hennepin History Museum

- The Hennepin History Museum has been collecting, preserving & presenting Hennepin Countys history since 1938
- Rotating exhibitions
- Extensive research library & archives
- Education & outreach programs
- Museum galleries available for private events

2303 3rd Ave. S.
Minneapolis, MN
(612)870-1329

00701155

The Bakken Museum

- The Bakken is a museum of electricity in life
- Explore interactive exhibits while learning about electricity & magnetism as you stretch your imagination & discover the possibilities of invention
- The Bakken offers invention programs & Family Science Saturdays, where families come together for hands-on activities & learn that science is fun!

3537 Zenith Ave. S.
Minneapolis, MN
(612)926-3878

00633358

entertainment.com — MOVIE TICKETS

REGAL ENTERTAINMENT GROUP

EDWARDS THEATRES · REGAL CINEMAS · UNITED ARTISTS Theatres

Present this coupon at the Theatre Box Office to purchase up to two (2) *VIP Super Saver Admission Tickets for only $6.00 each. Upgrade to an UNRESTRICTED Premiere Super Saver Admission Ticket for only $1.50 extra per ticket.

*Surcharge may be applied if redeemed at any Manhattan, NY location. Valid at all Regal Entertainment Group locations nationwide. *VIP Super Saver Admission Ticket is not valid during the first 12 days of selected new release films.*

G169

valid anytime

Offer validity is governed by the Rules of Use and excludes defined holidays. Offers are not valid with other discount offers, unless specified.

Valid now thru November 1, 2007

---

entertainment.com — MOVIE TICKETS

REGAL ENTERTAINMENT GROUP

EDWARDS THEATRES · REGAL CINEMAS · UNITED ARTISTS Theatres

Present this coupon at the Theatre Box Office to purchase up to two (2) *VIP Super Saver Admission Tickets for only $6.00 each. Upgrade to an UNRESTRICTED Premiere Super Saver Admission Ticket for only $1.50 extra per ticket.

*Surcharge may be applied if redeemed at any Manhattan, NY location. Valid at all Regal Entertainment Group locations nationwide. *VIP Super Saver Admission Ticket is not valid during the first 12 days of selected new release films.*

G170

valid anytime

Offer validity is governed by the Rules of Use and excludes defined holidays. Offers are not valid with other discount offers, unless specified.

Valid now thru November 1, 2007

---

entertainment.com — MOVIE TICKETS

REGAL ENTERTAINMENT GROUP

EDWARDS THEATRES · REGAL CINEMAS · UNITED ARTISTS Theatres

Present this coupon at the Theatre Box Office to purchase up to two (2) *VIP Super Saver Admission Tickets for only $6.00 each. Upgrade to an UNRESTRICTED Premiere Super Saver Admission Ticket for only $1.50 extra per ticket.

*Surcharge may be applied if redeemed at any Manhattan, NY location. Valid at all Regal Entertainment Group locations nationwide. *VIP Super Saver Admission Ticket is not valid during the first 12 days of selected new release films.*

G171

valid anytime

Offer validity is governed by the Rules of Use and excludes defined holidays. Offers are not valid with other discount offers, unless specified.

Valid now thru November 1, 2007

---

entertainment.com — MOVIE TICKETS

REGAL ENTERTAINMENT GROUP

EDWARDS THEATRES · REGAL CINEMAS · UNITED ARTISTS Theatres

Present this coupon at the Theatre Box Office to purchase up to two (2) *VIP Super Saver Admission Tickets for only $6.00 each. Upgrade to an UNRESTRICTED Premiere Super Saver Admission Ticket for only $1.50 extra per ticket.

*Surcharge may be applied if redeemed at any Manhattan, NY location. Valid at all Regal Entertainment Group locations nationwide. *VIP Super Saver Admission Ticket is not valid during the first 12 days of selected new release films.*

G172

valid anytime

Offer validity is governed by the Rules of Use and excludes defined holidays. Offers are not valid with other discount offers, unless specified.

Valid now thru November 1, 2007

---

entertainment.com — MOVIE TICKETS

REGAL ENTERTAINMENT GROUP

EDWARDS THEATRES · REGAL CINEMAS · UNITED ARTISTS Theatres

Present this coupon at the Theatre Box Office to purchase up to two (2) *VIP Super Saver Admission Tickets for only $6.00 each. Upgrade to an UNRESTRICTED Premiere Super Saver Admission Ticket for only $1.50 extra per ticket.

*Surcharge may be applied if redeemed at any Manhattan, NY location. Valid at all Regal Entertainment Group locations nationwide. *VIP Super Saver Admission Ticket is not valid during the first 12 days of selected new release films.*

G173

valid anytime

Offer validity is governed by the Rules of Use and excludes defined holidays. Offers are not valid with other discount offers, unless specified.

Valid now thru November 1, 2007

---

entertainment.com — MOVIE TICKETS

REGAL ENTERTAINMENT GROUP

EDWARDS THEATRES · REGAL CINEMAS · UNITED ARTISTS Theatres

Present this coupon at the Theatre Box Office to purchase up to two (2) *VIP Super Saver Admission Tickets for only $6.00 each. Upgrade to an UNRESTRICTED Premiere Super Saver Admission Ticket for only $1.50 extra per ticket.

*Surcharge may be applied if redeemed at any Manhattan, NY location. Valid at all Regal Entertainment Group locations nationwide. *VIP Super Saver Admission Ticket is not valid during the first 12 days of selected new release films.*

G174

valid anytime

Offer validity is governed by the Rules of Use and excludes defined holidays. Offers are not valid with other discount offers, unless specified.

Valid now thru November 1, 2007

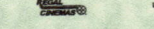

REGAL
ENTERTAINMENT
GROUP

www.REGMovies.com

00700463

Coupons void if purchased, sold or bartered.
Discounts exclude tax, tip and/or alcohol, where applicable.

REGAL
ENTERTAINMENT
GROUP

www.REGMovies.com

00700463

Coupons void if purchased, sold or bartered.
Discounts exclude tax, tip and/or alcohol, where applicable.

REGAL
ENTERTAINMENT
GROUP

www.REGMovies.com

00700463

Coupons void if purchased, sold or bartered.
Discounts exclude tax, tip and/or alcohol, where applicable.

REGAL
ENTERTAINMENT
GROUP

www.REGMovies.com

00700463

Coupons void if purchased, sold or bartered.
Discounts exclude tax, tip and/or alcohol, where applicable.

REGAL
ENTERTAINMENT
GROUP

www.REGMovies.com

00700463

REGAL
ENTERTAINMENT
GROUP

www.REGMovies.com

00700463

www.entertainment.com/tickets

Purchase movie tickets at
www.entertainment.com/tickets
or use the following forms for these theatres:

REGAL ENTERTAINMENT GROUP	amc THEATRES	CINEMARK The Best Seat in Town	NATIONAL AMUSEMENTS SHOWCASE CINEMAS cinema MULTIPLEX CINEMAS	Carmike Cinemas

AMC Theatres	Clearview Cinema	Malco Cinemas
Brenden Cinema	Consolidated Theatres	Mulone Cinema
Carmike Cinemas	Crown Theatres	National Amusements
Chakeres	Destinta Theater	Pacific Theatres
CinemaStar	Dipson Theater	Regal Entertainment Group
Cinemagic	Lockport Cinema	The Bridge
Cinemark		

- ✂

Movie Ticket Order Form

Theatre Chain and Movie Ticket Offer Experience*	Quantity		Price
AMC (Valid for up to TWELVE (12) GOLD EXPERIENCE TICKETS)	____ x $7.00 =	$ ____
AMC (Valid for up to TWELVE (12) SILVER EXPERIENCE TICKETS)	____ x $6.00 =	$ ____
AMC (Valid for up to TWELVE (12) DRINK SHOW SNACKS VOUCHERS)	____ x $2.25 =	$ ____
AMC Drink Show Snacks Vouchers are good for one small fountain drink or credit towards larger size		
AMC (Valid for up to TWELVE (12) POPCORN SHOW SNACKS VOUCHERS)	____ x $2.25 =	$ ____
AMC Popcorn Show Snacks Vouchers are good for one small popcorn or credit towards larger size		
Brenden Cinema (Valid for up to FOUR (4) ADMISSION TICKETS)	____ x $5.75 =	$ ____
Carmike (Valid for up to TWELVE (12) TICKETS)	____ x $5.50 =	$ ____
Chakeres (Valid for up to SIX (6) TICKETS)	____ x $4.50 =	$ ____
CinemaStar (Valid for an UNLIMITED NUMBER OF DISCOUNT ADMISSION TICKETS)	____ x $5.50 =	$ ____
Cinemagic (Enjoy up to FOUR (4) ADMISSIONS)	____ x $5.50 =	$ ____
Cinemark (Enjoy up to TWELVE (12) PLATINUM SUPERSAVER ADMISSION TICKETS)	____ x $6.75 =	$ ____
Cinemark Cinemas (Valid for up to TWELVE (12) CLASSIC SUPERSAVER ADMISSION TICKETS)	____ x $5.50 =	$ ____
Clearview Cinema (Valid for up to SIX (6) TICKETS)	____ x $5.00 =	$ ____
Consolidated Theatres - Hawaii (Valid for up to TWELVE (12) THEATRE ADMISSIONS)	____ x $5.75 =	$ ____
Crown Theatres (Valid for up to TWELVE (12) TICKETS)	____ x $6.50 =	$ ____
Destinta Theater (Enjoy up to SIX (6) ADMISSIONS)	____ x $5.50 =	$ ____
Dipson Theater (Valid for up to TEN (10) TICKETS)	____ x $5.50 =	$ ____
Lockport Cinema (Valid for up to EIGHT (8) TICKETS)	____ x $5.00 =	$ ____
Malco Cinemas (Enjoy up to FOUR (4) VIP TICKETS)	____ x $6.00 =	$ ____
Mulone Cinema (Enjoy up to FOUR (4) ADMISSIONS)	____ x $5.50 =	$ ____
National Amusements (Valid for up to TWELVE (12) TICKETS)	____ x $7.00 =	$ ____
Pacific Theatres (Valid for up to TWELVE (12) TICKETS)	____ x $5.50 =	$ ____
Regal/United Artists/Edwards (Valid for ONE (1) VIP SUPER SAVER)	1 x $6.00 =	$ ____
Regal/United Artists/Edwards (Valid for ONE (1) PREMIER SUPER SAVER - unrestricted ticket)	1 x $7.00 =	$ ____
Regal/United Artists/Edwards (Valid for ONE (1) ULTIMATE PREMIER MOVIE PACK - 2 unrestricted tickets and one $10 concession gift certificate)	1 x $24.00 =	$ ____
The Bridge (Philadelphia, PA) (Valid for up to TWELVE (12) TICKETS)	____ x $7.00 =	$ ____
The Bridge (Los Angeles, CA) (Valid for up to TWELVE (12) TICKETS)	____ x $9.00 =	$ ____

Subtotal $ ____
Handling $ ____
Total $ ____

*Tickets subject to surcharge in NYC Area.

Rules of Use and Order Instructions continued on back

Order Discounted Movie Tickets at www.entertainment.com/tickets

✂ -

■ Movie Ticket Rules of Use and Order Instructions ■

Movie Ticket Rules of Use:

- Mail-in Order Form is valid for redemption now through December 31, 2007. This form is not redeemable at the theatre box office.
- Ticket orders are fulfilled based on availability and prices are subject to change without notice.
- You will receive Ticket Vouchers to present at the box office for admission.
- Ticket Vouchers are not valid during the first two weeks of selected new films, special presentations and no-pass engagements; and they may contain additional restrictions and exclusions. Please read them carefully before redeeming at the box office.
- Ticket Voucher expiration dates will vary by theatre.
- Ticket Vouchers may not be exchanged, returned for refund, or resold.
- For theatre locations in your local area please consult your local newspaper.

Order Instructions:

- All checks or money orders must be made payable to: ENTERTAINMENT PUBLICATIONS, INC. Price per ticket is listed on the reverse side. Checks or money orders must include total cost of tickets ordered PLUS applicable shipping and handling charges of $2.50 for orders valued at $39.99 or less and $5.50 for orders valued at $40.00 or more. Please do not send cash.
- Mail payment and completed order forms to: Entertainment Publications, Inc., c/o Tickets, P.O. Box 539, Duncan SC 29334-5390.
- Allow three weeks for delivery of Ticket Vouchers. Please call (877) 814-5292 for orders not received within three weeks.

Name_____

Address_____

City_____ State_____ ZIP_____

Daytime Phone (_____)_____

Email Address_____

Movie Ticket Order Form

Theatre Chain and Movie Ticket Offer Experience*	Quantity		Price
AMC (Valid for up to TWELVE (12) GOLD EXPERIENCE TICKETS)	_____ x $7.00	=	$_____
AMC (Valid for up to TWELVE (12) SILVER EXPERIENCE TICKETS)	_____ x $6.00	=	$_____
AMC (Valid for up to TWELVE (12) DRINK SHOW SNACKS VOUCHERS)	_____ x $2.25	=	$_____
AMC Drink Show Snacks Vouchers are good for one small fountain drink or credit towards larger size			
AMC (Valid for up to TWELVE (12) POPCORN SHOW SNACKS VOUCHERS)	_____ x $2.25	=	$_____
AMC Popcorn Show Snacks Vouchers are good for one small popcorn or credit towards larger size			
Brenden Cinema (Valid for up to FOUR (4) ADMISSION TICKETS)	_____ x $5.75	=	$_____
Carmike (Valid for up to TWELVE (12) TICKETS)	_____ x $5.50	=	$_____
Chakeres (Valid for up to SIX (6) TICKETS)	_____ x $4.50	=	$_____
CinemaStar (Valid for an UNLIMITED NUMBER OF DISCOUNT ADMISSION TICKETS)	_____ x $5.50	=	$_____
Cinemagic (Enjoy up to FOUR (4) ADMISSIONS)	_____ x $5.50	=	$_____
Cinemark (Enjoy up to TWELVE (12) PLATINUM SUPERSAVER ADMISSION TICKETS)	_____ x $6.75	=	$_____
Cinemark (Valid for up to TWELVE (12) CLASSIC SUPERSAVER ADMISSION TICKETS)	_____ x $5.50	=	$_____
Clearview Cinema (Valid for up to SIX (6) TICKETS)	_____ x $5.00	=	$_____
Consolidated Theatres - Hawaii (Valid for up to TWELVE (12) THEATRE ADMISSIONS)	_____ x $5.75	=	$_____
Crown Theatres (Valid for up to TWELVE (12) TICKETS)	_____ x $6.50	=	$_____
Destinta Theater (Enjoy up to SIX (6) ADMISSIONS)	_____ x $5.50	=	$_____
Dipson Theater (Valid for up to TEN (10) TICKETS)	_____ x $5.50	=	$_____
Lockport Cinema (Valid for up to EIGHT (8) TICKETS)	_____ x $5.00	=	$_____
Malco Cinemas (Enjoy up to FOUR (4) VIP TICKETS)	_____ x $6.00	=	$_____
Mulone Cinema (Enjoy up to FOUR (4) ADMISSIONS)	_____ x $5.50	=	$_____
National Amusements (Valid for up to TWELVE (12) TICKETS)	_____ x $7.00	=	$_____
Pacific Theatres (Valid for up to TWELVE (12) TICKETS)	_____ x $5.50	=	$_____
Regal/United Artists/Edwards (Valid for ONE (1) VIP SUPER SAVER)	1 x $6.00	=	$_____
Regal/United Artists/Edwards (Valid for ONE (1) PREMIER SUPER SAVER - unrestricted ticket)	1 x $7.00	=	$_____
Regal/United Artists/Edwards (Valid for ONE (1) ULTIMATE PREMIER MOVIE PACK - 2 unrestricted tickets and one $10 concession gift certificate	1 x $24.00	=	$_____
The Bridge (Philadelphia, PA) (Valid for up to TWELVE (12) TICKETS)	_____ x $7.00	=	$_____
The Bridge (Los Angeles, CA) (Valid for up to TWELVE (12) TICKETS)	_____ x $9.00	=	$_____
		Subtotal	$_____
		Handling	$_____
		Total	$_____

*Tickets subject to surcharge in NYC Area.

Rules of Use and Order Instructions continued on back

Movie Ticket Order Form

Theatre Chain and Movie Ticket Offer Experience*	Quantity		Price
AMC (Valid for up to TWELVE (12) GOLD EXPERIENCE TICKETS)	_____ x $7.00	=	$_____
AMC (Valid for up to TWELVE (12) SILVER EXPERIENCE TICKETS)	_____ x $6.00	=	$_____
AMC (Valid for up to TWELVE (12) DRINK SHOW SNACKS VOUCHERS)	_____ x $2.25	=	$_____
AMC Drink Show Snacks Vouchers are good for one small fountain drink or credit towards larger size			
AMC (Valid for up to TWELVE (12) POPCORN SHOW SNACKS VOUCHERS)	_____ x $2.25	=	$_____
AMC Popcorn Show Snacks Vouchers are good for one small popcorn or credit towards larger size			
Brenden Cinema (Valid for up to FOUR (4) ADMISSION TICKETS)	_____ x $5.75	=	$_____
Carmike (Valid for up to TWELVE (12) TICKETS)	_____ x $5.50	=	$_____
Chakeres (Valid for up to SIX (6) TICKETS)	_____ x $4.50	=	$_____
CinemaStar (Valid for an UNLIMITED NUMBER OF DISCOUNT ADMISSION TICKETS)	_____ x $5.50	=	$_____
Cinemagic (Enjoy up to FOUR (4) ADMISSIONS)	_____ x $5.50	=	$_____
Cinemark (Enjoy up to TWELVE (12) PLATINUM SUPERSAVER ADMISSION TICKETS)	_____ x $6.75	=	$_____
Cinemark (Valid for up to TWELVE (12) CLASSIC SUPERSAVER ADMISSION TICKETS)	_____ x $5.50	=	$_____
Clearview Cinema (Valid for up to SIX (6) TICKETS)	_____ x $5.00	=	$_____
Consolidated Theatres - Hawaii (Valid for up to TWELVE (12) THEATRE ADMISSIONS)	_____ x $5.75	=	$_____
Crown Theatres (Valid for up to TWELVE (12) TICKETS)	_____ x $6.50	=	$_____
Destinta Theater (Enjoy up to SIX (6) ADMISSIONS)	_____ x $5.50	=	$_____
Dipson Theater (Valid for up to TEN (10) TICKETS)	_____ x $5.50	=	$_____
Lockport Cinema (Valid for up to EIGHT (8) TICKETS)	_____ x $5.00	=	$_____
Malco Cinemas (Enjoy up to FOUR (4) VIP TICKETS)	_____ x $6.00	=	$_____
Mulone Cinema (Enjoy up to FOUR (4) ADMISSIONS)	_____ x $5.50	=	$_____
National Amusements (Valid for up to TWELVE (12) TICKETS)	_____ x $7.00	=	$_____
Pacific Theatres (Valid for up to TWELVE (12) TICKETS)	_____ x $5.50	=	$_____
Regal/United Artists/Edwards (Valid for ONE (1) VIP SUPER SAVER)	1 x $6.00	=	$_____
Regal/United Artists/Edwards (Valid for ONE (1) PREMIER SUPER SAVER - unrestricted ticket)	1 x $7.00	=	$_____
Regal/United Artists/Edwards (Valid for ONE (1) ULTIMATE PREMIER MOVIE PACK - 2 unrestricted tickets and one $10 concession gift certificate	1 x $24.00	=	$_____
The Bridge (Philadelphia, PA) (Valid for up to TWELVE (12) TICKETS)	_____ x $7.00	=	$_____
The Bridge (Los Angeles, CA) (Valid for up to TWELVE (12) TICKETS)	_____ x $9.00	=	$_____
		Subtotal	$_____
		Handling	$_____
		Total	$_____

*Tickets subject to surcharge in NYC Area.

Rules of Use and Order Instructions continued on back

▪ Movie Ticket Rules of Use and Order Instructions ▪

Movie Ticket Rules of Use:

- Mail-in Order Form is valid for redemption now through December 31, 2007. This form is not redeemable at the theatre box office.
- Ticket orders are fulfilled based on availability and prices are subject to change without notice.
- You will receive Ticket Vouchers to present at the box office for admission.
- Ticket Vouchers are not valid during the first two weeks of selected new films, special presentations, and no-pass engagements; and they may contain additional restrictions and exclusions. Please read them carefully before redeeming at the box office.
- Ticket Voucher expiration dates will vary by theatre.
- Ticket Vouchers may not be exchanged, returned for refund, or resold.
- For theatre locations in your local area please consult your local newspaper.

Order Instructions:

- All checks or money orders must be made payable to: ENTERTAINMENT PUBLICATIONS, INC. Price per ticket is listed on the reverse side. Checks or money orders must include total cost of tickets ordered PLUS applicable shipping and handling charges of $2.50 for orders valued at $39.99 or less and $5.50 for orders valued at $40.00 or more. Please do not send cash.
- Mail payment and completed order forms to: Entertainment Publications, Inc., c/o Tickets, P.O. Box 539, Duncan SC 29334-5390.
- Allow three weeks for delivery of Ticket Vouchers. Please call (877) 814-5292 for orders not received within three weeks.

Name_____
Address_____
City_____ State_____ ZIP_____
Daytime Phone (_____)_____
Email Address_____

Order Discounted Movie Tickets at
www.entertainment.com/tickets

▪ Movie Ticket Rules of Use and Order Instructions ▪

Movie Ticket Rules of Use:

- Mail-in Order Form is valid for redemption now through December 31, 2007. This form is not redeemable at the theatre box office.
- Ticket orders are fulfilled based on availability and prices are subject to change without notice.
- You will receive Ticket Vouchers to present at the box office for admission.
- Ticket Vouchers are not valid during the first two weeks of selected new films, special presentations, and no-pass engagements; and they may contain additional restrictions and exclusions. Please read them carefully before redeeming at the box office.
- Ticket Voucher expiration dates will vary by theatre.
- Ticket Vouchers may not be exchanged, returned for refund, or resold.
- For theatre locations in your local area please consult your local newspaper.

Order Instructions:

- All checks or money orders must be made payable to: ENTERTAINMENT PUBLICATIONS, INC. Price per ticket is listed on the reverse side. Checks or money orders must include total cost of tickets ordered PLUS applicable shipping and handling charges of $2.50 for orders valued at $39.99 or less and $5.50 for orders valued at $40.00 or more. Please do not send cash.
- Mail payment and completed order forms to: Entertainment Publications, Inc., c/o Tickets, P.O. Box 539, Duncan SC 29334-5390.
- Allow three weeks for delivery of Ticket Vouchers. Please call (877) 814-5292 for orders not received within three weeks.

Name_____
Address_____
City_____ State_____ ZIP_____
Daytime Phone (_____)_____
Email Address_____

Order Discounted Movie Tickets at
www.entertainment.com/tickets

Out & About Index

Attractions

Minnesota

Duluth
- [kids] Carnival Thrillz G222-G223
- [kids] The Depot G245-G246
- [kids] Great Lakes Aquarium G276

Elk River
- [kids] The Depot G245-G246

Faribault
- [NEW] Faribault Family Aquatic Center G258

Saint Cloud
- [kids] Summerland G375

Scandia
- Eko Backen G252

Ontario

Ear Falls N.
- [NEW] Naughty Pines Fish Camp G329

Wisconsin

Somerset
- [kids] Apple Grand Prix G176
- [kids] River's Edge Tubing G352

Automotive

Minnesota

Forest Lake
- On Broadway Car Wash G333

Casual Dine

Minnesota

Annandale
- Fore Seasons at Southbrook Golf Club G264
- Lake Center Bar and Grill G304
- Thayer's Historic Bed n' Breakfast G379-G380

Byron
- [NEW] The Bears Den Sports Bar & Eatery G186
- [NEW] Rock 'N' Roll Pizza G356

Cannon Falls
- [NEW] Brewsters Bar & Grill G210

Carlton
- [NEW] Black Bear Grill G191

Carver
- Harvey's Bar & Grill G281

Cleveland
- Jocko's Bar & Grill G298

Cokato
- Daniel's Family Restaurant G240

Dassel
- Hojies Grill & Smokehouse G284

Delano
- Dave's Town Club G243

Duluth
- [kids] The Depot G245-G246
- Ground Round G277

Elk River
- [kids] The Depot G245-G246

Faribault
- [NEW] Banadir Restaurant G184
- Boxer's Bar & Grill G207
- [NEW] Signature Bar & Grill G363

Foley
- Mr. Jim's G327

Hastings
- RJ's Tavern on Main G347

Jordan
- Brewer's Bar & Grill of Jordan G209

Kasson
- Diggers Bar & Grill G247

Lake City
- Bronks Bar & Grill G213

Mankato
- Big Dog Sports Cafe G189
- Bobby Joe's Pub G200

Marine On Saint Croix
- Brookside Bar & Grill G214

Monticello
- [NEW] DeAngelo's G244
- Hawk's Sports Bar & Grill G282

[NEW] **New Merchants Added This Year**   [kids] **Great Place for Kids!**

OUT & ABOUT INDEX

Northfield
- J. Grundy's Rueb 'N' Stein G292

Owatonna
- Wings Tavern & Grille G394

Princeton
- Bud's Place Bar & Grill G215

Red Wing
- NEW Cheryl Ann's Bar & Grill G224

Rochester
- NEW Bon's Buffet G201
- NEW Brickyard Bar & Grille G211
- NEW Cuisine of India G237
- NEW El Carambas G253
- NEW Kabab Restaurant G300
- NEW Three Happiness G383

Saint Cloud
- Ground Round G277

Sartell
- Riverboat Depot G353

Stacy
- NEW Stacy Country Cafe G368

Sturgeon Lake
- NEW Doc's Bar & Grill G248

Taylors Falls
- Border Bar & Grill, The G205

Winsted
- Blue Note Supper Club G196

WISCONSIN

Centuria
- NEW McKenzie's Bar & Grill G323

Hudson
- Bob Smith's Sports Club G199
- NEW Stucci's Italian Food G374

FAMILY DINE

MINNESOTA

Albert Lea
- Turtle Dove Tea House & Gardens G389

Austin
- Harvest Buffet G280

- Zeppole's Pizza & Pasta G396

Cannon Falls
- Dudley's Pizza & Sandwich Shop G251
- Stone Mill Coffee House & Eatery G371

Elk River
- La Roses Pizza, Pasta & Ribs G303

Faribault
- NEW Aztlan Tortilleria Bakery & Eatery G177

Farmington
- B & B Pizza G178
- Fast Lane Pizza G262

Hutchinson
- Hutch Cafe G289

Le Sueur
- Le Sueur Diner G311

Mankato
- Choppers Bar & Grill G228

Montevideo
- Jake's Pizza G293-G294

Monticello
- Pizza Factory G342

North Branch
- Pizza Pub G343-G344

Owatonna
- Custom Coffee & Caffe G238

Pine City
- Pizza Pub G343-G344

Red Wing
- Marie's Casual Dining & Lounge G322

Rochester
- Garden Grill G268
- NEW Leo's Pizza Palace G312

Saint Cloud
- BoDiddley's Deli G198
- MC's Dugout Bar & Grill G319
- Pete's Place G341
- Zeppole's Pizza & Pasta G396

Saint Joseph
- BoDiddley's Deli G198

NEW New Merchants Added This Year   **kids** Great Place for Kids!

OUT & ABOUT INDEX

Saint Paul
    El Taquito Taco Shop Restaurant.... G254
Saint Peter
    Patrick's................ G338
Stewartville
    Sammy's G358
    Seth's Down Under Bar & Grill.... G362
Taylors Falls
    Chisago House Restaurant....... G225
Two Harbors
    The Rustic Inn............. G357
Waconia
    Island View Dining G291
Waverly
    Craig's Waverly Cafe G236
Willmar
    Jake's Pizza.......... G293-G294
    Zeppole's Pizza & Pasta........ G396
Winsted
    The Pantry G336
Wyoming
    Village Inn G392

WISCONSIN
Hudson
    Cafe' La Poste............. G221
New Richmond
    [kids] Pete's Pizza G340
River Falls
    Bo's 'N Mine............... G197
Saint Croix Falls
    Wayne's................. G393
Somerset
    Anne's Cafe G175

FINE DINE

MINNESOTA
Cannon Falls
    [NEW] Mill St. Tavern........... G324
Howard Lake
    Sunni's Grille G376

Sartell
    Blue Line Sports Bar & Grill...... G194
    G-Allen's Restaurant
      & Sports Bar............ G267

GOLF

MULTIPLE LOCATIONS
    [NEW] John Jacobs Golf Schools G299
IOWA
Webster City
    Briggs Woods Golf Course....... G212
MINNESOTA
Atwater
    Island Pine Golf Club G290
Battle Lake
    Balmoral Golf Course G183
Buffalo
    Buffalo Heights Golf Course...... G218
    Golfmasters Driving Range G271
Byron
    [NEW] The Links of Byron G314
Carlton
    [NEW] Black Bear Golf Course G190
Cokato
    Cokato Town & Country Club G234
Minneapolis
    [kids] [NEW] B&V Driving Range G179
North Branch
    North Branch Golf Course....... G331
Rochester
    [NEW] Rochester Indoor Golf Dome G355
WISCONSIN
Grantsburg
    Grantsburg Municipal
      Golf Course G275
Rice Lake
    Turtleback Golf & Country Club G390

[NEW] **New Merchants Added This Year**   [kids] **Great Place for Kids!**

Out & About Index

Health & Beauty

Minnesota

Becker
- (kids) Becker Community Center G187

Hotel

Minnesota

Annandale
- Thayer's Historic Bed n' Breakfast G379-G380

Museums

Minnesota

Duluth
- (kids) Glensheen G270
- (kids) Lake Superior & Mississippi Railroad G305

Saint Cloud
- (kids) Stearns History Museum G370

Music/Books/Video

Minnesota

Buffalo
- Buffalo Books G216

Minneapolis
- (kids) Personalized Children's Books G339

Quick Service

Minnesota

Albert Lea
- Bagels & Beans G181
- Lakeside Cafe & Creamery G306

Becker
- Cafe Pawz at Becker Furniture World G220

Belle Plaine
- The Bake Shop G182

Big Lake
- Tropical Brew G388

Buffalo
- Buffalo Books & Coffee G217

Cannon Falls
- Dairy Inn G239
- Hi-Quality Bakery G283

Carver
- Lisa's Place G316

Cokato
- The Grounds G278

Cold Spring
- Bagel & Brew G180

Cottage Grove
- Emily's Bakery & Deli G255

Elk River
- Nana's Chicken G328
- (NEW) Sarpino's Pizza G359

Ellendale
- (kids) Maggio's Pizza G320

Faribault
- Javalive! Community Coffeehouse G297

Farmington
- Bugaloo's Ice Cream Shoppe G219
- Farmington Bakery G259
- The Ugly Mug G391

Forest Lake
- On Broadway-Proudly Serving Dunn Bros. Coffee G334

Hastings
- Emily's Bakery & Deli G255
- Professor Java's G346

Hutchinson
- The Coffee Company G229
- (kids) Scoop's Frozen Custard G360

Isanti
- Rendezvous Coffee Shop G348

Le Center
- Evie's Soups & More G256
- Granny's Grill G274

Loretto
- Retro Roast & Fountain G349

(NEW) **New Merchants Added This Year**   (kids) **Great Place for Kids!**

Out & About Index

Mankato
    Coffee Creek Espresso & Eatery G231
    Coffee Klatsch. G232
    Fillin' Station G263

Mantorville
    The Chocolate Shoppe. G226

Maple Plain
  (kids) (NEW) Blackwater Coffee
        Company & Cafe G193

Montevideo
    Jake's Pizza. G293-G294

New Ulm
    Bookshelves & Coffeecups. G204
    Larkspur Market G308
    Three Sisters Tea Room G384

North Branch
    Koep's Village Bakery. G302
  (kids) O'Fudge Deli & Coffee. G332

Northfield
    James Gang
        Coffeehouse & Eatery G295
    Tacoasis G377

Red Wing
    Blue Moon. G195
    Good Life Nutrition Juice
        & Smoothie Bar G272
    Tale of Two Sisters Tea Room
        & Gift Shoppe G378

Rochester
  (NEW) The Chocolate Twist G227
    Coffee Mouse G233
    Double Click Coffee G249

Rockford
    Gathering Grounds G269

Rogers
    House of Beans G286

Rosemount
    Morning Glory's Bakery Cafe G325

Saint Cloud
    Java Joint G296
    Maid-Rite G321
    Serendipity G361

Saint Peter
    River Rock Coffee G351

Sartell
    Liquid Assets G315

Wabasha
  (kids) Papa Tronnio's Pizza G337

Waseca
    State Street Bistro. G369

Willmar
    Jake's Pizza. G293-G294

Winona
    Winona Island Cafe G395

Zimmerman
    Rise 'n Shine Coffee & Deli G350

WISCONSIN

Ellsworth
  (kids) Hollywood Video,
        Pizza & Tanning. G285

Hudson
    Commuter's Cup. G235
  (NEW) Hudson Bagel & Coffee Co. G287
    Knoke's Confections
        & Ice Cream. G301
    Lavender Thymes. G310

New Richmond
    Bean Bag Coffeehouse G185
    Douville Bakery. G250

Osceola
    Coffee Connection. G230
    Osceola Antiques
        & Ice Cream Parlor G335

River Falls
    Lighthouse Coffee. G313

Star Prairie
    BlackWater Coffee Co.. . . . . G192

RECREATIONAL SPORTS

MINNESOTA

Andover
  (kids) Ham Lake Lanes. G279

(NEW) **New Merchants Added This Year**   (kids) **Great Place for Kids!**

Out & About Index

Dassel
    Dassel Entertainment Center G242

Elk River
   (kids) FunCity G265-G266
   (NEW) Thunder Alley Indoor Paintball G385
   (NEW) Thunder Alley Indoor Speedway. . . . G386

Faribault
   (NEW) Faribault Bowling Center G257

Farmington
   (kids) Farmington Lanes G260-G261

Le Center
    Granny's Bowl G273

Montgomery
    Pla Mor Lanes G345

New Prague
    Strike Force Bowl G373

Norwood Young America
   (kids) Lano Lanes G307

Saint Cloud
   (kids) (NEW) Laser Storm at the Skatin' Place G309
   (kids) Skatin' Place G364

Wabasha
    Riverboat Lanes G354

Wisconsin

Eau Claire
    Bowl Winkles G206

Hudson
    Hudson Bowl G288

Turtle Lake
   (kids) (NEW) Speedy's Family & Fun Center G367

Retail

Minnesota

Austin
    Bone Appetit G202

Cannon Falls
   (NEW) Stone Mill Marketplace G372

Forest Lake
   (NEW) Daniela's G241

Red Wing
   (kids) (NEW) Tickle Yer Fancy G387

Rochester
    The Mouse G326

Wisconsin

Star Prairie
    This Old Store Etc. G382

Skiing

Minnesota

Lutsen
   (kids) Lutsen Mountains G318

Nisswa
   (kids) Ski Gull G365-G366

Special Events

Other
   (kids) Nelson's Apple Farm G330

Other

    Benton Station Bar & Grill G188
    Book-ems Bar & Restaurant G203
    Brass Rail Bar & Grill G208
    Little Dandy Sports Bar G317
    The Bayou G381

Register at
entertainment.com/register
to access even more of these great savings!

(NEW) **New Merchants Added This Year**   (kids) **Great Place for Kids!**

entertainment.com
Up To $12.00 Value

Anne's Café™
Home Cooking Done Right

Enjoy one complimentary ENTREE when a second ENTREE of equal or greater value is purchased.

valid anytime

Tipping should be 15% to 20% of TOTAL bill before discount

G175

Offer validity is governed by the Rules of Use and excludes defined holidays. Offers are not valid with other discount offers, unless specified.

Valid now thru November 1, 2007

---

entertainment.com
TICKETS

Apple Grand Prix
GO CARTS

Enjoy up to three complimentary TICKETS when you purchase the SAME NUMBER of equal or greater value.

valid anytime

G176

Offer validity is governed by the Rules of Use and excludes defined holidays. Offers are not valid with other discount offers, unless specified.

Valid now thru November 1, 2007

---

entertainment.com
Up To $7.00 Value

Aztlan Tortilla Bakery & Eatery

Enjoy one complimentary MENU ITEM when a second MENU ITEM of equal or greater value is purchased.

valid anytime

Tipping should be 15% to 20% of TOTAL bill before discount

G177

Offer validity is governed by the Rules of Use and excludes defined holidays. Offers are not valid with other discount offers, unless specified.

Valid now thru November 1, 2007

---

entertainment.com
Up To $6.00 Value

B&B PIZZA

Enjoy one complimentary MENU ITEM when a second MENU ITEM of equal or greater value is purchased or for those who prefer - any one pizza at 50% off the regular price - maximum discount $6.00.

Dine in only

valid anytime

G178

Offer validity is governed by the Rules of Use and excludes defined holidays. Offers are not valid with other discount offers, unless specified.

Valid now thru November 1, 2007

---

entertainment.com
Up To $6.00 Value

B&V DRIVING RANGE

Enjoy one complimentary BUCKET OF BALLS when a second BUCKET OF BALLS of equal or greater value is purchased.

valid anytime

G179

Offer validity is governed by the Rules of Use and excludes defined holidays. Offers are not valid with other discount offers, unless specified.

Valid now thru November 1, 2007

---

entertainment.com
Up To $6.00 Value

Bagel & Brew
& Gifts

Enjoy one complimentary MENU ITEM when a second MENU ITEM of equal or greater value is purchased.

valid anytime

G180

Offer validity is governed by the Rules of Use and excludes defined holidays. Offers are not valid with other discount offers, unless specified.

Valid now thru November 1, 2007

Apple Grand Prix

- Go Carts
- Bumper boats
- Pitching machine

Hwy 35 & 64
(1 mile west of downtown)
Somerset, WI
(715) 247-5621

00002293

Anne's Cafe
Home Cooking Done Right

- Home cooking done right
- Homemade omelets & a wide variety of breakfast entrees
- Call ahead with your order & it will be ready for you when you get here
- Sandwiches, burgers & wraps
- Delicious desserts
- All your favorites-pork chops, fish, chicken & steak

260 Main St.
(downtown Somerset)
Somerset, WI
(715) 247-5240

00613503

B&B Pizza

- We're more than a pizza place
- Serving strong beer & wine

216 Elm St.
Farmington, MN
(651) 463-4733

00493206

Aztlan Tortilla Bakery & Eatery

- Authentic Mexican cuisine
- Known for the best burrito
- We make our corn tortillas fresh on site

508 Central Ave. N.
Faribault, MN
(507) 334-1872

00701487

Bagel & Brew & Gifts

- Breakfast, lunch & dinner
- Full service restaurant
- Espresso, specialty coffees, pastas, sandwiches, soups, ice cream & more
- Open 7 days a week
- Wine & beer available
- Warm & cozy atmosphere
- Unique gift items for all occasions

200 Red River Ave. S.
Cold Spring, MN
(320) 685-7876

00522613

B&V Driving Range

- Full driving range
- 9 Hole golf course
- Grass tees
- Practice greens

4155 Hwy. 101
Plymouth, MN
(763) 478-6443

00591264

entertainment.com

Bagels & Beans — Up To $5.00 Value

Enjoy one complimentary MENU ITEM when a second MENU ITEM of equal or greater value is purchased.

valid anytime

G181

Offer validity is governed by the Rules of Use and excludes defined holidays. Offers are not valid with other discount offers, unless specified.

Valid now thru November 1, 2007

---

entertainment.com

THE BAKE SHOP — Up To $5.00 Value

Enjoy any BAKED GOODS ORDER at 50% off the regular price - maximum discount $5.00.

valid anytime

G182

Offer validity is governed by the Rules of Use and excludes defined holidays. Offers are not valid with other discount offers, unless specified.

Valid now thru November 1, 2007

---

entertainment.com

BALMORAL GOLF COURSE — Up To $30.00 Value

golfbalmoral.com

Enjoy ONE GREEN FEE when THREE GREEN FEES are purchased - maximum discount $30.00.

valid anytime

G183

Offer validity is governed by the Rules of Use and excludes defined holidays. Offers are not valid with other discount offers, unless specified.

Valid now thru November 1, 2007

---

entertainment.com

BANADIR RESTAURANT — Up To $8.00 Value

Enjoy one complimentary LUNCH OR DINNER ENTREE when a second LUNCH OR DINNER ENTREE of equal or greater value is purchased.

valid anytime

Tipping should be 15% to 20% of TOTAL bill before discount

G184

Offer validity is governed by the Rules of Use and excludes defined holidays. Offers are not valid with other discount offers, unless specified.

Valid now thru November 1, 2007

---

entertainment.com

THE BEAN BAG COFFEEHOUSE — Up To $5.00 Value

Enjoy any BEVERAGE ORDER at 50% off the regular price.

valid anytime

G185

Offer validity is governed by the Rules of Use and excludes defined holidays. Offers are not valid with other discount offers, unless specified.

Valid now thru November 1, 2007

---

entertainment.com

the bears den — sports bar & eatery — Up To $10.00 Value

Enjoy one complimentary LUNCH OR DINNER ENTREE when a second LUNCH OR DINNER ENTREE of equal or greater value is purchased.

valid anytime

Tipping should be 15% to 20% of TOTAL bill before discount

G186

Offer validity is governed by the Rules of Use and excludes defined holidays. Offers are not valid with other discount offers, unless specified.

Valid now thru November 1, 2007

THE BAKE SHOP

- Thanks for letting us bake for you!
- Our specialty is our made-from-scratch fried rolls
- Cookies, muffins & bars
- Baked from scratch buns & bread
- Wedding cakes, photo cakes & cakes for all occasions
- Hours Tues.-Fri. 6 a.m.-4:30 p.m. & Sat. 6 a.m-12 p.m.

**137 N. Meridian St.
Belle Plaine, MN
(952)873-2726**

00616567

Bagels & Beans

- Wide variety of coffees
- Breakfast sandwiches
- Baked goods
- Soups & salads
- Sandwiches
- Wraps
- Party trays

**152 Bridge Ave.
Albert Lea, MN
(507)377-7517**

00584762

BANADIR RESTAURANT

- Join us for authentic African & Somalian cuisine - try something new!
- Our restaurant is in the rear of the building & the market is in front

**211 Central Ave. N.
Faribault, MN
(507)209-1624**

00701430

BALMORAL GOLF COURSE

- Beautiful 18 hole par - 72 golf course located on the south east side of Otter Tail Lake

**28294 State Hwy. 78
Battle Lake, MN
(218)367-2055**

00491746

the bears den
sports bar & eatery

- Burgers, sandwiches, entrees, etc.
- Free popcorn
- Come watch the game on any of our 5 big screen TVs
- Lunch & dinner specials
- Full bar
- Happy hour Mon.-Fri. 3 p.m.-6 p.m.

**403 Frontage Rd.
Byron, MN
(507)775-2332**

00683110

THE BEAN BAG COFFEEHOUSE

- Espresso, coffee, tea & iced beverages
- Deli lunches
- Snacks
- Breakfast specials
- Relaxing atmosphere
- Meeting rooms available

**245 B S. Knowles Ave.
New Richmond, WI
(715)246-5800**

00609836

entertainment.com

Up To $5.00 Value

BECKER COMMUNITY CENTER

Enjoy one complimentary DAILY ADMISSION when a second DAILY ADMISSION of equal or greater value is purchased.

valid anytime

G187

Offer validity is governed by the Rules of Use and excludes defined holidays. Offers are not valid with other discount offers, unless specified.

Valid now thru November 1, 2007

---

entertainment.com

Up To $6.00 Value

Benton Station
BAR & GRILL

www.bentonstationbar.com

Enjoy one complimentary LUNCH OR DINNER ENTREE when a second LUNCH OR DINNER ENTREE of equal or greater value is purchased.

Delivery excluded

valid anytime

Tipping should be 15% to 20% of TOTAL bill before discount

G188

Offer validity is governed by the Rules of Use and excludes defined holidays. Offers are not valid with other discount offers, unless specified.

Valid now thru November 1, 2007

---

entertainment.com

Up To $9.00 Value

The BIG DOG Sports Cafe

Enjoy one complimentary LUNCH OR DINNER ENTREE when a second LUNCH OR DINNER ENTREE of equal or greater value is purchased.

valid anytime

Tipping should be 15% to 20% of TOTAL bill before discount

G189

Offer validity is governed by the Rules of Use and excludes defined holidays. Offers are not valid with other discount offers, unless specified.

Valid now thru November 1, 2007

---

entertainment.com

FREE GREEN FEE

Black Bear GOLF COURSE

www.golfatthebear.com

Enjoy one complimentary GREEN FEE when a second GREEN FEE of equal or greater value is purchased.

Valid Mon.-Fri.

Golf cart required

G190

Offer validity is governed by the Rules of Use and excludes defined holidays. Offers are not valid with other discount offers, unless specified.

Valid now thru November 1, 2007

---

entertainment.com

Up To $12.00 Value

Black Bear GOLF COURSE

www.blackbearcasinohotel.com

Enjoy one complimentary ENTREE when a second ENTREE of equal or greater value is purchased.

Dine in only; Specials excluded

valid anytime

G191

Offer validity is governed by the Rules of Use and excludes defined holidays. Offers are not valid with other discount offers, unless specified.

Valid now thru November 1, 2007

---

entertainment.com

Up To $6.00 Value

Black Water COFFEE CO.

Enjoy one complimentary MENU ITEM when a second MENU ITEM of equal or greater value is purchased.

valid anytime

G192

Offer validity is governed by the Rules of Use and excludes defined holidays. Offers are not valid with other discount offers, unless specified.

Valid now thru November 1, 2007

Benton Station
BAR & GRILL

- Dine in, take out & delivery available
- Live entertainment Wed.-Sun.
- Pool, darts & games
- Limo & bus service rental

303 N. Benton Dr.
Sauk Rapids, MN
(320)252-2410

Coupons void if purchased, sold or bartered. Discounts exclude tax, tip and/or alcohol, where applicable.

00652007

BECKER COMMUNITY CENTER

- Swimming Pool
- Water slide
- Rock climbing
- Racquet ball
- Sauna & hot tub
- Fitness center

11500 Sherburne Ave
Becker, MN
(763)261-5900

Coupons void if purchased, sold or bartered. Discounts exclude tax, tip and/or alcohol, where applicable.

00522950

Black Bear GOLF COURSE

- Championship 18 hole golf course
- Tee times required
- Close enough to get away from it all...just S. of Duluth
- Driving range
- On site bar & grill
- Pro shop
- GPS on all electric carts
- Golf lessons available

1791 Hwy. 210
(20 min. S. of Duluth on I-35)
Carlton, MN
(218)878-2483

Coupons void if purchased, sold or bartered. Discounts exclude tax, tip and/or alcohol, where applicable.

00701069

BIG DOG Sports Cafe

- Open 7 days a week for lunch & dinner
- Gift certificates available
- We accept Visa, MC, Discover
- Most items available for take out

1712 Commerce Dr.
North Mankato, MN
(507)386-8463

Coupons void if purchased, sold or bartered. Discounts exclude tax, tip and/or alcohol, where applicable.

00259708

Black Water COFFEE CO.

- Fresh roasted coffee
- Soups & salads
- Desserts

301 Main St.
Star Prairie, WI
(715)248-4800

Coupons void if purchased, sold or bartered. Discounts exclude tax, tip and/or alcohol, where applicable.

00609434

Black Bear GOLF COURSE

- Stomach growling for attention? Well we know how to satisfy it
- Grab a simple snack or hunker down for a hearty feast- the Bear has what you're craving
- Located inside Black Bear Casino
- Enjoy Poker, Black Jack, slots, Bingo & pull tabs
- Sign up for our Black Bear Casino Player Club Card

1785 Hwy. 210
(located inside Black Bear Casino)
Carlton, MN
(218)878-2445

Coupons void if purchased, sold or bartered. Discounts exclude tax, tip and/or alcohol, where applicable.

00701149

entertainment.com
Up To $6.00 Value

Blackwater Coffee Company & Cafe

Enjoy one complimentary MENU ITEM when a second MENU ITEM of equal or greater value is purchased.

valid anytime

G193

Valid now thru November 1, 2007

Offer validity is governed by the Rules of Use and excludes defined holidays. Offers are not valid with other discount offers, unless specified.

---

entertainment.com
Up To $12.00 Value

BLUE LINE
SPORTS BAR & GRILL

Enjoy one complimentary DINNER ENTREE when a second DINNER ENTREE of equal or greater value is purchased.

Dine in only; Specials excluded

valid any evening
Offers not valid holidays and subject to Rules of Use
Tipping should be 15% to 20% of the total bill before discount

G194

Valid now thru November 1, 2007

Offer validity is governed by the Rules of Use and excludes defined holidays. Offers are not valid with other discount offers, unless specified.

---

entertainment.com
Up To $5.00 Value

BLUE MOON

www.bluemoonrw.com

Enjoy one complimentary MENU ITEM when a second MENU ITEM of equal or greater value is purchased.

valid anytime

G195

Valid now thru November 1, 2007

Offer validity is governed by the Rules of Use and excludes defined holidays. Offers are not valid with other discount offers, unless specified.

---

entertainment.com
Up To $10.00 Value

BLUE NOTE
OF WINSTED

Enjoy one complimentary LUNCH OR DINNER ENTREE when a second LUNCH OR DINNER ENTREE of equal or greater value is purchased.

valid anytime
Offers not valid holidays and subject to Rules of Use
Tipping should be 15% to 20% of the total bill before discount

G196

Valid now thru November 1, 2007

Offer validity is governed by the Rules of Use and excludes defined holidays. Offers are not valid with other discount offers, unless specified.

---

entertainment.com
Up To $5.00 Value

Bo's 'N Mine

Enjoy one complimentary MENU ITEM when a second MENU ITEM of equal or greater value is purchased.

valid anytime

G197

Valid now thru November 1, 2007

Offer validity is governed by the Rules of Use and excludes defined holidays. Offers are not valid with other discount offers, unless specified.

---

entertainment.com
Up To $7.00 Value

Bo Diddley's DELI

Enjoy one complimentary SANDWICH when a second SANDWICH of equal or greater value is purchased.

Party subs excluded - not valid with delivery

valid anytime

G198

Valid now thru November 1, 2007

Offer validity is governed by the Rules of Use and excludes defined holidays. Offers are not valid with other discount offers, unless specified.

BLUE LINE
SPORTS BAR & GRILL

- Located in the heart of the state of hockey
- Come watch the game on one of our many TVs while dining on delicious food from a wide variety of appetizers & sandwiches to steaks, pastas & ribs
- We have something for everyone to enjoy

1101 2nd St. S.
Sartell, MN
(320)253-7825

00634848

Blackwater Coffee Company & Cafe

- Gourmet coffees, espressos, mochas & lattes
- Deli & toasted sandwiches
- Soups & salads
- Pastries, muffins, cakes & cookies
- Smoothies, iced coffees & tea drinks
- Wi-fi

5159 US Hwy. 12
Maple Plain, MN
(763)479-1313

00687024

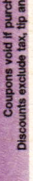

BLUE NOTE OF WINSTED

- The Blue Note is a dining experience that Winsted has enjoyed for years.
- We serve everything from hamburgers to great steak and seafood in an ultra-casual atmosphere.
- You can relax in the bar before/after dinner, and we have a ballroom available for weddings and events.
- See you at the Blue Note!

320 Third St. S
Winsted, MN
(320)485-9698

00274163

Blue Moon

- Serving great food with ambiance
- Antiques & gifts
- Live music
- Books, wine & beer

427 W. 3rd St.
Red Wing, MN
(651)385-5799

00583014

Bo Diddley's Deli

- A Relaxing Pub-like Atmosphere
- Pockets, Subs, Gyros, Beer & Wine
- Live Folk Music Concerts
- Voted Best Soup & Sandwich in Town
- Cribbage Capital of Minnesota
- 4 Area locations

6th Ave. & Division St., St. Cloud, MN
(320)255-9811

19 College Ave. N., St. Joseph, MN
(320)363-7200

00000115

Bo's 'N Mine

- Food service 11am-9pm
- Home of the Motherlode & other great burgers
- Homemade soups
- Complete sandwich menu
- Other daily specials

110 South Main Street
River Falls, WI
(715)425-9064

00000116

entertainment.com
Up To $10.00 Value

bob smith's Sports Club
"Hudson's Finest Steak House and Cocktail Lounge"
hudson, wis.

Enjoy one complimentary ENTREE when a second ENTREE of equal or greater value is purchased.

valid Saturday thru Thursday evenings
Tipping should be 15% to 20% of TOTAL bill before discount

G199

Valid now thru November 1, 2007

Offer validity is governed by the Rules of Use and excludes defined holidays. Offers are not valid with other discount offers, unless specified.

---

entertainment.com
Up To $5.00 Value

Bobby Joe's Pub

Enjoy one complimentary MENU ITEM when a second MENU ITEM of equal or greater value is purchased.

valid anytime

G200

Valid now thru November 1, 2007

Offer validity is governed by the Rules of Use and excludes defined holidays. Offers are not valid with other discount offers, unless specified.

---

entertainment.com
Up To $10.00 Value

Bon's Buffet
Mongolian Style Grill & Bar

Enjoy one complimentary LUNCH OR DINNER ENTREE when a second LUNCH OR DINNER ENTREE of equal or greater value is purchased.

valid anytime
Offers not valid holidays and subject to Rules of Use
Tipping should be 15% to 20% of the total bill before discount

G201

Valid now thru November 1, 2007

Offer validity is governed by the Rules of Use and excludes defined holidays. Offers are not valid with other discount offers, unless specified.

---

entertainment.com
Up To $25.00 Value

Bon Appétit
Canine Bakery

Enjoy 20% off the regular price of any PURCHASE (sale items excluded) - maximum discount $25.00.

valid anytime

G202

Valid now thru November 1, 2007

Offer validity is governed by the Rules of Use and excludes defined holidays. Offers are not valid with other discount offers, unless specified.

---

entertainment.com
Up To $6.00 Value

BOOK-EM'S

Enjoy one complimentary MENU ITEM when a second MENU ITEM of equal or greater value is purchased.

Dine in only

valid anytime
Tipping should be 15% to 20% of TOTAL bill before discount

G203

Valid now thru November 1, 2007

Offer validity is governed by the Rules of Use and excludes defined holidays. Offers are not valid with other discount offers, unless specified.

---

entertainment.com
Up To $5.00 Value

BOOKSHELVES & COFFEECUPS
Used Books and Espresso

Enjoy one complimentary MENU ITEM when a second MENU ITEM of equal or greater value is purchased.

valid anytime

G204

Valid now thru November 1, 2007

Offer validity is governed by the Rules of Use and excludes defined holidays. Offers are not valid with other discount offers, unless specified.

Bobby Joe's Pub

- Stop by for breakfast, lunch or dinner
- Specials & happy hour daily!

253 Belgrade
N. Mankato, MN
(507) 388-8999

Coupons void if purchased, sold or bartered. Discounts exclude tax, tip and/or alcohol, where applicable.

00080625

Bob Smith's Sports Club
"Hudson's Finest Steak House and Cocktail Lounge"
hudson, wis.

- Casual atmosphere
- Located next to the Phipps Center for the Arts
- Banquet & meeting rooms
- Sports TV, billiards, darts, lottery tickets & pull tabs
- Stop in, dine & have some fun

601 - 2nd St.
Hudson, WI
(715) 386-2962

Coupons void if purchased, sold or bartered. Discounts exclude tax, tip and/or alcohol, where applicable.

00089952

Bon Appétit
Canine Bakery

- Fresh baked dog treats
- Jewelry
- Elevated feeders
- Unique dog toys
- Gifts for dog lovers
- Clothing
- Plus much more

1211 4th St. N.W.
Austin, MN
(507) 434-5441

Coupons void if purchased, sold or bartered. Discounts exclude tax, tip and/or alcohol, where applicable.

00622878

Bon's Buffet
Mongolian Style Grill & Bar

- Buffet everyday
- Full menu
- Beer & wine available

1652 Hwy. 52 N.
Rochester, MN
(507) 281-9699

Coupons void if purchased, sold or bartered. Discounts exclude tax, tip and/or alcohol, where applicable.

00694071

BOOKSHELVES & COFFEECUPS
Used Books and Espresso

- We feature gourmet coffee, espresso, cappuccino, latte, chai & other beverages
- Bookshelves & Coffeecups has clean, quality used hard cover & paperback books
- Relax & enjoy your beverage with a book, small talk, or play a game of cribbage, chess, or backgammon

123 N. Minnesota St.
(downtown New Ulm)
New Ulm, MN
(507) 359-4600

Coupons void if purchased, sold or bartered. Discounts exclude tax, tip and/or alcohol, where applicable.

00620667

BOOK-EM'S

- Great selection of appetizers
- Sandwiches & salads
- Tacos
- Homemade pizza

823 W. St. Germain
St. Cloud, MN
(320) 259-6284

Coupons void if purchased, sold or bartered. Discounts exclude tax, tip and/or alcohol, where applicable.

00650404

Border Bar & Grill

Up To $6.00 Value

Enjoy one complimentary MENU ITEM when a second MENU ITEM of equal or greater value is purchased.

Dine in only

valid anytime

G205

Offer validity is governed by the Rules of Use and excludes defined holidays. Offers are not valid with other discount offers, unless specified.

Valid now thru November 1, 2007

BOWL Winkles
Bowling & Entertainment Center

50% OFF

Enjoy up to 4 GAMES (open bowling) at 50% off the regular price.

valid anytime

G206

Offer validity is governed by the Rules of Use and excludes defined holidays. Offers are not valid with other discount offers, unless specified.

Valid now thru November 1, 2007

BOXER'S BAR & GRILL

Up To $5.00 Value

Enjoy one complimentary MENU ITEM when a second MENU ITEM of equal or greater value is purchased.

valid anytime

G207

Offer validity is governed by the Rules of Use and excludes defined holidays. Offers are not valid with other discount offers, unless specified.

Valid now thru November 1, 2007

BRASS RAIL
BAR & GRILL

Up To $7.00 Value

Enjoy one complimentary MENU ITEM when a second MENU ITEM of equal or greater value is purchased.

valid anytime

Tipping should be 15% to 20% of TOTAL bill before discount

G208

Offer validity is governed by the Rules of Use and excludes defined holidays. Offers are not valid with other discount offers, unless specified.

Valid now thru November 1, 2007

Brewer's Bar & Grill
of Jordan

Up To $8.00 Value

Enjoy one complimentary LUNCH OR DINNER ENTREE when a second LUNCH OR DINNER ENTREE of equal or greater value is purchased.

valid anytime

G209

Offer validity is governed by the Rules of Use and excludes defined holidays. Offers are not valid with other discount offers, unless specified.

Valid now thru November 1, 2007

BREWSTERS Bar & Grill

Up To $11.00 Value

Enjoy one complimentary LUNCH OR DINNER ENTREE when a second LUNCH OR DINNER ENTREE of equal or greater value is purchased.

valid anytime

Tipping should be 15% to 20% of TOTAL bill before discount

G210

Offer validity is governed by the Rules of Use and excludes defined holidays. Offers are not valid with other discount offers, unless specified.

Valid now thru November 1, 2007

BOWL Winkles
Bowling & Entertainment Center

- 24 Lanes
- Thunder bowling
- Kid's birthday parties
- Leagues
- Game room
- Bumper bowling
- Synthetic lanes
- Company parties

1616 N. Clairemont Ave.
Eau Claire, WI
(715)552-0564

00612679

Border Bar & Grill

- Famous ground chuck "Border Burger"
- Open daily
- Families welcome
- On & off sale liquor
- Grill open 'til 12:30 a.m.

319 Bench St.
Taylors Falls, MN
(651)465-1011

00000731

BRASS RAIL
BAR & GRILL

- Happy hour Mon.-Fri. 4 p.m.-6 p.m.
- 2 For 1 every Thurs.
- Burgers, chicken & fish

101 W. Ash Ave.
Montgomery, MN
(507)364-7927

00650122

BOXER'S BAR & GRILL

429 Central Ave.
Faribault, MN
(507)334-0074

00493242

BREWSTERS
Bar & Grill

- Serving great food & drinks
- Open daily at 10 a.m.
- Entertainment on the weekends
- Pool tables, ping-pong tables & darts

115 S. 4th St.
Cannon Falls, MN
(507)263-5020

00672661

Brewer's Bar & Grill
of Jordan

- Happy hour 3 p.m.-6 p.m. & 10 p.m.-11 p.m.
- Children's menu
- 1/3 pound burgers made any way you want 'em
- Chicken sandwiches & other specialty sandwiches

350 Eldorado Dr.
Jordan, MN
(952)492-5022

00561286

entertainment.com — Up To $7.00 Value

THE BRICKYARD BAR & GRILLE

Enjoy one complimentary LUNCH OR DINNER ENTREE when a second LUNCH OR DINNER ENTREE of equal or greater value is purchased.

valid anytime

G211

Offer validity is governed by the Rules of Use and excludes defined holidays. Offers are not valid with other discount offers, unless specified.

Valid now thru November 1, 2007

---

entertainment.com — **FREE GREEN FEE**

BRIGGS WOODS GOLF COURSE

www.briggswoods.com

Enjoy one complimentary GREEN FEE when a second GREEN FEE of equal or greater value is purchased.

valid anytime

Golf cart required

G212

Offer validity is governed by the Rules of Use and excludes defined holidays. Offers are not valid with other discount offers, unless specified.

Valid now thru November 1, 2007

---

entertainment.com — Up To $8.00 Value

BRONK'S Bar and Grill
IT'S OUT OF THIS WORLD

Enjoy one complimentary LUNCH OR DINNER ENTREE when a second LUNCH OR DINNER ENTREE of equal or greater value is purchased.

valid anytime

Tipping should be 15% to 20% of TOTAL bill before discount

G213

Offer validity is governed by the Rules of Use and excludes defined holidays. Offers are not valid with other discount offers, unless specified.

Valid now thru November 1, 2007

---

entertainment.com — Up To $15.00 Value

Brookside Bar and Grill
MARINE ON ST. CROIX

Enjoy one complimentary LUNCH OR DINNER ENTREE when a second LUNCH OR DINNER ENTREE of equal or greater value is purchased.

valid anytime

Tipping should be 15% to 20% of TOTAL bill before discount

G214

Offer validity is governed by the Rules of Use and excludes defined holidays. Offers are not valid with other discount offers, unless specified.

Valid now thru November 1, 2007

---

entertainment.com — Up To $9.00 Value

Bud's Place
BAR & GRILL

Enjoy one complimentary LUNCH OR DINNER ENTREE when a second LUNCH OR DINNER ENTREE of equal or greater value is purchased.

Dine in only; Specials excluded

valid anytime

Tipping should be 15% to 20% of TOTAL bill before discount

G215

Offer validity is governed by the Rules of Use and excludes defined holidays. Offers are not valid with other discount offers, unless specified.

Valid now thru November 1, 2007

---

entertainment.com — Up To $25.00 Value

Buffalo BOOKS

Enjoy 20% off the regular price of any PURCHASE (sale items excluded) - maximum discount $25.00.

valid anytime

G216

Offer validity is governed by the Rules of Use and excludes defined holidays. Offers are not valid with other discount offers, unless specified.

Valid now thru November 1, 2007

BRIGGS WOODS GOLF COURSE

- Call ahead for reservations
- Iowa's greatest golf value
- Great course, great deal, nice people
- 18-Hole, par 72

2501 Briggs Woods Trail
Webster City, IA
(515)832-9572

00585283

Brookside Bar and Grill
MARINE ON ST. CROIX

140 Judd St.
Marine On St. Croix, MN
(651)433-5132

00613515

Buffalo BOOKS

- Featuring a wide selection of hardcover & paperback books
- Gift certificates available
- Free gift wrapping

6 Division St.
Buffalo, MN
(763)682-3147

00617522

THE BRICKYARD BAR & GRILLE

- Great appetizers
- Burgers & sandwiches
- Full bar service

1652 Hwy. 52 N.
Rochester, MN
(507)287-8736

00694120

BRONK'S Bar and Grill
IT'S OUT OF THIS WORLD

- The only smoke-free place in town where you'll find....
- Wonderful eats
- Musical beats
- Alcoholic treats
- Tues. & Thurs. 1/2 price margaritas
- Things you'll only find once in a blue moon!

101 E. Center St.
Lake City, MN
(651)345-2123

00583037

Bud's Place BAR & GRILL

- Great selection of appetizers
- Delicious burgers & sandwiches
- Salad bar
- Daily specials & happy hour
- Full bar
- Darts, pool & video games
- DJ or karaoke on weekends

2752 75th Ave.
Princeton, MN
(763)389-2153

00660979

entertainment.com — FREE MENU ITEM

Buffalo Books & Coffee

Enjoy one complimentary MENU ITEM when a second MENU ITEM of equal or greater value is purchased.

valid anytime

G217

Valid now thru November 1, 2007

Offer validity is governed by the Rules of Use and excludes defined holidays. Offers are not valid with other discount offers, unless specified.

---

entertainment.com — ONE ROUND OF GOLF

Buffalo Heights Golf Course

Enjoy one complimentary ROUND OF GOLF when a second ROUND OF GOLF of equal or greater value is purchased.

valid anytime

Please present ENTERTAINMENT® Membership Card to obtain discount. Not valid holidays & subject to Rules of Use. Not valid with other discount offers unless specified

G218

Valid now thru November 1, 2007

Offer validity is governed by the Rules of Use and excludes defined holidays. Offers are not valid with other discount offers, unless specified.

---

entertainment.com — Up To $5.00 Value

BUGALOO'S ice cream shoppe

Enjoy one complimentary MENU ITEM when a second MENU ITEM of equal or greater value is purchased.

valid anytime

G219

Valid now thru November 1, 2007

Offer validity is governed by the Rules of Use and excludes defined holidays. Offers are not valid with other discount offers, unless specified.

---

entertainment.com — Up To $8.00 Value

Café Pawz

SERVING DUNN BROS COFFEE at Becker Furniture World

www.cafepawz.com

Enjoy one complimentary MENU ITEM when a second MENU ITEM of equal or greater value is purchased.

valid anytime

G220

Valid now thru November 1, 2007

Offer validity is governed by the Rules of Use and excludes defined holidays. Offers are not valid with other discount offers, unless specified.

---

entertainment.com — Up To $7.00 Value

Café la Poste

Enjoy one complimentary MENU ITEM when a second MENU ITEM of equal or greater value is purchased.

valid anytime

Tipping should be 15% to 20% of TOTAL bill before discount

G221

Valid now thru November 1, 2007

Offer validity is governed by the Rules of Use and excludes defined holidays. Offers are not valid with other discount offers, unless specified.

---

entertainment.com — UNLIMITED RIDE PASS

THRILLZ

www.carnivalthrillz.com

Enjoy one complimentary UNLIMITED RIDE PASS when a second UNLIMITED RIDE PASS of equal or greater value is purchased.

valid anytime

G222

Valid now thru November 1, 2007

Offer validity is governed by the Rules of Use and excludes defined holidays. Offers are not valid with other discount offers, unless specified.

Buffalo Heights Golf Course

- Buffalo Heights Golf Course features a 9 hole golf course with PGA Pros on staff.
- We are open daily, April through October from 7 a.m. till 9 p.m.
- Reservations are recommended.

905 S. Hwy. 25
Buffalo, MN
(763) 682-2854

00154718

Buffalo Books & Coffee

- Best coffee in the area
- Fresh roasted coffee beans

6 Division St.
Buffalo, MN
(763) 682-3147

00616293

Café Pawz
SERVING DUNN BROS COFFEE at Becker Furniture World

- Follow your heart to Becker
- Our Cafe Pawz restaurant serves wood roasted pizzas, deli sandwiches, salads, wraps, soups & Dunn Bros coffee
- Play area with weekend supervision
- 2-Story Broyhill Showplace
- Natuzzi leather gallery
- Becker Outlet store
- Complete Thomasville store

13150 First St.
(Becker Furniture World, Hwy. 10)
Becker, MN
(763) 261-7299

00598039

BUGALOO'S ice cream shoppe

- We feature 32 flavors of hard ice cream
- Create your own ice cream sandwich
- All of our malts are made with premium ice cream & whole milk
- Gift shop
- Lunches daily - soups & delicious bread rolls

342 3rd St.
Farmington, MN
(651) 460-3085

00613668

THRILL!

- Northern Minnesota's only family entertainment center
- 50,000 Sq. feet of rides, games, food & fun
- Perfect for birthday parties, lock-ins, group outings & family events
- Rides include Laser Tag, Tilt-a-whirl, Mini-Golf, Trampoline, Spaceball, Nascar, Morphis Motion Ride & Merry Go Round
- Kiddie Land - special area for children under 54"

329 Lake Ave. S.
(Canal Park)
Duluth, MN
(218) 720-5868

00583909

Café la Poste

222 Locust St.
Hudson, WI
(715) 386-9330

00617535

entertainment.com — FREE RIDE

Thrillz

www.carnivalthrillz.com

Enjoy one complimentary RIDE when a second RIDE of equal or greater value is purchased.

valid anytime

G223

Valid now thru November 1, 2007

Offer validity is governed by the Rules of Use and excludes defined holidays. Offers are not valid with other discount offers, unless specified.

---

entertainment.com — Up To $8.00 Value

Cheryl Ann's Bar & Grill

Enjoy one complimentary LUNCH OR DINNER ENTREE when a second LUNCH OR DINNER ENTREE of equal or greater value is purchased.

valid anytime

Tipping should be 15% to 20% of TOTAL bill before discount

G224

Valid now thru November 1, 2007

Offer validity is governed by the Rules of Use and excludes defined holidays. Offers are not valid with other discount offers, unless specified.

---

entertainment.com — Up To $7.00 Value

Chisago House Restaurant

Enjoy one complimentary MENU SELECTION when a second MENU SELECTION of equal or greater value is purchased.

valid anytime excluding holidays, all you can eat buffets and daily specials

G225

Valid now thru November 1, 2007

Offer validity is governed by the Rules of Use and excludes defined holidays. Offers are not valid with other discount offers, unless specified.

---

entertainment.com — Up To $5.00 Value

The Chocolate Shoppe

Enjoy any ICE CREAM ORDER at 50% off the regular price.

valid anytime

G226

Valid now thru November 1, 2007

Offer validity is governed by the Rules of Use and excludes defined holidays. Offers are not valid with other discount offers, unless specified.

---

entertainment.com — Up To $5.00 Value

The Chocolate Twist

Enjoy one complimentary MENU ITEM when a second MENU ITEM of equal or greater value is purchased.

valid anytime

G227

Valid now thru November 1, 2007

Offer validity is governed by the Rules of Use and excludes defined holidays. Offers are not valid with other discount offers, unless specified.

---

entertainment.com — Up To $5.00 Value

Choppers Bar & Grill

Enjoy one complimentary MENU ITEM when a second MENU ITEM of equal or greater value is purchased.

valid anytime

G228

Valid now thru November 1, 2007

Offer validity is governed by the Rules of Use and excludes defined holidays. Offers are not valid with other discount offers, unless specified.

Cheryl Ann's Bar & Grill

310 Plum St.
Red Wing, MN
(651) 388-0028

Thrillz

- Northern Minnesota's only family entertainment center
- 50,000 Sq. feet of rides, games, food & fun
- Perfect for birthday parties, lock-ins, group outings & family events
- Rides include Laser Tag, Tilt-a-whirl, Mini-Golf, Trampoline, Spaceball, Nascar, Morphis Motion Ride & Merry Go Round
- Kiddie Land - special area for children under 54"

329 Lake Ave. S.
(Canal Park)
Duluth, MN
(218) 720-5868

The Chocolate Shoppe

- Ice cream
- Chocolates
- Candies

420 Main St.
Mantorville, MN
(507) 635-5814

Chisago House Restaurant

- Largest salad bar in the area
- Homemade pies & desserts
- Daily specials
- Delicious food
- Beautiful historic building
- Buffet Fri & Sat nights & all day Sun

361 Bench St.
Taylors Falls, MN
(651) 465-5245

Choppers Bar & Grill

521 S. Front St.
Mankato, MN
(507) 625-5090

The Chocolate Twist

- Fresh roasted coffee
- Premium ice cream
- Handmade chocolates
- Fine, imported chocolates & candy
- Fresh roasted nuts

104 17th Ave. N.W.
Rochester, MN
(507) 529-2922

the coffee company

entertainment.com — Up To $5.00 Value

Enjoy one complimentary MENU ITEM when a second MENU ITEM of equal or greater value is purchased.

valid anytime

G229

Valid now thru November 1, 2007

Offer validity is governed by the Rules of Use and excludes defined holidays. Offers are not valid with other discount offers, unless specified.

Coffee Connection — Osceola, WI. — Cascade Falls

entertainment.com — Up To $7.00 Value

Enjoy one complimentary MENU ITEM when a second MENU ITEM of equal or greater value is purchased.

valid anytime

G230

Valid now thru November 1, 2007

Offer validity is governed by the Rules of Use and excludes defined holidays. Offers are not valid with other discount offers, unless specified.

Coffee Creek — Espresso & Eatery

entertainment.com — Up To $5.00 Value

Enjoy one complimentary MENU ITEM when a second MENU ITEM of equal or greater value is purchased.

valid anytime

G231

Valid now thru November 1, 2007

Offer validity is governed by the Rules of Use and excludes defined holidays. Offers are not valid with other discount offers, unless specified.

Coffee Klatsch — Retail Beans · Café · Drive-Thru

entertainment.com — Up To $5.00 Value

Enjoy one complimentary MENU ITEM when a second MENU ITEM of equal or greater value is purchased.

valid anytime

G232

Valid now thru November 1, 2007

Offer validity is governed by the Rules of Use and excludes defined holidays. Offers are not valid with other discount offers, unless specified.

The Coffee Mouse

www.craftymouse.com

entertainment.com — Up To $6.00 Value

Enjoy one complimentary MENU ITEM when a second MENU ITEM of equal or greater value is purchased.

valid anytime

G233

Valid now thru November 1, 2007

Offer validity is governed by the Rules of Use and excludes defined holidays. Offers are not valid with other discount offers, unless specified.

Cokato Town & Country Club

entertainment.com — FREE GREEN FEE

Enjoy one complimentary GREEN FEE when a second GREEN FEE of equal or greater value is purchased.

valid anytime

Not valid during leagues and tournaments

G234

Valid now thru November 1, 2007

Offer validity is governed by the Rules of Use and excludes defined holidays. Offers are not valid with other discount offers, unless specified.

Coffee Connection
Osceola, WI
Cascade Falls

- Open year round
- Variety of foods, beverages, ice cream & more
- Live music Tuesdays June-August
- Friendly staff
- Enjoy sitting on our deck overlooking Cascade Falls!

107 N. Cascade St.
Osceola, WI
(715) 755-3833

the coffee company

- Gourmet coffee
- Coffee drinks, cappuccino
- Soups & sandwiches
- Pastries & delicious desserts
- Call ahead & we will prepare your drink or sandwich
- We can cater an event for you or supply an airport
- Meeting room available downtown
- Picnic lunches - basket & all!

18 Main St. S., Hutchinson, MN
(320) 587-8450
903 Hwy. 15 S., Hutchinson, MN
(320) 587-8420

Coffee Klatsch
Retail Beans · Café · Drive-Thru

- We specialize in international coffees
- World's Best Espresso...hands down!
- Sandwiches, soups
- Bars, cookies, muffins
- Perfectly prepared by our highly skilled baristas!

1625 Monks Ave.
(kitty corner from Jake's Pizza)
Mankato, MN
(507) 387-5282

Coffee Creek
Espresso & Eatery

- Espresso, coffee & smoothies
- Homemade soups & specials
- Made-to-order sandwiches

1400 Madison Ave. Ste. 604
(Madison East Center, rear entrance)
Mankato, MN
(507) 344-1441

Cokato
Town & Country Club

- 9 Holes, par 36
- 50 mi. W. on Hwy. 12 from Minneapolis
- Wed. league day
- Thurs. mornings junior golf 8 a.m.-noon

15246 U.S. Hwy. 12 W.
Cokato, MN
(320) 286-2007

The Coffee Mouse

- Soups, sandwiches & assorted bakery items
- Mary's famous homemade pies every Tues. & Thurs. - yum!
- Kathy's homemade ice cream sandwiches
- We roast our coffee beans daily
- Enjoy a gourmet coffee drink or a glass of wine
- A great place to host your next party - you pick the theme & we'll make it happen!

116 17th Ave. N.W.
(The Miracle Mile)
Rochester, MN
(507) 282-7711

entertainment.com

Up To $5.00 Value

COMMUTER'S CUP

Enjoy one complimentary MENU ITEM when a second MENU ITEM of equal or greater value is purchased.

valid anytime

G235

Offer validity is governed by the Rules of Use and excludes defined holidays. Offers are not valid with other discount offers, unless specified.

Valid now thru November 1, 2007

---

entertainment.com

Up To $8.00 Value

Craig's Waverly Cafe

Enjoy one complimentary ENTREE when a second ENTREE of equal or greater value is purchased.

Delivery excluded; Specials excluded

valid anytime

Tipping should be 15% to 20% of TOTAL bill before discount

G236

Offer validity is governed by the Rules of Use and excludes defined holidays. Offers are not valid with other discount offers, unless specified.

Valid now thru November 1, 2007

---

entertainment.com

Up To $15.00 Value

Cuisine of India

www.cuisineofindia.us

Enjoy one complimentary LUNCH OR DINNER ENTREE when a second LUNCH OR DINNER ENTREE of equal or greater value is purchased.

Dine in only

valid anytime

Offers not valid holidays and subject to Rules of Use. Tipping should be 15% to 20% of the total bill before discount

G237

Offer validity is governed by the Rules of Use and excludes defined holidays. Offers are not valid with other discount offers, unless specified.

Valid now thru November 1, 2007

---

entertainment.com

Up To $5.00 Value

Custom Coffee & Caffe

Enjoy one complimentary MENU ITEM when a second MENU ITEM of equal or greater value is purchased.

valid anytime

G238

Offer validity is governed by the Rules of Use and excludes defined holidays. Offers are not valid with other discount offers, unless specified.

Valid now thru November 1, 2007

---

entertainment.com

SANDWICH, BURGER OR HOT DOG

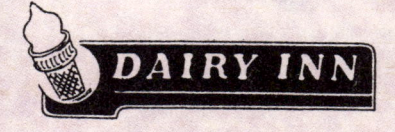

DAIRY INN

Enjoy one complimentary SANDWICH, BURGER or HOT DOG when a second SANDWICH, BURGER or HOT DOG of equal or greater value is purchased.

valid anytime

G239

Offer validity is governed by the Rules of Use and excludes defined holidays. Offers are not valid with other discount offers, unless specified.

Valid now thru November 1, 2007

---

entertainment.com

Up To $10.00 Value

Daniel's Family Restaurant

Enjoy one complimentary ENTREE when a second ENTREE of equal or greater value is purchased.

Dine in only; Specials excluded

valid anytime

Tipping should be 15% to 20% of TOTAL bill before discount

G240

Offer validity is governed by the Rules of Use and excludes defined holidays. Offers are not valid with other discount offers, unless specified.

Valid now thru November 1, 2007

Craig's
Waverly Cafe

- New menu
- Delicious homemade cooking!
- Soups, sandwiches, burgers & more
- All day breakfast
- Open early
- Dinner served Wed.-Sat.
- Catering & free local delivery

805 Pacific Ave.
(Hwy. 12)
Waverly, MN
(763) 658-6141

COMMUTER'S CUP

Plaza 94
Hudson, WI
(715) 386-9330

Custom Coffee & Caffe

- Gourmet coffee
- Espresso drinks
- Soups, salads & sandwiches
- Homemade caramel & cinnamon rolls
- Smoothies & Italian sodas
- Hours 6:30 a.m. - 5:00 p.m.

324 N. Cedar
Owatonna, MN
(507) 451-8775

Cuisine of India

- Soups & breads
- Tandoori
- Chicken, lamb & seafood specialties

7 12th St. S.E.
Rochester, MN
(507) 292-5775

Daniel's Family Restaurant

- Breakfast served all day
- Delicious appetizers and salad bar
- Salads, sandwiches, burgers, ribs, steaks & more
- Catering available
- Meeting rooms available
- Open daily

525 Cokato St. W.
(Hwy 12)
Cokato, MN
(320) 286-0007

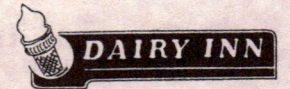

DAIRY INN

- Open year round, 10:30am daily
- Located on Hwy. 20 N., just 4 blocks north of Cannon Valley Bike Trail

1401 N. Highway 20
Cannon Falls, MN
(507) 263-4141

entertainment.com — Up To $25.00 Value

Daniela's
FOREST LAKE, MN

Enjoy 20% off the regular price of any PURCHASE (sale items excluded) - maximum discount $25.00.

valid anytime

G241

Offer validity is governed by the Rules of Use and excludes defined holidays. Offers are not valid with other discount offers, unless specified.

Valid now thru November 1, 2007

---

entertainment.com — UP TO 5 TOKENS

Dassel Entertainment Center

Enjoy UP TO 5 TOKENS at 50% off the regular price - maximum discount $5.00.

valid anytime

G242

Offer validity is governed by the Rules of Use and excludes defined holidays. Offers are not valid with other discount offers, unless specified.

Valid now thru November 1, 2007

---

entertainment.com — Up To $8.00 Value

Dave's Town Club

Enjoy one complimentary MENU ITEM when a second MENU ITEM of equal or greater value is purchased.

Dine in only; Buffet & lunch specials not included

valid anytime

Tipping should be 15% to 20% of TOTAL bill before discount

G243

Offer validity is governed by the Rules of Use and excludes defined holidays. Offers are not valid with other discount offers, unless specified.

Valid now thru November 1, 2007

---

entertainment.com — Up To $8.00 Value

DeAngelo's PIZZA & PASTA

Enjoy one complimentary DINNER ENTREE when a second DINNER ENTREE of equal or greater value is purchased or for those who prefer - any one pizza at 50% off the regular price.

Dine in only; Specials excluded

valid any evening

G244

Offer validity is governed by the Rules of Use and excludes defined holidays. Offers are not valid with other discount offers, unless specified.

Valid now thru November 1, 2007

---

entertainment.com — FREE ADMISSION

the Depot
ST. LOUIS COUNTY HERITAGE & ARTS CENTER

Enjoy one complimentary ADMISSION when a second ADMISSION of equal or greater value is purchased.

valid anytime

G245

Offer validity is governed by the Rules of Use and excludes defined holidays. Offers are not valid with other discount offers, unless specified.

Valid now thru November 1, 2007

---

entertainment.com — Up To $8.00 Value

The Depot
Elk River

Enjoy one complimentary LUNCH OR DINNER ENTREE when a second LUNCH OR DINNER ENTREE of equal or greater value is purchased.

Dine in only

valid anytime

G246

Offer validity is governed by the Rules of Use and excludes defined holidays. Offers are not valid with other discount offers, unless specified.

Valid now thru November 1, 2007

Dassel
Entertainment Center

- Batting cages
- Video rental
- Tanning
- Pizza
- Baseball equipment

640 Parker Ave.
Dassel, MN
(320)275-2916

00625050

Daniela's
FOREST LAKE, MN

- Fine chocolates from all over the world
- Truffles
- Other sweets
- Gelato
- Gifts & more

145 South Lake St.
Forest Lake, MN
(651)464-4696

00656069

DeAngelo's
PIZZA & PASTA

- All items are prepared daily in our kitchen
- 20+ Toppings & 3 crusts to choose from
- Great selection of fresh salads, homemade pastas & delicious pizza
- Enjoy our lunch buffet Wed.- Fri.
- Try our famous homemade garlic bread

9351 Cedar St.
(Hwy. 25 & School Blvd.)
Monticello, MN
(763)295-3882

00695471

DAVE'S TOWN CLUB

- Great sandwiches & burgers
- Buffet every Saturday
- Conveniently located on River St.

138 N. River St.
Delano, MN
(763)972-6815

00155797

---

the Depot
Elk River

- Homemade pizza
- Great selection of appetizers
- Flame grilled burgers
- Delicious salads & sandwiches
- Mexican entrees
- Daily happy hour & specials
- Kids menu

701 Main St.
Elk River, MN
(763)441-1371

00661118

---

the Depot
ST. LOUIS COUNTY HERITAGE & ARTS CENTER

- Train, historical & children's museums
- Art galleries & studios
- Special events
- Open daily
- Handicapped accessible

506 West Michigan Street
(Downtown Duluth)
Duluth, MN
(218)727-8025

00002211

entertainment.com — Up To $10.00 Value

Diggers Bar & Grill

Enjoy one complimentary LUNCH OR DINNER ENTREE when a second LUNCH OR DINNER ENTREE of equal or greater value is purchased.

valid anytime

G247

Valid now thru November 1, 2007

Offer validity is governed by the Rules of Use and excludes defined holidays. Offers are not valid with other discount offers, unless specified.

---

entertainment.com — Up To $8.00 Value

Doc's Sports Bar and Grill Bottle Shop

Enjoy one complimentary LUNCH OR DINNER ENTREE when a second LUNCH OR DINNER ENTREE of equal or greater value is purchased.

Dine in only

valid anytime

G248

Valid now thru November 1, 2007

Offer validity is governed by the Rules of Use and excludes defined holidays. Offers are not valid with other discount offers, unless specified.

---

entertainment.com — Up To $5.00 Value

Double Click Coffee
Rochester's Only Internet Cafe

www.doubleclickcoffee.com

Enjoy one complimentary MENU ITEM when a second MENU ITEM of equal or greater value is purchased.

valid anytime

G249

Valid now thru November 1, 2007

Offer validity is governed by the Rules of Use and excludes defined holidays. Offers are not valid with other discount offers, unless specified.

---

entertainment.com — Up To $5.00 Value

Douville Bakery

Enjoy any BAKED GOODS ORDER at 50% off the regular price.

valid anytime

G250

Valid now thru November 1, 2007

Offer validity is governed by the Rules of Use and excludes defined holidays. Offers are not valid with other discount offers, unless specified.

---

entertainment.com — 50% OFF

Dudley's Pizza and Sandwich Shop

Enjoy any one PIZZA at 50% off the regular price - maximum discount $5.00.

Dine-in or carry out

valid anytime

Tipping should be 15% to 20% of TOTAL bill before discount

G251

Valid now thru November 1, 2007

Offer validity is governed by the Rules of Use and excludes defined holidays. Offers are not valid with other discount offers, unless specified.

---

entertainment.com — FREE ADMISSION

The Call Of Eko Backen

www.ekobacken.com

Enjoy one complimentary SNO-TUBING OR WATERSLIDE ADMISSION when a second SNO-TUBING OR WATERSLIDE ADMISSION of equal or greater value is purchased.

valid anytime

G252

Valid now thru November 1, 2007

Offer validity is governed by the Rules of Use and excludes defined holidays. Offers are not valid with other discount offers, unless specified.

Doc's Sports Bar and Grill Bottle Shop

- Great selection of appetizers, sandwiches & burgers
- Delicious prime rib
- Live entertainment on Fri. & Sat.
- Happy hour Mon.-Thur.
- Best homemade chicken wild rice soup around!
- Wireless internet

34427 Majestic Pine Dr.
(Sturgeon Lake exit off I-35)
Sturgeon Lake, MN
(218)372-3040

Coupons void if purchased, sold or bartered. Discounts exclude tax, tip and/or alcohol, where applicable.

00695452

Diggers Bar & Grill

- Appetizers
- Salads
- Sandwiches
- Dinners

401 S.E. 8th St.
Kasson, MN
(507)634-7400

Coupons void if purchased, sold or bartered. Discounts exclude tax, tip and/or alcohol, where applicable.

00502605

Dowville Bakery

- Muffins
- Scones
- Cheesecakes
- Designer cakes
- Shortbread cookies
- Orange almond wedding cake
- Artisan breads
- Etcetera, etcetera, etcetera

137 S. Knowles Ave.
New Richmond, WI
(715)246-7036

Coupons void if purchased, sold or bartered. Discounts exclude tax, tip and/or alcohol, where applicable.

00609830

Double Click Coffee
Rochester's Only Internet Cafe

- Come on in to Double Click Coffee & enjoy a coffee drink while you use any of our 10 PC computers
- Located in downtown Rochester

317 S. Broadway
Rochester, MN
(507)536-0700

Coupons void if purchased, sold or bartered. Discounts exclude tax, tip and/or alcohol, where applicable.

00583078

The Call of EKO BACKEN

- Year round fun
- Great for company picnics, birthday parties & school outings
- Winter sno-tubing & summer waterslide!
- Miniature golf
- Call ahead for hours

22570 Manning Trail
Scandia, MN
(651)433-2422

Coupons void if purchased, sold or bartered. Discounts exclude tax, tip and/or alcohol, where applicable.

00000366

Dudley's Pizza and Sandwich Shop

- Dudley's features everything from soups & salads to lasagna to sandwiches & more

320 West Mill Street
Cannon Falls, MN
(507)263-4000

Coupons void if purchased, sold or bartered. Discounts exclude tax, tip and/or alcohol, where applicable.

00000284

entertainment.com — Up To $7.00 Value

EL CARAMBAS
AUTHENTIC MEXICAN FOOD

Enjoy one complimentary LUNCH OR DINNER ENTREE when a second LUNCH OR DINNER ENTREE of equal or greater value is purchased.

valid anytime

Offers not valid holidays and subject to Rules of Use. Tipping should be 15% to 20% of the total bill before discount.

G253

Valid now thru November 1, 2007

Offer validity is governed by the Rules of Use and excludes defined holidays. Offers are not valid with other discount offers, unless specified.

---

entertainment.com — Up To $9.00 Value

EL TAQUITO TACO SHOP
HOME COOKED MEXICAN TACOS

Enjoy one complimentary ENTREE when a second ENTREE of equal or greater value is purchased.

valid anytime

Tipping should be 15% to 20% of TOTAL bill before discount

G254

Valid now thru November 1, 2007

Offer validity is governed by the Rules of Use and excludes defined holidays. Offers are not valid with other discount offers, unless specified.

---

entertainment.com — Up To $5.00 Value

Emily's
BAKERY AND DELI

Enjoy one complimentary SANDWICH when a second SANDWICH of equal or greater value is purchased.

valid anytime

G255

Valid now thru November 1, 2007

Offer validity is governed by the Rules of Use and excludes defined holidays. Offers are not valid with other discount offers, unless specified.

---

entertainment.com — Up To $5.00 Value

Evie's
Soups & More

Enjoy one complimentary MENU ITEM when a second MENU ITEM of equal or greater value is purchased.

valid anytime

G256

Valid now thru November 1, 2007

Offer validity is governed by the Rules of Use and excludes defined holidays. Offers are not valid with other discount offers, unless specified.

---

entertainment.com — 50% OFF

Bashers
Sports Bar & Grill
Faribault Bowling Center

Enjoy up to 4 GAMES (open bowling) at 50% off the regular price.

valid anytime

G257

Valid now thru November 1, 2007

Offer validity is governed by the Rules of Use and excludes defined holidays. Offers are not valid with other discount offers, unless specified.

---

entertainment.com — FREE ADMISSION

Faribault Family Aquatic Center

Enjoy one complimentary ($5.00) ADMISSION when a second ($5.00) ADMISSION of equal or greater value is purchased.

valid anytime

G258

Valid now thru November 1, 2007

Offer validity is governed by the Rules of Use and excludes defined holidays. Offers are not valid with other discount offers, unless specified.

El Taquito Taco Shop
Home Cooked Mexican Tacos

- Authentic home cooked Mexican tacos
- Fajita's (beef), Al Pastor (pork chop), Chorizo (Mexican sausage), Tinga (shredded beef), Bistek Adobado (beef steak)
- Drive thru open Fri. & Sat. until 11 pm

**1434 S. Robert Street
West St. Paul, MN
(651) 455-4526**

00122897

El Carambas
Authentic Mexican Food

- Authentic Mexican food served in a festive atmosphere
- Choose from a wide variety of Mexican favorites
- Vegetarian entrees available

**1503 12th St. S.E.
Rochester, MN
(507) 281-3104**

00683182

Evie's
Soups & More

- Breakfast sandwiches
- Burgers & melts
- Panini
- Sandwiches, salads & soups
- Baked goods

**48 N. Park
Le Center, MN
(507) 357-4816**

00637356

Emily's Bakery and Deli

- Complete line of bakery products
- Homemade soups, salads & sandwiches
- Serving Hastings for over 50 years

8711 SE Point Douglas Rd *(Target Shopping Center)*, **Cottage Grove, MN
(651) 458-5075**

1212 Vermillion St *(Midtown Shopping Center)*, **Hastings, MN
(651) 437-3338**

00040582

Faribault Family Aquatic Center

- Water park open daily Memorial Day - Labor Day

**15 W. Division St.
Faribault, MN
(507) 334-2064**

00687025

Bashers Sports Bar & Grill
Faribault Bowling Center

- 16 lanes
- Thunder Alley Saturday nights
- Pro shop
- Non-smoking open bowling
- Full bar & restaurant

**1802 4th St. NW
Faribault, MN
(507) 334-3262**

00493238

entertainment.com

Up To $5.00 Value

Farmington Bakery

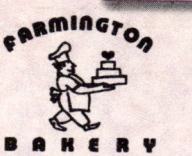

Enjoy any BAKED GOODS ORDER at 50% off the regular price.

valid anytime

G259

Offer validity is governed by the Rules of Use and excludes defined holidays. Offers are not valid with other discount offers, unless specified.

Valid now thru November 1, 2007

---

entertainment.com

50% OFF

Farmington Lanes

Enjoy UP TO 4 GAMES at 50% off the regular price.

valid anytime

G260

Offer validity is governed by the Rules of Use and excludes defined holidays. Offers are not valid with other discount offers, unless specified.

Valid now thru November 1, 2007

---

entertainment.com

50% OFF

Farmington Lanes

Enjoy UP TO 4 GAMES at 50% off the regular price.

valid anytime

G261

Offer validity is governed by the Rules of Use and excludes defined holidays. Offers are not valid with other discount offers, unless specified.

Valid now thru November 1, 2007

---

entertainment.com

Up To $6.00 Value

Fast Lane Pizza

Enjoy one complimentary LUNCH OR DINNER ENTREE when a second LUNCH OR DINNER ENTREE of equal or greater value is purchased or for those who prefer - any one pizza at 50% off the regular price - maximum discount $6.00.

valid anytime
Tipping should be 15% to 20% of TOTAL bill before discount

G262

Offer validity is governed by the Rules of Use and excludes defined holidays. Offers are not valid with other discount offers, unless specified.

Valid now thru November 1, 2007

---

entertainment.com

Up To $5.00 Value

The Fillin' Station

Enjoy one complimentary MENU ITEM when a second MENU ITEM of equal or greater value is purchased.

valid anytime

G263

Offer validity is governed by the Rules of Use and excludes defined holidays. Offers are not valid with other discount offers, unless specified.

Valid now thru November 1, 2007

---

entertainment.com

Up To $13.00 Value

Fore Seasons

www.southbrookgolf.com

Enjoy one complimentary LUNCH OR DINNER ENTREE when a second LUNCH OR DINNER ENTREE of equal or greater value is purchased.

Specials excluded

valid anytime

G264

Offer validity is governed by the Rules of Use and excludes defined holidays. Offers are not valid with other discount offers, unless specified.

Valid now thru November 1, 2007

Farmington Lanes

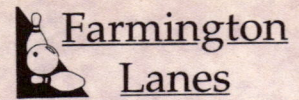

27 5th St.
Farmington, MN
(651)463-7811

00584506

Farmington Bakery

- Cookies
- Cakes for all occasions-wedding cakes
- Breads & buns
- Donuts
- Deli lunches
- Coffee
- Bars

212 Oak St.
Farmington, MN
(651)463-2242

00612535

Fast Lane Pizza

27 5th St.
Farmington, MN
(651)463-9611

00584491

Farmington Lanes

27 5th St.
Farmington, MN
(651)463-7811

00584506

Fore Seasons

- Open year round
- Sandwiches, salads, burgers, pastas, steaks
- Beautiful deck overlooking the golf course
- Check out our Southbrook golf coupon too!
- Banquet facilities

511 Morrison Ave. S.
(1 mile S.W. of Annandale)
Annandale, MN
(320)274-2341

00588805

The Fillin' Station

- Free wireless internet
- We serve a full line of fresh roasted coffees, espresso drinks, iced coffee & loose-leaf tea drinks
- Smoothies
- Muffins, pastries, cakes, cookies & bars
- Soups & sandwiches

634 S. Front St.
Mankato, MN
(507)344-0345

00637360

Coupons void if purchased, sold or bartered. Discounts exclude tax, tip and/or alcohol, where applicable.

entertainment.com

50% OFF

FunCity
Family Fun Center

Enjoy up to 4 RIDES at 50% off the regular price.

valid anytime

G265

Valid now thru November 1, 2007

Offer validity is governed by the Rules of Use and excludes defined holidays. Offers are not valid with other discount offers, unless specified.

---

entertainment.com

50% OFF

FunCity
Family Fun Center

Enjoy up to 4 ROUNDS of MINIATURE GOLF at 50% off the regular price.

valid anytime

G266

Valid now thru November 1, 2007

Offer validity is governed by the Rules of Use and excludes defined holidays. Offers are not valid with other discount offers, unless specified.

---

entertainment.com

Up To $12.00 Value

G-Allen's
RESTAURANT & SPORTS BAR

Enjoy one complimentary LUNCH OR DINNER ENTREE when a second LUNCH OR DINNER ENTREE of equal or greater value is purchased.

Dine in only; Specials excluded

valid anytime

Offers not valid holidays and subject to Rules of Use
Tipping should be 15% to 20% of the total bill before discount

G267

Valid now thru November 1, 2007

Offer validity is governed by the Rules of Use and excludes defined holidays. Offers are not valid with other discount offers, unless specified.

---

entertainment.com

Up To $13.00 Value

Garden Grill

Enjoy one complimentary DINNER ENTREE when a second DINNER ENTREE of equal or greater value is purchased.

valid any evening

G268

Valid now thru November 1, 2007

Offer validity is governed by the Rules of Use and excludes defined holidays. Offers are not valid with other discount offers, unless specified.

---

entertainment.com

50% OFF

Gathering Grounds

Enjoy any FOOD/BEVERAGE ORDER at 50% off the regular price - maximum discount $5.00.

valid anytime

G269

Valid now thru November 1, 2007

Offer validity is governed by the Rules of Use and excludes defined holidays. Offers are not valid with other discount offers, unless specified.

---

entertainment.com

GENERAL ADMISSION

Glensheen
The Historic Congdon Estate

www.d.umn.edu/glen

Enjoy one complimentary GENERAL ADMISSION when a second GENERAL ADMISSION of equal or greater value is purchased.

valid anytime

G270

Valid now thru November 1, 2007

Offer validity is governed by the Rules of Use and excludes defined holidays. Offers are not valid with other discount offers, unless specified.

FunCity Family Fun Center

- Mini Golf
- Godfather's Pizza, Nana's Chicken & Big Vinny's Subs
- Batting Cages
- Kiddie cars & bumper cars & boats
- Arcade
- Birthday party packages
- Use your Entertainment Card for 20% off future visits

9100 Park Ave.
Otsego, MN
(763) 441-8365

00524640

Coupons void if purchased, sold or bartered. Discounts exclude tax, tip and/or alcohol, where applicable.

FunCity Family Fun Center

- Mini Golf
- Godfather's Pizza, Nana's Chicken & Big Vinny's Subs
- Batting Cages
- Kiddie cars & bumper cars & boats
- Arcade
- Birthday party packages
- Use your Entertainment Card for 20% off future visits

9100 Park Ave.
Otsego, MN
(763) 441-8365

00292499

Coupons void if purchased, sold or bartered. Discounts exclude tax, tip and/or alcohol, where applicable.

Garden Grill

- Great appetizers
- Soups & salads
- Sandwiches
- Pastas & entrees
- Desserts

220 S. Broadway
Rochester, MN
(507) 288-3231

00504334

Coupons void if purchased, sold or bartered. Discounts exclude tax, tip and/or alcohol, where applicable.

G-Allen's Restaurant & Sports Bar

- We are proud to offer fine food without the stuffy atmosphere
- Our menu includes delicious pastas, fresh salads, great sandwiches, appetizers & more
- Come & relax after work at our full bar with pool, darts & games
- Children's menu available

116 Evergreen Dr.
(Hwy. 15, next to McDonalds)
Sartell, MN
(320) 230-9006

00637567

Coupons void if purchased, sold or bartered. Discounts exclude tax, tip and/or alcohol, where applicable.

Glensheen — The Historic Congdon Estate

- See the 39 room neo-jacobean estate on the shore of Lake Superior
- Minnesota's finest historic estate

3300 London Rd., Duluth, MN
(888) 454-GLEN
www.d.umn.edu/glen

00000426

Coupons void if purchased, sold or bartered. Discounts exclude tax, tip and/or alcohol, where applicable.

Gathering Grounds

- Gourmet coffee
- Espresso, cappuccino, mochas, lattes
- Fresh sandwiches

7951A Hwy. 55
Rockford, MN
(763) 477-7078

00516523

Coupons void if purchased, sold or bartered. Discounts exclude tax, tip and/or alcohol, where applicable.

entertainment.com — FREE BUCKET OF BALLS

Golfmaster Driving Range

Enjoy one complimentary BUCKET OF BALLS when a second BUCKET OF BALLS of equal or greater value is purchased.

valid anytime

G271

Offer validity is governed by the Rules of Use and excludes defined holidays. Offers are not valid with other discount offers, unless specified.

Valid now thru November 1, 2007

---

entertainment.com — Up To $5.00 Value

Good Life Nutrition

Enjoy one complimentary MENU ITEM when a second MENU ITEM of equal or greater value is purchased.

valid anytime

G272

Offer validity is governed by the Rules of Use and excludes defined holidays. Offers are not valid with other discount offers, unless specified.

Valid now thru November 1, 2007

---

entertainment.com — 50% OFF UP TO 4 LINES

Granny's Bowl

Enjoy up to 4 LINES (open bowling) at 50% off the regular price.

valid anytime

G273

Offer validity is governed by the Rules of Use and excludes defined holidays. Offers are not valid with other discount offers, unless specified.

Valid now thru November 1, 2007

---

entertainment.com — Up To $5.00 Value

Granny's Grill

Enjoy one complimentary MENU ITEM when a second MENU ITEM of equal or greater value is purchased.

valid anytime

G274

Offer validity is governed by the Rules of Use and excludes defined holidays. Offers are not valid with other discount offers, unless specified.

Valid now thru November 1, 2007

---

entertainment.com — FREE GREEN FEE

Grantsburg Municipal Golf Course

Enjoy one complimentary GREEN FEE when a second GREEN FEE of equal or greater value is purchased.

valid anytime

G275

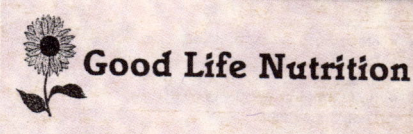

Offer validity is governed by the Rules of Use and excludes defined holidays. Offers are not valid with other discount offers, unless specified.

Valid now thru November 1, 2007

---

entertainment.com — FREE ADMISSION

Great Lakes Aquarium
Wonder. Explore. Discover.

www.glaquarium.org

Enjoy one complimentary ADMISSION when a second ADMISSION of equal or greater value is purchased.

Special events excluded

valid anytime

Not valid with any other discounts or promotions

G276

Offer validity is governed by the Rules of Use and excludes defined holidays. Offers are not valid with other discount offers, unless specified.

Valid now thru November 1, 2007

Good Life Nutrition

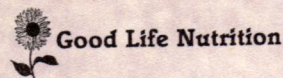

- Fresh fruit juices, delicious smoothies
- Vitamins, herbs
- Specialty foods
- Body building products
- Feng Shui items
- Bulk food

314 Main St. #316
Red Wing, MN
(651)388-8517

00468692

Golfmaster Driving Range

2561 Division St. E.
Buffalo, MN
(763)682-2842

00616370

Granny's Grill

- Great burgers & sandwiches
- Appetizers
- Daily specials Mon.-Fri.
- Soups

72 W. Minnesota St.
Le Center, MN
(507)357-2355

00637473

Granny's Bowl

- Automatic scoring
- Birthday party & group pricing available
- Arcade games & billiard table
- Bumper bowling available any time

72 W. Minnesota St.
Le Center, MN
(507)357-2355

00637450

Great Lakes Aquarium
Wonder. Explore. Discover.

- Discover freshwater fun!
- 70 species of fish & more than 30 critters
- Birthday party packages
- Gift shop on site
- Group rates & special event rates available

353 Harbor Dr.
Duluth, MN
(218)740-FISH

00540826

Grantsburg Municipal Golf Course

- Choose either 9 hole or 18 hole

333 West St. George Avenue
Grantsburg, WI
(715)463-2300

00002372

entertainment.com

Up To $10.00 Value

Ground Round Grill & Bar — EST. 1969

Enjoy one complimentary LUNCH OR DINNER ENTREE when a second LUNCH OR DINNER ENTREE of equal or greater value is purchased.

Dine in only

valid anytime

Not valid with any other discount offer
Tipping should be 15% to 20% of TOTAL bill before discount

G277

Offer validity is governed by the Rules of Use and excludes defined holidays. Offers are not valid with other discount offers, unless specified.

Valid now thru November 1, 2007

---

entertainment.com

Up To $6.00 Value

The Grounds

Enjoy one complimentary MENU ITEM when a second MENU ITEM of equal or greater value is purchased.

valid anytime

G278

Offer validity is governed by the Rules of Use and excludes defined holidays. Offers are not valid with other discount offers, unless specified.

Valid now thru November 1, 2007

---

entertainment.com

UP TO THREE LINES

Danny's — Ham Lake & Lounge

Enjoy UP TO THREE LINES of OPEN BOWLING when you purchase the SAME NUMBER at regular adult prices.

valid anytime

G279

Offer validity is governed by the Rules of Use and excludes defined holidays. Offers are not valid with other discount offers, unless specified.

Valid now thru November 1, 2007

---

entertainment.com

Up To $9.00 Value

Harvest Buffet

Enjoy one complimentary BUFFET when a second BUFFET of equal or greater value is purchased.

valid anytime

Tipping should be 15% to 20% of TOTAL bill before discount

G280

Offer validity is governed by the Rules of Use and excludes defined holidays. Offers are not valid with other discount offers, unless specified.

Valid now thru November 1, 2007

---

entertainment.com

Up To $11.00 Value

Harvey's Bar & Grill — EST 1937

Enjoy one complimentary ENTREE when a second ENTREE of equal or greater value is purchased.

valid anytime

Tipping should be 15% to 20% of TOTAL bill before discount

G281

Offer validity is governed by the Rules of Use and excludes defined holidays. Offers are not valid with other discount offers, unless specified.

Valid now thru November 1, 2007

---

entertainment.com

Up To $7.00 Value

Hawk's Sports Bar & Grill

Enjoy one complimentary LUNCH OR DINNER ENTREE when a second LUNCH OR DINNER ENTREE of equal or greater value is purchased.

Dine in only; Specials excluded

valid anytime

Tipping should be 15% to 20% of TOTAL bill before discount

G282

Offer validity is governed by the Rules of Use and excludes defined holidays. Offers are not valid with other discount offers, unless specified.

Valid now thru November 1, 2007

THE GROUNDS

- Specialty coffees
- Sandwiches, soups & salads
- Smoothies
- Ice cream
- Pastries

511 Cokato St. W.
(Hwy. 12)
Cokato, MN
(320) 286-2423

00610664

Harvest Buffet

- Breakfast, lunch & dinner
- Wide variety of items daily
- Chef carved meals
- Private meeting room available

1701 4th St. N.W.
(Inside the Holiday Inn & Conference Ctr)
Austin, MN
(507) 433-1000

00622860

Hawk's Sports Bar & Grill

- Great selection of appetizers
- Salads, sandwiches, burgers & steaks
- Kids meals
- Daily specials
- Pool, darts, volleyball & horseshoes
- Full bar

9697 Hart Blvd.
Monticello, MN
(763) 295-9990

00659147

Ground Round Grill & Bar
EST. 1969

- "Food & fun, a great time for everyone!"
- A large variety menu - steaks, seafood, pastas, Tex-Mex, sandwiches, etc.
- Daily happy hour & drink specials

2102 Maple Grove Rd., Duluth, MN
(218) 723-1776

2621 W. Division, St. Cloud, MN
(320) 252-7321

00106243

Ham Lake Lanes Lounge

- Birthday Parties
- Moonlight bowling
- Softball, volleyball & horseshoe leagues
- Bumper bowling
- Snack bar & full bar
- Bus trips to Vikings games!

16465 Highway 65 NE
Ham Lake, MN
(763) 434-6010

00077742

HARVEY'S BAR & GRILL
EST 1937

- Breakfast, lunch & dinner
- Come watch the game!
- Salads, steaks, sandwiches
- Full bar service
- Your small town bar just minutes from downtown
- 212 To Cty. Rd. 40, turn left, 1 blk. after the stop sign

220 N. Broadway
(historic Downtown Carver)
Carver, MN
(952) 448-2289

00585977

entertainment.com — Up To $5.00 Value

HI-QUALITY Bakery

Enjoy any BAKED GOODS ORDER at 50% off the regular price.

valid anytime

G283

Valid now thru November 1, 2007

Offer validity is governed by the Rules of Use and excludes defined holidays. Offers are not valid with other discount offers, unless specified.

---

entertainment.com — Up To $10.00 Value

Hojies Grill & Smoke House

Enjoy one complimentary ENTREE when a second ENTREE of equal or greater value is purchased or when dining alone - one ENTREE at 50% off the regular price - maximum discount $5.00.

valid anytime

Offers not valid holidays and subject to Rules of Use. Tipping should be 15% to 20% of the total bill before discount

G284

Valid now thru November 1, 2007

Offer validity is governed by the Rules of Use and excludes defined holidays. Offers are not valid with other discount offers, unless specified.

---

entertainment.com — 50% OFF

Hollywood Video Pizza & Tanning

Enjoy any one PIZZA at 50% off the regular price - maximum discount $7.00.

valid anytime

G285

Valid now thru November 1, 2007

Offer validity is governed by the Rules of Use and excludes defined holidays. Offers are not valid with other discount offers, unless specified.

---

entertainment.com — Up To $5.00 Value

House of Beans Coffee & Cafe

Enjoy one complimentary MENU ITEM when a second MENU ITEM of equal or greater value is purchased.

valid anytime

G286

Valid now thru November 1, 2007

Offer validity is governed by the Rules of Use and excludes defined holidays. Offers are not valid with other discount offers, unless specified.

---

entertainment.com — 50% OFF

Hudson Bagel & Coffee Co.

www.HBCC.biz

Enjoy up to TWO DOZEN BAGELS at 50% off the regular price.

valid anytime

G287

Valid now thru November 1, 2007

Offer validity is governed by the Rules of Use and excludes defined holidays. Offers are not valid with other discount offers, unless specified.

---

entertainment.com — 50% OFF

Hudson Bowl

Enjoy up to 4 GAMES (open bowling) at 50% off the regular price.

valid anytime

G288

Valid now thru November 1, 2007

Offer validity is governed by the Rules of Use and excludes defined holidays. Offers are not valid with other discount offers, unless specified.

Hojies Grill & Smoke House

- Welcome to Hojies Grill, we're glad to have you join us.
- We take pride in the food we serve, & our menu is a result of fine-tuning favorite recipes & serving foods from restaurants we've enjoyed & experienced throughout the years.
- Our "smoker" gives many of the foods we serve that unique wood-roasted flavor.
- We look forward to serving you.

841 Parker Ave.
Dassel, MN
(320)275-3885

00197755

HI-QUALITY Bakery

- We're more than just a bakery...we're a bakery tradition!
- All of our products are made from scratch
- Full line of bakery products: donuts, cookies, rolls, bread, buns & bars
- Cakes for all occasions - small cakes to large
- Beautiful wedding cakes
- Large seating area
- Open Tues.-Sat.

121 N. 4th St.
(Main St.)
Cannon Falls, MN
(507)263-2221

00583061

House of Beans Coffee & Cafe

- Specialty coffees
- Sandwiches & soups
- Pastries
- Warm friendly atmosphere
- Weekly live music
- Mon.-Fri. delivery available

12908 Main St.
Rogers, MN
(763)428-9900

00614024

Hollywood Video Pizza & Tanning

- Free lunchtime delivery 11 a.m. - 1 p.m.
- Pizza, specialty pizzas
- Wings & breadsticks

321 Main St.
Ellsworth, WI
(715)273-4383

00504031

Hudson Bowl

- 16 Lanes & bumpers available
- Karaoke Tues., Fri. & Sat.
- Full bar

1801 Ward Ave., #224
(Plaza 94)
Hudson, WI
(715)386-5121

00613646

Hudson Bagel & Coffee Co.

- Baked goods
- Wide variety of coffees
- Hot & cold sandwiches
- Soups & salads
- Great ambiance

800 Carmichael Rd.
Hudson, WI
(715)377-0938

00701075

HUTCH CAFE

Up To $4.00 Value

Enjoy one complimentary MENU ITEM when a second MENU ITEM of equal or greater value is purchased.

valid anytime
Tipping should be 15% to 20% of TOTAL bill before discount

G289

Offer validity is governed by the Rules of Use and excludes defined holidays. Offers are not valid with other discount offers, unless specified.

Valid now thru November 1, 2007

Island Pine Golf Club

Up To $23.00 Value

Enjoy one complimentary GREEN FEES when a second GREEN FEES of equal or greater value is purchased.

valid anytime

G290

Offer validity is governed by the Rules of Use and excludes defined holidays. Offers are not valid with other discount offers, unless specified.

Valid now thru November 1, 2007

Island View Dining

Up To $10.00 Value

Enjoy one complimentary ENTREE when a second ENTREE of equal or greater value is purchased.

Brunch included

valid Tuesday thru Sunday
Tipping should be 15% to 20% of TOTAL bill before discount

G291

Offer validity is governed by the Rules of Use and excludes defined holidays. Offers are not valid with other discount offers, unless specified.

Valid now thru November 1, 2007

J. Grundy's RUEB 'N' STEIN
Grueb's Restaurants, Inc

Up To $10.00 Value

www.ruebnstein.com

Enjoy one complimentary LUNCH OR DINNER ENTREE when a second LUNCH OR DINNER ENTREE of equal or greater value is purchased.

valid anytime

G292

Offer validity is governed by the Rules of Use and excludes defined holidays. Offers are not valid with other discount offers, unless specified.

Valid now thru November 1, 2007

Jake's Pizza
Willmar

Up To $5.00 Value

Enjoy one complimentary MENU ITEM when a second MENU ITEM of equal or greater value is purchased or for those who prefer - any one pizza at 50% off the regular price - maximum discount $5.00.

Dine in only; Specials excluded

valid anytime

G293

Offer validity is governed by the Rules of Use and excludes defined holidays. Offers are not valid with other discount offers, unless specified.

Valid now thru November 1, 2007

Jake's Pizza
Montevideo

Up To $6.00 Value

Enjoy one complimentary MENU ITEM when a second MENU ITEM of equal or greater value is purchased or for those who prefer - any one pizza at 50% off the regular price - maximum discount $3.00.

Dine in only

valid anytime
Tipping should be 15% to 20% of TOTAL bill before discount

G294

Offer validity is governed by the Rules of Use and excludes defined holidays. Offers are not valid with other discount offers, unless specified.

Valid now thru November 1, 2007

Island Pine Golf Club

- 18th hole Island green - par 3
- Large, rolling greens
- 40 acres of wild prairie grass
- 4 sets of tee boxes
- Driving range

1601 Wyoming Ave.
Atwater, MN
(320)974-8600

00292610

HUTCH CAFE

- We specialize in homemade soups & pies and are known for our broasted chicken
- Open Mon-Sat 6am-8pm, Sun 7am-2pm

122 S Main Street
Hutchinson, MN
(320)587-2438

00000723

J. GRUNDY'S RUEB 'N' STEIN
Grueb's Restaurants, Inc.

- Appetizers
- Great dinners
- Kid's Menu
- Pastas
- Soups & salads
- Burgers & sandwiches

503 Division St.
Northfield, MN
(507)645-6291

00493232

Island View Dining

- Sunday Brunch 10-2
- Our menu includes a great variety from Reubens to Salads to Stir-Fry
- Closed Monday

9150 Island View Rd.
(Island View Country Club)
Waconia, MN
(952)442-2956

00217798

Jake's Pizza
Montevideo

- Pizza, sandwiches, salad bar, soft drinks
- Lunch: 11am-2pm Tuesday-Saturday
- Evenings: 5-10:30pm Sun-Thurs, 5pm-12am Fri & Sat
- Party room for 70+ - call ahead
- Eat in or take out, we deliver after 5pm (dine in only with coupon)
- Conveniently located in downtown Montevideo

207 South 1st St.
Montevideo, MN
(320)269-2115

00060481

Jake's Pizza
Willmar

- Pizza sandwiches, salad bar, soft drinks
- Lunch Mon.-Fri., 11 a.m.-2 p.m.
- Evenings Sun.-Thurs., 5 p.m.-10 p.m.
- Fri. & Sat., 5 p.m.-11 p.m.
- Party room for 70+ people - call ahead
- Eat in, take out or delivery
- Dine in with coupon only

316 W. Litchfield Ave.
(Downtown Wilmar)
Wilmar, MN
(320)235-1714

00532678

James Gang Coffeehouse & Eatery

Up To $6.00 Value

www.jamesgangcoffeehouse.com

Enjoy one complimentary MENU ITEM when a second MENU ITEM of equal or greater value is purchased.

valid anytime

G295

Offer validity is governed by the Rules of Use and excludes defined holidays. Offers are not valid with other discount offers, unless specified.

Valid now thru November 1, 2007

The Java Joint

Up To $5.00 Value

Enjoy one complimentary MENU ITEM when a second MENU ITEM of equal or greater value is purchased.

valid anytime

G296

Offer validity is governed by the Rules of Use and excludes defined holidays. Offers are not valid with other discount offers, unless specified.

Valid now thru November 1, 2007

JavaLive! Community Coffeehouse

Up To $5.00 Value

Enjoy one complimentary MENU ITEM when a second MENU ITEM of equal or greater value is purchased.

valid anytime

G297

Offer validity is governed by the Rules of Use and excludes defined holidays. Offers are not valid with other discount offers, unless specified.

Valid now thru November 1, 2007

Jocko's Bar & Grill
Breakfast · Lunch · Dinner

Up To $7.00 Value

www.jockos-grill.com

Enjoy one complimentary LUNCH OR DINNER ENTREE when a second LUNCH OR DINNER ENTREE of equal or greater value is purchased or for those who prefer - any one pizza at 50% off the regular price - maximum discount $7.00.

valid anytime
Tipping should be 15% to 20% of TOTAL bill before discount

G298

Offer validity is governed by the Rules of Use and excludes defined holidays. Offers are not valid with other discount offers, unless specified.

Valid now thru November 1, 2007

John Jacobs' Golf Schools
The World Leader In Golf Instruction

Up To $25.00 Value

www.jacobsgolf.com

Enjoy 20% off one COMMUTER GOLF SCHOOL - maximum discount $25.00.

valid anytime

Mail coupon to Jacob's Golf Group at time of booking; For up to 2 students in same session

G299

Offer validity is governed by the Rules of Use and excludes defined holidays. Offers are not valid with other discount offers, unless specified.

Valid now thru November 1, 2007

Kabab Restaurant

Up To $9.00 Value

Enjoy one complimentary LUNCH OR DINNER ENTREE when a second LUNCH OR DINNER ENTREE of equal or greater value is purchased.

valid anytime
Tipping should be 15% to 20% of TOTAL bill before discount

G300

Offer validity is governed by the Rules of Use and excludes defined holidays. Offers are not valid with other discount offers, unless specified.

Valid now thru November 1, 2007

the java joint

- The original coffee house of St. Cloud
- Gourmet espresso drinks
- Teas
- Italian sodas
- Homemade baked goods
- Soups
- Internet
- Live music Fri. & Sat.

710 W. St. Germain
St. Cloud, MN
(320)656-5990

00650620

James Gang Coffeehouse & Eatery

- Come sit by the fire & enjoy coffee roasted on-site daily
- Relaxed family-friendly atmosphere
- Homemade soups, salads & sandwiches
- Freshly baked muffins, scones & desserts

2018 Jefferson Rd., Ste H
Northfield, MN
(507)663-6060

00617872

Jocko's Bar & Grill
Breakfast · Lunch · Dinner

- Breakfast, lunch & dinner
- Daily lunch specials
- Homemade soups & a variety of burgers & sandwich baskets
- Fri. night special, shrimp & fish
- Sat. night special, prime rib & pork rib
- Homemade pizza

325 Broadway
Cleveland, MN
(507)931-6637

00637275

JavaLive! Community Coffeehouse

- Wide variety of coffees
- Soups, salads, sandwiches
- Desserts

313 Central Ave.
Faribault, MN
(507)333-2979

00493248

Kabab Restaurant

- Come to Kabab Restaurant for the delicious cuisine of South Asia
- Try our Tandoori Chicken or Lamb Curry
- Wide variety of entrees

125 E. Center St.
Rochester, MN
(507)288-2181

00683106

John Jacobs' Golf Schools
The World Leader In Golf Instruction

Sun Ridge Canyon Fountain Hills, AZ
Canoa Ranch Golf Course Green Valley, AZ
Red Mountain Ranch/Painted Mountain Mesa, AZ
The Legacy Phoenix, AZ
Camelback Golf Course Scottsdale, AZ
Sanctuary Golf Course Arizona
Sedona Golf Course Sedona, AZ
Hilcrest Golf Course Sun City West, AZ
Indian Palms Country Club Indio, CA
Chardonnay Golf Course Napa, CA
Marriott's Desert Springs Resort Palm Desert, CA
Poppy Hills Golf Course Pebble Beach, CA
Riverwalk Golf Course San Diego, CA
Stevinson Golf Course Stevinson, CA
Sol Vista Golf Course Granby, CO
Inverrary Country Club Fort Lauderdale, FL
Lely Resort Naples, FL
Whisper Creek Golf Course Huntley, IL
Oak Terrace Resort Pana, IL
Brooks Golf Course Okoooji, IA
Tan-Tar-A Resort Golf Course & Spa Osage Beach, MI
Saint Croix Nat'l Golf Course St. Paul, MN
Stallion Mountain Country Club Las Vegas, NV
Scotland Run Golf Course Williamstown, NJ
Peek 'n' Peak Resort Findley Lake, NY
Pinewild Country Club Pinehurst, NC
Woodlake Resort & Golf Course Vass, NC
Hershey Golf Course Hershey, PN
Hidden Cypress Golf Course Hilton Head, SC
Rancho Viejo Rancho Viejo, TX
River Crossing Golf Course San Antonio, TX
Lake Lawn Resort Delavan, WI
The Okanagan Golf Course Kelowna, British Columbia

00511657

entertainment.com — Up To $5.00 Value

Knoke's Confections
a simply scrumptious experience

Enjoy any ICE CREAM ORDER at 50% off the regular price.

valid anytime

G301

Offer validity is governed by the Rules of Use and excludes defined holidays. Offers are not valid with other discount offers, unless specified.

Valid now thru November 1, 2007

---

entertainment.com — 50% OFF

KOEP'S VILLAGE BAKERY

Enjoy any BAKED GOODS ORDER at 50% off the regular price - maximum discount $3.00.

valid anytime

Please present coupon when order is placed

G302

Offer validity is governed by the Rules of Use and excludes defined holidays. Offers are not valid with other discount offers, unless specified.

Valid now thru November 1, 2007

entertainment.com — Up To $6.00 Value

LaRose's

Enjoy one complimentary MENU ITEM when a second MENU ITEM of equal or greater value is purchased or for those who prefer - any one pizza at 50% off the regular price.

Specials excluded

valid anytime

Not valid with any other discounts or promotions

G303

Offer validity is governed by the Rules of Use and excludes defined holidays. Offers are not valid with other discount offers, unless specified.

Valid now thru November 1, 2007

---

entertainment.com — Up To $5.00 Value

Lake Center Bar & Grill

Enjoy one complimentary MENU SELECTION when a second MENU SELECTION of equal or greater value is purchased or when dining alone - one MENU SELECTION at 50% off the regular price - maximum discount $3.00.

valid anytime

Tipping should be 15% to 20% of TOTAL bill before discount

G304

Offer validity is governed by the Rules of Use and excludes defined holidays. Offers are not valid with other discount offers, unless specified.

Valid now thru November 1, 2007

---

entertainment.com — FREE ADMISSION

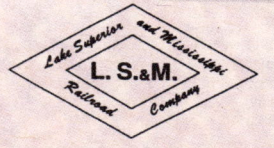

L.S.&M.
Lake Superior and Mississippi Railroad Company

www.lsmrr.org

Enjoy one complimentary ADMISSION when a second ADMISSION of equal or greater value is purchased.

valid anytime

G305

Offer validity is governed by the Rules of Use and excludes defined holidays. Offers are not valid with other discount offers, unless specified.

Valid now thru November 1, 2007

---

entertainment.com — Up To $7.00 Value

The Lakeside Cafe & Creamery

Enjoy one complimentary MENU ITEM when a second MENU ITEM of equal or greater value is purchased.

valid anytime

G306

Offer validity is governed by the Rules of Use and excludes defined holidays. Offers are not valid with other discount offers, unless specified.

Valid now thru November 1, 2007

KOEP'S VILLAGE BAKERY

- Come see our large variety of daily sweets & specials
- Remember our sandwiches for your lunches!
- Open Mon.-Fri. 6 a.m.-5 p.m., Sat. 6 a.m.-12 p.m., closed Sunday

**6372 Main St.
North Branch, MN
(651)674-4800**

00000719

Lake Center Bar & Grill

- Great food, fun times
- Outside seating
- Between Annandale & Clearwater
- Summer hrs. Mon-Thurs 11am-1am; Winter hrs. Mon 4pm-1am, Tue-Sun 11am-1am

**10480 Hwy. 24 N. E.
Annandale, MN
(320)274-5400**

00000799

The Lakeside Cafe & Creamery

- Espresso drinks
- 12 Flavors of hard ice cream
- Deli sandwiches
- 4 Soups daily
- Boxed lunches
- Patio seating

**408 Bridge Ave.
Albert Lea, MN
(507)377-2233**

00701478

Knoke's Confections
a simply scrumptious experience

- Handmade chocolates
- Fudge
- 150+ bulk candies
- Peanut brittle
- Hand-packed ice cream

**216 Locust St.
(Downtown Hudson - Locust St. off 2nd St.)
Hudson, WI
(715)381-9866**

00527052

LaRoses

- Home made pizzas with 3 sizes, 3 crusts & 13 toppings to choose from
- 19 pastas, appetizers, salads, broasted chicken, ribs & more
- Saturday night buffet
- Family owned & operated
- Dine in, carry out, delivery & catering
- Nightly specials

**508 Freeport Ave.
(next to the Elk River Movie Theater)
Elk River, MN
(763)441-3000**

00515376

L. S. M. Lake Superior and Mississippi Railroad Company

- 12 mile ride
- Beautiful scenery
- Vintage railroad cars
- Summer & Fall weekends
- 10:30 a.m. & 1:30 p.m.

**Fremont St.
Duluth, MN
(218)624-7549**

00529161

entertainment.com — UP TO THREE LINES

Lano Lanes

Enjoy up to THREE LINES OF OPEN BOWLING when you purchase the SAME NUMBER at regular adult prices.

valid anytime

G307

Valid now thru November 1, 2007

Offer validity is governed by the Rules of Use and excludes defined holidays. Offers are not valid with other discount offers, unless specified.

---

entertainment.com — Up To $5.00 Value

Larkspur MARKET

www.larkspurmarket.com

Enjoy one complimentary MENU ITEM when a second MENU ITEM of equal or greater value is purchased.

valid anytime

G308

Valid now thru November 1, 2007

Offer validity is governed by the Rules of Use and excludes defined holidays. Offers are not valid with other discount offers, unless specified.

---

entertainment.com — GAME PASS

LASER STORM — The Live-Action Laser Battle...

If you see the light, you're already dead!

Enjoy one complimentary GAME PASS when a second GAME PASS of equal or greater value is purchased.

valid anytime

G309

Valid now thru November 1, 2007

Offer validity is governed by the Rules of Use and excludes defined holidays. Offers are not valid with other discount offers, unless specified.

---

entertainment.com — Up To $5.00 Value

lavender thymes
BATH • HOME • CULINARY PROVISIONS

espresso bar • comfortable clothing

Enjoy any BEVERAGE ORDER at 50% off the regular price.

valid anytime

G310

Valid now thru November 1, 2007

Offer validity is governed by the Rules of Use and excludes defined holidays. Offers are not valid with other discount offers, unless specified.

---

entertainment.com — Up To $6.00 Value

Le Sueur DINER

www.lesueurdiner.com

Enjoy one complimentary MENU ITEM when a second MENU ITEM of equal or greater value is purchased.

valid anytime

Tipping should be 15% to 20% of TOTAL bill before discount

G311

Valid now thru November 1, 2007

Offer validity is governed by the Rules of Use and excludes defined holidays. Offers are not valid with other discount offers, unless specified.

---

entertainment.com — FREE PIZZA

LEO'S PIZZA PALACE

Enjoy any one complimentary PIZZA when a second PIZZA of equal or greater value is purchased.

valid anytime

G312

Valid now thru November 1, 2007

Offer validity is governed by the Rules of Use and excludes defined holidays. Offers are not valid with other discount offers, unless specified.

Larkspur MARKET

- Each day our staff prepares delicious soups, salads, sandwiches & amazing desserts
- We have a passion for preparing the perfect cup of coffee
- Larkspur is well known for its unique array of unusual gifts & ornaments
- Laughing at the ornaments & the cards is encouraged, especially with your friends

16 N. Minnesota St.
(downtown New Ulm)
New Ulm, MN
(507)359-2500

00620056

Lano Lanes

Hwy 212
Norwood, MN
(952)467-3500

00049246

lavender thymes
BATH • HOME • CULINARY PROVISIONS
espresso bar • comfortable clothing

- Unpredictable clothes, shoes & jewelry
- Homewares
- Bath luxuries
- Full espresso menu, whole beans

512 2nd St.
(Downtown Hudson)
Hudson, WI
(715)386-3866

00527073

LASER STORM — The Live-Action Laser Battle...

- The live-action laser battle
- "If you see the light, you're already dead"

3302 Southway Ind. Drive
St. Cloud, MN
(320)252-9768

00057678

Leo's Pizza Palace

- Pizza, breadsticks & salads
- Arcade games
- Ticket redemption games
- Prize redemption
- Birthday parties
- Kids play area
- Budweiser products

2280 Superior Dr. N.W.
Rochester, MN
(507)424-3711

00694658

Le Sueur DINER

- Family owned & operated
- Home cooked meals in a family-friendly environment
- Catering for business or private events

201 Valleygreen Sq.
Le Sueur, MN
(507)665-2080

00637298

entertainment.com — Up To $5.00 Value

Lighthouse Coffee

Enjoy one complimentary MENU ITEM when a second MENU ITEM of equal or greater value is purchased.

valid anytime

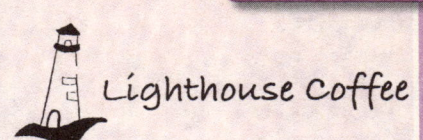

G313

Offer validity is governed by the Rules of Use and excludes defined holidays. Offers are not valid with other discount offers, unless specified.

Valid now thru November 1, 2007

---

entertainment.com — FREE GREEN FEE

The Links of Byron
Family Golf Center

Enjoy one complimentary GREEN FEE when a second GREEN FEE of equal or greater value is purchased.

valid anytime

G314

Offer validity is governed by the Rules of Use and excludes defined holidays. Offers are not valid with other discount offers, unless specified.

Valid now thru November 1, 2007

---

entertainment.com — Up To $6.00 Value

LIQUID ASSETS
COFFEE, SOUP & WINE BAR

Enjoy one complimentary MENU ITEM when a second MENU ITEM of equal or greater value is purchased.

valid anytime
Tipping should be 15% to 20% of TOTAL bill before discount

G315

Offer validity is governed by the Rules of Use and excludes defined holidays. Offers are not valid with other discount offers, unless specified.

Valid now thru November 1, 2007

---

entertainment.com — Up To $5.00 Value

Lisa's Place

Enjoy one complimentary MENU ITEM when a second MENU ITEM of equal or greater value is purchased.

valid anytime

G316

Offer validity is governed by the Rules of Use and excludes defined holidays. Offers are not valid with other discount offers, unless specified.

Valid now thru November 1, 2007

---

entertainment.com — Up To $7.00 Value

Little Dandy Sports Bar

Enjoy one complimentary LUNCH OR DINNER ENTREE when a second LUNCH OR DINNER ENTREE of equal or greater value is purchased.

Dine in only

valid anytime
Tipping should be 15% to 20% of TOTAL bill before discount

G317

Offer validity is governed by the Rules of Use and excludes defined holidays. Offers are not valid with other discount offers, unless specified.

Valid now thru November 1, 2007

---

entertainment.com — ALPINE SLIDE RIDE

LUTSEN mountains

www.lutsen.com

Enjoy one complimentary SINGLE ALPINE SLIDE RIDE when a second SINGLE ALPINE SLIDE RIDE of equal or greater value is purchased.

valid anytime

G318

Offer validity is governed by the Rules of Use and excludes defined holidays. Offers are not valid with other discount offers, unless specified.

Valid now thru November 1, 2007

The Links of Byron
Family Golf Center

- 9 Hole executive course
- 18 Hole championship miniature golf
- Driving range
- Group & private instruction

222 Second Ave. S.W.
Byron, MN
(507)775-2004

00694132

Lighthouse Coffee

- Coffee & tea
- Sandwiches
- Treats
- Casual, relaxed atmosphere

208 N. Main
River Falls, WI
(715)426-9392

00496643

Lisa's Place

- Open daily
- Great burgers & appetizers
- Live entertainment & karaoke
- Happy hour 3 p.m.-6 p.m. Mon.-Fri.

205 Broadway St. N.
Carver, MN
(952)448-7622

00585972

LIQUID ASSETS
COFFEE, SOUP & WINE BAR

- Gourmet espresso drinks & teas
- Sandwiches & panini
- Soups
- Muffins, scones & more
- Smoothies
- Upscale, warm environment
- Meetings
- Box lunches & catering
- Beer & wine available

1091 2nd St. # 600
(at 2nd St. S.)
Sartell, MN
(320)230-5201

00634865

LUTSEN mountains

- Ride to the highest vistas on the North Shore
- Fun for the whole family

On Lake Superior North Shore
Lutsen, MN
(218)663-7281

00532104

Little Dandy Sports Bar

- Private party room available

1070 E. Derrynane
Le Center, MN
(507)357-6062

00650230

Mc's Dugout Bar and Grill

entertainment.com — Up To $6.00 Value

Enjoy one complimentary ENTREE when a second ENTREE of equal or greater value is purchased.

valid anytime
Tipping should be 15% to 20% of TOTAL bill before discount

G319

Valid now thru November 1, 2007

Offer validity is governed by the Rules of Use and excludes defined holidays. Offers are not valid with other discount offers, unless specified.

Maggio's Pizza

entertainment.com — 50% OFF

Enjoy any one PIZZA at 50% off the regular price.
Dine-in or carry out

valid anytime

G320

Valid now thru November 1, 2007

Offer validity is governed by the Rules of Use and excludes defined holidays. Offers are not valid with other discount offers, unless specified.

Maid-Rite

entertainment.com — FREE SANDWICH

EAT MAID-RITE SINCE 1926

Enjoy one complimentary SANDWICH when a second SANDWICH of equal or greater value is purchased.
Delivery excluded; Specials excluded

valid anytime

G321

Valid now thru November 1, 2007

Offer validity is governed by the Rules of Use and excludes defined holidays. Offers are not valid with other discount offers, unless specified.

Marie's Casual Dining & Lounge

entertainment.com — Up To $7.00 Value

Enjoy one complimentary MENU ITEM when a second MENU ITEM of equal or greater value is purchased.

valid anytime excluding holidays, all you can eat buffet & daily specials
Tipping should be 15% to 20% of TOTAL bill before discount

G322

Valid now thru November 1, 2007

Offer validity is governed by the Rules of Use and excludes defined holidays. Offers are not valid with other discount offers, unless specified.

McKenzie's Bar & Grill

entertainment.com — Up To $7.00 Value

Enjoy one complimentary LUNCH OR DINNER ENTREE when a second LUNCH OR DINNER ENTREE of equal or greater value is purchased or for those who prefer - any one pizza at 50% off the regular price - maximum discount $7.00.

valid anytime

G323

Valid now thru November 1, 2007

Offer validity is governed by the Rules of Use and excludes defined holidays. Offers are not valid with other discount offers, unless specified.

Mill St Tavern

entertainment.com — Up To $12.00 Value

MILL ST · · · · ESTABLISHED 1998 · · · · TAVERN

Enjoy one complimentary LUNCH OR DINNER ENTREE when a second LUNCH OR DINNER ENTREE of equal or greater value is purchased.

valid anytime
Tipping should be 15% to 20% of TOTAL bill before discount

G324

Valid now thru November 1, 2007

Offer validity is governed by the Rules of Use and excludes defined holidays. Offers are not valid with other discount offers, unless specified.

Maggio's Pizza

- Mouth-watering gourmet pizzas baked in real stone hearth ovens
- Fresh & tasty vegetables used
- Smoke-free
- Bring in the family for dinner & watch your favorite show!
- Closed Mondays

301 5th Ave.
(between Albert Lea & Owatonna, 1.5 mi. west of 35WS)
Ellendale, MN
(507) 688-1050

00584263

Mc's Dugout
Bar and Grill

- Variety of salads, burgers, sandwiches & appetizers
- Full bar - great food & great fun!

501 W. Saint Germain St.
St. Cloud, MN
(320) 259-9862

00259858

Marie's
Casual Dining & Lounge

- Quality weeknight dining
- Wide variety of cocktails & refreshments
- Famous Friday Fish Fry & complete buffet
- Lunch served every day - eat in or take out
- Hours: Mon. - Sat. 11 a.m. - 9 p.m., closed Sunday

217 Plum St.
(Hwy 63 at the Armory Center, Downtown Red Wing)
Red Wing, MN
(651) 388-1896

00250191

EAT Maid-Rite
SINCE 1926

3267 Roosevelt Rd.
St. Cloud, MN
(320) 251-8895

00636070

MILL ST TAVERN
.... ESTABLISHED 1998 ....

- A short drive from The Cities, Cannon Falls is a quaint town with many offerings
- Visit Mill St. Tavern & enjoy our cool atmosphere
- Famous for our ribs
- Enjoy full bar service with happy hour from 3:30-5:30 p.m.
- Party specials
- Banquet facilities available

410 W. Mill St.
Cannon Falls, MN
(507) 263-9429

00672629

McKenzie's Bar & Grill

- Burgers & sandwiches
- Full bar
- Homemade "Uncle D's" pizza
- All our soup is homemade

75 State Hwy. 35
(inside McKenzie Lanes)
Centuria, WI
(715) 646-2228

00671966

entertainment.com — Up To $5.00 Value

Morning Glory's Bakery Cafe

Enjoy one complimentary MENU ITEM when a second MENU ITEM of equal or greater value is purchased.

valid anytime

G325

Offer validity is governed by the Rules of Use and excludes defined holidays. Offers are not valid with other discount offers, unless specified.

Valid now thru November 1, 2007

---

entertainment.com — Up To $25.00 Value

The Mouse

Enjoy 20% off the regular price of any PURCHASE (sale items excluded) - maximum discount $25.00.

valid anytime

G326

Offer validity is governed by the Rules of Use and excludes defined holidays. Offers are not valid with other discount offers, unless specified.

Valid now thru November 1, 2007

---

entertainment.com — Up To $5.00 Value

Mr. Jim's Food & Liquor

Enjoy one complimentary ENTREE when a second ENTREE of equal or greater value is purchased or when dining alone - one ENTREE at 50% off the regular price - maximum discount $3.00.

valid anytime

Tipping should be 15% to 20% of TOTAL bill before discount

G327

Offer validity is governed by the Rules of Use and excludes defined holidays. Offers are not valid with other discount offers, unless specified.

Valid now thru November 1, 2007

---

entertainment.com — Up To $5.00 Value

Nana's Chicken

Enjoy one complimentary MENU ITEM when a second MENU ITEM of equal or greater value is purchased.

valid anytime

G328

Offer validity is governed by the Rules of Use and excludes defined holidays. Offers are not valid with other discount offers, unless specified.

Valid now thru November 1, 2007

---

entertainment.com — UP TO $600.00

Naughty Pines Fish Camp

Enjoy one complimentary FISHING TRIP when a second FISHING TRIP of equal or greater value is purchased.

valid anytime

Surcharge applicable - $75 for all guests; Operating season - mid May thru mid October

G329

Offer validity is governed by the Rules of Use and excludes defined holidays. Offers are not valid with other discount offers, unless specified.

Valid now thru November 1, 2007

entertainment.com — APPLES

Nelson's Apple Farm
APPLES · BEDDING PLANTS · CHRISTMAS TREES

Enjoy 5 lbs. of FREE pick your own apples when you pick a second 5 lbs. of apples at regular price.

Offer not good towards other volume discounts or sale prices

valid during apple season

G330

Offer validity is governed by the Rules of Use and excludes defined holidays. Offers are not valid with other discount offers, unless specified.

Valid now thru November 1, 2007

The Mouse

- Mon.-Fri. 10 a.m.-9 p.m.; Sat. 10 a.m.-5p.m., Sun. 1 p.m.-5 p.m.
- Look for our extended holiday hours
- Unique gifts, candles, jewelry, gourmet & pantry dishes & fun cards
- Scrapbooking, stamping & card-making center
- Seasonal decor
- Red Hat society
- Visit our coffee shop

116 17th Ave. N.W.
(Miracle Mile Min. Mall)
Rochester, MN
(507)282-7711

00599665

Morning Glory's Bakery Cafe

- Gourmet coffee & tea
- Fresh muffins, scones, bars, cookies & other fabulous desserts
- Soups, salads & sandwiches
- Box lunches

14590 S. Robert Trail
Rosemount, MN
(651)322-1411

00283126

Nana's Chicken

- Nana's tender, juicy Broasted Chicken comes in convenient dinner packs along with delicious, home-styled side dishes
- Order by the piece to feed any crowd
- Stop in for a meal, take it home or have it delivered today

9100 Park Ave.
Otsego, MN
(763)241-9000

00524916

Mr. Jim's Food & Liquor

- Serving lunch weekdays at 11am
- Catering for weddings, class reunions or any special occasion

840 Hwy. 23
(on Hwy. 23, 6 blocks east of Hwy. 25, P.O. Box 668)
Foley, MN
(320)968-7543

00080642

Nelson's Apple Farm
APPLES • BEDDING PLANTS • CHRISTMAS TREES

- 23 varieties
- Farm animals
- Corn maze
- Mon.-Sat. 10 a.m.-6 p.m. & Sun. 1 p.m.-6 p.m.
- Start picking around Sept. 1 - call 461-3355

3270 Douglas Ave., Webster, MN
(952)461-3355 (I-35 south to Elko exit, west 2 mi. to Co. Rd. 91, south 2 mi. to Co. Rd. 86, then west 3/4 mi.)

00002306

Naughty Pines Fish Camp

- 7 day - 6 night cabin stays on world famous English River
- You will enjoy world class wilderness fishing & good times
- Canadian Walleye & Northern Pike, trophy Muskie & small-mouth fishing
- Boat & outboard motor rental included & insured
- Live bait for great fishing included

Wegg Lake, English River System
Ear Falls N., ON
(218)732-9385

00366581

entertainment.com

FREE GREEN FEE

North Branch Golf Course

Enjoy one complimentary GREEN FEE when a second GREEN FEE of equal or greater value is purchased.

valid anytime

G331

Valid now thru November 1, 2007

Offer validity is governed by the Rules of Use and excludes defined holidays. Offers are not valid with other discount offers, unless specified.

---

entertainment.com

Up To $5.00 Value

O'Fudge
Deli & Coffee

Enjoy one complimentary MENU ITEM when a second MENU ITEM of equal or greater value is purchased.

valid anytime

G332

Valid now thru November 1, 2007

Offer validity is governed by the Rules of Use and excludes defined holidays. Offers are not valid with other discount offers, unless specified.

---

entertainment.com

50% OFF

On Broadway Car Wash

Enjoy one ULTIMATE CAR WASH at 50% off the regular price.

valid anytime

G333

Valid now thru November 1, 2007

Offer validity is governed by the Rules of Use and excludes defined holidays. Offers are not valid with other discount offers, unless specified.

---

entertainment.com

Up To $5.00 Value

On Broadway Car Wash
Proudly Serving DUNN BROS COFFEE

Enjoy one complimentary MENU ITEM when a second MENU ITEM of equal or greater value is purchased.

valid anytime

G334

Valid now thru November 1, 2007

Offer validity is governed by the Rules of Use and excludes defined holidays. Offers are not valid with other discount offers, unless specified.

---

entertainment.com

Up To $5.00 Value

Osceola Antiques & Ice Cream Parlor

Enjoy one complimentary MENU ITEM when a second MENU ITEM of equal or greater value is purchased.

valid anytime

G335

Valid now thru November 1, 2007

Offer validity is governed by the Rules of Use and excludes defined holidays. Offers are not valid with other discount offers, unless specified.

---

entertainment.com

Up To $6.00 Value

THE PANTRY

Enjoy one complimentary ENTREE when a second ENTREE of equal or greater value is purchased.

Dine in only; Specials excluded

valid anytime
Tipping should be 15% to 20% of TOTAL bill before discount

G336

Valid now thru November 1, 2007

Offer validity is governed by the Rules of Use and excludes defined holidays. Offers are not valid with other discount offers, unless specified.

O'Fudge
Deli & Coffee

- Fresh, homemade fudge & candy
- Soups, sandwiches & salads
- Specialty coffee & smoothies
- 8 Flavors of ice cream
- Credit cards accepted

38500 Tanger Dr.
(Tanger Outlet Ctr.)
North Branch, MN
(651) 237-0706

Coupons void if purchased, sold or bartered. Discounts exclude tax, tip and/or alcohol, where applicable.

00573451

North Branch Golf Course

- 9 Hole, par 35
- Pro shop
- Snacks
- Challenging for all skill levels

38585 Forest Blvd.
(Old Hwy. 61/County Rd. 30)
North Branch, MN
(651) 674-9989

Coupons void if purchased, sold or bartered. Discounts exclude tax, tip and/or alcohol, where applicable.

00661001

On Broadway Car Wash
Proudly Serving Dunn Bros Coffee

- Drive thru
- Espresso
- Latte
- Pastries
- Coffee beans by the pound
- Chai tea
- Hours: Mon.-Fri. 7 a.m.-8 p.m., Sat. 8 a.m.-5 p.m., Sun. 9 a.m.-5 p.m.

955 W. Broadway
Forest Lake, MN
(651) 464-7001

Coupons void if purchased, sold or bartered. Discounts exclude tax, tip and/or alcohol, where applicable.

00527062

On Broadway Car Wash

- Soft cloth car wash
- Exterior wash only
- Coin operated vacuums
- Hours: Mon.-Fri. 7 a.m.-8 p.m., Sat. 8 a.m.-5 p.m., & Sun. 9 a.m.-5 p.m.

955 W. Broadway
Forest Lake, MN
(651) 464-7001

Coupons void if purchased, sold or bartered. Discounts exclude tax, tip and/or alcohol, where applicable.

00540896

THE PANTRY

- Breakfast, lunch & dinner served all day
- Tue.-Fri. lunch buffet
- Sun. breakfast buffet
- Delicious salads, sandwiches, burgers & more!
- Carry out orders available
- Open daily

121 2nd St. S.
Winsted, MN
(320) 485-4818

Coupons void if purchased, sold or bartered. Discounts exclude tax, tip and/or alcohol, where applicable.

00624887

Osceola Antiques & Ice Cream Parlor

- Kemps Supreme ice-cream
- Sandwiches, soups & salads
- Pastries
- N.W. Wisconsin's largest antique mall

117 Cascade St.
Osceola, WI
(715) 294-2886

Coupons void if purchased, sold or bartered. Discounts exclude tax, tip and/or alcohol, where applicable.

00609092

entertainment.com — 50% OFF

Papa Fronnie's Restaurant

Enjoy any one PIZZA at 50% off the regular price.

Dine in only

valid anytime

G337

Valid now thru November 1, 2007

Offer validity is governed by the Rules of Use and excludes defined holidays. Offers are not valid with other discount offers, unless specified.

---

entertainment.com — Up To $10.00 Value

Patrick's

Enjoy one complimentary LUNCH OR DINNER ENTREE when a second LUNCH OR DINNER ENTREE of equal or greater value is purchased.

valid anytime

Tipping should be 15% to 20% of TOTAL bill before discount

G338

Valid now thru November 1, 2007

Offer validity is governed by the Rules of Use and excludes defined holidays. Offers are not valid with other discount offers, unless specified.

---

entertainment.com — 25% OFF

Personalized Children's Books

Enjoy 25% off the regular price of any one PERSONALIZED CHILDREN'S BOOK.

valid anytime

G339

Valid now thru November 1, 2007

Offer validity is governed by the Rules of Use and excludes defined holidays. Offers are not valid with other discount offers, unless specified.

entertainment.com — Up To $7.00 Value

Pete's Pizza — EAT IN or TAKE OUT

Enjoy one complimentary MENU ITEM when a second MENU ITEM of equal or greater value is purchased or for those who prefer - any one LARGE at 50% off the regular price.

Sorry, no delivery with coupon

valid anytime

Tipping should be 15% to 20% of TOTAL bill before discount

G340

Valid now thru November 1, 2007

Offer validity is governed by the Rules of Use and excludes defined holidays. Offers are not valid with other discount offers, unless specified.

---

entertainment.com — Up To $8.00 Value

Pete's Place "HOME COOKING"

Enjoy one complimentary MENU ITEM when a second MENU ITEM of equal or greater value is purchased.

valid anytime

Tipping should be 15% to 20% of TOTAL bill before discount

G341

Valid now thru November 1, 2007

Offer validity is governed by the Rules of Use and excludes defined holidays. Offers are not valid with other discount offers, unless specified.

entertainment.com — 50% OFF

Pizza Factory

Enjoy any one PIZZA at 50% off the regular price - maximum discount $6.00.

Dine in only

valid anytime

One coupon per visit

G342

Valid now thru November 1, 2007

Offer validity is governed by the Rules of Use and excludes defined holidays. Offers are not valid with other discount offers, unless specified.

Patrick's

- World Famous Patty Melt
- Full bar service
- Hours: lunch 11am-4pm, dinner 4pm-10pm, Fri & Sat kitchen is open untill midnight
- Happy Hour 3pm-6pm
- Great food, good times & 16 taps

125 S. 3rd St.
St. Peter, MN
(507)931-9051

00474630

Pete's Pizza
EAT IN or TAKE OUT

- Pizza
- Subs
- Burgers
- Chicken
- Kids' menu
- Buffet

1230 North Knowles Avenue
New Richmond, WI
(715)246-2633

00002383

Pizza Factory

- Geared for perfect pizza

208 South Highway 25
(Just N. of 94 on Hwy. 25 at Broadway)
Monticello, MN
(763)295-5656

00002385

Papa Tronnie's Restaurant

- Full menu
- Sunday brunch
- Infamous pizza

218 Second St. W.
Wabasha, MN
(651)565-2626

00582421

Personalized Children's Books

- Make Your Child A Star
- Each storybook is personalized throughout with your child's name and other important information
- Call for the latest price listings

4513 - 14th Ave. S
Minneapolis, MN
(612)827-8168

00184780

Pete's Place
"HOME COOKING"

- Home cooking
- Best breakfast in town
- Burgers & sandwiches

413 9th Ave. N.
St. Cloud, MN
(320)259-6931

00636085

entertainment.com

Up To $12.00 Value

Pizza Pub
est. 1976

Enjoy any one PIZZA at 50% off the regular price - maximum discount $12.00.

Any size, any type

valid anytime

G343

Valid now thru November 1, 2007

Offer validity is governed by the Rules of Use and excludes defined holidays. Offers are not valid with other discount offers, unless specified.

---

entertainment.com

Up To $12.00 Value

Pizza Pub
est. 1976

Enjoy any one PIZZA at 50% off the regular price - maximum discount $12.00.

Any size, any type

valid anytime

G344

Valid now thru November 1, 2007

Offer validity is governed by the Rules of Use and excludes defined holidays. Offers are not valid with other discount offers, unless specified.

---

entertainment.com

50% OFF UP TO 4 GAMES

Pla Mor Lanes

Enjoy up to 4 GAMES (open bowling) at 50% off the regular price.

valid anytime

G345

Valid now thru November 1, 2007

Offer validity is governed by the Rules of Use and excludes defined holidays. Offers are not valid with other discount offers, unless specified.

---

entertainment.com

Up To $6.00 Value

PROFESSOR Java's

Enjoy one complimentary MENU ITEM when a second MENU ITEM of equal or greater value is purchased.

valid anytime

G346

Valid now thru November 1, 2007

Offer validity is governed by the Rules of Use and excludes defined holidays. Offers are not valid with other discount offers, unless specified.

---

entertainment.com

Up To $8.00 Value

RJ's Tavern on Main

Enjoy one complimentary LUNCH OR DINNER ENTREE when a second LUNCH OR DINNER ENTREE of equal or greater value is purchased.

valid anytime

G347

Valid now thru November 1, 2007

Offer validity is governed by the Rules of Use and excludes defined holidays. Offers are not valid with other discount offers, unless specified.

---

entertainment.com

FREE MENU ITEM

Rendezvous Coffee Shop

Enjoy one complimentary MENU ITEM when a second MENU ITEM of equal or greater value is purchased.

valid anytime

G348

Valid now thru November 1, 2007

Offer validity is governed by the Rules of Use and excludes defined holidays. Offers are not valid with other discount offers, unless specified.

Pizza Pub est. 1976

- Great family dining
- Enjoyable atmosphere for all
- North Branch location has fabulous antique decor & come to Pine City for a midevil adventure
- Award-winning pizza!
- Open 3 pm daily

6407 Main St., North Branch, MN
(651)674-1777

500 3rd Ave. E, Pine City, MN
(320)629-6468

00397410

Pizza Pub est. 1976

- Great family dining
- Enjoyable atmosphere for all
- North Branch location has fabulous antique decor & come to Pine City for a midevil adventure
- Award-winning pizza!
- Open 3 pm daily

6407 Main St., North Branch, MN
(651)674-1777

500 3rd Ave. E, Pine City, MN
(320)629-6468

00397410

Professor Java's

- Espresso drinks, cappucino, latte
- Deli sandwiches, soup, daily specials
- Desserts, ice cream, malts & floats
- Bulk coffee, tea & accessories
- Entertainment: Fri & Sat
- Open 7 days a week

202 E. 2nd St.
(Historic Downtown Hastings)
Hastings, MN
(651)438-9962

00143818

Pla Mor Lanes

- Automatic scoring
- Glow bowling, moonlight bowling, bumper bowling
- 8 Lanes
- Special parties welcome
- 2 Tanning beds available

314 1st St. S.
Montgomery, MN
(507)364-7762

00650229

Rendezvous Coffee Shop

- Drive-thru available
- Featuring homemade soups, sandwiches, candies & gourmet beverages
- Pastries
- Gift shop & meeting rooms
- Outdoor seating & a warm cozy atmosphere!

310 Dahlin Ave.
Isanti, MN
(763)444-3999

00610682

RJ's Tavern on Main

- Best burgers around!
- Happy hour: Mon.-Fri. 4 p.m.-6 p.m.
- Late night happy hour: Sun.-Thurs. 10 p.m.-close
- Karaoke on Wed. & Thurs.

106 2nd St. E.
(Downtown Hastings)
Hastings, MN
(651)437-8772

00549287

entertainment
entertainment.com

Up To **$5.00** Value

retro ROAST & FOUNTAIN
Generations of Fun!

Enjoy one complimentary MENU ITEM when a second MENU ITEM of equal or greater value is purchased.

valid anytime

G349

Valid now thru November 1, 2007

Offer validity is governed by the Rules of Use and excludes defined holidays. Offers are not valid with other discount offers, unless specified.

---

entertainment
entertainment.com

Up To **$5.00** Value

Rise'n Shine
Coffee & Deli

Enjoy one complimentary MENU ITEM when a second MENU ITEM of equal or greater value is purchased.

valid anytime

G350

Valid now thru November 1, 2007

Offer validity is governed by the Rules of Use and excludes defined holidays. Offers are not valid with other discount offers, unless specified.

---

entertainment
entertainment.com

Up To **$5.00** Value

RIVER ROCK coffee
ST. PETER, MN

Enjoy one complimentary MENU ITEM when a second MENU ITEM of equal or greater value is purchased.

valid anytime

G351

Valid now thru November 1, 2007

Offer validity is governed by the Rules of Use and excludes defined holidays. Offers are not valid with other discount offers, unless specified.

---

entertainment
entertainment.com

Up To **$15.00** Value

River's Edge
SOMERSET WISCONSIN

Enjoy one complimentary ALL DAY TUBING & WATERSLIDE COMBINATION TICKET when a second ALL DAY TUBING & WATERSLIDE COMBINATION TICKET of equal or greater value is purchased.

Not valid day of concert or special events

valid 7 days a week, Memorial Day thru Labor Day

G352

Valid now thru November 1, 2007

Offer validity is governed by the Rules of Use and excludes defined holidays. Offers are not valid with other discount offers, unless specified.

---

entertainment
entertainment.com

Up To **$6.00** Value

PORT OF SARTELL RIVERBOAT DEPOT
FOOD & SPIRITS

Enjoy one complimentary ENTREE when a second ENTREE of equal or greater value is purchased.

Dine in only; Specials excluded

valid anytime

Tipping should be 15% to 20% of TOTAL bill before discount

G353

Valid now thru November 1, 2007

Offer validity is governed by the Rules of Use and excludes defined holidays. Offers are not valid with other discount offers, unless specified.

---

entertainment
entertainment.com

UP TO 4 GAMES

Riverboat Lanes

Enjoy up to 4 GAMES (open bowling) at 50% off the regular price.

valid anytime

G354

Valid now thru November 1, 2007

Offer validity is governed by the Rules of Use and excludes defined holidays. Offers are not valid with other discount offers, unless specified.

Rise'n Shine Coffee & Deli

- Made to order sandwiches
- Wraps & salads with only the freshest ingredients
- Hot & cold espresso drinks, smoothies & hot & cold tea
- Try our delicious soup of the day!

12626 Fremont Ave.
Zimmerman, MN
(763)856-1122

00515380

Retro Roast & Fountain
Generations of Fun!

- Full espresso drink menu
- Drive thru
- Fresh roasted coffee for the home or office
- 50's Soda fountain ice cream and malts
- Bakery, soup, sandwiches & salads
- Free Wi-Fi

115 Railway St. W.
Loretto, MN
(763)479-1000

00579904

River's Edge
Somerset Wisconsin

Hwy. 64 east of Somerset
(River's Edge Apple River Recreation Area)
Somerset, WI
(715)247-3305

00082506

River Rock Coffee
St. Peter, MN

- Local treasure!
- Coffee, espresso & in-house bakery
- Full menu of soups, salads & sandwiches
- Try our world famous hermits!

301 S. Minnesota Ave.
(corner of Minnesota & Nassau)
St. Peter, MN
(507)931-1540

00637449

Riverboat Lanes

- 10 Lanes of bowling
- Thunder Alley
- Sports bar
- Infamous pizza

218 Second St. W.
Wabasha, MN
(651)565-2626

00586061

Riverboat Depot

- Where Good Friends Meet & Hungry Folks Eat!
- Open daily
- Great selection of appetizers
- Delicious burgers, sandwiches, chicken & fish
- Breakfast Sat. & Sun. 8 a.m.-11 a.m.
- Full bar
- Darts & pool

2 Riverside Ave. N.
Sartell, MN
(320)656-1150

00661201

FREE BUCKET OF BALLS

Rochester Indoor Golf Center

Enjoy one complimentary BUCKET OF BALLS when a second BUCKET OF BALLS of equal or greater value is purchased.

valid anytime

G355

Valid now thru November 1, 2007

Offer validity is governed by the Rules of Use and excludes defined holidays. Offers are not valid with other discount offers, unless specified.

FREE PIZZA

ROCK 'N' ROLL PIZZA

Enjoy any one complimentary PIZZA when a second PIZZA of equal or greater value is purchased.

Dine-in or carry out

valid anytime

Offers not valid holidays and subject to Rules of Use
Tipping should be 15% to 20% of the total bill before discount

G356

Valid now thru November 1, 2007

Offer validity is governed by the Rules of Use and excludes defined holidays. Offers are not valid with other discount offers, unless specified.

Up To $11.00 Value

THE RUSTIC INN

www.rusticinncafe.com

Enjoy one complimentary LUNCH OR DINNER ENTREE when a second LUNCH OR DINNER ENTREE of equal or greater value is purchased.

valid anytime

Offers not valid holidays and subject to Rules of Use
Tipping should be 15% to 20% of the total bill before discount

G357

Valid now thru November 1, 2007

Offer validity is governed by the Rules of Use and excludes defined holidays. Offers are not valid with other discount offers, unless specified.

Up To $6.00 Value

Sammy's

Enjoy one complimentary MENU ITEM when a second MENU ITEM of equal or greater value is purchased.

valid anytime

G358

Valid now thru November 1, 2007

Offer validity is governed by the Rules of Use and excludes defined holidays. Offers are not valid with other discount offers, unless specified.

Up To $16.00 Value

Sarpino's Pizzeria

www.sarpinos-usa.com

Enjoy any one complimentary PIZZA when a second PIZZA of equal or greater value is purchased.

Carry out only

valid anytime

G359

Valid now thru November 1, 2007

Offer validity is governed by the Rules of Use and excludes defined holidays. Offers are not valid with other discount offers, unless specified.

Up To $5.00 Value

Scoops Frozen Custard

Enjoy any ICE CREAM ORDER at 50% off the regular price.

valid anytime

G360

Valid now thru November 1, 2007

Offer validity is governed by the Rules of Use and excludes defined holidays. Offers are not valid with other discount offers, unless specified.

ROCK 'N' ROLL PIZZA

- All ingredients are chopped fresh!
- Dough & sauce made on site daily!
- Wide variety of unique & traditional pizzas
- Great service in our family - friendly atmosphere
- Check out our rock-n-roll memorabilia

518 2nd St. N.W.
Byron, MN
(507)775-6225

00683190

Rochester Indoor GOLF CENTER

- Discount golf superstore
- PGA instruction - group or private
- Expert club fitting & club repair
- Indoor practice facilities
- Open year-round

2700 Country Club Rd. W.
(1 mi. W. of St. Mary's Hospital)
Rochester, MN
(507)529-0223

00694125

Sammy's

- Take out available
- Banquet & catering services available
- Breakfast, lunch & dinner

115 S. Main
Stewartville, MN
(507)533-8966

00493231

THE RUSTIC INN

- Located on the beautiful North Shore near Gooseberry Falls at Castle Danger, open all year
- Breakfast, lunch & dinner 7 days a week
- Breakfasts, sandwiches, salads, burgers, pastas, steaks, seafood & more
- Seniors & kids menu, gift shop and delicious desserts, too

2773 Hwy. 61
(North of Two Harbors on Hwy. 61)
Two Harbors, MN
(218)834-2488

00502080

Scoops Frozen Custard

- Homemade ice cream made fresh all day
- Cones, sundaes, shakes, blasts & floats
- Delicious homemade waffle cones
- Open daily noon-10 p.m

19 Fourth Ave. N.W.
(intersection of Hwy. 7 & 15)
Hutchinson, MN
(320)587-0477

00592862

Sarpino's Pizzeria

9175 Quaday Ave. N.E.
Otsego, MN
(763)441-6200

00677747

entertainment.com
Up To $6.00 Value

Serendipity

Enjoy one complimentary MENU ITEM when a second MENU ITEM of equal or greater value is purchased.

valid anytime

G361

Offer validity is governed by the Rules of Use and excludes defined holidays. Offers are not valid with other discount offers, unless specified.

Valid now thru November 1, 2007

---

entertainment.com
Up To $7.00 Value

Seth's Down Under Bar & Grill

Enjoy one complimentary MENU ITEM when a second MENU ITEM of equal or greater value is purchased.

valid anytime

G362

Offer validity is governed by the Rules of Use and excludes defined holidays. Offers are not valid with other discount offers, unless specified.

Valid now thru November 1, 2007

entertainment.com
Up To $10.00 Value

The Signature Bar & Grill

Enjoy one complimentary LUNCH OR DINNER ENTREE when a second LUNCH OR DINNER ENTREE of equal or greater value is purchased.

valid anytime

G363

Offer validity is governed by the Rules of Use and excludes defined holidays. Offers are not valid with other discount offers, unless specified.

Valid now thru November 1, 2007

---

entertainment.com
FREE ADMISSION

Skatin' Place

Enjoy one complimentary SKATING OR LASER TAG ADMISSION when a second SKATING OR LASER TAG ADMISSION of equal or greater value is purchased.

valid anytime

G364

Offer validity is governed by the Rules of Use and excludes defined holidays. Offers are not valid with other discount offers, unless specified.

Valid now thru November 1, 2007

---

entertainment.com
Up To $17.00 Value

SKI GULL

Enjoy one complimentary LIFT TICKET when a second LIFT TICKET of equal or greater value is purchased.

valid anytime

G365

Offer validity is governed by the Rules of Use and excludes defined holidays. Offers are not valid with other discount offers, unless specified.

Valid now thru November 1, 2007

---

entertainment.com
Up To $17.00 Value

SKI GULL

Enjoy one complimentary LIFT TICKET when a second LIFT TICKET of equal or greater value is purchased.

valid anytime

G366

Offer validity is governed by the Rules of Use and excludes defined holidays. Offers are not valid with other discount offers, unless specified.

Valid now thru November 1, 2007

Seth's Down Under Bar & Grill

- Appetizers & burgers
- Full bar
- Where the drinks are cold, the talk is bold & there's always a cheerful smile
- When you're ready for fun, you gotta go Down Under!

115 S. Main
Stewartville, MN
(507)533-4329

00493219

Serendipity

- Espresso fine coffee
- Tea
- Soup & sandwiches
- Wine & desserts
- Gallery & unique gifts

1705 W. St. Germain
St. Cloud, MN
(320)230-7233

00636183

Skatin' Place

- 24 hour information hotline
- Laser tag - come see what it's all about!
- Fresh homemade pizzas that everyone raves about!

3302 Southway Drive
St. Cloud, MN
(320)252-9768

00499865

The Signature Bar & Grill

- You won't leave here hungry!
- Fresh cut quality meats & steaks
- Homemade soups
- Hot & cold sandwiches
- Burgers
- Casual, relaxed atmosphere
- Full service bar
- Happy Hour Mon.-Sat. 4 p.m.-6 p.m.

201 Central Ave.
Faribault, MN
(507)331-1657

00677979

SKI GULL

- 14 Runs (60% beginner, 20% intermediate, 20% advanced), snowboard park, 2 sledding hills, triple chair lift, 2 tow ropes & 1 T-bar
- New, top of the line rental equipment (Nautica & K2)
- Warm, cozy chalet & a wide variety of food from Judy's kitchen

County Rd. 77
(Hwy. 77 on Gull Lake)
Nisswa, MN
(218)963-4353

00276956

SKI GULL

- 14 Runs (60% beginner, 20% intermediate, 20% advanced), snowboard park, 2 sledding hills, triple chair lift, 2 tow ropes & 1 T-bar
- New, top of the line rental equipment (Nautica & K2)
- Warm, cozy chalet & a wide variety of food from Judy's kitchen

County Rd. 77
(Hwy. 77 on Gull Lake)
Nisswa, MN
(218)963-4353

00276956

entertainment.com — Up To $8.00 Value

Turtle LAKE RV Park & Speedy's Family Fun Center

Enjoy up to 4 RIDES at 50% off the regular price.

valid anytime

G367

Valid now thru November 1, 2007

Offer validity is governed by the Rules of Use and excludes defined holidays. Offers are not valid with other discount offers, unless specified.

---

entertainment.com — Up To $10.00 Value

STACY COUNTRY CAFE

Enjoy one complimentary ENTREE when a second ENTREE of equal or greater value is purchased.

Buffet excluded; Specials excluded; Dine in only

valid anytime

Tipping should be 15% to 20% of TOTAL bill before discount

G368

Valid now thru November 1, 2007

Offer validity is governed by the Rules of Use and excludes defined holidays. Offers are not valid with other discount offers, unless specified.

---

entertainment.com — Up To $6.00 Value

State Street Bistro

Enjoy one complimentary MENU ITEM when a second MENU ITEM of equal or greater value is purchased.

valid anytime

G369

Valid now thru November 1, 2007

Offer validity is governed by the Rules of Use and excludes defined holidays. Offers are not valid with other discount offers, unless specified.

---

entertainment.com — FREE ADMISSION

Stearns History Museum

www.stearns-museum.org

Enjoy one complimentary ADMISSION when a second ADMISSION of equal or greater value is purchased.

Special events excluded

valid anytime

Not valid with any other discounts or promotions

G370

Valid now thru November 1, 2007

Offer validity is governed by the Rules of Use and excludes defined holidays. Offers are not valid with other discount offers, unless specified.

---

entertainment.com — Up To $7.00 Value

STONE MILL Marketplace & Coffeehouse & Eatery

Enjoy one complimentary ENTREE when a second ENTREE of equal or greater value is purchased.

valid anytime

G371

Valid now thru November 1, 2007

Offer validity is governed by the Rules of Use and excludes defined holidays. Offers are not valid with other discount offers, unless specified.

---

entertainment.com — Up To $25.00 Value

STONE MILL Marketplace & Coffeehouse & Eatery

Enjoy 20% off the regular price of any PURCHASE (sale items excluded) - maximum discount $25.00.

valid anytime

G372

Valid now thru November 1, 2007

Offer validity is governed by the Rules of Use and excludes defined holidays. Offers are not valid with other discount offers, unless specified.

STACY COUNTRY CAFE

- Serving breakfast, lunch & dinner
- Fresh, homemade country cooking
- Gourmet coffee & desserts
- Appetizers, sandwiches, burgers, pastas, ribs, broasted chicken & more
- Kid's menu & senior discount
- Catering available

31100 Forest Blvd.
(downtown Stacy)
Stacy, MN
(651) 462-2227

00690604

Turtle LAKE RV Park & Speedy's Family Fun Center

- Go Karts
- Mini golf & driving range
- Bumper boats & cars
- Video game arcade
- Water wars
- RV Park & campground

750 US Hwy 8 & 63 S.
Turtle Lake, WI
(715) 986-4140

00494101

Stearns History Museum

- 2 floors of exhibits
- Hands on children's room
- Museum store
- Genealogy research center
- 100 acre nature park
- Open 7 days a week, all year round

235 33rd Ave. S., St. Cloud, MN
(320) 253-8424
(866) 253-8424

00525897

State Street Bistro

- Sandwiches
- Soups & salads
- Pasta
- Desserts
- Birthday/wedding cakes

118 S. State St.
Waseca, MN
(507) 833-6183

00650069

STONE MILL Marketplace & Coffeehouse & Eatery

- 12 Different shops under one roof with a wide variety of unique gifts & fun stuff
- Red Hat Society, handcrafted items, home decor & beautiful, original artwork
- Toll free: (888) 864-9190

432 W. Mill St.
Cannon Falls, MN
(507) 263-0171

00582545

STONE MILL Marketplace & Coffeehouse & Eatery

- We invite you to experience the friendly atmosphere of our European style coffee house
- Full menu
- Ask about our dinner theatre

432 W. Mill St.
Cannon Falls, MN
(507) 263-2580

00500889

entertainment
entertainment.com

50% OFF

STRIKE FORCE BOWL and ProShop

Enjoy up to 4 GAMES/LINES at 50% off the regular price.

valid anytime

G373

Valid now thru November 1, 2007

Offer validity is governed by the Rules of Use and excludes defined holidays. Offers are not valid with other discount offers, unless specified.

---

entertainment
entertainment.com

Up To $10.00 Value

Stucci's Italian Food

Enjoy one complimentary LUNCH OR DINNER ENTREE when a second LUNCH OR DINNER ENTREE of equal or greater value is purchased.

valid anytime

Tipping should be 15% to 20% of TOTAL bill before discount

G374

Valid now thru November 1, 2007

Offer validity is governed by the Rules of Use and excludes defined holidays. Offers are not valid with other discount offers, unless specified.

---

entertainment
entertainment.com

UP TO $3.00 VALUE

summer Land!
251-0940

Enjoy one complimentary ROUND OF MINI GOLF when a second ROUND OF MINI GOLF of equal or greater value is purchased or one GO-KART RIDE when you purchase a second GO-KART RIDE of equal or greater value.

valid anytime

G375

Valid now thru November 1, 2007

Offer validity is governed by the Rules of Use and excludes defined holidays. Offers are not valid with other discount offers, unless specified.

---

entertainment
entertainment.com

Up To $16.00 Value

Sunni's Grille
IN HOWARD LAKE

CLASSIC AMERICAN FAVORITES

Enjoy one complimentary ENTREE when a second ENTREE of equal or greater value is purchased.

Dine in only

valid anytime

Offers not valid holidays and subject to Rules of Use. Tipping should be 15% to 20% of the total bill before discount

G376

Valid now thru November 1, 2007

Offer validity is governed by the Rules of Use and excludes defined holidays. Offers are not valid with other discount offers, unless specified.

---

entertainment
entertainment.com

Up To $5.00 Value

TACO OASIS

Enjoy one complimentary MENU ITEM when a second MENU ITEM of equal or greater value is purchased.

valid anytime

G377

Valid now thru November 1, 2007

Offer validity is governed by the Rules of Use and excludes defined holidays. Offers are not valid with other discount offers, unless specified.

---

entertainment
entertainment.com

Up To $7.00 Value

tale of two Sisters

Enjoy one complimentary MENU ITEM when a second MENU ITEM of equal or greater value is purchased.

valid anytime

G378

Valid now thru November 1, 2007

Offer validity is governed by the Rules of Use and excludes defined holidays. Offers are not valid with other discount offers, unless specified.

Stucci's Italian Food

- Homemade Italian food with a touch of amore!

417 2nd St.
Hudson, WI
(715)381-7275

00701044

STRIKE FORCE BOWL and ProShop

- Bowl for the fun of it!
- Solar sonic & moonlight bowl on the weekends
- Food & beverages available
- Set-ups available
- Birthday parties
- Bumpers

309 W. Main St.
New Prague, MN
(952)758-5170

00616778

Sunni's Grille
IN HOWARD LAKE
CLASSIC AMERICAN FAVORITES

- Come to Sunni's Grille where you can enjoy classic American favorites, such as delicious burgers, sandwiches, salads & more
- Enjoy building your own pizza while you have a glass of beer or wine
- Visit us for breakfast, lunch, or dinner
- Children's menu available

728 6th St.
Howard Lake, MN
(320)543-3334

00609047

Summer Land!
251-0940

- St Cloud's most unique theme park. Attractive, clean family fun
- Go-karts, bumper boats & miniature golf
- Giant water slide, Indy karts
- Arcade center
- Picnic area, batting cages and much more!

Hwy. 23 E., 1 mile past Honda House
St. Cloud, MN
(320)251-0940

00000650

Sisters

- A kind & gentle place beckoning you to return again & again
- Homemade soups, salads, sandwiches & quiche
- Afternoon Tea - please call for reservations
- Tea, treasures & gifts
- Fresh Scones
- Closed Sunday & Monday

204 W. 7th St.
Red Wing, MN
(866)328-2300

00522649

TACOASIS

- Stop by the Tacoasis for our "super hot" deals

1140 South Hwy 3
Northfield, MN
(507)645-5340

00000760

Thayer's
Historic Bed 'n Breakfast

Up To $65.00 Value

www.thayers.net
Enjoy 25% off the regular price of any INTERACTIVE MYSTERY DINNER for up to 4 people.

valid anytime
Tipping should be 15% to 20% of TOTAL bill before discount

G379

Valid now thru November 1, 2007

Thayer's
Historic Bed 'n Breakfast

25% OFF

www.thayers.net
Enjoy any ROOM at 25% off the regular price.

anytime September thru May; Sunday thru Thursday June thru August

Reservations required; 72 hour cancellation policy; On availability basis; Not valid with packages or other discounts
Tipping should be 15% to 20% of TOTAL bill before discount

G380

Valid now thru November 1, 2007

The Bayou

Up To $6.00 Value

Enjoy one complimentary LUNCH OR DINNER ENTREE when a second LUNCH OR DINNER ENTREE of equal or greater value is purchased.

Dine in only

valid anytime
Tipping should be 15% to 20% of TOTAL bill before discount

G381

Valid now thru November 1, 2007

This Old Store Etc.

Up To $25.00 Value

Enjoy 20% off the regular price of any PURCHASE (sale items excluded) - maximum discount $25.00.

valid anytime

G382

Valid now thru November 1, 2007

Three Happiness
三喜

Up To $10.00 Value

Enjoy one complimentary LUNCH OR DINNER ENTREE when a second LUNCH OR DINNER ENTREE of equal or greater value is purchased.

Buffet excluded; Dine in only

valid anytime
Tipping should be 15% to 20% of TOTAL bill before discount

G383

Valid now thru November 1, 2007

Three Sisters Tea Room

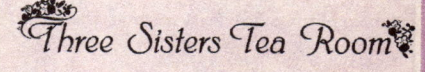

Up To $5.00 Value

Enjoy any FOOD/BEVERAGE ORDER at 50% off the regular price - maximum discount $5.00.

valid anytime

G384

Valid now thru November 1, 2007

Thayer's
Historic Bed 'n Breakfast

- Coupon used on bed & breakfast rack rate only
- Cocktail lounge featuring 43 scotches
- Mystery dinner packages
- Whirlpools, hot tubs, fireplaces, 2 cats!
- 4 course champagne breakfast
- 11 rooms each with private bath

60 W Elm
Annandale, MN
(800)944-6595

00319248

Thayer's
Historic Bed 'n Breakfast

- Reservations recommended at least 30 days in advance
- Interactive mystery dinners where you may be the killer or you might just be killed!
- Prefixed menu
- Plots, characters & settings change every time!

60 W Elm
Annandale, MN
(800)944-6595

00319147

This Old Store Etc.

- Antiques
- Collectibles
- Novelty items

301 Main St.
Star Prairie, WI
(715)248-4800

00609447

The Bayou

- Sandwiches, appetizers & soup
- Nightly drink specials
- Meat raffle every Sat.
- Live music
- Pull tabs, pool & darts

201 E. Broadway
Rockville, MN
(320)251-2397

00656369

Three Sisters Tea Room

- Tranquility begins with tea
- Fresh offerings from tea & scones to afternoon tea
- Light lunches, soups & salads
- Tea-related gift items

208 N. Minnesota St.
New Ulm, MN
(507)354-7087

00620597

Three Happiness
三喜

- Featuring Cambodian, Chinese & Thai cuisine
- Friendly service

1123 Civic Center Dr.
Rochester, MN
(507)252-5337

00683148

entertainment.com

FREE ADMISSION

Thunder Alley

Enjoy one complimentary ADMISSION when a second ADMISSION of equal or greater value is purchased.

valid anytime

G385

Valid now thru November 1, 2007

Offer validity is governed by the Rules of Use and excludes defined holidays. Offers are not valid with other discount offers, unless specified.

---

entertainment.com

ONE FAMILY TRACK TICKET

Thunder Alley

Enjoy one complimentary FAMILY TRACK TICKET when a second FAMILY TRACK TICKET of equal or greater value is purchased.

valid anytime

G386

Valid now thru November 1, 2007

Offer validity is governed by the Rules of Use and excludes defined holidays. Offers are not valid with other discount offers, unless specified.

entertainment.com

Up To $25.00 Value

TICKLE YER Fancy fine candies

www.tyfcandies.com

Enjoy 20% off the regular price of any PURCHASE (sale items excluded) - maximum discount $25.00.

valid anytime

G387

Valid now thru November 1, 2007

Offer validity is governed by the Rules of Use and excludes defined holidays. Offers are not valid with other discount offers, unless specified.

entertainment.com

Up To $5.00 Value

Tropical Brew coffee bar

Enjoy one complimentary MENU ITEM when a second MENU ITEM of equal or greater value is purchased.

valid anytime

G388

Valid now thru November 1, 2007

Offer validity is governed by the Rules of Use and excludes defined holidays. Offers are not valid with other discount offers, unless specified.

entertainment.com

Up To $9.00 Value

Turtle Dove Tea House & Gardens

www.turtledoveteahouse.com

Enjoy one complimentary ENTREE when a second ENTREE of equal or greater value is purchased.

valid anytime

Tipping should be 15% to 20% of TOTAL bill before discount

G389

Valid now thru November 1, 2007

Offer validity is governed by the Rules of Use and excludes defined holidays. Offers are not valid with other discount offers, unless specified.

---

entertainment.com

FREE GREEN FEE

Turtleback

www.turtlebackgolf.com

Enjoy one complimentary GREEN FEE when 3 GREEN FEES of equal or greater value are purchased.

valid anytime

Valid anytime Monday-Thursday; Friday-Sunday after 2 p.m.; Cart rental required

G390

Valid now thru November 1, 2007

Offer validity is governed by the Rules of Use and excludes defined holidays. Offers are not valid with other discount offers, unless specified.

Thunder Alley

- Nation's largest high speed indoor karting facility
- Banquet & meeting facilities
- Corporate events, bachelor parties, birthday parties, youth groups
- Catering available
- Indoor paintball, batting cages, billiards & arcade
- Full snack bar

1100 Northland Blvd.
Princeton, MN
(763) 631-7733

00680112

Thunder Alley

- Minnesota's largest indoor paintball facility
- Banquet & meeting facilities
- Corporate events, weddings, birthday parties & youth groups
- Catering available
- Indoor karting facility
- Batting cages, arcade & billiards
- Full snack bar

1100 Northland Blvd.
Princeton, MN
(763) 631-7733

00680103

Tropical Brew coffee bar

- Espresso drinks & teas
- Soups & sandwiches
- Smoothies
- Kids' drinks
- Pastries & desserts

450 Jefferson Blvd.
(Hwy. 10)
Big Lake, MN
(763) 263-3909

00633508

Tickle Yer Fancy fine candies

- Abdallah Chocolates - regular & sugar free
- JusTruffles
- Jelly Belly™ Jelly Beans
- Old fashioned candies & sodas
- Fresh, hot popcorn
- Shipping available
- (800) 864-1992

2000 W. Main St.
Red Wing, MN
(651) 388-1992

00522644

Turtleback

- A Golf Digest magazine Four Star Course
- Four sets of tees & strategically designed landing areas
- Clubhouse & conference center offers over 5000 sq. ft. of space for full service group events

1985 18 1/2 St.
Rice Lake, WI
(715) 234-7641

00585486

Turtle Dove Tea House & Gardens

- While you're waiting for the kettle to boil, feel free to browse the antiques, gifts & decor throughout the 1880's tea house
- Formal afternoon tea
- Visit our lovely garden & water landscape

510 W. Main
Albert Lea, MN
(507) 377-9381

00592552

entertainment.com — Up To $5.00 Value

The Ugly Mug
coffee bar & grill

Enjoy any FOOD/BEVERAGE ORDER at 50% off the regular price.

Dine in only

valid anytime

G391

Offer validity is governed by the Rules of Use and excludes defined holidays. Offers are not valid with other discount offers, unless specified.

Valid now thru November 1, 2007

---

entertainment.com — Up To $9.00 Value

Village Inn

Enjoy one complimentary ENTREE when a second ENTREE of equal or greater value is purchased.

Dine in only

valid anytime

Tipping should be 15% to 20% of TOTAL bill before discount

G392

Offer validity is governed by the Rules of Use and excludes defined holidays. Offers are not valid with other discount offers, unless specified.

Valid now thru November 1, 2007

---

entertainment.com — Up To $5.00 Value

Wayne's

Enjoy one complimentary MENU ITEM when a second MENU ITEM of equal or greater value is purchased.

valid anytime

G393

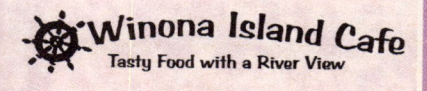

Offer validity is governed by the Rules of Use and excludes defined holidays. Offers are not valid with other discount offers, unless specified.

Valid now thru November 1, 2007

---

entertainment.com — Up To $11.00 Value

Wings
TAVERN & GRILLE

Enjoy one complimentary LUNCH OR DINNER ENTREE when a second LUNCH OR DINNER ENTREE of equal or greater value is purchased.

valid anytime

Tipping should be 15% to 20% of TOTAL bill before discount

G394

Offer validity is governed by the Rules of Use and excludes defined holidays. Offers are not valid with other discount offers, unless specified.

Valid now thru November 1, 2007

---

entertainment.com — Up To $6.00 Value

Winona Island Cafe
Tasty Food with a River View

Enjoy one complimentary MENU ITEM when a second MENU ITEM of equal or greater value is purchased.

valid anytime

G395

Offer validity is governed by the Rules of Use and excludes defined holidays. Offers are not valid with other discount offers, unless specified.

Valid now thru November 1, 2007

---

entertainment.com — Up To $10.00 Value

ZEPPOLE'S
PIZZA & PASTA
"The Original Italian"

Enjoy one complimentary ENTREE when a second ENTREE of equal or greater value is purchased.

valid anytime

Tipping should be 15% to 20% of TOTAL bill before discount

G396

Offer validity is governed by the Rules of Use and excludes defined holidays. Offers are not valid with other discount offers, unless specified.

Valid now thru November 1, 2007

Village Inn

- Good food, good feelings!
- Come sample our delicious sandwiches, soups, pies & dinners
- Breakfast anytime
- Conveniently located one block west of Hwy 35 on Country Rd. 22

4848 E. Viking Blvd.
Wyoming, MN
(651) 462-2669

00456660

The Ugly Mug
coffee bar & grill

- Full espresso bar
- Breakfast, lunch & dinner
- Bakery, desserts, ice cream & smoothies
- Great appetizers & kids menu
- Beer & wine
- NTN Trivia
- Live Music
- Non-smoking environment

18450 Pilot Knob Rd.
(In the Farmington Market Place)
Farmington, MN
(651) 463-6844

00562988

Wings
TAVERN & GRILLE

- 5 TVs
- Pool table
- Karaoke
- Buffalo wings, burgers, steaks & seafood
- Full bar service

1805 S. Elm
Owatonna, MN
(507) 444-9335

00622884

Wayne's

- Homemade soups piping hot & always delicious
- Our pastries, baked here & served to you at the peak of freshness

Hwy 8 & Hwy 35
St. Croix Falls, WI
(715) 483-3121

00477413

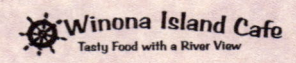

ZEPPOLE'S
PIZZA & PASTA
"The Original Italian"

Oak Park Mall, Austin, MN
(507) 433-1600

Crossroads Center, St. Cloud, MN
(320) 252-1791

1600 1st. St. N. *(Kandi Mall)*, **Willmar, MN**
(320) 235-7039

00217626

Winona Island Cafe
Tasty Food with a River View

- Espresso drinks
- Sandwiches, soups & salads
- Homemade cookies
- Scones
- Ice cream
- Smoothies

2 Johnson St.
Winona, MN
(507) 454-1133

00584613

RETAIL & SERVICES

Visit our "Top Web Deals" section online at www.entertainment.com

OVER 100 OFFERS

plus more at www.entertainment.com/shop

Home & Auto
Ace Hardware H50
American Blinds, Wallpaper & More H11
Ballard Designs H8
Bed Bath & Beyond H5
Brink's Home Security . . . HH13
Brookstone H21-H22
Frontgate H6
Grandin Road H44
HSN.com H47
Improvements Catalog . . .H46
Overstock.com H10
Pier 1 Imports H3-H4
Plow & Hearth H9
Sears.com H1
Smith + Noble H7
Target.com H2

Electronics, Communication & Investments
DirectStarTV H54
DISH Network H53
Gateway, Inc. H20
RadioShack H18-H19
ShareBuilder H52
SIRIUS Satellite Radio H51
The Sharper Image . . . H16-H17
Vonage H48

Toys, Games, Music & Pets
BLOCKBUSTER® H12-H15
K•B Toys H23-H26
PetSmart H55-H56

Apparel
Avenue H32-H33
Blair H49
Catherines H37-H40
eBags.com H70
Fashion Bug H35-H36
Garnet Hill H43
Growing Up with Garnet Hill . .H45
Lane Bryant. H34
Liz Claiborne H29-H31
New York & Company . . H27-H28
The Territory Ahead . . . H41-H42

Flowers
1-800-flowers.com H64
Blooms Today H66
Florist.com H65
From You Flowers H63
FTD H57-H58
Hallmark Flowers H61-H62
Jackson & Perkins H73
ProFlowers H59-H60
USAflorist.com H68

Gourmet Food & Gifts
à la Zing HH6
Candy Wholesale Company . . HH4
Cherry Moon Farms HH1
Cheryl&Co. HH7
From You Baskets H69
Harry and David H71-H72
Hickory Farms H74-H75
Omaha Steaks H76-H78
Personal Creations H67
Secret Spoon HH2

Photos & Portraits
JCPenney Portraits HH8
Kodak EasyShare Gallery . .HH14
Picture People HH9-HH10
Shutterfly HH15
Target Photo HH11
Target Portrait Studio HH12

Health & Beauty
Online Vitamin Outlet HH5
Pearle Vision HH16
SpaWish.com HH3

Sears

Save on everything from our Closeout Center

Closeouts

Top deals close to you! Visit www.entertainment.com/sears and select **"Closeouts"** to find the best deals in your area! Save 15-50% on Lawn & Garden, Appliances, Electronics, Tools, and Fitness products in your zip code. **Hurry!** Selection and quantities are limited and vary by area!

Valid now thru December 31, 2007

Offer validity is governed by the Rules of Use and excludes defined holidays. Offers are not valid with other discount offers, unless specified. Coupons void if purchased, sold or bartered. Discounts exclude tax, tip and/or alcohol, where applicable.

H1 **Visit www.entertainment.com/sears to find great deals and ongoing Entertainment® member specials from Sears.** You must register your Entertainment® book at www.entertainment.com to redeem these offers.

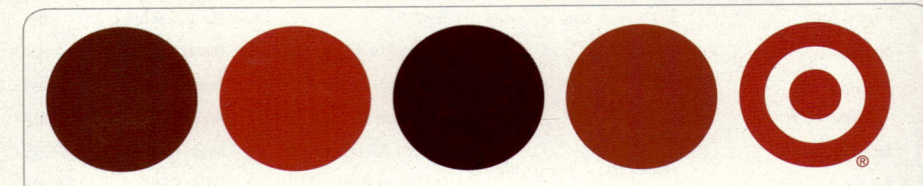

More great stuff.
Target.com

More products. More information. More fun. You'll also find exclusive offers just for Entertainment® members. Offers change monthly, so visit often: **Target.com/ent2007** Valid now thru December 31, 2007.

H2 Offer validity is governed by the Rules of Use. Coupons void if purchased, sold or bartered. ©2006 Target Stores. The Bullseye Design is a registered trademark of Target Brands, Inc. All rights reserved.

For the store nearest you, visit pier1.com or call (800) 245-4595.

Pier 1 imports®

Pier 1 imports®

$10 OFF

your next regular or sale price purchase of $50 or more at any Pier 1 store.

Coupon #2543

Valid August 1, 2006–March 31, 2007
See reverse side for details

H3

Pier 1 imports®

$10 OFF

your next regular or sale price purchase of $50 or more at any Pier 1 store.

Coupon #2545

Valid April 1–December 31, 2007
See reverse side for details

H4

Pier 1 imports®

For the store nearest you, visit pier1.com or call (800) 245-4595.

Bring this coupon to any Pier 1 store and save $10 on your next regular or sale price purchase of $50 or more. Offer does not apply to delivery or other service charges. Offer does not apply to prior purchases and cannot be used on Gift Card, Komen or UNICEF purchases. Coupon is valid at all Pier 1 company stores and participating franchise stores only, excluding pier1.com and phone purchases.

Coupon is not valid in combination with any other coupon or discount. Coupon must be redeemed at time of purchase.

Offer valid April 1 through December 31, 2007.

Offer validity is governed by the Rules of Use and excludes defined holidays. Offers are not valid with other discount offers, unless specified. Coupons void if purchased, sold or bartered. Discounts exclude tax, tip and/or alcohol, where applicable.

Bring this coupon to any Pier 1 store and save $10 on your next regular or sale price purchase of $50 or more. Offer does not apply to delivery or other service charges. Offer does not apply to prior purchases and cannot be used on Gift Card, Komen or UNICEF purchases. Coupon is valid at all Pier 1 company stores and participating franchise stores only, excluding pier1.com and phone purchases.

Coupon is not valid in combination with any other coupon or discount. Coupon must be redeemed at time of purchase.

Offer valid August 1, 2006 through March 31, 2007.

Offer validity is governed by the Rules of Use and excludes defined holidays. Offers are not valid with other discount offers, unless specified. Coupons void if purchased, sold or bartered. Discounts exclude tax, tip and/or alcohol, where applicable.

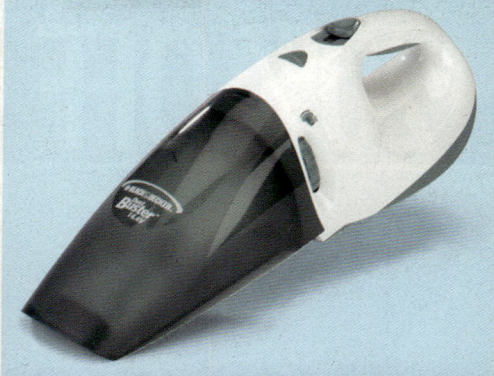

BED BATH & BEYOND

20% OFF
any single item*

Present this Certificate. Valid for in-store use only.

Valid now thru December 31, 2007

See reverse side for details

H5

20% OFF any single item*

Call 1-800-GO BEYOND® for locations Coast to Coast.
The Best Brands. Huge Selection.
Everything at or below sale prices every day.℠

BED BATH & BEYOND®

20% OFF

Take 20% off any single item.*
Present this certificate.
Valid for in-store use only.

Limit one to a customer per visit. No copies, please. *Not valid with any other offer. Coupon must be surrendered at time of purchase. Not valid for the purchase of gift certificates, gift cards, J.A. Henckels, All-Clad, Nautica®, Tempur-pedic®, Wusthof®, Little Giant Ladders and Ionic Breeze® Air Purifiers. Not valid for Wedgwood®, Lenox®, Waterford®, Vera Wang, Nambe®, Riedel, Royal Scandinavia, Viking, iJoy™, Frette Home, Miele, Capresso and Oreck® products (where available). See store for details.

5 71900 00000 6

Offer validity is governed by the Rules of Use and excludes defined holidays. Offers are not valid with other discount offers, unless specified. Coupons void if purchased, sold or bartered. Discounts exclude tax, tip and/or alcohol, where applicable.

FRONTGATE®

OUTFITTING AMERICA'S FINEST HOMES®

Call 1-800-626-6488 for a free catalog or shop frontgate.com.

FRONTGATE®

$10 off
any $50 purchase at frontgate.com

Keycode: **EB0610F**

$25 off
any $150 purchase at frontgate.com

Keycode: **EB0625F**

$50 off
any $300 purchase at frontgate.com

Keycode: **EB0650F**

Redeem online at frontgate.com by entering keycode at checkout.
Or, order by phone 1-800-626-6488 and mention keycode.

Offer is not valid with any other discount or promotional offer, or on prior purchases. Discount is applicable to merchandise only, excluding tax and shipping. Cannot be used towards gift certificates or on Bose® electronics. Coupon may be used one time per household. Expires December 31, 2007. Offer validity is governed by the Rules of Use and excludes defined holidays. Offers are not valid with other discount offers, unless specified. Coupons void if purchased, sold or bartered. Discounts exclude tax, tip, and/or alcohol, where applicable.

H6

smith+noble®

America's leading resource for window treatments™

$150 off
your purchase of $600 or more

$100 off
your purchase of $500 or more

$50 off
your purchase of $300 or more

Use offer code SAVE-6TCT when ordering.

Call 800.311.2438 today for a free catalog.
Go to smithnoble.com — get 10 Free Swatches.

Source Code: 60517031

Valid now thru December 31, 2007

H7 Offer validity is governed by the Rules of Use and excludes defined holidays. Offers are not valid with other discount offers, unless specified. Coupons void if purchased, sold or bartered. Discounts exclude tax, tip and/or alcohol, where applicable.

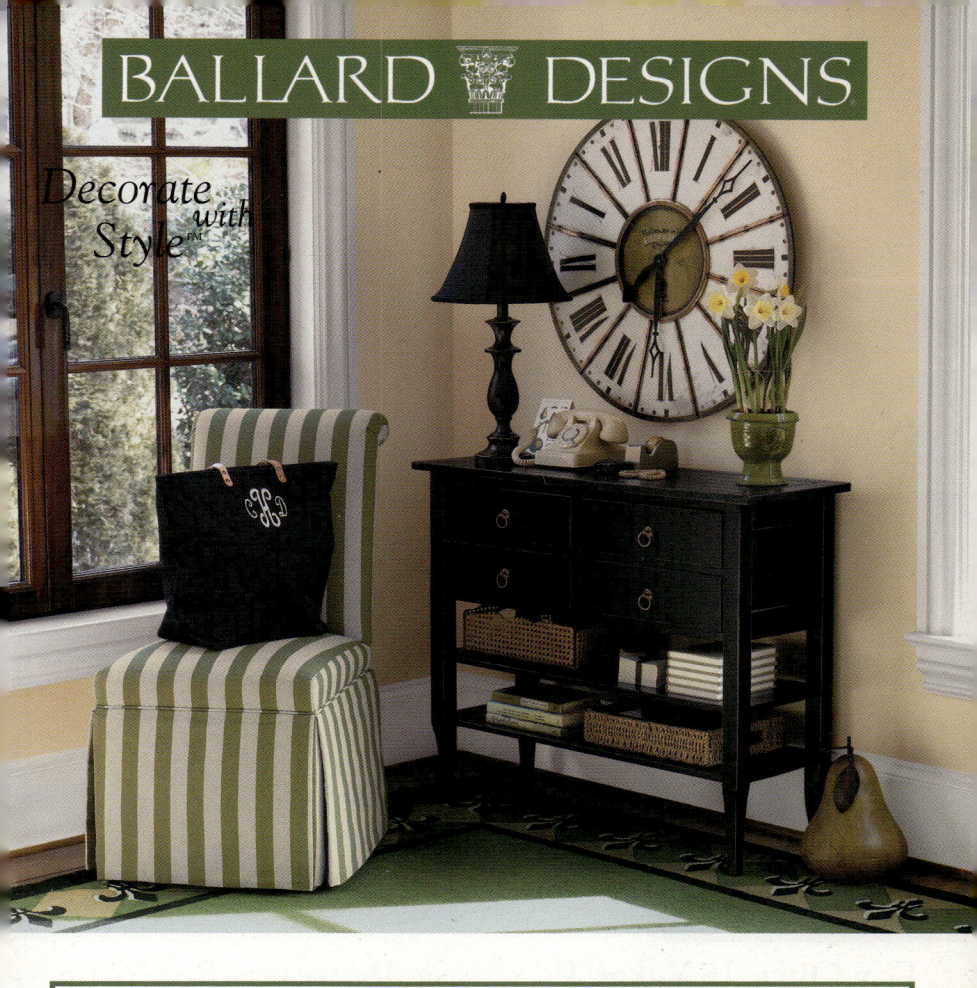

BALLARD DESIGNS

Decorate with Style™

SAVE $15 or SAVE $50
on your first purchase of $100 or more   on your first purchase of $250 or more

To Redeem:

By Phone: Call 1-800-367-2775 to request a catalog or place an order. Please mention code PHET2006 for your discount.

By Mail: Enter promotion code MLET2006 on your order form.

Online: Shop at ballarddesigns.com and enter special offer code WEET2006 at checkout.

At our Stores: Give this coupon to the Sales Associate for your discount.

Valid now thru December 31, 2007

Terms and Conditions: Only one coupon may be used per household. May not be combined with any other discounts. May not be used towards the purchase of gift certificates. May not be applied to previous orders. Reproductions will not be accepted. Void where prohibited by law. No cash value. Offer validity is governed by the Rules of Use and excludes defined holidays. Offers are not valid with other discount offers, unless specified. Coupons void if purchased, sold or bartered. Discounts exclude tax, tip and/or alcohol, where applicable.

H8

Plow & Hearth®

For Over 25 Years, Providing Products For Your
Home, Hearth, Yard & Garden

100% Satisfaction Guaranteed

Save $15
on orders of $100 or more
Promo code **EB2**

Save $50
on orders of $250 or more
Promo code **EB3**

Call:
800-627-1712

Order online:
plowandhearth.com

Visit A Store:
Locations listed online

Valid now thru December 31, 2007

Offer validity is governed by the Rules of Use and excludes defined holidays. Offers are not valid with other discount offers, unless specified. Discount is applicable to merchandise only, excluding tax and shipping. Coupons void if purchased, sold or bartered.

H9

Overstock.com®
Your Online Outlet™

Save up to 70% on brand names | Your entire order ships for $2.95 | Live customer service available 24-hours a day | 1-800-The-Big-O (843-2446)

- shopping
- books, music, movies & games
- bulk buys & business supplies
- auctions
- travel
- Home & Garden
- Jewelry & Watches
- Sports & Toys
- Electronics
- Apparel
- Worldstock
- Gifts
- Health & Wellness

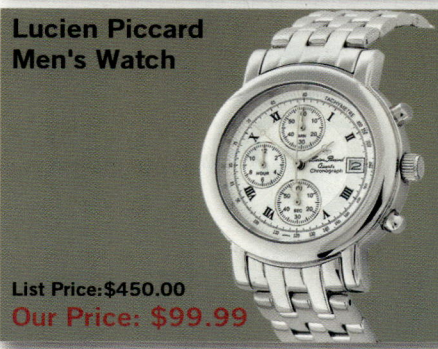

Black Leather Storage Bench
List Price: $615.00
Our Price: $279.99

Junior Plush Jacket
List Price: $50.00
Our Price: $22.99

6-inch Rainfall Showerhead
List Price: $39.99
Our Price: $19.99

Lucien Piccard Men's Watch
List Price: $450.00
Our Price: $99.99

10% OFF
any purchase of $45 or more.*
Excludes orders comprised only of media.

Enter promotional code 85721 at check out.
Valid now through December 31, 2007

Overstock.com Your Online Outlet™
BEST PRICE GUARANTEE

Offer validity is governed by the Rules of Use and excludes defined holidays. Offers are not valid with other discount offers, unless specified. Coupons void if purchased, sold or bartered. Discounts exclude tax, tip and/or alcohol, where applicable.
*Offer will appear on the billing page after you have entered the code. Offer code is limited to one use per customer. Discount is not to exceed $100. Ground Shipping only. Offer valid in the 48 continental U.S. only. Products limited to availability. Offer excludes Travel, Auctions & Affiliate Marketing Partners (offer must come through the Overstock site, not third-party links). Overstock.com & Your Online Outlet are registered trademarks of Overstock.com, Inc. All other trademarks are the property of their respective owners and are used only to identify products offered for sale by Overstock.com, and their owners are not affiliated with or sponsors of Overstock.com, Inc.

H10

BLINDS & WALLPAPER
Always SAVE 25%-85% off MOST RETAIL STORE PRICES

Hunter Douglas® • Levolor® • Duette® • Bali® • Waverly® • Imperial® • American® and more

3 ways to shop

Shop Our FREE Blinds Catalog
Call or email us at EN93@americanblinds.com for your FREE Blinds catalog.

Shop Online
Select from over 500,000 home decorating items on our website.

Shop Around, Then Call Us
If you see something you like elsewhere, call or log on for the Guaranteed Lowest Price!†

American
BLINDS, WALLPAPER & MORE
americanblinds.com
800-445-1735

†Call or visit our website for details.

PLUS...SAVE AN EXTRA 15% off*
any purchase enter or mention EN93 when ordering

and FREE SHIPPING

*Offers cannot be used in conjunction with other promotional offers or discounts. Previous orders are excluded.

Valid now thru December 31, 2007

Offer validity is governed by the Rules of Use and excludes defined holidays. Offers are not valid with other discount offers, unless specified. Coupons void if purchased, sold or bartered.

H11

SAVE UP TO 20%

Save up to 20% on your next movie rental from BLOCKBUSTER®!

Purchase BLOCKBUSTER® Movie Cards ("Movie Card") in advance through ENTERTAINMENT® and save on the hottest new releases, family favorites, and more. BLOCKBUSTER® Movie Cards are redeemable at over 5,500 participating BLOCKBUSTER stores nationwide.

Free Movie Rentals; Quantity of Rentals must be in increments of 10. See back for more details. (Face value - up to a $4.50 per average rental. Actual savings may vary.) Membership rules and certain restrictions apply for rental at BLOCKBUSTER. See Movie Card for details. Movie Cards are redeemable at participating BLOCKBUSTER store locations. BLOCKBUSTER name, design and related marks are trademarks of Blockbuster Inc. ©2006 Blockbuster Inc. All rights reserved.

Valid now thru December 31, 2007
See reverse side for details

H12

---

30 DAYS FREE

BLOCKBUSTER Online®

Get a 30-Day BLOCKBUSTER Online® Trial Subscription FREE.
Offer also includes 4 (four) FREE in-store rental coupons (one per week).

Sign up at blockbuster.com and enter promo code pmentpub07
(promo code is case sensitive)

Valid now thru December 31, 2007
See reverse side for details

H13

SAVE UP TO $4.75

Rent two (2) Movies and get one (1) Non New Release movie of equal or lesser value FREE.

VALID 8/1/2006 THROUGH 1/31/2007
See reverse side for details
H14

SAVE UP TO $7.99

Rent two (2) Movies or Games and get one (1) Movie or Game rental of equal or lesser value FREE.

VALID 2/1/2007 THROUGH 10/1/2007
See reverse side for details
H15

Order Form

Each BLOCKBUSTER® Movie Card will be valid for at least six months from the ship date.
Please complete this form with the number of rentals and attach a check or money order made out to: Entertainment Publications, Inc., for the total amount plus shipping and handling of $2.25 for orders valued at $39.99 or less and $5.50 for orders valued at $40.00 or more. Do not send cash. Mail to: Entertainment Publications, Inc.
c/o RENTAL CARDS
P.O. Box 539
Duncan, SC 29334-5390

Entertainment will fulfill the Movie Cards and approximately three weeks will be needed for delivery of Movie Cards. Movie Cards may not be exchanged or returned for a refund. Call 1-877-814-5292 only if you have ordered more than three weeks ago and have not received your order.

# of rentals		Cost per rental		Total
10	x	3.60	=	$36.00
20	x	3.60	=	$72.00
30	x	3.60	=	$108.00
_____	x	3.60	=	$_____
		shipping & handling	=	$_____
		TOTAL DUE	=	$_____

Name: _____
Address: _____
City: _____ State: _____ ZIP: _____
Daytime Phone: (_____) _____ x

BLOCKBUSTER® Movie Cards are subject to complete terms and conditions found on card. Membership rules apply for rental at BLOCKBUSTER®. Not valid with other discount offers. Any exchange for cash, sale, transfer or reproduction constitutes fraud and is prohibited. Must be relinquished upon redemption.

Sign up to receive a free thirty-day trial of the BLOCKBUSTER Online® Subscription, with up to 3 movies out at a time. Offer valid for new customers only; limit one free trial offer per household. You must have Internet access and provide a valid e-mail address and a valid credit card, check card or checking account number to participate in the free trial or to subscribe to BLOCKBUSTER Online. If you do not cancel your free trial membership before it expires, the credit or check card or checking account number provided will be charged the applicable monthly membership fee (plus taxes) beginning on the first day after the end of the free trial and continuing monthly thereafter until canceled. If you cancel your free trial, BLOCKBUSTER Online rentals must be returned no later than ten (10) days past the expiration date of your free trial to avoid additional charges. Separate membership required for in-store rentals, and in-store membership rules apply.

**Sign up at blockbuster.com and enter promo code
pmentpub07
(promo code is case sensitive)**

Membership rules apply for rental at BLOCKBUSTER®. Not valid with other discount offers. Any exchange for cash, sale, transfer or reproduction constitutes fraud and is prohibited. Must be relinquished upon redemption.

Actual savings may vary depending on item rented. Rental prices may vary by location. Free and paid rentals must be in same transaction. Excludes equipment and defensive driving rentals. Not valid with any other offers or discounts. This barcode only permits redemption of this coupon one time on one membership account. Limit one coupon of this type per membership account per day. Customer responsible for all applicable taxes and any charges other than the initial rental fee. See store for complete rental terms and conditions. Any exchange for cash, sale, transfer or reproduction constitutes fraud and is prohibited. Must be relinquished upon redemption. If customer rents multiple movies when redeeming this coupon, credit will be applied to lowest rental price. Membership rules apply for rental.

5610Z300014

Membership rules apply for rental at BLOCKBUSTER®. Not valid with other discount offers. Any exchange for cash, sale, transfer or reproduction constitutes fraud and is prohibited. Must be relinquished upon redemption.

Actual savings may vary depending on item rented. Rental prices may vary by location. Free and paid rentals must be in same transaction. Excludes game, equipment and defensive driving rentals. Not valid with any other offers or discounts. This barcode only permits redemption of this coupon one time on one membership account. Limit one coupon of this type per membership account per day. Customer responsible for all applicable taxes and any charges other than the initial rental fee. See store for complete rental terms and conditions. Any exchange for cash, sale, transfer or reproduction constitutes fraud and is prohibited. Must be relinquished upon redemption. If customer rents multiple movies when redeeming this coupon, credit will be applied to lowest rental price. Membership rules apply for rental.

5610UY00014

Membership rules apply for rental at BLOCKBUSTER®. Not valid with other discount offers. Any exchange for cash, sale, transfer or reproduction constitutes fraud and is prohibited. Must be relinquished upon redemption.

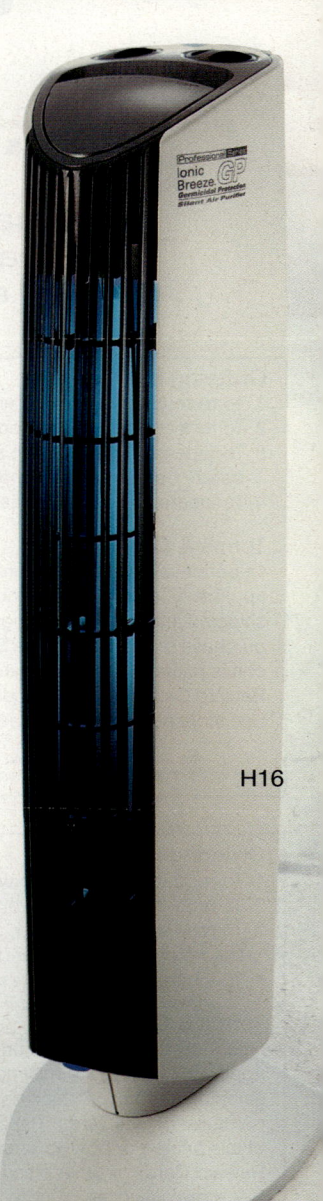

THE SHARPER IMAGE®

sharperimage.com™

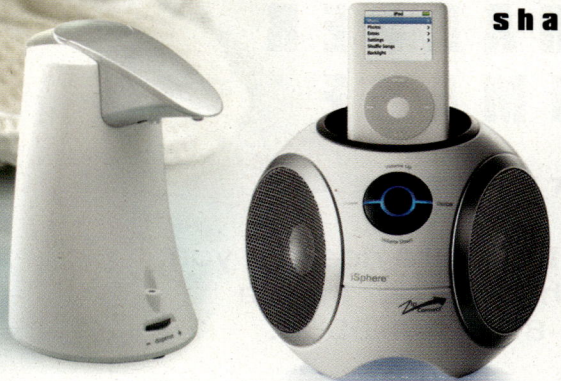

SHARPER IMAGE™
Save up to $50

Save $10 off any purchase of $50 or more or $50 off any purchase of $250 or more from The Sharper Image stores, catalog and Website.

The Sharper Image® shares the fun of discovering innovative products that make life better and more enjoyable. As America's premier specialty retailer, The Sharper Image is a great place to go for gifts and products for the home, office and travel.

POS CODE: EB7   Valid now thru December 31, 2007
See reverse side for details

©2006 Sharper Image Corporation

H16

SHARPER IMAGE™
Save up to $50

Save $10 off any purchase of $50 or more or $50 off any purchase of $250 or more from The Sharper Image stores, catalog and Website.

The Sharper Image® shares the fun of discovering innovative products that make life better and more enjoyable. As America's premier specialty retailer, The Sharper Image is a great place to go for gifts and products for the home, office and travel.

POS CODE: EB7   Valid now thru December 31, 2007
See reverse side for details

©2006 Sharper Image Corporation

H17

THE SHARPER IMAGE®

sharperimage.com™

To locate the store nearest you,
call The Sharper Image
at 1-800-344-5555.

Ordering Instructions
1. To redeem online, go to www.sharperimage.com/eb7 to receive your savings.
2. To redeem in store, surrender this coupon at the time of purchase.
3. To redeem by mail order, subtract the discount from the total merchandise amount before calculating tax and shipping and submit this coupon with the mail order form.
4. To locate the store nearest you, call The Sharper Image® at 1-800-344-5555.

Terms & Conditions
Offer not valid with phone orders or at any Sharper Image Auction site. The discount is applicable to, and the minimum purchase based on, merchandise prices only and excludes tax, shipping and tax on shipping. Not valid toward previously purchased merchandise or for the purchase of Gift Cards. The Sharper Image is not required to honor this coupon if any portion of it is printed or posted in error. Not valid with Price Matching Policy, Merchandise Certificates, Reward Cards or other discount/promotional offers. Not all products are eligible for discount. See store associate or individual product pages for details. Offer expires 12/31/2007.

Offer validity is governed by the Rules of Use and excludes defined holidays. Offers are not valid with other discount offers, unless specified. Coupons void if purchased, sold or bartered. Discounts exclude tax, tip and/or alcohol, where applicable.

Ordering Instructions
1. To redeem online, go to www.sharperimage.com/eb7 to receive your savings.
2. To redeem in store, surrender this coupon at the time of purchase.
3. To redeem by mail order, subtract the discount from the total merchandise amount before calculating tax and shipping and submit this coupon with the mail order form.
4. To locate the store nearest you, call The Sharper Image® at 1-800-344-5555.

Terms & Conditions
Offer not valid with phone orders or at any Sharper Image Auction site. The discount is applicable to, and the minimum purchase based on, merchandise prices only and excludes tax, shipping and tax on shipping. Not valid toward previously purchased merchandise or for the purchase of Gift Cards. The Sharper Image is not required to honor this coupon if any portion of it is printed or posted in error. Not valid with Price Matching Policy, Merchandise Certificates, Reward Cards or other discount/promotional offers. Not all products are eligible for discount. See store associate or individual product pages for details. Offer expires 12/31/2007.

Offer validity is governed by the Rules of Use and excludes defined holidays. Offers are not valid with other discount offers, unless specified. Coupons void if purchased, sold or bartered. Discounts exclude tax, tip and/or alcohol, where applicable.

RadioShack

The newest technology. The hottest brands. The best personal service. Have you visited your neighborhood RadioShack lately? Clip a coupon below and save today.

PRESENT THIS COUPON FOR
$10 OFF
A PURCHASE OF $40 OR MORE.

Must present this coupon to receive offer.

Valid now thru December 31, 2007
See reverse side for details

RadioShack

H18

PRESENT THIS COUPON FOR
$10 OFF
A PURCHASE OF $40 OR MORE.

Must present this coupon to receive offer.

Valid now thru December 31, 2007
See reverse side for details

RadioShack

H19

RadioShack®

Over 4,500 retail locations nationwide.
For a store near you, call 1-800-THE-SHACK®
or visit us at www.radioshack.com

$10 OFF A PURCHASE OF $40 OR MORE.

Must present this coupon to receive offer. Offer expires 12/31/07. Limit one coupon per person per visit. Services, online and phone orders excluded. May not be combined with any other discount offer. No cash value. No photocopies. Void where prohibited. Valid at participating stores only. Find the store nearest you at www.radioshack.com.

RSS Instructions: If the ticket total is $40.00 or more, use a Line Item Price Change to reduce the price of a product by $10.00. Select reason code "7.Promo/Coupon" and scan the barcode for the comment or type in the number under the barcode.

ENT2006

RadioShack®

Offer validity is governed by the Rules of Use and excludes defined holidays. Offers are not valid with other discount offers, unless specified. Coupons void if purchased, sold or bartered. Discounts exclude tax, tip and/or alcohol, where applicable.

$10 OFF A PURCHASE OF $40 OR MORE.

Must present this coupon to receive offer. Offer expires 12/31/07. Limit one coupon per person per visit. Services, online and phone orders excluded. May not be combined with any other discount offer. No cash value. No photocopies. Void where prohibited. Valid at participating stores only. Find the store nearest you at www.radioshack.com.

RSS Instructions: If the ticket total is $40.00 or more, use a Line Item Price Change to reduce the price of a product by $10.00. Select reason code "7.Promo/Coupon" and scan the barcode for the comment or type in the number under the barcode.

ENT2006

RadioShack®

Offer validity is governed by the Rules of Use and excludes defined holidays. Offers are not valid with other discount offers, unless specified. Coupons void if purchased, sold or bartered. Discounts exclude tax, tip and/or alcohol, where applicable.

Gateway®

TAKE AN EXTRA
$50 OFF

Visit **Gateway.com** and save even more when you combine your $50 coupon with specific limited time promotions on select award-winning **Desktop** and **Notebook** PCs.

Save today by entering **Coupon Code: GWENT001** when you check out.

Coupon only available at Gateway.com on Desktops $599 and up and Notebooks $799 and up.

Valid now thru December 31, 2007

Limited time offer to U.S. customers only with the purchase of up to two new desktops, notebooks or combination of systems. Qualifying desktops must be at least $599 and notebooks must be $799 before shipping/handling/tax. Offer can be combined with current advertising promotions including free offers and upgrades, instant and mail-in rebates, but cannot be combined with contractual or program discounts or coupon codes. Discount only available through Gateway.com with an expiration date of December 31, 2007.
Offer validity is governed by the Rules of Use. Coupons void if purchased, sold or bartered.

Ad code: 128508
H20

Brookstone
HARD TO FIND TOOLS™

UNIQUE SOLUTIONS FOR THE DISTINCTIVE HOME

Organize • Protect • Beautify

Call 1-800-926-7000 or shop brookstone.com

$10 off
any purchase of $75 or more
via Web and phone orders

Offer valid on Web and phone orders, not at retail stores. Use promo code TM2E175H at checkout or when placing phone orders. Minimum purchase does not include gift certificates, gift cards, gift wrap, shipping and handling, sales tax, Bose®, mattresses, game tables, or massage chairs. Limit one coupon per order. Cash value is 1/20 of one cent. Expires 12/31/07.

Promo Code: TM2E175H

Valid now thru December 31, 2007

H21   Offer validity is governed by the Rules of Use and excludes defined holidays. Coupons void if purchased, sold or bartered.

$20 off
any purchase of $150 or more
via Web and phone orders

Offer valid on Web and phone orders, not at retail stores. Use promo code TM3E215H at checkout or when placing phone orders. Minimum purchase does not include gift certificates, gift cards, gift wrap, shipping and handling, sales tax, Bose®, mattresses, game tables, or massage chairs. Limit one coupon per order. Cash value is 1/20 of one cent. Expires 12/31/07.

Promo Code: TM3E215H

Valid now thru December 31, 2007

H22   Offer validity is governed by the Rules of Use and excludes defined holidays. Coupons void if purchased, sold or bartered.

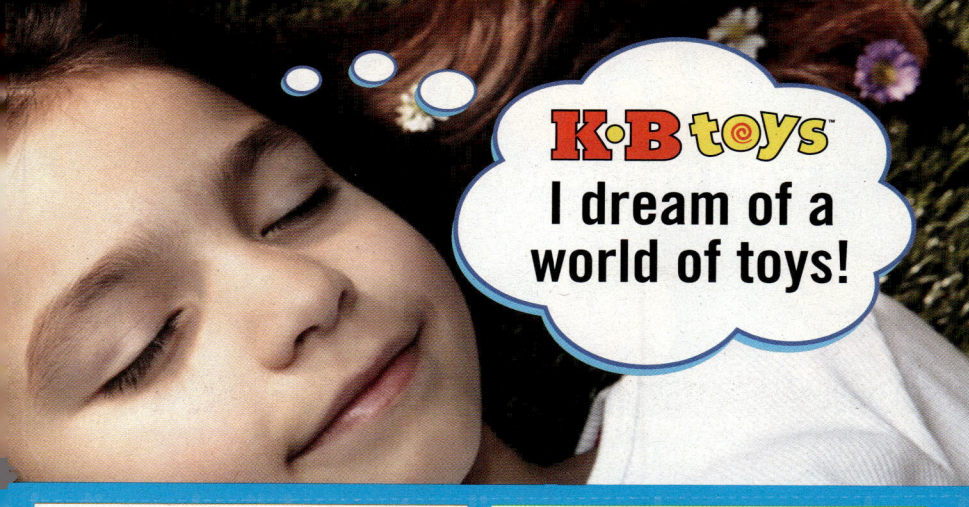

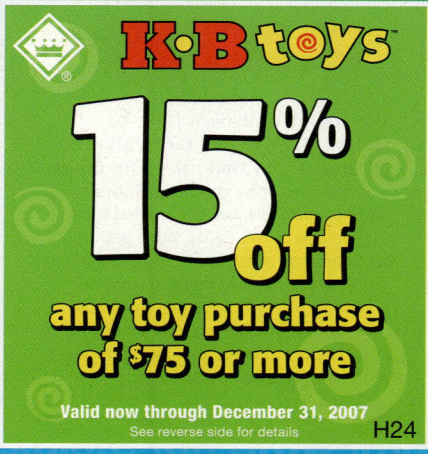

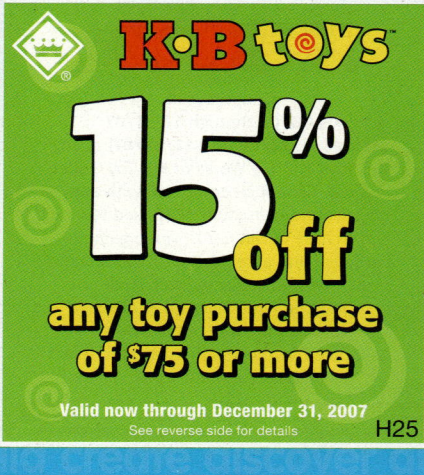

K·B toys
I dream of a world of toys!

K·B toys
$20 off
any toy purchase of $100 or more
Valid now through December 31, 2007
See reverse side for details
H23

K·B toys
15% off
any toy purchase of $75 or more
Valid now through December 31, 2007
See reverse side for details
H24

K·B toys
15% off
any toy purchase of $75 or more
Valid now through December 31, 2007
See reverse side for details
H25

K·B toys
$20 off
any toy purchase of $100 or more
Valid now through December 31, 2007
See reverse side for details
H26

K·B toys

To find the store nearest you, call toll-free:
1-888-4KB-TOYS (1-888-452-8697)

At K·B Toys, we know getting the right toy can be a dream come true for a child. Shopping for toys should be magical and at K·B Toys, it is.

K·B toys

Coupon valid 09/01/06 through 12/31/07 **(except 11/24/06 and 11/23/07)** at any K·B Toys, K·B Toy Works or K·B Toy Outlet store. Cannot be combined with any other coupon, discount or applied toward purchase of Gift Cards, video games, hardware and accessories. Discount taken off lowest prices at register. Limit one coupon per visit. Sales taxes not valid toward purchase requirement. Associates: to process the discount, select "Entertainment 15%".

Offer validity is governed by the Rules of Use and excludes defined holidays. Offers are not valid with other discount offers, unless specified. Coupons void if purchased, sold or bartered. Discounts exclude tax, tip and/or alcohol, where applicable.

K·B toys

Coupon valid 09/01/06 through 12/31/07 **(except 11/24/06 and 11/23/07)** at any K·B Toys, K·B Toy Works or K·B Toy Outlet store. Cannot be combined with any other coupon, discount or applied toward purchase of Gift Cards, video games, hardware and accessories. Discount taken off lowest prices at register. Limit one coupon per visit. Sales taxes not valid toward purchase requirement. Associates: to process the discount, select "Entertainment $20".

Offer validity is governed by the Rules of Use and excludes defined holidays. Offers are not valid with other discount offers, unless specified. Coupons void if purchased, sold or bartered. Discounts exclude tax, tip and/or alcohol, where applicable.

K·B toys

Coupon valid 09/01/06 through 12/31/07 **(except 11/24/06 and 11/23/07)** at any K·B Toys, K·B Toy Works or K·B Toy Outlet store. Cannot be combined with any other coupon, discount or applied toward purchase of Gift Cards, video games, hardware and accessories. Discount taken off lowest prices at register. Limit one coupon per visit. Sales taxes not valid toward purchase requirement. Associates: to process the discount, select "Entertainment $20".

Offer validity is governed by the Rules of Use and excludes defined holidays. Offers are not valid with other discount offers, unless specified. Coupons void if purchased, sold or bartered. Discounts exclude tax, tip and/or alcohol, where applicable.

K·B toys

Coupon valid 09/01/06 through 12/31/07 **(except 11/24/06 and 11/23/07)** at any K·B Toys, K·B Toy Works or K·B Toy Outlet store. Cannot be combined with any other coupon, discount or applied toward purchase of Gift Cards, video games, hardware and accessories. Discount taken off lowest prices at register. Limit one coupon per visit. Sales taxes not valid toward purchase requirement. Associates: to process the discount, select "Entertainment 15%".

Offer validity is governed by the Rules of Use and excludes defined holidays. Offers are not valid with other discount offers, unless specified. Coupons void if purchased, sold or bartered. Discounts exclude tax, tip and/or alcohol, where applicable.

Fashion that goes the distance.

take $**25** off
your purchase of $75 or more.
Doubles to $50 off a purchase of $150 or more.
See reverse side for details.

NEW YORK & COMPANY

Valid now thru December 31, 2007
See reverse side for details

H27

---

take $**25** off
your purchase of $75 or more.
Doubles to $50 off a purchase of $150 or more.
See reverse side for details.

NEW YORK & COMPANY

Valid now thru December 31, 2007
See reverse side for details

H28

take $25 off

your purchase of $75 or more.

Doubles to **$50** off a purchase of **$150** or more. Please visit us at **nyandcompany.com** for the store nearest you, or call 1-877-902-7521.

Only one certificate, coupon, or discount per purchase (pre-tax). Not valid on previous purchases, redlines, gift certificate or gift card purchases. Not redeemable for cash, nor accepted as payment for any credit card account. Certificate may be used only once. A percentage of the discount will be lost for each item returned that yields a balance below the required purchase amount. Not valid at New York & Company Outlet stores. Not valid at nyandcompany.com. Expires 12/31/07. **Ring 3573**

NEW YORK & COMPANY

Please fill out and return to store associate

NAME
ADDRESS

PHONE
EMAIL

By giving us your email address, you are agreeing to receive promotional emails from New York & Company. You can opt out anytime by clicking the 'opt-out' link in every email.

EB2007

Offer validity is governed by the Rules of Use and excludes defined holidays. Offers are not valid with other discount offers, unless specified. Coupons void if purchased, sold or bartered. Discounts exclude tax, tip and/or alcohol, where applicable.

---

take $25 off

your purchase of $75 or more.

Doubles to **$50** off a purchase of **$150** or more. Please visit us at **nyandcompany.com** for the store nearest you, or call 1-877-902-7521.

Only one certificate, coupon, or discount per purchase (pre-tax). Not valid on previous purchases, redlines, gift certificate or gift card purchases. Not redeemable for cash, nor accepted as payment for any credit card account. Certificate may be used only once. A percentage of the discount will be lost for each item returned that yields a balance below the required purchase amount. Not valid at New York & Company Outlet stores. Not valid at nyandcompany.com. Expires 12/31/07. **Ring 3577**

NEW YORK & COMPANY

Please fill out and return to store associate

NAME
ADDRESS

PHONE
EMAIL

By giving us your email address, you are agreeing to receive promotional emails from New York & Company. You can opt out anytime by clicking the 'opt-out' link in every email.

EB2007

Offer validity is governed by the Rules of Use and excludes defined holidays. Offers are not valid with other discount offers, unless specified. Coupons void if purchased, sold or bartered. Discounts exclude tax, tip and/or alcohol, where applicable.

$20 off
when you spend $80

$50 off
when you spend $200

liz claiborne

Liz Claiborne carries the latest fashions for women, men, kids, and for the home. We have thousands of styles from elegant to casual, from modern to classic. You'll discover fresh looks that offer mix and match opportunities to create your individual style.

Visit **LizClaiborne.com** for this web-exclusive offer, valid for single use only. Enter the following promotion codes at checkout: **ENTER20** to receive $20 off, or **ENTER50** to receive $50 off.

Valid now thru December 31, 2007
See reverse side for details

H29

ELiSABETH

Elisabeth is a boutique approach to dressing for women who are in sync with great style, drawn to quality and love options. We carry the latest plus-size and plus-size petite looks for women from five unique collections — Elisabeth, Liz Claiborne Woman, Sigrid Olsen, Ellen Tracy and Emma James. You'll discover fresh looks that offer mix and match opportunities to create your individual style.

Visit **Elisabeth.com** for this web-exclusive offer, valid for single use only. Enter the following promotion codes at checkout: **ENTER20** to receive $20 off, or **ENTER50** to receive $50 off.

Valid now thru December 31, 2007
See reverse side for details

H30

25% off
entire purchase

liz claiborne
OUTLET STORES

Liz Claiborne is redefining the Outlet Experience. In our Outlet Stores you can always expect the largest and finest selection of first-quality merchandise. Apparel, handbags, shoes, coats, jewelry, accessories, and much, much more — they're all there. So come in today, and experience for yourself — the true meaning of unparalleled assortment and unbeatable value.

Tear out this coupon and bring it to your nearest Liz Claiborne Outlet Store.

Valid now thru December 31, 2007
See reverse side for details

H31

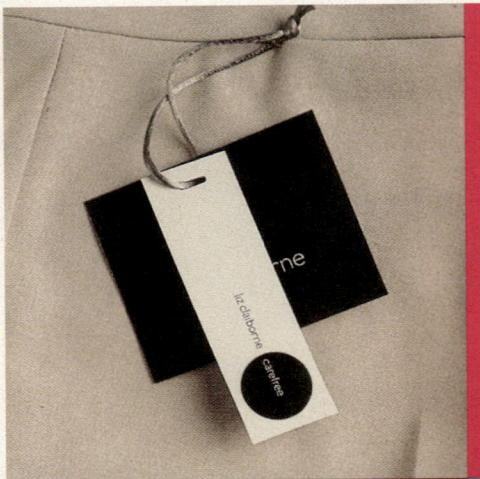

Receive $20 off of your $80 purchase or spend $200 and receive $50 off. This offer is available for one-time use only at LizClaiborne.com. Offer not valid towards the purchase of product for the Home, gift certificates, fundraising products or orders placed through group sales. Cannot be combined with any other offer. Offer not valid at outlet or departments stores. Cannot be used on previously purchased merchandise. No cash value. Void where prohibited. Employees of Liz Claiborne, Inc. and its subsidiaries are not eligible. Enter the following promotion codes: ENTER20 or ENTER50 at checkout. Orders must be placed by 12/31/07 11:59PM (EST) to qualify.

Receive $20 off of your $80 purchase or spend $200 and receive $50 off. This offer is available for one-time use only at Elisabeth.com. Offer not valid towards the purchase of gift certificates, fundraising products or orders placed through group sales. Cannot be combined with any other offer. Offer not valid at boutiques, outlet or departments stores. Cannot be used on previously purchased merchandise. No cash value. Void where prohibited. Employees of Liz Claiborne, Inc. and its subsidiaries are not eligible. Enter promotion code ENTER20 or ENTER50 at checkout. Orders must be placed by 12/31/07 11:59PM (EST) to qualify.

*Offer valid at Liz Claiborne Outlet Stores in the U.S.A. May not be combined with other offers or discounts. Not valid at specialty stores or online. Cannot be applied toward previous purchases or gift cards. One coupon per customer daily. This coupon may not be duplicated or reproduced and must be surrendered at time of purchase. Void where prohibited. No cash value. Purchases by employees of Liz Claiborne Inc. and its subsidiaries are not eligible.
Offer expires 12/31/07. Code ECB2006

For the nearest outlet store location, please visit www.lizclaiborne.com

420000004035

Offer validity is governed by the Rules of Use and excludes defined holidays. Offers are not valid with other discount offers, unless specified. Coupons void if purchased, sold or bartered. Discounts exclude tax, tip and/or alcohol, where applicable.

WOMEN'S FASHIONS IN SIZES 14 & UP

avenue®

LOOK GOOD FEEL GOOD!

100% FASHION

BOLD CONFIDENT SEXY UPBEAT

USE NOW THRU MAY 13, 2007
IN-STORE BONUS CARD
30% OFF*
ANY ONE ITEM
USE THIS CERTIFICATE
NOW THROUGH SUNDAY, MAY 13, 2007
AND RECEIVE 30% OFF* ANY ONE ITEM.
INCLUDING NEW ARRIVALS AND ITEMS ALREADY ON SALE.

avenue
nothing should stop you*
See reverse side for details   H32

VALID MAY 14, 2007 THROUGH DECEMBER 31, 2007
IN-STORE BONUS CARD
30% OFF*
ANY ONE ITEM
USE THIS CERTIFICATE
MONDAY, MAY 14, 2007 THROUGH
MONDAY, DECEMBER 31, 2007 AND RECEIVE
30% OFF* ANY ONE ITEM.
INCLUDING NEW ARRIVALS AND ITEMS ALREADY ON SALE.

avenue
nothing should stop you*
See reverse side for details   H33

WOMEN'S FASHIONS
SIZES 14 & UP

Experience the very newest styles to wear for work or play, we have everything you need or want.

Use these certificates at any Avenue® store and **save 30% off* any one item** including new arrivals and items already on sale.

To find an Avenue® store near you call 1-888-AVENUE-1 or visit avenue.com

SHOP IN-STORE
TO FIND A STORE NEAR YOU
CALL 1-888-AVENUE-1

SHOP ONLINE
VISIT US AT AVENUE.COM

SHOP BY PHONE
CALL 1-800-441-1362

Join our Email Club... New members receive a 20% off store certificate via their email. Sign up at www.avenue.com/email.html

---

30% OFF* ANY ONE ITEM

*This in-store card may be used toward new arrivals as well as merchandise already on sale. It is not valid toward "red star" items, "Special Edition" merchandise, previously purchased merchandise, gift certificates, gift cards, or Avenue.com purchases. It may not be redeemed for cash, used toward layaway purchases, or be combined with any other coupons or promotions. It may only be redeemed once throughout the duration of this promotion from Monday, May 14, 2007 through Monday, December 31, 2007. This offer is not available to Associates of United Retail, Inc. **Limit One Per Customer.**

928621820705140712310000 3072

avenue
nothing should stop you®   #862182

Offer validity is governed by the Rules of Use.
Coupons void if purchased, sold or bartered.

30% OFF* ANY ONE ITEM

*This in-store card may be used toward new arrivals as well as merchandise already on sale. It is not valid toward "red star" items, "Special Edition" merchandise, previously purchased merchandise, gift certificates, gift cards, or Avenue.com purchases. It may not be redeemed for cash, used toward layaway purchases, or be combined with any other coupons or promotions. It may only be redeemed once throughout the duration of this promotion now through Sunday, May 13, 2007. This offer is not available to Associates of United Retail, Inc. **Limit One Per Customer.**

928621810603150705130000 3071

avenue
nothing should stop you®   #862181

Offer validity is governed by the Rules of Use.
Coupons void if purchased, sold or bartered.

LANE BRYANT
Fashion for curvy women in sizes 14–28.

Valid through Dec. 31, 2007
See reverse side for details

Take $10 off any $50 purchase

in stores or online

LANE BRYANT
Shop lanebryant.com

H34

DISCOVER Lane Bryant

The latest looks…

amazing accessories…

must-have fashion at the

perfect price every day…

all you need is right here.

LANE BRYANT

For a store near you, call 1.800.940.6361 or visit lanebryant.com.

Take $10 off any $50 purchase

Use this coupon in stores or online.
To redeem online, enter promo code at checkout: **10008065**

Offer validity is governed by the rules of use. Coupons void if purchased, sold, or bartered. Only one coupon per customer. Not valid on permanently reduced, clearance or Perfect Price Every Day items. Wacoal, Natori, Bali or Spanx. Qualifying purchase is one minus discounts, promotions, purchased Gift Cards, shipping, tax and returns. May be used only once, can't be combined with other coupons or discounts, is not redeemable for cash, may not be applied to previous purchases, credit card payments or purchase of Gift Cards. If an item is returned which reduces the original purchase total to less than $50, a portion of the coupon value will be deducted from the refund. Valid in stores (except Lane Bryant outlet stores) and online through 11:59 PM EST December 31, 2007. Associates not eligible.

LANE BRYANT
Shop lanebryant.com

$10   LB806

Valid through
Dec. 31, 2007

1000 8065

FASHION BUG.
fashionbug.com

plus • misses • maternity • juniors • girls

enjoy
2 great ways to save…
one to use in stores,
one to use online.

IT'S BETTER AT THE
BUG

IN-STORE BONUS COUPON
FASHION BUG.
50% off
a single item
**Valid in any Fashion Bug store
now through Dec. 31, 2007**
More than 1,000 stores nationwide. Call 1.888.244.3347
or visit fashionbug.com for locations.
See reverse side for details. H35

ONLINE BONUS COUPON
FASHION BUG.
15% off
your fashionbug.com purchase
Valid now through Dec. 31, 2007
Just enter 776155707 at checkout to receive your discount.
See reverse side for details. H36

FASHION BUG®

fashionbug.com

plus • misses • maternity • juniors • girls

Be who you are. Love what you wear. Whatever your size, shape or style, Fashion Bug has great new looks that fit and flatter. All affordably priced.

06-0380A1 WK 6 © Charming Shoppes, Inc. 2006

FASHION BUG®
fashionbug.com

15% off

your fashionbug.com purchase

Valid now through Dec. 31, 2007

Just enter 776155707 at checkout to receive your discount.

15% discount valid online only. Good for one-time use. Offer valid until 11:59 P.M. EST on 12/31/07. Not valid in stores. Excludes "Priced Just Right" items and the purchase of Gift Cards. Cannot be combined with other promotion code offers. Not valid on purchases made at fashionbugcard.com.

Offer validity is governed by the Rules of Use. Coupons void if purchased, sold or bartered.

FASHION BUG®

50% off

a single item

Valid now through Dec. 31, 2007

Excludes "Priced Just Right" items. Coupon discount excludes sale offers of 40% or higher, Figure publications, prior purchases, layaways and the purchase of Gift Cards. Offer is redeemable one time only at any Fashion Bug store, and may not be combined with any other coupon or used as payment on your Fashion Bug Card. This offer is not valid for online purchases.

776155608

Offer validity is governed by the Rules of Use. Coupons void if purchased, sold or bartered.

CATHERINES®
PLUS SIZES

16W-26W • 16WP-26WP • 28W-34W

- **exclusive fashions** custom-designed to flatter
- **the perfect fit** feel as good as you look
- **more looks for less** with our legendary values

career | active | denim | accessories | social occasion | intimates

Two ways to save!
Shop now at catherines.com, or call 1.800.826.9649 for the store nearest you.

---

save at catherines.com!
10% off
your total purchase
enter promo code 444944664 at checkout

Valid now thru December 31, 2007
See reverse side for details
H37

---

save at catherines.com!
10% off
your total purchase
enter promo code 444841860 at checkout

Valid now thru December 31, 2007
See reverse side for details
H38

---

save in-store!
25% off
one reg. price item

Valid now thru December 31, 2007
See reverse side for details
H39

---

save in-store!
25% off
one reg. price item

Valid now thru December 31, 2007
See reverse side for details
H40

CATHERINES®
PLUS SIZES

16W-26W • 16WP-26WP • 28W-34W

- **exclusive fashions** custom-designed to flatter
- **the perfect fit** feel as good as you look
- **more looks for less** with our legendary values

career | active | denim | accessories | social occasion | intimates

Two ways to save!
Shop now at catherines.com, or call 1.800.826.9649 for the store nearest you.

---

save at catherines.com!

10% off
your total purchase
enter promo code 444841860 at checkout

Valid online only. Limit one coupon per customer. Cannot be combined with any other offer or used toward past purchases. Perfect Price items, 14K gold, handbags, Spanx® hosiery, gift cards and Perks memberships not included.

Offer validity is governed by the Rules of Use.
Coupons void if purchased, sold or bartered.

---

save at catherines.com!

10% off
your total purchase
enter promo code 444944664 at checkout

Valid online only. Limit one coupon per customer. Cannot be combined with any other offer or used toward past purchases. Perfect Price items, 14K gold, handbags, Spanx® hosiery, gift cards and Perks memberships not included.

Offer validity is governed by the Rules of Use.
Coupons void if purchased, sold or bartered.

---

save in-store!

25% off
one reg. price item

776754806

Must present coupon at time of purchase. Limit one coupon per customer. Cannot be used toward past purchases or layaways, online purchases or credit card payments. Perfect Price items, 14K gold, handbags, Spanx® hosiery, gift cards and Perks memberships not included.

Offer validity is governed by the Rules of Use.
Coupons void if purchased, sold or bartered.

---

save in-store!

25% off
one reg. price item

776754806

Must present coupon at time of purchase. Limit one coupon per customer. Cannot be used toward past purchases or layaways, online purchases or credit card payments. Perfect Price items, 14K gold, handbags, Spanx® hosiery, gift cards and Perks memberships not included.

Offer validity is governed by the Rules of Use.
Coupons void if purchased, sold or bartered.

THE TERRITORY AHEAD

Exceptional Clothing for Men & Women
Call 800-882-4323 for a FREE catalog
www.territoryahead.com

SAVE $10

WHEN YOU MAKE A PURCHASE OF $50 OR MORE.

Redeem online at territoryahead.com, by phone at 800-882-4323, or in one of our stores.
Visit our website to find a store location near you.

THE TERRITORY AHEAD
Exceptional Clothing for Life's Adventures

Limit one offer per coupon. Reproductions are not accepted. Void where prohibited by law. No cash value. Savings may not be combined with any other promotions, and discount is not valid on gift certificate purchases. May not be applied to previous purchases. Offer good now through December 31, 2007.

**Please mention Key Code 6G1100 if ordering by phone.
If ordering online, enter Key Code at checkout.**

Offer validity is governed by the Rules of Use and excludes defined holidays. Offers are not valid with other discount offers, unless specified. Coupons void if purchased, sold or bartered. Discounts exclude tax, tip and/or alcohol, where applicable.   H41

SAVE $20

WHEN YOU MAKE A PURCHASE OF $100 OR MORE.

Redeem online at territoryahead.com, by phone at 800-882-4323, or in one of our stores.
Visit our website to find a store location near you.

THE TERRITORY AHEAD
Exceptional Clothing for Life's Adventures

Limit one offer per coupon. Reproductions are not accepted. Void where prohibited by law. No cash value. Savings may not be combined with any other promotions, and discount is not valid on gift certificate purchases. May not be applied to previous purchases. Offer good now through December 31, 2007.

**Please mention Key Code 6G1100 if ordering by phone.
If ordering online, enter Key Code at checkout.**

Offer validity is governed by the Rules of Use and excludes defined holidays. Offers are not valid with other discount offers, unless specified. Coupons void if purchased, sold or bartered. Discounts exclude tax, tip and/or alcohol, where applicable.   H42

Garnet Hill

original design for home and fashion

- exclusive bedding
- home decor
- women's apparel
- designer footwear

Save $10 on any purchase of $50 or more

or

Save $50 on any purchase of $250 or more

at Garnet Hill, Growing Up with Garnet Hill or at garnethill.com.

To request a catalog, visit garnethill.com or call 1-800-622-6216.

How to Redeem: By Phone — Call 1-800-622-6216 and mention code G6KMENT when ordering.
By Web — Shop garnethill.com and enter G6KMENT in the catalog source code box during checkout.

This offer is valid on purchases from Garnet Hill. It is limited to one time use and cannot be combined with other discount offers. Qualified purchase amounts and discounts are based on merchandise prices only and exclude shipping, handling and taxes. There is no cash value to this offer and it cannot be used towards purchase of gift certificates or be applied to prior purchase. Offer void where prohibited.

Valid now thru December 31, 2007

H43   Offer validity is governed by the Rules of Use and excludes defined holidays. Offers are not valid with other discount offers, unless specified. Coupons void if purchased, sold or bartered. Discounts exclude tax, tip and/or alcohol, where applicable.

grandinroad
affordable style

Call 1-800-491-5194 for a free catalog—
or shop grandinroad.com
for hundreds of inspired ideas for
your home, garden, and more.

Valid now thru December 31, 2007
See reverse side for details

H44

---

a spirited collection of designs with kids in mind

Growing Up with
garnet hill

- colorful clothing
- home furnishings • fun accessories

Save $10
on any purchase
of $50 or more

or

Save $50
on any purchase
of $250 or more

To order, call 1-800-260-1926 or visit us
online at garnethill.com.

Valid now thru December 31, 2007
See reverse side for details

H45

Improvements®
Quick & Clever Problem-Solvers®

ImprovementsCatalog.com

**SAVE 20% on your first
purchase of $50 or more!**

- To redeem this coupon and receive your **20%** discount, enter the following Source Code when asked for it on your check-out screen: **ENT2007**
- You may also call 1-800-642-2112, and mention "Source Code **ENT2007**" to our operator to receive your **20%** discount.
- Discount is **20%** off any order with a merchandise total of $50 or more.
- Limit one order per coupon.
- Not valid with any other offer, discount or special promotion.
- Excludes shipping and processing fees, sales tax, clearance and sale-priced merchandise.

Valid now thru December 31, 2007
See reverse side for details

Exclusive **Lighted Travel Mirror** has dual, distortion-free glass mirrors that fold compactly for travel.

Just one example of the "Quick & Clever Problem-Solvers" you won't find anywhere else!

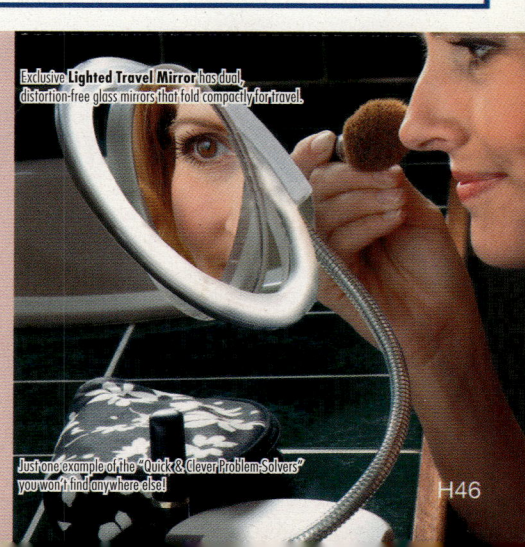

H46

grandinroad

$10 off
any $50 purchase at
grandinroad.com
Keycode: EB0610G

$25 off
any $150 purchase at
grandinroad.com
Keycode: EB0625G

$50 off
any $300 purchase at
grandinroad.com
Keycode: EB0650G

Redeem online at grandinroad.com by entering keycode at checkout.
Or, order by phone at 1-800-491-5194 and mention keycode.

Offer is not valid with any other discount or promotional offer, or on prior purchases. Discount is applicable to merchandise only, excluding tax and shipping. Cannot be used towards gift certificates or on Bose® electronics. Coupon may be used one time per household. Expires December 31, 2007.

Offer validity is governed by the Rules of Use and excludes defined holidays. Offers are not valid with other discount offers, unless specified. Coupons void if purchased, sold or bartered. Discounts exclude tax, tip and/or alcohol, where applicable.

---

a spirited collection of designs with kids in mind

Growing Up with garnet hill

To request a catalog, visit garnethill.com or call 1-800-260-1926.

How to Redeem: By Phone — Call 1-800-260-1926 and mention code **C6KMENT** when ordering.

By Web — Shop garnethill.com and enter **C6KMENT** in the catalog source code box during checkout.

This offer is valid on purchases from Garnet Hill. It is limited to one-time use and cannot be combined with other discount offers. Qualified purchase amounts and discounts are based on merchandise prices only and exclude shipping, handling and taxes. There is no cash value to this offer and it cannot be used towards the purchase of gift certificates or be applied to a prior purchase. Offer void where prohibited.

Offer validity is governed by the Rules of Use and excludes defined holidays. Offers are not valid with other discount offers, unless specified. Coupons void if purchased, sold or bartered. Discounts exclude tax, tip and/or alcohol, where applicable.

Improvements®
Quick & Clever Problem-Solvers!

When you shop at ImprovementsCatalog.com, you'll find over **1,700** handy and practical items that make life around your home, yard and car easier and less of a hassle.

And dozens of those problem-solvers are available **ONLY** from the Improvements® web site and printed catalog. The Lighted Travel Mirror is just one example, but of course there's more in store on our web site:

- Daily Specials!
- Bargain-Priced Outlet Mall!
- Internet-Only Special Buys!
- FREE Account Registration
- Much more than in our printed catalog!

Offer validity is governed by the Rules of Use and excludes defined holidays. Offers are not valid with other discount offers, unless specified. Coupons void if purchased, sold or bartered. Discounts exclude tax, tip and/or alcohol, where applicable.

SAVE 15%
on your first order

NEW CUSTOMERS SAVE 15% ON A SINGLE-ITEM PURCHASE WITH COUPON #990220.

Shop from the comfort of home for jewelry, beauty, fashion, cookware, fitness, sports, collectibles, home items and more. Order by phone or online and enjoy easy returns with our 30-day money-back guarantee.

For more great offers visit
www.hsn.com/entertainment

To order, visit hsn.com/entertainment or call 1.800.284.3100

SAVE $20
on any item over $100

All customers save $20 on any single-item purchase over $100. To receive your savings, refer to coupon #202099.

Coupon #990220 is for new customers only and is valid for 15% off your first single-item purchase with a maximum savings of $50 from HSN or hsn.com. Coupon #202099 is for all customers and is valid for $20 off any single-item purchase of $100 or more from HSN or hsn.com. Coupons are non-transferable and can only be used once per customer. Excludes shipping & handling, sales tax, Today's Special, clearance department and sale priced merchandise, electronics and computers. Coupons cannot be applied on HSN Protection Plus or combined with other coupons or offers, and coupons are not valid on purchases of alcoholic beverages and wine.com. We reserve the right to cancel orders when unexpected coupon system errors occur. Entertainment® membership card number required to redeem savings. Offer validity is governed by the Rules of Use and excludes defined holidays. Coupons void if purchased, sold or bartered. Offers valid through December 31, 2007.

HSN
hsn.com

VONAGE®
LEADING THE INTERNET PHONE REVOLUTION℠

Stop Paying TOO MUCH for Phone Service!

The **New Way** to Phone!

- Local & Long Distance Calling : **UNLIMITED!**
- Voicemail : **No Extra Cost!**
- Caller ID : **No Extra Cost!**
- Call Waiting : **No Extra Cost!**
- Call Return : **No Extra Cost!**
- Plus Many More Features!

Best Offer Yet!
$19.99/month
for 6 months†

Vonage 911 service operates differently than traditional 911. See www.vonage.com/911 for details. Service fee is $24.99 after 6 months. New subscribers only. † Rates exclude: broadband service, activation, regulatory recovery fee, 911 fees & cost recovery, premium services, equipment, Vonage compatible equipment, disconnect fee, taxes, and shipping. International calls billed/min. Credit card & high-speed Internet required. Satellite TV & alarm systems may require land line. See Terms of Service for details. ‡ 50% off claim based on 2/06 survey of competing land line service providers. For complete information see www.vonage.com/compare. ^Where available. Number transfer averages 10-14 days from customer authorization. ©2001-2006, Vonage Marketing, Inc., All Rights Reserved.

Save up to 50% or More on Your Phone Bill!‡

Keep Your Phone Number!^

Call: **1-800-846-4133**
Visit: **www.vonage.com/ent07**

Valid now thru December 31, 2007

H48 Offer validity is governed by the Rules of Use and excludes defined holidays. Offers are not valid with other discount offers, unless specified. Coupons void if purchased, sold or bartered. Discounts exclude tax, tip and/or alcohol, where applicable.

$15 off your $75 order
$20 off your $100 order
$30 off your $150 order

Shop our entire line — and save!

Find outstanding fashion values every day for women, men and home. Plus clearance buys at up to 70% off.

Save even more with this exclusive offer. To take advantage of the savings, go to www.blair.com/entertainment

BLAIR®

You must visit www.blair.com/entertainment for this special offer. You'll see your discount automatically at checkout with your merchandise order of $75 or more. This offer applies to online orders only and cannot be combined with other offers. Good through December 31, 2007.

Offer validity is governed by the Rules of Use and excludes defined holidays. Offers are not valid with other discount offers, unless specified. Coupons void if purchased, sold or bartered. Discounts exclude tax, tip and/or alcohol, where applicable.

H49

ACE®
The helpful place.

$5 OFF*
any $25 purchase

Valid now through December 31, 2007

See reverse side for details.

H50

Save Big on SIRIUS

15% OFF all Radios and Accessories.
Plus, get a FREE 7 Day Pass to listen to SIRIUS Music online.

SIRIUS Satellite Radio is 100% commercial-free music, plus the best news, sports and entertainment programming in all of radio.
Please visit **www.entertainment.com/sirius**
and have your Entertainment® membership number available.

- NFL
- NBA
- HOWARD STERN
- MARTHA STEWART LIVING RADIO
- BIG 80s
- COSMO RADIO

*15% discount cannot be combined with any other offer or discounts and is not valid for gift card purchases. Terms apply. © 2006 SIRIUS Satellite Radio Inc. "SIRIUS", the SIRIUS dog logo and related marks are trademarks of SIRIUS Satellite Radio Inc. The NFL Shield design is a registered trademark of the National Football League. The NBA silhouette logo is a registered trademark of NBA Properties, Inc. All other trademarks, service marks and logos are the property of their respective owners. All Rights Reserved. All fees and programming content are subject to change. Offer validity is governed by the Rules of Use and excludes defined holidays. Offers are not valid with other discount offers, unless specified. Coupons void if purchased, sold or bartered. Discounts exclude tax, tip and/or alcohol, where applicable.

Valid now through December 31, 2007

H51

$5 OFF*

ACE The helpful place.

any $25 purchase

Valid now through December 31, 2007.

$5.00 COUPON

8003 3547

*At participating Ace Hardware stores. Coupon not valid on sale and clearance priced Merchandise or in combination with any other coupon offer. May not be used toward rental items, in-store services, on-line purchases, for the purchase of the Ace Gift Card, or for previously purchased merchandise. Not redeemable for cash.
Cashier: Scan "$5 off" barcode in the body of the transaction or ring as in-store coupon.

Offer validity is governed by the Rules of Use and excludes defined holidays. Offers are not valid with other discount offers, unless specified. Coupons void if purchased, sold or bartered. Discounts exclude tax, tip and/or alcohol, where applicable.

125_103094_0106

Start Investing Online Today with **ShareBuilder**

Special Offer for Entertainment® Members

Get $30 Cash!* when you start investing

ShareBuilder Benefits:
- $30 account bonus*
- No account minimums
- Invest any dollar amount in the stocks you want
- 100% online service
- Free investment advice

Redeem $30 bonus now*

The easy, low-cost way to **invest** in the stock market

1. Visit www.sharebuilder.com/30entertain
2. Open a new ShareBuilder Individual, Joint or Custodial Account
3. Enter Promo Code: **30ENTERTAIN**

* $30 Account Bonus: You must open a new ShareBuilder Individual, Joint or Custodial Account and enter promo code 30ENTERTAIN to receive the $30 bonus offer. Please note the $30 credit will post to your account approximately 4-5 weeks after the first transaction executes. The $30 offer is not valid with IRA or Education Savings Accounts. Not valid with any other offers. ShareBuilder is not affiliated with Entertainment Publications.

© 2006 ShareBuilder Corporation. ShareBuilder is a registered trademark of ShareBuilder Corporation. Patent Pending. ShareBuilder Securities Corporation, a registered broker dealer, is a subsidiary of ShareBuilder Corporation and Member NASD/SIPC.

Please call (800) 215-4679 with any questions about ShareBuilder.

Valid now thru December 31, 2007
Offer validity is governed by the Rules of Use and excludes defined holidays. Coupons void if purchased, sold or bartered.

shareBuilder®

H52

AMERICA'S MOST ADVANCED TV AT THE LOWEST PRICE!

monthly rates as low as
$19.99 PER MONTH!*

CALL US FOR CURRENT PROMOTIONS

FREE 4-ROOM SYSTEM
FREE PROFESSIONAL INSTALLATION
FREE DIGITAL VIDEO RECORDERS
FREE LIFETIME WARRANTY

ASK US ABOUT HDTV!

dish NETWORK

Limited time offer expires soon. Certain restrictions apply. Please visit our website for current pricing, promotional information, and current terms and conditions.

WWW.SATELLITECOUPON.COM
ORDER BY PHONE (866) 423-1886

NOW WITH NEXT DAY INSTALLATION!*
when you order by 10:00 a.m. (excluding weekends)
Valid now thru December 31, 2007

Offer validity is governed by the Rules of Use and excludes defined holidays. Offers are not valid with other discount offers, unless specified. Coupons void if purchased, sold or bartered.

H53

SPECIAL DIRECTV OFFER!

DIRECTV

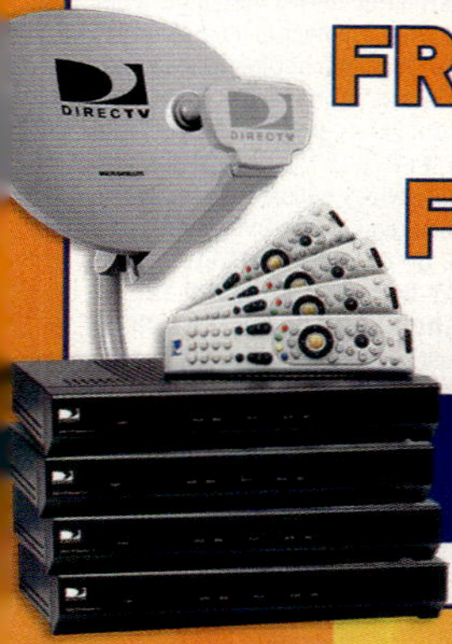

FREE INSTALLATION*
OF A DIRECTV® SYSTEM
*ON APPROVED CREDIT. PROGRAMMING COMMITMENT REQUIRED.
$19.95 HANDLING AND DELIVERY FEE APPLIES.

FREE DVR UPGRADE
After $100 mail-in rebate. While supplies last.

FREE IPOD® SHUFFLE™
From DirectStarTV. While supplies last. After mail-in rebate.

DIRECT ✷ STAR TV
An Authorized DIRECTV Dealer

CALL 1-866-747-7043
AND SCHEDULE YOUR INSTALLATION TODAY!

Valid now thru December 31, 2007   See reverse side for details

H54

PETSMART

Grooming

- PetSmart® safety-certified PetStylists trained in breed-specific and customized services
- Convenient hours— seven days a week and evenings
- Package includes bath, massage, blow dry, nail trimming, ear cleaning and bow or bandana

save $10
on our Bath, Brush & More package

Valid now thru December 31, 2007
See reverse side for details

H55

PETSMART

Doggie Day Camp℠

- All-day play and exercise
- PetSmart® safety-certified pet-loving professional caregivers
- Safe and clean environment
- Pawsitively Safe℠ health and temperament assessment

free day pass
(up to $23 value)

Valid now thru December 31, 2007
See reverse side for details

H56

iPod® Shuffle™ OFFER: iPod® Shuffle™ is provided by DirectStarTV and is not sponsored by DIRECTV. Limit one iPod® Shuffle™ and free system per household. To be eligible for the iPod® Shuffle™, you must be a new DIRECTV customer, have ordered a DIRECTV System from DirectStarTV via this offer, and complied with the following redemption instructions. Redemption instructions: To claim the iPod® Shuffle™, mail in an original copy of your first paid DIRECTV monthly bill and an original copy of this advertisement to iPod® Shuffle™, 14120 Ballantyne Corporate Place, Suite 200, Charlotte, NC 28277. Upon validation (which is the sole discretion of DirectStarTV), the iPod® Shuffle™ will be mailed to your billing address. Please allow 6-8 weeks for delivery. Offer void in Alaska and Hawaii, and where prohibited or restricted. May not be combined with any other offer. Apple® is not a sponsor or participant in this program. **HARDWARE LEASE:** Purchase of 12 consecutive months (24 consecutive months for advanced receivers) of any DIRECTV TOTAL CHOICE ($44.99/mo. or above) or DIRECTV PARA TODOS package ($29.99/mo. or above), or qualifying international services bundle required within 30 days of equipment lease. In certain markets, programming/pricing may vary. DVR service activation required for DVR and HD DVR lease. **FAILURE TO ACTIVATE DIRECTV SYSTEM WITHIN 30 DAYS MAY RESULT IN CHARGE OF $150 PER RECEIVER NOT ACTIVATED. IF YOU FAIL TO MAINTAIN YOUR PROGRAMMING COMMITMENT, DIRECTV MAY CHARGE PRORATED FEE OF UP TO $300. RECEIVERS ARE AT ALL TIMES PROPERTY OF DIRECTV AND MUST BE RETURNED UPON CANCELLATION OF SERVICE, OR ADDITIONAL FEES APPLY.** NEW CUSTOMER $100 MAIL-IN REBATE: Customer must complete and sign rebate form (sent automatically in first DIRECTV bill or in a separate mailing) and comply with the terms on the form. ©2006 DIRECTV, Inc. DIRECTV, the Cyclone Design logo and TOTAL CHOICE are registered trademarks of DIRECTV, Inc. All other trademarks and service marks are the property of their respective owners.

Subject to Rules of Use. Not valid with other discount offers, unless specified. Coupon VOID if purchased, sold, or bartered for cash.

DIRECT ★ STAR TV
An Authorized DIRECTV Dealer

PETSMART™ grooming

Please visit petsmartgrooming.com or call 1-877-4-PetSmart for current locations and more information. Simply call any of our locations to book your appointment and bring in this certificate to receive offer.

4 15108 36661 1

Valid through 12/31/07 only at PetSmart® in U.S. For new customers only. Must present coupon with purchase. Limit one coupon per customer and transaction. Not valid toward groom upgrade. Void if copied. Not redeemable for cash or credit. Non-transferable. Not valid with any other discount or offer. Based on availability. Current vaccinations required. Call or visit your local PetSmart store for more details. PetSmart reserves the right to refuse or limit this service. ©2006 PetSmart Store Support Group, Inc. All rights reserved.

Offer validity is governed by the Rules of Use and excludes defined holidays. Offers are not valid with other discount offers, unless specified. Coupons void if purchased, sold or bartered. Discounts exclude tax, tip and/or alcohol, where applicable.

PETSMART™ doggie day camp

Please visit petsmartdoggiedaycamp.com or call 1-877-4-PetSmart for current locations and more information. Simply call any of our locations to book your reservation and bring in this certificate to receive offer.

4 15108 36500 3

Valid through 12/31/07 only at PetSmart® in U.S. For new customers only. Up to $23 value. Must present coupon with purchase. Limit one coupon per customer and transaction. Void if copied. Not redeemable for cash or credit. No credit if purchase is less than coupon value. Non-transferable. Not valid with any other discount or offer. Based on availability. Current vaccinations required. Dogs must pass a health and temperament assessment and be at least five months old to participate. Call or visit your local PetSmart Doggie Day Camp for more details. PetSmart reserves the right to refuse or limit this service. ©2006 PetSmart Store Support Group, Inc. All rights reserved.

Offer validity is governed by the Rules of Use and excludes defined holidays. Offers are not valid with other discount offers, unless specified. Coupons void if purchased, sold or bartered. Discounts exclude tax, tip and/or alcohol, where applicable.

New and Improved Offer!

Same Day Delivery and the quality you trust!

Save $15 or 25% Order Now!

EVERYDAY SAVINGS:
Please retain coupon for repeat use

Save $15 on all Flowers
when you order online at www.ftd.com/ent2007

or Save $10
When you dial **1-800-SEND-FTD** and mention promo code **11967**

Valid now thru December 31, 2007　　See reverse side for details　　H57

EVERYDAY SAVINGS:
Please retain coupon for repeat use

Save 25% off all products
when you order online at www.ftd.com/entertainment

Valid now thru December 31, 2007　　See reverse side for details　　H58

SAVE UP TO $15
on all flowers when you order from FTD

To receive $15 off you must order online at www.ftd.com/ent2007 or
To receive $10 off dial 1-800-SEND-FTD and mention promo code 11967.
This offer cannot be combined with any other offer. Valid through December 31, 2007.

This coupon/coupon code is redeemable at face value only against the purchase price of merchandise plus applicable service fees and taxes, available at the time of redemption. Except where otherwise required by law, this coupon/coupon code is not redeemable for cash, cannot be returned for a cash refund, and will not be replaced if lost or stolen. Any resale or exchange for cash or other use of this coupon/coupon code for unauthorized advertising, marketing, sweepstakes or other promotional purposes is strictly prohibited. This coupon/coupon code cannot be used in conjunction with any other promotions, gift certificates, coupons, discounts or affiliate programs (including reward programs). FTD.COM reserves the right to change these terms and conditions from time to time at its discretion. In the event a coupon code number is non-functional, your sole remedy, and our sole liability, shall be the replacement of such coupon or coupon code.

©2006 FTD. All rights reserved.

Offer validity is governed by the Rules of Use. Coupons void if purchased, sold or bartered.

SAVE 25%
on all products when you order online

To receive this offer, you must order online at www.ftd.com/entertainment.
This offer cannot be combined with any other offer. Valid through December 31, 2007.

This coupon/coupon code is redeemable at face value only against the purchase price of merchandise plus applicable service fees and taxes, available at the time of redemption. Except where otherwise required by law, this coupon/coupon code is not redeemable for cash, cannot be returned for a cash refund, and will not be replaced if lost or stolen. Any resale or exchange for cash or other use of this coupon/coupon code for unauthorized advertising, marketing, sweepstakes or other promotional purposes is strictly prohibited. This coupon/coupon code cannot be used in conjunction with any other promotions, gift certificates, coupons, discounts or affiliate programs (including reward programs). FTD.COM reserves the right to change these terms and conditions from time to time at its discretion. In the event a coupon code number is non-functional, your sole remedy, and our sole liability, shall be the replacement of such coupon or coupon code.

©2006 FTD. All rights reserved.

Offer validity is governed by the Rules of Use. Coupons void if purchased, sold or bartered.

Save up to 50% Off Florist Prices

Join Over 4 Million People Who Have Found A Better Way To Buy Flowers

ProFlowers®
The Art of Fresher Flowers℠

2 Dozen Roses for $19.99 +S&H

A $60 value!

24 Red or Assorted Roses
(Availability and color dependent on time of year)

Order at: **www.proflowers.com/ENT**
or call: **1-800-627-6113** Reference Entertainment® Book

ProFlowers®
The Art of Fresher Flowers℠

Valid now thru December 31, 2007
See reverse side for details

H59

$10 OFF
Any product. Anytime.

Order at: **www.proflowers.com/ENT**
or call: **1-800-627-6113** Reference Entertainment® Book

ProFlowers®
The Art of Fresher Flowers℠

Valid now thru December 31, 2007
See reverse side for details

H60

Save up to 50% Off Florist Prices

ProFlowers
The Art of Fresher Flowers

Flowers For All Occasions
Anniversaries • Birthdays • Valentine's Day • Sympathy • Mother's Day

Awarded "Best Value" by Wall Street Journal

---

2 Dozen Roses for $19.99 +S&H

Two dozen red or assorted roses for $19.99 only applicable on PID 6338 and 8096 (color subject to availability). Offer not applicable on any other rose product. Offer not available between 12/29/06–2/16/07. Item cost exclusive of shipping & handling charges & taxes. Offer may not be combined with other offers or discounts. Offer expires December 31, 2007.

Order at: www.proflowers.com/ENT
or call: 1-800-627-6113 Reference Entertainment® Book

ProFlowers — The Art of Fresher Flowers

Offer validity is governed by the Rules of Use. Coupons void if purchased, sold or bartered.

$10 OFF

Does not apply to same-day, international delivery, or co-branded assortments with other merchants. Discount will appear upon checkout and cannot be combined with other offers or discounts. Offer expires December 31, 2007.

Order at: www.proflowers.com/ENT
or call: 1-800-627-6113 Reference Entertainment® Book

ProFlowers — The Art of Fresher Flowers

Offer validity is governed by the Rules of Use. Coupons void if purchased, sold or bartered.

Hallmark FLOWERS

HallmarkFlowers.com • 1-800-HALLMARK

Save on flowers for birthdays, special days, any day at all.

SAVE $10

on bouquets $39.95 and above.
Use code: IACEB10

H61

15% OFF

any bouquet, plant or wreath, every day!
Use code: IACEB15

H62

Valid now thru December 31, 2007
See reverse side for details

HallmarkFlowers.com • 1-800-HALLMARK

Hallmark.com • 1-800-HALLMARK

Say what you feel...with flowers.

Every Hallmark Exclusive bouquet comes with a *free*, full-sized greeting card, a distinctive vase and our 100% guarantee.

Flowers shown available while supplies last.

OUR GUARANTEE: 100% SATISFACTION.

SAVE $10

on bouquets $39.95 and above. Use code: **IACEB10**

$10.00 discount applies only to bouquets, plants and wreaths priced at $39.95 and above from Hallmark Flowers purchased with the qualifying promotion code, IACEB10, through our Web site, HallmarkFlowers.com, or on phone orders placed at 1-800-HALLMARK.

15% OFF

any bouquet, plant or wreath, every day! Use code: **IACEB15**

15% discount applies only to bouquets, plants and wreaths from Hallmark Flowers purchased with the qualifying promotion code, IACEB15, through our Web site, HallmarkFlowers.com, or on phone orders placed at 1-800-HALLMARK.

Offers valid on orders placed through 12/31/07. Discount will be applied to the order total prior to taxes and shipping and handling charges. Does not apply to products sold at any other Web site operated by Hallmark, its subsidiaries, affiliates or third-party merchants accessible from Hallmark.com. May not be combined with any other offer or applied to past purchases. Not valid with any other products sold on Hallmark.com. Not valid in stores. © 2006 Hallmark Licensing, Inc. Offer validity is governed by the Rules of Use and excludes defined holidays. Offers are not valid with other discount offers, unless specified. Coupons void if purchased, sold or bartered. Discounts exclude tax, tip and/or alcohol, where applicable.

from you FLOWERS

SAVE $15

say it with *color*

Product # TF68-3

fromyouflowers.com/entbook
800-758-9353
mention code 753

flowers & plants • balloons • gift baskets • chocolates • and much, much more!

Same-Day Delivery Until 3 PM!

Fast, easy ordering online or by phone!

SAVE $15 on a dozen long stem roses!

fromyouflowers.com/entbook
1-800-758-9353
mention code 753

SAVE $10 on all other flowers and gifts!

Valid now thru December 31, 2007
See reverse side for details

H63

SAVE $15
on a dozen long stem roses!
Save $10 on all other flowers & gifts!

from you FLOWERS

say it with *flowers*

Thinking of You • I Miss You • I Love You • Happy Anniversary • Just Because

fromyouflowers.com/entbook   or   **1-800-758-9353**   code 753

Save this coupon and order as often as you wish!

flowers & plants • gift baskets • balloons • chocolates • and so much more!

- Same-Day Delivery on all orders placed before 3 PM in the delivery time zone!

- Fast and easy ordering with a 100% Satisfaction Guarantee!

- Orders can be placed 24 hours a day, 365 days a year!

- Fast, easy ordering online at **www.FromYouFlowers.com/entbook** or call us at **1-800-758-9353** and mention code 753 to **SAVE $15** on a dozen long stem roses and **SAVE $10** on all other flower & gift purchases!

Offer validity is governed by the Rules of Use and excludes defined holidays. Offers are not valid with other discount offers, unless specified. Coupons void if purchased, sold or bartered. Discounts exclude tax, tip and/or alcohol, where applicable.

1-800-flowers.com℠
The freshest flowers same day, any day!

15%* OFF ALL YOUR PURCHASES ALL YEAR LONG!
Use **Promotion Code: ENTB7** at checkout

Trust 1-800-FLOWERS.COM®—your florist of choice℠ for 30 years—
with all your gifting occasions:

Birthdays	Anniversaries	Sympathy	Just Because
Thank You	New Baby	Congratulations	Wedding

**Call 1-800-FLOWERS® (1-800-356-9377)
or Click www.1800flowers.com!**

15%* off all your purchases!
Use **Promotion Code: ENTB7** at checkout

Call 1-800-FLOWERS® (1-800-356-9377) or Click www.1800flowers.com!

*Exclusive of applicable service and shipping charges and taxes. Items may vary and are subject to availability, delivery rules and times. Offers available online and by phone. Offers cannot be combined, are not available on all products and are subject to restrictions, limitations and blackout periods. Offer valid through 12/31/07. Prices and charges are subject to change without notice. Void where prohibited. © 2006 1-800-FLOWERS.COM®, INC.

🔒 1-800-FLOWERS.COM® uses Secure Socket Layer (SSL) encryption technology to secure its website.

1-800-flowers.com℠
Your florist of choice℠

Valid now thru December 31, 2007
Offer validity is governed by the Rules of Use. Coupons void if purchased, sold or bartered.

H64

FLORIST.COM

SAVE $10

Our goal is to deliver beautiful flower bouquets and plants at the best prices from expert FTD® Florists and carefully selected growers.

Save $10 when you order online every time at
www.florist.com/ent2007
Save $7.50 when you call **1-800-425-0622**
and mention promo code **11985**

This coupon/coupon code is redeemable at face value only against the purchase price of merchandise plus applicable service fees and taxes, available at the time of redemption. Except where otherwise required by law, this coupon/coupon code is not redeemable for cash, cannot be returned for a cash refund, and will not be replaced if lost or stolen. Any resale or exchange for cash or other use of this coupon/coupon code for unauthorized advertising, marketing, sweepstakes or other promotional purposes is strictly prohibited. This coupon/coupon code cannot be used in conjunction with any other promotions, gift certificates, coupons, discounts or affiliate programs (including reward programs). Florist.com reserves the right to change these terms and conditions from time to time at its discretion. In the event a coupon code number is non-functional, your sole remedy, and our sole liability, shall be the replacement of such coupon or coupon code. Offer validity is governed by the Rules of Use. Coupons void if purchased, sold or bartered.

H65   **Valid through December 31, 2007**

Save 25%
Send Flowers Today!

get well • sympathy • anniversary • birthday • congratulations • friendship

bloomstoday™

Family Owned & Operated • National & Local Delivery Guaranteed

Visit **bloomstoday.com** or call **1-800-521-6920**

Save 25%
on Florist Delivered Products
Use Coupon Code **78TA2**
www.bloomstoday.com
1-800-521-6920

Save 15%
on Boxed Flowers & Gift Products
Use Coupon Code **J5KR3**
www.bloomstoday.com
1-800-521-6920

Valid now thru December 31, 2007

Offer validity is governed by the Rules of Use and excludes defined holidays. Offers are not valid with other discount offers, unless specified. Coupons void if purchased, sold or bartered. Discounts exclude tax, tip and/or alcohol, where applicable.

H66

Personalized Gifts for Lifes Special Occasions

Personal
CREATIONS

A personalized gift always says it best!
Find unique, personalized gift ideas for all of life's special occasions on our web site or in our catalog. You'll find gifts for weddings, babies, birthdays and all the holidays. Our fast delivery and gift-boxing service make gift giving simple.

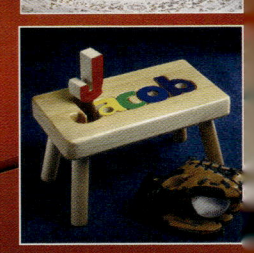

Click or Call Coupon

20% off your entire purchase

To redeem, just go to www.personalcreations.com (enter promo code 5426ENT) or call 800-326-6626 (mention code 5396PHN).

Cannot be combined with any other offer or promotion. Available for all online or phone orders. Offer validity is governed by the Rules of Use. Coupons void if purchased, sold, or bartered. Expires 12/31/07

www.personalcreations.com

Call 800-326-6626

H67

usaflorist.com

Save 20%
on all Floral and Gift Purchases!

Anything...Anywhere...Anytime!
- Flowers • Gift Baskets • Plants • Balloons • Champagne
- Wine • Chocolates...and so much more!

With same-day delivery! Save this coupon and order as often as you wish!

Order online at
www.USAFlorist.com/entbook
or call 1-800-236-1071
mention code 751

Valid now thru December 31, 2007
See reverse side for details

H68

Save this coupon and order as often as you wish!

fromyoubaskets.com/entbook

Save $10 on all Gift Baskets!
1-800-838-8853
mention code 752

Order 24 hours a day, 7 days a week!
Delivery anywhere in the country!
100% Satisfaction Guaranteed!

fruit & wine
gourmet
champagne
chocolates
spa baskets
cookies
flowers
much more!

Valid now thru December 31, 2007
See reverse side for details

H69

---

www.entertainment.com/ebags

eBags

$10 OFF
plus FREE SHIPPING on orders of $75 or more

$20 OFF
plus FREE SHIPPING on orders of $120 or more

$25 OFF
plus FREE SHIPPING on orders of $200 or more

Valid now thru December 31, 2007
See reverse side for details

H70

usaflorist.com

Visit www.USAFlorist.com/entbook
or call 1-800-236-1071 code: 751

~ Save 20% on all flower and gift purchases! ~

~ Same-day delivery available anywhere in the country on all orders placed before 3 p.m. in the delivery time zone! ~

~ Orders can be placed 24 hours a day, 7 days a week! ~

Offer validity is governed by the Rules of Use and excludes defined holidays. Offers are not valid with other discount offers, unless specified. Coupons void if purchased, sold or bartered. Discounts exclude tax, tip and/or alcohol, where applicable.

---

fromyoubaskets.com/entbook

Save $10 on all Gift Baskets!

1-800-838-8853

mention code 752

Choose from a wide variety of thoughtful gifts for any occasion and every sentiment! Gourmet Baskets, Fruit Baskets, Wine Baskets, Cookie & Chocolate Baskets, Spa Baskets, Custom Gift Baskets and so much more! Fast, easy ordering online or by phone! Order anytime, 24 hours a day, 7 days a week with 100% Satisfaction Guarantee!

Offer validity is governed by the Rules of Use and excludes defined holidays. Offers are not valid with other discount offers, unless specified. Coupons void if purchased, sold or bartered. Discounts exclude tax, tip and/or alcohol, where applicable.

---

eBags

eBags is the largest online retailer of bags, including luggage, backpacks, business cases, handbags, digital cases and travel accessories.

http://www.entertainment.com/ebags

Terms & Conditions: You must register your Entertainment® Book at www.entertainment.com to redeem offers. Discount cannot be used or combined with any other incentive or offer. Limit one per transaction. Not redeemable for cash. Shipping/Handling excluded. No change or store credit given for any unused portion. Not good on any previous purchases. Good for online purchases shipped to the US only. Gift Certificate purchases excluded from this special offer. Not valid at eBags Corporate Solutions (www.ebagscorporate.com) and does not apply to a select few brands.

Offer validity is governed by the Rules of Use and excludes defined holidays. Offers are not valid with other discount offers, unless specified. Coupons void if purchased, sold or bartered. Discounts exclude tax, tip and/or alcohol, where applicable.

Harry & David

Any Day Can Be a Celebration.℠
- Unique gifts for any occasion
- Delectable gourmet foods
- Easy entertaining ideas

Online, by phone or in any Harry and David store.

$10 OFF
your $75 purchase

Order online at harryanddavid.com/go/ent2007 or call 800-547-3033 and mention Quick Service Number 59726 and Coupon Code HDG. Or bring this coupon to any Harry and David store. Applies to merchandise total only (excluding shipping, handling and taxes). Cannot be applied to previous purchases or for gift card purchases, Same Day Delivery or We Deliver orders, nor in combination with any other offers, discounts or promotions. Limit: One per customer. For orders over $2500, please call our Corporate Sales Department at 800-248-5567.

Cash value: 1/20 of a cent. Offer ends 12/31/07

7 80994 65725 0

Offer validity is governed by the Rules of Use. Offers are not valid with other discount offers, unless specified. Coupons void if purchased, sold or bartered. H71

Online, by phone or in any Harry and David store.

$10 OFF
your $75 purchase

Order online at harryanddavid.com/go/ent2007 or call 800-547-3033 and mention Quick Service Number 59726 and Coupon Code HDG. Or bring this coupon to any Harry and David store. Applies to merchandise total only (excluding shipping, handling and taxes). Cannot be applied to previous purchases or for gift card purchases, Same Day Delivery or We Deliver orders, nor in combination with any other offers, discounts or promotions. Limit: One per customer. For orders over $2500, please call our Corporate Sales Department at 800-248-5567.

Cash value: 1/20 of a cent. Offer ends 12/31/07

7 80994 65725 0

Offer validity is governed by the Rules of Use. Offers are not valid with other discount offers, unless specified. Coupons void if purchased, sold or bartered. H72

Harry & David

AMERICA'S RAREST and FINEST

Visit us online for seasonal specials:
harryanddavid.com/go/ent2007

Jackson & Perkins
The best of everything for your ideal garden home

$10 OFF
your $60 purchase

The world's finest roses and exclusive outdoor furniture for garden-inspired living. Order online at jacksonandperkins.com/go/ent2007 or call 800-292-4769 and mention Quick Service Number 59650 and Coupon Code JDG. Applies to merchandise only (excluding shipping handling and taxes). Cannot be applied to previous purchases or used for gift card purchases, nor in combination with any other offers, discounts or promotions. Limit: One per customer. Cash value: 1/20 of a cent. Offer ends 12/31/07

2007 Rose of the Year® Sheer Magic

H73

Offer validity is governed by the Rules of Use. Offers are not valid with other discount offers, unless specified. Coupons void if purchased, sold or bartered.

Hickory Farms

SAVE
AT HICKORYFARMS.COM

Beef & Cheese Gifts    **Premium Meats**    **Gift Baskets**    **Gourmet Desserts**

ONLINE EXCLUSIVE
Save 15% Off Your Order

Birthdays • Get Well • Thank You • Mother's Day • Father's Day • Hostess Gift
Weekend Events • Christmas • Tailgating • Back-to-School

To redeem go to **www.hickoryfarms.com/ent**

Valid with online orders only. Not valid at mass merchandisers, grocery stores or Hickory Farms stores. Not valid on prior purchases, other discounts, promotions or on the purchase of gift certificates or Gourmet Rewards. This offer cannot be combined with any other offer. Offer validity is governed by the Rules of Use and excludes defined holidays. Offers are not valid with other discount offers, unless specified. Coupons void if purchased, sold or bartered. Discounts exclude tax, tip and/or alcohol, where applicable.

Valid now through December 31, 2007

H74

··· or ···

ONLINE EXCLUSIVE

FREE Shipping & FREE Gift!

Save 41%
On the Hickory Treasures Package

Includes Hickory Treasures Gift, **bonus gift** of 10 oz. bag of Strawberry Bon Bons and **FREE SHIPPING.** Total value $67.44, **Now $39.99**

To redeem go to **www.hickoryfarms.com/ent**

Valid with online orders only. Not valid at mass merchandisers, grocery stores or Hickory Farms stores. Not valid on prior purchases, other discounts, promotions or on the purchase of gift certificates or Gourmet Rewards. This offer cannot be combined with any other offer. Offer validity is governed by the Rules of Use and excludes defined holidays. Offers are not valid with other discount offers, unless specified. Coupons void if purchased, sold or bartered. Discounts exclude tax, tip and/or alcohol, where applicable.

Valid now through December 31, 2007

H75

OMAHA STEAKS
PREMIUM HEARTLAND QUALITY
SINCE 1917

www.omahasteaks.com/ent07

OMAHA STEAKS 100% GUARANTEE

Save 68%
The Entertainer Combo
- 2 (5 oz.) Filet Mignons
- 2 (5 oz.) Top Sirloins
- 4 (4 oz.) Boneless Pork Chops
- 4 (4 oz.) Boneless Chicken Breasts
- 4 (3 oz.) Gourmet Franks
- 4 (4 oz.) Omaha Steaks Burgers
- 10 Portions Potatoes au Gratin

That's 30 items...
Reg. $157.00,
Now Only......... $49.99

Save $107.01

Ask for Item 45003WKD   H76

Save 50%
The Steak that made us famous!
4 (5 oz.) Filets
Mild, delicious and so tender.
Reg. $65.00, Now Only...$32.50

Save $32.50

Ask for Item 1135WKD   H77

Save 54%
6 (6 oz.) Top Sirloin Steaks
Bold and Beefy!
Reg. $65.00, Now Only...$29.99

Save $35.01

Ask for Item 628WKD   H78

Call **1-800-228-9055** or Order Online at
www.omahasteaks.com/ent07

Limit of 2 of each package at these exclusive prices. Standard Shipping and Handling will be applied per address. Not valid with any other offer. Offer expires 12/31/07.

Offer validity is governed by the Rules of Use and excludes defined holidays. Offers are not valid with other discount offers, unless specified. Coupons void if purchased, sold or bartered. Discounts exclude tax, tip and/or alcohol, where applicable.

Cherry Moon Farms
FRESHEST QUALITY FARMS

We Deliver the Moon
100% Satisfaction Guarantee

THE FRESHEST QUALITY GIFTS FROM $29.99

SAVE 15%
& RECEIVE FREE CHOCOLATE
WITH EVERY ORDER

www.CherryMoonFarms.com/Fresh
1.888.378.2758 *Mention: "Entertainment® Book"*

Gourmet Snacks & Chocolate Gifts

Fruit Baskets & Organic Fruit

Delicious Samplers & Monthly Fruit Clubs

From the People Who Brought You *ProFlowers*

Save 15% & RECEIVE FREE CHOCOLATE WITH EVERY ORDER

Order online at CherryMoonFarms.com/Fresh
Or call **1.888.FRT.BSKT** *(1.888.378.2758)*
Mention code: "Entertainment® Book"

15% & Free Chocolate Discounts will appear at checkout. Discount may not be used in conjunction with other special offers, coupons, or discounts. Discount applies to item cost only and does not include discount on shipping and handling charges or taxes. Chocolate bar pictured subject to substitution, and may not be available with certain chocolate or gift basket orders. Offer expires December 31, 2007.

Offer validity is governed by the Rules of Use and excludes defined holidays.
Offers are not valid with other discount offers, unless specified. Coupons void if purchased, sold or bartered.

HH1

SECRET SPOON℠ Sweets

FROM THE PEOPLE WHO BROUGHT YOU ProFlowers®

SAVE 15%
ON EVERY ORDER

www.SecretSpoon.com/Fresh
1.888.673.2738

Mention: "Entertainment® Book"

From tasty sweets to chocolate-covered treats, SECRET SPOON has all the gourmet confections you could dream of.

SAVE 15%
ON EVERY ORDER

15% discount will appear upon checkout. Discount may not be used in conjunction with other special offers, coupons, or discounts. Discount applies to item cost only and does not include discount on shipping and handling charges or taxes. Offer expires December 31, 2007.

Order online at www.SecretSpoon.com/Fresh
Or Call 1.888.673.2738, Mention code "Entertainment® Book"

HH2

Secret Spoon Sweets

Offer validity is governed by the Rules of Use and excludes defined holidays. Offers are not valid with other discount offers, unless specified. Coupons void if purchased, sold or bartered.

Save $10
On Every SpaWish Gift Certificate Order
of $100 or More

Give more than a gift this year... give a pampering, relaxing experience

SpaWish Gift Certificates are the perfect way to say "Happy Birthday" or "Happy Anything."

Welcomed at over 1000 day spas nationwide, your gift recipients will enjoy selecting any spa and any services desired, from massages and facials, to pedicures and body wraps!

www.SpaWish.com
use savings code: **SETBK7**

SpaWish.com
1-888-SPA-WISH

SpaWish - The Best Way To Give the Gift of Spa!

Minimum purchase of $100 required before shipping. Offer cannot be combined with any other offer. Offer valid through 12/31/07.

Offer validity is governed by the Rules of Use and excludes defined holidays. Offers are not valid with other discount offers, unless specified. Coupons void if purchased, sold or bartered. Discounts exclude tax, tip and/or alcohol, where applicable.

HH3

Candy Wholesale Company™

$5.00 OFF YOUR ORDER OF $20.00 OR MORE.

♥ Candy Wholesale Company™. The largest online selection of candy, candy and more candy!

♥ Featuring over 1,250 delicious flavors and candy types…all available from one convenient and secure online shopping destination.

TO REDEEM GO TO:
www.candywholesalecompany.com/ent
Use Discount Code: **ENTCANDY** (gift certificates avail.)

Candy Wholesale Company™ is a registered trademark of Integrated Sales Group.
©2006 Integrated Sales Group. All Rights Reserved.

Valid now thru December 31, 2007
Offer validity is governed by the Rules of Use and excludes defined holidays. Offers are not valid with other discount offers, unless specified. Coupons void if purchased, sold or bartered. Discounts exclude tax, tip and/or alcohol, where applicable.

HH4

ONLINE VITAMIN OUTLET™

$10.00 OFF YOUR ORDER OF $40.00 OR MORE.

■ Online Vitamin Outlet™ is your premiere online shopping destination for all your vitamin and other related needs.

■ Only the very highest quality ingredients are used in our vitamin formulations.

■ Recommendations for children, adults and seniors!

TO REDEEM GO TO:
www.onlinevitaminoutlet.com/ent
Use Discount Code: **ENTWEB** (gift certificates avail.)

Online Vitamin Outlet™ is a registered trademark of Integrated Sales Group.
©2006 Integrated Sales Group. All Rights Reserved.

Valid now thru December 31, 2007
Offer validity is governed by the Rules of Use and excludes defined holidays. Offers are not valid with other discount offers, unless specified. Coupons void if purchased, sold or bartered. Discounts exclude tax, tip and/or alcohol, where applicable.

HH5

Introductory Offer - Save 58%
7 Super Suppers for Two, Just $49.99!
You'll Get 14 Total Servings, (each meal serves 2).

à la ZING

1. **Roast Chicken Rendezvous**
   Roasted Chicken Breasts, Red Roasted Potatoes, Broccoli & Cauliflower

2. **Meat Lasagna for Two**

3. **Gourmet Burger Buffet**
   Omaha Steaks Gourmet Burgers, Hamburger Rolls, Herb Roasted Potatoes, Sweet Corn

4. **Boneless Pork Chop Platter**
   Boneless Pork Chops, Twice Baked Potatoes, Roasted Vegetable Medley

5. **Stuffed Sole Suite**
   Stuffed Sole Fillets, Glazed Julienne Carrots, Whole Green Beans

6. **Beef Stroganoff for Two**

7. **Meatballs & Linguini Marinara for Two**

Reg. $120.45, Now $49.99

Roast Chicken Rendevous

Call 1-888-959-9464 (item 6756RFE) or
www.alazing.com/promo/ent2007

Offer validity is governed by the Rules of Use and excludes defined holidays. Coupons void if purchased, sold or bartered. Standard Shipping Rates Apply. Expires December 31, 2007.

HH6

DELICIOUS GIFTS FOR ALL OCCASIONS!

Take $10 off
any purchase of $75 or more.

Offer expires on 12/31/07. Valid only once.
Please use code 3B when ordering.
Not valid with any other offer.
Excludes shipping and handling charges.

Cheryl&Co.
Fresh-Baked Desserts & Gifts Since 1981

1.800.443.8124
www.CherylandCo.com

Offer validity is governed by the Rules of Use. Coupons void if purchased, sold or bartered.

HH7

Portraits you will love
from the family portrait experts

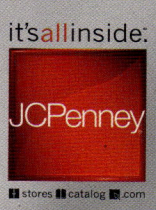

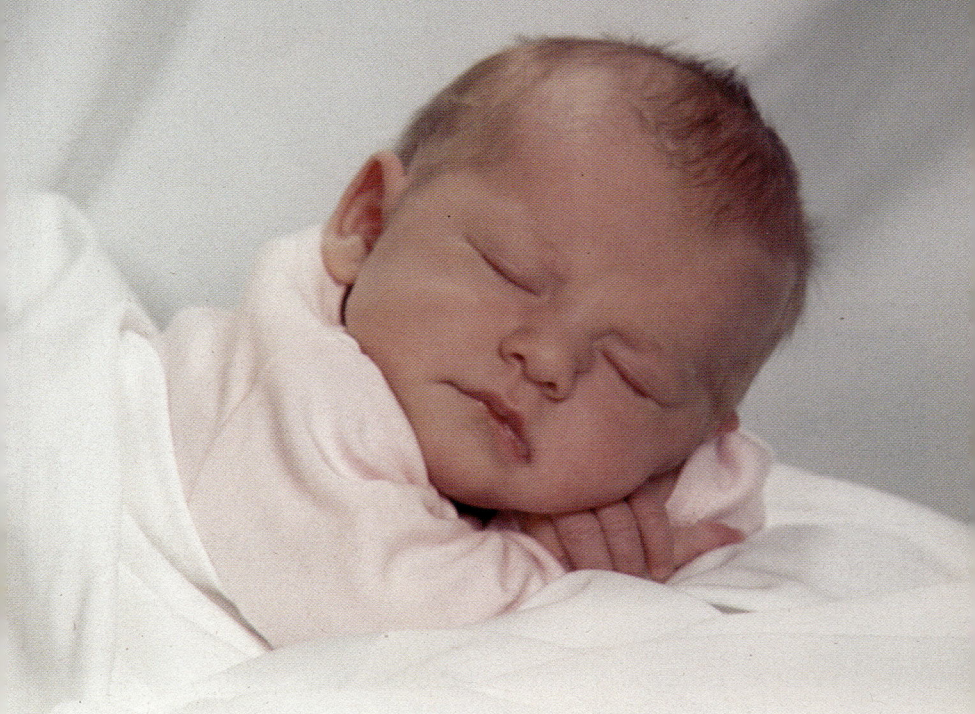

it's all inside:
JCPenney
stores · catalog · .com

Free 8x10 plus
50% Off
portrait purchase
(with $9.99 sitting fee)

Valid for 50% off entire portrait purchase including Enhancements, Collections, and fees
Call 1-800-59-SMILE for the location nearest you or visit jcpenneyportraits.com

Valid now thru December 31, 2007
See reverse side for details

it's all inside:
JCPenney portraits

HH8

it's all inside
JCPenney
stores ■ catalog ■ .com

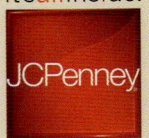

Creating memories for a lifetime®
with the family portrait experts at JCPenney Portraits

I Love You Grandma

Signature Enhancements

Anthony - 2½ y

Midnight Deja Vu Enhancements

Ryan Michael

Panoramic Light Enhancements

Visit jcpenneyportraits.com for more great portrait ideas!
Call 1-800-59-SMILE for the location nearest you or visit jcpenneyportraits.com

Free 8x10 plus
50% Off
portrait purchase
(including Enhancements and sitting fees)

Offer expires December 31, 2007. Valid for 50% off entire portrait purchase including Enhancements, Collections, and fees. Sitting fee $9.99 per person, FREE for Portrait Club members. Present at time of sitting. Not valid on reorders or studio events. Designs vary. Valid at participating locations. Cash value 1/20¢. PC1819286

it's all inside
JCPenney portraits

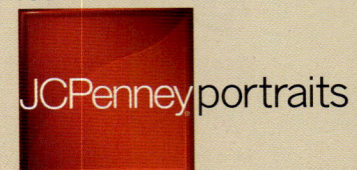

Offer validity is governed by the Rules of Use and excludes defined holidays. Offers are not valid with other discount offers, unless specified. Coupons void if purchased, sold or bartered. Discounts exclude tax, tip and/or alcohol, where applicable.

picture people

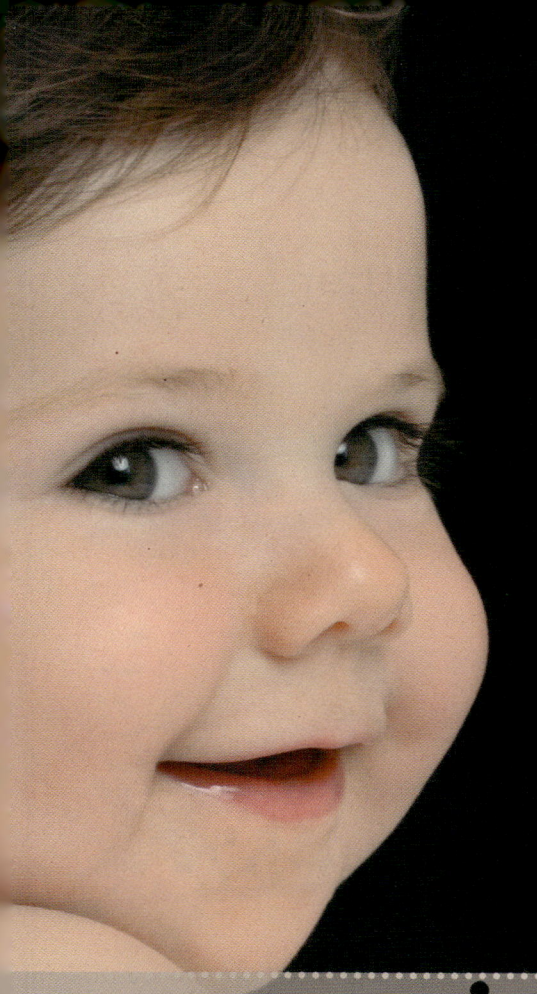

No Sitting Fees, Ever
100% Satisfaction Guaranteed
Portraits in One Hour

Because he's a different person every day

---

picture people

30% OFF
YOUR PORTRAIT PURCHASE

BOOK YOUR APPOINTMENT TODAY:
1-800-341-HOUR
www.picturepeople.com

Valid now thru December 31, 2007
See reverse side for details

HH9

---

picture people

FREE PORTRAIT
(8X10 OR 10X13)

UP TO A $20 VALUE
BOOK YOUR APPOINTMENT TODAY:
1-800-341-HOUR
www.picturepeople.com

Valid now thru December 31, 2007
See reverse side for details

HH10

picture people™

No Sitting Fees, Ever
100% Satisfaction Guaranteed
Portraits in One Hour

Every day there's another reason to smile.

Even the little things make you happy. Bring in a coupon for a free 8x10 or 10x13 portrait, or 30% off your portrait purchase, and we'll make you happy too.

Visit The Picture People for:

- No sitting fees, ever
- 100% satisfaction guaranteed
- Portraits in an hour

Book your appointment today:
1-800-341-HOUR

www.picturepeople.com

---

picture people™
No Sitting Fees, Ever

Free 8x10 or 10x13 Portrait:
Offer valid only for color portraits. Not valid on existing orders or reprints. Offer valid in-store only. Coupon cannot be used in combination with any other offer and must be presented at time of purchase. Limit one redemption per person (individually and/or as part of a group) and limit one offer per group. ODPMA (free 8x10) ODPMB (free 10x13)

Offer validity is governed by the Rules of Use and excludes defined holidays. Offers are not valid with other discount offers, unless specified. Coupons void if purchased, sold or bartered.

picture people™
No Sitting Fees, Ever

30% Off Portrait Purchase
Offer valid only for color portraits sized 10x13 and smaller. Not valid on existing orders or reprints. Offer valid in-store only. Coupon cannot be used in combination with any other offer and must be presented at time of purchase. Limit one redemption per person (individually and/or as part of a group) and limit one offer per group.
ODPMC (30% Off Portrait Purchase)

Offer validity is governed by the Rules of Use and excludes defined holidays. Offers are not valid with other discount offers, unless specified. Coupons void if purchased, sold or bartered.

Your Picture.

TARGET COUPON — EXPIRES 12/31/07

$3 off
One-Hour OR Next-Day Premium Processing

photo +digital

Valid now thru December 31, 2007
See reverse side for details

HH11

TARGET COUPON — EXPIRES 12/31/07

FREE
20 Basic Digital Prints
4x6"

photo +digital

Valid now thru December 31, 2007
See reverse side for details

HH11

Our Process.

⊙ photo + digital

Target Photo Lab, come see for yourself and improve your memories.

TARGET COUPON — EXPIRES 12/31/07

Offer available at One-hour Photo Labs. Go to Target.com/photo for the location nearest you. Limit one offer per coupon. One-hour service is limited to machine capacity. Void if copied, transferred, purchased, sold or prohibited by law. No cash value.

Cashier: Scan product, then scan coupon.

⊙ photo +digital

Offer validity is governed by the Rules of Use and excludes defined holidays. Coupons void if purchased, sold or bartered.

9 985239 074873   (8100) 0 05912

TARGET COUPON — EXPIRES 12/31/07

Offer available at One-hour Photo Labs. Go to Target.com/photo for the location nearest you. Limit one offer per coupon. Offer not available for prints made on Kodak Picture Maker kiosk. One-hour service is limited to machine capacity. Void if copied, transferred, purchased, sold or prohibited by law. No cash value. Maximum retail value $4 for combined free offer.

Cashier: Scan required products, then scan coupon.

⊙ photo +digital

Offer validity is governed by the Rules of Use and excludes defined holidays. Coupons void if purchased, sold or bartered.

9 985239 102019   (8100) 0 05915

making portraits just right for you

you get

Irresistible portraits
that speak to your heart

Quality
provided by our trained photographers & professional processing

Delivery in 7–10 business days!
(Portraits 10x13 or smaller)

Save
50% off
your portrait purchase

Valid for 50% off entire portrait purchase, including fees. The Studio at Target is located in select Target Stores. Call 1-888-887-8994 for the location nearest you or visit targetportraits.com. Present at time of sitting. Not valid with other offers, on reorders or studio events. PC24093

THE studio
family portraits at Target

Valid now thru December 31, 2007
See reverse side for details

HH12

more choices,
more smiles, more fun!

Delights
a 4x10
portrait with
personalization

Personalize portrait greeting cards
at no extra charge

Distinctions® portraits available — designs vary

Save
50% off
your portrait purchase

Valid for 50% off entire portrait purchase, including fees. The Studio at Target is located in select Target Stores. Call 1-888-887-8994 for the location nearest you or visit targetportraits.com. Present at time of sitting. Not valid with other offers, on reorders or studio events. PC24093

THE studio
family portraits at Target

Offer validity is governed by the Rules of Use and excludes defined holidays. Offers are not valid with other discount offers, unless specified. Coupons void if purchased, sold or bartered. Discounts exclude tax, tip and/or alcohol, where applicable.

Help protect your family with ||||BRINKS HOME SECURITY®

- You Could Save Up to 20% on Homeowners Insurance
- Dedicated to Rapid Response and Peace of Mind

PROTECTED BY ||||BRINKS HOME SECURITY®

Call Now!
1-800-706-0772

Standard System Installation ONLY $49*

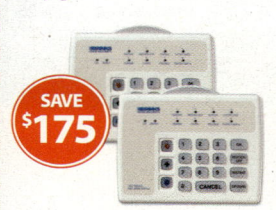

SAVE $175

Plus, call now and get a

FREE*

2nd Keypad Installation

That's a $175 value!

CONSUMERS DIGEST BEST BUY — ||||BRINKS HOME SECURITY® Standard & Premium Systems

Call Now! 1-800-706-0772
www.brinks.com

Call for information on Brink's® monitoring fees and other terms. OFFER REQUIRES ENROLLMENT IN BRINK'S EASYPAY℠ AUTO PAYMENT. Three-year monitoring agreement required. Applicable taxes and permit fees not included. Offer may not be combined with any other discount and is subject to change. Home ownership and credit approval required. Home must be located in a Brink's® service area. The Best Buy seal is a registered trademark of Consumers Digest Communications, LLC, used under license. ©2006 Brink's Home Security®, 8880 Esters Blvd., Irving, TX 75063. AL#333, AR#E93-29, AZ#ROC085024, AZ#ROC149890, CA#ACO3843, FL#EF0000921, GA#LVA004165, IL#127-000756, MA#7005-C, MD#107-319, MI — 11918 Farmington Rd., Livonia, MI 48150, NC#1633-CSA, NY#12000046324 - licensed by the NYS Department of State, OK#587, OR#44421, SC#BA-5249 and #FA-3273, TN Alarm Cert. #C-0053 and #00000234, TX#B04296, UT#325152-6501, DCJS#11-1964, WV#031960. Market Source: ENTER2

Offer ends December 31, 2007

Valid now thru December 31, 2007

Offer validity is governed by the Rules of Use and excludes defined holidays. Offers are not valid with other discount offers, unless specified. Coupons void if purchased, sold or bartered. Discounts exclude tax, tip and/or alcohol, where applicable.

HH13

Share, print and save at the Gallery.

20% off all Photo Greeting Cards or Calendars.

Buy one 8 x 10" print, and **get one** 8 x 10" print **FREE**.

Kodak EasyShare **Gallery**
www.kodakgallery.com

HH14

You went digital, so why not take your pictures to the next level? Sign up at the Gallery and give your smiles a home—organize albums, edit pictures and share without bulky emails.

Use coupon code ENTCARDCAL20 for 20% off all Photo Greeting Cards or Calendars, or ENTR8XTEN for Buy one 8 x 10" print, and get one 8 x 10" print free, at checkout to redeem.

Offer expires 12/31/07. Does not apply to shipping costs, film processing, Kodak Mobile Service subscription or applicable sales tax. One coupon redemption per customer. Cannot be combined with other offers. No substitutions, transfer rights or cash equivalents will be given.

Offer validity is governed by the Rules of Use. Coupons void if purchased, sold, or bartered.

Valid now thru December 31, 2007

---

30 FREE 4X6 PRINTS
FOR NEW CUSTOMERS

- Free photo storage
- Free online photo sharing
- Custom Photo Gifts

Already a customer?
SAVE 10% on your order of unique Photo Books, Photo Gifts and more.

Offer expires December 31, 2007

shutterfly®

Visit **www.shutterfly.com/ent2007**

The free prints and 10% off order cannot be combined with other offers. Shipping and handling charges will still apply. One coupon redemption per customer. Shutterfly reserves the right to cancel or modify this offer should the promotion be compromised in any manner.

HH15

Offer validity is governed by the Rules of Use. Coupons void if purchased, sold, or bartered.

Enjoy The New You

PEARLE VISION
Nobody cares for eyes more than Pearle®

Save $75
On Eyeglasses or RxSunglasses

PEARLE VISION

Valid now thru December 31, 2007
See reverse side for details

HH16

Many Great Benefits For You And Your Family:

- Thorough Eye Exams from Independent Doctors of Optometry*
- Most Vision Insurance Plans Accepted
- Contact Lenses Available
- 60-Day Complete Satisfaction Guarantee
- Huge Selection of Designer, Fashion and Value Frames

For a location near you, call 1-800-YES-EYES or visit www.pearlevision.com

*Eye Exams available by Independent Doctors of Optometry at or next to Pearle Vision, Inc. in most states. Doctors in some states are employed by Pearle Vision, Inc.

©2006 Pearle Vision, Inc.

PEARLE VISION
Nobody cares for eyes more than Pearle®

Complete pair (frame and lenses) purchase required. Cannot be combined with any other offer, previous purchases, most insurance programs, readers, non-prescription sunglasses and eye exams. Valid at participating locations. Savings applied to lenses.

Offer validity is governed by the Rules of Use and excludes defined holidays. Offers are not valid with other discount offers, unless specified. Coupons void if purchased, sold or bartered. Discounts exclude tax, tip and/or alcohol, where applicable.

PEP1

© 2006 LensCrafters, Inc. All Rights Reserved.

LensCrafters®

- **LensCrafters® Unconditional Happiness Guarantee**
  You have 30 days to make sure you love your new glasses. If you don't, exchange them until you do — or return them for a full refund.

- Thousands Of Frames, Latest Styles

- One-Hour Service Available On Most Glasses

Most locations open 7 days a week, including evenings.
Visit lenscrafters.com or call 1-800-522-5367 for store locations near you.

$75 OFF
ALL EYEGLASSES AND RXSUN®
ANY FRAME, ANY LENS, ANY RX

Valid on multiple pairs. Both frame and lenses purchase required with coupon. Cannot be combined with any other offer, previous purchases, insurance, readers, non-prescription sunglasses and eye exams. Savings applied to lenses.

Offer expires 12/31/07

19654399

LensCrafters®
Valid now thru December 31, 2007
See reverse side for details

HH17

© 2006 LensCrafters, Inc. All Rights Reserved.

LensCrafters®

- LensCrafters® Unconditional Happiness Guarantee
  You have 30 days to make sure you love your new glasses. If you don't, exchange them until you do — or return them for a full refund.

- Thousands Of Frames, Latest Styles

- One-Hour Service Available On Most Glasses

Most locations open 7 days a week, including evenings.
Visit lenscrafters.com or call 1-800-522-5367 for store locations near you.

$75 OFF
ALL EYEGLASSES AND RXSUN®
ANY FRAME, ANY LENS, ANY RX

Valid on multiple pairs. Both frame and lenses purchase required with coupon. Cannot be combined with any other offer, previous purchases, insurance, readers, non-prescription sunglasses and eye exams. Savings applied to lenses.

Offer expires 12/31/07   19654599

LENSCRAFTERS®

Offer validity is governed by the Rules of Use and excludes defined holidays. Offers are not valid with other discount offers, unless specified. Coupons void if purchased, sold or bartered. Discounts exclude tax, tip and/or alcohol, where applicable.

There's a *Walgreens* on a corner near you!

1-800-WALGREENS
(1-800-925-4733)
www.walgreens.com/findastore

Walgreens PHOTO COUPON

Good thru 12/31/07

19¢ ea.
With the purchase of 50 or more 4x6 in. digital prints!

From digital media only. Submit coupon with order. One coupon per order. Excludes Kodak Perfect Touch, APS and Panoramic Prints. Offer may not be combined with other offers. Customer pays any sales tax. Void if copied or where prohibited. Offer not valid in Puerto Rico.

Offer validity is governed by the Rules of Use and excludes defined holidays. Offers are not valid with other discount offers, unless specified. Coupons void if purchased, sold or bartered. Discounts exclude tax, tip and/or alcohol, where applicable.

HH18

Walgreens COUPON

Good thru 12/31/07

5/$1
Deerfield Farms™ Microwave Popcorn
1.4 to 1.6 oz. Assorted varieties.
Limit 5.

Limit one coupon per customer. Offer may not be combined with other offers. Customer pays any sales tax. Void if copied or where prohibited. Offer not valid in Puerto Rico.

Offer validity is governed by the Rules of Use and excludes defined holidays. Offers are not valid with other discount offers, unless specified. Coupons void if purchased, sold or bartered. Discounts exclude tax, tip and/or alcohol, where applicable.

HH19

Walgreens COUPON

Good thru 12/31/07

2/2.99
Buy 1 Get 1 Free
Vitamin C
100 pack, 500 mg
Gold Seal. Limit 4.

Limit one coupon per customer. Offer may not be combined with other offers. Customer pays any sales tax. Void if copied or where prohibited. Offer not valid in Puerto Rico.

Offer validity is governed by the Rules of Use and excludes defined holidays. Offers are not valid with other discount offers, unless specified. Coupons void if purchased, sold or bartered. Discounts exclude tax, tip and/or alcohol, where applicable.

HH20

Walgreens COUPON

Good thru 12/31/07

5/$1
Gentle Bar or Deodorant Soap
4.5 oz. Walgreens.
Limit 5.

Limit one coupon per customer. Offer may not be combined with other offers. Customer pays any sales tax. Void if copied or where prohibited. Offer not valid in Puerto Rico.

Offer validity is governed by the Rules of Use and excludes defined holidays. Offers are not valid with other discount offers, unless specified. Coupons void if purchased, sold or bartered. Discounts exclude tax, tip and/or alcohol, where applicable.

HH21

Walgreens

Walgreens— More Than A Pharmacy
Shop here for <u>all</u> of your needs!

Food Mart
Something for breakfast, lunch, dinner or snack.

One-Hour Photo
Can't wait to see those pictures? We'll get them back to you in a flash!

Cosmetics
The hottest trends and the latest styles.

Hallmark Aisle
Celebrating a friend's birthday? Get a card on your way to the party!

School Supplies
We have the coolest stuff for school.

Walgreens Brand
Same quality, lower prices— from aspirin to soda.

Our nearest location: the corner of your desktop!

Walgreens.com

- Upload photos and pick up prints in ONE HOUR at ANY Walgreens nationwide.
- Order prescription refills online.
- Get an e-mail when your prescription is ready.
- Print your prescription history— great for tax and insurance purposes.
- And so much more!

"If it's part of your car, it's part of my repertoire."

We're experts at oil changes, tire rotations and a lot more.

$10 off service over $100
$20 off service over $200
$30 off service over $300

Bonus Coupon

- Brakes • Exhaust • Factory Maintenance Service
- Radiators • Wheel Alignment • Suspension • Belts
- Hoses • Headlamps • Bulbs and More

MIDAS
Trust the Midas touch.
Expires 12/31/07

Most vehicles. Does not include tires or batteries. Coupon must be presented at time of purchase. One coupon per total invoice. Not good with any other offer. At participating shops only. Exclusive of taxes. Offer validity is governed by the Rules of Use and excludes defined holidays. Offers are not valid with other discount offers, unless specified. Coupons void if purchased, sold or bartered. Discounts exclude tax, tip and/or alcohol, where applicable.

HH22

$5.00 off

Oil Change

- Change engine oil
- New oil filter
- Lube chassis fittings
- Check fluid levels

MIDAS
Trust the Midas touch.
Expires 12/31/07

Discount off regular price. Most vehicles. Diesel vehicles extra. Other grades and synthetics available at extra cost. Coupon must be presented at time of purchase. Not good with any other offer. At participating shops only. Offer validity is governed by the Rules of Use and excludes defined holidays. Offers are not valid with other discount offers, unless specified. Coupons void if purchased, sold or bartered. Discounts exclude tax, tip and/or alcohol, where applicable.

HH23

$10.00 off

Midas Lifetime* Guaranteed Muffler
- Lifetime guaranteed muffler. You'll never have to buy another muffler for as long as you own your car.
- Nationwide lifetime guarantee on mufflers available at over 1800 shops across North America.

or

Catalytic Converter
- Designed to reduce emissions • 5-year/50,000 mile warranty
- Transforms pollutants into water vapor and less-harmful gases

Discount off regular price. Many vehicles. *Lifetime guarantee valid as long as you own your car. See manager for limited guarantee terms and details. Coupon must be presented at time of purchase. Not good with any other offer. At participating shops only. Offer validity is governed by the Rules of Use and excludes defined holidays. Offers are not valid with other discount offers, unless specified. Coupons void if purchased, sold or bartered. Discounts exclude tax, tip and/or alcohol, where applicable.

Expires 12/31/07   HH24

25% off

Lifetime*Guaranteed Brake Pads or Shoes
- Semi-Metallic brake pads
- Top off brake fluid • 45-point brake inspection
- Road test • Discount off parts only

LIFETIME GUARANTEE*

MIDAS
Trust the Midas touch.

Discount off regular price. Many vehicles. *Lifetime guarantee valid as long as you own your car. See manager for limited guarantee terms and details. Coupon must be presented at time of purchase. Not good with any other offer. At participating shops only. Offer validity is governed by the Rules of Use and excludes defined holidays. Offers are not valid with other discount offers, unless specified. Coupons void if purchased, sold or bartered.

Expires 12/31/07   HH25

Trust the Midas Touch to help keep you and your car going.

- America's leader in brakes and exhaust
- Oil changes, factory scheduled maintenance, batteries, and tires
- More than 1800 stores nationwide
- Expert service by over 3,000 certified mechanics

MIDAS

Trust the Midas touch.™

Call **1-800-GO MIDAS** or visit **www.Midas.com** to find a location near you.

©2006 Midas International Corporation

GAMEFLY.COM
Ready to Play™

Unlimited Game Rentals

- **OVER 3,500 TITLES**
- **FREE SHIPPING BOTH WAYS**
- **NO LATE FEES**

15-DAY FREE TRIAL

Sign up at **www.gamefly.com/promo**

Use code ▶ **1ENT5**

PS2 · XBOX · XBOX 360 · NINTENDO GAMECUBE · GAME BOY ADVANCE · NINTENDO DS · PSP

Valid now thru December 31, 2007
Offer validity is governed by the Rules of Use. Coupons void if purchased, sold or bartered.

HH26

The Popcorn Factory®

$5 off* your order

Use Promo Code ENT5.
Not valid with any other offer.

Delicious gifts for every occasion!

Choose a tempting tin of popcorn, a fresh batch of cookies, or a gift assortment for someone special, and SAVE $5!

Phone 1-800-541-2676
www.ThePopcornFactory.com

*Exclusive of applicable shipping charges and taxes. Items may vary and are subject to availability, delivery rules and times. Items available online, by phone, fax or by mail. Offers cannot be combined, are not available on all products and are subject to restrictions, limitations and blackout period. Prices and charges are subject to change without notice. Void where prohibited. ©2006, THE POPCORN FACTORY, INC. Offer validity is governed by the Rules of Use. Coupons void if purchased, sold or bartered.

Valid now thru December 31, 2007

HH27

THE BEST PRICES ON THE BEST SELECTION OF PHONES

FREE SHIPPING

EXCLUSIVE SELECTION OF **FREE** CELL PHONES*
*after rebates with 2-year contract on selected rate plans

FREE BLUETOOTH HEADSETS*
*on select phones and carriers

WIREFLY MOBILE

Call or visit web site to view current selection of discounted cell phones for every carrier. Offers are fulfilled by InPhonic, Inc., the leading authorized online agent for Alltel, AT&T Wireless, Cingular, Nextel, Sprint, T-Mobile and Verizon Wireless. Offer subject to availability at the time your order is approved, and to eligibility check by the selected carrier, which may include credit approval or deposit. Phone discount is based on the selected rate plan, and may be invalid if the rate plan is changed to a lower monthly service rate, or if this equipment is transferred to another line of service. Activation and early termination fees may apply. See web site for additional details, restrictions, terms and conditions. Availability is limited to the markets served by the selected carriers at the time your order is placed.

FIND THE BEST DEALS IN WIRELESS!
Visit www.wirefly.com/entertainment or call (866)-424-3950

alltel wireless — authorized agent
cingular raising the bar — Authorized Dealer
Sprint — Together with NEXTEL
verizon wireless — Authorized Agent

Valid now thru December 31, 2007
Offer validity is governed by the Rules of Use and excludes defined holidays.
Offers are not valid with other discount offers, unless specified. Coupons void if purchased, sold or bartered.

HH28

The ART of Portraits

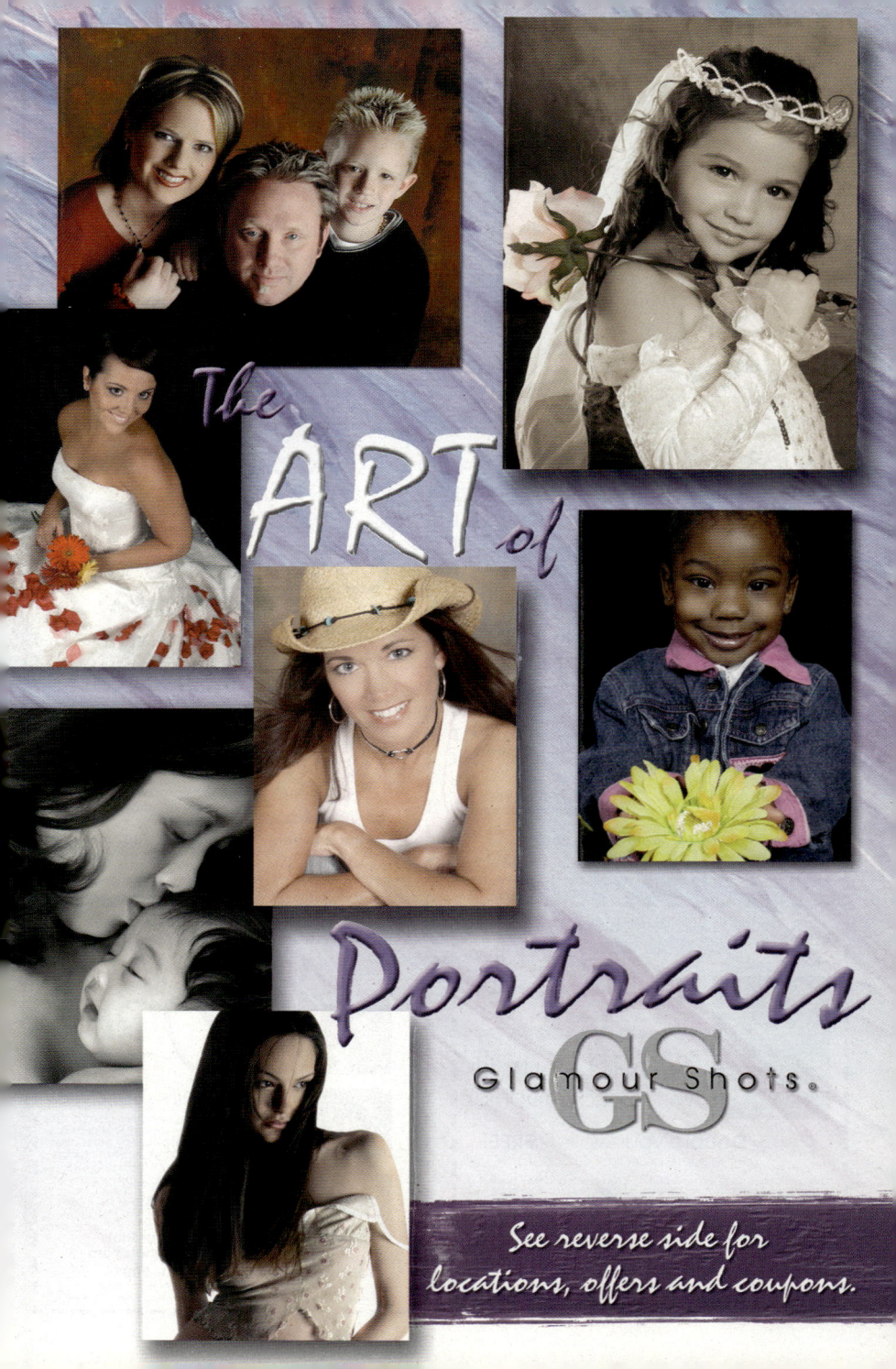

Glamour Shots.

See reverse side for locations, offers and coupons.

The ART of Portraits

Glamour Shots

Mall of America
952.858.8005

Rosedale Center
651.255.3041

FREE Session & 8x10 Portrait
Plus 10% off Glamour Touch Retouching Service

*Standard color finish and standard paper only. Limit one per session. Not valid with any other offer.

Glamour Shots 1.888.Glamour Shots
www.glamourshots.com

Valid now thru December 31, 2007
Subject to Rules of Use. Not valid with any other discount offers, unless specified. Coupons VOID if purchased, sold, or bartered for cash.   HH29

Kid's Special
9 Portraits $9 of your favorite pose* for

*Standard color finish and standard paper. Limit one per session. Not valid with any other offer. Makeup and hairstyling not included. Ages 12 & under. Must be accompanied by an adult.

Glamour Shots 1.888.Glamour Shots
www.glamourshots.com

Valid now thru December 31, 2007
Subject to Rules of Use. Not valid with any other discount offers, unless specified. Coupons VOID if purchased, sold, or bartered for cash.   HH30

HIGH SCHOOL SENIOR SPECIAL
FREE Senior Session & 8x10 Portrait with Grad Graphic

Plus Double your wallets **FREE!** (of the same pose, limit 48 wallets)

*Session includes up to 24 poses plus FREE makeover and FREE hairstyling. Limit one per session. Not valid with any other offer. Standard color finish and standard paper only.

Glamour Shots 1.888.Glamour Shots
www.glamourshots.com

Valid now thru December 31, 2007
Subject to Rules of Use. Not valid with any other discount offers, unless specified. Coupons VOID if purchased, sold, or bartered for cash.   HH31

Family Collage Special
$30 OFF Any Family Collage!

*Standard color finish and standard paper only. Limit one per session. Session fee additional. Not valid with any other offer. Mounting and framing available for an additional fee.

Glamour Shots 1.888.Glamour Shots
www.glamourshots.com

Valid now thru December 31, 2007
Subject to Rules of Use. Not valid with any other discount offers, unless specified. Coupons VOID if purchased, sold, or bartered for cash.   HH32

CAPTURE EVERY Precious Moment

FLASH!
digital · portraits
flashportraits.com

50% OFF
8x20 SPECIALTY PRODUCT

Not valid with other offers.
See studio for details.

FLASH!
digital · portraits
flashportraits.com

Valid now thru December 31, 2007
See reverse side for details

©2006 Flash Digital Portraits. All rights reserved. 70043-01

HH33

8x20 Specialty Product

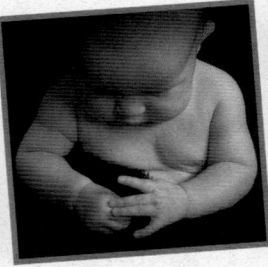

"Where there is love, there is life."
— Mother Teresa

FLASH! digital·portraits

flashportraits.com

FLASH! digital·portraits

50% OFF 8x20
SPECIALTY PRODUCT

Call the *Flash* Digital Portraits! studio near you for more information and to schedule a portrait session.

Oak Park Mall Overland Park, KS (913)888-3010	Westfield Shoppingtown Hawthorn
Coral Ridge Mall Coralville, IA (319)341-3403	Vernon Hills, IL (847)918-7844
Valley West Mall West Des Moines, IA (515)223-0591	Burnsville Center Burnsville, MN (952)892-5840
Florence Mall Florence, KY (859)372-0222	Eden Prairie Center Eden Prairie, MN (952)826-1111
Clackamas Town Center Portland, OR (503)654-4909	Ridgedale Center Minnetonka, MN (952)546-0539
Westfield Shoppingtown Vancouver, WA (360)254-0228	Polaris Fashion Place Columbus, OH (614)430-8610
Fox Valley Center Aurora, IL (630)978-3269	The Mall at Tuttle Crossing Dublin, OH (614)734-0566

Offer validity is governed by the Rules of Use and excludes defined holidays. Offers are not valid with other discount offers, unless specified. Coupons void if purchased, sold or bartered. Discounts exclude tax, tip and/or alcohol, where applicable.

PROEX Portraits

Fun in the tub!

PRO EX PHOTO & PORTRAIT

50% Off
PROEX Portrait Photocards

with the purchase of any PROEX Portrait Session.

Not valid Nov. 1, 2006 – Dec. 31, 2006
Expires October 31, 2007   CC4038

See reverse side for details

HH34

PRO EX PHOTO & PORTRAIT

$10 Off
Time-based Portrait Session

Frequent Foto members save an additional $5.

Not valid Nov. 15, 2006 – Dec. 31, 2006
Expires November 15, 2007   CC4039

See reverse side for details

HH35

PRO EX PHOTO & PORTRAIT

50% Off
Any Composite or Wall Portrait

with the purchase of a PROEX Portrait Session.

Not valid Nov. 30, 2006 – Dec. 31, 2006
Expires November 30, 2007   CC4040

See reverse side for details

HH36

PRO EX PHOTO & PORTRAIT

FREE!
Personalization of 48 wallets

with the purchase of any PROEX Portrait Session.

Expires November 30, 2007   CC4041

See reverse side for details

HH37

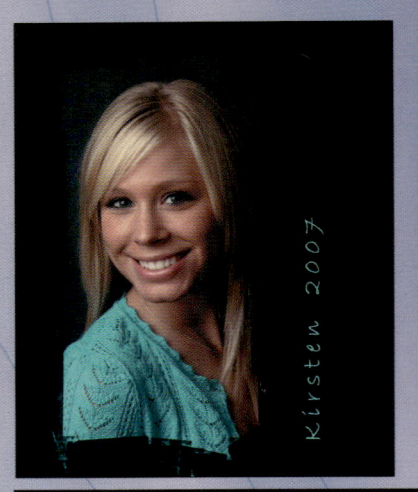

At PROEX you can have your portrait session, view your images and our new enhancement options just minutes after your session...then place your order, all in one trip! It all adds up to professional photography without the premium price.

Visit *www.proex.com* for a location near you.

Kirsten 2007

PRO EX
PHOTO & PORTRAIT

Valid for $10 Off Time-based Portrait Session. Frequent Foto members save an additional $5. May not be combined with any other offers.

Offer validity is governed by the Rules of Use and excludes defined holidays. Offers are not valid with other discount offers, unless specified. Coupons void if purchased, sold or bartered. Discounts exclude tax, tip and/or alcohol, where applicable.

PRO EX
PHOTO & PORTRAIT

Valid for 50% Off PROEX Portrait Photocards with the purchase of any PROEX Portrait Session. May not be combined with other photocard offers.

Offer validity is governed by the Rules of Use and excludes defined holidays. Offers are not valid with other discount offers, unless specified. Coupons void if purchased, sold or bartered. Discounts exclude tax, tip and/or alcohol, where applicable.

PRO EX
PHOTO & PORTRAIT

Valid for Free Personalization of up to 48 wallets (save up to $24 – $4 per eight wallets!) with the purchase of any PROEX Portrait Session. Regular price is $12.99 for eight personalized wallets.

Offer validity is governed by the Rules of Use and excludes defined holidays. Offers are not valid with other discount offers, unless specified. Coupons void if purchased, sold or bartered. Discounts exclude tax, tip and/or alcohol, where applicable.

PRO EX
PHOTO & PORTRAIT

Valid for 50% Off any Composite or Wall Portrait with the purchase of a PROEX Portrait Session. Available on 10x20 up to 30x40 sizes.

Offer validity is governed by the Rules of Use and excludes defined holidays. Offers are not valid with other discount offers, unless specified. Coupons void if purchased, sold or bartered. Discounts exclude tax, tip and/or alcohol, where applicable.

RAINBOW PLAY SYSTEMS

Finest Residential Play Equipment in America!

Sunshine Castle II Loaded

RAINBOW PLAY SYSTEMS®
FINE RESIDENTIAL PLAY EQUIPMENT

Visit Us Today!
900 West 80th Street
494 & Lyndale
South to American Blvd. (79th St.)
Bloomington, MN 55420

952-884-4040

$100 OFF the Best Price of a New RAINBOW PLAY SYSTEM Purchase

(Fiesta Systems Excluded)

RAINBOW PLAY SYSTEMS®
FINE RESIDENTIAL PLAY EQUIPMENT

Must present coupon at time of purchase.

Valid now thru November 1, 2007
See reverse side for details

HH38

RAINBOW PLAY SYSTEMS

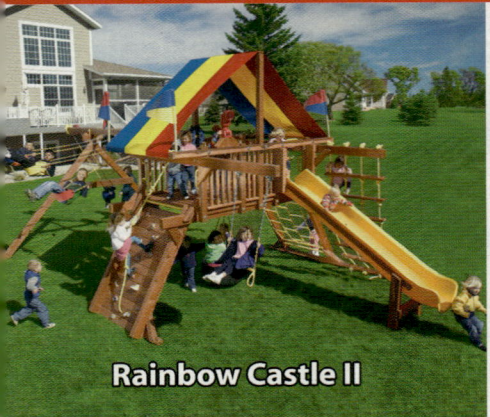

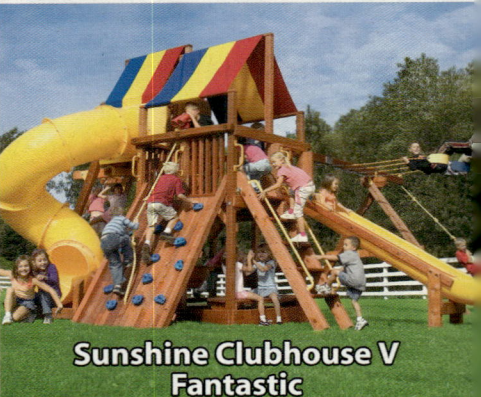

Rainbow Castle II

Monster Clubhouse

Spacesaver Playhouse

Carnival Cottage

Model 204

Sunshine Clubhouse V Fantastic

Visit Us Today!

RAINBOW PLAY SYSTEMS®
FINE RESIDENTIAL PLAY EQUIPMENT

952-884-4040

900 West 80th Street • 494 & Lyndale
South to American Blvd. (79th St.)
Bloomington, MN 55420

Offer validity is governed by the Rules of Use and excludes defined holidays. Offers are not valid with other discount offers, unless specified. Coupons void if purchased, sold or bartered. Discounts exclude tax, tip and/or alcohol, where applicable.

Retail & Services Index

Attractions

Minnesota
Minneapolis
- [kids] Underwater Adventures Aquarium I23

Automotive

Multiple Locations
- Bobby & Steve's Auto World I19
- Midas HH22-HH25
- Paradise Car Wash I28
- SuperAmerica I25
- SuperAmerica Car Washes I26

Minnesota
Chaska
- [NEW] Victory Lane Car Wash & Detail Center I36

Eden Prairie
- [NEW] Cloud 9 Car Wash & Detail Center I40

Minneapolis
- Brookdale Car Wash I32
- [NEW] Central Car Wash I34
- Don's Car Washes I31
- Galaxy Auto Centers I11
- [NEW] T & Y Car Wash I33

Saint Paul
- Downtowner Car Wash I29
- Heppner's Auto Wash & Detailing Center I30
- [NEW] River Bluff Car Wash I39

Savage
- [NEW] Classic Auto Spa & Detail Center I35

Other
- EZ Air Park I7

Car Rental

Minnesota
Minneapolis
- Golden Limousine I6

Dry Cleaning

Multiple Locations
- Clean 'n' Press I1
- Sew What! Midway Cleaners I38
- White Way Cleaners I37

Grocery

Multiple Locations
- Omaha Steaks ® H76-H78

Other
- Hickory Farms H74-H75

Health & Beauty

Multiple Locations
- Fantastic Sams I16
- It Figures I18
- LensCrafters HH17

Illinois
Geneva
- Pearle Vision HH16

Michigan
Saint Cloud
- Pearle Vision HH16

Minnesota
Minneapolis
- Ocean Waves Massage I20

Other
- Curves I10
- SpaWish.com HH3

Home & Garden Retail

Multiple Locations
- Brink's Home Security HH13
- [NEW] Sherwin Williams I21-I22

Other
- Ace H50
- American Blinds, Wallpaper & More H11

Other
- Ballard Designs H8

[NEW] **New Merchants Added This Year**   [kids] **Great Place for Kids!**

Retail & Services Index

- **NEW** Bed Bath & Beyond H5
- **NEW** Brookstone H21-H22
- Frontgate H6
- GrandinRoad H44
- Improvements Catalog H46
- **NEW** Pier 1 Imports I13-H4
- **NEW** Plow & Hearth H9
- RadioShack H18-H19
- Smith + Noble H7

Home & Garden Services

Colorado
Denver
- Qwest Communications 1

Michigan
Troy
- ShareBuilder H52

Minnesota
Minneapolis
- **NEW** SimonDelivers AA1

Washington
Bellevue
- ShareBuilder H52

Other
- **NEW** DISHNetwork H53
- **NEW** Maid Brigade I4

Miscellaneous

Minnesota
Osseo
- Boss Limo I2

Music/Books/Video

Multiple Locations
- **kids** **NEW** FYE I14
- The Sharper Image H16-H17

Other
- BLOCKBUSTER® H12-H15
- DirectStarTV H54
- **NEW** GameFly.com HH26

- **NEW** Sirius Satellite Radio H51
- VONAGE H48

Retail

Multiple Locations
- **kids** **NEW** Claire's I12-I13
- **kids** **NEW** Footlocker I5
- **kids** K B Toys H23-H26
- New York & Company H27-H28
- **kids** Once Upon a Child I8
- Sir Speedy I15
- Supermom's I27
- Target HH11-HH12

California
Emeryville
- KODAK EASYSHARE Gallery HH14

Connecticut
Old Saybrook
- **NEW** USAflorist.com H68

Illinois
Deerfield
- Walgreens HH18-HH21

Downers Grove
- Florist.com H65

Minnesota
Hopkins
- **kids** Games by James I17

Minneapolis
- **kids** Games by James I17
- Heavenly Shoes I24

Osseo
- **NEW** Lavish I9

New Jersey
Rochelle Park
- The Avenue H32-H33

Other
- 1-800-FLOWERS.COM ® H64
- A La Zing HH6
- **NEW** American Greetings / Carlton Cards . . . I3
- Blair H49

NEW New Merchants Added This Year   **kids** Great Place for Kids!

RETAIL & SERVICES INDEX

- **NEW** Blooms Today H66
- **NEW** Candy Wholesale Company® HH4
- **NEW** Catherine's H37-H40
- Cherry Moon Farms HH1
- **NEW** Cheryl & Co. HH7
- eBags.com H70
- **NEW** Fashion Bug H35-H36
- From You Baskets H69
- From You Flowers H63
- FTD.COM H57-H58
- Garnet Hill H43
- **NEW** Gateway H20
- Growing Up with Garnet Hill. H45
- Hallmark Flowers H61-H62
- Harry and David H71-H72
- HSN.com H47
- **NEW** Jackson & Perkins. H73
- **NEW** Lane Bryant. H34
- **NEW** Liz Claiborne H29-H31
- **NEW** Online Vitamin Outlet® HH5
- **NEW** Overstock.com H10
- Personal Creations H67
- **NEW** PetSmart® H55-H56
- Proflowers.com H59-H60
- **NEW** Rainbow Play Systems. HH38
- **NEW** Sears.com H1
- **NEW** Secret Spoon HH2
- Shutterfly HH15
- **NEW** Target.com H2
- The Territory Ahead H41-H42
- **NEW** The Popcorn Factory HH27
- **NEW** Wirefly.com HH28

SERVICES

MULTIPLE LOCATIONS
- JCPenney Portraits HH8
- **NEW** Picture People. HH9-HH10
- **NEW** Proex Photo & Portrait HH34-HH37

MINNESOTA
Eden Prairie
- **NEW** Flash Studios HH33

WISCONSIN
Luxemburg
- **NEW** Glamour Shots HH29-HH32

Register at
entertainment.com/register
to access even more of these great savings!

NEW New Merchants Added This Year   **kids** Great Place for Kids!

DON'T MISS OUT

FIND MORE OF THESE SAVINGS
at www.entertainment.com

- Print **50% off** and **2-for-1 discounts** not found in your book.

NEW
- Get **Repeat Savings**™. Save again and again at participating merchants.

NEW
- Access **savings from top online retailers**. We have added hundreds of offers, so when you shop online, start at entertainment.com.

- **Find it fast** — get driving directions, maps and offers near you. Search by merchant or by type of merchant.

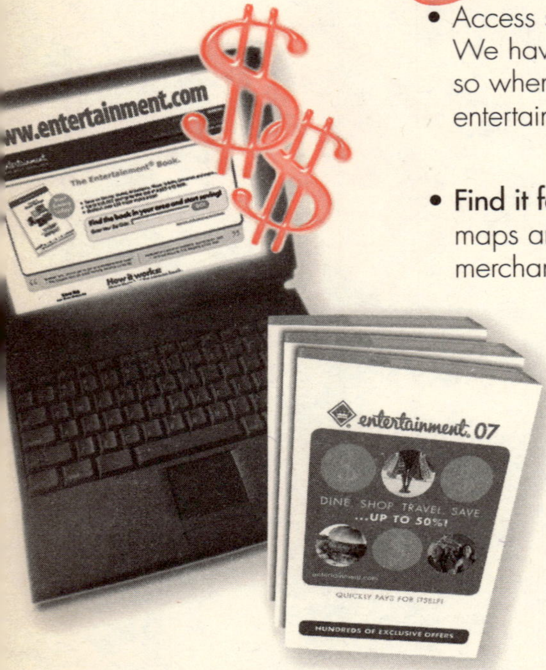

NEW DISCOUNTS ADDED DAILY!

You must register your membership card at
www.entertainment.com/register
to get these exclusive member benefits and savings!

Privacy Policy: Please see our Privacy Policy on www.entertainment.com.

One call gets you any or all of these Qwest services and VISA® GIFT cards good for up to $140!

Call 1 888-596-2467 today to order:

(Not an extension of credit)

Qwest Wireless® Service
- Affordable service plans that let you talk when you want, where you want (see qwest.com/map or a Qwest Solutions Center for nationwide coverage details)
- A selection of the latest and most popular phones
- FREE on-network calls to your primary Qwest® home phone number (with combined billing and qualifying plan)

Get a $50 Visa® Gift card

Qwest High-Speed Internet™
- Download speeds up to 5Mbps – no more waiting for dial-up
- Affordable pricing, so you get more of what you want from the Internet
- State-of-the-art MSN® Premium Security features at no additional charge
- Reliable 24/7 tech support

Get a $40 Visa® Gift card

Digital TV Service from Qwest
- 100% digital-quality picture and sound on every channel
- Access to more than 200 all-digital channels, including premium, pay-per-view and high-definition channels
- Including local channels where available

Get a $25 Visa® Gift card

Qwest Long-Distance Service
Unlimited nationwide or domestic long-distance and low per-minute domestic calling plans. Great International long-distance rates to Mexico.

Get a $25 Visa® Gift card

One call is all it takes!

Call **1 888-596-2467** | Click **qwest.com/ebook** | Visit **any Qwest store**

Qwest is your one-stop shop for all your communications and entertainment needs including state-to-state long-distance phone service, wireless, high-speed Internet, digital television services and more. **Offer valid through December 31, 2007.**

Qwest
Spirit of Service

Copyright © 2006 Qwest. All rights reserved.

Qwest Visa® Card Offer: Offer ends December 31, 2007. For Qwest local service customers ordering additional, qualifying new services. Customer must not have subscribed to qualifying services for at least 30 days. Offer void if qualifying service(s) cancelled within 90 days. Maximum value of cards issued under this offer is $140. Allow 4-6 weeks for delivery of card after eligibility period met. Offer not available to customers who have received a Visa Gift card from Qwest in connection with any other offer. Call for additional terms and conditions. Visa® gift card issued by West Suburban Bank of Lombard IL pursuant to a license from Visa® U.S.A. Incorporated. Not an extension of credit.

With approved credit. Services and combined billing not available in all areas. May require equipment purchase or rental at additional charge. Subject to applicable restrictions, tariffs and service agreements.
Contact Qwest for details.

Qwest Choice™ Unlimited: Requires Qwest local service (except in Montana). Cannot be used for business or Internet access. Usage may be monitored and customer may be required to show compliance if usage exceeds 5,000 minutes/mo. or non-compliance indicated. Services and combined billing not available in all areas. Prices exclude taxes, surcharges, and other fees. Bundle pricing and promotional discounts apply after first full month of billing. Subject to applicable restrictions, tariffs and service agreements.

Qwest DSL: Service not available in all areas. For Qwest residential local service customers only. Subject to applicable restrictions and service agreements. Requires compatible modem. Actual speeds vary depending on a variety of factors. MSN Premium also requires acceptance of MSN's terms and conditions. MSN is a registered trademark of Microsoft Corporation. All other trademarks are owned by their respective companies.

Free Calls Between Qwest Wireless(R) and Home Phones: Not compatible with all features and phone systems.

Digital TV Service: Service not available in all areas. Product availability and features vary by location. For residential use only. Additional equipment may be required. Subject to applicable restrictions and service agreements. Eligibility for local channels based on service address. For local channels availability by ZIP code, call Qwest. All trademarks are owned by their respective companies.

Copyright © 2006 Qwest. All Rights Reserved.

entertainment.com — Up To $5.00 Value

Clean'n'Press

Enjoy one complimentary GARMENT DRY CLEANED when a second GARMENT of equal or greater value is DRY CLEANED at the regular price.

valid anytime

Limit one garment per visit; Not valid with any other discounts or promotions; Leather excluded

I1

Offer validity is governed by the Rules of Use and excludes defined holidays. Offers are not valid with other discount offers, unless specified.

Valid now thru November 1, 2007

---

entertainment.com — 25% OFF

BOSS LIMO
VELVET RIDE · DIAMOND · KNIGHT RIDER

Enjoy 25% off the regular price of any LIMOUSINE SERVICE.

valid anytime

I2

Offer validity is governed by the Rules of Use and excludes defined holidays. Offers are not valid with other discount offers, unless specified.

Valid now thru November 1, 2007

---

entertainment.com — 25% OFF

AMERICAN GREETINGS
Fine Family of Stores
CARLTON CARDS

www.carltoncards.com

Enjoy 25% off your entire purchase of regular priced items.

Also redeemable at Card America, Gorant's, Social Expressions, & Yum Yum Tree; For participating locations call 800-679-8343 or visit carltoncards.com

valid anytime

Limit one coupon per customer purchase; Not valid on holidays, prior purchases, or sale/reduced items

I3

Offer validity is governed by the Rules of Use and excludes defined holidays. Offers are not valid with other discount offers, unless specified.

Valid now thru November 1, 2007

---

entertainment.com — Up To $25.00 Value

·MAID BRIGADE·

Enjoy 20% off any CLEANING SERVICES - maximum discount $25.00.

valid anytime

Please present coupon/card at time of purchase; New Customers only; Mention code XXEW0020P1

I4

Offer validity is governed by the Rules of Use and excludes defined holidays. Offers are not valid with other discount offers, unless specified.

Valid now thru November 1, 2007

---

entertainment.com — $10 OFF

foot Locker
America's Most Complete Athletic Footwear Store

Enjoy $10 off the regular price of ANY PURCHASE of $40 or more.

valid anytime

Not valid with any other discount or sale merchandise.; Valid at all Minnesota Footlocker® locations

I5

Offer validity is governed by the Rules of Use and excludes defined holidays. Offers are not valid with other discount offers, unless specified.

Valid now thru November 1, 2007

---

entertainment.com — 50% OFF

GOLDEN LIMOUSINE
& CHAUFFEUR SERVICE
"Serving With Distinction Since 1983"

Enjoy one LIMOUSINE SERVICE at 50% off the regular price.

valid anytime

I6

Offer validity is governed by the Rules of Use and excludes defined holidays. Offers are not valid with other discount offers, unless specified.

Valid now thru November 1, 2007

BOSS LIMO
VELVET RIDE · DIAMOND · KNIGHT RIDER

- It's Good To Be The Boss!

**6153 Eagle Lake Dr.
Maple Grove, MN
(763)536-0302**

Coupons void if purchased, sold or bartered. Discounts exclude tax, tip and/or alcohol, where applicable.

00686462

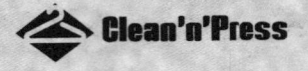

Clean'n'Press

- Years of top quality experience
- Environmentally friendly for over 10 years
- Modern state of the art pressing, finishing equipment
- Compare & save 30-50% off your dry cleaning with our everyday low prices!

Valid at All Participating Locations

Coupons void if purchased, sold or bartered. Discounts exclude tax, tip and/or alcohol, where applicable.

00281415

·MAID BRIGADE·

- Beneath the clean, you'll find sparkling customer service(SM)
- Serving the Greater Twin Cities Metro area
- Reliable & secure
- Cleanings inspected & guaranteed
- Background checked, uniformed, bonded & insured
- Regular, one-time move-in/out & home sale services

Maid Brigade (651)294-0019

Coupons void if purchased, sold or bartered. Discounts exclude tax, tip and/or alcohol, where applicable.

00689465

---

4 00000 50048 5

- Large selection of greeting cards & gift wrap for every occasion
- Earn FREE greeting cards with The Card Club!
- Fine gifts including collectibles, cuddly animals, & scented candles
- Stationery items include announcements, invitations, & "Thank You" notes for birthday, wedding, & baby

**For participating locations call
800-679-8343 or visit
www.carltoncards.com
Valid at All Participating Locations**

Coupons void if purchased, sold or bartered. Discounts exclude tax, tip and/or alcohol, where applicable.

00593960

GOLDEN LIMOUSINE
& CHAUFFEUR SERVICE
"Serving With Distinction Since 1983"

- We treat you golden
- Weddings, business, theatre & social occasions
- 6-10 Passenger stretch limousines
- In business since 1983
- Permit #167402

**8061 Zane Ave. N
Minneapolis, MN
(612)522-2939**

Coupons void if purchased, sold or bartered. Discounts exclude tax, tip and/or alcohol, where applicable.

00498071

---

foot Locker
America's Most Complete Athletic Footwear Store

- MANAGER: Keycode 27 (Stamp with store # and list in book.)

Valid at all Minnesota Footlocker® locations

Coupons void if purchased, sold or bartered. Discounts exclude tax, tip and/or alcohol, where applicable.

00002266

entertainment.com — Up To $9.00 Value

AIRPORT PARKING

EZ AIR PARK

Enjoy one complimentary DAY OF PARKING.

valid anytime

I7

Valid now thru November 1, 2007

Offer validity is governed by the Rules of Use and excludes defined holidays. Offers are not valid with other discount offers, unless specified.

---

entertainment.com — Up To $5.00 Value

Once upon a child
Kids' Stuff With Previous Experience™

Enjoy $5.00 off the regular price of A PURCHASE of $25 or more.

valid anytime

One coupon per customer per visit

I8

Valid now thru November 1, 2007

Offer validity is governed by the Rules of Use and excludes defined holidays. Offers are not valid with other discount offers, unless specified.

---

entertainment.com — Up To $25.00 Value

Lavish

Enjoy 20% off the regular price of any PURCHASE (sale items excluded) - maximum discount $25.00.

valid anytime

I9

Valid now thru November 1, 2007

Offer validity is governed by the Rules of Use and excludes defined holidays. Offers are not valid with other discount offers, unless specified.

---

entertainment.com — 50% OFF

Curves

www.curvesinternational.com

Enjoy 50% off the full price or 10% off the promotional rate of the SERVICE FEE.

valid anytime

I10

Valid now thru November 1, 2007

Offer validity is governed by the Rules of Use and excludes defined holidays. Offers are not valid with other discount offers, unless specified.

---

entertainment.com — Up To $25.00 Value

GALAXY AUTO CENTERS — ASE

Enjoy 20% off the regular price of any OIL CHANGE - maximum discount $25.00.

valid anytime

I11

Valid now thru November 1, 2007

Offer validity is governed by the Rules of Use and excludes defined holidays. Offers are not valid with other discount offers, unless specified.

---

entertainment.com — SAVE 20%

claire's®

Valid for 20% off one regularly priced item.

One coupon per customer per purchase. Excludes ear piercing, clearance and promotion merchandise, gift cards, and prior purchases

valid anytime

I12

Valid now thru November 1, 2007

Offer validity is governed by the Rules of Use and excludes defined holidays. Offers are not valid with other discount offers, unless specified.

Once Upon A Child
Kids' Stuff With Previous Experience™

- We buy & sell name brand clothing for teens & young adults
- No appointments necessary - no consignment - we pay outright!

Valid at All Participating Locations

00087381

AIRPORT PARKING
EZ AIR PARK

- "Celebrating 20 yrs. of service"

2804 Lexington Ave. (S. on 35E to Lone Oak Rd. E., then N. on Lexington), Eagan, MN
(651)777-7275
www.ezairpark.com

00069579

Curves

- A thirty minute fitness & weight loss center for women!
- Travel to over 5,000 locations worldwide
- Discover the power to amaze yourself
- Call 1-877-CURVES4U to find the Curves nearest you

Valid at All Participating Locations

00525041

Lavish

- Home decor
- Functional giftware
- Clothing, jewelry & accessories
- Free gift packaging
- Customer rewards program

7908 Main St. N.
(Main St., Arbor Lakes)
Maple Grove, MN
(763)493-2446

00683993

---

claire's

Valid at All Participating Locations.

00700430

GALAXY AUTO CENTERS

- Full service auto repair
- Oil changes, filters
- All fluid checks
- Maintenance programs

4309 85th Ave. N, Brooklyn Park, MN
(763)424-8888

5229 University Ave. NE,
Columbia Heights, MN
(763)572-8870

1111 81st Ave. N, Spring Lake Park, MN
(763)784-8000

00428164

claire's

SAVE 20%

entertainment.com

Valid for 20% off one regularly priced item.

One coupon per customer per purchase. Excludes ear piercing, clearance and promotion merchandise, gift cards, and prior purchases

valid anytime

I13

Valid now thru November 1, 2007

Offer validity is governed by the Rules of Use and excludes defined holidays. Offers are not valid with other discount offers, unless specified.

f.y.e.
for your entertainment
music • movies • games • more

$3.00 Value

entertainment.com

$3 off any CD OR DVD regularly priced $12.99 and up.

valid anytime

Limit 1 per transaction; Not to include electronics, game hardware, CD singles, gift cards/coins, sale items or special orders; Attention TWE Associate: Redemption instructions: Press discount key. Enter $3. Scan item. Select TWE coupon and enter promotion code 803800000000

I14

Valid now thru November 1, 2007

Offer validity is governed by the Rules of Use and excludes defined holidays. Offers are not valid with other discount offers, unless specified.

Sir Speedy
PRINTING • COPYING • DIGITAL NETWORK

Up To $25.00 Value

entertainment.com

www.sirspeedy.com

Enjoy 50% off the regular price of your next COPYING ORDER.

valid anytime

I15

Valid now thru November 1, 2007

Offer validity is governed by the Rules of Use and excludes defined holidays. Offers are not valid with other discount offers, unless specified.

Fantastic Sams

Up To $25.00 Value

entertainment.com

Enjoy 20% off the regular price of any SALON SERVICES - maximum discount $25.00.

valid anytime

One coupon/card per customer per visit

I16

Valid now thru November 1, 2007

Offer validity is governed by the Rules of Use and excludes defined holidays. Offers are not valid with other discount offers, unless specified.

GAMES by James

$5.00 Value

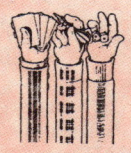

entertainment.com

Enjoy $5 off ANY PURCHASE of $25 or more.

valid anytime at listed locations

Coupon must be presented at time of purchase

I17

Valid now thru November 1, 2007

Offer validity is governed by the Rules of Use and excludes defined holidays. Offers are not valid with other discount offers, unless specified.

---

it figures!
Fast Fun Fitness for Women

SPECIAL OFFER

entertainment.com

www.itfigures.tv

Enjoy 50% off the regular price of one ENROLLMENT FEE or 10% off any promotional rate, whichever provides the best value to the consumer.

valid anytime

I18

Valid now thru November 1, 2007

Offer validity is governed by the Rules of Use and excludes defined holidays. Offers are not valid with other discount offers, unless specified.

f.y.e.
for your entertainment
music • movies • games • more

Valid at All Participating Locations

Coupons void if purchased, sold or bartered. Discounts exclude tax, tip and/or alcohol, where applicable.

00593867

claire's

Valid at All Participating Locations.

Coupons void if purchased, sold or bartered. Discounts exclude tax, tip and/or alcohol, where applicable.

00700430

Fantastic Sams

- Full service hair salon
- Cuts
- Colors
- Perms
- RedKen, American Crew, Nioxin, Sebastian, KMS, Biosilk, Matrix lines & Fantastic Sams hair care

Valid at All Participating Locations

Coupons void if purchased, sold or bartered. Discounts exclude tax, tip and/or alcohol, where applicable.

00665087

Sir Speedy
PRINTING • COPYING • DIGITAL NETWORK

- Full service printing
- Free pick up & delivery
- Oversize copies, Canon color copies
- Color output from disk, large format color output
- Graphic design & typesetting
- Major credit cards accepted

Valid at All Participating Locations

Coupons void if purchased, sold or bartered. Discounts exclude tax, tip and/or alcohol, where applicable.

00082758

it figures!
Fast Fun Fitness for Women

- Use this coupon for a FREE one day pass & body composition analysis!
- Fitness center designed for women of any size, any age, with any schedule
- The best adjustable hydraulic equipment in the industry

Valid at All Participating Locations

Coupons void if purchased, sold or bartered. Discounts exclude tax, tip and/or alcohol, where applicable.

00573402

GAMES by James

- Board Games
- Darts
- Puzzles

Mall of America, Bloomington, MN
(952)854-4747

2495 Southdale Mall, Edina, MN
(952)925-9656

Ridgedale Mall, Minnetonka, MN
(952)546-5446

Coupons void if purchased, sold or bartered. Discounts exclude tax, tip and/or alcohol, where applicable.

00150117

entertainment.com — 50% OFF

Bobby & Steve's Auto World
Auto Repair Experts — Minneapolis

Enjoy any CAR WASH at 50% off the regular price.

valid anytime

I19

Offer validity is governed by the Rules of Use and excludes defined holidays. Offers are not valid with other discount offers, unless specified.

Valid now thru November 1, 2007

---

entertainment.com — Up To $25.00 Value

Ocean Waves

Enjoy 20% off the regular price of any SPA SERVICES - maximum discount $25.00.

valid anytime

I20

Offer validity is governed by the Rules of Use and excludes defined holidays. Offers are not valid with other discount offers, unless specified.

Valid now thru November 1, 2007

---

entertainment.com — 15% OFF

SHERWIN-WILLIAMS
Cover the Earth

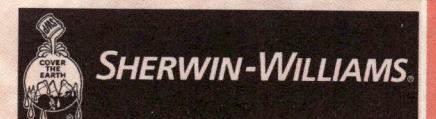

15% off regular price items.

valid anytime

RETAIL SALES ONLY; Sales tax excluded; Offer excludes Color to Go Paint Samples, Color Fan Decks & spray equipment; Present this coupon at time of purchase; Offer cannot be applied to charge card balance; Coupon has no cash value; Cannot be combined with any other offer; Void if copied, transferred, purchased or sold

I21

Offer validity is governed by the Rules of Use and excludes defined holidays. Offers are not valid with other discount offers, unless specified.

Valid now thru November 1, 2007

---

entertainment.com — 5% OFF

SHERWIN-WILLIAMS
Cover the Earth

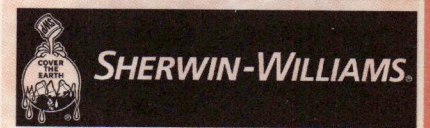

5% off sale priced items.

valid anytime

RETAIL SALES ONLY; Sales tax excluded; Offer excludes Color to Go Paint Samples, Color Fan Decks & spray equipment; Present this coupon at time of purchase; Offer cannot be applied to charge card balance; Coupon has no cash value; Cannot be combined with any other offer; Void if copied, transferred, purchased or sold

I22

Offer validity is governed by the Rules of Use and excludes defined holidays. Offers are not valid with other discount offers, unless specified.

Valid now thru November 1, 2007

---

entertainment.com — Up To $25.00 Value

Underwater Adventures
GIFT STORES — Mall of America

www.sharky.tv

Enjoy 20% off the regular price of any PURCHASE (sale items excluded) - maximum discount $25.00.

valid anytime

Not valid on admission purchases

I23

Offer validity is governed by the Rules of Use and excludes defined holidays. Offers are not valid with other discount offers, unless specified.

Valid now thru November 1, 2007

---

entertainment.com — Up To $25.00 Value

Heavenly Soles

heavenlysoles.com

Enjoy 20% off the regular price of any PURCHASE (sale items excluded) - maximum discount $25.00.

valid anytime

I24

Offer validity is governed by the Rules of Use and excludes defined holidays. Offers are not valid with other discount offers, unless specified.

Valid now thru November 1, 2007

Ocean Waves

- Oxygen bar
- Hydrotherapy water massage
- Shiatsu chair massage session
- Spinal exercise session
- Exixr herbal tonics bar
- Soothe your soul, calm your mind & ease your tension in our relaxing tropical environment

1570 Southdale Ctr.
(lower level, Southdale Mall)
Edina, MN
(952)922-3600

00630531

Bobby & Steve's Auto World
Minneapolis

3828 Central Ave. NE, Columbia Heights, MN
(763)788-1113
1221 Washington Ave. S., Minneapolis, MN
(612)333-8900
304 W. 61st St., Minneapolis, MN
(612)861-6133
7920 France Ave. S., Minneapolis, MN
(952)831-8833

00322480

SHERWIN-WILLIAMS

- "Ask how. Ask now. Ask Sherwin Williams.®"

Valid at All Participating Locations

00696079

SHERWIN-WILLIAMS

- "Ask how. Ask now. Ask Sherwin Williams.®"

Valid at All Participating Locations

00670237

Heavenly Soles

- Shoes for men & women
- Purses, bags & accessories
- Fun, unique barware
- Many, many gifts, cards, books & toys
- Open Mon.-Sat. 10 a.m.-8 p.m.; Sun. 12 p.m.-6 p.m.

615 W. Lake St.
(at Lyndale)
Minneapolis, MN
(612)822-2169

00665690

Underwater Adventures
GIFT STORES

- Touch real sharks & see over 4,500 animals at the world's largest underground aquarium
- Voted "World's Best Shark Encounter" by The Discovery Channel!
- Stop by Sharky's Treasure Chest or Sharky's Cove!

120 E. Broadway
(Mall of America)
Bloomington, MN
(952)883-0202

00485664

entertainment

REPEAT SAVINGS

SUPERAMERICA.

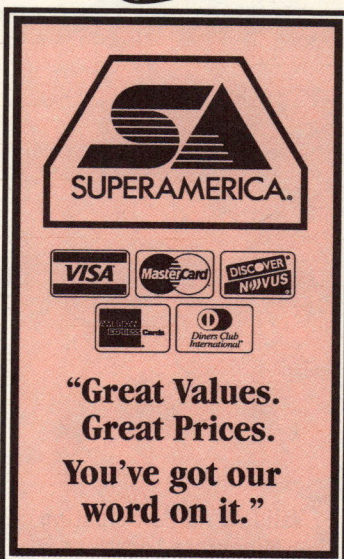

VISA MasterCard DISCOVER NOVUS
American Express Cards Diners Club International

"Great Values. Great Prices. You've got our word on it."

www.speedway.com
See Reverse Side For Locations

Enjoy $1.00 off any purchase of 8 GALLONS OR MORE, ANY GRADE.

(one coupon per month for 12 months)
Limit one coupon per visit
Valid at all participating Minnesota locations

Not valid holidays and subject to Rules of Use.   I25

Enjoy $1.00 off any purchase of 8 GALLONS OR MORE, ANY GRADE.
valid May 2007
Trancode EW
SuperAmerica

Enjoy $1.00 off any purchase of 8 GALLONS OR MORE, ANY GRADE.
valid Nov. 2006
Trancode EW
SuperAmerica

Enjoy $1.00 off any purchase of 8 GALLONS OR MORE, ANY GRADE.
valid June 2007
Trancode EW
SuperAmerica

Enjoy $1.00 off any purchase of 8 GALLONS OR MORE, ANY GRADE.
valid Dec. 2006
Trancode EW
SuperAmerica

Enjoy $1.00 off any purchase of 8 GALLONS OR MORE, ANY GRADE.
valid July 2007
Trancode EW
SuperAmerica

Enjoy $1.00 off any purchase of 8 GALLONS OR MORE, ANY GRADE.
valid Jan. 2007
Trancode EW
SuperAmerica

Enjoy $1.00 off any purchase of 8 GALLONS OR MORE, ANY GRADE.
valid Aug. 2007
Trancode EW
SuperAmerica

Enjoy $1.00 off any purchase of 8 GALLONS OR MORE, ANY GRADE.
valid Feb. 2007
Trancode EW
SuperAmerica

Enjoy $1.00 off any purchase of 8 GALLONS OR MORE, ANY GRADE.
valid Sept. 2007
Trancode EW
SuperAmerica

Enjoy $1.00 off any purchase of 8 GALLONS OR MORE, ANY GRADE.
valid March 2007
Trancode EW
SuperAmerica

Enjoy $1.00 off any purchase of 8 GALLONS OR MORE, ANY GRADE.
valid Oct. 2007
Trancode EW
SuperAmerica

Enjoy $1.00 off any purchase of 8 GALLONS OR MORE, ANY GRADE.
valid April 2007
Trancode EW
SuperAmerica

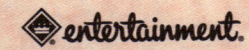

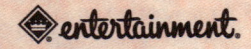

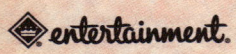

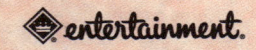

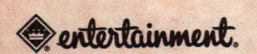

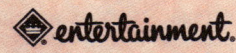

entertainment.
Please present coupon at time of purchase; Limit one coupon per visit; Trancode EW

entertainment.
Please present coupon at time of purchase; Limit one coupon per visit; Trancode EW

entertainment.
Please present coupon at time of purchase; Limit one coupon per visit; Trancode EW

entertainment.
Please present coupon at time of purchase; Limit one coupon per visit; Trancode EW

entertainment.
Please present coupon at time of purchase; Limit one coupon per visit; Trancode EW

entertainment.
Please present coupon at time of purchase; Limit one coupon per visit; Trancode EW

entertainment.
Please present coupon at time of purchase; Limit one coupon per visit; Trancode EW

entertainment.
Please present coupon at time of purchase; Limit one coupon per visit; Trancode EW

entertainment.
Please present coupon at time of purchase; Limit one coupon per visit; Trancode EW

entertainment.
Please present coupon at time of purchase; Limit one coupon per visit; Trancode EW

entertainment.
Please present coupon at time of purchase; Limit one coupon per visit; Trancode EW

entertainment.
Please present coupon at time of purchase; Limit one coupon per visit; Trancode EW

entertainment.
Please present coupon at time of purchase; Limit one coupon per visit; Trancode EW

entertainment.
Please present coupon at time of purchase; Limit one coupon per visit; Trancode EW

Valid At All Participating Minnesota Locations

Tran Code EW

entertainment

REPEAT SAVINGS

SuperAmerica Car Wash

"Great Values. Great Prices. You've got our word on it."

See Reverse Side For Locations

Enjoy one "THE WORKS" CAR WASH at 50% off the regular price.

(one coupon per two months for 12 months)
Not valid with any other discounts or offers

Not valid holidays and subject to Rules of Use.

Enjoy one "THE WORKS" CAR WASH at 50% off the regular price.

valid Nov. 2006 thru Dec. 2006
SuperAmerica Car Washes

Enjoy one "THE WORKS" CAR WASH at 50% off the regular price.

valid Jan. 2007 thru Feb. 2007
SuperAmerica Car Washes

Enjoy one "THE WORKS" CAR WASH at 50% off the regular price.

valid March 2007 thru April 2007
SuperAmerica Car Washes

Enjoy one "THE WORKS" CAR WASH at 50% off the regular price.

valid May 2007 thru June 2007
SuperAmerica Car Washes

Enjoy one "THE WORKS" CAR WASH at 50% off the regular price.

valid July 2007 thru Aug. 2007
SuperAmerica Car Washes

Enjoy one "THE WORKS" CAR WASH at 50% off the regular price.

valid Sept. 2007 thru Oct. 2007
SuperAmerica Car Washes

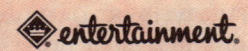

entertainment.
Please present coupon at time of purchase; Trancode IB

entertainment.
Please present coupon at time of purchase; Trancode IB

entertainment.
Please present coupon at time of purchase; Trancode IB

entertainment.
Please present coupon at time of purchase; Trancode IB

entertainment.
Please present coupon at time of purchase; Trancode IB

entertainment.
Please present coupon at time of purchase; Trancode IB

Valid at All Participating Minnesota Locations

Trancode IB

entertainment

REPEAT SAVINGS

SuperMom's RECIPE | SA SUPERAMERICA
Simek's

Valid at All Participating Minnesota Locations

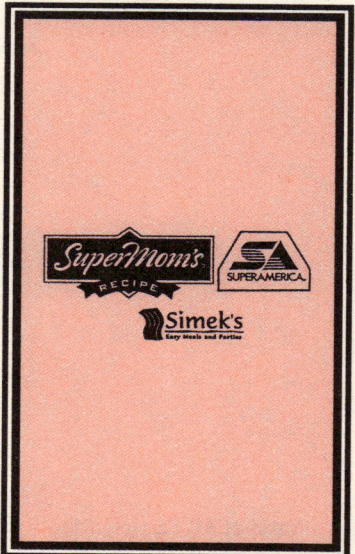

Enjoy $5.00 off a $10.00 or more Simek's, Supermom's or any in-store purchase.

(one coupon per three months for 12 months)

Simek's "Quality Foods for Busy People" now available at your local SuperAmerica

Call (651)459-CAKE (2253) to order Supermom's party trays, cakes & subs

Visit www.supermoms.com for Simek's party trays & all your other party needs

---

Enjoy $5.00 off a $10.00 or more Simek's, Supermom's or any in-store purchase.

valid Nov. 2006 thru Jan. 2007
Trancode EB
Excludes tobacco products, alcoholic beverages, lottery tickets & gasoline

Supermom's

Enjoy $5.00 off a $10.00 or more Simek's, Supermom's or any in-store purchase.

valid Feb. 2007 thru April 2007
Trancode EB
Excludes tobacco products, alcoholic beverages, lottery tickets & gasoline

Supermom's

Enjoy $5.00 off a $10.00 or more Simek's, Supermom's or any in-store purchase.

valid May 2007 thru July 2007
Trancode EB
Excludes tobacco products, alcoholic beverages, lottery tickets & gasoline

Supermom's

Enjoy $5.00 off a $10.00 or more Simek's, Supermom's or any in-store purchase.

valid Aug. 2007 thru Oct. 2007
Trancode EB
Excludes tobacco products, alcoholic beverages, lottery tickets & gasoline

Supermom's

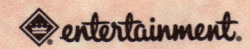

entertainment.

Excludes tobacco products, alcoholic beverages, lottery tickets & gasoline; Not valid with any other discount offer; One coupon per customer per visit; Trancode EB; Order on-line with coupon code ENTBOOK5

---

entertainment.

Excludes tobacco products, alcoholic beverages, lottery tickets & gasoline; Not valid with any other discount offer; One coupon per customer per visit; Trancode EB; Order on-line with coupon code ENTBOOK5

---

entertainment.

Excludes tobacco products, alcoholic beverages, lottery tickets & gasoline; Not valid with any other discount offer; One coupon per customer per visit; Trancode EB; Order on-line with coupon code ENTBOOK5

---

entertainment.

Excludes tobacco products, alcoholic beverages, lottery tickets & gasoline; Not valid with any other discount offer; One coupon per customer per visit; Trancode EB; Order on-line with coupon code ENTBOOK5

Valid at All Participating Minnesota Locations

entertainment

REPEAT SAVINGS™

PARADISE
CAR • WASH

See Reverse Side For Locations

Enjoy one SAVER WASH at 50% off the regular price.

(one coupon per month for 12 months)

Seats & floors vacuumed
Ashtrays emptied
Windows cleaned to a sparkle
Dash dusted off
Multi-coat protectant
Under chassis bath
Rust inhibitor
Air freshener
Outside wash bumper to bumper
Exterior towel dried

Not valid holidays and subject to Rules of Use.   I28

Enjoy one SAVER WASH at 50% off the regular price.
valid May 2007
Paradise Car Wash

Enjoy one SAVER WASH at 50% off the regular price.
valid Nov. 2006
Paradise Car Wash

Enjoy one SAVER WASH at 50% off the regular price.
valid June 2007
Paradise Car Wash

Enjoy one SAVER WASH at 50% off the regular price.
valid Dec. 2006
Paradise Car Wash

Enjoy one SAVER WASH at 50% off the regular price.
valid July 2007
Paradise Car Wash

Enjoy one SAVER WASH at 50% off the regular price.
valid Jan. 2007
Paradise Car Wash

Enjoy one SAVER WASH at 50% off the regular price.
valid Aug. 2007
Paradise Car Wash

Enjoy one SAVER WASH at 50% off the regular price.
valid Feb. 2007
Paradise Car Wash

Enjoy one SAVER WASH at 50% off the regular price.
valid Sept. 2007
Paradise Car Wash

Enjoy one SAVER WASH at 50% off the regular price.
valid March 2007
Paradise Car Wash

Enjoy one SAVER WASH at 50% off the regular price.
valid Oct. 2007
Paradise Car Wash

Enjoy one SAVER WASH at 50% off the regular price.
valid April 2007
Paradise Car Wash

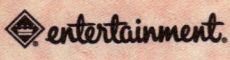

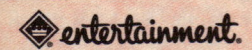

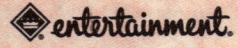

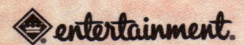

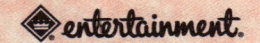

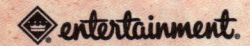

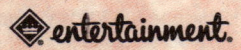

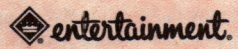

entertainment.
Not valid with any other discount offer

entertainment.
Not valid with any other discount offer

entertainment.
Not valid with any other discount offer

entertainment.
Not valid with any other discount offer

entertainment.
Not valid with any other discount offer

entertainment.
Not valid with any other discount offer

entertainment.
Not valid with any other discount offer

entertainment.
Not valid with any other discount offer

entertainment.
Not valid with any other discount offer

entertainment.
Not valid with any other discount offer

entertainment.
Not valid with any other discount offer

entertainment.
Not valid with any other discount offer

entertainment.
Not valid with any other discount offer

entertainment.
Not valid with any other discount offer

Apple Valley
7600 W. 145th St.
(952)431-4600

Bloomington
10820 Bush Lake Rd.
(952)944-9033

9201 Lyndale Ave. S.
(952)888-5388

Eagan
1355 Town Center Dr.
(651)456-0000

Savage
14324 Huntington Ave. S
(952)890-7755

entertainment

Repeat Savings

Downtowner Full Service Car Wash
COMPLETE CLEANING INSIDE AND OUT PROFESSIONAL Since 1978

www.downtownercarwash.com
See Reverse Side For Locations

Enjoy one GOLD WASH WITH CLEAR COAT PROTECTANT at 50% off the regular price.

One coupon per month for 12 months

Full service car wash

Most trucks & vans too!

Touchless equipment using soft cloth & only fresh water

Air & towel detail drying

Air freshener

Mon-Fri 7:30 a.m.-7 p.m., Sat 7:30 a.m.-6 p.m., Sun 8:30a.m.-5:30 p.m.

Not valid holidays and subject to Rules of Use.

I29

Enjoy one GOLD WASH WITH CLEAR COAT PROTECTANT at 50% off the regular price.

valid Apr. 2007

Downtowner Car Wash

Enjoy one GOLD WASH WITH CLEAR COAT PROTECTANT at 50% off the regular price.

valid May 2007

Downtowner Car Wash

Enjoy one GOLD WASH WITH CLEAR COAT PROTECTANT at 50% off the regular price.

valid Jun. 2007

Downtowner Car Wash

Enjoy one GOLD WASH WITH CLEAR COAT PROTECTANT at 50% off the regular price.

valid Jul. 2007

Downtowner Car Wash

Enjoy one GOLD WASH WITH CLEAR COAT PROTECTANT at 50% off the regular price.

valid Aug. 2007

Downtowner Car Wash

Enjoy one GOLD WASH WITH CLEAR COAT PROTECTANT at 50% off the regular price.

valid Sep. 2007

Downtowner Car Wash

Enjoy one GOLD WASH WITH CLEAR COAT PROTECTANT at 50% off the regular price.

valid Oct. 2006

Downtowner Car Wash

Enjoy one GOLD WASH WITH CLEAR COAT PROTECTANT at 50% off the regular price.

valid Nov. 2006

Downtowner Car Wash

Enjoy one GOLD WASH WITH CLEAR COAT PROTECTANT at 50% off the regular price.

valid Dec. 2006

Downtowner Car Wash

Enjoy one GOLD WASH WITH CLEAR COAT PROTECTANT at 50% off the regular price.

valid Jan. 2007

Downtowner Car Wash

Enjoy one GOLD WASH WITH CLEAR COAT PROTECTANT at 50% off the regular price.

valid Feb. 2007

Downtowner Car Wash

Enjoy one GOLD WASH WITH CLEAR COAT PROTECTANT at 50% off the regular price.

valid Mar. 2007

Downtowner Car Wash

entertainment
Not valid with other coupons or discounts

entertainment
Not valid with other coupons or discounts

entertainment
Not valid with other coupons or discounts

entertainment
Not valid with other coupons or discounts

entertainment
Not valid with other coupons or discounts

entertainment
Not valid with other coupons or discounts

entertainment
Not valid with other coupons or discounts

entertainment
Not valid with other coupons or discounts

entertainment
Not valid with other coupons or discounts

entertainment
Not valid with other coupons or discounts

entertainment
Not valid with other coupons or discounts

entertainment
Not valid with other coupons or discounts

entertainment
Not valid with other coupons or discounts

entertainment
Not valid with other coupons or discounts

MINNESOTA
St Paul
520 East 7th Street
(651)222-7045

Gold Wash with Clear Coat Protectant includes:

Outside washed bumper to bumper

Front & rear carpets vacuumed, ashtrays emptied

Litter bags emptied

Windows cleaned to sparkle, inside & out

Doorjambs wiped clean

Under chassis wash

Rust inhibitor

3 step ultra-shine wax

3 step clear coat protectant

Air freshener

entertainment

REPEAT SAVINGS

HEPPNER'S WOODBURY AUTO WASH

7776 Hudson Rd. (Radio Drive Exit off I-94 east)
Woodbury, MN
(651) 730-7808

Enjoy one SUPER WASH at 50% off the regular price.

One coupon per month for 12 months
Full service wash with vacuum
Ultra Shine® paint & clear coat treatment
Underchassis wash
Underchassis rust inhibitor
Vans & pickups $1.50 extra
Reconditioning & detailing services

Not valid holidays and subject to Rules of Use.   I30

Enjoy one SUPER WASH at 50% off the regular price. Valid Apr. 2007 Heppner's Auto Wash & Detailing Center	Enjoy one SUPER WASH at 50% off the regular price. Valid Oct. 2006 Heppner's Auto Wash & Detailing Center
Enjoy one SUPER WASH at 50% off the regular price. Valid May 2007 Heppner's Auto Wash & Detailing Center	Enjoy one SUPER WASH at 50% off the regular price. Valid Nov. 2006 Heppner's Auto Wash & Detailing Center
Enjoy one SUPER WASH at 50% off the regular price. Valid Jun. 2007 Heppner's Auto Wash & Detailing Center	Enjoy one SUPER WASH at 50% off the regular price. Valid Dec. 2006 Heppner's Auto Wash & Detailing Center
Enjoy one SUPER WASH at 50% off the regular price. Valid Jul. 2007 Heppner's Auto Wash & Detailing Center	Enjoy one SUPER WASH at 50% off the regular price. Valid Jan. 2007 Heppner's Auto Wash & Detailing Center
Enjoy one SUPER WASH at 50% off the regular price. Valid Aug. 2007 Heppner's Auto Wash & Detailing Center	Enjoy one SUPER WASH at 50% off the regular price. Valid Feb. 2007 Heppner's Auto Wash & Detailing Center
Enjoy one SUPER WASH at 50% off the regular price. Valid Sep. 2007 Heppner's Auto Wash & Detailing Center	Enjoy one SUPER WASH at 50% off the regular price. Valid Mar. 2007 Heppner's Auto Wash & Detailing Center

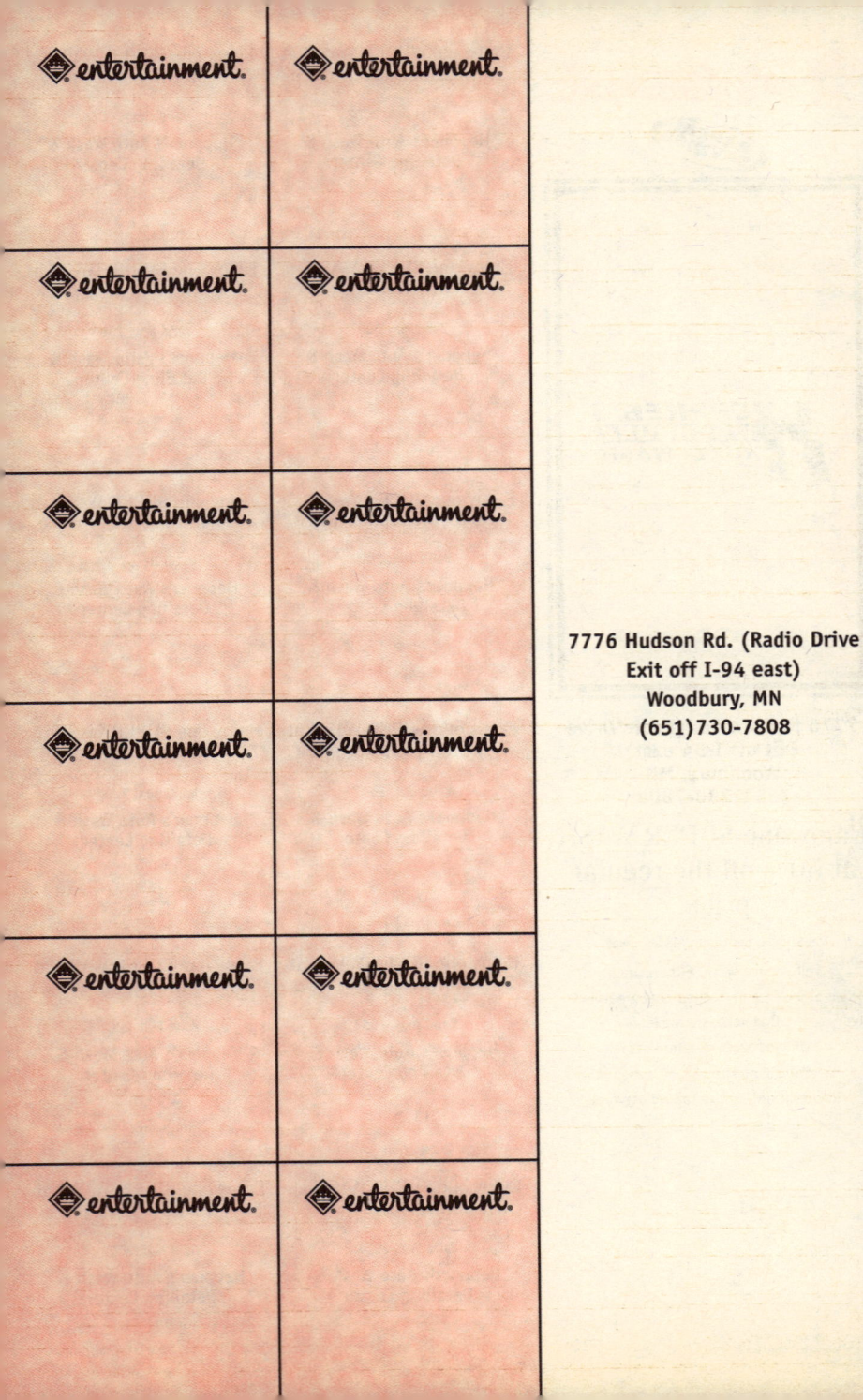

entertainment. entertainment.
entertainment. entertainment.
entertainment. entertainment.
entertainment. entertainment.
entertainment. entertainment.
entertainment. entertainment.

7776 Hudson Rd. (Radio Drive
Exit off I-94 east)
Woodbury, MN
(651) 730-7808

entertainment

REPEAT SAVINGS

Don's Car Washes

See Reverse Side For Locations

Enjoy one SUPREME WASH - Heights or DELUXE WORKS WASH - Apache at 50% off the regular price.

One coupon per month for 12 months

Supreme Wash valid at 4423 Central Ave. NE, Columbia Heights (763)788-1631

Deluxe Works Wash valid at 3725 Stinson Blvd., Minneapolis (Apache) (612)788-8689

Not valid holidays and subject to Rules of Use.   I31

Enjoy one SUPREME WASH - Heights or DELUXE WORKS WASH - Apache at 50% off the regular price. valid Apr. 2007 Don's Car Washes	Enjoy one SUPREME WASH - Heights or DELUXE WORKS WASH - Apache at 50% off the regular price. valid Oct. 2006 Don's Car Washes
Enjoy one SUPREME WASH - Heights or DELUXE WORKS WASH - Apache at 50% off the regular price. valid May 2007 Don's Car Washes	Enjoy one SUPREME WASH - Heights or DELUXE WORKS WASH - Apache at 50% off the regular price. valid Nov. 2006 Don's Car Washes
Enjoy one SUPREME WASH - Heights or DELUXE WORKS WASH - Apache at 50% off the regular price. valid Jun. 2007 Don's Car Washes	Enjoy one SUPREME WASH - Heights or DELUXE WORKS WASH - Apache at 50% off the regular price. valid Dec. 2006 Don's Car Washes
Enjoy one SUPREME WASH - Heights or DELUXE WORKS WASH - Apache at 50% off the regular price. valid Jul. 2007 Don's Car Washes	Enjoy one SUPREME WASH - Heights or DELUXE WORKS WASH - Apache at 50% off the regular price. valid Jan. 2007 Don's Car Washes
Enjoy one SUPREME WASH - Heights or DELUXE WORKS WASH - Apache at 50% off the regular price. valid Aug. 2007 Don's Car Washes	Enjoy one SUPREME WASH - Heights or DELUXE WORKS WASH - Apache at 50% off the regular price. valid Feb. 2007 Don's Car Washes
Enjoy one SUPREME WASH - Heights or DELUXE WORKS WASH - Apache at 50% off the regular price. valid Sep. 2007 Don's Car Washes	Enjoy one SUPREME WASH - Heights or DELUXE WORKS WASH - Apache at 50% off the regular price. valid Mar. 2007 Don's Car Washes

**MINNESOTA
Columbia Heights**
4423 Central Ave. NE
(763)788-1631

Mon-Fri 8:30am-6pm, Saturday 8am,-6pm at Columbia Heights

Mon-Fri 8:30am-6:30pm, Saturday 8am-6pm, Sunday 10am-5pm at Apache

entertainment

REPEAT SAVINGS

Brookdale Car Wash

See Reverse Side For Locations

Enjoy one SAVER WASH at 50% off the regular price.

One coupon per month for 12 months

Soft Cloth Wash System
Outside Washed & Towel Dried Bumper to Bumper
Carpets Vacuumed Front & Rear
Ashtrays Emptied
Interior Windows Cleaned
UnderChassis Flush
Rust Inhibitor Sprayed Under & Over Car
Two Step Wax Treatment: Clear Coat Sealer & Poly Foam Wax
Interior Air Freshener

Not valid holidays and subject to Rules of Use.

Enjoy one SAVER WASH at 50% off the regular price. valid Apr. 2007 Brookdale Car Wash	Enjoy one SAVER WASH at 50% off the regular price. valid Oct. 2006 Brookdale Car Wash
Enjoy one SAVER WASH at 50% off the regular price. valid May 2007 Brookdale Car Wash	Enjoy one SAVER WASH at 50% off the regular price. valid Nov. 2006 Brookdale Car Wash
Enjoy one SAVER WASH at 50% off the regular price. valid Jun. 2007 Brookdale Car Wash	Enjoy one SAVER WASH at 50% off the regular price. valid Dec. 2006 Brookdale Car Wash
Enjoy one SAVER WASH at 50% off the regular price. valid Jul. 2007 Brookdale Car Wash	Enjoy one SAVER WASH at 50% off the regular price. valid Jan. 2007 Brookdale Car Wash
Enjoy one SAVER WASH at 50% off the regular price. valid Aug. 2007 Brookdale Car Wash	Enjoy one SAVER WASH at 50% off the regular price. valid Feb. 2007 Brookdale Car Wash
Enjoy one SAVER WASH at 50% off the regular price. valid Sep. 2007 Brookdale Car Wash	Enjoy one SAVER WASH at 50% off the regular price. valid Mar. 2007 Brookdale Car Wash

entertainment.
Additional $1.50 charge for full size pickups, vans & Suburbans; Show coupon to service writer

entertainment.
Additional $1.50 charge for full size pickups, vans & Suburbans; Show coupon to service writer

entertainment.
Additional $1.50 charge for full size pickups, vans & Suburbans; Show coupon to service writer

entertainment.
Additional $1.50 charge for full size pickups, vans & Suburbans; Show coupon to service writer

entertainment.
Additional $1.50 charge for full size pickups, vans & Suburbans; Show coupon to service writer

entertainment.
Additional $1.50 charge for full size pickups, vans & Suburbans; Show coupon to service writer

entertainment.
Additional $1.50 charge for full size pickups, vans & Suburbans; Show coupon to service writer

entertainment.
Additional $1.50 charge for full size pickups, vans & Suburbans; Show coupon to service writer

entertainment.
Additional $1.50 charge for full size pickups, vans & Suburbans; Show coupon to service writer

entertainment.
Additional $1.50 charge for full size pickups, vans & Suburbans; Show coupon to service writer

entertainment.
Additional $1.50 charge for full size pickups, vans & Suburbans; Show coupon to service writer

entertainment.
Additional $1.50 charge for full size pickups, vans & Suburbans; Show coupon to service writer

MINNESOTA
Brooklyn Center
5500 Brooklyn Blvd.
(763)561-1123

Mon-Fri 8-8, Sat 8-6, Sun 9-5

entertainment

REPEAT SAVINGS

T & Y CAR WASH
Voted Best Carwash 02

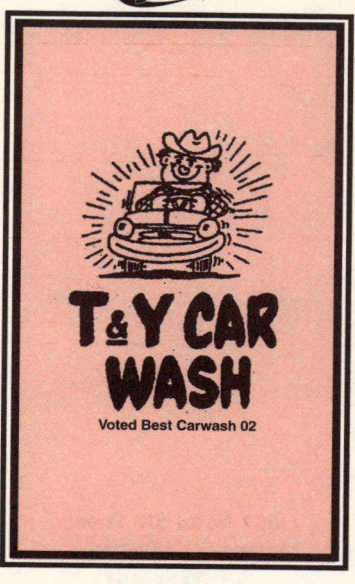

**601 North 5th Street
Minneapolis, MN
(612)338-8017**

Enjoy one ULTRA SHINE DELUXE or CLEARCOAT SUPREME WASH at 50% off the regular price.

(one coupon per month for 12 months)

Regular full service wash includes: interior vacuum, windows, dash, rear deck cleaned, blower & chamois dry detail exterior

Super wash includes: Blue Coral wax & polish, under chassis bath, dash, rear deck, windows & carpet cleaned, floor mats, scented air freshener, blower & chamois dry detail exterior

Vans, pickups & SUVs $1.00 extra

Not valid holidays and subject to Rules of Use.   I33

Enjoy one ULTRA SHINE DELUXE or CLEARCOAT SUPREME WASH at 50% off the regular price. valid May 2007 T & Y Car Wash	Enjoy one ULTRA SHINE DELUXE or CLEARCOAT SUPREME WASH at 50% off the regular price. valid Nov. 2006 T & Y Car Wash
Enjoy one ULTRA SHINE DELUXE or CLEARCOAT SUPREME WASH at 50% off the regular price. valid June 2007 T & Y Car Wash	Enjoy one ULTRA SHINE DELUXE or CLEARCOAT SUPREME WASH at 50% off the regular price. valid Dec. 2006 T & Y Car Wash
Enjoy one ULTRA SHINE DELUXE or CLEARCOAT SUPREME WASH at 50% off the regular price. valid July 2007 T & Y Car Wash	Enjoy one ULTRA SHINE DELUXE or CLEARCOAT SUPREME WASH at 50% off the regular price. valid Jan. 2007 T & Y Car Wash
Enjoy one ULTRA SHINE DELUXE or CLEARCOAT SUPREME WASH at 50% off the regular price. valid Aug. 2007 T & Y Car Wash	Enjoy one ULTRA SHINE DELUXE or CLEARCOAT SUPREME WASH at 50% off the regular price. valid Feb. 2007 T & Y Car Wash
Enjoy one ULTRA SHINE DELUXE or CLEARCOAT SUPREME WASH at 50% off the regular price. valid Sept. 2007 T & Y Car Wash	Enjoy one ULTRA SHINE DELUXE or CLEARCOAT SUPREME WASH at 50% off the regular price. valid March 2007 T & Y Car Wash
Enjoy one ULTRA SHINE DELUXE or CLEARCOAT SUPREME WASH at 50% off the regular price. valid Oct. 2007 T & Y Car Wash	Enjoy one ULTRA SHINE DELUXE or CLEARCOAT SUPREME WASH at 50% off the regular price. valid April 2007 T & Y Car Wash

entertainment entertainment
entertainment entertainment
entertainment entertainment
entertainment entertainment
entertainment entertainment
entertainment entertainment

601 North 5th Street
Minneapolis, MN
(612) 338-8017

entertainment

REPEAT SAVINGS

Central Car Wash

1814 Central Ave. N.E.
Minneapolis, MN
(612) 781-6924

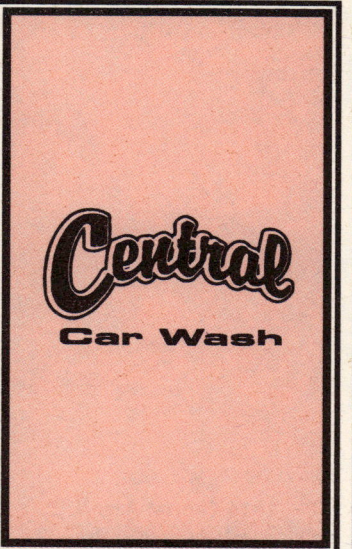

Enjoy one THE WORKS CAR WASH at 50% off the regular price.

One coupon per month for 12 months

Full Service Wash
Ultra Shine® RAINBOW WAX
Ultra Shine® Paint & Clear Coat Sealer
Underbody Flush
Underbody Rust Inhibitor
Air Freshener

Not valid holidays and subject to Rules of Use.

Enjoy one THE WORKS CAR WASH at 50% off the regular price.
valid Apr. 2007
Central Car Wash

Enjoy one THE WORKS CAR WASH at 50% off the regular price.
valid Oct. 2006
Central Car Wash

Enjoy one THE WORKS CAR WASH at 50% off the regular price.
valid May 2007
Central Car Wash

Enjoy one THE WORKS CAR WASH at 50% off the regular price.
valid Nov. 2006
Central Car Wash

Enjoy one THE WORKS CAR WASH at 50% off the regular price.
valid Jun. 2007
Central Car Wash

Enjoy one THE WORKS CAR WASH at 50% off the regular price.
valid Dec. 2006
Central Car Wash

Enjoy one THE WORKS CAR WASH at 50% off the regular price.
valid Jul. 2007
Central Car Wash

Enjoy one THE WORKS CAR WASH at 50% off the regular price.
valid Jan. 2007
Central Car Wash

Enjoy one THE WORKS CAR WASH at 50% off the regular price.
valid Aug. 2007
Central Car Wash

Enjoy one THE WORKS CAR WASH at 50% off the regular price.
valid Feb. 2007
Central Car Wash

Enjoy one THE WORKS CAR WASH at 50% off the regular price.
valid Sep. 2007
Central Car Wash

Enjoy one THE WORKS CAR WASH at 50% off the regular price.
valid Mar. 2007
Central Car Wash

1814 Central Ave. N.E.
Minneapolis, MN
(612) 781-6924

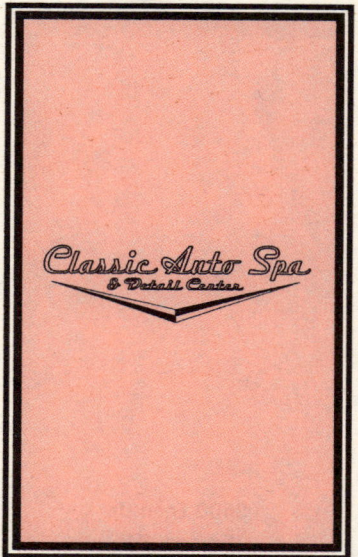

entertainment

REPEAT SAVINGS

Classic Auto Spa & Detail Center

8600 Egan Dr.
Savage, MN
(952) 233-5585

Enjoy one FLEETWOOD CAR WASH at 50% off the regular price.

(one coupon per month for 12 months)

Full service car wash & detail center
Soft cloth & fresh water
We can detail any car/SUV, H2's, lowered cars, Porsches, Corvettes & motorcycles
Perfection is our only acceptable standard

Not valid holidays and subject to Rules of Use.

Enjoy one FLEETWOOD CAR WASH at 50% off the regular price.
valid May 2007
Classic Auto Spa & Detail Center

Enjoy one FLEETWOOD CAR WASH at 50% off the regular price.
valid Nov. 2006
Classic Auto Spa & Detail Center

Enjoy one FLEETWOOD CAR WASH at 50% off the regular price.
valid June 2007
Classic Auto Spa & Detail Center

Enjoy one FLEETWOOD CAR WASH at 50% off the regular price.
valid Dec. 2006
Classic Auto Spa & Detail Center

Enjoy one FLEETWOOD CAR WASH at 50% off the regular price.
valid July 2007
Classic Auto Spa & Detail Center

Enjoy one FLEETWOOD CAR WASH at 50% off the regular price.
valid Jan. 2007
Classic Auto Spa & Detail Center

Enjoy one FLEETWOOD CAR WASH at 50% off the regular price.
valid Aug. 2007
Classic Auto Spa & Detail Center

Enjoy one FLEETWOOD CAR WASH at 50% off the regular price.
valid Feb. 2007
Classic Auto Spa & Detail Center

Enjoy one FLEETWOOD CAR WASH at 50% off the regular price.
valid Sept. 2007
Classic Auto Spa & Detail Center

Enjoy one FLEETWOOD CAR WASH at 50% off the regular price.
valid March 2007
Classic Auto Spa & Detail Center

Enjoy one FLEETWOOD CAR WASH at 50% off the regular price.
valid Oct. 2007
Classic Auto Spa & Detail Center

Enjoy one FLEETWOOD CAR WASH at 50% off the regular price.
valid April 2007
Classic Auto Spa & Detail Center

entertainment. entertainment.
entertainment. entertainment.
entertainment. entertainment.
entertainment. entertainment.
entertainment. entertainment.
entertainment. entertainment.

8600 Egan Dr.
Savage, MN
(952) 233-5585

entertainment

REPEAT SAVINGS

www.victorylanecw.com
**1301 Crystal Ln.
Chaska, MN
(952)368-0085**

Enjoy ONE WINNERS CIRCLE WASH at 50% off the regular price.

(one coupon per month for 12 months)

- The latest in hi-tech car care equipment
- Equipped with a soft cloth cleaning system & a fully trained pit crew
- Not just another car wash - It's a complete car care experience

Not valid holidays and subject to Rules of Use.   I36

Enjoy ONE WINNERS CIRCLE WASH at 50% off the regular price.
valid May 2007
Victory Lane Car Wash & Detail Center

Enjoy ONE WINNERS CIRCLE WASH at 50% off the regular price.
valid Nov. 2006
Victory Lane Car Wash & Detail Center

Enjoy ONE WINNERS CIRCLE WASH at 50% off the regular price.
valid June 2007
Victory Lane Car Wash & Detail Center

Enjoy ONE WINNERS CIRCLE WASH at 50% off the regular price.
valid Dec. 2006
Victory Lane Car Wash & Detail Center

Enjoy ONE WINNERS CIRCLE WASH at 50% off the regular price.
valid July 2007
Victory Lane Car Wash & Detail Center

Enjoy ONE WINNERS CIRCLE WASH at 50% off the regular price.
valid Jan. 2007
Victory Lane Car Wash & Detail Center

Enjoy ONE WINNERS CIRCLE WASH at 50% off the regular price.
valid Aug. 2007
Victory Lane Car Wash & Detail Center

Enjoy ONE WINNERS CIRCLE WASH at 50% off the regular price.
valid Feb. 2007
Victory Lane Car Wash & Detail Center

Enjoy ONE WINNERS CIRCLE WASH at 50% off the regular price.
valid Sept. 2007
Victory Lane Car Wash & Detail Center

Enjoy ONE WINNERS CIRCLE WASH at 50% off the regular price.
valid March 2007
Victory Lane Car Wash & Detail Center

Enjoy ONE WINNERS CIRCLE WASH at 50% off the regular price.
valid Oct. 2007
Victory Lane Car Wash & Detail Center

Enjoy ONE WINNERS CIRCLE WASH at 50% off the regular price.
valid April 2007
Victory Lane Car Wash & Detail Center

entertainment. entertainment.

entertainment. entertainment.

entertainment. entertainment.

entertainment. entertainment.

entertainment. entertainment.

entertainment. entertainment.

**1301 Crystal Ln.
Chaska, MN
(952)368-0085**

entertainment

REPEAT SAVINGS

White Way

See Reverse Side For Locations

Enjoy any DRY CLEANING ORDER at 50% off the regular price - maximum discount $5.00.

One coupon per month for 12 months

Not valid holidays and subject to Rules of Use.   I37

Enjoy any DRY CLEANING ORDER at 50% off the regular price - maximum discount $5.00. valid April 2007 White Way Cleaners	Enjoy any DRY CLEANING ORDER at 50% off the regular price - maximum discount $5.00. valid October 2006 White Way Cleaners
Enjoy any DRY CLEANING ORDER at 50% off the regular price - maximum discount $5.00. valid May 2007 White Way Cleaners	Enjoy any DRY CLEANING ORDER at 50% off the regular price - maximum discount $5.00. valid November 2006 White Way Cleaners
Enjoy any DRY CLEANING ORDER at 50% off the regular price - maximum discount $5.00. valid June 2007 White Way Cleaners	Enjoy any DRY CLEANING ORDER at 50% off the regular price - maximum discount $5.00. valid December 2006 White Way Cleaners
Enjoy any DRY CLEANING ORDER at 50% off the regular price - maximum discount $5.00. valid July 2007 White Way Cleaners	Enjoy any DRY CLEANING ORDER at 50% off the regular price - maximum discount $5.00. valid January 2007 White Way Cleaners
Enjoy any DRY CLEANING ORDER at 50% off the regular price - maximum discount $5.00. valid August 2007 White Way Cleaners	Enjoy any DRY CLEANING ORDER at 50% off the regular price - maximum discount $5.00. valid February 2007 White Way Cleaners
Enjoy any DRY CLEANING ORDER at 50% off the regular price - maximum discount $5.00. valid September 2007 White Way Cleaners	Enjoy any DRY CLEANING ORDER at 50% off the regular price - maximum discount $5.00. valid March 2007 White Way Cleaners

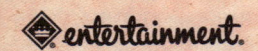

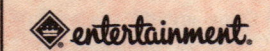

entertainment.
Present with incoming order; Not valid with any other discount offer; One coupon per customer per day; Route service excluded; Not valid on laundry

entertainment.
Present with incoming order; Not valid with any other discount offer; One coupon per customer per day; Route service excluded; Not valid on laundry

entertainment.
Present with incoming order; Not valid with any other discount offer; One coupon per customer per day; Route service excluded; Not valid on laundry

entertainment.
Present with incoming order; Not valid with any other discount offer; One coupon per customer per day; Route service excluded; Not valid on laundry

entertainment.
Present with incoming order; Not valid with any other discount offer; One coupon per customer per day; Route service excluded; Not valid on laundry

entertainment.
Present with incoming order; Not valid with any other discount offer; One coupon per customer per day; Route service excluded; Not valid on laundry

entertainment.
Present with incoming order; Not valid with any other discount offer; One coupon per customer per day; Route service excluded; Not valid on laundry

entertainment.
Present with incoming order; Not valid with any other discount offer; One coupon per customer per day; Route service excluded; Not valid on laundry

entertainment.
Present with incoming order; Not valid with any other discount offer; One coupon per customer per day; Route service excluded; Not valid on laundry

entertainment.
Present with incoming order; Not valid with any other discount offer; One coupon per customer per day; Route service excluded; Not valid on laundry

entertainment.
Present with incoming order; Not valid with any other discount offer; One coupon per customer per day; Route service excluded; Not valid on laundry

entertainment.
Present with incoming order; Not valid with any other discount offer; One coupon per customer per day; Route service excluded; Not valid on laundry

Minneapolis
200 S. 6th St.
(US Bank Bldg., Skyway)
(612)332-4372

222 S. 9th St.
(Campbell Mithun, Skyway)
(612)338-2006

40 S. 7th St.
(City Center, Block E Skyway)
(612)338-3220

811 La Salle Ave.
(Highland Bank Ct., Skyway)
(612)338-9001

St. Paul
286 W. 7th St.
(651)224-1391

444 Cedar St.
(Town Square, Skyway)
(651)291-7344

510 N. Robert St.
(The Rossmor)
(651)224-8348

678 Grand Ave.
(Crocus Hill)
(651)291-1683

entertainment

REPEAT SAVINGS

Sew What! Midway Cleaners

See Reverse Side For Locations

Enjoy any DRY CLEANING ORDER at 50% off the regular price - maximum discount $5.00.

(one coupon per month for 12 months)

Not valid holidays and subject to Rules of Use.

Enjoy any DRY CLEANING ORDER at 50% off the regular price - maximum discount $5.00. valid May 2007 Sew What! Midway Cleaners	Enjoy any DRY CLEANING ORDER at 50% off the regular price - maximum discount $5.00. valid Nov. 2006 Sew What! Midway Cleaners
Enjoy any DRY CLEANING ORDER at 50% off the regular price - maximum discount $5.00. valid June 2007 Sew What! Midway Cleaners	Enjoy any DRY CLEANING ORDER at 50% off the regular price - maximum discount $5.00. valid Dec. 2006 Sew What! Midway Cleaners
Enjoy any DRY CLEANING ORDER at 50% off the regular price - maximum discount $5.00. valid July 2007 Sew What! Midway Cleaners	Enjoy any DRY CLEANING ORDER at 50% off the regular price - maximum discount $5.00. valid Jan. 2007 Sew What! Midway Cleaners
Enjoy any DRY CLEANING ORDER at 50% off the regular price - maximum discount $5.00. valid Aug. 2007 Sew What! Midway Cleaners	Enjoy any DRY CLEANING ORDER at 50% off the regular price - maximum discount $5.00. valid Feb. 2007 Sew What! Midway Cleaners
Enjoy any DRY CLEANING ORDER at 50% off the regular price - maximum discount $5.00. valid Sept. 2007 Sew What! Midway Cleaners	Enjoy any DRY CLEANING ORDER at 50% off the regular price - maximum discount $5.00. valid March 2007 Sew What! Midway Cleaners
Enjoy any DRY CLEANING ORDER at 50% off the regular price - maximum discount $5.00. valid Oct. 2007 Sew What! Midway Cleaners	Enjoy any DRY CLEANING ORDER at 50% off the regular price - maximum discount $5.00. valid April 2007 Sew What! Midway Cleaners

entertainment

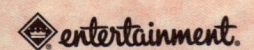

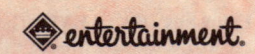

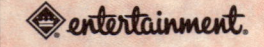

Coupon must be presented with incoming order; Not valid on clean only, leather, fur or laundry; Not valid with any other discount offer; Not valid on household items; One coupon per customer per visit; Valid once per month for 12 months

(Coupon repeated 14 times in two columns)

Bloomington
4019 W. Old Shakopee Rd.
(952)881-3813

Burnsville
13706 Nicollet Ave. S.
(952)890-6737

Columbia Heights
2313 37th Ave. N.E.
(763)788-2760

Edina
4953 Xerxes Ave. S.
(612)920-9159

Minneapolis
4049 Minnehaha Ave.
(612)724-1410

801 Marquette
(TCF Skyway)
(612)340-0073

New Hope
2722 Winnetka Ave. N.
(763)544-4285

Richfield
416 W. 65th St.
(612)866-0877

Shoreview
161 W. Country Rd. E.W.
(Hwy. 694 & Rice St.)
(651)633-8195

St. Paul
1802 St. Clair Ave.
(651)699-2445

1818 St. Clair Ave.
(651)699-0381

224 N. Cleveland
(651)644-4983

318 Norwest Bank Skyway
(651)224-9570

St Louis Park
6001 Excelsior Blvd.
(952)922-7470

West St. Paul
1200 S. Robert St.
(651)451-9966

White Bear Lake
4746 Banning Ave.
(651)426-1807

entertainment

REPEAT SAVINGS

River Bluff Car Wash & Buff 'n' Shine Center

1340 W. 7th St.
St. Paul, MN
(651) 222-6264

Enjoy one ULTIMATE CAR WASH at 50% off the regular price.

(one coupon per month for 12 months)

Specializing in full service washes

Ultimate wash includes: full interior vacuum, windows cleaned, dash & steering column cleaned, Blue Coral triple coat wax & clear coat, hand & air dried & much more

Full interior & exterior detailing available

Oil changes

Enjoy one ULTIMATE CAR WASH at 50% off the regular price.
valid June 2007
River Bluff Car Wash

Enjoy one ULTIMATE CAR WASH at 50% off the regular price.
valid Dec. 2006
River Bluff Car Wash

Enjoy one ULTIMATE CAR WASH at 50% off the regular price.
valid July 2007
River Bluff Car Wash

Enjoy one ULTIMATE CAR WASH at 50% off the regular price.
valid Jan. 2007
River Bluff Car Wash

Enjoy one ULTIMATE CAR WASH at 50% off the regular price.
valid Aug. 2007
River Bluff Car Wash

Enjoy one ULTIMATE CAR WASH at 50% off the regular price.
valid Feb. 2007
River Bluff Car Wash

Enjoy one ULTIMATE CAR WASH at 50% off the regular price.
valid Sept. 2007
River Bluff Car Wash

Enjoy one ULTIMATE CAR WASH at 50% off the regular price.
valid March 2007
River Bluff Car Wash

Enjoy one ULTIMATE CAR WASH at 50% off the regular price.
valid Oct. 2007
River Bluff Car Wash

Enjoy one ULTIMATE CAR WASH at 50% off the regular price.
valid April 2007
River Bluff Car Wash

Enjoy one ULTIMATE CAR WASH at 50% off the regular price.
valid Nov. 2007
River Bluff Car Wash

Enjoy one ULTIMATE CAR WASH at 50% off the regular price.
valid May 2007
River Bluff Car Wash

Not valid holidays and subject to Rules of Use.

entertainment. entertainment.
entertainment. entertainment.
entertainment. entertainment.
entertainment. entertainment.
entertainment. entertainment.
entertainment. entertainment.

**1340 W. 7th St.
St. Paul, MN
(651) 222-6264**

entertainment

REPEAT SAVINGS

Cloud 9 DELUXE CAR WASH
DETAIL CENTER

**8916 Aztec Dr.
Eden Prarie, MN
(952)947-0817**

Enjoy any WORKS CAR WASH at 50% off the regular price.

(one coupon per month for 12 months)

Full service car wash including: tri-foam polish/wax; underbody flush, rust buster, wheel brite, fragrace, floor mats cleaned & tire dressing

Additions fee for vans & SUVs

Not valid holidays and subject to Rules of Use. I40

Enjoy any WORKS CAR WASH at 50% off the regular price. valid May 2007 Cloud 9 Car Wash & Detail Center	Enjoy any WORKS CAR WASH at 50% off the regular price. valid Nov. 2006 Cloud 9 Car Wash & Detail Center
Enjoy any WORKS CAR WASH at 50% off the regular price. valid June 2007 Cloud 9 Car Wash & Detail Center	Enjoy any WORKS CAR WASH at 50% off the regular price. valid Dec. 2006 Cloud 9 Car Wash & Detail Center
Enjoy any WORKS CAR WASH at 50% off the regular price. valid July 2007 Cloud 9 Car Wash & Detail Center	Enjoy any WORKS CAR WASH at 50% off the regular price. valid Jan. 2007 Cloud 9 Car Wash & Detail Center
Enjoy any WORKS CAR WASH at 50% off the regular price. valid Aug. 2007 Cloud 9 Car Wash & Detail Center	Enjoy any WORKS CAR WASH at 50% off the regular price. valid Feb. 2007 Cloud 9 Car Wash & Detail Center
Enjoy any WORKS CAR WASH at 50% off the regular price. valid Sept. 2007 Cloud 9 Car Wash & Detail Center	Enjoy any WORKS CAR WASH at 50% off the regular price. valid March 2007 Cloud 9 Car Wash & Detail Center
Enjoy any WORKS CAR WASH at 50% off the regular price. valid Oct. 2007 Cloud 9 Car Wash & Detail Center	Enjoy any WORKS CAR WASH at 50% off the regular price. valid April 2007 Cloud 9 Car Wash & Detail Center

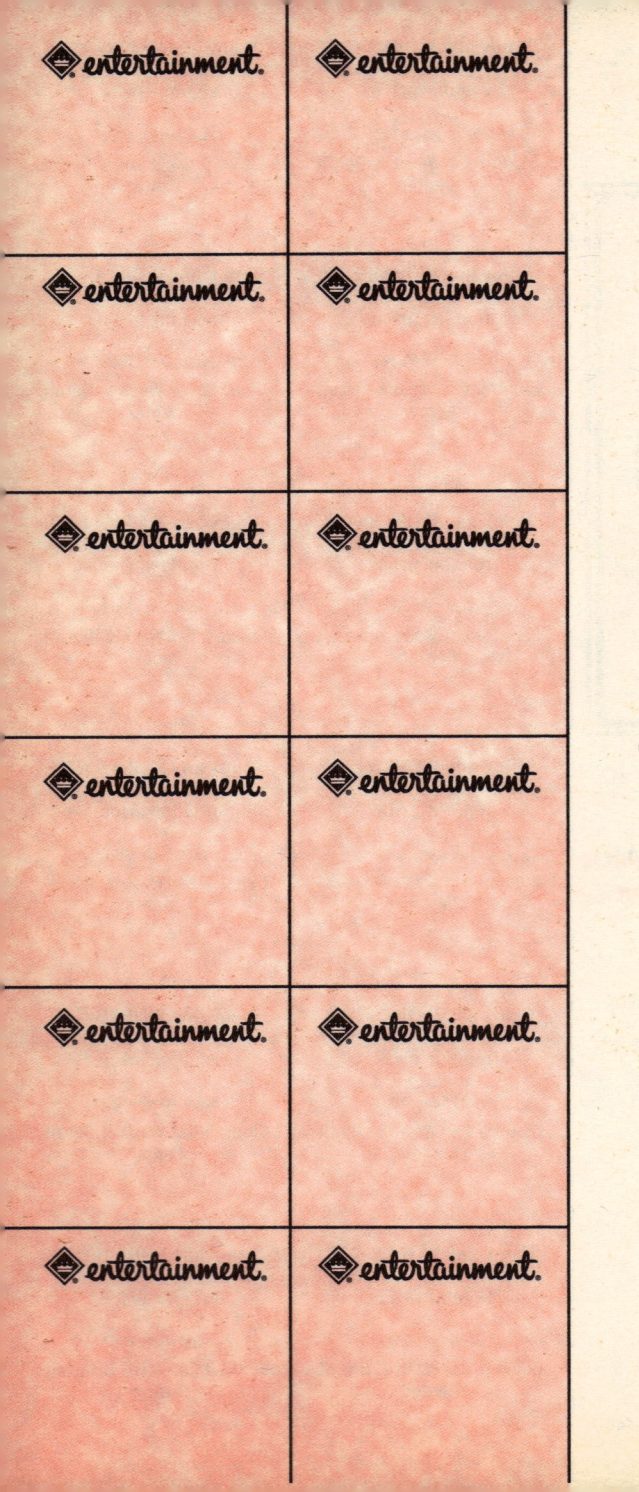

8916 Aztec Dr.
Eden Prarie, MN
(952)947-0817

FIND IT FAST!

HELPFUL TOOLS TO ACCESS YOUR FAVORITE DISCOUNTS IN A FLASH...

Neighborhood Index
Find offers near you. Also look for these helpful symbols:

- **NEW** — New merchants added
- **kids** — Great place to take the whole family
- **Online** — Print these offers at www.entertainment.com

Alphabetical Index
Search alphabetically for your favorite offers.

Information Pages
Find valuable information in the last pages of your book.

- *Membership Information*—Find the answers you need quickly
- *Rules of Use*—Detailed directions on how to use your book
- *Ordering Information*—Purchase additional books at special member prices

Also go to www.entertainment.com for even more tools, discounts and helpful hints.

Neighborhood Index

Multiple Locations

	A & W	B52-B54
kids	AMC Theatres	GG
	Angeno's	B60
	Au Bon Pain	B34-B36
	Baja Sol Tortilla Grill	B16-B18
	Ben & Jerry's Ice Cream	B28-B30
	Big Apple Bagels	B100-B101
kids	Blimpie Subs & Salads	B48
	Bobby & Steve's Auto World	B288,I19
kids NEW	Brenden Theatres	GG
	Camille's	B31-B33
NEW	Carbone's	B61-B63
NEW	Carmike Cinemas	GG
kids	CEC Theatres	G13-G15
kids NEW	Chakeres Theatres	GG
	Chanticlear Pizza	B19-B21,B308
kids NEW	Cinemark Theatres	GG
kids NEW	CinemaStar	GG
kids NEW	Claire's	I12-I13
	Clean 'n' Press	I1
NEW	Cold Stone Creamery	B13-B14
kids	Crown Theatres	GG-G10-G11
kids	Culver's Frozen Custard	B4-B6
NEW	Destinta Theatres	GG
kids NEW	Dipson Theatres	GG
kids NEW	Disney Live	G38
	Domino's Pizza	B7-B9
	Eddington's	B46-B47
kids	Embers America Restaurant	B72
	Fantastic Sams	I16
NEW	Figaro's Pizza	B145
kids NEW	Footlocker	I5
kids NEW	FYE	I14
	Golden Tan	Online
	The Great Frame Up	Online
	It Figures	I18
NEW	John Jacobs Golf Schools	G299
kids	KarmelKorn	B43-B45
NEW	Krispy Kreme Doughnuts	B15
NEW	Linwood Pizza	B168
	Long John Silver's	B257-B258
NEW	Malco Theatres	GG
kids	Mann Theatres	F5,G1-G5
kids	Marcus Theatres	G7-G9
kids	McDonald's®	A1-A3,B1-B3
kids NEW	National Amusements	GG
NEW	Nick-N-Willy's Take-N-Bake	B195
kids	Once Upon a Child	I8
kids	Orange Julius®	B25-B27
NEW	Handle With Care Packaging Store	Online
	Pannekoeken Huis	B71
	Papa John's Pizza	B22-B24
	Paradise Car Wash	I28
	Pizza Man	B204
	Pizza N' Pasta	B37-B39
	Pizza Ranch	B206
	PostNet	Online
NEW	Pump It Up	G133
NEW	Quizno's Sub®	A5
kids	Ramsey County Parks & Recreation	G100
kids NEW	Regal Entertainment Group	GG-G169-G174
	Rocco's Pizza	B222
	Roly Poly	B42
	Sew What! Midway Cleaners	I38
NEW	Sherwin Williams	I21-I22
NEW	SimonDelivers	AA1
	Sir Speedy	I15
kids	Smuckers Stars on Ice	G39
kids	Snuffy's Malt Shop	B228
kids	Steak Escape	B40-B41
	SuperAmerica	I25
	SuperAmerica Car Washes	I26
	Supermom's	I27
kids	Taco Bell®	A4
kids	Taco John's	B10-B12
NEW	Taystee	Online
kids	TCBY	B232-B233
NEW	Texaco Express Lube	Online
	Totally Tan	Online
NEW	USA Karate	G92
	White Way Cleaners	I37
	Wild Birds Unlimited	Online
	Wing Street	B254

California

Chatsworth
kids	Winnetka 21	GG

Lakewood
kids	Lakewood Center South 9	GG

Los Angeles
kids	The Grove	GG

NEW New Merchants Added This Year   **kids** Great Place for Kids!

Online... Print This Offer at www.entertainment.com

Neighborhood Index

Manhattan Beach
- (kids) Manhattan Village 6 .... GG

Northridge
- (kids) Northridge 10 .... GG

Pasadena
- (kids) Paseo 14 .... GG

Rohnert Park
- (kids) Rohnert Park 16 .... GG

Iowa

Webster City
- Briggs Woods Golf Course G212

Minnesota

Afton
- Afton House Inn C23

Albert Lea
- Bagels & Beans G181
- Lakeside Cafe & Creamery G306
- Turtle Dove Tea House & Gardens G389

Albertville
- (kids) Rosetti's Pizza & Pasta B223

Alexandria
- Arrowwood Golf Club G74

Andover
- (NEW) Adventure Park G128
- Big Bite Pizza B277
- (kids) Bunker Beach G30
- (kids) Ham Lake Lanes G279
- (NEW) Home Fireplace .... Online
- (NEW) Marco's Pizza B175
- The Meadows Restaurant & Sports Bar B183
- (NEW) Ollie & Co. Indoor Skate Park G131
- State of Bean B456
- (NEW) Tanners Steakhouse & Bar C4
- Tasty Pizza B231

Annandale
- (kids)(NEW) Annandale Video & Tanning ..... Online
- Fore Seasons at Southbrook Golf Club G264
- Lake Center Bar and Grill G304

- Southbrook Golf Club G71
- Thayer's Historic Bed n' Breakfast G379-G380

Anoka
- (NEW) Anoka Coffee Shop B91
- Diamonds Sports Bar & Grill B132
- Durkin's Pub B135
- (NEW) Fatso's B142
- Jackson Street Grill & Bar B162
- (NEW) Lily Pad Ceramics .... Online
- (NEW) Main Street Central Perk B392
- Spectators Grille & Bar B68
- (NEW) Super Bowl G114
- Zebra Pizza & Tacos B479

Atwater
- Island Pine Golf Club G290

Austin
- Bone Appetit G202
- Harvest Buffet G280
- Zeppole's Pizza & Pasta G396

Battle Lake
- Balmoral Golf Course G183

Becker
- (kids) Becker Community Center G187
- Cafe Pawz at Becker Furniture World G220

Belle Plaine
- The Bake Shop G182
- Duets B134
- Valley View Golf Course G59

Bethel
- (NEW) Fatboys Bar & Grill B141

Big Lake
- Tropical Brew G388

Buffalo
- Buffalo Books G216
- Buffalo Books & Coffee G217
- Buffalo Heights Golf Course ... G66, G218
- Golfmasters Driving Range G271
- (NEW) Golfmasters Golf Lessons ..... Online

Burnsville
- (kids) Adventure Zone G93
- (kids) Burnsville Ice Center G97
- Chinese Gourmet Restaurant B311

(NEW) New Merchants Added This Year **(kids)** Great Place for Kids!

Online... Print This Offer at www.entertainment.com

NEIGHBORHOOD INDEX

Dakota County Steakhouse C44
NEW Deck The Walls . . . . Online
kids Eric the Juggling Magician . . . . . . Online
kids Honeybaked Ham B365-B367
J's Family Restaurant B376
Maya Mexican Restaurante B180
NEW Nina's Grill B414
kids Pro-Kart Indoor Racing G33
Q-Sharks G104
Q-Sharks Cafe. B431
NEW Renegades Bar & Grill. B218
Shooters Billiard Parlor & Cafe B447
Shooters Billiards G106

BYRON
NEW The Bears Den Sports
    Bar & Eatery G186
NEW The Links of Byron G314
NEW Rock 'N' Roll Pizza G356

CAMBRIDGE
Cafe Caffeine B297

CANNON FALLS
NEW Brewsters Bar & Grill. G210
Dairy Inn G239
Dudley's Pizza
    & Sandwich Shop G251
Hi-Quality Bakery. G283
NEW Mill St. Tavern. G324
Stone Mill Coffee
    House & Eatery G371
NEW Stone Mill Marketplace G372
The Summit Golf Club G69

CARLTON
NEW Black Bear Golf Course G190
NEW Black Bear Grill G191

CARVER
Harvey's Bar & Grill. B79,G281
Lisa's Place G316

CEDAR
NEW Hunter's Inn Bar & Grill B371

CHAMPLIN
5-8 Grill & Bar B86
El Toro. C15
Enjoy China B140

CHANHASSEN
NEW Aroma Cafe'. B265

Chanhassen Fireside Theatre G41
Chanhassen Dinner Theatre G42
NEW CJ's Coffee & Wine Bar B113
NEW MaggieMoo's B51
Pizzaioli Pizzamaker B428

CHASKA
Chaska Bakery B309
kids Chaska Community Center G145
NEW Coffee Cats Cafe. B315
Dahlgreen Golf Club. G54
Golf Zone G81
NEW Heartbreakers Bar & Grill B155
Minnesota Landscape
    Arboretum. G157
NEW Pine Street Grille C39
Playoffs Sports Bar & Grill C40
NEW Rain, Snow or Shine Golf
    Center - Chaska . . . . Online
NEW Seasons Restaurant C8
NEW Victory Lane Car Wash
    & Detail Center I36

CIRCLE PINES
Miller's on Main B186

CLEVELAND
Jocko's Bar & Grill G298

COKATO
Cokato Town & Country Club G234
Daniel's Family Restaurant G240
The Grounds. G278

COLD SPRING
Bagel & Brew G180

COLOGNE
NEW J & D's 212 Club. B375

COTTAGE GROVE
All Seasons Golf. . . . . Online
Emily's Bakery & Deli G255

DASSEL
Dassel Entertainment Center G242
Hojies Grill & Smokehouse G284

DELANO
Dave's Town Club G243

DULUTH
kids Carnival Thrillz G222-G223
kids The Depot. B130,G245-G246

NEW **New Merchants Added This Year**   kids **Great Place for Kids!**
Online... Print This Offer at www.entertainment.com

Neighborhood Index

(kids)	Glensheen	G270
(kids)	Great Lakes Aquarium	G276
	Ground Round	G277
(kids)	Lake Superior & Mississippi Railroad	G305

Eden Prairie

	Brunswick Zone	G108
NEW	Cloud 9 Car Wash & Detail Center	I40
	Coffee Oasis	B317
NEW	Detello's Pizza & Pasta	B131
	Eden Prairie Community Center	G94
NEW	Eden Restaurant	B136
	Golf Usa	Online
	Higher Grounds	B362
NEW	Leonardo's	B64-B66
NEW	Little Sushi on the Prairie	B169
NEW	Naar	C6
	Qdoba Mexican Grill	B67
	Red Moon Restaurant	B214

Elk River

NEW	Anytime Fitness	Online
	Big Vinny's Subs	B281
(kids)	The Depot	B130, G245-G246
(kids)	FunCity	G265-G266
	The Grille at Elk River Country Club	B154
	La Roses Pizza, Pasta & Ribs	G303
	Nana's Chicken	G328
NEW	Northwoods Bar & Grill	B198
NEW	Sarpino's Pizza	B225, G359
NEW	Shandi's Scrapbooking	Online
NEW	Thunder Alley Indoor Paintball	G385
NEW	Thunder Alley Indoor Speedway	G386

Ellendale

(kids)	Maggio's Pizza	G320

Excelsior

NEW	Cafe Lettieris	B298
(kids) NEW	Country Club Lanes	G111
	Pizza Prima	B205

Faribault

NEW	Aztlan Tortilleria Bakery & Eatery	G177
NEW	Banadir Restaurant	G184
	Boxer's Bar & Grill	G207
NEW	Dusek's Bakery	B342
NEW	Faribault Bowling Center	G257

NEW	Faribault Family Aquatic Center	G258
	Javalive! Community Coffeehouse	G297
NEW	Signature Bar & Grill	G363

Farmington

	B & B Pizza	G178
	Bugaloo's Ice Cream Shoppe	G219
	Farmington Bakery	G259
(kids)	Farmington Lanes	G260-G261
	Fast Lane Pizza	G262
	Southern Hills Golf Club	G61
	The Ugly Mug	G391

Foley

	Mr. Jim's	G327

Forest Lake

NEW	Brick House Eatery	B108
	Castlewood Golf Course	G64
	Country Home Bakery & Deli	B325
NEW	Daniela's	G241
	On Broadway Car Wash	G333
	On Broadway-Proudly Serving Dunn Bros. Coffee	G334

Gaylord

NEW	Woody's Grille	C2

Glencoe

	Glencoe Country Club	G55

Hamel

NEW	Medina Entertainment Center	G129
	Medina Lanes	G113
NEW	Rascal's Bar & Restaurant	B213
	Rose Garden	B440

Hastings

	Emily's Bakery & Deli	G255
	Professor Java's	G346
	RJ's Tavern on Main	G347

Hopkins

	Boston Garden	B289
	Country Glazed Ham Shop	B324
(kids)	The Depot	B130, G245-G246
(kids)	Games by James	I17
(kids)	Honeybaked Ham	B365-B367
	Jack Yee's Restaurant	B378
	Munkabeans & Sunshine	B410
	Nick's Ice Cream & Popcorn	B196
	Stacy's Grille	C26

NEW New Merchants Added This Year   **(kids)** Great Place for Kids!
Online... Print This Offer at www.entertainment.com

NEIGHBORHOOD INDEX

[NEW] Stages Theatre Company G136
[NEW] Tuttle's Bowling, Bar & Grill G137
[NEW] Tuttle's Shady Oak Grill B244
Wanderer's Chinese Cuisine B251

HOWARD LAKE
Sunni's Grille G376

HUTCHINSON
The Coffee Company G229
Hutch Cafe G289
[kids] Scoop's Frozen Custard G360

INVER GROVE HEIGHTS
In the Spirit of Coffee,
  Cards & Gifts B372-B373
Jersey's Bar & Grill B381
[NEW] Lastrack Family Restaurant B166
[NEW] Turitto's Pizza & Subs B242

ISANTI
Rendezvous Coffee Shop G348
Wintergreens C42
Wintergreens Indoor Golf G90

JORDAN
Brewer's Bar & Grill of Jordan. G209
Cup of Knowledge. B328

KASSON
Diggers Bar & Grill G247

LAKE CITY
Bronks Bar & Grill. G213

LAKELAND
Common Grounds Coffee House. . . . B320

LAKEVILLE
Babe's Sports Bar & Grill B93
Blue Sky Creamery B105
[NEW] Cafe' Pierre B302
Daddio's Take-N-Bake. B332
[NEW] Pizza Prima & Pasta. B427
[kids] Tacoville. B462

LE CENTER
Evie's Soups & More. G256
Granny's Bowl. G273
Granny's Grill G274
Little Dandy Sports Bar G317

LE SUEUR
Le Sueur Diner G311

LESTER PRAIRIE
Shadowbrooke Golf Course G70

LONG LAKE
The Red Rooster. B216

LORETTO
Retro Roast & Fountain G349

LUTSEN
[kids] Lutsen Mountains G318

MANKATO
Big Dog Sports Cafe. G189
Bobby Joe's Pub. G200
Choppers Bar & Grill G228
Coffee Creek Espresso & Eatery. . . . G231
Coffee Klatsch. G232
Fillin' Station G263
Roadhouse 169 Bar & Grill B220

MANTORVILLE
The Chocolate Shoppe. G226

MAPLE PLAIN
[kids] [NEW] Blackwater Coffee
  Company & Cafe G193
[kids] Pete's Pizza B423,G340

MARINE ON SAINT CROIX
Brookside Bar & Grill G214

MINNEAPOLIS
101 Blu B69
[NEW] 1st of Thai Restaurant. B85
Acme Comedy Co. G43
Adrian's Tavern B259
Airport Bowl. G109
[NEW] Ambrosia Coffee B260
America's Harvest. C58
[kids] American Pie B87,B261
American Swedish Institute G158
Amy's Classic Confections B262
Anodyne @ 43rd B264
[NEW] Antoine's Creole Maison. C28
Arthur Murray Dance Studios . . . . . Online
Athen's Cafe. B92
Atlas Grill C19
Audubon Coffee. B268-B269
Auntie Em's B270
[NEW] Auto Pro. . . . . Online
[kids] [NEW] B&V Driving Range G179
[NEW] B&V Golf Course. G79

[NEW] **New Merchants Added This Year**   [kids] **Great Place for Kids!**
Online... Print This Offer at www.entertainment.com

NEIGHBORHOOD INDEX

NEIGHBORHOOD INDEX

The Backyard Bar & Grill	B94
[NEW] Bahn Thai Cuisine	B273
The Bakken Museum	G167
[NEW] Bargain Seeker	Online
Be-Bop Sports Bar & Grill	B96
Beach House Bar & Grille	C12
Begin Oaks Driving Range	Online
Begin Oaks Golf Course	G80
The Bell Auditorium	G162
The Bell Museum of Natural History	G159
Betsy's Back Porch Coffee	B274
Betty's Bikes & Buns	B275
Beyond Juice	B99
Big Daddy's Pizza	B278
[NEW] Big Dipper	B279
[NEW] Big Stop Deli	B280
Blondies Sports Grill and Bar	B104
[NEW] Bloomers Floral & Gifts	Online
[NEW] Blue Eyes Cafe	B286
Blue Moon Coffee Cafe	B287
[kids] [NEW] The Book Hive	Online
[NEW] Boston's	B481-B484
Braemar Golf Dome	G68
Brave New Workshop	G165
Brookdale Car Wash	I32
[kids] Brooklyn Center Community Center	G135
[NEW] Bruck's Espresso Bar	B293
The Bulldog Restaurant	B110
Bunkers Music Bar & Grill	B111
Bunny's	B112
C. McGee's Deli	B294
[NEW] Cafe Limon	B299
Cafe Northstar	C29
Cafe of the Americas	B301
Cafe Tatta Bunna	B300
[NEW] Cafe' of Americas Catering	Online
Camden Coffee Company	B304-B305
The Cardinal Restaurant & Bar	B115
[NEW] CardSmart	Online
Cedar Inn Bar & Grill	B306
Cedar Market & Deli	B307
[NEW] Central Car Wash	I34
Charley's Grilled Subs	B118
[NEW] Charly's Polleria Restaurant	B116
[kids] Cheap Skate	G98
Chez Daniel Bistro	C30
Chicago Deli Cafe & Grille	B117
[NEW] Cinema Grill	B123
[NEW] Cinema Grill Theater	G51
Classic Bowl	G115
Coffee & Tea LTD	B124
Col. Muzzy's Texas BBQ	B319
ComedySportz	G123
Cornell's	C43
Creekside Cafe	C55
Crescent Moon Bakery	B327
[NEW] Crystal Bistro	C48
[NEW] Crystal Cafe & Grill	B126
[kids] Crystal Recreation Dept.	G147
Cupcake	B127
Cuppa Java	B329-B330
Cuzzy's	B331
da Afghan	C50
Daily Grind	B333
[NEW] Daisy Nails	Online
Dashen Ethiopian Restaurant & Bar	C31
[NEW] Dave's Sport Shop	Online
[NEW] Deck The Walls	Online
Denny's 5th Ave. Bakery	B336
Diamonds Coffee Shoppe	B337
The Dinkytowner	B133
[NEW] Dinosaur Walk MOA	G36
The District	B84
Don's Car Washes	I31
East African Taste Restaurant	B343
[NEW] Easy Tanning	Online
8th Street Grill	B137
El Azteca	C14
[NEW] El Nuevo Rodeo	B138
[NEW] El Paraiso Mexican Restaurant	B139
El Rey Bakery	B344
El Tequila Restaurante	B345
[NEW] Eli's Food & Cocktails	B77
[NEW] Elsie's Restaurant & Bar	C25
Erte	C17
Espresso 22	B346
Espresso Royale Cafe	B348
Fat Boy Billiards	Online
[NEW] Fire Roast Mountain Cafe	B349
The Fish House	B350
[NEW] Flashback Cafe & Cocktail Lounge	B144
Franklin Market & Deli	B352
Franklin Street Bakery	B353
Fresco Juice Company	B146

[NEW] **New Merchants Added This Year**   [kids] **Great Place for Kids!**

Online... Print This Offer at www.entertainment.com

Neighborhood Index

Merchant	Page
(kids) Freshens	B147
Fridley Crab House	C13
Gabby's Saloon & Eatery	B148
Galaxy Auto Centers	I11
(kids) Games by James	I17
Gameworks	G34
Golden Limousine	I6
Grand Rios Indoor Water Park	G27
Grand Slam U.S.A.	G82
(kids) Great Steak & Potato Co.	B153, B360
(kids) Greater Twin Cities Youth Symphonies	G124
The Guthrie Theater	G45
Harmony's	C33
Harold's Chicken	B361
Harvey's Bar & Grill	B79, G281
Heavenly Daze Coffee	B156
Heavenly Shoes	I24
(NEW) Hennepin History Museum	G168
(NEW) Hollywood Scoops	B363
(NEW) Hollywood Tans	Online
Holy Land Deli	B364
(NEW) Home At Last	Online
Hopscotch Grill	C11
House of Java	B369
Hunan Restaurant	B370
Imperial Room	B76
(NEW) Insomniac Beads	Online
(NEW) International Business Cafe	B374
Jamaica Jamaica	B163
Java Restaurant	B380
Jerusalem's Restaurant	B382
Jewel of India	C21
Jimbo's	B383
Jimmy's Pro Billiards	Online
JJ's Clubhouse	B161
jP American Bistro	C5
(NEW) JT's Restaurant & Pizza Parlor	B377
(kids)(NEW) Kids' Time of Northtown	G95
Kikugawa at Riverplace	C3
KinhDo Restaurant	B165
(NEW) Kips An Authentic Irish Pub & Restaurant	C53
Kokomo's Island Cafe	C10
(NEW) Koyi Sushi	C35
La Bodega Tapas Bar	B78
(NEW) La Casita	B70
La Pinata	B386
(kids) Lariat Lanes	G112
Legends Bar & Grill	B167
Little Tel-Aviv Cafe & Restaurant	C45
Lombard's	C46
Lone Tree Bar & Grill	B170
Loring Park Coffee House & Wine Bar	B172
Lyn-Del Lanes	G139
MacKenzie	B75
MacTavish's	C49
(kids) Mady's Bowl and Lounge	Online
(NEW) Mairin's Table Neighborhood Bistro	C36
Mama Donato's	B393
(NEW) Mama Taught Me How To Cook Soul Food Eatery!	B394
(NEW) Mama's Bakery, Pizza & Salad Bar	B395
Manny's Tortas	B396
(kids) Marble Slab Creamery	B174
Margarita Bella	B176
(NEW) Marina Grill & Deli	B397
Marino's Deli	B398
(NEW) Marla's Indian & Caribbean Cuisine	B177
Martini's	B178
Marysburg Books	B399-B400
Maxwell's	B179
Mayslack's	B181
(kids) Mel-O-Glaze Bakery	B401
Mell's Beauty Bar	B80
(NEW) The Melting Pot	C1
(NEW) Memory Lanes	G138
(NEW) Merle Norman	Online
Mexico Y Mexico	B402
Mias Pizza	B403
Milda's Cafe	B185
Ming's Palace	B406
Mings Garden Restaurant	B187, B407
Minneapolis Town Hall Brewery	B188
Minnesota Dance Theatre	G125
(kids) Minnesota Lynx	G17-G18
Mochalini's	B189
Mojos Pizza	B408
Moose Bar & Grill	B190
Muddy Paws Cheesecake	B191
(NEW) My Music Store	Online
(kids) Nascar Silicon Motor Speedway	G32
The Neighborhood Ice Cream Shoppe	B411-B412

(NEW) **New Merchants Added This Year**

(kids) **Great Place for Kids!**

Online... Print This Offer at www.entertainment.com

NEIGHBORHOOD INDEX

Nestle Tollhouse
  Cafe by Chip. B193-B194
NEW Nghia's Auto Service . . . . Online
Nic's on Nicollet C38
Nino's Pizza Plus B197
North Country Co-op B415
NEW Northern Espresso Cafe B416
Northern Shores. C22
Oak Street Cinema . . . . Online
Ocean Waves Massage I20
kids Old Fashion Donut Shoppe B417
Pair of Dice Pizza B419
Panaderia El Rey B421
NEW Papa's Pizza and Pasta B199
The Park at MOA G22
Park Cafe B422
kids Park Tavern
  Lounge & Lanes. B200,G117
Pasquale's Sports
  Bar & Restaurant B201
NEW Pavek Museum of Broadcasting . . . . Online
kids Personalized Children's Books. . . . . Online
Ping's Szechuan Star B202
NEW Pizza Flame B203
Pizza Magic B424
Pizzeria Uno B207
Plan B Coffeehouse B429
NEW PlayZone Arcade G23
NEW Plymouth Ice Center. G132
Plymouth Playhouse G126
Porter's Bar and Grill B210
NEW Pretzel Time. B211
Pupuseria El Rincon
  Salva Doreno B430
Qdoba Mexican Grill. B67
Queen Of Cakes B432
Rail Station Bar & Grill B212
NEW Rail Station Catering . . . . Online
Rand Deli & Catering B433
The Red Pepper B215,B435
Red Sea Restaurant B217
The Refuge B83
Restaurante Guayaquil B219,B436
Richfield Adventure Gardens
  Miniature Golf. . . . . Online
Richfield Municipal
  Pool & Waterslide. G163
Riverside Restaurant B438
Riverview Theater. G52

NEW Rix Bar & Grill. C59
Rocky Rococo B439
kids Roller Garden G101
kids Rollerdome G102
Rosen's City Tavern B82
NEW Royal Nails of Golden Valley . . . . . Online
Rudolph's Bar-B-Que C9
Sally's Saloon & Eatery B224
Scandia Bake Shop B441
Scoops Pub B226
Scoreboard Pizza B442
2nd Moon Coffee Cafe. B443
Shaw's Bar & Grill. B445
Shell's Cafe B446
Sindbad Cafe & Market B448
kids Skateville G103
NEW The Soaring Spirit . . . . Online
kids Soho Cafe B451
The Sportsman's Pub B229
kids Spring Lake Amusement Park G88
Spring Street Tavern. B230
kids Square Peg Diner B454
St. Louis Park Outdoor
  Aquatic Park G149
kids St. Louis Park Rec Center G150
St. Petersburg Restaurant
  and Vodka Bar C41
NEW Sun Ray Restaurant B457
Sweet Taste of Italy B458-B460
NEW T & Y Car Wash I33
NEW Tangerine Dreams. . . . . Online
NEW Tans Plus . . . . Online
Taraccino Coffee. B463
The Tea Garden B235
Tea Source B236
kids Texa-Tonka Lanes G120
kids 3rd Lair G96
TJ's of Edina. B234
Tortilla Ria Mexican Cafe B466
NEW Toy Store G24
NEW Tropic Tan . . . . Online
Tropicana B241
NEW Twisted Shamrock Pub & Grill B467
NEW Two Stooges Billiards G107
NEW Two Stooges Sports Bar & Grill B245
U of M Athletics G153-G156
Ubah Restaurant B468
kids Underwater Adventures
  Aquarium F7-F8,I23

NEW New Merchants Added This Year   **kids** Great Place for Kids!
Online... Print This Offer at www.entertainment.com

Neighborhood Index

[NEW] Uptown Pizza B246
Vescio's B247
Vientiane Restaurant B470
Villa Pizza B249
Village Blend B472
[NEW] Violin-A-Gram . . . . Online
Waberi Somalian Restaurant B474
The Wagon Grill B250
Waldo's Bar & Grill B475
[kids] Walker Art Center G47
Water Park of America F6
[NEW] The Well Sports Tavern & Grill B252
Wing Joint B477
Wolves Den Native Coffee B255
[NEW] Woody's Grille C2
Youth Performance Co. . . . . Online
Zebra Pizza & Tacos B479

Minnetonka
The Bunker Indoor Golf Center G65
General Store Cafe B150
Glen Lake Coffee Co. B356-B357

Montevideo
Jake's Pizza G293-G294

Montgomery
Brass Rail Bar & Grill G208
Montgomery Golf Club G73
Pla Mor Lanes G345

Monticello
[NEW] DeAngelo's G244
Hawk's Sports Bar & Grill G282
Pizza Factory G342
[NEW] Riverwood National
     Driving Range G141
[NEW] Riverwood National Golf Course . . . G60
[NEW] Vintage Driving Range G89
[NEW] Vintage Golf Course G75

Mound
[NEW] Big Stone Mini Golf
     & Sculpture Garden . . . . Online
[NEW] Tokyo Express B465

New Prague
Strike Force Bowl G373

New Ulm
Bookshelves & Coffeecups G204
Larkspur Market G308

Three Sisters Tea Room G384

Nisswa
[kids] Ski Gull G365-G366

North Branch
Koep's Village Bakery G302
North Branch Golf Course G331
[kids] O'Fudge Deli & Coffee G332
Pizza Pub G343-G344

Northfield
J. Grundy's Rueb 'N' Stein G292
James Gang
     Coffeehouse & Eatery G295
Tacoasis G377
The Mock Turtle B464

Norwood Young America
[kids] Lano Lanes G307

Onamia
Izatys Golf & Yacht
     Club - The Sanctuary G57

Osseo
Boss Limo 12
[NEW] Boston's B481-B484
[NEW] Chin Yung B120
Country Glazed Ham Shop B324
[NEW] Dave's Sport Shop . . . . Online
[NEW] Eddies Billiards G140
Gator's Garden Cafe B149
[NEW] Kay's Wine Bar & Bistro C34
[NEW] Lavish I9
The Lookout Bar & Grill B171
[NEW] MaggieMoo's B51
[kids] Maple Grove Community Center . . . G91
Mongkok B409
[kids] Pro-Kart Indoor Racing G33
Qdoba Mexican Grill B67
[NEW] Rocky Mountain
     Chocolate Factory . . . . Online
Segue Cafe B444
[kids] Sundance Golf and Bowl G119
Yarn Cafe B478

Owatonna
Custom Coffee & Caffe G238
Hidden Creek Golf Club G56
Wings Tavern & Grille G394

[NEW] **New Merchants Added This Year**   [kids] **Great Place for Kids!**

Online... Print This Offer at www.entertainment.com

Neighborhood Index

Pine City
   Pizza Pub G343-G344

Princeton
   Bud's Place Bar & Grill G215

Prior Lake
   City Perks Coffee House. B313
   Trigger's. C18
   The Wilds Pub. C54

Red Wing
   Andy's Sports Bar & Grill B263
   [kids] Bev's Cafe. B276
   Blue Moon. G195
   [NEW] Cheryl Ann's Bar & Grill. G224
   [NEW] The Galley Room B354
   Good Life Nutrition Juice
      & Smoothie Bar G272
   [NEW] Life's Little Oasis . . . . Online
   Marie's Casual Dining & Lounge. . . . G322
   Tale of Two Sisters Tea Room
      & Gift Shoppe G378
   [kids][NEW] Tickle Yer Fancy. G387

Redwood Falls
   Redwood Falls Golf Club. G58

Rochester
   [NEW] Bon's Buffet. G201
   [NEW] Brickyard Bar & Grille. G211
   [NEW] The Chocolate Twist G227
   Coffee Mouse G233
   [NEW] Cuisine of India G237
   Double Click Coffee G249
   [NEW] El Carambas. G253
   Garden Grill. G268
   Grand Grill C32
   [kids] Great Steak & Potato Co. B153,B360
   [NEW] Kabab Restaurant. G300
   [NEW] Leo's Pizza Palace. G312
   Lord Essex Tavern C56
   The Mouse. G326
   [NEW] Rochester Indoor Golf Dome . . . G355
   Shady Hill Grille. C57
   [NEW] Three Happiness G383
   [NEW] Westfire Grille C60

Rockford
   [NEW] American Hair Design . . . . . Online
   Gathering Grounds G269

Rockville
   The Bayou. G381

Rogers
   House of Beans G286
   [NEW] Luna Blu B389
   Northern Palms Driving Range G85
   [NEW] Northern Palms Mini Golf . . . . Online
   [NEW] Northern Palms Paintball . . . . Online

Rosemount
   [NEW] Master Transmission. . . . . . . Online
   McDivot's Sports Pub & Eatery . . . B182
   Morning Glory's Bakery Cafe G325

Saint Cloud
   BoDiddley's Deli. G198
   Book-ems Bar & Restaurant. G203
   [NEW] Diamond Vogel Paint Center. . . Online
   Ground Round. G277
   Java Joint G296
   [NEW] Java Joint Live Entertainment. . . Online
   [kids][NEW] Laser Storm at the Skatin' Place. . . G309
   Maid-Rite G321
   MC's Dugout Bar & Grill. G319
   Pete's Place G341
   Serendipity G361
   [kids] Skatin' Place G364
   [kids] Stearns History Museum G370
   [kids] Summerland G375
   Zeppole's Pizza & Pasta G396

Saint Francis
   Boulevard Coffee B290
   Tasty Pizza B231

Saint Joseph
   BoDiddley's Deli. G198

Saint Paul
   5-8 Tavern & Grill. B81
   [NEW] Abbey Carpet . . . . Online
   [NEW] All The Best . . . . Online
   [NEW] Ambrosia Coffee B260
   American Sports
      Cafe & Nightclub B88
   [kids] Andy's Garage B89
   [kids] Aroma's Pizza & Cafe B266
   Arthur Murray Dance Studios . . . . Online
   [NEW] Artists' Grind B267
   Aurelio's. B271

[NEW] **New Merchants Added This Year**   [kids] **Great Place for Kids!**

Online... Print This Offer at www.entertainment.com

NEIGHBORHOOD INDEX

Avalon Tearoom & Pastry Shoppe.	B272
Bascali's Brick Oven.	B95
Battle Creek Waterworks Family Aquatic Center.	G146
NEW The Bean Factory	B97
The Bird Nightclub.	B102
Black Bear Crossings	B282
Blink Bonnie	B283
Blondies Cafe	B103
NEW Blue Cat Coffee & Tea	B284-B285
Boca Chica.	B106
NEW Brewberry's Coffee Shop	B107
Brightwood Hills.	G67
Brothers Coffee	B291
Bru House Coffee Shop	B292
The Bunker Indoor Golf Center	G65
Cabin Fever	B295
Capital City Market Cafe & Bar	B114
Carousel Restaurant.	C24
Cascade Bay Water Park	G28
China Wok Restaurant.	B310
Chocolat Celeste.	B121
NEW Chula Vista	B122
Cinema Espresso	B312
Classic Pizza.	B314
Coffee Cottage	B316
NEW Coliseum Billiards.	Online
Como Park Golf Course	G87
NEW Como Town	G29
Copper Dome Restaurant	B321
Cora's Best Chicken Wings.	B322
Cosmic's Cafe	B323
NEW Creative Catering	B326
CuppaChiodo's	B128
NEW Dar's Double Scoop	B335
Don Panchos Bakery	B338
Dorothy Ann Bakery & Cafe.	Online
Downtowner Car Wash	I29
Dugout Bar	B341
kids Eagles Nest Indoor Playground	G148
NEW Easy Tanning	Online
El Taquito Taco Shop Restaurant. . .	G254
Espresso Donut Co.	B347
NEW Fitness Haven for Women	Online
5 Star Cafe	B351
Flaherty's Arden Bowl.	G110
kids Flaherty's Pub & Grill	B143
Fort Snelling	G160
NEW Genghis Grill	B151-B152
kids Gibbs Museum of Pioneer & Dakotah Life	G161
Giuseppe's	B355
Golden's Cafe & Deli	B358
kids Goodrich Golf Dome & Putting Links	Online
kids Grand Slam U.S.A.	G82
Grandma Rita's Cafe	B359
Great American History Theatre. . . .	G40
kids Great Clips IMAX Theatre	G6
Heppner's Auto Wash & Detailing Center.	I30
kids Honeybaked Ham	B365-B367
Hong Wong	B368
Hunan Garden Chinese Restaurant	B158
In the Spirit of Coffee, Cards & Gifts	B372-B373
Island Lake Golf Center	G84
NEW Island Lake Golf Lessons	Online
J.R. Mac's Bar & Grill	B159-B160
Jade Island Cuisine	B379
kids John Rose Minnesota Oval	G99
Kalli's Popcorn Shop.	B384
NEW La Casita	B70
kids Lava Links.	G77
NEW Leonardo's	B64-B66
Limu Coffee	B387
NEW Lori's Coffee House	B388
McGuires	C37
The Mediterranean Cruise Cafe . . .	B184
kids Midway Pro Bowl	G116
NEW Midway Rendezvous Cafe	B404
NEW Mim's Cafe	B405
kids Minnehaha Lanes	Online
The Minnesota Opera	G46
Minnesota Swarm.	G25
kids Minnesota Thunder Pro Soccer . . .	G21
Minnesota Zoo	G26
NEW Mounds Theatre	G130
Muddy Paws Cheesecake	B191
NEW The Neighborhood Cafe	B192
New York Burrito	B413
Nickelby's Maplewood Grill	C51
Ordway Center for the Performing Arts	G48-G50
Over The Rainbow.	B418
Paisano's Pizza & Hot Hoagies	B420

NEW **New Merchants Added This Year**   kids **Great Place for Kids!**

Online... Print This Offer at www.entertainment.com

Neighborhood Index

Phalen Park Golf Course	G72
Pizza Pazza	B425
Pizza Planet	B426
Plums Neighborhood Grill & Bar	B208-B209
NEW Razs Cafe	B434
Rice And Arlington Batting Cages	G152
NEW River Bluff Car Wash	I39
Roberts Sports Bar & Entertainment	B221
Roseville Cedarholm Golf Course	G86
Saint Paul Chamber Orchestra	G44
NEW Salsarita's Fresh Cantina	B58-B59
Skinners Pub & Eatery	B227
The Smooth Grind	B449
NEW Snelling Cafe	B450
Sojourner's Cafe	B452-B453
kids St. Bernard's Bowling Lanes	G118
St. Paul Bagelry & Deli	B455
NEW Starting Gate Productions	G134
kids Tamarack Nature Center	G151
NEW Tangerine Dreams	Online
The Tea Garden	B235
Tea Source	B236
Tiffany's Sports Lounge	B238
Transmission Doctor, Inc.	Online
kids Tropics Indoor Water Park	G31
Valley Sports Pub & Grill	B469
kids Vertical Endeavors	G76
Villa Pizza	B249
Villa Roma Pizzaria	B471
kids Wabasha Deli	B473
kids West Side Lanes	B476, G121
The Whiskey Rack	B253
NEW Whitehouse Furniture	Online
NEW The Woodbury Broiler Bar	C7
kids Wooddale Recreation Center	G142
kids NEW Zobota Cafe	B256

Saint Paul Park
Harborside Restaurant & Lounge	C20

Saint Peter
Patrick's	G338
River Rock Coffee	G351

Sartell
Blue Line Sports Bar & Grill	G194
G-Allen's Restaurant & Sports Bar	G267

Liquid Assets	G315
Riverboat Depot	G353

Sauk Centre
Greystone Golf Club	G83

Sauk Rapids
Benton Station Bar & Grill	G188

Savage
Buffalo Tap	B109
NEW Cactus Grill Mexican Buffet	B296
NEW Classic Auto Spa & Detail Center	I35
Spectators Grille & Bar	B68
Tin Shed Tavern & Pizza	B239
NEW Tropical Smoothie Cafe	B240

Scandia
Eko Backen	G252

Shakopee
Canterbury Park	G37
Coffee Ta Cream	B318
Rack N' Roll Billiards	G105
Taco Loco	B461
NEW Thailand View	B237
Turtle's Bar & Grill	B243
Zuppa Cucina	B480

South Saint Paul
NEW The Coop Restaurant	B125
kids Judes Coffee & Eatery	B164
NEW Restaurante La Rancherita	B437

Spring Park
NEW Shape Up for Women	Online

Stacy
NEW Stacy Country Cafe	G368

Stewartville
Sammy's	G358
Seth's Down Under Bar & Grill	G362

Stillwater
Angel O'Malley's	B90
NEW ArtRageous	Online
Charlie's Irish Pub	B119
The Daily Grind	B129, B334
Darla's Grill & Malt Shop	B73-B74
Dreamcoat Cafe	B340
kids NEW Grand Games	Online
NEW Mai Thai Cafe	B173
NEW Murasaki Japanese Restaurant	C16

NEW New Merchants Added This Year   **kids** Great Place for Kids!

Online... Print This Offer at www.entertainment.com

NEIGHBORHOOD INDEX

[NEW] Nacho Mama's C47
St. Croix Crab House Music Cafe. C52
Water Street Inn. C27

STURGEON LAKE
[NEW] Doc's Bar & Grill. G248

TAYLORS FALLS
Border Bar & Grill, The G205
Chisago House Restaurant. G225

TWO HARBORS
The Rustic Inn G357

VICTORIA
Victoria House. B248

WABASHA
[kids] Papa Tronnio's Pizza G337
Riverboat Lanes. G354

WACONIA
[NEW] Beef 'O' Brady's Family
Sports Pub. B485
Hopper's Bar & Grill. B157
Island View Dining G291

WAITE PARK
[NEW] Anytime Fitness. . . . . Online

WASECA
The Daily Grind B129, B334
[NEW] Katie O'Leary's Beef & Brew B385
State Street Bistro. G369

WAVERLY
Craig's Waverly Cafe G236

WAYZATA
Beanhaven Cafe. B98
Caffe de Lago B303
[NEW] The Good Life . . . . Online
Maggie's Restaurant B391
Orono Golf Course. G62

WILLERNIE
[kids] Wildwood Bowl G122

WILLMAR
Jake's Pizza. G293-G294
Zeppole's Pizza & Pasta. G396

WINONA
Winona Island Cafe G395

WINSTED
Blue Note Supper Club G196
The Pantry G336

WYOMING
Village Inn G392

ZIMMERMAN
Rise 'n Shine Coffee & Deli G350

NEW JERSEY

CHATHAM
[kids] [NEW] Clearview Cinemas . . . . GG

NEW YORK

LOCKPORT
[kids] [NEW] Lockport Cinema 8 . . . . GG

ONTARIO

EAR FALLS N.
[NEW] Naughty Pines Fish Camp G329

PENNSYLVANIA

PHILADELPHIA
[kids] [NEW] The Bridge . . . . GG

PITTSBURGH
[kids] [NEW] Cinemagic Theatre . . . . GG

WISCONSIN

CENTURIA
[NEW] McKenzie Lanes. G53
[NEW] McKenzie's Bar & Grill. G323

EAU CLAIRE
Bowl Winkles G206

ELLSWORTH
[kids] Hollywood Video,
Pizza & Tanning. G285

GRANTSBURG
Grantsburg Municipal
Golf Course G275

HUDSON
Bob Smith's Sports Club G199

[NEW] **New Merchants Added This Year**   [kids] **Great Place for Kids!**
Online... Print This Offer at www.entertainment.com

NEIGHBORHOOD INDEX

Cafe' La Poste G221
Commuter's Cup. G235
Darla's Grill & Malt Shop . . . B73-B74
NEW Hudson Bagel & Coffee Co. G287
Hudson Bowl G288
Knoke's Confections
  & Ice Cream G301
Lavender Thymes G310
NEW Stucci's Italian Food G374

NEW RICHMOND
Bean Bag Coffeehouse G185
Douville Bakery G250
kids Pete's Pizza B423, G340

OSCEOLA
Coffee Connection G230
Osceola & St. Croix
  Valley Railway G143
Osceola Antiques
  & Ice Cream Parlor G335

RICE LAKE
Turtleback Golf & Country Club G390

RIVER FALLS
Bo's 'N Mine G197
NEW Cue's From Nature . . . . Online
Kilkarney Hills Golf Course G63
Lighthouse Coffee G313

SAINT CROIX FALLS
NEW St. Croix Falls Mini Golf
  & Go-Karts G144
Wayne's G393

SOMERSET
Anne's Cafe G175
kids Apple Grand Prix G176
kids River's Edge Tubing G352

STAR PRAIRIE
BlackWater Coffee Co. G192
This Old Store Etc. G382

TURTLE LAKE
kids **NEW** Speedy's Family & Fun Center. . . . G367

OTHER
NEW American Greetings / Carlton Cards. . . . I3
NEW Auntie Anne's B55-B57
kids **NEW** Consolidated Theatres. . . . . GG
Curves I10

Dairy Queen® B49-B50
Dodge's World's
  Toughest Rodeo G127
EZ Air Park I7
NEW Maid Brigade I4
Metropolitan Boys
  Choir & Choralaires G164
kids Minnesota Renaissance Festival G35
kids Minnesota Timberwolves F1-F2, G16
kids Minnesota Twins F3-F4, G19-G20
kids **NEW** Mulone Theatres . . . . GG
kids Nelson's Apple Farm G330
kids Pizza Hut A6
kids Trail of Terror G166

Register at
entertainment.com/register
to access even more of these
great savings!

NEW New Merchants Added This Year   **kids** Great Place for Kids!
Online... Print This Offer at www.entertainment.com

Alphabetical Index

1

1-800-FLOWERS.COM ®	H64
101 Blu	B69
1st of Thai Restaurant	B85

5

5-8 Grill & Bar	B86
5-8 Tavern & Grill	B81

A

A & W	B52-B54
A La Zing	HH6
Ace	H50
Acme Comedy Co.	G43
Adrian's Tavern	B259
Adventure Island	D68
Adventure Park	G128
Adventure Zone	G93
Afton House Inn	C23
Airport Bowl	G109
Alamo	D33-D42
All Seasons Golf	G78
Ambrosia Coffee	B260
America's Harvest	C58
American Airlines	D1
American Blinds, Wallpaper & More	H11
American Greetings / Carlton Cards	I3
American Pie	B87, B261
American Sports Cafe & Nightclub	B88
American Swedish Institute	G158
Amy's Classic Confections	B262
Andy's Garage	B89
Andy's Sports Bar & Grill	B263
Angel O'Malley's	B90
Angeno's	B60
Anne's Cafe	G175
Anodyne @ 43rd	B264
Anoka Coffee Shop	B91
Antoine's Creole Maison	C28
Apple Grand Prix	G176
Aroma Cafe'	B265
Aroma's Pizza & Cafe	B266
Arrowwood Golf Club	G74
Artists' Grind	B267
Athen's Cafe	B92
Atlas Grill	C19
Au Bon Pain	B34-B36
Audubon Coffee	B268-B269
Auntie Anne's	B55-B57
Auntie Em's	B270
Aurelio's	B271
Avalon Tearoom & Pastry Shoppe	B272
The Avenue	H32-H33
Avis	D3-D12
Aztlan Tortilleria Bakery & Eatery	G177

B

B & B Pizza	G178
B&V Driving Range	G179
B&V Golf Course	G79
Babe's Sports Bar & Grill	B93
The Backyard Bar & Grill	B94
Bagel & Brew	G180
Bagels & Beans	G181
Bahn Thai Cuisine	B273
Baja Sol Tortilla Grill	B16-B18
The Bake Shop	G182
The Bakken Museum	G167
Ballard Designs	H8
Balmoral Golf Course	G183
Banadir Restaurant	G184
Bascali's Brick Oven	B95
Battle Creek Waterworks Family Aquatic Center	G146
Be-Bop Sports Bar & Grill	B96
Beach House Bar & Grille	C12
Bean Bag Coffeehouse	G185
The Bean Factory	B97
Beanhaven Cafe	B98
The Bears Den Sports Bar & Eatery	G186
Becker Community Center	G187
Bed Bath & Beyond	H5
Beef 'O' Brady's Family Sports Pub	B485
Begin Oaks Golf Course	G80
The Bell Auditorium	G162
The Bell Museum of Natural History	G159
Ben & Jerry's Ice Cream	B28-B30

Alphabetical Index

Benton Station Bar & Grill	G188
Betsy's Back Porch Coffee	B274
Betty's Bikes & Buns	B275
Bev's Cafe	B276
Beyond Juice	B99
Big Apple Bagels	B100-B101
Big Bite Pizza	B277
Big Daddy's Pizza	B278
Big Dipper	B279
Big Dog Sports Cafe	G189
Big Stop Deli	B280
Big Vinny's Subs	B281
The Bird Nightclub	B102
Black Bear Crossings	B282
Black Bear Golf Course	G190
Black Bear Grill	G191
BlackWater Coffee Co.	G192
Blackwater Coffee Company & Cafe	G193
Blair	H49
Blimpie Subs & Salads	B48
Blink Bonnie	B283
BLOCKBUSTER®	H12-H15
Blondies Cafe	B103
Blondies Sports Grill and Bar	B104
Blooms Today	H66
Blue Cat Coffee & Tea	B284-B285
Blue Eyes Cafe	B286
Blue Line Sports Bar & Grill	G194
Blue Moon	G195
Blue Moon Coffee Cafe	B287
Blue Note Supper Club	G196
Blue Sky Creamery	B105
Bo's 'N Mine	G197
Bob Smith's Sports Club	G199
Bobby & Steve's Auto World	B288,I19
Bobby Joe's Pub	G200
Boca Chica	B106
BoDiddley's Deli	G198
Bon's Buffet	G201
Bone Appetit	G202
Book-ems Bar & Restaurant	G203
Bookshelves & Coffeecups	G204
Border Bar & Grill, The	G205
Boss Limo	I2
Boston Garden	B289
Boston's	B481-B484
Boulevard Coffee	B290
Bowl Winkles	G206
Boxer's Bar & Grill	G207
Braemar Golf Dome	G68
Brass Rail Bar & Grill	G208
Brave New Workshop	G165
Brewberry's Coffee Shop	B107
Brewer's Bar & Grill of Jordan	G209
Brewsters Bar & Grill	G210
Brick House Eatery	B108
Brickyard Bar & Grille	G211
Briggs Woods Golf Course	G212
Brightwood Hills	G67
Brink's Home Security	HH13
Bronks Bar & Grill	G213
Brookdale Car Wash	I32
Brooklyn Center Community Center	G135
Brookside Bar & Grill	G214
Brookstone	H21-H22
Brothers Coffee	B291
Bru House Coffee Shop	B292
Bruck's Espresso Bar	B293
Brunswick Zone	G108
Bud's Place Bar & Grill	G215
Budget Car Rental	D13-D22
Buffalo Books	G216
Buffalo Books & Coffee	G217
Buffalo Heights Golf Course	G66, G218
Buffalo Tap	B109
Bugaloo's Ice Cream Shoppe	G219
The Bulldog Restaurant	B110
Bunker Beach	G30
The Bunker Indoor Golf Center	G65
Bunkers Music Bar & Grill	B111
Bunny's	B112
Burnsville Ice Center	G97
Busch Gardens Tampa Bay	D67

ALPHABETICAL INDEX

C

C. McGee's Deli B294
Cabin Fever B295
Cactus Grill Mexican Buffet B296
Cafe Caffeine B297
Cafe Lettieris B298
Cafe Limon B299
Cafe Northstar. C29
Cafe of the Americas B301
Cafe Pawz at Becker Furniture World G220
Cafe Tatta Bunna B300
Cafe' La Poste G221
Cafe' Pierre B302
Caffe de Lago B303
Camden Coffee Company B304-B305
Camille's. B31-B33
Candy Wholesale Company® HH4
Canterbury Park. G37
Capital City Market Cafe & Bar B114
Carbone's B61-B63
The Cardinal Restaurant & Bar B115
Carmike Cinemas G12
Carnival Cruise Line D63-D65
Carnival Thrillz G222-G223
Carousel Restaurant. C24
Cascade Bay Water Park. G28
Castlewood Golf Course G64
Catherine's H37-H40
CEC Theatres. G13-G15
Cedar Inn Bar & Grill B306
Cedar Market & Deli. B307
Central Car Wash I34
Chanhassen Fireside Theatre G41
Chanhassen Dinner Theatre G42
Chanticlear Pizza B19-B21, B308
Charley's Grilled Subs B118
Charlie's Irish Pub B119
Charly's Polleria Restaurant. B116
Chaska Bakery B309
Chaska Community Center. G145
Cheap Skate. G98
Cherry Moon Farms HH1
Cheryl & Co. HH7

Cheryl Ann's Bar & Grill G224
Chez Daniel Bistro. C30
Chicago Deli Cafe & Grille B117
Chin Yung B120
China Wok Restaurant. B310
Chinese Gourmet Restaurant B311
Chisago House Restaurant. G225
Chocolat Celeste. B121
The Chocolate Shoppe G226
The Chocolate Twist G227
Choppers Bar & Grill. G228
Chula Vista B122
Cinema Espresso. B312
Cinema Grill B123
Cinema Grill Theater G51
City Perks Coffee House B313
CJ's Coffee & Wine Bar B113
Claire's I12-I13
Classic Auto Spa & Detail Center. I35
Classic Bowl G115
Classic Pizza B314
Clean 'n' Press. I1
Cloud 9 Car Wash & Detail Center I40
Coffee & Tea LTD. B124
Coffee Cats Cafe B315
The Coffee Company G229
Coffee Connection G230
Coffee Cottage B316
Coffee Creek Espresso & Eatery G231
Coffee Klatsch G232
Coffee Mouse G233
Coffee Oasis B317
Coffee Ta Cream. B318
Cokato Town & Country Club G234
Col. Muzzy's Texas BBQ B319
Cold Stone Creamery B13-B14
ComedySportz. G123
Common Grounds Coffee House B320
Commuter's Cup G235
Como Park Golf Course G87
Como Town G29
CondoDirect. D86
The Coop Restaurant B125

Alphabetical Index

Copper Dome Restaurant B321
Cora's Best Chicken Wings B322
Cornell's C43
Cosmic's Cafe B323
Country Club Lanes G111
Country Glazed Ham Shop B324
Country Home Bakery & Deli B325
Craig's Waverly Cafe G236
Creative Catering B326
Creekside Cafe C55
Crescent Moon Bakery B327
Crown Theatres G10-G11
Cruise America D76
Crystal Bistro C48
Crystal Cafe & Grill B126
Crystal Recreation Dept G147
Cuisine of India G237
Culver's Frozen Custard B4-B6
Cup of Knowledge B328
Cupcake B127
Cuppa Java B329-B330
CuppaChiodo's B128
Curves I10
Custom Coffee & Caffe G238
Cuzzy's B331

D

da Afghan C50
Daddio's Take-N-Bake B332
Dahlgreen Golf Club G54
Daily Grind B333
The Daily Grind B129, B334
Dairy Inn G239
Dairy Queen® B49-B50
Dakota County Steakhouse C44
Daniel's Family Restaurant G240
Daniela's G241
Dar's Double Scoop B335
Darla's Grill & Malt Shop B73-B74
Dashen Ethiopian Restaurant & Bar . . . C31
Dassel Entertainment Center G242
Dave's Town Club G243
DeAngelo's G244

Denny's 5th Ave. Bakery B336
The Depot B130, G245-G246
Detello's Pizza & Pasta B131
Diamonds Coffee Shoppe B337
Diamonds Sports Bar & Grill B132
Diggers Bar & Grill G247
The Dinkytowner B133
Dinosaur Walk MOA G36
DirectStarTV H54
DISHNetwork H53
Disney Live G38
The District B84
Doc's Bar & Grill G248
Dodge's World's Toughest Rodeo G127
Domino's Pizza B7-B9
Don Panchos Bakery B338
Don's Car Washes I31
Dorothy Ann Bakery & Cafe B339
Double Click Coffee G249
Douville Bakery G250
Downtowner Car Wash I29
Dreamcoat Cafe B340
Dudley's Pizza & Sandwich Shop G251
Duets B134
Dugout Bar B341
Durkin's Pub B135
Dusek's Bakery B342

E

Eagles Nest Indoor Playground G148
East African Taste Restaurant B343
eBags.com H70
Eddies Billiards G140
Eddington's B46-B47
Eden Prairie Community Center G94
Eden Restaurant B136
8th Street Grill B137
Eko Backen G252
El Azteca C14
El Carambas G253
El Nuevo Rodeo B138
El Paraiso Mexican Restaurant B139
El Rey Bakery B344

Alphabetical Index

El Taquito Taco Shop Restaurant	G254
El Tequila Restaurante	B345
El Toro	C15
Eli's Food & Cocktails	B77
Elsie's Restaurant & Bar	C25
Embers America Restaurant	B72
Emily's Bakery & Deli	G255
Enjoy China	B140
Enterprise Rent-A-Car	D23-D32
Erte	C17
Espresso 22	B346
Espresso Donut Co.	B347
Espresso Royale Cafe	B348
Evie's Soups & More	G256
EZ Air Park	I7

F

Fantastic Sams	I16
Faribault Bowling Center	G257
Faribault Family Aquatic Center	G258
Farmington Bakery	G259
Farmington Lanes	G260-G261
Fashion Bug	H35-H36
Fast Lane Pizza	G262
Fatboys Bar & Grill	B141
Fatso's	B142
Figaro's Pizza	B145
Fillin' Station	G263
Fire Roast Mountain Cafe	B349
The Fish House	B350
5 Star Cafe	B351
Flaherty's Arden Bowl	G110
Flaherty's Pub & Grill	B143
Flash Studios	HH33
Flashback Cafe & Cocktail Lounge	B144
Florida Vacation Station	D85
Florist.com	H65
Footlocker	I5
Fore Seasons at Southbrook Golf Club	G264
Fort Snelling	G160
Franklin Market & Deli	B352
Franklin Street Bakery	B353
Fresco Juice Company	B146
Freshens	B147
Fridley Crab House	C13
From You Baskets	H69
From You Flowers	H63
Frontgate	H6
FTD.COM	H57-H58
FunCity	G265-G266
FYE	I14

G

G-Allen's Restaurant & Sports Bar	G267
Gabby's Saloon & Eatery	B148
Galaxy Auto Centers	I11
The Galley Room	B354
GameFly.com	HH26
Games by James	I17
Gameworks	G34
Garden Grill	G268
Garnet Hill	H43
Gateway	H20
Gathering Grounds	G269
Gator's Garden Cafe	B149
General Store Cafe	B150
Genghis Grill	B151-B152
Gibbs Museum of Pioneer & Dakotah Life	G161
Giuseppe's	B355
Glamour Shots	HH29-HH32
Glen Lake Coffee Co.	B356-B357
Glencoe Country Club	G55
Glensheen	G270
Golden Limousine	I6
Golden's Cafe & Deli	B358
Golf Zone	G81
Golfmasters Driving Range	G271
Good Life Nutrition Juice & Smoothie Bar	G272
Grand Grill	C32
Grand Rios Indoor Water Park	G27
Grand Slam U.S.A.	G82
GrandinRoad	H44
Grandma Rita's Cafe	B359
Granny's Bowl	G273
Granny's Grill	G274

Alphabetical Index

Grantsburg Municipal Golf Course	G275
Great American History Theatre	G40
Great Clips IMAX Theatre	G6
Great Lakes Aquarium	G276
Great Steak & Potato Co.	B153, B360
Great Vacation Destinations	D83
Greater Twin Cities Youth Symphonies	G124
Greystone Golf Club	G83
The Grille at Elk River Country Club	B154
Ground Round	G277
The Grounds	G278
Growing Up with Garnet Hill	H45
The Guthrie Theater	G45

H

Hallmark Flowers	H61-H62
Ham Lake Lanes	G279
Harborside Restaurant & Lounge	C20
Harmony's	C33
Harold's Chicken	B361
Harry and David	H71-H72
Harvest Buffet	G280
Harvey's Bar & Grill	B79, G281
Hawk's Sports Bar & Grill	G282
Heartbreakers Bar & Grill	B155
Heavenly Daze Coffee	B156
Heavenly Shoes	I24
Hennepin History Museum	G168
Heppner's Auto Wash & Detailing Center	I30
Hertz	D53-D62
Hi-Quality Bakery	G283
Hickory Farms	H74-H75
Hidden Creek Golf Club	G56
Higher Grounds	B362
Hojies Grill & Smokehouse	G284
Hollywood Scoops	B363
Hollywood Video, Pizza & Tanning	G285
Holy Land Deli	B364
Honeybaked Ham	B365-B367
Hong Wong	B368
Hopper's Bar & Grill	B157
Hopscotch Grill	C11
Hotwire	D2
House of Beans	G286
House of Java	B369
HSN.com	H47
Hudson Bagel & Coffee Co.	G287
Hudson Bowl	G288
Hunan Garden Chinese Restaurant	B158
Hunan Restaurant	B370
Hunter's Inn Bar & Grill	B371
Hutch Cafe	G289

I

Imperial Room	B76
Improvements Catalog	H46
In the Spirit of Coffee, Cards & Gifts	B372-B373
International Business Cafe	B374
Island Lake Golf Center	G84
Island Pine Golf Club	G290
Island View Dining	G291
It Figures	I18
Izatys Golf & Yacht Club - The Sanctuary	G57

J

J & D's 212 Club	B375
J's Family Restaurant	B376
J. Grundy's Rueb 'N' Stein	G292
J.R. Mac's Bar & Grill	B159-B160
Jack Yee's Restaurant	B378
Jackson & Perkins	H73
Jackson Street Grill & Bar	B162
Jade Island Cuisine	B379
Jake's Pizza	G293-G294
Jamaica Jamaica	B163
James Gang Coffeehouse & Eatery	G295
Java Joint	G296
Java Restaurant	B380
Javalive! Community Coffeehouse	G297
JCPenney Portraits	HH8
Jersey's Bar & Grill	B381
Jerusalem's Restaurant	B382
Jewel of India	C21
Jimbo's	B383

Alphabetical Index

JJ's Clubhouse	B161
Jocko's Bar & Grill	G298
John Jacobs Golf Schools	G299
John Rose Minnesota Oval	G99
jP American Bistro	C5
JT's Restaurant & Pizza Parlor	B377
Judes Coffee & Eatery	B164

K

K B Toys	H23-H26
Kabab Restaurant	G300
Kalli's Popcorn Shop	B384
KarmelKorn	B43-B45
Katie O'Leary's Beef & Brew	B385
Kay's Wine Bar & Bistro	C34
Kids' Time of Northtown	G95
Kikugawa at Riverplace	C3
Kilkarney Hills Golf Course	G63
KinhDo Restaurant	B165
Kips An Authentic Irish Pub & Restaurant	C53
Knoke's Confections & Ice Cream	G301
KODAK EASYSHARE Gallery	HH14
Koep's Village Bakery	G302
Kokomo's Island Cafe	C10
Koyi Sushi	C35
Krispy Kreme Doughnuts	B15

L

La Bodega Tapas Bar	B78
La Casita	B70
La Pinata	B386
La Roses Pizza, Pasta & Ribs	G303
Lake Center Bar and Grill	G304
Lake Superior & Mississippi Railroad	G305
Lakeside Cafe & Creamery	G306
Lane Bryant	H34
Lano Lanes	G307
Lariat Lanes	G112
Larkspur Market	G308
Laser Storm at the Skatin' Place	G309
Lastrack Family Restaurant	B166
Lava Links	G77

Lavender Thymes	G310
Lavish	I9
Le Sueur Diner	G311
Legends Bar & Grill	B167
LEGOLAND	D77
LensCrafters	HH17
Leo's Pizza Palace	G312
Leonardo's	B64-B66
Lighthouse Coffee	G313
Limu Coffee	B387
The Links of Byron	G314
Linwood Pizza	B168
Liquid Assets	G315
Lisa's Place	G316
Little Dandy Sports Bar	G317
Little Sushi on the Prairie	B169
Little Tel-Aviv Cafe & Restaurant	C45
Liz Claiborne	H29-H31
Lombard's	C46
Lone Tree Bar & Grill	B170
Long John Silver's	B257-B258
The Lookout Bar & Grill	B171
Lord Essex Tavern	C56
Lori's Coffee House	B388
Loring Park Coffee House & Wine Bar	B172
Luna Blu	B389
Lutsen Mountains	G318
Lyn-Del Lanes	G139

M

MacKenzie	B75
MacTavish's	C49
Mady's Bowl and Lounge	B390
Maggie's Restaurant	B391
MaggieMoo's	B51
Maggio's Pizza	G320
Mai Thai Cafe	B173
Maid Brigade	I4
Maid-Rite	G321
Main Street Central Perk	B392
Mairin's Table Neighborhood Bistro	C36
Mama Donato's	B393
Mama Taught Me How To Cook Soul Food Eatery!	B394

Alphabetical Index

Mama's Bakery, Pizza & Salad Bar B395
Mann Theatres F5,G1-G5
Manny's Tortas B396
Maple Grove Community Center. G91
Marble Slab Creamery. B174
Marco's Pizza B175
Marcus Theatres. G7-G9
Margarita Bella B176
Marie's Casual Dining & Lounge. G322
Marina Grill & Deli B397
Marino's Deli B398
Marla's Indian & Caribbean Cuisine B177
Martini's. B178
Marysburg Books B399-B400
Maxwell's B179
Maya Mexican Restaurante B180
Mayslack's. B181
MC's Dugout Bar & Grill G319
McDivot's Sports Pub & Eatery. B182
McDonald's® A1-A3,B1-B3
McGuires C37
McKenzie Lanes G53
McKenzie's Bar & Grill. G323
The Meadows Restaurant
    & Sports Bar B183
Medina Entertainment Center G129
Medina Lanes G113
The Mediterranean Cruise Cafe B184
Mel-O-Glaze Bakery. B401
Mell's Beauty Bar B80
The Melting Pot C1
Memory Lanes. G138
Metropolitan Boys
    Choir & Choralaires G164
Mexico Y Mexico. B402
Mias Pizza. B403
Midas HH22-HH25
Midway Pro Bowl G116
Midway Rendezvous Cafe B404
Milda's Cafe B185
Mill St. Tavern G324
Miller's on Main B186
Mim's Cafe B405
Ming's Palace B406

Mings Garden Restaurant B187,B407
Minneapolis Town Hall Brewery B188
Minnesota Dance Theatre G125
Minnesota Landscape Arboretum G157
Minnesota Lynx G17-G18
The Minnesota Opera G46
Minnesota Renaissance Festival G35
Minnesota Swarm G25
Minnesota Thunder Pro Soccer. G21
Minnesota Timberwolves F1-F2,G16
Minnesota Twins. F3-F4,G19-G20
Minnesota Zoo. G26
Mochalini's B189
Mojos Pizza B408
Mongkok B409
Montgomery Golf Club G73
Moose Bar & Grill B190
Morning Glory's Bakery Cafe G325
Mounds Theatre G130
The Mouse. G326
Mr. Jim's. G327
Muddy Paws Cheesecake B191
Munkabeans & Sunshine B410
Murasaki Japanese Restaurant C16

N

Naar. C6
Nacho Mama's. C47
Nana's Chicken G328
Nascar Silicon Motor Speedway G32
National Car Rental D43-D52
Naughty Pines Fish Camp G329
The Neighborhood Cafe B192
The Neighborhood
    Ice Cream Shoppe. B411-B412
Nelson's Apple Farm. G330
Nestle Tollhouse Cafe by Chip B193-B194
New York & Company H27-H28
New York Burrito B413
Nic's on Nicollet C38
Nick's Ice Cream & Popcorn B196
Nick-N-Willy's Take-N-Bake B195
Nickelby's Maplewood Grill C51
Nina's Grill B414

Alphabetical Index

Nino's Pizza Plus	B197
North Branch Golf Course	G331
North Country Co-op	B415
Northern Espresso Cafe	B416
Northern Palms Driving Range	G85
Northern Shores	C22
Northwoods Bar & Grill	B198

O

O'Fudge Deli & Coffee	G332
Ocean Waves Massage	I20
Old Fashion Donut Shoppe	B417
Ollie & Co. Indoor Skate Park	G131
Omaha Steaks ®	H76-H78
On Broadway Car Wash	G333
On Broadway-Proudly Serving Dunn Bros. Coffee	G334
Once Upon a Child	I8
Online Vitamin Outlet®	HH5
Orange Julius®	B25-B27
Ordway Center for the Performing Arts	G48-G50
Orono Golf Course	G62
Osceola & St. Croix Valley Railway	G143
Osceola Antiques & Ice Cream Parlor	G335
Over The Rainbow	B418
Overstock.com	H10

P

Pair of Dice Pizza	B419
Paisano's Pizza & Hot Hoagies	B420
Panaderia El Rey	B421
Pannekoeken Huis	B71
The Pantry	G336
Papa John's Pizza	B22-B24
Papa Tronnio's Pizza	G337
Papa's Pizza and Pasta	B199
Paradise Car Wash	I28
The Park at MOA	G22
Park Cafe	B422
Park Tavern Lounge & Lanes	B200, G117
Pasquale's Sports Bar & Restaurant	B201
Patrick's	G338
Pearle Vision	HH16
Personal Creations	H67
Personalized Children's Books	G339
Pete's Pizza	B423, G340
Pete's Place	G341
PetSmart®	D75, H55-H56
Phalen Park Golf Course	G72
Picture People	HH9-HH10
Pier 1 Imports	H3-H4
Pine Street Grille	C39
Ping's Szechuan Star	B202
Pizza Factory	G342
Pizza Flame	B203
Pizza Hut	A6
Pizza Magic	B424
Pizza Man	B204
Pizza N' Pasta	B37-B39
Pizza Pazza	B425
Pizza Planet	B426
Pizza Prima	B205
Pizza Prima & Pasta	B427
Pizza Pub	G343-G344
Pizza Ranch	B206
Pizzaioli Pizzamaker	B428
Pizzeria Uno	B207
Pla Mor Lanes	G345
Plan B Coffeehouse	B429
Planet Hollywood	D79-D80
Playoffs Sports Bar & Grill	C40
PlayZone Arcade	G23
Plow & Hearth	H9
Plums Neighborhood Grill & Bar	B208-B209
Plymouth Ice Center	G132
Plymouth Playhouse	G126
Porter's Bar and Grill	B210
Pretzel Time	B211
Pro-Kart Indoor Racing	G33
Proex Photo & Portrait	HH34-HH37
Professor Java's	G346
Proflowers.com	H59-H60
Pump It Up	G133
Pupuseria El Rincon Salva Doreno	B430

Alphabetical Index

Q

Q-Sharks	G104
Q-Sharks Cafe	B431
Qdoba Mexican Grill	B67
Queen Of Cakes	B432
Quizno's Sub®	A5
Qwest Communications	1

R

Rack N' Roll Billiards	G105
RadioShack	H18-H19
Rail Station Bar & Grill	B212
Rainbow Play Systems	HH38
Ramsey County Parks & Recreation	G100
Rand Deli & Catering	B433
Rascal's Bar & Restaurant	B213
Razs Cafe	B434
Red Moon Restaurant	B214
The Red Pepper	B215, B435
The Red Rooster	B216
Red Sea Restaurant	B217
Redwood Falls Golf Club	G58
The Refuge	B83
Regal Entertainment Group	G169-G174
Rendezvous Coffee Shop	G348
Renegades Bar & Grill	B218
Restaurante Guayaquil	B219, B436
Restaurante La Rancherita	B437
Retro Roast & Fountain	G349
Rice And Arlington Batting Cages	G152
Richfield Municipal Pool & Waterslide	G163
Rise 'n Shine Coffee & Deli	G350
River Bluff Car Wash	I39
River Rock Coffee	G351
River's Edge Tubing	G352
Riverboat Depot	G353
Riverboat Lanes	G354
Riverside Restaurant	B438
Riverview Theater	G52
Riverwood National Driving Range	G141
Riverwood National Golf Course	G60
Rix Bar & Grill	C59
RJ's Tavern on Main	G347
Roadhouse 169 Bar & Grill	B220
Roberts Sports Bar & Entertainment	B221
Rocco's Pizza	B222
Rochester Indoor Golf Dome	G355
Rock 'N' Roll Pizza	G356
Rocky Rococo	B439
Roller Garden	G101
Rollerdome	G102
Roly Poly	B42
Rose Garden	B440
Rosen's City Tavern	B82
Rosetti's Pizza & Pasta	B223
Roseville Cedarholm Golf Course	G86
Rudolph's Bar-B-Que	C9
The Rustic Inn	G357

S

Saint Paul Chamber Orchestra	G44
Sally's Saloon & Eatery	B224
Salsarita's Fresh Cantina	B58-B59
Sammy's	G358
Sarpino's Pizza	B225, G359
Scandia Bake Shop	B441
Scoop's Frozen Custard	G360
Scoops Pub	B226
Scoreboard Pizza	B442
Sears.com	H1
Seasons Restaurant	C8
SeaWorld Adventure Parks	D66
2nd Moon Coffee Cafe	B443
Secret Spoon	HH2
Segue Cafe	B444
Serendipity	G361
Sesame Place	D69
Seth's Down Under Bar & Grill	G362
Sew What! Midway Cleaners	I38
Shadowbrooke Golf Course	G70
Shady Hill Grille	C57
ShareBuilder	H52
The Sharper Image	H16-H17
Shaw's Bar & Grill	B445
Shell's Cafe	B446
Sheraton Vacation Ownership	D84

Alphabetical Index

Sherwin Williams	I21-I22
Shooters Billiard Parlor & Cafe	B447
Shooters Billiards	G106
Shutterfly	HH15
Signature Bar & Grill	G363
SimonDelivers	AA1
Sindbad Cafe & Market	B448
Sir Speedy	I15
Sirius Satellite Radio	H51
Skateville	G103
Skatin' Place	G364
Ski Gull	G365-G366
Skinners Pub & Eatery	B227
Smith + Noble	H7
The Smooth Grind	B449
Smuckers Stars on Ice	G39
Snelling Cafe	B450
Snuffy's Malt Shop	B228
Soho Cafe	B451
Sojourner's Cafe	B452-B453
Southbrook Golf Club	G71
Southern Hills Golf Club	G61
SpaWish.com	HH3
Spectators Grille & Bar	B68
Speedy's Family & Fun Center	G367
The Sportsman's Pub	B229
Spring Lake Amusement Park	G88
Spring Street Tavern	B230
Square Peg Diner	B454
St. Bernard's Bowling Lanes	G118
St. Croix Crab House Music Cafe	C52
St. Croix Falls Mini Golf & Go-Karts	G144
St. Louis Park Outdoor Aquatic Park	G149
St. Louis Park Rec Center	G150
St. Paul Bagelry & Deli	B455
St. Petersburg Restaurant and Vodka Bar	C41
Stacy Country Cafe	G368
Stacy's Grille	C26
Stages Theatre Company	G136
Starting Gate Productions	G134
State of Bean	B456
State Street Bistro	G369
Steak Escape	B40-B41
Stearns History Museum	G370
Stone Mill Coffee House & Eatery	G371
Stone Mill Marketplace	G372
Strike Force Bowl	G373
Stucci's Italian Food	G374
Summerland	G375
The Summit Golf Club	G69
Sun Ray Restaurant	B457
Sundance Golf and Bowl	G119
Sunni's Grille	G376
Sunterra	D82
Super Bowl	G114
SuperAmerica	I25
SuperAmerica Car Washes	I26
Supermom's	I27
SuperShuttle	D74
Sweet Taste of Italy	B458-B460

T

T & Y Car Wash	I33
Taco Bell®	A4
Taco John's	B10-B12
Taco Loco	B461
Tacoasis	G377
Tacoville	B462
Tale of Two Sisters Tea Room & Gift Shoppe	G378
Tamarack Nature Center	G151
Tanners Steakhouse & Bar	C4
Taraccino Coffee	B463
Target	HH11-HH12
Target.com	H2
Tasty Pizza	B231
TCBY	B232-B233
The Tea Garden	B235
Tea Source	B236
The Territory Ahead	H41-H42
Texa-Tonka Lanes	G120
Thailand View	B237
Thayer's Historic Bed n' Breakfast	G379-G380
The Bayou	G381
The Mock Turtle	B464
The Popcorn Factory	HH27

Alphabetical Index

3rd Lair	G96
This Old Store Etc.	G382
Three Happiness	G383
Three Sisters Tea Room	G384
Thunder Alley Indoor Paintball	G385
Thunder Alley Indoor Speedway	G386
Tickle Yer Fancy	G387
Tiffany's Sports Lounge	B238
Tin Shed Tavern & Pizza	B239
TJ's of Edina	B234
Tokyo Express	B465
Tortilla Ria Mexican Cafe	B466
Toy Store	G24
Trail of Terror	G166
TravelSmith	D87
Trigger's	C18
Tropical Brew	G388
Tropical Smoothie Cafe	B240
Tropicana	B241
Tropics Indoor Water Park	G31
Turitto's Pizza & Subs	B242
Turtle Dove Tea House & Gardens	G389
Turtle's Bar & Grill	B243
Turtleback Golf & Country Club	G390
Tuttle's Bowling, Bar & Grill	G137
Tuttle's Shady Oak Grill	B244
Twisted Shamrock Pub & Grill	B467
Two Stooges Billiards	G107
Two Stooges Sports Bar & Grill	B245

U

U of M Athletics	G153-G156
Ubah Restaurant	B468
The Ugly Mug	G391
Underwater Adventures Aquarium	F7-F8, I23
Universal Orlando Resort	D70-D73
Uptown Pizza	B246
US Airways	D81
USA Karate	G92
USAflorist.com	H68

V

Valley Sports Pub & Grill	B469
Valley View Golf Course	G59
Vertical Endeavors	G76
Vescio's	B247
Victoria House	B248
Victory Lane Car Wash & Detail Center	I36
Vientiane Restaurant	B470
Villa Pizza	B249
Villa Roma Pizzaria	B471
Village Blend	B472
Village Inn	G392
Vintage Driving Range	G89
Vintage Golf Course	G75
VONAGE	H48

W

Wabasha Deli	B473
Waberi Somalian Restaurant	B474
The Wagon Grill	B250
Waldo's Bar & Grill	B475
Walgreens	HH18-HH21
Walker Art Center	G47
Wanderer's Chinese Cuisine	B251
Water Park of America	F6
Water Street Inn	C27
Wayne's	G393
The Well Sports Tavern & Grill	B252
West Side Lanes	B476, G121
Westfire Grille	C60
Westgate Resorts	D78
The Whiskey Rack	B253
White Way Cleaners	I37
The Wilds Pub	C54
Wildwood Bowl	G122
Wing Joint	B477
Wing Street	B254
Wings Tavern & Grille	G394
Winona Island Cafe	G395
Wintergreens	C42
Wintergreens Indoor Golf	G90
Wirefly.com	HH28
Wolves Den Native Coffee	B255

Alphabetical Index

The Woodbury Broiler Bar C7
Wooddale Recreation Center G142
Woody's Grille C2

Y

Yarn Cafe B478

Z

Zebra Pizza & Tacos B479
Zeppole's Pizza & Pasta G396
Zobota Cafe B256
Zuppa Cucina B480

Register at
entertainment.com/register
to access even more of these
great savings!

When One Just Isn't Enough!

Buy a Second Membership Card for Only $15.00

Share Additional Savings With an Associate Family Membership!

An additional Membership Card gives you Double Savings on:

- many dining offers
- online printable coupons
- online retailer discounts
- many hotel discounts
- car rental savings

Call now to take advantage of this special offer!
1-888-231-SAVE (7283)

XCS7AM

Be the first to get the Entertainment® Book every year!

JOIN THE ENTERTAINMENT® RENEWAL PROGRAM TODAY!

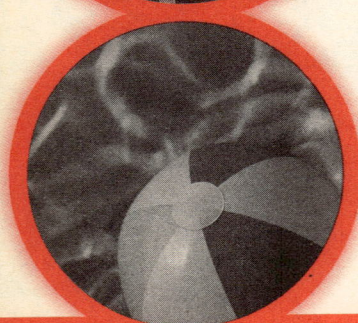

The Entertainment® Renewal Program is a convenient way to maximize your savings! Join the Renewal Program and have future years' books shipped to you as soon as they are published. You'll be among the first to get the book and will have the maximum amount of time to use as many of the great Entertainment® offers as possible. All this and shipping and handling is totally **FREE!**

Best of all…you can credit a fundraiser with up to 50% of the purchase price every year you receive delivery of the book. Convenience, extra time to save, free shipping, and credit for your favorite fundraiser—you just can't lose!

Just sign up during membership card registration at
www.entertainment.com/register

Making a Difference...Every Day!

The Minnesota Timberwolves FastBreak Foundation and the Minnesota Lynx want to positively impact the lives of the youth in our Minnesota communities, enabling them to make responsible decisions, and helping them to contribute to their own future and experience lifelong memories. For more information, log on to www.timberwolves.com.

One for the Community®

Rules of Use

The membership card and coupons are valid now through November 1, 2007, unless otherwise stated on the discount offer.

1. **Entertainment® Membership Card...** Remove your membership card from the front of this book and register online at www.entertainment.com/register to receive full membership benefits and begin using the membership card right away. The membership card is used to obtain the offers found in the Dining Out section that have [icon] in the upper right-hand corner of the offer page and with car rentals and select hotels.

2. **Additional Conditions...** Read the offer carefully for stated conditions, restrictions, and exclusions. All offers are valid anytime except on defined holidays or unless the offer states otherwise. Certain offers are restricted to one offer per party, per visit. These additional conditions supersede other Rules of Use.

3. **How To Redeem Discount...** Present your coupon/membership card to a participating merchant at the time you request your bill to receive your discount. The merchant will retain your coupon or remove the card number from the back of your membership card to indicate you have used the discount offer. The least expensive item(s), up to the maximum value stated, will be deducted from your bill, or you will receive a percentage off the designated item(s), up to the maximum value stated, depending on the discount offer. For restaurants offering one complimentary "menu item" when a second is purchased, a "menu item" is a main course or entrée item. You may only use an offer once, and you may not combine the offer with any other discount or awards program/offer.

4. **Valid Dates and Times/Holidays...** Read the offer carefully for valid dates and times. Major holidays, including those defined below, and regional holidays observed by participating merchants, are excluded, even if the offer states "valid anytime":

New Year's Eve/Day	Valentine's Day	St. Patrick's Day	Easter
Mother's Day	Father's Day	Thanksgiving	Christmas Eve/Day

   Please check with the merchant regarding other holidays.

5. **Dining Discount Details...** Only one coupon/membership card may be used for every two people, up to a maximum of three coupons/membership cards per party, and separate checks are not allowed. Some restaurants include a "when dining alone" option in their offers. These offers are valid only when dining alone. Dining offers cannot be applied to children's menu items, discount-priced daily specials, senior citizen rates, Early Bird specials, carryout/takeout (except in the Casual Dining & Fast Food section), and buffets, unless otherwise noted. Discounts on alcohol are prohibited. The discount will be applied only to the food portion of the bill.

6. **Tipping...** Tipping for satisfactory service should be 15–20% of the total bill **before** the discount amount is subtracted.

7. **Discounts...** Discounts exclude tax, tip and/or alcohol, where applicable.

8. **Hotel Discounts...** Please see the "Hotel Rules of Use" located in the Travel & Hotels section.

9. **Movie Theater Discounts...** Some movie theaters are obligated by studio contracts to exclude discounts on certain movies. Please see individual offers for theatre exclusions, restrictions and conditions or review the "Movie Ticket Rules of Use" located in the Entertainment & Sports section for mail-in or online ordering information..

10. **Repeat Savings™...** You must register your card at www.entertainment.com/register to receive this monthly benefit. Just look for [icon] on coupons in the book for participating merchants. Then, go to www.entertainment.com to print additional coupons for the merchant. Most offers may be printed one time per month. Offer value may vary and certain conditions and restrictions may apply. Simply click, print and redeem at these merchants. Coupons may not be reproduced, altered, traded or sold. Offers expire 14 days after printing.

11. **Printable Offers...** Print coupons on www.entertainment.com for merchants not found in your book, for newly added offers and for Repeat Savings™ merchants. Offers expire 14 days after printing. You must register your card and be logged into your membership to access these offers.

12. **Free Offers...** In most cases, to qualify for a free offer or complimentary item, you must purchase goods or services from the merchant making the offer. Such offers may not be used in conjunction with any other discount or awards program/offer.

13. **Merchant Information...** All merchant information is valid as of May 1, 2006. Go to www.entertainment.com for important updates.

The barter, trade, sale, purchase, or transfer for compensation of this book, in whole or in part or any of its offers, is strictly prohibited, unless expressly authorized by ENTERTAINMENT PUBLICATIONS, INC. This book and its offers are intended for the personal use of the individual purchaser of this book and are not valid with other discount offers or in other cities unless otherwise specified. The use of this book or any of its offers for advertising purposes, in any form or fashion, is strictly prohibited. Any use of an offer in violation of these Rules will render the offer VOID and ENTERTAINMENT PUBLICATIONS, INC. will pursue all legal remedies available to it by law. Offers may not be reproduced and are void where prohibited, taxed or restricted by law.

ENTERTAINMENT PUBLICATIONS, INC., and or its parent or subsidiaries, will not be responsible if any establishment breaches its contract or refuses to accept the membership card/coupons; however, it will attempt to secure compliance.

ENTERTAINMENT PUBLICATIONS, INC. disclaims all alleged liability for bodily injury or property damage resulting from any accident, event or occurrence on, or resulting from the use of, the premises of the participating businesses. ENTERTAINMENT PUBLICATIONS, INC. disclaims a warranties express, implied or otherwise imposed by law, regarding the condition of those premises or the safety of same. ENTERTAINMEN PUBLICATIONS, INC. disclaims all alleged vicarious liability for bodily injury or property damage resulting from the acts or omissions of th participating businesses.

Membership Information

www.entertainment.com
Your comprehensive source for information about your Entertainment® membership and related products.

MEMBER SERVICES
(You must register your Entertainment® Membership Card and log in to access these services.)

TO REGISTER YOUR BOOK/MEMBERSHIP CARD
Go to www.entertainment.com/register

FOR QUESTIONS REGARDING YOUR ENTERTAINMENT® MEMBERSHIP AND ITS MANY BENEFITS
Go to www.entertainment.com/questions

TO PURCHASE ADDITIONAL ENTERTAINMENT® BOOKS AT MEMBER-ONLY PRICES (FOR GIFTS OR TRAVEL)
Go to www.entertainment.com/books

FOR OUR HOTEL PROGRAMS, GUARANTEED BEST RATE, OR HOTELS AT HALF PRICE
Go to www.entertainment.com/travel

FOR THE LATEST MEMBER UPDATES AND OFFER INFORMATION
Go to www.entertainment.com/hotline

FUNDRAISER/BUSINESS SERVICES

IF YOU ARE INTERESTED IN SELLING OUR PRODUCTS AS A FUNDRAISER
Go to www.fundraising.entertainment.com/2007

IF YOU ARE INTERESTED IN ADVERTISING IN THIS BOOK OR ON OUR WEB SITE
Go to www.entertainment.com/advertise

IF YOU ARE INTERESTED IN CREATING A CUSTOM COUPON BOOK OR ONLINE SAVINGS PROGRAM
Go to www.entertainment.com/pmd

If our web site does not address your question, or if you need to speak to one of our customer care representatives, please call
1-888-231-SAVE (7283)

Published by: Entertainment Publications, Inc. • International Headquarters
1414 E. Maple Road • Troy, MI 48083

Order Extra Editions & Out-of-Town Editions

Prices listed below reflect regular retail price and are shown in U.S. dollars. When calling **1-866-592-5991** toll free to order extra editions, you will receive $5 off the prices listed below. If you choose to order online at **www.entertainment.com**, you will receive $5 off the price listed below plus **FREE SHIPPING** (a $5 value). You must have registered your membership at www.entertainment.com/register and be signed in to take advantage of this free shipping offer. Please refer to the 3-digit code and edition name below when ordering.

Regular Retail Price listed below.

ALABAMA
106	Birmingham	$25

ARIZONA
047	Phoenix	$30
068	Tucson	$40

ARKANSAS
082	Little Rock	$25

CALIFORNIA
104	Bakersfield	$25
055	East Bay Area	$30
086	Fresno/Central Valley	$30
097	Inland Empire/Riverside/ Palm Springs	$30
110	Lake Tahoe/Reno	$30
016	Los Angeles West	$30
102	Modesto/Stockton	$35
084	Monterey Peninsula	$30
014	Orange County	$40
042	Sacramento/Gold Country	$45
017	San Diego	$45
012	San Fernando Valley	$30
073	San Francisco/San Mateo	$30
096	San Gabriel Valley	$30
010	San Jose/Santa Clara	$30
088	Santa Barbara/Ventura	$30
126	Sonoma/Marin	$30

COLORADO
141	Colorado Springs	$30
038	Denver	$30

CONNECTICUT
080	Fairfield County	$30
046	Hartford	$35
144	New Haven	$30

DELAWARE
157	Delaware	$35

FLORIDA
137	Brevard County	$30
035	Ft. Lauderdale/ West Palm Beach	$35
075	Ft. Myers/Naples	$35
037	Gainesville	$30
036	Jacksonville	$25
154	Miami/Florida Keys	$35
153	Orlando	$30
118	Sarasota	$30
139	St. Petersburg/Clearwater	$30
045	Tampa	$30

GEORGIA
028	Atlanta	$25
201	Augusta	$30

HAWAII
146	Hawaii	$35

IDAHO
085	Boise	$30

ILLINOIS
008	Chicago North/Northwest	$25
027	Chicago South/Southwest	$25
015	Chicago West/Central	$25

INDIANA
078	Ft. Wayne/NE Indiana	$30
039	Indianapolis/ Central Indiana	$25
056	Louisville/Southern IN	$25
058	Northwest Indiana	$25
159	South Bend/Michiana	$30

IOWA
053	Des Moines	$25
302	Quad Cities	$25

KANSAS
105	Kansas City	$25
057	Wichita	$30

KENTUCKY
122	Lexington	$30
056	Louisville/Southern IN	$25

LOUISIANA
202	Baton Rouge	$30
321	Lafayette	$30

MARYLAND
024	Baltimore	$30
022	Washington, D.C/ Maryland	$30

MASSACHUSETTS
030	Boston	$30
124	Springfield/Western MA	$30
108	Worcester County/ Central MA	$30

MICHIGAN
001	Detroit Area	$25
150	Grand Rapids	$30
303	Saginaw	$25

MINNESOTA
091	Twin Cities	$35
123	Twin Ports	$30

MISSISSIPPI
304	Jackson	$25

MISSOURI
105	Kansas City	$25
134	Springfield/Branson	$25
013	St. Louis	$30

NEBRASKA
138	Omaha/Lincoln	$30

NEVADA
149	Las Vegas	$25
110	Reno/Lake Tahoe	$30

NEW HAMPSHIRE
128	Southern New Hampshire	$30

NEW JERSEY
048	Central/Middlesex	$30
094	Central/Monmouth	$30
052	North/Bergen	$30
026	North/Essex	$30
093	North/Morris	$30
076	NJ South	$35

NEW MEXICO
083	Albuquerque/Santa Fe	$40

NEW YORK
060	Albany	$35
109	Binghamton	$15
011	Buffalo	$30
111	Cortland/Ithaca	$15
033	Long Island/ Nassau/Suffolk	$25
087	Mid-Hudson Valley	$35
004	New York City	$30
044	Rochester	$30
074	Syracuse	$30
040	Westchester/ Lower-Hudson Valley	$35

NORTH CAROLINA
043	Charlotte	$30
222	Fayetteville	$30
113	Greensboro	$20
112	Raleigh/Durham	$30

OHIO
006	Akron	$35
069	Canton	$35
002	Cincinnati Area	$25
004	Cleveland	$30
003	Columbus/Central OH	$25
005	Dayton/Springfield	$30
018	Toledo/NW Ohio/ SE Michigan	$35
131	Youngstown	$30

OKLAHOMA
160	Oklahoma City	$30
151	Tulsa	$25

OREGON
051	Oregon	$35
029	Portland/Vancouver	$35

PENNSYLVANIA
136	Erie	$30
162	Harrisburg	$30
072	Lancaster/York	$30
062	Lehigh Valley	$30
156	NE Pennsylvania/Poconos	$30
031	Philadelphia North	$30
079	Philadelphia West	$30
007	Pittsburgh	$30
120	Pittsburgh and East	$30
081	Reading/Pottsville	$30

RHODE ISLAND
155	Providence	$30

SOUTH CAROLINA
261	Charleston	$30
021	Columbia	$30
129	Greenville/Spartanburg	$30

TENNESSEE
116	Memphis	$25
064	Nashville	$25
205	Tri-Cities	$25

TEXAS
142	Austin	$25
140	Corpus Christi	$30
145	Dallas	$25
125	El Paso	$30

###		
147	Ft. Worth	$25
019	Houston Area	$25
152	San Antonio	$25

UTAH
092	Utah	$25

VERMONT
095	Vermont	$35

VIRGINIA
063	Norfolk/VA Beach	$30
070	North Virginia/ Washington, D.C.	$3
158	Richmond	$3

WASHINGTON
143	N. Puget Sound	$3
050	S. Puget Sound	$3
023	Seattle/Eastside	$3
090	Spokane/N. Idaho	$3

WEST VIRGINIA
115	Charleston Area	$3
117	Huntington	$3

WISCONSIN
077	Appleton/Green Bay	$3
049	Madison	$3
032	Milwaukee	$4

CANADA
065	Calgary	$
066	Edmonton	$3
130	Halifax	$
059	Hamilton/Burlington/ Oakville	$
089	Montréal et environs	$
101	Okanagan Valley	$
067	Ottawa/Outaouais	$
135	Saskatchewan	$
054	Toronto Area	$
025	Vancouver	$
107	Victoria/ Mid Vancouver Island	$
161	Winnipeg	$

PUERTO RICO
100	San Juan	$

AUSTRALIA
327	Adelaide	$
326	Brisbane	$
332	Canberra	$
387	Geelong	$
410	Gold Coast	$
324	Melbourne	$
330	Newcastle	$
388	Parramatta/ Blue Mountains	$
336	Perth	$
328	Sydney	$

NEW ZEALAND
331	Auckland	$
400	Christchurch	$
338	Wellington	$

Some editions will not be available until 11/1/06. Offer subject to availability. Credit card transactions are processed in U.S. funds and are subject to applicable exchange rates. Offer expires 9/1/07.